The New
Making
of a Cook

The New Making of a Cook

The Art, Techniques, and Science of Good Cooking

Madeleine Kamman

WILLIAM MORROW AND COMPANY, INC.
New York

Library of Congress Cataloging-in-Publication Data

Kamman, Madeleine.
    The new making of a cook : the art, techniques, and science of
good cooking / Madeleine Kamman. – 1st ed.
        p.   cm.
    Includes bibliographical references and index.
    ISBN 0-688-15254-6
    1. Cookery.   I. Title.
TX714.K356   1997   96-37452
641.5–dc21   CIP

Printed in the United States of America

First Edition

1   2   3   4   5   6   7   8   9   10

BOOK DESIGN BY LAURA HAMMOND HOUGH

I dedicate this book, with deep gratitude, to

Pam Hoenig, my editor,
and her staff who produced this book,

Ruth Tanner, professor of chemistry at the
University of Massachusetts, Lowell,
who polished the language of the food chemistry
sections, so every cook could understand them,

Patricia Hart, RD, MS, who reviewed parts of the
manuscript with the rigor of the dedicated dietician,

Joe Heitz, founder and principal owner of
Heitz Cellar in St. Helena, California,
who checked the accuracy of the section on wines, and

To anyone who wishes to discover that there is much happiness and many
opportunities for learning and becoming oneself in what is still considered
by too many the least important room in a home or even in a restaurant,
the humble and all-important kitchen.

Acknowledgments

IT TAKES MANY YEARS AND MANY PEOPLE TO HELP SHAPE A PROFESSIONAL IN any art or technique and I would like to thank here all the people who over many many years have, in one way or another, contributed to make and keep me a passionate cooking teacher.

In my French family: Marie Pin, Marguerite-Charlotte and Charles Alexandre Pin, Simone and Charles Georges Pin, Georgette Ordonneau, Claire Robert, Marie Becker, and Marie Labarrière, who nurtured me, taught me to read, sew, and cook, run a small restaurant kitchen and dining room, and foremost, to analytically taste what came on my plate and in my glass and always be grateful for both.

During my years of schooling: Professors Bergeron, Claude, Jarillon, Colville, Grappin, Labarrière, Pelizaeus, and Pochard, who taught me to think and reason in French, German, and English, and passed on to me a font of historical and artistic knowledge that, years later, I was able, in turn, to pass on to my students.

During my business years: Georges Ulmer, executive vice-president of the Swissair Office in Paris, who taught me real-life business procedures and personnel management and issued those wonderful free intercompany air tickets, which opened the whole world to me; and the leaders of the professional seminars of the Société Suisse des Commerçants, affiliated with the Hotel School at Lausanne.

In my American family: Alan Bertram Kamman, Alan Daniel Kamman, and Neil Charles Kamman, who gave me the love that in the life of anyone must balance the intellect. Ann Pollender, who gave me Aliza and Sawyer Pollender Kamman, and Carla Mayo, who gave me Rowan Atkins Kamman. Our friends Neil Gebhardt, who donated some of his personal funds to establish my first school, Wilhelmine, George, and Albert Rieger, who besides kindness also brought spirituality to my life.

In my teaching work: The boards of education of the States of Massachusetts and New Hampshire, especially Dr. Rachel K. Winer; the board of directors of the Philadelphia Gasworks, and that of the Cheltenham Adult Education Center in the greater Philadelphia area; Northeastern University, Boston University, Johnson & Wales University, and the Cornell University School of Hotel Management, as well as all the privately owned cooking schools that welcomed me as a guest teacher across the nation; E. Michael

Moone, Walter Klenz, and Tor Kenward, who as president of the board, chief executive officer, and vice-president of public relations at Wine World Inc. in St. Helena, California, created for me at Beringer Vineyards the scholarship program known as the School for American Chefs, where for each session, I establish a different curriculum which answers the specific questions each chef-recipient of a scholarship brings to class; Antonia Allegra, who brought many visitors from the press to the school; Debra Murphy and Teresa Aldama, who are to this day my co-operators at the school, and all those who were up to now my assistants during the sessions, particularly Michelle Gilardi, Pamela Hogan, Gabriella Petrick, Patrick Mulvaney (whose great knowledge of food chemistry was particularly appreciated), and Kathleen Orme.

In my restaurant-teaching work: Jacqueline Cattani, June and Thomas Connors, Gary Danko, Deirdre Davis, Judith Flewelling, Brett Frechette, Kendra Horstmeyer, Ethel Goralnick, Linda Marino, our much missed friend Lynn McManus, Rebecca Reilly, and Jimmy Schmidt, who were my personal assistants; Richard Kzirian, who was a superb cellar master, and all the student-chefs who worked with me at Chez la Mère Madeleine in Newton Centre and at L'Auberge Madeleine in Glen, New Hampshire, or in Annecy, France, especially Richard and Cindy Black, Tom Connors, Chris Evans, Roy Palmeri, Bruce and Pat Tillinghast, and Ruth Tanner Isaks.

In the press: All the newspaper and magazine writers who interviewed me at all the schools where I taught over the years, with very special thanks to Craig Claiborne of the *New York Times*, whose article in the early 1960s heralded the serious start of my career as a cooking teacher; Elaine Tait of the *Philadelphia Inquirer*, Lane Palmer from *Farm Journal*, the late Anthony Spinazzola, whose generous articles made my first restaurant an instant success, Marian Burros both of the *Washington Post* and the *New York Times*, Florence Fabricant of the *New York Times*, Phyllis Richman of the *Washington Post*, Beverly Bennett of the *Chicago Sun Times*, Bill Rice of the *Chicago Tribune*, Harvey Steiman of the *Wine Spectator*, Michael Bauer of the *San Francisco Chronicle*, and Robin Mather of the *Detroit Free Press*. Gratitude also goes to Jane Matyas, formerly of *Bon Appetit* magazine, the staff of the late *Cuisine* magazine, to Kathy Fliegel, who wrote a glowing review of my restaurant in *Boston* magazine; the editors of the *Boston Globe Sunday Magazine*; and Susan Costner, who now produces and edits *Tables*, the magazine of Beringer Wine Estates. In France, thanks go to Odette Kahn, former owner of *Cuisine et Vins de France* and of *La Revue du Vin de France*, for whom I wrote for years, and more recently to Monsieur Bonhommet, who published my article on the Napa Valley in the French magazine *Saveurs*.

In the book publishing world: Charlotte Sheedy, who, having read Craig Claiborne's article, offered me a book contract and magazine work; Pat Knopf of Atheneum Publishers, who gave me a contract for *The Making of a Cook*, which was edited by Dorothy Parker; Judith Kern who, while still at

Atheneum, was the delightful editor of *When French Women Cook, In Madeleine's Kitchen*, and *Madeleine Kamman's Savoie*; Maria Guarnaschelli, who edited *Madeleine Cooks* as a companion book to the television series at William Morrow and asked me to write the book on chicken cookery that is now being edited; Pam Hoenig, my valued editor of this *New Making of a Cook* at Macmillan and now at William Morrow; and my literary agent, Susan Lescher.

In the television world: WCVB Channel 5 in Boston, where for almost three years, I learned to direct my own seven-minute show on live camera; the staffs of the *Mike Douglas Show* in Philadelphia and of the *Today* show on NBC; Mike Styer of Maryland Public Television, who agreed to produce the fifty-two *Madeleine Cooks* shows that appeared on most public television stations in the United States; Charles Pinsky, who directed the production of the series and taught me how to pause and speak slowly, and all those who worked behind the cameras and in the makeup room, especially Gary Danko, Ethel Goralnick, and the late Maria Hausmann, who did the preparation for the dishes that I cooked and styled on camera.

In the French community in California: Monsieur le Consul de France Yvon Roe d'Albert, who was kind enough to recommend my name for recognition of my work by the French Ministry of Culture in the form of a Knighthood in the Order of French Arts and Letters, as well as Jean-Michel Jeudy and André Fournier, who were my sponsors in that nomination.

In the food and wine community at large, my acquaintances, friends, and colleagues: Ned Atwater, Antoinette Benjamin, Johanna Borenstein, Dan Bowe, Joan Brett, Giuliano Bugialli, Linda Burgess, Ann Carpy, Laura Chenel, Phyllis Cherry, Barbara Colleary, Jerry Comfort, Joseph Costanzo, Marion Cunningham, Shirley Corriher, Chris Diamond, Andrew Dornenberg, Mark Dirkheising, Anita Eisenhower, Mary Goodbody, Ruth Gresser, Elwin Greenwood, Beverly Gruber, Gwen Gulliksen, Carolyn and Sam Gusman, Amelia Hard, Patricia Hart, Karen Hess, Peter Hesse, Joe and Alice Heitz, Libby and Betty Hillman, Diane Holuigue, Paul Inveen and Maureen Pothier Inveen, Gayle Jolley, David Hagedorn, Cathy Kaufmann, Todd Kawachi, Christopher Kimball, Peter Kelly, Oliver Kita, Barbara Lang, Jan Longone, Harold McGee, Willinda McRea, Margriet Biever Mondavi, Sara Monick, Mary Etta Moose, Weezie Mott, Barbara Gibbs Ostmann, Chris Ostlund, Ann Palmer, Brian Patterson, Toula Patsalis, Peggy Rahn, Kerry Romaniello, Robert Reynolds, Mary Risley, Geri Rinschler, Gwenda Robb, Ann Rosenzweig, Roxsand Scocos, Martha Shaw, Dawn Simms, Pat Skillman, Andre Soltner, Bonnie Stern, Renie Steves, John Schwartz, Blake Swihart, John Taylor, Jeremiah Tower, Barbara Tropp, Jeffrey Tuttle, Phyllis Vacarelli, Jeanne Voltz, the late Maggie Waldron, Bill Wallace, Alice Waters, Joanne Weir, Paula Wolfert, Susan Wyler, Martin Yan, and, in a very special way, Julia Child and Susan Breger. I apologize if, because like my computer my memory has quirks, I have forgotten someone who has been helpful to me.

Many of the people mentioned here are not of this world anymore and neither are these last two, but it seems fitting that they both put the final point to this tribute:

James Beard, who was so generous to me and who, during the last two years of his life, was my frequent telephone friend, and Peter Kump, who always had a place for me as a teacher in his school and for reasons he and I knew well and always kidded about, named one of his kitchens "Madeleine's kitchen."

Contents

From Cook to Cook

Dear Cook,

I picture you in a bookstore, standing in front of the cookbook section with this new big book in hand and thinking, "Ah . . . this one has a funny title and it is huge; it is probably too complicated for me." Not a bit so. I am Madeleine, its author. Perhaps you have seen me cook on PBS or other channels over the past several years; as a matter of fact, if you have not seen me there too often during the last few, it is because I was busy rewriting this book for you, and also for myself.

The first edition of *The Making of a Cook* was published in 1971, a long time ago for those of you who were perhaps just born and are now active young adults. One of its many reviewers made a joke about its title. Since this was the time when Mr. White wrote books about the "Making of the President," my reason for sparing the public from yet another cookbook preceeded by an unknown name, this time mine, was that if politicians could make presidents, why should I not, as a cooking teacher, think and write about making cooks? It was, after all, what I was doing for a living at the time, and I have not stopped doing so for the last thirty-five years.

I wrote this book at the height of the latest French phase in American cooking. The fact that I was born and educated in France, but became a naturalized American citizen in 1963 gave me two countries and made my point of view on French cuisine in America a different one. As I told my readers in the first version of this book twenty-five years ago, I immediately realized that, having cooked extensively in France both at home and in a restaurant, it would be totally impossible to fully duplicate the French tastes and textures with American ingredients. I decided to use the French techniques of cooking and apply them to American ingredients.

Did I ever have a great time, using corn and sweet potatoes, pecans, Meyer lemons and avocados, plenty of citrus fruits and juices, American freshwater and ocean fish and Rocky Mountain–raised meats accompanied and cooked with American wines from California and New York State, flambéed with Wild Turkey and Jack Daniel's instead of Cognac and Armagnac.

Why did I decide to rewrite this book and make it larger than it already was? It may at first sight appear to be madness, but there has been reasoning to my madness.

First as the years went on, I realized that the first edition contained quite a few imperfections, and that, like all young cooks with a passion, I had given in to the "passion" first and then only to reasoning. I simply had written it too soon, when I still thought I knew so much. If indeed I was quite strong on techniques, my kitchen chemistry was at that point the result of reading only, rather than of deep reasoning. I remedied that by enormous amounts of "reading with reasoning" during the last twenty-five years. Still, since I have reached the stage where I know I shall never know enough, I asked my friend, former student, and restaurant co-operator Ruth Tanner, who is a professor of chemistry at the University of Massachusetts, Lowell, to review every word I have written on this subject in this new edition. She systematically went over the vocabulary of the sections explaining food chemistry, so they read scientifically correct, but are expressed in everyday language, an insurance that all cooks can understand and enjoy every word without needing a degree in chemistry.

Why that insistence on food chemistry? Because the most important question I was ever asked in my career as a cooking teacher was the first one, and it began with "Why," way back in 1962, which, if I remember correctly, came from Carolyn Gusman. It threw me back to my school days when my revered teacher of Greek and Roman history had explained the whys of democracy during the German occupation of France, at the risk of her life. It was like a revelation. This is the question that makes a good teacher, that makes one able to point to the reasons for one's answers, be it in history or in simple cooking. In cooking the importance of understanding the whys is economically most important for home finances and restaurant success; it means reasoning one's techniques so the dish comes out successfully and no waste of good ingredients results. Some of my former students may remember how I answered their question, "Should I throw it away?" My answer was always, "Think it out first; can you salvage it?"

But there were more reasons for rewriting this book. Quite a few of my colleagues who run small but important professional training programs for future chefs were using the book as a class textbook, and that necessitated a large and serious revision on my part, so no imprecision was left and the text would be entirely usable and modernized. There are just a few of the recipes of what I call "the old book" remaining in this second version; the others are all new.

The significant changes in eating habits that have taken place in the United States, and in all developed Western countries, over the past ten years were caused by the knowledge of the consequences of eating too much, and including too much of the wrong fats and oils in our diet. It was necessary that this book reflect these changes. You will find me to be on the side of moderation; I say "yes" to using the right types of fats in the correct quantity, but vehemently "no" to using no fats at all. After all, our brains are predominantly made of fat.

So you will find the dishes offered in this book prepared mostly with monounsaturated (olive oil) or polyunsaturated oil (corn, safflower, and grapeseed oils) and some butter often added last for taste, but only when necessary. In dishes designed for entertaining or for restaurant use, there may be more butter, but certainly not the large amounts that they contained in the first edition. Butter remains a taste treat unlike any other, and as you minimize its presence in your everyday life, you will appreciate its lovely flavor even more when you allow yourself a special indulgence.

For the cook's convenience, the recipes have each been coded with three letters: FFR represents a full-fat recipe containing saturated fats in the form of butter, cream, bacon fat, lard, and/or duck fat; FCR represents a fat-controlled recipe in which the fat used is an unsaturated oil; LFR represents a recipe containing only a small amount of fat; and NFR is a recipe with only a very small percentage of fat.

However, as you read these headings, bear in mind that they are indicative only of the rough quantity of fat included in the recipe and represent in no way the precise measurements a nutritionist would bring to a complete and precise analysis of each recipe in grams of fat, proteins, and carbohydrates. It will be easy for you to subtract fat or enrich any recipe as you please by changing the type of fat used in the text. If you object to the taste or use of oil in one recipe, simply change over to the same amount or a little more of butter; if, on the other hand, heavy cream is too rich for you, simply change to light cream, half-and-half, or even, in a case where total lack of fat is essential, a mixture of nonfat milk blended with nonfat cream cheese.

The recipes are, with a few exceptions, easy to execute and the portions are reasonably small. I am a firm believer in training cooks and chefs to cook and taste on small-quantity production rather than on large quantity; it is easier to learn to season and appreciate texture when one can prepare a small, manageable dish. I have trained all the young people who have passed through my kitchens this way and those who have had enough physical energy to remain in the difficult "kitchen professions" are still doing very well. No one has had any difficulty making the move from small quantity to large quantity in the transition from our school sessions to restaurant operation.

All in all, this book represents the basic technical culinary knowledge a cook and future chef must have assimilated before taking a position in a professional kitchen. However, learning emphatically cannot stop with its last page; it must continue daily, way beyond the content of this book.

Yet another reason I rewrote this book is because our world is a troubled one, and many members of the new generations worry about their futures and whether they will have energy resources to survive. As you will see throughout the book, I am a great believer in teaching cooking as an interdisciplinary art—or technique, if you prefer, but certainly not just a craft—involving some science and history in the process.

I have found it necessary to describe numerous basic techniques that can be done by hand, without the help of electric implements. I believe in teaching to work by hand first, so the cook can function under any circumstance; machines are wonderful, and I use them, but the world cooked without them before they were invented and probably still will after they disappear, and/or electricity becomes scarce.

I had the proof of this theory in September 1989, when a nasty thunderstorm cut our electric power in the Napa Valley from early morning to four o'clock in the afternoon; dinner, prepared entirely by hand by graduates of my diverse professional classes, for about ninety guests was served at six o'clock sharp, without the slightest delay.

What I stated in the 1971 introduction to *The Making of a Cook* remains valid. There are born cooks, people of great imagination and taste, who can start dancing at the stove with any ingredient and end up putting masterpieces on the dinner table. They do it without apparent effort, not a piece of paper, book, or recipe in sight, enlisting the mere help of what I have called for years in my classrooms "the Holy Trinity" of the kitchen: the brain, the heart, and the hands.

That would seem to leave stranded all those who are not born cooks, wouldn't it? Rest assured that it does not, for there are many good books to hold the hand of those who know how to read and follow instructions. Think at all times; that is what that wonderful brain in your head is for: If something goes wrong, stop what you are doing, calm down, and try to reason through what is happening.

I am sure that you have seen the words "tested recipe" on many recipes. We all test recipes; some of the people whose profession it is to test recipes do this with the greatest and most admirable care, testing with stopwatches to establish exact cooking times. Unfortunately, that is not failproof. I remember one of my cooking buddies testing the cooking of mushrooms to figure out exactly how many minutes it would take for them to lose their vegetative water. I did the same in a different type of skillet. His mushrooms took four minutes, mine just two. The next time, the results were switched; his took just two minutes, mine at least six. My skillet conducted heat better than his the first time and his mushrooms contained less moisture than mine the second time.

This type of problem will happen with many other ingredients; flour, for example, can be a major offender if you do not learn to feel it between your fingers to appreciate the fineness of its texture and the way it cakes. There is a cake in this book that I made perhaps twenty-five times; not once did its texture turn out exactly identical because the flours I used over several years, although labeled "cake flour" or "unbleached all-purpose flour," felt different each time I made it, even if the flour was of the same brand. Besides the flour, I am sure that the quality of the eggs, the accuracy of the oven thermostat, and the variation of my own deftness with each try had something to do with the observed differences.

I have tested all over the United States and France, from Paris to Philadelphia, back to New Hampshire and California, and every time there have been slight differences due to the climate and the texture of the flour, meat, or vegetables. What is valid for me is valid for you. Rather than go by time alone, look for the texture that is indicated in the recipe and taste often; you will know yourself when the dish is just right for you, because it tastes and feels the way you like it. That last sentence is key; if it feels and tastes the way you like it, it is successful. We all have different tastes and there is no way that each of us can satisfy everyone completely every time we cook a dish. In the long run it comes down to being tolerant of other people's tastes. It took me years to understand just that.

I first improvised each of the new recipes in this book at the stove for an everyday dinner, then redid each recipe at least twice during the four years it took me to write the book. Some of the formulas come from the kitchens of relatives and friends, although I have reinterpreted them; I have given credit to all in the introduction of each recipe.

Your goal should be to start cooking with recipes at first, then, after a couple of years, to trust your newly acquired knowledge and to start improvising on your own. How will you get there? First, by understanding the proper techniques, mastering them, cherishing them, and, if you can, never forgetting to apply them. Success comes with the proper techniques of preparation for any given ingredient. One of my young colleagues insists on telling me that what counts first and foremost is the quality of the ingredient. Why, of course, the higher the quality, the better the meal, but if you have not mastered the technique to cook that beautiful piece of meat or that "fragrant truffle from Italy" or that "amazing foie gras," let me tell you, cook, you are not only in great trouble from the start but you are also in great danger of seriously damaging that beautiful ingredient. That applies to the everyday ingredients of our daily fare as well; overcooked carrots taste no better than undercooked, grassy, crunchy green beans. So, sit down and read before your start cooking.

All the classic formulas of the western cuisines are to be found here, often presented with different personal techniques that have made their execution easier for many of my students. My point of view is not the only one existing, and you may also want to find out what other authors are recommending. There is something instructive to be found everywhere and the more points of view you allow yourself to understand, the more you will become truly yourself by keeping what you like and discarding what you do not.

Once you have applied a technique and successfully cooked a dish, you have to learn to correct its final seasoning properly. Yes, emphatically yes, you must taste a dish before serving it; there is no possible way that the recipe writer can know how much salt your combination of ingredients finally needs. That can be difficult for some because there are two trends of thinking about salt in this country. Either the cook in your family is of the old school and salts everything "to the finish," or she/he is of the new school and believes that salt is akin to poison. There is a very rational way to deal with this problem. There is salt in your blood and in your saliva; you can be very sure that if a dish is not salted enough for your taste, you obviously salted below the level of salt in your saliva, and that if you perceive any degree of saltiness in it, you have salted above it. How much above it you should salt is entirely your personal choice.

Remember that anything that is too flat or too acid can be rebalanced with salt, and anything too salty can be rebalanced with an acid such as lemon juice. It is as simple as that, because you taste both salt and acid in two parallel regions located on each side of your tongue. You may make some mistakes at the beginning of your cook's life, but you will get used to it so fast that you will not believe it yourself. Also, some peppers have wonderful fragrances and aftertastes, but take it easy with them. Some are so hot that the taste of all other foods entering the composition of a dish will disappear in their diabolical heat and the flavors of the most expensive wines will be lost irretrievably in them.

Fats and oils help lower the intensity of most acids by coating the taste buds and palate and, as they go into emulsion in our saliva, give our foods the pleasant slip that we know and miss so much when we really must restrict our fat intake. You will soon find out that for the very same reason, vegetables that must be seasoned with a minimal amount of fat are much more enjoyable when they have been pureed. If they cannot be pureed, you will find homemade low-fat salad dressings prepared with a tad of unsaturated oil to be acceptable replacements for oil or melted butter.

You may want to make a point of comparing the seasoning of dishes that are from the Mediterranean world, in which salt is abundant both as a seasoning and through the use of anchovies, pancetta, and preserved olives, with the seasoning of northern and eastern European countries, where the sour taste seems to predominate, as in the sauerkraut of the Germanic countries. Also notice the sweet-sour sauces of the Slavic and Scandinavian countries. It will take you no time to understand that classic cuisine as practiced in France and the traditional cuisine of the United States are poised somewhere in the middle, with moderate uses of salty or sour ingredients. As you investigate the Orient, you will note the enormous differences existing between the seasonings of India and those of China. Japan will seem either the strangest or the most interesting of all, with its almost unsalted preparations dipped and/or sauced in concentrated preparations such as shoyu, mirin, or ponzu.

It seems as if, during the last thirty years, cooks have made the ultimate effort to elevate their techniques to the level of true art, as in painting and music compositions. Many styles have surfaced in rapid succession, veritable fashions, which have bred their lions, stars, talents, geniuses, and fakes as well as political caucuses at least as powerful as those of any world power government. However interesting all these happenings may seem, it remains a fact that food is cooked to be eaten and enjoyed by the palate and that the taste balance of a dish is a lot more important than its final look.

The complete lack of color photographs in this book will, considering the present trends, surprise many a reader. It is mostly due to my belief that it is essential for a cook's plate presentations to be as personal as she or he wishes. Developing a personal style of plate decoration is absolutely necessary. Decorate as much or as little as you wish, but make certain that the eye appeal is not to the detriment of the taste appeal, for the longer it takes to "style" a plate or platter, the longer the food must wait to be served and the more its final taste will suffer. I have found, over my fifty years of cooking, that simplicity in presentation, using the natural colors of meats, vegetables, herbs, nuts, and small unobtrusive flowers, yields the very best results.

It is probable, as you gradually become a dedicated cook, that over the years you will develop other related passions, such as for beautiful table appointments. There is yet another whole world of discovery and knowledge to be acquired in porcelain or pottery, crystal, table linens, and related flower arrangements.

I wish you much fun in your kitchen and at the table, and, to those of you who will be working with this book during your schooling hours, much success. May the kitchen be a place of happiness in your home or at work and may the trinity of the hands, heart, and brain always be your "protecting kitchen witch."

Madeleine Kamman

Tools of the Trade

Kitchen Equipment
and How to Use It

NO EXTRAVAGANTLY EXPENSIVE ARRAY OF EQUIPMENT IS NEEDED TO COOK well. Many of the essential items can be purchased for very little in a local shop, but if you purchase some of your equipment in a hotel or restaurant supply store, it will be sturdier, longer lasting, and often obtainable at better prices than in smaller stores or even department stores.

The list of items that follows may seem enormous, but if you are equipping your first kitchen, there is no necessity to acquire all the items mentioned at once. If you are what is commonly known as a gadgeteer, anything not listed here is not absolutely necessary.

Pots and Pans

The best pots and pans were said to be the old French copper beauties, because they were heavy and conducted heat evenly; but they were expensive and during a lifetime of frequent use, they required several retinnings. Modern manufacturers remedied this situation by creating copper pots and pans lined with stainless steel and nickel that never need relining.

As a cook with many years of experience both at home and in the food professions, I have come to the conclusion that in our days of hurried life, it is wiser for a young cook to first acquire practical, sturdy pots and pans that are easy to take care of. The pace of life has become so very quick that the little time cooks have left for leisure is better spent resting than polishing copper pots, which look absolutely terrible if they are not shined regularly. If you have no steady help who will be able to take proper care of coppers in your household, choose another style of pot. If, on the contrary, you have enough funds and leisure time to afford coppers, by all means buy some, but beware of the quality. The best and heaviest come from France and Switzerland; other countries produce some, but they are of lighter weight and do not conduct heat any more efficiently than other modern pots and pans.

The choice of pots and pans made from aluminum and steel is wide and interesting. Some of these pans are made in France, but most of the pans manufactured in the United States deserve to be investigated. Among them are heavy cast-aluminum pots and pans, stainless steel pans with "dressed" (copper-lined) bottoms and professional nonheat-conductive hollow handles. The thicker the pot, the sturdier it will be and the better it will retain heat.

There are also several lines of so-called nonstick pots and pans which will allow the cook to utilize a minimum of fat in cooking and can be cleaned in a jiffy. In purchasing these, bear in mind that the darker the coating and the thicker the pot, the better the heat conduction will be. If you acquire nonstick pots and pans, make it a personal "religion" never to use metal utensils to stir preparations or turn pieces of meat over, and never to cut meat in them, as this will scratch and damage the coating irreparably and cause it to start peeling. There is a whole line of wood or soft plastic implements especially devised for working with these pans. If a nonstick pot is damaged because you have used it for many years, call the manufacturer's customer service, and they will be able to tell you where you can have it recoated; it may be less expensive to recoat than to buy a brand new pan.

To braise or stew, think of that wonderful cast-iron pot you may have inherited from your grandmother or great grandmother. I still use my mom's *cocotte*, an old-fashioned cast-iron oval pot which is by now a good sixty-five years old and in which I prepare all my family's winter stews.

If an older or a new cast-iron pot "sticks," reseason it as follows: Heat 2 to 3 tablespoons oil in it. Turn the heat off and add 2 tablespoons coarse or kosher salt. Rub and scrub the pot with the salt using a thick wad of paper towels. The towels will become stained as the pot is cleaned. Discard the salt and towels and wipe the oil off with a new wad of paper towels, then store the pot. Wipe the pot off again just before you use it, and repeat this quick operation after each use.

If no family inheritance is available, purchase one of those great French enameled cast-iron pots, round or oval, which come in bright red, brown, or blue and conduct heat evenly and slowly, to allow you to produce stews on which you will build the reputation of a great cook. Such cast-iron pots require no seasoning.

If you cannot afford any high-quality heavyweight equipment right now, please do not give up. For years, I have cooked professionally out of thin stainless steel and thin aluminum pots and pans with the best of luck and very good results. Regulate the heat according to the thickness of the pot and remember always that the pot is not cooking, *you* are; do not let a piece of metal ruin your enjoyment of food preparation.

Here are a few tips to solve some of the common equipment difficulties met by new cooks:

Basically, all pots and pans of any kind should be washed with soapy water, rinsed and dried, but

- If you have copper pans, never scrub them with abrasive cleanser or a soapy metal pad; rather, soak them in water, flush the remnants of food out with water, and wash the pans with plain soap and water.

- If food has scorched at the bottom of a pot or pan, do not scrub it; add baking soda to the pan in the ratio of 1 tablespoon per cup of water and bring to a boil; simmer until the crust of food lifts off by itself. This will save any pot.

- Aluminum pans should preferably not be used for cooking white sauces or creams that require constant stirring. The soft aluminum is actually scraped off the bottom of the pan in tiny flakes which will tint the preparation gray. If you own only aluminum pots, stir with a wooden spoon which will not scratch the bottom and remove the sauce or cream from the pan to a nonreactive vessel as soon as it is finished.

- All preparations containing an acid such as vinegar, tomatoes, a citrus juice, or wine should be cooked in a nonreactive pan; aluminum and cast-iron pans are reactive, stainless steel and enamel pans are not.

- Stir with wooden or plastic implements. To wash these utensils, rinse them thoroughly, then stack them in the upper tray of the dishwasher to sterilize them. If you have no dishwasher, soak the thoroughly rinsed implements in simmering water for five minutes, then air dry them.

Which Size Pots and Pans?

This is a list of what you basically should have. Again, if you are not given the whole collection as a present all at once, gradually acquire pots and pans as you can, piece by piece, buying the most practical sizes first, which are marked below with an asterisk.

- ½-quart (2-cup) saucepan
- 1-quart (4-cup) saucepan
- 2-quart saucepan*
- 1½-quart braising pot
- 4-quart braising pot, very thick bottom, preferably made of enameled or plain cast iron*
- 9- and 10-inch(*) sauteuse pans, sautoirs, or rondeaux made of copper-bottomed stainless steel for stews such as Brunswick stew or for the meat dishes originating from France and called sautés (see pages 840–44)
- Double boiler and hot water bath; both can be improvised, the first with a smaller bowl fitted over a larger pot containing water, the second with any heatproof dish half filled with boiling water.
- Roasting pan fitted with a rack; the rack is essential to prevent the roast from frying and overcooking on the bottom.
- Broiling pan fitted with a rack; this can be improvised with a jelly-roll pan fitted with a cake rack.
- Small saucepan, capacity 1 to 1½ cups to melt gelatin, dissolve coffee powder, etc.
- 9- and 10-inch skillets and/or frying pans, nonstick or regular. To limit

Sauteuse with lid on

Sautoir, lid off

Rondeau

Improvised double boiler

Kettle

Large steamer for steaming 6 portions. It is fitted with a dome lid and a steaming basket with a handle and feet that sits above the water and is pierced with holes to let the steam through.

Small steamer for 2 to 3 portions

the amount of fat needed in cooking, use nonstick pans made of thick aluminum

- 8-inch nonstick skillet or frying pan to prepare omelettes, crepes, or any of their relatives. If you have inherited an old-fashioned cast-iron or steel French omelette pan from your mother or grandmother, you can still use it but you will need more butter or oil to cook in it. See page 4 on how it should be reseasoned.

- 5-quart copper-bottomed kettle, preferably made of stainless steel. If you have inherited one made of cast-iron or thick aluminum, you can use it to cook broth, stock, or soup, but do not store these in the pan. Rather, strain into stainless or glass bowls to prevent a metallic taste in the broth and unhealthy aluminum leaching.

- Steamer with rack to steam meats and vegetables. (No special steamer is needed to steam shellfish open; you can use a sauteuse or a 5-quart pot.)

Especially for Frying

- Electric deep fryer with frying basket to lower the foods into the hot oil bath
- Frying thermometer
- Electric frying pan. An electric frying pan is arguably the most versatile piece of equipment in everyday cooking, as in it you can not only fry chicken, but make a small soup, prepare some sautés of chicken and veal, panfry steaks or chops, prepare small stews, stir-fry mixed vegetables and small pieces of meat in the Chinese manner, poach eggs, make omelettes and pancakes, and even bake soufflés (see page 173) and cakes.

Other Larger Pieces of Equipment

- A large plastic or stainless steel colander to drain pasta, rice, etc.
- As soon as you can afford one, purchase a food processor, coming as it does with an array of slicing and grinding disks and much more; it slices vegetables, grinds nuts, makes bread crumbs, purees certain vegetables, purees raw meat and fish for some classic European and Oriental dishes, quickly shreds and cuts into sticks of several sizes most vegetables.
- A blender. It purees anything to a perfectly smooth liquid or semi-liquid texture, which the food processor does not always do as well.
- An electric mixer. Invest in an electric mixer to save time and energy in making not only cakes and desserts but in doing such things as whipping cream or chilled skim milk. The larger, the better, as the sturdy ones last for decades; if your budget restricts you to a hand mixer, choose the stur-

diest one, as, again, it will last a good number of years and can be replaced by a larger model later.

Flimsy hand electric mixers are not a good investment and they are legion, so beware. There is still nothing that an old-fashioned rotary beater cannot beat, so if you have to use one, do so; it will just take a little more time.

- Meat grinder. The food processor does not grind really; it reduces anything from meat to nuts from large particles to medium and small ones, then to an imperfectly smooth or very smooth puree, depending on the length of time you process. For that reason, an old-fashioned meat grinder still has its uses for preparations such as sausage and European-style terrines. If you purchase a larger electric mixer, it is a good idea, for just a little more money, to purchase an electric meat grinder attachment at the same time.
- A food mill. The old-fashioned food mill can still make wonderful mashed potatoes and grind tasty vegetable soups.
- Vegetable slicer. If you do not own a food processor, a French-style mandoline will slice vegetables just as well. That humble little piece of equipment sold as a "feemster" will cost you a minimum amount of money for a maximum amount of service; mine is thirty years old and still functions as it did on the day I purchased it.
- A hand grater is absolutely necessary to grate hard cheeses finely and some citrus rinds; the simplest models are fine. See page 53 on grating citrus rinds.
- Chopping boards. It is advisable to own two chopping boards both made of excellent well-jointed heavy maple wood. Rinse the boards thoroughly, then wash them with soap and water, rinse them again under hot water, and air dry them.

One of these boards should be reserved for foods such as onions, shallots, leeks, or other vegetables, and uncooked fish and meats. On the edge of this first board write in indelible ink "fish" followed by an upward arrow to indicate which side is for fish. On the other end of the edge write "meats-vegies" followed by a downward arrow to indicate that the other side of the board is reserved for these categories of foods.

The second board can be used for the preparation of fresh or dried fruit, biscuit dough, pastry dough, noodle dough, etc. Note that if you have a good Formica or other nonporous countertop, you can prepare any pastry as well on a sanitized counter. If you have tiled counters as is common in the western states, it is advisable to use boards instead, as the grout between the tiles is almost impossible to clean completely and deeply.

- A marble slab can be very useful to prepare pastry, especially if you live in a warm climate, but it is by no means an essential piece of equipment. If you do not own one and cannot find one—which is not rare—use a well-sanitized nonporous countertop. Only some chocolate work can be done well only on a marble slab.

This blade fits on the bottom, attaching to the handle.

Food mill

Mandoline

1 American liquid tablespoon of any

liquid equals ½ liquid ounce

¼ of an American liquid cup measures

4 tablespoons, or 2 liquid ounces

½ of an American liquid cup measures

8 tablespoons, or 4 American

liquid ounces

¾ of an American liquid cup measures

12 tablespoons, or 6 American

liquid ounces

1 American liquid cup measures 16

tablespoons or 8 American

ounces

There are 2 pints in an American

liquid quart and 2 cups in an

American liquid pint.

Balloon whisk

Regular whisk

- Clock and timer if your stove does not have one; even if it does, it does not hurt to own an additional timer, so as to be able to mind what is in the oven and what is on the stove at the same time.

For Storing and Freezing

- 2 dozen each 1- and 2-cup glass jars with dome lids
- 4½-ounce baby food jars
- Food-quality plastic containers
- Freezer tape
- Food-quality plastic wrap
- Heavy-duty aluminum foil

Small Utensils

Of the following list of small implements, except the timer, have as many of them as you wish and can afford and keep them in a large cylindrical ceramic or metal container by the side of your stove burners:

- Wooden spoons
- Square end—often called blunt end—wooden spatulas; they will be used to reduce gravies and sauces rapidly in shallow skillets or sauteuse pans
- Rubber spatulas large and small for scraping that last spoonful of whatever out of pans and bowls. A word of warning: American-made rubber spatulas have no taste, but some of the European ones have a nasty bitter taste which can taint the flavor of your good food, so choose well.
- Long-handled kitchen fork
- Turners; select metal ones for working in regular metal skillets and frying pans but buy those made of plastic for nonstick pans
- Oval slotted spoons and sauce spoons; sauce spoons are the same size as slotted spoons, but have no holes and are generally used to sauce meats or skim fat from the surface of stocks and stews
- Tongs (long two-pronged instruments used to remove pieces of meats or vegetables from a hot pan)
- Skewers for skewered foods, for testing the doneness of meats, and for applying aspic decorations (see pages 231 and 856)
- Potato and vegetable peelers
- Melon-ball scoop; this implement is called a Parisian spoon by some fancy cooks and by French cooks
- 12-inch balloon wire whip for beating heavy cream; it allows better control of the texture of the cream than does an electric mixer (optional)
- 14-inch balloon wire whip (the larger the better) for whipping egg whites; it provides better textured egg whites than an electric mixer (optional)

Other useful equipment to be kept stored in quickly accessible drawers or cupboards or on a shelf:

- 12-inch unlined copper bowl in which to whip egg whites; this can nowadays be replaced by a copper liner which fits inside the regular bowl of most electric mixers (optional)
- Small stainless steel wire whisk to prepare or finish sauces
- A small mortar and pestle for grinding some herbs and making the best "pesto style" preparations; it still gives a much nicer texture than the blender, so have one if you want
- Two sauce conical strainers made of stainless steel fine mesh
- A so-called chinois or China cap which chefs use to strain refined sauces is optional; whereas strainers are easy to find and should be in each and every kitchen, the China cap can be found only in restaurant equipment stores, is pricey, and not easy to find in good quality superfine stainless steel mesh. You can work without it until you become a champion at making great sauces.
- A serious pepper mill that grinds pepper from coarse to very fine. Having one dark-colored wooden one for black pepper and one light-colored wooden one for white pepper seems practical.
- A meat baster, which can also be used as an inexpensive gravy separator. The graduated glass model is the best and most practical.
- Plastic pot scrubbers for cleaning mussels and clams
- Crackers for shelling lobsters, crabs, and nuts
- Several sets of measuring cups for dry ingredients and several for liquid ingredients
- One each 1-quart and 2-quart measuring bowls with pouring spouts
- Several sets of measuring spoons

Conical strainer

China cap or chinois

Why You Should Have a Kitchen Scale

Kitchen scales are very useful and do not cost much. In spite of all our measuring cups, we often run into difficulties with proportions in recipes because the dry measuring cups do not take into consideration the fact that the density of solid ingredients varies. A small kitchen scale activated by two small batteries can be switched from the ounces of the American avoirdupois (AVP) system of measurement to the grams of the metric system, so you can use any type of foreign cookbook accurately. Older cookbooks coming from any part of the former British Empire offer measurements in British Imperial measures. The old British Imperial measurement system for liquids, contrary to our American volume measurement system, corresponds exactly to the metric system for liquids.

$$\frac{\text{New required \# of portions}}{\text{Number of portions recipe serves}} = ?$$

? × the amount of each ingredient = the new required amount of each ingredient

Converting Cup Measurements to Metric Measurements

The mistake commonly made in quite a few cookbooks written by authors who have been kitchen educated in the regular American measuring cup system is to use liquid measures to measure dry ingredients, so that one can sometimes see onions, flour, or other solid or ground ingredients measured in milliliters, which is a total impossibility since in the metric system, a milliliter is a measure for liquid ingredients, not for solid ones; proceeding this way is heading for disaster because solid ingredients all have different densities. There are many types of flours which do not all fill the same volume; not all chopped onions or shallots will fill the same volume, since no one onion or shallot ever contains the exact same amount of water.

Solids in the metric system are measured in kilograms, pounds, hectograms, grams, centigrams, and milligrams. One kilogram weighs 1,000 grams, 1 pound 500 grams, ½ pound 250 grams, ¼ pound 125 grams, and 1 hectogram 100 grams, while 1 centigram weighs 1/100 of a gram and 1 milligram 1/1,000 of a gram. Milligrams are used by chemists and druggists for measuring out the dosage of medications or other very precise mixtures of chemical ingredients, and are almost never used in the kitchen.

BEWARE: One American avoirdupois pound weighs a little over 454 grams, while a metric pound weighs 500 grams.

Also, an American ounce equals a little over 28 grams. Round that to 30 grams for easier calculation; this simple little bit of knowledge and your ele-

TO CONVERT LARGER WEIGHTS FROM AVP TO METRIC AND VICE VERSA

AVP to Metric

Multiply the number of AVP pounds by 0.454 (since 1 AVP pound weighs 454 grams, you will find the weight of your beef in

kilograms)

Example: 6 pounds of beef

6 × 0.454 = 2.724 kg

which corresponds to 5.448 metric pounds weighing 500 grams each.

Metric to AVP

Multiply the number of kilograms by 2.24 since there are 2.24 AVP pounds per kilogram

Example: 240 kilograms of breast of veal

240 × 2.24 = 537.60 AVP pounds

TO CONVERT FROM AVP SYSTEM TO METRIC SYSTEM; SOLIDS, OUNCES TO GRAMS

Ounces	Grams	Ounces	Grams
1	28.35 (often rounded to 30g)	9	255.15
2	56.70	10	283.50
3	85.05	11	311.85
4	113.40	12	340.20
5	141.75	13	368.55
6	170.10	14	396.90
7	198.45	15	425.25
8	226.80	16	453.59 (often rounded to 454g)

*Source *Encyclopaedia Britannica*

To convert the weight of an ingredient listed in metric grams to AVP weight in ounces, divide the number of grams indicated by 28.35 (you may round up to 30 if that is easier for you).

mentary school arithmetic will allow you to convert a recipe from ounces into grams or vice versa.

REMEMBER: In the avoirdupois system, a pint of water (2 cups) weighs 1 pound; the same situation exists in the metric system where a liter of water weighs a kilogram or 2 pounds. This information can be important in baking and confectionary. Many professional books which you will probably use at some point in your cooking life measure water by weight instead of volume.

TO CONVERT AVP SYSTEM TO METRIC SYSTEM; SOLIDS, AVP POUNDS TO KILOGRAMS AND GRAMS TO METRIC POUNDS

AVP	METRIC		AVP	AVP	METRIC		AVP
Pounds	Kilograms	Grams	Pounds	Pounds	Kilograms	Grams	Pounds
1	0.454	454	0.454	6	2.72	2.720	5.450
2	.91	910	1.450	7	3.18	3.180	6.360
3	1.36	1.360	2.360	8	3.63	3.630	7.260
4	1.81	1.810	3.310	9	4.08	4.080	8.160
5	2.27	2.270	4.540	10	4.54	4.540	9.080

*Source *Encyclopaedia Britannica*

Ounces	Milliliters	Deciliters	Liters		Ounces	Milliliters	Deciliters	Liters
1	29.573	0.29	0.029		10	295.73	2.95	0.295
2	59.15	0.59	0.059		11	325.30	3.25	0.325
3	88.72	0.88	0.088		12	354.87	3.54	0.354
4	118.30	1.18	0.118		13	384.24	3.84	0.384
5	147.87	1.47	0.147		14	413.82	4.13	0.413
6	177.44	1.77	0.177		15	443.39	4.43	0.443
7	207.02	2.07	0.207		16	472.96	4.72	0.472
8	236.59	2.36	0.236		24	709.55	7.09	0.709
9	266.16	2.66	0.266		32	946.14	9.46	0.946

*Source *Encyclopaedia Britannica*

To measure liquid ingredients in the metric system, one uses the liter which contains 10 deciliters, or 100 centiliters, or 1,000 milliliters, the milliliter again almost never used in kitchen measurements. More often than not liquids in recipes from countries using the metric system are measured in deciliters, with the exception of liquors used in the flavoring of sauces and desserts, which are measured in centiliters.

Please, please, get used to the metric system; sooner or later the United States is going to have to adopt it to end the state of measuring isolation in which it finds itself right now. Rest assured from an old kitchen buff that the metric system is mastered very quickly and, once assimilated, is much easier and much more accurate than the cup-volume system.

The following examples will make things clear for all cooks. First, remember the basic rule:

- If a measurement is given in ounces or grams, you must weigh the ingredient on a scale. There is no other way.
- If a measurement is given in cups, parts of a cup, or tablespoons, you must use a cup or a spoon set. There is no other way.

Imagine that you want to cook from a European recipe requiring 125 grams of finely chopped onion (¼-inch cubes) and want to know how much this represents in the cup-volume system:

1. Chop the onion exactly as described into ¼-inch cubes.
2. Weigh it to obtain 125 grams of onions.
3. Transfer to a measuring cup and read the result.

Ounces	Spoons	Cups	Milliters	Deciliters	Liters
⅙	1 teaspoon		4.92	0.049	0.0049
½	1 tablespoon	¹⁄₁₆	14.78	0.147	0.014
1	2 tablespoons	⅛	29.573	0.29	0.029
2	4 tablespoons	¼	59.15	0.59	0.059
3	6 tablespoons	⅓	88.723	0.88	0.088
4	8 tablespoons	½	118.30	1.18	0.118
6	12 tablespoons	¾	167.446	1.67	0.167
8	16 tablespoons	1	236.60	2.36	0.236

*Source *Encyclopaedia Britannica*

Now imagine that the weight of the onions is given to you in ounces. Proceed exactly the same way but weigh the onions to obtain 8 ounces.

If you write a recipe yourself and test the recipe in the cup- or table-spoon-volume system and want to give the weight both in AVP measures and metric measures, chop the onion, measure it in volume, then empty into the scale tray and weigh with a set of AVP weights, then with a set of metric weights.

You will find that 125 grams of chopped onions weigh 4.3 ounces AVP, and fill just about 1 dry measurement cup. It will, however, vary with the season (more or less water in the onions) and the type of onion, some containing more water than others.

Equipment Needed for Making Breads and Desserts

- Flour sifter, unless you decide as I did a long time ago to use a small conical stainless steel sauce strainer
- Two sets of mixing bowls made of either stainless steel or heatproof glass or ceramic, one set of each being ideal
- One set of pastry bags with conical nozzles. A professional set is a better investment than the flimsy sets found in hardware stores. My nozzles are forty-five years old and I purchased plastic bags which can be washed carefully and so far they have lasted more than fifteen years.

1 Pastry scraper; also used to cut
   through doughs in the making
2 Pastry spatulas
3 Plain
4 Offset
5 Pastry bag fitted with nozzle
6 Pastry cutters for puff pastry and
   biscuits
7 Charlotte mold
8 Bavarian cream mold
9 Soufflé mold

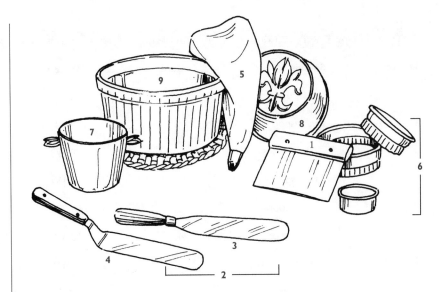

- Four pastry brushes 1 inch wide, made of natural bristles (keep two for pastry making and two for brushing meats)
- One wire pastry cutter, but with the food processor and your capable hands, you may not even need one (optional)
- One pastry scraper with a wooden holder to transfer doughs from the countertop or work board into a bowl
- One candy thermometer
- A 4-cup Charlotte mold
- Diverse molds of your choice for Bavarian creams, mousses, or other molded desserts
- One each 3-cup and 6-cup soufflé mold (see the section on soufflés on page 173)
- Long wooden- or plastic-handled pastry spatulas for icing cakes or transferring them to platters
- One each 8- and 9-inch pie plates, the best are made of porcelain; one each 8-, 9-, and 10-inch cake pans, the best are made of heavy aluminum or a nonstick material
- Cookie sheets; the best are made of heavy unbendable black steel
- One each large and small jelly-roll pan made of heavy aluminum. Investigate the professional so-called half sheet pans; they are heavy, fit in the smallest home ovens, and last a lifetime.

The All-Important Knives

You need very few knives; if you decide on owning more, that's great, but the four essential knives are:

- A 9- to 10-inch chef's knife for chopping vegetables

- A 2½- to 3-inch blade paring knife for paring and boning. While professional hands with long practice can bone with those menacing-looking boning knives, be content at home to use a very sharp paring knife; it is much safer.
- A slicing knife with a 12- to 14-inch blade for slicing meats, cooked or uncooked (for cutting uncooked meats, please read the section on sanitation on page 19)

The old-fashioned carbon steel blades used to stay much sharper a longer time than the modern stainless ones. The best stainless blades are made in Germany, so investigate German knives, and make sure that you use your knives only on cutting boards to protect their fine edges.

Wash and dry knives carefully and put them out of the reach of curious little hands, either on a magnetic board affixed way up on a wall out of their reach, or inserted in a knife carrier to be put away in a drawer or cupboard inaccessible to children. Knife carriers come in all sizes and materials, so your choice is wide.

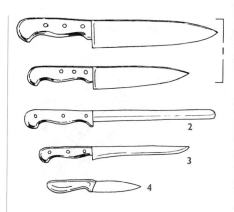

1 **Chef's knives**

2 **Slicer**

3 **Bendable-blade fileting knife used for flatfish; also called filets de soles**

4 **Parer**

How to Use Knives

Take hold of the handle of the knife in your working hand (the right hand if you are right-handed or the left if you are left-handed); the tip of your thumb should rest on the right-hand corner of the blade where it joins with the handle. *Resist the impulse to extend your index finger onto the blade*; it may look chic, but it is unsafe.

TO SLICE VEGETABLES, such as carrots and onions, first cut a slice from any round vegetable, so it can lie flat on the cutting board without wobbling; cut from the back of the blade, as close as possible to the handle of the knife, using a guillotine motion; as the blade slices, its tip should never leave the surface of the board. Your left hand rests on the vegetable, all fingers together and rounded; the blade of the knife comes and meets your rounded fingers before cutting; you determine the thickness of the slice

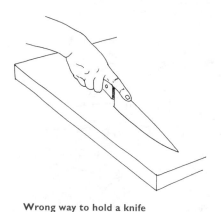

Wrong way to hold a knife

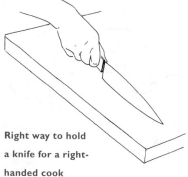

Right way to hold a knife for a right-handed cook

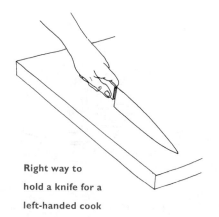

Right way to hold a knife for a left-handed cook

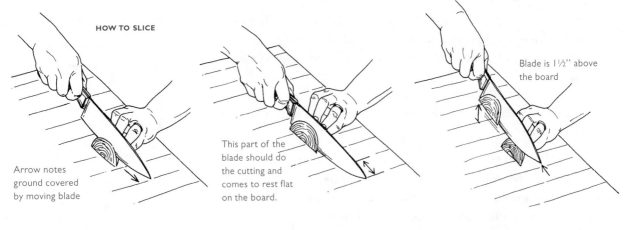

HOW TO SLICE

Arrow notes
ground covered
by moving blade

This part of the
blade should do
the cutting and
comes to rest flat
on the board.

Blade is 1½" above
the board

Beginning of downstroke (note positioning of the hands)   **Completion of downstroke**   **Upstroke**

by putting your middle finger either ¹⁄₁₆, ⅛, or ¼ inch away from the blade and moving down along the vegetable.

TO DICE VEGETABLES, such as onions and shallots, cut each onion or shallot in half. Put each half flat side down on the chopping board with the root end to the left or right of your working hand, depending on whether you are right- or left-handed. Cut ⅛- to ¼-inch-thick slices parallel to the board, not cutting through the root end to keep the slices together.

Next, cut ⅛- to ¼-inch-thick slices at a right angle to the board, with the point of the knife pointing toward the root end, but again, do not cut through the root. Now slice across and you will obtain a diced shallot or onion.

TO CUT VEGETABLES INTO JULIENNE STRIPS (this applies to all root vegetables), cut the vegetables into slices of the desired thickness, then into small sticks. For a fine julienne, cut the sticks ⅛ inch wide, for a large julienne, cut sticks ⅙ to ¼ inch wide.

TO CUT VEGETABLES INTO SALPICON, MIREPOIX, OR BRUNOISE, using the same motion as for slicing, cut a small bundle of julienne pieces

HOW TO DICE

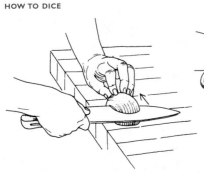

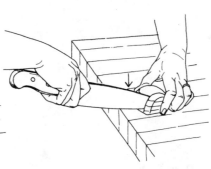

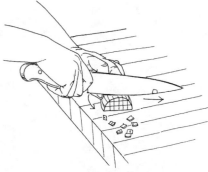

Making cut parallel to the board   **Making cut at right angle to the board**   **Slicing across to make the dice**

into small cubes. Cubes ⅓ inch are called a salpicon, cubes ¼ to ⅙ inch are called a mirepoix, and cubes ⅛ inch are called a brunoise. These diverse cuts are used in sauce making, stews, and pasta garnishes.

TO CUT LETTUCE OR OTHER LEAFY VEGETABLES INTO CHIF-FONNADE, devein the leaves, then stack them on top of one another and roll them into cigars no thicker than 1 inch in diameter. Slice the cigars crosswise at ⅛- to ⅙-inch intervals. The long, curly strips obtained are the chiffonnade (from the French *chiffonner* meaning to crumple).

TO MINCE OR CHOP INTO VERY SMALL PIECES (this technique applies to herbs, mushrooms, nuts, hard cheeses, and chocolate since the knife in many cases does a more even job than the food processor), hold the knife handle with your working hand in the way instructed on page 15. With your second hand, apply pressure to the back of the blade tip, using the "mounds" separating your fingers from the palm of your hand and *leaving the fingers extended straight ahead* (if you hold the tip of the blade between the tips of your fingers, you can eventually cut yourself). Lift the blade with your working hand and press down in rapid chopping motion, pressing firmly with both hands to reduce the food to very small particles.

Pay particular attention to the fact that the part of the blade that should be chopping is that closest to the handle, which, again, works by the principle of the guillotine, and gives the best results with the greatest speed. Avoid chopping with your blade moving in a fanlike motion or you will chop irregularly. Center the material to be chopped at the center of the chopping board on a width of 2 to 3 inches and chop forward, moving toward the opposite side of the board. Bring the coarser particles back toward the front of the blade and repeat. Stop chopping when the chopped particles have reached the size you desire and appear even.

Do not chop herbs until they are liquefied; they are ready when the board starts turning light green from their juices.

Rolled-up lettuce leaf being cut into chiffonnade

Other Kitchen Necessities

- Kitchen string to tie meat, preferably thin rather than thick, but you may have to take what you find. If you cannot find thin string, simply unwind several ply from a thicker string.
- So-called parchment paper
- Cheesecloth
- Kitchen towels. Although paper towels can be used for almost everything, cloth towels are more economical and environmentally sounder. You will need two dozen of those so-called kitchen towels. Purchase the inexpensive flour sack ones in your supermarket and wash them often to

prevent bacterial development in their fibers. There is nothing more dangerous to the health of a family than dirty kitchen towels; you can wash towels in a detergent called Ecover, the formula of which is ecologically sound.

The Refrigerator and Freezer

A refrigerator is by now taken for granted and a freezer is almost as familiar a piece of equipment and an important aid to economy in the modern kitchen. I do not agree with the general statement that "frozen foods are dead foods." Some foods should never be frozen (cheeses, oysters, shellfish of diverse types), but frozen and carefully defrosted meats are perfectly fine. As a help to your budget, buy whole chickens when they are on sale and cut them up yourself (see page 726). If you are using only the breasts for cutlets, freeze the remainder. Buy large joints of meat in the same way; the bones and scraps can be made into almost cost-free stock or broth. With the freezer to help, you can use every scrap.

Have both a primary veal stock and a secondary stock (see pages 219 and 220) bone and scrap bag in the freezer and keep accumulating for your stock/broth sessions. In the same way, store leftover vegetables; when blended together with a secondary stock, they will make a much better than average vegetable soup. Stocks and sauces take a long time to prepare, but with the help of the freezer you can prepare large amounts at one time and freeze it in smaller containers holding diverse numbers of portions.

Clarified and compound butters, some meat and fish sauces, as well as completed dishes can be frozen; you will find many examples in the recipes that follow.

Stoves

Either gas or electric stoves can be used. Obviously the more efficient the stove outfitted with more burners, the better. But I do not see any advantage if you do not ever intend to become a professional cook or baker to clutter your home kitchen with one of those large professional gas stoves which heat a small kitchen unreasonably and often make work more uncomfortable than it should be. Very large stoves are for very large kitchens with proper ventilation. A four-burner stove is most adequate for a home kitchen. I ran my first restaurant with home kitchen stoves simply because I could not afford to purchase larger ones; it did not prevent me from having one of the most respected kitchens in the Northeast at the time. As mentioned above regarding pots and pans, you are cooking, the stove is not. When cooking on electric burners, always use heavy pots and pans with a dressed (plated) bottom for even heating of the contents of the pot.

Electric stoves present one problem; it takes time for a burner to heat to the proper temperature and more time again for a burner to cool down to a lower temperature. As a result, if you are preparing a recipe that requires more than one temperature, you will have to have two or three burners pre-set at different temperature levels to be able to switch a pot from one to another. This is important for delicate dishes, especially those prepared with eggs.

Preparation Trays

Recipes can be simple and be prepared in one step, or they can be more involved and require several.

Read the ingredients and the method used for each recipe or step of a recipe, then measure and place the ingredients for each recipe or step on a tray until you are ready to use them.

This method of work corresponds to what is known as *mise en place* (French for setting up) in professional kitchens and is the only efficient way to work. Do not get caught with your chocolate still solid when it needs to be melted or some such silly situation; simply be prepared.

Sanitation and Safety

For one reason or another the word *sanitation* generally frightens a lot of cooks; it should not frighten you at all; rather, you should consider sanitation a routine discipline, which, once acquired, remains with you for life. When you are finished working, wash your counters and boards with soap and water, rinse them well, and wipe them dry with a clean kitchen towel or, better yet, air dry them. If you have worked on meat on a board or counter, do not hesitate after you have rinsed the counter to dry it and rub it with lemon juice which destroys some harmful bacteria.

If your chopping board is dishwasher safe, pass it through the dishwasher to sterilize its surfaces. A board simply rinsed under hot water may look clean, but it is not necessarily sanitary. It becomes so only after being washed in the dishwasher or, if hand washed with soap and water, after being rinsed under hot water and preferably air dried.

Your worst enemy in food preparation is the unavoidable presence of bacteria in whatever you may prepare; bacteria are nothing to be scared of—our immune system is there to keep them at bay—but our immune system needs to be sustained by our understanding that sanitation is not a luxury but an absolute necessity.

There is a rule that cannot ever be broken in a kitchen, that of avoiding *cross contamination*.

Cross contamination happens, for example, when you clean raw vegetables on a board or, even worse, raw meat, then use the same unwashed board to slice bread, cooked meat, or cheese for a sandwich. By doing so, you expose yourself and your family to the presence in the sandwich of all kinds of harmful bacteria. It is your role as a cook to protect family or guests by either sanitizing your board or using another clean and uncontaminated board.

Since this book is not only used by home cooks but by many teaching chefs as a training tool for future professional cooks, I cannot insist enough on the importance of understanding fully the concept of cross contamination, which in professional kitchens can lead to multiple cases of food poisoning and eventual lawsuits in food businesses.

Besides sanitation, one should also pay attention to safety:

- Shoes should be low heeled and offer good support for the feet; I have found nurses' shoes in their feminine and masculine versions to be the most comfortable and easiest to keep clean. *Do not work in bare feet*; a drop of hot fat is painful and dangerous.
- Tight-fitting slacks can soak up hot spilled liquids and loose overblouses catch on fire. A long apron covering you from just below the shoulders to midcalves is the only fitting garb in a kitchen.
- Do use pot holders and mittens and certainly do not try to lift that very heavy pot full of hot food by yourself; call a member of the family or a colleague to help you. In all professional kitchens, even the strongest men work in teams of two when removing their pots of hot food from stoves.

Good Ingredients for Good Dishes

THIS IS A COOKBOOK, ALBEIT A DIFFERENT ONE, AND ALTHOUGH I DO NOT PLAN to write a whole section on nutrition per se, I truly believe that it should contain information on the basic fats that enter all the foods we prepare.

You are an intelligent person, born with the ability to think. Information on the all-important subject of fats and oils will allow you to understand the importance of limiting the consumption of saturated fats.

If you practice *moderation*, you will have the pleasure of continuing to enjoy a dollop of whipped cream on an occasional piece of delicious butter cake or a bit of butter spread on crispy bread without your cholesterol level showing one iota of difference. A good "fat philosophy" consists in having a wedge of butter-made pie or a brownie with ice cream only once a month, for example; you will be surprised to realize how much more your pleasure will be enhanced by their relative rarity in your life. The same will go for a good piece of cheese from Wisconsin or Normandy; one ounce of true Camembert or Brie with a glass of good red wine is heavenly and will become even more so if you enjoy the combination at regular intervals rather than every day. So much for nutritional discussions—I am sure that you have caught the zest of what I am saying and that your doctors will not disagree with these principles; mine never have.

A Simplified Explanation of Fats and Cholesterol

Because it is so important to understand the difference between saturated and unsaturated fats, the next pages will contain as simple an explanation of each as possible. Skip these pages if you know all about saturation or if you find that bit of chemistry difficult to understand right now, but come back to it later, again and again, until it makes sense to you.

But if you are responsible for feeding and nourishing a family or are about to enter one of the food professions, you must read and understand these few pages now and learn to recognize the difference between saturated fats, which could be called the "not-so-good fats," and unsaturated fats, which could be called the "better fats."

Lipids is the name given to a group of organic substances that are fat soluble, in other words nonwater soluble; to this group belong, among other compounds, the solid fats, the liquid oils, and sterols, with which a cook should be well acquainted.

Fats and Oils

All the fats and oils we use for cooking are formed by glycerol (a water-soluble alcohol) and organic acids, the famous "fatty acids."

Here is a very short and condensed explanation of saturation, simplified to the nth degree of simplification; it includes three drawings illustrating and hopefully elucidating the difference between saturated and unsaturated fats.

Molecules of naturally occurring fatty acids contain an even number of atoms of carbon which can vary from four to as many as more than twenty.

When a fatty acid is saturated, each of its carbon atoms is linked to two other atoms of carbon and to two atoms of hydrogen, except at the beginning and at the end of the molecule. The shape of saturated fatty acids is described as linear, meaning that all the molecules of carbon form a continuous line. Look to the left at the formula representing butyric acid, the fatty acid that gives butter its typical flavor and aroma; it has four carbon atoms lined up in a single chain, one after the other.

Saturated fats, which contain a high percentage of saturated fatty acids, are mostly of animal origin, but a few of vegetal origin are also saturated, coconut oil, for example. Saturated fats are solid at room temperature, with each and every one of them showing a different degree of solidity.

When fatty acids are unsaturated, the number of atoms of hydrogen they contain is less; one or several of their atoms of carbon are not each attached to two hydrogen atoms; rather, they are linked to one atom of hydrogen only and to another atom of carbon by a double bond represented in chemical formulas by two parallel lines (looking like an elongated = sign). There are monounsaturated fats and polyunsaturated fats. Unsaturated fatty acids are found in plants and fish.

When a fatty acid is monounsaturated, only one carbon atom in its formula is linked to the next carbon atom by one double bond. Fatty acids in which several of those double bonds exist are called polyunsaturated fatty acids. In all unsaturated fatty acids, the alignment of the molecules of carbon bends slightly out of shape at the point of each double bond; this bending, which some food chemists relate to the shape of a horseshoe, is characteristic of the "cis" form of unsaturated fatty acids. This bend in the shape makes any double bond fragile and it lowers the melting point of the molecule, giving you an "oil," which is liquid instead of being a solid fat and is more susceptible to oxidative damage.

Saturated butyric acid

Immediately below you can see two formulas, each representing the monounsaturated oleic acid. The first is written fully; the other is in chemists' shorthand. Oleic acid has eighteen carbon atoms and lacks two atoms of hydrogen. Notice how the shape of the molecule bends where the two center atoms of carbon are bound to each other by a double bond, showing a slightly bowlike form:

$$\begin{array}{ccccccccccccccccccc}
\mathrm{H} & \mathrm{H} & \mathrm{H} & \mathrm{H} & \mathrm{H} & \mathrm{H} & \mathrm{H} & \mathrm{H} & & \mathrm{H} & \mathrm{H} & \mathrm{H} & \mathrm{H} & \mathrm{H} & \mathrm{H} & \mathrm{H} & & \\
| & | & | & | & | & | & | & | & & | & | & | & | & | & | & | & & \\
\mathrm{H-C-C-C-C-C-C-C-C-C=C-C-C-C-C-C-C-C-C} & & & & & & & & & & & & & & & & & \nearrow^{\mathrm{O}} \\
| & | & | & | & | & | & | & | & | & | & | & | & | & | & | & | & \searrow_{\mathrm{OH}} \\
\mathrm{H} & \mathrm{H} & \mathrm{H} & \mathrm{H} & \mathrm{H} & \mathrm{H} & \mathrm{H} & \mathrm{H} & \mathrm{H} & \mathrm{H} & \mathrm{H} & \mathrm{H} & \mathrm{H} & \mathrm{H} & \mathrm{H} & \mathrm{H} & &
\end{array}$$

Monounsaturated oleic acid—"cis" configuration

A fatty acid is called essential when the body needs it to function properly but cannot make it from any other substance. Essential fatty acids must be found in foods.

Linoleic acid is a polyunsaturated essential fatty acid which lacks four atoms of hydrogen and has two double bonds; when the formula of this fatty acid is fully written, much space is needed for its bow shape is much more accentuated than that of oleic acid. Chemists developed a sort of shorthand to write all these formulas, which you may want to look up in a science book; below you can see the formula for linoleic acid written in shorthand in which each angle represents one carbon and its two attached molecules of hydrogen.

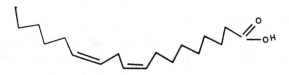

Polyunsaturated linoleic acid—"cis" configuration

Try to relate this to the physical state in which a fat is naturally found and it will make sense. Butter is solid, unless warmed or heated, because it contains a large amount of saturated fatty acids, which have higher melting points than the unsaturated fatty acids. An oil, on the other hand, which contains large amounts of unsaturated fatty acids will remain fluid with more or less viscosity at diverse temperatures, because one or several of its fatty acids are unsaturated and have the bent "cis" configuration, which lowers its melting point.

You will read in the section on margarine that margarine and vegetable shortening are hydrogenated; both are solid but softer than butter, becoming as hard as the saturated cold butter or lard only if kept at a low enough temperature. The term "hydrogenated" as applied to a fat or shortening means that hydrogen has been added under pressure and in the presence of tiny amounts of nickel or platinum to the oil it was made from; these act as catalysts to help some of the hydrogen bond to the molecule. The softness or hardness of a hydrogenated fat is a matter of the ratio between its content of saturated and unsaturated fatty acids. In hydrogenated fats the configuration of the molecules is of the "trans" type in which the hydrogen atoms are attached on opposite sides of the carbon atoms across from each other, as in the drawing below of the shorthand formula of elaidic acid:

Elaidic acid

It is important to know that in the process of assimilation of nutrients, the body recognizes all "trans" fatty acids as saturated fatty acids.

Sterols

Sterols are lipids (another scientific term for any type of fatty substance) with a structure different from that of fats. They are found in plants and animals. Sterols found in plants are called phytosterols. Phytosterols are not easily absorbed by the body but are powerfully important to our nutrition.

CHOLESTEROL AND VITAMIN D

Cholesterol, of which we hear much more than we would like, is a sterol found in all dairy products, in all meats, organ and gland meats such as brains, sweetbreads, kidneys, liver, etc.—and in shellfish and egg yolks. Cholesterol is not found in plants.

The fact that an excessive intake of foods containing cholesterol is dangerous has been challenged by some scientists, but there seems to be agreement on the fact that too many saturated fats in the nutrition are a source of excessive blood cholesterol, which will deposit itself along the arteries and eventually clog them. These clogs are one of the reasons for the numerous cardiovascular incidents known as heart attacks.

It is our liver that makes cholesterol as a precursor to other compounds our body needs. For example, cholesterol is an intrinsic component of cell membranes and is a precursor for vitamin D and other steroids, such as the sex hormones and the bile salts. The body's production of cholesterol is such that a dietary intake of cholesterol is not required under normal circumstances because the body makes all the cholesterol it needs.

Cholesterol is not metabolized at the same rate by any two human beings; some of us are born with a tendency to make more cholesterol than needed, others with a tendency to make less. So it is up to each and every one of us to find out what our personal tendency is and to act accordingly.

As long as you avoid consuming too large amounts of meats, saturated fats, hydrogenated fats, cheese, whole milk, and refined sugars, drink wine and alcohol moderately, exercise, preferably do not smoke, and have a diet containing a lot of cereals, fresh vegetables, and fruits, chances are (barring any genetic predispositions to high cholesterol) that the level of total cholesterol in your blood will remain steady. Also the respective levels of VLDL and LDL (very low-density and low-density lipoproteins, a.k.a. bad cholesterol) and HDL (high-density lipoproteins, or good cholesterol) will have a good chance to remain in balance through a lifetime.

There is a lot more to know about fats and oils than the information I have offered here; if you are interested, please consult the bibliography.

Dairy Products
Milk

Milk, unhomogenized and as it comes from the cow, contains all the elements that give us those other wonderful ingredients: cream, butter, and cheeses. Regular milk contains 3.3 to 4 percent butterfat; semi-skim milk, also called low-fat milk, 2 percent; and milk containing only 1 percent butterfat is known as extra light milk and, although it still contains traces of fat, skim milk is called nonfat milk or skim milk.

Milk is homogenized when it is passed through a very fine nozzle which projects the milk onto a hard surface, so that the globules of butterfat are reduced to a tiny size (1/100th of a millimeter). These tiny particles of butterfat stay in suspension in the milk instead of separating from it and traveling to its surface, where they would agglomerate as cream. Homogenized milk is particularly rich in saturated butterfat and obviously is not as healthy as partially skimmed or completely skimmed milk. On the other hand, desserts prepared with full-fat homogenized milk taste better, so they should be reserved for special occasions.

Creams

After the milk is drawn out of the cow's udder and left to stand under refrigeration, cream, which is a thick emulsion of butterfat globules in milk, comes to its top and can be separated to be commercialized as heavy cream (also sometimes called manufacturing cream) which contains 36 to 42 percent butterfat or whipping cream which contains 30 to 36 percent butterfat;

neither are homogenized, so they can be whipped. Light cream, which contains 18 to 20 percent butterfat, is homogenized and cannot be whipped, as is the case with half-and-half which is a mixture of pasteurized milk and cream containing 10.5 to 18 percent butterfat and is not considered a cream.

It is possible that in very remote areas you may be able to find only ultra-homogenized pasteurized cream which whips with difficulty or sometimes not at all. To use this cream for whipping, scald it first, then deep chill it and it will whip like any other unhomogenized cream, producing only a bit less foam volume.

CRÈME FRAÎCHE AND SOUR CREAM

Much has been said and written over the past twenty years about preparing a crème fraîche at home using methods that resulted in a product that was satisfactory in texture, but certainly not in taste. Finally, in the last five years, several brands of good and natural tasting crèmes fraîches have come to market, properly made of heavy cream safely soured by inoculation with the proper lactic bacteria. These creams are pricey, but again, once in a while, why not, as long as the taste and texture correspond to the cost. Search your area for good crème fraîche; you should be able to find some. California, as always in the lead of good food production in the United States, has a steady supply of it in better grocery stores. Some crème fraîche from California may reach 38 to 40 percent butterfat.

Sour cream is prepared pretty much like crème fraîche, but with light cream instead of heavy cream, so that it contains approximately 14 to 18 percent butterfat only.

Crème fraîche and sour cream must be added to finish sauces after the heat has been turned off, because of their high acid contents, which make them curdle when exposed to high temperatures. It is important to slightly over-reduce sauces which will receive a final addition of any soured cream, since the cream will dilute the sauces further, and it is equally important, when bringing the sauce to its final serving temperature, not to allow it to reboil to avoid the curdling. Recipes usually are explicit and mention "reheat without boiling." Crème fraîche can take a higher temperature than sour cream because of its higher fat content (200°F compared to 185° to 190°F).

WHIPPED CREAM   When you whip cream, you build up a foam as air bubbles get trapped and are surrounded by thin protein walls intermingled with butterfat globules, both acting as foam stabilizers. The more butterfat a cream contains, the more stable the whipped cream will be, and the more you whip, the stronger and firmer the walls become. Eventually, as all beginners in the kitchen know all too well, if you beat too much and too long, the phospholipid membranes which enclose the butterfat will break and the fat molecules will cling to one another to make butter; the protein walls also collapse, and release true buttermilk containing acids and proteins in suspension.

Before you whip cream, keep it chilled in the refrigerator so that the butterfat is quite firm; also, freeze the bowl and the whip or beaters for two hours before whipping. If the butterfat in the cream warms up and becomes fluid, the cream will neither foam nor thicken. If you feel that a cream ready to be whipped is too warm and fluid, do not hesitate to add a few ice chips to it. If the surrounding temperature is above 80°F—and only then—beat the cream in a bowl set in another bowl containing ice. As you whip with your working hand, rotate the bowl containing the cream in the ice bath with your second hand to expose the whole mass of the cream as much as possible to the steadily cooling effect of the ice.

Sweetened and flavored whipped cream. If you add sugar to whipped cream, use granulated or superfine sugar in the last few seconds of whipping, as confectioners' sugar contains cornstarch which can be felt on the tongue and will interfere with the smoothness of the cream.

If you flavor the cream with a liqueur or an extract, add either or both only after the cream has started thickening, using 1 to 2 tablespoons of liqueur per cup of cream, or the flavoring extracts as indicated in the recipes or to your personal taste.

Stabilizing whipped cream. After many tries over many years, I have come to the conclusion that the best stabilizer for satisfactorily textured and natural tasting whipped cream is the addition, per cup of the plain cream, of 2 level measuring teaspoons of nonfat dried milk.

A hand whisk will give more volume to the beaten cream than an electric mixer because it introduces more air more gradually. Follow the instructions of the maker if you wish to use an electric mixer, but the best whipped cream is hand fluffed to this day. For cooks who have to whip large amounts of cream but have no professional extra large mixer at their disposal, a better volume is obtained if the cream is whipped in successive smaller batches, rather than in one large quantity. Beat cream preferably in a chilled glass bowl (Pyrex) or a top-quality stainless steel bowl, *never* in a copper bowl which must be reserved for egg whites.

Whipped cream for decoration. To decorate cakes, fruit cups, or custards, whip cream stiff, that is until it holds a "flag" that stands at a 90-degree angle at the end of the whisk or beater. Place this stiff cream in a pastry bag and pipe rosettes of the needed size on pieces of parchment paper set on a sheet pan, then freeze until solid and cover with plastic wrap. To decorate the desserts, remove the frozen rosettes and put them on the dessert where they will defrost in no time and never weep or oversoften.

Folding whipped cream into desserts. If whipped cream is to be folded into a mousse, Bavarian cream, or frozen soufflé, whip it only to what is called the Chantilly stage, i.e., until it barely mounds and still flows, if quite heavily so, from the whisk or beater.

Butter

PLAIN BUTTER

Plain butter is the result of overwhipping—in technical terms—churning cream; the agitation of churning breaks the phospholipid membranes which keep the fat globules separated in unchurned cream and brings the molecules of butterfat together. Everyone who has overwhipped cream on a hot day has made butter.

FRESH BUTTER

So, from now on, if you want a small batch of fresh butter, whip two cups of cream with an electric mixer on medium-high speed until it turns to butter. Rinse a thin towel in cold water, squeeze it dry, empty the churned cream on it, and close it into a package which you then must rinse under cold water, kneading the butter until the water runs clear; continue kneading a few minutes to extract most of the water. Two cups of cream yield between 6½ and 8 ounces of fresh butter, depending on the butterfat content of the cream. It keeps fresh as long as any other butter if kept well wrapped.

Also, if you overwhip a batch of cream by mistake, do not throw the whole thing away, continue overwhipping and proceed exactly as just mentioned. If the cream was already sweetened and/or seasoned with some sugar or liqueur, keep the butter for morning toast, French toast, and pancakes or to butter a soufflé mold or custard molds, etc.

COMMERCIALLY AVAILABLE BUTTER

Both unsalted (sometimes called sweet) and salted butter are offered for sale. Whether you prefer one or the other is often a function of which butter your mother gave you while growing up.

Besides the question of taste, there is one of freshness. Butter is naturally almost totally unsalted and as a result must be kept very well packaged and at an extremely cold temperature (even frozen) to remain fresh. Any butter that is unsalted is probably fresher than one that is salted, for it makes sense that unsalted butter that has not been sold within the prescribed time limits provided by law would then be salted and sold as salted butter. This is sensible merchandising.

So, if you are a true butter lover, buy only unsalted butter and if you prefer salted butter, salt it yourself by creaming it with as much salt as you like either in a mixer or a food processor. The best butters in America come from Vermont, Wisconsin, and California.

BUTTER MEASUREMENT EQUIVALENTS

AVP Pounds	AVP Ounces	Grams	Cups and Tablespoons
I pound	16 ounces	454	2 cups
¾ pound	12 ounces	339	1½ cups
½ pound	8 ounces	227	I cup
¼ pound	4 ounces	115	½ cup or 8 tablespoons
	3 ounces	85	⅓ cup or 6 tablespoons
	2 ounces	56	¼ cup or 4 tablespoons
	I ounce	28	⅛ cup or 2 tablespoons
	½ ounce	14	I tablespoon

It is essential that you learn as soon as you start cooking the weights of the sticks of butter you buy in a package. Each ½-pound package contains two "sticks" of butter and each 1-pound package four. A stick, however, is not a measurement, so here is a chart that you can follow. When you first start cooking, photocopy it and post it by your stove or on your refrigerator; it will take you only a few days to memorize it. The grams have been rounded to avoid useless decimals.

Fresh, unadulterated butter can look either white if it is made from winter milk when the cows feed on hay in barns or enclosures, or deep yellow when the cows graze freely in the fields or on mountain slopes during the good weather months of the year. The difference of color comes from carotenoid pigments that color yellow and orange many of the summer flowers. Very fresh yellow butter is most likely richer in vitamin A than white butter, unless the latter has been artificially colored with annatto, which unfortunately can happen. Annatto is the usual yellow coloring agent for butter; it is extracted from the pulp surrounding the fruit of the bush *Bixa orellana* which grows in the tropical zones of the Americas.

RANCID BUTTER

Another reason for butter to be deep yellow is oxidation or loss of some of its hydrogen by exposure to the oxygen in the air. I strongly advise you to smell the butter you are buying; if it is old, your nose will tell you immediately as even the most slightly rancid butter can be detected through several layers of paper. Once rancidity has started, it cannot be stopped; indeed it becomes a chain reaction called auto-oxidation. Any of the food chemistry books listed in the bibliography at the end of this book will describe this chemical change in detail.

CLARIFIED BUTTER

Although butter is washed before being packaged, some whey and milk solids, among which is casein, remain in suspension in it. When food is sautéed or panfried in hot butter, the milk solids precipitate to the bottom of the pan and turn brown; often they even burn, so that sautéed food can look pitted with many brown flecks and black dots. Clarifying butter solves this problem. Clarified butter is called *ghee* in India and when made from ripened naturally soured cream in the North African countries, it is given the name of *smen*, and tastes somewhat stronger than *ghee*.

Melt the butter over medium heat, then let it stand for 20 minutes. With a spoon remove the foamy crust of casein from the top. *Do not pour or strain the butter*, even through cheesecloth, but rather spoon the deep yellow liquid butterfat into a jar or glass tub and store. The casein may be used in vegetable dishes or to flavor and enrich bread doughs. The whey remains at the bottom of the pot mixed with a bit of melted butterfat. To avoid losing that small amount of butter, pour the mixture into a custard cup and refrigerate it; when the butter has solidified at the surface of the whey, lift it off in one solid piece, rinse it well under cold water, pat it dry in a paper towel, and add it to the jar of clarified butter. You can then discard the whey, although it can be used instead of milk to make crepe or pancake batters.

Clarified butter is also known as butter grease and when used for panfrying will give you gorgeous, clean-looking food. Clarifying butter is an old-fashioned procedure seldom used now in our butter-lean days. To skip the clarification step, cooks add unmelted butter to hot oil or simply panfry and sauté in plain olive oil or any of the unsaturated oils such as canola, sunflower, or corn oil. Do what pleases you the most. Using all clarified butter once in a while is a feast for the palate and certainly not unreasonable. Clarified butter can be kept frozen in small jars a relatively long time without oxidating since the whey and casein, both subject to bacterial transformation, have been removed. How long it really keeps depends on the efficiency of your freezer, but at least 6 to 8 months.

NOISETTE BUTTER AND BLACK BUTTER

When butter is cooked to the point of turning russet brown, it acquires a slightly hazelnutlike taste from the toasted milk solids and is known as noisette butter, *noisette* being the French word for hazelnut. Black butter is a butter which has cooked beyond the noisette stage and has started to burn. From a nutritional point of view it is not recommended to ingest black butter, although a fish with black butter is acceptable every so often.

To make noisette butter, cook your butter in a saucepan over medium heat and whisk it occasionally to prevent the casein and other proteins from depositing on the bottom of the pan and burning. Continue cooking and whisking until the butter acquires the depth of color you prefer, then strain it through an extremely fine strainer or through several layers of clean cheesecloth to discard the browned casein. The best color for maximum taste is dark russet.

CREAMING BUTTER

Creaming introduces quite a bit of air into butter, causing it to become whiter and lighter; creaming also distributes the whey evenly through the butterfat. When sugar is added to creamed butter, the whey mixes with the sugar to form a syrup which is emulsified into the butterfat. The whey contained in the butter is a helpful sugar-melting agent in the preparation of simple butter-creams.

Creaming is an important process in old-fashioned cakes such as the poundcakes and all the modern butter cakes, in which the recipe always starts with the words "cream the butter." When I was growing up, we creamed butter with a wooden spoon or a small wire whisk; now the electric mixer gives the very best results. When creaming butter, it is not only important to bring it to room temperature before starting, but to make sure it doesn't go to the other extreme, turning too warm and oily. If you have forgotten to bring the butter to room temperature, rinse the mixer bowl in very hot water, cut the butter into tablespoon-size pieces, and cream right away; you should encounter no difficulty.

OTHER FATS AND MARGARINES

As I mentioned earlier, I have made it a habit of using only unsaturated oils and butter. The fact that I prefer a blend of these two natural ingredients does not mean that you should not use other fats or margarine if you so prefer. Tolerance is after all of the essence, but still I suggest that before completely replacing butter with margarine, even margarine made from polyunsaturated vegetable oils, you read for yourself in serious food science books how margarine is manufactured.

You will realize first that it contains as much fat as butter and as a result generates just as many calories. Also, you may want to consult the particularly interesting and thorough book called *Fats That Heal and Fats That Kill*, authored by Udo Erasmus (see bibliography). In this book the author gives an easy to understand explanation of what happens when margarine is made. Like vegetable shortening, margarine results when hydrogen is injected into refined oils at a relatively high temperature, under pressure and in the presence of metal catalysts; this treatment causes the oils to turn solid and opaque. Even if, in the making of margarine, the hydrogenation of the oils is only partial, it is sufficient to allow the "cis" type fatty acids in the oils to acquire some of the characteristics of "trans" type fatty acids, so that many margarines (not all though) have ratios of polyunsaturated to saturated fats that are closer to those of animal fats than vegetable fats. This type of information cannot be derived from a margarine's list of ingredients, but if you want to know the exact amount of those "trans" type fatty acids in any margarine, do not hesitate to question the manufacturer's consumer service on the polyunsaturated/saturated ratio of the ready-to-eat margarine, not of the oils from which it is prepared.

Margarine being a French idea, it is interesting to note that shortly after its invention, the French legislature passed a law restricting its marketing to cube-shaped packages rather than the customary rectangular cakes reserved for butter, so that no one could make a mistake when buying it.

Homemade "Butter Spread" for Fat-Controlled Diets

I POUND
¾ cup unsalted butter
I envelope unflavored gelatin
¼ cup nonfat milk
½ cup low-fat buttermilk
Salt (optional)
¾ cup pure olive oil or polyunsaturated oil of your choice

Cream the butter with an electric mixer. Meanwhile, place the gelatin in a small pot, add the nonfat milk, and soften completely on slow heat until the particles of gelatin are no longer visible on the bottom of the saucepan. Blend in the buttermilk and let stand until the mixture starts to set.

To the creamed butter, slowly add the gelatinized milks. Add salt to your taste if you like salted butter. When all the buttermilk has been absorbed by the butter, it will have the consistency of a stiff buttercream.

Gradually whisk in the oil until it has been totally homogenized. Whip a few seconds on high speed and immediately turn into eight 2-ounce ramekins or custard cups. Refrigerate one container for immediate use and cover the remainder with plastic wrap and aluminum foil, and freeze. Because the buttermilk is perishable, defrost each cup as you need it; once defrosted it will keep fresh for seven days in the refrigerator; keep frozen no more than three months.

The color of this spread is as white as snow. If you object to that, you can add one drop of red food coloring and two drops yellow food coloring while beating it. If you object to food colorings, soften in water and crush lightly ½ teaspoon annatto seeds, then soak the crushed seeds in water until the yellow color leaches out of them. Add as much of this natural coloring to the buttermilk as you need to obtain the yellow tinge you desire. Annatto seeds can be found on market shelves offering Latin American foods or in health food stores.

This butter spread is for people for whom pure butterfat represents a true danger. Spread it on bread and crackers or toss it into steamed or boiled fresh vegetables. Please note that you will not be able to sauté or panfry with it, as the buttermilk solids will burn.

I developed this spread while in France writing a book. I bought a new "butter-reduced" spread for my breakfast, and liked it because it really tasted of butter. I studied its list of ingredients carefully, and realized that it was just another saturated oil margarine-type spread that also contained hydrogenated oil, but I also realized that its butter taste came from the addition of buttermilk.

I developed this entirely natural breakfast spread, with a taste so "civilized" that it almost tastes like very fresh "just made" unpasteurized butter still containing a bit of its natural buttermilk. It is easy to prepare and contains exactly one third each butter, nonfat milk and buttermilk mixture, and mono- or polyunsaturated oil. Salt it as much as you like or sweeten with confectioners' sugar to use on pancakes and waffles.

Oils for Daily Use

I have separated the diverse types of oils available according to the cooking technique for which they are best suited. Opinions vary, so if you feel that the oils you have been using work better for you than those I recommend, by all means continue using the oils you prefer. As you will see, I use unsaturated oils. Most of these vegetable oils undergo a process called winterizing during which they are chilled between 40° and 50°F; this causes the larger crystals of fat to turn solid and precipitate. They are then filtered out so the oils can stand cold temperatures and remain limpid and fluid.

FOR DEEP-FRYING Any of the oils containing a large amount of unsaturated fatty acids will work well. Use either corn, sunflower, canola, cottonseed (though beware of possible pesticide content), grapeseed oil, or pure olive oil.

FOR COOKING AND SALAD DRESSINGS Grapeseed oil, corn, sunflower, canola, or safflower oil will work. You can use the two safflower oils (one is high in oleic acid, the other in linoleic acid), but purchase those two in small bottles only since they oxidate very quickly and easily become rancid.

FOR ANY TECHNIQUE OF COOKERY Olive oil expressed from several types of olives harvested in California or the Mediterranean is appropriate for any kind of cooking.

Olive oil, which is the base of most of the cuisines of the Mediterranean basin, was maligned for years before nutritionists and physicians finally agreed on its immense nutritional value. It is monounsaturated.

Good olive oil is expensive. Most expensive are the extra virgin olive oils from France, Italy, and Spain with an acidity of 0.5 to 0.75 percent and are "cold pressed." In the "cold-pressed" process the olives are crushed between huge, finely chiseled stones to produce a pulp which is subsequently layered on mats of straw or other resistant fine-meshed material. Metal disks are placed between the mats and up to four hundred tons of pressure are applied to extract the oil. These oils are also unfiltered and you can often see a slight deposit of semisolid material at the bottom of the bottle. Taken on an empty stomach every morning for six weeks, one teaspoon of cold-pressed extra virgin olive oil will close stomach ulcers with as much speed as any modern medicine.

Very few of these oils are found in supermarkets; you usually must go to a specialty shop to find them. If you visit olive oil producers in the French, Italian, or Spanish countryside, you may sample these oils and find them extremely fruity and perhaps a little strong for your taste. If this is the case, go to the next less expensive and very affordable grades which are:

- Extra fine virgin olive oil (1 percent acidity or less in the best European oils)

- Fine virgin olive oil (1.5 percent acidity)
- Regular virgin olive oil (no more than 3 percent acidity)

All of these can be found in supermarkets.

Beware, if an olive oil labeled "virgin" is bright emerald green and turns even more toward emerald while heating in the pan; it may have been artificially colored.

The most commonly found olive oil in supermarkets is pure olive oil which contains no colorants and is generally yellow golden. Pure olive oil is as good an all-purpose oil as all the unsaturated oils mentioned above.

At the bottom of the olive oil list is light olive oil which can be pure or a mixture of pure olive oil and any other unsaturated oil.

I cannot encourage you enough to try all kinds of olive oils in order to find out which you like best, for there is no better oil for the good health of both adults and children. Also consult the bibliography for an interesting and detailed book on olive oil.

FOR SPECIAL SALADS OR PASTRY WORK   Heavy oils such as walnut and hazelnut oils are made from English walnuts and hazelnuts respectively. Both are expensive since at this point they are imported, for the most part, from France. They are extremely delicious when very fresh. Be choosy and use your nose before you use walnut or any other nut oil; their rancidity is very aggressive to the sense of smell and you should return any bottle in which the oil has an off smell.

Many a cook lives for the day when American-made oils will be produced regularly in the many states of the United States where those two nuts are available. I have been hoping for Oregon to present us with a good hazelnut oil for years and the southern States with a delicious pecan oil. Use walnut and hazelnut oils sparingly as they are most flavorful; you can even blend them with another neutral-tasting unsaturated oil if you like to stretch them a bit.

A very delicious pistachio oil exists, made with California pistachios. It is of high quality and I have used it with great success in the tempering of chocolate and a few delicious dressings.

Avocado oil is one of California's treats. It comes in small bottles, is still very pricey, and spoils quickly but makes the most wonderful melon and shellfish salads. To prolong the life of avocado oil, wrap the bottle in aluminum foil to protect it from light, even more than the colored glass bottle in which it comes.

THE SMOKING AND FLASHING POINTS OF OILS

It is important to impress on the cook the absolute necessity to stay by and always watch a pan or container in which oil is heating.

The smoke point comes when the oil releases a bluish smoke. If the smoke develops to the point of irritating eyes and throat, acroleine has formed and you must remove the oil from the fire and let it cool rapidly, because you are very close to the flash point, which is reached when the mixture of smoke and air spontaneously ignite. The smoke point is followed by the fire point in which the combustion of the oil is uncontrollable. Heat oil just below the smoking point, where it starts rippling slightly.

Flavored Oils and Their Pitfalls

Flavored oils are not, as may be believed, an invention of our century; they have been produced all over the Mediterranean basin for centuries. One of the most famous and most used of all is the *olio santo* of Tuscany in which basil leaves and fiery hot peppers are steeped in the best virgin olive oil for two weeks.

These paragraphs are meant to be only an introduction to those oils, which will be explained in detail in the chapter on sauces. Flavored oils present a problem which is not understood well enough, and which I mention here and again in the sauce chapter to underline its importance. Oil is dense, poorly aerated, and has very little acidity, so that the famous bacterium *Clostridium botilinum*, if carried by any kind of vegetable matter mixed into the oil, will find a comfortable home there, at the same time contaminating the oil with its extremely dangerous toxin, the *botulin*. Botulin has killed again and again, a fact that must be squarely faced.

When buying already bottled flavored oils, you have little to worry about, since the manufacturers of the oils, very aware of this serious problem, add enough acid to the oil to suppress the problem or prepare the oil in such a manner that only the extracted flavors of the vegetables ever come in contact with the oil. Flavored oils must be kept refrigerated and wrapped in aluminum foil to prevent oxidation after their bottles have been opened.

When you work at home or in a restaurant where you pride yourself in making delicious flavored oils with entirely fresh herbs, spices, or shellfish, the problem is different and very real, and you will have to follow the directions which are given in the sauce chapter on pages 304–8.

Vinegars

The word *vinegar* is the English version of the French and Norman French *vinaigre*, which means *vin aigre*, or sour wine. Vinegars are made not only from wines but from substances as diverse as pure white dilute of alcohol, pure fruit juices fermented from apples, pears, or berries, and from fermented rice or other cereal mashes.

Homemade Vinegar

If you look at the bibliography, you will find the title of a book written by Lawrence J. Digg which will give you all the information you need to make your own vinegar from any source at home. It is not a difficult process at all.

The most elementary home method consists of taking a large jar fitted with two tubes, one going down into the jar to bring air into the developing vinegar and another fitted with a plastic tube which will allow you to siphon the finished vinegar into small bottles for aging. Fill the jar two thirds up with leftovers of good red or white wine (use either red or white) or unpasteurized apple or pear cider as you prefer.

Leaving at least one third of the jar unfilled provides the necessary large supply of air for the bacterium *Mycoderma aceti* to slowly develop and form a skin on the surface of the wine—the famous Mother of vinegar. Store the jar in a dark cupboard where it is not cold but not hot either and wait. In about six months you will have good homemade vinegar. It may take even longer than six months; let it take its time and do not try to rush the process; it will do what it likes to do anyhow, however impatient you may become with it. The best thing to do is forget the jar until the liquid looks clear with a sediment resting at the bottom and, sometimes, but not always, the thin white blanket of the Mother floating on the surface of the vinegar.

Expert Digg explains that the sulfur dioxide added to wines by vintners to stabilize them is not detrimental to the formation of the vinegar Mother, having, as it did, destroyed both useless yeasts during the fermentation of the wine and lactic acid bacteria afterward. It is a good idea, if you start with fresh unpasteurized cider, to mix into it an almost imperceptible pinch of sulfur dioxide once the fermentation has taken place, shaking the jar well to mix the sulfur compound well into the cider. It will help the juice clear quickly. Ask your druggist for a small amount of sodium meta-bisulfite or, if you live in a wine-producing area, go to the specialized wine-making equipment store.

Commercially Prepared Vinegars

While you wait for your own vinegar to shape up, you can always purchase many interesting vinegars in stores. The label will indicate the degree of acetic acid the vinegar contains, which is usually between 4 and 7.5 percent. The best is somewhere in between. If you have only very strong vinegar on hand, use less than you would of a mellower one; some people like to cut it with reduced wine, others with uncooked wine. The reduced wine will taste better since most of the alcohol will have evaporated.

Wine vinegar has approximately 6 percent acetic acid, cider vinegar from 4.5 to 5 percent.

SHERRY VINEGAR

Sherry vinegar has 7.5 percent acetic acid depending on the producer. Unfortunately, there is a dearth of in-depth documentation on this vinegar and how it is prepared. All bottles carry the proud name of sherry producers that make the beautiful sherry wines in and around Jeres de la Frontera in Spain.

All one can do, failing availability of more technical information, is pour a bit of this vinegar in a glass, taste it, and appreciate this wonderful condiment. It is made with the same wines that are refined into sherries. From its beautiful color, as appetizing as that of the best amontillado, and its wonderful aftertaste of flor (see page 99 for an explanation of flor), one can definitely establish the fact that it has been aged in casks in which wines have been aged for many years.

ORIENTAL RICE WINE VINEGAR

Rice wine vinegar is made all over the Orient following many different personal techniques. Basically, rice is soaked for approximately fifteen hours in water until it is well saturated. After then being steamed below the boiling point for eighty minutes, it is cooled and transferred to clean vats, and *Aspergillus oryzae*, a bacteria that transforms the starch in the rice into sugar, is added to it. Instead of aspergillus, an enzyme extract can be used.

The rice is then drained of all its liquid, which will ferment, and undergo an alcoholic fermentation, then turn into a soft vinegar low in acetic acid, about 4 to 4.3 percent. In Japan rice vinegar is called *su*.

BALSAMIC VINEGAR

Aceto balsamico is the Italian name for balsamic vinegar, the soothing mellow vinegar which originated centuries ago in the Emilia Romagna region of northern Italy, and is to this day *the* gastronomical specialty, among many other excellent specialties, of the old city of Modena. Some are also made in the vicinity of the city of Reggio. The shape of the small bottles in which it is sold—a round one for Modena vinegars and a more vertical bulbous one for Reggio vinegars—will allow you to distinguish one from the other. Reggio vinegars are somewhat sweeter than Modena vinegars.

Balsamic vinegar was originally made in homes by women following some of the ancient Latin techniques of blending reduced fresh must of (Trebbiano) grapes (possibly the *mulsum* of the Latins) with very small quantities of strong vinegars and fermenting these blends in *botti della batteria,* a collection of small barrels made of diverse woods, over long periods of time. As each barrel carried its own culture of *Mycoderma aceti,* and contributed its individual wood essence, the flavors obtained varied; the texture of the vinegar was syrupy, coating spoons or glass visibly. The aging went on from ten to one hundred years and no residue at all of alcohol was present in this elixir which was used parsimoniously in desserts and savory dishes.

This type of balsamic vinegar, called *aceto balsamico tradizionale*, still exists and can be purchased at prices which will surprise the neophyte, but which are entirely justified considering the time it takes to age these vinegars and the very small production obtained from each barrel.

There is a second modern and more affordable type of balsamic vinegar which is prepared following the very different technique of blending larger quantities of finished wine vinegar with must and sometimes caramel coloring; such vinegars are sold in many of our supermarkets in larger half pint or pint bottles under diverse labels. These vinegars have variable residues of alcohol and absolutely nothing in common with the traditional vinegars. But one can work quite well with them.

If you feel like experimenting a bit and have a lot of fresh red grapes at your disposal, do as I did five years ago. I blended such a vinegar with fresh red grape juice reduced by 75 percent and sweetened with a little honey. This mixture has been resting peacefully in my cellar in a small French vinegar barrel; I am still waiting patiently to see what the results will be.

The subject of balsamic vinegar is vast and there is much more to know about it. Consult the bibliography for the text available on it, in expert Emilia-Romagna cook Lynne Rossetto Kasper's book *The Splendid Table*. Or request a brochure from Corti Bros. in Sacramento.

Flavored Vinegars

Flavored vinegars offered for sale catch quite handsome prices, which you can avoid by taking any regular vinegar of your choice and adding flavorings to it yourself.

Note that flavored vinegars should be made only with "finished" vinegar that has reached a level of acidity varying from 5.5 to 7.5 percent. There is no danger of the development of botulin in such vinegar, as it is too acid for the bacterium to live in.

There are two methods used to flavor vinegars:

THE QUICK METHOD

Bring the vinegar to a boil and add the finely chopped flavoring(s). The more finely the flavoring agent is chopped, the faster it will lose its flavor to the vinegar. This method works well for any vinegar flavored with dried herbs, garlic, shallots, and garlic and fresh rosemary mixed. Watch that the rosemary does not become too pungent, as a little goes a long way.

THE SLOW METHOD

For flavored vinegars made with fresh herbs, I prefer the slow method of steeping the herbs in the fresh unpasteurized vinegar. By not cooking it, the vinegar retains all of its own natural flavor.

All fruit vinegars are made by this slow method. It is easy to produce any berry or fruit vinegar by first macerating the berries or diced unpeeled fruit in a few tablespoons of the vinegar for two days at room temperature. The mixture must be covered with cheesecloth or the vinegar fly (we know it better by its common name of fruit fly), the little brown *Drosophila*, will find its way into your bowl. Once the maceration is finished, remove ¼ cup vinegar from the bottle you plan to use and add the macerated berries to the bottle. Seal the bottle again and let macerate a good six months.

People who have large homes may prefer to use a barrel to make plain or flavored vinegars, but since most people have limited space at their disposal, bottles are much more "user friendly" and less cumbersome than barrels.

Being European born, I prefer "slow process" flavored vinegars to be prepared with cider or wine, but there is no real reason for any cook to follow my line of thinking; following one's own taste is most important.

Here is a list of the best combinations of fruit, herbs, and vinegars:

- *Steep in red wine vinegar:* raspberries, strawberries, cranberries, blackberries, and blueberries.
- *Steep in white wine or apple cider vinegar:* basil, tarragon, chervil, dill, fresh coriander/cilantro, peaches, nectarines, pears of all types (especially Bartlett and ripe Bosc), rose petals, salmon berries, cloudberries, and all plums.

All steeped vinegars must be gently shaken upside down once a week. After five months of steeping, periodically try a drop or so of the vinegar to test whether the flavor of the steeped material comes through well; if not, continue the steeping until it does and be patient.

Verjus

In two of my books, I gave old-fashioned recipes for *verjus*, the very mellow vinegar made from unripe grapes. *Verjus* was used all through the Middle Ages in cities and in the countryside of France where it was made from sorrel leaves and from the juice of the many plums which never ripen completely in some of the colder regions of France. In regions producing apples and pears it was made from the juices of those unripened fruits.

Grape-made *"vert-jus,"* although mentioned in the medieval book called *Le Ménagier de Paris*, probably did not become popular until the sixteenth century and may have come about as a result of the right given to peasants to pick the unripe grapes from the second growth which were left on the vine by the vineyard owners and never ripened. *Verjus*, which in French simply means "green juice" and translates into the English word verjuice, is made not only with the juice of white grapes but with that of red and black grapes.

Verjus

ABOUT 4 BOTTLES

10 pounds fresh red or white grapes, juicy but still frankly acid (17 to 18 Brix)

½ teaspoon active dry yeast

3 tablespoons warm water

¼ cup liquid honey

Brandy of your choice as needed

This is the method of making verjus I have used since I came to live in the wine country of California; you can make verjus out of any grape, with varieties grown for wine making as well as those raised for fruit consumption. I made an excellent one with Muscat Cannelli grapes.

Stem and crush the grapes well with your hands. Dissolve the yeast in the warm water and stir it into the crushed grapes. Melt the honey in a small, heavy saucepan and let it cool. Stir the honey into the juice and cover the bowl or container with a layer of cheesecloth to keep the fruit flies away. Let the mixture ferment until it finishes bubbling, 6 to 8 days, pushing the cap of grape skins into the juice once a day. Strain the sour juice into a container and add just enough brandy so that the taste of the brandy becomes ever so slightly detectable.

Store at least 2 months in a cool, dark cupboard before using exactly as you would any vinegar. A sediment will slowly fall to the bottom of the container; this is normal—you can transfer the clear *verjus* to small cup-size containers as you like. Keep them well sealed, in a refrigerator or freezer. Do not keep at room temperature.

Verjus can be used to prepare sauces; you will find several of these in the recipes for meats.

Mustard

Mustard is prepared with the ground seeds of the yellow mustard flower which one can see blooming all over the countryside in temperate climates come the first days of spring. Two of the many species of wild mustard, *Sinapis alba* and *S. nigra*, were domesticated to produce respectively white and black mustard seeds. All ancient and medieval mustards were prepared with white mustard, with the exception of the famous Meaux mustard or *moutarde à l'ancienne* which was made of mixed crushed white and black mustard seeds. Black mustard by itself was mostly reserved for medicinal purposes and it is only after the advent of antibiotics that the torture of mustard poultices and plasters for the treatment of chest colds disappeared.

It is interesting to note that the names given mustard in Germany and Italy are respectively *Senf* and *senape*, each a derivative of *Sinapis*. The word *mustard* came from the Medieval French *mostarde* which has become *moutarde* in modern French; all three terms are derived from the Latin *mustum ardens*, which means "burning" (as in hot to the palate) must. The

Romans loved their mustard; a celebrated text written by the poet Columella shows the ado which, for him, could surround the process of preparing mustard. However, Columella was a poet and historians insist that Roman mustard was nothing more than a paste of mustard seed, flour, and vinegar.

The most famous European mustards are the French Dijon which is made with must and white wine, the proportions varying with the manufacturer and remaining a well-kept secret in each house; the peppy English Colman; and the serious German Düsseldorf. The farther north one travels, the more sweet-sour the mustards become, probably to better offset the often salty fare such as sauerkraut and gravlax.

Many cooks like to prepare their own basic mustard blend and passions run high on which is best: Should the paste be made with water alone or with vinegar, wine, or must? Discussions go on forever. I rarely make my own basic mustard, happy with the basic Dijon of my native country. But if you want to make your own mustard, I suggest that you follow a great little technique I found in the Rodale herb book (see the bibliography), in which the mustard is never exposed to heat, either on the stove or in a double boiler. The heat used to thicken the mustard is that of a reduction of wine, juice, and vinegar as it comes from the stove.

Basic Homemade Mustard

ONE 8-OUNCE JAR

1½ cups white grape juice, preferably fresh

1 cup dry white wine

1½ tablespoons white wine vinegar

1 teaspoon salt

¼ teaspoon white pepper from the mill

1 large shallot, extremely finely chopped

⅔ cup mustard powder (Colman or other)

1 tablespoon mono- or polyunsaturated oil of your choice

Liquid honey if desired and to your taste

This makes a strong white Dijon-style mustard.

In a saucepan over medium heat reduce together by two thirds 1 cup of the grape juice, the white wine, vinegar, salt, pepper, and chopped shallots. In another small pot bring the remaining grape juice to a boil and simmer for 5 minutes. Set the latter aside.

Remove the mixture of reduced wine and juice from the heat. Put the mustard powder in a blender; start the blender on mix, and using a fine strainer strain in the wine and juice reduction through the lid opening. Add the oil, then blend a few more seconds. Let stand 1 hour before tasting. Correct the texture and seasoning by adding more of the reserved pure grape juice and more salt if desired. If the mustard is too pungent for you, add honey to your taste.

Store the mustard in a small container; seal it and let it age for about 10 days; keep well refrigerated when not in use. It keeps well for 2 months, but tastes best if consumed within one.

Flavored Mustards

There is so much interest in mustards these days that the number of books on the subject is impressive. Even in France, where for years one saw nothing more than *moutarde de Dijon*, the last twenty years have seen a surge of new products prepared by blending diverse purees of herbs or aromatics and even honey with the basic Dijon. The American taste for sweetness has popularized numerous honey-flavored mustards coming from all over the United States and Hawaii.

When I was growing up in the 1930s, the old-fashioned fancy grocery stores of Paris still sold mustard flour compacted into small slabs, like chocolate, and I remember vividly my great grandmother crying behind her iron-rimmed glasses while she was crushing one of those with some freshly squeezed *verjus* of Cabernet Franc. The purple-red color was unbelievably attractive, tempered as it was with fresh cream and chopped parsley; the condiment was meant to pep up leftover cold chicken.

Mustard was always present on medieval tables because its acid pungency offered a welcome relief from too many salted meats. At the time of the Renaissance, when all the new peppers began arriving from America, many of them, sweet and hot, found their way into the mustards used in princely households. In the mid-seventeenth century, the *précieuses*—the literary Parisian ladies whom Molière chided in his comedies—required their mustard to be flavored with orange flower water, violet water, or even vanilla.

MAKING FLAVORED MUSTARD AT HOME

As I have mentioned in my earlier book *In Madeleine's Kitchen*, it is easy to make flavored mustard out of any basic prepared mustard you like by simply adding to it any puree of cooked or blanched vegetables or vinegared fruit. The section on mustard in that book offers recipes for tarragon mustard, green herb mustard, red pepper mustard, green pepper mustard, as well as raspberry mustard, pear and apple mustard, and Italian plum mustard. Here is a new idea:

Quince Mustard

I TO 2 CUPS

2 medium-size ripe quince, peeled, seeded, and coarsely chopped

⅓ cup firmly packed brown sugar of your choice

¼ cup tarragon Dijon mustard

I tablespoon balsamic vinegar

Cider as needed

Salt as needed

Place the quince and water to cover in a saucepan. Bring to a boil, turn down to a simmer and cook over low heat, uncovered, until the quince is very tender, anywhere from 30 minutes to an hour. Add the sugar and cook until the water has mostly evaporated, mashing the quince as you do so. The mixture will be dark brown. Off the heat, blend the prepared mustard into the hot quince mash; add the balsamic vinegar and cider if needed to get the consistency you want; salt to your taste. The mixture can be blended for complete smoothness.

In the chapter on meat, particularly in the sections on poaching and steaming, you will find a use for this and other fruit mustards and you will see the salt in those mustards replaced by meat glaze.

COOKING WITH MUSTARD

When using prepared mustard or mustard powder in sauces or in dishes, add it to the sauce at the last minute, after the temperature of the preparation has dropped down just below the boiling point by putting the mustard in a small cup, blending a few tablespoons of the sauce into it, then reversing the process and whisking the mustard mixture back into the hot sauce. A sauce containing cream and mustard must never reboil after the addition of mustard to prevent alteration of the texture as the cream is coagulated by the acid in the mustard.

Starches

Pure starches—cornstarch, potato starch, arrowroot, and modified starches from manioc—are extracted from seeds and roots and make possible the rapid thickening of quick sauces, meat gravies, and dessert puddings. Their behavior in the pot can be quite interesting; more details on this subject can be found in the chapter on basic sauces on pages 268–71.

Flours

You can prepare just about any baked product using all-purpose flour. In the earlier edition of this book, I used exclusively all-purpose flour, but since a number of different and very useful flours have become available in markets, it is important to learn how to recognize their different properties and to know what each of them does best and why. Please refer to the following pages to learn about:

- All-purpose flour (page 1014)
- Bread flour (page 1014)
- Cake flour (page 1015)
- Pastry flour (page 1015)

Sugar and Sugar Substitutes

When you cook, you use sugar in its most commonly sold forms:

- Confectioners' sugar, also called 10-X sugar, for icings
- Superfine sugar for dessert sauces, beverages, and fruit preparations
- Granulated sugar for all-purpose use
- Light and dark brown sugars

Unless otherwise mentioned in a recipe, sugar means granulated sugar. Granulated sugar is cooked with water to prepare sugar syrups. For a complete discussion about cooking sugar and sugar syrups, see page 936.

In line with my philosophy of using only natural ingredients, this book does not contain any recipe prepared with chemically produced sugar substitutes; but you will find the recipes for all the familiar classic pastries and dessert compositions prepared with half the amount of sugar originally called for in the classic cookbooks. Many books have been written about cooking with sugar substitutes. They are easy to find.

I have battled long and hard to master my sweet tooth, and it has taken many years to remove confections and desserts from my life. In the beginning, it was really annoying not to indulge in a delicious piece of chocolate or candy the moment I felt the urge to. Since I have discovered that sweets can be even more delicious when they are a rarity in one's life, I truly enjoy and savor sweet treats the very few times that I decide to indulge; slowly I have adopted the same discipline with all confections from cookies to Danish.

Craving sweet things is generally a barometer of your fatigue level. Try taking a walk if your profession leaves you time enough for that, or before going to bed have a cup of yogurt and a cup of herb tea; it relieves the sugar craving with total efficiency and provides the most delightful night's sleep.

And think of what you are doing when, after having the most delicious dinner in a restaurant and enjoying more often than not a nice salad dressed with olive oil, a rich piece of beef followed by the fattest baked potato slathered with sour cream and chives, you go and spoil your excellent cup of coffee with an envelope of sugar substitute; you might as well enjoy the eighteen little calories of a teaspoon of real sugar.

Gelatin

Unless otherwise directed in a recipe, use 1 envelope unflavored gelatin to gel 2 cups of liquid. To add gelatin to a preparation, mix it with 2 table-spoons cold water and melt the mixture in a small pot placed over simmer-ing water.

TO BLEND GELATIN INTO A CUSTARD, add some of the custard to the gelatin, then reverse the process and pour the gelatinized cream back into the bulk of the preparation.

GELATIN IN SHEETS It is now possible to find gelatin in sheets as used in European countries. Many pastry chefs and cooks prefer the sheets which are easier to use since after being first dipped into cold water to be softened, they are simply dripped lightly and stirred into any hot cream or custard. See the section on custard desserts on page 140 for details.

Cocoa Powder and Chocolate

On the threshold of the twenty-first century, America is experiencing the most amazing obsession with chocolate; there is not a restaurant menu that does not offer at least one chocolate dessert, often more.

Cocoa is extracted from the pods of the cocoa tree (*Theobroma cacao*), which grows in many tropical forests. Both cocoa and chocolate were brought to Spain by Cortez after he enjoyed the *tchocohatl* drink that was offered to him by Moctezuma. The Aztec drink may very well have been quite bitter and spicy because of the addition of hot peppers and cinnamon. Spanish cooks quickly added sugar to temper the bitterness of the product, keeping, only occasionally, a shade of cinnamon.

The beans—called nibs—are extracted from large orangy colored pods that contain 50 to 75 nibs, depending on the geographical location of the tree. The beans are removed from the pods and allowed to ferment, which facilitates the removal of their skins. The average composition of a cocoa bean is 3.5 percent water, 51.5 percent cocoa butter (a saturated fat), 10 percent starches, 21 percent cellulose, 5 percent acid, an 8-percent mixture of tannins and sugar, and between 1 and 1.5 percent of a stimulant called theobromine, plus traces of caffeine. This composition makes cocoa and its derivative chocolate true foods, as opposed to coffee which is a stimulating beverage only.

The best cocoa beans come from Venezuela and Costa Rica. Some very good ones are produced in Trinidad, Equador, Brazil, and Africa. The beans are delivered to factories already dried, but must be sorted by size and quality, cleaned of all insects, and scrubbed in special brushing machines. They are then torrefied (roasted like coffee beans), cooled, broken up, and mashed into cocoa paste. Some of these pastes will become cocoa powder, others chocolate.

To obtain cocoa powder one first separates the cocoa butter from the cocoa paste. Alkali is added to reduce the astringency of the product and to allow the cellulose in it to swell. The separation stage can last as long as 24 hours at 212°F. The paste is only partially defatted, then broken down into a lumpy powder. Successive grindings and siftings will take place until the paste has been turned into the very thin powder we find in the box of cocoa to be found in markets.

There are many brands of cocoa powder to choose from; the darker the color, the more flavor the beans will have acquired and the more bitter the cocoa beverage will be. As a matter of interest, try the following brands: Hershey, Nestlé, Van Houten, Droste, and Valrhona. This will give you an idea of the range of taste that can be obtained.

To test these cocoas, prepare a really good cup of each by mixing ¼ cup cold water with 2 tablespoons of the unsweetened cocoa powder, whisking well; put over medium heat and bring just below the boiling point, stirring constantly. Meanwhile, scald ¾ cup milk and, over low heat, blend into the hot cocoa mixture, whisking as much as you can until the mixture foams heavily. Sweeten to taste while whisking.

A cocoa drink is high in fat and gives a lot of good energy. Some defatted cocoas are starting to appear in health food stores and you may want to investigate them. The oversweetened cocoa drinks mass-produced and sold in supermarkets are pleasant on a cold day but never carry the same level of flavor as a drink made from unsweetened cocoa powder.

Chocolate is a mixture of nondefatted cocoa paste with additional cocoa butter and sugar, plus any aromatic element the manufacturer chooses. The mixture is put through successive machines which will mellow the cocoa butter, then work the chocolate paste until its particles are no more than 25 micromillimeters. The final operation, called conching, is done in large machines known as conchers, which keep the paste in motion from many hours to several days, depending on the quality of the beans used and the grade of the chocolate being manufactured. Small amounts of cocoa butter are added all through the conching to maintain the fluidity of the paste and help keep the temperature constant.

The finished chocolate is tempered by slowly lowering the temperature to 113°F to ensure as fine a crystallization of the cocoa butter as possible. The paste is reheated once more by just a few degrees to allow molding.

After the machines pour the chocolate into the molds, the molds are gently agitated to allow any air bubbles to dissipate, then passed through refrigerated chambers at approximately 34°F. This allows the chocolate bars to contract and unmold easily.

Plain dark chocolate contains from 43 to 71 percent cocoa depending on the manufacturer. Milk chocolate receives an addition of either condensed, powdered, or fresh milk, the proportion of milk varying with the regulations proper to the country of manufacture. White chocolate is a mixture of sweetened milk and a large amount of cocoa butter.

The glut of excellent chocolates one can purchase nowadays is a true pleasure; what is not, is the price one must often pay for it. The same philosophical theme comes to mind, though, have chocolate rarely, but have the best.

Among the best and the most expensive are French Valrhona, Belgian Caillebaut and Côte d'Or, Swiss Lindt and Tobler, and American Van Lear and Ghirardelli. All come in many grades and tastes which depend on their content of cocoa, their texture, and last but not least, the origin of the cocoa beans used to prepare them. Less expensive chocolates of good quality at more reasonable prices are prepared by Nestlé, Baker's, and Hershey.

In the recipes given in this book, I indicate the amount of cocoa contained in the chocolate for each given recipe rather than the brand name and leave to my reader the pleasure of investigating which brand they prefer; there is too much fun and pleasure involved in that little bit of research for me to impose my personal taste.

Nuts

Nuts are extremely expensive and if you bake a lot or are a professional cook, it is much more advantageous to purchase them shelled but unpeeled in large quantities. Nuts must be stored in the freezer in sealed plastic containers until needed to prevent oxidation of their oils and consequent rancidity.

Almonds

TO BLANCH AND PEEL ALMONDS, bring a pot of water to a boil, then add the almonds and turn off the heat. Let the nuts steep for 3 minutes. Drain and rinse them under cold water. Squeeze the kernel out of the brown skin between your thumb and index finger. Spread the nuts on a baking sheet or jelly-roll pan and let dry for several hours; to accelerate the drying, you can put the nuts in a preheated 150°F oven for 30 minutes.

TO CHOP ALMONDS, do so with a chef's knife; it does the best and most regular work. See page 17 for instructions.

TO GRIND ALMONDS AND OTHER NUTS, use a food processor, adding 1 to 2 tablespoons sugar to the processor bin; it will prevent the formation of almond paste, as the sugar will absorb the almond oil pressed out of the nuts by the blades. Subtract those 2 tablespoons of sugar from the total amount of sugar needed in the recipe.

TO TOAST ALMONDS AND OTHER NUTS, spread whole blanched almonds evenly in a single layer on a cookie sheet. Roast in a preheated 350°F oven 6 to 10 minutes, shaking the pan at regular intervals. Continue roasting to the desired color, staying in the vicinity of the oven so you can smell the progression of the toasting.

To pan toast nuts, heat them in a heavy pan over medium heat to slowly draw their natural oil out. Shake the pan often until you reach the depth of color you are looking for. Best flavor is indicated by an even beige color.

TO PREPARE ALMOND MILK
- *With milk:* The amount of nuts and milk will vary with the composition of the dessert, but it is generally 1 cup whole blanched almonds per quart of boiling milk. Chop the almonds coarsely in a blender. Pour boiling milk over the almonds and grind until smooth. Turn into a bowl and let steep 2 hours. Squeeze through two layers of damp cheesecloth. Add ⅛ teaspoon pure almond extract per cup of almond milk.
- *With water:* Use 1 cup whole blanched almonds per quart of boiling water following the procedure above. Squeeze the almond milk through two layers of damp cheesecloth. Add ⅛ teaspoon pure almond extract per cup of almond milk, then store it in 1-cup containers and keep frozen until ready to use. The milk keeps 2 to 3 months.

Hazelnuts, Filberts, and Avelines

These all belong to the genus *Corylus* which has eleven different species. In the mountainous regions of Europe one still can find the small wild hazelnuts, which are usually peeled, separated into two cotyledons, and either sautéed in butter to garnish chicken breasts or added plain to salads or desserts.

Cultivated trees in the United States (*Corylus cornuta* and *C. californica*) produce the same nuts called filberts, for St. Philibert, whose day falls on the 22nd of September, which heralds the gathering of hazelnuts. *Avelines (C. avellana)* is one of the many mysterious French names for hazelnuts; it comes from the Latin *abellana*—the nut from Abella—an ancient city in the Italian Campania. Two other French names may also be encountered in cookbooks: *noisettes* and *croquemolles*.

TO SKIN HAZELNUTS, place the shelled hazelnuts on a cookie sheet and bake in a preheated 375°F oven until the skins fall off when you rub the nuts between the hands, about 10 minutes. Again, stay close to the oven and use your nose to evaluate the roasting process. Empty the nuts onto a clean old terry towel and rub the nuts against one another to remove the skins. Pick the cleaned nuts out and shake the towel into the trash bin.

Walnuts, Pecans, and Hickory Nuts

These nuts are all of the same family and will oxidate faster than almonds or hazelnuts. It is best to use them during their year of harvest and to keep them frozen at all times if you want them to stay fresh and not develop extra pungent brown skins.

To minimize the tannin in their skin and concentrate their flavor, toast them lightly in a preheated 350°F oven or cook, stirring them, in a tablespoon or so of unsaturated neutral-tasting oil over medium heat for about 10 minutes.

Rare and Expensive Nuts

Whereas pistachio nuts, which were so expensive when they came from Iran and the Mediterranean only, have become more accessible pricewise since such good ones are produced in California and the Southwest, pignoli nuts or pine nuts (which come from pinecones) and the native Australian macadamia nuts, which are now produced almost as abundantly in Hawaii, remain expensive because of the difficulty of removing them whole from their very hard outer shells.

Cashews are always sold shelled because their shell contains an irritating oil. Some cashews come plain, while others are already toasted and salted or unsalted. Expect to pay a large amount of money for top-quality cashews, but they adorn an oriental chicken dish like no other nut will.

The quantity of Brazil nuts one finds in a can of premium nuts is indicative of their rarity. If you are not familiar with Brazil nuts, hurry and taste at least one, for few of those large and fatty nuts are produced. They are native to the Amazon; with the devastation of the natural forest growth in Amazonia and the few small plantations existing only in Brazil, we can only hope that Brazil nuts are not soon to become an endangered species. Brazil nuts are very fatty and only one generates as many as 150 calories.

Praline Powder

2½ CUPS

2 cups granulated sugar

1 cup water

2 cups chopped nuts of your choice

Praline powder is a delicious caramel and nut powder often used in European and now more and more in American pastry cooking.

To make it, you must first prepare a very sweet nut brittle with the nuts or mix of nuts of your choice. The nuts may be blanched or unblanched, as you prefer. Almonds and hazelnuts are usually blanched and skinned respectively, but walnuts or pecans are not.

Mix the sugar and water together in a heavy saucepan. Let stand 1 hour, stirring occasionally, then slowly bring to a boil and cook to 290°F, measuring the temperature of the syrup with a candy thermometer. Meanwhile, heat the nuts in a slow oven and add them warm to the sugar syrup once it reaches 290°F. Let cook over medium heat to as dark a caramel as you like (see page 154), but not to the point where the caramel is black, otherwise the nuts will burn and the brittle will taste bitter. Pour and spread the mixture onto a lightly buttered cookie sheet or, better yet, a marble slab and let it cool: It will look like a nut brittle.

Break the brittle into pieces and pulverize those in a food processor. Store the praline powder in well-sealed jars in a dry place to prevent caking. The powder tastes best when made fresh for each and every use. You may want to compare the taste of your homemade product to that of praline sold in cans.

Dried Fruit

Traditional dried fruit includes raisins, currants, dates, figs, apricots, prunes, pears, and apples. In the last few years, dried cherries both sweet and sour as well as cranberries and blueberries of all types have joined the collection at our disposal.

If you read the information on a box of currants, you will see "Zante Currants." Zante is an island on the western coast of Greece where those lovely little grapes called Zante grapes—now known as Champagne grapes—probably originated. The dried currants that you purchase are not really currants but dried Zante grapes, because in many states true currants are illegal, for agricultural reasons. The name currant may also be a colloquial deformation of the name of the Greek city of Corinth where small grapes identical to the Zante were ancestrally grown and sun dried. European cookbooks use the expression "Corinth raisins" for dark raisins which are indeed small if not as small as Zante raisins.

All fruit as they dry naturally turn brown through oxidation. Dark raisins may be either white or red grapes that have been dried; they are not treated with sulfur dioxide. Golden raisins (sultanas), however, are treated with sulfur dioxide to prevent them from turning brown. This fact is important and deserves great attention. Many people are allergic to sulfur in its many forms and most commercially offered dried fruit is treated with sulfites to preserve their color. Health food stores offer dried fruit which is unsulfured and consequently brown.

If you want to avoid sulfur, consider purchasing a small dehydrator in which you can dehydrate fruit yourself, rapidly and without losing the bulk of the color. All fruit dehydrates well, including tomatoes, and can be rehydrated in water, wine, fruit juice, or even liqueurs.

To cook dehydrated fruit, see page 933.

Flavorings for Desserts and Dessert Sauces

Citrus fruit extracts may be used to flavor creams or custards, but a finer taste results if strips of fresh citrus peel lifted from the citrus fruit with a potato peeler, so that no trace of the white pith is left on the skin, are added to scalded milk and left to infuse, covered, for about 2 hours; the flavored milk is then used to prepare the cream or custard.

If you candy citrus rind, blanch it first one minute in boiling water to force the large amount of bitter citrus oil out of it. There will be just enough left in the skins for a mild flavor (see page 936).

When freshly grated citrus rind is called for to flavor frozen dessert in which the flavor cannot be extracted in a liquid, do not lift the peel with a potato peeler from the fruit and chop it; rather, use the fine blade of a hand grater to grate the fruit peel over a sheet of parchment baking paper, then simply lift up the paper and scrape the rind and visible oil of citrus into the preparation.

Orange flower water distilled from orange blossoms and rosewater distilled from rose petals, both imported from France, can be purchased in specialty shops; their dark bottles prevent them from denaturing by exposure to light. They are used as are other extracts, by the teaspoon or more if desired.

The flavor of almonds can be given to a mixture by adding ground almonds or almond milk, prepared as described on page 50, or a few drops of bitter almond extract. The extract is used to replace bitter almonds, which are no longer available in our markets because they often contain too much of the toxic hydrocyanic or prussic acid.

Coffee flavor for desserts in our modern days is obtained by dissolving instant coffee granules in a very small amount of water. Even strong prepared coffee is often not strong enough; the old-fashioned method of steeping coffee ground directly in the scalded milk which will be used to prepare a custard remains the very best but takes more time (it should steep for 30 minutes). You can also purchase commercially produced coffee extract; its quality then is of the essence.

Tea flavor in desserts was a favorite in Victorian times and has been neglected ever since—probably due to the birth of the illustrious tea bag. To extract tea as a dessert flavoring, steep 1 tablespoon black tea for 2 minutes in ¼ cup boiling water, then add 1¼ cups boiling whole milk. Let steep another 2 minutes to extract maximum flavor with *no* bitterness.

Vanilla Comes in Two Forms

The original vanilla bean from the Bourbon Islands gives the very best extraction of flavor and taste. Cut the bean in half lengthwise. Scrape the seeds of one half into 2 cups of scalded milk for single vanilla flavor or, if you prefer a double vanilla flavor, use the seeds of both sides of the bean. Let steep 30 minutes to 1 hour before using the milk. You can make vanilla sugar by storing vanilla bean shells in granulated sugar; the longer the two remain together, the better the flavor.

Pure vanilla extract costs twice as much as the artificial extract made with synthetic vanillin. Please use the pure extract. One teaspoon usually is sufficient to flavor 1 cup of milk for a custard or an 8- to 10-inch cake, but you certainly may use more if you prefer. For vanilla ice cream, the low temperature of the product will interfere with the perception of the flavoring, and you will have to use the seeds of two vanilla beans or 2 tablespoons pure extract to flavor a batch of ice cream made with 1 quart of milk or cream.

For a list of liqueurs used in cooking, see pages 116–17. To flavor custards and creams one usually uses 2 tablespoons of liqueur per each cup of liquid in the recipe. When using a liqueur to flavor ice cream, do not use more than ½ cup for each quart of milk or cream used to prepare the ice cream; more alcohol would prevent the ice cream from freezing.

Seasonings: Minerals, Aromatics, Herbs, and Spices Used for Seasoning

Salt

Our best known and universally used seasoning is salt, or sodium chloride, which is a mineral extracted from seawater to obtain the prized sea salt or from mineral salt deposits left within the earth's layers by dehydrated ancient seas; mineral salt is mixed with a number of other elements that are industrially extracted. During this purification process mineral salt loses quite a bit of its flavor.

Try this experiment: Prepare some mashed potatoes, divide them into three equal portions, and flavor one with pure sea salt, one with mineral salt (common table salt), and the last with kosher salt. This will give you an idea of the existing or nonexisting differences in their respective flavors and you can choose the one you prefer.

It is obvious enough to think of adding salt to meats, fish, vegetables, and so on, but salt is also important in desserts. Any sweet dish should contain a small amount of salt to counterbalance and enhance the sweetness of the sugar. Use ⅛ to ¼ teaspoon according to your taste, *never more*. If you bake cakes or pastries with salted butter, omit that small amount of salt called for. Recipes for cooked desserts such as creams, soufflés, and some mousses do not always call for salt because it is considered customary for a cook to remember the "pinch" of salt, so add it yourself.

Another seasoning is monosodium glutamate, or MSG, to which quite a few people thought they were allergic until recent research established that MSG is not accountable for the discomfort known as the Chinese syndrome. MSG should never enter into the composition of authentic traditional western foods; a classic French dish or an Italian risotto from Milan or Venice, for example, should never contain any MSG. On the other hand, authentic Chinese dishes often contain MSG. It is a fact that MSG added in minute quantities (never by as much as a half teaspoon, only by the pinch) to a stock makes it taste fuller. Many bouillon cubes contain MSG and using some of those to very lightly season stocks is a good idea (see details on page 210).

OTHER "SALTS"

Other products and preparations are used as salt. I call them in plain language "body salt" because they are often used as correctors of preparations already salted, but which do not seem to have enough body to fill the mouth with a full enough flavor.

SOY SAUCES In the United States where so many culinary traditions meet, it is not rare to see western foods seasoned with soy sauce. Japanese soy sauce is made by fermenting a mixture of soybean and wheat meal in the presence of enzymes for as long as two years. It can be dark and contain about 18 percent salt or be light and less salty.

In America and China, soy sauces are made by hydrolizing vegetable proteins and adding quite a bit of caramel coloring and preservatives. These sauces are somewhat thicker than the Japanese products.

Again, try both types and see which fits your personal taste better. All keep fresh for years at room temperature.

MEAT GLAZE AND MEAT EXTRACTS Meat glaze can be produced in professional and home kitchens by reducing stocks to a very thick consistency; the glaze boils so long that its shelf life in the refrigerator is several weeks. See page 215 for complete details on how to prepare and keep it.

Meat extracts are prepared industrially, sold in diverse forms, and called bases; they come semiliquid, viscous and thick, semisolid, powdered, or compacted into cubes. See pages 212 and 287 for their proper use in sauces. If you want a great sauce, it is a good idea to prepare your own stock and to use the extracts or bases *only* as correcting agents if the taste of your stock is not strong enough. All these products keep at room temperature because of their high salt content.

MASHED ANCHOVIES   In Mediterranean cuisines, mashed anchovy is very often added to preparations to create a most delicious concentration of taste and literally an explosion of flavor on the palate. This habit is derived from the use in ancient Rome of a condiment made from fermented fish and called *garum* or *liquamen*; if you want to know exactly what *garum* tasted like, try to find on the French Riviera and in the backcountry of Nice a true *pissalat*, which by now has become a rare form of true *liquamen*. Although less rare, Worcestershire sauce with its anchovy and vinegar base could be considered a descendant of the *oxygarum*, the ancient Roman mixture of vinegar and *garum*. See the bibliography for more information.

Any of these taste enhancers should be used with great discretion and added very gradually. Do not trust the measurements given in any recipe since the people who tested the recipe possibly were not using the same product as you, with the very same content of salt and proteins. *Trust your own palate*.

Pepper

All peppercorns, the green ones sold very rarely fresh but more often in brine, and the dried black and white ones, are one and the same peppercorn, produced by a vine called *Piper nigrum*.

The fresh green peppercorns can be found only in the fanciest grocery stores of very large cosmopolitan cities such as Paris, New York, and the Far East. They must be blanched before being used in any dish to prevent excessive heat on the palate.

The same green peppercorns also come in small cans preserved in a fiery brine. This brine is not to be used ever; it is so hot that it ruins any dish, unless you use only tiny, tiny amounts of it. Another problem is that this brine often tastes metallic. The peppercorns can be used as they come out of the can for major heat, or for a more refined and flowery taste, you can place them in a strainer and run cold water over them until the outer skin has disintegrated; you are left with the pale green cores of the peppercorns, which are delicate and flavor seafood beautifully.

The same relation between the whole peppercorn and its core exists when peppercorns have been dried. The whole green peppercorn when dried slowly shrivels to become the whole black peppercorn. And the whole fresh peppercorn left to ripen until red, then stand and ferment, then rubbed of its outer skin, becomes the milder white peppercorn. Both have their virtues. Some people hate white peppercorns, some black peppercorns. Make up your own mind on what you personally prefer by trying each type in a row.

When a text instructs you to use *mignonette*, it means coarsely cracked white pepper.

Pink peppercorns are not true peppercorns of the *Piper* genus; they come from a bush that grows in the Bourbon Islands under the name of pink pimento. I have a large tree growing in my garden where it luxuriates in the

California climate. These peppercorns are sold freeze-dried in small jars. Used in very large quantities they may be toxic.

Szechuan peppercorns are one of the most delightful Chinese seasonings. Another common name for it is fagara. In China the corns are toasted to destroy the dried shell that surrounds its hot black little kernel, thus allowing the heat of the peppercorn to develop more fully.

In western dishes, I like to use Szechuan pepper's dried shells and corns ground together, and add it to dressings, sauces, and vegetable dishes to make use of its lovely flowery flavor and smell.

AROMATIC PEPPER   I like to have three pepper mills: a dark wood one containing black corns, a light-colored wood one containing white corns, and a larger one of any other colored material containing a mixture of black and white peppercorns plus a few berries of allspice, making a blend I call aromatic pepper. By weight, I usually use 45 percent each black and white peppercorns plus 10 percent allspice berries.

CAYENNE PEPPER   is a powder made from dried *Capsicum annuum* var. *annuum* "cayenne," a fingerlike pepper that is extremely hot. Often it is also made from the small pepper harvested from C. *frutescens* var. *tabasco* from which Tabasco sauce is prepared, or even from the Carribean bird pepper dear to the Martinique people and known under the name of *piment oiseau*.

Whichever the origin of the cayenne powder, *please use it with utmost discretion*; it is really hot, as is Tabasco sauce.

There are other peppers and chiles that are becoming more familiar to us through the traditions of Mexican and Central and South American cookery. They will be explained in the recipes in which they are used.

It is a mistake to believe that peppercorns and chiles are only used in savory dishes; they make excellent additions to some desserts.

Aromatics

Aromatics are basic garden vegetables that communicate their individual flavors to broths, stocks, sauces, and other diverse dishes.

The most common aromatics are onions of all kinds, shallots, leeks, and garlic, as well as the popular aromatic Thai, Vietnamese, and Far East seasonings—lemongrass, ginger, and/or galangal.

ONIONS, SHALLOTS, SCALLIONS, LEEKS, AND GARLIC
All of these vegetables belong to the Liliaceae family.

It is important to use the proper onions to obtain a particular flavor in a dish. For example, only the mean "crying" yellow onion should be used to flavor cooked dishes of European origin; the red onion should go mostly in salads or compotes.

The sweeter white, Spanish, Bermuda, and Vidalia onions will taint anything with their sugars. Cook several types of onions separately in a bit of oil or butter and establish which corresponds best to your own personal taste. In ethnic recipes, you can generally trust the author who wrote a recipe to know the ethnic background of the written recipe and use the proper onions; but if you think that your personal taste knows better than the author, use the onions you like—you will obtain a personal dish that will suit your palate, but just know that a degree of authenticity will have been lost in the process. That question of authenticity is academic anyhow, for no food ingredient produced far away from the origin of a food specialty can taste as it does where it originated because the quality of the soil in which a vegetable or fruit is grown is as responsible for its taste as the climate. Onions grown in Texas, California, Virginia, Massachusetts, and Hawaii will never quite adequately replace the onions of the Emilia Romagna or the European Alps. This seems sustained by the fact that most of the shallots sold in this country arrive from Brittany in their original orange bags; it is impossible to obtain the true French taste of certain French specialties without using shallots.

There are gray shallots (*échalotes grises*) which are always used in the lower Loire Valley to prepare the famous *beurre blanc,* and red shallots (*échalotes roses*) and both have some of the mixed characteristics of onions, garlic, and leeks. Shallots of both kinds grow in clusters and each bulb, after being peeled, can be separated into two half bulbs. If a recipe reads "1 shallot," it means both of those half bulbs.

Shallots mold quickly if kept in too moist a refrigerator. Place them in a plastic container with a tight-fitting lid before storing in the vegetable bin of the refrigerator.

Finely chopped scallions can be used if no shallots can be located; you can safely use one and one half times more scallions than the quantity indicated for shallots in any recipe. The white part of 6 to 8 scallions, depending on size, replaces 1 large shallot.

It is essential that you know how to tell the difference between leeks and scallions. Leeks are flat leaved with a visible crease in their leaves; they look as if they had been ironed. Leeks are bigger in diameter than scallions and vary, when ready for harvest, from ¾ to 1 fat inch in diameter. Beware of huge old leeks, the center of which is already a solid ligneous flower stem and unusable if you want to prepare a leek salad. I prefer the smaller more tender leeks. Nothing gives a stock a better flavor than leeks; use their light green part for stocks and keep the white part for a vegetable dish.

Scallions are often called green onions since scallions are onion family plants too young to have formed a bulb; there are scallions from onions, shallots, leeks, and garlic. The scallions offered for sale come mostly from onions and they have round tubular leaves about ⅓ inch in diameter, never more.

According to a legend floating around, scallions would cause a stock to spoil. In areas where leeks do not grow, scallions in large quantity are used to prepare stocks and soups, which is perfectly all right. The taste of a stock will not be the same when prepared with leeks or scallions, but the only thing that can make a stock spoil is poor management of it and poor sanitation practices; see pages 215–16 for details on this important subject.

The odoriferous lily known as garlic is the soul of many ethnic cookeries. The smell of its large bulbs is rather faint; one has to remove the outside membranes, separate a few cloves from the bulb, peel, and chop them for the inimitable pungent smell to invade your kitchen and to permeate the skin of your hand and your hair. Its very recognizable taste—dear to many and hated by a few—gives any food, raw or cooked, an unmistakable flavor. I am a pro-garlic cook who has been successful in slipping more than one garlic clove into the food offered to garlic haters.

Cooked and raw garlic, which for this cook provide two of the glorious tastes in this world, is good only if it is used with discretion. "Tons" of garlic, as the expression goes, is not necessarily good; as for any other vegetable, the taste of garlic varies with the origin and the soil in which it grows. Smell, taste, and dose the garlic used in your dish so that it does not dominate the dish; for example, do not serve garlic with ratatouille instead of ratatouille with garlic.

A few garlic tricks:

- To peel a clove rapidly that will then be chopped, place it under your knife blade and give a good rap on the blade with your other hand; the peel will be easier to separate from the clove. If the cloves are to be used whole, immerse them a minute or two in boiling water and they will peel easily.
- To chop raw garlic into very small particles, add a tiny pinch of salt to it; the salt helps extract the water rapidly from the bulb to make the garlic turn into the finest particles without sticking to the knife blade.
- If you wish to obtain a garlic paste, the best way is to repeatedly flatten the chopped garlic under the tip of your knife blade so that the juice and pulp become evenly mixed into a smooth paste.
- Garlic which is to be consumed raw must be peeled, then chopped on an impeccably clean board as close as possible to the time it is to be consumed.

BEWARE: Garlic, in cloves or chopped, is often sold preserved in oil, a medium which is deprived of oxygen. The very dangerous bacterium *Clostridium botilinum* finds a very hospitable home in jars of oil-preserved garlic where it can secrete a deadly toxin called botulin. If you use garlic preserved in oil, please use it for cooking exclusively, since a simmering of 20 minutes renders the toxin inactive. There is no doubt that when you purchase the jar, the manufacturers of the product have taken every precaution to offer you safe merchandise for sale, but one never knows what happens between the time the product leaves the factory and the time it arrives in your kitchen in a seemingly normal-looking jar. Botulin is undetectable by look or smell.

WHY YOU CRY WHEN CHOPPING ONIONS AND RELATED VEGETABLES

Onions, shallots, and, for some, chives, scallions, and garlic are known for their lachrymogenic capabilities, meaning some of us "cry buckets" when chopping them. This is due to the presence in the vegetables of sulfur compounds which, with the help of enzymes, are released as soon as the vegetables are cut open. The more you cut and chop, the more oils that are released, the more you will cry. People potentially allergic to sulfur compounds will cry more abundantly.

Helpful remedies to this annoying problem include:

- Holding a small piece of bread between your teeth to keep your mouth open will make you breathe mostly through your mouth and retard the arrival of the sulfur-based compound to your nose and lachrymal canal.
- Putting your cutting board as close as you can to the stove without it being unsafe and keeping a burner on while you chop. This way the volatile sulfur-based compound will dissipate faster close to a source of heat.
- If worse comes to worst and you are one of those people who are most sensitive, wear a small pair of goggles—special ones are sold from catalogues.

Lemongrass

I have included lemongrass (*Cymbopogon citratus*) among the aromatics since it is often steeped in broth or cooked in meat stews of Thai and Vietnamese inspiration. Not to be confused with its relative citronella (*Cymbopogon nardus*), it belongs to the sedge family and consists of fibrous spears with a soft and juicy bulb. It can be found in Oriental markets and in many western and better eastern vegetable markets and supermarkets.

Ginger and Galangal

Both of the family of the Zingiberaceae, ginger and galangal are used generously in Far Eastern cuisines. *Zingiber officinale* is plain garden ginger and often called king ginger in Thailand. In China, a freshly sliced piece of fresh ginger root is browned lightly in the oil used to stir-fry vegetables and meats not only to flavor the oil but also because it is supposed to make whatever is stir-fried in it more digestible. Very fresh ginger root has a pink hue; older ginger root, as we usually find it in supermarkets, is used only during the rainy season in the Far East. Grated ginger can be used as a part of a marinade to give flavor to any meat.

Galangal was the name given during the European Middle Ages to the rhizome now respectively called *laos* or *ka* in Thailand and Indonesia. It is a rather large root, basically light yellow with large pink sprouts. In *Le Ménagier de Paris* (published in 1392), it is stated that the purpler the sprouts, the more delicate the meat.

Both ginger and galangal can be turned into spices when the rhizomes are dried and powdered. Please note that unless it is used as a flavoring for dessert creams, powdered ginger cannot quite adequately replace the taste of fresh ginger.

Fresh ginger or galangal clabber milk, so that there is no way to infuse either in milk when preparing ice cream or ginger custard. To remedy this problem, the ginger or galangal must be peeled, diced, and candied in sugar syrup. The sugar syrup is then used to sweeten the custard and the diced pulp can be used as a garnish inside or on top of the ice cream.

Herbs

If you want to experience the taste of all the families of herbs mixed into one great big enjoyable blend, treat yourself to a small sip of Chartreuse verte, a liqueur prepared in the distilleries of the two Carthusian monasteries in Voiron, France, and Saragossa, Spain. A mixture of more than one hundred herbs is macerated in alcohol in huge vats, then distilled into an extract which is used to prepare the Grande Chartreuse liqueur. Each and every one of the herbs listed below, plus a great many others, are contained in this liqueur.

Cooking and flavoring herbs are usually classified in families within which diverse herbs will show similar botanic characteristics as well as somewhat related tastes. If you are interested in herbs, refer to the bibliography in which you will find excellent titles on the subject of herbs. The following information represents a primer of the very basics of a subject so vast that it can offer a lifetime of studies.

THE MINT OR LABIATAE FAMILY

1. All the mints, of course—spearmint and peppermint, as well as the many hybrid mints such as chocolate mint that fill gardens all over the United States.
2. All the rosemaries, from the original wild rosemary that grows in the pine forests of the Mediterranean to the California rosemary which blooms early and blue in the spring. Use the Mediterranean rather than the California rosemary for cooking and baking, and use very small amounts in any meat dish and in breads.

3. Marjoram, which grows wild in the pine forests of the Mediterranean, and the sweet cultivated marjoram. Wild marjoram is also called oregano and grows abundantly on the slopes of the Lycabettus which overlook the city of Athens. Its flowers give its wonderful flavor to the delightful Lycabettus honey. Mexican oregano tastes and smells a bit like the French verbena which grows in the Alpine gardens of western Europe precisely because it belongs not to the mint but rather the verbena family which is neither well known nor used at all in the United States; this is a shame because it makes the most delightful ice cream and lovely dressings for salads and for steamed fillets of fish and chicken cutlets.

4. Savory is available as summer savory or winter savory. Summer savory is best and can be used in meat dishes as well as vegetarian dishes, especially those with a Mediterranean character such as ratatouille. Winter savory is much less attractive.

5. Sage is the American herb—par excellence—very often used to flavor pork roasts and stews as well as turkey stuffings. A little bit goes a long way, so be discreet with the quantity to prevent your dishes from turning all too pungent. There are many different sages, the two best known being the ordinary green-leaved sage and the variegated golden sage.

6. The best thyme grows wild in the pine forests of the Mediterranean, but many different types are grown in American gardens. There is French thyme, lemon thyme, caraway thyme, nutmeg thyme, etc. French thyme is one of the components of a bouquet garni (see page 65). All can flavor stocks, soups, sauces, and stews and enter many a meat marinade as well as the ubiquitous bouquet garni.

To this family belong all the basils. For the people of Provence and the Greeks basil is the herb among all herbs. In India it is a sacred plant. For young ladies of centuries gone by in Provence, basil leaves were chewed as an early form of chewing gum to achieve sweetness of breath.

There are many basils: sweet basil with its large green leaves, the tiny leaved Greco-Roman bush basil used to prepare the true pesto made in the Italian Liguria, the purple-leaved so-called Thai basil, and some ten other varieties which are not commonly used in the United States.

Besides preparing pesto, try any basil in salads, adding a few small leaves with other kinds of greens for a very special perfume and taste, also in soups and stews as well as in sauces. Basil leaves slipped into sandwiches bring a delightful refreshing nuance to everyday lunch favorites, and, infused at length in vinegar, yields the best ever salad dressings.

THE CARROT OR UMBELLIFERAE FAMILY
Wild carrots, which you can see blooming all over the countryside, develop large umbrella-shaped flowers called ombellae. The flowers of the following

herbs also bloom in the shape of umbrellas and produce large amounts of seeds, which can be used fresh or dried in many culinary preparations:

1. Parsley, the most common of our herbs, is available in the curly leaves of curly parsley and with the broad flat leaves of Italian parsley. Use curly parsley for dishes from temperate climates and flatleaf parsley for dishes of Mediterranean origin. Parsley roots are one of the tastiest vegetables existing. Parsley ingested in extremely large doses can be toxic.

2. Called angelica (*Angelica archangelica*) because it blooms every year on the 8th of May, which is St. Michael's Day, this delicious herb should be used only when cultivated, never when collected in the wild for it can be confused easily with the wild water hemlock by which Socrates died; water hemlock looks like Queen Anne's lace but with white, ever so lightly greenish flowers. In small quantities angelica can flavor everything nicely from soups to vegetable dishes, stews, and salads. Its ribs can be candied and used for decorating cakes and desserts. If unavailable, angelica can be replaced by fennel stalks, which, when candied, will taste almost the same.

3. Chervil. Until very recently, chervil was not used in the United States, but in France it is one of the most prized herbs and one of the components of the four *fines herbes*. Its light licorice flavor is delicate, never overpowering, and beloved by all those who prepare fish and shellfish sauces and dishes, salads, etc. Rather pricy, it is now available in many supermarkets.

4. Coriander. Both the fresh leaves and seeds of coriander are used. Also called cilantro or Chinese parsley, coriander is a major component in many Asian and Mexican dishes. The French rediscovered the leaves in the last ten years, but since the Renaissance the Carmelite Order used the seeds to make a cordial known as Eau de Carmes. It does not exist anymore, but is still made in many French country homes. A scented water is made with it nowadays and is simply called *Coriandre*.

5. Cumin seeds crushed or powdered are used in Europe in the making of the *chef*, or leaven of a bread (see page 1049) to promote its slight souring. The ground seeds are used in a number of Indian and Mexican dishes.

6. Fennel grows wild all over the Mediterranean and California; if you decide to collect its seeds, do so in areas close to river edges rather than roads to prevent its contamination by the hydrocarbons of car exhaust. Fennel seeds make a wonderful flavoring for Provençal olive oil bread and lamb roast; the bulbs of cultivated fennel are one of the most enjoyable vegetables.

7. Anise is used widely in Europe, especially in such liqueurs as the Greek ouzo, the Marseilles pastis, and the beloved French pernod which are commonly used in Mediterranean dishes. Aniseeds can be crushed into a powder by those who do not use alcohol and want to replace its flavor in such

dishes. It does marvels for vegetables such as spinach and especially carrots. In some of the confections left behind by the Arab incursions in the southeast of France, a wonderful flavoring mixture of anise and saffron is used.

8. Dill was a common sight in ancient Greco-Roman gardens. The Middle English name dill is derived from the old High German Tilli. The Latin name *Anethum graveolens* is shortened in French into the lovely *aneth*, which is one of the rages of the modern French cuisine. Dill is a wonderful herb which can be used in all kinds of preparations for fish, meats, and vegetables and blends extremely well with tomatoes of all colors. Taken as a tea, it induces sleep.

THE COMPOSITAE, OR DAISY, FAMILY

The delightful tarragon, the *estragon* of the French, the fourth, along with chervil, parsley, and chives, of the four *fines herbes*, is the best-known representative of the composite, or daisy, family. Tarragon received its name from the dragonlike form of its roots. Its propagation is accomplished by dividing those root clumps in the spring and replanting them, since the seeds of the plant are not fertile.

If tarragon were used only for one dish, a roasted tarragon chicken, it would be enough to justify its existence, for the dish is utterly delicious. Tarragon is also steeped in vinegar to make tarragon vinegar and pureed into mustard to flavor it most pleasantly.

It is good to note that tarragon can be either almost tasteless when it is of the Russian kind to almost too pungent when it is of the narrow-leaved French type. Be discreet with French tarragon, it can overpower a dish more effectively than any other herb.

THE FAMILY OF THE LAURACEAE

Bay is indigenous to the Old and New Worlds. In the Old World all kinds of legends are attached to it, such as that of the lovely Daphne who escaped the unwelcome amorous pursuit of Phoebus, by being transformed into a bay tree by her father. Phoebus was the first "laureate" as he swore to wear a crown of bay leaf at all times in reverence to his lost love. "Laureates," when I was still a young girl, were still given laurel crowns when graduating from high school or other undergraduate schools.

The European bay leaf and Turkish bay leaf come from large bushes, while the American bay found in the redwood forests in California are large trees. If a recipe calls for one bay leaf, use one whole Turkish bay leaf, but only half of a California bay leaf to obtain the same flavor.

SPECIAL HERB COMBINATIONS

The three following herb combinations have come to us from the repertory of the classic or provincial French cuisines in which they are still very much in use:

FINES HERBES This typically French *quatuor* of herbs has passed happily into the modern American kitchen and is used in many of the simple dishes of the American cuisine. The four *fines herbes* are chives, tarragon, chervil, and parsley. They are chopped together until the board on which you are working starts to barely turn green.

HERBES DE PROVENCE or Provençal herbs is a mixture of rosemary, thyme, and savory, which grow wild in the Provençal *garrigue* (the natural underforest of Provence) with the four *fines herbes,* plus mint and whatever else catches the fancy of the cook, including lavender flowers. Many combinations of these dried herbs are sold in small clay pots or in colorful little bags made out of Provençal materials. You can make your own combinations to your heart's content. Balance the taste well so no herb dominates the other; often the dried mixtures offered for sale contain too much wild savory and oregano.

BOUQUET GARNI A bouquet garni is a bunch of herbs tied together; usually it includes bay leaf, thyme, fresh or dried, and fresh parsley stems. It flavors all stocks, and some sauces and gravies. All these elements are tied together, to allow easy lifting of the bundle of herbs out of the pot at the end of the cooking.

Please do not enclose your bouquet garni in cheesecloth or tie it to one of the handles of the pot; on the contrary, let it float freely in the pot, so that it releases all of its flavor in whatever preparation or dish you are making.

Note that in cuisines other than French, the bouquet garni often contains a piece of celery. I prefer not to use any celery, for its presence becomes dominant when stocks are reduced to prepare modern meat sauces.

FRESH HERBS VERSUS DRIED
Even if it has become easier to find fresh herbs, they may not be available in all parts of the country all year round and in remote areas one may have to use dried herbs.

When flavoring a large amount of liquid (a sauce, soup, stock), add the dried herbs directly to the liquid. When flavoring a preparation with a low moisture content (a hollandaise-type sauce, for instance), revive the dried herbs first by pouring a small amount of boiling water or broth over them; it will restore their elasticity and help them blend delicately into any fine composition. If one tablespoon of chopped fresh herbs is required in a recipe, you can use one teaspoon of the dried herb instead.

Hothouse fresh herbs look very good, but since nothing can replace true sunshine, do not expect them to be as flavorful as garden-grown herbs. Use a little more of a hothouse herb than you would of a garden-grown one.

Spices

Whereas herbs consist of fresh leaves and stems or crumbled or powdered dried leaves, spices consist of many other parts of the plants—seeds, stems, roots, and berries which have been dried—and can be offered for sale either whole, ground (more or less coarsely), or powdered. Spices can go stale rather quickly. Smell each spice before using it; your nose can tell the tale, and indicate whether or not you need to purchase a fresh jar.

SAFFRON Saffron, the most expensive spice, belongs to the Iridaceae family, which includes irises and crocuses and is a fall-flowering crocus (*Crocus sativus*) with six petals, which can be white, purple, or purplish red.

The spice known as saffron consists of the deep orange-colored stamens of these flowers, and since it takes approximately 35,000 flowers to produce a pound of saffron, the price of that pound of dried threads oscillates between $4,250 and $4,500. You can be assured that you have pure saffron only when you purchase saffron threads and crush them yourself. Powdered saffron does not necessarily contain other bulk material, but at such prices, there is no need to take a chance. The price of the powder is usually indicative of the purity of the product. The smell and taste of saffron is irreplaceable, although quite a few thrifty cooks replace its color by using the gorgeous deep orange petals of safflowers and sometimes turmeric.

It is important to realize that saffron cannot ever be boiled or reduced in sauces or another liquid without losing a large percentage of its lovely fragrance; on the other hand, too much saffron tastes medicinal, so be parsimonious. To develop the flavor, soak the threads or powder in a small amount of warm broth for a few minutes and just before serving add the mixture to the prepared dish. Saffron is traditionally used in the Milanese osso bucco and risotto, in the Marseilles bouillabaisse, and many related fish soups.

COMMON SPICES

We use a number of spices and spice mixtures which smell wonderful and give our food preparations hints of exotism; the following are generally favored and used by many cooks:

ALLSPICE The fragrant allspice powder that you can buy in small spice jars comes from the ground berries of a tree which grows in Jamaica and belongs to the Myrtaceae family. Confusion ensued in many minds when it was given the Latin name of *Pimenta dioica*—in French *piment de la Jamaïque*—by the botanist Linné in 1753, *piment* meaning pepper. Allspice does not belong to the capsicum/pepper family at all. It is one of the ingredients of the famous French *quatre épices* (see page 71). Added to a mixture of black and white pepper it communicates to any dish a faint but delightful flavor. See Aromatic Pepper, page 57.

CARDAMOM *Elettaria cardamomum*, a member of the ginger or Zingiberaceae family, is one of the most expensive and most intriguing of spices. It comes from southeast India and has been adopted not only by the cuisine of Thailand where it is always part of the Muslim curry powder, but it is also used with great enthusiasm by the cuisines of Scandinavia where it enters several pastries and the famous Swedish limpa bread. In India it flavors many a rice pilaf and a large majority of the sweets prepared in this, its place of origin.

Cardamom can be sold as pods, seeds, or powder; the pods are either white, green, or black and contain only a few seeds each which, once ground, would barely fill an eighth of a teaspoon; this explains the high price of a jar of ground cardamom. Keep cardamom away from the light and you will be surprised how long it keeps fresh. Also watch the quantity you use, as a little bit goes a long way.

CINNAMON This member of the so-called sweet spices, called sweet because of their lovely perfumes, is usually available powdered in a jar and in different colors. The reason for the variations is that there are two cinnamons and that often the two find themselves mixed in jars for reasons of economy.

Cinnamomum zeylanicum, a member of the laurel or Lauraceae family, grows on the island of Sri Lanka and along the southwestern coast of India; the inner bark of the tree yields the "bark cinnamon" sold in scroll-like sticks packed in small glass jars. If you want absolutely true cinnamon powder, break those scrolls in as small pieces as possible and grind them in a spice mill or cleaned coffee mill.

Cinnamomum cassia is the bark of another lauraceus tree growing in South China and Vietnam; it is mostly sold powdered but can also be found in bark form which bears no resemblance to the large scrolls of true cinnamon; instead of the pronounced mildness of true cinnamon, cassia has slightly bitter undertones. Try adding some to the most ordinary chocolate ice cream and you will have the most pleasant surprise.

CLOVES *Syzygium aromaticum* is responsible for the wonderful irrespressible smell of your pantry; one clove can fill any closet or armoire with its mysterious smell. I still remember the smell of the *bonnetières* (a special small armoire in which women stored their bonnets, coifs, and *chapeaux* in France) which filled the rooms of my childhood; in each and all of them hung a pomander made of an orange stuck with many, many cloves.

The spice known as clove is the unopened flower bud of a tree which grows in many of the warmer regions of the globe such as Madagascar, India, Malaysia, the Philippines, Sumatra, and Brazil.

Cloves are so strong that a tiny bit will be sufficient to flavor a great deal of prepared food. Some prefer to use only the tip of the bud which is the unopened flower, others use the whole clove, including the stem. It is easier to use whole cloves than the powder. Be extremely discreet with the powder, as it dominates any dish if used in too large amounts. Two cloves steeped in a quart of chicken stock give it a most pleasant flavor.

MACE AND NUTMEG Nutmeg is the fruit of *Myristica fragrans*, a tree sixty feet high which is native to the Moluccas. The fruit is a false fruit, or drupe—like cherries or apricots—the flesh of which is used as food in the islands. Below the flesh is a seed which consists of two parts, the crimson-colored aril, or outer membrane, which is flattened, dried, and slowly roasted to become mace. Freed from the mace, the seeds, still surrounded by their seed coat, are then sun dried and turned twice daily. After the nutmeg has shrunk away from the seed coat, the latter is broken open and the brownish nutmegs are picked, cleaned, and processed for sale.

Good nutmeg is always better when used whole and is grated either with a special small nutmeg grater or simply with a paring knife. If you purchase already grated nutmeg, you may be shortchanged, for often the nutmeg is mixed with mace and its taste is seriously diluted. Both nutmeg and mace contain an essential oil which can bind with the fat of melted butter or of neutral-tasting oils if you want to produce your own oil of nutmeg or oil of mace.

SPICE MIXTURES

The following are the most popular mixes of spices usually found in modern kitchens:

CHINESE 5-SPICE POWDER Chinese 5-spice powder has the distinction of containing star anise, fennel seeds, and Szechuan peppercorns. I truly enjoy it and have used it in many terrines, *pâtés*, and other meat preparations. If there is a choice between two or several powders, be sure always to purchase the most expensive; the powder should be extremely finely ground and pale compared to others offered for sale. Since 5-spice contains cinnamon, it is possible that the slight bitterness in the least expensive powders may be due to the use of cassia instead of true cinnamon. (See Cinnamon, page 67.)

The three Chinese cookbooks I own and that were printed in China do not give a formula for 5-spice powder; it is probable that Chinese chefs both in Mainland China and in Taiwan compose their own powder as French cooks compose their own *quatre épices*.

GARAM MASALA Garam masala comes from north India where it is home-ground from three to eight of the spices known as "warm" spices in the Ayur Veda book of medicine. These are dried chiles, black peppercorns, cinnamon, mace, nutmeg, cloves, coriander seeds, and cumin seeds.

As with Chinese 5-spice powder, garam masala varies with the cook, who will tend to use the spices originating in their own province and location. The spices are ground, then toasted at least 5 minutes to intensify flavor. It is not rare that a masala will also contain a small amount of powdered dried bean or pea (*dal*).

For examples of excellent masalas coming from diverse parts of India see the bibliography.

CURRY POWDERS OR PASTES You may think of curry as the deep mustard yellow powder you can purchase in spice jars, but there are many curries in the eastern countries and each and every cook prides her/himself with a personal blend prepared by hand in a mortar just a few minutes before being used.

The English word *curry* comes from the Tamil word *kari* which means sauce, because curry powders flavor mostly sauces. In India the curries, once powdered, belong to the general category of "masalas" or spice blends which are prepared from ground ingredients indigenous to the diverse regions of the country. Where in India curries always contain a certain amount of sweet spices, in Thailand, only the Muslim curry contains some of those, in addition to a relatively large amount of hot chiles and strong spices. In Thailand the mixture of curry spices is always combined with some liquid to become a paste before being added to a food preparation. If you purchase curry powder, chose one imported from India.

As curry powders contain all kinds of starchy and ligneous material, it is essential to cook them gently in oil or clarified butter to tame the raw taste of some of them. *Never* add curry powder to any dish without precooking it in a fat or making a paste of it with water or broth.

As a matter of interest, turmeric, which is one of the major components of curries, has strong antiseptic powers; a little dusting of it on chicken or other meat cooked outdoors will keep the flies away.

Special beverages must be served with dishes containing hot curries; see the section on Wine and Food Pairing on page 109.

MIDDLE EASTERN SPICES AND RAS EL HANOUT It makes sense that the Arabs, who for centuries caravaned the branches of the Silk Road through China and India all the way to the ports of Syria and Lebanon where they delivered their exotic goods, would use in their own cookery a spice powder reminiscent of the Asian compositions.

As for the Asian powders, the taste varies with the country in which it is used. In Lebanon the powder contains cinnamon, paprika, and hot peppers. During the Ramadan, out of each and every home in the Arab countries escapes the smell of the *taklia*, the mixture of ground coriander seeds and garlic. *Ras el hanout* is used primarily in Morocco and all over the Maghreb (the north coast of Africa). It is a wonderfully fragrant powder without which the traditional couscous has no soul. Depending on which country you are looking at, Morocco, Algeria, or Tunisia, the *ras el hanout* (its name means "the best the shop has to offer") will vary in composition, from twelve spices in Algeria to twenty to twenty-four spices in Morocco. In Tunisia, the spices are fewer but one adds dried pulverized rosebuds.

CHILI POWDER   You already know its very special flavor if you have enjoyed a southwestern chili con carne. The chili powder gives this delicious American dish its dominant flavor.

Chili powder is a mixture of ground spices and dried herbs, a commercial version of which can be found on the spice rack of any supermarket. You will, however, obtain a much brighter flavor if you prepare this composition yourself each and every time you need it and, before adding the mixture to a dish, you slowly cook it in the fat or oil of your choice.

You may use all or only part of the following components of chili powder in the quantities and ratios you prefer:

- Allspice
- Black pepper
- Cayenne pepper
- Ground coriander
- Ground cloves

- Ground cumin
- Dried oregano
- Turmeric
- Ground mustard seeds
- Paprika

Some formulas exist which recommend using garlic powder. I prefer to omit the garlic powder and use fresh garlic in the dish I am cooking. Also I have occasionally added finely chopped dried pasilla peppers because I am very fond of their taste.

For a uniform texture, process all the ingredients in a mortar or spice mill to obtain a well-blended powder.

Please refer to the bibliography to find more information on the diverse compositions described above.

FRENCH SPICED SALT AND FOUR SPICES   Due to the influences of the Romans and, through them, of the ancient Greeks, and the Arab invasions of several parts of what is now the French Territory, spices were used extremely early in France for their flavor-enhancing as well as their antiseptic qualities. Both Taillevent's *Viandier* and *Le Ménagier de Paris* from the fourteenth century often recommend seasoning with *épices à foison*—a wealth of spices. The word *wealth* was not used lightly, for only the wealthy could afford spices; magistrates and lawyers in the French Parliament were offered bags of pepper called *épices* as a gratuity, besides their fees, as late as 1789.

The use of spices in French cookery began to diminish at the time of the Renaissance and steadily declined until 1970. Certain spices and herbs such as fresh ginger and fresh coriander leaves have regained some popularity in the last twenty years. But to this day, the sel épice(spiced salt) and the mixture known as *quatre épices* (so-called four spices) are still used in charcuterie, terrines, and *pâtés*. There is no set formula for either of these preparations; although the base of both mixtures is somewhat identical, it changes with the taste of the person who composes it. Every spice firm in Europe has its own formula and American spice firms have made their own versions in the last two decades (sometimes sold under the name Spice Parisienne).

In the recipes that follow, the balance of salt and pepper follows the recommendations of Auguste Escoffier. The spice mixture is my own since Escoffier mentions only "spices."

Spiced Salt
SEL ÉPICE

½ CUP

⅓ cup fine sea salt

4 teaspoons black or white pepper from the mill to taste

2 teaspoons ground coriander

2 teaspoons ground allspice

I teaspoon ground cinnamon

I teaspoon freshly grated nutmeg

½ teaspoon ground cardamom

⅛ teaspoon ground cloves

Mix the salt and all the spices in a blender and blend on high speed until finely powdered. Put the mixture in small jars that can be tightly sealed.

Four Spices
QUATRE ÉPICES

2 TABLESPOONS

I teaspoon ground cinnamon

2 teaspoons ground allspice

⅛ teaspoon ground cloves

½ teaspoon ground cardamom

I teaspoon freshly grated nutmeg

2 teaspoons ground coriander

2 teaspoons finely crumbled dried tarragon

½ teaspoon finely crumbled dried marjoram

Mix the spices and dried herbs in a blender and blend on high speed until finely powdered. Put the mixture in a small jar that can be tightly sealed.

MUSHROOM POWDER Many different kinds of mushrooms are sold dried, the most common being the porcini (*Boletus edulis*) and the spring morel (*Morschella esculenta*). You can powder these mushrooms in the blender, or any other dried mushroom of your choice, and use the powder to reinforce the taste of soups, stews, gravies, and sauces. Prepare the amount of powder you need as needed, not ahead of time; insects of all sorts are extremely fond of them. If you made too much powder, jar it, wrap the jar in aluminum foil, and freeze so as not to lose such a precious ingredient.

Fresh mushrooms of all sorts will be used in many of the recipes of all chapters. See the chapter on vegetables, pages 355–454, for more details.

OTHER HERBS AND SPICES There is a multitude of other herbs and spices not mentioned in this chapter. Please consult the bibliography for interesting and very complete volumes on these two subjects.

A Cheese Primer for the Cook

There is so much to say about cheese that it seems almost an overwhelming task to try to sort through and organize one's thoughts. This present listing of the major types of cheeses from diverse countries of the world is by necessity incomplete, for if I had to list all those existing nowadays, it would make a chapter of several hundred pages. Though abbreviated, this listing represents fairly accurately what we have at our disposal to enjoy as a cheese course or to introduce as an ingredient in recipes.

I come from a country where cheese is an obsession, a passion about which many serious books have been written, one of the most interesting and personal being the lovely book Pierre Androuet wrote for his daughter. It has been translated into English and I cannot encourage you enough, if you are interested in cheeses, to read this charming and well-documented little volume (see the bibliography).

The first artifacts attesting to the presence of cheese in human life have been dated to the sixth millennium B.C. with the find of vessels with holes, which were identified as cheese strainers and drippers (*faisselles* in French).

It is generally recognized that very early in the history of man, as social organization progressed, women first, then monks after the Christian communities were established, had a major part in the creation of many of the smaller-size cheeses existing in Europe. The large Gruyère-type cheeses—its name derived from the little city on the Swiss plateau around which it originated—are all roughly 700 to 1,000 years old and date from the times when the Cistercian monks helped the peasants of the Alpine countries rebuild the large but neglected meadow domain that the Celts had developed a millennium before on the slopes of the Alps, at altitudes varying from 5,500 to 7,000 feet.

The techniques of making those wheels of cheese weighing a little over a hundred pounds each spread all over the Alpine chain by way of Swiss immigrants. These large cheeses are the result of "man's" work only, probably because of the large weight of each wheel, and were prepared by crews of shepherds cooking within a strictly organized hierarchy.

Having grown up in a Europe where refrigeration in the home was still a rarity and pasteurized milk was sold side by side with unpasteurized milk, I still can remember my great grandmother, grandmother, and mother leaving big batches of milk covered with cheesecloth to curdle in the heat of July and August. It happened naturally in a matter of twenty-four hours; the beautiful fat milk first sealed its liquid part with a thick layer of cream which was carefully lifted off to make butter or cream cookies, then the curd formed overnight. When solid, it was then cut with a knife to help the liquid whey escape, and carefully, with a ladle, the curd was transferred from the bowl in which it had fermented into a colander lined with cheesecloth. Depending on what one wanted to prepare, the curd was allowed to drip a short or long stretch of time.

To produce this type of fresh natural cheese now, I have to use rennet or junket tablets. Junket can be found in good supermarkets and is also excellent for preparing light custards and ice creams. Rennet can be ordered from a drugstore. Its smell can be discouraging as opposed to the odor-free junket. I encourage you, if you are interested in making cheese at home, to purchase either and follow the recipes given inside for the making of such fresh cheeses as cottage cheese. Here is the recipe for preparing your own fresh white cheese to enjoy in the summer with berries or to transform into a few nice hors d'oeuvres such as the famous *Cervelle de Canut* of the French Lyonnais.

Fresh Soft White Cheese

FFR—ABOUT 1 QUART
1 gallon milk of your choice
½ rennet tablet
2 tablespoons water
½ cup buttermilk

Pour the milk into a large stainless steel container and heat it to 75° to 78°F. While it heats, mix the rennet tablet and water together, breaking and crushing the rennet well with a spoon. Stir the rennet mixture into the buttermilk, then pour that mixture, stirring well, into the warm milk. Be sure that it is stirred carefully through the whole mass of the milk or the cheese will be thicker on the surface than it will be at the bottom of its clabbering bowl or pot.

Pour the milk into a glass vessel, cover it with cheesecloth to prevent

This cheese can be prepared with all kinds of milks: cow's, goat's, or ewe's. The best-tasting cow's milk cheese will of course be the full-fat one made with homogenized milk containing 4 percent butterfat, but 2 percent, 1 percent, or nonfat milk can yield a fresh cheese which is the very best source of protein and calcium besides yogurt. Use full-fat or low-fat buttermilk as you prefer.

Goat's milk can now be found in most California supermarkets and in most health food stores in the nation. Ewe's milk is not so easy to come by, but anyone interested in it can inquire at any farm which produces lambs anywhere in the country.

insects from falling into the cheese, and let set unrefrigerated until the curd is solid, 12 to 18 hours; the most practical way is to prepare the cheese overnight. As soon as the curd pulls away from the sides of the fermenting vessel, use a large stainless steel knife to cut square-inch cubes through the curd and release the whey.

Line a colander with a fresh length of cheesecloth rinsed in cold water and squeezed almost dry and ladle the curd into the colander placed over another larger bowl if you want to keep the whey, or in the sink if you plan to discard it. Ladling rather than pouring is important, resulting in a better texture in the finished cheese. Let the curd drip until the cheese forms a ball of soft-textured protein to its center.

To obtain a harder cheese, let the just renetted cheese sit for 1 hour over a large bowl of water maintained at 170°F, stirring occasionally. The cheese proteins will "denature" further and harden as the water they contain is squeezed out of them. The cheese you get will not taste as silky but rather slightly chalky on the tongue.

There are many ways to utilize this cheese. First you can salt it as much as you desire, or sweeten it, or both. Try it with berries and a puree of raspberries, or a cooked compote of apricots or plums; since it is recently clabbered, it is refreshing and sweet-tasting from all the lactose it still contains. If you try to make a cheesecake with it, you will obtain the same peasant-type cake that is made in Alsace and western Germany, slightly dry compared to our American idea of a rich cheesecake, but lighter. The whey can be used to prepare pancakes or crepes.

If you have a cellar or cool basement, you can age this cheese to allow its remaining lactose to turn slowly into lactic acid and its casein to denature all through the process of fermentation. I aged some of this fresh cheese in my cool New Hampshire cellar after shaping the clabber into little patties about 3 inches in diameter and 1 inch thick and salting them lightly all around. Not having at my disposal the little wire cage that all the women in my family had, I lined an old sanitized birdcage with cheesecloth to prevent insect visits, arranged a small cake rack in it as a shelf and put the cheese on it to age for two months. It developed at first a small white crust of local molds which curled up and became thicker as time went on. We enjoyed this cheese thoroughly; it tasted as a pasteurized milk cheese would, nice without too much personality, but certainly it was a pleasure since nothing like it could be purchased in the supermarket.

Another time, I soaked the crust of an unpasteurized Camembert brought back from Europe in 1½ cups water for several days and kept the mixture in the cellar; I then sprayed this water all around the curd cakes to obtain cheeses that tasted slightly of Camembert and ripened somewhat like true Camembert would. That was great fun even if it required some time turning the cheeses twice a day. If you want to give this a try, remember that a goodly amount of moisture in your cellar is important. The same experiment was made with the alpine Reblochon.

The same applies to goat cheeses: They age beautifully provided the moisture of the cellar is constant and relatively high. If you live in a climate where this is not the case, do not hesitate to age the goat cheese in a relatively moist refrigerator; you can provide the moisture yourself by setting a large pan full of water on the bottom shelf, making certain to refill it regularly.

I have been successful in aging a goat cheese to taste a bit like French Valençay by first letting a French Valençay develop a deep blue mold, cutting its crust, soaking it in water for several days, and spraying that water all around the cakes of goat cheese. This was done in California and as a result I had more difficulty due to the dryness of the climate.

The recipe that follows, made with fresh homemade cheese, will offer a very different dip.

Cervelle de Canut

FFR— 8 SERVINGS

2 cups well-dripped fresh white cheese as made on page 73 with 4% milk

¼ cup unsaturated oil of your choice, preferably pure olive oil

1 tablespoon wine vinegar

⅓ cup dry white wine

Salt

Pepper from the mill

1 very large shallot, finely chopped

2 small cloves garlic, mashed

2 tablespoons finely chopped fresh parsley leaves

1 tablespoon each chopped fresh tarragon, chives, and chervil leaves

¼ cup crème fraîche

Break the cheese into pieces in a small bowl and beat it with a spoon until it forms a thick paste. With a whisk mix together the oil, vinegar, wine, and salt and pepper to your taste, then blend it into the cheese, stirring well to rehomogenize the mixture.

Squeeze the shallots in the corner of a towel to extract the hard juices; add the shallots, garlic, herbs, and crème fraîche to the cheese. Beat until the mixture is smooth, then let rest, refrigerated, until ready to serve with whole wheat crackers and a nice bottle of Saint Véran wine.

In the French city of Lyon, the silk-workers—or canuts—of the nineteenth century were in the habit of preparing a white cheese and cream mixture flavored with herbs and wine, which they called in self-mockery Cervelle de Canut, or canut's brain. "Regular" people in Lyon called this preparation claqueret *because it was beaten "as if it would be your wife" (a* claque *being a slap in the face). There is still plenty of this preparation to be found in Lyon nowadays.*

Goat Cheese Timbales

I often have to pair Cabernet wines with different cheese and salad compositions. Here is a nice little timbale of goat cheese which tastes delicious either after a light meal or as an appetizer. The idea of the crouton soaked with mushroom-flavored meat glaze is that of my student Denny Hillin who, at the writing of this recipe, is the chef de cuisine at Restaurant L'Órangerie in the Biltmore Hotel in Phoenix, Arizona.

FFR — 12 SERVINGS

Loaf of French bread

½ cup chopped wild mushrooms of your choice

1½ cups Primary Veal Stock (page 219)

1½ tablespoons unsalted butter

1 cup well-packed fresh homemade goat cheese, or other fresh goat cheese

4 large eggs

1 cup heavy cream

Salt

Pepper from the mill

1 cup Cabernet Sauvignon or Merlot

1 large shallot, finely chopped

1½ teaspoons sweet yellow mustard

6 tablespoons pure olive oil

2 cups frisée leaves, washed and spun dry

Out of the center of slices of the French bread, cut twelve croutons ⅓ inch thick and of the same diameter as the ramekins. Toast them lightly under the broiler. Add the mushrooms to the stock and reduce to ½ cup over high heat; strain and brush the mixture over the croutons. Set the croutons aside.

Preheat the oven to 325°F. Bring a kettle full of water to a boil. Butter twelve 2-ounce porcelain ramekins. Place the cheese, eggs, and cream into a blender and season with salt and pepper. Blend until smooth and pour into the prepared ramekins.

Place the ramekins in a large baking dish so they do not touch. Put the dish on the oven rack and pour the boiling water into the dish so it reaches ¼ inch below the rims of the ramekins. Cover with a sheet of parchment paper. Bake until a skewer inserted two thirds of the way into a ramekin comes out clean, 15 to 20 minutes. Cool to lukewarm in the water bath. In a small saucepan, reduce the wine and shallot over medium heat to 2 tablespoons, then empty the mixture into the blender; add the mustard, salt and pepper, and oil; process into a dressing. Dress the frisée very lightly with it.

To serve, unmold each ramekin onto a crouton and surround with a few sprigs of the dressed frisée.

The Main Types of Cheeses

Such fresh white cheese as made above is known as "fresh cheese" or "white cheese"; in France it is the famous *fromage blanc.*

In all countries such fresh cheeses are consumed fresh or turned into the two categories of cheeses listed below:

SOFT PASTE CHEESES WITH A FLOWERY CRUST

These cheeses are made by simply spraying the entire surface of the white cheese with a solution of *Penicillium candidum* mold. As the lactose turns into lactic acid, mold develops and thrives around the cheese, absorbing moisture from its center, and the cheese "ripens" gradually over a period of one to two months; the ripening is brought on by an increasing softening of the casein in the curd under the influence of the lactic acid.

To this family of cheeses belong:

- Camembert, from Normandy and imitation Camembert from everywhere (United States, Denmark, Germany, etc.)
- All the Bries whether made in Melun or Meaux and Coulommiers, all three located on the large plain of the Brie southeast of Paris, and all the imitations made in Europe and the United States
- Fougeru, also from the Brie plain
- Chaource from the French Champagne
- Farm Munster from the French Alsace (not Dairy Munster)

"Double crème" and "triple crème" cheeses are made by adding enough cream to the milk, before making the cheese, for the final paste to contain, respectively, at least 60 and 75 percent butterfat. To this category belong:

- Explorateur, Brillat Savarin, Boursault, Boursin, and Saint André

All these cheeses were originally sold in small wooden boxes which in more modern times are sometimes replaced by strong cardboard boxes. Depending on the region in which it is made, the same cheese can acquire different tastes because of the different microclimates and traditional local conditions of ripening. The taste will differ considerably when the milk is pasteurized and when it is not. I suggest that if you visit France, you purchase an unpasteurized Camembert or piece of Brie, for it is a totally different experience from the pasteurized cheeses of this name we can purchase in the United States. As they ripen, these cheeses develop rinds which turn from white in a young cheese to reddish and smelling of ammonia in very old cheeses. In between is the stage where the cheese is just right, when, under gentle pressure of the thumb, it feels soft *à coeur*, which means to the heart. The rind of such cheeses should always be removed before eating the cheese or its taste will interfere with the quality of the good wine you have chosen to accompany it. The same rule applies when you use one of them in a dish of pasta or rice.

With these cheeses, serve a nice red wine such as a light Cabernet Sauvignon from California, a good Zinfandel, or light Bordeaux or young Pinot Noir from Europe.

SOFT PASTE CHEESES WITH A WASHED CRUST

These cheeses are made from the same type of paste as the Camemberts, Bries, etc., but their rinds are washed with different liquids such as cider, wine, whey, beer, brandy, or oil to keep them soft and moist, and the rinds must be removed before eating the cheese. Note that the cheese rinds must be moist when you remove the paper in which the cheese is wrapped and that most of these cheeses are still sold in wooden boxes.

Among the soft paste washed cheeses are:

- Pont l'Évêque from French Normandy
- Livarot from French Normandy
- Maroilles from the north of France
- Limburger from Belgium, Holland, Germany, and a few U.S. states
- Dairy Munster from the French Vosges mountains

Resist the temptation not to buy these cheeses because of their powerful smell, for once their smelly crust is removed, they offer the most delicious of tastes, which will vary, of course, with the location and the time each cheese comes into season. With the exception of the Maroilles, Livarot, and Munster which are round, all the others are square or rectangular.

These washed soft pastes definitely have more pronounced flavors than the Camemberts, Bries, and triple crèmes and should be served with round, mature but still fruity wines such as California Cabernet Sauvignon or Merlot and the lighter French Côtes du Rhône.

UNCOOKED PRESSED CHEESES

Halfway between the washed crust cheeses and the uncooked pressed cheeses one can find the Vacherins from Switzerland and France. To enjoy a Vacherin one must first heat it in its opened wooden box in a very slow oven, then remove its top crust, and spoon the melted cheese on slices of bread.

The Raclette, another half-breed, originally came from the Swiss Valais but is now also prepared in France. Weighing 8 to 9 pounds, it presents an inner paste that will flow like that of the Vacherin when exposed to heat, and is generally melted over potatoes.

The pressed uncooked cheeses come mostly from cold or mountainous climates. Their crusts may be washed, as for the Reblochon, or be entirely natural like the Saint Nectaire, or oiled like the English Cheshire and cheddar and the French Morbier. The milk used to make these cheeses is heated just enough to bring on clabbering, but not long enough to result in elasticity of the curd. The set curd is ladled into molds lined with cheesecloth and pressed strongly by hand or with a heavy board fitting exactly into the mold. The smaller ones are often sold wrapped (Reblochon and Beaumont), the larger ones "as is," and the Vacherins in their typical wooden boxes.

The most famous of these cheeses are listed here with their country of origin:

- Asiago from Vicenza, Padua, Verona, and Trento in Italy
- Taleggio from Bergamo in Italy
- Stracchini from Lombardy in Italy
- Fontina from the Valle d'Aosta in Italy
- Reblochon and Beaumont from Savoie in France
- Morbier from the Jura in France
- The many Tommes from Savoie and Dauphiné in France
- Cheshire from Cheshire and cheddar from Somerset in England
- Saint Paulin from several western and northwestern regions of France
- Saint Nectaire and Cantal from the Auvergne in France
- Aged Mimolette from the north of France, and many more

These cheeses require white wines with a bit of freshness and acidity such as the Savoie wines from Entremont and Abymes, Swiss Fendant du Valais, Dézaley, etc., and Pinot Grigio from the Italian South Tirol, but light red wines such as Mondeuse and some Gamays are not to be disdained with them.

COOKED PRESSED CHEESES

In these cheeses clabbering is done as in white cheese and soft paste cheeses, but, after 30 minutes, the curd is stirred for 1½ to 2 hours and heated during the last 45 minutes. As the stirring and heating progress through the large mass of milk, a large curd forms which, through the stirring, separates into millions of small particles no larger than one eighth of an inch.

After the curd has been cooked, a large cheesecloth is stretched under the large mass of curds which is then lifted by two men working together; the curd is left to drain before being molded into very large wooden or steel drums. The cheeses are then pressed heavily to extract all moisture from them and to force the grains of curd to adhere to one another; that last operation will turn the grainy curd into a smooth, homogeneous paste that will harden with age. After several hours under pressure, the wheels of cheese are removed from the press, brined in a salt solution for several days to two weeks, then put to dry on shelves where they will develop a thickish rind, which, as it dries, becomes thicker and harder.

Gruyère-type cheeses fermenting and aging in warmer temperatures at lower altitudes develop a lot of holes as does the Emmenthal; those fermenting and aging at higher altitudes and colder temperatures will have only occasional holes, as is the case with true Gruyère, and some even have no holes at all, but rather horizontal splits called lainures; "lainured" Beauforts are said to taste better than those with a perfect paste.

The Grana-type cheeses from the Po Valley and the Emilia Romagna of Italy will retain an infinitely small graininess, hence their generic name of

Grana; the finest of all the Grana cheeses is the Parmigiano-Reggiano; see the bibliography for more interesting details.

A visit to an aging room of the producer of one of these cheeses in any country is quite an experience, as one can almost hear the large wheels live and release their powerfully nice smell into the atmosphere. Attached to any Gruyère farm or plant is always a large building containing a herd of pigs which is fed solid food mixed with the whey from the cheese production; in the Italian Emilia, these pigs will provide the hams for the famous prosciutto di Parma.

To this category of cheeses belong:

- All true Swiss cheeses: Gruyère from Fribourg, Neuchâtel, and Vaud; Emmenthal from all the central cantons of Switzerland; Appenzell, the namesake of its canton of production; Sbrinz from Schwyz; the French Comté from the Jura mountains; and Beaufort from the Beaufortain mountains of the Savoie.
- All the Alpine-style cheeses, such as Jarlsberg from Norway, and all the Austrian and Finnish Swiss cheeses to be found in all our supermarkets.
- The true great Parmigiano-Reggiano, the very best of all Grana-type cheeses; other Grana cheeses such as Padano from Padua, Lodigiano from Lodi, Lombardo from Lombardy, and Reggiano from Reggio nel Emilia which are Parmigiano-Reggiano wheels weighing less than the required weight or wheels that have developed into a paste neither fine nor regular enough in texture to be classified as true Parmigiano-Reggiano. True Parmigiano is identified by its own name written all over its surface in dots, plus other important information; Grana cheese is recognizable by its large metal seal giving the place of origin of each wheel.
- All the Pecorino cheeses of Italy: Romano from the Lazio, Sardo from Sardinia, and Canestrato from Sicily are made with ewes' milk instead of cows'. These cheeses are also known as hard grating cheeses and are used for the flavoring of pasta and macaroni in their regions of production.

BLUE CHEESES

Blue cheeses are prepared very simply: Besides the rennet which turns it into curd, the milk also receives an addition of blue molds from two different strains, *Penicillium glaucum* and *P. roqueforti*, which is stirred into the milk before clabbering takes place. The fermentation occurs in two stages, a shorter anaerobic one and a second, longer and aerobic one during which the cheese wheels are pierced with steel needles to let oxygen penetrate the cheese and start the development of the blue mold. In blue cheeses the development of the mold progresses from the center toward the outside of the cheese.

Blue cheeses are made with all kinds of milks: cows', ewes', and goats'. Here is a list of those that are most beloved and can be found easily in the United States. The type of milk and mold is indicated for each cheese:

- Roquefort: Born in the fourteenth century in the small town of Roquefort, this cheese is made with ewes' milk and seeded with *Penicillium roqueforti*, which grows naturally in the caves of Roquefort (see bibliography for interesting details and history). A good Roquefort has very little blue visible at its center and at least one inch of perfectly white cheese along its sides, bottom, and top.
- Stilton comes from Stilton in Lancastershire, England. It is an exquisite cheese made with cows' milk and seeded with *Penicillium glaucum* mixed with *P. roqueforti,* the making of which started around 1750. The perfect companion to great ports.
- Gorgonzola: Dating back to the last quarter of the ninth century A.D., this cheese is the probable ancestor of all European large blue cheeses and is made with cows' milk seeded with *Penicillium glaucum;* its real name is Stracchino di Gorgonzola (from the word *stracco,* or tired, referring to the large herds of cows overnighting in the small Lombardy town of Gorgonzola, in the Po Valley, during the summer-fall alpine transits up and down the mountains); see bibliography for details on techniques and history.

  Non-mold-seeded Gorgonzola remains white and is known as Gorgonzola Dolce, Pannarone, or Stracchino.
- The remaining blue cheeses are, from Denmark, Danish Blue, Sago Blue, and Blue Castello; from France, Fourme d'Ambert, Bleu d'Auvergne, and Persilles des Alpes from Savoie and Dauphiné; and from the United States, a variety of American blue cheeses.

OTHER CHEESES MADE WITH
DIFFERENT MILKS OR WHEYS

There are thousands and thousands of cheeses made across the world; some of the most interesting are those made with goats' milk. In the last fifteen years very nice and serious goat cheese farms have developed in the United States which has resulted in the welcome arrival of goat cheese pies, soufflés, salads, and cakes on our restaurant menus. Too many Americans still have not made friends with goat cheese, probably because its taste is much more pronounced than that of cows' milk cheese.

If you want to get used to goat cheese, start slowly by enjoying first fresh white cheeses such as *fromage blanc* (see page 76), our regular cottage cheese which is nothing more than curdled milk recooked and stirred until larger semihard curds form, then regular Camembert and Brie, then fresh goat cheese which is quite sweet, then graduate slowly to goats' milk Camembert and the drier semi-aged goat cheeses. Proceed slowly and you will be surprised to see your dislike melt away.

Some of the best goat cheeses are made in California by Laura Chenel in her dairy on Route 121 from Napa to Sonoma. Try her specialties which are sold across the United States. Laura's was truly pioneer work, and her cheeses compare favorably with some of the French goat cheese production.

Among the favorite French goat cheeses are:

- Sainte Maure from the Loire and Cher valleys
- Valençay from the village of the same name in the Indre
- Chabichou from the farms of the Poitou or Vienne Valley
- Crottins from the region of Sancerre and the neighboring village of Chavignol
- Saint Marcellin-Chèvre from the Isère Valley in the French Dauphinian Alps (beware, there is also a St. Marcellin-Vache made with cows' milk)

It is not rare in Europe for the same type of cheese to be made with ewes' milk in the very early spring, then with goats' milk around Easter, and finally with cows' milk starting in June and for the remainder of the year; this is especially the case with the Banons of Provence which are recognizable by the chestnut leaves in which they are wrapped and the Brousse of the Nice countryside, called also Broccio in Corsica.

Pure ewes' milk cheeses include the blue Roquefort described on page 81 and a number of very well-known cheeses from Greece such as feta and Kasseri, both of which have very pronounced flavors, but are oh so excellent in the typical Greek salad.

A few cheeses are made by the method known as *recuite* in French which corresponds to ricotta in Italian. Some of the whey derived from previous cheese makings is mixed with fresh milk, which is then mixed with rennet and recooked. Slowly the mixture is heated until the "flowers" of curd rise to the surface of the pot, from which they are lifted with a fine meshed strainer-type spoon. You can make your own ricotta this way if you are interested, mixing 3 quarts each of whey from the *fromage blanc* recipe on page 73 with 3 quarts of fresh whole or skim milk. In Savoie such a cheese is prepared in large wheels and is known as Sérac.

PASTA FILATA CHEESES

To this very special category of cheeses belong:

- *Mozzarella di bufala*, made in the Italian Campania with milk from the water buffalo, which is snow-white, soft, and retains the wonderful taste and flavor of fresh milk as long as it is kept in its whey. The presence of water buffalo in southern Italy is attributed by some to the Greeks who themselves acquired the animals from India. Others think the Longobards, a northern Germanic tribe which invaded Italy in A.D. 568, would have brought them from the then marshy Baltic shores. These cheeses are shaped into layer cakes 2½ to 3 inches in diameter or into bite-size miniatures called bocconcini (see page 83).

- The caciocavallo, made in the same region with cows' milk curdled with sheep or goat rennet, which gives it a strong flavor.
- The scamorza of the Abruzzi made from cows' milk, which over the last few decades has come to be called *fior di latte* (flower of the milk). Scamorza is often smoked, its color turning ivory and its texture much harder than it is in the fresh state.

  Provola is another form of the Scamorza that comes from the region of Molise.
- Provolone is made in the Campania from cows' milk and is aged two to six months, thus developing a thin smooth skin and a strong taste. Provolone is imported to the United States in large salami-like loaves, but it can have other shapes in Italy; it is usually sold sliced very thinly for sandwiches or to garnish antipasto plates.

The technique used to prepare these cheeses consists of curdling the milk, and cooking it so the curds become ever so slightly elastic, then removing the curds from the heat in large blocks and letting them cool on a slanted table to allow the whey to drain. When the cheese maker is ready to shape the cheese, it is cut into strips; those strips will be immersed in hot water, which will soften the curd again. Pieces will be torn out of the strips (the Italian verb for tearing is *mazzare* and it gives its name to the cheese) and manipulated into the shape appropriate to each cheese: 2½- to 3-inch balls for mozzarella, 1-inch balls for bocconcini, irregularly shaped brioche for scamorza and caciocavallo. Caciocavallo will be hung to dry and age by a string attached between the smaller upper and the larger lower part of the briochelike cheeses.

If you cannot go to Italy to taste the wonderful true Italian mozzarella, which itself is so rare that it must be eaten fresh, you can find fresh scamorza made at the restaurant Tra Vigne in St. Helena, California, by the expert hands of chef Michael Chiarello. Large dairies make scamorza all over the United States and sell it under the name of mozzarella, but to experience one that is closer in taste and texture to the original you may want to investigate the mozzarella produced by the Mozzarella Company in Dallas, Texas. An infinite number of details surrounds the making and shaping of these cheeses. For more information, see the bibliography.

MARINATED CHEESES

In the Provence it is not rare to find small goats' or ewes' milk cheeses soaking and continuing to ferment in olive oil flavored with herbs.

And all over the cheese-producing countries, there exist not very well-known preparations known as *fromage fort,* or strong cheese, which are made by mixing peeled leftovers of any cheese you may have with any brandy of your choice and letting the whole thing mellow into a homogeneous mass.

Please keep this kind of mixture in the refrigerator, and well covered, and be warned that it is not called strong cheese without reason.

Cooking with Cheese

Cheeses containing large amounts of proteins cannot be exposed to high temperatures or you will see the butterfat melt out of the cheese and come floating to the surface of whatever sauce or gravy you are enriching at the same time the proteins turn stringy, grainy, and elastic and often bond together in large clumps. These changes are due to the protein completely denaturing, hardening further and losing all of its water and fat content. The only solution to this problem is to avoid it. Apply a slow heat progressively, to a cheese melting into a sauce or a cheese melting on a pizza. If you want to avoid a layer of fat flooding the top of your pizza, bake the pizza to set and brown the dough, and add the cheese on top later, so it melts thoroughly without browning excessively.

Do not limit yourself forever to using the sempiternal Grana-type, Gruyère-type, or cheddar-type cheeses in pasta dishes; you can also melt some Camembert, Brie, Munster, or Pont l'Évêque after removing the crust.

In using pasteurized versus unpasteurized cheeses in cooking, you will notice that the pasteurized cheeses are more stable and less liable to break down as the temperature increases; on the other hand, unpasteurized cheeses have so much more flavor that it is well worth being a little more careful when submitting them to heat to obtain a tastier final product. Although unpasteurized cheeses are not made in the United States, many of them are available imported from other countries.

A Wine
Primer
for Cooks

IN THE LAST TWENTY YEARS THE CONSUMPTION AND MAKING OF FINE WINES IN the United States has increased considerably. I am dedicating this small chapter to wine, because, besides being a pleasure to drink, it enters the composition of so many basic dishes of all ethnic backgrounds, that it is important to know what wine is, where it comes from, how it should be tasted, and, especially, how it should be used in cooking.

Making and Perfecting Wine

Wine is made with the juice of many fruits. There is peach wine, wines made from berries of all types, apple wine, which is also called cider, and pear wine, which in some regions of France is more popular than cider; all of these so-called wines can be alcoholic or nonalcoholic. What is most commonly understood as wine, however, is the fermented juice of grapes. As it has just been pressed and/or in fermentation, the juice is called *must*.

The making of wine is very simple in principle: Pick excellent grapes (because the quality of the wine will be directly proportional to that of the grapes), stem, and crush them. Use white grapes and remove the skins quickly if you are making white wine; use red grapes and leave the skins on for a few hours or one full night if you are making rosé wine, or use red or black grapes and leave the skins on for one to two weeks if you are making red wines. (Note that there are some instances when white wines are made with red grapes, the most celebrated case existing in Champagne, see page 102.) Then wait until the fermentation happens, which it does all by itself and naturally. If you "ferment dry," that is, until no sugar is left at all in the finished wine, you will obtain a wine containing the maximum degree of alcohol the particular grapes you crushed can produce for the climate in which they were grown. If you want a certain amount of sugar to remain in the wine, you must stop the fermentation by increasing the dosage of sulfur dioxide, lowering the temperature of the must, and filtering the finished wine through sterile filters; all of these operations will result in such mellow wines as the famous white Zinfandel or white Cabernet in which the alcohol is never more than 10 percent and which so many people with a sweet tooth absolutely love.

How does fermentation work and what, roughly, happens while the grape juice ferments? The fruit sugar, or fructose, contained in the juice is consumed by the natural yeasts which live on the skin of the grape berries; the yeasts (*Sacchoromyces ellipsoideus*) are assisted in this fermentation process by an enzyme (zymase). Through their life cycle, the yeasts produce waste products, carbon dioxide, and alcohol. While in red wines, because the skins stay in contact with the juice a long time, one can use exclusively the wild yeasts existing on the skin to ferment, in white wines, the natural yeasts are partly destroyed by the addition of sulfites which will keep the juice from browning, and special fermenting yeasts prepared in laboratories are used. It is not rare to see selected yeasts also added to red wines made in large quantities.

While they are fermenting, white wines look as if they were boiling; red wines are covered by what is called a cap, which is made of the skins, pips, and sometimes a few of the grape stems included to give the red wine a certain amount of body (this is done with Pinot Noir grapes, for example). The cap prevents you from seeing the fermenting juice, over which a thick layer of carbon dioxide develops; the layer of gas pushes the cap upward. To give color to a red wine, the cap is punched down into the juice twice a day and the juice mixed very well to help the coloring pigments contained in the skins (anthocyanins) leach into the fermenting juice. As one punches, the fermenting bubbling purple juice comes rushing to the surface and covers the cap, which over the next few hours will again rise to the top and completely cover the juice. In large tanks, the juice is pumped from the bottom of the tank over the top of the cap.

New white wines are greenish cloudy and new red wines are purplish cloudy for both contain a lot of yeast residues in suspension. When finished or almost finished fermenting, the new wines are put in stainless steel tanks, wood casks, or oak barrels and after the fermentation has been completed, they are "racked" several times during their first year of life. That means they will be partly clarified by being drawn from the top of each container into clean containers; the dead yeasts which have fallen to the bottom of the barrel (called lees) are discarded. The mysterious French expression *sur lies*—in English, on the lees—refers to certain very young and fresh white wines, especially the lower Loire Valley Muscadet wines, which are bottled in the month of March following their birth directly from barrels still containing lees and consequently may sometimes contain a few "floaters." Tanks, casks, and barrels are scrubbed and washed with intense care to prevent them from acquiring off tastes and being contaminated by bacteria.

High quality wines, both white and red, which show the promise of being able to age are put in aging barrels which are generally made of oak; in certain Mediterranean countries chestnut wood is still used. In early California wine making, redwood vats were used, but they have been replaced by French and American oak tanks and barrels and, in Châteauneuf-du-Pape in Provence, friends of mine still ferment and age their powerful red wines in huge old Hungarian oak vats.

When wines are young, they contain tannins (astringent phenolic substances) acquired from the skins of the grapes and from the wood of the barrels; tannins derived from the wood feel raspy on the tongue and sometimes make one pucker when one tastes the young wine. This is not a taste reaction, but rather a tactile reaction on the tongue, palate, and sides of the cheeks. A well-made wine ready to drink may still show traces of raspiness in the mouth but the sensation never reaches further than the middle of the tongue. This small raspiness comes from the so-called fruit tannins contained in the skins of the grapes used to make the wine; the perception of those will disappear as the wine ages and the tannins precipitate to the bottom of the bottle over the years as a "sediment." Any wine older than three years and leaving a raspy feeling all the way behind the teeth has been "oaked" too long and loses some of its varietal taste characteristics. If oak is perceived at all, it should not be on the tongue but through the nose (see below in the pages on tasting). Some people relish oak to the point of pronouncing certain wines as great which I think are rather unpleasant and will never age properly. Taste is taste, though, and we all feel and taste differently and tolerance is of the essence in wine tasting as in anything else in life.

When, after multiple rackings and tastings the wine maker decides that the wine has rested long enough in wood, it is fined—or cleaned and cleared—of all the matter it holds in suspension by way of the small addition of such clarifying media as egg white or, in large quantities, such powders as bentonite, so that its color—or "robe"—becomes brilliantly pale green or pale golden for white wines, and clear purplish or bright garnet for red wines. Once brought to total clarity, the wine is finally bottled. Some wine makers choose not to filter their wines which may then result in a slighter darker hue than the same wines filtered.

Any good to great bottle of wine is closed by a cork which allows the wine to breathe all the while it rests in the bottle. Metal caps are for mass-produced wines and nowadays are replacing the old corks and clamps used to seal sparkling wines. As the wine ages, you will see its level go down into the neck of the bottle, the result of slow evaporation. The distance between the cork and the surface of the wine is called *ouillage*, whether in French or English. For great wines which age in their bottles for a number of years, the *ouillage* is brought back to the correct position ¾ inch below the cork by adding some of the same wine from one or several other bottles. When I was growing up this was a delicate operation done carefully and slowly to prevent the air, as much as possible, from getting to the wine; nowadays vintners can rent a vacuum machine in which the transfer is done, so the racked wines never come in contact with any trace of oxygen.

As white wines age, their color turns from greenish yellow to frank yellow, then over the years slowly to deeper and deeper gold. Very old white wines will turn light brown and "maderize," which means that they lose their acidity completely; the wine feels all round in the mouth, then acquires, when one smells and tastes it, some of the characteristics of the wines made on the island of Madeira, hence the term. Sweet dessert white wines do not maderize as fast as dry white wines, because of the large percent of sugar they contain.

The aging of red wines is irregular in length and depends very much on many factors such as the type of grapes and correct temperature of cellaring. Any first quality wine made from Cabernet Sauvignon, Pinot Noir, or Syrah grapes will make you really understand what a great wine is. Just vow to forget a bottle each of good California Pinot Noir and California Cabernet Sauvignon for twenty years in the proper conditions of cool cellaring and you will one day have the most amazing surprises. You will see that the purplish color has changed to a light garnet in the Pinots and somewhere between light brown casts or amber and tawny tints in the Cabernets, and I leave you to find out for yourself about the tastes; just know that the fruit will still be there but with different characters than it had when young, and that the wine will fill your mouth and nose with the most amazing tastes, aftertastes, smells, and aromas, the combination of these last two often called the bouquet.

How can you afford some of these old wines? Simply by buying them when they are young and less expensive; you do not have to buy more than a few bottles, but you have to find a cool place to store them, usually in your basement, and then forget about them. You will be grateful you did. Most people who buy great wines are not possessed with enough patience to let the wines age properly, which accounts for the fact that the majority of great wines made in the world are drunk much too soon and are never quite appreciated for what they really can become. Ah, you will say, it is just wine after all. Sure, but wine is alive and like anything alive, it develops, as it ages, qualities which are not to be missed. You like old ladies and gentlemen with character, wisdom, a bit of crustiness, and a twinkle in their eyes, don't you?

All that sounds pretty straightforward, ideal, and easy, doesn't it? In reality, it is not as simple as all that. Making and perfecting wines is a true art that rests not only on understanding fully the chemical reactions that go on in the fermenting vat, but also on the extreme care one has to bring to its upbringing. The same joke is made in all wine countries of the world where the question is, meant of course in jest, what is most costly to raise, fine wines or children? The economics of the wine industry can be very complicated, to say the least, especially during hard times.

Some wines can be indifferent albeit very drinkable. Some wines can truly be an experience to make and to drink; most great wines are the result of many factors, such as knowledge of the soil and climate in which the grapes are grown, of the techniques to be applied to make the wine, and, last but not least, the techniques, the little personal tricks and quirks of the wine maker, her or his temperament, taste, gift, and intuition. Wines, which have a life of their own, can, like people, become ill from childhood on, so the wine maker must also be a doctor who knows which treatment to apply to the wine in order not to lose it.

Wine as Food

In the old European world, and at all levels of society, wine is not something special for Sunday dinner, it is an everyday happening as the bottle of wine is put on the table side by side with the loaf of bread. In my family, where wine was made in very small quantities, each parent, aunt, and uncle would put away a few bottles for everyone to enjoy at the banquet following their funeral, a tradition that was meant to celebrate the continuation of life in the family; it was also a custom to moisten the lips of all young children with a drop or so of the wine so that they would participate in the ritual.

As a result of this ancestral attitude toward wine, in Europe it is always drunk in great moderation and is considered part of the daily diet, as it really should be everywhere the climate allows the growing of grapes.

The many mentions of alcoholism in Europe come from the times when life for the poor was so harsh that all one could afford to survive on was a piece of bread and cheap wine in the middle of a fourteen-hour work day. A look at American history will show that the temperance movement in the United States was brought on by somewhat identical problems at the time of the heavy industrialization of the country. Poverty and the sense of having been uprooted still comes with alcoholism as its companion.

Alcoholism is and remains a treatable disease to which some people are prone because of their personal makeup. It is understandable that persons suffering from such a sensitivity should not drink wine or any other alcoholic beverage such as beer or hard liquor once their problem has been discovered and treated.

For those who do not suffer from such a hereditary predisposition, wine is food, and good food it is. It contains many of the elements so many people are looking for on the shelf in a drugstore in the form of vitamin pills: calcium, iron, phosphorous, and magnesium to name a few, plus zinc and vitamin P. Wine has been recognized as being helpful in the strengthening of the arteries and in preventing heart attacks. There seems to be quite a resistance to accepting this fact, which is not a really modern fact; it has been recognized over the ages. Wine was the only medicine for centuries; it healed the wounds of many a warrior in the Middle Ages and was for thousands of years the only antiseptic available and the very best tranquilizer. Why take Valium or a sleeping pill when you can have a little glass of wine with a cracker or biscuit just before going to bed? I remember the scandalized faces of many food writers when a few years ago I ventured to say so at a food conference. The key to wine enjoyment is *moderation* as it is in the enjoyment of anything else. Anyone "OD-ing," as the colloquial modern expression goes, on anything, be it wine, ice cream, or chocolate, will be sick and mighty uncomfortable.

Persons suffering from any ailment of the alimentary tract should consult their physicians before having wine. Also some people have a sensitivity to sulfur and since wine contains sulfites, they may be made uncomfortable or sick by its intake. Please consult your physician.

Where Is Wine Produced?

Mostly in the temperate and Mediterranean climates everywhere on the planet.

Wines are produced in many European countries: France, Italy, Spain, Portugal, Greece, Germany, Austria, Switzerland, and Hungary. In the United States, excellent wines have come from California, more precisely from the Napa and Sonoma valleys, since the middle of the nineteenth century. Prohibition very nearly destroyed the western wine production, but after the ban on alcoholic beverages was lifted, it displayed a strong comeback, extending from its already known areas of production to the north toward Mendocino, to the south toward the central and southern coasts, and into the Central Plain. From California it extended to the states of Texas, Oregon, and Washington. The grapes used in the West were brought there by the Spanish Franciscan fathers and European immigrants; they were and remain of the European genus *Vitis vinifera*.

Wine has also been made in the eastern United States since the second half of the nineteenth century. They were mostly made from grapes of the many varieties of the native American genus *Vitis labrusca*. All *labrusca* grapes have an extremely fruity taste which not everybody likes and which in wine circles is called foxy. A similar expression is used in France for describing the taste of older Champagnes, which are said to have "*un goût en queue de renard*" (tasting like the tail of a fox!). Even if you find out that you are not extraordinarily fond of wines made from *labrusca* grapes, try them, they are interesting and go very well with fresh strawberries and are quite good in a wine cream to accompany winter fruit (see page 943).

Since the 1960s eastern wine production has considerably revived. The introduction of *Vitis vinifera* in New York State by Dr. Konstantin Frank has provoked a slow replacement of the indigenous *labrusca* and French hybrid grapes by a proportion of *vinifera* grapes. Good table wines are made in New York, Ohio, Kentucky, Virginia, and Tennessee.

I cannot encourage you enough to get interested in wines. They need not be exceptional wines, nor very expensive ones to be enjoyable. All the wine houses in the country produce very good and affordable wines besides their productions of premium wines. From simple bottles you can slowly graduate to an occasional excellent bottle which will demonstrate to you the immense and fascinating variety in the American production.

Many other countries in other hemispheres also produce excellent wines; try a bottle or two from Chile, Australia, New Zealand, and South Africa, for in each and every country you will experience different tastes, textures, and personalities.

Whichever wine you try, taste it for itself; resist the temptation of pitting the productions of one country against those of another. By the very fact that each and every vineyard in any country in the world has a different soil in a different climate, it is futile and useless to make comparisons in an attempt to know "which is the best." There has forever been a great need in wine circles to compare the great Bordeaux wines against the great Cabernet Sauvignons of California; I find this a useless exercise, for those wines will never be comparable. Bordeaux has been Bordeaux for centuries and Napa will forever be Napa; everything from soil to climate, to the methods of vinification will always make those wines different. Taste wines made from the same grape in different countries to experience how different they can be, never to find out whether one surpasses the other in any way.

Comparisons between wines become interesting only when two or several different wines are produced in the same district in identical soil and climate, in the same year, but by different wine makers. In this case, one can really focus on the personal style and art of the wine makers. The same exercise can be carried out between wines produced by one wine maker in different years.

Types of Wines

There are many types of wines; the most important for the cook are:

- Table wines
- Fortified wines
- Sparkling wines

Each and every one of these types of wine is made following a different process, but all first go through the fermentation steps described above before any special treatment takes place.

Table Wines

Table wines are made to contain any desired degree of alcohol up to a maximum of 14 percent, this upper limit being regulated by law in most countries. There are two types of table wines: generic table wines and varietal table wines.

In the United States, many of the inexpensive table wines are generic. A generic wine is made by blending a variety of wines made from different grape types to obtain a commercial blend (as opposed to the more noble "assemblage," see in the discussion of varietal table wines) which is often given a name such as American Chablis, Mountain White, Burgundy, Sauterne, but does not contain a trace of true Chablis from Chablis nor Burgundy wine from Burgundy, nor true Sauternes from the Bordeaux region. It is important to note, right here and now, that Sauternes, when referring to the sweet white dessert wines coming from the Sauternes district around Bordeaux, always ends with an "s" while American generic wines called Sauterne without an "s" are a blend of ordinary, nondistinctive, and uncharacteristic white wines, sold mostly in jugs, generally drinkable, but lacking personality and character.

Generic wines are not necessarily bad; some of them are quite drinkable and I think you should try one or two before you drink some of the varietal wines described below; you will immediately understand the difference. Generic wines are not just an American phenomenon, they are legion in France where the wine brokers have a merry old time mixing and blending to their hearts' content; as in America, French generic wines are generally pleasant, but they are never great.

VARIETAL TABLE WINES

Varietal wines are wines that are made completely from one variety of grape or from a very high percentage of one grape "assembled"—or blended—with one or more varieties of other grape types. The percentage of the dominating grape, the name of which appears on the label, is regulated by law in the United States. Great wines are always varietal.

The Major Red Grapes Used in Varietal Wines

- *Cabernet Sauvignon* is one of the primary grapes used to make all the red wines of the Medoc district of Bordeaux, most of the California premium red wines, and many of the red wines of Australia, New Zealand, and South Africa. It is a magnificent grape, which tasted right from the vine immediately reveals its strong varietal characters; as you bite through the skin, the juice is good but it is the aftertaste left in your mouth by the skin which reveals what is usually called a "cedarlike" quality. When Cabernet wine is well made, the same quality is so present in the glass that no one needs to be an expert to identify it immediately by nose and palate. In colder, more temperate climates Cabernet may be clear and transparent, hence its English name of Claret, but in warmer climates its color evokes dark crimson velvet.

- *Cabernet Franc* is used in the making of Bordeaux wines in the district of Saint Emilion, and it is also the grape from which the Bourgueil and Chinon wines of the Loire Valley are made. In other districts of the Bordeaux region Cabernet Franc is used in small percentages to soften tannins and allow shorter ripening times in wines made mostly from the long ripening Cabernet Sauvignon; any wine of this type is said to be an "assemblage." The practice of "assembling" wines from the two Cabernets and Merlot is spreading in California, where such wines are called Meritages.

- *Merlot.* In the extraordinary district of Bordeaux known as Pomerol, the wines are made from Merlot grapes which are sometimes assembled in relatively small quantities with both Cabernets. In California pure Merlot is being produced more and more extensively.

- *Pinot Noir,* known in Germany and Switzerland as *Burgunder,* is the red grape of Burgundy and some German and Swiss valleys, and the grape used to make the clear pale red wines of Alsace. It is extending its domain to many of the American areas of production such as the Carneros district in California and the Willamette Valley in Oregon. Much less typical in taste when tasted as a fresh grape than Cabernet Sauvignon, Pinot Noir is very difficult to turn into great wine and requires an immense amount of care. The goal of all of the better Burgundian producers is to obtain a nonfiltered wine which is clear and somewhere between ruby and garnet in color. Try some Pinots Noirs from Burgundy, California, and Alsace, so you can appreciate different wines from different climates with different robe colors.

  Pinot Noir is also the grape used to make the Champagnes known as *blancs de noirs,* which means white wines made from black grapes; see page 102 under Sparkling Wines for details.

- *Syrah* is the dominant red grape of the French Rhône Valley where its propagation began after having been brought back from the Holy Land by the Crusaders. It is present in all the wines of Hermitage and Châteauneuf-du-Pape which must be aged a very long time. In Australia Syrah is called Shiraz or Hermitage. In South Africa it is called Hermitage and can be blended with Pinot Noir to obtain what is called a Pinotage. Right now Syrah is being introduced on a larger scale in the valleys of California.

- *Gamay* was also brought back from the Holy Land by the Crusaders and is the grape used to make the famous Beaujolais wines of France, a region adjacent to the large city of Lyon on the Rhône, where it yields the fruitiest and nicest wines because of the mixed clay and granite of the different soils in which it is grown. In Burgundy Gamay is much less successful and usually crushed together with lesser grade Pinot Noirs to obtain a type of wine called Passetoutgrain, which is inexpensive and of no particular distinction.

  In the United States, especially in the Napa Valley, the "Gamay Beaujolais" in its better presentations is a very nice wine which, as they say, "goes down easy." Gamay grapes blended with Pinot Noir grapes are made into a young purplish red wine that smells of candy by a natural method called carbonic maceration, in which the grapes are not crushed but rather are allowed to ferment in a closed vat where they eventually pop open naturally by simple carbonic pressure, releasing their beautifully colored juices.

- *Zinfandel.* Considering that Zinfandel is the most planted red grape in California, I have been wondering ever since I arrived in the United States why wine writers do not pay more attention to the delicious wines made from this grape and why, when they do, they are so persistent in comparing it to the French Beaujolais.

  As indeed there are multiple types of Beaujolais wines made in France, there are as many Zinfandels made in California where it seems to produce a most popular wine, possibly as popular as Beaujolais, but this is really where the comparison must stop; ask a group of wine makers what they like to drink after a long day of work and the majority of them will tell you Zinfandel. I am writing here of course about the red Zinfandel, not the sweetish white Zinfandel. There is absolutely nothing wrong with a glass of white Zinfandel if you like sweet wines, but I really prefer a nice dry red wine and Zinfandel is first and foremost a very nice dry red wine.

  No one really knows for sure where the Zinfandel grapes now produced in the United States came from; they seem to have been in California before the wine industry started. Some believe that they came from Hungary, while others will tell you they are related to Carignan, one of the thirteen grapes used to make Châteauneuf-du-Pape. All of this, however plausible, is only conjecture.

  Certain, though, is the fact that most of the wines produced from Zinfandel range from pleasant in the lighter versions, to extremely delicious in the more serious ones where the wine maker has fully brought out its fruit and body. And yes, in spite of many statements to the contrary from many wine professionals, Zinfandel certainly can age, for I have enjoyed several very old Zinfandels which would have put to shame more than one good Cabernet Sauvignon. Probably because of the current high prices for Cabernet Sauvignon, Zinfandel is experiencing quite a renaissance, which is very welcome.

The Major White Grapes Used in Varietal Wines

- *Chardonnay* is the white grape from which the great white wines of Burgundy are made; in Burgundy the grape is still quite often called Pinot

Chardonnay. It is also the great white grape of California. Everywhere, it is utterly charming when very young, sending to one's nose its inimitable fresh aromas, and quite awesome when aged, and, its acid tones having melded into a well rounded but still extremely fruity wine, it rolls lusciously in the mouth. The variations in Chardonnay wines are extreme and the variety of styles absolutely mind boggling. The prices are also interesting in that they can vary from the most affordable to nothing short of a fortune per bottle. One Chardonnay made in southern Burgundy is called Pouilly-Fuissé; I mention it here especially to avoid it being confused with the Pouilly-Fumé mentioned in the next paragraph.

- *Sauvignon Blanc* is used to produce white wines in the Graves district of the Bordeaux area of production. Its variations are amazing; in the upper Loire Valley, its juice becomes the racy Pouilly-Fumé, and the fruity Sancerre. California produces some excellent Sauvignon Blanc which, being raised in a rather warm climate, has completely different characteristics from the French wines. French and American Sauvignons are two different entities, never to be compared, but drunk side by side a bottle of each will teach much about climate and soil effects on wine.

  In the Sauternes and Graves districts of Bordeaux the Sauvignon is often assembled with the Sémillon grape which mellows it considerably, for Sémillon can, depending on the climate in which it grows, have a trace of sweetness.

  Both Sauvignon and Sémillon grapes in the Bordeaux area and in a few areas of California can develop what is called the "noble rot" in English, *edelfäule* in German, and *pourriture noble* in French. Called *Botrytis cinerea* in Latin, it develops slowly on grape berries through the foggy European fall until the berries are completely covered with a white mold which gradually turns gray. The mold absorbs the water in the grape juice and leaves in the berries a very concentrated and flavorful juice which is pressed late in November. From this juice one obtains very sweet wines containing as much as 14 percent alcohol and residual sugar as high as 12 to 16 percent. The best known and most celebrated botrytised wine is Château d'Yquem, which is in a class all by itself and the price of which is always justified, because of the intense labor that it requires and the wonderful flavors brought out by the contact of the juice with the molds.

- *Riesling* is the white grape variety of the German Rhine Valley where it unequivocably originated. It produces excellent wines, not only in Germany but also in the French Alsace, Switzerland, Austria, and northern Italy as well as in California where it is given the name of either white Riesling or Johannisberger Riesling; in Chile the Sylvaner (see below) seems to be called Riesling. In all these countries the wines obtained are totally different in style and all merit investigation; they are most affordable when it comes to price, unless they are left to botrytise and are transformed into wines called in Germany Beerenauslese or

Trockenbeerenauslese, which require the same lengthy care as the making of French Sauternes.

- *The Sylvaner* is also a grape of the Germanic countries and the French Alsace; it produces wines that are light and soft, fresh, fruity, and eminently drinkable. In most of its areas of production it is served in charming little pitchers of two, five, or ten deciliters; it goes well with all those wonderful Germanic sausages.
- *Traminer and Gewürztraminer* are grown in Alsace, the Rhine Valley, the South Tirol of Italy, and California. In Europe Traminer is mostly cultivated in its best version, the Gewürztraminer, which is usually fermented dry, but because of its spiciness it is wrongly perceived as containing residual sugar. In California, more and more Gewürztraminers are fermented dry but many are still fermented with lower alcohol degrees and larger sugar residues.
- *Chenin Blanc* is cultivated and vinified almost exclusively all along the Touraine and Anjou parts of the Loire Valley; it can be vinified dry or in different degrees of sweetness, the heat and ripeness of a given year often determining the style for that year. All the great middle Loire wines such as Vouvray, Montlouis, Saumur, Savennières, etc., are made with Chenin Blanc. In California it also yields very good white wines with a small but frank degree of sweetness.
- *Viognier*, grown and vinified up to now only in the northern Rhône Valley, is an exceptional grape that produces exquisite wines such as Château-Grillet and Condrieu in France. Many attempts have been made to make Viognier wines in California with more or less success, but slowly a few are emerging that show the beautiful floral, citrus, peach, and apricot flavors this grape can display when the climate and grape are compatible.

There are quite a few other varieties of grapes. For more information see the bibliography on page 1175.

Fortified Wines

A wine is said to have been fortified when the wine maker interrupts its natural fermentation between 7 and 10 percent alcohol with an addition of pure ethyl alcohol from distilled grape wine or younger brandy, which raises the final alcohol content of the wine to anywhere between 15 and 18 percent, or even, in certain cases, higher.

The most important, better known, and most widely consumed fortified wines include sherry, Madeira, Marsala, and port. Each of them, plus quite a few other fortified wines which are more regional and not as well known worldwide, deserve special reading, for the making of each of them is technically different and quite involved. The information I give here is nothing but a wide generalization, meant as very elementary and basic information for the cook. Hugh Johnson, in his first book, *Wine*, gives enthusiastic, fascinating, and very informative reports on each of the fortified wines (see the bibliography).

SHERRY

Any true sherry comes from Spain around a city called Jerez de la Frontera; any sherry produced in the United States, Australia, and South Africa can only be considered a sherry-type wine. True sherries come from several types of Spanish soils, each producing a different quality of wine, from many different grapes.

The bone dry fino and the slightly more mellow Amontillado, which are both served as before-dinner drinks, are produced mostly from Palomino grapes grown in the white, chalky so-called *albariza* soil. The rare Pedro Ximénez grapes undergo a sun-drying period before being crushed, the result being sweet and weighty wines used mostly in the artful blending of the darker sweet sherries called *olorosos*.

Sherries are fermented in 150-gallon butts (large vats) made of American white oak and, in the month of December immediately following the vintage, they are already cleared (meaning the sediment has dropped to the bottom). Specialists determine the quality of the wines by the presence or absence on their surface of a blanket of yeast which thickens over the months, and is called the *flor*. If *flor* is present on its surface, the new wine becomes either a fino which is pale and straw yellow (*muy pálido*), or an Amontillado, which has slightly more color (*pálido*) and is slightly less dry. Both are fortified to reach 15.5 percent alcohol, raised from one to three years in separate storage rooms called *criaderas*, or nurseries, and then finally bottled.

Manzanilla, with its 15.5 to 17 percent alcohol, is the wine of the bullfighters. It is very dry, and one of the very few wines in the world that gives the impression on the palate of being ever so slightly salty; it is made in a region which borders the Jerez vineyards and is said to gather its special taste from the winds blowing over the vines from the Atlantic Ocean.

Sweet sherries are called *olorosos*, or cream sherries in English. The best are sweetened by using wines made from grapes dried almost to the point of raisins before being pressed (*PX vino dulce*), the more ordinary ones by being blended and sweetened with grape juices which have been reduced to their own quintessence (*vino de color*); most of the sweet sherries are wines which, in the first few months of their life, did not develop the *flor*. The results are diverse wines of medium to full sweetness which can contain 18 to 21 percent alcohol, with different caramel accents, making them perfect dessert wines.

All sherries are aged according to the system of the *solera*. Barrels are lined up in a cellar or stacked on top of one another to form two to three rows or tiers; the wines in one *solera* are from year to year blended into one another, passing slowly from the top tier to the lowest tier, the wines ready for bottling coming always from the bottom tier. Only one third to one half of the wines of the lowest tier are bottled in a single year; the others continue being blended and aged as the second tier becomes the last and a new tier of barrels containing younger wines is added on top of the second. Because of this system of aging there are no vintages in sherries.

MADEIRA

Madeira is a large island which is territorially part of Portugal and lies almost at mid-Atlantic. It produces wines that are fortified to 18 to 20 percent alcohol by the addition of brandy.

Many wines are made on Madeira and their names are usually the same as that of the grapes from which they were made. The driest Madeira is the Sercial, which is often compared to a fino sherry. If you can find a fino and a Sercial, it would be a good idea to taste both side by side to appreciate the difference. The Verdelho is also extremely dry and with a remarkable bouquet; since it is becoming hard to find, keep any bottle you may find for drinking and cook with Sercial or Rainwater.

Rainwater is the name given to a very dry, pale yellow Madeira for its American creator, "Rainwater" Habisham, who invented a special way to fine (clarify) his wines. It is imported by the French in huge quantities for the finishing of their fine sauces.

The deep sweet golden wines are made from the Malvasia, Malmsey in English, grape which originally came from Greece and has been thriving for some four hundred years on the island. As a matter of interest, the much maligned French king, Louis XVI, loved Malmsey, his *vin de malvoisie* as he gently called it. Another extremely lovely and extremely sweet Madeira is the Bual, or Boal, which is one of the very best dessert wines.

Like sherry, Madeira wines are raised in *soleras*, but the rooms in which they are kept, called *estufas*, are intensely heated for a number of months, resulting in the distinctive "cooked," caramel-like, and ever so slightly, smoky flavor the wines have.

MARSALA

Scaloppine di vitello al Marsala is the dish responsible for most American cooks knowing Marsala wine so well. The wine is made on the island of Sicily and bears an Arabic name derived from the name of a port, Marsah el Allah (the port of Allah) which had been known before as the Lilibeo of the Carthaginians, who founded it in mid-300 B.C.

The production of Marsala as we know it today started in the late eighteenth century with the thought of making a wine less expensive than sherries and ports. Marsalas are made into dry wines which are fortified to 17 to 18 percent alcohol; some are then sweetened with *mosto cotto*, or strongly concentrated grape juice, which is the most direct descendant of the Latin *mustum* so important in the ancient Latin kitchen.

The driest Marsala, called Marsala Vergine or Marsala Solera, is bone dry and unsweetened, then comes the Garibaldi or Colli, which is barely sweet, then the Italia with which one usually cooks in Italy, which is fortified to 17 percent alcohol and contains 5 percent sugar.

PORT

There is so much to write on port that I have had to choose to either write just the essentials or leave to my readers the pleasures of reading about port themselves in Hugh Johnson's *Wine,* where you will find the most delightful general description of the area of production of the true Portuguese ports, the valley of the Douro and its surrounding mountains. There are many port-type wines made in many countries other than Portugal; for example, we have our American ports—New York State port or California port—and Australia produces several excellent port-type wines, but none can ever disguise its non-Portuguese lineage.

Red port has been made since 1450 by crushing an assortment of red grape varieties and allowing them to progress halfway through the fermentation process. At that point the juice is drawn off and a significant amount of high-proof brandy is added to it. This stops the fermentation and fortifies the wines between 19 and 21 percent alcohol. White port is made the same way, using white grape varieties. Up to very recently the crushing of the grapes was done by men and older boys exclusively by foot and was part of a true tradition. The custom continues only in very small vineyards.

Great ports are always red ports and they come in two categories:

VINTAGE PORTS In great years of production, certain lots of wines are selected, left unblended, and fortified, then they are bottled, but not necessarily in Portugal; many are bottled in England. A vintage port will barely be drinkable before it has been in the bottle for fifteen to eighteen years, often much longer. It is really ready for drinking at its peak of life and quality, around thirty years. For example, the ports of the vintage of 1963 are delicious right now, and those of 1977 are by now coming of age. Some port aficionados will tell you, sometimes with a funny kind of snobby sneer, that a port is not "worth drinking" unless it is sixty years old. Why yes, of course, it will always be better, but what if one does not live that long? For me and millions of others of my generation, vintage port is a treat that comes into my life maybe once every five years, so I accept it gratefully, even if the port is not all that old.

Vintage ports are put to age label up; in the old days, ports were not labeled, but simply marked with a white strike of paint to indicate the side opposite to that where the sediments of the wine had deposited. Such bottles still exist and cost small fortunes. Vintage ports must be left to stand several days, for their sediment, or the "crust" that clings to the sides of the bottle, to break down into small particles and settle at the bottom of the bottle. It is sometimes recommended to filter the wine through a piece of muslin. I prefer to pour the uppermost two thirds to three quarters of the bottle most carefully directly into glasses and leave the remainder to settle again; then I filter it.

OTHER PORTS "Ports of a vintage" are blended wines that have been made in a certain year in which a vintage has been declared, but instead of being bottled and aged in the bottle, they are aged in casks. As a result, all the sedimentation happens in the cask and when the wines are bottled, usually after an average of twelve years in cask, very often more, they are clear and have acquired the most gorgeous and seductive color. The very best tawny ports are ports of a vintage.

The ports offered for sale as ruby port and tawny ports sold in retail wine stores are blends of many cask-aged wines, prepared by the shippers in huge blending lodges.

If you decide to drink port, get used to it progressively, starting with the more humble ones, so you can build gradually toward the great vintage ports and appreciate all the work that went into their production.

There are many other fortified wines, less well known but often just as delicious; please consult the bibliography.

Champagne and Sparkling Wines

There are two ways of making sparkling wines. The inexpensive way is to use the "bulk process method" in which indifferent white wines are fermented in large closed tanks and bottled under pressure. Such wines are sold for much lower prices. Such wines can lose their bubbles quite quickly and be very unsatisfactory to drink.

True Champagne in France and a number of extremely well made and delicious sparkling wines in the United States and Australia are produced by the other technique, called the *méthode champenoise*. In Champagne the weather is quite cold and even fully mature grapes are not always full of sugar; add to this the fact that the soil of Champagne is pure chalk, and you will understand that the wines one obtains to make the sparkling wines are anything but mellow. In California, where the weather is extremely hot and the grapes not grown in the typical chalky terrains, the grapes are collected by the middle of August as soon as their content in sugar is 18 Brix, Brix being a measurement of sugar in the grape juice. Chardonnay and Cabernets, for example, are picked at 23 to 24 Brix.

Whether in Champagne or anywhere else where a good sparkling wine is made, the grapes are collected, pressed, and the vinification started all in one day. When a sparkling wine is made entirely with red or black grapes such as Pinot Noir and Pinot Meunier, it will be called a *blanc de noirs*; *blancs de noirs* are pressed with the greatest care so that none of the color of the skins finds its way into the juice. If a wine is made with white grapes from Chardonnay, which always gives the best white sparkling wines, or other white grapes, the wine is called a *blanc de blancs*.

All sparkling wines made by the *méthode champenoise* undergo a double fermentation. The first one takes place in barrels or vats; when it is finished, the wine maker will assemble wines from different vineyards to obtain the particular balance of flavors he/she thinks represents the best qualities of the yearly vintage; that blend is called the *cuvée*. The second fermentation will start after a certain amount of sugar syrup mixed with yeasts (called *liqueur de tirage*) is added to each bottle of wine. The yeasts will ferment in the bottle, producing carbon dioxide and alcohol, and, as they die, will deposit on the bottom part of the bottle belly. Sparkling wines are, as you may know, bottled in extremely thick dark green glass; it is believed by some authorities that the modern thick bottles were created by the British early in the seventeenth century when they realized the wine could not be kept in barrels without becoming fizzy and that regular bottles could not take the pressure of the developing gas. The pressure of the carbon dioxide is so high, indeed, that some bottles will simply explode. When you visit a sparkling wine cellar you sometimes can hear one of these explosions and its shattering of glass.

Most quality sparkling wines nowadays are finished in three years; great sparkling wines are finished in five years or longer. The length of time involved in producing them is responsible for the final cost of the wine. Lesser quality *méthode champenoise* sparkling wines can certainly be produced in less time but the quality of the wines will be from average to good only, for it is the length of time the wine remains in contact with the lees in the bottle that gives a Champagne its particular flavor. Some Champagne and high quality sparkling wines remain in contact with the lees a very long time and are disgorged just before being released for sale; the bottles in which they are sold will carry the mention "recently disgorged." What then does the word *disgorged* mean?

The dead yeasts that have fallen to the inner-lying side of each bottle form a layer of sediment which must be removed. To complete total clarification of the wine, the bottles are put to rest in the oval holes of racks called *pupitres*. Each day a *rémueur* turns the bottles a quarter of a turn in opposite directions, using a motion of the wrist which slowly sends the yeast down toward the neck of the bottle; the *rémueur* gradually raises the angle of the bottle in doing so, so that when the yeast arrives in the neck, the bottles are upside down, which is called *sur pointe* (tipped over). This operation is still done by hand for the high-class Champagnes and the best California and Australia sparkling wines, but, for those that are less expensive, it is done in special computerized cubic racks called *gyropalettes*. Hand *rémuage* requires three months versus two weeks when done in *gyropalettes*.

To remove the yeast from the neck of the bottle, one freezes the yeast by passing the bottles through a bath of high-power refrigerant and as one opens the bottle with a clamp, the frozen block of yeast is expelled by the pressure of the carbon dioxide; this operation is called *dégorgement,* or disgorgement. A few specialists in France can still disgorge by hand or, according to the French expression, *à la volée* (the wine explodes out of the bottle so fast that it appears to fly—*voler*—hence the term "*à la volée*"); it is an admirable technique and you will feel like cheering if you are lucky enough to be able to see Champagne disgorged by hand for the specialist rarely loses one drop more than he should.

Finally, the space left in the bottles by the expulsion of the sediments is refilled with a second mixture of sugar syrup called the *liqueur de dosage,* or sugar dosage. The wine being quite dry, up to 1.5 percent sugar is added to obtain a Brut Champagne which remains the driest and is the favorite of the French; extra dry Champagne, which contains up to 3 percent dosage, is made almost exclusively for exportation to the Anglo-Saxon countries, including the United States. The French really prefer their Champagne Extra Brut, which means that no dosage at all is added to the wine; in Extra Brut the primary characteristic of the wine is the presence on the roof of the mouth of that dry chalk aftertaste that comes from the soil.

The French are extremely particular and constantly send reminders all over the world that only French sparkling wines made by the *méthode champenoise* in Champagne can, by law, be called Champagne. The reason is that the Province of Champagne received its name from a geological type of soil called in French a *champagne*. A *champagne* is a dry chalky soil sparsely covered with vegetation. In the same vein, the term Fine Champagne is used for great Cognacs grown in this same type of soil. Sparkling wines produced in other wine areas of France are called *vins mousseux,* their labels always mentioning the fact that they were made by the *méthode champenoise*. *Mousseux* sold with labels not mentioning this last fact are ordinary bulk process wines.

Whereas some European countries have found other names for their sparkling wines, such as *Spumante* in Italy and *Sekt* in Germany, the United States uses the word *Champagne,* followed by the area of production whenever the fermentation is finished in the bottle. Each bottle made in America must show the geographic origin of its "Champagne" and on all bottles you can read the statement "fermented in this bottle." There are some remarkably good California "Champagnes" produced by American vintners in the Napa Valley from Chardonnay and Pinot Noir grapes.

The history of Champagne is particularly interesting and romantic; you can find out more fascinating facts by reading some of the books listed in the bibliography.

Tasting Wine

To taste wine and perceive all of its flavors and aromas, you must put not only your tongue and palate to work but also your nose and your eyes.

I was introduced to wine tasting as a very very young woman by my grandfather, on my fourteenth birthday, as I irritated him by—as he so aptly put it—"using half of my nose" only. Great panic on my part, of course. Half of my nose? Which, the right or the left? Well, both actually.

Here you are with a glass of wine in front of you; the first thing you will do is use not your mouth or your nose, but your eyes. Place the glass on your white napkin, or use the white tablecloth or place a piece of white paper under the glass and look into the glass from the top. You will see the color of the wine and its clarity or lack of clarity; there may be a few small things floating in a young white wine; most of the time they are tiny particles of lees. In an older wine, red or white, there may be some tiny crystals of tartrate (tartaric acid deposits on barrels in which wines age); in a very old red wine improperly decanted, some of the sediment can cloud the wine. As time goes by and you drink more and more of very different wines, you will learn to distinguish these particles. Most of the wines you will drink will be perfectly clear; wines which have been fined but not filtered will be darker in color but they should be neither murky nor cloudy. A wine is fined when it is clarified using egg white or bentonite. It can then be filtered which will remove some of the anthocyanins and make it appear lighter in color.

Next, use your nose: Smell the wine as soon as it has been poured. Try to determine what you smell: It can be flowers, fruit of one sort or another, tobacco, candy, pepper, a tiny trace of the sulfur dioxide used to make sure that the wine remains healthy, etc. Swirl the wine around your glass and smell again; the aromas you first detected will have changed; they will either have intensified or disappeared to let other aromas surface. Try to identify what they remind you of. Your nose does nothing more than send the information it detects to that part of your lower brain known as the olfactory bulb, which analyzes the received information and tells you which fruit or other aroma you recognize.

After you have swirled and once again inhaled the wine's aroma, put your eyes to work again. All around the surface of the glass you will see the wine falling back into the glass in long so-called legs. The longer the legs are and the slower they take to blend back into the wine, the more alcohol the wine contains. Do this exercise with a white Zinfandel and with a red Zinfandel each in its turn and you will see that the pink wine has such short legs, they are called tears.

Now put your mouth to work: Take a regular mouthful of the wine and roll it on your tongue, pursing your lips as you aspirate and pass air over the wine. Now close your mouth and swish the wine all around your mouth: Any sweetness you perceive will be just behind the tip of your tongue, any acidity or sourness on the very edges of your tongue on the right and left, and a lot of strong acidity or even bitterness will be perceived toward the back center of your mouth where the very large papillae are.

Any such roughness, perceived on the sides of your cheeks and toward the large papillae, is due to the presence of the phenolic compounds—the tannins—in suspension in the wine. These are especially evident in opulent red wines made from Cabernet Sauvignon, Syrah, and Pinot Noir grapes when they are very young.

This strong assault of your taste buds will diminish as the wine ages. Tannins of "middle-aged wines" soften to the impression of a very light powder coating the tongue and mouth.

In very old red wines the tannins disappear, giving way to the most wonderful blend of dried fruit flavors, such as raisins, mixed with faint wood flavors. As you do this exercise, it is important that you do not confuse sour, as in acid lemon juice, with bitter, as in bitter barely sweetened dark chocolate.

This part of tasting is done in a matter of seconds; now, by reflex action, you will swallow. *Immediately reopen your mouth* approximately one half inch and inhale air; *immediately close your mouth tightly* and breathe out through your nose. This is the part that my grandfather meant by using the other half of my nose; as you breathe out, the whole aroma of the wine will pass through your nose again, to pass more information to the olfactory bulb. The fruit that you first smelled will come back mixed with all the essences of the wood barrel in which the wine was aged; if the wine was aged only in stainless steel, you will know it immediately, for all you will have is a remnant of fruit or flower aromas. If the wine has been aged in wood, the fruit/flower and wood aromas will be mixed together; since you already know from your first sniffings which aromas come from the fruit, the new nuances you discover while breathing out are coming from the wood.

This is all there is to tasting a wine; it is simple and unpretentious. If you become really interested and fascinated by wine, go to any continuing education class at a university—a university is important—where a true wine professional will put his/her expertise to work and help you go further by learning to taste in a totally objective manner. A few too many people taste wines using an obfuscating elitist vocabulary that is immensely discouraging to the new wine drinker. Tasting and drinking wine must be joyous; do not let your pleasure be spoiled by anyone and make up your mind according to your own taste because *a good wine is a wine that you like and that you enjoy drinking* and with all the good wines made across the world, the world is your oyster.

Cooking with Wines

I have described in detail how to taste wine because it is absolutely essential that you taste the wines with which you plan to prepare all dishes calling for wine. Any wine that is too acidic before being put in a pan to reduce will yield a sauce or gravy which will taste even more acid than the wine and will spoil the dish.

The Cardinal Rules of Cooking with Table Wines

1. All table wines used in cooking must undergo a slow reducing process to allow the alcohol they contain to evaporate. The wine, most of the time mixed with aromatics (see page 57 for a definition of aromatics), is first brought to a boil, immediately turned down to a *simmer,* and slowly cooked down, or reduced, to the point where only the concentrated flavor of the wine remains, if modified somewhat by the aromatics. Reduced *separately* from the sauce or gravy to which it will be added, wine, red or white, will give it individuality and incomparable taste. The notion applied by some French chefs that wine should be boiled rapidly is not correct and leads to the demise of many a potentially good sauce; so does the notion that wine and stock can be reduced together.

2. *Do not* at any time succumb to the temptation of adding raw, unreduced table wine to a sauce that is finished or you will see your good, tasty sauce turn into a rough, unpalatable one, due to the presence of alcohol.

3. If a recipe calls for dry white wine without mentioning the type of wine, use any good dry white wine such as Sauvignon Blanc, if you are a complete beginner, or a Chardonnay if you are a little more experienced and know how to cope with the relatively larger degree of acidity surfacing when Chardonnay wine is reduced. If Sauvignon and Chardonnay are too expensive, use a generic wine that tastes round in the mouth just after opening the bottle.

4. Champagne in cooking is treated as a table wine and must be reduced exactly as any Chardonnay would be; because of the tiny percent of sugar contained in the *liqueur de dosage* (see page 104), fish sauces made with Champagne are more mellow than those made with still Chardonnay.

5. If a recipe calls for a dry red wine, you can use:
   - That most understated red wine in America, the wonderful Zinfandel, which always results in smooth and full-bodied sauces for the minimum amount of cost. Another red wine of Italian origin called Grignolino does well when used in light Italian-style sauces. The one American Grignolino produced in the Napa Valley "outcooks" all of its Italian cousins.

- A French Côtes-du-Rhône, which is an excellent reducer, especially those sold under the labels Châteauneuf-du-Pape or Gigondas. For Italian and Mediterranean dishes, consider besides a light Barolo (never a Valpolicella which drinks beautifully and cooks poorly) or a lighter Spanish Rioja or Penedès.
- For serious dishes where a great sauce is needed, use an American Cabernet Sauvignon or a Bordeaux with body and depth. For my taste, an average American Cabernet Sauvignon reduces with more depth and body than an average French Bordeaux. Cooking with great Bordeaux or the greatest American Cabernets gives equally excellent results in two different styles but should be reserved for special occasions and perhaps, also, for the day when you have attained total proficiency in the kitchen.
- A French and American Pinot Noir reduce with equal depth and provide red wine sauces that are lighter than those prepared with Cabernet-based wines, but excellent.

6. Whereas in everyday dishes generic wines can be used, it is a good idea, if a bit pricy, to use the same wine to cook a dish as you plan to serve with it at dinner to appreciative company.

7. A dry vermouth never quite adequately replaces a good dry white wine because it is a cooked wine in which woodruff (*Artemisia absinthium*) has been steeped. The woodruff surfaces after reduction and renders any sauce or gravy anywhere from slightly to quite bitter. The only place dry white vermouth should have in a kitchen is as an aperitif blended with a bit of black currant or cassis liqueur to sustain the efforts of the cook. In an emergency, if no white wine is available, vermouth may be used as a replacement in the making of fish stock, using only half as much vermouth as you would wine in this instance. Also, to be fair, if you like the taste of vermouth and wish to use this type of steeped and cooked wine to prepare a dish, the wine then should become the star in the sauce and the sauce can be called vermouth sauce; the slightly bitter taste is then to be expected and savored for itself.

The Rules of Cooking with Fortified Wines

1. In cooking, fortified wines may be allowed to reduce slowly, never at a full boil, mixed in modest proportions with a sauce or gravy. Or they may be added in small amounts without boiling to finished brown sauces or soups; this type of addition will depend on the preparation and is done at the very last minute as an adjustment. The quantity of wine added varies between one tenth and one eighth of the total quantity of sauce or soup to be flavored.

2. It is not necessary to choose and use very expensive fortified wines for cooking; all serious brands have fortified wines which give a lovely flavor to dishes and sauces without costing an absolute fortune. It goes without saying that vintage ports and very old tawny ports should be reserved for drinking.

The Marriage of Wine and Food

The subject of "pairing" or "marrying" wine and food has become a burning one. So that I can give you an idea of how it works, I want you to do some basic exercises with me. You will notice that all the while we are working, we will be weighing the effects of acid, salty, sweet, and bitter components in foods on the wine, often modifying one to raise the other and always trying to make sure that the wine is not damaged by the food.

THE BASIC RULE OF WINE AND FOOD PAIRING

The taste of a wine is what it is in each particular bottle you are serving and cannot be changed; since the elements of taste in the food will act either to enhance the wine or damage it, the role of the cook consists of:

- Presenting combinations of foods seasoned in a way that is in harmony with the taste and flavor of the wine and, if the harmony is not correct,
- Modifying the composition or the seasoning of the dish to bring harmony and allow the wine to be served with its integral taste and/or its mouth feel modified in such a way that its best characteristics are enhanced and its weaknesses minimized.

BASIC EXERCISE

PHASE 1 Buy a bottle of light, extremely reasonably priced Cabernet Sauvignon of a recently released vintage from the Napa Valley. If you are a total novice, you are going to have fun. Simply ask the wine merchant to give you one of those fruity wines with a pleasant aroma of blackberries and strawberries, which leaves the palate asking for more wine, because you want to try to understand how to pair wine and food. The wine merchant will understand perfectly and send you home with a nice rounded wine, not strong enough to conflict with almost any food, yet robust enough to show off well with a number of foods.

Also buy a quarter pound in one solid piece, not grated, of true Parmigiano-Reggiano cheese. Go home and open your bottle fifteen minutes before you start the tasting and pairing session and taste your wine alone first. Look for the fruit aromas by smelling the wine and tasting it in depth, appreciate if there may be some tannins coming to rest on the sides and back of your tongue, but hopefully not all the way behind your teeth when you swirl it in your mouth; remember to open your mouth after you swallow, breathe in with your mouth opened half an inch, and finally close your mouth and breathe out through your nose only.

IMPORTANT: When you taste wine and food, remember to alternate wine and food and never let them mix on your palate or you will not taste each of them correctly. This may sound silly, but I have been asked this question a number of times.

Now take a paper-thin sliver of cheese, not a piece, only a sliver, chew it well, and allow it to completely coat your mouth before you swallow it; now take a sip of wine again and repeat your normal tasting procedure; you will notice that the wine tastes completely different. It will fill the mouth more broadly at the same time its fruitiness will be somewhat overwhelmed by the lactic flavors of the cheese; as you breathe out after drinking the wine, you will perceive both the lactic flavors of the cheese and the alcoholic redolence of the wine well mixed and well blended, but the lovely fruitiness will have been so minimized by the cheese that you will immediately think that a Cabernet Sauvignon with a heftier body, more pronounced fruit, and more intense wood essences would have been better with such a flavorful cheese.

PHASE 2 On another day, buy a steak, remove any fat, cut it in half, and panfry one half of it in a bit of butter or oil, and at the same time grill the other half. The panfried meat will be much more complementary to the wine, because in the grilled meat, the slightly bitter aftertaste of the burned outside layers of the steak will completely destroy the fruit and bond on your tongue with any tannins present in the wine, allowing for a not very pleasant final taste. There are two things you can do to solve this problem: Grill your steak more lightly outside and a little longer, or choose a fruitier wine such as Pinot Noir, Beaujolais, or a light Zinfandel.

PHASE 3 Choose a white wine such as Chardonnay. Try pairing it first with an ordinary grilled chicken, the skin of which has been generously salted, and note what happens to the white wine; to your taste, is that wine good with the chicken or would you prefer a different white wine containing a little more acid and from a colder climate?

If, however, you roast a plain chicken with salt added to its cavity rather than on the skin, and taste it with the Chardonnay or, even better, a Sauvignon Blanc, you will realize that the marriage is much more pleasant than it was with the grilled chicken.

So what did these little exercises tell you? Simply that wine and food pairings rest on the way you learn to balance or successfully contrast the four fundamental flavors: salty, sweet, sour, and bitter. It is no more mysterious than that and you will become so proficient at it so fast that you will not believe it.

Trying to determine exactly which is the absolutely right wine to accompany a dish and to engage in longish discussions about it is somewhat silly. Unless you have a cellar and know the wines in it well, you will, like the majority of people, go buy a bottle of wine for dinner and have the wine specialist in the store recommend a wine for the dish you are preparing. If you find out that the wine does not work with your dish, the onus is on you to modify the dish, since the wine will not change to please you; it is the way it is. Work patiently to adjust the taste of your dish so that the bottle of wine you purchased is shown as well as it can be. Most wines accused of being "terrible wines" really are not; they are simply not treated properly by the cook; it is as simple as that. As the colloquial expression goes, the monkey is entirely on your back.

WORKING IN DEPTH WITH WHITE WINE

Sole is a soft, bland, very delicate fish that requires strong seasoning to become really tasty. Buy a few small fillets of sole and a bottle of Chardonnay and try the following experiments.

1. First, taste a piece of plain cooked fish unseasoned and follow it with a mouthful of the wine; your reaction will be, whoever said that fish goes well with dry white wine? Indeed, the bland fish meat will bring out the refreshing acidity of the wine so completely that it will maximize it all too much and suggest to you that the wine is sharp when it really is not.

2. Salt a piece of the cooked fish lightly and eat it, then taste the wine again; its acidity will have lessened to the point of giving you the impression that the wine flattens toward the center of your tongue, while still being pleasant and well balanced on the sides of your tongue. Remember where you taste acid? At the very edges of your tongue on both sides, but you taste salt in the spaces immediately between the edges of your tongue and the center of it. Salt spreads its work from that zone toward the center of your tongue as it dissolves in your saliva and appears to modify the taste of the wine over the whole tongue and palate.

3. Now take another piece of fish, salt it, and spoon over it a good dab of dill-flavored oil; nice taste to the fish, indeed, but, as you taste the wine it literally sinks and disappears into your mouth as it hits against not only the salt, but the oil which coats your tongue and keeps it from really perceiving the fruit and acidity of the wine. The conclusion of this experiment is that the combination of salt with one of those modern flavored oils, so popular nowadays, does not do all that much for the enjoyment of a fine white wine with fish.

4. Salt another piece of fish and spoon over it a dab of warm melted butter. Butter contains only 80 percent fat, which is less dense than oil, and approximately 20 percent of slightly acidic whey. This combination will preserve the integrity of the wine more than the heavier, more strongly flavored oil. Now, taste the fish, then the wine and appreciate how the

wine continues to show its natural fruit and acidity in a pleasant balanced manner.

In order to show a wine beautifully when serving a dish seasoned with a flavored oil, two things must be added to it:

- A small quantity of lemon juice or an excellent vinegar that is not too sharp, as the acid in emulsion in the oil will interfere with the total coating action of the pure oil on the palate and,
- Salt, which will both lift the taste of the fish and prevent the different acidities in the dressing and the wine from fighting one another.

5. In yet another experiment: Butter a fillet of sole and charcoal grill it rapidly; it will take you no time to recognize the regrettable fact that, again, the tongue is assaulted by the wine as the slight bitter edge of the grilled fish bonds with the acidity of the wine and intensifies it.

6. In a last experiment with the sole, give a fillet a few minutes of cold smoking, then cook it in a small amount of melted butter. As you taste it and then drink the wine, you will discover that at the same time the salt tempers the acidity of the wine, the light smoky taste latches on to the wine's fruit flavors and its delicate wood essences.

For another fun exercise, why don't you repeat this series using salmon? You will find that the fat in the salmon and the texture of its fibers will lead you to different conclusions, as it would also with swordfish or a fillet of red snapper.

For yet another exercise, repeat the exercise using two Chardonnays, one aged in stainless steel and one aged in wood having undergone the malolactic fermentation, and judge the differences between both.

WORKING WITH AN OLDER WHITE WINE

Older white wines require a lot of care when matching them with food. Without having oxidized to the point of being brownish and having acquired a frank Madeira-like taste, some older wines develop a deep golden color accompanied by a faint aftertaste of sherry, and their acidity is greatly reduced, sometimes barely existent.

The best way to show off such a wine is to present it with a dish prepared with a touch of fino sherry, so that if we were to prepare a fillet of sole again, it would be a nice idea to sauté it lightly in butter, remove the fillet to a plate, whisk a dash of sherry into the butter in the hot pan and dribble the mixture on top of the fillet. Going one step further, you could mix a dab of cream with the sherry and reduce it lightly for a smooth sauce that would blend like silk with the older wine.

WORKING IN DEPTH WITH RED WINE

The principles established for white wines apply to red wines with one added variable: The age of the wine is even more important than it is for white wines.

Young red wines of good quality made to drink within two to four years, such as light Pinots Noirs, Zinfandels, and Gamay Beaujolais, have a pleasant light acidity which helps bring out their intense fruit.

In a young Cabernet Sauvignon aged in oak barrels, the presence of tannins coming both from the skins and pips of the grapes and from the barrels in which the wine was aged will be perceived immediately on the large back papillae of the tongue, making the drinker slightly pucker.

Red wines are for red meats is a statement that should be reconsidered, for if you care to prepare salmon or tuna with a red wine butter or sauce, you will be surprised to discover how delicious it tastes and that it can be accompanied without hesitation by the same wine as was used to prepare the butter or sauce. Which red wines with fish then? A wine that is smooth, that has already lost a large amount of its tannins, or a wine that never had enough tannins: A soft Pinot Noir or a light Zinfandel is just fine. But if you are lucky enough to own older Bordeaux wines, never hesitate to drink some with a nicely panfried salmon, somewhat crisp outside with a soft and moist center.

Great attention should be paid to tannins when one cooks meat, as already explained in the basic exercise on page 110. Using a compound butter containing the well-reduced wine to be drunk with the meal or a small sauce made from a reduction of the same wine and some good stock helps build a bridge between the meat and the wine.

But, you will say, what if you do not like a sauce with your meat? What then? More than ever you will have to season the meat very well with salt but lightly with pepper, or the astringency of the tannins will latch on to the heat of the pepper and the wine will positively scream in your mouth. Also, cook the meat in a frying pan rather than on the grill to avoid the bonding of tannins and charcoal, both of which are detrimental to the balance of the wine.

When you drink a great opulent Cabernet, be very careful of the quantity of salt you use in your dish. There seems to be a threshold not to be crossed, for too much salt can destroy the wine completely by bringing out the tannins with a vengeance for a few seconds. This probably happens because the sites of perception of acid and salt are side by side on both edges of your tongue, and for one second you will perceive the high salt and the high tannin side by side, until by reflex your saliva will help blend the two flavors exactly in the middle of your tongue and relieve the problem somewhat but never completely. The best way to avoid such little jolts is to season "just right." You will get used to this and after a very little while have no problem whatsoever salting meat for lighter or for more opulent wines.

To vary this last exercise, redo it with a Cabernet side by side with a full-bodied Zinfandel, a Barolo, a Châteauneuf-du-Pape, or a Pinot Noir from France.

RED WINES AND CHEESES A cardinal rule of cheese eating is always to remove the rind of any cheese, which, even if the cheese is very fresh, may contain tiny amounts of ammonia which is *the* wine killer par excellence. Just as important is the fact that cheese contains fat, which coats the palate significantly, and can hide the fruit of a wine at the same time as it minimizes its tannins. Cheeses such as Camembert or Brie usually go very well with red wines, even those that are a bit young and slightly tannic, but think of the blue cheeses where the high salt and the mold can latch on to tannins. As an exercise, try different blue cheeses: a drier indifferent Danish Blue, a Stilton, a Roquefort, a Gorgonzola, and a very buttery Danish Sago Blue with different red wines such as Cabernet Sauvignon, Syrah, Châteauneuf-du-Pape, and Barolo. You will see vast changes occur when you drink each wine with each cheese and you will have no difficulty determining which wine goes best with each cheese.

WINE AND SPICY FOODS

It is generally a good idea to respect bands of climates and to serve Mediterranean-style foods with Mediterranean or hot climate wines and colder climate foods with colder climate wines.

With the arrival on our tables of many foods from hot climates which are highly spiced with hot peppers, great efforts have been made to pair these foods with wine. This is, of course, tempting, for certainly some softer or spicier white wines may eventually work, but my philosophy is the following:

If, for centuries, hot foods have been served in hot climates where no grapevines are grown and if, for centuries, people there have served beer or tea with their hot dishes, is their taste not to be trusted? Far from not wanting to be adventurous and creative in wine and food pairing, I am first and foremost dedicated to not damaging wines that have required quite a bit of work and thinking. My personal opinion is to stay with beer when enjoying hot and spicy foods; the bubbles of carbon dioxide in the beer diffuse the heat from the taste buds and allow the diner to further enjoy a dish which, should it be served with wine, would continue building heat on the palate and destroy the palate and the wine.

Having much tolerance for other peoples' tastes, I certainly don't want to be categorical and pull anyone away from their wine experiments, but such is my personal conclusion.

WORKING WITH DESSERT WINES

Sweet dessert wines are usually served with a sweet dessert which most of the time overwhelms the wine. It is important to understand why this happens.

Desserts are usually prepared with a large amount of regular sugar, or sucrose, which, chemically speaking, is a double sugar. Since the largest quantity of sugar contained in a dessert wine is fructose, which is a simple sugar and less sweet, the wine is completely overshadowed by the dessert and one could say that it "sinks" into the dessert.

It may be a good idea if you serve a dessert wine with a prepared dessert to use honey in the latter's preparation rather than plain sugar. But I personally prefer to serve the dessert wine after the dessert has been consumed and after the plates have been removed, so the lovely wine can be appreciated for itself and be the delicious conclusion of the meal.

Spirits and Liqueurs

Brandies

Brandy originated in that part of Spain occupied by the Moors, who apparently invented the distillation process as early as the tenth century, probably in the region of Jerez de la Frontera, home of the great sherries. The fact that spirits and brandies are distilled in an alembic—from the arabic *al ambic,* for "the distilling vase"—tends to confirm the fact, however contradictory it may seem, since the Arab countries consume no alcohol nowadays. From Spain the process made its way north.

A brandy—*Brandwein* or burnt wine in German, *eau-de-vie* in French from the Latin *aqua vitae* or aquavit in Scandinavia—is a transparent liquid resulting from the distillation of wine, fruit, or grain. By distilling ten bottles of wine, one bottle of clear brandy is obtained. Young brandy is colorless, but as it ages in barrels, the wood slowly gives it a brown color and wonderful flavors. Some very good brandies come from Spain where they are aged in barrels used for the making of sherry.

The most famous brandies distilled from wines are Cognac, made from white wines (Ugni Blanc, Saint-Emilion, and Folle Blanche) grown in the area around the French city of Cognac, and, Armagnac, distilled from the Picpoul—another name of the Folle Blanche—wines from the Gers *département,* also in France.

Marc is a brandy distilled from the pomace of skins and pits left after the wine has been pressed. A marc is named after the wine produced from the juice of those same grapes, which produced the pomace out of which it is distilled, so that a bottle label will read Marc de Champagne, Marc de la Romanée-Conti, or Marc de Pommard, for example. In Italy, marc is called grappa when distilled from grapes and/or when made from fruit; the bottle label will indicate from which fruit the grappa was made.

Brandies distilled from fruit are aged in crocks and remain white and colorless. They are usually called simply by the name of the fruit. Fruit liqueurs such as cordials are made by blending fruit syrups with alcohol or a clear brandy. Chartreuse is a 115 proof brandy distilled from more than one hundred herbs. Aquavit is distilled from grain, and vodka may be distilled from grain and/or potatoes, Scotch whisky from rye, and bourbon whiskey from a mash containing a minimum of 51 percent corn, its name deriving from Bourbon County, in Kentucky.

The following is a partial list of the brandies that are mostly used in the preparation of desserts and some main dishes, with the names of the countries from which they are imported:

Grapes (wine)	Cognac and Armagnac from France
	Brandies in all other countries
Grape pomace	Marc in France
	Grappa in Italy
Apples (Cider)	Calvados in France
	Applejack in the United States
Prune Plums	Quetsch in France
	Slivovitz in Slovakia
Raspberries	Framboise in France
	Himbeere in Switzerland and Germany
	Raspberry brandy in California
Strawberries	Fraise in France
	Erdbeere in Switzerland and Germany
Cherries	Kirsch in France
	Kirschwasser in Switzerland and Germany
Pears	Poire in France
	Birnengeist in Switzerland and Germany
Sugarcane	Rums of all colors from all the Caribbean islands

In cooking, domestic brandies may certainly replace imported brandies and applejack can replace Calvados. Brandies and applejack are used to flambé meats and sauces and to flavor *pâtés* and terrines while colorless high-proof fruit brandies are used mostly to flavor desserts, but can occasionally be used in flavoring sauces.

A special word about rum: Rum is the pastry spirit par excellence; it can be chosen according to your own taste, but you may find that with almond-flavored desserts light white rum is better while lime-flavored desserts are enhanced by dark rum.

Liqueurs

Liqueurs are mixtures of plain sugar syrup or pure fruit syrups with pure spirits. They are used as after-dinner drinks equally as much as they are to flavor desserts and an occasional meat sauce. The following imported liqueurs carry the predominant flavors listed; for each of them there is an equivalent domestic liqueur and either may be used. Beware, though, that a number of domestic liqueurs are made from chemical extracts, not distilled spirit of fruit.

- Apry—apricots
- Cherry Marnier, Cherry Heering, and Cherry Rocher—cherries
- Cointreau and Curaçao—orange
- Crème de cacao, white or brown—chocolate
- Noyeau de Poissy—almonds
- Amaretto—almonds of apricots (the seeds extracted from apricot pits)

Certain other imported liqueurs have no domestic substitutes; you must use the original to obtain the exact flavor:

- Grand Marnier—orange and brandy
- Mandarine Napoleon—tangerine
- Tía María from Jamaica, Kahlúa from Mexico, and Kona from Hawaii—coffee
- Chartreuse verte—mountain herbs from Savoie or Spain
- Chartreuse jaune—a sweeter mountain herb brandy
- Benedictine—a sweet herb brandy from Normandy
- B&B—a blend of benedictine and brandy

Cooking with Brandies and Liqueurs

The amount of alcohol contained in any high-proof brandy (marc, Cognac, Armagnac, bourbon, whisky, vodka, gin, etc.) must be burned off before it is added to any dish.

Heat the brandy in a small saucepan, light it carefully with a match, and stir it flambéing into a sauce, or pour it, also flambéing, over a piece of fish or meat. Keep your face away from the flames as you flambé; you are responsible for your own safety.

Brandies can be added to prepared desserts in small quantities without being preflambéed, as can liqueurs with lower alcohol content. Proper proportions vary with the strength of the brandy or liqueur and means that there will be just enough liqueur added so the dessert is agreeably flavored without the taste buds being burned by the raw alcohol. Two tablespoons of liqueur per cup of dessert sauce usually represents the maximum amount. Cakes are said to be "punched" when they are made to absorb a mixture of 50 percent plain sugar syrup and 50 percent of any liqueur.

Cooking with Beer

Beer contains an average of 7 percent alcohol only. To cook with it, it is either used pure, which yields a slightly bitter sauce, or blended half and half with water or stock. Beer should not be reduced by itself as the bitter taste will be unpleasantly accentuated.

Cooking with Cider

When cooking with cider, one should preferably use English or French cider which is tart and contains 7 percent alcohol. One can use straight cider or a mixture of half cider and half water or stock. Unfermented sweet cider that is alcohol-free will have to be corrected with lemon juice or cider vinegar.

Miracles
in a Shell

The Techniques of Egg Cookery

IT IS NOT CONVENTIONAL TO WRITE ABOUT EGGS SO EARLY IN A COOKBOOK, but if you have an early knowledge of the culinary possibilities of the egg, you will acquire better insight into the making of many savory and sweet preparations.

The Nutritive Value of Eggs

The egg yolk contains every vitamin except vitamin C; the deeper the color of the yolk, the higher its carotene content, which is converted to vitamin A in the human body. Of the multiple minerals present in the yolk, iron and phosphorus are the most abundant; calcium is totally absent. In some under-developed countries, though, the pounded shells of eggs are often incorpo-rated into the diet as a source of calcium. Egg yolk also contains, along with a large amount of protein, 33 percent fat and about 50 percent water.

Present in the composition of the egg yolk is the infamous, oh so vexing cholesterol. At this point, it is safe to say that so much has been written about cholesterol and its effects that all of us are more or less scared "stiff" about eating even an egg once a week. The egg industry has had to advertise seriously that "four a week is safe" and mercifully smart egg farms have started producing eggs with considerably reduced amounts of cholesterol by feeding the hens strictly vegetable matter. Look for eggs from hens on a veg-etarian diet—the boxes are labeled clearly—and you can safely have your favorite eggs twice a week, going back to natural, nonpresweetened cereals on the other days without feeling guilty in any way. Everything in modera-tion. People with cholesterol levels that are difficult to control must follow their physician's advice in this matter.

Egg white, also called albumen, contains more than ten different proteins, each of them playing a very important role in the future development of the chicken. A globulin known as lysozyme has an antibiotic power to protect the chicken embryo against infection; the still-active lysozyme allows refrig-erated egg whites to keep for a relatively long time without spoiling. Of all the vitamins contained in the white, the B-complex riboflavin is the most valuable; it gives the egg white its yellow-greenish tinge. Egg white contains as much as 87 percent water, which is useful in baking.

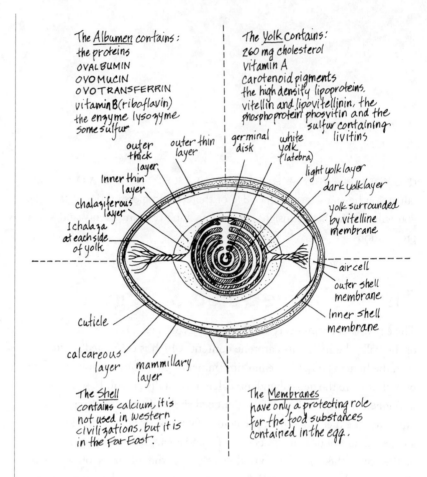

The Albumen contains:
the proteins
OVALBUMIN
OVOMUCIN
OVOTRANSFERRIN
vitamin B (riboflavin)
the enzyme lysozyme
some sulfur

The Yolk contains:
260 mg cholesterol
vitamin A
carotenoid pigments
the high density lipoproteins,
vitellin and lipovitellinin, the
phosphoprotein phosvitin and the
sulfur containing livitins

outer thin layer
outer thick layer
Inner thin layer
chalaziferous layer
1 chalaza at each side of yolk
germinal disk
white yolk (latebra)
light yolk layer
dark yolk layer
yolk surrounded by vitelline membrane
air cell
outer shell membrane
Inner shell membrane
Cuticle
calcareous layer
mammillary layer

The Shell
contains calcium, it is
not used in western
civilizations, but it is
in the Far East.

The Membranes
have only a protecting role
for the food substances
contained in the egg.

In centuries past eggs were the protein of the European poor who ate them almost daily for lunch or dinner, which explains why there are so many recipes for egg dishes in the western European cuisines. Also, as recently as ten years ago, they were "lean" fare for the important meatless religious days of most Christian churches, so it was important to prepare them attractively. The Anglo-Saxon and some of the Germanic and Scandinavian countries prefer eggs at breakfast, but in most of Continental Europe, especially in the Mediterranean, they still are considered main course fare.

Egg Grades

Lucky the farmer who raises chickens and has day-old eggs! In large cities, fresh eggs are more of a rarity nowadays than is ever realized. The best quality eggs found on the market are Graded AA, Fresh Fancy quality. If at all possible, these should be used for feeding infants and young children and for poaching since they were graded within the past ten days.

• Grade AA eggs are more than ten days old.

- Plain Grade A may be as old as three weeks or more.
- Grade B, in my opinion, should not be used, even in the making of dishes in which the eggs are mixed and cooked with other ingredients.

A fresh egg is easily recognizable. Whole and in its unbroken shell, it will fall to the bottom of a pan of water immediately, because its content is dense, compact, and heavy. The egg has not been in contact with the surrounding atmosphere long enough to allow air to penetrate the porous shell and accumulate in the air pocket. Conversely, an older egg, full of air, bobs to the surface of the water and even floats.

Evaluating the Freshness of an Egg

When broken, a fresh egg eight to ten days old shows an air pocket the size of a dime at the bottom of the rounded part of its shell. The size of the air pocket increases to that of a penny from two weeks on. Break a Grade B egg and try to figure out how old the poor thing is! A Grade AA, Fancy Fresh quality egg has a raised plump yolk the color of which will vary with the diet of the hen from darker yellow to lighter yellow, depending on the type and amount of carotenoid pigment the feed contains. No matter how deep yellow this color is, it is not indicative of how much vitamin A the yolk contains since all of the pigments in the yolk may not be precursors to vitamin A (beta-carotene will be, lycopene and xanthophyll will not). The albumen is thick and barely spreads in a pan.

Keeping Eggs Fresh and Safe

To preserve their freshness, you should store eggs in the refrigerator, but never on the open shelf built by refrigerator makers for that purpose; the shell, being porous, absorbs all sorts of odors when stored that way. Keep eggs well separated from cheeses and pungent fruit such as melon. On the contrary, should you have truffles or fresh boleti, you could make a truffle or boleti omelette by simply interspersing the eggs among the mushrooms.

Keep eggs in the carton in which they are sold, and as they are sold, which is blunt end up. This keeps the yolk centered, making for a better looking cooked egg, especially when hard cooked. If you pay no attention to the centering of the yolk, you may be interested to know that French farm lore maintains that when the eggs are stored pointed end up, the weight of the egg presses on the air pocket, thus keeping it small.

Eggs cook better when they are at room temperature. However, because of the recent problem of contamination by salmonella bacteria, which can cause severe intestinal disturbances and sickness, it is essential to keep eggs refrigerated as long as possible. Warm eggs for ten minutes in warm water, if necessary, if they are too cold before cooking them, then cook them immediately. Salmonella is a problem only if you do not cook the eggs to the temperature at which all bacteria will be destroyed, which is at least 160°F or when the egg is not runny anymore. So unless you are absolutely certain that the eggs are free of any contamination—which is not easy to ascertain, since most of us do not produce our own eggs—start cooking eggs a little deeper than you did before all that talk about contaminated eggs came around. By the time this new text is published, the egg industry, which is working very hard on the problem, will hopefully have been successful in producing salmonella-free eggs. Meanwhile, prepare your Caesar salad with egg yolks mixed with salted water and foamed over heat to at least 160°F as is done for hollandaise and béarnaise sauces (see pages 350 and 352).

If an egg is left to reach room temperature outside of its shell even for the shortest time, the membrane of its yolk, exposed to the air, dehydrates, shrivels, and hardens; this hardened part will form unpleasant specks which will not whip properly, or will have to be strained out of custards, or will remain in cake batters or omelettes. If out-of-shell eggs must wait unrefrigerated more than a few minutes but no more than thirty, a length of plastic wrap stretched over them will alleviate this problem by trapping the moisture lost by the egg yolks and bouncing it back and forth between their surfaces and that of the plastic film.

When using eggs it is a good practice to break each egg individually into a small cup before adding it to any preparation. Some eggs contain large splotches of bright red blood; they must be discarded since they indicate a sick hen. Some eggs, which have been fertilized, will contain a tiny embryo; remove it with a spoon before you use the egg.

SALMONELLA, A NASTY ORGANISM

Because the eggshell is porous it can be infiltrated by the live bacteria existing in any of the soiling media to be found in egg nests or in the possibly contaminated water in which fresh eggs may have been washed before being boxed.

Among these bacteria is the very dangerous salmonella which in anyone who is tired, sick, or physically weakened in any way can bring on two to seven days of debilitating sickness characterized by the most excruciating abdominal pains and diarrhea. There is no way to know just by looking at either the unbroken shell of an egg or any egg just broken and dropped into a bowl whether that egg is contaminated by this organism or not. The most recent research has established that the contamination of eggs by salmonella can happen within the ovaries or oviduct of any infected laying hen. For more information on this subject, contact the Egg Board.

For safety's sake, take the following precautions:

- If you have your own egg-laying hens, keep the nests clean. After you gather the fresh eggs, put on rubber gloves and rinse off any soil on the eggshells under running cold water. Change to a new pair of rubber gloves, then scrub the eggs in water at 140°F and dry with a clean towel.

Store the clean eggs in a plastic container with a tight-fitting lid and use them within a few days.

- If you buy your eggs in a supermarket, buy the best possible grade of eggs, most recently boxed, checking the expiration date carefully on the box. Examine each egg for hairline cracks. *Do not use cracked eggs ever, even if the crack is barely visible.* Storebought eggs have already been washed; keep them either in their original carton or in a plastic box with a tight-fitting lid.
- If you operate any type of food operation, purchase and use exclusively *pasteurized eggs*.

The Size of Eggs

It is preferable to use large rather than jumbo or medium-size eggs. A large egg weighs about 2 ounces or 55 to 60 metric grams. It contains barely three tablespoons of white and barely one tablespoon of yolk. If large eggs are not available, use the following measurements to compensate adequately:

One measuring cup contains:

- 5 large eggs
- 4 extra large (jumbo) eggs
- 6 medium-size eggs
- 7 small eggs

It may happen that a recipe calls for one half egg. To measure half an egg accurately, break an egg into a cup and beat it just to mix. Measure the tablespoons of beaten egg contained in the small cup and use half that amount.

The Use of the Chemical and Physical Properties of Eggs in Cookery

Once you are aware of the properties of eggs, you will be more efficient in egg cookery.

1. *Be aware of sulfides.* The taste of semispoiled, semistale eggs, too often present in cooked eggs, is caused by hydrogen sulfide, which is released from the sulfur contained in the white if the egg is cooked at too high a temperature.

   In addition, that discouraging-looking gray ring around the yolk of a hard-cooked egg, combined with the unpleasant smell it has, would not be there if the egg had not been overcooked, giving time for the iron in the yolk to combine with the sulfur in the white to produce iron sulfide, and the gray ring.

2. *Be aware of protein denaturation and coagulation when cooking eggs.* Cookery utilizes the capability of egg protein to denature and coagulate. Viscous in the raw state, egg proteins progressively denature when submitted to heat and end up coagulating completely:

- Egg white becomes firm between 145° and 150°F
- Egg yolk coagulates between 144° and 150°F
- A whole egg is completely coagulated by 180°F

The expression "She doesn't even know how to cook an egg" generally applied to a young inexperienced woman-cook is, to say the least, unfair, for all methods of cooking eggs, both as savory dishes or desserts, are tricky and require attention, even experience.

Bear in mind at all times that unless you know for a fact that the eggs you are using are totally free of contamination by salmonella, the yolks of coddled, shirred, and fried eggs must reach at least 150°F, which, from the temperature information given above, will give you well-done eggs.

The description given below is for eggs that are bacteriologically sanitary and which can be cooked without worry; it is up to you to ascertain this fact.

Techniques Using the Coagulating Properties of Eggs

In the following paragraphs, the techniques explained will all illustrate the different ways of partially or completely coagulating eggs to obtain:

1. Savory egg dishes
2. Custard sauces, semisolid custards, and solid custards that can be inverted from their pans

Savory Egg Dishes Prepared by the Partial or Complete Coagulation of Eggs

Cooked eggs are often presented in croustades; indeed, many of the egg preparations described below will acquire an added attractiveness if the eggs are served in a croustade, which may be a pastry shell, but more often is made out of white bread. An American-style croustade is easy to make: Remove the crust from a regular slice of white bread. Pass a rolling pin over the bread once to flatten it and butter or lightly oil the bread on one side. Gently bend the bread to fit it, buttered side out, into a muffin tin. Bake in a preheated 350°F oven until golden.

Another more interesting croustade can be obtained by buttering half a sheet of phyllo dough lightly, folding it into a square, and fitting the square of dough into a muffin tin. Bake in a preheated 325°F oven until pale golden.

CODDLED EGGS

There are at least five different ways of coddling, or soft-cooking, an egg. This is the easiest:

Use at least 1½ cups water per egg; bring the water to a boil in a saucepan. Immerse the whole egg(s) in their shell(s), in the rapidly boiling water. Remove the pot from the heat, cover it, and keep it tightly closed for 4 to 6 minutes, depending on the doneness you desire. Then immerse the eggs in cold water to stop the cooking.

Coddled eggs are to be enjoyed without garnish, just with bread and butter. They make a royal meal.

SHIRRED EGGS

Shirred eggs are usually baked in individual round shallow dishes just large enough to contain one or two eggs. Shirred eggs taste better without garnish, but they may be sprinkled with grated cheese or 1 tablespoon or so of the cream of your choice may be spooned over them before cooking. A very aromatic shirred egg is obtained when the dish is first rubbed with a cut garlic clove.

Shirring eggs is easy, but watch that timer! Heat 1 teaspoon butter in each shirred-egg dish; break each egg into a small cup and empty the cup into each of the "shirrers." Set all the dishes on a large baking sheet. Bake in the upper third of a preheated 500°F oven for 1½ minutes. Baste each yolk with another teaspoon of melted butter, unless you have used cream, and bake for another minute. The intensity of the heat is such that the albumen is coagulated immediately without having time to harden.

Eggs in ramekins, or *cocottes*, are another version of shirred eggs. A glass custard cup or a deep round ramekin is used instead of a shirrer. Since a ramekin has thicker walls than a shirrer, the eggs need to be cooked at a lower temperature for slow, even penetration of the heat. Set the buttered custard cups in a hot water bath filled just before cooking with boiling water, and bake in a preheated 375°F oven for about 12 minutes.

Celebration Succotash Ramekins

FFR— 6 SERVINGS

One 10-ounce package frozen succotash

Pinch of granulated sugar

Salt

Pepper from the mill

1 tablespoon unsalted butter or unsaturated oil of your choice

⅔ cup heavy cream, scalded

6 large eggs

⅔ cup shredded cheddar cheese of your choice

This shouldn't be for every day; keep this presentation for a Sunday when friends or family are coming for breakfast or brunch. In winter this also can make a pleasant lunch first course.

Preheat the oven to 325°F. Cook the succotash until tender in boiling water to cover seasoned with the sugar, salt, and pepper. Drain well. Butter six 3-ounce custard cups with the butter. Place an equal amount of the vegetables into each custard cup. Add 2 tablespoons of the scalded cream to each cup. Break each egg into a teacup and transfer to each ramekin, salt and pepper lightly, and cover each with 2 tablespoons of the cheddar.

Set the ramekins in a baking dish. Bring a kettle of water to a boil and after setting the baking dish on the middle oven shelf, pour the boiling water into it. Bake 12 to 14 minutes, until the white is firm, which you may test by inserting a skewer into the thickest part of the white. If the skewer comes out clean, serve without delay.

FRIED EGGS

Fried eggs may be panfried or deep-fried. Deep-fried eggs, a garnish of some stews in the old French cuisine, are seldom used anymore. This is no great loss, since a deep-fried egg is surrounded by a golden but tough layer of over-cooked egg white, most unattractive to the taste buds.

The fried eggs we are familiar with are those cooked in fat in a frying pan. Taste intervenes here; some people like their eggs sizzled, some not. To obtain sizzled eggs, fry them in the fat of your choice over medium heat. Cover the pan during the last few minutes of cooking to solidify the upper layers of egg white. To obtain unsizzled fried eggs, cook them as you prefer, in butter or a dab of pure olive oil, over very low heat. Also cover them during the last 2 minutes of cooking to finish firming up the top; when eggs are fried this way, they are very close to shirred eggs.

Another way to firm up the top white of fried eggs is to flip them over once gently using a turner, hence the expression "once over lightly" or "over easy". Do this little flipping without hesitation; the less you hesitate, the less you break the yolks.

Eggs Prepared in the Valley Dosta
UOVA ALLA VALDOSTANA

A deep winter warm antipasto from the old Hôtel de la Source in Saint Vincent d'Aosta in the Italian Piemonte, which is much appreciated for brunch in our family.

FFR—6 SERVINGS

2 tablespoons olive or other unsaturated oil of your choice

2 cloves garlic, finely chopped

2 tablespoons chopped fresh parsley leaves

6 large eggs

2 anchovy fillets, finely mashed

I teaspoon finely grated lemon rind

6 small ¼-inch-thick slices Fontina cheese, large enough to cover an egg

Heat the oil in the skillet, then add the garlic and parsley and cook over medium heat, stirring, until brown. Spread the mixture evenly over the entire bottom of the pan. Add the eggs one at a time and allow their bottoms to lightly sizzle; keep their tops soft. Top each egg yolk with a dab of the mashed anchovy, a tiny sprinkle of the lemon rind, and one slice of the Fontina. Turn the heat down to low and cover the skillet a few minutes, until the Fontina starts melting. Serve in the skillet.

POACHED EGGS

Poaching eggs can be fun if the eggs are not more than three days old, but who can be sure except the farmer? With older eggs, poaching is not that much fun anymore, since the older, too-fluid white produces stragglers in the water.

To make things easier, butter a large frying pan and add about 2 quarts water to it; the water should be 2 inches deep. Bring the water to a boil and add 2 tablespoons vinegar and 2 teaspoons salt; they will help coagulate the egg faster. Reduce the heat until the water is barely simmering. Break an egg into a lightly buttered or oiled teacup. Tilt the cup and lower it into the water; count slowly to fifteen, then let the egg gently slide down into the water. If stragglers appear, bunch them on top of the egg with a slotted spoon. Cook the egg 4 minutes, then remove it from the water with a slotted spoon; immerse the egg in a bowl of warm salted water if you are serving the eggs immediately, or cold water if you wish to refrigerate them. To reheat them, simply reheat the water in which you refrigerated them.

Drain the eggs on a clean thick towel before saucing and garnishing them. Should you find it difficult to poach eggs—and the age of your eggs will be more responsible for difficulty than your skills—break each of them into individual buttered custard cups of the smallest size; set the custard cups in a baking dish. Just before baking in a preheated 375°F oven, pour boiling water into the baking dish, so that the water reaches just below the rim of each cup, and bake about 12 minutes. When unmolded, the eggs will look unnaturally regular in shape, but they will fit neatly on buttered toast.

Klaus's Hungarian Poached Eggs

For a fall Sunday morning, when the last tomatoes of the season are coming in from the lightly frosted garden. This was prepared for me by a Hungarian friend from Vienna; he called the sauce gulyas sauce.

FFR — 6 SERVINGS

3 large, preferably sun-ripened tomatoes

2 large green bell peppers

3 large onions

¼ cup unsalted butter

½ teaspoon caraway seeds

1 tablespoon Hungarian paprika of your choice, sweet or hot

Salt

Pepper from the mill

6 slices white bread, lightly toasted and crusts removed

6 poached eggs, warm or reheated (page 129)

½ cup sour cream of your choice

6 tablespoons grated Austrian "Swiss" cheese

Prepare the sauce as much as 24 hours ahead of time: Remove the stem end of each tomato and immerse all of them in boiling water for 2 minutes. Remove the tomatoes from the water, rinse them under very cold water, then peel, seed, and dice them.

Preheat the broiler. Broil the peppers, turning them at regular intervals to char their skins. Remove the peppers to a brown paper bag, and let them steam for a few minutes. Remove the pepper skins and seeds, derib the peppers very well, and dice finely.

Turn the oven temperature down to 375°F. Peel and dice the onions coarsely. Melt half the butter in a large skillet and brown the onions, add the tomatoes and peppers, caraway seeds, and paprika. Cook gently over medium-low heat until the mixture is well bound and has the texture of applesauce. Correct the final seasoning with salt and pepper.

Using a 2-inch biscuit cutter, cut a circle out of each slice of bread. Butter a baking dish; add the toasts and place one reheated poached egg in the center of each of them. Mix the sour cream into the hot gulyas, top each egg with an equal amount of it, and sprinkle each egg with the grated cheese. Bake until the cheese has melted and starts browning, about 5 minutes.

MOLLET AND HARD-COOKED EGGS

Another kind of egg, cooked in the shell, is the 6-minute, or "*mollet*," egg; *mollet* in Old French means softish. Mollet eggs can replace poached eggs in various dishes and were often used in the famous eggs in aspic so dear to the French and to which I stopped being partial after canned bouillon or powdered jelly replaced the very sapid homemade veal stock aspic of my young days.

So that mollet eggs all cook for the same length of time, place them in a frying basket and lower them into the boiling water all together. Simmer for exactly 6 minutes. Remove the basket from the hot water and immerse it immediately in cold water. The contact with the cold water produces a layer of steam between egg and shell, which makes peeling easy.

The very same method is used for hard-cooked eggs, which should be left to simmer for 10 minutes, no more, to avoid the formation of iron sulfide as mentioned on page 125.

To peel a mollet or hard-cooked egg, roll it at its center against the sharp angle of a table or counter; remove the soft cracked shell belt first. The top and bottom of the shell will come off with just a little pull, and the egg will show no scar.

Grandmother Charlotte's Eggs and Mushrooms

FFR—6 SERVINGS

½ pound fresh mushrooms of your choice, white or brown

1 tablespoon unsalted butter or pure olive oil

Salt

Pepper from the mill

1 clove garlic, finely chopped

1½ tablespoons chopped fresh Italian parsley leaves

6 hard-cooked eggs (page 130)

Several gratings of fresh nutmeg

6 tablespoons finely grated Gruyère cheese

Clean and dice the mushrooms coarsely. Heat the butter or oil in a skillet. Add the mushrooms, salt, pepper, garlic, and parsley. Mix well and sauté 2 minutes over medium-high heat. Cover and cook the mushrooms over medium heat until their juices run into the pan.

Meanwhile, cut the eggs into halves, remove all the yolks, and coarsely mash three yolks only. Remove the lid of the skillet, add the nutmeg, stir, and let half of the mushroom juices evaporate. Off the heat add the mashed egg yolks; mix until a homogeneous paste forms. Correct the seasoning carefully.

Cut a fine sliver from the bottom of each half hard-boiled egg white to allow each to sit in a heatproof baking dish. Fill the half shells evenly with the mixture of mushrooms and yolks. Sprinkle with an equal amount of the cheese and broil a few minutes, until the cheese is golden. Serve piping hot.

SCRAMBLED EGGS

Scrambled eggs are mis-scrambled by the millions every morning in America, perhaps because most people do not like "wet" eggs or because most were served dry eggs in their home and believe that this is the only way scrambled eggs can be prepared.

A wonderful memory from my paternal grandmother's kitchen. This dish, which was always prepared for my three cousins and me when we were children to replace whatever we may not have been too fond of on the adult menu of the day, taught me to love garlic.

NOTE: *My grandmother added a bit of butter, sugar, flour, and vanilla to the remaining three mashed egg yolks to make us a few shortbreads.*

Please give yourself, your family, or guests the chance to taste a truly scrambled egg just once. Use a thick pan; a heavy aluminum pan with a Silvertone coating is the best since it allows the cook to use either no fat or less fat than other pans.

Beat the eggs well, but do not liquefy them. Only if you desire—and on Sunday only—add ½ tablespoon heavy cream per egg. Add very little salt before cooking, for it hardens the egg proteins and you can always add more for perfect taste after cooking.

For the sake of excellent taste, since we do not eat so many scrambled eggs anymore, use 1 tablespoon butter per egg for a celebration breakfast or 1 teaspoon of unsaturated oil for an everyday breakfast. Melt the butter or heat the oil, add the beaten eggs and, stirring *constantly* with a whisk or large fork, cook over low heat. The eggs soon form a slightly granular custard. Keep breaking the curds; the smaller the curd, the softer and creamier the eggs. As soon as the eggs are two-thirds solidified, remove the pan from the heat. The heat retained in the pan is sufficient to finish cooking the eggs. If you leave them over heat longer, they will start drying up.

The higher the heat you use, the drier the eggs, so that if you prefer dry scrambled eggs with large curds, all you have to do is whisk slowly over relatively high heat. Scrambled eggs at their best still have a shiny appearance. Scrambled eggs have a tendency to lose their creamy custardlike consistency when milk, water, or any water-producing food is added to them before scrambling; any vegetable addition (tomatoes, mushrooms) should be presautéed until dry. Some cheeses with a high level of lactic acid (such as Parmesan-style cheeses not made in Italy) will have a disastrous effect on the egg proteins, often causing them to lose their water; they should be added during the last stages of cooking, after the pan has been removed from the heat. Cold scrambled eggs are considered a delicacy by some, but rather unattractive by others.

A Scrambled Eggs Treat

FFR—6 TO 8 SERVINGS

6 sheets frozen phyllo dough, thawed

6 tablespoons unsalted butter

2 medium-size Oregon truffles, scrubbed

½ cup Primary Veal Stock (page 219) or Secondary Stock (page 220)

2 tablespoons Sercial Madeira or fino sherry

12 large eggs

½ cup heavy cream

Salt

Pepper from the mill

1½ tablespoons chopped fresh chives

Now that the discovery of the effects of cholesterol has ruined our happiness in eating eggs with abandon, it is essential that we insist on enjoying a dish of them once in a while. This is for Christmas morning and in memory of all those lovely times reading Dr. Seuss's Scrambled Eggs Super! *to my children and looking forward to doing the same*

Preheat the oven to 325°F. Cut the phyllo sheets in half crosswise. Melt 2 tablespoons of the butter and brush the phyllo sheets with it. Fold the phyllo halves into squares and fit into twelve muffin cups. Bake on the middle shelf of the oven until the phyllo cups have turned pale beige. Set aside.

Slice the truffles without peeling them—their skins are very thin. Melt another tablespoon of the butter in a skillet. Add the slices of truffles and gently heat until the mushrooms develop a good earthy smell. Add the stock and wine and reduce slowly until only a glaze surrounds the slices of truffle.

Heat the remaining butter in a Silverstone-coated skillet until it turns brown and smells of hazelnuts (see noisette butter, page 32) and beat the eggs with the heavy cream. Salt and pepper to your taste. Add the eggs to the pan and cook over medium-low heat, stirring or whisking them constantly until they form a lovely soft custard. During the last few minutes of cooking, add the chives, then spoon the eggs into the phyllo cups. Top each cup with a few slices of the truffles and their juices. Fast to the table so the eggs do not continue cooking and turn hard. Try a bottle of Champagne with that and you will be feeling on top of the world for the whole day.

OMELETTES

Yet another old favorite, the humble omelette, which for centuries was the daily fare of millions of the poor in all western countries, and which in our hunger-filled world would be a luxurious dish for many a child, has to be considered a treat only for those of us who are lucky enough to be the beneficiaries of a normal nutrition. Unless one makes it with a majority of egg whites, an omelette should be an occasional pleasure in order to avoid the daily intake of too much cholesterol. The recipe for a one-egg plus two-egg-whites omelette given on page 136 will be of help for those who must pay stringent attention to any cholesterol problem.

How was the first omelette born? Who knows? If we believe Prosper Montagné in *Larousse Gastronomique*, many people were involved, from the Romans to a mythical king of Spain. The truth is probably that an involuntary breakage and scrambling became, along the centuries, a technique to be mastered. The French word *omelette* itself is a metathesis for *alemette* or *alumette* which in Old French means "sheet." The etymology given by Harold McGee in his wonderful book *On Food and Cooking* makes sense, if one realizes that all omelettes in the Latin countries are flat (Italian *frittate* and Spanish tortillas) and look indeed like a flat plate, called in Latin *lamella*.

Making an omelette used to be almost a romantic endeavor. I remember how much I enjoyed writing all the details of the making of omelettes in the first edition of this book. One had to have an old-fashioned cast-iron French omelette pan, which needed to be conditioned with salt and oil when brand new, and never was supposed to be washed. And indeed it was not, the heat took care of any sterilization problem. I remember my despair when a well-intentioned baby-sitter cooked dinner for one of my children in my omelette

with my grandchildren. Use Oregon truffles which can be found all through the winter at reasonable prices.

pan, which from then on became sticky for several months, no matter what I tried to do to recondition it properly. A true drama in the kitchen! Little did I know that within five years modern technology would change all that, removing all the love for one's omelette pan, but in exchange allowing one to produce the best omelette in fifteen to twenty seconds. I have kept my old cast-iron omelette pans as treasures, for in classes for training professional chefs, I never allow the use of plastic-coated pans until each student has mastered all omelette cooking methods in the old cast-iron ones.

Thick aluminum pans lined with Teflon, Silverstone, or other fibrous coatings allow us to produce omelettes that are just the best and can be prepared with very little butter. Clarified butter (see page 32) is no longer necessary and you can even skip butter altogether if you wish; however, I tend not to be so happy with this because butter is integral to the taste of a good omelette.

Preparations for omelettes nowadays are pretty basic. Get your pan out; the making of a one-, two-, or three-egg omelette per person remains preferable to the making of a six- or seven-egg omelette for three to four persons. But since all thick plastic-coated aluminum pans are relatively inexpensive nowadays, have two pans, one 8-inch for small omelettes and one 9- to 10-inch for larger ones.

TO OBTAIN MAXIMUM VOLUME IN MAKING OMELETTES It could be argued from the food science point of view that omelettes should be explained in the section on using egg foams. Since the foam in an omelette batter should barely start to develop, I prefer to leave omelettes here.

Break the eggs into a small bowl, add a large pinch of salt, several turns of the peppermill, and beat thirty strokes with a fork, so only a minimal foam made of very large bubbles forms. Do not overbeat, otherwise it will overliquefy the eggs which will develop less volume than they should while cooking, the result being "skinny" omelettes that never reach that wonderful "fat" and satisfying look on the plate. Beat the eggs enough so that the little bit of foam you have produced is trapped in the batter when you cook the eggs.

Heat the pan over medium heat, adding to it ½ teaspoon to 1 tablespoon butter, as you see fit. When the butter sizzles, the pan is ready; raise the heat very high and add the beaten eggs. From here on the key word is *speed*: the faster, the better. An omelette is the result of a combination of speed and high heat affecting an egg mixture, scrambling it into large curds. The curds coagulate in the shortest possible amount of time and, as a result of and in spite of the higher heat, stay soft. The bottom layer of the omelette is exposed a few seconds longer to the heat of the pan and hardens just enough to form a casing for the bulk of the eggs.

There used to be three different ways of making an omelette: scramble it, beat it, or shake it. With the modern pans, shaking remains the most efficient and the fastest and also provides excellent volume.

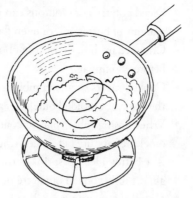

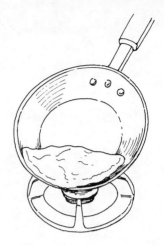

Hold the pan at a 45-degree angle to throw the eggs against the lip of the pan, then shake pan back and forth.

Set the pan flat on the burner, rotating it right to left and vice versa to bring the cooked egg toward the center and the uncooked egg toward the perimeter of the pan.

Omelette ready to turn onto a plate

TO PREPARE A SHAKEN OMELETTE   Pour the omelette mixture into the pan; count "one" exactly as the beaten egg hits the pan; continue counting to five, then immediately grab the handle of the pan with your working hand and raise the pan so it forms a 45-degree angle with the burner. Rapidly shake the pan back and forth so that the egg mixture is thrown against the front lip of the pan and coagulates there. *Do not be afraid or hesitant;* the angle at which you hold the pan and the speed with which you work make it impossible for you to spill the batter. Very soon, the batter forms a dam enclosing still-liquid egg; let the pan lie flat on the burner for one second and quickly give a circular motion to the pan to let the liquid portion pour out back into the pan. Return to shaking and from then on, alternate circular motions and shaking until the eggs have scrambled in superimposed sheets; the whole operation requires 15 to 20 seconds. The "lip of the pan" portion of the omelette will fold upon itself, forming the first flap. Raise the pan a little higher and fold the larger portion of the omelette over that first flap with a spatula; the little time spent on this last operation will allow the bottom of the omelette to shape and coagulate; immediately invert the omelette onto a serving plate or platter.

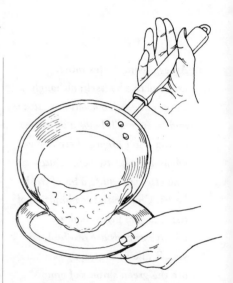

Position of the hand on pan handle to turn omelette over

TO INVERT AN OMELETTE   Open your hand *palm up*, close it around the pan handle, and turn the pan upside down over a plate. What was the bottom of the omelette in the pan becomes its top on the plate. Rub the top of the omelette with a small piece of cold butter stuck on the tines of a fork; this will make it glisten and look attractive. No additional butter desired? Simply skip this step.

OMELETTE FILLINGS   A plain omelette becomes an elegant dish when filled. However, any filling containing either protein or water should not touch the pan, or the mixture will start flowing into the pan and a mush of eggs and filling may result.

- Diced potatoes or croutons can be sautéed in the omelette pan in a small amount of butter, oil, or even flavored oil before adding the eggs.
- Chopped fresh herbs of your choice can be added to the beaten egg batter before cooking it.
- Cooked meats or any combination of sauce and meats should be laid on the flat, yet unfolded omelette, and encased between the two flaps.
- When using fiber plastic-coated pans, grated cheese added to the omelette mixture before cooking will not make the omelette stick; still, it is a better idea to sprinkle the grated cheese down the center of the almost fully cooked omelette only one or two "shakes" before folding it.
- No filling of any type will escape from an omelette if it is set at its very center before folding.

Lower Cholesterol Omelette

FCR — I SERVING

½ cup **Primary Veal Stock** (page 219), completely defatted

I large egg from vegetarian hens

2 large egg whites from vegetarian hens

2 teaspoons each chopped fresh parsley, tarragon, and chervil leaves

I tablespoon chopped fresh chives

Salt

Pepper from the mill

I½ teaspoons unsaturated oil of your choice (olive, canola, grapeseed, sunflower, or corn)

An egg white tastes rather unattractive by itself; although it can produce an omelette, its taste and texture will leave a lot to be desired. So I propose here a one-whole-egg plus two-egg-whites omelette with quite a bit of fresh herbs. Change the combination of herbs as you prefer and use whichever ones are available to you. Scallions are very good, as are the green sprouts of onions and shallots that shoot up when they sense that spring is arriving and so are garlic and mint mixed together in the Arab way. This omelette must be beaten, so follow my directions precisely. The meat glaze on top of the omelette is strictly optional and is there to disguise the slightly dominant taste of the egg whites.

Over medium heat, reduce the veal stock to 2½ tablespoons; keep warm. Beat the whole egg and additional whites together with a fork until the mixture is full of very large bubbles and lightened, *but not* until it starts really foaming heavily. Beat in the herbs, and salt and pepper to your taste.

Brush the oil on the bottom of a nonstick pan. Heat the pan to medium-high only, not on very high, to prevent any sulfur taste from developing and the egg white protein-loaded mixture from hardening excessively. Pour the egg mixture into the hot pan and beat until the mixture forms large curds. Shake the pan back and forth on the burner to smooth and equalize the texture of the omelette bottom. Bring the curd to the lip of the pan by raising the handle at a 45-degree angle and, with a spatula, fold the top part of the omelette over the part already resting in the lip of the pan. Invert onto a plate as you would a regular omelette. Spoon the meat glaze over the omelette. *Serve and consume very fast;* you should wait for this omelette, it should never wait for you or a slight sulfur taste will start developing as it sits on the plate and continues cooking inside.

Regular Whole-Egg Omelettes

FFR— I SERVING

2 large eggs

Pinch of salt, varying to your personal taste from a real pinch to ⅛ teaspoon

Pepper from the mill

I tablespoon heavy cream (optional)

Mix together the ingredients, simply follow the general directions on page 135, and have fun.

All the formulas for omelettes given below are calculated for one person. As the number of guests at a table increases, the number of eggs per person needed to serve them diminishes. You can, for example, serve eight people with six eggs if the filling is substantial, seven if made with herbs and consequently less substantial. The amount of filling will also not be as large proportionally for a large omelette for six people as it would be for a smaller omelette for one person.

Here are a few omelette recipes for you to enjoy, plus a recipe for a lovely Italian frittata and one for a Spanish tortilla.

This is all you need to prepare a basic full-fat omelette for one person.

Potato and Scallion Omelette

FFR— I SERVING

I tablespoon unsalted butter or unsaturated oil of your choice

I small potato of your choice, peeled and diced into ⅓-inch cubes

2 large eggs from vegetarian hens

Pinch of salt

5 turns of the pepper mill or to taste

2 tablespoons finely slivered scallions (white and light green parts only)

I tablespoon crème fraîche or heavy cream (optional)

Preheat the omelette pan over medium-high heat. Add the chosen fat or oil and sauté the potatoes in it until nice and golden all around. Beat the eggs with the salt, pepper, and slivered scallions. Pour the mixture into the omelette pan over the potatoes and shake until the omelette has shaped up as instructed on page 135. Fold over and invert onto a warm plate.

Spoon the crème fraîche over the top of the omelette and serve immediately.

This is certainly basic food, but it remains one of the great favorites of all the French provincial cuisines. This version is often made in Normandy when the shallots are sprouting at the end of winter.

The Devil's Omelette

FFR — I SERVING

I slice white bread

2 teaspoons prepared Dijon mustard

2 large eggs from vegetarian hens

Salt

Pepper from the mill

I ½ teaspoons unsalted butter or olive oil

½ to I tablespoon crème fraîche or heavy cream (optional)

My great grandmother called it "l'omelette du Diable," confusing le diable—the devil—with diablotins, or tiny mustard-flavored croutons. Speed is of the essence so the effect of the acid mustard does not damage the egg texture as the cooking proceeds.

Remove the crust from the bread. Toast it on both sides, then let cool. Spread the cooled bread on both sides with a very thin film of the mustard, then dice the bread into ⅓-inch cubes. Beat the eggs, salt, and pepper together well. Just before cooking, add the butter to the pan and heat over medium-high. Add the mustard croutons to the batter. Pour the egg-and-crouton mixture into the pan and cook the omelette as rapidly as possible as instructed on page 135. Invert onto a plate. If used, mix the crème fraîche with the remaining mustard and spread it over the top of the finished omelette.

Creamed Salmon Omelette

FFR — 2 SERVINGS

3 tablespoons crème fraîche

3 slices Nova Scotia salmon, coarsely chopped

I teaspoon beluga caviar

Pepper from the mill

4 large eggs from vegetarian hens

Salt

I tablespoon unsalted butter or unsaturated oil of your choice

Greens to your taste for decoration

This omelette is inspired by the great breakfast fare I sampled at the Beverly Hills Hotel on my first visit there . . . too many years ago.

Mix the crème fraîche, chopped salmon, and caviar together; these three ingredients should not cook. Season the mixture with pepper to your taste.

Beat the eggs with a small dash of salt. Heat the chosen fat in a 9-inch omelette pan over medium-high heat and pour in the eggs. Shake the mixture until it has curdled as instructed on page 135 and spread the salmon mixture over the whole surface of the omelette, then fold the omelette quickly and invert it onto a platter. Decorate with the greens.

Gallo Roman Frittata

FFR — 6 SERVINGS

3 large yellow onions, sliced

Salt

Pepper from the mill

2 tablespoons unsalted butter or olive oil

2 tablespoons chopped fresh parsley leaves

½ teaspoon grated lemon rind

2 small cloves garlic, finely chopped

1 or 2 anchovy fillets, finely mashed or to your personal taste

8 large eggs from vegetarian hens

Balsamic vinegar of your choice

Toss the onions with salt and pepper. Heat the butter in the pan until foamy, then add the onions and toss them well in the butter over medium heat, uncovered, until they start to brown. Cover the pan for a few minutes until the onions have softened. Remove the lid and continue to toss the onions occasionally until golden. Blend in the parsley, lemon rind, garlic, and anchovy.

Beat the eggs, then season them with salt and pepper. Pour the egg mixture into the pan containing the onions and mix well. Turn the heat down to low and let the frittata cook, gently shaking back and forth until the first side has browned lightly. Flip the frittata or, if you are not so brave, slide it onto a plate and invert it back into the pan to cook the second side. When the frittata is done on both sides, cut it into six wedges and serve it forth with a bottle of balsamic vinegar. Some people like to shake a few drops of the vinegar over their portion of the frittata.

The flavoring of this frittata, the Italian gremolata, *appears every so often in dishes of old, predominantly Gallo Roman parts of France, especially in some dishes of the Lyon area and surrounding countryside. You will need a 10-inch nonstick pan.*

Federico's Tortilla

FFR — 6 SERVINGS

2 tablespoons virgin olive oil

2 large onions, finely chopped

½ cup tomato sauce of your choice

¼ cup dry sherry

Salt

Pepper from the mill

1 pound crabmeat, picked over carefully for cartilage

8 large eggs from vegetarian hens

Heat half the olive oil in a 10-inch skillet. Add the onions and sauté over medium-high heat until they brown at their edges. Add the tomato sauce

Federico was born in Spain and raised by a French family after he lost his parents in the Spanish Civil War. Besides being a frustrated matador, practicing "veronicas" with a red cape around his adoptive parents' dining room chairs, he was also one of the most inspired cooks I have ever met. You will need a 10-inch nonstick pan.

and sherry, season with salt and pepper to your taste, and simmer until the liquid ingredients have been absorbed by the onions. Remove the mixture to a bowl, cool to warm. Blend in the crabmeat, set aside, and keep warm.

Wipe the pan clean. Beat the eggs with a dash each of salt and pepper. Heat the remainder of the oil in the skillet over medium-high heat. Pour the beaten eggs into the pan, turn the heat down and gently cook the tortilla until the bottom of the cake is cooked to your taste, either pale or lightly browned. Flip or invert the tortilla back into the pan and finish cooking its second side. Serve quickly topped with the crab mixture.

Dessert Custards Prepared by Partial or Whole Coagulation of the Eggs

Some custards can be made into dessert sauces or into ice creams, others, known as *pots de crème*, can be baked into soft dessert confections served in small ramekins; others yet can be made into firmer confections which, once inverted upon a shallow dish, offer royal look, taste, and texture. All of these custards are made based entirely on techniques using the coagulating capacity of egg proteins.

ENGLISH OR STIRRED CUSTARD (CRÈME ANGLAISE)

The principle of making a stirred custard is that of poaching egg yolks in scalded milk or different types of cream. Here is the way to make a perfect custard without trauma and trepidation. Start with the medium amount given below for a first exercise, then, when you feel secure, move on to a larger batch and make yourself some real ice cream.

Have at hand a flat-bottomed, wide, and low-sided pan known as a sauteuse, a wooden blunt-end spatula or a wooden spoon with a wide spoon end, and a medium-size whisk, as well as, if you wish, an instant thermometer and a big bowl full of ice cubes, just in case you feel insecure for your first try. Once you have made this custard, you will need neither thermometer nor ice again.

The formula I use here is all-purpose and if you have made custard before, you will notice the four egg yolks per cup of milk instead of the classic three. Do not start thinking "Oh that is bad, so many egg yolks." Instead, stop feeling guilty and "Think moderation" again. Be smart, you're not going to prepare such a custard every day, are you? Since you only make it once in a while, prepare it with all its good taste and flavor. Of course, you can diminish the number of egg yolks to three per cup, replace the whole milk with any leaner milk such as 2 pecent, 1 percent, or nonfat. You can also choose to go in the other direction and instead of whole milk use half-and-half, light cream, or heavy cream. The decision is in your capable hands and should reflect what is best for the health of those you are nurturing and the texture you want for your dish.

For example, make the custard thin if you plan to use it to soak a cake, and keep it thick and rich as the base of a Bavarian cream (see page 149), and somewhere in between if you want to freeze it into an ice cream.

Basic Crème Anglaise

FFR—3 CUPS

Ice cubes

Pinch of salt

2 cups milk of your choice

8 large egg yolks

½ cup granulated sugar

I teaspoon pure vanilla extract

Any other flavoring of your choice

You will need a saucepan to scald the milk, one large bowl for the ice cubes, a sauteuse to cook the custard, a strainer, and a second bowl to receive the cooked custard.

Half fill the large bowl with ice cubes, toss salt generously among the cubes, and add a bit of water.

In the saucepan, scald the milk.

Directly in the sauteuse—*not in another bowl*—mix together the egg yolks, sugar, and a pinch of salt well with the wooden spoon. You must mix very well, but contrary to everything you have been told or read so far, *do not foam the mixture heavily.* All you have to do is bring out the air hiding between all the crystals of sugar.

The reason for not whisking heavily at this stage is precisely to avoid the development of a large amount of foam at the surface of the custard, so the novice cook is able to control the cooking, it would be impossible for all the air integrated into a heavy foam to reintegrate into the atmosphere, and the custard would, unseen by the cook, start coagulating and become granular under its blanket of foam.

By simply mixing the egg yolks and sugar, you will quickly obtain a silky mixture. Lift the wooden spatula or spoon about 2 inches above the surface of the mixture and you will see that it forms a very short and breaking stream. The egg yolks and sugar are now mixed enough so the yolks will not curdle on contact with the scalded milk. Also, the layer of tiny air bubbles extracted from the sugar is thin enough so that it will be absorbed by the time the mixture reaches a temperature of 165° to 170°F. Very slowly, in small additions, add the still scalding hot milk, stirring well. *Notice the thin white layer of foam* floating on the surface of the uncooked custard.

Put the sauteuse on high heat (*yes, you read correctly, I really mean high heat*) without being afraid. With the same wooden spatula or spoon, and using motions which will bring your spatula every second to scrub the bottom of the sauteuse, describe the two letters V and O. Write V starting at 11 o'clock, going down to 6 o'clock, and going back up to 1 o'clock; next write a large O that goes all around the edges of the sauteuse from 12 o'clock to 12 o'clock. Continue this way until the foam starts lightening. If you dip your instant thermometer into the custard, you will see that it registers 140° to 150°F. Gradually you will see the millions of tiny air bubbles consolidate into larger ones. At 165° to 170°F, steam will start rising out of the custard and its surface custard will become smoother and smoother, until there is no more foam on its surface and only a few larger bubbles at the edges of the pan. The foam disintegrated under the effect of the increasing pressure in the pan as the custard got warmer and warmer.

Remove the pan from the heat and *only now*, using the whisk, foam the custard as strongly as possible, to cool it by introducing as much air as possible into it and to stop the poaching of the eggs. Heavy whisking at this stage is essential as the partial coagulation of the eggs will not stop in the next few seconds; on the contrary, the temperature of the custard may continue to increase all the while you are whisking "madly," because your pan is still very hot, hotter than the custard, and transmitting heat to the custard. You may see your custard reach toward 175°F; this is no problem, the custard can take it. Only if it heats above 180°F would it be in danger of potential "curdling" followed by full coagulation. That the custard mixture reaches such a high temperature before coagulation occurs is due to the fact that the egg yolks are mixed with milk and sugar, which surround the protein molecules and keep them apart. The protein molecules now need more energy (heat) to move, to come in contact and bond with each other (coagulation).

Dip the spatula for a second back into the custard. You can see it coats the spatula thickly. Pass your index finger through the custard; you will see it separate to form a passage that remains clear and dry on the spatula. In France, I was told to call this the "parting of the Red Sea" and to remember that the custard was not thick enough until it happened. I use the same expression with my students.

Now check the temperature again with your instant thermometer; it will soon start to go down; as soon as it reaches 155°F, add the vanilla and any other flavoring you may have chosen. Notice that I use both vanilla and another flavoring that varies with the recipe and its use. The vanilla is there only to temper the taste of the yolks. If you were to flavor the custard with vanilla only, use pure vanilla extract in the ratio of 2 teaspoons to 1 tablespoon per cup of custard. (If you want to use a vanilla bean, split it in half and scrape its seeds into the scalded milk before you make the custard.)

The total cooking time is no more than 4 minutes; and the larger the batch you are preparing, the faster it will cook proportionally,* because the larger the mass of the custard, the faster it heats up proportionally. Strain through a regular conical strainer into a clean cold bowl.

For sanitary reasons, it is essential to cool the custard rapidly, so place the bowl of finished custard in the prepared bowl full of ice and stir it occasionally to prevent the formation of a skin. When the custard is cool, cover it with a plastic wrap and refrigerate it. Serve within 24 hours, unless it is made into ice cream which will be frozen.

Remember the following important points:

- Do not whisk while you cook the custard, rather stir, scraping quickly and constantly, the entire bottom of the sauteuse with a broad spatula.
- Whisk hard only after the custard is cooked to prevent it from curdling.
- Do not use cornstarch; since the custard does not boil, the cornstarch would not cook and would remain raw and regrettably tastable as such in the custard. The custard will continue to thicken by itself as it cools and you will be surprised how silky and thick it becomes.
- Keep the custard refrigerated at all times unless you serve it. The refrigerator shelf life of the custard is no more than 48 hours at 41°F.

STABILIZING STIRRED CUSTARD Stirred custard can be stabilized with gelatin. Use ½ envelope unflavored gelatin per cup of milk or cream. Melt the gelatin in 3 tablespoons water in the top of a double boiler over simmering water. Add to the custard when you have removed it from the heat. As you whisk the mixture to cool it, the gelatin will be completely mixed with the custard and melt into it. You can achieve the same effect by adding to the custard 2 sheets of European-style gelatin presoaked in water and well drained. Stabilized custard is what is meant when some recipes use the culinary jargon *crème anglaise collée*. Stabilized custard is also sometimes called Spanish cream in English.

VARIATIONS

ALMOND: Replace the milk with the almond milk on page 50, and make the custard as usual, or add 1 teaspoon pure almond extract per cup of finished custard.

BUTTERSCOTCH: Replace the sugar with the same amount of firmly packed dark brown sugar.

CHOCOLATE: Melt as much chocolate as you wish and gradually whisk the hot just finished custard into the melted chocolate, whisking well.

CITRUS FRUIT: Bring the milk or cream to a boil, then add and infuse

---

*8 yolks and 2 cups of milk cook in about 4 minutes. Twice that amount may take 4½ to 5 minutes and 2 dozen yolks mixed with 2 quarts of milk about 5 to 6 minutes.

1 teaspoon finely grated lemon, lime, orange, tangerine, or grapefruit rind per cup of milk or cream an hour before making the custard. Strain well. Or, use citrus extracts of your choice, added with the vanilla after cooking.

COFFEE: Add 1½ teaspoons, or more to taste, of a good instant coffee powder to each cup of scalded milk before making the custard.

LIQUEURS: Add 2 tablespoons of the liqueur of your choice per cup of custard when the custard temperature is between 140° and 155°F.

PRALINE: Replace half the sugar with praline powder (see page 51).

Here are some simple recipes using flavored stirred custard.

Molded Scarlet Custard

This was always a favorite of the children in our family, the scarlet raspberry custard being extremely attractive to curious little eyes and fingers.

FFR—6 SERVINGS

1 tablespoon finely grated lemon rind
1½ cups milk or cream of your choice, scalded
6 large egg yolks
6 tablespoons granulated sugar
Pinch of salt
2 teaspoons unflavored gelatin
2 tablespoons water
2 teaspoons neutral oil (such as canola or corn)
One 10-ounce bag frozen raspberries in syrup, thawed and drained (reserve half the syrup)
Fresh lemon juice

Infuse the lemon rind for 1 hour in the scalded milk. Make a custard with the egg yolks, sugar, salt, and milk following the directions on page 141. Melt the gelatin in the water and add to the hot custard.

Rub six 3-ounce custard cups with the oil over their whole inner surface. Strain an equal amount of custard into the cups and chill.

Place the raspberries and the reserved syrup in a blender container and puree. Strain through a fine strainer to remove the seeds. Add lemon juice to your taste.

When ready to serve, unmold the custards onto plates and serve dressed with the raspberry sauce.

Strawberries in Custard

FFR—6 SERVINGS

I vanilla bean

I½ cups milk of your choice, scalded

I quart fresh strawberries, hulled and washed

¼ cup kirsch, Grand Marnier, Mandarine Napoléon, or yellow Chartreuse

6 large egg yolks

6 tablespoons granulated sugar

Pinch of salt

24 pistachios, peeled and coarsely chopped

This is a good way to utilize all the super-ripe berries of the strawberry season. If liqueur is not on your program, use a tablespoon of balsamic vinegar on the strawberries as well as sugar to your taste.

Add the vanilla bean to the scalded milk, cover the pan, and let infuse for 1 hour.

Meanwhile, stand the berries in a lovely crystal dish; add half the liqueur, and let macerate while you prepare and cool the custard.

Remove, rinse well, and store the vanilla bean in a small jar of sugar for later reuse (the vanilla sugar can be used in another recipe). Reheat the milk to scalding. Mix the egg yolks, sugar, and salt in a sauteuse pan and gradually add the milk to the mixture. Cook the custard according to the instructions on page 141, then whisk it to cool; strain into a bowl and chill it completely over ice to accelerate the process. Add to it the remaining 2 tablespoons of liqueur and chill. Just before serving, spoon over the strawberries. Decorate with the chopped pistachios.

A FEW ICE CREAM RECIPES

Ice creams are nothing more than flavored stirred custards which are churned in ice cream freezing machines.

You will notice quite a number of egg yolks in the formulas that follow. Large amounts of egg yolks result in:

- A large amount of lecithin in the cream, which limits the size of air bubbles. Lecithin is one of the lipids to be found in egg yolks; it acts naturally as an emulsifier for the fat.
- A better texture with tiny ice crystals.
- A lower melting point.
- A better body and texture due to a well-balanced "overrun," overrun being the increase in volume due to the air introduced into the custard by churning, i.e., if you have a 100 percent overrun, the volume of the mix is doubled.

If you prefer another basic ice cream formula, by all means replace mine with yours; remove egg yolks and cream if you want. You may use only milk and fewer egg yolks, but you can still flavor the custard with the same ingredients as I propose in the recipes below.

Once again, make ice cream once in a while, but make it so it is worth enjoying and radically better and more original than any of the commercial brands, even the better ones. I am giving you different formulas with more or fewer egg yolks. If you have no ice cream machine, talk to your friends and see who could lend you one. Or, with the healthy modern point of view, I hardly dare mention this point, you can increase the number of egg yolks and "still-freeze" the ice cream without a machine; if you are interested, refer to page 140 and make certain that you enjoy this type of parfait no more than once a year and in a very small quantity. Which brings to mind an anecdote. If you are ever in the Decorative Arts Museum in Paris, do not miss admiring the tiny Mennecy Villeroy porcelain cups in which this type of ice cream was served; you will realize from their size that our preoccupation with waistlines is not a modern obsession.

Note that to preserve its fresh taste and full sanitary state, ice cream must be kept frozen until ready to be consumed and must be consumed within 48 hours of its making. I cannot insist enough on the fact that each and every tool or implement coming in contact with any ice cream must be thoroughly sanitized.

To scoop out ice cream easily, let it mellow in the refrigerator no less than 20 minutes before serving it. If you have a party or dinner with numerous guests, line sheet pans with parchment paper, scoop the ice cream into portions, cover with plastic wrap, and return it to the freezer. When ready to serve transfer the solidly frozen portions to chilled plates or bowls. By the time you set the plates in front of guests, the ice cream will be "just right."

Verbena Ice Cream with Manyaberry Compote

Verbena grows in our California gardens; if you cannot find some, replace it with basil, it will work just as well. If lavender honey is not available, use any other flower honey. For the berries, use a small amount each of raspberries red and white, tiny garden strawberries, blueberries, red currants, black berries, boysenberries, etc.

FFR— 12 TO 18 SERVINGS

2 cups 4% milk

½ cup packed, very finely chopped fresh verbena or basil leaves

2 cups heavy cream

8 large egg yolks

I cup granulated sugar

2 pinches of salt

I tablespoon pure vanilla extract

I quart mixed red and white berries

2 cups Beaujolais or Zinfandel

Lavender honey to your taste

Scald the milk in a saucepan. Remove from the heat, add the verbena, and let steep 2 hours. Strain. The milk should be green. Blend in the cream.

In a sauteuse pan, mix thoroughly the egg yolks and sugar. Add the salt. Reheat the milk-cream blend to scalding and gradually blend it into the yolks, stirring well. Thicken on high heat following the instructions on page 141. Whisk to cool, then add the vanilla. Strain through a China cap into the sterilized (washed and dried in the dishwasher) container of the ice cream maker and chill overnight.

The next day churn the ice cream in the ice cream maker according to the manufacturer's instructions. Ripen for 12 to 24 hours in the freezer well packed and sealed in a sanitized plastic container. Let soften in the refrigerator before serving.

To prepare the compote, place the berries in a crystal dish. Reduce the wine to ¼ cup over medium-high heat; dissolve as much honey as you like into it and cool. Dribble over the berries just before serving with the ice cream.

Cardamom, Rose Petal, and Pistachio-Praline Ice Cream

FFR—12 SERVINGS

2 cups milk of your choice

2 cups heavy cream

12 large egg yolks

Pinch of salt

¾ cup granulated sugar

1½ teaspoons pure vanilla extract

1 tablespoon ground cardamom

For the garnish

½ cup fresh unsprayed rose petals of your choice

½ cup granulated sugar

¼ cup water

2 drops fresh lemon juice

⅔ cup peeled pistachios

1 teaspoon unsalted butter to grease the jelly-roll pan

3 ounces 61%-cocoa bittersweet chocolate

With this lovely ice cream serve some really nice lace cookies of your choice. I offer this recipe with a big thank you to my friend and student Karl Weller, otherwise known as "Wyoming Karl," for pouring chocolate over my white pistachio pralines.

In a saucepan, scald the milk and cream together. In a sauteuse pan, mix the egg yolks, salt, and sugar together, then gradually blend the hot liquid mixture into the egg yolks and thicken on high heat according to the instructions on page 141. Whisk to cool, then strain into a bowl, add the vanilla and cardamom, mix well, and chill overnight in the refrigerator.

The next day, just before churning the ice cream, using scissors, cut the rose petals into slivers and keep them refrigerated.

Heat the sugar with the water and lemon juice until it cooks to the hard crack stage (see page 143), add the pistachios, and stir constantly with a spatula until the sugar hardens around the nuts and turns white and sandy. Cool the nuts completely on a lightly buttered baking sheet or jelly-roll pan.

Melt the chocolate over hot water, stirring it well until it looks reddish. Pour the hot chocolate over the nuts in a zigzagging motion to cover them. Cool until the chocolate is cold and hard, then separate the nuts.

Churn the ice cream in the ice cream maker according to the manufacturer's instructions; when it is almost done, add to it the rose petals and chocolate-covered pistachio pralines. Pack into a well-sealed sanitized plastic container and ripen in the freezer 12 to 24 hours. Soften in the refrigerator before serving.

Moctezuma's Ice Cream

FFR — 12 to 18 servings

2 cups each 4% milk and heavy cream mixed together
8 to 10 large egg yolks, as you please
¾ cup granulated sugar
4 ounces bittersweet chocolate, preferably Valrhona 57% cocoa, chopped
1 ounce bitter unsweetened chocolate, preferably Valrhona 61% cocoa, chopped
½ teaspoon ground cassia (page 67) or cinnamon
1 teaspoon grated lime rind
1 teaspoon red pepper flakes
Pinch of salt

Scald the mixture of milk and cream in a saucepan. In a sauteuse pan, mix the egg yolks and sugar together. Dilute the mixture with the scalded milk and cream and thicken on high heat according to the instructions on page 141. Remove from the heat and whisk to stop the cooking. Strain, then immediately whisk in while still hot the chocolates, cassia, lime rind, red pepper flakes, and salt. Stir well until the chocolate has entirely melted.

Chill overnight in the refrigerator and strain; churn in the ice cream maker according to the manufacturer's instructions on the same day as you are going to serve. Enjoy by itself; there are enough flavors mixed in this composition to keep the palate interested.

Jimmy Schmidt, my former student, and I pretty much came up with the same idea at the same time, and both presented it during the events of the Book and the Cook of 1988 in Philadelphia. But it wasn't such a new idea, though; didn't Moctezuma, his real name Motecozuma, drink such a hot chocolate brew? So why not freeze it and tame the heat? The pepper in this composition is not strong; rather, it comes on as a pleasant piquant aftertaste.

Kona Macadamia Velvet

FFR—24 SERVINGS

4 cups heavy cream

I cup milk of your choice

I cup medium-ground coffee beans, preferably pure Kona

I cup granulated sugar or more to taste

24 large egg yolks

I tablespoon pure vanilla extract

8 ounces Swiss Lindt or Tobler milk chocolate

I cup very coarsely chopped macadamia nuts

Scald the heavy cream and milk together in a saucepan, then add the ground coffee. Remove from the heat and let steep an hour. Strain through a fine tea strainer or China cap, then reheat the flavored cream to scalding.

Mix the sugar and egg yolks together in a sauteuse pan, then slowly mix in the hot cream. Thicken on medium heat—not high heat; there are too many egg yolks—according to the instructions on page 141. Strain and add the vanilla. Rapidly cool to room temperature by placing the bowl of custard in another larger bowl filled with ice cubes and salt, and stir occasionally until cold.

Melt the chocolate in the top of a double boiler over barely simmering water and toss the macadamia nuts into the chocolate until coated. Pour onto a lightly buttered baking sheet or jelly-roll pan and let harden. Chop into coarse pieces and stir into the custard. Pour the custard into a shallow sterilized (washed and dried in the dishwasher) container and "still-freeze," meaning pop it in the freezer, without churning. Serve in very small prechilled ramekins without bringing back to refrigerator temperature.

BAVARIAN CREAMS

Bavarian creams were called *fromages bavarois* by Carême although they have nothing to do with cheese, probably because he made them with crème fraîche and no eggs. Escoffier, who gave us many excellent recipes for Bavarian creams in the first edition of his *Guide Culinaire*, explained in the last edition (1927) that the term "cheese" was dropped because it was thought unaesthetic for a dessert; he added that the word *Bavarian* was illogical and that he replaced it with "Muscovite," which he deemed to be more logical and rational, though he neglected to explain why that was the case. Were Bavarian creams, made with or without eggs, extremely popular in Imperial Moscow? Or was it—as Helena, one of my Paris friends of Russian descent suggested to me—because the Russian émigrés living in Paris after 1917 came in large part from Moscow and relished this type of dessert?

This "parfait" reflects the immense pleasure that is mine when I visit Maui and is dedicated to my former student James Rheaux, former executive chef of the Westin Maui Hotel. Do not hesitate to add more sugar if, when you taste the cooled cooked custard, you think it is too bitter for you, for I love an edge of bitter in sweet things.

The Russian kisels, made originally of fruit puree sugar and thickened with a starch, may have been frozen in Bavarian molds when they reached Paris, for I remember several of those on my plate as a child, prepared by one of my very old great aunts who had many friends in the Paris Russian colony of the thirties; see page 149.

Whichever type of a preparation a Muscovite may have been, it was a popular one, for Prosper Montagné tells us that the shape of the mold used for a Muscovite had to be hexagonal, and a kümmel (caraway liqueur) and almond Bavarian cream as well as a frozen vanilla pudding both carry the name "Muscovite" in his work.

A true Bavarian cream contains *no egg whites*; it is a stirred custard stabilized with gelatin and enriched with a very light foam of heavy cream, beaten only very lightly until it barely starts mounding. The heavy cream is the one and only ingredient responsible for the light texture of the preparation. If many chefs and cooks replace some of the cream with egg whites, it is not for dietetic reasons, but simply because the cream in Bavarians is almost always overwhipped, which gives the finished product the approximate texture of lead.

A Bavarian cream is a perfect dessert for entertaining or ordering in restaurants because, since it should be kept no longer than 24 hours, it both suppresses last-minute preparations and is always fresh. If a Bavarian cream that has been kept in a refrigerator 24 hours is not used and cannot be used, melt it, reheat it to 165°F, chill it over ice, and freeze it immediately in an ice cream maker; it must then be served that very same day or discarded.

A new and personal basic technique for making Bavarian cream:

In the old days, the custard was stabilized with gelatin and stirred over ice until it started to set, then the cream, beaten to a full Chantilly (see page 30), was folded into the custard base. What a scramble to have a beginner finish this without traces of tiny gelatinized lumps in the finished cream! Seeing one of my students struggle with this problem, I told her to finish the *bavarois* by whipping the remainder of the heavy cream into the gelatinized custard. Hers was the best-textured *bavarois* the school had ever seen, so I changed the technique of making the cream. Here is the new sequence as I have been teaching it since 1980:

1. Beat the cream so it barely starts mounding and keep it refrigerated.
2. Cook the stirred custard.
3. While it is hot, stabilize the custard with dissolved and melted powdered gelatin, or gelatin sheets softened in water.
4. Cool the custard over ice, stirring occasionally with a rubber spatula, until the gelatin barely starts to thicken at the edges of the bowl.
5. Whip the prepared lightly whipped cream into the cool custard; the cream will finish stiffening as it blends into the stabilized custard.
6. Mold or pour the *bavarois* into dessert cups.

BAVARIAN CREAM TEXTURES Bavarian cream can be made with two different textures.

1. By using a whole envelope of gelatin or four leaves of European-style gelatin per recipe made with 1 cup milk for the custard and 1 cup heavy cream for the foam, one can mold the Bavarian cream and turn it upside down.

   The procedure for unmolding is easy. Before you mold the cream, very lightly oil the mold with your well-washed fingertips, then turn the mold upside down on paper towels. Fill the mold and deep chill the finished cream. When chilled and ready to serve, run the tip of a knife around the edges of the cream, center the mold upside down over a platter prerinsed with cold water, and invert. It is possible, because quite a vacuum builds between the sides of the mold and the cream, that unmolding will be difficult. If you have problems, cover the mold with a hot damp towel, *but do not dip into hot water* or half the cream will melt and your beautiful Bavarian will pitifully swim in its own melted half self. Because you rinsed the platter or plate in cold water, the Bavarian can be gently nudged for recentering in case it comes out off-kilter while unmolding.

2. I prefer not to mold the cream and use only half an envelope of gelatin, or two leaves of European gelatin for the same proportion of liquids and serve the cream in old-fashioned Champagne cups. The texture is lighter and the taste brighter.

   Here are a few recipes to practice with.

Thai-Flavored Bavarian Cream

FFR—6 TO 8 SERVINGS

I cup heavy cream

1¼ cups milk of your choice

⅓ cup sweetened small coconut flakes

One 2 x ½-inch strip lime rind

I stick cinnamon, broken into pieces

⅓ teaspoon ground cardamom

¼ teaspoon freshly grated nutmeg

1½ teaspoons unflavored gelatin or 2 leaves European gelatin

3 large egg yolks

1¼ cups granulated sugar

Pinch of salt

2 limes

I cup water

I love the flavors of Thai food, but they always seem to me to evoke luscious desserts. As a result, here is a Bavarian cream with a different spicing.

Whip the cream until it barely starts to mound and keep it refrigerated.

Bring the milk to a boil in a saucepan, add the coconut, lime rind, cinnamon, cardamom, and nutmeg and let steep for 45 minutes off the heat. Strain and bring the milk back to scalding. Meanwhile, dissolve or soften the gelatin in a tad of water.

In a sauteuse pan, mix the egg yolks, ¼ cup of the sugar, and the salt well together, then gradually whisk in the perfumed milk and thicken over high heat according to the instructions on page 141. Whisk the softened or melted gelatin into the hot custard off the heat. As soon as the gelatin has completely melted (it will do so almost instantly), strain the custard into a bowl and stir it over ice until it starts to thicken.

Whip the prepared heavy cream into the cold custard until both have homogenized into each other. Gently ladle into glass serving cups and chill overnight, covered with plastic wrap.

With a potato peeler, lift off the rind of each lime without including any white pith and cut into ⅛-inch-wide strips; put the rinds in a small saucepan, cover with water and bring to a boil; discard the water.

Mix the remaining cup of sugar with the water in a saucepan and add the rinds to the cold syrup; slowly bring to a boil and simmer until the rinds are translucent and the syrup has thickened.

Squeeze the juice from the limes and add as much lime juice to the syrup as you personally like. Decorate the top of each Bavarian cup with a spoonful of the lime sauce just before serving.

Sauternes and Roquefort Bavarian Cream with Baked Figs

FFR — 12 SERVINGS

1 cup heavy cream
4½ teaspoons almond or hazelnut oil
One 750 ml bottle botrytised white wine of your choice
4 large egg yolks
⅓ cup liquid plus ¼ cup honey of your choice
1 envelope unflavored gelatin softened in 2 tablespoons water or 4 leaves gelatin
1 to 1½ tablespoons well-crumbled Roquefort
2 dozen fresh Black Mission or white honey figs

Whip the cream until it barely mounds and keep it refrigerated. Wash your hands carefully and with the tip of a finger lightly coat twelve 2-ounce custard cups with some of the oil. Turn them upside down on paper toweling.

Pour 2 cups of the white wine in a small saucepan over medium heat and reduce to 1 cup to concentrate the flavors. In a sauteuse pan mix the egg

Sauternes (see page 94) being expensive, you may use any other botrytised wine of your choice that is more affordable. It is important that the figs be ripe; purchase them a little early and keep them in a paper bag with a ripe banana for two days if they are still too firm.

yolks with ⅓ cup of honey then gradually blend in the reduced wine. Thicken on medium-high heat as instructed on page 141. Whisk in the softened gelatin off the heat, cool over ice, and, as the custard starts setting, remove from the ice and whisk in the prepared heavy cream; during the last few strokes add the crumbled cheese. Ladle into the prepared little cups. Chill at least four hours or, better yet, overnight.

Rub a stainless steel or glass baking dish with the remainder of the oil. Slice the figs lengthwise from the root end toward the stem, stopping where the stem starts so it remains intact. Fan the figs opened and place them in the baking dish. Sprinkle them with the remaining ¼ cup of honey. Bake in a preheated 350°F oven for 15 to 20 minutes.

When the figs are done, transfer them to a platter, add the remainder of the wine to the baking dish and scrape the fig juices to mix them well with the wine. Strain into a small saucepan and over medium heat reduce to about ½ cup. Cool completely.

To serve, unmold the creams onto chilled plates; fan a fig open on top of each cream and spoon a bit of the sauce over each of their tops.

BAKED CUSTARDS

There are many types of baked custards:

1. Dessert custards are made with egg yolks or whole eggs mixed with milk or cream and sugar; they are explained in the paragraphs that follow.
2. Savory custards made with mixtures of meat, eggs, and cream are given the names of mousses, mousselines or loaves, and puddings; you will find them in the chapters on fish and meat, pages 686–98 and 886–92.
3. Custards made with mixtures of vegetable puree, eggs, and cream are called timbales and you will find them in the vegetable chapter on page 442.

GENERALITIES ON BAKED DESSERT CUSTARDS Dessert custards being very rich, they are baked in very small cups or containers immersed in a hot water bath. The old-fashioned and "oh so pretty" little cream "pots" of the eighteenth and nineteenth century have more or less disappeared, which is too bad aesthetically, but may be salutary from a nutritional point of view since they were still a tad too large for a modern portion. I have taken to the habit of baking these delicious creams in the type of stainless steel containers that are used in restaurants to present the drawn butter accompanying steamed lobster. They do not look as elegant as the old porcelain and faience pots but arranged on a large dish decorated with herbs and flowers, they do their deed very well indeed. Such little containers are readily available at extremely reasonable prices from restaurant supply houses and will last a lifetime. Larger molds or small baking cups in which custards are baked are either caramelized or greased.

TO CARAMELIZE A CUSTARD MOLD Wash a skillet with soap and water. Rinse it abundantly with clear water and do not wipe it dry. Add sugar and one third of the volume of the sugar in water. Bring rapidly to a boil then turn the heat down slightly and cook until the sugar starts to turn brown. Tilt the pan back and forth to homogenize but do not stir with a spoon! From now on, be careful not to let the caramel get too dark; it happens very quickly because making caramel consists of removing most of the water contained in sugar. The darker a caramel becomes, the less sweet it is and the more bitter it turns. If you burn a caramel, it will be unmercifully bitter and if it starts smoking, you can expect it to turn into a crust of cinder which is pure carbon.

Remember that the heat accumulated in the metal of the pan will continue heating and cooking the sugar even after you remove the pan from the heat, so remove it a minute or so before the caramel has reached the color you desire, as it will darken in the last few seconds before you pour it into the mold(s) and cool it. Note that in order to obtain a frank caramel taste in an ice cream or custard, the caramel must turn quite dark brown but not ever start smoking.

If the caramel is used to line a mold, pour it directly from its cooking pan into the mold to be coated and, holding the mold with a towel, tilt it back and forth to coat all its sides evenly. Turn the mold upside down over a greased plate to allow the caramel to dribble evenly all over the sides of the mold. Grease lightly whichever part of the mold(s) has not been covered with caramel for easier unmolding.

GREASING MOLDS NOT TO BE CARAMELIZED If the mold or molds are not caramelized, they must be rubbed either with a piece of soft butter or with a bit of oil. Use your well-washed fingers for that; they work better than a brush which is no more sterile than your fingers. And forget that piece of parchment paper lining your fingers, it does a nasty job by forgetting a lot of nooks and crannies that the sensitive skin of your fingers will never miss.

If you strongly object to using your fingers, fill a small spray bottle fitted with a fine mist nozzle with oil and spray the mold(s) with a thin coating of it. Nut oils are especially recommended for this, hazelnut, pistachio, and almond being especially delicious.

MIXING THE CREAM, FILLING THE MOLD, AND BAKING THE CUSTARD Always scald the milk or cream (sweetened when applicable) and beat it into the yolks or eggs very gradually while hot, so as to prepare the egg proteins for the heat of the oven. Avoid overbeating the milk-and-egg mixture to prevent a layer of foam from forming on top of the custard.

While scalding the milk preheat the oven to 325°F and bring a kettle full of water to a boil. The water must be boiling, not just hot, for the custard to cook in the minimum amount of time possible.

Strain the custard mixture into its container(s) and fill completely to within ⅙ inch of the rim. Line a baking dish large enough to hold all the containers with a kitchen towel, which will temper the heat at the bottom of the baking dish and prevent the custards from boiling.

Arrange the custard containers in the baking dish so they do not touch one another. Set the dish on the middle oven rack and only then pour the boiling water into the dish in which the custard containers are set, so they will be immersed in the water to within ¼ inch of their rims.

Cover the baking pan or dish with a large lid or a baking sheet so that the heat of the oven cannot solidify the top of the custard too fast and thus build a hard crust. If you are still using some of those lovely cream pots, do not use their small lids; they are too thick to let the heat through fast and gather condensation which falls back into the custard. Instead cover the baking dish with a large lid or a sheet of parchment paper and cover the pots with their own little lids only after the custard is cold and ready to chill.

TESTING DONENESS Egg yolk custards (there will be more egg yolks than whole eggs) are done when, tapping them with a knife blade, they shake nicely and lightly, but are not liquid anymore.

Whole egg custards (there will be more whole eggs than egg yolks) are done when a nonreactive skewer (the stem of an instant-read thermometer is best) inserted two thirds of the way into the center of the cream comes out clean. Nonreactive is necessary because a reactive material like aluminum could stain the custard or give it an unpleasant taste.

Even if the center of a custard does not look quite completely firm, remove the water bath from the oven and cool the custard in the water bath. The same reaction will occur as in the stirred custard; the temperature will continue to increase toward the center of the cream and finish coagulating it. The speed of penetration of the heat into a custard is proportionally faster in larger molds than in smaller ones; you will be able to verify this fact when, having filled a large mold and poured a small remainder of the custard into a smaller cup, both will be done almost at the same time.

Beware of molds that have a hole in their center such as tube and small-size Bundt molds; since the water carries heat from the outside of the mold and from the inside of the tube, the custard will cook extremely fast. I remember baking a large custard in a large Bundt mold in 15 minutes. Stay close when you bake custards.

OVERCOOKED CUSTARDS AND SYNERESIS If overheated or cooked too long, a custard separates, i.e., the protein-water mesh which gives the custard its texture and structure breaks. The milk and egg proteins bond tightly to each other, releasing the loosely held water. The overheated custard is grainy (protein clumps) and watery. The physical phenomenon is called *syneresis*.

You may have seen some custard recipes recommending a small addition of starch to the custard; this starch is meant precisely to prevent the water effect of syneresis, as it will absorb the released water. However, dessert custards must be made without starch; since the custard does not come to the boiling point, the starch does not bind with the water in the mixture and remains unpleasantly tastable in the cooked custard.

COOLING AND REFRIGERATING CUSTARDS Remove the custard from the water bath when the water cools to barely lukewarm and refrigerate to chill it. Egg yolk custards to be served in their baking vessels must be refrigerated at least 4 hours before consumption; whole egg custard to be unmolded must be refrigerated overnight. *Keep all custards refrigerated at all times until ready to serve.* The shelf life of all custards, even well refrigerated, is never more than 48 hours.

POTS DE CRÈME OR POTTED CREAMS
These small custards, served always in cups or small containers, are prepared exclusively with cream, and more egg yolks than whole eggs, which firms up the custard. In our fat-conscious times, they are certainly to be considered very sinful and probably not too healthy; but again, they represent one of the pleasures of life and a little custard once or twice a year is as acceptable as such a little custard every day would be dangerous.

The basic proportions to be used for egg yolk custards are:

½ cup granulated sugar

Pinch of salt

2 cups heavy cream, scalded

8 large egg yolks

I small egg

which is not that different from the stirred custard on page 141; the difference is that the cream is scalded, the sugar is melted in it, and then the yolks are gradually diluted with the scalded sweetened cream and the mixture is strained into a greased custard cup or pot and baked.

To flavor these custards, you can add extracts to the cream or infuse citrus rinds in it or add liqueur. If you'd like a chocolate baked custard, add 2 to 3 ounces chocolate and decrease the number of egg yolks to achieve a ratio of 3 egg yolks (not including the one in the whole egg) per cup of cream.

Here are the recipes for three rich egg yolk-based potted creams.

For a dinner for twelve persons, I have presented mixed small containers of all three of these custards on a large platter with great success. Guests consider these a real treat.

Creole Potted Cream

FFR — 10 SERVINGS

1½ tablespoons hazelnut oil or a neutral oil

3 ounces Swiss Lindt or Tobler milk chocolate

2 ounces bittersweet chocolate of your choice

1¾ cups heavy cream

¼ cup dark molasses

Pinch of salt

4 large egg yolks

2 tablespoons dark rum

This is a variation on my mother's crème au chocolat; *it gave me a true liking for this kind of confection.*

Wash your hands carefully and, using a finger, carefully coat ten small custard cups with the oil. Set aside. Preheat the oven to 325°F.

Melt the chocolates together over hot water, then remove them from the heat and let them cool slightly but not harden.

Mix the cream and molasses together in a saucepan and scald, but do not boil. Add the salt. Using a wooden spoon, whisk the egg yolks together until homogeneous but not foamy; slowly and very gradually blend in the cream-and-molasses mixture. Now blend the egg-and-cream mix with the chocolate mixture; the chocolate may thicken, but do not worry, continue blending very slowly to obtain a smooth mixture. Finally, blend in the rum.

Bring a kettle full of water to a boil. Meanwhile, strain the mixture through a conical strainer into the prepared custard cups. Line a baking dish large enough to hold the custard cups without touching with a folded kitchen towel, then add the custard-filled cups. Set the baking dish on the middle oven shelf and pour the boiling water into it. Bake, covered, until properly set, 18 to 20 minutes, then remove from the oven and let cool in the water bath. Chill. Serve as is.

Viennese Caramel Potted Creams

FFR — 10 SERVINGS

1½ tablespoons neutral-tasting oil of your choice

1 cup granulated sugar

3 tablespoons water

2 cups heavy cream, scalded

Pinch of salt

8 large egg yolks

2 teaspoons pure vanilla extract

From a Viennese friend and colleague at Swissair forty years ago. It was served with a great big rosette of Schlag (whipped cream) flavored with coffee liqueur, which I do not use because it dilutes the taste of this lovely custard too much.

Preheat the oven to 325°F. Bring a kettle full of water to a boil. Using the tip of a finger, coat ten small custard containers very lightly with the oil and set aside.

Mix half the sugar and the water together in a small skillet. Quickly bring the mixture to a boil, then cook it to a dark, almost bitter caramel (see page 154). Let the mixture cool completely. Add the scalded cream and reheat slowly, stirring to completely dissolve the caramel; add the salt.

Stir the egg yolks and the other half of the sugar in a large bowl with a wooden spoon until completely broken and smooth, then gradually add the caramel-flavored mixture and the vanilla extract. Strain through a conical strainer into the prepared cups and set into a kitchen-towel-lined baking dish large enough to hold the cups without touching. Put the dish on the middle oven rack, pour in the boiling water, and bake, covered, until properly set, 18 to 20 minutes. Remove from the oven, let cool in the water bath, then chill before serving.

Bergamot Potted Cream

Oil of bergamot, which is usually used for this type of dessert, is difficult to find and I have replaced it with a mixture of rinds; its taste is still intriguing.

FFR — 8 SERVINGS

1 tablespoon neutral-tasting oil or pistachio oil

2 cups heavy cream

½ teaspoon each finely grated orange, lemon, lime, and grapefruit rind

½ cup granulated sugar

Pinch of salt

10 large egg yolks

Wash your hands very carefully and, with one of your fingers, rub the custard cups with the oil. Preheat the oven to 325°F.

Bring the cream to a boil; add the rinds and let steep off the heat for 45 minutes. Strain the mixture into a saucepan through a conical strainer, then add the sugar and salt. Reheat to scalding.

Stir the egg yolks, then gradually dilute them with the flavored cream. Strain again into the custard cups, set in a kitchen towel-lined baking dish big enough to hold all the cups without touching, and put on the middle oven rack. Pour in the boiling water and bake, covered, until properly set, 18 to 20 minutes. Remove from the oven, cool in the water bath, and refrigerate to deep chill before serving.

WHOLE-EGG UPSIDE-DOWN CUSTARDS

Whole-egg baked custards may be served in the vessel in which they have been baked, as in the plain whole-egg, milk, and sugar custards known as *oeufs au lait* made by generations of mothers all through Europe as a dessert for their children or as a good protein source for the sick. A version of this used to be sold by the now disappeared Horn & Hardart stores in the East when I arrived in America in the early sixties; on the label was written the old-fashioned, naive, and nice motto "Less Work for Mother." Also to this category belong all the ordinary or extraordinary and varied flans of the Mediterranean countries and those of Spain which crossed the oceans on their way to a fabulous enrichment in Mexico and the islands of the Caribbean.

When the custard is to be unmolded, it is more often than not lined with caramel (see page 154 for instructions on how to do this) and then the number of whole eggs increases or is even mixed with additional egg yolks to give the custard a lot of "slip," or richness on the palate.

You can make any custard with the flavoring of your choice by using the following proportions:

For an ordinary, everyday family-style custard (considered unworthy of being unmolded because of its coarser texture and pale appearance):

4 large eggs
4 cups milk of your choice
I cup granulated sugar

For a richer custard that can be unmolded:

6 large eggs
4 cups milk of your choice
I cup granulated sugar

For a very rich and opulent custard that can be unmolded:

6 large eggs
4 large egg yolks
4 cups milk of your choice
I ¼ cups granulated sugar

How many eggs you use is entirely your decision.

For people on strict diets for cardiovascular problems, you can make an entirely different egg white custard pudding, for which you will find a recipe on page 170.

The Kids' Custard

FCR — 8 SERVINGS

2 cups milk of your choice
½ vanilla bean, sliced open
½ cup granulated sugar
Pinch of salt
2 large eggs

Scald the milk in a saucepan; scrape the tiny seeds of the vanilla bean into the milk and add the pod; let steep off the heat for 45 minutes. Strain

This was the treat of my young days, prepared with love by my dear mother, and because she had made this dessert for me, I made it many times for my children. With it came a compote of fresh fruit or homemade shortbread (see page 1076).

through a conical strainer, add the sugar and salt, and reheat to scalding. Preheat the oven to 325°F and bring a kettle full of water to a boil.

Beat the eggs without making too much foam. Gradually beat in the hot milk and strain into small ungreased custard cups or ramekins. Set the cups in a baking dish large enough to hold the cups without touching and lined with a kitchen towel. Put the dish on the middle oven rack and pour the boiling water into it. Bake, covered, until a nonreactive tester inserted two thirds of the way into the custard comes out clean, 20 to 25 minutes. Remove from the oven, cool in the water bath, refrigerate, and chill. Serve as is.

Pistachio Upside-Down Custard

FFR—8 TO 10 SERVINGS

I tablespoon pistachio oil or a neutral-tasting oil

2½ cups milk of your choice

I cup peeled pistachios

½ cup granulated sugar

Pinch of salt

¼ cup kirsch

3 large eggs

2 large egg yolks

For the apricot sauce

8 ounces fresh apricots

½ cup granulated sugar

½ cup water

2 tablespoons kirsch

Wash and dry your hands, then rub a 3-cup soufflé dish with the oil using your fingertips. Preheat the oven to 325°F. Bring a kettle of water to a boil.

Scald the milk. Put the nuts in a food processor or blender and pour the hot milk over them. Process until the nuts are ground finely. Let steep 1 hour. Strain through a China cap, pushing on the nuts to extract all the milk. Discard the nuts.

Add the sugar and salt to the nut milk; reheat until they dissolve, then add the kirsch. Beat the whole eggs and egg yolks together lightly and, still beating, blend in the hot pistachio milk. Strain the custard into the prepared dish through a fine-meshed China cap. Set the dish in a kitchen towel-lined baking dish and place on the middle oven rack. Pour in the boiling water, cover, and bake until a nonreactive tester inserted two thirds of the way into the custard comes out clean, 40 to 45 minutes. Remove from the oven, let cool in the water bath, and chill overnight.

For the apricot sauce, place the apricots, sugar, and water in a saucepan and cook over medium heat, stirring occasionally, until the apricots have fallen apart, about 40 minutes. Strain them through an ordinary strainer to discard the skins and add the kirsch. If the sauce is too thick, lighten it up with a drop or so of water until you reach the desired consistency.

To serve, unmold the custard; serve basted with the apricot sauce.

Coconut Caramel Flan

FFR—8 SERVINGS

1 1/4 cups granulated sugar

1/4 cup water

2 1/4 cups milk of your choice

Finely grated meat of 1 fresh coconut or 3/4 cup packed dried unsweetened
    coconut flakes

4 large eggs

2 large egg yolks

1/2 cup dark rum

1 fresh pineapple, peeled and core removed

Inspired by the Haupia of Hawaii. Beware of the fact that coconut contains plenty of saturated fats.

Put 1/2 cup of the sugar and the water in a skillet. Bring rapidly to a boil and cook to a medium dark caramel (see page 154). Evenly coat a 3-cup soufflé mold with the caramel and let cool.

Scald the milk, then place it and the coconut in a blender or food processor, and blend until smooth. Let stand for 30 minutes at room temperature, then refrigerate for 2 hours.

Preheat the oven to 325°F. Bring a kettle full of water to a boil. Skim the coagulated coconut oil from the top of the milk and rub some of it on the sides of the prepared dish where the caramel has not reached. Strain the coconut milk through a fine-mesh China cap and reheat with the remaining sugar to the scalding point. Beat together the whole eggs and egg yolks, then gradually beat in the hot coconut milk and half the rum. Strain through a fine-mesh strainer directly into the prepared soufflé mold. Set the mold in a baking dish lined with a kitchen towel and place the dish on the middle rack of the oven. Pour in the boiling water, cover, and bake the custard until a nonreactive tester inserted two thirds of the way through the custard comes out clean, 40 to 45 minutes. Remove from the oven, let cool in the water bath, and chill overnight.

To prepare the pineapple sauce, cut half the pineapple into tiny triangular bits. Sauté them in a nonstick pan over medium-high heat until browned on both sides. Puree the remaining pineapple in a blender or food processor, then strain the puree through a conical strainer over the tidbits. Cook until well bound, add the remainder of the rum, simmer another 5 minutes, and let cool.

Serve the room-temperature sauce over the chilled unmolded custard.

Using the Foaming Capacity of Eggs in Cooking and Desserts

The foaming capacity of egg proteins is used in making soufflés, meringue-type preparations, savory sauces such as hollandaise (see page 350), and dessert sauces such as sabayons (see page 195). Egg foams are also used in the preparation of cakes, a discussion of which you will find on page 1130.

Both egg yolks and egg whites foam when subjected to the mechanical action of a hand beater, whip, or electric mixer.

Separating Eggs

Egg whites and egg yolks are used separately to achieve different purposes. With your working hand, crack the shell on the countertop—not on the edge of the bowl you are using—and quickly drop the whole egg into the hollow of your other hand. Let the white run out between your fingers into the bowl below. Pinch the ligaments (called chalazas or chalazae) on either side of the yolk between your fingers and drop the yolk into another bowl. Try not to break the yolks; any loss of yolk means loss of foam volume.

This is not the only way to separate an egg, but when you get used to it, you will find it the quickest and easiest. An egg separator or the familiar method of passing the yolk from one half shell to the other can also be used, but I do not recommend the latter, for, when the eggs have been brought to room temperature, the membrane surrounding the yolk is softened and any angular shell piece can pierce it too easily, thus letting yolk and white mix, which is costly since any egg white mixed with even a small trace of yolk loses part, if not its entire, capacity to foam.

As for the chalazas, it does not matter whether they are left in the white or not; they are just thickened albumen that is pulverized by any whisking or electric beating.

Keeping Egg Whites Safely

It certainly is a good idea not to discard all the egg whites you don't use and to keep them, especially for those of us who pay attention to cholesterol. Too often, however, I hear about egg whites being tossed into a "pit," as it is known in the food business, topsy-turvy, with no care for dating, some even being kept at room temperature.

I would like to recommend keeping egg whites in containers of six, which represents roughly a volume of one cup, if you cook only at home, and in one-quart containers if you work in a food business, and to **positively keep these whites refrigerated at all times between cooking or baking sessions;**

egg whites should be at room temperature only during the time they warm up for use, which is never more than one hour.

If you make soufflés without egg yolks, which is particularly recommended for people with cardiovascular problems, bring your egg whites to room temperature approximately 30 minutes before you use them.

I know that egg whites can be frozen; however, I have always found that they must be brought to room temperature for quite a long time if you want them to whip as well as recently separated whites, which really isn't recommended in these days of salmonella contamination.

To measure egg whites from a bulk quantity of egg whites, just tilt the container over a bowl or measuring cup and let the egg whites drop one by one, remembering that one egg white from a large egg fills a volume of about 3 tablespoons.

Foaming Egg Yolks: The Ribbon

Egg yolks whipped without the addition of another ingredient can be foamed to prepare a number of savory dishes such as soufflés or souffléed omelettes for which you will find recipes in the following pages. But most of the time, yolks are foamed with sugar to prepare desserts.

In dessert recipes, you will often be given the instruction to "beat the egg yolks and sugar until thick and lemon colored." This direction is misleading; it would be more specific to instruct to "beat the egg yolks and sugar until they form a *ribbon*."

To make a ribbon consists of combining the capacity of the yolks to foam and trap air when submitted to mechanical action with the capacity of sugar to attract moisture. The beater slightly denatures (unfolds) the protein in such a way that it traps air while at the same time the sugar absorbs the moisture contained in the yolks, thus forming an extremely heavy and viscous syrup. The result is a pale yellow, bulky, sticky mixture in which the air remains trapped within the protein structure which keeps expanding as the beating goes on. When the beating stops, the mixture falls from whisk or beater—lifted no higher than 4 inches above the foam—in a broad flat band that folds upon itself as a silk ribbon would if dropped onto a table. A *"ribbon" is never straight and round;* if it is, you have either not beaten enough, or you are testing from too high above the foam.

If you prepare a dessert, add the sugar to the eggs slowly and in regular small additions when you mix by hand or rotary beater. If you use a modern electric mixer, you may add the total amount of sugar at once in one slow steady stream. The power of the motor will break down the mixture quickly and effortlessly.

If you ribbon too long, so that about two thirds of the sugar has turned to syrup, with no moisture left to dissolve the remaining third, the mixture will turn granular from undissolved sugar. To prevent this from happening, recipes will often direct to add from 1 teaspoon to 1 tablespoon lukewarm water to the ribboning mixture. If this happens to you when you experiment with a personal recipe, remember to add lukewarm water whenever your ribbon turns granular to dissolve the sugar.

Ribboning ensures an even dispersion of the lightened yolks through a batter; the air enclosed in the yolks' protein mesh dilates as soon as it is reached by the oven heat. Without that air, the heavy yolks would bear down on the batter and coagulate too fast. A cake made with a yolk mixture that has not been ribboned properly has the definite taste of hard-boiled egg yolk and does not rise as it should; one can usually see a layer of hard-boiled egg on the bottom of the cake pan.

Use a ribboned mixture without delay although the mixture is capable of waiting a bit, but using the ribboned mixture quickly prevents the protein walls from collapsing. Although an egg yolk ribbon can reform when beaten again, a considerable amount of air is lost and the ribbon will reform only if a small amount of lukewarm water is added to the partly collapsed mixture.

Whole eggs and sugar are also ribboned in the famous *génoise* cake batter described on page 1134. In the making of this particular cake it is essential to bear in mind how important it is that a ribbon is never straight and that one should not beat either below or beyond this particular stage. See the special explanations given in the cake section on page 1135.

Beating Egg Whites

Egg whites will acquire a better volume if they have reached room temperature when you start beating them, because their proteins will expand more rapidly. The white of older eggs will also whip easier because of the chemical changes in the albumen that have occurred over time.

The beating bowl and whisk or beaters must be free of fat and moisture for a film of water on the inside of a metal bowl prevents the rapid development of a foam.

The whites should not contain the slightest trace of yolk, or some yolk proteins will bind with the proteins of the whites and weaken the coagulated network of the foam, at the same time as the fat coming from the yolks will interfere with the formation of the air pockets or "cells" which constitute the foam.

The addition of an acid (cream of tartar, or one or two drops of lemon juice or vinegar) stabilizes egg white foams and retards their disintegration when the beating stops. Acids also turn the pigments known as flavones in the egg whites from yellow to white. A pinch of salt firms up the proteins.

The structure of foams is easier to understand when one works up an egg white foam, because one can see that structure develop much better than in an egg yolk foam.

The beating action of the mixer or hand whisk disperses bubbles of air into the viscous egg white, which chemically is plain water containing proteins in suspension. The result is a foam made of a continuous phase of thin liquid layers called lamellae separated by millions of air bubbles.

After the beating stops, a foam can disintegrate for different reasons:

- When the foam waits to be used, drainage of the lamellae liquid occurs by virtue of gravity; the liquid is heavy and is simply and normally pulled downward.

- As the lamellae drain downward, the air bubbles coalesce—or join—to produce larger air bubbles which break more easily; the larger the bubbles become, the more easily they break and the more the foam deflates, which eventually leads to complete collapse.

- The more prolonged the whipping, the more numerous the bubbles and the firmer the foam. Excessive beating of egg white proteins, however, can result in problems because overbeating provokes partial aggregation and coagulation of the egg white proteins where air bubbles and liquid meet (the air/water interface) and the viscosity of the liquid lamellae becomes insufficient for the foam to remain stable. The proteins have bonded to each other (coagulation) and have released their water and the air. You have seen this happen in your own egg white bowl, when, wanting to make meringues, you have beaten the whites just a few seconds too long and the foam starts falling apart as it releases a thin layer of liquid all around the bowl.

BEATING EGG WHITES IN A COPPER BOWL WITH A HAND WHISK

Beating egg whites by hand produces one third more volume of foam but is only worth the effort if the correct instruments are at hand:

- either a 10-inch unlined copper bowl and an 18- to 20-inch-long whisk with a 3½- to 5-inch balloon wire, or
- a copper liner for the KitchenAid mixers K5A or K45 models.

CLEANING A COPPER BOWL   Never wash a copper bowl with soap and water. Instead, mix ¼ cup vinegar and 1 tablespoon salt in it and rub with a wad of paper toweling until the inner surface is perfectly pink. Rinse under clear running water and dry with paper towels, not a regular kitchen towel, which, having been washed with a detergent, is liable to contain microscopic fat particles or droplets in suspension in its fibers, even after it has been rinsed properly.

Mixer Type	Add	Beat Stage 1	Add	Beat Stage 2	Add	Beat Stage 3
Mixmaster	Salt	1 minute, speed 2	Acid	2½ minutes, speed 9	Sugar	30 seconds, speed 11
KitchenAid	Salt	1 to 4 whites, 1 minute, speed 3	Acid	3 minutes, speed 8	Sugar	15 seconds, speed 8
		5 whites and more, 2 minutes, speed 3	Acid	3 to 4 minutes, speed 6	Sugar	15 seconds, speed 6
Electric hand mixers	Salt	2 minutes, medium speed	Acid	2 minutes, high speed	Sugar	30 seconds, high speed

THE STAGES OF BEATING EGG WHITES

Start beating the whites the minute they are in contact with the bowl; if they must wait, let them do so in a china bowl.

1. With your wrist or elbow, beat without interruption slowly for 45 seconds. It will introduce air in the albumen, and produce large air pockets. Add a pinch of salt. You need no other acids than the natural acidity of the copper enhanced by the vinegar already used to clean the bowl. The copper bowl itself will also help to produce the foam.
2. Continue beating for 3½ minutes at 250 strokes per minute to break the large air pockets and multiply the small air bubbles. Continue beating in this manner until the eggs are about seven times their original volume.
3. Give the whisk six good turns around the bowl, scraping well against its sides. This procedure, called *forcer* in French culinary jargon, homogenizes the foam by forcing out possible larger air pockets. This is the stage at which you will add a large pinch of sugar if your foam does not look stable.

THE ROLE OF OVOTRANSFERRIN ON
EGG WHITES BEATEN IN A COPPER BOWL

One of the proteins contained in the egg whites is called conalbumin. Conalbumin, also called ovotransferrin, has the capability of attaching metal ions to itself and it does just that when the whites are beaten in copper. This property produces a foam that is much more stable and less susceptible to the effects of overbeating than a foam produced with cream of tartar in a china or stainless steel bowl. This is a very important point that has been studied in depth and proven by Harold McGee. Please go directly to Mr. McGee's text in his book *On Food and Cooking* listed in the bibliography. It is detailed and most interesting and explains why the copper bowl does produce such wonderful egg white foams; there is no need for me to paraphrase his words—no one can express a personal conception better than the author of that conception.

BEATING EGG WHITES WITH AN ELECTRIC MIXER

Please see the list of speeds for different mixers at different stages of beating egg whites on the opposite page.

When beating egg whites with a large standard mixer, run a spatula along the edges of the bowl to push the whites back into the mixer blades. This keeps the centrifugal force generated by the beaters from throwing too much air out of the whites and whipping them too hard at the center of the bowl and too soft around the edges.

With an electric hand mixer, turn the mixing bowl from left to right (or vice versa if you are left-handed) as you beat and keep moving the beaters up and down the sides of the bowl to make sure that the whole bulk of whites is constantly kept in movement.

In both cases and for each 4 to 6 egg whites, use ⅛ teaspoon cream of tartar as acid, a pinch of salt before stage 2, and 1 tablespoon sugar before stage 3, the last only if needed.

THE SUGAR FIX

The "sugar fix" is a repair method for egg whites that are on the verge of being overbeaten or were just overbeaten. It will very rarely, if ever, be needed when using a copper bowl. But in all other types of bowls, to prevent it from happening and *only* if you are making a dessert, add 1 tablespoon or so of sugar to the foam just before the end of the beating. You will see the change of texture in the foam as the sugar mixes with the water seeping slowly from the proteins to form a syrup viscous enough to rehomogenize and restabilize the foam for a few minutes. Use the foam *immediately,* for if it is left standing, it will break down again in the worst of ways.

WHEN ARE EGG WHITES BEATEN ENOUGH?

Whether beaten by hand or by electric mixer, egg whites are beaten enough when:

- *First and foremost* an uncooked egg in its shell sinks only ¼ inch deep into the foam. The foam is overbeaten if the same egg sits on top of it without sinking at all.
- The foam does not slide down when the bowl is turned upside down.
- The foam retains the trace of a knife or spatula pulled through it.
- The foam forms a *toupe,* a tuft, that slightly bends over on the whisk or beaters when they are withdrawn from the bowl, the stiff but not dry peaks many recipes call for.

WHICH FOAM WAITS FOR THE OTHER?

Unfortunately, it is common to see recipes instructing the reader to beat the egg whites first and to keep them waiting for the egg yolk foam into which

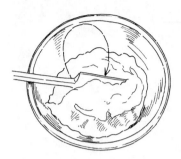

Cut at the center down to the bottom of the bowl.

Bring the spatula from the bottom up, scraping the side of the bowl. Left hand turns the bowl toward the right while right hand folds the mixture following the arrows at the center of the bowl.

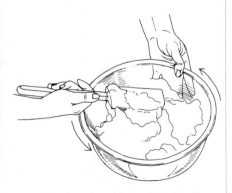

Turning your wrist, not the handle of the spatula, bring the batter over the egg white; continue until the mixture is uniformly pale yellow.

they are to be folded. From what I have mentioned in all the paragraphs above, you can well understand that this is incorrect procedure and that it is definitely smarter to keep the egg yolk foam waiting for the egg whites. Simply stretch a light towel over the bowl in which the yolks wait for you to be ready with the whites. The heavy egg yolk foam can stand a wait of 3 to 4 minutes.

If you can afford to have two beaters and two bowls, even two simple hand beaters and two glass bowls will do well, it will be easy to beat the yolks first, then beat the whites and immediately fold them into the yolks. Should the yolks show the least little bit of dehydration, add to them a teaspoon of water and give them three to four additional little turns of the beaters before folding the egg whites into them.

FOLDING FOAMS INTO OTHER FOAMS OR BATTERS

Folding is the procedure used to incorporate egg foams into batters or dry ingredients into egg foams. It is done with a large long-handled spatula. The cardinal rule of folding is:

When you fold, the heaviest ingredient must be at the bottom of the bowl.

1. *To incorporate a foam into a heavy moist base of batter or ribboned egg yolks,* first mix about one fourth to one third of the total volume of the egg white foam into the heavier mixture to lighten it and bring its consistency closer to that of the foam.

    Place the remaining egg whites on top of the batter and, with a large spatula, cut through both the whites and yolks or batter *at the dead center of the bowl and down to its bottom,* lifting the yolks or batter upward. As you do so, turn your wrist so its inner side is forced to face toward the outside by the folding motion and in doing so deposits yolk or batter on top of the egg white foam. As you fold, your other hand should turn the bowl rhythmically. Continue this folding of the foam and turning of the bowl until no traces of egg white are to be seen anymore and you are left with a perfectly homogeneous mixture.

    The first time you fold a batter, it would be a good idea to do so in a glass bowl, so you can see through the bowl and monitor your work. As you direct the spatula back upward, it must scrape the side of the bowl. When the spatula comes out of the mixture, gently deposit the yolk or batter on top of the whites; do not throw it with force or into a wild *toupe,* which will result in a loss of volume—keep as calm a rhythm as you can. This long description represents all of a maximum of 90 seconds of rapid work.

    The second most important rule is:

Be as fast as you possibly can.

Observe the following tips:

- Never fold from one edge of the bowl to the other; the batter will liquefy and turn heavy because, in essence, you will be stirring horizontally instead of folding.
- Never turn the handle of the spatula in your hand, and never let the spatula rest on the batter at any time, or you will lose an appreciable amount of air.

2. *To incorporate dry ingredients into an egg white foam*, sprinkle or strain their total volume on top of the foam and fold until the dry ingredients are completely incorporated.

If ground nuts and powdered material such as flour or starch are to be incorporated into ribboned yolks (see page 163) along with beaten egg whites, start by mixing together the nuts and flour. Lighten the egg yolk foam first by mixing in one quarter of the total volume of the beaten whites into it. Top the ribboned mixture with the remainder of the beaten whites, sprinkle the mixed nuts and flour on top of the whites, and fold at once the lightened yolks, whites, and dry ingredients into one another. For more details, see the cake section on page 1135. This Swiss method of working, which I learned in Zurich at Lindt Spruengli, is far superior to the French method of adding alternately the whites and the dry ingredients.

Different Uses of Egg White Foams

Egg white foams are used for the following preparations:

- Low-calorie and low-cholesterol desserts based on a simple cornstarch pudding lightened with an Italian meringue for people with serious cardiovascular problems.
- Soufflés of all kinds, including the "puffy" omelettes.
- Preparations such as slow-baked French meringue shells and the famous floating island–style custard desserts.
- Sabayons warm and cold.
- Frozen soufflés and mousses.

Fat-Free Puddings for Cardiovascular Patients

I am, as I already stated, against the idea of substituting ingredients; I personally prefer a fresh fruit to a dessert loaded with agar-agar or other gums to finish my meal, but I well understand that many people, who have been accustomed to sweet desserts all of their lives, have great difficulties renouncing them when health problems develop and feel deprived. The following three desserts will please a sweet tooth without any guilt.

Orange and Cranberry Pudding

LFR—6 TO 8 SERVINGS

1 tablespoon cornstarch

1 cup cold skim milk

Pinch of salt

2 tablespoons Grand Marnier

1 cup coarse-cut orange marmalade

¼ cup water

3 large egg whites

1 cup prepared whole-cranberry sauce

Use any jam you like to flavor the egg whites; I use marmalade here, but you could just as well use strawberry preserves in the custard and top the finished pudding with a fine diced strawberry compote or any other jam/preserve/fruit compote combination you like. This dessert must be consumed within 24 hours of its making.

Mix the cornstarch and cold milk with the salt in a saucepan. Bring to a boil, reduce the heat to medium, and cook, stirring constantly, until the mixture has boiled and acquired the consistency of a light pudding. Cool completely. Whisk in the Grand Marnier. Cover with plastic wrap to prevent the formation of a skin.

Melt the marmalade in a saucepan over medium heat, strain the rinds out, chop them, and set them aside. Mix the marmalade and water together, bring to a boil, and cook to 238°F.

Start beating the egg whites in a large bowl and as soon as they reach a light foam, gradually add the hot marmalade; continue beating until the whites are stiff, glossy, and almost cold.

Mix a large sauce spoon's worth of the egg white mixture into the custard to lighten it, then fold in the remainder together with the reserved chopped rind until the mixture is homogeneous. Turn into a serving dish and deep chill.

Just before serving, melt the cranberry sauce in a saucepan over medium heat, and turn it into a small bowl. Pass the warm sauce with the chilled pudding.

Cappuccino and Walnut Crunch Pudding

LFR—6 to 8 servings

2 teaspoons cornstarch

I cup cold skim milk

Pinch of salt

I ½ tablespoons dark roast instant decaffeinated coffee granules

½ teaspoon ground true cinnamon or cassia (page 67)

I ½ cups granulated sugar

¼ cup water

3 large egg whites

½ tablespoon corn oil

⅓ cup coarsely chopped walnuts

Gradually mix the cornstarch and cold skim milk together in a saucepan. Bring to a boil, reduce the heat to medium, and cook until thickened to the consistency of a light pudding. Off the heat, stir in the salt, instant coffee, and cinnamon and cool completely.

Mix 1 cup of the sugar with the water, bring to a boil and cook to 238°F. Meanwhile, start beating the egg whites in a large bowl; as soon as they start to foam, pour in the hot sugar syrup and continue beating until the egg whites turn glossy and have almost completely cooled. Stir 1 large sauce spoon full of the egg white mixture into the coffee base. Fold in the remainder of the whites until the mixture is homogeneous. Turn into a serving dish and deep chill.

Grease a baking sheet or jelly-roll pan very lightly with a wad of paper toweling moistened with the oil. Melt the remaining sugar in a 1-quart saucepan with a bit of water and cook to a light caramel (see page 154). Add the walnuts and finish cooking until the caramel has darkened. Pour onto the oiled sheet and let harden completely. Lift the sheet off and chop the walnut praline coarsely.

To serve, sprinkle the praline on top of the pudding.

Caramel Eggs in the Snow

NFR—6 to 8 servings

I cup granulated sugar

2 cups skim milk

Pinch of salt

4 teaspoons cornstarch

I tablespoon pure vanilla powder or any other vanilla flavoring of your choice

4 large egg whites

The same type of preparation with the same shelf life of twenty-four hours

My mother prepared this mixture in 1945 when we received a distribution of powdered egg whites and a supplementary pound of sugar for the Easter holidays. We took it as a great omen that "Things were getting better." Cook's vanilla powder is a good American brand; the French Vahine, when to be found, is more aromatic.

Melt and caramelize ½ cup of the sugar to a rather dark but not black color (see page 154). Cool the caramel, then slowly dissolve it with the skim milk over low heat in a saucepan; add another 2 tablespoons of the sugar to the milk and the salt and let cool completely.

Put the cornstarch in another saucepan, then gradually stir in the caramel milk; thicken it over medium heat. Add the vanilla powder and strain the custard through a conical strainer into a crystal dish.

Bring a skillet full of water to a boil, then turn it down to a bare simmer. Beat the egg whites in a large bowl with another 2 tablespoons of the sugar until they can carry the weight of a raw egg in its shell. With a large sauce spoon, shape as many "eggs" from the beaten egg white foam as you can and drop these into the barely simmering water to poach them 3 minutes on each side; use a slotted spoon to flip the "eggs" over. Drain the eggs on paper toweling.

Pile the eggs to float on top of the custard. Cook the remaining sugar in a saucepan to a golden caramel and dribble it over the eggs. Keep refrigerated until ready to use.

Souffléed Omelettes and Soufflés

There is nothing more fun to prepare than a souffléed omelette. The technique is simple and consists of foaming egg yolks and egg whites separately, then folding them into each other. These omelettes are wonderful budget-wise, for four eggs can easily provide six servings, especially if there is a nice little filling at the center of the omelette. Here is a pleasant example.

La Bella Scarolata

This recipe is from the backcountry of Nice, way up in the hills, where one can see the Mediterranean glistening in the distance. The name comes from the fact that an old Niçoise friend of the family always looked at this omelette saying "bella" (it is beautiful). Since it was filled with escarole, I called it "La Bella Scarolata," the pretty thing filled with escarole!

Use a 10-inch nonstick skillet.

FFR or FCR—4 TO 6 SERVINGS

2 large heads escarole

Salt

Pepper from the mill

2 tablespoons virgin or other olive oil of your choice

2 cloves garlic, finely chopped

I ounce pancetta, cut into ¼-inch cubes

I tablespoon chopped fresh parsley leaves

I tablespoon chopped fresh chives

I teaspoon crushed fennel seeds

Large pinch of dried orange peel

I anchovy fillet, rinsed and mashed

4 large eggs

Wash the escaroles carefully. Bring a pot of water to a boil, season with salt and pepper, and blanch the greens 2 minutes. Drain, cool completely, and squeeze dry in a towel. Chop the escarole very finely. Heat half the olive oil in a skillet, add the chopped garlic and toss until beige, then add the pancetta and toss 1 minute, on high heat, then add the escarole, parsley, chives, fennel seeds, orange peel, mashed anchovy, and pepper to your taste. Let cook over low heat until the mixture is reduced to a small puree that is still mellow and can be spread. Correct the salt and pepper and remove to a plate; keep warm. Wipe the pan clean.

Separate the eggs. Salt, pepper, and foam the egg yolks in a large bowl until they form a very short ribbon (see page 163). Beat the egg whites until they can carry the weight of an uncooked egg in its shell without it sinking into the mass of the whites by more than ¼ inch. Fold the whites into the yolks until the mixture is homogeneous.

Brush the pan with a tiny bit of the remaining olive oil. Heat the pan until very hot, maintaining it on high heat. Pour the egg foam into the pan; count to three, then, using a spatula, continue folding the foam onto itself to cook it thoroughly. Shake the pan to smooth the bottom of the omelette at regular intervals. Turn the heat off, spread the escarole mixture on the omelette, lift the pan to a 45-degree angle and roll the omelette closed. Invert on a serving dish, brush the remainder of the olive oil over the top of the omelette, and enjoy.

To make this a fat-controlled omelette, reduce the egg yolks to two and omit the pancetta.

ALL ABOUT SOUFFLÉS

Ah, you will say, why soufflés nowadays, who has the time to make them anyhow?

First, for the sake of preserving techniques which should not be lost because they constitute a tradition that has been developed over centuries and deserve preserving. Also, because there is nothing wrong with a nice treat after a light supper with fun company.

If your objection to soufflés is the amount of work they represent, may I suggest that you read this section from beginning to end and you will have the nice surprise of finding out that soufflés can be made way ahead of time, frozen, and baked still frozen, coming out of the oven looking as graceful as they would if they had just been made.

Soufflé is the past participle of the French verb *souffler*, which means "to blow up"; it has become a noun designating a culinary preparation, other than a cake, that contains a large amount of beaten egg whites and is baked in the oven. The cold soufflé, or *soufflé glacé*, is not a baked dish and consequently not a true soufflé, but a kind of frozen mousse. You will find out all about this type of soufflé in the next section.

A soufflé is made of two parts:

- The base (made from beaten egg yolks, sauce, puree), which contains all the elements giving the soufflé its taste and flavor, and

- The whipped egg whites, which constitute the active part. A soufflé puffs up when baked because the air beaten into the egg whites and trapped in the foam walls dilates when subjected to the heat of the oven. This dilation is further helped by the pressure applied on the foam walls by the steam produced when the water present in the batter boils.

GENERALITIES OF SOUFFLÉ MAKING Many soufflés can be made without egg yolks, thus answering our modern need of lightening our nutrition.

After you have chosen a soufflé recipe, prepare all your ingredients. Make sure that you are familiar with the following basic techniques all involved in the preparation of the soufflé:

- Making a basic white flour-bound sauce (see pages 271–75), or a bouillie (page 187)
- Ribboning the eggs and sugar (page 163)
- Folding (page 168)
- Whipping egg whites (page 164)

And remember one of the most important rules of soufflé making: A soufflé, whether savory or sweet, should always contain at least one more egg white than egg yolks.

USING AN ELECTRIC FRYING PAN AS AN OVEN Sometimes a cook would like to prove to him- or herself that they can make a soufflé and feel the urge to experiment but are stopped by lack of an oven, which is not a rare occurrence in many a modern apartment. In this case, be smart, and preheat your electric frying pan to 325°F for savory soufflés or 400°F for dessert soufflés. Placing the dome lid on the pan transforms it into an oven. I used such a frying pan to prepare soufflés many times at the beginning of my career, when I was doing demonstrations to women's groups in locales where no ovens were available. If you want the sides of the soufflé to remain soft, fill the pan with water and preheat to 325°F. If you prefer them to turn crispy, bake the soufflé in an empty pan that has been preheated to 425°F.

SOUFFLÉ DISHES If at all possible, use a classic round soufflé dish with striated sides. The striations, together with the perfectly straight sides of the dish, ensure even penetration of the heat through the entire batter. However, many dishes such as heatproof glass casseroles and Charlotte molds may be used instead. The most practical dish to acquire is a 1¾-quart round Corning Ware soufflé dish, the white model with the straight sides. Soufflés to serve large numbers of guests can be baked in plain rectangular baking dishes, then cut into square portions.

COLLAR OR NO COLLAR? COLLAR MATHEMATICS As the soufflé bakes, it rises. If your dish is just the right size for your batter, the soufflé will rise in the dish, making a beautiful crown. If your dish is not large enough, the batter will rise out of the dish and spill over before it is firm enough to hold its shape. In such a case, quite a few cooks would think a collar is needed.

I am not partial to collars because the temperature of the oven is not carried through paper at the same rate as through the ceramic material of the soufflé dish; as a result, after going to the trouble of making a collar, when you remove it, the soufflé collapses a solid inch into itself because it is not cooked as deeply where the collar was attached as on its top.

But what if you do not own a dish that is large enough for the recipe?

Decide for yourself by using the following collar mathematics. Add together:

- The volume of the base
- The volume of each egg yolk when beaten (2½ tablespoons per yolk)
- The volume of each egg white beaten, then folded into the mixture (the original volume per egg white is 1 cup which is reduced to a final ⅔ cup after folding).

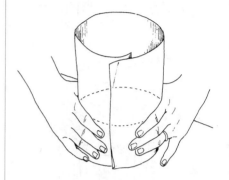

Collar for a frozen soufflé (don't use collars for hot soufflés)

The actual volumes listed above will probably be a little less if this is your first try because of your relative inexperience with egg foams. Measure the volume of the dish you own by filling it with water and compare it with the probable volume of the batter. As an exercise, choose any of the soufflé recipes listed below and calculate the volume of its batter and compare it with the volume of your soufflé dish. The volume of the batter should be lower than that of the dish by about 1¼ cups.

If you need it and want it, make a collar. Measure a piece of parchment paper 1⅓ times as long as the diameter of the soufflé dish and twice as high. Butter or oil it well. Wrap the paper around the dish, its lower edge *resting on the countertop*. Doing this gives the paper rigidity and makes it easier to handle than a shorter piece of paper that sits just under the lip of the dish. The buttered side of the paper should face the center of the dish. Secure the paper at the top with a paper clip and tie a length of kitchen string around the waist of the dish.

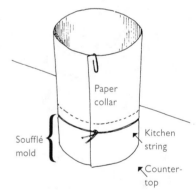

Paper collar

Soufflé mold

Kitchen string

Counter-top

Finished collar

Basic Soufflé Sequence

1. Preheat the oven to the desired temperature.
2. Butter or lightly oil the dish and collar, if using one.
3. Sprinkle the dish lightly with grated cheese, bread crumbs, or sugar, whichever is appropriate.
4. Cook the base; add the egg yolks one by one and whisk well.
5. After adding the egg yolks, reboil the batter if you like a very firm soufflé that will hold a long time. Do not reboil it if you prefer a regular light consistency.

Cutting vents in the soufflé top

Cooked round hat soufflé

6. Correct the seasoning now, before you mix one fourth of the whites into the *warm*, not hot, base and then fold in the remainder. Fill the dish and bake.

FILLING A SOUFFLÉ DISH *Do not pour* a soufflé into its baking dish; *spoon* it in using a large sauce spoon. You will lose less air this way and be able to control the thickness of the successive layers of batter, which must be even throughout the dish.

If the soufflé contains a heavy garnish (diced meat, cake, candied fruit), do not mix it into the batter. Spoon half of the batter into the dish, add the garnish, then cover it with the rest of the batter.

SOUFFLÉ TOP STYLES To obtain a "*round hat*" soufflé (medium heat cookery only—see the next section on oven temperatures), shape the top of the batter so it mounds slightly toward the center. One inch away from the sides of the dish and at 1-inch intervals, cut ½-inch-deep openings in the batter with a pair of scissors. The cuts will form the round hat.

To obtain a "*top hat*" soufflé (high heat cookery only—see the next section on oven temperatures), fill the mold up to the brim, allowing the batter to mound a little. Scrape the excess batter out of the mold with one stroke of a long spatula to obtain a perfectly smooth surface. Slide the thumb of your working hand between the dish and the batter; turning the dish from left to right or vice versa with your other hand, trace a rim all around the top of the batter. The soufflé will rise straight out of the mold and look like a top hat.

OVEN TEMPERATURES If you desire a soufflé evenly cooked to the center, bake it in a medium oven (325°F). All savory soufflés must be cooked at this temperature. Heavy batters need slow ovens. When baking a soufflé at 325°F shape its top to obtain a round hat (see above).

If you desire a French soufflé with about two inches of cooked batter enclosing a slightly creamy center, bake at a high temperature (400°F). When baking a soufflé at 400°F, shape it to obtain a top hat (see above).

The arrows inside the cone indicate the soft part of the soufflé. The arrows outside the cone indicate the fully cooked part.

Flatten the top of the soufflé with a cake spatula.

Trace the rim of the mold with your thumb.

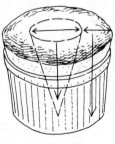

Cooked top hat soufflé

Light dessert batters can be baked according to either method.

Warning: With proper sanitation in view, in spite of the fact that light, soft-centered soufflés are moister and more pleasant, it is safer to use the deep-cooking method for all soufflés, unless you are absolutely sure that the eggs you are using are totally free of any contamination. You are responsible for establishing this fact.

The goal when baking a soufflé is to coagulate the proteins as soon as the batter is pushed out of the dish by the oven heat. In a *too low oven*, the soufflé will flatten at its top and spill over the edges of the dish. In a *too high oven*, the soufflé will build a hard crust on the outside and stay liquid in the center.

To obtain a "mushroom" top, place the soufflé in a preheated 400°F oven and turn the heat down immediately to 350°F; the soufflé top will show the difference in temperatures.

Always bake a soufflé on the lowest rack of the oven or as close as possible to the source of heat. For crisp sides, bake directly on the rack. For firm but unbrowned sides, bake in a hot water bath.

PREPARING SOUFFLÉS AHEAD AND FREEZING THEM UNCOOKED
All uncooked soufflés, unless otherwise mentioned in the recipe, may be frozen. I am always met with a lot of incredulity when I state this little fact in school. I learned it myself way back in 1962 while my French-born eyes incredulously came to rest upon the label of a Stouffers' frozen corn soufflé. It suddenly hit me that if Stouffers could do it, there was no reason why I could not. I rushed home to try and it worked the first time out.

Set your freezer for half an hour at its coldest setting. Cover the soufflé dish with clear plastic wrap. Set the dish flush on the bottom of the freezing unit so that the batter stays level during freezing. Let the batter freeze solid, then wrap it in aluminum foil.

Best Methods for "Defrost While Baking" Soufflés

- If the soufflé is in a Corning Ware dish, place it directly in the preheated oven; a Corning Ware dish is worth its price for being able to do that. Bake the soufflé twice the normal, unfrozen, baking time, less 5 minutes.
- If the soufflé is in a regular china dish, let it stand unwrapped at room temperature for 30 minutes and bake twice the normal, unfrozen, baking time.

You will help yourself a great deal if, at the time you prepare and freeze the soufflé, you label it with the date on which it was prepared and its expected baking time.

The shelf life of a frozen soufflé is only one month, but in catering and restaurants or for large parties at home, it is ample time to be of great help.

SERVING A SOUFFLÉ To serve, break the soufflé top open with two large serving spoons with their convex sides facing each other. Slide one spoon between the batter and dish and, with the help of the other, lift portions out of the dish.

If you are working with larger quantities, remember that soufflé batters can be baked in plain rectangular baking dishes and cut into square portions.

Generally, a savory soufflé baked in:

- A 6-cup mold will make 6 servings as a first course, 4 servings as a main course.
- An 8-cup mold will make 8 servings as a first course, 6 servings as a main course.
- A 1-quart baking dish will make a soufflé for 12 first courses or 8 main courses.
- A 2-quart baking dish will make a soufflé for 24 first courses and 16 main courses.

As for dessert soufflés, if baked:

- In a 4-cup mold, you can expect 4 servings; 6 servings from a 6-cup mold; 8 servings from an 8-cup mold.

These are not precise guidelines, but they are a general indication of what you can expect.

Types of Soufflés

There are three types of soufflés: savory soufflés, roulades, and dessert soufflés. They all can be prepared with whole eggs separated or with plain egg whites, the latter being extremely useful in fat-restricted diets.

ROULADES

A roulade is a soufflé baked flat, either in a baking pan or in a large skillet, and rolled to enclose cooked vegetables, diced ham, chicken, shrimp, mushrooms, either plain or bound with a small sauce. You may vary them according to your own taste.

Ham and Mushroom Roulade

FCR — 6 SERVINGS

As little olive or other unsaturated oil as needed

⅔ cup soy flour (available in health food stores)

I cup fat-free chicken broth of your choice

Salt

Pepper from the mill

I pound mushrooms, finely chopped

I clove garlic, finely chopped

I tablespoon each chopped fresh parsley, chives, chervil, and tarragon leaves

6 large egg whites

12 thin slices cooked ham, finely chopped

Very lightly oil a 15¼ × 10 × 1-inch jelly-roll pan or a professional half sheet pan. Line with parchment or baking paper, letting 1½ inches of paper protrude over the edge of one of the long sides of the baking sheet; you will use this "tab" to roll the roulade. Oil the baking paper very evenly so the roulade will not stick to it once it is cooked. Set aside. Preheat the oven to 325°F.

Mix the soy flour and broth together in a large saucepan and bring to a boil, stirring constantly, over medium heat until the mixture has thickened. Season with salt and pepper to your taste.

Heat a dab of oil in a nonstick skillet. Sauté the chopped mushrooms over high heat with a bit of salt and pepper until dry and brown. Add half the garlic and chopped herbs. Mix the mushrooms into the soy base. In a large bowl, beat the egg whites until they can carry the weight of a raw egg in its shell without sinking into the foam by more than ¼ inch. Fold them into the mushroom base. Turn into the prepared baking pan and bake 15 to 18 minutes, or until a skewer inserted at the center of the pan comes out clean. Do not overbake; the roulade must stay moist or it will break when rolled.

Mix the chopped ham with the remainder of the garlic and chopped herbs. As soon as the roulade is cooked, loosen it from the paper on all sides with the tip of a paring knife and spread the chopped ham over its surface. Roll the roulade lengthwise around the ham and, as you go along rolling, detach the paper from the bottom of the roulade, which will become its top. Let the roulade roll onto a long serving dish and cut into desired size portions. Serve surrounded with the vegetables of your choice.

I use soy flour because of its good content in proteins and its nutritiousness. In case of an allergy to soy, replace it with 3 tablespoons of regular whole wheat flour. This roulade does not freeze gracefully, so prepare it fresh and, as a vegetable, consider stir-fried sliced zucchini flavored with chopped fresh basil (see page 392).

SUGGESTED WINE:
Grignolino, either Italian or from California

Ricotta Roulade

FFR—6 SERVINGS

3 tablespoons unsalted butter or unsaturated oil of your choice

1 pound fresh spinach leaves, well washed and dried, stems removed

Salt

Pepper from the mill

2 tablespoons unbleached all-purpose flour

¼ cup milk of your choice (optional), scalded

6 large eggs, separated

1 pound very fresh ricotta cheese

½ cup freshly grated Parmigiano-Reggiano, Grana, or similar local cheese

3 tablespoons fresh mint leaves, finely chopped

2 small cloves garlic, finely chopped

1½ to 2 cups tomato coulis (page 308) or sauce of your choice, kept warm

This is a full-fat recipe. You can lighten it—a euphemism for defatting it—by using skim ricotta and Alpen Lace cheese instead of any of the full-fat cheeses mentioned below. As a vegetable accompaniment consider the sautéed mushrooms on page 414.

SUGGESTED WINE: *Italian or California Grignolino, Valpolicella, or any other light Italian red wine*

Lightly oil a 15¼ × 10 × 1-inch jelly-roll pan or professional baking half sheet and fit it with a piece of parchment paper, letting 1½ inches of paper protrude over the edge of one of the long sides of the baking sheet; you will use this "tab" to roll the roulade. Oil it with 1 tablespoon of the chosen fat or oil. Set aside. Preheat the oven to 325°F.

Chop the spinach leaves coarsely. Over medium-high heat, heat another tablespoon of the chosen fat in a skillet and add the spinach; stir-fry it a few seconds, season with salt and pepper. Reduce the heat to medium, cover, and let the juices exude from the spinach; do not let them evaporate. Cool the mixture completely. Sprinkle the flour over it and mix well. Reheat slowly until the mixture thickens, adding the milk only if needed. Remove the pan from the heat and add the egg yolks, one at a time, stirring and mixing very well.

Remove the mixture to a large bowl. In another large bowl, beat the egg whites until they can carry a raw egg in its shell without it sinking into the foam by more than ¼ inch. Fold the whites into the spinach base. Spread evenly into the prepared pan and bake until fully set, 20 to 25 minutes.

While the roulade is baking, lightly mix the cheeses together with half the mint and garlic and a dash each of salt and pepper. When the roulade is cooled, spoon an even layer of the mixture, lengthwise, over three quarters of the surface of the roulade and roll up the roulade, also lengthwise, letting the part not covered by the cheese mixture become the bottom of the roulade; transfer the roulade to a long heatproof serving dish. Cut into the desired number of portions. Let the roulade reheat to its core in a slow oven.

Season the hot tomato *coulis* or sauce with the remaining garlic and mint and spoon over the roulade.

A SELECTION OF CLASSIC AND LIGHTENED SAVORY SOUFFLÉS

If, perhaps, you hesitate to make a soufflé because you think it is too rich, please reconsider; you will soon realize there is much you can do to lighten it.

The base of a savory soufflé can be a puree of meat, fish, or vegetables, a thick *béchamel* or velouté sauce (see page 276), or a combination of vegetable puree or cheese with any of these sauces. If the base of the soufflé is a white sauce, you can cut out all the butter or oil by thickening the base with a slurry of flour, cornstarch, or potato starch instead of the classic butter-and-flour roux. All savory soufflés otherwise follow the rules explained on the preceding pages.

As a basic rule, you can make up your own savory soufflé combinations by using:

¼ cup of base per egg

Do not forget the basic rule of adding one more egg white than the number of egg yolks contained in the batter.

For the sake of even lighter nutrition, all savory soufflés can be made with egg whites only. And I'd like to point out that this is not a brand new idea; in the old-fashioned French cookbook known as *La Bonne Cuisine de Madame St. Ange*, which has been the bible of the majority of French home cooks for a century and a source of information for this cook and a few other well-known cooks, there is a recipe for an excellent Gruyère cheese soufflé made of a base of Gruyère and *béchamel* sauce leavened with egg whites only.

Soufflés made of an uncooked meat or fish base are not made anymore because they are simply too rich; they require cream in the soufflé formula and cream in a small sauce to accompany the soufflé. Cheese soufflés are rich enough by themselves and do not require a sauce.

Savory soufflés are excellent main courses for vegetarians and for luncheons, formal and informal. I do not recommend serving soufflés as a first course, as was done up to the 1950s, as they are too substantial when offered before a regular meat portion accompanied by vegetables.

BEWARE: Work in one saucepan large enough for you to prepare the base of the soufflé and in which you can also fold in all of the beaten egg whites without their overflowing. You will save time and obtain a better soufflé if you fold the egg white foam into a pot which is still warm from the cooking of the base; the air in the batter will begin to slightly dilate even before you put the soufflé in the oven.

Here are a few recipes for experimentation; notice that in each of them I have opted for a different way of making the soufflé, so that the reader can see some of the possible variations. Notice the dietetic code of each recipe.

Baked Yam and Ham Soufflé

FCR — 6 SERVINGS

1 tablespoon unsaturated oil of your choice

3 tablespoons fresh bread crumbs

6 large yams or sweet potatoes, scrubbed

1 small can evaporated skim milk

3 ounces baked fat-free ham, finely diced

Pepper from the mill

6 or 7 large egg whites, as preferred

Rub the sides of a 6-cup soufflé mold with the oil. Sprinkle the crumbs all around the sides and bottom of the mold. Preheat the oven to 325°F. Bake the potatoes until their skins are almost black and shriveled, about 1 hour. Cut them into halves, remove the pulp, and mash it as finely as possible. Mix the puree of potatoes with the milk and ham in a large bowl. Season the mixture with pepper.

Beat the egg whites until they can carry the weight of a raw egg in its shell without its sinking into the whites by more than ¼ inch. Mix in one quarter of the whites, then fold in the remainder. Spoon the soufflé batter into the prepared mold and bake until a thin nonreactive skewer inserted at the center of the soufflé comes out clean, about 40 minutes. Serve immediately.

Hickory-Smoked Cheddar Soufflé

FFR — 6 SERVINGS

6 ounces hickory-smoked cheddar cheese

1 tablespoon unsalted butter or unsaturated oil of your choice

¼ cup cornstarch

1½ cups cold milk of your choice

¼ teaspoon freshly grated nutmeg

8 slices bacon, cooked until crisp, drained, and finely crumbled

Salt

Pepper from the mill

6 large egg whites

Grate two thirds of the cheese; dice the remaining third of it into ¼-inch cubes. Rub an 8-cup soufflé mold with 1 tablespoon of butter or oil; sprinkle the sides and bottom with 1 tablespoon of the grated cheese. Preheat the oven to 325°F.

Put the cornstarch in a large saucepan. Using a wooden spoon, gradually stir in the cold milk until the mixture is completely smooth. Thicken over medium heat, stirring constantly and making sure that the mixture comes to

A good main course recipe for people on a low-cholesterol or fat-controlled diet. For a more substantial soufflé, use only 6 whites, but use 7 for a lighter one.

SUGGESTED WINE: A California Chenin Blanc

A true American flavor, smoked cheddar is not used enough in cooking; here is a good opportunity to showcase a delicious product in any of its regional versions.

SUGGESTED WINE: Zinfandel

a complete boil. Off the heat, add the grated and diced cheese, nutmeg, and bacon. Add salt and pepper as needed.

Beat the egg whites until they can carry the weight of a raw egg in its shell without its sinking into the whites by more than ¼ inch. Mix one quarter of the whites into the batter; fold in the remainder. Spoon into the prepared mold. Bake until a thin, nonreactive skewer inserted at the center of the soufflé comes out clean, about 45 minutes. Serve immediately.

Moussaka Soufflé

FFR— 6 SERVINGS

2 small eggplant, peeled and cut into large dice

Salt

6 tablespoons olive oil of your choice

3 tablespoons each freshly grated Parmigiano-Reggiano and Pecorino cheeses

I large onion, finely chopped

½ pound freshly ground lamb meat

¼ cup red Retsina wine or dry red wine

2 tablespoons tomato paste

Pinch of dried thyme

I clove garlic, mashed

½ teaspoon ground coriander

Pepper from the mill

3 tablespoons unbleached all-purpose flour

I cup milk of your choice, scalded

2 to 5 large egg yolks, as preferred

6 large egg whites

All the elements of the Greek moussaka in a soufflé dish. A very substantial soufflé which will require only a lightly dressed salad to become a full meal.

SUGGESTED WINES: *Red Retsina from Greece or a small French Côtes-du-Rhône or a California Zinfandel*

Sprinkle the diced eggplant with salt and let stand for 1 hour in a bowl. Drain off the water extracted by the salt. Rinse in cold water and pat very dry. Meanwhile, rub an 8-cup soufflé mold with 1 tablespoon or so of olive oil and sprinkle with 1 tablespoon of the mixed cheeses. Set aside.

Heat 2 tablespoons of the olive oil in a large skillet over medium-high heat. Add the onion and sauté to light golden. Add the lamb and brown well, then discard all the fat by lifting the handle of the pan to a 45-degree angle, bringing the meat close to the pan handle side of the pan, then letting the fat drain completely into its lip and sponging the fat off with paper towels. Add the wine, tomato paste, thyme, garlic, coriander, and salt and pepper. Cover and simmer until all the liquids have evaporated, about 20 minutes.

Heat the remaining 3 tablespoons of olive oil in a large skillet over low heat, cook the eggplant, stirring, over low heat, letting the vegetable soften slowly and fall apart. Add the flour and cook for a few minutes. Add the milk in two additions, stirring each time until smooth and let cook until thickened over medium heat. Add the egg yolks one by one, mixing well after each addition. Preheat the oven to 325°F.

Beat the egg whites until they can carry the weight of a raw egg in its shell without its sinking into the whites more than ¼ inch. Mix one quarter of the whites into the eggplant base; fold in the remainder. Spoon half the soufflé batter into the prepared dish, then spread the lamb mixture over this layer. Top with the remainder of the soufflé batter. Bake until a thin, nonreactive skewer inserted at the center of the soufflé comes out clean, 50 to 55 minutes. Serve immediately.

Any Blue Cheese Soufflé

FFR—6 SERVINGS

1 tablespoon unsalted butter or unsaturated oil of your choice

3 tablespoons fresh bread crumbs

2 teaspoons caraway seeds

4½ tablespoons unbleached all-purpose flour

1½ cups cold milk of your choice

3 to 5 large egg yolks, as preferred

1 cup crumbled blue cheese

Salt

Pepper from the mill

6 large egg whites

Butter an 8-cup soufflé mold. Sprinkle the bread crumbs on its sides and bottom. Set the mold aside. Preheat the oven to 325°F.

In a large saucepan, mix the caraway seeds and flour together. Using a wooden spoon, gradually stir in the cold milk until the mixture is smooth. Cook until thickened over medium heat, making sure that the mixture comes to a complete boil. Off the heat, add the egg yolks one by one, whisking well between additions, then reboil the mixture to give it more solidity. Let the mixture cool to lukewarm, then add the crumbled cheese. Mix well. Correct the seasoning with salt and pepper.

Beat the egg whites until they can carry the weight of a raw egg in its shell without its sinking more than ¼ inch into the whites. Mix one quarter of the whites into the batter, then fold in the remainder. Spoon into the prepared soufflé mold and bake until a thin nonreactive skewer inserted at the center of the soufflé comes out clean, about 45 minutes. Serve immediately.

In spite of the fact that I removed 4 tablespoons of butter from the original recipe, this formula remains a full-fat recipe because of the yolks and the cheese. The yolks are necessary to give the soufflé sufficient solidity. Use any blue cheese of your choice, bearing in mind that the very fat ones do not work as well as the drier ones. Optimum choices are Wisconsin blue and Danish blue.

SUGGESTED WINES:

California Pinot Noir, Syrah or Petite Syrah, or French Gigondas

Any Crab Soufflé

FFR — 6 SERVINGS

6 tablespoons unsalted butter

2 tablespoons fresh bread crumbs made from French bread

8 ounces fresh crabmeat, picked over for cartilage and shredded

2 tablespoons Cognac or brandy of your choice

4½ tablespoons unbleached all-purpose flour

½ cup hot fish fumet (page 543)

1 cup light cream, scalded

4 large egg yolks

1 tablespoon fino sherry

5 large egg whites

Salt

Pepper from the mill

This recipe can be applied to Maryland crab, Dungeness crab, or Alaskan king crab as well as to shrimp and lobster. This is a celebration dish, which, because of the quality of its ingredients, I have kept purposefully in its full-fat version. Great for a late spring luncheon or even an old-fashioned first course for six.

SUGGESTED WINES:

Virginia or California Chardonnay or a French Meursault

Rub a 6-cup soufflé mold with a tablespoon of the butter and coat its sides and bottom with the bread crumbs. Melt another tablespoon of the butter in a skillet over low heat, then add the crabmeat and heat it through. Preheat the oven to 325°F.

Pour the Cognac into a small saucepan. Holding the pan away from yourself, light the spirit with a match, then pour it, flambéing, over the crabmeat. Shake the pan with the crabmeat back and forth until the flames die away, working at all times away from yourself. You are responsible for your own safety during this operation.

In a medium-size saucepan, melt the remainder of the butter, then add the flour and cook, stirring, over medium heat until golden, about 4 minutes. Off the heat, whisk in the hot fish stock, then the light cream, and cook until thickened over medium-high heat and the mixture comes to a complete boil. Off the heat, add the egg yolks one by one, whisking well after each addition. Add the sherry and crabmeat and season with salt and pepper.

Beat the egg whites until they can carry the weight of a raw egg in its shell without its sinking more than ¼ inch into the whites. Mix one quarter of the whites into the base, fold in the remainder, and turn the batter into the prepared soufflé mold. Bake until a thin, nonreactive skewer inserted at the center of the soufflé comes out clean, about 40 minutes. Serve immediately.

DESSERT SOUFFLÉS

Sweet dessert soufflés are made according to no less than four different methods; each of these methods will be considered here and developed in one recipe type. In all these recipes—with the exception of the true fruit soufflés—the original, and rich, amount of egg yolks and fat has been respected since a soufflé for dessert has always been considered a treat and is prepared only for special occasions. There is absolutely no doubt that dessert soufflés have become "just a little too much" after a full meal, which is my reason for including only one recipe to illustrate each technique.

ABOUT FOLDING EGG WHITES INTO DESSERT SOUFFLÉS

The rule of mixing one quarter of the total amount of the egg whites into the base of a sweet soufflé applies only if that base consists of a relatively heavy material such as a flour pudding or melted chocolate blended with egg yolks. If the base consists only of whipped egg yolks, you can fold the egg white foam directly into the egg yolk foam.

UNCOLLAPSIBLE DESSERT SOUFFLÉS

No soufflé is totally "uncollapsible"; eventually the change of pressure between the oven and the kitchen will slowly but surely provoke the demise of your work of art. However, you can limit the damage and coerce a soufflé into waiting on a sideboard by simply reboiling any soufflé base containing a flour or starch after adding the egg yolks. It is easy to understand what happens: The egg yolks hard-boil and give the soufflé base a solidity which is akin to mortar. Some find the texture of the soufflé "creamier" after it bakes, perhaps, but it is also noticeably heavier and loses finesse. Be adventurous and try both to see what happens and decide which is to your personal taste.

METHOD 1: EGG YOLK BASE These soufflés are the easiest and the fastest to prepare, often, but not always, using the same number of yolks and whites. Make the base by ribboning the yolks (see page 163) heavily with the sugar and the flavoring, and finish the batter by folding the whites into the mixture. This is so perfect for a soufflé "to order" in a restaurant or prepared at the "tip of a hat" in a family kitchen that the French call it a "minute" soufflé. Bake at 350°F until the soufflé is done within one inch of its center; it will finish cooking to its very center by the time you have brought it to the table.

You can improvise any such soufflé using one separated egg per person, unless you are making the following chocolate soufflé, in which there is an additional egg white because of the solidity given to the batter by the starch in the chocolate.

Chocolate Soufflé

FFR—6 SERVINGS

1 tablespoon unsalted butter

1½ tablespoons plus ½ cup granulated sugar

6 ounces bittersweet chocolate of your choice

1 ounce unsweetened chocolate of your choice

6 large egg yolks

Pinch of salt

2 tablespoons heavy cream

1½ teaspoons instant espresso coffee granules

3 tablespoons Cognac, rum, Grand Marnier, or green Chartreuse

7 large egg whites

1 recipe Stirred Custard (page 140), flavored with 2 tablespoons of the liqueur used in the soufflé

The typical example of a minute soufflé is a chocolate soufflé, because there is enough starch in the chocolate itself to obtain a good and solid soufflé without adding corn- or potato starch. A very rich dessert, especially with the addition of the custard, but incomparable as an occasional treat.

Butter an 8-cup soufflé mold, then sprinkle the sides and bottom with 1½ tablespoons of the sugar. Preheat the oven to 350°F.

Melt the chocolates together over hot water; cool. Ribbon the egg yolks, the remaining sugar, and the salt very heavily (see page 163). Blend the cooled chocolate, heavy cream, instant coffee powder, and liqueur into the ribboned yolks until the mixture is smooth.

Whip the egg whites until they can carry the weight of a raw egg in its shell without its sinking more than ¼ inch into the whites. Mix one quarter of their volume into the base, then fold in the remainder. Turn into the prepared soufflé mold and bake on lowest shelf of the oven until set within a generous inch of the center, 14 to 16 minutes. Serve immediately with the warm stirred custard as a sauce.

METHOD 2: BOUILLIE, OR STIRRED FLOUR PUDDING BASE The base of a homemade soufflé is more often than not a bouillie, or stirred flour pudding, in which the raw flour is mixed with sugar and cold milk, then brought to a boil. The bouillie can be used for a soufflé base because the flour has time to finish cooking while the soufflé bakes.

You can create your own combinations by using the following proportions per egg yolk:

1 tablespoon granulated sugar

1½ teaspoons flour of your choice

2 tablespoons milk of your choice

See "Collar or No Collar? Collar Mathematics" on page 174, and remember that you need one more egg white than the total number of egg yolks. Bake at 400°F for a soft creamy center if you are certain of having totally healthy eggs or at 325°F for a firmer center. As an example, here is:

Rum Raisin Soufflé

A fond memory of a demonstration for the Alliance Française of Philadelphia in 1963.

FFR—6 SERVINGS

3 tablespoons each dark and golden raisins

5 tablespoons white rum

I tablespoon unsalted butter

1½ tablespoons plus ¼ cup granulated sugar

¼ cup flour of your choice

½ cup light cream

Pinch of salt

4 large egg yolks

5 large egg whites

I recipe Stirred Custard (page 140), flavored with 2 tablespoons rum

Soak the raisins in ¼ cup of the rum for 24 hours, turning them several times.

Butter a 6-cup soufflé mold and coat it well with 1½ tablespoons of the sugar. Preheat the oven to 325°F.

In a large saucepan, mix together the remaining sugar, the flour, cream, and salt and bring to a boil over medium heat. Off the heat, add the egg yolks one by one, whisking well. Flavor the batter with the remaining 1 tablespoon of rum and any rum left in the raisin dish. Whip the egg whites until they can carry the weight of a raw egg in its shell without its sinking more than ¼ inch into the whites. Mix one quarter of their volume into the base, then fold in the remainder. Turn half the batter into the prepared mold. Sprinkle the raisins on top and add the remainder of the batter. Bake 10 to 25 minutes, depending on the temperature used. Serve immediately with the rum-flavored custard.

METHOD 3: PASTRY CREAM BASE This method is really a fat one, but you should know that it exists. As a matter of fact, it is, most probably, what you are served in a restaurant, where you can almost be sure that the pastry chef has used a small amount of pastry cream to make your soufflé, after blending it with more egg yolks and flavorings. Use basic pastry cream on page 1107 unfinished, that is, without the additions of egg whites and cream. For a 6-cup dish to serve six persons use:

¼ cup warm **Basic Pastry Cream** (page 1107)

3 large egg yolks

3 tablespoons granulated sugar

5 large egg whites

Bake at 325°F for a firm center and at 400°F for a creamy one, but only if you are certain that your eggs are healthy. As an example, here is:

Amaretto Soufflé

FFR — 6 SERVINGS

1 tablespoon unsalted butter

3½ tablespoons granulated sugar

12 dry Italian amaretti cookies, crumbled

6 tablespoons amaretto liqueur of your choice

3 large egg yolks

¼ cup warm Basic Pastry Cream (page 1107) without the egg whites and cream added

5 large egg whites

A typical restaurant-type soufflé.

Butter a 6-cup soufflé dish, then sprinkle it with 1½ tablespoons of the sugar. Preheat the oven to the desired temperature.

Soak the crumbled cookies in ¼ cup of the liqueur to obtain almost a paste. Ribbon heavily the egg yolks and remaining sugar (see page 163) in a large bowl, and blend in the warm pastry cream. Add the paste of cookies and liqueur and beat until smooth. Beat the egg whites until they can carry the weight of a raw egg in its shell without its sinking more than ¼ inch into the whites. Mix one quarter of their volume into the base, then fold in the remainder. Turn into the prepared mold and bake 15 to 20 minutes, depending on the chosen oven temperature. Serve immediately.

METHOD 4: SOUFFLÉED PUDDINGS These soufflés *cannot* collapse and *can* be unmolded; their flavoring can be varied to your choice. Use the same amount of yolks as whites. Use per egg:

1 teaspoon cornstarch

1 to 1½ tablespoons sugar

¼ cup cold milk or cream of your choice

Mix the cornstarch, sugar, and cold milk together in a saucepan and cook over medium heat until the dough leaves the sides of the pan and forms a ball. Beat in the egg yolks one by one. Whip the egg whites until they can carry the weight of a raw egg in its shell without its sinking more than ¼ inch into the whites. Mix one quarter of their volume into the base, then fold in the remainder. Turn the batter into a heavily buttered dish. Bake in a hot water bath in a preheated 325°F oven until a thin nonreactive skewer inserted into the center of the soufflé comes out clean, 40 to 45 minutes. Let the pudding cool in the cooking vessel. Push the top lightly back down into the mold. Invert on a platter and serve covered with a stirred custard. As an example here is a:

Dried Fruit Pudding

Use any kind of dried fruit: apricots, pears, prunes, etc.

FFR—8 SERVINGS

12 ounces dried fruit of your choice

1 tablespoon unsalted butter

⅔ cup light cream

2 tablespoons cornstarch

½ cup firmly packed brown sugar of your choice

4 large eggs, separated

1 teaspoon pure flavoring: almond extract for apricots; vanilla extract for pears; lemon extract for prunes

1 recipe English Custard (page 140), flavored with 2 tablespoons liqueur: kirsch for apricots; pear brandy, kirsch, or Grand Marnier for pears; rum or slivovitz for prunes

Soak the fruit 2 hours in lukewarm water to cover. Discard the water. Cover with enough fresh lukewarm water to just cover the fruit and let soak overnight. The fruit should have absorbed all the water. Puree in a blender or food processor.

Butter an 8-cup soufflé mold. Boil a kettle full of water. Preheat the oven to 325°F.

In a large saucepan, mix together the fruit puree, cream, cornstarch, and brown sugar and cook, stirring, over medium heat until the mixture has boiled and thickened. Add the egg yolks, one by one, whisking well after each addition. Add the chosen flavoring.

Whip the egg whites until they can carry the weight of a raw egg in its shell without its sinking more than ¼ inch into the whites. Mix one quarter of their volume into the base and fold in the remainder. Turn the batter into the prepared soufflé mold. Place the mold in a baking dish lined with a kitchen towel and put the dish on the center oven rack. Pour the boiling water into the baking dish to reach ¼ inch below the rim of the soufflé mold and bake until a thin, nonreactive skewer inserted into the center of the soufflé comes out clean, 40 to 45 minutes.

Remove the soufflé from the oven and from the water bath. Cool 10 minutes, then gently push the pudding top down until level with the rim of the soufflé mold; unmold onto a shallow serving dish. Ladle the custard over its top. Serve warm.

METHOD 5: SUGAR SYRUP AND FRUIT PUREE BASE If you plan to prepare this type of fruit soufflé, you can, during fruit season, prepare large amounts of fruit purees and freeze them in ½-cup containers for use the rest of the year.

Before cooking a sugar syrup, refer to page 199 for detailed instructions. Per egg white, use:

¼ cup granulated sugar

½ cup fruit puree

Plus one additional egg white to compensate for loss of foam while folding

Blend the total amount of sugar with just enough water to moisten it in a saucepan; cook to 264°F (the soft crack stage). Blend the syrup with fruit puree and reheat together for a few minutes.

Beat the egg whites until they can carry the weight of a raw egg in its shell without its sinking more than ¼ inch into the whites. Mix one quarter of the whites into the puree, then fold in the remainder. Bake in a preheated 400°F oven. A buttered 6-cup mold bakes in 13 to 14 minutes and will be firm in the center. Since fruit soufflés are not heavy in fats, here are two recipes to practice on.

Apricot Soufflé

FCR—6 SERVINGS

½ pound dried apricots

1 tablespoon unsalted butter

1½ tablespoons plus 1 cup granulated sugar

2 tablespoons Cognac, rum, or kirsch

5 large egg whites

Crème fraîche, sour cream, or light sour cream (optional)

A year-round recipe. Use fresh apricots when in season.

Soak the dried apricots in cold water to cover overnight. Drain off the water, barely cover with fresh water, and cook in a saucepan until soft, over medium-low heat. Puree in a blender; strain only if desired.

Butter a 6-cup soufflé mold. Sprinkle the sides and bottom with 1½ tablespoons of the sugar. Preheat the oven to 400°F. Mix the remainder of the sugar with just enough water to moisten it in a saucepan. Cook to 264°F without stirring over medium heat. Blend with the apricot puree, then reheat well together. Flavor with the chosen liquor.

Beat the egg whites until they can carry the weight of a raw egg in its shell without its sinking more than ¼ inch into the whites. Mix one quarter of their volume into the base and fold in the remainder. Turn into the prepared soufflé mold, bake until firm in the center, 20 to 25 minutes. When done, spoon servings onto plates and top each portion with a dollop of the chosen cream if desired.

Raspberry Soufflé with Strawberry Compote

FCR—6 SERVINGS

2 cups sliced fresh strawberries

2 tablespoons kirsch or Framboise

I tablespoon unsalted butter

3 tablespoons granulated sugar

Three 10-ounce boxes frozen raspberries, thawed

4 large egg whites

Steep the sliced strawberries in the liqueur for 2 hours; keep chilled.

Butter a 6-cup soufflé mold and sprinkle the sides and bottom with 1 tablespoon of the sugar. Preheat the oven to 400°F.

Do not drain the syrup from the raspberries. Puree the raspberries in a blender and strain to remove the seeds. Cook the puree down to ½ cup in a saucepan over medium heat. Beat the egg whites until they can hold the weight of a raw egg in its shell without its sinking more than ¼ inch into the whites, adding the remaining 2 tablespoons sugar toward the end of the beating. Mix one quarter of the egg whites into the puree and fold in the remainder. Turn the batter into the prepared mold. Bake until firm in the center, 12 to 14 minutes.

Serve the liqueur-macerated strawberries unsweetened over the soufflé, for the soufflé is sweet enough.

Meringues in Their Most Common Uses

Because of their intense sweetness, meringues are not used much anymore; still, they allow the cook to prepare delicious desserts, which need not be excessively rich.

FRENCH MERINGUE

French meringues are made very simply: The egg whites are beaten to a good foam, able to carry the weight of a raw egg in its shell without its sinking more than ¼ inch into the whites, and the sugar is then *folded* into the egg white foam. The baking is slow and long and necessitates almost no special care; as each sugar crystal melts into the egg foam, it leaves a supplementary bubble of air in the foam, which makes the meringue especially light.

French meringues are barely beige outside and are cooked, but still soft, inside. This is achieved by cooking them a long time in a slow oven. The making of French meringue is particularly well illustrated in the recipe that follows for the famous Australian Pavlova, but if you try to top a lemon meringue pie with French meringue, you will have a nice surprise.

Melbourne Pavlova

FFR — 6 SERVINGS

6 large egg whites

Pinch of salt

⅛ teaspoon cream of tartar

1¼ cups granulated sugar

1 teaspoon pure vanilla powder or 1½ teaspoons pure vanilla extract

Confectioners' sugar for sprinkling

1 cup heavy cream

3 mangoes, peeled, pitted, and sliced

6 passion fruit

I discovered this wonderful dessert in Melbourne in the company of my friend Diane Holuigue in the lovely atmosphere of midmorning October Australian sunshine, while parrots and parakeets were sending their love calls from gum tree to gum tree. If passion fruit and mangoes are not available or too costly, which they can be, use any diced fresh fruit of your choice.

Preheat the oven to 100°F. Whip the egg whites with the salt and cream of tartar until almost stiff peaks form, then beat in a tablespoon of the sugar. Mix the remainder of the sugar with the vanilla powder, then fold into the egg whites.

Line a large baking sheet with parchment paper. Spoon the meringue foam into a pastry bag fitted with a plain nozzle and pipe twelve meringue shells onto the paper. Place some confectioners' sugar in a tea strainer and sift or sprinkle the sugar over the meringues.

Bake the meringues, sliding a stainless steel knife between the door and the oven frame to allow steam to evaporate. The meringues are done when they separate from the parchment by themselves. Be patient, it can take as much as 2½ hours.

Beat the cream to a firm foam (see page 28). Assemble six pair of meringues into sandwiches by piping a thick layer of unsweetened cream between them. Top with the mango slices. Scrape the juice and seeds of one passion fruit on top of each confection and serve immediately.

Old-fashioned Floating Island

FFR — 6 TO 8 SERVINGS

For the custard

8 large egg yolks

½ cup granulated sugar

Pinch of salt

2 cups 4% milk, scalded

2 tablespoons pure vanilla extract

This was one of my mother's glorious desserts and remains the one favorite dessert of all French people. It is, to this day, served in many Michelin three-star French restaurants. The combination of ice-cold custard and warm almond meringue island with the slightly bitter caramel is particularly attractive.

For the island

1 tablespoon unsalted butter

1 cup granulated sugar

4 large egg whites

Pinch of cream of tartar

Pinch of salt

2½ ounces almonds, chopped and toasted (page 50)

To make the custard, mix together the egg yolks, sugar, and salt in a sauteuse pan; gradually add the scalded milk and thicken over medium-high heat, stirring constantly to obtain a custard (see techniques on page 140). Add the vanilla and strain into a bowl. Stir at regular intervals until cool to prevent the formation of a skin. Deep chill.

Butter a 3-cup soufflé mold, then sprinkle the sides and bottom with 1 tablespoon of the sugar. Preheat the oven to 325°F. Beat the egg whites, cream of tartar, and salt with another tablespoon of the sugar until the foam can carry the weight of a raw egg in its shell without its sinking more than ¼ inch into the whites. Mix the almonds with half the remaining sugar and fold the mixture into the egg whites. Turn the batter into the prepared mold and bake until a nonreactive skewer inserted into its center comes out clean, 20 to 25 minutes. Invert the warm "island" into a 1-quart shallow crystal serving dish and gently pour the chilled custard all around the island.

Melt the remaining sugar with a few drops of water in a small saucepan and cook to a darkish caramel (see page 154). Drizzle over the top of the island and serve immediately.

ITALIAN MERINGUE

Italian meringue is more often than not prepared for inclusion in foamed desserts such as buttercreams. It is also what you really prepare when making a fruit soufflé as already explained on page 190; you beat a sugar syrup, plain or fruit-flavored, into egg whites.

The technique consists of adding hot syrup to beating egg whites so as to obtain a very dry meringue with millions of tiny foam bubbles, which will have a long shelf life. A flame tamer—a double-layered, round sheet of metal with many holes and a handle which does not heat up—is useful in this operation. If your gas burner cannot be turned way down as it should, place a flame tamer between the flame and the bowl in which you are beating the eggs.

Italian Meringue Mushrooms

NFR—2 DOZEN

I tablespoon unsalted butter

I tablespoon sifted flour of your choice

2⅔ cups sifted confectioners' sugar

4 large egg whites

Pinch of salt

I tablespoon pure vanilla extract or I teaspoon pure vanilla powder

Unsweetened cocoa powder

Butter a baking sheet or jelly-roll pan evenly with the butter and coat evenly with the flour. Set aside. Preheat the oven to 100°F.

Place the sugar, egg whites, salt, and vanilla in a mixing bowl of copper or stainless steel. Using a hand whip or an electric hand beater if preferred, start beating the eggs until the sugar starts dissolving. Put a flame tamer over a low flame burner. Set the mixing bowl on the flame tamer and continue beating until the mixture makes a stiff *toupé* (a peak, see page 167) that holds straight on the wire whisk.

Stuff the meringue batter into a pastry bag fitted with a ½-inch nozzle. Pipe 24 round buttons 1 to 1¼ inch in diameter; these will become the caps of the mushrooms. Then pipe twenty-four 1- to 1¼-inch-high columns ending in a sharp point; these will be the stems. Bake the meringues, sliding a stainless steel knife between the door and the oven frame to allow steam to evaporate, until the pieces of meringue can be detached from the sheet without difficulty, 1 to 2 hours.

Using a paring knife, carve a hole in each mushroom cap large enough to fit into the pointed part of each stem. Add a tiny amount of the butter to each hole and gently force a stem into each opening. Line the mushrooms up on the baking sheet again and sprinkle them very lightly with cocoa, using an extra-fine tea strainer; the cocoa imitates the dirt often found on mushrooms.

The best example of Italian meringue is probably the meringue mushrooms I saw Chef Pasquet whip, shape, and bake at the Cordon Bleu in Paris in the late fifties. These attractive little confections can be used to decorate any cake; they look so true to life that they have fooled many people. These confections keep a long time in a tin; keep button tops and stems separately and put them together as described just before use.

Sabayons, Warm and Frozen

Sabayon is the French name of the truly Italian *zabaglione* which has been imitated the world over. Its variations are multiple. *Zabaglione* can be a sauce or a dessert custard. In Italy it is mostly served warm—foamy, ethereal, and flavored with great dry Marsala, but many a cook has brought one's grain of salt to *zabaglione*, so that by now, it comes in all flavors and is served either warm or cold. When prepared for chilling or freezing, it must be stabilized with gelatin, ½ teaspoon for every 4 egg yolks, to avoid separation in the refrigerator. Some *zabaglione* recipes are so similar to recipes for mousses that it is difficult to see a difference, which is why I am listing frozen sabayons just before the mousses.

It is not absolutely necessary to own one of those lovely Italian pans with a round bottom in which the whisk can turn and spin without encountering the angles it would in an ordinary pot. But if you are fortunate enough to own such a pan, use it over a bath of simmering water. The bottom of the pan must be held 2 inches above the surface of the water; the pan is heated only by the steam.

If you do not own a *zabaglione* pan, an enameled cast-iron pan will do very well, and will allow you to work directly on a very low burner. The *zabaglione* you make will be slightly thicker.

Classic Zabaglione

FFR — 12 SERVINGS

8 large egg yolks
½ cup granulated sugar
½ cup dry Marsala

Ribbon the yolks and sugar heavily (see page 163) in a saucepan. Place the pan over the source of heat. While continuing to beat, slowly add the Marsala. Continue beating until the mixture is thick, foamy, and spinning a fat ribbon. It should feel warm to the touch, 165° to 170°F.

Two applications:

- Poured into sherbet glasses and served immediately as is.
- Poured onto sliced juicy fresh fruit and passed a few minutes under the broiler to obtain a "fruit gratin" as popularized by Chef Fredy Girardet.

VARIATIONS

The following variations are all designed for a recipe based on 8 large egg yolks. The technique is the same as in the above recipe. Whip any liqueur into the finished sauce off the heat to retain the alcohol.

ALMOND: ½ cup granulated sugar, ½ cup almond milk (page 50), 1 to 2 ounces almond-flavored liqueur or to taste.

CHOCOLATE: 6 tablespoons unsweetened cocoa powder, ⅔ cup granulated sugar, ⅔ cup scalded light cream, 1 to 2 ounces crème de cacao, rum, or Grand Marnier, to taste.

CITRUS: Generally, for all citrus flavors, remove 1 tablespoon of the sugar from the total amount. Mash that sugar together with citrus rind until the sugar has acquired the color of the rind. Dissolve the citrus sugar in a mixture of citrus juice and wine and let steep for 2 hours; strain. Make the zabaglione as usual with the egg yolks, the remainder of the sugar, and the flavored juice-wine mixture.

COFFEE: ⅔ cup granulated sugar, ½ cup brewed coffee, 2 teaspoons good instant coffee granules, 1 to 2 ounces Tía María or Kahlúa, to taste.

GRAPEFRUIT: Pink grapefruit is preferable. Use 4 teaspoons finely grated rind, ⅔ cup granulated sugar, ⅓ cup dry white wine, 6 tablespoons grapefruit juice, and 1 ounce rum.

LEMON OR LIME: 1 cup sugar, 1 tablespoon finely grated rind, 6 tablespoons white wine of your choice, 2 to 3 tablespoons lemon or lime juice, to taste, and 1 or 2 ounces rum, to taste.

ORANGE OR TANGERINE: ⅔ cup granulated sugar, 1 tablespoon finely grated orange or tangerine rind, ¼ cup each orange juice and sweet Marsala, and 1 to 2 ounces Grand Marnier, Curaçao, or Triple Sec, to taste.

As applications here are a few recipes:

Frau Pelizaeus Weinsauce

FFR—6 SERVINGS
4 large eggs
4 large egg yolks
¾ cup granulated sugar
Pinch of salt
1½ cups Spätlese Riesling

In an enameled cast-iron saucepan ribbon the whole eggs, egg yolks, sugar, and salt together with an electric mixer (see page 163). Place over low heat and gradually add the wine. Continue beating until the mixture is thick and feels warm to the finger (165° to 170°F). Pour into sherbet glasses and serve warm or chilled.

In Old French this type of recipe was called a chaudeau (meaning, warm water) because it was made over warm water. This version of the German chaudeau comes from a dear friend in the Saargebiet, who taught it to me when I was all of seventeen.

California Black Cherries with Cabernet Port Sabayon

This is almost a mousse; compare it with the mousse recipes in the following section. *Prepare during cherry season only; canned cherries have lost too much of their flavor.*

FFR—6 TO 8 SERVINGS

¾ cup heavy cream

2 large eggs

5 large egg yolks

½ cup granulated sugar

Pinch of salt

½ cup Cabernet port

I teaspoon unflavored gelatin softened in I tablespoon water

2 ounces maraschino liqueur

½ pound dark sweet cherries, pitted

Whip the cream until barely mounding and keep refrigerated until ready to use.

Ribbon the whole eggs, egg yolks, sugar, and salt together (see page 163) in a cast-iron enameled saucepan with an electric mixer; gradually add the port and beat until the mixture feels warm to the finger (165° to 170°F). Whisk in the gelatin, remove from the heat, and blend in half the maraschino. Transfer to a bowl over ice and continue beating until cold. Fold in the whipped cream and turn into sherbet glasses. Chill.

Mix the pitted cherries with the remaining maraschino and let macerate until ready to serve. Serve the cold sabayon topped with the cherries.

Frozen Pear Caramel Sabayon

I presented this dessert during one of my tours of demonstrations across the nation; it was so well received that it went on the menu of my restaurant in New Hampshire.

FFR—6 SERVINGS

I tablespoon plus 2 teaspoons unsalted butter

6 large ripe Bosc pears, peeled, cut in half lengthwise, and cored

I cup granulated sugar

¾ cup dry Marsala or Amontillado

I cup heavy cream

8 large egg yolks

Pinch of salt

Johnny-jump-up pansies

Butter a baking dish with 1 tablespoon of the butter and place the pears flat side down. Preheat the oven to 350°F. Sprinkle well with ⅔ cup of the sugar. Place the pan in the oven. When the sugar has melted and begins to brown, turn the pears over and bake, until tender, basting several times with the pear caramel; the pears will be done in about 45 minutes. Remove the cooked pears to a glass dish lightly greased with the remaining butter. Dissolve the caramel in the baking dish with the chosen wine.

Beat the cream until it just starts foaming, almost without mounding, and keep chilled until ready to use. In a stainless steel saucepan, ribbon the remaining sugar with the egg yolks and salt until a very heavy ribbon forms (see page 163). Place over medium-low heat and continue whisking until the mixture has reached 165° to 170°F, and spins a heavy ribbon.

Place the pan in a bowl filled with ice and cool, stirring until the sabayon starts to thicken. Immediately whisk in the prepared cream and churn in the freezer bin of an ice cream machine according to the manufacturer's instructions. Serve the pear halves each filled with an equal amount of the frozen sabayon and decorated with the edible flowers and leaves of those small pansies called Johnny-jump-ups.

Mousses and Frozen Soufflés

Mousses and frozen soufflés are preparations built on proteins which are whipped to build foam walls: eggs, heavy cream, or combinations of both. A frozen soufflé is made, in French culinary language, from *appareil de mousse à la crème,* which means "batter for creamed mousse," so you can easily see that mousses and frozen soufflés are closely related.

A PRACTICAL HEALTH VIEW OF MOUSSES AND FROZEN SOUFFLÉS
If you are absolutely certain that your eggs are salmonella-free, you can ribbon the egg yolks with plain sugar.

If you are not, it is essential that you poach both the egg yolks and whites in a sugar syrup cooked to 232°F, adding half of it bright hot to the egg yolks while ribboning them and the other half, bright hot, to the egg whites while whipping them. Both the foams must be whipped until cold after receiving the hot sugar syrup before they are folded into each other and before they receive the addition of cream.

Immerse the unbroken eggs in a bowl of warm water before starting to whip them up. This warming will provide better extension of the egg proteins and prepare them for receiving the hot syrup without damage.

This modern uncertainty about egg quality has not made life easy for cooks. Since it is not very practical to prepare small amounts of syrup each and every time one needs to prepare a mousse or frozen soufflé, I have gotten into the habit of preparing a larger amount of syrup with:

½ granulated sugar and ½ water by volume (which is the same as equal weights of
   sugar and water)
Plus a good pinch of cream of tartar or 2 drops of lemon juice

Cook the mixture in a saucepan to 212°F and keep refrigerated no more than 2 weeks. When I am ready to prepare mousses or frozen soufflés, I reheat 1½ to 1⅓ cups of this syrup, recook it to 232°F, and whip half into the egg yolks and half into the egg whites. The hot syrup makes the egg yolks and egg whites safe by raising their temperature within the 140° to 165°F range. Also after recooking the syrup to 232°F it is made of pure melted sugar in the quantity usually used in a mousse.

To make the immediate work of ribboning and whipping easier, it may be a good idea to have two identical mixer bowls and two sets of whisks, or to beat the yolks in the mixer bowl and the whites by hand in a copper bowl, which is what I do.

DESSERT MOUSSES

These may be served chilled or frozen. The flavor of a mousse is contained in a base into which foamed egg whites and whipped cream, used as lighteners, are folded, exactly as described on pages 168–69 in the section on soufflés.

The base may consist of:

- A puree of uncooked fruit or a sweetened puree of cooked fruit. For such fruit purees and their basic proportions, see the chapter on fruit, page 943.
- A ribboned mixture of egg yolks or a mixture of whole eggs with additional egg yolks and sugar syrup cooked to 232°F, flavored with a liqueur, a citrus fruit rind, unsweetened cocoa powder, or coffee, and sometimes stabilized with a small amount of gelatin.
- Melted chocolate, sometimes mixed with melted butter. The cocoa butter in the chocolate acts as a stabilizer for the mousse and replaces gelatin.

MOUSSE "MUSTS"   Before you start making a mousse, you must be familiar with the following techniques:

- Cooking a sugar syrup (page 199)
- Ribboning (page 163)
- Folding (page 168)
- Whipping cream (page 28) or egg whites (page 164)

The base must be completely cold before you add the egg whites and/or whipped cream, or you will obtain nothing more than a sweet sauce.

POACHING BOTH THE EGG YOLKS AND WHITES   Up to the beginning of this century, the egg yolks used in mousses were ribboned with a hot sugar syrup because at that time sugar came in loaves which could never be broken up, crushed, or ground enough to obtain the small and even sugar crystals needed to yield a perfectly smooth ribbon after whisking. The modern processing of sugar into fine crystals changed all that and the preparation of egg yolk foams by the simple whipping of the uncooked egg yolks and sugar became customary until recently. The possible presence of salmonella bacteria in eggs and its health concerns has resulted in the movement back to sugar syrups which will heat the eggs to the right temperature to destroy any bacteria.

BASIC PROPORTIONS FOR MOUSSES You may make up your own mousses with the flavors of your choice. To fill a 3-cup dish or 6 large sherbet glasses, use the following mixtures:

- For fruit puree-based mousses, no yolks are used, but more egg whites are added.
- For liqueur-flavored mousses, use 3 to 8 large egg yolks (this is your choice).
- If using salmonella-free eggs, ⅔ to ¾ cup sugar.
- ¾ cup sugar syrup recooked to 232°F (page 199).
- 1 to 2 cups of heavy cream, whipped, as you prefer.
- Never more than 3 large egg whites for liqueur mousses, more for fruit mousses.
- ½ to 1 envelope unflavored gelatin; the more cream the recipe contains, the more gelatin you should use.

THE FOLDING OF SEVERAL FOAMS INTO ONE ANOTHER A mousse consists of several foams folded into one another. The only details you must pay attention to are the following: If there are egg whites, they will always be added before the whipped cream; if the egg yolk base is rendered heavy by the presence of chocolate, one quarter of the egg white foam must be mixed into the heavier base before the remainder is folded in. If the base consists only of egg yolks and sugar syrup, you can fold the egg white foam directly into it without lightening it further. Finally, fold the cream into the base you just lightened with the egg white foam.

WHIPPING CREAM FOR MOUSSES AND FROZEN SOUFFLÉS Beat the cream so that it barely mounds and remains no stiffer than the Chantilly stage (see page 30). It is essential to keep the cream soft since folding it into the base stiffens it further. Cold mousses made with over-beaten cream will be heavy because the cream starts separating during the folding and the texture of the dessert presents very visible small blocks of butter hardened by the cold of the freezer and separated by ice crystals if the mousse is frozen, or the very same butter blocks with seepage of liquid at the bottom of the dish if the dessert is only deep chilled. If the mousse has been stabilized with gelatin, no seepage will occur, but the pesky little butter blocks will certainly be there.

Here are a few formulas to practice on:

New Orleans French Quarter Coffee Mousse

It is essential to use New Orleans roast or espresso coffee granules or the taste will be too flabby. See page 199 for a complete explanation of the sugar syrup technique. This mousse has the nice, barely sour taste of the old-fashioned French mousses prepared with diluted crème fraîche, as they were before the French developed the same type of heavy cream we have in America for use in pastries and desserts.

FFR — 10 TO 12 SERVINGS

¾ cup crème fraîche

¼ cup plus 2 tablespoons milk of your choice

1⅓ cups sugar syrup cooked to 212°F (page 199)

1½ teaspoons unflavored gelatin

3 large eggs from vegetarian hens

3 large egg yolks from vegetarian hens

3 rounded tablespoons plus 1 teaspoon very dark roast instant coffee granules

Pinch of salt

⅓ cup dark rum

Dilute the crème fraîche with ¼ cup of the milk and beat until barely mounding. Refrigerate until ready to use. Pour the syrup into a small pan and recook it to 232°F over medium heat. Dissolve the gelatin in the top of a double boiler over simmering water in the remaining milk to avoid tiny gelatin lumps in the mousse.

Meanwhile, put the whole eggs and yolks into a large bowl and beat until thick and foamy. Add 3 tablespoons of the coffee to the mixture and beat until dissolved; stop the mixer, remove a small ladleful of the mixture, stir it into the dissolved gelatin until homogeneous, then whip it back into the bulk of the eggs. Continue beating until the mixture spins the heaviest ribbon (see page 163). Gradually add the sugar syrup, the salt, and rum and keep beating until the ribbon has reformed again and the mixture is cold.

Finally, give the cream a few strokes of a hand whip to make sure no seepage of whey has happened at the bottom of the bowl and immediately fold it into the mousse base. Turn into a bowl and deep chill or freeze. Serve sprinkled with the remaining coffee granules.

Maple Mousse

This mousse is very sweet, but the relatively large amount of walnuts provides a contrast between totally opposite tastes and textures.

FFR — 8 SERVINGS

½ cup amber grade A maple syrup

1½ teaspoons unflavored gelatin

3 tablespoons water

6 large egg yolks from vegetarian hens

Pinch of salt

¼ teaspoon pure maple extract

1 cup heavy cream

½ cup chopped walnuts

In a saucepan, heat the maple syrup to 232°F. Dissolve the gelatin in the water in the top of a double boiler over simmering water. Put the yolks and salt in a large bowl and start beating with an electric mixer on medium-low speed until a foam forms and whip to the ribbon stage (see page 163). Increase the mixer to foaming speed, then pour in the hot syrup in a thin stream. Remove a large spoonful of the ribboned yolks, mix it with the gelatin, and return the mixture to the bulk of the ribboning yolks. Beat the yolk foam until cold.

In a medium-size bowl, whip the cream until it starts mounding, then fold it into the base of flavored egg yolks. Turn into a serving dish and deep chill or freeze. To serve, cover with a thick layer of chopped walnuts.

FROZEN SOUFFLÉS, FROZEN MOUSSE CAKES
Frozen soufflés are extremely rich mousses frozen in one or several soufflé dishes fitted with a collar. When the collar is removed, the dessert stands frozen above the rim of the dish, giving the illusion of a soufflé.

To fit the collar and calculate the capacity of your mold, study "Collar or No Collar Mathematics" on page 174. Lightly oil the side of the paper that will be in contact with the batter. You can expect all your ingredients to double in volume; also expect a one-third loss of volume when folding. Before freezing, turn the refrigerator to its coldest freezer setting to obtain small crystals.

To remove the collar, let the soufflé stand at room temperature for 5 minutes, then gently pull off the paper. If for any reason the sides of the soufflé have been damaged in the freezer and do not look perfectly smooth, cover them with crushed praline powder (see page 51) or crumbled macaroons.

Frozen mousse cakes are nothing more than frozen soufflé batters poured into cake pans and garnished with diverse nuts or crumbs. They can be inverted and cut into sliver-size portions.

Basic Proportions

FOR EACH 2 CUPS OF HEAVY CREAM, WHIPPED, USE

8 to 9 large egg yolks

1½ cups sugar syrup cooked to 212°F (page 199)

1 envelope unflavored gelatin or 4 leaves European gelatin

3 large egg whites

½ cup liqueur of your choice

Here are a few recipes to practice on:

Chocolate Chip Frozen Mousse Cake

I served this frozen mousse cake in my restaurant in Boston. Use any liqueur you prefer. Green Chartreuse is perfect, but there is nothing wrong with a coffee or orange liqueur. You need parchment paper, a 10-inch cake pan, and a cookie sheet to cook the meringue layers.

FFR — 16 SERVINGS

For the meringue layers

butter

flour

3 large egg whites

2 tablespoons unsweetened cocoa powder

1 cup finely ground almonds

⅓ cup granulated sugar

For the mousse

2 cups heavy cream

Pinch of salt

½ cup green Chartreuse or other liqueur of your choice

1½ cups sugar syrup cooked to 212°F (page 199)

1 envelope unflavored gelatin

9 large egg yolks

3 large egg whites

2 ounces bittersweet chocolate, chopped

Confectioners' sugar

To prepare the meringue layers, preheat the oven to 325°F. Butter and flour the cookie sheet, then trace two circles on it using the bottom of the 10-inch pan as a pattern. Whip the egg whites until they can carry the weight of a raw egg in its shell without its sinking into the foam by more than ¼ inch. Mix the cocoa powder, almonds, and sugar and fold into the beaten whites. Spread half of the mixture ¼ inch thick over both the circles traced on the cookie sheet. Bake until set and dry, about 20 minutes. Lift from the baking sheet with a long spatula as soon as it comes out of the oven. Cool completely on a rack and trim the edges carefully so the layers will be able to fit into the 10-inch pan.

Line the 10-inch cake pan with a circle of parchment paper on its bottom and another long one covering its sides completely. Fit the best-looking circle of meringue into the bottom of the pan, flat side down. Reserve the other.

To make the mousse, beat the cream, salt, and half the liqueur until barely mounding. Keep refrigerated.

Recook the sugar syrup to 232°F over medium-low heat. Melt the gelatin in the top of a double boiler over simmering water. In a large bowl with an electric mixer, ribbon the egg yolks (see page 163) with half this syrup. Mix the dissolved gelatin with a large spoonful of the ribboned egg yolks and blend the mixture back into the bulk of the yolks. Beat in the remainder of the liqueur and finish ribboning the yolks until the foam is cold. Beat the egg whites with the remaining syrup until the whites are glossy, able to stand without breaking down, and cold.

Fold the egg whites into the egg yolk foam, beat the cream to lightly rehomogenize it, and fold it into the mixture.

Turn half the mixture into the pan; set in the freezer for 15 minutes. Sprinkle the solidified layer with the chocolate chips; cover with the remainder of the mousse. Smooth the top carefully and fit the second layer of meringue on top of the mousse. Wrap in plastic wrap and deep freeze.

To serve, invert the mousse cake onto a cake platter and remove the parchment. Set a paper doily on top of the inverted cake and sprinkle with confectioners' sugar. Remove the doily to obtain a nice stenciled pattern of sugar. Cut the mousse cake into 16 to 24 portions.

Blueberry Frozen Soufflé

FFR — 8 SERVINGS

Unsaturated oil of your choice

3 cups fresh blueberries, picked over for stems

¾ cup granulated sugar

1½ tablespoons fresh lemon juice

1½ cups heavy cream

3 large eggs from vegetarian hens

2 large egg yolks from vegetarian hens

Pinch of salt

½ teaspoon grated lemon rind

2 teaspoons unflavored gelatin

2 tablespoons water

3 drops blue food coloring

¼ teaspoon red food coloring

2 tablespoons bourbon

Confectioners' sugar

This soufflé is a prototype for all fruit soufflés, in that the sugar is melted and cooked in the fruit puree and used boiling hot to poach the eggs. This frozen soufflé tastes better if you use wild berries such as huckleberries or even, if you can find them, black currants. Do not strain the berry puree; the skins will melt while cooking. If using the food colorings bothers you, omit them; they are only there to correct the not too attractive color taken on by blueberries when mixed with egg yolk.

Oil a large band of parchment able to circle completely a 3-cup soufflé mold; tie it around the mold (see page 175 for details).

Puree the berries in a blender. Mix with the sugar and lemon juice in a saucepan and cook down over medium-low heat to 1½ cups. Whip the cream until barely mounding and keep chilled.

Beat the whole eggs, egg yolks, salt, and lemon rind until a ribbon as stiff as possible forms (see page 163). Dissolve the gelatin in the water in the top of a double boiler over simmering water, then add it to the hot blueberry puree and stir well to melt it completely. Pour the hot blueberry puree into the egg mixture and bring back to as stiff a ribbon as possible, continuing to beat until cold. Add both food colorings and the bourbon during the last few minutes of beating. Fold the whipped cream into the mousse and turn it into the collared soufflé mold, smoothing the top of the mixture as level as possible.

Freeze immediately. To serve, remove the paper collar and sprinkle evenly with confectioners' sugar.

Cooking Techniques Using the Capacity of Eggs to Act as Emulsifiers

Hollandaise and her sister sauces, as well as mayonnaise and her sister sauces, represent a special group of sauces in which egg yolks are used as emulsifiers.

The concept of emulsions is explained in detail in the chapter on sauces; see page 325.

Happy Marriages

Vegetable Broths, Meat Stocks and Consommés, and All Types of Mixed Vegetable and Meat Soups

IT IS BELIEVED THAT ONION SOUP WAS CREATED BY THE FRENCH KING LOUIS XV from a bottle of flat Champagne and a few onions on an occasion when he came back famished from a joyous night in eighteenth-century Paris. It may be, but onion soup made with plain water and onions has been the fare of the poor from time immemorial, not only in France but all over the Old World, where it could be indifferently served as breakfast, dinner, or supper fare.

Over the last century, *la soupe à l'oignon* became the specialty of all the bistros and cafés around the old "Halles" or central market of Paris, now transferred to the modern functional market of Rungis. The soup remains, though, and Parisians, after a late and happy night, still enter the same old bistros in the wee hours of the morning for an invigorating plate or bowl of their ancestral awakener.

Les Halles French Onion Soup

FFR to FCR — 6 SERVINGS

3 tablespoons unsalted butter or 2 tablespoons olive oil

6 very large yellow onions, thinly sliced

1 cup dry white wine (optional)

6 cups cold water

Small bouquet garni of parsley stems, 1 bay leaf, and 1 sprig fresh thyme

Salt

Pepper from the mill

6 slices French bread, cut at a slant and lightly toasted

Six 3-inch-square ⅛-inch-thick slices Gruyère

In a large saucepan, melt the butter until its foam starts receding or the oil until it starts shimmering, then add the onions and sauté quickly over medium-high heat to remove most of their moisture. Turn the heat down to medium and continue cooking, tossing occasionally, until the onions are uniformly brown. Add the wine and let it completely evaporate.

Cover the onions with the water and bring slowly to a boil, then add the bouquet garni. Simmer, uncovered, until 5 cups of mixed solids and liquid are left, about 45 minutes. Salt and pepper to your taste. Taste the broth and continue cooking if not tasty enough. Add boiling water and a bit more seasoning if needed.

Ladle an equal volume of soup into 6 fireproof casseroles, and set the casseroles on a large jelly-roll or baking sheet. Float one slice of bread on top of the soup in each casserole and top with a cheese slice. Broil 2 minutes to melt and serve piping hot.

Now try to experiment a bit with that basic soup. For example, try adding a bouillon cube or two; it will taste fuller and rounder. Try making the soup with canned beef or chicken broth, or a combination of both instead of water, and the taste will change and may be better still, but you will immediately notice that in this latter case, no additional salt is necessary since the broth used was already strongly salted at the cannery.

By covering the onions with water and simmering both together, you have made a broth. There is a difference between a broth and a stock. According to *Webster's*, both are defined as the liquid in which meat, fish, cereal grains, or vegetables have been cooked. However, when it comes to defining stock, *Webster's* adds that stock is used as a basis for soups, stews, gravies, or sauces. In that last statement resides the basic difference between the products.

A broth is lighter in texture because it is generally made with a whole bird and/or the carcasses of barnyard birds, or odd pieces of lean meat containing little connective tissues. A broth can be used as a comforting hot drink in the cold of winter, to make a light soup because it is light in taste and does not hide the taste of the vegetables used in the soup, or to cook grains because it is easily absorbed by starches, and because it smells appetizing. But if you try to prepare a great sauce with it, it will prove too light and yield a final product that will be too bland and not roundly fill the mouth. True cooks usually prefer using a meat stock when preparing a great classic sauce or a rich soup.

If you wish to taste and evaluate the differences between broth and stock, take the time to taste and compare a canned chicken broth, a homemade vegetable broth, a homemade turkey stock, and a homemade veal stock. You will recognize immediately fundamental differences, which are measurable in taste, flavor, and aroma. Be aware—taste, flavors, and aroma are different.

The taste of a stock will be evaluated by your taste buds only, so that you will find the stock to taste salty, sour, sweet, or bitter and feel that it is thin or thicker on or between your tongue and palate. Since we taste not only with our taste buds but also with our nose as we breathe in or out after having tasted any food, we shall then be able to appreciate the flavors of the stock as they were released into it by vegetables containing certain acids (citric, tartaric, and oxalic, for example) and diverse amino acids extracted from the meats by the cooking liquid. The aroma of a broth or stock is important, for it is the "great appetizer" par excellence; we perceive it strictly with our nose as broths and stocks simmer and send their lovely smells all over the kitchen and house or when stocks have been used to prepare great sauces and stews.

For this cook, the main difference between a broth and a stock resides most definitely in the thicker and more viscous texture of the latter, which is obtained after cooking a well-balanced mixture of meats, bones, and vegetables in liquid for a nice long time. A stock will jell deeply when refrigerated and will still be flavorful when consumed cold and jellied. A broth generally will not; it will, at most, be viscous when chilled and be really tasty only when its flavors are enhanced by heating.

As late as the 1960s, stocks were all-important in cookery and all chefs and cooks followed the advice of Auguste Escoffier in his book *Le Guide Culinaire* to use the best possible stocks and broths for the best possible results. Starting in the 1970s, stocks came under fire and their role as the "base of the pyramid" of cookery found itself under strong attack, even in France, where some prophets of doom for their National Cuisine presented their country with "natural" food cooked with—water. I had the opportunity of tasting such presentations in several restaurants in France and in demonstrations by "great" chefs in the United States and though I could not say that these food offerings were downright bad, I certainly could not say they were examples of perfection. I want all my readers to know that this opinion was not mine only, but that of many people, "regular" people and chefs alike, who could find enough in those super "lightened" foods to satisfy their appetites but certainly not fully satisfy their palates.

What to do? The battery of stocks available to the cook prior to the seventies was impressive; there was white chicken stock and brown chicken stock, beef stock, white veal stock and brown veal stock, combination stocks of chicken and veal, general poultry stocks such as turkey stock and duck stock—some people even made lamb stock. The discussion about "stocks forever" in cooking classes was endless and confusing and certainly not in line with the apparent modern simplification of food preparation brought on by the nutrition revolution and the rapid rhythm of life and work at the end of our twentieth century. So, having to be a leader for many students entering the food professions, I decided to adopt a system which would be practical and economical, and to apply it at home and in my restaurants.

Before examining a practical home or restaurant system, I wish to give an outline of the existing commercially produced broths and stocks and comment on them, with the goal of explaining to those beginner cooks who cannot or do not wish to prepare their own broths and stocks how commercial products can best be tapped.

Quick Commercially Available Broths

Different types of packaged products can be used to make quick broths.

1. *Dry meat and vegetable extracts like bouillon cubes and/or granules.* These are best dissolved according to the package directions. They can be used for soups or for cooking grains, but certainly not to prepare the few sauces we still present on our plates nowadays.

2. *Semisolid meat extracts sold in jars.* These are commercially made stocks partially dried and concentrated by slow cooking or by vacuum processing. They contain concentrated proteins of meats and vegetables and are highly salted for preservation. They can be a boon in household kitchens and certainly are generously used by many a hotel kitchen, where they are called bases.

   When carefully diluted with water, they can replace freshly made stock for the "cook in a hurry." How much extract should be used is entirely up to the cook's taste. Some cooks use as much as a teaspoon of extract per cup of liquid; when faced with having to use these products, I use barely ½ teaspoon. A typical example of overgenerous use of meat extract can be found in almost any average American restaurant where the onion soup is oversalted and burns the throat. Whatever the commercial product chosen, great care must be taken so that the pungent taste of the extract cannot be detected in the finished dish. This requires a bit of personal experimentation, always. The same restriction applies as for cubes: No great sauce can be made with broth reconstituted from extracts.

3. *Canned stocks,* be they made with beef or chicken, are not bad for certain dishes, although they contain too much salt and celery. As I write this, a pure vegetable broth has just come on the market which is quite pleasant, except for a slightly accentuated taste of bell pepper. For the onion soup on page 209, for example, any canned stock will serve well because the characteristic taste of the onions takes over that of the stock. Any curried soup may also be made successfully with canned broth, for what other spice could hold its own against curry? A braised dish of beef or any other meat will taste adequate but never great if prepared with canned stocks, but when a subtle sauce is involved, canned stock still gives results that are short of perfection. To be used in average-quality sauces, canned stocks and broths have to be upgraded by being mixed with unsalted vegetable broth in the proportions of 12 ounces (1½ cups) vegetable broth for each 10 ½-ounce can of condensed stock.

4. *Commercially prepared frozen broths* sold in 8-ounce plastic containers and prepared by diverse smaller businesses. These broths are quite pleasant, if not totally potent; their taste is clean and their seasoning sensible, which

makes them the choice of commercially available stocks. Their biggest drawback is, of course, their overall cost, since they are made with good fresh ingredients. I have used them on several occasions and liked—not loved—the results.

A Philosophy of Stocks for the Twenty-First Century

So now, what does a modern cook do, who, whether in a well-organized home or in a restaurant situation, wishes to have solid stocks with texture and taste, requiring the least amount of work?

Here are the descriptions of the stocks I have used for the last twenty years and with which I have functioned most efficiently at home and in my profession, followed by a commentary on their management and storage.

Vegetable Broth

The vegetable broth given below is used for pure vegetarian dishes and for most effectively diluting commercial concentrated canned broths, when the latter is used.

Since vegetable broth contains many nutritive elements, it is like any broth or stock, subject to spoilage and will, as a matter of fact, very rapidly turn sour if left standing too long in a hot kitchen. Like any meat stock, vegetable broth must be at all times in use, or refrigerated, or frozen in sanitary containers which have been washed and dried in a dishwasher, or, if cleaned by hand, washed in soapy water, rinsed in water at 180°F, and air dried.

Pure Vegetable Broth

NFR—5 QUARTS

1½ pounds carrots, cut up

2 pounds medium-size yellow onions, cut up

3 bunches scallions, chopped

10 leeks, white and light green parts, well washed and sliced into ¼-inch slivers

1 celery rib from the center of the heart

5 quarts cold water

Large bouquet garni of parsley stems, 1 bay leaf, and 1 sprig fresh thyme

Salt

This recipe may be multiplied by two, four, six, etc. It is the famous bouillon de légumes, *the French nectar of health, cure for the* crise de foie, *a general malaise across the French nation caused by overindulgence in great food at an occasional celebration dinner, after weeks, even months, of generally frugal meals.*

Note that this is a neutral basic stock which can be used for all ethnic cuisines. You can add whatever other vegetables you feel like tasting in such a stock: more celery, for example; the tops of red, green, or yellow bell peppers; any hot pepper; and, of course, tomatoes. I have avoided all these to keep the stock from having any ethnic tendencies.

Wash and drain all the vegetables well. Put them in a large stockpot. Cover with the cold water and slowly bring to a boil; skim if necessary, then add the bouquet garni and simmer until the volume of liquid is reduced to 8 cups and the broth tastes good, about 1½ hours. Strain through a conical strainer lined with cheesecloth. Salt to taste.

Microwaving is not recommended for vegetable broth if you want to obtain the deep taste and flavor that comes from vegetables that have cooked at some length. This is a personal opinion, though; please use your microwave if you prefer and do not mind the lighter texture and taste.

Store in the refrigerator for up to 1 week or freeze for up to 2 months in 16-ounce (2-cup) freezer containers at home or in 32-ounce (1-quart) containers in restaurant operations.

Meat Broths and Stocks

Before giving any recipe, I would like you to understand how very important the good management and sanitation of stocks is nutritionally and economically and to understand your responsibilities as a stock maker. The following description of what happens when you prepare a stock will make you understand why there must be rules in stock making and storing.

THE PRINCIPLES OF MAKING MEAT BROTHS
Meats are made of muscle fibers surrounded and held together by connective tissues. Two different types of connective tissue exist. The most important for the cook is *collagen*, which varies in texture from a thick liquid surrounding fascicles of meat fibers to ultra-thin membranes that are barely visible, and to very noticeable, white, mostly thin, but sometimes thicker membranes surrounding a muscle. The white membrane surrounding any large muscle, which is called silverskin in everyday language or aponeurosis scientifically, is mostly made of collagen. Collagen has the capacity of hydrolizing, that is, liquefying, when submitted to heat. When collagen hydrolizes, gelatin is released, which explains why stocks and gravies turn progressively to a solid gel when they cool and are refrigerated.

The second connective tissue, called *elastin*, which can be seen in the large tendons attaching muscles to bones, has very little interest for the cook, for it has no hydrolizing capacity and remains rubberlike even after long cooking.

When meats are immersed in water, various products are released into the water and form the stock. A few proteins and enzymes are freed by the cold water. As the water is slowly brought to a boil and a long simmering follows, a larger amount of proteins is released together with vitamins, fats, the gelatin produced by the liquefied collagen, mineral salts, and a few substances called extractives (lactic and amino acids).

Similarly, while cooking, aromatic vegetables and spices release such elements as pectin, starches, acids (citric, tartaric, and oxalic), and sulfur compounds, which help to give the stock its taste, flavors, and aroma.

METHODS AND TECHNIQUES FOR MAKING MEAT STOCKS

AT HOME Since making a true stock every week at home would be extremely time-consuming, consider instead two or three stock-making sessions a year at six- or four-month intervals, which will concentrate time and work. Whether you decide on two or three sessions a year depends entirely on your style of cooking and whether you entertain a lot. Pull out your soup kettle, make your stock, and freeze it in larger freezing jars or containers.

You know how much stock you need for your own household, so it is up to you to consider acquiring a 10-, 20-, or 40-quart stockpot. They all work very well on home-size burners.

The stock will cook by itself; you can let it simmer without constant attention, except for an occasional replenishment of water when necessary. But as soon as the stock if finished, immediate attention is needed to handle it in a sanitary manner.

IN A SMALL TO MEDIUM-SIZE RESTAURANT Depending on the requirements of the menu, it is a good idea to have two stock sessions a week, one for the primary stock, one for the secondary stock, each session yielding enough stock to last the whole week for all categories of food presented in the dining room. The executive chef will know how to set up the stock preparation sessions properly to follow the rhythm of business. It is a good idea always to have a three-week supply of stock frozen and ready to defrost and use to avoid surprises, and to be strictly disciplined and organized as to the regular replacement and rotation of that stash.

SANITATION FOR HOME AND RESTAURANT USE When it comes to storage vessels for stock or anything else that is perishable, the word *clean* means not only clean but always and foremost *sanitized*. To sanitize containers, wash and dry them in the dishwasher, or wash them by hand in soapy water, rinse with water heated to 180°F, and air dry them.

Finished stocks must be treated in the strictest sanitary manner. As soon as the cooking is finished, turn the heat off and let the stock cool to a more manageable heat level, but *never* lower than 160°F. *The critical temperatures not only for stock but for any other perishable food are 40° to 140°F, which represents the range of bacterial development in all foods.*

Removing the pot to a wooden board placed in a cooler, remote corner of the kitchen is the easiest. Keep children away from the hot stock at home and put a conscientious apprentice in charge of the guard and care of it in a restaurant.

As soon as the temperature of the pot contents approaches 160°F, strain the stock into several sanitized storage containers. It will by then be very close to the limit temperature of 140°F. Half fill the sink with cold water and lower its temperature by adding to it as large a batch of ice cubes as possible and some salt; immerse the storage containers into the chilly water until the stock is completely cold. Immediately refrigerate, covered. Keep refrigerated without using it until the fat has not only come to the top, but hardened into a flat, hard cover; break that fat cover and discard it. The stock is now fully usable or can go into final storage.

Make sure the temperature of the refrigerator is steady. If the stock is kept only refrigerated, it should be reboiled at regular intervals of 3 to 4 days to prevent spoilage, though this interval will depend on the efficiency of your refrigerator or walk-in refrigerator to keep a steady 35°F temperature. A stock that shows signs of liquefaction around the edges of its container is on its way to spoiling. Be strict with your reboiling schedule and do not let this liquefaction happen because, as you reheat the whole batch of stock with the goal of reboiling it, you may stand there powerless as you smell it turn sour. If you are not sure that your work schedule will allow proper management of refrigerated stock, consider the freezer your best storage bet; it is indeed better to freeze, if only for a few days, than to lose a whole batch of expensive material.

TO FREEZE AND DEFROST STOCK

There is no doubt that for purists, the freezing of anything is not the ideal solution. But let us be practical. Life at the end of our twentieth century has become exceedingly difficult; our food chain is highly disrupted, the quality of the foods we can purchase is often below standard, especially where our main sources of protein are concerned, so let us put any guarantee on our side that whatever food we prepare will be kept fresh and safe.

When freezing, do so in containers that have been sanitized and are of no more than 1-quart capacity for home use and no more than 1-gallon capacity for restaurant use. Always leave enough space for expansion during freezing; seal the containers with sterilized lids and label them with the name of the stock and date on which you froze it; it will allow you to know that it must be used two months later.

Example: Primary stock 12.5.94

When defrosting frozen stocks, *don't ever leave the containers at room temperature*. If you have a microwave, defrost the stock in it. Then continue heating the stock long enough for it to boil a full 5 minutes, and use it immediately.

If you have no microwave, loosen the stock from the sides of its freezing container by dipping it into hot water, then immediately turn the block of solidly frozen stock into a pot and bring it to a full boil over high heat: The stock should barely have the time to melt before it's already boiling. *Always reboil a stock that has been frozen a full five minutes before using it.*

FREEZING IN ICE-CUBE TRAYS FOR CONVENIENCE To obtain immediately available stock straight from the freezer, freeze the stock in sanitized ice cube trays, then loosen the cubes and store them in plastic food bags. Frozen stock cubes can be added directly to skillets or roasting pans to be "deglazed" to obtain a nice gravy at maximum speed. The reboiling of the stock happens at the same time as the deglazing of skillet or roasting pan.

Any Meat Stock in a Hurry

FCR— I GENEROUS QUART

2 pounds chopped or ground meat of your choice, as lean as possible

I envelope unflavored gelatin

5 to 6 cups cold water

2 small carrots, coarsely chopped

2 large yellow onions, coarsely chopped

2 cloves

3 large leeks, well washed and coarsely chopped

Small bouquet garni of I crushed bay leaf, I sprig fresh thyme and
**   10 parsley stems**

⅓ teaspoon salt

3 black peppercorns

Gravy Master (optional)

Top of the stove method: Put the meat in a large saucepan or small stockpot, sprinkle it with the gelatin, and add the cold water. Bring to a boil very slowly, then add the vegetables and seasonings. Skim and simmer for 1 hour. Strain carefully; the stock is ready to use. If brown beef or veal stock is desired, color the finished stock with Gravy Master as needed. Note that Gravy Master is not a flavoring agent in my opinion, but a very good-tasting coloring agent.

Microwave method: Chop all the vegetables finely instead of coarsely and add 1 tablespoon oil to the recipe. You will need 6 cups water.

Place all the vegetables and the oil in an 8-cup soufflé dish or Pyroceram casserole and mix well. Cover loosely with microwave-grade plastic wrap and cook 4 minutes on medium power. Dissolve the gelatin into 1 quart of the cold water. Add to the casserole. Cover again and cook 20 minutes on high power. Add 2 cups of boiling water to the casserole and finish cooking another 45 minutes on medium power. Strain; the stock is ready to use.

Keep any part of this stock not used immediately in the refrigerator or for 3 to 4 days. It will keep in the freezer for 2 to 3 months.

This recipe is my mother's; she worked all her life and could produce it in 1½ hours from start to finish. You can top her by cooking this nice stock in only two thirds the time in a microwave oven; it tastes fresh, keeps the kitchen in its relative normal state, and is usable immediately.

This stock is for people who would not consider using a great stock in any case, people who work too many hours and too hard to take the time to make long-cooking stocks, people who live in small apartments with no storage possibilities, or people who live by the microwave oven. This stock will cook any grain dish excellently, it will make a nice stew and soup, and adequately deglaze pans in which steaks, chops, or cutlets are cooked. It will not make a great sauce, whether classic, neoclassic, or modern.

Use ground turkey or chicken for a lean light stock and ground beef or veal for a richer stock, or a mixture of half-and-half.

PRIMARY BROWN OR "GOLDEN" VEAL STOCK

The advantages of using veal stock are the following: Its texture is gelatinous and rich on the palate, and its taste is full but neutral enough that, when used with chicken, it acquires a definite chicken flavor, and when used with beef it becomes very rich and beefy and, used with any other meat, it will acquire the taste of that meat. It freezes well up to six months without losing more than 5 percent of its flavor.

I call this stock "primary" veal stock because it is very important to use it exclusively for the making of all sauces, be they classic, neoclassic, or modern, or for the cooking of expensive pieces of meat or birds for entertaining at home, or for the "à la carte" service of small to medium-size restaurants. The two chicken bouillon cubes replace salt and provide that tiny amount of monosodium glutamate to the stock which perks up its taste and flavor. If you are sensitive to MSG in any quantity, do not use the cubes; rather, replace them with 1 teaspoon salt per each 5 quarts of water used.

Note that using no salt at all in the preparation of stock results in sauces which lack quite a bit of depth of taste. This, of course, is a personal opinion, but I have such a passion for really great sauces that you can trust me.

THE MEAT   Please do not use exclusively those ugly long veal bones that are sold scraped clean of any trace of meat and veal knuckles. They make such a very gelatinous stock that if you reduce that stock to make what is called demi-glace by some chefs or what I call a good "essence," all you will taste and feel is gelatin on your palate, so much of it that your lips will often stick together. A good stock must be opulent, unctuous, and have the right balance of taste and texture.

The piece of meat most capable of giving you the best results is the breast because it contains meat, bones, and cartilage. If you investigate the price of the bones against that of the breast bought in larger quantities you will find that there is not that much of a difference, and the difference in price is certainly worth the difference in taste and texture even if you work at home. Call a meat purveyor rather than a local butcher.

If the breast is really too expensive for your budget, use one third veal bones and two thirds veal breast; it will be better than only bones. Also, any meaty scraps coming from chops, roasts, the ends of osso buco, and trimmings from the shoulder and legs used for stews and scaloppine are also good material and can replace the breast partly so as to perhaps reach the ratio of one third veal bones, one third meaty scraps, and one third veal breast. You will know how to do the best possible for your budget.

WINE IN PRIMARY STOCK   Notice that the wine called for in this recipe is optional. You can, if you prefer, not use wine; rather, deglaze the pan(s) in which the meats are roasted with the same amount of boiling water.

If you use wine, *use white wine only*, not red wine; using red wine is fine if you are going to use the stock only for sauces finished with another addition of red wine, but if you are going to prepare a sauce that will contain no other wine, or a white wine, an underlying taste of red wine will be present in your sauce even if you did not intend it to be there, and it may also clash with some of the meats you will be using.

TOMATOES IN PRIMARY STOCK In order to keep the stock as compatible as possible for use with all kinds of meats and in all styles of cookery, I never use tomatoes; they give the stock a slightly acid taste foundation, even if the tomatoes have been cooked before being added to the stock. I leave you freedom to do what you please as far as this is concerned. I prefer to use a tomato *coulis* (see page 308) when making a sauce rather than putting tomato in the basic stock. Some may retort that the tomato is there for color, to which I say, brown your meats correctly to just the wonderful deep russet gold that is needed and you will need no extra color enhancement. And might I also point out that most of the great contemporary French chefs use no tomato in their stocks.

A GREAT STOCK IS A FAT-FREE STOCK
Because stocks—including this golden veal stock—came basically from France, there is that somewhat peculiar tendency nowadays to kill the value of "rich" stock in culinary matters and to characterize French cuisine as "fat"; I have even heard "greasy." Again, moderation please! Just take a look at French women; most of them are not fat and they consume just about everything they want on a daily basis. The reason: Everything they eat is precisely defatted, from stocks to sauces to boiled ham, etc. This principle began in France around 1950 under the guidance of extremely progressive nutritionists and the tendency has continued to this day. So defat your stock.

Primary Veal Stock

FCR — MAKES 10 QUARTS

10 pounds veal breast or other meats as described on page 218

2 cups dry white wine, preferably Sauvignon Blanc (optional), or water

10 quarts water

6 medium-size yellow onions, quartered

4 medium-size carrots, coarsely cut up

10 large leeks, white and light green parts, well washed, cut up

1 center pale yellow celery rib with leaves

4 cloves

Large bouquet garni of 30 parsley stems, 2 large sprigs fresh thyme and 2 small European or 1 large California bay leaf

Two ½-inch chicken bouillon cubes or 2 teaspoons salt

You can multiply this recipe by two, four, six, eight for larger quantities and divide it the same way for smaller quantities.

Preheat the oven to 400°F. Cut the meat into large chunks and remove as much fat as possible. Place the meats in a large roasting pan(s). Roast until golden and all the juices in the pan have browned to a deep golden russet color, about 45 minutes. Do not roast too long and allow the meat juices to burn at the bottom of the roasting pan or the stock will have a bitter aftertaste.

Transfer the meats to a stockpot. Discard the fat in the roasting pan. Place the roasting pan over medium heat and add the wine or the same volume of water; "deglaze" the pan by scraping up the golden brown glaze at the bottom of the pan. Add this to the stockpot together with the 10 quarts of water. Bring to a boil, add the vegetables, cloves, bouquet garni, and bouillon cubes or salt. Return to a boil, then turn down to a simmer. Simmer until the bouillon tastes good, the number of hours depending on the quality of your meat, leaving the pot lid ½ inch askew for evaporation. Skim off any scum or fat at regular intervals; also add warm water to the pot at regular intervals to keep the water level approximately even. If after 4 hours the stock does not taste deeply flavored, pursue the cooking as long as needed to obtain a good concentrated taste. Do not overcook to prevent the taste of bone and calcium from leaching into the stock.

Once the stock is finished, pay special attention to cooling, straining, and especially defatting and storing, as explained in the management of the stock on pages 215–17. *Reminder: This stock must be defatted completely to be as healthy as it is delicious.* Refrigerate up to 4 days, then reboil, and reboil every fourth day. Freeze up to 6 months.

Secondary Stock
A LIGHTER WHITE VEAL AND POULTRY STOCK

FFR—VARIABLE YIELD

This stock corresponds roughly to what was called a rémuage in the old days, when, after the freshly finished stock had been poured away, one filled the pot with water again and cooked again. Only it is cleaner in look and taste, because already cooked meats and bones are not indiscriminately used.

You will discard old vegetables and bones, keeping only those large blocks of gelatin to be found between the floating ribs and any piece of meat that still appears moist, instead of being fully stringy.

There is no list of ingredients for secondary stock; you make it up with whatever scraps you have stored in your freezer. Take to the habit of saving: uncooked chicken carcasses, uncooked duck carcasses, game birds, quail carcasses, veal chop bones, small scraps of veal, etc. Poultry giblets are fine also, with the exception of livers which will turn the stock gray and can be used to better advantage in other preparations.

Do not brown duck or other poultry carcasses; the stock will not taste as good if you do, for these bones are small and lose a lot of their taste-giving properties as they brown. If you do not believe me, try both browning the carcasses and not browning them and compare both tastes; notice also the very small amount of glaze left in the roasting pan once you are finished roasting the carcasses.

Add new soup vegetables, such as two large yellow onions, a very small carrot, as many leeks as you can afford, a medium-size bouquet garni. Cover the stock with enough water to cover all the meats and vegetables, plus 2 inches. Bring to a boil, turn down to a simmer, and skim well during the first hour of cooking, then simmer until the stock tastes good; it will take at least 2 hours. You will have to taste to know when the stock is done, for its taste and length of cooking will again depend on the amount of nutrients contained in the meats you used. Cool, strain, defat, and store the stock as explained on pages 215–17. The color of this stock is more white than dark, even if it contains duck and a bit of lean beef.

USES OF SECONDARY STOCK Secondary stock is used for soups or potages requiring a true broth, for cooking grain dishes, etc. If it turns out quite rich, which it is quite liable to do, you will have to dilute it when using it for risotto, which should have a light stock.

WHAT ABOUT PLAIN AND SIMPLE
CHICKEN STOCK?
If you never make veal stock and do not consider it worth your while to make it, obviously it would be impossible for you to reuse the gelatin still attached to the veal bones; and you may still want to have good poultry stock at your disposal. In this case, simply prepare chicken or turkey stock, as instructed in any meat stock in a hurry on page 217, or if you plan to use it in large quantities, prepare a white stock using exclusively unbrowned chicken and turkey, or a golden poultry stock by oven browning the same meats before making the stock.

CONCENTRATING A LIGHT STOCK If any stock does not taste concentrated enough after being cooked properly, strain it, defat it, and reduce it over medium heat until it has acquired the desired texture and taste.

AN OLD-FASHIONED CONCEPT: MEAT GLAZE
The old-fashioned, very heavily reduced stock called meat glaze, in the western cuisines of the past, need not be made anymore if you adopt the system of stocks outlined above. However, for the sake of knowledge and documentation it will be explained in the next chapter on sauces on page 286.

Fish Stocks

All the fish and shellfish stocks are listed in the chapter about fish on page 540.

Soups

While in our practical America a soup is a soup—sometimes a bisque or a chowder—I can offhand think of fifteen different words for soup in French. They all make sense to French people, since I have yet to meet one French person who has not been "raised" on soup.

A soup was originally a broth or a *coulis*—itself a broth mixed with a thin puree of meat or vegetables—thickened by pouring it onto slices of bread. The onion soup at the beginning of this chapter is the classic example. In fact the origin of the word *soup* is to be found in the old German *soppen*, which meant to drink and by extension to absorb. Nowadays, all denominations of soup have become more fluid and the name "soup" is widely used for preparations served with or without bread slices.

Soup is not as ancient a nourishment as grilled or roasted meats, but it can be linked to the discovery of pottery-making. Soup was probably even being made before pottery and metal smithing, when early man boiled water in skin- and stone-lined holes dug into the ground. Water added to these holes was kept boiling by immersing in it other stones that had been heated directly in the main hearth. Soups and *coulis* reached their peak of glory in the late Middle Ages; it is said that Joan of Arc subsisted on them while her companions at arms feasted on much more terrifying fare (instances of cannibalism, left over from the famines of the Middle Ages, continued to occur up to the beginning of the fifteenth century). From way back, soups have come to us from all over the world and all civilizations.

Categories of Soups

1. Vegetarian soups, which are made with water and enriched either with a compound butter or oil or any milk or cream, or not enriched at all.
2. Whole-meal meat and vegetable soups, cooked in water and sometimes thickened with a grain; they are so substantial that they are considered main courses, especially if they are further enriched with grated or shredded cheese, or followed by a cheese course.
3. Clear or so-called clear soups, which consist of a clear broth lightly garnished with vegetables or grains or a combination of both; those called consommés are considered elegant enough to become the first course of a formal dinner.
4. Several subcategories of creamed soups, which are enriched with different types of cream.
5. I am not forgetting fish soups and chowders; you can find them all in the chapter about fish on page 540, together with the special fish stock which is used as their base.

The Basic Rules to Serving Soups

1. Unless you use extraordinary ingredients, a soup is always a much less expensive first course than any fish or shellfish.
2. Since making a large amount of soup requires hardly more time or energy than making a smaller amount, it is a good idea to prepare a double or triple batch and freeze what is not needed immediately, unless otherwise directed in the recipe. Freeze only the plain soup base and, for the sake of freshness, garnish with a fresh garnish of your choice just before serving.
3. The type of soup you should serve will depend on the remainder of the meal. If the main course is to be sauced with a rich white sauce or emulsified butter sauce, the best soup is a clear consommé; if, on the contrary, the main course is a lean piece of broiled fish or meat, or a simple roasted chicken, either a cream soup or a pure vegetarian soup is perfectly fine.
4. Serving wine with soup: No wine is usually served with soup, but, of course, there are exceptions:
   - In England one often meets with the most pleasant custom of being served a glass of Madeira or dry sherry with one's potage.
   - If a soup is sturdy enough to become a main meal, that is, if it contains a lot of vegetables including legumes and some meat or meat replacement such as tofu, and/or is garnished with grated and shredded cheese, you may want to serve a wine with it. In this case, choose the one you like best; if the meat in the soup is red, it can be a red wine such as a Pinot Noir, Gamay Beaujolais, or even any Rosé or, if the meat is a poultry, a white wine such as Sauvignon Blanc, Riesling, or Gewürztraminer.
   - Fish soups are usually served as a full-course meal, and accompanied by a dry white wine.

Vegetarian Soups

Vegetable soups may contain anything—potatoes or no potatoes, any type of vegetable—but they are all made according to the age-old principle: Bring *water*—not stock—to a boil, add the vegetables, bring back to a boil, and turn down to a simmer as long as you like. That's *all*. To transform a pure vegetable soup into a whole meal, serve it with a good loaf of bread and garnish it with grated cheese.

As possible enrichments for any vegetable soup, you can use additional butter, crème fraîche, whipped cream, or any of the soured creams available nowadays, from the richest to the leanest; whether or not you enrich the soup is entirely your decision.

Pure vegetable soups can be served "chunky" or pureed. The pureeing implement used is important and will depend on whether the soup contains potatoes or not. Potatoes contain proteins which, if pureed in a blender or food processor, acquire a filmy texture as these proteins have already been denatured by cooking, and are further denatured by the strong action of the machines. It is preferable to puree any soup containing potatoes through an old-fashioned food mill. Vegetable soups containing no potatoes can be pureed in a blender or in a food processor without hesitation.

Kamman's Onion Soup

FFR — 6 SERVINGS

This full-meal onion soup—richer than the bistro type on page 209—is good enough for entertaining friends on a cold night. It is made by replacing the water in Les Halles French onion soup with veal stock and flavoring the finished onion broth with ¼ cup dry Madeira or sherry. If you want, you can also double the amount of cheese melted over the bread.

Spring Country Soup

This is a chunky soup that comes from my mother's kitchen and became a favorite in my Boston restaurant. Fresh and healthy, serve it with a crusty bread flavored with fennel seeds.

NFR — 6 TO 8 SERVINGS

8 cups water

2 large red beets, peeled and diced into ⅓-inch cubes

I tablespoon fresh lemon juice

2 large carrots, diced into ⅓-inch cubes

3 medium-size purple-top turnips, peeled and diced into ⅓-inch cubes

I small rutabaga, peeled and diced into ⅓-inch cubes

I small celery root, peeled and diced into ⅓-inch cubes

3 medium-large leeks, white and light green parts, well washed and cut into slices

I cup baby peas

Salt

Pepper from the mill

½ cup chopped fresh chervil leaves

Crème fraîche or sour cream of your choice (optional)

Bread of your choice (optional)

Bring the water to a boil in a large soup pot, then add the beets and lemon juice and cook until half tender. Add the carrots, turnips, rutabaga, celery root, and leeks. Bring back to a boil, then reduce the heat and simmer until all the vegetables are tender and the broth tastes good. Add the baby peas, correct the seasoning, and finish cooking, another 5 minutes. Add the chopped chervil and serve immediately. Pass the bowl of chosen cream around the table to let family or guests help themselves as they wish. Serve the bread on the side.

Radish Greens Soup

FCR—6 SERVINGS

I tablespoon unsalted butter or unsaturated oil of your choice

3 cups chopped radish greens from 3 bunches of radishes

4 cups water or Secondary Stock (page 220)

2 large Idaho potatoes, peeled and diced into ⅓-inch salpicon (page 16)

12 red radishes, sliced ⅛ inch thick

I tablespoon cider vinegar

Salt

Pepper from the mill

I tablespoon Dijon mustard

⅓ cup sour cream of your choice

Bread of your choice (optional)

Grated Gruyère-type cheese or crumbled ripe goat cheese (optional)

Heat the butter or oil in a soup pot over medium heat. Toss the radish greens for 1 minute in the hot butter. Cover with the water and bring to a boil. Add the potatoes and simmer until the soup tastes good, 20 to 30 minutes. Strain through a food mill.

Meanwhile, place the radish slices and vinegar in a small pot, add water to cover, and bring to a boil. Season with salt and pepper, simmer 3 to 4 minutes, and drain. Add the slices of radishes to the strained soup. In a small bowl, mix the mustard with the chosen sour cream. Mix two ladlesful of the soup into this mixture, then whisk that mixture back into the bulk of the soup. Correct the final seasoning and serve immediately, with bread on the side and cheese passed in a bowl.

Do not throw away those wonderful radish greens; they are an excellent source of iron and taste just as good as expensive watercress.

Six-Onion Soup

FFR—6 SERVINGS

½ pound slab bacon

1½ tablespoons unsalted butter or unsaturated oil of your choice or confit fat (page 785)

6 leeks, white part only, well washed and thinly sliced

6 scallions, thinly sliced

2 large yellow onions, thinly sliced

3 shallots, minced

6 cloves garlic, coarsely chopped

6 cups water or Secondary Stock (page 220)

2 large Idaho potatoes, peeled and diced into ⅓-inch salpicon (page 16)

Salt

Pepper from the mill

2 tablespoons chopped fresh chives

⅔ cup crème fraîche or sour cream of your choice (optional)

This soup is the favorite of all the men in our family after a cold hike. This version has been somewhat defatted but remains opulent in taste and nutritional value.

Dice the bacon, discarding the fat as you work. Melt the butter in a large saucepan over low heat, toss in the bacon meat, and cook slowly until it starts coloring. Add the leeks, scallions, onions, shallots, and garlic and toss into the meat until soft. Add the water and bring slowly to a boil. Add the potatoes, salt, and pepper and simmer until the broth tastes good, 30 to 40 minutes. Strain through a food mill.

Serve the soup piping hot sprinkled with the chives and, if you want, pass a bowl of crème fraîche for family or guests to help themselves as they please.

Chunky Summer Tomato Soup

FCR— 6 SERVINGS

¼ pound dried **Great Northern** beans, soaked overnight in 6 to 8 cups water

6 cups cold water

Small bouquet garni of 1 bay leaf, 1 sprig fresh thyme, and 10 parsley stems

Salt

Pepper from the mill

1 tablespoon olive or other unsaturated oil of your choice

3 large cloves garlic, finely chopped

2 large leeks, white part only, well washed and finely chopped

12 large sun-ripened tomatoes, peeled, seeded, and cut into chunks

2 tablespoons chopped fresh parsley leaves

¼ pound cheese of your choice (optional), grated

All gardens and farmers' markets across the United States offer, come late summer, the wonderfully ripe and warm tomatoes that we all fancy. Here is how to use those that may have a spot of overripeness here or there. To make this soup faster, you can heat a can of cannellini beans in 3 cups of water seasoned with the bouquet garni, then add the tomatoes. The choice of cheese is yours; use any of the Gruyère- or cheddar-type cheeses, Parmigiano-Reggiano, or Pecorino.

Drain and sort the soaked beans, then cover them with 4 cups of the water; bring slowly to a boil with the bouquet garni, then add salt and pepper to your taste and cook until the beans are three quarters done, 35 to 40 minutes.

Heat the olive oil in a large saucepan, then add two thirds of the garlic and sauté over medium-high heat until beige. Add the leeks and sauté until wilted. Add the chunky tomatoes and sauté until their juices start running into the pan. Finally, add the cooked beans, their broth, and the remaining water and simmer together, uncovered, until the mixture tastes good, about another 40 minutes. Correct the final seasoning. If the soup turns too thick, lighten with boiling salted water or the hot broth of your choice.

Just before serving, chop the remaining garlic and parsley together and add to the soup. Serve with a loaf of crusty bread and pass the grated cheese in a bowl for family and guests to help themselves as they wish.

Whole-Meal Vegetable and Meat Soups

Although there is a definite freshness to a soup of vegetables simply boiled in water and properly seasoned, there is a school of cookery that prefers to use meat in vegetable soup to obtain a broth that is stronger in taste and more nutritious. Do not hesitate to do just that if this is your pleasure; your soup will become a complete meal instead of a first course only. Though these soups, if prepared for only two to four persons, can be microwaved or pressure cooked to save time, let me emphasize the fact that they will never develop the deep, complex taste they will have when slowly cooked on top of the stove.

Occitanian Soup

FFR — 6 SERVINGS

I cup dried navy beans, soaked overnight in 8 cups water

4 cups cold water

Salt

Pepper from the mill

¼ cup confit fat (page 785) or 2 tablespoons each walnut and corn oils

2 ounces pancetta, as old as possible, diced into ⅓-inch cubes

4 medium-size yellow onions, finely chopped

I large head Savoy cabbage

6 leeks, white and light green parts, well washed and thinly sliced

3 medium-size carrots, diced into ⅓-inch cubes

3 large purple-top turnips, peeled and diced into ⅓-inch cubes

Small bunch celery leaves from the center of the heart, finely chopped

Large bouquet garni of 20 parsley stems, I large Mediterranean bay leaf, and
    I very large sprig fresh thyme

For the filling

2 quarts water

Salt

½ pound ground turkey, goose, or duck meat

½ pound Italian sausage, removed from its casing

3 large cloves garlic, finely chopped

¼ cup finely chopped fresh parsley leaves

I large egg or I large egg white plus I cup fresh bread crumbs

Pepper from the mill

3 ounces hard grating cheese of your choice, grated

Drain and sort the beans. Place them in a large saucepan and cover with the fresh cold water. Bring slowly to a boil, add salt and pepper, and

This is a whole-meal soup from the Occitania, as French poets have always called the southwest part of the country, where the language is sonorous and the food as powerfully tasty as it is deliciously odoriferous. To obtain an authentic taste, use confit fat or a fifty-fifty mixture of walnut oil and corn oil when browning the onions, cook the vegetables deeply so they almost start falling apart, and add the second part of the mixture of garlic and parsley (called the persillade) to the soup raw at the last minute and just before serving. For the most authentic taste in cheese, use any dry sheep's milk cheese from the French or Spanish Pyrenees or Pecorino Romano.

Do not be discouraged by the long list of ingredients; once on the stove it takes care of itself.

Lighten the soup by boiling the pancetta and vegetables without tossing in any fat, plus using all turkey meat and the egg white in the filling of the cabbage leaves.

cook until semi-tender, about 35 minutes. Set aside in the cooking water.

Melt and heat the chosen fat in a large soup pot, then add the pancetta and onions and brown both well over medium heat. Meanwhile, remove six of the large outer green leaves of the cabbage, set them aside, and shred the cabbage heart. Wash the shredded cabbage well and add it to the pot together with the leeks, carrots, turnips, celery leaves, and bouquet garni. Toss together, salt and pepper lightly, and cover 10 minutes to let the vegetables wilt. Uncover, add water to cover the vegetables by 2 inches and cook until semi-tender. Add the beans and their water, and continue cooking until all the vegetables are fully tender (not crunchy), about 35 more minutes.

Meanwhile, prepare the sausage mixture. Bring the water to a boil, add a dash of salt and blanch the reserved cabbage leaves for 2 minutes in the boiling water. Remove the leaves from the water and cut out the center ribs. Mix the turkey and sausage meat with half the chopped garlic and parsley and the whole egg or egg white plus bread crumbs, and salt and pepper to your taste until homogeneous. Divide into six patties, then wrap each patty in a large cabbage leaf and tie into packages with kitchen string. Add the packages to the soup and finish cooking together, 30 to 40 minutes. If the soup becomes too thick, add boiling water and salt as needed to your personal taste. Just before serving, remove the string of the meat packages and stir the remainder of the persillade into the soup. Serve piping hot with a small bowl containing the grated cheese.

La Marmite

FFR — 12 SERVINGS

1 large center-cut 1-inch-thick slice veal shank

1 center-cut 1-inch-thick slice beef shank

1 shoulder lamb shank

2 cups dry red wine or water

One 5-ounce slab smoked bacon

5 medium-size carrots, thickly sliced

12 small white onions, peeled

2 rutabagas, 3 inches in diameter, peeled and diced into 1-inch cubes

12 leeks, white and light green parts, well washed and tied in a bundle with kitchen string

Large bouquet garni of 20 parsley stems, 1 large Mediterranean bay leaf, and 1 large sprig fresh thyme

Salt

1 roasting chicken, about 4 pounds, cleaned and trussed

12 small potatoes, peeled

Pepper from the mill

12 half slices walnut bread

The marmite was the black pot that hung over the fire in the hearth of my great grandmother and the name given to the soup she cooked in it on her Poitou farm. My great grandmother, having migrated to Paris, prepared this soup on the top of the stove, always complaining that it "just does not taste the same," although it tasted good to me. Again, this is relatively long-cooking winter "stick to the ribs" soup which is certainly feasible in the microwave or pressure cooker but "just does not taste the same" as when prepared on the stove top.

1 large clove garlic, mashed

1 tablespoon each finely chopped fresh basil, savory, parsley, and chives

3 tablespoons unsalted butter or walnut oil

Dijon or other mustard of your choice

Preheat the oven to 350°F. Remove as much fat from the veal, beef, and lamb as possible and place all three meats in a small roasting pan; roast until golden brown, about 45 minutes. Remove the meats to a soup pot and discard the fat in the roasting pan. Add the red wine to the roasting pan, place the pan for a few minutes over a hot burner, scrape well to dissolve the browned deposits, and reduce the wine to 1 cup. Add this liquid to the soup pot. Also add the bacon slab, carrots, onions, rutabagas, leeks, bouquet garni, and enough water to cover plus 2 inches. Bring to a boil, salt to taste, and simmer until the meats are half done, about 1 hour, skimming occasionally.

Add the chicken and, if necessary, more hot water and salt. Cook until the chicken is three fourths done, about 40 minutes, then add the potatoes and pepper to taste; cook another 20 minutes or so. Remove the soup meats and chicken and cut them into serving portions. Arrange them in a country dish surrounded by all the vegetables. Keep hot.

Strain the bouillon and defat it completely. Toast the slices of walnut bread and spread each evenly with an equal amount of the garlic, herbs, and butter well mixed into a paste. Place each slice into a soup bowl. Ladle the clear soup over the slices of bread and serve; then serve the meats and vegetables as a main course with a jar of the mustard of your choice.

Clear Soups

Clear soups start with the good stocks described at the beginning of this chapter to become simple or double consommés. Such soups may be served plain or with a garnish.

The old favorite consommé in its original form seems to have vanished from home and restaurant tables to be replaced by canned and processed products. For a change from the uniform taste of the canned, try making your own consommé. It does not involve as much work as you might expect, and when prepared ahead of time a consommé can wait well refrigerated until you are ready to use it. Follow the rules of refrigeration described for stocks on pages 215–17. Preferably organize your time so you need not freeze the consommé, since freezing it may bring a slight haze to its clarity.

There are two types of consommé. The first one, called simple consommé, is perfect for modern life; it is simply a good stock clarified and garnished with fresh vegetables or other pleasant additions. The second one is veal stock enriched with more meats and vegetables, pretty much following the techniques for any meat stock in a hurry on page 217 but using different types of meat to add complexity to the finished product.

CLARIFICATION

In the recipes that follow, egg whites and eggshell will attract all the particles that would normally make a stock cloudy and will "clarify" the stock as their large protein molecules bond with the tiny protein molecules held in suspension. The addition of egg white, though, forces the cook to stay at the stove and continue whipping the consommé until it comes to a boil; if this beating is omitted, the egg white can fall to the bottom of the pan, attach, and possibly burn there, thus spoiling the taste of the consommé.

There are two paths to follow once you have brought the mixture of egg whites, stock, and vegetables to a boil and lowered it to a simmer:

If you are in a hurry, strain the consommé immediately; if you are not, let the consommé cool to 160°/150°F; you will see, as the consommé cools, the "cap" of egg whites submerge and fall to the bottom of the pan. You can then ladle out the clarified stock without straining it.

If you must work fast—as is usually the case—strain the consommé. To do so, line a China cap or other fine strainer with a double layer of previously boiled cheesecloth that has been twisted dry; ladle the consommé and its egg-white cap into the lined strainer placed over a deep pot; *leave undisturbed* to drip at its own rhythm. Resist the impulse to push down on the ingredients resting in the strainer to accelerate the process, for there are tiny, tiny protein particles still floating free in the broth which have not been captured by the egg white; they will remain trapped in the spent meats and egg whites while straining, but if you push on those, they will pass into the finished soup and your consommé will show a small haze.

If you cannot spare the time for clarifying, omit the egg white and simply strain through cheesecloth, then garnish the finished soup with a small dollop of seasoned whipped cream; no one short of an expert wise to the trick will know that under the cream your soup is cloudy rather than clear.

GARNISHES FOR HOT OR WARM CONSOMMÉS

In the days when soup and consommé were still an all-important part of a meal, elaborate garnishes were prepared such as small cubes of savory herb custards known as *royales*. Nowadays the following light garnishes are preferably used:

- Juliennes of vegetables or vegetables cut into fancy shapes with Japanese or Chinese cutters
- Juliennes of crepes
- Soup noodles
- Instant tapioca
- Minced very flavorful mushrooms such as Oregon truffles
- Blanched juliennes of lettuce
- Blanched watercress
- Minced herbs, etc.

FORTIFIED WINE AND OTHER ADDITIONS TO JELLIED CONSOMMÉS

Cold jellied consommés have become outdated. Still, I remember with fondness my grandmother's consommé cups with the small silver spoons poised on their underliners, as they waited on her kitchen table for her to fill them halfway with jellied consommé. She loved to add some dry sherry or Madeira to give zest and taste to that then-elegant summer first course.

If you decide to serve a jellied consommé and want to add any fortified wine, be careful, as they contain a small amount of acid which, if added to the consommé while still very hot, will further denature the natural gelatin which makes the consommé gel and produce a slight haze through it. So wait and add the wine when the consommé has completely cooled. Jellied consommé can be served completely clear with a simple spray of chopped chervil leaves or other herbs on its top. It can also be garnished with small cooked shrimp and herbs, or even cooked diced vegetables and herbs. In this last case, ladle in half the already jellied consommé, add the garnish, then ladle the remainder of the jellied consommé on top.

OTHER USES FOR JELLIED CONSOMMÉ

Some preparations called aspics and *chaud-froids*, which were made for great occasions such as weddings and formal parties and were put on display on long decorated tables, have now fallen in desuetude in modern cuisine. The only people who persist in preparing these dishes are the chefs who compete and execute decorative food displays for food competitions; in our days of deep hunger in many parts of the planet, I believe strongly that such displays, in which the food is not used for consumption, should be abandoned and that the only culinary competitions to remain should be for hot food and desserts, in which the food can be consumed or, if not used, donated to people who need it badly.

Just so you know how such compositions are prepared, see the section on poached meats on pages 855–56 for a simple recipe for chicken breasts in aspic.

Simple Consommé

In the Paris of the thirties, this was a very popular Sunday dinner presentation which was often called Instantané *because it was done rapidly.*

FCR—6 TO 8 SERVINGS

6 ounces each fat-free ground turkey, beef, and veal

2 small carrots, finely diced

2 large yellow onions, finely chopped

2 large leeks, white and light green parts, well washed

Small bouquet garni of ½ bay leaf, pinch of dried thyme, and 2 parsley stems, chopped,
    tied together in a piece of cheesecloth

2 cloves

1 teaspoon salt

3 black peppercorns

1 large egg white

1 eggshell, crushed

6 cups cold water

Mix together the ground meats and vegetables in a large pot. Add the seasonings. Beat the egg white very lightly and add to the pot. Crumble the eggshell over the other ingredients. Cover with the water and, beating *constantly*, bring to a boil. Reduce the heat to very low and simmer for 1 hour. When done, turn the heat off and let stand 30 minutes.

Strain the soup through a fine strainer lined with a cheesecloth and let drip until the solids are dry as instructed on page 230; do not push on them to extract more broth. Serve the well-reheated consommé garnished as you choose.

Double Consommé

Use the primary veal stock and beef meat for beef consommé, or the secondary stock and half turkey meat and half chicken meat for poultry consommé.

FCR—6 TO 8 SERVINGS

1½ pounds ground fat-free meat of your choice

2 small carrots, finely chopped

2 leeks, white and light green parts, well washed and finely chopped

1 large yellow onion, finely chopped

3 black peppercorns

Small bouquet garni of ½ bay leaf, pinch of dried thyme, and 2 parsley stems, chopped,
    tied together in a piece of cheesecloth

1 large egg white, slightly beaten

1 eggshell, crushed

6 cups Primary Veal Stock (page 219) or Secondary Stock (page 220)

Mix the ground meat, vegetables, peppercorns, bouquet garni, egg white, and the eggshell together in a large pot. Cover with the cold stock and, beating constantly, bring to a boil. Reduce the heat to very low and simmer for 1 hour. Let stand 5 minutes and strain through a deep strainer lined with cheesecloth as instructed on page 230 and let drip without pressing down on any of the solids. Reheat well and serve garnished as you choose.

Creamed Soups

Creamed soups fall into three different categories:

1. Purees
2. Veloutés
3. True cream soups

The puree is, as its name indicates, based on a puree of vegetables; the velouté is built on a base of chicken or other poultry broth thickened with a roux; and the true cream soup on a base of cream sauce or *béchamel* sauce in which the liquid used to bind the base is milk or cream.

ACHIEVING SMOOTHNESS IN CREAMED SOUPS A fine creamed soup should contain no trace of vegetable skins or fibers and a puree should be very smooth:

1. *Creamed soups containing potatoes*. Such soups should be strained through a large drum sieve or *tamis* with the help of a large rigid plastic scraper. The procedure is not time-consuming provided only small amounts are strained at a time and the skins and fibers of vegetables other than potatoes are discarded after each and every stroke of the scraper. If no *tamis* is available, the same result can be obtained by using a large, deep conical strainer and a wooden pestle or even a thick highball glass, the bottom of which can crush potatoes fast and efficiently.

    Whichever implement you use, *do not go back and forth* with the mashing implement you are using; rather, push the potatoes—or the potatoes mixed with other vegetables—straight from the center of the *tamis* toward its rim or from the top of the strainer toward its bottom *in one decisive stroke* so as not to provoke the usual gumminess caused by the presence of proteins in the potatoes. The use of a blender or food processor is not acceptable for soups containing potatoes, as their blades shear through the potato pulp and agitate it in a manner that gives it a filmy and unpleasant texture.
2. *Creamed soups containing no potatoes*. Both blender and food processor can be used to puree vegetables containing no potatoes, but the soup must be strained after the blending or processing to remove all tiny traces of skins or fibers that may be left in the puree.

ENRICHING CREAMED SOUPS These soups have been from long tradition enriched with butter, plain cream, or a liaison of egg yolks and cream. But in our modern times, conscious as most of us are of the consequences of too much fat intake, these enrichments have been seriously curtailed and most of the time reduced to a tablespoon or so of lightened sour cream or crème fraîche in each plate or bowl at the most. The crème fraîche may seem extravagant, but 1 tablespoon of it is reasonable for anyone on a regular diet; it represents only ½ ounce of cream per person, compared with the 1⅓ ounces of heavy cream previously used. The efficiency of our electrical equipment in achieving extremely silky textures helps the cook limit enrichments.

PUREES

Purees are thickened with a puree of vegetables; in the old days they may have been thickened also with a puree of meat. If the vegetables are very starchy (potatoes, lima beans, beans, chestnuts, peas), they will adequately thicken the soup themselves. If the vegetable starch is not strong enough to produce a good binding, another starch is used as a thickener; it may be cornstarch in the modern style or rice in the old-fashioned style or even a roux, but one may, even today, find a puree thickened with bread crumbs.

The old-fashioned enrichment of a "liaison" consisting of one or several egg yolks mixed with heavy cream has not been used in the last twenty years or so.

Puree of Cauliflower

FCR—6 SERVINGS

2 medium-size perfectly white heads cauliflower

**8 cups Secondary Stock (page 220), chicken broth of your choice, or Pure
   Vegetable Broth (page 213)**

¼ cup fresh bread crumbs from French bread

½ cup finely chopped watercress leaves

Salt

Pepper from the mill

6 tablespoons crème fraîche or sour cream of your choice

The garnish of watercress refreshes the taste of the cauliflower which must be overcooked for this preparation. Do not blanch the watercress; the heat of the soup will do it.

Clean the cauliflowers; cut them into medium-large florets. Peel the stems. Bring a large pot of water to a boil, add the cauliflower, and blanch 2 minutes.

Bring the chosen stock to a boil, add the blanched cauliflower, bring back to a boil, then turn down to a simmer. Add the bread crumbs and continue simmering, uncovered, until the cauliflower falls apart, 20 to 25 minutes. Puree in a blender or food processor. Reheat well. Stir in the chopped watercress and correct the final seasoning. Serve garnished with the crème fraîche. The basic unenriched soup freezes well for up to 4 months.

Puree of Carrot

FCR — 6 SERVINGS

2 tablespoons unsaturated oil of your choice

I large yellow onion, chopped

3 shallots, chopped, or white part only of 6 scallions, sliced

I pound carrots, shredded

6 cups Secondary Stock (page 220), chicken broth of your choice, or Pure
    Vegetable Broth (page 213)

Salt

Pepper from the mill

½ cup light sour cream

½ cup chopped fresh chervil leaves

This soup is for everyday use and the butter has been replaced by oil to give its texture some smoothness. It can be made totally fat free by eliminating the oil and simmering the onions and shallots in the broth with the carrots; the taste, though, is less interesting.

Heat the oil in a large saucepan, then add the onion and cook, stirring, over medium heat until light golden. Add the shallots and carrots and toss a few minutes. Add the chosen stock and bring to a boil. Salt and pepper to your taste and simmer, uncovered, until the carrots are soft, 20 to 25 minutes.

Puree in a blender, adding the sour cream at the end of the blending. Reheat to very warm, correct the final seasoning and serve sprinkled with a thin blanket of chervil which your family or guests can stir themselves into the soup.

Puree of Succotash

FCR — 6 SERVINGS

8 cups Secondary Stock (page 220)

One 24-ounce package frozen large lima beans

½ teaspoon granulated sugar

½ teaspoon rubbed sage

Salt

Pepper from the mill

½ cup crème fraîche or light sour cream of your choice

½ cup light cream

1½ cups fresh Silver Queen corn kernels

The classic American combination of corn and lima beans becomes elegant in this pureed soup which tastes best when fresh corn is in season.

Bring the stock to a boil, then add the frozen limas, sugar, sage, salt, and pepper. Bring back to a boil, then turn down to a simmer; cook, uncovered, until the beans are very tender and discolored, about 15 minutes. Puree in a blender or food processor until the skins are well broken, then strain to discard all the skins. Mix the chosen sour cream with the light cream and add to the soup, stirring, and reheat to just below the boiling point. Add the fresh corn to poach for 2 to 3 minutes in the soup. Correct the seasoning to taste and serve.

If you wish to freeze the soup (up to 4 months), freeze only the soup base and add cream and fresh corn just before serving in order not to lose the fresh corn flavor.

Mexican Pea Puree

FCR—6 SERVINGS

2 tablespoons unsalted butter or corn oil

I large sweet onion, finely chopped

I head Boston lettuce, washed, dried, and chopped

2 tablespoons chopped cilantro leaves and stems

½ teaspoon ground cumin

5 cups Secondary Stock (page 220)

One 24-ounce bag frozen large peas

Salt

Pepper from the mill

I cup half-and-half, regular milk, or 2% milk

I to 4 tablespoons chopped cilantro leaves, to your personal taste

I teaspoon grated lime rind

I tablespoon fresh lime juice

Melt the butter in a large saucepan over medium-low heat, then cook the onion, stirring, until soft and translucent. Add the chopped lettuce and toss until softened. Add the cilantro leaves and stems and cumin and cook a few minutes. Add the stock and bring to a boil. Add the peas and salt and pepper and bring back to a boil, then turn down to a simmer, cooking until the peas are very soft and discolored, 30 to 35 minutes. Puree the soup in the blender or food processor and strain to discard all traces of skins. Add the half-and-half and reheat just below the boiling point. Just before serving, stir in the cilantro, lime rind, and lime juice. Correct the final seasoning with salt and pepper.

Puree of Chestnut Soup

A holiday soup for Thanksgiving and Christmas. If you have no time for shelling and peeling the chestnuts, use one jar of imported peeled chestnuts. Otherwise, cut a slit into the bottom end of each chestnut. Bring a pot of water to

FFR—6 SERVINGS

3 cups shelled and peeled chestnuts

6 cups Secondary Stock (page 220) or more if needed

One 3-inch piece celery rib

½ teaspoon coriander seeds

Salt

Pepper from the mill

¼ cup Sercial Madeira

¾ cup light cream

2 tablespoons fresh minced celery leaves

Cover the chestnuts with the stock in a large saucepan. Bring to a boil and add the piece of celery rib, coriander seeds, and salt and pepper to your taste. Reduce the heat and simmer until the nuts crumble, 40 to 45 minutes. Remove the celery rib and puree the soup in the blender or food processor. Add the Madeira, cream, and more seasoning if needed. Add more stock if too thick and reheat to just below the boiling point. Serve sprinkled with a dab of minced celery leaves.

a boil, add the chestnuts, and turn the heat off. Remove 3 chestnuts at a time from the hot water and, using a towel to hold each nut and not burn yourself, remove both the shell and inner brown skin completely.

VELOUTÉS AND TRUE CREAM SOUPS

Up until twenty years ago, the veloutés, as their name indicates, were made from a base of velouté sauce, a white sauce made with a white roux and white stock. The creams were made with *béchamel* or a plain white sauce made with a white roux and milk. You can find all the information you wish on these sauces on pages 275–82.

These types of soups used to be thickish; where the veloutés used to retain some vegetable flavor, it was not rare for the flavor of the vegetables to be drowned in the milkiness of the basic cream or *béchamel* sauce in the true cream soups.

VELOUTÉS AND TRUE CREAM SOUPS FOR REGULAR DIETS

Nowadays, veloutés and true cream soups are prepared more and more rarely and then with a plain velouté or white sauce, made on the spot, using for the roux the proportions of 1 tablespoon unsalted butter plus 1 tablespoon flour cooked for a few minutes and bound with 1 cup of secondary stock or other poultry stock of your choice for a velouté, or milk of your choice for a cream soup.

It is never quite possible to indicate the exact amount of stock or sauce to be used in a velouté or cream, since the vegetables used for a given preparation may yield very different textures and consistencies from one batch of vegetables to the next. It is up to the cook to judge whether, to her/his taste, the soup needs additional stock or milk for a thinner consistency. Based on the proportions given above, the soups are rarely too thin.

The use of canned or commercially prepared and frozen stock is, unless otherwise indicated, perfectly acceptable; the taste of the vegetables usually masks the "canned" taste. No unreasonably long simmering being necessary, the salt concentration is diluted by the large addition of different creams, sour creams, crème fraîche, or half-and-half used for the final enrichment.

VELOUTÉS AND TRUE CREAM SOUPS FOR SPECIAL DIETS

Vegetarians will use vegetable broth instead of a meat broth in any cream soup and perk up the final seasoning with a few additional herbs and/or spices of their choice.

People on fat-controlled diets will use secondary stock (see page 220) or pure vegetable broth (see page 213) and thicken the soups with cornstarch in the proportions of: 2 teaspoons cornstarch for each cup of finished soup, that is, the finished soup plus the light cream used to enrich it.

The cornstarch will be added by slurrying it (see page 269) in some cold stock or vegetable broth and adding that to the simmering soup base to finish it.

SEASONS FOR VELOUTÉS AND TRUE CREAM SOUPS Veloutés and true cream soups are generally served warm in the winter and chilled during the summer months. Adapt the soups to follow the vegetables in season.

Corn Milk Velouté

To be served warm garnished with the mushrooms or cold garnished only with chopped chives. The butter is necessary here for the final good taste of the soup. If that's too fat for you, then make the soup infrequently as a treat—do not substitute oil.

FFR—6 SERVINGS

8 ears fresh sweet corn

2½ cups water

Pinch of granulated sugar

Salt

White pepper from the mill

¼ cup unsalted butter

¼ cup unbleached all-purpose flour

2 cups Secondary Stock (page 220)

I cup light cream, scalded

⅓ cup cooked baby peas

2 Oregon black truffles, peeled and cut into ¼-inch cubes, or 3 ounces
    black chanterelles, chopped and cooked (optional)

I½ tablespoons chopped fresh chives (optional)

Using a chef's knife, remove all the kernels from the corn. Set aside. Using a fork, scrape the cobs, reaching into the sockets of the kernels to release the sweet milk. Put each cob into a soup pot and add the water. Add the sugar and salt and pepper to your taste; bring to a boil, then turn down the heat to a simmer and cook until the water is reduced to 2 cups or so and is white and milky.

In a large saucepan, melt the butter until the foam starts to recede. Off the heat, add the flour and mix well; return to medium heat and cook 3 to 4 minutes. Remove from the heat again and whisk in the corn milk, then the stock. Bring back to a boil, then reduce the heat to a simmer and cook until reduced to 3 cups. Strain into a clean pot.

Put 1 cup of the velouté in a blender or food processor together with the corn kernels and the hot cream; process until a thick puree results. Strain this puree into the remaining velouté; if too thick, dilute with additional cream or stock, as you prefer. Correct the final seasoning carefully.

For a warm presentation: Add the peas and diced truffles or chopped chanterelles to the soup, reheat just below the boiling point, and ladle into six soup cups.

For a cold presentation, add only the peas and ladle into six soup cups. Sprinkle the top of each cup with the chives.

Fresh Sorrel Velouté

FFR—6 SERVINGS

¼ cup unsalted butter

3½ tablespoons unbleached all-purpose flour

3½ cups Secondary Stock (page 220) or other poultry stock of your choice

5 ounces (about 3 cups) sorrel leaves, well washed, tough stems removed, and cut into chiffonnade

I cup cream of your choice

Salt

White pepper from the mill

I tablespoon chopped fresh chervil leaves

This recipe, because of the sourness of the sorrel, must remain a full-fat one executed with either regular heavy cream or crème fraîche. Make only for a treat if you have to, but use a high-percent fat cream.

Melt the butter in a large saucepan until the foam starts to recede. Off the heat, add the flour and mix well; return to medium heat and cook 3 to 4 minutes. Remove from the heat again and whisk in half the stock, then the other half. Bring to a boil and cook until thickened over medium-high heat, stirring constantly.

Place the sorrel chiffonnade in a blender or food processor. Add 1 cup or more if needed of the velouté and process until smooth and bright green. Strain this puree into the remaining velouté. Put the chosen cream in a large bowl and gradually blend a cup of the soup into the cream, then gradually blend this mixture back into the remainder of the soup. Whisk well and correct the seasoning very carefully, balancing the sourness with the right amount of salt and pepper for your taste. Reheat the soup to just below the boiling point if the soup is served warm.

Ladle into six soup cups, dot with the chervil leaves, and serve either warm or chilled.

Sauerkraut Velouté

FFR — 6 SERVINGS

½ pound fresh sauerkraut

4½ tablespoons unsalted butter or canola oil

I large yellow onion, finely chopped

2 cloves garlic, crushed

I cup dry Riesling or Sylvaner

½ sour apple, peeled, cored, and finely chopped

3 juniper berries, crushed

Salt

Pepper from the mill

3 tablespoons unbleached all-purpose flour

4½ cups Secondary Stock (page 220) or other poultry stock of your choice, or more if
    needed, scalding hot

3 ounces smoked bacon in one thick slice

I cup crème fraîche

2 tablespoons chopped fresh curly parsley leaves

In the Alsatian part of my family this soup was made with leftovers of a big sauerkraut feast. It is easier in the United States to cook a small batch of sauerkraut from scratch; please follow the directions carefully. The Riesling or Sylvaner must be dry and fruity. This recipe requires full-fat treatment and is a perfect treat, which ski guests, winter house guests, or other cold weather friends will relish.

Empty the sauerkraut into a large bowl of water and rinse it well. Repeat this operation three times. After the last rinse, squeeze the sauerkraut in your hands, so it remains only damp.

Melt 1½ tablespoons of the butter in a small braising pot until the foam starts to recede; add the onion and garlic and sauté until the onion is translucent; add the wine and reduce until almost dry. Add the sauerkraut, chopped apple, and juniper berries, salt and pepper to your taste, and toss well together. Cover the pot with a sheet of parchment paper and the pot lid. Cook over low heat until the cabbage shreds are dry and glisten with the butter or oil, at least 1½ hours. Stir the sauerkraut several times during the cooking so it does not attach to the bottom of the pan.

Melt the remaining butter in a large saucepan until the foam starts receding; off the heat, add the flour and mix well; cook 3 to 4 minutes over medium heat. Off the heat again, whisk in half the stock, then the remaining stock and bring to a boil, stirring. Pour this velouté over the sauerkraut and simmer together 30 to 40 minutes. Pour the soup into a blender or food processor and puree well. Strain into a clean saucepan.

While the soup reheats, cut the bacon into ⅓-inch-wide "lardons" and cook it gently in a skillet until most of its fat has rendered. Discard the fat, completely mopping it up with a wad of paper towels. Cut out all the remaining visible bacon fat and discard it. Dice the cooked lean meat into ⅛-inch cubes. Add the crème fraîche to the skillet and over very low heat, deglaze the pan well with it so as to lift all the glazed bacon juices off its bottom. Add about 1 cup of the soup to the cream, then reverse the process adding the mixture to the bulk of the soup, and reheat it to just below the boiling point. If the soup seems too thick, add enough stock to dilute it to your taste.

Serve in bowls or cups dotted with chopped parsley.

Spanish Cream of Tomato

FFR — 6 SERVINGS

4½ tablespoons olive oil of your choice

2 large sweet onions, finely chopped

2 cloves garlic, finely chopped

2 pounds fresh sun-ripened tomatoes, peeled, seeded, and chopped

Salt

Pepper from the mill

Pinch of granulated sugar

1 Mediterranean bay leaf

1 small sprig fresh thyme

2½ tablespoons unbleached all-purpose flour

1½ cups full-fat milk, scalded

2 cups Secondary Stock (page 220), scalding hot

¼ teaspoon freshly grated nutmeg

1 large or 2 medium-size green bell peppers

3 tablespoons dry fino sherry

2 teaspoons chopped fresh Italian parsley leaves

This is an old-fashioned soup as a Spanish-born friend of mine used to prepare it in the days when food offerings were always seasonal and prepared as close as possible to dinnertime. The blender is your best friend as it instantly pulverizes any curd which could possibly form when the acid of the tomatoes and the milk proteins come in contact.

Preheat the oven to 325°F. Heat 2 tablespoons of the olive oil in a small braising pan. Add the onions and sauté over medium-high heat until golden, then add the garlic and continue cooking until the garlic is beige. Add the tomatoes and toss well together. Add salt, pepper, sugar, bay leaf, and thyme. Bake, uncovered and stirring occasionally, until the tomatoes have completely lost their liquid and taste sweet and delicious, 25 to 30 minutes. Puree in the blender and strain through a conical strainer.

Meanwhile, heat the remaining oil in a saucepan. Off the heat, add the flour and mix well; return to the heat and cook 3 to 4 minutes over medium heat. Remove from the heat again, whisk in the milk, then the stock, and bring to a boil, stirring constantly. Add the nutmeg and season well.

Preheat the broiler. Put the green pepper(s) on the broiler rack and broil, turning it as necessary until its skin is charred all around. Place the pepper(s) 5 to 10 minutes in a small bag, then peel and seed, also removing the inner ribs of the vegetable. Dice the pepper into ¼-inch cubes and combine with 2 tablespoons of the sherry in a small bowl. Let steep until the soup is ready to serve.

Pour the hot cream sauce into a blender or food processor and very gradually add the tomato puree through the feed tube while on high speed.

Strain back into a clean saucepan and add the sherry-steeped green pepper cubes. Correct the final seasoning with salt and pepper and by adding the last tablespoon of sherry if needed. If the soup is too thick for your taste, correct its texture with some more stock. Serve in cups sprinkled with the chopped parsley.

A Modern Oxtail Soup

FCR — 6 TO 8 SERVINGS

Oxtail soup used to be a rich and heady concoction which pleased the gentlemen in the family enormously when we could still afford to garnish this potage with fresh truffles. Here is a lightened recipe garnished with more affordable mushrooms; prepare the stock twenty-four hours ahead of time for proper and complete defatting.

3 oxtails, cut into chunks

2 small carrots, peeled

3 medium-size yellow onions, peeled

1 cup water

3 leeks, white and light green parts, well washed and chopped

One 3-inch piece celery rib, chopped

6 cloves garlic, crushed

Large bouquet garni of 12 parsley stems, 1 Mediterranean bay leaf, and 1 large sprig fresh thyme

3 cloves

2 teaspoons salt

1 pound mushrooms of your choice, coarsely chopped (black chanterelles and Boleti eduli—porcini—being the best)

10 black peppercorns

Meat extract, if needed

¼ cup dry sherry or Madeira (optional)

1½ tablespoons cornstarch or more as needed

1 cup light cream or half-and-half

2 tablespoons chopped fresh chives

Preheat the oven to 350°F. Remove all visible traces of fat from each piece of oxtail; put the pieces of meat, the carrots, and onions in a roasting pan and roast until golden brown, about 45 minutes. When done, discard all the liquid fat in the pan and blot off the last traces of it on the meat and in the pan with wads of paper towels, taking care not to dislodge the browned gravy on the bottom of the pan.

Transfer the pieces of oxtail, carrots, and onions to a soup pot. Add the water to the roasting pan, place it over a hot burner, and scrape well to dissolve the meat juices into the water. To the soup pot add this deglazing, along with the leeks, celery, garlic, bouquet garni, cloves, and salt plus enough water to cover the solid ingredients by 1 inch. Bring to a boil, skim, if necessary, then turn down the heat to a simmer, add one third of the chopped mushrooms and cook until tasty, at least 2½ to 3 hours; add enough boiling salted water through the cooking to maintain the liquid level with the solids. During the last 10 minutes of cooking, add the peppercorns.

When the soup is done, strain it and taste it carefully. If it does not feel strong enough, reduce it until it tastes the way you like. If you find the taste to be still too light after reduction, do not hesitate to add the meat extract of your choice to correct the final seasoning. Strain the soup through a China cap into a deep pot and cool rapidly in a sinkful of iced water; then refrigerate overnight and when ready to use, remove any traces of solid fat on top of the stock.

To finish the soup, add the remaining mushrooms and the sherry and bring to a boil; reduce the heat and simmer 10 minutes. Put the cornstarch in a small bowl and gradually whisk in the light cream until smooth. Stirring constantly, add the cornstarch mixture (see page 269 for details on doing this) to the simmering stock. Stir constantly until the mixture comes back to a boil and thickens slightly, which will happen in a matter of minutes. Correct the final seasoning and add half the chives to the soup.

Ladle the soup into six to eight heated soup bowls and serve piping hot, sprinkling the top of each soup bowl with a bit of the remaining chives.

A Lighter Cream of California Wheat

FCR — 6 SERVINGS

¾ cup **California hulled wheat (available in health food stores)**

5½ cups **Secondary Stock (page 220) or Pure Vegetable Broth (page 213)**

Salt

Pepper from the mill

⅛ teaspoon **ground cardamom**

⅛ teaspoon **ground coriander**

⅛ teaspoon **freshly grated nutmeg**

2½ cups **low-fat or nonfat milk, scalding hot**

2 tablespoons **cornstarch**

1½ cups **light cream**

3 tablespoons **dry fino or Dry Sack sherry**

¼ cup **pine nuts, toasted (page 51)**

2 teaspoons **finely chopped cilantro leaves**

California hulled wheat is unpolished whole grains of wheat, not cracked wheat or bulgur. If you cannot find the whole grains, this soup can be made with cracked wheat, but the texture and character of the soup will be different.

Cover the wheat with the broth of your choice in a large saucepan and bring to a boil. Add salt, pepper, and the spices, reduce the heat, and simmer until all but ½ cup of the stock has been absorbed. Stir in the hot milk. Bring back to a simmer.

Place the cornstarch in a small bowl and gradually whisk in the light cream, making sure that there are no lumps. Stir the mixture into the cream soup (see the instructions for doing this on page 269). Add the sherry of your choice and the toasted pine nuts. Correct the final seasoning.

Ladle into six cups and serve topped with a tiny spray of the chopped cilantro.

Modern Cream of Leek

FCR—6 SERVINGS

This soup used to be made with a generous amount of cream and egg yolks and butter-browned croutons. Not so this lean little concoction which still tastes awfully good, thanks to the delicious leeks. Do not use a fruity virgin olive oil; its taste would dominate the soup.

12 large leeks, white and light green parts, well washed

2 tablespoons pure olive, canola, or corn oil

4 cups Secondary Stock (page 220) or Pure Vegetable Broth (page 213),
    scalding hot

⅛ teaspoon freshly grated nutmeg

Salt

Pepper from the mill

Cornstarch as needed

I to 2 cups light cream to your personal taste

I tablespoon chopped fresh chives

Slice the leeks paper thin. Heat the oil in a small soup pot, then add the leeks and sauté a few minutes over medium-high heat until well coated with the oil. Cover the pot, reduce the heat to medium, and let the leeks soften completely without coloring. Add the chosen stock, bring to a boil, season lightly with the nutmeg, salt, and pepper and turn the heat down to a simmer; cook until tasty. Puree completely in a blender or food processor.

Measure the volume of soup and measure out 2 teaspoons of cornstarch per cup, plus another 2 teaspoons per cup of cream. Put the cornstarch in a small bowl and whisk in the cold cream, making certain there are no lumps. Bring the soup to a boil, then turn it down to a simmer and stir in the starched cream until the soup comes back to a boil and has thickened lightly (see page 269 for instructions on doing this). Simmer another 20 minutes or so. Correct the final seasoning and ladle into six soup bowls or cups. Serve sprinkled with the chives.

A Multinational Society

Sauces from All Over the World

THE SAUCE "JUNGLE" IN THESE LAST FEW YEARS OF THE TWENTIETH century has become extremely diversified. As you may have noticed, I purposefully avoid the word *complicated*, which I shall leave to the many prophets of doom who would like us to believe that sauce making is indeed difficult, and that sauces as prepared by the French, the Bolognese, the Swiss, and some of the very best chefs in all of the western world are full of fat and unhealthy. As a cook and chef who is not content with writing about food and cooking and also still cooks professionally and teaches the culinary arts the only way the culinary arts should be taught, which is with passion, I feel compelled before starting this very important chapter to take a personal stand as to the preparation of sauces.

Preparing a sauce, any sauce, be it cooked or uncooked, ancient or modern, French, Italian, Greek, American, Indian, or Far Eastern, is not complicated provided one takes the time to learn to prepare it with care from the very start, so that one's understanding of the techniques involved results in a true work of art, not a pale and unpalatable imitation of the real thing. Perhaps in no other culinary preparation is corner cutting more dangerous than in sauce preparation, be it in the most refined of French sauces or in the most fragrant and well-balanced of Indian chutneys. Trust your intelligence and palate to be capable of helping you produce excellent sauces of the right quality in the correct quantity. Not only are sauces too often severely lacking in quality, but they are served in huge quantities that are absolutely unnecessary.

To make things interesting for the cook and reader, I shall first give a retrospective of sauces as they have existed in the western world for two millennia and go through some of their successive transformations. Some sauces, not used in our century anymore, will only be mentioned; some of the sauces, still usable nowadays, will be presented in recipe form as written by their creators, in case the reader would like to know what its taste and texture may have been; of course, there will be one major discrepancy: Ingredients from times gone by are not the same as ours. The information given here is not only interesting as reading material for anyone who likes the history of food and the culinary arts, but necessary knowledge for future chefs, professional cooks, and teachers of the culinary arts at any level.

The word *sauce* as we use it today is derived from *salsus*, a Latin adjective which meant salted; as the Latin language deteriorated into Low Latin, *salsa*, the feminine form of *salsus* became a substantive meaning something sharp or witty or, if concerned with food, something sharp or briny. My old Latin dictionary states: "Hence the old French 'Saulce.'" *Salsa*, a word with which we are very familiar today, passed directly from Low Latin into Italian and Spanish; in French it passed through the different forms of *saulce* in the Middle Ages, *sausse* in the seventeenth and eighteenth centuries, before reaching its modern form of *sauce*. Modern English, as we all know, uses the same form as the French.

A sauce is a fluid to semifluid composition that has been thickened by diverse means and contains elements which give "salt," that is, bring added savor and piquancy to foods such as meats, fish, vegetables, and fruit.

Lessons from Roman Sauces

It is wise, for the sake of a plain and simple understanding of western sauce heritage to go straight to ancient Rome and investigate rapidly the Roman way with sauces. Looking at Rome will also give us a window on the ancient Greeks since the Roman way to cook was strongly influenced by Greek slaves and Greeks manumissioned to Roman citizenship. There were as many Greek cooks in ancient Rome as there were Greek teachers and artists.

To better understand Roman food and the Roman way with sauces, here is the formula for a sauce, extracted directly from the Apicius Roman cookery book, compiled sometime between the fourth and fifth century A.D. To accompany a roast meat, the writer advises to make a sauce containing:

> One quarter ounce each of pepper, lovage, parsley, celery seed, dill, asafetida root [see page 250], hazelwort [perhaps the root of a hazel bush or an infusion of hazel leaves?], a little pyrethrum [aromatic leaves of a type of chrysanthemum], cyperus [an edible tuber?], caraway, cumin, ginger, 2 generous cups of *liquamen* [see page 56] and finally 8 ounces of oil.

No technique is indicated for this particular formula; it is not impossible that all the elements were mixed together to obtain a very fragrant mixture of spices and herbs, seasoned highly with the pungent—simultaneously sulfuric and oniony—smell and taste of the asafetida, the high salt of the *liquamen*, and the fruity olive oil of Italy, which was probably whipped into the mixture to provoke an emulsion identical to those we make when we prepare salad dressings. To be a true dressing this mixture would have to contain an acid, which it does not, but perhaps some of the spices and herbs used were acid. Other sauces in the book contain plenty of vinegar and/or mustard and really are what we call salad dressings.

Of the components of this sauce, most of the herbs, the ginger, and the oil are still part of our daily larder. *Liquamen* may be unfamiliar; it was a preparation which today would belong to the family of fermented fish sauces of ancient China, and the modern fish sauces of Thailand and Vietnam.

The little Greco-Roman city of Antipolis, still in existence as Antibes on the French Riviera, used to be one of the greatest centers of the production of *liquamen*. As I mentioned in the general chapter on ingredients (see page 56), I strongly believe that the Provençal *pissalat*—a fermented mixture of salt, anchovies or sprats, and artificial mercury sulfide—is a direct descendant of *liquamen*. In Greek it was called *garon* or *haimation*. After fermenting fish in salt for two months in the sun, most of it liquefied, lost its smell of fish, and acquired the smell of cheese. It was strained through fine-weave baskets and the solid residues were used to prepare yet another type of fish sauce called *hallec*. *Liquamen* could be cut, mixed, or reduced with water to become *hydrogarum*, with wine to become *oenogarum*, or with vinegar to become *oxygarum*.

Why all this information on a product that does not exist anymore? Because we continue to employ the concept in the fermented fish sauces *nuoc mam* and *nam pla*, and those sauces prepared with mashed anchovies preserved in salt and/or oil. We can assume that the use of anchovies in sauces in Provençal and some Italian styles of cooking is the most modern replacement of the Roman *liquamen*. Which brings to mind the question of where *liquamen* really came from; did the technique of making it follow the Silk Road all the way to the Mediterranean or have all the fish sauces naturally and separately evolved in various coastal communities of the seas of China and Japan and of the Mediterranean?

Other ingredients that appeared in Roman sauces were:

- *Vinum* or *merum*, which was simple wine. The rule in Rome was to always reduce wine before adding it to a sauce; we still do this today, either separately, away from the other elements of a sauce, or together with them, when we prepare the reductions of the classic and some of the modern French-style sauces (see page 298).

- Must, or the juices of fresh grapes before or during fermentation. The must could be reduced to different degrees to become *defrutum* which was thick and sweet, *caroenum* which was reduced by one third of its original volume and must have been slightly sweet-sour, and *sapa* which was reduced by two thirds. Opinions varied greatly among Latin authors as to the true and real ratio of reduction of *defrutum*, *caroenum*, and *sapa*. We still use must when we add *verjus*/verjuice (see page 41) to our food, the fermented juice of green grapes.

- *Passum* was a type of sweet wine used relatively often in sauces; it was made by first drying grapes in full sun, then macerating them in fresh must for six days. The mixture was then pressed and fully fermented for twenty to thirty days. Such wines are still made in the Piemonte of Italy; to their style belongs the Caluso Passito made from the beautiful Erbaluce grape.

- And then there was *mulsum* which really could be called *enomel*—or wine and honey mixture—since it was made with 3 gallons of wine (preferably dry) in which 10 pounds of honey was dissolved and fermented. *Hydromel* was prepared in the same manner, honey being dissolved in twice its own weight of water, then fermented. It seems to have been used to glaze pieces of meat which had been browned in a *patella*, the Roman round frying pan.

Besides the herbs and liquids mentioned, other important and expensive aromatic ingredients could be found in the Roman kitchen. The most expensive was sylphium, a plant purchased at great expense from the northeastern province of what is now Lybia, the Cyrenaica. Sylphium was so overused that it had disappeared from Cyrenaica by the first century B.C. and had been replaced by Persian asafetida. Asafetida is still used extensively in small quantities in the modern East Indian cuisines; I used it only once, its strong sulfur smell filling my kitchen. Added to foods and sauces, asafetida has such a strong smell of onions that, exactly like in modern Indian sauces, Latin sauces did not ever seem to contain onions and asafetida at once. It is interesting to note that all through the Apicius book, only two recipes contain a small amount of garlic; on the contrary, onions of all types, shallots, and leeks are well represented. We continue to use those in large quantities in our modern concoctions.

The Latins gave their sauces the name of *Ius* which may immediately evoke for the modern cook the French *jus*, but the two are different. We have no way of really knowing what the respective textures of the different sauces of the Latin kitchen were, because the book of Apicius mentions weight and proportions only in two of the many formulas it contains. Some were uncooked and carried the name of *Ius crudum*, meaning uncooked sauce. Such a sauce was the *Ius crudum* poured on a boiled chicken, which contained pepper, lovage, cumin, Welsh onions (perhaps scallions or shallots or true baby onions?), oregano, pine nuts, Jericho dates, honey, vinegar, *liquamen*, mustard, and a little oil. It probably looked and tasted like a highly seasoned, thickish honey-mustard vinaigrette. A few other vinaigrette-type sauces contained chopped hard-boiled egg yolks, which probably gave them the smoother texture of our modern hard-boiled egg mayonnaises, more specifically the remoulade.

In the chapter on fish one finds this sauce prepared to accompany grilled young tuna:

Pepper, lovage, oregano, fresh coriander, onion, and pitted raisins mixed with *passum*, vinegar, *liquamen*, *defrutum*, and oil.

Think of it; you can make this sauce without difficulty, using ingredients which are in all our kitchens: Pepper is one of our staples; lovage is in many gardens, fresh coriander in all our supermarkets, as are onions, our raisins are made from seedless grapes, we can imitate *passum* with *oloroso* sherry mixed with balsamic vinegar, replace *liquamen* with *nuoc mam* or mashed anchovies, replace the *passum* with fresh grape juice reduced to a thick texture, and whisk some of the best Italian, Greek, Spanish, or French olive oil into the mixture.

How about proportions? Refer to the modern sauces on pages 557–59 in the fish chapter and you will be surprised at the similarity of ingredients and soon realize that some of the modern western vinaigrettes as well as some of the modern reduction-type sauces are made pretty much as the Latin sauces were. I served a number of such sauces on fish in my Boston restaurant twenty years ago, and they were very successful.

Many of the warm Latin sauces used on birds and meats and also quite a few Latin fish sauces were bound with *amulum*, a special wheat starch thickener made by a complicated process, explained in one of Pliny's texts. *Amulum* probably thickened sauces as well as our cornstarch does (see starch slurry on page 269). Some other Latin sauces were thickened by an addition of pastry; which type of pastry was used eludes me completely, as it seems to have eluded the diverse translators of Apicius, but could it have been some crumbled *pizza dolce*, in existence today but sweetened at the time with honey? Or some *pâte à choux*?

Among the Latin dishes with descendants to be found in modern European cuisine are leeks in vinaigrette; the *tians* of the Provence, early forms of the many vegetable gratins of the lower and upper Alps; the Italian frittata, sometimes translated by Latinists as "turnover," probably because, if made in a frying pan, a frittata is turned over; the fried fish with vinegar dear to Londoners; fricassees of meatballs and apples; duck with turnips; birds in pastry; and many meat stews.

Sauces in the Middle Ages

The sauces of the Middle Ages we have seen well documented by two authors of the time. The first was Taillevent (his real name was Guillaume Tirel) and he lived between 1310 and 1395. He was the *queux* (cook) to several highborn persons until 1373, when he became the chef of King Charles V of France, then, in (possibly) 1380, the executive chef to Charles VI of France, and in 1392 the "Master" of his entire kitchen personnel. He is either the author or one of the authors of *Viandier*, a cookbook written in the mid-fourteenth century and of which four manuscripts exist. One copy of the *Viandier* is in the Valais Archives of Sion in Switzerland, one at the French Bibliothèque Nationale in Paris, one in the Mazarine Bibliothèque in Paris, and one at the Vatican Library. The Terence Scully edition I own, in modern transcription, does not mention the exact date of any of them.

The second author is not known by name; he is the charming *Ménagier de*

Paris (*The Good Man of Paris*), an anonymous Paris bourgeois, who between 1392 and 1393 wrote for his new, quite young wife-to-be, a large book in two parts. Over the years I have developed such a friendship with the *Ménagier* that I put a whole menu on the tables of my Boston restaurant, in which his dishes were adapted into modern offerings; it is probable that my Cameline sauce bound with bread cooked in spiced Châteauneuf du Pape would have tasted deficient in cinnamon to the *Ménagier*. I love his Old French; for a French woman living at the end of the twentieth century, it is touching and charming at once, although, from the advice the dear man gave to the young lady, I always wondered how she enjoyed taking care of his household.

As in the Latin world, the *saulces* of the two medieval authors come cooked or uncooked, uncooked in the summer and cooked in the winter. Also as in the Latin world, spices are used *à foison*, even *à grand foison*, meaning in the largest quantities possible, probably larger than those of the Latins.

When one tries to prepare these concoctions exactly as written, the results range from unpalatable to downright revolting. The uncooked Cameline of the *Viandier*, which by the way may have been originally called Canneline because it contained a lot—oh but a lot—of cinnamon, which was and still is called *cannelle* in French, and also ginger, ground cardamom pods (*graine*), mastic (a resin lentisk tasting of tar), long pepper (cayenne) for those who wanted to use it, and bread soaked in vinegar, all of this strained and salted "properly."

Why such strong and acid preparations? Probably because since all cattle were killed in the summer and had to be salted for keeping over the winter, the spices and the vinegar made a pleasant opposition to the salty meat served day in and day out and, of course, because, even when one could buy fresh meats, they were more often than not anything but fresh due to complete lack of cold storage.

The Jance (a sort of white sauce) of the *Ménagier* is boiled and thus reads as being a bit more palatable. It is thickened with some of the ground peeled almonds dear to the Persian/Arabic cuisines, mixed with two roots of ginger, also ground, spice powder, a little garlic, a little more white bread than almonds softened with *verjus* from white grapes and one quarter as much more white wine. All of this is boiled very well, and thanks to the starches in the bread crumbs, bound before being ladled into dishes. Chances are that it somewhat resembled the wine *panade*—or wine and bread soup—that my great grandmother brought from her native Poitou.

The dear *Ménagier* also offers a formula for a *Jance au lait de vache* or cow's milk Jance which makes the reader hope for some ancestor to what was to become the white cream or *béchamel* sauce. No such luck. Fresh ginger is mixed with egg yolks and milk and "well boiled" so that, the fresh ginger having curdled the milk as the heat curdled the egg yolks, what went to the table in sauce dishes must have been the messiest, ugliest mixture upon which to set one's eyes and the most unpalatable to pass across one's palate.

On the other side, Taillevent tells us to roast pork, putting garlic, onions, wine, and *verjus* in the roasting pan so they mix and cook with the lard dripping from the roast, and make a sauce with all these elements. This sounds at the same time delicious and interesting since this will constitute a form of sweet-and-sour gravy as the meat juices fall into the dripping pan, mix with the other liquid ingredients, and reduce together in the heat of the fire burning in the hearth.

I have purposefully used this example of a true gravy to touch on what has been discussed by each and every food historian since the medieval manuscripts were studied in depth in the nineteenth century. There exist in both books what the two writers call *potaiges lyants* or bound soup/stews. So you understand what was meant, here is a version of the same recipe adapted from each manuscript:

GRAINNE OF SMALL BIRDS (ADAPTED FROM TAILLEVENT, FROM THE MAZARINE MANUSCRIPT)

Take small birds of your choice and fry them very well; then take toasted bread and soak with beef broth, strain to liquefy, and add with your grain; then season with ginger, cinnamon, and a little verjuice and boil all together. This should not be bound too thickly.

Here is, as a matter of comparison, the recipe appearing in the *Ménagier*, probably adapted by its author from the Vatican manuscript of Taillevent. The text may appear not to make sense to the modern reader, but it is quoted here in direct translation from *Le Ménagier*.

GRAVE OF SMALL YOUNG BIRDS

The birds being plucked dry, put them in a frying pan with fat bacon cut into cubes and let them fry to remove the fat and fry them crisp. Then put [the birds] to cook in meat broth. Then take toasted bread or crumbs of bread soaked in meat broth and a bit of wine; then take ginger, cloves, cardamom and cinnamon, and the livers and mash them; then pass your bread and broth mixture through muslin, adding the spices at the end and without straining them; and put to boil with your birds and a little verjuice. If you have no broth, add a pea puree. Should not be too thick, but lighter and clear; hence only bread and livers should be used to bind the broth.

As you see in the first version, the broth is thickened with grain and bread, in the second with bread and liver. One is called *grainne* (it can be also *graine* or *grene*), the other is called *grave*.

There is much confusion in all books about these two words which almost describe the same dish. *Grane* seems to have been used considerably more than *grave* even though the word *grave* did exist. Many experts have examined this question in detail; being just a cook interested in history I probably should not venture an opinion, but also being French-born and having received some training in philology, I have a sense of my own language in both its old and new forms.

I believe that, as is discussed in the Terence Scully edition of the *Viandier* on page 64, Note 2, *grene* is akin to the Italian *granato*—as in *brodo granato*—which when applied to a broth, defines one that contains some small lumps of something; in the *grane* the small lumps may be the grain or lumps of bread that may not have dissolved completely in the liquid part of the *potage*. It would be consistent with the meaning of the word *grave*—with a "v," not an "n"—also existing as *grève* (the first as in the Graves terrains of the Bordeaux vineyards, the other as in the Place de Grève in Paris because it was covered with natural gravel) which in Middle French referred to a terrain of mixed sand and small stones.

In any case, the word *gravey* in Medieval English is indicated in *Webster's* as being derived from the Medieval French *grane* and has probably become gravy in modern English. Though they both started from the same type of medieval preparation, English gravy and French sauces developed into two very different culinary entities in the centuries to come.

The Renaissance and the Italian Connection

Italy brought the Renaissance to Europe, not only in all the fine arts but also in the culinary arts. As the ancient roads of commerce between Asia and Europe fell into the hands of the Ottoman Turks, culminating in the Fall of Constantinople in 1453, it became more and more difficult for spices to reach the important centers of resale in Genoa and Florence. Although Venice was able to hold on to its spice monopoly for another few years, Italy accepted the challenge of gradually learning to cook without the spices that had been part of its culinary heritage since Roman times, before any other European nation, and went on to build new, more direct and brighter styles of cuisine. The Italians also benefited very early on from the important consequences of the domination of the eastern Mediterranean by the Turks, the opening by the great discoverers of ocean routes circumnavigating the globe, and the beginning of the huge exchange of food products between the Old Worlds of Europe and Asia and the New World.

And between 1494 and 1559, life in Italy was neither more peaceful nor any easier than it was in France at the time. The so-called Italian wars conducted between several successive French kings and a number of Italian principalities in coalition with two successive emperors of Austria were probably as much a burden on the economy of all the Italian principalities involved as they were on that of the French kingdom. However, the Italians seem to have made as much use of these wars as they had of their art to radiate their culture over all of Europe through the sixteenth century and a good part of the seventeenth. Leonardo da Vinci came to live at the court of Francis I of France and many Italian families important in the world of banking moved to France in the wake of the two Medici princesses who became queens of France, Catherine in 1536 and Marie in 1600. The Italian influence on French food presentations and style continued way beyond the death of Marie de Medici's husband, Henry IV, in reality until that of Italian-born Cardinal Mazarin in 1661. Sixteen sixty-one is the year in which a young Louis XIV, very much in love with Italian Marie Mancini, niece of Mazarin, renounced his passion and inner feelings to marry the Infanta Marie Thérèse of Spain for strictly political reasons. Sixteen sixty-one saw the beginning of his role of absolute monarch over France and started the domination of the French over the kitchens of Europe.

There is a school of historians that thinks the influence of the Medici princesses on the development of French cuisine is somewhat of a myth. As a teacher of the culinary arts, I have been asked my opinion many times on this subject. It is indeed truly improbable that the princesses themselves ever had anything to do with the kitchens, but the many Italian cooks who came to France in their wake to serve the wealthy Italian banking families worked side by side with French chefs in the only French professional kitchens existing then, those of the noble and/or wealthy houses of France and those of the *rôtisseurs* and *pâtissiers*, as the caterers were called in those days.

According to Giuliano Bugialli's *The Fine Art of Italian Cooking*, the binding of sauces with flour—even with the cooked butter-and-flour paste known as roux—finds its beginnings in fifteenth-century Italy. It makes sense that a country that had enough flour to feed itself on pasta and bread would not hesitate to use flour to thicken sauces, and more so when one considers these were the direct descendants of the Romans, who had thickened sauces with wheat starch. Sauces remained bound with bread in other countries much longer than they did in Italy, probably because flour had to be reserved for the baking of bread, was precious and not to be wasted. Another example of this conservation can be found at a later date in Austria when cakes were—and in some instances still are—prepared with bread crumbs instead of flour.

Bugialli cites the name of Chef Pantanelli, who, arriving in France in 1533 with Catherine de Medici's train of servants, may have brought the roux to sixteenth-century French kitchens; Bugialli mentions that Pantanelli knew the roux since he used it in the Italian *pasta soffiata* which became in French *pâte à chaud*, known now as *pâte à choux*. *Pâte à choux* in its modern version is prepared by first heating water, seasonings, and diced cold butter to a boil, then, off the heat, adding the flour and drying the mixture on the stove before adding the eggs. So, for Chef Pantanelli really to have been the one who brought roux to France, he must have had to start his *pasta soffiata* by mixing hot butter with flour, then binding the mixture with water.

In any case, either through Pantanelli, or through one of several other Italian chefs, the roux passed from Italian cooks to French apprentices, and slowly became the thickener of choice, and was first published by La Varenne in 1651 as we shall see shortly. This all makes sense for me as a practicing chef, since this is the way the art is passed from master to student.

I believe that, with so many modern chefs receiving good academic educations, it is not only going to be trained historians who will be involved in the study of food history through the examination of ancient texts, but also practitioners, who daily are manually and mentally involved in professional kitchens, and participating in the production of meals for the public at large. The writer-chef's perception of the quick or slow changes which contribute to the modernization of a style of cuisine will definitely be of help to analyze and evaluate past cooking concepts from the practitioner's point of view, not only from the researcher's point of view.

As a French-born chef and writer who has practiced and taught the art of cooking both in the French and American contexts, I can say, from what I saw happen in my own kitchens over the last twenty years, that some new concepts were accepted only very slowly because they were difficult for apprentice cooks to understand and assimilate, while others, which a certain ease of execution rendered attractive, were readily accepted and rapidly adopted. That very same rhythm of work and assimilation must have happened during the sixteenth century between the Italian masters and their French students. There is no doubt that it took a good hundred years for the French apprentices and chefs to take from the Italians what was new and attractive in their techniques and adapt those to the French taste. The princesses were responsible for the masters coming to France, and the French chefs were ultimately responsible for the assimilation and transformation of the Italian concepts.

The Emergence of French Sauces

François de La Varenne published in 1651 the renowned *Cuisinier François* (François, which was his first name, is also the old form of what is now the adjective *français*, which translates as French in English, and some have suggested a pun in the title of the book), the first French cookbook since the fourteenth-century *Viandier* of Taillevent. This book offers both old-style sauces made of vinegar, *verjus*, and bread crumbs and new-style sauces thickened with probably the first roux ever used in French cuisine. His roux is made of lard and flour, and the sauce is bound with bouillon; the flavorings differed from dish to dish, but onions and mushrooms were favored.

The list of French chefs who in the seventeenth century would have captured the fancy of our modern newswriters and food reviewers is long. Nothing has changed in the way people have opinions and dispense them and it is interesting to see how nobles, bourgeois, chefs, cooks, food merchants, and diners had as many opinions on food preparation and chefs as we seem to have nowadays. For some, La Varenne was the light of the seventeenth century; but, not only then but now quite a few practitioners of the art of cooking seem to prefer Pierre de Lune, a chef and contemporary of La Varenne, who still sweetened some of his sauces but also had some splendid ideas and may very well have been the first to prepare an early version of the classic brown sauce known as Spanish sauce. Pierre de Lune may have been born in Spain, a fact that has never been proved.

I feel compelled to give Pierre de Lune credit for his *paquet*, which we now call a bouquet garni (see page 65), which, said one of his detractors, he used "all the time." De Lune should be blessed for having thought of it, for without it, no stew can ever taste just right; Escoffier and all the chefs of the nineteenth and twentieth centuries certainly thought so and I would not dare to ever forget it myself.

The *coulis* used as a sauce became "*à la mode*" by the last quarter of the seventeenth century. At first it was a very tasty, but rough-textured concentrated stock made from one or several meats mixed, pounded in a mortar, returned to a saucepan, covered with bouillon, and simmered further. Its texture, however, was a problem. The first chef-writers to use this technique did not instruct to strain the concoction, so that it must have been grainy, somewhat like the ragù of Bologna. It would take a few more years for chefs to start passing *coulis* through an *étamine*—a very finely woven material such as silk or very finely woven horsehair mounted onto a circle of wood as are our drum sieves nowadays—before using it as a sauce or adding it to a *potage* to give it more body. We still use all kinds of *coulis* today, most made of vegetables and fruit, though, and what the eighteenth century called a *coulis* has been refined into an "essence" (see page 308).

As the eighteenth century dawned, François Massialot, a celebrated chef-writer, rose on the French culinary horizon. Massialot prepared *jus de veau* by cooking slices of veal in an earthenware pot sealed with a flour-and-water paste for two hours on low heat. But he also recommended something which has been very important for me as a modern cook: the preparation of essences (see pages 293–98).

Here is Massialot's formula for a ham essence, as he gives it in his book *Le Cuisinier Roial et Bourgeois* (*The Royal and Bourgeois Cook*), published in 1705. The ham Massialot used was what we call country ham in the United States in its cured uncooked state. If you want to prepare this essence, you can use the veal stock on page 219 instead of the old *jus de veau*, and obtain a very rich essence. The lemon and vinegar are here to cut the high salt of the ham. I have provided essential missing information in brackets:

ESSENCE OF HAM, TRANSLATED FROM MASSIALOT

Have some small slices of "raw" [country] ham, pound them well with a meat bat, lightly sear them in a sauteuse pan in a small amount of lard: put on the stove, toss in a little flour and let color. Once ham and flour have lightly browned, one adds some good *Jus de Veau*, a small bouquet of chives and fine herbs, (2) cloves, one clove of garlic, a few slices of lemon, a handful of chopped mushrooms, some chopped truffles, a few bread crusts and a small jigger of vinegar. When all this is cooked, strain carefully through a muslin, and store this *jus* in such a place as it will not boil anymore: it will be useful for all kinds of preparations containing ham.

Here is a recipe for a strained *coulis* from the book of Louis Liger, published in 1739 by Christian David in Paris, and called *Le Ménage des Champs et de la Ville ou Nouveau Cuisinier François* (*The Country and City Household or New French Cook*). Where Massialot used both flour and bread crusts to thicken the *coulis*, Liger twenty-four years later uses only bread crusts:

PARTRIDGE COULIS, TRANSLATED FROM LIGER

Take a partridge, roast it two thirds of the way; once roasted, pound it in a mortar together with the bands of fatback in which it was wrapped, a few truffles, mushrooms, melted lard, chives, fine herbs and bread crusts; once everything is pounded, add a spoonful* of veal *jus*, let simmer a little while, then strain through a muslin and use.

As you can see, the techniques of cooking show improvement over the medieval *grave*, especially in the taste. Abundant spices have been replaced by aromatic vegetables, which will give the *coulis* and essences concentrated texture and flavor but not necessarily clarity and translucency; also, the use of pork fat from lard or diced fresh brisket of pork is still prominent. In French *lard*, also called *lard frais*, is fresh unsalted, unsmoked brisket of pork; what we call lard in English is either *lard fondu* or *saindoux* in French. Our bacon is *lard fumé*, and the French equivalent of salt pork is *lard salé*.

Not yet owning a copy of either Vincent La Chapelle's or François Marin's books, I am unable to give examples of the works of these authors, which is too bad since Marin made essences reduced to the "quintessence," which means reduction of the stock to one fifth its original volume (for more details, refer to the technique of preparation for multiple essences on page

---

*The spoon Liger is talking about is a large tin ladle which I remember fondly hanging from one of the shelves of the hearth of my old friend Victoire in the Auvergne, way back in the thirties. Such ladles may have contained a half liter of stock, perhaps even more and were used also to ladle soup into the rimless, often round-bottomed country plates called *écuelles*, which fitted into the holes carved into thick farm wood tabletops. Such a sauce as cited above can, to this day, be tasted at the lovely old-fashioned Auberge Bressanne in Bourg-en-Bresse, where it is generously ladled upon Bresse chicken.

293). Adding aromatic vegetables to an essence while it reduces, as was practiced in the eighteenth century, would perhaps give you an idea of Marin's work.

The most prolific author of the eighteenth century was Menon, whose work, according to several historians, is quite inspired by Marin's *Dons de Comus* (*The Gifts of Comus*). Menon published a number of books, several of them addressing the chefs of wealthy houses, one written for the home cook. That last book, called *La Cuisinière Bourgeoise* (*The Bourgeois Cook*), was reedited many times between 1746 and 1845. I work from its 1774 Brussels edition and from a facsimile edition of the 1755 edition of *Les Petits Soupers de la Cour* (*The Small Suppers at the Royal Court*), received as a present from a dear student.

Menon's sauces are important for some of them are true precursors to the modern French/western classic sauces. For example, the formula for the *coulis général* in *Les Petits Soupers* still calls for some "slices of ham, a little fresh pork brisket, and a sufficient amount of round of veal for the quality and quantity of the *coulis* one would like to prepare"; all the aromatics are present plus a touch of spice. All these elements are sweated in a large saucepan until the *jus* has been extracted and is allowed to slightly brown at the bottom of the pot, so the *coulis*, says the author, will be a pretty "cinnamon color." The roux of flour and good butter is made directly over the caramelized meat juices in the bottom of the pan and the veal pieces, moistened with bouillon, so that we now have a sauce containing both pork fat and butter. The mixture simmers over a slow fire and is defatted from time to time. Two major modern technical steps are represented in this recipe: the use of butter in the roux and the defatting of the *coulis* while it cooks.

Though Menon does not give a formula for *coulis à la bourgeoise* in *La Cuisinière Bourgeoise*, he does so in *Les Petits Soupers de la Cour*, possibly to show the difference between the two styles of cuisine. Here is that *coulis à la bourgeoise*, which resembles a thoroughly modern preparation:

COULIS BOURGEOIS FROM MENON

Put in a saucepan a piece of butter with flour in the proportions which you will judge necessary for the quantity of *coulis* you wish to prepare; cook on the fire turning constantly until the flour is a pretty golden color; moisten with some bouillon, some *jus* (*de veau*) and a glass of white wine, a bouquet of parsley, chives, a clove of garlic, one bay leaf, thyme, basil, two cloves, a touch of nutmeg, a few mushrooms, salt, a bit of pepper. Cook one hour on low fire, defat and strain through a muslin; this *coulis* will be fat or lean depending on the bouillon you will use.

The need for fat or lean *coulis* can be explained by the fact that in deeply Catholic France, fat bouillons were prepared with meat stocks, lean bouillons for Fridays or meatless High Holidays with fish fumet or vegetable broths.

Notice how much simpler the bourgeois recipe is. It demonstrates also what is meant by *cuisine bourgeoise:* It is a way of cooking which is a mere simplification of the involved and too-rich style of the cuisine prepared for the upper classes, is much less expensive, and prepared twice as fast. I must insist on this fact, for too many authors have failed to understand that *cuisine bourgeoise* is not a provincial cuisine at all, but a simpler version of the classic French cuisine for upper middle class to middle class households, be they in Paris and its surroundings, in larger provincial cities, or in the well-to-do households of the countryside. The fact that the different provinces have mixed the techniques of the classic cuisine with the use of their local ingredients has probably caused this misunderstanding.

Menon refers to *coulis* containing a certain amount of pounded meats as *restaurants*, a word which within fifty years would have changed its meaning altogether to mean a restaurant as we know it today. (The first French "restaurant" was opened in Paris in 1765 on the rue des Poulies. Its owner, Monsieur Boulanger, served precisely rich bouillons to restore one's vitality. Above the entrance one could read in Latin: "Come to me if you are hungry, I shall restore your strength.") Menon's sauces have some of the same names they bear nowadays; here is the recipe for the *sauce à l'espagnole* in *La Cuisinière Bourgeoise* which you may want to compare with the Escoffier-style *espagnole* and the demi-glace recipes on pages 284 and 285; this is a direct translation from Menon's text:

SAUCE À L'ESPAGNOLE FROM MENON

It is prepared by putting some *coulis* into a saucepan with a good glass of white wine, as much bouillon, a bouquet of parsley, chives, two cloves garlic, two cloves, one half of a bay leaf, a pinch of ground coriander, two tablespoons of oil, one sliced onion, one carrot and half a parsnip. Bring to a boil and simmer on very low heat; then defatten and strain through a *tamis*. Season with a bit of salt and coarsely ground pepper. You can use this *coulis* for whatever you like.

One of Menon's sauce recipes in *La Cuisinière Bourgeoise* is particularly interesting because the author uses the juice of sorrel as a base; it shows that the "new" idea of using vegetable juices in contemporary sauces is not all that new at all (see more on this subject on page 310).

The twenty years that preceded the national cataclysm that was the French Revolution of 1789 were, so to say, empty of new culinary work. This situation might have been due in part to the difficult political, social, agricultural, and climatic conditions of the French kingdom from 1785 on. Eyewitness to these times, the Alsatian Baronne of Oberkirsch writes in her memoirs:

One dines at three in the afternoon and dinners have become so rapid, that gastronomes and raconteurs complain bitterly. It seems as if one would be in the greatest haste not to eat but to merely nourish oneself, then quickly run along. The oldest among us call this practice undignified; as for the cuisiniers they are in a quasi-insurrectional mood.

The fact that the only small culinary text published during the reign of Louis XVI came out in 1786 and was only an almanac containing 200 recipes may be read as a proof that minds had turned toward preoccupations other than those two national pastimes of France: good fare and refined cuisine.

The violence and excesses of the Revolution sent many of the "cuisiniers" into exile in foreign countries, where they followed their masters and would, by their mere presence either in London or in many German cities, spread the gospel of French cuisine. When the horrors of the Revolution and the Terror were over, some of these exiles, following an idea that had germinated shortly before the Revolution, opened establishments which continued to be called restaurants. This is how Beauvilliers, a chef who had emigrated to England, opened a restaurant called "The Great London Tavern," where he regaled French palates with *machepotettes* and vegetables "*à l'anglaise*." To know what that curious first dish was, simply pronounce mashed potatoes with a French accent. Beauvilliers's recipe for *sauce à l'espagnole*—possibly served on *machepotettes* as we serve gravy—is three times as long as Menon's and not half as good. His prize comment that "with the wine the sauce can turn sour overnight if not used completely during the day" shows the depth of ignorance of the relation of bacterial development to temperature in 1814.

The greatest reputation of the first third of the nineteenth century was bestowed upon the famous Carême, who was to practice his art in the *grandes maisons* of the Prince of Talleyrand-Périgord and later of the Tsar of Russia. Trained as a pastry chef, Carême established his reputation with his book *Le Pâtissier Royal Parisien* (*The French Pastry Chef*), published in Paris in 1815, the year of the defeat of Napoleon at Waterloo.

Carême was an extraordinary saucier, one who, after living through the disorders of the French Revolution and the wars of the Napoleonic Empire, insisted on observing again with care the distinctions between what is still known as *cuisine en maigre* (meatless cuisine) and *cuisine en gras*, containing meats and meat broths (in many parts of France the rules of abstinence from meats and meat products are still observed on Fridays and during Lent). When one reads Carême, the distinction between those two cuisines is clearly outlined and what we now call a fish velouté is called a *sauce espagnole en maigre* and made with generous quantities of whole fresh fish, most of which are not at our disposal anymore.

It was Carême who initiated the basic organization of sauces into categories (brown and white sauces), with a basic so-called mother sauce at the head of each category. The mother sauce of the brown sauces is the *espagnole* (brown roux and brown stocks). Any other brown sauce made by adding to *espagnole* either wine or aromatics or a combination of both and a certain amount of stock or veal *jus* and reducing all these ingredients together will become a "small" brown sauce. After Carême and for a good century, all good professional or well-to-do kitchens in France and, for that matter, in most developed countries in Europe, would keep an "inexhaustible" supply of *espagnole* to use as a base for the preparation of the many derivative small brown sauces.

The very same system is used for the white sauces, the velouté (white roux and white stock) or the *béchamel* (white roux and milk or cream) being the mother sauce of all white sauces.

This system existed all through the nineteenth century, and was finally codified perfectly by Auguste Escoffier, as you will see later.

Carême's *sauce espagnole en gras* as translated into English by William Hall (*French Cookery*, A. Carême, London: John Murray, Albemarle Street, 1836) is thirty-one lines long, and a tight little discourse which leaves the modern cook somewhat breathless at the enormous amount of work the master used to go through to produce a good sauce on an old-fashioned stove. Carême used a technique known as *tombage à glace,* in which he covered two slices of lean ham, a whole round of veal, and two partridges with excellent veal stock and let the stock reduce to the point of half glaze, then cut the meats into pieces, covered the pot, and steamed the meat over the glaze "so the gravy of the meats mixes with the glaze." Then, he let this cook again until it returned to the glaze stage. Having prethickened "consommé or beef stock with roux" he poured it over the meats and let the preparation simmer another hour and a half, skimming off fat (and probably also flour proteins) as the sauce simmered. Finally, the sauce was brought to perfection by being passed through a *tamis*.

Dedicated cook that I am, I always end up intellectually exhausted when reading Carême, for he communicates his passion and eagerness at doing great work very clearly and efficiently. At the same time I feel very sorry that that wonderful culinary artist could not benefit from our wonderful modern technical means of cooking.

If you feel like spending a little time in your kitchen with Carême, here is my direct translation of his recipe for a financière sauce, where the brown-tinged *espagnole* sauce clearly assumes its role as the basic or so-called mother sauce as explained above.

From Carême's time on, the *espagnole* sauce became a true work of art, so shiny after being completely skimmed of all fat, flour protein, and fiber traces, that I remember being instructed to skim "until the sauce could be used as a mirror"; this in-depth work of clarification by skimming and straining several times is reflected in the French word *travaillée*—or crafted—often used by Carême.

This financière sauce was so expensive that it is affordable only to a financier, hence its name. In the translation, the comments in brackets are mine. All the techniques which enter into the making and perfecting of a *grande sauce,* a perfectly prepared sauce,

- Proper blending of a wine-and-aromatics reduction with a rich stock and the same volume of finished *espagnole,*
- Proper reduction and skimming of the mixture, and
- Proper tying of the basic taste of the sauce to that of the meat which it will accompany,

are demonstrated in the recipe that follows.

CARÊME'S FINANCIÈRE SAUCE

Put in a saucepan, some minced lean ham, a pinch of mignonette [see page 56], a bit of thyme and bay leaf, mushroom and truffle trimmings and two glasses of dry Madeira; bring to a boil and turn down to a simmer, add 2 ladlesful each of consommé and finished and skimmed [here Carême writes *travaillée*] *espagnole.* When this sauce has reduced by one half, pass it through a muslin, then put it back on the fire adding half a glass of Madeira; reduce to the correct consistency. After which you pour the sauce [into a container and keep it] in a bain-marie.

It is important to observe that in this sauce, being prepared for a dish of venison "*à la financière,*" one should omit the poultry consommé and replace it by a "fumet" [double stock made by cooking game trimmings and bones in regular stock] of the game it will be saucing.

This sauce as prepared here reflects the abundance of workers in a time when apprentices were literally "a dime a dozen" and the poor children, having for the most part no home to go back to at night, more often than not slept on the lower shelf of the large kitchen worktables. If this sauce appears time-consuming and complicated, it is even more important to realize that the work for this dish does not stop at cooking the meat and saucing it. *Quenelles* of the proper composition to blend with the game were made, small mushroom caps turned and *étuvéed,* cockscombs and kidneys, each requiring special care, cleaned and cooked, truffles smothered in stock, and blanched olives pitted.

When Carême passed away in 1833, his employer of many years, the Prince de Talleyrand, wrote to a friend "Carême passed away today, consumed by the flame of his genius and the fires of his stoves." He was only forty-nine; his student Plumerey finished the books he left uncompleted at his death.

Through the remainder of the nineteenth century, the sauce techniques of Carême were more or less respected and practiced. Chef Jules Gouffé, who had been his apprentice, seems to have been the most faithful to his techniques in the preparation of the mother sauces. But in the 1867 edition of his *Livre de Cuisine,* besides an *espagnole* still very visibly influenced by Carême, he published also a "*Jus de Veau* for the Home," which heralded a simplification of Carême's work and resembles very much the modern brown veal stock, adding at the end of the recipe: "Should one have trimmings of beef, rack of veal and lamb, one should add them to the *jus de veau*." This is a good idea that you will find used, if in a slightly different manner, in the modern essences explained on pages 293–98.

I was particularly lucky in having been able to work when I was younger with a woman who had apprenticed in the kitchen of a castle under the tutelage of one of the last of Carême's students. I have often thought in retrospect of her incredibly perfect techniques, and after having read thousands of pages on classic French cuisine, I realize that the wonderful influence on her work was Carême's, even if he had reached her, so to say, "secondhand" only.

For most of the chefs of my generation, the master, however, remains Auguste Escoffier who, born in 1847, died only in 1935, six years after Paul Bocuse was born. His name was constantly cited in my family; somewhere in one of my many cookery books hides an old yellowed newspaper cutout, coming probably from my grandfather whose profession as a master coppersmith brought him into all the kitchens of Paris to care for copper pots and pans. It describes the banquet given by President Herriot in 1928 in honor of Escoffier receiving the Legion of Honor.

The difference of vision between Carême and Escoffier is very well explained in the four successive introductions of Escoffier's *Le Guide Culinaire*, which any modern cook should read. Carême worked in *grandes maisons*, Escoffier in restaurants and in luxury hotels; each of them knew a different world with different preoccupations. These preoccupations resulted in changes in the techniques of cooking and especially sauce making.

With Carême we were still catching a glimpse of the pre-1789 world; with Escoffier, we are solidly grounded in a new world order, a world that has changed from horse-drawn carriages to automobiles, which has known social unrest and brought on social reforms and in which capitalism has taken on a definitely modern and aggressive form. The way Escoffier finally organized the world of classic sauces reflects the technical changes that came to the kitchen with the Industrial Revolution.

His classification of sauces, in which he follows the groundwork of Carême, is clear and simple and should be read by every present-day cook in the words of the master himself. All texts of the successive editions of his *Le Guide Culinaire* are available, some for sale in the original French or in diverse English translations. The best edition to read for modern cooks is the 1927 French edition. For those who would find the professional texts all too long and drawn-out, the home version Escoffier wrote under the title *Ma Cuisine* is far more accessible.

The relationship between Escoffier and capitalist hotel owner César Ritz gave him an extraordinary visibility that his contemporaries did not enjoy, although they were, without a doubt, as proficient in the kitchen as he was.

Prosper Montagné especially comes to mind as a perfect professional, acknowledging visibly his debt to Carême in his *Grand Livre de la Cuisine*, written in cooperation with Prosper Salles.

Both Escoffier and Montagné used the very descriptive word *fonds* when writing about what we call a stock nowadays. Both Escoffier and Montagné, besides using the *espagnole*, velouté, and *béchamel* as mother sauces, also used the lighter *fonds de veau lié* as described on page 292 and the *fonds de veau tomaté* (with tomatoes added), which many of my French colleagues still use nowadays. Both added tomato puree, well reduced to lessen the acidity of the fruit, to their basic *espagnole*.

The great "simplifier" chef of the early to mid-twentieth century was Henri Paul Pellaprat, who taught at the famous Cordon Bleu School of Cookery in Paris. He still observed the important rules, which were respected scrupulously by most of his apprentices and students up to 1939.

During the World War II years (1939 to 1945), French chefs had the worst of challenges for the French system of cuisine to survive the six long years that food shortages made plain good food a rarity. Great food in those days was nonexistent for what I always called regular people. The psychological effects of the war were responsible for what I remember as a fabulous resurgence of French cuisine from 1945 through 1960. Wow! Did everything taste and look good and were the sauces that we had missed so much ever so grand! . . . or were they really? So why the great changes of the 1960s? In the late sixties "modern cuisine" with its simplified sauces arrived and with it came a gigantic clash of styles, which some consider a breakthrough and others a disaster.

The truth, as usual, probably lies in between. Let us see what the world of sauces is like nowadays in modern France and America and decide each for ourselves what we like best.

French and Western Sauces in the Twentieth Century

There is a difference between a gravy and a sauce, although many cooks tend not to pay attention to this detail.

A gravy can be made two ways:

1. An abundant gravy usually results from the liquid in which a meat is pot roasted or braised; more often than not, it must be reduced to concentrate its taste, and since reduction gives such gravies the texture of a sauce, most people will use the terms *gravy* and *sauce* interchangeably.
2. When birds and roasts are oven roasted and steaks, chops, escalopes, cutlets, or medallions of any meat are panfried, a concentrated gravy builds at

the bottom of the roasting or frying pan. After removing the fat from the pan, these concentrated, extremely browned juices are *deglazed,* which consists of diluting the dehydrated and partly solidified meat drippings with stock, wine, or water, reducing a bit, and seasoning properly to obtain maximum good taste.

The gravies of roasted, pan-roasted, and panfried meats acquire their deep brown color through a chemical reaction known as the Maillard reaction, Maillard being the name of the French scientist who first understood and explained the reaction. To put it simply, this reaction occurs among proteins, amino acids, and their products as well as various sugars. At the same time, the sugars caramelize as they cook and the mixture, Maillard reaction plus caramelization, teams up to give a great combination of color and aroma in the gravy.

As you will see in other chapters, the same reaction can happen in other foods such as bread (see page 1034). For more detailed explanations of this reaction, see the bibliography under Food Chemistry and Food Science.

Sauces are prepared differently. A basic sauce, also called a mother sauce, is made from a stock or broth that has been thickened and flavored and usually garnishes a piece of meat or, sometimes, vegetables. Brown sauces are prepared with brown stocks and white sauces with white stock or milk. Often sauces for vegetables are prepared with a mixture of vegetable broth and milk or cream.

Any good cook, of any western nationality, will finish any white or brown sauce by adding to it the "deglazing" of any roast, steak, chop, or other dry-cooked piece of meat, and perhaps a pat of butter, herbs, mustard, reduced wine, cream, etc., thus transforming the basic sauce into a "small sauce" and tying the taste of the particular meat prepared to the sauce that accompanies it. Here are two examples:

1. A beef steak has been panfried, the fat is discarded, the dehydrated meat drippings at the bottom of the pan are "deglazed" with brown stock, reduced by two thirds, and added to enough *espagnole* sauce or enough excellent reduced veal stock. The small sauce obtained acquires the depth of taste of the beef and relates better to the steak than plain thickened veal stock or *espagnole* sauce alone would.
2. A beautiful veal chop has been panfried. The fat is discarded, the pan deglazed with veal stock and a dash of sherry; the deglazing is added to the proper amount of any cream sauce and the sauce becomes better related to the piece of meat it will be saucing.

The better the liquid used to make a sauce and/or to deglaze a pan, and the tastier the flavorings added to it, the more flavorful the sauce or gravy will be.

- The different liquids used to make brown sauces and deglaze brown gravies vary from plain water to brown stocks and/or broths made from poultry, veal, beef, lamb, or any other meat such as game and venison.
- Those used to prepare white sauces range from water to white stock made from poultry or veal, to milk of any butterfat content, and occasionally to light cream.

In all cases, the texture of the stock as well as its depth of flavor affects the final taste of the basic sauce. The difference between a delicious sauce and an indifferent or even unpleasant one resides also in the plain and simple *skill* of the cook. The majority of people who complain about "overly rich French sauces" have probably never tasted a truly beautifully crafted sauce, nicely textured, seasoned with precision to accent the meat and the wine served with it, and dispensed on the plate in the proper small quantity that will just enhance and season the meat, not send it and its accompanying vegetables swimming all over the plate.

Thickeners for Gravies and Sauces

Sauces and gravies are thickened or, in culinary jargon, *bound* in several ways:

- With pure starches such as potato starch, cornstarch, or arrowroot
- With plain flour, as in the basic American roast beef gravy,
- With a roux, a mixture consisting of flour cooked in a fat such as butter, oil, or any other animal or vegetable fat
- With reduced heavy cream blended with reduced meat broth or gravy, or vegetable juices; such sauces often cover pasta offerings (see page 295 for important nutritional details on such sauces)
- Without starch or flour, but rather by plain and simple reduction of meat stock, sometimes followed by enrichment with a fat such as butter, or a natural or flavored oil
- Without starch or flour, using a reduction of a pure acid, such as lemon juice or vinegar, or a reduction of an acid and fish or meat broth, thickened with an addition of butter
- With lightly cooked proteins such as egg yolks

Each of these thickening agents results in a different consistency, texture, appearance, and taste and is used on different types of foods, each adapted to its texture.

Neutral Sauces

Another kind of sauce is the neutral sauce, which is prepared without meat or meat stock. All the meatless tomato sauces and the presently extensively used sauces made with reduced vegetable juices, as well as all the chutneys and related vegetable-based sauces of Far Eastern and American origin belong in this category (see pages 308–14).

Starch-Bound Sauces

I will explain the principles of starch-bound sauces as simply as possible; I am aware that some scientists may think my approach too simplistic, but my goal is for everyone with a high school education, consequently with a very simple background in chemistry, to understand what approximately happens in a pot when one binds a liquid with a starch to make a sauce. Understanding what one is doing and how chemical elements behave as a result of one's manner of working can save a lot of money wasted on failed dishes that can be put to otherwise good use. In home economics as well as in restaurant economics, there are no small savings; every little bit saved through good understanding of the work is money put in the bank. Besides, it is much more interesting being a cook who tries to figure out "what happens" rather than follows a recipe blindly; it provides wonderful exercise for the brain.

A starch can be used to bind sauces because, when mixed with a liquid and subsequently heated, the mixture acquires a gellike texture, which is pleasant and fills the mouth better than the pure liquid.

As an exercise, mix 2 tablespoons cornstarch with 1 cup cold water without heating it. The starch will absorb some of the water; other than that, no further change will occur, and within 30 minutes the total amount of starch in suspension in the liquid will have settled to the bottom of its container.

If, continuing the exercise above, you stir the cornstarch back into its water, empty the mixture into a saucepan, and heat it gradually, stirring constantly, the starch granules will gradually swell. A starch may absorb 300 percent of its own weight in water by the time its temperature reaches 60°F and 1,000 percent by the time it reaches 70°F. The starch granules will swell still more, approaching a maximal swelling capacity of some 25 times its own weight. As the heat continues to increase, the water continues to be absorbed and the swelling of the starch granules increases, until the granules rupture, releasing some of their starch molecules. As soon as they are released, these starches increase the viscosity of the liquid as they bind more of the water.

The cooked starch paste now consists of large swollen granules in suspension in hot water, in which molecules of starches are dispersed, which themselves have bound with some of the water. The thickening is due to the fact that the water has been trapped in the starch matrix and/or bound by the granules and the starch and is no longer able to flow freely. The liquid is now said to have been thickened.

Different degrees of thickening of such cooked starch-liquid mixtures can be obtained after cooking, depending on the kind of starch and the amount of it used as well as the amount of liquid used. If the mixture is still liquid it is called a *sol* and will be used as a sauce most of the time. If the paste obtained is thickish, the mixture is a *gel* and will be used mostly as a pudding or the base for a soufflé (see pages 173–74).

Thickening Starch-Bound Sauces: The Slurry

Starch-bound sauces, due to the varying degree of stability of the starch used, should be thickened just before serving; they present no major timing problem for the cook since they thicken within seconds.

Cornstarch, potato starch, and arrowroot are usually called pure starches since they contain very little or no proteins at all. The opacity of a starch-bound sauce reflects the amount of protein the starch contains. For example, cornstarch contains more proteins than potato starch and arrowroot and as a result produces more stable but also more opaque sauces than potato starch or arrowroot.

The best way to thicken a sauce with any of these starches is to separate the starch granules by dispersing them in a small amount of the cold liquid, then adding this mixture (known as a slurry) while stirring constantly, to the *simmering*—not boiling—remainder of the total amount of liquid needed to prepare the sauce. Constant stirring ensures an even swelling of the granules and prevents them from sticking to one another and making lumps. Once the thickening has happened, stir gently. Any vigorous whisking will cause the swollen starch granules to break and the sauce to lose its thickened consistency. Starch slurries are popular in modern cuisine because they thicken sauces in a matter of minutes with a minimum amount of work.

CHANGES OF TEXTURE

It has been my personal experience over many years of cooking that both a sol and a gel may, if heated too long or too hard too fast, never thicken properly or begin to liquefy again, especially if an acid (tomato or lemon juice, for example) has been added before the gel has finished forming. The mixture remains liquid even upon cooling and acquires a sweet taste, which means that the starch molecules have reacted with water and have broken down into smaller starchlike units and various sugars, some of which are soluble in water. Adding lemon or another acid juice or liquid as well as tomato products off the heat to a starch-bound sauce immediately after it has completely thickened will minimize this problem.

A starch and/or flour sol may also lose its thickness—and this is much less well known or recognized—in the presence of egg yolks which have not been cooked at a high enough temperature to destroy the enzymes they contain (see page 281). Like sauces made with acids, starch-bound sauces made with egg yolks require special care (see the techniques of the liaison, on page 281).

A starch-bound sauce that has undergone such liquefaction as described above will taste sweetish and no amount of salt and/or acid added to it will ever be able to fix its taste for the best. It has also been my personal experience that once a starch-bound sauce has liquefied upon standing, the only way to rethicken it is to change the starch, using potato starch, for example, if the starch originally used was cornstarch or vice versa. If the same starch is used for rethickening the sauce, it seems that the sauce will, on standing and waiting to be served, turn soupy again. I have discussed this problem with several scientists who did not seem to understand how this could happen. But, I can assure all cooks, this unpleasant little adventure having happened to me several times through years and years of sauce making, that I tried everything I could think of to repair the damage and changing the starch was the only positive and stable solution.

Stir starch-bound thick sauces with a wooden spoon preferably. In the making of thicker sauces used as a base for soufflés, the wires of any whisk will shear through the gel and liquefy it just as you are ready to use it. Letting the gel stand will allow it to reform in about fifteen minutes, but you will lose time that is not available. A gel that has been liquefied by whisking with a wire whisk is called a *thixothropic gel*. Be aware of the difference between a hydrolyzed sol or gel which does not rethicken unless one recooks it with a different starch and a thixothropic gel which results from hard whisking and will reform on standing and cooling.

BASIC PROPORTIONS OF STARCH TO LIQUID;
AVERAGE THICKENING TEMPERATURES

The thickening power of each and every starch will show slight variations from brand to brand and from package to package, but the approximate proportions to thicken one cup of liquid are indicated below. The temperature at which starches gelatinize varies from 138° to 176°F.

Sauce Consistency	Cornstarch	Potato Starch	Arrowroot
Thin	2 teaspoons	1¼ teaspoons	1 teaspoon
Medium	1½ tablespoons	2½ teaspoons	2 teaspoons
Thick	2½ tablespoons	1⅓ tablespoons	3 teaspoons

THE THICKENING EFFECT OF COOLING

To fully understand the following paragraph, bear in mind that any liquid other than plain water (stock, broth, etc.) used to prepare a starch-bound sauce contains a large percentage of water.

The cooling of starch-bound sols or gels is accompanied by a visible thickening. This thickening is called retrogradation and happens as the starch molecules rebond to one another and to the swollen starches of the outer edges of the starch granules, creating a network. As this occurs, water fills the network formed between the blocks of cooled starches and the sides of the vessel that contains it. If a starch sol or gel has been frozen, this water is turned into ice crystals which, as the sol or gel defrosts, seeps from the interstices. This squeezing of water out of a sol or gel is called syneresis. For the water to reassociate with the starch, the defrosted gel must be brought back to a boil.

A special technique must be applied to reheat cold starch-bound sauces in any quantity. Start by reheating a large tablespoonful of the sauce on very low heat; when it is warm, not hot, gradually stir in the remainder of the sauce, by spoonfuls at a time until the total volume of the sauce is smooth and lukewarm. Finish warming up very gradually, stirring constantly and gently until the sauce is warm, then hot, then finally reboils. Gradual reheating will bring the sauce back to its original sol or gel texture.

You may wonder why commercial products containing starch sols and gels remain bound very nicely when reheated according to the directions on the package. It is simply because the manufacturers use special starches known as "modified-cross-linked" starches, which have been chemically modified to reheat at a relatively high temperature without going into syneresis and/or resist hydrolysis with acids. For more information on this subject, see the bibliography on page 1175.

Flour-Bound Sauces

Flours are mixtures of starches, proteins, and fibrous materials such as bran and other parts of the wheat kernel's endosperm. While cooking in sauces, flours will behave partly as any starch will, that is to gelatinize, but their proteins will also be coagulated by the heat and turn the sauces opaque. Different flours will thicken differently, depending on their ratios of starches and proteins. Cake flour, the richest in starches, will thicken relatively rapidly and produce a clearer sauce than pastry flour, which in turn will produce a clearer sauce than all-purpose flour. Bread flour should not be used for thickening a sauce because it contains strong gluten-forming proteins which result in a gummy and unpleasant texture. All-purpose flour, the easiest to buy, is, to my personal taste, the best, provided the sauce is well "finished," that is skimmed of all proteins prior to serving.

In the making of a regular all-American roast beef gravy, raw unsifted flour is "slurried" with cold water or cold broth and added to the roasting pan to deglaze it, so that the pan is deglazed at the same time as the slurry of flour thickens. The resulting gravy is robust and not especially refined and all cooks, young and old, are familiar with its texture and taste.

Thickening with a Roux

It is better when using flour to use it in the form of a roux, which is a cooked mixture of fat and flour. Depending on how long the roux cooks, it takes on more or less coloration and is called a *white, golden*, or *brown roux*.

Making a roux has a purpose. If you taste a bit of raw flour, you will notice how sour, almost bitter, your palate becomes. The precooking of the flour in fat removes that unpleasant taste, replacing it with a pleasant toasted flavor; also it initiates the swelling of the starch granules in fats such as butter which contains 20 percent water. It also deactivates the many enzymes present in the flour, which might hydrolyze the starch when the liquid is added, thinning the sauce.

Cooking a roux is a more delicate process than is often realized. It should be done over medium and very even heat. If the fat is too hot, it will overtoast and shrink the starch granules, which will harden and lose their ability to absorb water. A sauce made with an overcooked roux thickens half as much as expected or even barely; a white sauce in these conditions will remain thin, though still look palatable, but a brown sauce will hardly bind at all and the burned starch granules will be seen settling at the bottom of the container as the sauce stands.

COOKING A WHITE OR GOLDEN ROUX

Use a heavy-bottomed pot that carries heat evenly (copper, enameled cast-iron, copper-dressed-bottom saucepan). If you own only a thin saucepan, you must place a heat tamer (see page 194) between the heat and the saucepan. Some people use a double boiler, which is also a possibility.

Heat the fat, preferably butter, until the foam recedes; you can also use clarified butter or, for a controlled-fat diet, corn or sunflower oil. When using any oil which can heat to high temperatures, and can damage the flour, heat it over moderate heat.

Add the unsifted flour *off the heat*; mix well and return the pot to medium-low heat, stirring occasionally, for a suitable length of time, using the chart below as a guideline. A white roux looks straw yellow, a golden roux, golden yellow.

Amounts		Cooking Time	
Fat/Oil	Flour	White Roux	Golden Roux
2 tablespoons	2 tablespoons	2 minutes	4 minutes
3 tablespoons	3 tablespoons	3 minutes	6 minutes
¼ cup	¼ cup	4 minutes	8 minutes
½ cup	½ cup	8 minutes	12 minutes

COOKING A BROWN ROUX

A heavy-bottomed pot is a must, since a flame tamer of any kind will not prevent the flour from burning in a thin saucepan when set over the heat for as long as this will be. A black or an enameled cast-iron pot gives the best results. For larger quantities, start the cooking on the stove and finish it in a 275°F oven; stir often during the last stages of cooking. Clarified butter results in a much better tasting sauce, for the milk solids in the butter have been removed and do not burn as the roux cooks at length.

It is essential that you understand what is going to happen. In order to obtain a nice hazelnut brown color, you need to cook the flour deeply, and in doing so you are going to destroy three quarters of its thickening power. So that you do not burn the whole amount of flour, leaving shrunken, deep-toasted starch cells that cannot absorb liquid anymore, it is essential that you proceed very slowly. The proportions and cooking times are as follows:

Fat/Oil	Flour	Cooking Time
¼ cup	3 tablespoons	10 minutes
7 tablespoons	6 tablespoons	15 minutes
½ cup	½ cup	15 minutes on the stove, plus 5 minutes in the oven

ADDING LIQUID TO A ROUX

The amounts of liquid necessary to prepare the basic flour-bound sauces appear in the section on each sauce. What follows is important information about adding liquid to a roux.

Have the liquid very hot. *As soon as the roux is cooked, remove the saucepan from the heat* and whisk half the hot liquid into the hot roux until the mixture is homogeneous. It will thicken immediately. Whisk in the remainder of the liquid until smooth. Whisking *hot* liquid into a *hot* roux ensures constant temperature for the starch granules which have begun to swell and gelatinize. Return the mixture to the heat and, now using a wooden spoon, bring to a boil, stirring constantly. Stirring prevents the formation of lumps in the sauce, as well as precipitation of the not fully swelled starch cells to the bottom of the pot where they can burn; finally, it cools the progressively thickening starch sol by introducing some air into it, so that its granules are submitted as gradually as possible to the increase of temperature, which finally results in the sauce boiling.

SKIMMING A FLOUR-BOUND SAUCE

IN A SAUCE MADE WITH STOCK OR BROTH As soon as a stock-based flour-bound sauce boils, a skin forms at its surface; the skin thickens as the sauce simmers and becomes scum. This scum is made of some of the proteins and fibers contained in the flour. Below the scum is a layer of liquid fat;

it is the butter, fat, or oil used to prepare the roux; first thrown into emulsion in the sauce by the strong boiling motion, it now breaks out of emulsion as the sauce slowly simmers, and accumulates in a large puddle, under the scum.

The immediate reaction of a brand-new cook will be to stir both scum and fat back into the sauce, which is the worst thing to do, for this is precisely what results in one of those heavy sauces responsible for people thinking that classic sauces are heavy, fat, and unhealthy. Unskimmed sauces have a gummy texture and appear greasy and dirty, and damage the properly prepared foods they accompany.

Using the long "belly" side, *not the tip* of a large sauce spoon, and starting from the center of the pot out toward its sides, lift both scum and fat and discard both if you want or, if you have used butter, add it to a pot in which you have poured some fat-free tomato puree or tomato sauce of your choice and simmer all this together while you finish your sauce. The result is two sauces at once:

- A high-class flour-bound sauce that is lean, appealing, and delicious, and
- A tomato sauce for spaghetti or any pasta that tastes awfully good if not looking really great, and costs very little, since the butter will have been used twice, which is an economy of material at home and in a restaurant. People have raved about such tomato sauces in my restaurants.

IN A SAUCE MADE WITH MILK OR CREAM Flour-bound sauces made with milk or cream need not and cannot be skimmed, because the scum and fat are trapped in the very viscous milky sol and cannot be disassociated from it.

FREEZING COOKED ROUX

Roux may, if desired, be prepared in bulk and frozen, although this practice does not save that much time. If you find it useful, make a roux with 1 cup clarified butter and 1 cup unsifted flour, and cook to the degree of coloration desired.

Pour the finished roux into an 8-inch-square cake pan. Cool and freeze in a perfectly horizontal position to obtain even thickness throughout the pan. When solid, cut into 16 equal-size squares, and store these in a freezer bag in the freezer. Each square has the thickening power of 1 tablespoon flour. Before using frozen roux, let it defrost completely in the same pot where you plan to warm it and reheat it very gently.

In larger quantities, proceed by weight; for example, if you use 1¼ pounds butter to each pound of flour, you will obtain 2¼ pounds of roux. Poured into an 8-inch-square pan, the roux will solidify when frozen; it then can be cut into 16 equal pats of mixture, each containing 2 ounces of flour.

Flour-bound sauces may be frozen. As I mentioned earlier, as they defrost to room temperature, syneresis, or the weeping of water out of the starch sol, occurs, and the sauce looks curdled. Empty a small amount of the sauce into a pan, reheat it slowly, stirring, and gradually add more of the sauce; bring slowly to the boiling point while stirring well with a wooden spoon to restore the sauce to its normal consistency.

Classic Flour-Bound Mother Sauces

These are the basic sauces that were prepared on a daily basis from the time of Carême on through the nineteenth and twentieth centuries until about 1970; these sauces were last codified and listed for commercial as well as home use by Auguste Escoffier. Adding diverse flavorings to a mother sauce, one can obtain a world of small sauces.

As those readers who have used the first edition of this book will find out, the many variations of the mother sauces which were offered in it can be abandoned nowadays, since most represent unnecessary simplifications. In short, if any chef or cook is going to prepare flour-bound sauces at this stage of our culinary history, these sauces should reflect the very best of existing techniques, not oversimplified shortcut methods resulting in average to poor sauces.

Classic White Sauces

The basic or "mother" white sauces are the veloutés and the *béchamel*. Before you start preparing either of them, please read all the material concerning the theory of starch- and flour-bound sauces on pages 268–75, if you have not already done so.

VELOUTÉS

The name *velouté*, a French adjective meaning "possessing the texture of velvet," is given to any sauce made with white roux plus a classic white stock, whichever white stock you choose to prepare it with: white poultry stock, white veal stock, a mixture of both, the secondary stock on page 220, or a fish fumet (see page 543). As a result, one can make a velouté of chicken, veal, turkey, or fish, depending on the stock used.

Veloutés are made with different consistencies, using the following proportions of unsifted unbleached all-purpose flour to stock:

Consistency	Amounts (Home Use)	Amounts (Professional Use)
Thin, for cream soups	1 tablespoon flour per 1 cup stock	1 ounce flour per 1 quart stock
Medium, for sauces	1½ tablespoons flour per 1 cup stock	1½ ounces flour per 1 quart stock
Thick, for soufflé bases	¼ cup flour per 1 cup stock	4 ounces flour per 1 quart stock

Any velouté may be made in larger quantity and frozen, or it may be made on the spot, as needed. If you decide on making velouté in bulk, do so using the proportions for sauces and following the recipe below. The skimming of a velouté is an absolute necessity if one wishes to obtain the very best taste, texture, and appearance.

Basic Velouté

FFR — 2½ QUARTS MEDIUM TEXTURE

1 cup butter, preferably unsalted

1 cup unsifted unbleached all-purpose flour

3 quarts hot classic white stock of your choice, or Secondary Stock (page 220), or fish fumet (page 543)

1 cup chopped mushroom stems

Small bouquet garni

4 white peppercorns

2 cups classic white stock of your choice, at room temperature

Make a white roux with the butter and flour (see page 272), cooking 10 to 12 minutes. Off the heat, whisk in the 3 quarts of hot stock in two separate additions. Bring back to a boil over medium heat, stirring constantly with a wooden spoon. Add the mushrooms, bouquet garni, and peppercorns. Simmer for 30 minutes, skimming 2 to 3 times.

Add the 2 cups room temperature stock and, without stirring, bring to a boil again. Turn down to a simmer, skimming again at regular intervals until totally fat- and scum-free. Let the velouté reduce to the consistency you personally prefer. Strain through a China cap into 1½-cup freezer containers. Cool to 140°F, then to room temperature in a cold water bath; seal well and immediately freeze or refrigerate. Will keep refrigerated, 2 days; frozen, 3 months.

BÉCHAMELLE OR BÉCHAMEL

The name of this sauce has two origins, depending on whether one is an Italian or a French citizen.

Here is the Italian explanation as given to me so nicely by my pleasant colleague Giuliano Bugialli. The Italian word *balsamo* means balm. As a soothing balm—we would nowadays say a mask—for the tender skin of their lovely faces, genteel Italian ladies of the fifteenth century made a *balsamo* with milk, flour, and perhaps also some butter; hence the name given to the Italian white sauce made with butter, flour, and milk: *balsamella*.

The white sauce which became the *béchamelle* for the French was prepared approximately as the modern Italian *balsamella* still is nowadays, using white roux plus scalded milk.

French-born as I am, I have no difficulty giving the Italians credit for having created that white milk sauce. But, if there is one thing that characterizes most French cooks (and I take the blame personally for having this trait myself), it is that they always want to rearrange original ideas for food preparations to make them taste the way they would personally prefer them to taste and the way they think they would appeal to the French palate.

There were some milk sauces in the cookery of the Middle Ages (refer to the information on the Jance on page 252), but the French *béchamel* sauce was created in the seventeenth century; legend has it that it was the high wire financier Louis de Béchameil (or Béchamel), secretary or steward to Louis XIV—in America we would say he was the food and beverage manager(!)—who "created" the sauce that now carries his name, by either adding cream to a velouté or, as La Varenne and Bonnefons indicate, making the sauce with sautéed shallots, a white roux, and fresh cream, most probably the lighter, thin fleurette-type cream. The existence of a related sauce in France before Béchameil is reflected in the terse comment of the Duke d'Escars, which I can only hope to be authentic. Monsieur le Duc, up in years and irritated at the somewhat pompous Béchameil exclaimed: "How lucky that little Béchameil. I was making minced chicken in cream sauce twenty years before he was born, but never was lucky enough to give my name to any sauce." Both duke and financier achieved fame and notoriety by way of a sauce.

In France, at the present time, the name *béchamel* is used to refer to white sauce although there are cooks who still make the distinction between the milk-based *béchamelle* and the cream-based *béchamel*. The sauce is made with a salpicon of aromatic vegetables sautéed in butter over which flour is sprinkled, then cooked into a white roux. The liquid used is scalded milk, which makes the sauce a descendant of the Italian *balsamella,* and also a first cousin to the American cream sauce, only the presence of aromatic vegetables distinguishing the French sauce from them. Up until fifty years ago, I remember my mother flavoring a *béchamel* with veal scraps and a salpicon of vegetables (see page 16); in most modern European (non-French) cookery books, these have been replaced by a lonely little onion and a small dash of nutmeg.

Because it requires no skimming and is relatively easy to make, *béchamel* is still used quite extensively in modern cuisine: in macaroni and cheese, for example, in America, in dishes of lasagne in Italy, in moussaka in Greece, in some of the delicious Spanish tapas, and as a base for many a good soufflé.

A good *béchamel* properly prepared must be flavorful and always contain that salpicon of vegetables and/or that dash of nutmeg which makes it palatable; otherwise, its taste is certainly not very assertive. Here are the three possible textures for the sauce, as well as the respective quantities of ingredients required for each of them.

Consistency	Amounts
Thin, for cream soups and creamed vegetables	2 teaspoons to 1 tablespoon flour per cup milk
Medium, for sauces	4 to 4½ teaspoons flour per cup milk
Thick, for soufflés	3 to 4 tablespoons flour per cup milk

Béchamel

FFR–FOR 1 QUART

1 small yellow onion, peeled

1 small carrot, peeled

⅓ celery rib

½ cup unsalted butter

⅓ cup unsifted unbleached all-purpose flour

4½ cups milk of your choice, scalded

Salt

Pepper from the mill

Good pinch of freshly grated nutmeg

Small bouquet garni

FOR 5 QUARTS

2 large yellow onions, peeled

2 large carrots, peeled

1½ celery ribs

2½ cups unsalted butter

2¼ cups unsifted unbleached all-purpose flour

6 quarts milk of your choice, scalded

Salt

Pepper from the mill

½ teaspoon freshly grated nutmeg

Large bunch parsley stems

Large sprig fresh thyme

2 small Turkish bay leaves

Cut the vegetables into a salpicon (see page 16). Heat the butter in a large saucepan over medium heat until the foam subsides. Add the vegetables and sauté until the onions are translucent. Off the heat, stir in the flour, then cook 5 to 7 minutes (10 to 12 for the larger recipe), stirring occasionally. Off the heat, gradually whisk in the scalded milk. Bring back to a boil, stirring with a wooden spoon or paddle; add salt, pepper, and nutmeg to taste, and the bouquet garni, or all the herbs for the larger recipe. Simmer for 35 minutes for the small recipe and 45 for the larger one. Strain without pushing on the vegetables to prevent the sauce being dotted with tiny pieces of carrot. Cool to 140°F, then cool completely to room temperature in a cold water bath (see page 141) and immediately store in the refrigerator for 2 days or in the freezer up to 3 months.

PREPARATION OF SMALL WHITE SAUCES

The two "mother" white sauces become small white sauces when different ingredients are added to them. For example, a chicken velouté reduced to medium-thick consistency and thinned again with cream becomes the classic suprême sauce, while a fish velouté simmered with a mixture of reduced white wine and shallots becomes a bercy sauce.

Tomato sauce or puree added to a *béchamel* sauce turns it into an aurore sauce, while a mixture of grated Gruyère and Parmigiano-Reggiano cheeses makes it a mornay sauce.

These are just a few simple examples. To find complete collections of small white sauces consult all the books on classic French and Italian cuisine and other European cuisines listed in the bibliography. You will find interesting differences of style between renowned chefs. Some will prefer the exquisite work of Prosper Montagné, others that of celebrated Auguste Escoffier, others yet the simplified work of Pellaprat.

Also in the section on poultry and other poached or steamed white meats, you will find a few classic small white sauces (see pages 849–56).

ENRICHING AND FINISHING WHITE SAUCES

A small amount of fortified wine, butter, cream, or a mixture of cream and egg yolks, called a *liaison*, can be added to a white sauce to enrich it and give it a better texture, color, and taste. The sauce is then said to be *finished*, with whatever element has been used. Follow these directions carefully:

WITH FORTIFIED WINE Add 1 to 2 tablespoons ruby, tawny, or white port, fino sherry or Amontillado, Sercial, or Rainwater Madeira, or Marsala per cup of sauce when it is ready to serve.

WITH TABLE WINE Add white table wine reduced by half, always with aromatics. The amount of table wine will vary in each recipe.

WITH BUTTER PLAIN OR FLAVORED Whisk raw, unmelted butter to taste into the ready-to-serve sauce. As you whisk, the butter will be dispersed into the sauce, go into emulsion in it, and thicken it further, as well as make it look shiny and velvety.

Be careful . . . you may reheat the sauce once it has been buttered, but:

- You either reheat the sauce just below the boiling point, stirring, or bring it to a rolling boil, for slow simmering of the sauce after the butter has been added will cause the emulsion to break down and the butter will come floating to the surface of the sauce.

WITH REGULAR FLUID HEAVY CREAM (30 TO 32% BUTTER-FAT) Choose one of these three methods:

- Gently reduce the sauce until thick, then thin to the desired consistency with the desired and/or required amount of cream. Beware: Because each sauce is composed of ingredients that taste different and is thickened with flour from a different origin each time (even if you use the same brand with each and every sauce), the amount of cream you use each time to attain the same consistency will not be the same, but will change with each particular sauce. *You must be the judge* . . . some like a lot of cream, others do not.
- Or, bring the sauce to a high boil in a sauteuse pan. Stirring constantly with a blunt-end wooden spatula, add the cream 3 to 4 tablespoons at a time; continue stirring over high heat after each addition of cream until the sauce coats the spatula.

    As you add the cream, stir, forming a V on the bottom of the sauteuse by going from 11 o'clock down to 6 o'clock, then back up to 1 o'clock. Then run the spatula all around the edges of the pot describing a circle, then go back to writing another V followed by another circle, etc., until the cream coats the spatula to a thickness of one eighth of an inch.

    This technique is called *reduction on high flame*. If you choose this method, which yields the best results, be sure to stir constantly or the sauce will scorch at the bottom of the pot.

    If you overreduce the sauce, *do not add more cream*; rather, add stock to lighten the sauce again.
- Or, mix the sauce and cream together, bring to a boil, stirring, then let simmer gently over low heat until the mixture coats the back of a spoon. Keep at a simmer only and give a stir occasionally to prevent the sauce from "sticking" too thickly to the bottom of the pot.

WITH RIPENED CRÈME FRAÎCHE (32 TO 34% OR MORE BUT-TERFAT) Whisk the cream into the hot, just-off-the-stove sauce. Reheat but do not simmer or boil the sauce; this type of cream, having been cultured, contains lactic ferments which will curdle sauces made with milk when brought to a simmer and give them an ugly texture, with small, readily visible curds. Remove immediately from the stove and use.

WITH REGULAR OR LIGHT SOUR CREAM (18 TO 8% BUTTER-FAT) OR YOGURT OF ANY FAT CONTENT Add any sour cream or yogurt enrichment just before serving; adding it any earlier will turn the sauce into a large culture of sour cream. I remember enriching a velouté of leek soup, which is the same type of preparation as a sauce, and finding myself richer by 15 quarts of leek-flavored yogurt.

WITH A LIAISON A liaison is a mixture of egg yolks and cream added to a sauce to enrich it and enhance its color. It is quite delicious, quite old-fashioned in our present day of low cholesterol, but again with the rule of moderation, why not use a liaison once in a while?

The technique used to add a liaison is important: Put the yolks and cream in a large cup or bowl; mix well. Whisk half of the hot sauce *bit by bit* into the liaison to heat the yolks *very slowly*. Reverse the process and very slowly whisk the warmed liaison into the remainder of the hot sauce. Reheat the sauce slowly until you can see a few boils at the surface of the sauce, then remove it from the heat.

Most cooks will be shocked by the instruction to boil the sauce, but these few boils *are a must*. Without them the sauce will hydrolize and stay liquid or, if it thickens as its temperature reaches 180°F but has to wait to be served, the sauce will reliquefy. The reason why remains mysterious, an enzyme or enzymes in the egg yolks possibly being the culprit, provoking hydrolysis of the starch or flour in the sauce in the same manner as the amylase of saliva liquefies a sauce when the cook tastes it with the spoon used for stirring and puts the spoon back into the saucepan instead of into the sink.

Those few boils for a brief period of time ensure that the overall temperature in the pot reaches 190°F, the temperature at which most enzymes become inactive.

Remember the basic rules for the liaison:

1. A starch- or flour-bound sauce not only can, but must boil for a brief period of time when enriched with egg yolks.
2. On the contrary, a sauce that contains neither starch nor flour and is enriched with a liaison cannot be boiled or the eggs will curdle and ruin the texture and taste of the sauce.

The important step is to heat the enriched sauce slowly, stirring constantly, so that the yolks have no chance to harden and pit the sauce with millions of tiny particles of hard-boiled egg yolk, as they do when the sauce is submitted to any sudden burst of heat.

Auguste Escoffier in *Le Guide Culinaire* (Crown Publishers, 1969), is very explicit on this point. Please refer to the recipe for allemande sauce, where, on page 15, the master directs his readers to " . . . mix velouté, egg yolks and stock . . . bring to a boil and reduce by one third on full flame, stirring constantly with a spatula."

Very rich sauces, containing a goodly amount of cream, egg yolks, and butter alone or combined, may start separating if they stand in a hot kitchen. Tiny puddles, or floccules, of fat appear at the edges of the sauce. Avoid this possibility by never letting a finished egg-enriched sauce stand at a temperature higher than 140°F. To stop flocculation, make sure that the temperature is an even 140°F and give a few strokes of a whisk to the sauce; you will see the fat go back into emulsion in the sauce.

However, if the sauce really becomes too hot and the tiny butter puddles become larger and larger and then start joining together or in more scientific terms *coalesce*, not only should you whisk, but you should, as you whisk, add *cool stock* to the sauce until it replaces any liquid that may have evaporated and the smooth texture of the sauce has been reinstated. This addition of liquid restabilizes the emulsion of the fats in the sauce. Resist the temptation to add any more cream or butter; if you have no stock, use room-temperature salted water. For more details, see the emulsified sauces on page 325.

Classic Brown Sauces

This section of the sauce chapter is for cooking buffs, student chefs, and apprentices only, because it is still essential for them to learn properly how to execute these by now "old-fashioned" sauces and to understand the logistics of a brown roux and the principles of the reduction of these sauces. Home cooks whose goal is only to prepare a delicious brown sauce can refer instead to the modern brown sauces on page 287, which are quicker and just as good, if not better.

There were, as recently as twenty years ago, a number of ways of making flour-bound brown sauces, so that when French cuisine came into preeminence in the United States in the 1960s, one could see all kinds of inferior brown sauces published in many books and food magazines. The word was shortcuts, shortcuts, and more shortcuts and the result on the plate was about as satisfying as a shortcut can be. The first edition of this book, in which I unfortunately gave in to the shortcut mania, and other celebrated volumes of the period are still in existence and can be consulted for these shortcuts.

In this edition, I have made the decision to suppress anything having to do with shortcuts, since the results were not satisfying, and to give the purely classic method for making the two mother brown sauces: the *espagnole* and the demi-glace.

I also decided to give only the chef's method for the *espagnole* since it is, by far, the best and no more arduous to execute, nor time-consuming, than the much less satisfying simplified methods.

There is no doubt that flour-bound sauces have in the last thirty years fallen into complete disrepute. Too rich, too time-consuming, too this, too that. But a true and good cook/chef worthy of his/her title should under no circumstances be ignorant of the preparation of *espagnole* or demi-glace. What is nowadays called demi-glace is not demi-glace, as will become clear after reading the section on modern brown sauces.

This is the *espagnole* as it came down to us from the eighteenth century and was refined by the classic chefs of the nineteenth and twentieth centuries into the demi-glace sauce.

PRINCIPLES OF THE CLASSIC ESPAGNOLE AND DEMI-GLACE SAUCES

A classic brown sauce must not be thick. Its consistency should be somewhere between that of light cream and heavy cream. A brown sauce can be served with a meat roasted at high temperature, which has no or almost no natural gravy, or it can be used in small quantities as a binder for the deglazed and reduced pan juices of panfried and pan-roasted meats. In truly classic cuisine, brown sauces were used as part of the liquid for properly braised meats (see page 286), so that the braising juices were properly bound after the meat had finished cooking, and needed much less reduction before service. Examples of such braises and sautés are to be found in the English translation of Auguste Escoffier's *Le Guide Culinaire*.

For small pieces of meat such as steaks, tournedos (as tenderloin steaks are often called), chops, escalopes, medallions, etc., the average serving of a brown sauce is 2 tablespoons, at most three; but three in my opinion is already bordering on too much. Many restaurants in Europe and the United States still serve their versions of *espagnole* in quantities, which, unfortunately, are much too large, flood the plate, and are responsible for giving the sauces their poor reputation, which they emphatically do not deserve. Well-prepared *espagnole* and demi-glace sauces are lean, tasty, totally fat free, and beautiful to look at, all because of the techniques used to prepare them.

Here is the recipe for *espagnole* sauce, prepared as I was taught in the 1940s and 1950s. The techniques and methods I use here are a combination of those of several classic French chefs. After you have read the recipe, please read the comments on what happens as the elements of the sauce are added to one another and cook together.

Espagnole Sauce

The use of primary veal stock is absolutely necessary.

FCR — 1½ QUARTS

2 medium-size carrots, peeled

2 yellow onions, peeled

3 tablespoons unsalted raw butter

¾ cup clarified butter (page 32)

1¼ cups unsifted unbleached all-purpose flour

4 quarts hot Primary Veal Stock (page 219)

2 tablespoons tomato paste

Bouquet garni of 1 bay leaf, 1 sprig fresh thyme, and 5 parsley stems

1 cup dry white wine

6 cups cold Primary Veal Stock (page 219)

⅓ cup Sercial or Rainwater Madeira

Stage one: Cut the carrots and onions into mirepoix (see page 16). Heat the raw butter over medium-high heat until the foam starts to recede, then add the mirepoix and sauté until the onions are golden brown. Meanwhile, in another saucepan, heat the clarified butter over low heat. Add the flour and cook, stirring, until the mixture is the color of a hazelnut shell; it will smell nice and toasty. Off the heat, whisk the *hot* stock into the *hot* roux; bring to a boil, stirring constantly. Stir in the browned mirepoix, tomato paste, bouquet garni, and white wine. Bring to a boil, reduce the heat to a simmer, and let cook for 2½ hours, skimming off as much scum as possible. Strain into a large mixing bowl; cool to 140°F, then to room temperature in a cold water bath (see page 141); refrigerate overnight.

Stage two: Remove the layer of butter solidified on the surface of the sauce; it may be reused for seasoning vegetables. Return the sauce to a large pot, mix in the *cold* stock, and bring to a boil, stirring. The cold stock will replace the moisture lost the day before and allow for further skimming, clarifying the sauce even more. Reduce the heat to a simmer and let cook until reduced to about 6 cups, skimming at regular intervals. The length of the time required depends on the richness of the stock. The finished sauce is fat free and so clean you can use it as a mirror; it coats the back of a spoon like a thick sticky syrup. No correction of color should be necessary. See page 286 if the sauce is not dark enough. Add the Madeira and strain through the finest China cap strainer into storage containers of the desired size. Again, cool to 140°F, then to room temperature in a cold water bath. Keep refrigerated 1 week or frozen up to 6 months.

Demi-glace Sauce

FCR — 3⅞ CUPS

4 cups finished Espagnole Sauce (page 284)

4 cups Primary Veal Stock (page 219)

2 tablespoons Sercial or Rainwater Madeira

Mix the finished *espagnole* and stock together in a medium-size saucepan. Bring to a boil, then reduce to a simmer, skimming again at regular intervals, until the sauce is reduced to 3⅞ cups. Add the Madeira. Strain through the finest China cap strainer. The sauce is ready to use. Keep refrigerated up to 1 week or frozen up to 6 to 8 months.

Working as it was done up until 1960, we obtained these two sauces, which we now know can be prepared and be just as tasty using other, more time-efficient methods.

So why demand such an exercise anymore? Because it is important for *each and every* well-educated chef to know how a brown roux works, why one uses so much flour to start with and ends up having such a small quantity of relatively thin sauce. The fact that we do not use roux in brown sauces anymore does not mean that no one does, as every Cajun or French Canadian chef will attest to. As long as someone, somewhere utilizes a technique, this technique is worth investigating—if not using because of personal taste and philosophy—but at least investigating and understanding.

WHAT HAPPENED DURING THE COOKING OF THE ESPAGNOLE

The mirepoix as well as the bouquet garni are present in the sauce to give it flavor; so are both wines. They will add their own flavors to the veal stock as they cook in it, give it depth and multiple layers of taste.

The tomato paste will add some taste to such a large amount of liquid, but foremost, as the sauce reduces, it will add to it a certain depth of color which it would not show without its presence.

What about the brown roux? If you look at the amount of flour used in the roux, you will realize that there is just 1 tablespoon of flour per each cup/8 ounces of stock. So why are the 6 cups of finished sauce just the right consistency? Because as you cooked the roux in clarified butter to the correct color of hazelnut shells, you lost some of the thickening power of the flour starches by deeply toasting the starch cells; between 70 and 80 percent lost their ability to absorb liquid and gelatinize. That amount of starch that was not destroyed gelatinized normally and thickened the sauce by the time the stock had reduced to 6 cups. Also, the toasted flour brings a small additional dimension of taste to the sauce. Since the sauce contains particles from the overcooked starch and flour, stringent straining through the finest strainer is absolutely necessary to remove them.

This was, when I grew up, the "crème de la crème" of brown sauces. I often helped prepare it for the "grands dîners" in my aunt's restaurant; it was prepared only twice in my home, for my first Holy Communion and my wedding dinners.

USING THE ESPAGNOLE FOR BRAISES

The few times we prepare braised meats nowadays, we simply braise them in the best possible stock. In the days of the *espagnole*, chefs used a fifty-fifty mixture of stock and *espagnole*, so that by the time the braise was finished, they obtained a delicious, well-reduced sauce that, once defatted, was shiny and splendidly coated the cooked meats. That sauce, as you can see, is equivalent to a demi-glace and I remember those beautiful braises vividly on the plates of my aunt's restaurant and other restaurants during the 1940s and 1950s.

The demi-glace, reduced and skimmed again as it is after being blended with its own volume of stock, was probably created to obtain that same glazy, shiny effect when used with panfried and pan-roasted meats, which produce very little gravy of their own. Whatever protein fractions in the flour are still contained in the *espagnole* will be removed when you skim a demi-glace; the scum, instead of being bulky and abundant as it was in the *espagnole*, is much lighter, but still accumulates on the surface of the sauce in a noticeable way. By the time you have reduced the sauce to one quart, the sauce will be clear and mirrorlike again.

DEEPENING THE COLOR AND TASTE OF ESPAGNOLE AND DEMI-GLACE; MEAT GLAZE

The color of *espagnole* and demi-glace should be a gorgeous russet–reddish brown, as shiny as a lacquer. Sometimes if the stock is not brown enough, it is necessary to deepen the color of the sauce to prevent it from appearing a nondescript brownish beige on the plate.

Poor cooking techniques for *espagnole* and demi-glace are not only reflected in a poor color but in a disappointing taste and too thin and soupy a texture. What to do?

- Try first to reduce the sauce until its taste and color start to deepen. Often this will be sufficient and the sauce will "turn around" all by itself.
- If the sauce does not turn around, the best solution is to prepare meat glaze; reduce the sauce a little and add as much meat glaze as is needed to round up its flavor.

Meat glaze is made by reducing primary stock (see page 219 for the recipe) by at least three quarters; three quarters should be sufficient, but if it is not, pursue the reduction a little further. It is necessary to skim the stock as it cooks down and the finished glaze should coat the back of a spoon by at least one tenth of an inch. Store the glaze in small jars.

Meat glaze looks like a piece of brown rubber when cold; it stays refrigerated for weeks without spoiling. It is a good idea, because of the cost of the glaze (in time and ingredients), to reboil the glaze every so often. Every third week the glaze should be checked for mold. If there is some, it should be removed with a clean spoon and the glaze should be reboiled to destroy any remaining mold spore. Once reboiled it can again be kept refrigerated. Check it each and every week.

And if no meat glaze is available? It is well understandable that nowadays, preparing meat glaze is just not practical because it is too expensive; to replace it you may use a semiliquid meat extract, adding drops of it at a time once the sauce has reached its proper texture. *Remember that semiliquid meat extract can be used only as a corrector or taste reinforcer* (see page 212 for details).

THE ENRICHMENT OF BROWN SAUCES

Brown sauces are mostly enriched with raw butter, plain or flavored. The butter must be whisked into the ready-to-serve sauce. How much butter one adds to a sauce is entirely left to the personal taste of the cook or chef. Brown sauces prepared as described in this book are good enough to be used without butter enrichment. However, it is sometimes necessary to use a bit of butter to pair the dish in which the sauce is used with the wine that is meant to accompany it.

If cream is used in brown sauces, it is mostly crème fraîche or sour cream.

SMALL BROWN SAUCES

The repertory of small brown sauces of the French and other European cuisines is extremely rich. Please consult the bibliography and also see the sections on panfried and pan-roasted meats in this book for a nice collection of small brown sauces which can be executed either with the classic *espagnole* and demi-glace sauces or, as we will see below, with the quicker modern brown sauces.

Twentieth-Century French/Western Brown Sauces

Between the 1930s and 1960, chefs devised all kinds of ways to prepare brown sauces which involved much less labor than the two classic brown sauces and their derivatives.

BEURRE MANIÉ, THE QUICK THICKENING FOR MEAT GRAVIES

Beurre manié, or kneaded butter, is ancient (mention of it can be found in eighteenth-century cookbooks.) It is used as a thickener for a number of sauces, especially fish sauces. A mixture of butter and flour is well "kneaded" together to obtain a perfectly homogeneous mixture that is not cooked like a roux but rather whisked, uncooked, into a simmering liquid. The liquid, usually, is the gravy of a braised or stewed meat and/or the poaching liquid of poultry or fish. In the last edition of the *Le Guide Culinaire*, Escoffier suggested it as suitable for *matelotes*, the freshwater fish stews of the French provinces. Not all chefs of the period mentioned it in their books, but it is very well explained in such books as *La Bonne Cuisine de Madame Saint Ange* which home cooks have used as a standard cooking guide since the beginning of the twentieth century. *Beurre manié* is also the great redeemer of sauces that turn out too thin, for it can, in a matter of seconds, bring a sauce back to the correct texture.

Beurre manié is used in the following proportions and according to the following technique:

- *For a thin sauce:* 1 tablespoon each flour and butter per cup of liquid
- *For a medium sauce:* 2 tablespoons each flour and butter per cup of liquid

To thicken the sauce, whisk the kneaded butter very fast into the sauce while it is maintained at a good and steady simmer all through the pot; the butter separates the starch granules in the flour and delays their cooking by the few seconds it takes the butter to melt. A few seconds more, and the flour starches gelatinize and the sauce thickens almost instantly.

At this point, *be careful:*

- Stop the cooking as soon as the sauce has completely thickened or the sour/bitter taste of the imperfectly cooked flour will permeate the dish.
- The color of a brown sauce thus thickened will lighten considerably and should be darkened with a dab of a proper coloring (see page 217).
- If the sauce of a dish has been thickened with a *beurre manié* and the dish must wait more than five minutes before being served, you are in danger of serving a sauce tainted with the taste of raw flour; do not hesitate to simmer the sauce a full twenty minutes to fully cook the flour rather than running that risk. This last remark illustrates the fact that it is always preferable to use a roux to thicken a flour-bound sauce, however enticing the *beurre manié* technique may seem.

Contemporary French/European Sauces Thickened by a Reduction of Gravies or Stocks
White Sauces

Around the late 1920s, European chefs and cooks started to thicken white sauces made with white stocks of poultry or fish with cornstarch rather than flour, while the United States still made quite a number of flour-bound cream sauces up until the 1970s. The considerable nutrition documentation now available on the problem of cholesterol finally sounded the death knell for cream sauces. This is not too much of a loss, for the *béchamel* is excellent in an occasional dish of lasagne or moussaka, but no one would like to see it on the dinner plate every night.

Since quite a few people still like a nice little cream sauce once in a while, this is the way it can be done without making a white roux.

"UNIVERSAL SAUCES" MADE WITH LIGHT CREAM

I give this name in jest to all sauces obtained by moistening cornstarch with light cream and using the resulting slurry to thicken the deglazed and partially reduced deglazings of panfried and roasted meats, or the reduced juices of braised, stewed, or sautéed fish, meats, sweetbreads, etc. "Universal" seemed to be the most appropriate adjective I could find since there is not a bistro or "nice" quick food restaurant anywhere in the western world which does not serve such a sauce in some dish or other.

The proportion of cornstarch is approximately 1 to 1½ teaspoons cornstarch per cup of *finished* sauce. When you calculate the amount of starch needed, you must first add the deglazed or reduced meat/fish juices to the cream. A good mixture is at least one third meat or fish juices and two thirds cream. Some prefer half-and-half. The more you reduce the gravy, the tastier the sauce will be, but then the more cream you will need to add to reinstate a well-balanced taste and achieve the volume of sauce you need, so do not overreduce the deglazing.

For such a white sauce to be its most flavorful, the stock used to deglaze the gravy or to braise the meat must be of the best quality.

For fish: Use fish fumet, or a fifty-fifty mixture of clam juice and the secondary stock (page 220) or chicken broth of your choice. Chicken broth, as is often suggested in magazine recipes, is not recommended for saltwater fish and should be used only for freshwater fish such as trout, pike, crayfish, etc.

For meats: Use secondary stock or any good pure chicken or turkey stock or broth of your choice. For the very best taste, use primary veal stock (page 219), but expect a deeper color (see below under "Color").

DEPTH OF TASTE Some universal sauces, especially those for white meats, often come out a bit bland and it is necessary to correct and deepen their flavor. Use the following ingredients to round them out, added very gradually and in the smallest possible quantity to the finished sauce:

For fish: Mashed anchovies or soy sauce.

For beef and lamb: A dab of meat extract, or some mashed anchovies, or any concentrated Oriental sauce such as soy, hoisin, oyster sauce, or plum sauce.

For veal and chicken: A very small dab of meat extract, mashed anchovies only in Mediterranean recipes, and soy or other concentrated Oriental sauces in East-West dishes.

PORTION SIZE   Rather than serve a regular portion of white sauce, which is a hefty ¼ cup, spoon 1½ tablespoons of the sauce on top of each portion of meat or fish and serve the remainder of the sauce in a sauce boat, or a small ramekin if you serve individually; this will allow each guest to decide how much more sauce she/he wishes to enjoy.

COLOR   The color of universal sauces is rarely white but rather beige to light taupe or, at their deepest, russet, because all of them acquire their color from the depth of shade of each particular deglazing or braising gravy. Such sauces made on a base of deglazing in which the Maillard reaction occurs (see page 266) are a much deeper shade than those made on a base of reduced braising juices.

THICKENING TECHNIQUE
- *At home:* For the best results, deglaze the pan or reduce the braising juices. If needed, reinforce the flavor as suggested on page 289. Add as much cream as needed to obtain the taste you like; bring the mixture to a simmer. Dilute the starch in 2 tablespoons cream and add, stirring constantly, to the simmering sauce until it thickens.
- *In a restaurant operation* (this technique applies only to the deglazing of panfried meats): For the sake of speed, have a larger amount of a thick cornstarch slurry ready in a stainless steel pitcher; add cream in the desired proportions to the gravy or reduced braising juices, then thicken with as much of the slurry as needed, simmering and stirring until well bound. Correct the depth of flavor in each portion, since it may vary each time.

In either situation, strain through a conical strainer, then flavor with any herb or spice of your choice.

For a recipe using this method, see page 771.

WHITE SAUCES THICKENED WITH
REDUCED HEAVY CREAM
In professional kitchens, many chefs—and not only the older ones—still keep a tin of already reduced heavy cream, some of which is added to deglazings and reduced cooking juices to thicken sauces. No slurry is needed as the reduced cream acts as a thickener.

Such sauces are the very best tasting, but must be kept for very special occasions, since there is no doubt that, enjoyed on a daily basis, they will have a negative effect on health, due to the large butterfat content of the heavy cream.

I leave the resolution of this personal problem to cooks and chefs. Here is how it is done.

PROPER CREAM TEXTURE   If you are going to have a party, or if you have a restaurant, reduce the cream ahead of time for convenience; it evaporates water from the cream and concentrates the mixture of butterfat, proteins, and lactose. Lactose is the sugar found in milk and is about one third as sweet as sucrose. As a result, reduced heavy cream is much sweeter than raw heavy cream.

Never reduce cream by more than 50 percent or the cream will acquire that cooked milk taste particular to all cooked dairy products (it's a concentrated and condensed milk taste). Such a flavor does very little for a white sauce. If you reduce by more than 50 percent, you will also see the butterfat break out of emulsion and the color change to an unattractive light beige as a result of the Maillard reaction (see page 266). Adding liquid will fix the texture but nothing can fix the taste or look.

A more pronounced taste is obtained in home cooking than in quantity cooking when plain raw cream is used to deglaze the pan-reduced meat juices, then is allowed to simmer a few minutes more. All there is to do is to reduce the cream to a light coating texture and add the taste reinforcer, if needed.

PORTION AND TASTE   You are on your own as to the quantity of cream added to the quantity of deglazing or reduced braising juices at your disposal for each particular dish. Proceed slowly, adding the cream or reduced cream until you obtain the flavor you prefer. For the portion size, follow my suggestion on page 289, since the same rules apply as for the slurried light cream sauces.

The same rules also apply for the deepening of the taste with meat extract, mashed anchovies, or any concentrated Oriental sauce (see page 289).

For specific recipes using white sauces thickened with reduced heavy cream see pages 596, 850, and 887.

CREAM SAUCES THICKENED WITH A LIAISON
These sauces could also be called *custard sauces*, since, containing egg yolks, as they cook, they thicken exactly as a stirred custard would around 160° to 165°F, *and should never be overheated or boiled*. Since, unlike a dessert custard, a savory custard sauce does not contain any sugar, it thickens even faster than a dessert sauce. See the English custard techniques on page 140 for a refresher.

As you can read on page 281, a liaison is a mixture of egg yolks and cream added to a classic flour-bound velouté to enrich it. The same liaison, only richer in egg yolks was used in classic cuisine, and is still used very occasionally, to thicken the gravy of such delicious dishes as braised sweetbreads, or braised fish and shellfish such as turbot, Chilean sea bass, and lobster.

THE TECHNIQUE OF CUSTARD SAUCES   The technique is not difficult at all, but you must be alert and keep your eyes wide open, so that as soon as the thickening occurs, you remove the pan from the heat. Should you fail to do so, you will see the custard thicken too much, the egg yolks eventually curdling into a mess of watery scrambled eggs.

After deglazing a pan or reducing braising juices, return them, along with whichever meat, fish, or shellfish you are preparing, to a sauteuse pan or large skillet. Mix together the egg yolks and cream, usually 4 egg yolks per cup of cream (less to taste, but never more) and add to the pan. Immediately start shaking the pan back and forth over medium-high heat. Within 2 or 3 minutes, you will see the sauce coat the food. Remove the pan from the heat at once, still shaking it to cool off the sauce, and serve immediately.

Nutritionally these sauces are too rich to be prepared any more often than once a year for a great treat, and should be served as a very small luxurious appetizer in 2-ounce ramekins.

Modern Western Flourless Brown Sauces Thickened by the Reduction of Stock

By 1965 it had become customary in French/European high gastronomic circles to make fun of the poor "fools" who still worked enthusiastically with the classic techniques, those who still served *espagnole* and demi-glace.

I think it is necessary to know every possible way to make brown sauces, to chose one's own favorite, and simply be tolerant of the way other people prepare them. It is natural enough for any cook to enjoy one's own brown sauce style better than anyone else's. *De gustibus non disputandum* remains a truth, even if half the population does not believe in this tenet, that of taste one neither discusses nor disputes.

The following paragraphs are dedicated to the different ways you can prepare a very good to excellent brown sauce nowadays without spending hours skimming.

Jus de veau lié means "thickened brown veal stock." It is made by reducing primary veal stock and it is up to you to decide how much that stock should be reduced, since the degree of reduction will depend on the quality of the stock you made.

To evaluate the stock, pour some into a small jar and refrigerate it overnight; if it still trembles when cold, reduce the stock by one quarter. If it is solid and can be cut with a knife, use it as is. *Jus de veau lié* is prepared as needed on a daily basis and used to deglaze the gravies of steaks, chops, roast beef, roast leg of lamb, roast veal, and any roasted bird.

Be careful: Do not prepare *jus de veau lié* with any ordinary or secondary stock or reduced canned stock; the ordinary or secondary stock will give you a sauce that lacks body, the canned stock a sauce that lacks body and is radically oversalted, a double jeopardy.

Jus de Veau Lié

FFR

FOR I CUP:

¼ cup cold Primary Veal Stock (page 219), fat free, reduced or not as needed

1⅓ teaspoons potato starch

¾ cup Primary Veal Stock (page 219), heated to a simmer

1 tablespoon Sercial Madeira or fino sherry

FOR I QUART

¾ cup cold Primary Veal Stock (page 219), fat free, reduced or not as needed

5¼ teaspoons potato starch

3 cups Primary Veal Stock (page 219), heated to a simmer

¼ cup Sercial Madeira or fino sherry

Mix the cold stock and starch into a slurry. Stir this into the simmering stock until thickened. Remove from the heat and add the wine. Use as recommended above.

Prepared with excellent primary veal stock, jus de veau lié is one of the modern replacements for espagnole sauce. Do not freeze jus de veau after it has been bound with the starch. Keep refrigerated only for up to 2 weeks and reboil any that is left over at three-day intervals.

Modern Replacements for the Classic Demi-glace:
The Essences

I never abandoned the making of *espagnole* and demi-glace, and taught those two classic sauces to all chefs-in-training who came under my tutelage. If I were still teaching, I would continue to do the same.

But, after going into the restaurant business, it became obvious that preparing *espagnole* even just twice a week was much too expensive, and I investigated other possibilities which would be better than *jus de veau lié* and the equivalent of the classic demi-glace.

After spending an afternoon in the company of Messieurs Carême, Gouffé, Urbain Dubois, and Escoffier at the Schlesinger Library in Boston, reading all about their ways with brown sauces, I came back and tried the following essences. I have stayed with them ever since because, as far as I am concerned, they are the best brown sauces that can be made. They may cost a bit but they are well worth the investment and I can vouch for the fact that guests do not mind the additional dollar for their plate.

The Principle of Essences

In the making of essences, the ratio of reduction of the stock is the same as for the *espagnole* and the demi-glace: The stock will reduce by three quarters by the time the sauce is finished. *The stock must be primary stock* (see page 218). If no primary stock is available, you may use double strength turkey stock. Do not use beef stock with beef as the essence will be too beefy; do not make a special stock for lamb, as it is useless (see below).

The great advantage of essences is that they can either be made as needed or in advance and refrigerated or frozen as you prefer; because of their high level of taste, they lose practically no flavor.

QUANTITY AND PORTION SIZE

To obtain the quantity of essence listed in the left column, you will need the quantity of primary stock listed in the right column.

Finished Essence	Quantity of Primary Stock Needed
I cup	I quart
I pint	2 quarts
3 cups	3 quarts
I quart	I gallon
I gallon	4 gallons

For larger quantity production, you can start with one gallon stock to obtain one quart essence. The stockpot is usually left on very low heat to keep it sanitary and the cook dips directly into it to prepare as much essence as is needed.

The portion size for an excellent essence is 2 to 3 tablespoons per person, more so two than three.

STORAGE

Essences remain sterile for a long time because, cooking for such a relatively long time, they lose a large proportion of their moisture which makes them less susceptible to bacterial spoilage. Their shelf life in the refrigerator is two weeks; since they contain no starches at all, they can be frozen without syneresis occurring, and when well sealed last up to eight months in the freezer.

It is a good idea to prepare larger amounts of essence at once and to freeze them in sterilized 8-ounce freezer containers at home and half-quart or quart containers in the restaurant. Essences must be reboiled immediately after defrosting, but they lose none of their flavor from having been frozen.

NUTRITION

Essences contain a tiny amount of fat, coming from the browned pieces of meat. It is a good idea to prepare an essence ahead of time, and to allow it to sit to let that tiny bit of fat come to the surface. Once the essence is cold and solid, scrape the fat off with a clean stainless steel or silver spoon, and the essence will be fat free. The spoon must have been washed and sterilized in a dishwasher. Do not use a wooden spoon ever, to prevent bacterial contamination of the essence.

Essences are extra rich in proteins and very nutritious; the only people who need be careful not to consume them on a daily basis or in large quantities are those subject to attacks of gout.

OBTAINING MAXIMUM TASTE FROM EACH TYPE OF MEAT

The problem with the *jus de veau lié* lies in its almost always uniform taste, whether it sauces a piece of chicken or a piece of beef; even if the cooking gravy of that meat has been added to it, it often remains *jus de veau*. To address this, I decided on the following method:

1. Whether using chicken, turkey, rabbit, beef, lamb, veal, any game bird, or venison, always reserve the giblets (no livers, though; they would muddy the essence) and wingtips of all types of birds, the defatted trimmings and meaty rib bones of all red meats and venison, and the many unusable pieces of rabbits such as belly flaps, riblets, and necks; completely remove the fat from them and cut them into ½-inch cubes or as close as possible to this size. Using a sauteuse pan, initially sear these cubes in unsaturated oil on all sides over a high flame, then reduce the heat to medium to obtain a nice even brown glaze around the pieces of meat, and on the bottom of the pan. Do not cook over too high a heat or the glaze will turn bitter, which would spoil the taste of the essence.

2. Once the meat trimmings are nicely browned, remove all the fat in the sauteuse completely by tilting the sauteuse forward and wedging a sauce spoon under it on the handle side. Let the sauteuse stand in this angled position for 5 minutes while you bunch the meat pieces against the handle side of the pan so the lowest part of the pan is free; you will see all the fluid fat surrounding the pieces of meat flow down into the lip of the pan.

   Using a wad of paper towels, sponge all the fat off; *do not scrape or touch the glaze* at the bottom of the pan yet.

3. Place the sauteuse over a medium flame again. Add enough primary stock to barely cover the meats, scrape the bottom of the pan well to dissolve the glaze, and let the stock reduce to a thicker glaze that will coat the meats by one sixteenth of an inch, if not more.

There are then three different ways to proceed, depending on the meat used:

THE SINGLE ESSENCE This is used for veal only because the veal stock is reinforced by the juices of veal meat. After the first glaze is finished, add all the remaining stock and let slowly reduce to the final quantity of essence you need (see page 294). Strain through a China cap or conical strainer. I call the obtained essence a single essence because the larger part of the stock has been added in one last addition.

THE MULTIPLE ESSENCES

For lamb: After the first glaze, add ½ teaspoon of fennel seeds for each quart of primary stock used. The fennel accentuates the taste of the lamb and prevents you from having to make a special lamb stock. Divide the remaining stock into three equal parts; add to the sauteuse in three separate additions, reducing each time over medium-low heat to a consistency such that it coats the back of a sauce spoon with a lacquer about one tenth of an inch thick. After you are finished with the last addition, you should have between ⅔ and 1 cup of finished multiple essence of lamb per quart of stock used.

For all other meats: Proceed exactly as for lamb, but do not add the fennel seeds. It is essential to prepare a multiple essence with meats other than veal to accentuate the taste of the particular meat used and minimize the veal taste in the finished essence. A single essence is not quite successful enough at doing that.

The principles of single and multiple essences outlined above offer the best results in texture and taste for each meat considered. But, trust me, as one who has worked with hundreds of apprentices, the quality of the finished essence will depend on two things:

The quality of the primary stock: You will find the quality of a stock to vary with the quality of the veal you use to make it, and the perseverance of the cook who browns the veal meat used in the making of the stock.

So before starting, taste your stock and appreciate the depth of its color (check for bitterness), taste (taste for the presence of unwanted aromatic notes such as celery which increase enormously as the essence reduces), and its texture (are your lips sticking to each other because the stock is overcooked and it has a nasty taste of bones?).

If the stock is too thin, you will need to make a multiple essence to obtain the texture you are looking for. If it is just right, follow the recommendations above. If it is too thick and sticks to your lips, dilute it with enough hot water until the stock, still tasting very good, does not feel sticky to the lips anymore. This is very important, for a good essence should be opulent and unctuous, but never stick to the lips, for if it does, it will congeal on the plate as the plate starts to cool off.

You should never cook the essence until the meats shred and fall apart or the essence will acquire the taste of overcooked meat, which is horrible. This is even more the case if the meats are on bones, which leach a nasty taste of bones into the essence. The pieces of meats used to prepare the essence should remain nice and tender and you should be able to prepare the following dish of pasta and mixed vegetables with them.

Essence Leftovers Stretcher Pasta

FCR — 6 SERVINGS

½ **pound macaroni, boiled according to package instructions until al dente**

I **tablespoon olive or other unsaturated oil of your choice**

2 **cups mixed vegetables cut as for stir-fry**

Salt

Pepper from the mill

Meats left over from essence making

½ **cup Secondary Stock (page 220)**

Chopped fresh herbs of your choice

Grated cheese of your choice

Drain the pasta. Meanwhile heat the oil, then stir-fry the vegetables for a few minutes to the degree of doneness you like. Season with salt and pepper. Toss the pasta and meats into the vegetables, add the stock and reheat for 1 minute. Correct the seasoning and add the herbs. Sprinkle with cheese and enjoy; it is great—ask all the chefs who trained with me.

Vegetables and Essences

No tomato puree is added to essences, as their color is very deep and mahogonylike without the tomato, and adding it would give the essences a slight acid taste.

Avoid adding aromatic vegetables to any essence while it cooks. It is often believed that chopped onions, mushrooms, and other aromatic vegetables give great taste to an essence. It has been my experience that, on the contrary, the vegetables detract from the clarity and meaty taste of the essence because they shrink in the gelatin-loaded stock instead of losing their juices slowly as they should. If you desire the taste of vegetables in an essence, *étuvé*—the French word for smother—the vegetables to extract all their juices. To do this, add to the vegetables one of the portions of stock you plan to use to make the essence and let the vegetables simmer for 5 minutes, then steep in it, then strain that vegetable-flavored stock into the simmering essence. Or, if you are going to blend wine into your essence, simmer the vegetables in the wine to flavor it, then strain the flavored wine into the finished essence. In either case, finish by simmering the mixture 5 to 10 minutes to blend the flavors together.

Small Sauces Made from Mixed Essences and Reductions

It is not a good idea to add wine to a cooking essence; some red wines (not the exceptional growths of Bordeaux and Burgundy, nor the California Cabernets and Pinots Noirs) will turn purple and give the sauce a muddy bluish hue. If you want to flavor an essence with wine, prepare a reduction by reducing the wine and the aromatics you prefer (shallots, garlic, onions, scallions, leeks, etc.) together by at least one half and strain that into the *finished* essence. Then simmer together an additional 10 to 12 minutes to blend the flavors. The result is a modern small brown sauce.

Be sure to make a clear distinction in your mind between:

- *Essences*, which are reductions of excellent stock in the presence of defatted browned meat scraps,
- *Jus de veau lié*, which is primary veal stock reduced and bound with a pure starch, and
- *Reductions*, which are mixtures of wine and/or vinegar or fruit purees reduced *slowly* with or without aromatic vegetables, then strained into either essences or *jus de veau lié* to change the basic character of their flavor.

THE ENRICHMENT OF JUS DE VEAU LIÉ AND ESSENCES

Essences may be enriched with sour cream, crème fraîche, or butter, plain or flavored. They may be turned into small brown sauces by adding herbs, reductions of different wines with aromatics, condiments such as mustard, or a small amount of any prepared Oriental sauce such as soy sauce, the Chinese hoisin, oyster, or plum sauce, the Vietnamese *nuoc mam*, or the Thai *nam pla*. For a deeper understanding of the enrichment of essences with oil or butter, see the theory of emulsions on page 325.

For examples of many essences finished with many different herbs or condiments, see the chapter on meats starting on page 699.

Compound Butters, Flavored Butters, and Flavored Oils as Sauces or Finishing Touches to Sauces

The European love for plain and compound butters can be easily explained historically. Butter was used by the Celts who were great cattle raisers, but the later dominance of the Romans over western Europe made lard and olive and walnut oils the fats mostly used in western Europe through the early Middle Ages. The Viking invasions brought the use of butter back and deeper toward the center of Europe. Butter, which was hardly used in famous medieval French cookbooks, became very popular by the fifteenth century, so much so that the Church had to declare it unsuitable for consumption during Lent. The frustration of many western Europeans, kept from eating their favorite fat during Lent, led to quite a commerce of papal indulgences for the right to eat butter on lean days. Luther fulminated at the Roman cardinals for forcing Christians "to eat an oil they themselves would not use to grease their slippers."

Europe produces mountains of butter, a problem that has probably plagued the economy of some of its nations for the last fifty years; special inexpensive but delicious butter goes on sale in all supermarkets at Christmastime, so that many a family will buy plenty of it and prepare not only Christmas cookies and cakes, but also keep some frozen and at hand for use all through the year.

Compound Butters

The term *compound butter* is usually applied to creamed raw butter flavored with different spices and aromatics. Compound butters are quite old preparations. Their origin can probably be found in the Latin habit of pounding mixtures of herbs and spices, called in Low Latin *moretaria*, in rough-surfaced bowls called *mortaria*. Latin *mortaria*, a few of which can still be found offered for sale in village antique shops all over Provence, were obviously the ancestors of our classic mortars, and the Ligurian pesto and its cousin the Provençal pistou are probably modern descendants of *moretaria* made with a mixture of herbs containing a large amount of basil and some olive oil. It only makes sense to assume that when, north of the Loire River, butter became more plentiful and popular than olive oil or walnut oil, the cooks immediately thought of adding pounded herbs and spices to butter as had been previously added to oils for centuries, and thus compound butters were born. A few compound butters found a place in the kitchens of France toward the end of the seventeenth century and, by the end of the nineteenth, French cookbooks offered full collections of them.

THE BEST USES FOR COMPOUND BUTTERS

Compound butters have seen a comeback with the change of styles in cooking during the last twenty years and they may be used either on grilled fish and meats, or on steamed vegetables; those chefs and cooks who still go to the trouble of preparing true sauces with a base of stock often add some compound butter to a good sauce to finish and change it into a fragrant small sauce.

In these days of cholesterol "obsession," compound butter can also be prepared with half oil and half butter or with the lightened butter on page 34.

Anything tasty can be added to butter to make it a compound butter: herbs and spices singularly or in combination, strong spicy and hot peppers in small quantity, plain or reduced juices of citrus fruit, purees of fruit, cheeses, aromatics such as garlic, chopped shallots, etc.

MAKING COMPOUND BUTTERS

Use only the best *unsalted* butter and add salt to your taste; unsalted butter as sold in stores is always fresher than salted butter. Keep the butter at room temperature until it has turned waxy but not oily.

Chop any herb or aromatic you intend to use into very, very small pieces, especially garlic and shallots. Cream or process the butter, then add the herbs and/or other flavorings and let stand at room temperature for 2 hours before using in order to dissolve the salt and let the tastes of all the components blend into one another. If you work in larger quantities, use the food processor, but avoid processing too long to prevent the herbs from turning into a mash.

STORAGE OF COMPOUND BUTTERS

Because the vegetables used in the making of compound butters are used mostly in their raw state, they can contaminate the butter with bacteria if the butters are kept too long in the refrigerator or frozen for a longer time.

- To *minimize* bacterial development, wash herbs several times under cold running water and dry in paper towels. To *eliminate* bacterial development, blanch herbs for 2 minutes in boiling water. Squeeze dry and process with the butter in a blender or food processor.
- Do not keep at length or freeze butters containing any uncooked element, *unless* it contains a strong acid such as lemon, lime, or reduced orange juice or an acid fruit such as cranberries, which retard bacterial development.
- If the butter is flavored with cooked or blanched elements, you may freeze it. To do so, roll the butter in plastic wrap and form a small sausage about ¾ inch in diameter by twisting both ends of the plastic in opposite directions. Refrigerate the butter first, cut it into slices of the desired thickness, then freeze it if you want.

- When frozen, compound butters must be stored either in a plastic container with a lid or in a self-sealing bag.
- Compound butters kept more than one month in the freezer start oxidating as the herbs lose their flavor and the butter slowly turns rancid. The best-tasting compound butter is made and consumed the same day.

Here are four modern recipes as examples:

Cranberry and Chive Butter

FFR — ⅔ CUP

½ cup fresh cranberries

¼ cup water

½ cup unsalted butter, at room temperature

1 tablespoon finely chopped shallots

Salt

Pepper from the mill

1 to 2 tablespoons chopped fresh chives to your personal taste

Use primarily on all grilled fish, but it also tastes very good on plain macaroni. If you do not object to a rougher texture, you can skip the straining.

Put the cranberries and water in a small pot and bring to a boil. Cook until the cranberries have popped open. Cool completely. Put the berries and butter in a food processor and process 1 minute, pulsating several times. Strain through a conical strainer if desired.

Put the chopped shallots in the corner of a clean towel and squeeze the strong juices out into the trash can or sink. Add the shallots, salt, pepper, and chives to the cranberry butter, mashing them into the butter with your knife blade. Shape into a sausage-shaped roll, wrap in plastic, and refrigerate. Cut into slices of desired size, rewrap, and freeze if desired since the acidity of the cranberries will retard bacterial development.

Chipotle Butter

FFR — ABOUT ½ CUP

1 canned chipotle chile

½ dried ancho chile, coarsely chopped

1 tiny clove garlic, crushed

Salt

½ cup unsalted butter, at room temperature

1½ tablespoons chopped cilantro leaves

Excellent on grilled steak or grilled butterflied leg of lamb. It is best prepared in the smallest Cuisinart or an "Oscar" food processor.

Put the chiles and garlic into a food processor with salt to taste and the butter. Process until well homogenized. Remove from the processor to a bowl and cream in the chopped cilantro.

Let stand 1 hour at room temperature, covered. Roll into plastic wrap and refrigerate. When solid, cut into slices of the desired size and rewrap. This butter must be used within a day of its making and cannot be frozen.

Tangerine Gremolata Butter

FFR—ABOUT ½ CUP

2 tangerines

Tangerine rind

½ cup unsalted butter, at room temperature

Salt

Pepper from the mill

I small clove garlic, crushed

I teaspoon finely grated lemon rind

I anchovy fillet, coarsely chopped

2 tablespoons finely chopped fresh Italian parsley leaves

The Italian gremolata is probably the ancestor of the French remoulade; the anchovy reveals its ancient Latin origin. This works well with grilled chicken cutlets (see page 739), or veal or lamb chops; it's also excellent on snapper and any white fish steak such as monkfish, Chilean sea bass, and yellowtail.

Squeeze the juice of both tangerines and reduce in a small stainless steel saucepan over medium-high heat to 1 tablespoon; place in a food processor. Remove the white pith from a piece of tangerine rind the size of a quarter and add the rind to the food processor together with the butter, salt and pepper to taste, garlic, grated lemon rind, and anchovy and process until smooth. Using a knife blade, blend in the chopped parsley.

Let stand at room temperature for 1 hour. Roll into plastic wrap. Refrigerate until solid, then cut into slices of the desired size. Rewrap in plastic and keep refrigerated. Despite the acid of the tangerine juice, this butter is best used fresh as it loses quite a bit of its flavor in the freezer.

Pistou Butter Oil

FCR—⅔ CUP

½ cup packed fresh basil leaves

Pepper from the mill

2 tablespoons freshly grated Pecorino Romano or mashed fresh goat cheese

5 fresh rosemary leaves

Large pinch of chopped fresh savory leaves of your choice

Large pinch of fresh thyme leaves

I tablespoon pine nuts

I large clove garlic, crushed

4 to 5 tablespoons unsalted butter, at room temperature, or to your personal taste

3 to 4 tablespoons virgin olive oil or to your personal taste

You can proceed as described here using either olive oil, or the lightened butter on page 34. Good for grilled chicken legs, thighs, and breasts, to spread on bread served with fish chowders, and to add to pasta dishes and soups. It is not firm enough to cut, but rather should be spooned onto whichever offering you choose.

Bring a small saucepan of water to a boil; immerse the basil leaves in it for 2 minutes; this sterilizes the leaves. Drain and pat completely dry.

Place the basil leaves, pepper to taste, the cheese, rosemary, savory, thyme, pine nuts, garlic, and butter in a small food processor or Oscar and process until smooth. Add the oil very gradually. The texture will depend on the cheese you have used and the density of the olive oil. If the butter oil is too thin to shape, pack it into a small bowl. Ripen at room temperature for 1 hour, then refrigerate. Spoon onto or into the desired food. *Do not freeze*.

Other Butter Ideas

Using the proportions of butter given in the recipes above, you can make compound butters with:

- Chopped shallots and the four *fines herbes*
- Chopped fresh parsley leaves and lemon juice
- Chopped fresh parsley leaves, lemon juice, and melted meat glaze
- Minced shallots, minced garlic, minced fresh parsley leaves, and a dash of freshly grated nutmeg
- Dijon mustard
- Minced fresh tarragon leaves
- Tomato paste and chopped fresh basil leaves
- Tabasco sauce and diced green bell pepper

Flavored Butters

Unlike a raw compound butter, a flavored butter is melted at a high enough temperature, so that whichever flavoring is added to it will leach its fatty components and/or pigments into the butter grease and color and flavor it strongly. Flavored butters are made with spices, herbs, and also roasted shellfish shells.

Noisette Butter

Noisette butter with its toasted milk solids taste is absolutely delightful when blended with lemon juice and salt and pepper. It is probably the very best accompaniment to grilled fillets of sole and, in fact, grilled fish of any kind except the fat "blue" species such as tuna, mackerel, bluefish, etc. Noisette butter is also excellent as a finishing touch in some fish and shellfish sauces and is indescribably delicious on spätzle (see page 49). The instructions for making noisette butter are on page 32.

Shellfish Butter

FFR — About 60% of the weight of the butter used

Any amount of small legs and/or shells of any shellfish such as freshwater crayfish, shrimp, prawns, and lobsters of any type

The same weight in unsalted butter

Menon, in the mid-eighteenth century, already used this delicious, beautiful butter, which can be the soul of many a fine sauce or dressing.

Not only must the shellfish shells be dry, but they must still contain some meat in order to obtain a full-bodied taste.

At home, prepare shellfish butter as you need it; it is a preparation which should only be made for celebration dishes. In a small restaurant operation, prepare it each and every week and refrigerate no longer than 24 hours and keep frozen no more than one week.

Preheat the oven to 350°F. Crush the shellfish as small as you can using the back of a very large knife or, if the shellfish are small, a food processor. Place the shells in a baking dish; dry the shells 30 minutes, tossing them several times. Cut the butter into small pieces and distribute it evenly over the shells. Bake until the shells are brittle, have turned pale orange, and the butter at the bottom of the baking pan is deep orange, about 40 minutes. *Do not overbake!*

Strain through several layers of cheesecloth that have been boiled, cooled, and squeezed dry. Since only a few tablespoons are sufficient to deeply flavor a sauce, store in baby food jars filled only halfway and seal well. To freeze place the jars in a tightly sealed larger plastic container.

Recipes using shellfish butter can be found in the fish chapter, starting on page 517.

Pecan Butter

FFR — 1¼ CUPS

¾ cup pecans, finely chopped

1½ cups unsalted butter

This butter can be prepared with many other nuts and is especially delicious with walnuts and hazelnuts. It complements any pasta very well.

Mix the pecans and butter together in a small skillet. Slowly heat until the butter turns a nice hazelnut shell color. Turn the heat off, let steep until lukewarm, then strain into a small sterilized container through a sterilized tea strainer, pushing on the mesh with a sterilized spatula to extract as much butter as possible. Any leftovers of this or any nut butter can be kept frozen for 2 weeks. It will go rancid faster sitting in the refrigerator.

Nut butters are excellent used on vegetables, veal, and white meat of chicken or turkey.

Flavored Oils

Flavored oils are not a new concept but an updated one. The Egyptians made flavored oils from all kinds of herbs and flowers and taught us the process, called in French *enfleurage*, the word for extracting and transferring the oil, containing the perfumes of flowers and/or herbs into a nutritional or medicinal oil. The contemporary Alsatian chef Jean-Georges Vongerichten has initiated the use of flavored oils in the kitchen and vastly popularized them in the United States.

Flavored oils, when prepared with unsaturated oils, are excellent for use in dressings and can replace the saturated classic flavored butters on pastas, grilled fish, etc.

MAKING FLAVORED OILS

Do not be frightened by the rules as explained here; as a teacher and food handler, it is my duty to teach how to be safe and avoid contamination.

If you are in any way put off by my explanations, simply go to a grocery store or purveyor and purchase oils that have been rendered safe by the addition of ascorbic or citric acid, which raises the level of acid in the oil and ensures that no dangerous bacteria can live in it. Purchase small bottles which can be used quickly and keep unsealed bottles well corked on the lower shelf of your refrigerator for as short a time as you can to prevent oxidation and rancidity.

THE CHOICE OF OILS

Use a neutral-tasting polyunsaturated oil such as corn or grapeseed oil, or pure olive oil. Do not invest in the best virgin olive oil for this process; there may be a clash between the fruitiness of the olive oil and the flavor of the spice or herb. For example, virgin olive oil is a perfect choice to prepare garlic or basil oil, but not to prepare carrot or lavender oil.

TO PREPARE SAFE FLAVORED OILS

Imagine yourself preparing a bottle of *olio santo,* that lovely Italian oil flavored with sprigs of fresh basil, several cloves of garlic, and fresh tiny hot peppers. The skins of all these vegetables are liable to be contaminated, even after you wash and dry them well, with many kinds of bacteria, which of course are undetectable since they are microscopic.

Clostridium botulinum is one of these bacteria, and especially nasty, because it can survive anywhere there is no oxygen and very little acid. As part of its life cycle, *Clostridium botulinum* secretes a deadly toxin called botulin, which kills with certainty by paralyzing the vital centers of the brain. Since botulin has been detected in jars of garlic preserved in olive oil, you must assume that, if it can happen with garlic, it can happen with any other vegetal matter.

To begin, sterilize the blender and all its parts, the jar(s) in which you will store any flavored oil, the spatula with which you will scrape the blender, and any colander or strainer used to drain or strain the herbs and flavored oil by passing all of them through the full sanitizing cycle of the dishwasher before using them.

Since you will have to squeeze water out of the herbs after blanching them, wash your hands with soap and water, rinse them, then rub them with lemon juice, which destroys the bacteria, and let your hands air dry. You can, if you prefer, use surgical gloves.

Boil, cool, and squeeze absolutely dry any cheesecloth through which you may want to strain a finished flavored oil, after you wash your hands as described above or using surgical gloves.

RULES FOR STORING FLAVORED OILS

- Do not keep flavored oils at kitchen temperature, where bacteria can find them and contaminate them since bacteria grow best between 86° and 99°F and their lowest temperature for growth is 50°F.
- **Keep them refrigerated at all times and use each and every home-prepared oil within 48 hours of its making,** not only for safety reasons but also because the flavor of homemade oils starts deteriorating after this time.
- Any freshly made flavored oil not used after 48 hours can be used to brown the vegetables for meat stews or soups, replacing butter.
- Either pour the oil directly from its jar or bottle, or spoon it out using a sterilized spoon.

PREPARING A FLAVORED OIL WITH SPICE

Heat enough of the oil to cook the chosen spice in it until you release all of its flavor, then blend in the remainder of the cold oil; let steep 24 hours on the lower shelf of your refrigerator before using. **Keep the oil refrigerated at all times in between uses.**

Oil of Curry

FFR — ½ CUP

½ cup unsaturated oil of your choice

1 heaping tablespoon fresh curry powder

This oil is particularly excellent for dishes of rice and small macaroni pasta.

Heat 3 tablespoons of the oil in a small skillet over medium heat, then add the curry and cook until the kitchen fills with its smell, 2 to 3 minutes; do not burn the curry. Pour the remainder of the oil into the pan. Mix well, using a sterilized spatula, and scrape into a small sterilized jar. Keep refrigerated 24 hours on the lowest shelf of the refrigerator. Strain through several layers of sterilized cheesecloth. Use within 48 hours of its making.

PREPARING A FRESH HERB OIL

Be certain that the herbs are free of soil and that their roots have been completely removed. Wash and dry the herbs well.

Bring a pot of water to a boil, put the herbs in a colander and immerse in the rapidly boiling water for 2 minutes to sterilize them. Refresh the herbs under cold water so they do not turn color by overcooking, nor burn your hands.

Squeeze the herbs between your cleaned or gloved hands (see above) until absolutely no water comes out of them anymore. Add the herbs to the sterilized blender, pour the oil over them, and blend until they are thoroughly pureed.

Pour the unstrained oil into sterilized jars and let infuse 24 hours *in the refrigerator*. Use within 48 hours whether used in cold or hot dishes. **Keep the oil refrigerated at all times within those 48 hours,** unless in use.

The puree of the flavor-giving herbs will have deposited at the bottom of the jar; do not use it for dressings or sauces, add it to vegetable soups for more flavor.

PREPARING GARLIC OIL

Peel and remove the root end of as many garlic cloves as you wish. Crush and heat them gradually in a small amount of the oil so they are sterilized by the heat and release all their flavor into it; then pour the remainder of the cold oil over the heated oil and let infuse in a sterilized jar. **Keep refrigerated while the oil is steeping and use within 48 hours.** The garlic cloves can be used in a soup.

Mint and Garlic Oil

FFR — ½ CUP

½ cup packed fresh mint leaves

¾ cup unsaturated oil of your choice

2 large cloves garlic, root end completely removed and crushed

An excellent oil for salad dressings or as an addition to any sauce for poached chicken breasts or legs and Mediterranean fish dishes.

Wash the mint leaves in several successive changes of water, drain, and pat them dry.

Bring a small pot of water to a boil; put the mint leaves in a small colander, immerse in the rapidly boiling water, and blanch for 2 minutes to sterilize them. Drain and rinse under cold water. Squeeze dry.

Put them into a blender and add ½ cup of the oil. Blend until pureed, then scrape into a 1-cup jar.

Heat the remainder of the oil in a small saucepan over medium-high heat, add the garlic and cook until it starts to brown lightly and smells good. Scrape into the jar containing the mint oil and let infuse for 24 hours on the lowest shelf of the refrigerator. Strain through several layers of sterilized cheesecloth and use as desired within 48 hours. Keep refrigerated when not using.

Shellfish oils are made exactly like shellfish butter, by baking shells in oil in the oven until the shells are perfectly dry and brittle. They are more sterile than herb oils and have a longer shelf life. Also, because of the deep flavoring they communicate to the oil, they lose less of their flavor when kept in the freezer.

Shellfish oil prepared in larger quantities must be strained through sterilized strainers into sterilized baby food jars and well sealed. Their shelf life is 2 to 3 days well refrigerated and 10 days to 2 weeks frozen.

The technique for making shellfish oil is the same as for making shellfish butter (see page 304).

USING FLAVORED OILS

Flavored oils are used to decorate plates, prepare dressings, and as an enrichment to sauces, replacing butters. Cooks and chefs have very diverse opinions when it comes to their utilization. Please refer to the discussion on the seasoning and fine tuning of sauces containing flavored oils and vegetable juices on page 299, and in diverse meat and fish recipes in which they are used.

Neutral or Vegetarian Sauces

A "neutral" sauce is a sauce that contains absolutely no trace of meat or meat broth. To these belong the classic tomato sauces and the newfangled vegetable-juice sauces.

Tomato Sauces

Making a bad tomato sauce is easy. Unripe tomatoes, too much or insufficient cooking, and too many seasonings and herbs are the main offenders.

The primary ingredient of a truly good tomato sauce is, of course, sun-ripened fruit full of sunshine, offering a nice balance of acid and sweetness. Do not even think of using the hothouse fruit; rather, limit yourself to the September tomatoes if you have to because of your geographic location, and gather or buy as many tomatoes as you can and prepare that long-cooking essence of tomato recommended by Prosper Montagné. This sauce cooks gently all by itself for four hours; the result is delicious, as the natural acidity of the raw fruit mellows considerably. The obtained *coulis* is all-purpose and can be either transformed into diverse sauces of different ethnic origins or used as a plain seasoning for pasta, rice, and grains.

In the recipe that follows, you will see that the strained essence is thickened with a bit of potato starch. If you plan on freezing the essence, *do not thicken it until you have defrosted it*; otherwise, syneresis of the starches will occur in the freezer and you will have to rethicken the sauce anyway.

Essence of
Fresh Sun-Ripened Tomatoes

FCR — 3 QUARTS ALL-PURPOSE ESSENCE OF PURE TOMATOES

20 pounds fresh sun-ripened tomatoes, unpeeled

½ cup olive oil of your choice

4 small yellow onions, chopped

4 teaspoons granulated sugar

2 teaspoons salt

Pepper from the mill

Potato starch as needed

Wash and halve the tomatoes; do not peel them, but squeeze out all traces of seeds and water. Chop coarsely.

Heat the oil on medium-high heat in a large ovenproof braising pot, then add the onions and sauté until translucent. Add the tomatoes, sugar, salt, and pepper to taste; mix well. Cook, covered, over medium heat for 1 hour.

Preheat the oven to 300°F. Uncover the pot and place it in the oven for 3 hours, stirring at regular intervals. Strain through a conical strainer into a large stainless steel saucepan. If you want to freeze the essence or part of it, do so now.

Cool 1 cup of the sauce rapidly in a cold water bath (see page 141). Place 1 tablespoon potato starch for each quart of finished essence in a small bowl and dilute with the cooled sauce. Bring the bulk of the essence to a boil, turn down to a simmer, and gradually blend in the slurry of starch until the essence has come back to a boil and has very lightly thickened.

Ladle into sterilized glass jars of the preferred size. Keep refrigerated 1 week or frozen up to 9 months.

Baking this essence of tomatoes ensures an even heat all around the pot and eliminates any "sticking" at the bottom of the pot which could happen on a stove burner.

Essence of Tomato Prepared with
Canned Tomato Puree

FCR — 4 CUPS

2 tablespoons olive oil of your choice

2 large yellow onions, chopped

4 cups water or vegetable broth

4 cups tomato puree

1 teaspoon granulated sugar

¼ teaspoon salt

Dash of pepper from the mill

Read the list of ingredients on the puree you buy: The puree should contain nothing but tomatoes and citric acid. The finished essence will have turned orangy red by the time it has finished baking. It is up to you to judge whether it needs thickening or not. If it does, prepare a slurry of potato starch and thicken as indicated in the recipe above.

Preheat the oven to 350°F. Heat the oil in a medium-size ovenproof saucepan over medium heat. Add the onions and cook, stirring, until translucent. Add the remaining ingredients. Bring to a boil, turn down to a simmer, immediately transfer to the oven, and bake, uncovered, for 1 hour. Strain through a conical strainer. Keeps 1 week refrigerated and up to 9 months frozen.

VEGETARIAN TOMATO SAUCES

By adding aromatic vegetables, herbs, spices, and wine of your choice to a tomato essence, you can vary its taste and prepare dishes from all over the Mediterranean. Here are a few ideas:

- *From Catalonia in Spain:* Sautéed chopped celery and chopped green bell pepper, reduced red wine, and cayenne pepper to taste
- *From Provence in France:* Chopped garlic and fresh parsley leaves fried in olive oil, chopped fresh Provençal herbs, and mashed anchovy fillets
- *From Toscana in Italy:* A handful of vinegar-soaked bread crumbs, chopped garlic to your taste, and chopped fresh tarragon leaves to your taste
- *From Liguria in Italy:* A pesto made in the blender with lots of fresh basil leaves, a small handful of grated Pecorino cheese of your choice, a heaping teaspoon of pine nuts, and olive oil to your taste
- *From Emilia-Romagna in Italy:* Chopped garlic and fresh parsley leaves sautéed in butter, and olive oil and balsamic vinegar to your taste
- *From Basilicata in Italy:* Chopped celery, fennel bulb, and garlic sautéed in olive oil
- *From Greece:* Red wine reduced with ground cinnamon, and chopped fresh parsley and basil leaves

For additional ideas, see the chapter on pasta and rice on page 455.

Modern Vegetable-Juice Sauces

Although an occasional recipe prepared with vegetable juice can be found in the classic cuisine, they are not numerous enough to have been at any time as important as Jean-Georges Vongerichten has made them in the last ten years. It was a brilliant idea to extract the juice from different vegetables using an electric juicer, then reduce the juices to a less vegetal and more well-rounded taste and use them as extra light sauces.

The use of vegetable juices as sauces necessitates careful thinking on the part of the cook to harmonize the elements of the dishes in which they are used; the taste of the meat, the vegetal taste of the vegetable juice, and, if wine is served with the dish, the character of the wine must be balanced against one another or the dish will be unsatisfying as the flavors contained in each element, so to say, "bump" against one another.

THE EXTRACTION

The easiest way to extract the juices from vegetables is to use a juicer, but this requires ownership of a relatively expensive piece of equipment. Follow the directions given by the manufacturer of the machine for juice extraction.

If a juicer is not available, use a blender to pulverize the vegetables, then squeeze the juice out through several layers of sterilized cheesecloth. Work over a bowl fitted with the finest possible strainer or drum sieve, which will catch extra fine particles of cellulose that might still be in the juice.

Since the juice will be reduced after being extracted, one may think that there is no need to blanch the vegetables before extracting their juice; there is no difficulty indeed as far as bacterial content is concerned, but an ultra rapid blanching of *green* vegetables will fix the color as it does for the preparation of the flavored oils explained on page 304. This will apply to very well-washed zucchini, celery ribs, Savoy cabbage, asparagus, Swiss chard greens, sorrel, spinach, scallions, leek greens, etc., in which oxidation combined with enzymatic reactions will change the color toward green-brown.

Bring a large pot of water to a boil and add a large pinch of salt. Cut solid vegetables into medium-size chunks; use whole leaves and stems of leafy vegetables. Put the vegetables in a colander. Immerse the vegetables in the boiling water, count to three, remove the vegetables from the water, and rinse them under cold running water. Pat dry in a kitchen towel and *immediately* process in juicer or blender.

REDUCING THE JUICES

Although they contain pectin, all vegetable juices are thin and raw tasting after extraction. Put any of them in a saucepan and reduce with a tiny pinch of salt until they lose their watery texture and taste harmonious.

As some juices reduce, they throw off a thin layer of foamy material which gathers at the surface; this is cellulose; skim it with a spoon as you would any classic sauce.

THE NUTRITIONAL VALUE OF VEGETABLE JUICES AS SAUCES

Vegetable juices can be very tasty and are very lean, but at the same time, it is necessary to realize that the mere fact that they are reduced disposes completely of the vitamins they contain. So their only nutritional advantage— and it is not a negligible one—resides in their low calorie content.

TEXTURIZING AND HARMONIZING VEGETABLE JUICES WITH DIFFERENT DISHES

It is often necessary to change the status of a vegetable-juice sauce from neutral—which, remember, means containing no meat—to non-neutral, that is, containing a certain amount of fish or meat broth to make sure that, taste-wise, the sauce blends with the food it accompanies.

Vegetable juices are best used as sauces and binders for the following categories of foods:

- Pasta, rice, and grain dishes, whether vegetarian or not.
- Poached fish and shellfish; for these dishes it will be a good idea—I would even say, it is a must—to add to the vegetable juice a small amount of reduction of fish or shellfish fumet and wine to tie the fish to the vegetal taste of the juice. This small bit of reduction will, at the same time, form a bridge between the sauced dish and the wine eventually presented with it.

Another tie between fish and shellfish and a vegetable-juice sauce can be provided by adding a tablespoon or so of shellfish oil or butter to the sauce (see pages 308 and 304). Beautiful visual effect, but not as effective as a taste blending, can be achieved by dotting a green vegetal sauce with bright orange shellfish oil.

One very important restriction applies when a shellfish such as lobster, shrimp, or scallops is served with a sweeter vegetable juice such as carrot juice. The sweetness of the pure carrot juice fights the natural sweetness of the shellfish and the two clash miserably. It is important in this case to acidify the carrot juice either with a small amount of mixed fumet and wine reduction or to add a good squeeze of lemon juice to the carrot juice.

- Grilled fish and panfried fish are not complemented as well with vegetable juices as is poached fish because the slightly bitter edge of grilled fish does not blend well with the vegetal essences; blanched, sliced grilled or fried vegetables will do better in each case.
- Poached white meats of chicken, turkey, etc., are very well complemented by vegetable juices.
- Panfried white meat such as chicken cutlets, turkey cutlets, and veal chops can be sauced with such juices as zucchini and bell pepper juices, but again, as is the case with the fish, it will be necessary to tie the concentrated taste of the meat to the juice by seasoning the juice so its level of salt is the same as that of the deglazing coming from the pan in which the meat cooked. This can be achieved by using either plain salt or a small amount of meat essence. This balance of seasoning will tie the meat to the vegetable taste and act as a bridge for any wine served with such a dish.

CALCULATING QUANTITIES FOR JUICING AND ACHIEVING THE RIGHT TEXTURE

The vegetables used to prepare vegetable-juice sauces must be of the very freshest and best quality. Using organic vegetables always gives the tastiest results. Since all vegetables, in any category, will always vary in quality in regard to the length of time elapsed since they have been picked, the fresher the vegetable is, the better and more abundant the juice yield. There is no doubt that cooks working in the cold eastern and northern regions will have a much tougher time finding the right vegetables for juices outside of the summer months than southerners, southwesterners, and Californians.

To determine how much juice a particular type of vegetable will yield, weigh out one pound of the chosen vegetable. Blanch it if needed, then juice or puree and squeeze the juice out directly into a measuring cup; this will give you an idea of how much the batch of vegetables available to you will yield. I have seen significant differences between batches of zucchini, for example, where one pound of large supermarket-bought zucchini rendered half as much juice as small dark green farm-purchased zucchini. So, *test* the vegetables you will be using before you embark on a juicing adventure.

Bear in mind when preparing that test juice that you will need to reduce it by at least one half its original quantity. So purchase wisely—if one pound yields 1 cup of juice and you need 1 cup of reduced juice for your dish, purchase two pounds of vegetables.

As you can see, these sauces are healthy but they also will not be inexpensive, since fresh vegetables can cost almost as much as meats.

The texture of the juice is entirely to your taste. If you like it thin and natural, by all means use it as is after reduction. If you prefer it a little thicker, you can add a tiny amount of the pure starch of your choice, introduced to the simmering juice in the form of a slurry (see Starch-Bound Sauces, page 268).

Cooked and Uncooked Neutral Vegetable, Fruit, and Herb Relishes

These relishes which, in the last ten years, have often replaced true sauces are divided into the chutneys, pickles, and raitas of the Far East and the salsas of Latin America, especially Mexico.

Chutneys, pickles, chowchows, and piccalillis, originating from all over the Far Eastern world from India to Thailand, have become increasingly popular as time has become more and more scarce for working cooks and as the health movement has progressed.

Made of vegetables and/or fruit combined with spices, aromatics, and sometimes herbs, these relishes can be ready in very little time and used not only on grain dishes, but on many grilled fish and meats. They are perfect for barbecued meals served with beers and sodas rather than wine, for their content of strong aromatics and spices tends to make wines show poorly, whereas the bubbles of beers and sodas have the pleasant advantage of diffusing the heat of exotic chiles and of different types of gingers.

The problem with these little sauces is that it is so difficult to make a frank distinction between each category. According to Harvey Day, a long-time resident of India who published a book on curries in India, the distinction between a chutney and a pickle is that, whereas chutney contains one or several sweet ingredients such as white sugar, brown sugar, molasses, or chopped dried fruit and presents a jamlike texture, pickles contain only fruit and vegetables cut into large chunks or kept whole if of a small size. Also, in India, mustard oil always enters the composition of a pickle but is never part of a chutney.

After reading this interesting statement, I proceeded to read all the recipes that followed only to discover that several chutneys contained mustard oil, while a pickle was made from a combination of five different chopped dried fruits and ¼ pound of sugar . . . What is a French cook and longtime resident of the United States of America to make out of such a contradiction? Probably forget about all rules, do what she pleases, and encourage all of her readers/cooks to do exactly the same. In the bibliography, I have listed several very nice and interesting books offering chutneys and pickles. The intent is not to create a chutney or pickle that is authentically Far Eastern or a salsa authentically Mexican, but to create one that you personally like.

Because differences of texture and taste are bound to exist in the fruit and vegetables available in the different regions of the United States, you should consider the proportions given in the recipes below definitely as guidelines only, corresponding to the basic texture and taste of the fruit or vegetables as well as to the basic taste and acetic acid content of the vinegar used.

It is essential to remember that you should initially use minimal amounts of salt, sugar, and vinegar with the idea that more of each can be added to adjust the final taste of each preparation, so it relates best to the basic taste of the meat, fish, or grain it will accompany, as well as to your personal taste.

Pickles

The pickles that follow are mostly "short" pickles which can be made today and will last just the few hours necessary to prepare and enjoy them. So that you can see the great difference between short- and long-term pickles, I will start with the authentic recipe for French cornichons which undergo long pickling.

True French Cornichons

LFR—ONE 1½-QUART JAR

1 pound pickling cucumbers, 2 inches x ⅓ inch

Sea salt for sprinkling the cucumbers plus 1 tablespoon

6 small purple shallots, peeled and separated into single bulbs

12 silverskin onions, peeled

12 tiny cloves garlic, peeled

4 cups white wine vinegar, 5 to 6% acetic acid

5 large leafy sprigs fresh French tarragon, washed and dried

12 white peppercorns

12 black peppercorns

Cornichons are tiny pickling cucumbers preserved in pure vinegar without a trace of sugar, although some sugar is provided by the silverskin onions and shallots. Cornichons are present on all French tables to enjoy with cold cuts, hamburgers, and grilled chicken—they are the most beloved condiment for "zhe barbeque."

Using a small brush, scrub all the small spines off the surface of the cucumbers. Put them in a bowl and sprinkle them abundantly with sea salt. Cut a cross into the root ends of the shallots, onions, and garlic cloves. Toss them into the bowl of salted cucumbers and let stand 1 hour. Rinse all the vegetables under cold running water and pat dry in a kitchen towel.

Over medium heat, bring the vinegar to a boil in a stainless steel medium-size saucepan and add the tablespoon of salt; turn the heat off. Pack the cucumbers, shallots, onions, and garlic into a sterilized glass jar, tucking the tarragon sprigs and peppercorns in between. Pour the hot vinegar into the pickling jar to cover the contents by ½ inch; taste, using a clean stainless steel spoon and, after each test, add more salt if needed. Seal the jar and shake well. Place on the lowest shelf of the refrigerator to age. Shake once a day for the next week. The cornichons, onions, shallots, and garlic cloves are ready to enjoy after 6 months in the brine.

Red Radish Pickle

LFR—ABOUT 2 CUPS

1 bunch red radishes, diced into ⅛-inch cubes

½ medium-size red onion, diced into ⅛-inch cubes

Salt

Cider vinegar

1 very large clove garlic, finely chopped

3 tablespoons chopped fresh Italian parsley leaves

This short pickle must be enjoyed within a few hours of its making. It is excellent with fresh oysters.

Place the radishes and onion into a bowl, sprinkle generously with salt, and add just enough vinegar to balance the salt, so that neither of them dominates the other. Toss in the garlic. Let stand 30 minutes, then toss in the parsley and use immediately.

Green Tomato Chowchow

LFR—ABOUT 2 CUPS

3 pounds green tomatoes, sliced ⅓ inch thick

Salt

¼ teaspoon ground cloves

I teaspoon ground cinnamon

I or 2 dried Thai chiles to your personal taste, finely powdered

I large Bermuda onion, cut into small dice

I cup vinegar of your choice

¼ cup firmly packed brown sugar or to taste

Sweet yellow mustard

This chowchow is good with grilled and poached turkey breast, poached whole chicken and chicken breasts, and grilled rabbit, as well as roast pork and rice dishes.

Place the tomato slices on a large stainless steel rack placed over a jelly-roll or sheet pan. Salt on one side only and let stand for 2 hours.

In a large stainless steel saucepan mix together the tomatoes, cloves, cinnamon, chiles, onion, vinegar, and brown sugar. Bring to a boil, then reduce the heat to medium-low and simmer until thickened and compotelike. If the mixture is too dry, add water as needed. Add mustard to taste and correct the final seasoning of salt and sugar. Turn into a small compote dish. Keep refrigerated and consume within 4 days.

Kiwicranpickle

LFR—2 CUPS

2 Valencia oranges, cut into halves and seeded

I ½ cups fresh dark red cranberries

½ teaspoon finely grated lemon rind

I tablespoon balsamic vinegar or to taste

Granulated sugar

Salt

4 large kiwi, peeled and diced into ¼-inch cubes

This uncooked relish is most popular with Thanksgiving turkey.

Slice the orange halves, then chop them into large chunks. Put the cranberries into a food processor and pulse 15 seconds twice. Add the oranges and pulse another 15 seconds. The particles of cranberries and orange should not be smaller than ⅛ inch. If the mixture is uneven, remove the larger pieces and finish them by hand. Avoid overprocessing to prevent the mixture from liquefying.

Turn into a small bowl, add the lemon rind, vinegar, sugar, and salt to your personal taste, and mix well to homogenize. Keep refrigerated and just before serving, mix in the diced kiwi to prevent it from bleeding its juices. This relish is to be consumed on the same day as it is made.

Lime Chowchow

NFR — ABOUT 1½ CUPS

12 limes as large as possible

Salt

½ cup sweet rice vinegar

½ cup cider vinegar

Brown sugar

3 tablespoons chopped dark raisins

6 very soft dates, chopped

2 large cloves garlic, finely chopped

Red pepper flakes

Quarter the limes; set them pulp side up on a stainless steel rack placed over a jelly-roll or sheet pan and salt them. Let stand overnight in a warm kitchen, covered with cheesecloth. Chop very finely, rind and pulp.

Place the limes, vinegars, brown sugar to taste, raisins, dates, garlic, and as much pepper flakes as you like into a large stainless steel saucepan and bring to a boil; reduce the heat to medium and simmer 10 to 15 minutes. Do not overcook to prevent bitterness from leaching out of the lime rinds. Correct the final seasoning with salt and sugar and turn into a small bowl. Keep refrigerated and consume within 4 days.

For all grilled white meats, especially pork and chicken.

Wilted Cucumber and Tomato Pickle

LFR — ABOUT 2 CUPS

1 to 2 tablespoons olive or other unsaturated oil of your choice

8 large, firm sun-ripened tomatoes (about 3 pounds), sliced ⅓ inch thick and seeded

Salt

Pepper from the mill

1 large European cucumber, peeled, seeded, and diced into ¼-inch cubes

½ cup chopped fresh dill

Cider vinegar

Rub one or two stainless steel cake racks with the oil, then set the tomato slices on the racks, set over a large glass baking dish to collect the juices they will lose. Reserve the juice. Dry the tomatoes at least 4 hours in a very low oven.

Salt and pepper the cucumber dice; let stand until all the juices have leached out, about 1 hour. Then drain them and set aside.

Remove the skin from the oven-dried tomato slices; cut into small dice and mix them with the cucumber and dill. Add just enough vinegar to bind the mixture, which should be moist but not soupy. Reduce the tomato col-

The French chef who had the great idea of oven drying tomatoes did a great service to all cooks and chefs who cannot obtain sun-ripened tomatoes. This pickle is excellent on all poached and grilled fish and tossed through hot macaroni just before serving to replace butter or oil dressings. When used on pasta, do not let the pasta stand once the relish has been added or the vinegar will penetrate the pasta and give it the most unpleasant sour-bitter taste.

lected water in a stainless steel 1-quart saucepan over medium heat until it is concentrated to 2 tablespoons. Add as much of that essence as you like to add flavor to the pickle; also add more plain salt, if needed. Mix well. Serve without delay. Keeps well but does not taste quite as good on the second day.

New South Wales Mint Relish

LFR—ABOUT 1½ CUPS

1 medium-size white onion, diced into ⅛-inch cubes

Salt

½ cup packed washed and dried fresh mint leaves

Red pepper flakes

1 large clove garlic, finely chopped

⅓ cup water

½ cup sherry vinegar, 7% acetic acid

⅓ cup sweet rice vinegar

Pinch of granulated sugar (optional)

Fresh lemon juice (optional)

From Australia, where it was served with a delicious long-cooked and well-done leg of lamb.

Spread the chopped onion on a plate and sprinkle with salt. Let stand 30 minutes, then drain into a conical strainer.

Mix the onion, mint, pepper flakes, garlic, water, and vinegars together well. Let stand 15 minutes, then if needed add more salt and a pinch of sugar and/or lemon juice if needed. Serve within the next 15 minutes.

Chutneys

These sweet-sour, low-sugar, jamlike preparations are often so pleasant that one feels like taking a spoon and just digging in . . . a thing not to do, for a small amount goes a long way, especially with curried meats, grilled or broiled poultry, pork roasts, etc.

Pear Chutney

FCR—ABOUT 2 CUPS

6 Bartlett or Anjou pears, as ripe as possible

½ teaspoon grated lemon rind

Juice of 1 lemon

½ cup granulated sugar or to taste

2 teaspoons peeled and grated fresh ginger or galangal

You must pay particular attention to the choice of pears; half of them must be at the peak of ripeness, the other, somewhat under-ripe and crunchy. Unfinished with the eastern spices, this would be a

6 Bosc pears, firm and under-ripe

Balsamic vinegar (optional)

Salt

Coarsely cracked white pepper from the mill

2 scallions, green part only, finely sliced

Peel, core, and coarsely dice the ripe pears. Put them in a blender, add the lemon rind, lemon juice, sugar, and ginger, and process until a coarse puree results. Turn into a large stainless steel saucepan and bring to a boil. Reduce the heat to medium-low and simmer until reduced by one third, stirring occasionally to prevent sticking.

Meanwhile, preheat the oven to 350°F. Set the Bosc pears in a baking dish, prick each fruit with a trussing needle or cake tester, and bake until the needle inserted to their center comes out quite warm. Cool the pears, then peel, core, and dice them coarsely. Mix them into the reduced puree, then add the balsamic vinegar if desired, salt, and several generous turns of the pepper mill. Simmer until the mixture is well bound. Turn into a serving bowl and when cold stir in the scallions. Keeps up to a week refrigerated.

Mango-Apricot Chutney

NFR—ABOUT 2 CUPS

12 dried apricot halves, soaked in water to cover overnight

3 very ripe mangoes, peeled, pitted, and mashed

6 very soft and sticky dates, pitted and mashed

3 tablespoons whisky or bourbon of your choice

¼ cup firmly packed brown sugar

½ cup sweet rice vinegar

1 teaspoon ground cardamom

3 unripe mangoes, peeled, pitted, and diced into ⅓-inch cubes

2 to 4 tiny dried Tabasco peppers or to your personal taste

Salt

Drain and discard the apricot soaking water; rinse the apricots in two more changes of water and drain well. Place the apricots, mashed ripe mangoes, dates, whisky, brown sugar, rice vinegar, and cardamom in a large stainless steel saucepan. Bring to a boil, reduce the heat to medium-low and simmer until the mixture starts to thicken. Add the diced unripe mangoes, and as many Tabasco peppers as desired; continue cooking, stirring occasionally to prevent sticking, until the mixture looks and feels like jam, then salt it to your taste. Turn into a small bowl and cool. This keeps 2 weeks well refrigerated.

plain European compote. Galangal is a cousin to ginger and is used a lot in Thai and Vietnamese dishes.

Delicious with all kinds of roasted and grilled poultry. The peppers used here are the tiny Capsicum frutescens *"Tabasco," sometimes labeled "Piments Oiseaux."*

Curried Many-Tomato Chutney

FCR—ABOUT 2 CUPS

8 large sun-ripened red tomatoes, peeled and seeded

8 large sun-ripened orange tomatoes, peeled and seeded

8 large sun-ripened yellow tomatoes, peeled and seeded

2 tablespoons unsaturated oil of your choice

I large Bermuda onion, diced into ⅓-inch cubes

I heaping tablespoon curry powder of your choice

⅓ cup granulated sugar

⅔ cup vinegar of your choice

Sweet yellow mustard

4 large under-ripe green tigerskin tomatoes, peeled, seeded, and cut into ½-inch cubes

Salt

If you can find the green tigerskin tomatoes now grown in California and the warmer states, use them; the visual effect is lovely. You can use your own home-ground curry powder. Good on couscous, rice, millet, and spätzle.

Chop the red tomatoes until almost liquid; cut the orange and yellow tomatoes into ½-inch chunks. Heat the oil in a sauteuse pan, then add the onion and cook, stirring, over medium heat until light brown. Add the curry and cook over medium-low heat until the smell develops powerfully, then add the red tomatoes and bring to a boil. Add the orange and yellow tomato chunks, the sugar, and vinegar, reduce the heat to medium-low, and simmer, stirring occasionally to prevent sticking, until the mixture is jamlike. Add as much sweet yellow mustard as you wish. Reheat just below the boiling point and add the cubes of green tomatoes and salt to your taste; keep warm over very low heat for 15 minutes. Turn into a bowl and serve. Keeps up to 4 days in the refrigerator.

Raitas

Raitas do not quite qualify as neutral sauces since their base is yogurt which is of animal origin, but this is a good place to draw attention to them and how interesting and refreshing they are. Raitas are made with thick yogurt, what we would call in the United States "yogurt cheese," which you can make yourself, and in which vegetables, herbs, or fruit and nuts, and always spices are blended.

There are two theories to the origin of the word itself. In India, some believe it is derived from *rai,* which is the word for mustard seeds; indeed, some western India raitas contain some mustard seeds. Others believe that the name comes from the second syllable "ta," which would be an abbreviation of the word *taat,* which means hot, as in hot pepper, and, in fact, some raitas from other parts of India contain hot peppers.

The raitas may have traveled with the Arabs along the Silk Road, and I have included the laban of Saudi Arabia and the tzatsiki of Greece in the recipes below so cooks can see the similarities. There is even a *raito* or *reito* in the Provençal cuisines, but since it contains neither yogurt nor hot peppers, the origin of the word may be different, although I have tasted at least one version which was very peppery.

Raitas usually accompany very, very hot dishes and act as a soother and refresher of the palate.

ABOUT THE YOGURT Use only *natural* yogurt that contains absolutely no stabilizers such as carageenan or gelatin, or the cheese will not drip; so, read the list of contents very closely. If you make your own yogurt, of course use it.

Dried Papaya Raita

FFR — 1 ½ CUPS

2 cups full-fat natural plain yogurt

¼ cup crème fraîche or 2 tablespoons each heavy cream and sour cream

6 ounces dried papaya

1 tablespoon caraway seeds

⅓ cup shelled pistachios

½ teaspoon garam masala

Salt

2 dashes Tabasco sauce

2 tablespoons chopped cilantro leaves

This is nice with rice or couscous which has been highly seasoned with Tabasco or hot chiles, with spice-seasoned grilled chicken, and with grilled lamb. The same raita can be made using chopped dried apricots. In this case use unsulfured dried fruit to prevent irritation of the mouth.

Line a large conical strainer with cheesecloth rinsed under cold water and squeezed dry. Empty the yogurt into the strainer; let it drip at room temperature until it has lost half its volume, about 4 to 5 hours. Place the resulting yogurt cheese in a bowl and beat in the crème fraîche or other creams.

Rinse the dried papaya under cold running water to dissolve the layer of sugar on its surface. Pat dry in paper towels and dice into ¼-inch cubes. Add to the yogurt cheese.

Toast the caraway seeds until lightly browned and fragrant in a frying pan over medium heat, being careful not to burn them. Add to the yogurt cheese. Toast the pistachios in the same pan; when they are very hot and smell good, empty them into a kitchen towel and rub well to discard the skins. Chop coarsely and add to the yogurt mixture together with garam masala, salt to your taste, and Tabasco. Add the cilantro and mix well. Keep refrigerated until ready to serve. Serve within 24 hours.

Arabic Laban

There are many versions of laban, some thick, some light to the point of being almost liquid. This is laban prepared as I enjoyed it as the guest of a Saudi Arabian family whose mother was originally from Lebanon. It was brushed over a medium-rare spit-roasted leg of lamb that was then cooked until well done and crisp with browned milk solids; the remainder of the laban was served in a small bowl.

FFR— I ½ CUPS

2 cups full-fat natural plain yogurt

I large white onion, chopped

Salt

⅓ cup chopped dark raisins

⅓ cup packed, coarsely chopped fresh mint leaves

Line a conical strainer with cheesecloth rinsed under cold water and squeezed dry. Empty the yogurt into the strainer; let drip until it has lost one quarter of its volume, 30 to 40 minutes. Place the resulting yogurt cheese in a bowl.

Meanwhile, place the onion on a plate, salt it, and let it drain off all its water, about 1 hour. Drain in a colander and pat dry.

Add the onion, raisins, and mint to the yogurt cheese, mix well, and keep refrigerated until ready to use. Use the same day as prepared.

Tzatsiki

This tasty sauce or condiment was placed on my table at the onset of lunch one glorious sunny day in Piraeus, accompanying the biggest, most succulent grilled Mediterranean prawns. Tzatsiki came to Greece from the Middle East and is usually hardly salted; add salt if you prefer it less acid. Also excellent as a less fat salad dressing.

FFR— I ½ CUPS

3 cups full-fat natural plain yogurt

I European cucumber

2 small cloves garlic, mashed

I tablespoon fresh lemon juice

I tablespoon extra virgin olive oil

I ½ tablespoons chopped fresh mint leaves

I ½ tablespoons chopped fresh dill

Large pinch of salt

Line a colander with cheesecloth rinsed in cold water and squeezed dry. Empty the yogurt into it and let drip until the yogurt has lost half its volume, 4 to 5 hours. Turn into a bowl.

Peel and seed the cucumber, then grate it through the coarse side of a grater directly into the bowl of yogurt cheese; stir in the garlic, lemon juice, olive oil, herbs, and salt. Mix well, cover with plastic wrap, and store overnight in the refrigerator to blend the flavors. Use the next day only and make it fresh as needed.

Salsas

There is hardly a cook, beginner or sophisticated, who does not know about salsas, since the shelves of our supermarkets are well stocked with all kinds of salsa variations, cooked and uncooked. The following salsas are formulas which I have put together myself with ingredients from Mexico which I particularly like and in the small quantities I like them. These salsas need a maximum of an hour of standing time before being served to blend the flavors, but it is a good idea to enjoy them before they have lost their slight crunchiness.

It is essential that the ingredients for a good salsa be hand cut with a knife, as small as possible. The French rule of "the smaller the aromatics are cut, the deeper the taste of the sauce they flavor" also applies without a doubt to Mexican-style salsas. Refrain from using any mechanical implement or you will obtain, at best, indifferent vegetable pap instead of salsa. You will notice the small amount of salt, added only after the ingredients have sat together for a while; this way of salting prevents the salt from drawing out the juices from the vegetables.

Not only are salsas good as tidbits to be picked up on crunchy tortilla chips, but they are wonderful as condiments with rice, small-size pastas, etc., and they help lose many a pound when used as a salad dressing.

Citrus and Jícama Salsa

LFR—2 CUPS

1 large juice orange

12 fresh kumquats

1 small jícama, 3 inches in diameter, peeled

1 small sweet onion, peeled

1 dried pasilla chile

¼ cup packed, washed, and dried cilantro leaves

⅓ teaspoon salt

Pepper from the mill

I owe this idea of citrus and jícama salsa to Elizabeth Lambert Ortiz, and I enjoy it so much that I have prepared multiple variations on it. Try all kinds of oranges and tangerines and you will find a different variation of taste every time. This is excellent with cold shrimp, cold pâté of scallops, grilled shrimp, etc.

Remove the ends of the orange, slice it into ¼-inch slices, and remove all the seeds. Fold each slice over into a half moon and cut crosswise into ¼-inch-wide pieces; push the chopped fruit into a corner of the cutting board. Slice the kumquats the same way, removing all seeds. Bring the mixture back to the center of the board and chop 1 minute or so until the pieces of citrus turn into roughly ⅛-inch cubes. Push the citrus and all its juice into a bowl. Cut the jícama into ⅛-inch-thick slices, then cut slices into ⅛-inch-wide julienne sticks. Cut the sticks into ⅛-inch cubes. Add to the bowl containing the citrus and mix well.

Chop the onion into ⅛-inch cubes; chop the pasilla, seeds and all, into a very fine powder. Add the onion and pasilla to the bowl. Chop the cilantro leaves and add to the mixture. Mix well without adding the salt and let the flavors blend together for an hour in the refrigerator. Salt and pepper to your taste only 10 minutes before serving to preserve the crunch. Serve on the same day as prepared.

Tomato Chipotle Salsa

FCR — 1½ CUPS

6 medium-size sun-ripened tomatoes

1 teaspoon grated lime rind

1 teaspoon unsweetened cocoa powder

½ large sweet onion, diced into ¼-inch cubes

Salt

2 tablespoons olive oil of your choice

2 canned chipotle chiles, finely chopped

This is my personal taste; if you prefer something more authentically Mexican, see the bibliography for a list of excellent books offering many authentic concoctions. Excellent with all grilled meats.

Place the tomatoes on a baking sheet. Turn on the broiler and grill the tomatoes until their skins char, a few minutes on each side. Remove from the oven and peel. Cool, seed, and cut the pulp only into ¼-inch pieces. Place the pulp in a bowl. Mix in the lime rind and sift and mix in the cocoa.

Meanwhile, place the onion cubes into a stainless steel strainer set over a bowl, salt lightly, and let the juice render for 15 minutes. Mix the onion, then the olive oil, then the chipotles into the tomatoes and mix well. Let stand 30 minutes at room temperature and serve. Use the same day as prepared.

Salsa Maddalena

FCR — 3 CUPS

1 large, ripe Haas avocado, peeled, pitted, and diced into ¼-inch cubes

1 tablespoon fresh lime juice

1 recipe Tomato Chipotle Salsa (above)

⅓ cup cooked black beans

⅓ cup roasted corn kernels

Salt

This salsa was born on a day when half a bowl of the above salsa was mixed with leftovers of avocado, black beans, and corn salad and ended up on plates side by side with great hamburgers.

Toss the avocado with the lime juice. Add it to the salsa, then add the black beans and corn. Keep chilled 15 to 20 minutes, then salt lightly. Serve with hamburgers on the same day as prepared.

Far Eastern Cuisines and Sauces

Many young cooks nowadays use various sauce ideas coming from Japan, China, Thailand, and Korea. This is certainly wonderful and brings a lot of diversity to the table. I have myself, as you can see all through this book, made use of many ingredients from foreign countries and civilizations, and blended them in a very western manner in my preparations. From the two sections above, you can see that I fully appreciate the cuisines of India and the Arab countries; since most of these nations speak a language I can fully understand besides their own native languages, I can communicate at least three quarters of the way with their cooks and food writers.

I am, after more then fifty years of in-depth study of all the French cuisines, still learning important details about them and I am a strong believer in the fact that it is better to be an expert in one discipline than to be a dabbler in many. I have never felt adequate to present really original ideas coming from China, Japan, or Korea, for sheer lack of true deep personal knowledge and documentation. This is why, in spite of many requests, I have steadily and totally refused to teach any Chinese, Japanese, Thai, or Korean techniques and dishes; I simply lack the emotional language and education of the palate to assimilate them deeply enough to be able to teach them.

All cooks fascinated by the food of China and other Far Eastern nations should refer to the bibliography and consult the books written by those of my colleagues who have lived, studied, married, and cooked in one part or another of China, Japan, or any other Far Eastern country, and mastered the national language or local languages in depth, for they have been able to truly communicate with the people and ask the key questions which, alone, could unravel the mysteries of their tables.

You will find some of the western sauces garnishing several meat and fish dishes finished with classic Chinese soy, plum, and oyster sauces as well as such classic ingredients of Japan as wasabi, sake, and mirin, but they will always be part of an "East meets West" dish; I have prepared plenty of these dishes since 1973 and have included some in my book *In Madeleine's Kitchen*.

Emulsified Sauces

Let's take a cook's look at emulsions. It is important for any cook to understand how they function, for they are part of our work in many preparations, from cakes to egg and cream foams, and especially in sauces.

An *emulsion* is a suspension or dispersion of one liquid into another, the two liquids being mutually insoluble, or immiscible. The first example that comes to mind is, of course, oil and water. Pour some of each onto the same plate and you will end up with two well-delineated puddles skirting each other, but never mixing. If the puddles are mixed, observe, as in one way or another, smaller puddles of water will come to join one another again and so will the puddles of oil; in this inevitable rejoining of each element, each is said to *coalesce*. In opposition to oil and water, think of wine, vinegar, or brandy and how each of them mixes with water to become one liquid. The immiscibility of water and oil is such a natural fact of life that in many cultures, two people who obviously are not compatible elicit the comment: "Those two get along like oil and water."

There are different types of emulsions. Some are unstable, which means that their components will always remain immiscible and will separate quickly when mixed; some are semipermanent, which means that by mixing them with certain molecules or at certain temperatures one can render them stable but they will eventually separate over a period of time. Some are permanent and will remain stable, or mixed, and will not separate because they contain an *emulsifier*.

An Unstable Emulsion

The typical unstable emulsion used in cookery is the *vinaigrette*, the oil-and-vinegar dressing millions of us use daily as a dressing on salads.

Repeat the experiment above, replacing water with vinegar or lemon juice and putting the vinegar in a small jar with at least twice as much oil as vinegar. Add salt and pepper, agitate the jar as quickly as you can, and you have a plain vinaigrette, an opaque mixture in which the oil has been dispersed into the vinegar into millions of microscopic droplets which are temporarily suspended into the vinegar. You have made an *oil-in-water* emulsion. As you well know, the oil and vinegar each will go its way and after a few minutes they will separate into two layers, or *phases*. The oil, being the lighter, will be the top layer; the vinegar, being the heavier, will be the bottom layer in the jar.

THE PHASES OF AN EMULSION;
PHASE SEPARATION

Now, continuing your experiment, add a finely chopped shallot and some finely chopped herbs, and shake the jar again to emulsify the dressing again. It is even easier now to observe the emulsion breaking down and to see how the herbs and shallot stay just below the oil, on the surface of the vinegar. The line at which they seem to float is called the *interface* between the *oil phase* and the *water phase*. The fact that the water has been acidified with acetic acid is unimportant for the terminology; vinegar is 95 percent water and is referred to as the water phase. If butter were melted and used, it would be the oil phase (even though it consists of 20 percent water, it is also 80 percent fat). Butter as a solid is referred to as a water-in-oil emulsion. The surface of the oil that is exposed to the air is called the *oil/air interface*.

As you let the dressing stand and the phases of the emulsions separate, it is easy for you to observe that *phase separation*; the oil phase will travel upward and the water/vinegar phase will travel downward, doing what nature wants them do, which is to separate.

An emulsion of oil and water is an *unstable emulsion* because it will never be able to stay emulsified and will always separate. Keep the dressing 24 hours in the refrigerator and you will soon see that the aromatics and herbs added to the dressing have absorbed some of the vinegar at the same time as, by osmosis, they rendered some of their juices into the vinegar, giving it additional flavor. When they are saturated they will settle at the bottom of the jar.

VARIATION OF COMPOSITION OF THE BASIC VINAIGRETTE

The proportion of acid used in a vinaigrette is strictly a matter of personal taste. Some like a very acid vinaigrette, some a very mellow one. Use the following proportions as a guide:

- For a very acid vinaigrette, use 50 percent each oil and vinegar
- For a medium-acid vinaigrette, use 35 to 40 percent vinegar and 60 to 65 percent oil
- For a mellow vinaigrette, use 25 percent vinegar and 75 percent oil

These are the proportions generally accepted by the Old World and Latin American countries. The Romans express their predilection for mellow vinaigrette in that cute little saying: "It takes four persons to make a salad: a wise one to add the salt, a miser to add the vinegar, a spendthrift to add the oil, and a crazy one to toss the salad."

The vinegar can be replaced by any citrus juice, plain or reduced, or a blend of vinegar and citrus juice. The amount of salt needed will vary with the volume and type of vinegar used; the more acid the vinegar or juice, the more salt will be needed to obtain a perfect balance of taste between the two.

Pepper can be black pepper, white pepper, or any chile of your choice, whether American or Thai, powdered cayenne or Szechuan, toasted or untoasted; the choice is wide and yours.

Aromatics can include finely chopped onion, chopped shallot, mashed garlic, grated fresh ginger, etc. They are added to the vinegar together with the salt.

Fresh herbs are added to the dressing just before mixing the emulsion, which itself should be done just before serving. If, on the contrary, the herbs used are dried, they should be revived in a tiny bit of warm water and then added to the vinegar.

Here is a nice dressing very popular in the Maghreb; it was brought back to the French Riviera by the Pieds Noirs families when they left Algeria at the time of its independence. "*Pieds Noirs*" was the name given to French people born in Algeria during the colonial era when this nation was occupied by France.

Vinaigrette des Pieds Noirs

FFR—I CUP

3 tablespoons fresh lemon juice

Salt

Pepper from the mill

½ cup plus I tablespoon virgin olive oil

I clove garlic, mashed or whole

3 tablespoons chopped fresh mint leaves

The garlic can, if you prefer, be omitted from the dressing and rubbed against the sides of the bowl. The taste of the salad will be more subtle. To be used with crackling Romaine.

Mix the lemon juice, salt, and pepper well to start dissolving the salt. Whisk in the oil until the dressing turns completely opaque. Toss in the garlic and mint. Use within 15 minutes after reemulsifying well.

Slowing Down the Speed of Separation of the Phases—Semipermanent Emulsions

There are several ways of slowing down the speed of the separation of an emulsion, to the point where the emulsion will remain stable for a length of time, if held at the correct temperature.

MECHANICAL AGITATION

Many cooks and chefs advocate the use of machines such as the blender or food processor to prepare a vinaigrette-type dressing, because the dressing becomes more viscous and thicker and presents a uniform color; also, such a dressing coats salad greens far more evenly than the handmade dressing.

It is easy to understand why. The extreme speed of the machine helps disperse the oil into the vinegar in infinitely tiny droplets, much, much smaller than a hand whisk could ever make them. The two phases of the emulsion become totally invisible and the resulting dressing takes on an even color that is one of the paler shades of the vinegar color. At the same time as it disperses the phases into one another, the machine churns quite a bit of air into the dressing in the form of microscopic bubbles. These bubbles, interspersed between the droplets of oil, interfere with the latter coalescing and slow their motion considerably.

As a small experiment, calculate the total volume of the ingredients put into the machine and check the difference once the dressing is finished; it is measurable.

All that, of course, does not mean that the emulsion prepared in a machine will never separate; it will, but the coalescing will be slow and you can actually see it take place slowly but surely. But for at least 30 minutes the dressing will be stable, which is a great help in quantity work, when a cook has to ready a large number of salad plates at once. It is actually a great idea to leave the dressing in the blender or processor so you can fully reemulsify it quickly every so often.

Blender Orange Vinaigrette

FFR

FOR 1¼ CUPS

Juice of 2 large Valencia oranges

½ teaspoon finely grated orange rind

2 tablespoons balsamic vinegar

2 tablespoons white wine vinegar

I shallot, finely chopped

Salt

Pepper from the mill

¾ cup unsaturated oil of your choice

1½ tablespoons chopped fresh tarragon leaves

FOR 4 CUPS

Juice of 8 large Valencia oranges

2 teaspoons finely grated orange rind

½ cup balsamic vinegar

½ cup white wine vinegar

4 shallots, coarsely chopped

Salt

Pepper from the mill

3 cups unsaturated oil of your choice

⅓ cup packed chopped fresh tarragon leaves

Here are small and large proportions. Compare the texture and taste of each emulsion, in a small dressing for home use and in the blender quantity for large party or restaurant use. As a choice of oil, may I suggest one third corn oil and two thirds hazelnut oil; it blends deliciously with the orange juice.

Place the orange juice and rind in a stainless steel saucepan and reduce by three quarters over medium-high heat.

For the small recipe: Empty the juice with the rind into a bowl. Blend with the vinegars, shallot, and salt and pepper to taste. Whisk in the oil and tarragon.

For the large recipe: Place the reduced juice and rind into a blender or food processor with the vinegars, shallots, salt and pepper to taste, and the oil of your choice. Liquefy, then turn into a jar with a lid and shake in the tarragon.

Correct the seasoning of machine-made dressings very carefully; more seasoning will be needed than for handmade dressings because the bubbles of air they contain help reduce the perception of the intensity of seasonings on the tongue.

BY THE ACTION OF STABILIZERS SUCH AS GELATIN

In sauces made with reduced stock such as the essences described on pages 293–98, the gelatin contained in the stock acts as a temporary stabilizer for the emulsion taking place when these sauces are enriched with butter or a flavored oil, because it slows down the water mobility in the sauce, by trapping it in the gelatin network, somewhat in the same way as starches trap water when one thickens with a starch.

WHEN YOU ADD THE BUTTER AT FULL BOIL If you bring the sauce to a full boil and add butter or oil, the boiling motion will emulsify the butter or oil into the sauce in millions of droplets; there may be an ever so slight change of texture of the sauce, but it is not so remarkable that you can really notice it.

WHEN YOU ADD THE BUTTER OFF THE HEAT If, on the contrary, you remove the saucepan from the heat, wait a few seconds for all motion to be stilled within the saucepan, and whisk cold butter into the sauce, you will see the color of the sauce lighten as it refracts the light differently after receiving the yellowish white butter.

The texture will change also and become slightly but visibly thicker. It will coat pieces of meat better because, due to the stillness of the sauce, its lower temperature, and the moderate agitation of the whisk (compared to the frantic agitation of the rapidly boiling motion), the butterfat will be less fluid and more plastic.

An essence is a very stable reduced double stock, which becomes a semipermanent emulsion after one enriches it with butter or oil. The cook must be careful not to let the essence stand unattended at length over heat, even over a pilot light, or a tension skin will develop on its surface. As the heat accumulates in the pan and the water mobility very gradually accelerates, the oil phase will break from emulsion, travel upward, and coalesce under the tension skin.

The best way to keep the sauce warm is to set it in a water bath at 140°F and to whisk it at regular intervals to keep the oil phase in emulsion.

If a tension skin develops, you can reinstate the semipermanent emulsion and fix the texture of the sauce by, first and foremost, removing the pan from the source of heat, and whisking. Whisking, most of the time, is sufficient to bring back the correct texture.

If whisking is not enough and the butter/oil keeps breaking to the surface of the sauce, extend the water phase by gradually adding stock in small amounts until you see the sauce lighten in color and the emulsion reinstated. At this point the layer of butter/oil will have disappeared and the oil phase will again be in emulsion in the viscous essence.

The breakage of the butter out of emulsion corresponds also to overconcentration of the sauce, which often becomes oversalted; as soon as you add the stock, the taste deconcentrates.

You will have the opportunity to experiment with these principles to your heart's content when you prepare essences.

BY THE ACTION OF A STABILIZER SUCH AS STARCH

Why spend money on bottled dressing which is full of preservatives when your grandmother showed you how to make "cooked dressing"— remember her German potato salad? There were all kinds of good things in there, but basically she started by making a white sauce, because the white sauce allowed her to "spend less on oil."

Any salad dressing based on a starch slurry or a roux is basically identical to a good number of commercial bottled salad dressings and can be produced at home in a matter of minutes.

Low-Cal Fat-Controlled Dressing

LFR — ½ CUP

⅔ cup cold water

2½ teaspoons cornstarch

Salt

Pepper from the mill

1½ teaspoons prepared mustard of your choice or more to taste

2½ teaspoons vinegar of your choice or more to taste

2 tablespoons unsaturated oil of your choice

Chopped fresh herbs of your choice

Mix the water and cornstarch together in a small saucepan. Bring to a boil and thicken over medium-high heat. Pour into a small bowl and stir occasionally until barely lukewarm. Add salt and pepper to taste, the mustard, vinegar, and oil, homogenizing well, then finally add the herbs of your choice.

If some dressing is left, store it in a baby food jar and shake well before using the remainder. Refrigerate and use within 24 hours.

This dressing can be as fat free as you like; you can add as little or as much oil as you desire. The cornstarch gives the dressing almost as much slip on the palate as a regular vinaigrette made with two thirds oil and one third vinegar. The mustard plays a role in this dressing besides giving the dressing a little more taste; try to think what it can be or see below on page 333. Add the herbs in the quantity you like just before tossing the salad.

OF MILK AND BUTTER: OIL-IN-WATER AND WATER-IN-OIL EMULSIONS

The two emulsions we just described are semipermanent oil-in-water (O/W) emulsions. So is milk in which tiny droplets of butterfat are dispersed in protein-laden water. The protein-laden water is the *dispersion phase* of the emulsion; the butterfat droplets are the *dispersed phase*. Because of the body temperature of the cow, the butterfat is plastic and fluid up to the time it is drawn from the animal; as the milk cools, the butterfat becomes semisolid.

When my generation was growing up, the milk delivered at the door of the kitchen by the milkman or bought in any market had "creamed," meaning that the butterfat-laden part had traveled to the top of the bottle and the protein-laden, pure white, partially defatted milk (we call it skim milk nowadays) could be seen, sometimes as low as three inches below the neck of the bottle. The separation happened gradually over a period of 24 hours.

Nowadays, as soon as it reaches the dairy plant, the great majority of the milk sold in markets is homogenized to eliminate creaming. The homogenizer forces the milk under pressure through infinitely small holes which divide the globules of butterfat into such tiny particles (averaging 2 micrometers in diameter) that they can float in the milk and will not separate because they are coated all around by the milk protein casein. This protein increases the weight of the milk particles and forces them to remain suspended in the milk rather than rise to the surface. This process is what makes homogenized milk nutritionally too fat. Our mothers lifted the cream and made cookies with it for Sunday dinner, or transformed the cream into butter, so that we drank partly skimmed milk all the time.

Butter is also made in those big dairy plants exactly as our mothers made it, but in gigantic quantities. As the milk stands, ever so slowly creaming, the butterfat globules start "clustering" or "flocculating," or gathering in larger and larger clusters which end up clinging to one another in their upward travel to the top of the container.

Cream is milk chocked with fat globules. It is still an oil-in-water emulsion, but the oil phase is large and when you agitate the cream, the clusters of fat globules become larger and larger until they release the water they contain and you are left with large butterfat globules floating in whey. If you try churning one 8-ounce cup of cream in the blender or food processor, you will obtain roughly 5 ounces of butter (see page 30). After you gather all the butter clusters into one, the butter has become the dispersion phase for the approximately 20 percent of whey remaining in emulsion in it. Butter is a water-in-oil (W/O) emulsion.

Permanent or Stable Emulsions; Emulsifiers

Mayonnaise, which we all know for having seen it in jars bought in the supermarket, is a stable or *permanent emulsion,* in which the large amount of oil it contains is emulsified in a small amount of liquid which is either vinegar or lemon juice, thanks to the egg yolks which act as an *emulsifier.* The role of the egg yolks is to keep the oil-and-acid solution in a colloidal dispersion that will not break.

An emulsifier is a molecule with two ends:

- One of them is water soluble, consequently attracted to water and said to be *hydrophilic* (meaning loving water).

- The other is soluble in oil; it is repulsed by water, and attracted to oil/fat. It is said to be *hydrophobic* (meaning disliking water).

As the hydrophilic end of the molecule bonds with water and the hydrophobic one with fat/oil, the surface tension between the two phases is relieved and the emulsion will not separate.

Egg yolk is one of the best-working emulsifiers thanks to its large content of phospholipids such as lecithin. Lecithin is the most active and useful of all emulsifying agents contained in egg yolk, but it is not the only one; cholesterol is another one. The two do not work the same way (if you want to read interesting details on the subject, please consult the bibliography). Eggs are used in cookery as emulsifiers in sauces, cakes, creams, and mousses.

Egg yolks are not the only emulsifiers; there are many others such as sour cream, crème fraîche, mustard, gelatin, and starches. The natural pectin contained in vegetables and fruit also can act as an emulsifier and, in the manufacture of foods, common emulsifiers are carageenan and agar-agar, which you will find on the list of ingredients of many stabilized products such as yogurt, low-fat sour cream, and diet mousses.

In the paragraphs that follow, you will find an explanation of all the emulsified sauces; as you will see some are eggless, others contain eggs. Their primary characteristic is that they contain a large amount of fats and for that reason they should be consumed only occasionally. For most of these sauces, there are no real and true replacements; I am adamantly opposed to hollandaise or béarnaise in a foil packet that a cup of water is supposed to turn into one of those miraculous "none of the calories, all of the taste" sauces. Once again, have the real sauce as it should be made once in a while, but have the real thing; it is essential for your palate and for the children you raise and educate to know the difference between true food and trumped food. A spoonful of rich butter sauce is not a sin; it only becomes so if it is consumed in unreasonable amounts as part of the daily diet.

WARM EGGLESS EMULSIFIED SAUCES
THE BEURRE BLANC: ITS TECHNIQUES AND VARIATIONS
Beurre blanc Nantais, shortened to *beurre blanc*, in which the final "c" is never pronounced, translates in English to plain and simple "white butter" and is a lukewarm sauce prepared originally in the middle to lower Loire Valley of France to accompany the pike of that river and its tributaries. It is often attributed to the city of Nantes, but it is prepared all the way up the valley as far as Saumur, even Tours.

During the 1970s, *beurre blanc* was adopted widely by United States cooks and chefs who found a home for a variation of it or another, on just about everything from any type of fish to even lamb, a use that would make all food aficionados in France cry for mercy, but which was quite popular from Boston to San Francisco. *Beurre blanc* is a sauce so rich in butter that it should be reserved for very lean white fish and for shellfish and used only once in a while for an extremely delicious and opulent celebration treat. In France it is a celebration sauce usually found in good restaurants only or in wealthy homes with a house cook or chef.

From the chemical point of view, *beurre blanc* is an oil-in-water emulsion of room temperature butter into a relatively strongly acidified reduction of vinegar—or vinegar and white wine mixed—and extremely finely chopped shallots. The shallots used are the French gray shallots which are much rarer that the pink shallots cultivated in this country or imported from Brittany in five-pound bags. The *beurre blanc* made in the United States is always slightly rosy, the French one always yellow because of the large amount of carotene in French butter.

The first condition for success with *beurre blanc* is the use of the *freshest butter*; the best would be an unpasteurized butter, but we all know it is not to be found in the United States. That, however, should not keep you from making fresh butter by churning some heavy cream in a blender or food processor (see page 30).

Other major conditions of success are:

- When you are about to whisk it into the reduction, the butter should have been at room temperature for about 10 minutes and still be plastic. That means it should retain the trace of a finger when you push on it, but should be neither hard nor soft and oily.
- A pot that will transfer heat gently. I have used a nickel-lined hollandaise copper saucepan, Le Creuset pots of enameled cast iron, and several stainless steel saucepans with copperclad bottoms equally successfully. Making this sauce is one of those instances where you will know that *you* are cooking, not the pot. Use your head to keep the heat low in any way you can.
- Keeping the temperature between 130° and 140°F maximum.
- Working on a small power burner on an electric stove or a burner with a thermostat on a gas stove.
- Whisking *madly*; indeed, the more you whisk, the more tiny air bubbles you trap in the building sauce, the more staying power the sauce will have since the air bubbles will interfere with and delay the coalescing of the butter globules. Your first allies are the natural emulsifiers contained in the butter which were originally part of the milk from which the butter was made and the pectin of the shallots contained in the reduction.

    As you whisk more and more butter into the reduction, you will see the sauce turn pinkish ivory if you use pink shallots and frankly ivory if you use gray ones.

The finished sauce should not be a mass of nearly cold butter, but a fluid true sauce, surprisingly well bound and creamy enough to coat a piece of fish with a thin but shiny laquer; a *beurre blanc* must be strained through a fine conical strainer, pushing strongly on the shallots to extract all their flavorful juices. Do not use a super-fine China cap which may help break the emulsion.

REPAIRING A BEURRE BLANC Repair work of the sauce is difficult because the water phase is so very small. If you are the slightest bit afraid that the sauce is going to break, do not hesitate to whisk in a tablespoon or so of crème fraîche or buttermilk. Now if it breaks, do not get nervous. Using clam juice or fish fumet if you are working with fish or shellfish or the broth of your choice if you are working with white poultry, mix 2 tablespoons of the chosen liquid with 1/4 teaspoon potato or cornstarch. Add another tablespoon of the chosen broth to the broken *beurre blanc*, whisk well as you heat, and gradually add a few drops of the slurry. The sauce will come back "together" between 138° and 154°F with potato starch, or 144° and 162°F with cornstarch. Should it ultimately turn out too thick, add as much of the chosen broth as you need to reinstate the correct texture, and correct the taste with lemon juice, salt, and pepper as needed.

Over the last thirty years, I have prepared many variations of this basic sauce. Here is the basic sauce formula, followed by some of them.

Classic French White Butter
BEURRE BLANC ANGEVIN

FFR— I CUP

⅓ cup white wine vinegar or cider vinegar

⅓ cup dry white wine, preferably Muscadet or California
    Fumé Blanc

2 large shallots, very finely chopped

⅓ teaspoon salt or to taste

Pepper from the mill

¾ to I cup unsalted butter or to your personal taste

I tablespoon buttermilk (optional)

Reduce the vinegar, wine, shallots, salt, and pepper in a saucepan over medium heat to ¼ cup of mixed solids and liquids. Remove the pot from the heat. Cool the mixture to 140°F. Return the pot to extremely low heat and whisk in the butter tablespoon by tablespoon. If used, whisk in the buttermilk until it disappears into the sauce. Strain into a sauce boat heated to lukewarm. Serve immediately.

This is the recipe I used when learning to make the sauce under the tutelage of my chef aunt Claire Robert. This formula is the Anjou-Touraine beurre blanc containing some white wine; the Nantes butter would be prepared entirely with vinegar.

This pairs well with yellow or walleye pike, shad, all trout, steelhead, Arctic char, salmon, and any shellfish from shrimp to crab, lobster, and scallops.

Virgin Butter

For vegetables and poached or steamed fish.

FFR—ABOUT 1 CUP

⅓ cup water

2 tablespoons fresh lemon juice

⅓ teaspoon salt or to taste

⅛ teaspoon white pepper from the mill or to taste

½ cup unsalted butter

⅓ cup unsweetened lightly whipped heavy cream

Mix and reduce water, lemon juice, salt, and pepper in a saucepan over medium heat to 2 tablespoons. Whisk in the butter over very low heat tablespoon by tablespoon. Fold in the whipped cream. Strain into a sauce boat heated to lukewarm.

Black Virgin Butter

This is especially delicious as a dip for lobster grilled in its shell and seared scallops.

FFR—ABOUT 1 CUP

⅓ cup water

2 tablespoons fresh lemon juice

⅓ teaspoon salt or to taste

⅛ teaspoon white pepper from the mill

⅓ cup unsalted butter, at room temperature

⅓ cup lukewarm Noisette Butter (page 32), strained through a very fine tea strainer

2 tablespoons unsweetened lightly whipped heavy cream

In a saucepan over medium heat, mix and reduce the water, lemon juice, salt, and pepper to 2 tablespoons. Whisk in the room-temperature butter over low heat tablespoon by tablespoon. Then whisk in the noisette and finish by folding in the whipped cream. Strain into a sauce boat heated to lukewarm.

Note: In any sauce containing butter at room temperature and noisette butter, the cold butter is always added first because the whey it contains helps to initiate the emulsion.

Geneva Butter

A modern replacement for the time-consuming Genevoise sauce, which is ever so delicious on salmon. For all poached or broiled fish.

FFR—ABOUT 1 CUP

4 shallots, very finely chopped

2 tablespoons red wine vinegar

½ cup water

½ cup dry red wine

2 tablespoons chopped fresh parsley leaves

1 tablespoon each chopped fresh tarragon, basil, and chervil leaves

1 ½ to 2 teaspoons anchovy paste or to your personal taste

Pepper from the mill

¾ cup unsalted butter

Mix all the ingredients together in a saucepan except the butter. Reduce over medium heat to 3 tablespoons. Whisk in the butter tablespoon by tablespoon over very low heat. Strain into a lukewarm sauce boat.

For other white butter–style sauces, please consult the fish chapter.

COLD EMULSIFIED EGG YOLK SAUCES

MAYONNAISE AND ITS VARIATIONS Our much used mayonnaise is the prototype or "mother" of the cold, stable emulsion sauces. It has existed from great antiquity, for if one reads the book of Apicius, enough sauces contain eggs and oil in their list of ingredients that they could have been prepared pretty much as we prepare mayonnaise nowadays. In the most recent French book on food history by Maguelonne Toussaint Samat, the author wonders whether mayonnaise might have started as *moieulnoise*, from the old French word *moieulx* meaning egg yolks; others support the Port Mahon theory because the sauce would have been served after the battle of Port Mahon in 1756. In a word, no one knows for sure.

Personally I believe that the sauce existed in one form or another, from antiquity on, as there are too many "olive oil" sauces in the Mediterranean basin for that not to have been the case, some stabilized with the soft center of bread, others with the liver of fish such as the famous rascasse, others yet with egg yolks or even the relatively modern potato, all of them accompanying some fish soup or other, and there is no doubt that fish soup is the ancestral food of the seafarers of the eastern Mediterranean. On the coasts of Greece, Provence, and the Languedoc, I have been served the modern forms of Greek *skordalia* and *rouille* prepared sometimes with bread (even with potatoes in Greece), sometimes with egg yolks; only aïoli is always made with egg yolks, although once it had been made with the mortar-pounded gelatinous skin of a poached cod towering on the aïoli platter. Besides bread, eggs, or codskin, each sauce contained the most fragrant virgin olive oil. So much for mayonnaise history; for more information, follow the latest discoveries in the food history department.

SAFETY AND NUTRITION As for every preparation containing uncooked egg yolk, you must remember the problem of salmonella in the eggs and check that your source of eggs is not contaminated. Unfortunately, for the time being, this remains your responsibility. Hopefully by the time this book appears the problem of salmonella contamination will have been solved at large in the country; much work has been going into eliminating it. Besides the classic techniques and recipe for true mayonnaise, you will find one for an always safe boiled egg yolk mayonnaise on page 341.

Poor, lovely, deliciously addictive mayonnaise has joined the rank of the no-nos of modern nutrition and we all have gone out of our way to find a replacement product that is both nutritionally sound and totally sanitary. Again, at the risk of being a bore, I would rather have a true mayonnaise less often, but enjoy the real thing. However, I have included recipes for mayonnaises that are restricted in either eggs or oil.

THEORY AND BASIC TECHNIQUES OF MAKING MAYONNAISE
Mayonnaise is a stable or permanent emulsion in which a large amount of oil is emulsified in a small amount of liquid, which is either vinegar or lemon juice, mixed with egg yolks, which act as emulsifier. The role of the egg yolks is to keep the oil and acid in a colloidal dispersion that will not break; within the egg yolk, the emulsifying role is held mostly by the phospholipid lecithin.

True mayonnaise does not contain any emulsifier other than egg yolks, but many people like to add a bit of mustard which is not only helpful in promoting the emulsion, but also adds piquancy to the taste of the sauce.

The implements. Use a small bowl that is as cylindrical in shape as possible, such as the 1-quart bowl of an electric mixer. Rinse the bowl with hot water and dry it before starting. Use a whisk; it is more efficient than a wooden spoon. A perfectly good emulsion can be obtained with a wooden spoon, it just does not form as fast as it does with the whisk and when one works with a wooden spoon, one must add the oil twice as slowly at the beginning.

The ingredients and their temperature. All ingredients should be at *room temperature*. Cold ingredients retard the formation of the emulsion, the viscosity of the oil is such that it resists being broken up into droplets and does not flow well into the yolks and thus has a problem being accepted by them. Cold ingredients straight from the refrigerator should be kept at room temperature for at least 30 minutes before starting the sauce. In some cold climates it still may not be enough to warm the eggs and oil to room temperature; in this case, warm the oil and eggs in their shells in a small bowl of warm water, then dry the eggs before separating them. If, because of time limits, you have to start a mayonnaise with oil that is just a bit too cold, warm the bowl with warm water and dry it well.

The choice of oil. The choice of oil is important but is basically a question of personal taste. If you do not like the taste of olive oil, use corn oil or half corn and half olive oil. Extra virgin olive oil alone, however, should be used for the making of the Provençal *aïoli* or the *skordalia* of Greece. The modern heavy oils such as walnut, hazelnut, and pistachio oils can of course be used but always cut them with a lighter neutral-tasting oil which will lighten their viscosity; the exact quantity of the heavy oil depends very much on the texture and taste of the oil at your disposal. Always start with the lighter oil, then continue and finish the sauce with the heavier one. Flavored oil can also be used; you will have to taste to find out how much when you use each particular oil.

Whichever oil you use, you will have an easier time if it has been *winterized* (see page 633 for a full explanation), for if it is cold, tiny crystals of fat in a nonwinterized oil will not allow the emulsion to form as the hydrophobic ends of the lecithin molecules have difficulty making contact with the crystals. Nonwinterized oils, such as extra virgin olive and other heavy nut oils, must be at room temperature for a full hour before being used.

Handmade mayonnaise. Place the egg yolks in a bowl with salt, pepper of your choice, and vinegar or lemon juice; whisk well to break all the yolk membranes. The egg yolks should lighten to a much paler yellow.

Add the oil drop by drop at the beginning, to allow the lecithin enough time to go to work; start adding more oil, that is, about a teaspoon at a time, only after you see the sauce thicken visibly. Then increase to a tablespoon at a time, then finally, once the emulsion is well formed, add up to 3 tablespoons or more at a time.

The more oil you add, the stiffer the mayonnaise becomes; it can become so thick that you can put it into a pastry bag and pipe it for decoration at the edge of a platter, as is done in all French charcuteries.

Lightening the sauce. For lightness's sake, cut the sauce with as much lightly salted water and/or lemon juice as you wish as you go along. Each egg yolk has the capacity of emulsifying a very large amount of oil (2 to 3 cups) in laboratory work but in kitchen work, it is essential, if only for good taste and appearance, to limit the amount of oil and lighten the sauce with these additions.

Stabilizing the sauce with boiling water. Mayonnaise is finished with a good tablespoon of boiling water which gives the sauce a reserve of water, so that, on standing, the sauce will not "bleed" oil drops through the thin tension skin that builds when the sauce stands uncovered at room temperature. You can skip this addition nowadays by covering the sauce with a film of plastic wrap which will keep the water bouncing back and forth between the air/oil interface of the sauce and the plastic stretched over it. But it never hurts to add that tablespoon of boiling water; do not worry about the sauce thinning; it will thicken again and mound beautifully after a two-hour stay in the refrigerator.

IF THE MAYONNAISE SEPARATES Mayonnaise separates for two reasons:

- Either the oil was very cold and did not flow well and/or the lecithin molecules in the existing egg yolk did not function properly,
- Or, and this is the most common reason, you simply added too much oil at once.

Be sure to prepare mayonnaise plenty of time in advance to avoid last-minute scrambling in case of its "breaking." Once a handmade mayonnaise separates, and you see the particles of yolk floating in what will look like an "ocean" of oil, please stay calm and do not pitch out the contents of the bowl. Put your mind to work, and you can redeem the whole thing without difficulty.

1. Let the separated sauce stand for 30 minutes; the egg yolks will collect at the bottom of the bowl and the oil will come floating to the top, as usual.
2. Using a large sauce spoon or a small ladle, gently remove to another bowl all the oil you can possibly remove. If some of the oil is still visible in the egg, that is fine, but make sure it is as little as possible.
3. Whisk the yolks at the bottom of the bowl until you have an emulsion again; do not doubt that it will happen, *it will*. If it does not, you have not removed enough oil and must wait again for it to separate before beginning the process again. As soon as the emulsion is reinstated, begin adding the oil very gradually this time, so the emulsion does not break again.

STORING MAYONNAISE You can keep regular mayonnaise refrigerated the day you make it and the next, but no longer.

Never let mayonnaise stand at room temperature; if it is not in use or being served at the table, it must be in the refrigerator, covered with plastic wrap. Otherwise you run the risk of bacterial contamination.

Basic Mayonnaise

Before you start, remember that it is your responsibility to make sure that your eggs are not contaminated by salmonella. If you have the slightest doubt, use a yolk-free recipe (see page 342).

FFR — ABOUT 1½ CUPS

2 large egg yolks

¼ teaspoon salt

Pepper from the mill

I teaspoon fresh lemon juice plus more as needed

1½ to 2 cups unsaturated oil of your choice or to your personal taste

Cold salted water as needed

I tablespoon boiling water

With a whisk, mix the egg yolks, salt, pepper, and lemon juice in a tall 1-quart glass bowl until the egg yolks lighten in color. Add the oil drop by drop, stirring vigorously until the emulsion forms. As the sauce thickens, add progressively more oil and as much lemon juice as desired. Also as the sauce thickens, lighten it with some of the salted water. Add the boiling water last and refrigerate 2 hours, tightly covered with plastic wrap, before using. This will keep, covered, for 2 days in the refrigerator.

Quantity Production Mayonnaise

FFR — ABOUT 4 CUPS

3 tablespoons instant powdered skim milk

3 to 4 tablespoons water

3 large eggs

I teaspoon salt or to taste

Pepper from the mill

I tablespoon prepared mustard of your choice

3 cups or more as needed unsaturated oil of your choice

2 to 3 tablespoons fresh lemon juice or to your personal taste

Dissolve the skim milk in the water until smooth, then pour in the food processor. Boil the eggs in water to cover for 6 minutes; shell them, open the whites, and spoon the yolks out, adding them to the blender container with the salt, pepper, and mustard. Discard the whites. Blend well. Set the machine on medium-high speed and gradually add ¾ cup of the oil. Process until the emulsion has formed, then add the remainder of the oil in a thin stream. Add lemon juice to taste. Correct the final seasoning. Refrigerate 2 hours, tightly covered with plastic wrap, before using. It will keep, covered, in the refrigerator for 2 days.

The replacement of the raw egg whites with skim milk and the heat treatment of the yolks make this mayonnaise bacteriologically safe for large parties or professional service. Use the blender or the larger model food processor.

Hard-Cooked Egg Yolk Mayonnaise

FFR — ABOUT 2 CUPS (BACTERIOLOGICALLY CONTROLLED)

3 hard-cooked eggs, cooled

3 tablespoons skim milk

I tablespoon Dijon mustard

¼ teaspoon salt

Pepper from the mill

1½ cups unsaturated oil of your choice

Fresh lemon juice

Shell the eggs, remove the whites, and reserve if desired; mash the yolks, then push them through a strainer directly into the blender. Add the skim milk, mustard, salt and pepper to taste, and 3 tablespoons of the oil; blend on medium speed. Gradually add the remainder of the oil in a steady stream. Add lemon juice to taste and correct the seasoning. This will keep, refrigerated and covered tightly with plastic wrap, for 5 days.

The direct ancestor of this sauce is the recipe for Ius in Copadiis, numbered 286 on page 164 of the Flower and Rosenbaum translation of Apicius; from the list of ingredients alone it is possible to see that the combination could only end up as a mayonnaise-textured sauce. It is a sweet-sour sauce containing honey and recommended as an accompaniment to sliced boiled meats.

For this modern version, use the blender. You can either discard the egg whites or, to make volume, chop some or all of the hard-cooked whites very small and add them to the mayonnaise. If you do this, intensify the seasoning of the sauce.

Cooked Mayonnaise

Please do not use the blender for
this mayonnaise; the blades will
shear through the starch and yolk
gel and the emulsion will not form
properly. The finished mayonnaise
may appear somewhat fluid, but
after refrigeration it will thicken
properly. You can use chicken
broth instead of water, but the
taste will not be neutral enough to
be used on fish and vegetables.

FFR—ABOUT 2 CUPS (BACTERIOLOGICALLY CONTROLLED)

¾ cup cold water

I tablespoon cornstarch

2 large egg yolks

¼ teaspoon salt or to taste

Pepper from the mill

2 teaspoons Dijon mustard or to taste

I cup unsaturated oil of your choice

Fresh lemon juice

Mix the water and cornstarch together in a small saucepan, bring to a boil, and thicken over medium-high heat. Meanwhile, beat the yolks with a whisk until they appear white and foamy. Add some of the cornstarch gel to the yolks, stirring constantly; then reverse the process, blending the warmed yolk mixture into the bulk of the starch gel. Season with salt and pepper and bring back to a boil over medium heat. It is essential that the mixture reboil; however, do not let it boil until very thick. Turn into a small mixer bowl.

Cool the gel completely, then whisk in the mustard on medium speed and gradually add the oil, proceeding exactly as for a regular mayonnaise. Add as much lemon juice as you prefer. Strain into a small bowl and refrigerate 2 hours before using. Should the finished mayonnaise start separating, stir in a teaspoon of water at a time until it is well bound again. Correct the seasoning again. This will keep, refrigerated and covered tightly with plastic wrap, for 3 days.

Egg-Free Pseudo-Mayonnaise

This is cholesterol free and made
on a base of gelatinized seasoned
water. You can use chicken stock
if you prefer, but it will not be as
neutral in taste and consequently
not so universally usable for fish
and/or vegetables because of the
meaty flavor. The mustard here
plays an important role as
emulsifier.

FFR—ABOUT 2 CUPS

½ cup cold water

I teaspoon unflavored gelatin

Large pinch of salt

Pepper from the mill

I tablespoon Dijon mustard

I to I¼ cups unsaturated oil of your choice or to your personal taste

Skim milk as needed

Fresh lemon juice as needed

Put the water in a small saucepan, sprinkle with the gelatin and salt, and slowly heat to the boiling point over medium heat, then reduce the heat to low and simmer until the gelatin has completely dissolved. Pour into a small mixer bowl and cool until the gel starts to thicken and has the texture of virgin olive oil. Season with pepper and beat on medium speed until the gelatin is foamy. Add the mustard, homogenize well, and start adding up to ¼ cup of the oil bit by bit until you obtain a very nice mayonnaiselike mixture, which is not mayonnaise but tastes quite good. Gradually add more oil, alternating it with skim milk and lemon juice as needed for taste and texture. If salt is needed, dissolve some in skim milk and add as much of the solution as needed. Refrigerate 2 hours before using to allow the gel to firm up. The sauce mounds nicely when served. This will keep, refrigerated and tightly covered with plastic wrap, for 1 week.

VARIATIONS

Any of these basic mayonnaise recipes can have their flavor changed by adding the following ingredients. All recipes indicated call for 2 cups of mayonnaise:

HERB MAYONNAISES: Add any chopped fresh herbs of your choice, alone or in combination.

AÏOLI: Add mashed garlic to your taste, saffron if desired, and extra virgin olive oil.

GRIBICHE: Add 2 tablespoons minced cornichon (page 315), 2 tablespoons minced capers, and chopped fresh parsley, tarragon, and chives to taste.

MOUSQUETAIRE: Add ⅓ cup dry white wine, 1 tablespoon chopped shallots, and 2 tablespoons meat glaze (page 286) reduced by half over medium heat.

CAVIAR AND LOBSTER MAYONNAISE: Add 2 tablespoons cooked lobster tomalley and 1½ tablespoons caviar of your choice (watch out for the artificially colored lumpfish caviar, which will leach its coloring into the sauce).

AVOCADO MAYONNAISE: Add ½ teaspoon finely grated lime rind, ½ cup finely mashed avocado, and 1 tablespoon fresh lime juice.

SWEDISH APPLE MAYONNAISE: Add 2 tart apples, peeled, cored, and cooked to a puree with 1 tablespoon fresh lemon juice in a small saucepan over low heat.

ARTICHOKE MAYONNAISE: Add 5 cooked artichoke bottoms, pureed, plus 1 tablespoon finely chopped fresh tarragon leaves.

PEPPER MAYONNAISE: Add any cooked and mashed chile(s) or bell peppers of your choice, in the quantity you prefer.

SHALLOT AND MUSHROOM MAYONNAISE: Add mushroom duxelles as on page 1064 in the quantity you prefer.

REMOULADE: Add 1 tablespoon each chopped cornichons (page 315), capers, fresh chives, tarragon, parsley, and chervil leaves, 1 teaspoon Dijon mustard, 1 teaspoon anchovy paste, and a dash of Tabasco sauce.

CUCUMBER AND DILL MAYONNAISE: Add 1 cucumber, peeled, seeded, cut into cubes, blanched 1 minute and squeezed dry, then pureed, plus 3 tablespoons finely chopped fresh dill.

WARM EMULSIFIED EGG YOLK SAUCES

HOLLANDAISE SAUCE AND ITS VARIATIONS Hollandaise is the "mother" sauce of the warm stable emulsion sauces; warm emulsified sauces are permanent emulsions in which a rather large amount of warm butter is emulsified into a small amount of warm acidulated or even acidified liquid and mixed with poached egg yolks, which act as an emulsifier. In essence, hollandaise and its variations are diversely flavored warm mayonnaises, but because they are warm they are somewhat more difficult to prepare than the mayonnaises.

Some American authorities seem to believe that the French sauce béarnaise (not bernaise, which would mean that it originated in Bern, Switzerland, which it did not) is in a category all by itself, which it is not. There is no difference between the preparation techniques of hollandaise and those of béarnaise; the only difference resides in the composition of the reduced liquid base or reduction which is part of each sauce. Also it seems that the hollandaise had been in existence a while before the béarnaise was created.

There are still a few people in France who believe that béarnaise really came from the Béarn, a small provincial kingdom which bordered Spain in the early seventeenth century and became part of France with the advent of King Henri IV, where it would have been prepared with olive oil, rather than butter. My first thought was to question "Olive oil in Béarn?" Simin Palay, an expert on Béarn cuisine, dismisses that theory categorically in his book *La Cuisine du Pays* (Pau, France, 1978). He also confirms that the sauce was first made at the Pavillon Henri IV, a wonderful hotel built in 1836 in the park of Henri IV's castle at St. Germain, near Paris. The restaurant of the hotel is called Le Grand Béarnais, in honor of the king, and I can honestly say that I was served the very best béarnaise I ever tasted in its dining room. According to many sources, the sauce was created there in the 1830s, but there is another stumbling point, mentioned by Prosper Montagné in *Larousse Gastronomique* (Paris, 1938) and noticed before him by Bertrand Guégan in *Le Cuisinier Francais* (Paris, 1934). A chef by the name of Louis-Eustache Audot already published a béarnaise in his book, *La Cuisinière de la Campagne et de la Ville* (Paris, 1818).

So, here is what I believe happened. Audot did use the name béarnaise, but his sauce contains only a reduction of vinegar and shallots, egg yolks, butter, and meat glaze, which is delicious and gives depth of flavor to the sauce and salts it nicely. But there is no trace of the tarragon and other aromatics used in what we now know as béarnaise. So, the Pavillon Henri IV probably added those herbs to Audot's sauce and was credited with the name. Whatever happened, we probably shall never know; but most important is the sauce, which is so delicious and well worth all the calories it generates.

THE INGREDIENTS FOR WARM EMULSIFIED SAUCES The eggs must be of extreme freshness (Grade AA Fresh Fancy quality). The butter must be extremely fresh and unsalted. If you cannot find excellent butter, this is a good opportunity to prepare your own (see page 30). The butter can be clarified or not; since I churn my own butter for the rare hollandaise-style sauces I prepare, I personally prefer to melt the butter and instead of using water to lighten the sauce, I use some of the fresh whey, which accentuates the buttery taste of the sauce.

The vinegar must be of prime quality. If you have difficulty finding truly distinguished vinegar, use half dry white wine and half vinegar to avoid a harsh flavor in the reduction on which the sauce is based.

PREPARING WARM EMULSIFIED SAUCES In the first edition of this book, I gave four different methods for making warm emulsified sauces: the blender method, the cold butter method, the double boiler method, and the professional method.

In this edition, I have, due to the reduced consumption of such rich sauces, settled on explaining only the professional method which is used by all chefs and taught in all professional cooking schools. This method is no more difficult than any of the other so-called easier methods and yields a product that is far superior in taste and lightness of texture. Its successive steps are:

The proper saucepan. Use the proper type of saucepan.
- It can be a special copper nickel-lined hollandaise pan which, being very thick, diffuses the heat very well.
- It can be a Le Creuset enameled cast-iron saucepan. I find these quite nice because you can cook the reduction in one of them, let the reduction cool somewhat and still use the heat accumulated in the pan to poach your egg yolks, thus having greater control over them. If the yolks remain a bit too supple, put the pan over very low heat and whisk until the yolks stiffen just enough.
- For larger quantities: A first quality sauce is never prepared with more than 9 to 10 egg yolks; to fluff them you can use any 9- to 10-inch sauteuse pan or a small rondeau with a dressed copper bottom. The heat conduction will be better than in a bowl, the semiconical shape of a metal bowl preventing the even poaching of the yolks.

The reduction. The base of the sauce is a reduction of water with an acidifier such as vinegar or lemon juice. The reduction is often called an *infusion* in French books. The reduction fulfills a double goal:

1. It is a taste carrier. An emulsified sauce acquires its particular taste from the reduction or simmered mixture of aromatics in acidulated or acidified water or wine.

   If *acidulated*, the water is mixed with a small proportion of an acid such as vinegar or lemon juice. If *acidified*, it is mixed with a larger proportion of either or a combination of both of those acids. How much acid is used is entirely up to the taste of the cook. In hollandaise the acid is either vinegar or lemon juice, depending on the author of the recipe. In béarnaise the acid can be pure tarragon vinegar or a mixture of plain vinegar and dry white wine mixed with chopped fresh tarragon leaves or stems.

   The reduction must also contain some salt (not too much, you can adjust later), pepper, and, eventually, the herbs and aromatics which, while simmering, will lose their essences to the reduction.

   The reduction is simmered until reduced by at least half but never more than three quarters of its original volume, so all the flavors have time to blend into one another. Reducing by more than three quarters or, as the expression goes, "*à sec*," is not a good technique for hollandaise, since it means that you reduce until almost all the liquid has evaporated. Reducing *à sec* is looking for trouble you are in no need of.

   Please proceed slowly and respect the simmering rule; the slower the reduction is prepared, the better the sauce will taste. Also, maintain a reasonable ratio of reduction, so you really extend the water phase of the emulsion you are trying to prepare.

2. It acts as an extender of the water phase. Besides giving taste to the sauce, the reduction extends the amount of water contained in the egg yolks, so the yolks can be cooked gradually, without overcooking too rapidly.

The poaching of the yolks. Always proceed over direct, low to very low heat, without being scared; thousands of gallons of these sauces are prepared this way every day all over the world. The double boiler spells nothing but trouble, for while you concentrate on the whisking of the sauce with intensity, the water may start boiling at the bottom of the double boiler without your being aware of it. Over direct heat, you are in charge, not the double boiler.

By whisking the infusion and egg yolks together very fast over low heat, you will obtain a very foamy, custardlike mixture containing millions of bubblets of air. Slow and progressive heating of the yolks over low heat is a must; too much heat too fast invariably brings on overcooking of the yolks and a grainy texture. Even if you strain the sauce to correct its texture, the quantity of sauce obtained will be much smaller than you expected since you will have lost a good number of egg yolks.

It is essential that you do not cook the yolks until thick and deep yellow. Keep the foam light, fluffy, and pale yellow. In so doing you are guaranteeing that the sauce will not separate or, according to the vernacular, "curdle" later.

While you whisk the yolks over direct, low heat, you will slowly cook their proteins and gently *denature* them.

The compact globules of protein will unfold into long chains forming an open network with liquid filling the spaces within the network. The proteins within the yolks help trap the water around the fat globules, acting as an emulsifier. This is the point at which you will see the sauce thicken; the temperature of the sauce will be between 160° and 165°F.

Should you cook the yolks above this temperature at this early stage of the sauce making, the egg proteins will coagulate. The long chains will bind to one another, aggregate, and no longer retain the water in their network. You will now have hard-cooked egg yolks floating in fat.

The role of the acid in the reduction seems to be one of preventing the coagulation of the egg proteins when they are overheated, which means that the more acid you use to prepare the reduction, the less likely you are to scramble the yolks if you happen to subject them to too high a temperature. This is why some people use straight lemon juice.

If you realize that your yolks are deep yellow, thick, and heavy, try adding a bit of water first and if the mixture turns pale yellow again and remains smooth, you can proceed. If the yolks form a granular slush with the water you just added, it is better to start all over again with new ingredients and not lose any more time on yolks which have lost probably a good three quarters of their emulsifying power.

By general consensus, the yolks are ready to accept the butter when, cutting with your whisk into the bulk of the yolks at the center of the saucepan, you can catch a glimpse of the pan bottom for a split second before the egg foam closes right back over it.

To achieve correct foaming:

- Keep whisking the yolks energetically with your working hand as you keep passing the handle of the saucepan from east or west successively to the north and south with your other hand. This regular three quarter rotation insures that the volume of the yolks is exposed to the warmth of the pan.
- If you feel insecure on your first try, slightly undercook the yolks; you can always finish cooking them later after you have added the butter or oil.

The emulsion—adding the butter or oil. Yes, oil, for indeed you could use olive oil instead of butter. Try half butter and half pistachio oil, for example, or half butter and half hazelnut oil; you may like it.

Many an old chef whose hair has turned gray making "buckets" of hollandaise over forty plus years of professional work will tell you that making hollandaise is an art and they would be right, for in preparing it one definitely combines reasoned hand techniques with scientific reasoning to obtain not only optimum taste but optimum texture, somewhat in the way still-life painters can give color and relief to a painting so vividly that the onlooker can perceive the smells of the room and the objects painted.

Here are the keys to the art: First, test the temperature of butter or oil; it should not be hot, but warm and preferably at the same temperature as the egg yolk foam. Very gradually add the butter or oil, whisking well; proceed *drop by drop* at the beginning. There is a few seconds' delay before the emulsifiers go to work and too much butter at once results in an emulsion that does not form well. From drops go to a teaspoon and from a teaspoon to a tablespoon. Rejoice, those slow, calculated additions of a beginner will, over the years, turn into a well-understood automatic addition of the right amount of butter for the foam.

The best beginner's method is to divide the butter or oil into successive batches, one to be added in increasingly large drops, then by teaspoons, one by tablespoons, and the last in increasingly larger amounts after the sauce has thickened visibly.

Between each of those batches of butter, add 1 or 2 teaspoons of lightly salted water or the whey at the bottom of the butter container; it will be absorbed by the cooking egg proteins, retard their coagulation, and allow the emulsifiers to remain active at each of their water friendly ends. One egg yolk can easily absorb 4 ounces of butter and even much more.

A finished warm emulsified sauce such as hollandaise should not be so thick and stiff as to *sit* on a plate or a piece of fish like a bump on a log; it should be a thickish semifluid preparation, the temperature of which, when measured with an instant thermometer is between 160° and 170°F, maximum.

Correcting the final seasoning; holding the sauce for service. Taste the finished sauce. It will need more salt because you added just a little to the reduction as salt tends to destabilize (break) an emulsion, making it more difficult to form. Do not add plain salt to such a fat/oil heavy sauce, as it will not melt properly; instead, dissolve it in a bit of water or butter whey. Other seasonings need no such special treatment.

To hold the sauce for service, you must remember first and foremost that the minimum temperature that must be maintained to avoid bacterial development in the sauce is 150°F. Your finished sauce will be at approximately 160° to 165°F. To keep it safe and at serving temperature at all times, fill an electric frying pan with water and bring it to 155°F. Put the panful of hollandaise in it; it will sit there happily waiting for you.

However, do remember to pay some attention to it; every so often, give it a good whisk, especially if you notice that the color of the mixture is getting a shade darker yellow and a bit too thick. Also add a bit of lightly salted water to maintain a well-balanced water phase. Do not keep the finished sauce in any kind of high and narrow container, in which whisking the sauce at regular intervals would prove awkward and the contents of which is cooler at the top than at the bottom unless continually stirred.

Rather than prepare huge batches of sauce which will sit around dehydrating and thickening while waiting to be served, prepare the sauce with no more than 10 egg yolks and 2 pounds of butter (30 modern servings) and have plenty of reduction ready to prepare more sauce if you notice that you are going to run out of it. Any professional will know how to whip up a batch, even in the midst of dinner service.

CLUSTERING; REPAIRING A SEPARATING EMULSIFIED SAUCE
As the sauce stands in the warm kitchen, it may begin to warm up and while you are busy doing something else, start to separate (the correct technical term is cluster or flocculate). The globules of butter start congregating and moving in groups, which means that the proteins in the sauce are dehydrating and getting very thirsty. Whisk in enough cool, lightly salted water, definitely lower in temperature than the sauce, until you see the sauce snap right back to its texture.

COALESCING OF THE BUTTER OR OIL; BREAKING OF THE SAUCE If the temperature keeps increasing in the very warm kitchen, instead of the fat (or oil) droplets remaining separated, they will coalesce without your noticing it, since the sauce still looks nice and foamy on the surface; but all around the sides of the holding vessel and on its bottom the egg has started hard cooking and the underside of the sauce is floating on a puddle of butterfat or oil as large as the bottom of its container. The sauce is really separating this time and it may be difficult to save it. Try adding water first and taste the sauce. If it has not acquired a slight taste of overcooked egg, you can still serve it; reemulsify it by whisking well after adding the water and strain the sauce into a cooler container through a fine conical strainer.

If the sauce has acquired that slight sulfur taste, immediately strain the sauce through a China cap placed over a deep container; the butter or oil will drip through and separate from the offending egg mass. This butter can be reused to prepare another hollandaise, *provided* it has not acquired the same sulfur taste as the eggs. Usually it has not, if you catch the separation in time.

In some very large kitchens, the chef will add fresh egg yolks and water to such an endangered sauce, whisking to rebuild it and then strain the resulting repaired sauce. Such a rescued hollandaise is certainly far from perfection, but where there is a budget and plates to be filled in great numbers at very reasonable prices, the technique is excusable. Being faced with such a problem one night in my restaurant, I preferred to rescue the failed sauce as follows:

To rescue hollandaise for use with salmon. Thicken 3 cups fish fumet with a white roux made of 6 tablespoons butter and 4 tablespoons flour. Add the hollandaise to the obtained velouté and blend the whole thing in the blender. This sauce will taste of hard-cooked egg yolks; to temper that flavor, add more lemon juice to taste, plenty of very finely chopped fresh parsley, a dab of mashed anchovy, and some very finely diced hard-cooked egg white.

I called this a Scottish sauce, served it on the salmon medallions on the menu, and everyone liked it. I mentally thanked my Scottish landlady in Edinburgh, who had served me such a sauce twenty years before. If in home cooking you have no fish fumet, use a mixture of 50 percent clam juice and 50 percent chicken broth to prepare the "rescue velouté."

SERVING HOLLANDAISE AND ITS VARIATIONS In classic service, hollandaise is set on the plate beside the piece of fish it accompanies, *not on the fish.*

In contemporary service, offer the hollandaise in a sauce boat at home for each and everyone to enjoy as large or as small a serving as desired, and in restaurant service, offer the sauce in a 2-ounce ramekin for your guests to decide on their own allowance.

Here is hollandaise, followed by a small collection of variation ideas:

Basic Hollandaise

FFR — FOR SMALL RECIPE (ABOUT 2 CUPS)

$\frac{1}{3}$ **cup plus 2 tablespoons water**

Fresh lemon juice to taste

Salt as needed, up to $\frac{1}{2}$ teaspoon

White pepper from the mill, up to $\frac{1}{4}$ teaspoon

3 large egg yolks

$\frac{1}{2}$ **pound unsalted butter, melted**

FOR LARGE RECIPE (ABOUT 4 CUPS)

1 $\frac{1}{4}$ cups plus 2 tablespoons water

Fresh lemon juice

Salt as needed

White pepper from the mill, up to $\frac{3}{4}$ teaspoon

9 large egg yolks

1 $\frac{1}{4}$ to 2 pounds unsalted butter, melted

Mix $\frac{1}{3}$ cup of the water for the small recipe, 1 cup for the large, the lemon juice, a pinch of salt, and pepper together in an enameled cast-iron pan and reduce over medium heat to 2 tablespoons for the small recipe and 6 tablespoons for the large recipe. Cool the reduction and whisk in the egg yolks. Continue whisking over direct low heat until the mixture turns into a thickish pale yellow foam. Remove from the heat and dribble in the warm melted butter; add the remaining water teaspoon by teaspoon alternately with the butter. When all the butter and water have been incorporated, strain into a lukewarm container and keep in water bath set between 140° and 155°F.

VARIATIONS

One recipe basic hollandaise can be modified in the following ways:

HORSERADISH HOLLANDAISE: For boiled beef and tongue, poached chicken, and grilled mackerel. Include 1 tablespoon prepared horseradish in the reduction and add 1 teaspoon Dijon mustard to the finished sauce.

ANCHOVY HOLLANDAISE: For poached salmon. The anchovy will salt the sauce, so be careful not to add too much salt. Add 1 to 2 mashed anchovy fillets to the finished sauce.

CAPER HOLLANDAISE: For blanched caulifower, broccoli, poached salmon, poached chicken and turkey, and English boiled leg of lamb. Drain the preserving juice of a 2-ounce jar of tiny capers into the saucepan and use as a reduction, adding pepper and a dash of salt. Prepare the hollandaise the usual way and stir as much of the capers into the finished sauce as you enjoy.

MUSTARD HOLLANDAISE: For all poached and boiled white meats and grilled chicken; in very small quantity, on deep-fried, panfried, or breaded fish. Add 1 tablespoon Dijon mustard for every 3 egg yolks and lighten with 1 additional teaspoon water for each tablespoon mustard.

MOUSSELINE SAUCE: Generally served on asparagus, both green and white. For every 3 egg yolks, add ¼ cup lightly salted heavy cream, whipped until barely mounding, to the finished sauce. To any mousseline, you can also add any of the following:

- A small tablespoon of finely crumbled Roquefort cheese for braised lettuce and escarole
- A small tablespoon of best possible caviar for poached or grilled salmon
- 1 tablespoon very finely chopped fresh mint leaves for English boiled leg of lamb

MALTAISE AND MIKADO SAUCES: These two sauces are served exclusively with white and green asparagus. For the Maltaise Sauce, replace the amount of water in the reduction by the same amount of tart orange juice mixed with 1 teaspoon fresh lemon juice and finely grated orange rind to your taste. Prepare both the reduction and sauce as you would a hollandaise.

For the Mikado Sauce, replace the amount of water in the reduction by the same amount of tangerine juice mixed with 1 teaspoon fresh lemon juice and a ½ × 2-inch strip of tangerine rind. Prepare both the reduction and sauce as you would hollandaise.

KEY LIME SAUCE: Especially good with grilled pompano, this sauce is prepared exactly like hollandaise, replacing the lemon juice in the recipe with lime juice and ½ teaspoon very finely grated lime rind.

Béarnaise remains probably the most delicious of all French sauces for grilled steaks, grilled South American sea bass, etc. In its modern version it is not stiff at all and could not, as the old version did, sit stiff and stultified on top of a fillet steak. The maximum portion of béarnaise is 3 to 4 tablespoons served in a small ramekin for the diner to use as desired. I have never seen a ramekin of béarnaise come back to the kitchen with more than tiny traces of the sauce left.

The recipe is presented in two parts, a bulk reduction which can be prepared both at home and in a restaurant kitchen. Keep the finished *unstrained* reduction refrigerated in a tightly sealed glass jar. Each and every time you would like to have a quick béarnaise, remove one small tablespoon of the reduction (aromatics and all) per egg yolk to be used; rewarm the reduction and proceed to make the sauce as you would a hollandaise. The sauce will be ready in half the time and taste better, because the reduction ages and mellows as it sits in the refrigerator. If you operate a restaurant, do not hesitate to multiply the recipe for the reduction as many times as you think you will use within a two-month period.

When only one third to one quarter of the reduction is left, prepare a new bulk reduction and blend the old and the new together for consistency of taste, and reboil a few minutes.

Bulk Béarnaise Reduction

This quantity of reduction is enough to prepare ten recipes each using 3 egg yolks and ½ pound butter.

FFR — ABOUT 10 SERVINGS

1 bottle dry white wine

2 cups cider vinegar

½ cup finely chopped shallots

⅓ cup packed mixed chopped fresh tarragon stems and leaves

⅓ cup packed mixed chopped fresh chervil stems and leaves

3 tablespoons chopped fresh parsley stems

1 Mediterranean bay leaf

1 teaspoon dried thyme

Salt as needed

2 teaspoons cracked white peppercorns

Mix all the ingredients together. Bring to a boil, reduce to medium-low, simmer until reduced by one half to two thirds. Cool and store, covered, in the refrigerator.

There are two ways of proceeding:

If you have the reduction ready in the refrigerator:

3 small tablespoons prepared reduction

3 large egg yolks

3 teaspoons lightly salted water

$\frac{1}{2}$ to $\frac{3}{4}$ pound unsalted butter as desired, melted

Cayenne pepper

2 tablespoons each chopped fresh tarragon and chervil leaves

Place the reduction in a saucepan and reheat to warm. Off the heat, add the egg yolks one at a time; with a whisk foam heavily. Return the pan to low heat and continue whisking until the foam has quadrupled in bulk and starts to stiffen a bit. At regular intervals mellow the foam with a teaspoon of the salted water. Very gradually whisk in the desired quantity of butter. Strain through a conical strainer, add cayenne pepper to your taste and the fresh herbs. Correct the final seasoning. Serve on the day it is prepared only.

If you do not keep a jar of ready reduction in the refrigerator:

$\frac{1}{2}$ cup dry white wine

$\frac{1}{3}$ cup cider vinegar

2 tablespoons very finely chopped shallots

I tablespoon finely chopped fresh tarragon leaves and stems plus 2 teaspoons chopped fresh leaves

I tablespoon finely chopped fresh chervil leaves and stems plus 2 teaspoons chopped fresh leaves

I tablespoon finely chopped fresh parsley stems plus 2 teaspoons chopped fresh leaves

$\frac{1}{4}$ Mediterranean bay leaf

$\frac{1}{3}$ teaspoon salt

$\frac{1}{2}$ teaspoon cracked white peppercorns

2 large egg yolks

$\frac{1}{2}$ pound unsalted butter, melted

Pinch of cayenne pepper

Put the wine, vinegar, shallots, tarragon and chervil leaves and stems, parsley stems, bay leaf, and a pinch of salt in an enameled cast-iron pan. Reduce over medium-low heat until only 5 teaspoons of the reduction are left. Cool the saucepan to lukewarm. Off the heat whisk in the egg yolks one by one until the foam has quadrupled in bulk. Return the egg yolks to low heat and, rapidly whisking, stiffen them a little; remove the pan from the heat again and very gradually whisk in the melted butter. Strain into a warm bowl, stir in the chopped herb leaves and the cayenne pepper, and correct the final seasoning with salt and pepper.

VARIATIONS

CHORON SAUCE: Like the béarnaise this is excellent on grilled red meats. Reduce $\frac{1}{2}$ cup tomato essence (page 309) to 3 tablespoons and whisk into a finished béarnaise. Use the herbs or not as you prefer.

BÉARNAISE BRAZIER: Madame Brazier, one of the mères of Lyonnaise cuisine, used to serve this sauce on a poached chicken with truffles under the skin. It was so wonderful. Try using the Oregon black truffles, which are almost affordable. Prepare the béarnaise and add to it 1 generous teaspoon creamed horseradish.

VALOIS SAUCE: Reduce 1 cup primary veal stock (page 219) to 3 tablespoons of thick meat glaze (page 286) and blend into the finished béarnaise. If no primary stock is available, panfry your red meat; discard the frying fat, then deglaze the pan with secondary, chicken, or turkey stock. Add to the sauce.

Colors on Your Plate

Cooking Vegetables

THE PRETTIEST COLORS ON YOUR PLATE ARE THE VIVID GREEN, ORANGE-RED, and yellow shades and hues of vegetables. Unfortunately, because of the way they are sometimes prepared, they aren't always that vivid and pretty. Read on and bid good-bye forever to soggy, pallid, and tasteless vegetables.

So that you can read to your heart's content about vegetables, I have included in the bibliography a list of excellent books that approach the subject from all possible angles. The following information is what you should try to remember at all times without having to check it in any manual.

Plant cells, like animal cells, are the structural and functional units which compartmentalize the materials necessary for their living functions. Certain structures and functions are common to both plant and animal cells, but there are many very important differences. One of these differences is the rigidity of the outer cell walls in plants. The thickness of the cell wall largely determines the texture of a vegetable. Plant texture is also determined by the inner water pressure of the cells, or turgor. As water diffuses into the plant cells, it swells and exerts pressure against other cells, which results in rigid tissue. This turgidity gives the crisp texture to plant materials. Water is the single most abundant constituent of vegetables and represents about 96 percent of its total weight. If the water supply to a plant is suppressed, say, because of natural drought, the vegetable will lose its firmness, gradually wilt, and eventually die of dehydration.

Plant cells are kept together by what are called pectic substances (pectin, protopectin, and the two acids pectinic acid and pectic acid), which in essence play the same role as collagen in meats (collagen keeps the muscle cells and fibers tightly packed against one another, see page 1159).

As plants age, an amorphous material called lignin comes to be deposited in the cell walls and hardens them considerably. You can see lignin if you cut across a large stem of broccoli. Also, when you bend an asparagus stem, you will see it break at the place where the lignin has stopped depositing; the older the asparagus, the shorter the edible part of the stem is. When I was growing up in France, it often happened that the summer pears we had preserved for the Christmas season by dipping their stems into wax would develop very small round pelletlike inserts of lignin.

Within the walls of each cell is the cytoplasm. The cytoplasm is very viscous, actually jellylike; besides containing the nucleus of the cell, it includes a number of plastids, or very small bodies, each endowed with a special metabolic function within the cell. One such type contains pigments and is referred to as chromoplast. The most common chromoplast is the chloroplast, which stores fats in droplets, as well as two thirds of the green chlorophyll pigments and one third of the yellow to deep orange carotenoid pigments. They are present in all green tissues.

Photosynthesis takes place in the chloroplasts; it is the process by which plants, during the sunlight hours, transform carbon dioxide from the air and water they absorb from the soil into carbohydrates, and release oxygen into the atmosphere as a by-product. During the dark hours plants utilize some of the carbohydrates they have stored during sunlight hours and release carbon dioxide. We use the plants' carbohydrates (simple and compound sugars, fibers, glycogen, and starches) for our nutrition and the oxygen they release.

There are other chromoplasts, which can be yellow, orange, or red and which contain only carotenoid pigments, as well as colorless plastids called leucoplasts which are also called starch grains because they produce starch granules.

Each cell contains one or several interstices filled with air or either sweet or acidic sap that are called vacuoles. Besides sap, vacuoles contain the plant pigments, polyphenolic compounds such as tannins, and many vitamins, enzymes, and sugar. As plants age, the vacuoles slowly fill with sap and push the cytoplasm more and more toward the cell walls.

Colors in Plants and Vegetables

The compounds responsible for color or pigments in plants and vegetables fall into three main groups: carotenoids, chlorophyll, and the flavonoids (anthocyanins and anthoxantins).

When you cook certain vegetables, you will sometimes see the butter or oil in which they were cooked or which garnishes them turn the same color as the vegetables. This is an indication that their color comes from carotenoids and chlorophylls (those pigments which are respectively yellow, orange and red, or green) as they are fat soluble.

Carotenoids

The depth of yellow, orange, or orange-red color in a vegetable depends on the carotenoid pigments it contains; carrots are colored by xanthophylls and carotene, orange skins by cryptoxanthin, tomatoes by lycopene, and red peppers with capsanthin. Those carotenoids are quite heat stable. In the fall when the leaves turn color in a matter of a few days, notice that it occurs after one or two very cold nights; the cold rapidly destroys the chlorophyll in the leaves so that they turn from deep green to translucent chartreuse green at first, then to the yellow or orange, or, for maples, red, colors, which through the summer months, have been masked by the dark green color of the chlorophyll.

Chlorophyll

There are two types of chlorophyll, both fat soluble. All chlorophyll molecules are structured so that they contain an atom of magnesium enclosed within a hydrocarbon ring. The hydrocarbon ring shows variations of structure depending on whether the chlorophyll is of the type A and blue-green or of the type B and olive-green.

All chlorophylls are unstable in the presence of heat and acid, which remove the magnesium from the chlorophyll molecules. When vegetables are cooked too long and the organic acids contained in their vacuoles are forced into the water as the vegetable cell walls soften and collapse, their color will turn to the olive then brownish green of another pigment called pheophytin (also sometimes written phaeophytin).

It is well known that adding baking soda, which reacts to acid, to water will preserve the bright green color of green vegetables. Unfortunately, this is a big mistake as baking soda promotes the loss of cellulose and pectin material in the cell walls, breaking them down and turning them to mush; so, do not ever use baking soda when cooking vegetables. There are other techniques (read on) that you can employ to preserve coloring.

Flavonoids

These water-soluble pigments are divided into anthocyanins and anthoxanthins. Anthocyanins are violet, blue, and red pigments; each vegetable and fruit color corresponds to a particular anthocyanin, each with a most attractive name, such as cyanin for cherries.

When cooked in water, vegetables colored by anthocyanins will change color and the new color depends entirely on the chemicals contained in the water. An acid is always used to keep bluish red vegetables a stable brighter red; the acid can be vinegar, lemon juice, or even currant jelly. Indeed, when we make jelly, we add lemon juice to prevent the color of our red fruit jam from turning brown during storage. A base (alkali) like baking soda would accentuate the blue.

Anthoxanthins are colorless, white, or very pale yellow. You must have seen onions turn yellow when blanched in boiling water; this is due to the presence of alkali in the water. I personally like my potatoes to turn yellow when I cook them, but if you prefer them to stay white, you must add a few drops of lemon juice toward the end of their cooking time.

A red vegetable which may be thought to contain anthocyanin is the red beet. Such is not the case; beets contains a mixture of pigments very particular to them which are called betacyanins and betaxanthins and are stable to changes in acidic conditions.

The Organic Acids in Vegetables and Fruit

All vegetables and fruit contain two types of acids: volatile and nonvolatile.

Nonvolatile acids leach into the cooking water of vegetables and the juices of fruit. Taste different fruit and vegetables with the goal of investigating the different degrees of acidity.

Apples, apricots, cherries, peaches, pears, and also broccoli, turnips, and green beans contain malic acid. Grapes contain tartaric acid. All citrus fruit, tomatoes, raspberries, and pineapple contain citric acid. Sorrel, spinach, and rhubarb have a heavy content of oxalic acid.

The volatile acids contained in some vegetables escape into the microscopic droplets of the steam rising from boiling water in which vegetables are cooking, or even from the steam produced by the natural water content of the vegetables if they are cooked without water. Volatile acids are the main reason that green vegetables should not be covered while they cook, for if they are, the acids deposit on the inside of the pot lid, mix with the condensation, and as the condensation falls back into the pot, change the bluish-green of chlorophyll to the brownish green of pheophytin. The unattractiveness of the vegetables, however, is sometimes directly inverse to their delicious taste (see the recipe for green beans on page 393).

Enzymes and the Oxidation of Vegetables

You know all about and have already noticed the browning of some vegetables and fruit once they are cut into pieces and left to stand at room temperature. If the cut stays exposed to the air long enough, it will turn almost completely brown.

The browning is the work of enzymes called phenolases. The phenolases react with oxygen and the phenolic compounds in the vegetable or fruit pulp, resulting in the formation of grayish brown compounds belonging to the pigments called melanins. The enzymes and the phenolic compounds are both present in the cells, but each is compartmentalized in a different part of the cell. Cutting or disrupting the cells exposes them to oxygen and allows the enzymes and phenolic compounds to mix. This reaction does not take place in citrus fruit, because the enzymes are not present in their cells. Highly acidic conditions, such as the presence of vitamin C, or ascorbic acid, will retard this enzymatic browning reaction. This browning reaction is important, however, in the production of coffee, tea, and particularly cider, which is brown.

In the commercial drying of fruit, the sulfur compound known as sulfur dioxide is used to prevent this reaction and to maintain an appetizing color in the fruit or vegetable pulp. Compare the color of fruit preserved with sulfur dioxide with that of fruits that have been dried without such prior treatment as can be bought in health food stores.

We use sugar in a similar manner when we cook and candy fruit in a syrup or succession of syrups. In this case, the boiling syrup coats the fruit and prevents oxygen from reaching it at the same time the high temperature inactivates the browning enzymes and dehydrates microorganisms that could make the preserve unstable.

Potentially Dangerous Fruit and Vegetables

The following is a partial list of nutritional problems and sicknesses that can result from ingesting certain vegetables and fruit.

Allergies and Sensitivities

Dried fruit treated with sulfur dioxide to prevent browning can be dangerous for people who are sensitive to the sulfites that form on the surface of the fruit. The fruit must be soaked in water and washed several times to reduce the sulfites to a minimal amount. Also, be careful of giving such treated fruit to babies and toddlers, whose nutritional sensitivities are not yet known and who may be allergic. Give toddlers only brown raisins, which are simply dehydrated and safe, as opposed to golden raisins, dried apricots, dried pears, etc.

Toxins

Some of the following toxins are deadly and you must know where and how they develop.

IN WILD MUSHROOMS

Phallotoxins, amatoxins, and muscarine are serious poisons (the first two are deadly, the third causes serious illness) existing in some species of the

Amanita genus of mushrooms. The snow-white spring amanitas called *A. verna* and *A. virosa* and the light green *A. phalloides* have been responsible for more deaths than any other mushroom, though all but a few of the other *Amanitas* species are dangerous. The poison does not start acting in the system until at least twelve hours after ingestion and it is active whether the mushrooms are consumed uncooked, cooked, or dried.

Another wild mushroom, *Coprinus atramentarius*, of the family of the "inky caps," should never be consumed with any beverage containing the slightest amount of alcohol. If you decide to enjoy a dish of any type of coprini, treat yourself if you know them very well, but abstain from alcohol during the meal and for three full days after it to avoid being subjected to the effects of disulfiram, a chemical that interferes totally with the absorption of alcohol by the human system. The symptoms are a deeply flushed face and a rapid pulse accompanied by weakness and cold extremities.

Do not pick or eat any wild mushrooms that you do not know to be safe, nor accept any from anyone else, unless the person who gives them to you is a recognized and learned expert. It is essential to be able to recognize each and every type with complete accuracy to prevent mistakes such as confusing the delicious true chanterelle (*Cantharellus cibarius*) with the false chanterelle, also called jack o' lantern (*Clytocibe illudens*). To inexperienced eyes, both can look identical.

Before you collect mushrooms in forests, read the books listed in the bibliography carefully and study for years by joining a mycological club on its foraging parties.

IN CANNED FOODS

Clostridium botulinum, an anaerobic bacterium which, as its name indicates, lives without oxygen, finds a great haven in canned nonacid foods. There it secretes the toxin botulin, which is deadly in approximately 65 percent of the cases. This individual is especially dangerous in home-canned foods, where it is totally undetectable by taste, smell, or appearance. Also watch for gas in jars and deformed swollen commercial cans. In principle, do not taste any part of a can that has not been previously reboiled for a full 20 minutes. These twenty minutes of boiling destroy the toxin.

Botulin may also be present in compound vegetable and pasta salads in which the contaminated canned vegetables have been added straight from the can, thus contaminating other ingredients.

Also, if you do not positively hear the hiss of air reentering a can of vegetables or fruit as you open it, make it your policy to discard that can.

IN POTATOES THAT HAVE TURNED GREEN

Potatoes exposed to sunlight turn green and develop the alkaloids solanine and chaconine, which accumulate directly under the skins of the tubers and leave an extremely unpleasant bitter taste on the large back papillae of the tongue. If potatoes have turned green, simply peel them until no trace of the suspect color is visible and use what remains; if the tuber is green halfway to the center, discard it. It would take quite an amount of green potatoes for the solanine to be poisonous, but the cumulative taste is unbearably nasty.

IN FRESH LIMA BEANS AND BAMBOO SHOOTS
Lima beans as cultivated in the United States contain a very small amount of cyanoanhydrins, the same potential inhibitor of the respiratory system as found in apple, pear, apricot, peach, plum, and citrus seeds. This presents no danger in this country, for we boil the beans with the lid off and allow the hydrogen cyanide that might have been produced by disrupted cells to escape into the atmosphere, thus discarding all traces of potentially poisonous material. Fresh bamboo shoots, if you can find them, should be cooked the same way for the very same reason.

IN INSUFFICIENTLY COOKED RED BEANS
Insufficiently cooked red beans are sometimes served in modern salads in some restaurants for the sake of "texture." The only acceptable texture for a rehydrated dried bean is soft and well done, otherwise the bean can contain a residue of fiber (composed of cellulose and hemicellulose) which can bring on uncomfortable intestinal symptoms within three hours of ingestion. Cook dried beans sufficiently; they will not develop all their flavor otherwise.

IN PRODUCTS CONTAINING MONOSODIUM GLUTAMATE (MSG)
According to recent studies, the reaction known until now as the Chinese restaurant syndrome is not due to monosodium glutamate (MSG). However, do not pour MSG into a dish; using a very tiny quantity is sufficient.

FROM IMPROPERLY STORED GRAINS OR NUTS
Claviceps purpurea is a fungus that develops on improperly stored grains, especially rye, exposed to humidity. It was one of the scourges of the Middle Ages and manifested itself in what was called St. Anthony's fire, which would cause a form of gangrene in which the skin turned black and blue, accompanied more often than not by hallucinogenic episodes. This problem had disappeared for centuries but reappeared in 1951 in the small French village of Pont-Saint-Esprit; it was traced to rye flour contaminated with *Claviceps*, which in older times was called rye ergot, because the seeds of rye suffering from this fungus develop ergots. The sickness is called ergotism; it is very serious and due to the effects of a derivative of lysergic acid. For more information, read a book called *The Day of St. Anthony's Fire* by John G. Fuller.

Molds can settle and feed on nuts and secrete toxins. Such is the case of *Aspergillus flavus*, which secretes an aflatoxin on nuts, seeds, and some dried fruit not protected by sulfur dioxide (like imported figs). The controls against these types of contamination have been tightened by government agencies and occurrences are almost nonexistent in the United States. It is important to know, though, that aflatoxins can be passed on to milk and meats if animals ingest contaminated material, and ultimately to man if man ingests the contaminated meat or dairy products. The consequences can be very serious.

IN FOODS LEFT STANDING TOO LONG AT
ROOM TEMPERATURE

Infections can result from food contaminated with diverse *Salmonella* bacteria and *Clostridium perfringens* in salads containing a certain amount of meats and mayonnaise, or poached eggs either as a garnish or in a dressing; see pages 123–24 for a longer discussion of salmonella infections.

Intoxications can result from leaving vegetables at room temperature after they have been contaminated by *Staphiloccocus aureus* carried by sick food handlers and *Bacillus cereus*, which both produce toxins resulting in food poisoning. The vegetables involved can be plain or part of composed salads. The results are diarrhea and vomiting starting about a half hour after ingestion and lasting for six hours.

Also responsible for the same type of illness is *Shigella*, transferred to foods by food handlers whether they are infected themselves by the bacteria or not. It can be found in contaminated vegetable and fruit salads.

Keep cooked vegetal foods refrigerated at all times, as you do for meats and dairy products. The dangerous temperature range is the same for all, between 40° and 140°F.

The Nature and Wherefrom of Common Vegetables

We all know the different parts of a plant. As a seed germinates some of its shoots are drawn to sunlight and become stems and branches, while others are attracted into the soil to search for moisture and become the roots of the plant. As the plant grows, it will produce flowers, which will each contain a reproductive system and in its turn produce seeds in an eternal cycle of life. A plant may produce two types of flowers, one female and another male. In this case it will live in symbiosis with an animal—though most probably an insect—which by its fluttering around the flowers will carry pollen on its wings and thus transfer it to the female flowers while looking for nectar. We consume all parts of certain plants but only some parts of most of them.

The following lists the part of the vegetable which is edible and its most probable origin.

Old World Vegetables

- *Artichoke.* Botanically a flower. We consume the base of all the bracts, which we call leaves, and base of the flower, which we call the bottom. In Mediterranean climates artichokes flower; the bracts open up to expose the choke, which in the strong sunlight opens into a glorious purple flower. Origin: southern Europe and North Africa.
- *Asparagus.* When young, they have a purple tip and green stem, which later will thicken and can be made to blanch white by piling sand about it as it continues to grow. Origin: southern central Europe, western and central Asia, North Africa.
- *Beets* (root, called the hypocotyl, and leaves). Origin: western Europe and North Africa.
- *Cabbages.* Wild, white, Savoy, red cabbage (leaves). Origin: central and western Europe and western Asia.
- *Napa cabbage and bok choy* (leaf stalk and leaves). Origin: China.
- *Cardoon* (swollen stems). Origin: southern Europe and North Africa.
- *Carrot* (taproot). Origin: Mediterranean Basin.
- *Cauliflower and broccoli* (so-called florets and peeled stems). Origin: central and western Europe.
- *Celery* (leaves—for seasoning—and stalks). Origin: Europe.
- *Celery root* (large swollen rootstock). Origin: Europe.
- *Chenopodium*—Bon Henri or wild mountain spinach (leaves, also see page 486). Origin: central and western Europe.
- *Chestnuts* (nuts). Now scarce in North America due to a blight, but still to be found imported, mostly from Italy. Origin: the Mediterranean.
- *Chick peas* (seeds). Origin: the Mediterranean and India.
- *Collard greens* (leaves). Origin: exact origin not available, probably central and western Europe.
- *Cow peas*, also called black-eyed peas (seeds). Origin: Iran and India.
- *Cucumber* (botanically a fruit, used as a savory vegetable). Origin: India and tropical Asia.
- *Eggplant* (botanically a fruit, used as a savory vegetable) is a member of the nightshade family. Origin: said to be India.
- *Fava beans* (preferably peeled cotyledons). Origin: probably North Africa (Algerian backcountry) and southwestern Asia.
- *Fennel*, erroneously called anise in many supermarkets (swollen leaf stalks and—as a seasoning—leaves and seeds). Origins: There are several; Greece (it gives its name, *marathon*, to the same city), the Canary Islands, and England all had different varieties.
- *Kohlrabi* (swollen stem). Origins: western and central Europe and western Asia.
- *Lablabs* (seeds), another name for the Far Eastern black bean. Origin: probably China.

- *Leeks* (bulb and flatly creased pale green leaves). Origin: Its ancestor *Allium ampeloprasum* comes from the Mediterranean.
- *Lettuce, chicory, escarole, curly endive* (leaves) were known to the ancients of the Mediterranean; pointed whitloof, or modern Belgian or French endive, dates from 1850. Origin: developed from a common ancestor called *Lactuca scariola* found originally in Asia, Europe, and North Africa. Some scientists also say that it was found in Siberia.
- *Nettles* (leaves) are found only in the wild and make a nice substitute for spinach. Use gloves when picking the leaves as they carry numerous irritating small spikes. Origin: central and western Europe.
- *Okra* (botanically a fruit, used as a vegetable) was used by the ancient Egyptians. Origin: either Africa or Asia and brought to the New World by African slaves.
- *Olives* (drupes). The olive is ancient and originated in the eastern Mediterranean and was brought eastward toward present-day France and Spain by the Greeks. We consume olive oil, or whole olives that have been brined, cured in deep salt, and stored in olive oil. A lye treatment is also used which produces olives for hors d'oeuvres and salads; these are often sweet to the point of blandness. Origin: the ancient Fertile Crescent from where it went to Syria, Palestine, Greece and the whole Mediterranean.
- *Onions, shallots, garlic, chives* (bulb and long hollow leaves). Origin: Iran, Afghanistan, and Baluchistan.
- *Parsnips* (taproot). Origin: the whole of Eurasia.
- *Peas* (depending on the variety, either the shucked seeds, or the seeds—peas—in their edible pods). Origin: possibly Italy where they grow wild; in any case Europe.
- *Radishes* (root, called the hypocotyl, and leaves, which are excellent with mixed greens and in soups). Origin: uncertain; already known and used in ancient China and Egypt.
- *Rhubarb* (stalks) is very high in oxalic acid and usually used for the preparation of desserts. It also makes an excellent fish sauce because of its acidity. The leaves contain a poison as yet unidentified and should never be consumed. Origin: Tibet and northern Asia.
- *Salsify and scorzonerae* (taproots). The small hearts of the leaf stems also make a delicious addition to salads. Origin: southern Europe, Caucasus, Crimea, and central Asia.
- *Soybeans* (seeds, sprouts, and fermented as bean curd). Origin: southwest Africa.
- *Spinach* (leaves), of the family of Chenopodiaceae (see page 486). Origin: Persia (modern Iran).
- *Turnips and rutabagas* (roots and top leaves are good for vegetable soups). Origin: Europe.
- *Yams* (tuber) flowered all over Pangaea, the original single continent on

Earth. It is found now on all continents and was cultivated very early; however, some Old World species contain poisonous alkaloids.

New World Vegetables

- *Chayote* (curcurbit fruit used as a vegetable, containing only one large delicious seed). The meat is edible and a choice vegetable. Origin: probably the Caribbean islands.
- *Corn* (see page 481). Origin: developed from *Euchlaena mexicana* (teosinte) found wild in the Mexican highlands and some of South America.
- *Haricot beans* (seeds and pods). The French *haricots verts* are barely 1/4-inch-wide babies of several types of haricot beans. Origin: Central and South America.
- *Jerusalem artichoke* (tuber) should really be called sunchoke because it definitely has nothing to do with Jerusalem. Disliked by Europeans, especially the French, because it was the only vegetable available during World War II; it was sold frozen, which renders it saccharin sweet. Origin: North America.
- *Lima beans* (seeds). A large South American bean equivalent in size to the broad European fava bean, but with a thinner skin. Origin: Central America.
- *Manioc* (root), also called cassava, originated in Central and South America and is the staple starch food of these areas. The root is grated or ground, put in a bag, pressed, and squeezed until its milky juices, which are poisonous, have been completely extracted. The tapioca we use to make puddings is made from manioc.
- *Peppers*, sweet bell peppers as well as the hot chiles, all belong to the genus *Capsicum*, of the nightshade family. The fruit is used once cleaned of its seeds and inner ribs for fresh vegetable dishes. Both the pulp and seeds are used when hot peppers are dried, the pulp finely powdered and the seeds, whole.
- *Potatoes* (tubers). There are many varieties all originating in the Peruvian Andes, all having adapted very well to Europe. Some varieties are very starchy, while other are waxy, containing as they do somewhat more protein. A member of the nightshade family. Origin: Peru and Bolivia.
- *Summer squashes* (botanically a fruit, used as a vegetable) include zucchini and the yellow crookneck.
- *Sweet potatoes* (roots), although resembling yams, are not related. Origin: disputed; some scientists say Asia.
- *Tomatoes* (botanically a fruit, used as a vegetable) are filled with cavities containing an acid jell that serves as food for the very small seeds. Tomatoes come in all shades of green, yellow, orange, and red. Their foliage is poisonous; they belong to the nightshade family. Origin: South America,

probably Peru, as one of its names, Peruvian apple, seems to indicate.

- *Winter squashes* (botanically a fruit, used as a vegetable) are available in at least twenty-five varieties; they are sweet and most of the seeds are fleshy and can be toasted and used for garnish on any dish but particularly Meso-American dishes. Origin: Americas.

About the Nightshade Family

Everyone seems to wonder and worry about the "deadly nightshade" without knowing exactly what it is. You have noticed that I have indicated all the vegetables belonging to the nightshade family. The tomato remained unused a long time by most of Europe, except in Italy, because it was believed to be poisonous. In reality only its leaves are.

The plant that deserves the common name of deadly nightshade is belladonna. It has the most beautiful red flowers, maturing into shiny obsidian-black berries, and is still to be found on country lanes all over Europe. Its root is particularly poisonous, producing the alkaloid atropin. Atropin is used medicinally in minute doses to dilate the pupils and as an antispasmodic.

A Vegetable Cooking Philosophy

There are many philosophies when it comes to cooking vegetables. Some people like to make extraordinary, complicated mixtures, others make sauces, while others yet seem to prefer the vegetable as plain and simple as possible. I belong to the last group; I believe that vegetables are on a plate not only to bring vitamins and nutrition, but to refresh the palate from the strong tastes of meats, be it simply grilled as is the pleasure in the United States, or roasted, boiled, and stewed as is the pleasure in England, or sautéed, braised, or roasted as is the pleasure in Continental Europe. I like the way the cuisines of the Far East present their vegetables, still brightly colored and slightly crunchy under the tooth, but not downright grassy and all too vegetal-tasting, as is often the case nowadays, where crunchy potato salads and half-cooked dried beans are happily sold by many delicatessens for the sake of a "crispness" which is nothing more than "underdoneness."

Each and every vegetable reaches a point of doneness where it is perfectly delicious, when the fibers have softened just enough and the natural vegetable juices have not totally escaped into the boiling water or the sauté pan. All the techniques described below follow this philosophy.

By all means, disagree if you feel you have to and do what you like best. If you are a "crisper," just cook less than I direct in the following techniques; if you are a "vegie-softy," simply cook more. It is really a case of personal taste.

Vegetable Cooking Techniques

In spite of being separated from their moisture-gathering root system, vegetables remain alive after picking. This is why you should store them in the vegetable bin of your refrigerator where they will not dehydrate half as fast as they would on one of its shelves.

As soon as they are subjected to heat, vegetable cells cease all activity; with the help of heat, water, and steam, the cellulose softens, the pectic substances melt into pectin (which thickens the cooked juices of vegetables lightly), the starches swell and absorb moisture. Like meat and fish, vegetables are cooked by moist-heat and dry-heat cookery techniques.

Each of the techniques outlined in the following pages contains recipes for vegetables which adapt particularly well to this technique, and each technique constitutes the basic way to cook this vegetable. There are many others and many combinations as you will be able to see if you consult all the vegetable cookbooks listed in the bibliography.

The Moist-Heat Cooking Procedures

PARBOILING, BLANCHING, AND BOILING
There is a definite difference between these three techniques.

PARBOILING This is an initial precooking of a vegetable in boiling, preferably salted, water, when one intends to finish cooking it using a second, different technique. Parboiling is also done simply to remove an all too pungent flavor from a strong vegetable. If the vegetables are very pungent (brussels sprouts, large older cabbage, spinach) the blanching can also be started in cold water in an attempt to minimize any strong taste.

For example, if you wish to sauté or panfry some potatoes in butter or oil but cannot invest all the time it takes to cook the potatoes in fat from the raw stage, peel, then parboil the potatoes until half cooked, dry them well, keep them stored, and finish cooking them in fat in a frying pan about 15 minutes before serving them.

This second case is also common: If a cabbage family vegetable or other pungent vegetable is too strong for your taste, you can parboil it to remove a large part of the strong taste, and finish cooking the vegetable in a second pot of fresh water or smother it in a tightly closed pot.

General rules of parboiling. Parboil older vegetables until half cooked, but young vegetables only 2 to 3 minutes. The real length of time depends on the size of the vegetable. Larger vegetables will need more time than smaller ones. This technique is empirical and depends entirely on your personal judgment.

BLANCHING   Blanching is slightly different, but, as you will see, not that much. Blanching is the equivalent of the French *faire blanchir*, which means whitens. Why whitens? Because cooks of former centuries, as yet unaware of enzymatic reactions, discovered that by preboiling certain vegetables, their color would be fixed and that they could wait a nice long time to be finished for serving without darkening. If the vegetable is finished cooking immediately in another pot, use it hot from the blanching water. If its final cooking is postponed, rinse it in cold water and store it in a plastic bag.

But blanching can also be used with the exact same meaning as parboiling when one precooks a pungent vegetable to remove its initial strong taste. Also, in many French books of classical times, especially those of the late nineteenth and early twentieth centuries, the term blanching was synonymous with fully cooking in boiling water.

FULLY COOKING A VEGETABLE BY BOILING IT   Boil only young and tender vegetables containing little cellulose since it takes a relatively long time to soften the cellulose of older vegetables; other techniques are better adapted to this goal.

You may use either of two methods when boiling.

The vitamin method. This is the method used by most home economists who cover the vegetables to cook them faster. Drop the vegetables into a pot containing only a small amount of boiling water; cover and cook until tender but still crisp. The premise is that the less water there is, the fewer vitamins are inactivated; however, if the vegetables are not very closely watched their texture and color can be damaged beyond repair. Salt after cooking, the salt contributing to the loss of color when a vegetable is cooked by this method.

The texture method. Immerse the vegetables in a large amount of rapidly boiling water seasoned with 1½ teaspoons salt per quart. Salting the water is essential for the vegetables contain natural salts which, if not replaced by table salt, will leave them tasteless.

Bring to a second boil. Keep at a rolling boil, *uncovered*, until the desired doneness has been reached. Drain and serve, or, if the vegetable is prepared ahead of time, drain and rinse in ice water to stop the cooking. You will retain fewer vitamins using this method, but you will be able to better control the taste, texture, and color.

For best results:

- Never cover the vegetables while cooking; let the volatile acids evaporate, as it will preserve the color of all vegetables, but especially the green ones.
- Cook purplish red vegetables in water containing either an apple or a small amount of vinegar, to prevent them from turning an unappetizing grayish blue.

- *Never add baking soda to the cooking water;* it bites through the outer layers of the vegetables, renders them mushy, and completely destroys thiamin, one of the B-complex vitamins.
- Never attempt to keep vegetables warm after boiling them; they will become mushy and gradually lose color and texture. Cool them completely in ice water, roll them in a towel to absorb excess moisture, and reheat them in the butter or oil with which you have chosen to season them. Correct their final salt level just before serving and add any herb or spices you like.

CREAMING VEGETABLES Although one does not cream vegetables too much anymore, you must know how to do it well for those lovely Thanksgiving creamed onions; use cream or a light cream sauce made in one of the following ways.

Cream Sauce for 6 Servings of Boiled Vegetables

FFR — 1 CUP

Reduce ⅔ cup heavy cream by one half in a saucepan over medium heat. Add the vegetables and dilute the sauce with as much of the boiling water of the vegetables as you like. Or, thicken light cream with cornstarch (see page 289), or mix ½ cup heavy or light cream with ½ cup of the cooking water from the vegetables or ½ cup of secondary stock (see page 220). Bind with a white or blond roux made of 2 tablespoons butter or light oil and 1½ tablespoons sifted unbleached all-purpose flour (see page 272 for more detailed instructions on making roux and introducing the liquid into it).

In all cases, the sauce should be light and there should be just enough of it to barely coat each vegetable, *not drown them,* as is too often done.

SEASONING BOILED VEGETABLES WITH COMPOUND BUTTERS, BUTTER OILS, OR FLAVORED OILS Please refer to the sauces chapter to find those preparations in which you can toss freshly boiled vegetables, or use those indicated after each technique. You can make up any compound butter or flavored oil with any herbs and spices you like. Be creative!

Baby Artichokes

The directions are given for baby artichokes as found in California or in Italian markets during the early months of the year. If you cannot find them, use the frozen artichoke hearts sold in 10-ounce boxes, trimming the hard leaves after cooking.

VARIATIONS

You can also use ½ cup Hollandaise or Mousseline Sauce (page 350 or 351) or toss the artichokes in ⅓ cup mayonnaise (page 340) of your choice.

FCR—6 SERVINGS

Juice of 2 lemons

36 baby artichokes or three 10-ounce packages frozen baby artichokes

3 quarts water

4½ teaspoons salt

For the dressing

¼ cup unsweetened pineapple juice

¼ cup fresh orange juice

1 tablespoon balsamic vinegar

1 teaspoon salt, more or less to taste

1 large clove garlic, positively mashed

½ cup olive oil of your choice

2 tablespoons minced fresh mint leaves

1 tablespoon minced fresh tarragon leaves

Pepper from the mill

1 head Romaine lettuce, cleaned and hand torn into half leaves

Strain the juice of the lemons into a large bowl. Cut off the stems of all artichokes and remove the leaves, leaving just enough center leaves to obtain a small artichoke heart ¾ inch large. Cut a ½ inch off the top of the remaining center leaves. Toss the prepared artichokes into the lemon juice, making sure to coat all the cut surfaces to prevent browning. Bring the water to a boil; add the salt, artichokes, and lemon juice. Cook at a rolling boil, until fork tender, 6 to 8 minutes.

Meanwhile, in a small, nonreactive saucepan reduce the pineapple and orange juices, vinegar, and salt over medium heat to ¼ cup. Add the mashed garlic and whisk in the olive oil. Let stand while the artichokes finish cooking.

Drain the artichokes, stop the cooking under cold running water, pat dry, and add to the dressing together with the chopped herbs and pepper. Correct the final seasoning. Arrange the artichokes on the romaine leaves and spoon the dressing over them. Serve lukewarm.

Removing the top of an artichoke

Trimmed artichoke, seen from its top

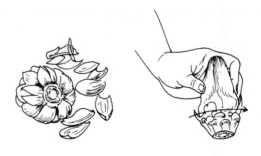

Stem and leaves removed

Artichoke Bottoms Filled with Peas and Shrimp

FFR to FCR—6 MAIN-COURSE OR 12 APPETIZER SERVINGS

3½ quarts plus ½ cup cold water

¼ cup unsifted unbleached all-purpose flour

¼ cup corn oil

Juice of 2 lemons

½ teaspoon salt

6 very large artichokes

I lemon, cut in half

½ cup bright green cooked baby peas

½ pound cooked tiny bay shrimp

Mayonnaise of your choice as needed

2 teaspoons each chopped fresh parsley, chervil, chives, and tarragon leaves

Salt

Pepper from the mill

Salad greens of your choice

12 cherry tomatoes

Bring 1½ quarts of the water to a boil; in a small bowl, whisk together the ½ cup of water, the flour, oil, the juice of 1 lemon, and salt, until the mixture looks like a crepe batter. When the large pot of water boils, turn it down to a simmer and whisk in the prepared slurry. Bring back to a boil, reduce the heat to low, and let simmer while you prepare the artichokes. In a large bowl, mix 1½ quarts of the cold water and the remaining lemon juice. Using surgical gloves so as not to damage your hands, remove the top, stems, and all leaves of each artichoke until you can see the rim of the bottom. Rub the bottom with half of the lemon to prevent browning. Using your paring knife, contour this rim and lift out the cone of yellow leaves. Pull out all the chokes and,

The goal of this recipe is to teach the preparation of artichoke bottoms for filling as appetizers or as meat garnish. If served in a salad, artichoke bottoms will be sliced. I am giving here a filling made with whole peas and small shrimp, but you can use any filling you prefer, such as purees of vegetables, foie gras, whipped liver mousse, snails, shellfish in mayonnaise, etc. In this particular recipe, you can also cook the artichoke leaves, scrape their meat out with a spoon, mash it, and place it under the shrimp.

The liquid in which these artichoke bottoms will cook is called a blanc; it contains flour, oil, lemon juice, and just a tad of salt. The combination of the starch gel with the oil in emulsion and the citric acid in solution makes this liquid perfect to prevent discoloration of the artichoke meat.

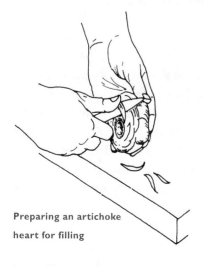

Preparing an artichoke heart for filling

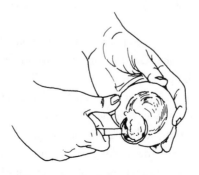

Contouring the bottom of the heart with a paring knife

Finished bottom ready for filling

using a melon baller, remove all the visible little dots, which are the root beds of the chokes. Also trim the outside, using nice rounded movements, without cutting off too much, so the bottoms remain nice and round inside and outside. Keep the artichokes immersed in lemon water until ready to be cooked.

When all artichokes are ready, add them to the *blanc* and cook until a needle inserted into the largest artichoke bottom comes out freely; test several times. Immediately add the remaining half quart of cold water to the *blanc* to stop the cooking, and keep the artichokes in it until ready to serve. If using for a large party, keep the whole pot refrigerated until ready to use. When ready to fill, pat the artichoke bottoms very dry.

Mix the peas and shrimp together and add mayonnaise to taste, diluting it with a tad of the *blanc* to make it more fluid. Add half the herbs, then season with salt and pepper carefully. Just before serving, fill the artichoke bottoms with an equal amount of the shrimp-and-pea mixture and sprinkle with the remainder of the herbs. Serve chilled on a plate decorated with the greens of your choice and a few cherry tomatoes.

Boiled Jumbo Green Asparagus with Kumquat and Pistachio Dressing

FCR — 6 SERVINGS

3 dozen large to jumbo asparagus

I dozen kumquats or the grated rind of I orange

I shallot, very finely chopped

I tablespoon balsamic vinegar

I tablespoon cider vinegar

Salt

Pepper from the mill

2 tablespoons grapeseed or other unsaturated oil of your choice

¼ cup pistachio oil

2 tablespoons chopped fresh chervil leaves

To prepare asparagus, bend the stalks head to stem; the stem will break at exactly the place where the fibers stop being edible. Peel—this is a must or you will lose half of the delicacy of the vegetable—with a potato peeler or a parer from the blossom end down, starting just under the close crop of leaves. Assemble the stalks in bundles of small, medium, or large asparagus.

If the asparagus is to be used as a vegetarian first course or as one of the vegetables of a main course, use the jumbo asparagus which are so delicious; pencil-thin Italian-style asparagus is never peeled and mostly used in salads.

Bring a large pot of water to a boil. Have all the asparagus ready to cook in bundles. Cut the kumquats into halves, discard the acid centers, and chop the peels into ⅛-inch cubes. Place the chopped shallot in the corner of a kitchen towel and press hard to remove the strong juices. Mix the kumquats and shallot together in a small bowl. Add the vinegars, season with salt and pepper, and whisk in both oils until a delicious dressing results.

Salt the cooking water for the asparagus with 1½ teaspoons of salt per quart of water and cook the vegetables as follows:

- 2 minutes for tinies
- 4 minutes for smalls
- 5 minutes for mediums
- 6 minutes for large
- 7 minutes for jumbos

Keep the pot lid off at all times and keep the water at a rolling boil. When crisp-tender, drip well over a towel and put on *cold* plates without rinsing under cold water. Spoon an equal amount of the dressing over the stalks and sprinkle with the chopped chervil.

Green Beans

FFR to FCR—6 SERVINGS

3 quarts water

Salt

1 pound young green beans, ⅛ to ¼ inch wide

1 clove garlic, peeled

12 large fresh basil leaves

Pepper from the mill

2 tablespoons unsalted butter or 1½ tablespoons pure olive oil

Bring 3 quarts water to a rolling boil and add the salt, then the beans. Boil for 6 to 7 minutes. Keep the lid off at all times and taste often for desired crispness. Meanwhile, mash the garlic and basil leaves together in a mortar. Drain the beans, refresh them under cold running water, and shake them well. Toss the beans over high heat in a hot skillet until most of the moisture has evaporated, then turn the heat off and add salt, pepper, the butter, and the herb mixture. If you prefer to use oil instead, mix it into the garlic and basil first, then add to the beans and toss well. Serve promptly.

VARIATIONS

- You can also use the tangerine gremolata on page 302, chipotle butter on page 301, and shallot and fines herbes butter on page 303. Blend those butters with an oil of your choice if you prefer, or even use only oil.
- Prepare exactly the same recipe using wax beans. For a nice effect, use half green beans and half wax beans, taking care to cut and trim each vegetable to exactly the same size.

We finally can find the same little haricots verts (say Harryko vair, not "virts," as I have heard a few cooks say) as are sold in France, at unheard of prices. Be smart, go to your supermarket on the day the fresh beans arrive and dig down toward the bottom of the heap; the little ones always slip downward. Such small beans are at the peak of flavor because their sugars have not yet turned to starches.

To use larger beans, french them, which means remove the strings on both sides of the pod with a paring knife.

You need 3 quarts water and 4½ teaspoons salt per pound of beans; if you have more, cook by increments of 1 pound only. Boil larger frenched beans 6 minutes and young baby beans ¼ inch or less wide a maximum of 7 minutes, and large whole beans up to 12 minutes.

Chinese Long Beans

FCR — 6 SERVINGS

Chinese long beans are unusual but absolutely delicious. You will not need more than three per person and you will weave them around other little groups of diversely colored vegetables to obtain a very different look on your plate.

Simply boil the beans in water salted with 1½ teaspoons salt per quart for 5 to 6 minutes, until crisp-tender, no more; drain and pat dry before buttering lightly.

Candy-Striped Baby Beets

FFR — 6 SERVINGS

2 dozen each yellow-striped and red-striped baby beets

Salt

¼ cup vinegar of your choice

Unsalted butter as needed

Pepper from the mill

These lovely little beets—also called Chioggia beets—are as delightful to look at as they are to eat, provided you cook them fully; otherwise, they will have an unpleasant mineral taste, the result of the large amount of iron they contain. You can cook them whole, then peel and slice them, or peel and slice them raw, then cook them (in any case wear gloves); the two looks and tastes are different; judge for yourself. If mixed with tiny green beans or if Chinese long beans are curled around one or several islands of beets, you will obtain an elegant plate. Good with any meat but looks absolutely delightful with two plump little quail, nice and shiny brown (see page 769 or 807).

To cook them whole: Scrub the beets well, then cut the tops leaving ½ inch of the greens on to prevent the beet color from leaching into the cooking water. Salt with 1½ teaspoons salt per quart of water and add the vinegar (to prevent discoloration) to a large bath of water and bring to a boil. Cook the yellow beets first until tender. Remove then add the red beets to the same water and also cook until tender. The cooking time varies from 10 to 15 minutes. Rinse under ice cold water just as soon as each is done and peel. You can leave them whole or slice them. Butter to taste and season well.

To cook them sliced: Scrub and peel the beets, removing all blemishes (of which there are plenty because earth bugs love their sugar). Cut into ⅛-inch slices and cook in a large bath of boiling salted water to which you have added the vinegar. Cook until tender, 8 to 10 minutes. Drain and rinse under ice cold water; the beet slices will be pastel pink and yellow. Season with the butter, salt, and pepper.

Harvard Beets

FCR — 6 SERVINGS

¼ cup vinegar of your choice

6 large beets, scrubbed and trimmed leaving on 2 inches of stems

Salt

The large red beets known as Harvard beets are, I think, better suited to become a warm salad than an accompaniment to meats.

Pepper from the mill

2 celery ribs, very thinly sliced on the bias

1 fennel bulb, thinly sliced

2 tablespoons chopped fresh lemon balm leaves or chives

½ cup nonfat plain yogurt

2 tablespoons grapeseed or other unsaturated oil of your choice

Bring a large pot of water to a boil, add the vinegar and beets, season with 1½ teaspoons salt per quart of water and pepper, and cook until the beets are tender, 35 to 40 minutes. Reserve 2 tablespoons of the cooking water. Preheat the oven to 325°F and immediately transfer the drained beets to the oven to dry for another 40 to 50 minutes. Peel and slice.

Make separate piles of the beet, celery, and fennel slices, and half the chopped lemon balm leaves. Mix the yogurt, the reserved cooking water, and the oil together in a small bowl. Chop the remainder of the lemon balm and add it to the dressing. Spoon half the dressing over the bottom of a small platter. Alternate the slices of each of the three vegetables, and sprinkle the lemon balm leaves over the salad. Salt and pepper well and dribble the remainder of the dressing all around the vegetables. Serve chilled.

Do as the women of northern France do; once they are fully cooked in water, bake them in a slow oven for another hour to reconcentrate their flavor. Serve the salad lukewarm or chilled, as you prefer.

Broccoli

FCR — 6 SERVINGS

2 bunches broccoli

Juice of 1 lemon

Salt

1½ tablespoons unsalted butter

1 tablespoon walnut oil

3 tablespoons chopped walnuts

1 clove garlic, finely chopped

2 tablespoons finely chopped fresh Italian parsley leaves

Grated rind of ½ lemon

Separate the broccoli into florets. Peel the stems; if the stems are very large, cut a cross ½ inch deep into each of their bottoms. Soak the florets in water acidulated with the lemon juice to discourage any insects from staying in place. Parboil for 2 minutes if desired, in boiling salted water.

Bring a large pot of water to a boil, add 1½ teaspoons salt per quart of water and the broccoli; cook, uncovered, until the florets are bright green and the stems have turned almost translucent, like apple green jade, 4 to 6 minutes. Drain in a colander, florets down, and rinse under cold running water.

While the vegetables cook, heat the butter in a small pan, then add the

Usually no one likes broccoli for the simple reason that it is often overcooked, mushy, and strong. The secret is to peel the stems so the flower and the stem cook evenly in the same time span and both look attractive. Also, leave the cheese and the cheese sauce in the refrigerator for pasta. Instead, use the fresh little mixture recommended below. If you still do not relish the taste of broccoli, try parboiling it 2 minutes, then change over to a new bath of boiling salted water. This is a good accompaniment for a pork roast.

oil, walnuts, and garlic and toss together over medium heat until a nice smell develops. Add the parsley and lemon rind and mix well. Add the broccoli to the pan and turn them over several times to coat them with the mixture. Serve promptly.

Brussels Sprouts

FCR—6 SERVINGS

1 ½ pounds small brussels sprouts

Salt

2 tablespoons walnut or hazelnut oil

Celery salt

Pepper from the mill

This is another vegetable usually disliked for two reasons: too strong in taste and most of the time cooked so "crisp" that it is hard as a rock and indigestible. Great in the winter to accompany a big roast or turkey. Make sure to use only small sprouts. You can find only large sprouts? Remove the outer leaves until they are smaller; those big outer leaves full of strong oil are offenders anyhow.

In a large pot of boiling unsalted water, parboil the sprouts 3 minutes. Change the water, bring it to a boil, salt with 1½ teaspoons per quart of water, and cook the sprouts another good 6 to 8 minutes.

What if the sprouts are a tad overcooked? If it happens, remove the over-cooked leaves and separate all those that are not; with their different colors, the separate leaves are extremely attractive and gather a lot more of the seasoning. Toss them with the chosen oil seasoned with as much celery salt and pepper as you like.

Carrots

FFR—6 SERVINGS

1 pound fresh tiny carrots

Salt

Pepper from the mill

2 tablespoons unsalted butter creamed with freshly grated nutmeg to taste or
   2 tablespoons plain unsalted butter

½ teaspoon granulated sugar

¼ cup Secondary Stock (page 220) or other stock of your choice

1 good squeeze fresh lemon juice

2 tablespoons brandy, whisky, or bourbon

Use fresh carrots. The excuse that fresh ones are too large has disappeared with the appearance of tiny fresh carrots in the supermarket. Good with any meat.

Immerse the carrots in boiling water salted with 1½ teaspoons salt per quart and peppered to taste, and boil, until crisp-tender, not mushy, about 5 minutes. Serve tossed either in the nutmeg butter or, while the carrots cook, mix the butter, sugar, stock, lemon juice, and liquor of your choice together in a small saucepan and reduce to 3 tablespoons over medium-high heat. Toss the bright hot carrots in this small glaze and serve immediately.

Glorious Boiled English Baby Peas

FFR — 6 SERVINGS

2 pounds sweet peas in shells

4 cups water

3 thick fresh mint stems

Salt

Pepper from the mill

2 tablespoons unsalted butter

Pinch of granulated sugar

1 ½ tablespoons chopped fresh mint leaves

Shell the peas. Bring the water to a boil, add the mint stems, and season with salt to taste and pepper. Simmer 10 minutes, then remove the mint stems, add the peas, and cook until just tender and still bright green, 4 to 5 minutes. Drain and immediately toss with the butter, sugar, more salt and pepper if needed, and the chopped mint leaves. Serve immediately while so very nice and fresh.

Peas remain a problem; they are still not to be found tiny and delicious in their pods, which is just as well, since when they were years ago, we always ended up eating half of them uncooked, so never enough of them were left for dinner. Good by themselves or with roast chicken.

Boiled Coeurs de Pigeons Potatoes

FCR to FFR — 6 SERVINGS

1 pound coeurs de pigeons

Salt

2 tablespoons extra virgin olive oil

1 clove garlic, finely chopped

1 ½ tablespoons finely chopped fresh parsley leaves

Several fresh thyme leaves, chopped

Wash the tiny potatoes well. Immerse them in cold water to cover. Bring to a boil, add 1½ teaspoons salt per quart of water, and simmer until tender, about 18 minutes. In a small skillet, heat the oil, garlic, parsley, and thyme over medium heat. Roll the tiny potatoes in this mixture and serve nice and hot.

Coeurs de pigeons or pigeon hearts are tiny potatoes that farmers used to replant in the old days, but which now have become a little luxury item. Go to a farmers' market; I have seen them everywhere from Massachusetts to New Hampshire, Michigan to California. If unavailable use Red Bless or Yellow Finnish potatoes as small as possible. Especially good with guinea fowl.

Boiled Rutabagas

FFR — 6 SERVINGS

3 large rutabagas

Salt

Pepper from the mill

½ cup excellent Primary Veal Stock (page 219)

6 Chinese mustard leaves, coarsely chopped

I tablespoon unsalted butter or unsaturated oil of your choice

Here is another not-well-liked vegetable that is positively delicious if, again, one cooks it properly. It needs to be cooked very tender and is best coated in a mixture of reduced stock garnished with coarsely chopped Chinese mustard leaves. Enjoy with pork tenderloin or chops or cutlets.

Peel the rutabagas, then cut them into sticks 2 inches long and ½ inch wide. "Turn"—that means remove all the angles of each stick so they do not break off in the water and make the vegetables look mushy. Turning the vegetables will also allow them to roll into the glaze once in the skillet.

Bring a large pot of water to a boil. Season with 1½ teaspoons salt per quart of water, and pepper, add the rutabagas, and cook until tender, 20 to 25 minutes. Meanwhile, reduce the veal stock by half in a large skillet over high heat. When the rutabagas are done, drain them well. Add them immediately to the veal stock, reduce the heat to medium, and roll the pan back and forth on the burner to coat them. Add the chopped mustard leaves and butter or oil which will prevent the vegetables from sticking to one another. Toss well together and serve on a very hot plate.

Jardinière of Boiled Vegetables

FFR — 12 SERVINGS

½ pound boiled baby carrots (page 378)

½ pound boiled cut rutabagas (page 380)

½ pound boiled baby green beans (page 375)

½ pound each sliced cooked red- and yellow-striped beets (page 376)

½ pound boiled medium-size asparagus stalks, sliced into I-inch pieces on a slant (page 374)

1½ cups Secondary Stock (page 220)

2 tablespoons unsalted butter

Several fresh rosemary leaves, chopped

Several fresh lemon thyme leaves

Salt

Pepper from the mill

This is practical for a larger dinner party. Boil all the vegetables in water salted with 1½ teaspoons per quart of water, and store them away in your refrigerator as much as two days ahead of time. Reheat and serve with any meat from poultry to beef.

Bring all the vegetables to room temperature while you reduce the secondary stock to approximately ⅔ cup over high heat. Toss and reheat all the vegetables a few minutes in the stock, add the butter and herbs and season with salt and pepper. Swirl the vegetables in the pan to coat them well.

STEAMING VEGETABLES

Steaming vegetables has become extremely popular in the last twenty years because, not ever being in contact with the water, they lose a lot less of their vitamins than boiled vegetables.

The most inexpensive steamer is the little French folding steaming basket which every French homebody absolutely treasures. However, it is not always the best since it is so small that, more often than not, the vegetables are piled on top of one another, unless one does several steamings, which takes a lot more time.

Excellent, more modern steamers of larger sizes exist in which the vegetables can be spread in one single layer and cook almost as fast as they would in boiling water. Steaming usually requires a few more minutes than boiling but the concentration of the flavor in steamed vegetables easily compensates for that small difference in time. If a steamer has several tiers as is often the case, you can steam a whole dinner at once. In this case some cooks like to place the meat over the vegetables so they can be basted with the natural meat juices and acquire an added degree of taste.

Even if you do not own a proper steamer, you can easily improvise one with a drum sieve, or one of those large mesh draining covers fitted with a long handle; either can rest easily over a pot containing boiling water and both are wide enough to allow the vegetables to be spread in a single layer. As a cover to trap the steam you can use any lid which can stand 2 inches above the vegetables, even a large glass or metal bowl placed upside down over the vegetables.

I do not recommend steaming green vegetables, for the volatile acids which escape from them will condense on the lid and fall back upon them, bleaching them ever so lightly. But all white and yellow vegetables—white asparagus, cauliflower, peeled new potatoes, carrots, cut-up butternut squash, sliced pattypan squash—do very well and taste absolutely glorious. Peels of zucchini and crookneck yellow squash do very well steamed as you will see further along.

It is a good idea to flavor the steaming water with aromatics because not only will it flavor the surface of the steaming vegetables, but if you use some of the water to prepare a small sauce, it will be in harmony with the steamed vegetables.

As a garnish try some of the new-fangled flavored oils (see page 304 for some suggestions). You can prepare them in a frying pan in just the small quantity you need.

CARDINAL RULES OF STEAMING

- With very few exceptions, the steamer must be covered.
- The water in the bottom of the steamer must boil throughout the steaming.

- The water must not come in contact with the vegetables, or they will boil instead of steam.

White Asparagus with Fennel Butter

FFR— 6 SERVINGS

3 dozen white asparagus with stems as thick as possible

1 fennel bulb with greens on, sliced, or 1 tablespoon fennel seeds, crushed

Juice of 1 lemon

Salt

Pepper from the mill

½ cup unsalted butter, at room temperature, cut into tablespoons

1 tablespoon fresh wild fennel flowers (optional)

Bend the asparagus stalks head to stem; the stem will break where the fibers stop being edible. Peel the stalk from the blossom end down, starting just under the close crop of leaves. Put 3 inches of water at the bottom of the steamer and add the sliced fennel bulb or half the fennel seeds. Bring to a boil, covered. Arrange the asparagus in a single layer in the steamer basket, set over the boiling water and cover with the lid. Steam until mellow, 8 to 10 minutes.

When the asparagus is half done, remove ½ cup of the steaming water to a saucepan. Add the lemon juice and season with salt and pepper. Reduce to 3 tablespoons over medium heat. Remove the pan from the heat and whisk in the butter tablespoon by tablespoon. Strain the sauce through a conical strainer into a small bowl or pitcher. Add the fennel flowers if available.

When the asparagus is done, lift out the steamer basket and let it rest a few minutes on a folded kitchen towel to absorb the excess moisture. Arrange the asparagus on plates or a small platter and serve basted with the lemon-and-fennel butter. Serve no cooler than lukewarm.

Steamed Cauliflower

FCR— 6 SERVINGS

1 large head cauliflower

1 large yellow onion, finely chopped

1 large clove garlic, finely chopped

Sprig fresh thyme

1 bay leaf

1 ½ teaspoons cornstarch

If you cannot find a fresh fennel bulb, simply crush some fennel seeds and use them instead, or if wild fennel grows in your area, use the greens and some of the tiny yellow blossoms in the butter sauce. White asparagus cannot be cooked crisp-tender but must be served "mellow" (read well done); otherwise, it will remain somewhat bitter and disappointing. The purple tips will turn green while steaming. Serve by itself as an excellent first course.

The hot pepper flakes will give a bit of "zing" to that very discreet white sauce. Especially good served as a vegetarian dish in combination with a pilaf of orzo (see page 466).

3 tablespoons nonfat milk

⅓ cup crème fraîche

2 tablespoons chopped fresh Italian parsley leaves

¼ teaspoon red pepper flakes

Salt

Pepper from the mill

6 sprigs fresh Italian parsley

Trim the cauliflower into florets and peel the stems so they can cook as fast as the florets. While you do so, bring 3 inches of water to a boil in the bottom of a steamer. Add the onion, garlic, thyme, and bay leaf and let boil 10 minutes. Place the cauliflower in the steaming basket, cover, and steam until crisp-tender, 6 to 8 minutes.

Halfway through the cooking, remove ¾ cup of the water from the steamer to a small saucepan and simmer. Dilute the cornstarch in the milk, then add the slurry to the simmering water and thicken over medium heat. When the sauce has thickened, add the crème fraîche, chopped parsley, and pepper flakes.

Remove the cauliflower from the steamer and season with salt and pepper. Place them upside down in a small bowl, reshaping the head as best you can. Turn onto a small platter and pour the sauce over. Decorate all around with Italian parsley sprigs.

Steamed Cucumbers in Dill Oil

FCR—6 SERVINGS

½ cup grapeseed or other unsaturated oil of your choice

¼ cup plus 1 tablespoon chopped fresh dill

3 American cucumbers, peeled, cut into halves lengthwise, and seeded

1 tablespoon dillseeds

Salt

Pepper from the mill

Prepare the dill oil before you make the cucumbers so it has time to infuse. Especially good with salmon.

Slowly heat the grapeseed oil over medium heat. Meanwhile, blanch (see page 370) the dill 1 to 2 minutes in a small pot of boiling water. Drain, pat dry, and put in a blender. Pour the hot oil over the dill and process until the dill is completely pureed. Refrigerate overnight and the next day strain the oil through a fine tea strainer into a ramekin; let drip without pushing on the dill to keep the oil clear.

Bring 3 inches of water to a boil in the bottom of a steamer. Add the dillseeds, bring to a simmer, and cook, covered, for 10 minutes. Place the cucumber halves in one layer in the steaming basket, cover, and steam until crisp-tender or fully tender, as you prefer, 3 to 4 minutes, over the dill water. Season well with salt and pepper as soon as done and toss with as much of the prepared dill oil as you wish.

Steamed Potatoes

I usually serve these potatoes with a steamed or poached fish such as trout. The potatoes should be waxy enough that they do not fall apart. Keep the potato trimmings to make potato cakes (see page 417).

FFR — 6 SERVINGS

3 very large Yellow Finnish, or Yukon Gold potatoes, or Red Bliss potatoes, peeled

Large bouquet garni

2 scallions, sliced on a slant

Salt

Pepper from the mill

2 tablespoons unsalted butter, melted

Cut the potatoes into ½-inch-thick slices, then again into halves in the other direction. "Turn" each small piece so as to carve seven even faces out of each; this will make the potatoes look very even and like small torpedoes.

While you do so, bring 3 inches of water to a boil in the bottom of a steamer. Add the bouquet garni and scallions and simmer, covered, until the potatoes are ready to cook. Set the potatoes in one layer in the steamer basket and steam, covered, until fork tender, 18 minutes or so. The potatoes will be nicely perfumed with the aromatics. Season them well with salt and pepper and roll them in the melted butter before serving.

"Turning" potatoes; each finished potato has seven faces.

Pattypan and Carrot Slices in Anise and Saffron Oil

Particularly enjoyable with breaded scaloppine of turkey or breaded chicken cutlets. Cook to crisp-tender or tender, as you prefer.

FCR — 6 SERVINGS

¼ cup pure olive oil

Large pinch of saffron threads

2 teaspoons aniseeds

6 yellow baby pattypan squash, 1½ inches in diameter

6 green baby pattypan squash, 1½ inches in diameter

2 very large, very fresh carrots, peeled

Salt

Pepper from the mill

Heat the olive oil in a small pan, then pour over the saffron threads and ½ teaspoon of the aniseeds in a small bowl and let steep overnight in the refrigerator. Bring back to room temperature 1 hour before using. Do not strain.

Cut the pattypans and carrots into ¼-inch-thick slices, making the pattypan slices round and the carrot slices slanted and elongated. Put 3 inches of water in the bottom of a steamer, bring to a boil, and add the remainder of the aniseeds. Simmer, covered, for 20 minutes. Bring the water to a boil again. Steam the carrots first in a single layer for about 6 minutes, then remove to a large skillet. Then steam the pattypans, each color separately, about 4 minutes each. Remove to the same skillet and mix well. Add the prepared oil and toss together, reheating very well on medium heat and seasoning with salt and pepper. Serve promptly.

Two Zucchini and Carrot Spaghetti

FCR — 6 SERVINGS

¼ cup virgin olive oil

2 cloves garlic, very finely chopped

6 large yellow zucchini, cut into spaghetti

6 large green zucchini, cut into spaghetti

4 large carrots, cut into spaghetti

2 tablespoons unsalted butter

Salt

Pepper from the mill

Fresh basil leaves

Heat the olive oil, then add the garlic, letting it turn a nice beige color over medium heat, stirring occasionally. Remove from the heat and cool completely. Store overnight in the refrigerator. When you are ready to steam, bring the oil to room temperature and strain it into a large skillet.

Mix the zucchini and carrot spaghetti together, then divide among six plates. Place 3 inches of water in the bottom of a steamer and bring to a boil. Rub 1 teaspoon of the butter on your hands, grasp the contents of the first plate of spaghetti and toss it over the steam until completely heated through and hot. Season with salt and pepper while you steam. Remove to the skillet containing the saffron-and-anise oil and keep warm over medium heat. Repeat with the other five portions. Toss all the spaghetti together for 1 minute, divide among the plates again, and serve surrounded with fresh basil leaves.

I like to present this under a brace of brown quail. The spaghetti can be done the easy way, using the famous Japanese vegetable cutter with a handle or the not so hard way by peeling all the vegetables with a potato peeler along their lengths and slicing the thin strips lengthwise into ⅛-inch-thick spaghetti.

The second technique retains more natural taste in the vegetables because the knife bruises the vegetables a little less and cuts them a little thicker. Be careful; the cooking of the "spaghetti" is done in a matter of seconds. Divide the batch into six equal portions. You will steam one at a time using no lid and only your hands as an instrument. If your hands are not used to heat and are sensitive, wear surgical gloves. If you don't think your hands can stand the heat, put the spaghetti in a conical strainer, immerse it in boiling salted water, and pat dry in paper towels before final seasoning. Don't expect the same taste, though.

Steamed Whole Artichokes

FCR—6 SERVINGS

Bring 3 inches of water to a boil in the bottom of a steamer. Trim the stems and tops of the leaves of the artichokes. Steam upside down until a skewer inserted at the center of the heart comes out freely, 25 to 30 minutes. Consume lukewarm with the dressing of your choice, made with an unsaturated oil.

Steamed Corn on the Cob

This takes all of 3 minutes and is the essence of good fresh corn. You need not cook the corn; it is enough to heat it through.

FFR—6 SERVINGS

6 fresh ears Silver Queen corn, just picked
Salted butter

Remove all the husks and silk. Bring 3 inches of water to a boil in the bottom of a steamer. Place the ears in the steamer basket and steam 3 to 4 minutes. Remove from the steam and rub with salted butter.

VEGETABLE PUREES

There are purees and there are *coulis*. Those vegetables containing enough starches will turn into purees that are solid enough to hold their shape on a plate. Those vegetables that are not solid enough will not turn into true purees but rather thick *coulis*. These are better served as a sauce on starches such as pasta and rice or as a filling for other vegetables such as artichoke bottoms. If mixed with a protein that can give it body, a *coulis* can become a custard poached in elegant little timbales. This section is dedicated to true purees; *coulis* can be found on page 397 and timbales on page 442.

Of all the starchy vegetables, only potatoes must really be strained through a food mill or fine sieve (*tamis*), in spite of all the electric equipment we have nowadays. Passed through a high speed electric machine (more so the blender than the food processor), the pulp of potatoes, which contains proteins comparable to those in wheat flour, becomes stringy and gummy. So truly, the old-fashioned food mill or sieve still delivers the best-textured mashed potatoes.

Since green vegetables and some of the yellow contain mostly cellulose and water they produce purees that are saucelike *coulis*. You can, however, turn them into more solid purees if you blend them with mashed potatoes. If you choose this solution, add the plain unseasoned and unenriched potato puree, then finish the blend with seasonings or an enrichment of butter or cream or both.

ABOUT POTATO PUREES Never use a back-and-forth motion to puree potatoes; rather, apply a one-direction motion that does not give the proteins the opportunity to develop any glutinous elasticity. If you work with a *tamis*, put only two or three pieces of potatoes on it at once and always push toward yourself with a wooden mallet or a highball glass to flatten the potatoes into the mesh. Lift the mallet or glass and go back to the starting point of your stroke each and every time you give a stroke. The same applies when you use a large conical strainer. Put a few pieces of potatoes in the bottom of the strainer and using a highball glass push upward toward yourself until the potatoes pass through the mesh and lift the glass, returning to the bottom of the strainer for your next stroke. The food mill is certainly a little faster and the food processor is certainly useful, but neither quite yields that same fluffy texture as a *tamis* or conical strainer. How about a masher? Use it if you don't mind a bit of lumpiness in your daily meal purees, but if you prepare a great meal for company, the masher is a no-no.

Any liquid—stock, milk, cream—that is added to a puree containing a small or large amount of potatoes must be hot, or the finished preparation will acquire a definite taste of stale potato starch. The cold liquid changes the taste of the starches, so an unpleasant slight aftertaste of cardboard suffuses the puree. Try both ways to convince yourself.

The starches in potatoes have a tendency to liquefy if submitted to bursts of heat (see starch-bound sauces, page 268). Therefore, it is imperative to reheat a potato puree very gradually; if you proceed too quickly, the puree will become rather liquid and soupy. "Dry" any puree containing potatoes by flattening it against the bottom of the pan, as is explained for cream puff dough on page 1105, over medium heat. If the mashed potatoes are to be blended with moist vegetables, evaporate any moisture in the moist vegetables before you blend them with the puree of potatoes.

Potato Puree or Mashed Potatoes

FFR—6 SERVINGS

6 large older Maine or Idaho potatoes (the starchier the better), peeled

Salt

⅓ cup heavy cream, scalded

¾ cup unsalted butter

Pepper from the mill

Freshly grated nutmeg (optional)

If you want to avoid the large amount of butter, reverse the process and instead add twice as much heavy cream and only 2 tablespoons butter. Try both, use the one you like best. Or use the next recipe made with olive oil.

Cut the potatoes into large pieces, place in a large saucepan, cover with cold water, and add 1 teaspoon salt per quart of water. Bring to a boil and boil until you can crush them with a fork, 18 to 20 minutes; drain, reserving the water.

Pour the cream and butter into a large sauteuse pan placed over very low heat. Set a *tamis* over the opening of the pan and strain the potatoes directly into the scalded cream. Homogenize with a wooden spoon; if the mixture is too stiff, add a few tablespoons of the cooking water. Season with salt and pepper as needed, and add the nutmeg if desired. Homogenize well by stirring for 1 minute, no longer.

Medmadmash

FCR — 6 SERVINGS

2 heads garlic

6 tablespoons extra virgin olive oil

6 large older Maine or Idaho russet potatoes (the starchier the better) or Red Bliss
    potatoes, peeled

Salt

Pepper from the mill

⅓ cup chopped hazelnuts

3 sprigs fresh sage

These are very "Mediterranean Mad Mashed Potatoes," perfect for the current food trends.

Preheat the oven to 350°F. Cut off top and root of each garlic head. Set in a small baking dish with ½ inch of water and 2 tablespoons of the olive oil. Bake until the garlic is soft and the pulp can be squeezed out of the skin, about 45 minutes. Place the garlic pulp in a conical strainer.

Meanwhile, cut the potatoes into large pieces, place in a large saucepan, cover with cold water, and add 1 teaspoon of salt per quart of water. Bring to a boil and simmer, covered, until the potatoes are fork tender, about 20 minutes. Drain, reserving the water.

Set the strainer over a large sauteuse pan and strain the potatoes together with the garlic cloves directly into the pan. When all the potatoes have been strained, add the olive oil in which the garlic cooked and a few additional tablespoons of potato-cooking water if needed. Correct the salt and pepper. Arrange the potatoes in a serving dish, mounding their tops. Heat the remaining olive oil with the hazelnuts and the sage sprigs over medium-low heat for 3 to 4 minutes. Spoon over the top of the potatoes and make sure that each guest receives a bit of that delicious topping to stir into her/his portion. Serve piping hot with a roast pork flavored with Mediterranean herbs.

Yam, Sweet Potato, or
Any Winter Squash Puree

FFR—6 SERVINGS

6 large yams or sweet potatoes or 2 large winter squash such as butternut or
    kabocha
¼ cup heavy cream, scalded
2 to 3 tablespoons dry sherry or to your personal taste
3 to 8 tablespoons unsalted butter or to your personal taste
Salt
Pepper from the mill
Scalded milk, if and as needed

Bake the yams, sweet potatoes, or squash in a preheated 375° to 400°F oven until tender, about 1¼ hours. Place the cream in a food processor or blender with the sherry and butter. Scoop out the meat of the vegetables and add to food processor or blender. Process together until the mixture is smooth and homogeneous. Season with salt and pepper. If too stiff, add a few tablespoons of hot milk as needed. If too soft, reduce over gentle heat until thickened.

The proteins in these vegetables not being of the same nature as those in white potatoes, you can process the puree in the food processor or blender.

Puree of Peas in
Artichoke Bottoms

FFR—6 SERVINGS

Two 24-ounces bags frozen large peas
Large bouquet garni of fresh chervil, stems and leaves separated and finely chopped
Salt
⅓ cup unsalted butter
⅓ teaspoon granulated sugar
¼ teaspoon freshly ground white pepper or more to taste
6 cooked large artichoke bottoms (page 373)

Mix the peas and chervil stems in a large pot, cover with water reaching 1 inch above the peas, add salt to taste, bring to a boil, and cook until the peas start to discolor, which is a sign that their starch has completely developed. Drain, then process the peas and chervil stems together in a food processor or blender only long enough to break the skins. Strain the pea mixture through a conical strainer or *tamis* directly into a sauteuse pan. Add the chopped chervil leaves together with the butter, sugar, pepper, and however much salt is needed. Reheat and homogenize well. Pipe into the cooked artichoke bottoms using a pastry bag to make a beautiful vegetable garnish.

Excellent with roast chicken and roasted or panfried veal.

Chestnut Puree

FFR — 6 SERVINGS

3 pounds chestnuts in their shells, to obtain 1¾ pounds shelled nuts

3 to 4 cups cold Secondary Stock (page 220)

Yellow center leaves of 1 celery heart, chopped

Salt

Pepper from the mill

⅓ cup heavy cream, scalded

2 tablespoons dry Madeira or sherry

¼ to ½ cup unsalted butter, to your personal taste, or ¼ cup hazelnut oil

Chestnuts as purchased in American markets (having traveled from Europe) can be more or less dry and will absorb more or less stock to soften properly, hence the variable amount of stock called for in the recipe.

To be served with wintry meals of roast turkey, goose, or venison.

NOTE: *Since chestnuts require so much time to peel, you may use the whole chestnuts canned in glass jars, but they are pricier than fresh chestnuts and also not so fresh-tasting. Reheat the processed nuts slowly in a bit of stock.*

To shell the nuts, cut a gash ⅛ inch deep under the lighter-colored root patch of each nut. Immerse the nuts in boiling water. Remove from the heat and lift out a few nuts at a time to remove the shells and skins with a paring knife. Keep any unpeeled nut in the warm water until ready to be peeled, or the skin will not come off.

Cover the shelled and peeled nuts with the cold stock in a large saucepan; bring to a boil. Add the celery leaves and season with salt and pepper. Simmer over medium-low heat until the stock has been completely absorbed and the nuts are falling apart; how long this will take depends on the dryness of the chestnuts at the time of purchase. Puree the nuts in a food processor. Return to a sauteuse pan and toss the puree over medium-high heat to dry it out a bit. Blend in the cream, Madeira, and butter. Correct the seasoning.

Artichoke Puree

FFR — 6 SERVINGS

6 large or 9 smaller cooked hot artichoke bottoms (page 373)

1½ cups hot mashed potatoes (½ recipe on page 387)

¼ cup unsalted butter

⅛ teaspoon finely grated lemon rind

1 heaping tablespoon finely chopped fresh tarragon leaves

Salt

Pepper from the mill

Serve with veal and poultry.

Puree the artichoke bottoms in a blender or food processor. Blend with the mashed potatoes. Stir in the butter, lemon rind, and tarragon and season with salt and pepper.

Puree of Carrots or Rutabagas

FFR—6 SERVINGS

1 pound cooked large carrots or yellow turnips (page 378 or 380)

½ cup heavy cream

1 cup unbuttered hot mashed potatoes (page 387)

¼ cup unsalted butter, cut into pieces

Salt

Pepper from the mill

Serve with poultry, veal, or ham.

Place the hot vegetables in a large skillet and add the cream. Shake the pan back and forth over low heat until the cream has reduced and coats the vegetables. Remove them to a blender or food processor and puree. Return to the skillet and blend with the puree of potatoes. Stir in the butter until melted and season with salt and pepper.

Puree of Celeriac

FFR—6 SERVINGS

2 pounds net weight cleaned celeriac (4 medium-size or 3 very large roots), cut into large cubes

2 large older Maine or Idaho potatoes (the starchier the better), peeled and cut into large cubes

Salt

Pepper from the mill

½ cup crème fraîche

2 tablespoons unsalted butter or more to taste

Celeriac is the swollen rootstock of a kind of celery. It is incomparable as a winter vegetable served with a roast chicken. When the first edition of this book was published it was difficult to find, but now it is displayed in every supermarket. This puree of celeriac has always been a great favorite in my restaurants and we had to prepare tons of it, for we always had requests for seconds. Preferably use dense celeriacs, which do not sound hollow when knocked on with a finger. Put gloves on to peel the celeriacs and remove every bit of dirty surface as well as any cellulose formed inside the root. Serve this with roast chicken or turkey, lamb, veal, magrets of duck, or beef.

Place the celeriac and potatoes in a large saucepan with cold water just to cover and season with 1½ teaspoons salt per quart of water and pepper. Cover and boil over medium heat until both are fork tender, 20 minutes. Drain, reserving the cooking water.

Place the crème fraîche and butter in a sauteuse pan. Strain the vegetables through a *tamis* or conical strainer directly over the enrichments. Stir well and correct the seasoning.

ÉTUVÉED VEGETABLES (POT-ROASTED OR SMOTHERED VEGETABLES)

This technique is left over from the days when our grandmothers still cooked on the hearth; the pot was buried in hot ashes and the vegetables cooked gently and evenly.

In the first edition of this book, this technique was called pot-roasting, because I could no more come to terms with the evil-sounding term "smothered" than I could with its French equivalent *à l'étouffée*, neither sounding more "charming" than the other. I prefer the French term *étuvée* which means exactly the same thing: a dish of vegetables cooked covered, in their own juices, without any liquid added or, if any, very little.

This method should only be used for young vegetables which contain new cellulose that can soften in a relatively short amount of time in the vegetables' own relatively large amount of moisture.

Zucchini, summer squash, young peas mixed with young lettuce, young green beans, young carrots, young cabbage of the Savoy type, bell peppers, and tomatoes can be cooked in this manner. Slightly older vegetables containing more cellulose and less moisture can be cooked in this manner provided a small amount of liquid is added to the pot to help the cellulose soften.

All you need to do is heat a small amount of butter or oil, add the raw vegetables—sliced, shredded, or diced—and season with salt and pepper. Cover the pot tightly and cook over very low heat until just tender, tossing every so often. The color will not be bright since the volatile acids dissolved into the condensation on the pot lid will fall back into the pot, but you may love the taste so much that you will gladly exchange taste for color. Overcooking, however, will result in mushy vegetables.

For this method of cooking vegetables, in which they need to be tossed once or twice during cooking, the best cooking pot is either a heavy skillet with a lid or any thick pot with two handles which can be grasped to toss the vegetables. (Le Creuset round stew pot, for example, or a Cuisinart sautoir or sauteuse with one long handle on one side and a round one on the other, will do very well.)

This method is a good way to prepare vegetable *coulis*, which can be used as sauces on vegetarian dishes or on pasta and rice dishes.

Étuvée of Green and Yellow Zucchini

Use the very small green or bright yellow zucchini barely one inch across. If yellow zucchini are not available, replace them with crookneck squash. This is good with all meats.

FCR—6 SERVINGS

6 small green zucchini, washed and dried

6 small yellow zucchini, washed and dried

2 tablespoons virgin olive oil

Salt

Pepper from the mill

2 tablespoons chopped fresh Italian parsley leaves

1 tablespoon finely scissored fresh basil leaves

1 tiny clove garlic, finely chopped

Cut the zucchini into ⅓-inch-thick slices. Heat the olive oil on medium heat, then toss both squash in it to coat them evenly and very well. Season with salt and pepper. Cover and cook 5 minutes over medium heat. Toss, cover again, and cook another 5 minutes. Do not cook more than 12 to 14 minutes altogether. When tender, toss the herbs and garlic into the vegetables, correct the final seasoning if needed, and turn into a vegetable dish.

Étuvéed Shredded Carrots

FFR to FCR—6 SERVINGS

2 tablespoons unsaturated oil of your choice

2 small yellow onions, very finely chopped

1 ½ pounds carrots, shredded into fine julienne

¼ teaspoon freshly grated nutmeg

Salt

Pepper from the mill

1 tablespoon fresh lemon juice

Dry white wine or apple cider, if needed

2 to 4 tablespoons whipped or heavily creamed unsalted butter or to your personal taste (optional)

1 to 2 tablespoons finely chopped fresh Italian parsley leaves or to your personal taste

2 tablespoons chopped fresh chervil leaves

Heat the oil in a large pot over medium heat. Add the onions and cook, stirring, until soft. Add the carrots and nutmeg and season with salt and pepper. Cover tightly, and cook over low heat until tender, 15 to 20 minutes. Add the lemon juice and wine or cider and toss the carrots to blend all the elements well. Add the butter and chopped herbs and toss again to blend well. Turn into a vegetable dish.

If the carrots seem to need a tad of moisture at any time during the cooking and if you have some mellow white wine left over, add a bit to the pot; the final taste will be most delicious. You can replace the wine with apple cider.

The best carrots are obtained when you add 2 to 4 tablespoons of butter to the julienne after the cooking is completed. Excellent with all meats, especially the white ones.

Marie Becker's Green Beans

FFR—6 SERVINGS

¼ pound slab bacon

1 pound small Blue Lake green beans

Salt

Pepper from the mill

1 to 2 tablespoons water, if needed

3 small Yellow Finnish potatoes, cut into chunks, angles turned if you wish

Cut the bacon into ⅓-inch-thick lardons (see page 1165). Render the bacon slowly in a skillet over medium-low heat until golden. Discard the bacon fat completely but not the bacon, which stays in the skillet throughout the cooking. Trim and wash the beans, drain them well, and add them to the

From the Lorraine kitchen of my stepgrandmother who used to cook these beans in the ashes of her hearth as late as 1945. To "unsaturate" this dish, suppress the bacon and use unsaturated oil; walnut oil would be excellent. If you double the ingredients this dish can make a nice supper by itself; offer a measured amount of cheese afterward and abundant fruit.

skillet. Season with salt and pepper and toss well together. Cover tightly and cook 15 minutes over very low heat. Add the water if necessary. Let cook another 15 minutes.

Add the potatoes, hiding them among the beans. Continue cooking on very low heat, covered, until the potatoes are tender, about 20 more minutes. The beans will be completely discolored, but the taste of both vegetables will be delicious. Serve without delay.

Ragout of Peas and Artichokes

FCR — 6 SERVINGS

2 tablespoons pure olive oil

Two 10-ounce packages frozen artichoke hearts thawed, or 18 fresh artichokes, trimmed as on page 372

1 dime-size piece lemon rind

1½ tablespoons chopped fresh tarragon leaves

2 tablespoons Pure Vegetable Broth or Secondary Stock (page 213 or 220) or broth of your choice

Salt

Pepper from the mill

One 10-ounce package frozen baby peas (without butter sauce)

1½ teaspoons chopped fresh Italian parsley leaves

1½ teaspoons chopped fresh mint leaves

For the proper taste, both the vegetables must be overcooked. You must trim the harder leaves from the artichokes. The amount of stock needed will depend on the size of the artichokes used. And unfortunately frozen baby peas are still the best unless you grow your own. Excellent for chicken cutlets and veal chops or scaloppine.

Heat the olive oil; add the artichokes, lemon rind, tarragon, and stock and season with salt and pepper. Cover the pot tightly and cook 10 minutes over low heat. Defrost the peas under cold running water, drain well, and mix with the artichokes. Toss well, cover again, and continue cooking until the vegetables are very tender, 10 to 15 minutes. Remove the lemon rind and correct the final seasoning. Add the parsley and mint and serve rapidly.

Sour Yellow Turnips

SURI RUWI

FFR — 6 SERVINGS

4 pounds rutabagas, to obtain 8 cups packed fine julienne

4 teaspoons sea salt

1½ teaspoons caraway seeds

¼ pound slab bacon

Pepper from the mill

2 tablespoons unsalted butter

This Alsatian dish is quite delicious. It is best served with smoked pork chops. You will need to keep the turnips in a cool basement or refrigerator to be successful with the souring.

Peel the rutabagas, then cut them into ⅛-inch-thick slices. Pile the slices on top of one another and cut into ⅛-inch-wide matchsticks. Put those in a glass bowl. Mix with the salt, kneading and mixing with your hands until the juices of the turnips start running out of the pulp. Pack into a 6-cup plastic container, alternating layers of turnip with caraway seeds. Place a triple layer of parchment paper flush on the surface of the turnips and snap the container lid on. Store in the warmer part of your refrigerator and let sour for 3 weeks.

When sour, wash the rutabagas twice and drip well in a colander. Cut the bacon into ⅓-inch-thick lardons and render it in a large skillet until golden but not crisp; discard the bacon fat completely. Add the turnips, put the pot lid on, and cook over low heat until very tender; the cooking time will vary with the age of the turnips, from 35 minutes to 1 hour. When done, add pepper to your taste and, if you wish, more salt and the butter.

Mixed Vegetable Ragout

FCR — 6 SERVINGS

2 tablespoons unsaturated oil of your choice

1 cup button mushrooms

1 head Boston lettuce, finely chopped

2 leeks, white and light green parts only, washed and thinly sliced

Salt

Pepper from the mill

2 green zucchini, sliced ⅓ inch thick

2 yellow crookneck squash, sliced ⅓ inch thick

1 cup baby carrots, peeled

1 cup small white turnips, 1 inch in diameter at the most, or 4 larger turnips, peeled and
    quartered

½ cup fresh lima beans, unpeeled, or fava beans, peeled

½ cup fresh large peas

1 cup 1-inch pieces Blue Lake green beans

1 to 1½ cups Secondary Stock (page 220) or chicken broth of your choice as needed

1 tablespoon unsalted butter

1 tablespoon unbleached all-purpose flour

1 tablespoon each chopped fresh chervil, chives, parsley, and cilantro leaves

I liked to serve this dish with a large pilaf or plain risotto of rice (see page 461 or 466) when I lived in climates that were not reputed for their sunshine and young vegetables. The vegetables need not be of the most tremendous quality to still taste good.

Heat the oil in a two-handled pot over medium heat; add the mushrooms, lettuce, and leeks, toss well in the oil, season with salt and pepper, and cover for a few minutes. Add the remaining vegetables, season again, toss well together, and cook, covered, until tender, another 25 to 30 minutes.

Add the stock to the pot and bring to a boil. Mash the butter with the flour and stir quickly through the vegetables to bind them lightly together. Use as a topping for the rice of your choice, then sprinkle with the herbs.

So much has been said and written about ratatouille but I find it is usually either overcooked to puree, a lesser sin, or undercooked to the point that the eggplant tastes like warm, wet cotton balls, a major sin. This dish is the epitome of étuvéing: Simply cook the vegetables covered in a heavy pot until there is only enough of the wonderful natural vegetable juices mixed together to coat them lightly. If you want a crunchy ratatouille, then you don't want a ratatouille. Instead, take the same vegetables, less the eggplant, and make yourself a stir-fry (see page 407).

The latter name is in Provençal; I prefer it to the French name. This recipe is for ratatouille as prepared in Nice. It is preferable to:

• Use the long, thin, light purple eggplant known in this country as Naples early eggplant or Japanese eggplant. These need no or very little salting. If you can find only the larger ones, salt them to extract the bitter juices.

• Use the ripest tomatoes you can find and only sun-ripened. I have suggested using two different types, the first for juice and sugar, the second for texture; if you cannot find them, use the best available in your part of the country.

• Do not use red onions for this dish even if they are used in the Italian cousin of ratatouille, caponata. The onions used for this dish in Nice are mostly the yellow ones and not too large at that.

Ratatouille or Ratatouia

FCR—6 SERVINGS

This is a hot weather dish; it should be enjoyed at room temperature, whatever it may be on the day you are making the dish.

Let the ratatouille ripen overnight, refrigerating it (my French friends put it in the cellar overnight, well covered) to let the flavors blend well and bring it *completely* back to room temperature before serving it.

Salt

2 eggplants, peeled and diced into ½-inch cubes

6 tablespoons extra virgin olive oil

3 large cloves garlic, finely chopped

3 tablespoons chopped fresh Italian parsley leaves

2 large onions, diced into ½-inch cubes

3 small zucchini, ½ inch wide and 4 inches long, cut into ½-inch chunks

3 yellow or crookneck summer squash, as small as possible, cut into ½-inch cubes

2 large green bell peppers, charred over a flame, peeled, seeded, and cut into ½-inch squares

4 large red bell peppers, charred over a flame, peeled, seeded, and cut into ½-inch squares (or 2 each red and yellow)

2 large sun-ripened Big Rainbow tomatoes, peeled, seeded, and coarsely chopped

6 large sun-ripened Roma or red plum tomatoes, peeled, seeded, and coarsely chopped

Pepper from the mill

Salt the eggplant cubes if needed. Let stand 30 minutes, then pat dry, or, if you prefer, wash and pat dry. Meanwhile, heat 3 tablespoons of the olive oil in a heavy pot and brown the garlic in it until golden. Add the parsley and crisp 1 minute, then add the onions and let cook gently over medium-low heat until they are translucent. Stir occasionally. Remove the mixture to a plate.

Heat the remaining olive oil in the same pot. Add the eggplant cubes and brown them until golden all around; they will at first absorb all the oil, then, as they brown, render almost all of the oil at once. As soon as the eggplant renders the oil, add the zucchini, then the yellow squash, and cook a few minutes.

Return the onion mixture to the pot; add the peppers and tomatoes. Mix well, season with salt and pepper, and cook, covered, leaving the lid slightly askew for evaporation, until the juices are completely reduced and just coat all the vegetables without separating from them. Stir gently—passing a rubber spatula under the vegetables—several times during the cooking time of at least 1¼ hours. The vegetables are "candied" in their own juices with limited loss of color and a big concentration of taste.

Coulis of Bell Peppers

FCR — 2 CUPS

1 large onion, finely chopped

6 large red bell peppers, seeded and cut into strips

6 large yellow bell peppers, seeded and cut into strips

6 large sun-ripened tomatoes, seeded and finely chopped

1 cup Secondary Stock or Pure Vegetable Broth (page 220 or 213) or stock of your
   choice

Salt

Pepper from the mill

2 tablespoons dry sherry or a few red pepper flakes

2 scallions, very thinly sliced on a slant

Put all the ingredients except the scallions in a 2-quart saucepan. Cover and cook slowly over low heat until all the vegetables have positively liquefied; the length of time varies from 30 to 45 minutes depending on the content of water in the peppers. Pour into a blender and process on the liquefying cycle. Strain through a very fine China cap to discard all traces of skins. Just before serving, add the scallions and serve in a gravy boat.

Because of the astronomical price of peppers, try to make this only in the summer when you can grow the peppers yourself or charm your neighbor into giving you some of his.

This is a great coulis to use on plain pasta, rice, or even to add in small quantity to the deglazing of pans in which veal and lamb chops have cooked.

Étuvéed Red Cabbage

FFR — 6 SERVINGS

2 tablespoons unsalted butter

1 large red onion, finely chopped

2 heads red cabbage, cored, ribs removed, and shredded

3 tablespoons cider vinegar

Salt

Pepper from the mill

Heat the butter in a large saucepan over medium heat and toss in the red onion. Add the shredded cabbage and vinegar and season with salt and pepper. Toss again, cover, and cook on very low heat until the cabbage is "candied" in its own juices. The length of time of the cooking is variable, anywhere between 45 minutes and 1 hour.

This is the best with pan-roasted pork tenderloin or pork roast, but also good with roasted goose, duck, or even chicken.

Étuvéed Celery Ribs

FFR — 6 SERVINGS

2 tablespoons unsalted butter

2 large white onions, finely chopped

Ribs of 1 heart of celery, peeled and sliced ½ inch thick on a slant

2 tablespoons chopped fresh dill

Salt

Pepper from the mill

Stock or broth of your choice as needed if making a coulis

Heat the butter in a two-handled pot. Add the onions and cook, stirring, 1 minute. Toss in the celery and cook covered until fork tender, 30 to 35 minutes. If you wish to use as a vegetable, sprinkle with chopped dill, season with salt and pepper, and serve.

If you wish to make a celery *coulis*, put the étuvéed celery in a blender, process to a puree, and dilute with stock to the consistency you prefer. Strain through a China cap and add the chopped dill.

The goal in cooking this dish is to have the celery lose all of its moisture into the pan without totally losing its color. The addition of chopped fresh dill saves the day if the latter happens.

Étuvéed Mixed Greens or Spinach

FFR — 6 SERVINGS

One 3-ounce piece pancetta, cut into ⅓-inch cubes (optional)

1 tablespoon virgin or pure olive oil

2 large cloves garlic, finely chopped

1 large onion, finely chopped

12 cups coarsely chopped greens of your choice

1½ teaspoons fennel seeds

Salt

Pepper from the mill

1 to 2 tablespoons butter of your choice (optional) or to your personal taste

If used, render the pancetta over medium heat in a very large pot; discard most of its fat but not the meat and blend in the oil. Add the garlic and cook until light golden; add the onion and cook, tossing over medium heat until soft. Add the greens and fennel seeds, season with salt and pepper, and cook covered with the lid kept slightly askew until the greens are reduced to approximately 2½ cups and all the vegetal water has evaporated. Add the butter if you like and serve.

VARIATION

This is a higher protein variation used with spinach by my friend Wilhelmine Rieger. Add 2 tablespoons well-seasoned cottage cheese of your choice directly to the very hot greens before serving.

Use a large pot and pile in all the coarsely chopped greens you can possibly save: leek greens, large leaves of any lettuce too unattractive for a fresh salad, older spinach that has started to look thirsty, any leftover herbs, the green tops of beets and Swiss chard, even the shells of fresh young peas. African American and American Indian cooks have done this type of vegetable dish for centuries, as did the pioneer women who came over from Europe. Here is a formula, but feel free to elaborate on it each and every time you cook. If you are cooking for a heart patient, remove the pancetta, but serve a different dish of this elixir of health daily. It is excellent with brown rice or any grain dish.

BRAISED VEGETABLES

In braising, which is very close in principle to the braising of red meats (see page 819) there is a constant exchange of fluids between the vegetable tissues and the cooking liquid. The vegetables will not retain their color since the volatile acids are given ample time to dissolve in the steam and cooking juices. The vitamins are completely destroyed, and the texture is softer than in étuvéed vegetables. However, the taste is delicious, since the vegetable essences are mixed with a reduced meat stock. You can, of course, do this with the vegetable broth on page 213 or any vegetable broth you enjoy.

Braise only vegetables containing a large amount of cellulose and fibers. Line the braising pot or dish with bacon slices or rub it with butter or oil. Blanch (parboil) the vegetables, starting in cold water if the vegetable is extremely pungent; drain well. Failure to blanch pungent vegetables will cause their pungency to become accentuated during the braising and reduce what could have been a delicious dish to something quite unpleasant. Put the vegetables in the braising pot or baking dish; add enough stock to barely cover, and season with salt and pepper. Cover with a greased sheet of parchment paper forming an inverted lid, then with the pot lid or tight-fitting aluminum foil if the vegetable is nonreactive (acid vegetables containing a lot of oxalic acid have to be covered with parchment paper). A parchment paper or aluminum foil inverted lid is used to collect the condensation water which would make the vegetables boil instead of braise. The lid can be lifted with the condensation water in it if need be and the water discarded.

Braise in a preheated 325°F oven or over low direct heat.

If the cooking juices do not completely reduce by the time the vegetables are tender—and this happens—pour the juices into a skillet and quickly reduce them to a glaze. Spoon the glaze over the vegetables.

Braised Belgian Endives

FFR—6 SERVINGS

12 Belgian endives
2 tablespoons unsalted butter
1 cup water
1 tablespoon fresh lemon juice
Salt
Pepper from the mill
½ cup Primary Veal Stock (page 219; optional)

Do not blanch the endives. Remove their root cones if they are very large. Wash them quickly under cold running water. Butter the baking dish, arrange the vegetables in it side by side and root to tip, and add the water

Removing the root cone of Belgian endive with a paring knife

Endives should always be perfectly white with barely yellow tips. Visible green means bitterness. To ensure endives stay sweet, keep them tightly wrapped in dark paper in the vegetable bin of your refrigerator until you are ready to use them or they will turn green and bitter. Remove the root cone with a paring knife and, if the tips show blemishes, shave them lightly with the tip of the knife.

You may be surprised to see water used instead of stock but endives contain a lot of sugar and if they cook in stock, the combination of the gelatin in the stock and the sugar in the endive often results in too much caramelizing of the juices, which will become very bitter. Use a heavy white Pyroceram or fireproof porcelain dish.

and lemon juice. Bring briskly to a boil and season with salt and pepper. Turn the heat to low, cover with a greased sheet of parchment paper and a lid, and cook until very tender, 35 to 45 minutes, depending on size. Turn the endives often so they cook evenly and baste them with their own cooking juices which should reduce regularly. When the endives are cooked, rapidly evaporate any water that may be left over in the dish, and let them color ever so lightly. Meanwhile if you wish to use the veal stock, reduce it to a medium glaze in a separate little saucepan; pour over the endives, then roll them in the glaze.

Braised Radicchio

FCR—6 SERVINGS
Serve with veal, chicken, or duck magret.

6 heads radicchio

2 apples, cored, peeled, and each cut into 6 wedges

Salt

Pepper from the mill

2 tablespoons extra virgin olive oil

3 tablespoons balsamic vinegar

I cup Pure Vegetable Broth or Secondary Stock (page 213 or 220)

⅓ cup Primary Veal Stock (page 219; optional)

Clean the heads of radicchio of all blemished leaves. Remove the large outer leaves and set them aside. Cut each head in half, cut a wedge out of the center of each piece with a parer and slide an apple slice into the cut. Season each half well with salt and pepper and wrap it in one of the reserved outer leaves. Preheat the oven to 325°F. Rub a baking dish with the olive oil, arrange the packages of radicchio in the dish, then pour over the balsamic vinegar and half the vegetable broth. Bring to a boil on top of the stove, cover with a greased sheet of parchment paper and a lid. Bake the radicchio until a skewer inserted into one of the packages comes out freely, 30 to 35 minutes or longer if necessary. Remove the dish from the oven; transfer the packages of radicchio to a small round platter. Add the remainder of the vegetable broth to the baking dish together with the veal stock and reduce to a few tablespoons of glaze over high heat. Spoon over the radicchio and serve.

Braised Fennel

FFR to FCR—6 SERVINGS

6 fennel bulbs

2 tablespoons unsalted butter or virgin olive oil

Salt

Pepper from the mill

¾ cup boiling Pure Vegetable Broth, Secondary Stock (pages 213 or 220), or any light
chicken broth of your choice

¼ cup grated Gruyère or other Swiss-type cheese

2 tablespoons freshly grated Parmigiano-Reggiano cheese

Preheat the oven to 325°F. Trim away the cores and the tough outer layer of the fennel bulbs. Cut each in half. Blanch in lightly salted boiling water 2 to 3 minutes. Drain well. Rub the butter on the bottom and sides of a 1½-quart baking dish. Arrange the fennel in the dish alternating them top to root. Season with salt and pepper. Add the vegetable broth. Cover with a greased sheet of parchment paper only and bake until fork tender, 1 hour or so. Remove the parchment paper, sprinkle with the mixed grated cheeses and bake until melted, 15 minutes more.

Another extremely expensive, but incomparably fitting vegetable with a leg of lamb. Keep the outer layers, stalks, and greens, as they make a lovely soup to which any macaroni product can be added for a second inexpensive meal. Excellent with lamb roast or chops, chicken cutlets, and veal chops or scaloppine.

Braised Leeks

FFR to FCR—6 SERVINGS

12 medium-large leeks

1½ tablespoons unsaturated oil of your choice or 2 tablespoons unsalted butter

⅔ cup boiling Pure Vegetable Broth, Secondary Stock (page 213 or 220), or chicken
broth of your choice

Salt

Pepper from the mill

4 thin strips bacon, cooked until crisp, then crumbled, or 1 tablespoon chopped fresh
savory leaves

Preheat the oven to 325°F. Cut off dark green tops of the leeks (reserve them for broth) keeping only the light green and white parts. Cut vertically down into the middle of each leek, leaving the 2 inches above the root uncut. Wash the leeks, letting the water run freely through the leaves to dislodge any dirt. Blanch 2 to 3 minutes in lightly salted boiling water. Drain well.

Grease a 1½-quart baking dish with the oil. Arrange the leeks alternating root to top and cover with the boiling broth. Season with salt and pepper. Cover with a greased sheet of parchment paper and bake 35 minutes. Remove the parchment paper and finish cooking, until the broth just coats the vegetables. Serve sprinkled with the crumbled bacon.

Instead of using bacon, you can use any hard grating cheese of your choice; sprinkle it on the leeks so the cheese gratinés as the leeks finish cooking. Excellent with all meats red or white.

Braised Lettuce

FFR — 6 SERVINGS

For the lettuce

3 large heads Boston or Lola Rossa red lettuce

1 tablespoon unsalted butter, softened

½ cup boiling Secondary Stock (page 220) or other broth of your choice

Salt

Pepper from the mill

For the mushroom topping

½ cup finely minced mushrooms

½ cup dry white wine or Pure Vegetable Broth (page 213) or other broth of your choice

2 tablespoons minced scallions, white and green parts mixed

1 tablespoon fresh lemon juice

Salt

Pepper from the mill

¼ cup heavy cream, whipped until barely mounding

Trim the root ends of the lettuce and cut each head in half. Wash under cold running water. Wrap the lettuce hearts in the larger outer leaves to make tight bundles. Preheat the oven to 325°F. Rub a baking dish with the butter, add the lettuce, and cover with the boiling stock. Season with salt and pepper. Cover with a greased sheet of parchment paper and the pot lid and bake 30 to 35 minutes. Pour off the cooking juices in a small saucepan and reduce them to 2 tablespoons. Set aside.

Meanwhile, prepare the mushroom garnish. Mix the mushrooms, wine or broth, scallions, and lemon juice together in a small saucepan. Season with salt and pepper. Reduce to a thick *coulis* over medium-low heat; add the reserved lettuce juice and fold in the heavy cream.

Spoon the mushroom garnish over the lettuce heads.

VARIATIONS

Braise escarole and top with grated mozzarella. Braise green curly endive (chicory) and top with grated Parmigiano-Reggiano cheese. Lightly color the cheese under the broiler.

Braised White Onions

FFR — 6 SERVINGS

1 pound small silverskin onions

1½ tablespoons unsalted butter, melted

1⅓ cups Primary Veal Stock or Vegetable Broth (page 219 or 213)

Salt

Pepper from the mill

Soft leaf lettuce is one of the best for braising but escarole is also wonderful. See the note below for more suggestions. Excellent with any poultry or veal dish.

These sweet little onions can be prepared as a garnish for any meat or in any savory pie, or mixed with any other boiled or braised vegetables.

Drop the unpeeled onions in boiling water, remove the pot from the heat, and let stand 1 minute. Drop the onions into cold water until cool enough to handle, then squeeze them out of their skins. Cut off any trace of roots and cut a tiny cross in the root end of each onion so that moisture can penetrate evenly on both sides of the vegetable; this keeps the onions from breaking open while cooking.

Mix the melted butter and stock together, in a heavy-bottomed medium-size pot, then add the onions and season with salt and pepper. Cover with a greased sheet of parchment paper and pot lid and cook over medium to low heat until tender, 35 to 40 minutes.

Alsatian-Style Sauerkraut

FFR—6 SERVINGS

6 pounds sauerkraut processed without sugar

⅓ cup rendered goose fat or confit fat (page 785) or unsalted butter

3 large onions, chopped

1½ cups dry Riesling

2 cups veal or chicken broth of your choice

10 juniper berries, crushed

6 black peppercorns

1 bay leaf

1½ teaspoons caraway seeds

One 1-pound piece slab bacon, blanched in boiling water for 3 minutes

6 smoked pork chops

6 pure pork frankfurters

¾ cup whipped unsalted butter

Salt only if necessary

Pepper from the mill

6 Yellow Finnish or Yukon Gold potatoes, peeled and boiled or steamed until tender and kept warm

Preheat the oven to 325°F. Wash the sauerkraut under cold running water three times; spread on a thick towel and squeeze dry. Heat the fat in a large pot over medium heat. Add the onions and cook, stirring occasionally, until translucent. Add the sauerkraut, wine, and stock and bring to a boil. Add the spices, then cover with a greased sheet of parchment paper and the pot lid. Bake for 2 hours.

Add the bacon and chops and bake another hour. Uncover the pot and add the franks and butter. Let steep over extremely low heat on top of the stove for approximately 10 minutes. Correct the seasoning with salt and pepper. Pile the cooked sauerkraut on a platter; cut the bacon into thick

Use a large enameled cast-iron braising pot to make this. If you do not care to use the ingredients indicated here, simply boil the sauerkraut in water to your personal taste, or étuvée the sauerkraut with several sautéed onions; you will obtain a much lighter product. The ingredients in this recipe represent a very typical style of cooking which I cannot transgress.

To make sauerkraut from scratch, go back to page 394 and apply the recipe for making Sour Yellow Turnips to finely shaved cabbage using two tablespoons sea salt. You can save time by purchasing large bags of coleslaw containing no carrot strips. In big cities with large German and Alsatian colonies, you may be able to find that delicious piece of smoked pork called a schiffela, which is the center of the shoulder. In this recipe it is replaced with pork chops.

SUGGESTED WINE:

*Alsatian Sylvaner, Riesling,
Pinot Blanc, or from California,
Stony Hill White Riesling*

slices, top the sauerkraut with the meats, and surround it with the potatoes. There should not be any juices left in the pot, but if there are, boil them down quickly to 2 tablespoons and spoon them over the kraut.

MARINATED VEGETABLES

This technique is known generally as vegetables in the Greek style, but many vegetable presentations from around the Mediterranean are cooked in this very same manner: Mix together the same volume of water and wine, add lemon juice, all the seasonings, and the raw vegetables, and cook over medium-high heat until the vegetables are tender. The vegetables should then steep overnight in the refrigerator. In Italy and Greece eggplant is poached in a hot oil bath, then covered with what is more a dressing than a marinade, in which it will also steep overnight.

Marinated vegetables are almost always served as appetizers or cocktail tidbits. The latter occasion makes it quite awkward to serve vegetables in such a relatively large amount of liquid, and I have taken to the habit of removing the vegetables from the marinade, setting them on a dish or on a platter, and reducing their marinade to a few concentrated tablespoons of acid glaze which I spoon over the vegetables.

A common restaurant way of serving these vegetables "à la Grecque" is to present along with the platter of vegetables a dish of unsweetened cream puffs into which guests can spoon them, preventing many a stain on good clothing. See page 1105 for a recipe for cream puffs, but leave out the sugar.

You will notice that vegetables prepared this way are mostly those that won't lose their green color. You can use green vegetables such as zucchini, which will lose their color; that would disturb no one in the Mediterranean, where all vegetables are overcooked and utterly delicious.

Greek-Style Artichokes

FCR — 6 SERVINGS

¾ cup dry white wine

¾ cup water

Juice of 1 lemon

¼ cup virgin or extra virgin olive oil

2 Turkish bay leaves or 1 California bay leaf

1 large sprig fresh French thyme

⅓ teaspoon salt or more to taste

10 black peppercorns

2 dozen fresh small artichokes, turned and leaf tops cut off (page 372), or three 10-
   ounce packages frozen artichokes, thawed

2 anchovy fillets, rinsed and completely mashed

In a large nonreactive pot, mix the wine, water, lemon juice, olive oil, bay leaves, thyme, salt, and peppercorns together. Mix in the artichokes. Bring to a boil and cook until tender, 12 to 15 minutes. Let the vegetables steep overnight in the refrigerator covered with plastic wrap. When ready to serve, drain them and reduce the marinade with the anchovy paste to no more than 3 to 4 tablespoons. Toss well with the artichokes. Serve at room temperature.

VARIATIONS

The exact same recipe can be used with: florets from a large head of cauliflower; 3 medium-size celery roots peeled and cut into ½-inch cubes; 3 large or 4 medium-size fennel bulbs; quartered and sliced; 3 large zucchini cut into ½-inch cubes; 1 pound cleaned button mushrooms; or 1 pound silverskin onions, peeled. Or make a lovely medley of all these vegetables for a large party.

Marinated Eggplant

FFR—6 SERVINGS

Unsaturated oil of your choice for deep-frying

3 large Japanese eggplant, peeled and cut into ¼-inch-thick slices

¼ cup wine vinegar of your choice

2 cloves garlic, thinly sliced

Salt

Pepper from the mill

Heat 3 inches of oil to 350°F (see page 632). Immerse three or four slices of eggplant at once in the bath and let cook until soft, 2 to 3 minutes. Remove from the oil and drain on crumpled paper towels. Repeat with the remaining eggplant. Arrange in a deep dish. Put the vinegar and garlic in a small saucepan, season with salt and pepper, and bring to a boil. Add 6 to 8 tablespoons of the frying oil to the saucepan and pour the mixture bright hot over the eggplant slices. Let marinate in the refrigerator overnight covered with plastic wrap. Serve at room temperature from the marinade.

This is an Italian specialty to be found all along the Riviera dei Fiori, on the eastern side of the Gulf of Genoa, and in many other regions. The oil bath must be fresh and never have been used before. In the last step of the recipe, keep your face away. The mixture of vinegar and oil may splatter—you are responsible for your own safety.

Broccoli in Pinzimonio

FCR—6 SERVINGS

I pound broccoli florets

I tablespoon fresh lemon juice

Salt

Pepper from the mill

¼ cup virgin olive oil

I large clove garlic, cut into paper-thin slivers

Pinzimonio is one of my very favorite Italian preparations, a creamy mixture of a trace of lemon juice with a wealth of olive oil and a lot of wonderful little slivers of garlic that gives so much taste to the vegetables.

Blanch the broccoli for 2 minutes in lightly salted boiling water, keeping them slightly crunchy. *Do not rinse under cold water.* While the broccoli blanch, mix together the lemon juice and salt and pepper to taste, then energetically whisk in the olive oil until the dressing has turned creamy and looks like pale green milk. Remove the broccoli to a deep dish, sprinkle the slivers of garlic over them, and pour over the marinade. Let marinate several hours in the refrigerator covered with plastic wrap. Serve at room temperature. The broccoli will discolor. The oil bath must be fresh and never have been used before.

Marinated Red Peppers

FCR — 6 SERVINGS

6 large red bell peppers

Unsaturated oil of your choice for deep-frying

3 tablespoons sifted unbleached all-purpose flour

1 teaspoon salt

Pepper from the mill

2 oil-cured olives

2 tablespoons tiny capers plus 2 tablespoons of their canning vinegar

2 cloves garlic, cut into paper-thin slices

Cut the peppers open lengthwise. Remove the seeds and the foamy cellulose tissues which line their flesh. Cut the peppers into 1-inch-wide strips. Mix the flour with the salt. Put the flour and pepper strips in a bag and shake well; it will coat the side of the peppers that is slightly moist.

Meanwhile heat 3 inches of oil to 350°F (see page 632). Deep-fry 4 or 5 pepper strips at a time until tender, 2 to 3 minutes, and remove to crumpled paper towels to drain. Repeat with the remaining strips. Arrange in a deep dish. Pit and chop the olives coarsely, then sprinkle them over the peppers. Mix the capers and their vinegar and the garlic with ¼ cup of the frying oil. Pour over the peppers and let marinate overnight in the refrigerator covered with plastic wrap. Serve at room temperature in the marinade.

Pickled Striped Beets

FCR—6 SERVINGS

1 cup sherry vinegar

1 pound yellow-striped beets, scrubbed

1 pound red-striped beets, scrubbed

3 tablespoons granulated sugar

12 allspice berries

2 white Belgian endives

2 red Belgian endives

¼ pound mizuna leaves

¼ cup walnut or hazelnut oil

Salt

Pepper from the mill

This is a nice lean item to make part of a buffet. Remember to cook the beets until well done so they lose their strong mineral taste.

Bring water to a boil in a large nonreactive pot, add 1¼ teaspoons salt per quart of water, then add ¼ cup of the vinegar. Cut the top of the yellow beets off, leaving ½ inch of stem and the root on each beet to prevent discoloration while cooking. Add to the water and cook until tender, 20 to 25 minutes. Remove from the water with a skimmer, then peel and slice into ⅙-inch-thick slices. Store the beet slices covered with plastic wrap.

Repeat exactly the same operation using the same water with the red beets storing them in their own bowl. Each beet will render some juice while stored, hence the need to keep them separate.

Mix another ¼ cup of the vinegar with 1½ tablespoons of the sugar and 6 of the allspice berries in a small nonreactive saucepan. Bring to a boil and pour over the red beets. Repeat the very same operation with the yellow beets. Let marinate overnight.

When ready to serve, remove the beets from their marinade. Alternate leaves of red and yellow endives around a dish. Alternate the beets in the same manner, making sure that each red beet rests against a yellow endive and each yellow beet against a red endive. Fill the center of the dish with the mizuna tossed with a dressing made of 2 tablespoons of the vinegared beet juice mixed with the oil of your choice and seasoned with salt and pepper.

The Dry Heat Cooking Techniques
STIR-FRIED VEGETABLES

This technique used to be strictly Chinese but not so anymore; we are all stir-frying because this is the best way we know to cook vegetables quickly, retaining most of their vitamin content and their beautiful colors.

The technique is clear enough from the name: You fry as you stir. Some Chinese cooks call this technique toss cooking, which is pretty much the same thing; you toss the vegetables in hot oil and cook them at the same time.

THE STIR-FRY PAN AND THE HEAT SOURCE The pot in which you will cook these marvels is most important. If you have a wok, perfect; set it over your gas burner and you are in business.

If you do not own a wok, use an old-fashioned cast-iron skillet; I still use mine, given to me by my sweet husband thirty-five years ago and it still works very well. I have always cooked my stir-fries over the hottest electric burners of my home stoves with great success but when a few months ago, after thirty-five years as a professional and home cook, I finally acquired the high-electric BTU burner I needed, I could not believe my palate when I tasted my first stir-fry. Absolutely wonderful with each and every vegetable just as tasty and crunchy as possible.

The solution if your burners are not as effective as you would wish, is to exchange large amounts of BTU for smaller amounts of vegetables, and everything will work out all right. You will notice that the recipes are calculated for four instead of six. If you have six guests at your table, prepare eight portions and stir-fry twice. While the first four help themselves, you can quickly stir-fry the second batch.

COOKING MEDIUM The choice of oil is also most important; I like peanut oil for Chinese combinations but I also use corn, canola oil, grapeseed oil, and the reputed "impossible to use" olive oil, making vegetables well flavored with the famous Provençal persillade.

Make certain that the pan is well coated with oil. Whether using a wok or a skillet pour oil all around the rim of the pan so it works its way down to the bottom; turn the skillet in your hand protected with a mitten to coat its whole surface with oil.

BE SYSTEMATIC Have each vegetable ready in a pile to be added as its turn comes, and have a long-handled blunt-end spatula (the same as used for reducing sauces) at your fingertips.

If you like herbs in your stir-fries, they must be added after all the vegetables are cooked and the pan is already off the fire, so they remain fresh and do not cook in the intense heat of the fire. Contrary to Chinese cooks, I use no sauce on my stir-fries, but if you feel like having one, this is how you should proceed:

Have ⅓ cup light vegetable or chicken broth ready mixed with ½ teaspoon cornstarch. During the last minute of cooking, add this mixture, stirring a few times, and watch it coat the vegetables with a glistening little sauce.

The choice of vegetables is yours; those vegetables which naturally contain a lot of water will, if you cook them one minute too long, see their cellular walls collapse and fill the bottom of your pan with water. If this happens, use the slurry described above and the dish will be perfectly good.

Finally, start with the vegetable which takes the longest time to cook and end with the one needing the shortest time, with all the others coming in between in decreasing order of cooking time. Avoid long lists of vegetables;

otherwise, by the time vegetable number "ten" comes to the pan, number "one" will be totally deflated.

Salt is added during the last stirrings where it melts fast but pepper is added only when the stir-fry has been emptied into the serving dish so it does not burn.

HOW ABOUT USING FROZEN PREPARED STIR-FRIES? If you work and have a lot more to do once you get home, I understand your predicament, so yes, use prepared stir-fry combinations. All you have to do is bring the oil to the edge of smoking—*mind you, not really smoking*—hot enough that when the still-frozen vegetables hit the pan the water that surrounds them evaporates instantly. Remember: Frozen vegetables have already been blanched, so they are, so to say, already cooked and all your stir-frying will do is defrost and reheat them very quickly. Also, only stir-fry two portions at a time as the more surface area you have, the faster the water will evaporate and the quicker the vegetables will be reheated.

MEAT AND GRAIN ACCOMPANIMENTS Below each plain vegetable recipe I have indicated a meat that would blend particularly well with the combination, as well as a grain you can cook besides. By mixing all three, you can obtain a "center of the plate" mixture for good nutrition. Stir-fry the meat in a frying pan as soon as the vegetables are done and add it and the precooked and hot grain or pasta. See page 809 for a more detailed discussion of stir-frying meats.

All Green Stir-fry

FCR— 4 SERVINGS

Vegetable oil of your choice

3 celery ribs, cut into ¼-inch-thick slices on a slant

1 large zucchini, halved, then cut into ¼-inch-thick half moons

1 medium-size head bok choy, ribs and leaves sliced ¼ inch thick

1 European cucumber, halved, seeded, and cut into ¼-inch-thick half moons

Salt

¼ cup chopped walnuts

Pepper from the mill

FOR CENTER OF THE PLATE DINNER DISH: *Add 2 ounces slivered chicken breast meat per person, stir-fried separately and well seasoned, and warm cooked brown or wild rice.*

Heat the wok or pan very well over high heat. Drizzle in just as much oil as needed to cover the sides and bottom of it. When the oil is hot, add the celery and stir-fry 30 seconds; add the zucchini and stir-fry another 45 seconds. Add the bok choy, stir-fry another 30 seconds, and finally add the cucumber and stir-fry another minute. Season with salt, add the walnuts and stir to mix. Empty into a serving dish, season with pepper, and serve.

Red, Orange, and Yellow Stir-fry

FOR CENTER OF THE
PLATE DINNER DISH: *Add
2 ounces slivered beef tenderloin
or sirloin strip per person, stir-
fried separately, and well
seasoned, and warm cooked
cracked wheat.*

FCR—4 SERVINGS

2 large yellow bell peppers

2 large orange bell peppers

2 large red bell peppers

Vegetable oil of your choice as needed

Salt

⅛ teaspoon red pepper flakes, more or less to taste

2 tablespoons coarsely chopped cilantro leaves

Cut all the peppers from top to bottom into quarters, remove all the seeds and the thickest part of the foamy cellulose inner ribs, then cut each quarter into ½-inch-wide strips.

Heat the wok or pan very well over high heat. Drizzle in just as much oil as needed to cover the sides and bottom of it. When the oil is hot, stir-fry the yellow peppers 1 minute, add the orange peppers and stir-fry another minute, then finally add the red peppers and stir-fry another 30 seconds, also adding salt to taste. Off the heat, add the pepper flakes and cilantro, stir once, and turn into a serving dish.

Colors of Italy Stir-fry

FOR CENTER OF THE
PLATE DINNER DISH: *Add
2 ounces strips of veal loin or
tenderloin per person, stir-fried
separately, and warm cooked
ribbon egg pasta seasoned with a
sparse sprinkling of Parmigiano-
Reggiano cheese.*

FCR—4 SERVINGS

Virgin olive oil as needed

2 garlic cloves, crushed in their peel

1 cup sliced fresh water chestnuts or canned if unavailable

1 cup snow peas, strings removed

3 large Roma or pear-shaped tomatoes, peeled, quartered, and seeded

Salt

Pepper from the mill

1 tablespoon mixed chopped fresh basil, oregano, and mint leaves

Heat the wok or skillet very well over high heat. Drizzle in as much oil as needed to just cover the bottom and sides of it. When the oil is hot, add the garlic cloves and stir them until the smell develops grandly. Remove the cloves, add the water chestnuts, and stir-fry 1 minute. Add the snow peas, stir-fry 30 seconds, then the tomatoes and stir-fry 1 minute more. Remove from the heat, season with salt (added now so as not to draw the juices out of the tomatoes) and pepper, stir in the mixed herbs, and turn into a serving dish.

Viking Stir-fry

FCR—4 SERVINGS

Vegetable oil of your choice

2 medium-size onions, cut in half and sliced ¼ inch thick

I large European cucumber, peeled, halved, seeded, and cut into ¼-inch-thick half moons

I head Romaine lettuce, cut into I½-inch pieces, ribs included

⅓ cup bottled clam juice mixed with ½ teaspoon cornstarch

Salt

Pepper from the mill

2 tablespoons chopped fresh dill

Heat the pan or wok very well over high heat. Drizzle in as much oil as needed to just cover the bottom and sides of it. When the oil is hot, add the onion slivers and toss 1 minute; add the cucumber and toss another minute. Add the Romaine and toss another 30 seconds. Season with salt and pepper and pour the slurry into the pan; it will thicken instantaneously. Off the heat, blend in the dill. Turn into a serving dish.

PANFRIED VEGETABLES

The term panfrying is interchangeable with the French term sautéing. In this context its use is totally legitimate since most vegetables are tossed in the frying pan to expose their sides to the heat of the pan and the cooking fat or oil.

There are set rules for panfrying vegetables. Each type is panfried following the procedure best adapted to its texture. The goal in panfrying is to seal the moisture inside the vegetables. If the vegetable is starchy there will be no problem in achieving this goal. If the vegetable is filled with moisture, there is the danger that it will be released by the breaking of cellulose cell walls and interfere with the formation of a crust. Use these guidelines:

STARCHY VEGETABLES Use either clarified butter or unsaturated oil. Keep the initial heat high so as to build a crust and seal the moisture inside the vegetable. Turn the heat down to give the starches time to absorb the sealed-in moisture and soften. Raise the heat to high again to brown, then and only then salt and pepper just before serving to prevent the brown crust from softening. This procedure applies to raw potatoes, raw butternut squash, and cooked white and sweet potatoes.

MOIST VEGETABLES Use oil only. Butter, even clarified, would burn on the high heat. Slice the vegetables ¼ to ⅓ inch thick, flour the slices, and sauté, keeping the heat rather high. Salt and pepper only after the frying and browning are completed. This applies to tomatoes green or ripe, zucchini, summer squash, and eggplant.

FOR CENTER OF THE PLATE DINNER DISH: *Add either cooked lobster or 1 dozen or more cooked shelled medium shrimp and, as a starch, serve on the Yulland Leek Cakes (see page 420).*

BLANCHED STARCHY OR FIBROUS OR SEMIFIBROUS VEGETA-BLES Carrots, turnips, either white or yellow-fleshed, celery, cauliflower, and broccoli must be blanched and completely dried before being panfried. Each vegetable will be blanched a longer or shorter time depending on its age and texture. The average blanching time is 3 to 4 minutes.

MUSHROOMS, A SPECIAL CASE Use butter, oil, or a mixture of both. The abundant moisture contained in fresh mushrooms must be removed, or the dish will be flooded and thinned without remedy. Whether they be added to a stew or served by themselves, mushrooms must be added to hot fat in a frying pan, seasoned with salt and pepper, and sprinkled with lemon juice. You will see the water pour out of the mushrooms as the salt draws it out and the lemon juice lightens the color of the mushrooms; if you want to keep this water to be part of a stew, gather it in a small bowl. If you don't want it, keep cooking the mushrooms over high heat until the juices have completely evaporated. Turn the heat down and continue browning slowly. Season as you please and serve.

Sautéed Apples, Pears, Asian Pears, Medium Ripe Peaches, and Nectarines

FFR to FCR—6 SERVINGS

6 Fuji, Red Delicious, or Golden Grimes apples

¼ cup clarified butter (page 32) or unsaturated oil of your choice

½ teaspoon granulated sugar

Salt

Pepper from the mill

2 tablespoons applejack, Calvados, or other brandy of your choice

These fruits are often used in the same way as vegetables to accompany poultry or game and venison. The seasonings recommended here are added before the browning and can be replaced by the same amount of brown sugar or no sugar at all, and the brandy can be any one you like with the fruit you are using. This is an example of how to proceed with apples. You can also use other fruit. This is excellent with roast or sautéed chicken, roast pork, and roast fresh ham.

Peel and core the apples and cut into 6 slices each. Heat the clarified butter in a skillet until it bubbles well, then add the apples and sauté over high heat. Add the sugar and a little salt and pepper and continue sautéing until the apples are browned and all their moisture has evaporated, 12 to 15 minutes. Add the brandy and continue sautéing until it has all evaporated.

Sautéed Butternut Squash

FFR—6 SERVINGS

2 small butternut squash

3 tablespoons unsaturated oil of your choice

Salt

Pepper from the mill

1 to 2 tablespoons unsalted butter or to your personal taste

2 tablespoons chopped pecans

2 tablespoons fino sherry

Excellent with turkey, duck, or veal.

Peel the squash and cut them into ⅓-inch-thick slices. Heat the oil in a large skillet over high heat. Add the squash and cook until brown on one side; turn over and brown the second side. By the time the second side is brown the squash will be done. Season with salt and pepper. Remove to a warm serving platter.

Discard the oil from the pan and replace it with the butter over medium heat. Toss the pecans in the hot butter; turn off the heat and add the sherry. Mix well and spoon over the slices of squash.

Sautéed Eggplant

FCR—6 SERVINGS

2 Japanese eggplant or best available

Salt, if needed

½ cup unbleached all-purpose flour

⅓ cup light olive oil

2 tablespoons chopped fresh parsley or basil leaves

1 small clove garlic, minced

Excellent for all grilled red or white meats.

Peel the eggplant and cut them into ⅓-inch-thick slices. If you are using Japanese eggplant, proceed with the recipe. If you are using other eggplant, sprinkle the slices with salt and let stand at least 35 to 40 minutes in a non-reactive colander. Drain off the water that has been extracted by the salt, rinse the slices quickly, and pat them dry.

Flour the eggplant slices. Heat the oil just below the smoking point in a large skillet over high heat. Brown the eggplant slices 3 to 4 minutes on each side. It will seem as if the vegetable absorbs all the oil and retains it, but as it dries, it will eventually release the oil. Transfer the cooked slices to a platter. Add the parsley and garlic to the pan, toss without letting them brown too much, and spoon over the eggplant slices.

Sautéed Mixed So-Called Wild Mushrooms

The mushrooms that we buy as wild—shiitake, porcini, morel, crimini, oyster, portobello—are sometimes truly wild, but mostly come from spores that have been acclimated to special commercial cultivation benches. They are still very nice but many have lost the intense flavor of their ancestors, missing as they do the forest floor. This preparation is excellent with red meats.

FFR to FCR—6 SERVINGS

1½ pounds medium-size wild mushrooms of your choice

2 tablespoons unsalted butter or unsaturated oil of your choice

1 tablespoon fresh lemon juice (except if using morels; the lemon juice destroys their wonderful flavor)

Salt

Pepper from the mill

Clean the mushrooms as well as you can, using either water or a paper towel if they do not contain too much sand and mulch. Cut off the dirty ends of their stems. Place a layer of paper toweling on a baking sheet and set the mushrooms, well separated from one another, to dry in the refrigerator for 24 to 48 hours before you cook them; this allows some of their excess water to evaporate before you sauté them and they will not lose their shape.

Cut the mushrooms only if they are large (1½-inch caps and above). The stems are good to eat and can be left on small mushrooms, only the dirty ends being removed. Large boleti stems are delicious and can be diced with the caps.

Heat the chosen fat or oil in a large skillet over high heat. Add the mushrooms and season with lemon juice, salt, and pepper. Keep tossing over high heat until the mushrooms are brown and dry.

VARIATION

Stir 1 tablespoon Dijon mustard, 2 tablespoons chopped fresh parsley leaves, and 1 very small garlic clove, finely chopped, into the sautéed mushrooms.

Creamed Mushrooms

Excellent with veal chops, chicken, turkey, or ham.

FFR—6 SERVINGS

⅔ cup heavy cream

1½ pounds mushrooms, sautéed (recipe above)

2 tablespoons dry Madeira or sherry

2 to 3 tablespoons stock of your choice or water, if needed

To the sautéed mushrooms, add the cream and sherry and shake the pan back and forth over medium heat until the cream coats the mushrooms well. Do not overcook or the cream will separate into proteins coating the mushrooms and butter coating the pan. In case of separation add the stock or water to reinstate the cream to its semiliquid coating state.

SAUTÉED PRECOOKED POTATOES For the diverse variations indicated here, start with potatoes boiled in their jackets. Wash and scrub medium-size Yellow Finnish, Yukon Gold, Red Bliss, or Maine potatoes. Cover them with cold water. Bring the water slowly to a boil. Add 1 teaspoon salt per quart of water and boil uncovered for about 20 minutes. Peel when cool enough to handle.

Home Fries

FFR — 6 SERVINGS

¼ cup clarified butter (page 32) or unsaturated oil of your choice

2 cups ⅛-inch-thick boiled potato slices

Salt

Pepper from the mill

2 tablespoons chopped fresh parsley leaves

Heat the butter or oil in a large skillet over medium-high heat. Add the potatoes and sauté until golden on both sides. Drain on paper towels. Season with salt and pepper and sprinkle with the parsley. Serve immediately for best flavor.

In spite of the possibility of using unsaturated oil, this must be considered a full fat recipe because the potatoes will retain some of the fat.

Lyonnaise Potatoes

FFR — 6 SERVINGS

¼ cup unsaturated oil of your choice

2 cups ⅛-inch-thick boiled potato slices

2 tablespoons unsalted butter

1 cup minced yellow onions

1 teaspoon vinegar of your choice or more to taste

Salt

Pepper from the mill

2 tablespoons chopped fresh parsley leaves

Best with eggs and red meats.

Heat the oil in a large skillet over medium-high heat. Add the potatoes and sauté until golden on both sides. At the same time melt the butter in a smaller skillet over medium heat. Add the onions and sauté until golden. Add the vinegar and a little salt and pepper to the onions only. Drain the cooked potatoes on paper towels, then toss the onions and potatoes together. Serve immediately, sprinkled with the parsley and more salt and/or pepper if needed.

Swiss Roesti

FFR — 6 SERVINGS

¼ cup lard, unsalted butter, or unsaturated oil of your choice

1½ cups shredded boiled potatoes

Salt

Pepper from the mill

Serve with white bratwurst, eggs, or red meats.

Heat the chosen fat in a 9-inch nonstick or well-seasoned cast-iron skillet over medium heat. Add the potatoes and brown slowly and regularly, pushing them down with a turner to form a cake, until a golden crust has formed. Flip the cake over or, if you are not so brave, slide it onto a plate and invert it back into the pan. Fry the second side to the same golden color. Holding the cake in the pan with an inverted plate, drain as much of the fat as you can onto crumpled paper towels. Season with salt and pepper and serve.

SAUTÉED UNCOOKED POTATOES In all cases use enough large red, new California, Yellow Finnish, Yukon Gold, or Maine potatoes to obtain 3 cups cut and trimmed potatoes ready to cook. All the potato recipes that follow are best executed with *uncooked* potatoes.

However, for the sake of speed in handling larger groups, the potatoes can be parboiled. Put them in cold water to cover, bring them to a boil over medium heat, and simmer for 4 to 5 minutes, which starts cooking them, and fixes their color. Since the potatoes are partly cooked, they will be done faster when you panfry them just before serving. Keep the potatoes rolled in a kitchen towel until they are to be fried; the towel will completely absorb their superficial moisture and they will brown rapidly.

Classic Noisette, Château, and Parisienne Potatoes

FFR — 6 SERVINGS

½ cup clarified butter (page 32)

3 cups cut and trimmed potatoes

Salt

Pepper from the mill

2 tablespoons meat glaze (page 286), for Parisiennes only

2 tablespoons chopped fresh parsley leaves, for Parisiennes only

All these small potatoes are exquisite and to be used exclusively for special meals; they work particularly well with grilled steak and chicken and châteaubriand. Since they are a treat, they are in pure butter.

Noisette potatoes are cut into small ¾-inch balls with a Parisian spoon or melon baller. Château potatoes are given seven faces by turning them with a parer into 1½

Heat the butter in a large skillet over medium-high heat until bubbly and deep yellow. Raise the heat to high, add the potatoes, and sear them well on all sides to obtain a crust that should be visible but not golden. Reduce the heat to medium to let the starches cook and dilate slowly, 10 to 12 minutes, until one potato can be pierced easily when tested with a skewer.

Pan finishing: Raise the heat again to high and, shaking the pan back and forth, finish cooking the potatoes in any case until uniformly golden. Drain on crumpled paper towels and season with salt and pepper just before serving.

Oven finishing: The cooking may be finished in an oven preheated to 350°F if this is easier for you and especially if the potatoes will have to wait before being served. In any case, they should be uniformly golden and crisp, finished with no trace of blackness from heat spots. Sprinkle with salt and pepper just before serving.

Finishing Parisienne potatoes: Drain the butter completely, turn the heat down to low, and dribble the meat glaze over the potatoes as you shake the pan back and forth. Sprinkle with the chopped parsley.

Shredded Potato Pancakes

FFR — 6 SERVINGS

6 medium-size Yukon Gold potatoes, peeled

Salt

Pepper from the mill

½ cup clarified butter (page 32) or unsaturated oil of your choice

Shred the potatoes directly into a bowl of cold water to keep the pulp from darkening. Drain and wash in two more changes of water, until no starch is visible in the water. Drain well and pat dry in kitchen towels. Season with salt and pepper, then shape the shreds into 6 large or 12 small cakes. Heat the butter in a large skillet over medium-high heat until bubbling. Add the potato cakes and cook until golden on both sides, 15 to 20 minutes. You may have to cook them in several batches. Drain the cakes on paper towels before serving.

Whole Glazed Onions

FFR to FCR — 6 SERVINGS

1 pound small silverskin onions

⅓ cup clarified butter (page 32) or unsaturated oil of your choice

⅓ teaspoon granulated sugar

Salt

Pepper from the mill

× ½-inch torpedoes (see page 384). Parisienne potatoes are identical to noisette potatoes, but after they have been sautéed, they are rolled in 2 tablespoons of melted true meat glaze (no meat extract can replace the glaze here) and sprinkled with finely chopped parsley.

In large quantity preparation, these potatoes should be precooked in hot oil until the first crust has formed and finished to order or in batches which follow table service for their second cooking and browning. The trimmings of these potatoes can be used in a soup or for mashed potatoes, or for potato cakes.

Served plain with a green salad, these cakes make a royal meal for a weekend dinner; also good as garnish for steaks, chops, eggs, or grilled chicken.

NOTE: *Beginners can feel free to add a beaten egg to the potatoes if they are unsure of the quality of the potatoes; it will make their life much easier.*

Use as a garnish for browned stewed or braised meats.

Blanch the silverskins in lightly salted boiling water for 2 minutes. Drain well, then peel and cut a cross in their root ends. Heat the butter in a large skillet over medium heat. Add the onions and cook, stirring, until golden. Add the sugar; it will caramelize and accentuate the brown color of the onions. Season with salt and pepper, reduce the heat to medium low, and cook until the onions are golden brown, shaking the pan back and forth occasionally to prevent the onions from attaching to its bottom.

Caramelized Onions

(ALSO CALLED CONFITED ONIONS OR CONFITURE D'OIGNONS)

FFR to FCR—6 SERVINGS

½ cup clarified butter (page 32) or unsaturated oil of your choice

4 cups minced onions of your choice, white, yellow, or red

2 teaspoons granulated sugar

2 tablespoons red wine vinegar (only if using red onions)

Hot water as needed

Salt

Pepper from the mill

Good as a garnish for all meats and omelettes. If using red onions, you will need the vinegar to set their color.

Heat the butter in a large skillet over medium-high heat. Add the onions and sauté until golden. Add the sugar and vinegar (if needed) as soon as the onions have been coated with butter. Continue cooking until the onions are deep brown and candied; this will take up to 45 minutes. Add an occasional tablespoon of hot water if the pan becomes too dry. Season well with salt and pepper.

Panfried Tomatoes

FCR—6 SERVINGS

1 large Evergreen tomato

1 large Carmello tomato

½ cup olive oil of your choice

Unbleached all-purpose flour as needed

Salt

Pepper from the mill

This is a mixture of red and green tomatoes. For the green tomatoes use Evergreen tomatoes (green ripened) and for the red ones Carmellos; both are huge tomatoes and they should be ripe but not dripping with juices and sugar. An excellent garnish for grilled steaks and chops.

Remove the stem end of the tomatoes. Immerse each whole fruit separately in boiling water for 2 minutes; rinse under cold running water and peel immediately. Cut into ⅓-inch-thick slices. Heat the oil in a large skillet until bristling hot over high heat. Flour the tomato slices and immediately place them in the oil; fry each slice 2 to 3 minutes on each side. Transfer to a platter. Sprinkle with salt and pepper and any of the following garnishes:

- 1 tablespoon chopped fresh parsley leaves mixed with ½ very small garlic clove, minced
- Finely grated Parmigiano-Reggiano
- A small gremolata made of 2 tablespoons chopped fresh parsley, half an anchovy, mashed, 1 teaspoon each finely grated lemon and orange rinds, and 1 small clove garlic, minced.

VEGETABLE CAKES

This is a wildly popular and economical formula that uses up good leftover vegetables and grains. You may use any type of cooked vegetables, especially corn kernels, diced peppers presautéed or charred, peas, diced presautéed zucchini, presautéed leeks, or mixtures of several onions, herbs, aromatics, and cooked grains or a combination of whatever you like.

This is easy to prepare ahead of time too for larger crowds. Cut a sheet of parchment paper in as many square pieces as you have cakes and slightly larger than the cake. Cook the cakes on one side only; they will be almost cooked through after the first side anyhow. Remove each cake to one of the prepared pieces of paper and set on a baking sheet; cover the sheet with plastic wrap or parchment and refrigerate until ready to finish cooking.

If your dinner is formal, do not hesitate to round the cakes off now by shaping them with a sharp pastry cutter. At dinner time, invert the cakes into a hot buttered or oiled pan, flip them over once to refresh the already cooked side, and serve them freshly cooked side up.

Southwestern Cakes

FFR — 12 CAKES; 6 SERVINGS

1 whole large egg plus 1 large egg white

½ cup milk or your choice

½ cup unbleached all-purpose flour

1 teaspoon baking powder

Salt

¼ cup plain cooked cracked wheat (page 477)

¼ cup cooked black beans

⅓ cup cooked corn kernels

1 red bell pepper, charred over a flame, seeded, and cut into ¼-inch squares

1 green bell pepper, charred over a flame, seeded, and cut into ¼-inch squares

1 large zucchini, cut into ¼-inch cubes and sautéed in a little oil until tender

1 or 2 canned chipotle chiles, finely chopped, or to your personal taste

2 tablespoons chopped cilantro leaves

1 large egg white

Unsaturated oil of your choice as needed

Separate the whole egg and dilute the yolk with the milk. Reserve the egg white. Mix the flour and baking powder together in a large bowl and season with salt. Make a well in the center and gradually add the milk-egg mixture. Whisk until smooth. Mix in the wheat and all the vegetables and seasonings. In a medium-size bowl, beat the two egg whites to stage 3 foam (see page 166) and fold into the vegetable mixture.

Cover the bottom of a large skillet with a thin layer of oil. Heat it over high heat just below the smoking point and drop large spoonsful of batter to obtain cakes 2½ to 3 inches in diameter. Reduce the heat to medium high; when one side is crisp and golden, turn over and finish cooking the other side. Drain the cakes on paper towels if desired.

Yulland Leek Cakes

FFR—12 CAKES; 6 SERVINGS

5 tablespoons unsalted butter

12 large leeks, white and light green parts only, washed and sliced ¼ inch thick

Salt

Pepper from the mill

I whole large egg

½ cup milk of your choice

½ cup unbleached all-purpose flour

I teaspoon baking powder

I large egg white

3 tablespoons chopped fresh dill

These are Danish; some cooks blanch the leeks before étuvéing them, some do not. Here is the direct version which I have encountered more often than the blanched one.

Heat 3 tablespoons of the butter over medium-high heat in a large sauteuse. Add the leeks and mix until the vegetables are well coated with the butter. Season with salt and pepper and étuvée (see page 391) over low heat until the leeks are almost completely tender but retain a tiny bit of firmness. Turn into a bowl and cool.

Separate the whole egg. Dilute the yolk with the milk. Mix the flour with the baking powder in a large bowl, make a well in it, gradually add the milk-yolk mixture to it, and stir until homogeneous. Blend into the leeks. Beat the two egg whites in a medium-size bowl to stage 3 foam (see page 166) and fold into the leek base.

Heat the remaining 2 tablespoons butter in a large frying pan or skillet over high heat and drop large spoonfuls of the batter into it to obtain cakes 2½ to 3 inches in diameter. Reduce the heat to medium and cook until golden, then turn over and cook until light golden on the other side. Keep warm in a low oven. Serve, sprinkled generously with the chopped dill.

DEEP-FRIED VEGETABLES

For a general discussion of the techniques of deep-frying, please refer to pages 632–34.

Starchy vegetables should be deep-fried without being floured, while vegetables with a relatively high moisture content, such as eggplant or zucchini, must be floured, so the flour can absorb their surface moisture. Very moist vegetables like tomatoes are enclosed in a fritter batter (see page 635).

Deep-fried vegetables cook as the heat of the oil bath raises the temperature of the water they contain, which, eventually, vaporizes, thus softening the cellulose and swelling the starches. Notice the large amount of steam that escapes when you cut through a hot deep-fried potato.

Drain all deep-fried vegetables on crumpled paper towels. Salt them just before serving only, or the salt will attract, through the hardened fried crust, the moisture contained in the vegetables and render it soggy.

Remember, before you add vegetables to an empty frying basket, dip the basket in the oil to prevent the vegetables from sticking to the basket weave or mesh.

Deep-fried Onion Rings

FFR — 6 SERVINGS

1 ½ pounds medium-size sweet onions (6 to 8 onions), peeled

½ cup sifted cake flour

½ cup sifted corn flour (the superfine cornmeal used for breading fish)

1 teaspoon baking powder

Salt

1 large egg, lightly beaten

½ cup nonfat milk

½ cup light beer

½ cup sifted unbleached all-purpose flour

Unsaturated oil of your choice for deep-frying

Cut the onions into ¼-inch-thick slices. Separate the slices into rings. Spread them on baking sheets lined with parchment paper or on a kitchen towel.

Mix the cake and corn flours, the baking powder, and salt to taste together in a medium-size bowl. Make a well in the mixture and in it put the egg and milk. Whisk, gathering the flour from the center and sides of the bowl. Add the beer and finish the batter by whisking until smooth, homogeneous, and slightly foamy.

Pour 3 inches of oil into a frying kettle; preheat it to 350°F. Put the all-purpose flour in a brown or plastic bag. Add a few rings at a time to the bag and shake to coat them well. Remove the rings from the bag to a large mesh conical strainer and shake again to discard any excess flour.

Immerse the frying basket in the hot oil. Dip the rings in the frying batter; shake any excess batter from the rings. Lift the basket out of the oil, then add the rings and fry them until golden and crisp. Remove to crumpled paper towels to drain and salt just before serving. Repeat with the remainder of the onion rings.

Cauliflower or Broccoli Fritters

FFR— 6 SERVINGS

1 head cauliflower or 1 bunch broccoli
½ cup unbleached all-purpose flour
1 recipe Savory Fritter Batter (page 635)
Unsaturated oil of your choice for deep-frying
2 cups warm tomato sauce of your choice or any chutney of your choice

Delicious as appetizers. There is enough fat in the batter; please do not put a funny cheese sauce on these. The large stems can be peeled, cut up, and used in a soup. These fritters can also be served as vegetables with red meats and grilled chicken.

Clean the cauliflower or broccoli, trim into florets, and peel the small stems. Blanch in boiling water salted with 1¼ teaspoons per quart of water until crisp-tender. Cool completely and pat dry.

Preheat 3 inches of oil to 370°F. Flour the florets. Dip into the fritter batter and deep-fry in the oil bath until golden. Drain on paper towels and serve with the condiment of your choice.

Deep-fried Eggplant

FFR— 6 SERVINGS

2 medium-size eggplants
Salt
Unsaturated oil of your choice for deep-frying
½ cup unbleached all-purpose flour
1 recipe Savory Fritter Batter (page 635; optional)
Pepper from the mill

Serve with red meat.

Peel the eggplants and cut them into ⅓-inch-thick slices. Sprinkle with salt and let stand in a colander for 1 hour.

Preheat 3 inches of oil to 370°F. Drain off any water extracted from the eggplant by the salt; rinse, pat completely dry, and dredge in the flour. Dip into the batter if desired and deep-fry, or fry only in its flour coating until golden and crisp. Drain on paper towels and sprinkle with salt and pepper just before serving.

Deep-fried Mushroom Caps

FFR — 6 SERVINGS

1 pound medium-size button mushrooms

2 tablespoons fresh lemon juice

Salt

Pepper from the mill

½ cup unbleached all-purpose flour

1 recipe Savory Fritter Batter (page 635)

Unsaturated oil of your choice for deep-frying

Remove the stems from the mushrooms; they can be used in a soup or to prepare duxelles (see page 1064). Marinate the caps in the lemon juice with a little salt and pepper for 15 minutes. Preheat 3 inches of oil to 370°F.

Pat the mushrooms dry, dredge in the flour, and dip into the batter. Deep-fry until golden. Drain on paper towels and sprinkle with salt and pepper before serving.

These are strictly appetizers.

Deep-fried Tomatoes

FFR — 6 SERVINGS

Unsaturated oil of your choice for deep-frying

4 large tomatoes, peeled and cut into ⅓-inch-thick slices

½ cup unbleached all-purpose flour

Salt

Pepper from the mill

1 recipe Savory Fritter Batter (page 635)

Preheat 3 inches of oil to 370°F. Coat the tomato slices with flour seasoned lightly with salt and pepper. Dip into the fritter batter, immerse in the oil bath, and fry until golden. Drain on paper towels and serve.

Use firm-fleshed tomatoes, ripe but not "dripping-juice-ripe." Try Ultra Big Boy, which always works well. Serve with beef, lamb, or veal.

Zucchini Shoestrings

FFR — 6 SERVINGS

Unsaturated oil of your choice for deep-frying

½ cup unbleached all-purpose flour

6 small zucchini, cut into sticks 2 × ¼ inches

Salt

Preheat 3 inches of oil to 370°F. Flour the zucchini sticks, then put them in a large strainer and shake well to discard any excess flour. Dip the frying basket into the hot oil to coat it well. Add one third of the zucchini sticks to

This preparation works better for a small group of friends than a formal dinner party or reception as the zucchini should almost be prepared at most two portions at a time for the sake of crispness. Prepare them for large groups only if you have the necessary help. The fewer strings you prepare at once the more successful they will be.

the basket and dip into the hot oil until golden. Remove from the basket and serve immediately. Repeat twice more. Guests should salt their portions themselves.

Fried Stuffed Zucchini Blossoms

FFR — 12 PIECES; 6 SERVINGS

3 small marrow zucchini, sliced paper thin

Salt

Pepper from the mill

Fresh lemon juice

Virgin olive oil to taste

Large pinch of grated orange rind

12 deep orange zucchini blossoms

Unsaturated oil of your choice for deep-frying

3 tablespoons fresh goat cheese

3 tablespoons freshly grated Pecorino Romano cheese

2 tablespoons pignoli nuts, toasted (page 50) and finely chopped

2 cloves garlic, finely mashed

2 tablespoons chopped fresh Italian parsley leaves

½ cup milk of your choice

2 tablespoons bread crumbs as needed

½ cup unbleached all-purpose flour

1 recipe Savory Fritter Batter (page 635)

Two fritters will be served per person as an appetizer with a small zucchini salad. Prepare the salad first by mixing the zucchini slices, salted, peppered and tossed with a small dressing made by mixing together to your taste lemon juice, virgin olive oil and orange rind. Set aside.

Using small scissors, snip off the pistil of each blossom. Preheat 3 inches of oil to 375°F. Mix together both the cheeses, the nuts, garlic, and parsley and season with salt and pepper. The mixture should be neither stiff nor too soft. If too stiff, add a tablespoon or so of the milk; if too soft, add bread crumbs as needed. Stuff the mixture into the flowers using a tiny spoon. Fold the tips of the petals over the filling. Brush lightly with the milk, flour lightly, and dip into the fritter batter. Dip the frying basket into hot oil to coat it well. Deposit 4 blossoms at a time in the basket and immerse immediately. Deep-fry until golden. Drain on paper towels. Repeat with the remaining blossoms and serve.

True French Fries

FFR — 6 SERVINGS

Unsaturated oil of your choice for deep-frying

4 large Maine, Yukon Gold, Yellow Finnish, or California White Rose potatoes

Salt

Preheat 3 inches of oil to 370°F.

Meanwhile, peel the potatoes and cut them into sticks ⅓ inch wide. Wash the sticks in 3 successive rinses of water, until no trace of starch is visible in the water. Pat very dry and wrap tightly in clean kitchen towels to avoid browning while waiting, even just a few minutes.

Dip the frying basket into the hot oil to coat well. Add 1 cup of the potato sticks at a time to the basket and immediately dip into the hot oil. Cook 6 to 7 minutes. Remove the fried potatoes to paper towels and spread them out into a single layer. Repeat with the remaining potatoes, 1 cup at a time. This precooking may be done as early as 1 hour before service.

Just before serving, reheat the oil to 380°F. Immerse about 1 cup of potatoes at a time until golden and crisp, no more than 1 to 2 minutes. Drain on paper towels again and sprinkle with salt just before serving.

Straw Potatoes

FFR — 6 SERVINGS

These directions are for both white and sweet potatoes.

Use four large potatoes and prepare them as for french fries (see preceding recipe) but cutting them into only ⅙-inch-wide matchsticks. Measure 4 cups of straws. Immerse the potatoes 2 cups at a time in oil preheated to:

- 370°F for white potatoes
- 300°F only for sweet potatoes, which contain more sugar and would caramelize and darken too fast at the higher temperature.

Raise the temperature respectively to 380°F and 320°F after immersion. Cook the straws until golden. *A second immersion is not necessary.*

Serve the white potatoes with red meats and the sweet with wild birds, chicken, or turkey.

Potato Baskets

Small frying baskets can be purchased in kitchen supply stores. Potato baskets are usually filled with a quail (see pages 769 and 807) or bunches of greens.

FFR—6 BASKETS

Use the special double frying basket.

Prepare 4 cups of straw potatoes (see preceding recipe) no thicker than ⅛ inch. Use a metal potato or noodle nest frying basket. Line the larger basket with ⅔ cup potato straws. Put the small basket in place over the potatoes and clamp the handles shut. Heat the oil to 370°F. Immerse the basket in the oil and let cook 7 to 8 minutes. Unclamp the basket handle and deposit the potato nest on crumpled paper towels. Repeat with the remaining potato straws.

Reheat the oil bath to 380°F and immerse two baskets at a time, without the metal frame, until golden, about 2 minutes. Keep pushing the baskets down with the bottom of an araignée or skimmer to keep them immersed. Do this last operation just before serving.

Baskets can also be made with sweet potato straws but the temperature must then be 300°F for the first immersion and 310°F for the second.

Potatoes Dauphine

Although mixed with all the "wrong" ingredients by modern nutrition concepts, these little potatoes are truly delicious and deserve to be enjoyed at least two or three times a year for a nice Sunday family dinner. This is the nicest classic accompaniment to red meats. For the complete technique of cream puff dough, see pages 1104–7.

FFR—6 SERVINGS

2 very large Idaho russet potatoes
¼ cup unsalted butter
½ cup cold Secondary Stock (page 220) or broth of your choice
½ teaspoon salt
Dash of pepper from the mill
Dash of freshly grated nutmeg
½ cup unbleached all-purpose flour
2 large eggs, beaten separately

Preheat the oven to 400°F and bake the potatoes 1 hour. Keep warm. Dice the butter into the cold stock. Add the salt, pepper, and nutmeg. Bring slowly to a boil over medium heat. Remove from the heat. Add the flour and stir until a ball forms. Return the pot to medium-high heat and dry. Remove from the heat again and add the eggs one at a time.

Mash the potato pulp directly into the pot of paste and mix intimately. Correct the final seasoning of the paste.

Preheat the oil to 370°F. Drop the batter by teaspoons into the oil and cook until golden. Drain on crumpled paper towels. Salt lightly just before serving.

ROASTED VEGETABLES

This seems a new concept, but didn't all our mothers used to roast potatoes for Sunday dinner, side by side with birds of all feathers or roast beef?

Nowadays, roasted vegetables are all over the menus of modern restaurants, always very tasty, but not all of them are really roasted. One chef will roast peppers on the open grill two minutes on each side, which to me is called charring, while another will oven-roast garlic at a very low temperature for a number of hours, which I call baking.

So let's tune our culinary violins and remember that roasting means cooking in an oven at a medium-high to high temperature, that is, between 350° and 450°F.

Vegetables, to be roasted successfully, should be young and succulent, exactly as is the case for meats. The technique? Roll the new vegetables in a bit of your favorite oil or butter, add the aromatics you like, and roast at 375° to 400°F and you will obtain vegetables with a concentrated taste.

Most of us only have access to mature vegetables since this is what supermarkets usually have to offer. Older vegetables can also be roasted, but they must be cut into smaller pieces and parboiled first to soften their fibers; otherwise, those fibers, made partly of tough lignin, will harden, due to the relatively rapid evaporation of their water content in the hot oven.

Another nice technique is to blanch or parboil the vegetables, then sear them in oil on top of the stove and do what is usually done for meats: finish roasting them in the oven. This ensures good appetizing color.

In recipes containing tomatoes I have recommended new breeds which may not be available in markets but farmers' markets may offer them. If not, use whichever tomatoes grow locally in your area.

Roasted Tiny Carrots

FFR—6 SERVINGS

I pound tiny carrots

½ pound baby silverskin onions, parboiled for 3 minutes and peeled

2 tablespoons unsaturated oil of your choice

Salt

Pepper from the mill

2 tablespoons broth of your choice or salted water (optional)

I tablespoon chopped fresh chervil leaves

Great with chicken and veal.

Preheat the oven to 375°F. In an ovenproof dish mix together the carrots, onions, and oil and season with salt. Roast until very tender, about 35 minutes. When the carrots are done, season with pepper from the mill, then add the broth and swirl it together with the vegetables to dislodge any vegetable juices. Turn into a serving dish, sprinkle with the chervil, and serve.

Mixed Roasted Roots and Squashes

Keep all the vegetable trimmings and store in a bag to make a soup. Serve with turkey and other birds.

FFR to FCR—6 SERVINGS

Salt

6 small carrots, peeled

6 baby purple-top turnips, peeled

1 medium-size rutabaga, peeled and cut into balls with a large melon baller

1 large celery root, peeled and cut into balls with a large melon baller

2 parsnips, peeled, cut in half lengthwise, then again into quarters crosswise

2 to 3 tablespoons unsalted butter or unsaturated oil of your choice or to your personal taste

Neck of 1 large butternut squash, peeled and cut into sticks 1½ × ½ inch

⅛ teaspoon ground allspice

Pepper from the mill

2 tablespoons Pure Vegetable Broth (page 213) or water (optional)

1½ teaspoons finely chopped fresh savory leaves

Preheat the oven to 375°F. Bring a large pot of water to a boil and season it with 1½ teaspoons salt per quart. Add all the root vegetables and parboil 3 minutes. Drain. Spread the butter all over an ovenproof dish and toss in the vegetables, adding the squash. Salt the vegetables again and sprinkle them with the allspice. Roast until tender, 30 to 35 minutes. Season with pepper and add the vegetable broth or water only if desired, to dissolve any caramelized vegetable juices. Turn into a vegetable dish and sprinkle with the savory.

Roasted Baby Zucchini and Tomatoes

Good with grilled London broil.

FCR—6 SERVINGS

2 tablespoons virgin or pure olive oil

4 small zucchini, cut into 1-inch chunks

12 baby yellow pear tomatoes

12 red cherry tomatoes

Large sprig fresh rosemary

2 cloves garlic, crushed in their peels

Salt

Pepper from the mill

Preheat the oven to 375°F. Heat the olive oil in a skillet, then add the zucchini pieces and brown them over medium-high heat until deep golden on all sides. Empty into an ovenproof dish and add both tomatoes, rosemary, and garlic. Toss together well. Roast until the zucchini are fully tender and the tomato skins tense, 12 to 15 minutes. Season well with salt and pepper. Remove the aromatics and turn into a vegetable dish.

Roasted Crumbed Tomatoes

FFR — 6 SERVINGS

6 medium-size sun-ripened Ultra Pink tomatoes

6 tablespoons fresh bread crumbs from French or Italian bread

¼ cup freshly grated Parmigiano-Reggiano cheese

2 teaspoons chopped fresh curly parsley leaves

1 clove garlic, very finely chopped

Salt

Pepper from the mill

2 tablespoons virgin olive oil

Great with any meat.

Preheat the oven to 375°F. Remove the stem end of each tomato and cut a small sliver off the top of each also. Cut each fruit in half crosswise. Mix the bread crumbs, cheese, parsley, and garlic together and season with salt and pepper. Sprinkle an equal amount of the mixture on the large cut side of each tomato half and dribble ½ teaspoon of the oil on top. Roast until golden, about 15 minutes.

Roasted Peppers of All Colors

FCR — 6 SERVINGS

3 large green bell peppers

3 large yellow bell peppers

3 large orange bell peppers

3 large red bell peppers

2 tablespoons pure or virgin olive oil

2 cloves garlic, finely chopped

2 tablespoons finely chopped fresh Italian parsley leaves

Salt

Expensive but delicious with chicken sausage, pork, and veal, and just about any other meat.

Char the peppers on all sides over a gas flame using a long fork or under a broiler on a baking sheet, turning to blacken them on all sides. Place the peppers in a paper bag; remove one pepper at a time to stem and peel it. Cut each pepper into four strips and remove all their seeds.

Preheat the oven to 400°F. In a small skillet heat the oil over medium-high heat. Add the garlic and parsley and sauté until the garlic is brown. Sprinkle the mixture over the bottom of a 1-quart glass baking dish.

Arrange the peppers in the dish, alternating colors, and salt them well.

Roast until the peppers are tender and have browned lightly. The peppers must have lost most of their juices and those must have then mostly evaporated. The time will vary with the quality and freshness of the peppers, 25 to 30 minutes.

Roasted Fennel

FCR — 6 SERVINGS

6 small fennel bulbs, cut in half
Salt
2 tablespoons virgin or light olive oil
2 tablespoons Pure Vegetable Broth (page 213) or salted water
Pepper from the mill

Preheat the oven to 375°F. Bring a large pot of water to a boil, salt it with 1½ teaspoons per quart of water, and parboil the fennel halves 7 to 8 minutes. Drain and pat dry. Heat the olive oil in a heavy-bottomed skillet, place the fennel halves in the oil flat side down, and brown them until golden over medium heat. Transfer the fennel bulbs to a 1-quart glass baking dish browned side up, salt and pepper them, pour the olive oil leftover in the pan along the sides of the dish, and roast until tender, 12 to 15 minutes longer or more if needed. Remove the fennel to a serving dish, add broth to the baking dish, mix well, and sprinkle evenly over the fennel.

Roasted Celery Hearts and Pears

FCR — 6 SERVINGS

Salt
Center yellow small ribs and leaves of 6 celery hearts
3 tablespoons unsalted butter or unsaturated oil of your choice
3 not too ripe Anjou pears, peeled and cut into quarters
Pepper from the mill

Preheat the oven to 375°F. Bring a large pot of water to a boil, salt with 1½ teaspoons per quart of water, and parboil the celery hearts 3 minutes; drain well in a colander. Rub a 1-quart baking dish with half the butter.

Cut the core out of each pear quarter in one straight line so there is no cavity and the piece can lie flat in the bottom of the dish. Heat the remainder of the butter in a large skillet and over medium heat brown the cut side of each pear first, then the skin side, then the celery hearts. Transfer the pears and celery hearts to the baking dish, placing one celery heart between

Compare this with the braised fennel on page 401. If you roast a boned leg of lamb, put the fennel halves in to roast with it. Also good with grilled chicken.

This is best with a roast pork well coated with spices.

Keep the ribs of the celery hearts to stir-fry, add to salads, or for the preparation of an Italian brodo or for braising. The pears should not be rock-hard.

two pieces of pear. Scrape the remaining butter from the skillet over the pears and celery hearts; salt well. Roast until the pears are tender and the celery hearts golden and tender, about 40 minutes. Pepper well and serve from the baking dish.

GRILLED VEGETABLES

What to do to grill vegetables well? First do so on an outdoor grill; it is there that the charm of this type of preparation reveals itself, not on those inside grills, too small in a home kitchen and too large and powerful in professional kitchens, where the vegetables are marked so deeply that they acquire charred lines which irremediably destroy their natural taste by rendering them bitter. That complaint of bitterness is heard all over the land and is to be avoided at all cost. So, if you grill vegetables, use the outer rim of your grill rack, where the heat is far from intense, but hot enough to cook the vegetables reasonably slowly.

First prepare a dressing, which can be varied. If you make only one, make it the Italian pinzimonio (see page 405), or a mixture that is one part acid (be it lemon juice, lime juice, balsamic vinegar, or another low-acid vinegar) to four parts olive oil with salt and pepper to taste. Whisk the dressing well and marinate the vegetables in it or, if you prefer, simply brush the mixture on the vegetables.

Some vegetables are better suited to being grilled than others, such as those possessing a lot of juice, like peppers, eggplant, and, my favorite, zucchini. Root vegetables would seem difficult to grill, but most of them come out from under that hood tasting grand, especially old rutabagas, big carrots, and parsnips.

Here are my simple grilling guidelines:

1. *Never wrap any vegetable in aluminum foil; it destroys the true taste of the vegetable.* This is, of course, a very personal opinion, but one that seems valid for many of my friends and colleagues also.
2. *Beware of vegetables that are naturally bitter.* If you char them at all, their bitterness will be intensified and they will be almost painful to eat.

In this section, I feel like writing happily instead of technically and seriously. So here are my ideas only because, when it comes to grilling, there is no need for organized recipes with those sempiternal lists of ingredients and measurements to be respected. Your fire is your fire, not mine, and it will be different each and every time you light it, depending on the weather mostly, so take my suggestions and by all means feel free to rearrange them your way; grilling is for fun.

For **root vegetables,** such as carrots, turnips, rutabagas, parsnips, and beets, you are better off using the whole vegetable rather than slices, which tend to dry out quite fast. Scrub larger, older roots so that no dirt, and not a "hair" is left on them. Dry and brush them parsimoniously with oil and put them on to cook at the edge of the grilling rack just as soon as the smoke has stopped and the fire is giving forth good heat with clear flames. You will see them change face and gradually wrinkle; brush them again with a tad of oil, salt them a bit, and turn them for even cooking. They will take a good half an hour to 40 minutes to cook to tender and you will enjoy their very concentrated taste. You will not simply eat those roots, my friends; your enjoyment will be a "dégustation," the more so if you take a great pat of butter and rub it all around the root.

Beets are the greatest, but you must boil them first so they are four fifths done when you put them at the edge of your grill. Forget them there all the while the fire is burning and let their skins wrinkle as much as possible. Turn them over at regular intervals. They smell so good, you will feel like gobbling them up in one bite, especially if they are small, but patience. Let them cool a little, dribble a dab of a pinzimonio made with balsamic vinegar, dip them into chopped parsley and garlic, and enjoy.

If your **potatoes** are small—we can find those tiny babies here in California at the farmers' market but you can use the small red ones in the supermarket, well scrubbed—skewer the little things and brush them with garlic-flavored olive oil. Let them cook at the edge of the rack, 15 minutes for the puny ones and 35 to 40 minutes for a normal small potato.

The large tubers have thicker skins and run the risk of burning on the outside and staying too firm on the inside. If you turn them regularly, they should be good. White potatoes, sweets, and yams will take a great while, almost as much as their usual hour when in the oven, so choose them smaller rather than larger. For my personal taste I like the California whites or the Yellow Finnish which taste grand even without butter or salt. On the sweets' side, I am partial to sweet potatoes, served with cool sour cream.

Try **Jerusalem artichokes,** they were the discovery of my life, because I was used to them tasting terrible from the old days in Europe when they came to us all frozen and saccharin sweet. They will come tender off the grill in 35 to 40 minutes tasting like not too sweet chestnuts, and salted butter is their best accompaniment.

For **eggplant**—they should be the Japanese type—and **zucchini,** which should be the nice young ones, 6 inches long maximum, prepare a dressing with lemon juice, a scratch or two of lemon rind, and a generous amount of garlic. Mix that all together with olive oil and let the ⅓-inch-thick slices you are going to cut along the length of each vegetable marinate in it for a good 30 minutes. Shake the slices in the marinade, then let them cook till tender, 5 to 6 minutes for the zucchini and 8 to 10 for the eggplant, turning them over once. These are two fellows that under no circumstances should be allowed to char, for charring ruins them forever.

There is a little trick which I like dearly and which I do with long slices of grilled eggplant. Brush ⅓-inch-thick wedges of nice and ripe tomatoes with virgin olive oil, then dip them into mixed chopped fresh basil, parsley, and a tad of garlic and grill them side by side with eggplant slices. When done, roll each wedge of tomato into one slice of eggplant. That, Mom, is a bit fancy, sure, but talk about taste, kid.

For **mushrooms,** you have the choice of portobellos or shiitakes. I prefer the portobellos; just butter them and grill them slowly so they concentrate their juices. Then cut up two of them on top of a little mound of fresh polentina. Or cut open a roasted potato, mix it well with butter, and bury those pieces of mushrooms in its hot pulp. Pam, who edited this book, put in a plug for domestic white mushrooms brushed with olive oil, so I pass the trick on to you.

For the **onion family,** remember to cook with the cover up, for if you put it down, they all will starve your fire of oxygen and you will get nowhere. I still have not found what chemical is responsible for this, but I can tell you it happens for we used to starve chimney fires in the farmhouses by throwing onions in the burning coals and closing the lid of the stove tightly.

I like my grilled onions only one way: nice ⅓-inch-thick slices marinated in true lemon pinzimonio for the yellow ones and the whiter Vidalias, and in balsamic vinegar pinzimonio for the red ones. I grill onions, a bit more rapidly than anything else, just until they start to lose their crunchiness and start to mellow. Then they get piled on hamburgers or grilled chicken cutlets served in homemade rolls.

Shallots and **garlic** get cooked in their skins after being sprayed generously with olive oil. They are left to cook a nice long time, all by themselves at the edge of that rack, starting when the smoke has subsided. Slice some sourdough bread, grill it, spread it with butter (those of you whose ancestors came from Italy will call that a *bruschetta*—my French ancestors called it a *rôtie*), then spread either the overcooked shallots or the overcooked garlic on top. Good? I think so, but find out for yourself.

There are two other **squash** that I like particularly, butternut and chayotes. Butternut is sliced into thick slices, buttered, lightly salted, and grilled slowly—simply exquisite. As for the chayotes, I commit a dietetic heresy that came to me from Martinique, passing first through Normandy. I halve them and cook them deeply on the grill, covered with a fig leaf or several chestnut leaves or whichever nontoxic leaf you have that smells good. When the pulp is good and as soft as it can get, I mash it with butter and chopped toasted hazelnuts. Compliments of old friend Yvonne, who has relatives in Saint Pierre de la Martinique. Count 15 to 20 minutes for the butternut and 35 for the chayotes.

Bell peppers are particularly difficult to grill well for their sugar content often makes them char very quickly; they must be watched with an eagle's eye.

Prepare the pepper by removing both its ends, opening each pepper like one long scroll and removing the seeds and inner cellulose. I personally like to peel the peppers with a potato peeler and spray them with olive oil, then grill them a few minutes on each side, just long enough so they warm up through the whole thickness of their pulp and have only superficial grill markings to prevent bitterness at their surface. Once the pepper scroll is cooked, you can cut it into diverse-size pieces. For a treat, roll a piece of mozzarella di buffala into a hot grilled pepper of any color. Peppers can also be grilled whole slowly until their skins are charred, turning them regularly to cook each face evenly. But then they will have an edge of bitterness and you will have to provide a small plate to serve them, for when your guests open the pepper, the inner juices will run out abundantly.

That leaves us with the likes of the white part of **leeks** and **fennel bulbs.** You will have to blanch the leeks 2 minutes, or they will taste too pungent—though feel free to disagree. Blanching is not needed for the fennel. Cut each vegetable in half lengthwise, spray with olive oil, and grill at the edges of the rack, turning and turning them again until they are both soft and concentrated; count 35 minutes to reach that delicious point.

That leaves us with fruit used as vegetables. If you grill pineapple slices, you can char them ever so lightly; they are delicious when the sugar in their juices caramelizes a bit. So are nectarine halves, not yet too too ripe, and peaches, not yet too too ripe either. But keep apple and pear slices well buttered and watch them carefully for they cook fast, charring rapidly, and lose a lot of their charm and good taste; for them go back to slow cooking.

For additional information on grilling vegetables and fruit, see the bibliography.

BAKED VEGETABLES, GRATINS

We usually bake vegetables that contain enough natural moisture to swell their starches and soften their cellulose but, at the same time, contain enough cellulose to retain their shape. Such vegetables can be baked in their own skins, as is the case for potatoes and eggplant; to avoid explosions in the oven we usually prick the skin with a needle or skewer to allow steam to escape.

Potatoes, white or sweet as well as yams, are cooked whole. Some cooks like to rub them with oil; this is good in a way because it allows the skin to remain aesthetically more pleasing, but an oiled potato skin does not taste half as good as one that has been allowed to dry slowly, wrinkle a bit, and that can be delectably filled with butter, melting cheddar, or Fontina cheese and bacon, etc., etc. And, of course, an emphatic *no* to an aluminum jacket around any baking potato for several reasons, the most important being taste.

The large vegetables of the nightshade family, tomatoes and eggplant, are cut into halves, their cut side seared in a skillet; they finish cooking in a low oven in diverse manners. Tomatoes can be filled with meats, as the French and Italians like to do, or with bread crumbs and cheese, or other chopped vegetables.

Scalloped vegetables are first sliced, then baked in cream in a very slow (300° to 325°F) oven. In French cuisine such dishes are called gratins and are baked in French pottery dishes, heatproof glass, or Pyroceram. They will keep a long time in a 150°F oven without acquiring the unpleasant taste of cooling starches.

Each cup of heavy cream used can be replaced with 1 cup light cream or 1 cup milk bound with 1 tablespoon flour. The quality of the dish is not the same, of course, but it is still good.

In the production of scalloped potatoes in cream for large groups, the French manner consists of precooking the potato slices in milk, which starts dilating their starches and allows them to cook faster. The taste is pleasant but does not in any way rival that of a home-style gratin where the uncooked potato slices bake ever so slowly in cream until the butter breaks out of the cream. Some prefer a golden crust at the bottom of a gratin; to get this, bake the gratin directly on an oven rack. If you prefer a soft bottom, the dish must be set in a bain marie filled with boiling water. The taste obtained with the first method is best. Any gratin left over will reheat very well the next day by simply panfrying the portions left over in a nonstick skillet.

BAKED POTATOES The choice of potatoes for baking has become rather large. The very best bakers used to be the Maine russet and the California new potato, but with all the recently introduced tubers, the choice extends to the Yellow Finnish (often shortened to Yellow Finn, which makes you think the potato may be related to some finfish), the Yukon Gold, the Prince Edward Island, and, of course, the beautifully moist russet from Idaho.

The basic technique: There is no secret to baking a good potato. Scrub it, punch 5 to 6 holes in it with a skewer so it won't explode from the mounting internal steam pressure, and bake it in a preheated 400°F oven until the skin is crisp and delicious, which is just about 1 hour.

The possible garnishes are multiple:

NONFAT GARNISHES

- Low-fat sour cream or, better yet, make yogurt cheese with nonfat yogurt poured into cheesecloth, set in a colander, and allowed to drip until still slightly moist. Mix that with chopped fresh chives or any other herb of your choice. Or, to the same dripped yogurt, add the mustard of your choice and a tablespoon of chopped fresh tarragon leaves.
- Chopped fresh herbs mashed into the potato pulp.
- Caramelized garlic: Peel 30 cloves of garlic. Brown them lightly over medium heat in a tablespoon or so of unsaturated oil. Add ¾ cup light broth of your choice—vegetable broth is excellent—and cook until the

garlic falls apart. Mash the cloves with as much "light butter" (see page 34) as you wish.

FULL-FAT GARNISHES (ON THE RICHER SIDE AND TO GARNISH 6 BAKED POTATOES)

- Crisp 3 slices of bacon over medium heat. Discard the bacon fat, crumble the bacon, and add 1 cup heavy cream to the pan. Reduce to ½ cup over medium heat, then let cool slightly. Season with salt and pepper, and use a generous tablespoon of this mixture per person.
- Parmigiano-Reggiano cream with basil: Reduce 1 cup heavy cream by half in a saucepan over medium heat. While still hot, add 1 heaping tablespoon of finely scissored fresh basil leaves, 3 tablespoons finely grated Parmigiano-Reggiano cheese, and coarsely ground pepper to taste. Let cool and spoon 1½ tablespoons of this mixture into each baked potato.

Baked Stuffed Potatoes

This dish belongs to the very interesting cuisine of the nineteenth-century silk workers of Lyon. It makes a plentiful supper when supplemented with a green salad.

SUGGESTED WINE:
Beaujolais of your choice, which is the wine always served with this dish.

FFR—6 SERVINGS

I tablespoon unsalted butter

3 large baking potatoes of your choice

6 links Italian fennel sausage

I large yellow onion, very finely chopped

2 shallots, very finely chopped

I clove garlic, extremely finely chopped

I tablespoon chopped fresh tarragon leaves

I large egg, beaten

Salt

Pepper from the mill

2 cups Primary Veal Stock (page 219)

Six ⅓-inch-thick slices Gruyère, tome de Savoie, or Reblochon cheese

Rub a 1-quart baking dish evenly with the butter. Peel the potatoes, then cut them in half *lengthwise*. Remove a sliver of pulp from the rounded side of each half so it can sit firmly in the baking dish.

Remove the sausage from its casings and place in a bowl. Scoop the potato pulp out of each potato half to form a container uniformly ⅓ inch thick all around. Grate the scooped out potato pulp into the sausage meat; add the chopped onion, shallot, garlic, and tarragon. Mix until homogeneous, then add the egg and mix again. Season with salt and pepper. Divide the filling into six equal portions and fill each potato boat with one portion.

Preheat the oven to 325°F. Pour the veal stock in the bottom of the baking dish. Bake 1 to 1¼ hours, basting the tops of the potatoes with the veal stock in the dish every 15 minutes. The potatoes when fully baked are glazed, light brown, and very appetizing and have an internal temperature of 180°F. Set one slice of cheese over each of them just before serving.

BAKED SQUASH Two of the best bakers in the squash world are the spaghetti squash, which is so lean and delicious, and the butternut. Baking is the best technique for preparing winter squash, because their flavor concentrates deeply during baking, resulting in excellent texture and taste.

Spaghetti Squash

FFR — 6 SERVINGS
2 large spaghetti squash

Prick each squash and bake them 1 to 1½ hours in a preheated 325°F oven. When they are tender cut a lid in their top and from each squash extract the pale yellow strings indeed resembling spaghetti. Season these with:

VARIATIONS
FOR SAGE CREAM: Season 1 cup heated heavy cream with a tad of salt and pepper and 1 leaf of fresh sage very, very finely chopped. Spoon 2 tablespoons of this cream over each portion of spaghetti.

FOR PARMESAN CREAM: Add ½ cup freshly grated Parmigiano-Reggiano or Grana cheese to 1 cup heated heavy cream and several good gratings of pepper. Spoon over the spaghetti.

Baked Butternut, Buttercup, Kabocha, and Delicata Squash and Pumpkin

6 SERVINGS
You will have to decide for yourself how many squash you need to obtain six portions, depending on their size. There are usually three good portions in each butternut, buttercup, or kabocha squash, one in each delicata, and six in half a medium-size pumpkin.

All must be baked a nice long time in a preheated 325°F oven until a skewer inserted at the thickest part of the vegetable comes out clean. You will see pumpkins lose a lot of moisture; let it concentrate in the bottom of the baking dish as the meat bakes, then dilute it with sherry and add to one of the following garnishes. You can serve the squashes with a spoon after removing the seeds, and the pumpkins can be sliced or cut into large cubes.

FOR SHERRY AND PECAN (OR OTHER NUT) CREAM: Reduce 1 cup heavy cream to ½ cup in a saucepan over medium heat. Add 1 tablespoon dry sherry, salt, pepper from the mill, and 2 tablespoons chopped pecans, plain or lightly oven toasted to intensify their flavor. Lightly toasted walnuts, pistachios, pignoli nuts, and hazelnuts can also be used.

FOR CITRUS CREAM: Reduce 1 cup heavy cream mixed with 2 gratings each of orange, lemon, lime, and grapefruit rinds to ½ cup in a saucepan over medium heat. Strain the cream over the squash or pumpkin meat.

Maghumma

This dish is the Arab ancestor of Sicilian caponata and Provençal ratatouille. Use young Japanese eggplants; these need not be salted. If you can only find the large ones, salt them 45 minutes to extract their strong juices, then rinse and pat them dry before you proceed as instructed.

FCR—6 SERVINGS

Unbleached all-purpose flour as needed

4 to 5 Japanese eggplant, cut into ¼-inch-thick slices lengthwise

3 tablespoons pure olive oil plus more as needed

Salt

Pepper from the mill

4 large, sun-ripened tomatoes, peeled and sliced ¼ inch thick

3 medium-large zucchini, sliced ⅛ inch thick

¼ cup chopped fresh Italian parsley leaves

3 tablespoons chopped fresh mint leaves

2 cloves garlic, minced

I cup cooked chick peas

¼ cup plain bread crumbs

Preheat the oven to 325°F. Flour the slices of eggplant, tapping off any excess. Heat 3 tablespoons olive oil in a skillet over medium-high heat and fry the slices until light golden on both sides. Rub a baking dish with olive oil and line it with half the eggplant slices. Then add, salting and peppering each layer, one layer of tomatoes and one layer of zucchini slices. Sprinkle half the herbs and garlic on them, top with the chick peas, then repeat with a second layer each of tomatoes and zucchini. Cover with the remainder of the eggplant slices and sprinkle with the remainder of the herbs and garlic mixed with the bread crumbs. Drizzle olive oil to taste over the topping and bake 1½ hours or more; the dish must be one solid layer of vegetables fused into one another, still mellow and moist, but not wet and drippy.

Stuffed Tomatoes

FFR — 6 SERVINGS

6 large tomatoes, unpeeled

2 tablespoons virgin or pure olive oil

2 large yellow onions, finely chopped

2 large cloves garlic, finely chopped

2 anchovy fillets, rinsed and mashed

½ cup fresh bread crumbs made from French bread

1½ cups chopped cooked veal or beef or ¾ cup chopped cooked meat mixed with

  ¾ cup finely chopped boiled ham

1 link Italian fennel sausage, removed from its casing and crumbled

4 oil-cured black olives, finely mashed

¼ teaspoon grated lemon rind

Large pinch of dried thyme

Several fresh rosemary leaves, finely chopped

1 large egg, beaten, or more if needed

Salt

Pepper from the mill

This is the popular French way to use leftover meats from Sunday roasts during the summer months. The usual accompaniment for this dish is a pilaf of rice, as on page 461.

Remove a lid ⅓ inch thick from the top of each tomato. Place a strainer over a bowl. Using the tip of your finger, gently remove the seeds from each tomato, letting them fall into the strainer as well as the tomato juice. Cut the center ribs out without cutting through the outside of the fruit. Repeat this operation with each tomato. Set the tomatoes upside down in the strainer and let the juices drip while you prepare the filling. Set aside.

Heat the olive oil in a large skillet over medium-high heat. Then add the onions and garlic and sauté until golden. Add the anchovies, bread crumbs, meat, sausage, olives, lemon rind, herbs, and egg and mix until very homogeneous. The mixture should be mellow rather than stiff; add more egg if needed or, if you prefer, some of the tomato juice gathered from the cleaning of the tomato insides.

Salt and pepper the inside of each tomato and fill with one sixth of the forcemeat. Cover with the tomato lid. Rub a baking dish with olive oil, then set the tomatoes in it and pour over the reserved strained juices.

Preheat the oven to 325°F. Bake the tomatoes 1 to 1½ hours, until the vegetables have taken on a lovely brown color and the filling is well set. If there is a large amount of juice in the baking dish, empty it into a pan and reduce to ⅓ cup of gravy. If there is no juice, only a brown tomato glaze, transfer the tomatoes to a serving dish and add ¼ cup hot water to the dish. Deglaze the baking dish and strain the deglazing over the tomatoes through a conical strainer.

Melanie's Stuffed Zucchini

This is a summer French Alps recipe.

FFR—6 SERVINGS

2 cups warm thick Béchamel Sauce (page 278) or plain cream sauce (page 371)

6 small zucchini, 1 inch in diameter and about 6 inches long

Salt

½ cup chopped boiled ham

2 large cooked artichoke bottoms (page 373), mashed with a fork, or 4 cooked Jerusalem artichokes (page 432), mashed with a fork

¼ cup ¼-inch cubes Gruyère cheese

2 hard-cooked egg yolks, mashed

¼ cup chopped almonds

Pepper from the mill

½ cup fresh bread crumbs

½ cup freshly grated Parmigiano-Reggiano cheese

1 tablespoon unsalted butter, melted

Keep the béchamel sauce warm.

Cut the zucchini in half lengthwise. Using the small scoop of a melon baller or a Parisian spoon empty each half, leaving ¼ inch of pulp to form a boat. Chop up the pulp removed from each half.

Bring a pot of water to a boil and salt it with 1½ teaspoons per quart of water. Add the zucchini halves and parboil 3 to 4 minutes; drain and arrange them side by side in a 1-quart baking dish rubbed with butter.

Preheat the oven to 350°F. To prepare the filling, mix the béchamel sauce with the chopped zucchini pulp, the ham, artichokes, Gruyère, egg yolks, and almonds. Salt and pepper well, stuff the mixture evenly into the zucchini boats. Mix crumbs and cheese together and sprinkle an equal amount over the top of each zucchini boat. Drizzle the melted butter over the crumbs. Bake until golden brown, about 1 hour. Serve hot.

Gratin of Potatoes

FFR—6 SERVINGS

1 clove garlic, crushed

2 tablespoons unsalted butter

4 large Yellow Finnish potatoes, peeled and sliced ⅛ inch thick

Salt

Pepper from the mill

Freshly grated nutmeg

1½ to 2 cups heavy cream or to your personal taste

Rub the garlic clove all around the bottom and sides of an ovenproof 1-quart baking dish. Discard the garlic and butter the dish with *all* the butter.

Preheat the oven to 325°F. Place the potato slices in a bowl. Season with salt and pepper and dust with nutmeg. Toss together well, then layer in the baking dish, pouring the cream over the potato layers. Shake the dish back and forth until the salt has dissolved. Taste the cream. It should be salted through.

Bake until the cream has reduced completely and breaks into butter at the edges of the dish, about 1½ hours. During the baking the crust will build rather rapidly. Break it several times so the brown cream is submerged by the yet unbrowned cream. The last crust should be a deep, darker brown.

The cooked gratin will keep at least 2 hours in a low oven.

VARIATIONS

LOW-CALORIE GRATIN OF POTATOES: Use the same ingredients and techniques replacing the cream with the milk of your choice. Each cup of milk should be stabilized with 1 teaspoon of flour.

MUSHROOM-POTATO GRATIN: Separate two equal layers of potatoes with 1½ cups sautéed mushrooms mixed with 2 tablespoons chopped fresh Italian parsley leaves.

GRUYÈRE GRATIN: Separate 2 equal layers of potatoes with ¾ cup grated Gruyère cheese mixed with ¼ cup minced fresh Italian parsley leaves. Top the dish with another ¼ cup grated Gruyère.

BLUE CHEESE GRATIN: Use no garlic on the baking dish. Cream 3 tablespoons unsalted butter with ⅓ cup well-crumbled Gorgonzola, Roquefort, Stilton, or Bleu de Bresse, and separate two equal layers of potatoes with one layer of cheese.

ONION GRATIN: Separate two equal layers of potatoes with 2 cups minced yellow onions sautéed in butter.

LEEK GRATIN: Use no garlic on the baking dish. Separate two equal layers of potatoes with 2 cups white part of leeks, blanched for 2 minutes, then étuvéed in butter (page 391).

CELERIAC GRATIN: Peel, slice, wash, and blanch 1 root of celeriac about 2½ inches in diameter for 5 minutes. Separate two equal layers of potatoes with one layer of celeriac and use a little more cream if needed.

FENNEL AND POTATO GRATIN: Stir-fry until quite tender 2 small fennel bulbs, sliced. Separate two equal layers of potatoes with one layer of the fennel. Season well. You may need a tad more cream.

Butternut Squash Gratin

FFR—6 SERVINGS

2 medium-size butternut squash

2 tablespoons hazelnut oil plus extra as needed

1 cup heavy cream, scalded

½ cup dry Sercial Madeira

Salt

Pepper from the mill

½ cup fresh bread crumbs

½ cup chopped hazelnuts

Peel the squash and cut into enough ¼-inch-thick slices to fill 3 cups. Heat the 2 tablespoons of hazelnut oil in a large skillet over medium heat. Add the squash and cook gently on each side until golden; or, if you prefer, parboil the slices 3 to 4 minutes in lightly salted boiling water.

Preheat the oven to 325°F. Rub a 1½-quart baking dish with the hazelnut oil and place a layer of squash in the bottom. Mix the cream and Madeira together and pour half of it over the slices. Season with salt and pepper, then add another layer of squash. Pour over the remaining cream mixture, then sprinkle the top with the crumbs and hazelnuts mixed together. Bake until the cream breaks into butter at the edges of the dish, about 1 hour.

VEGETABLE TIMBALES

A timbale, to be pronounced any way you feel like pronouncing it, is a small oval or conical 2- to 3-ounce container in which the French oven poach dainty vegetable puddings. Inverted, a timbale looks extremely nice on a plate, not only because of its fresh color(s), but because it represents a true change of pace in the vegetable world. To be really good, timbales must be made with a lot of cream and eggs, which is why their size is always so small; quality replaces quantity.

The texture of a timbale can be varied by pureing the chosen vegetable or shredding it before cooking. Also, the eggs can be used whole for a true pudding texture or separated and whipped for a souffléed appearance and texture.

Timbales can be served as a fancy vegetable on a plate or as a first course accompanied by a small sauce. Don't worry about not owning any real timbales; 2-ounce porcelain ramekins do just fine. Here are two examples: The first can be adapted to all root vegetables, the second to all greens.

Timbale of Carrots with Chervil Oil Vinaigrette

FFR—6 SERVINGS

I large bunch fresh chervil or 2 smaller ones

¼ cup corn oil

3 tablespoons unsalted butter

I large yellow onion, very finely chopped

½ pound large carrots, peeled and shredded

Salt

Pepper from the mill

4 large eggs

I teaspoon cornstarch

I cup heavy cream

I tablespoon fresh lemon juice

6 small yellow pansies

As presented here this timbale will be an hors d'oeuvre, but it could be served warm with a roasted loin of veal. A chervil pluche is a group of three chervil leaves attached to a tiny stem. The chervil oil must be prepared one day before the timbales.

Wash the chervil very well. Blanch half of it for 1 minute in boiling salted water. Drain and pat dry. Place in a 1-cup blender jar. Pour the oil over the chervil, seal the jar, and immediately process to a smooth puree on high speed. Let stand at room temperature 30 minutes, shaking the oil several times, then refrigerate overnight.

Butter the timbale containers with 2 tablespoons of the butter. They must be well buttered for the timbale to unmold without difficulty.

Heat the third tablespoon of butter in a sauteuse pan and in it cook the onion over medium heat, stirring, until translucent. Add the shredded carrots and season them with salt and pepper. Toss them well in the butter, cover, and cook over low heat until very tender, 25 to 30 minutes. Cool completely.

Preheat the oven to 350°F. Transfer the carrots to a blender or food processor. Add the eggs, cornstarch, and heavy cream and process until smooth. Correct the seasoning. Strain the pudding through a conical strainer into the prepared timbales. Cover the top of the timbales with a square of parchment paper to prevent the formation of a skin.

Bake in a hot water bath (see page 693) until a skewer inserted in the center comes out clean and feeling hot to the top of the hand, 30 to 35 minutes. Let stand in the hot water bath for 5 minutes, then unmold onto a round dish and let cool completely. Chill overnight covered with plastic wrap.

Sort the remaining chervil leaves and separate into tiny *pluches*, store in a glass bowl, and cover with plastic wrap.

An hour before serving the timbales, strain the chervil oil through a tea strainer placed over a bowl. Let drip until all the oil has passed through. Add the lemon juice, season with salt and pepper, and whisk into a dressing. Transfer each timbale to a lunch-size plate, dribble some of the chervil dressing over it, and decorate with chervil pluches and one pansy.

Escarole Souffléed Timbales with Parma Cream

For all dishes of veal, turkey, and chicken.

FFR—6 SERVINGS

For the timbales

3 tablespoons unsalted butter

4 cups chopped escarole leaves, blanched for 5 minutes, squeezed dry, and finely chopped

Salt

Pepper from the mill

½ teaspoon cornstarch

¼ cup light cream

3 large eggs, separated

For the sauce

1 tablespoon unsalted butter

1 large onion, finely chopped

⅓ cup light cream

1 tablespoon cornstarch

⅓ cup cold broth of your choice

⅓ cup freshly grated Parmigiano-Reggiano cheese

Salt

Pepper from the mill

1 carrot, diced into ⅛-inch brunoise (page 16)

6 fresh Italian parsley leaves

Heat the butter in a 2-quart enameled cast-iron pan. Toss the escarole into the pot. Season with salt and pepper and cook over medium-low heat, covered, until the greens are soft, about 35 minutes. There should be approximately 1 cup of cooked greens. Cool the cooked greens to lukewarm.

Meanwhile, butter six timbales and preheat the oven to 325°F. Prepare a hot water bath (see page 693). Place the greens, cornstarch, cream, and egg yolks in a blender, season with salt and pepper, and process to a puree.

In a medium-size bowl, beat the egg whites to stage 3 foam (see page 166). Mix one third of their volume into the escarole puree, then fold in the remainder. Turn into the prepared timbales and bake until a skewer inserted at the center comes out clean and hot, 20 to 25 minutes.

While the timbales cook, prepare the sauce. Heat the butter in a small skillet over medium-high heat and sauté the onion until deep golden and dry. Add the cream and bring to a simmer over medium heat. Mix the cornstarch with the cold broth, then blend into the simmering cream, stirring until the mixture comes back to a boil. Simmer another 5 minutes. Off the heat, blend in the grated cheese. Correct the seasoning, adding salt if needed and freshly ground pepper.

Put the carrot brunoise in a conical strainer. Bring a small pot of water to a boil, add a pinch of salt, and immerse the strainer in the water for 3 minutes. Drain and pat dry.

Spoon a sauce spoon of sauce on each plate. Unmold the timbale at the center of the sauce. Sprinkle some diced carrots over its top and decorate with a parsley sprig.

Savory Salads of Greens and Fruit

Whichever greens you use in a salad, wash the whole head. Separate the leaves, wash them individually, shake or spin them well in a salad spinner, and roll them up in a kitchen towel before refrigerating to crisp them well.

You may tear the greens with your hands into bite-size pieces or cut them with a stainless-steel knife to prevent the oxidation carbon-steel blades normally cause at the edges of the salad leaves.

There is no reason why you cannot use salad greens mixed with fruit of your choice. The best example of this is the favorite salad seen in so many magazines and on television—red- and yellow-striped beets, endives or watercress, and blood oranges. This is an exquisite salad, though somewhat pricey.

In the stir-fried vegetable section, I mentioned the "center of the plate" dishes containing mostly vegetables, a little grain and a little meat as being good examples of good nutrition. Salads offer the same opportunity; see the fennel and carrot salad (see page 449).

Salad Dressings

Modern salad dressings are divided into full-fat vinaigrettes and low-calorie dressings. The creamy dressings made with cream must be given up for they are too fat, especially if the meals contain a meat. They can be replaced by the mango dressing on page 448.

VINAIGRETTES AND THEIR DIFFERENT BASES
The basic oil-and-vinegar dressing is called vinaigrette. The oil for the dressing can be olive, corn, grapeseed, canola, peanut, walnut, hazelnut, or even the delicious pistachio oil. You may also use any infused oil of your choice. Please go to pages 35–41 for more details on oils and vinegars and how to make vinegar flavored many ways. For the making of flavored oils see page 304.

Oil and vinegar can be combined to make an acid dressing using 1 part vinegar or other acid to 2 parts oil, measured by volume; or it can be made into a mellow dressing using ½ or 1 part vinegar to 3 to 3½ parts oil. Make the dressing by hand or in the blender, as you prefer.

In recent years it has proved somewhat risky to use raw egg in dressings, as called for in the classic Caesar dressing. The egg yolk and whole egg can be replaced easily by reduced stock which will provide almost as much protein as the egg yolk and smooth out any acid taste because of its intensely concentrated taste.

Combine the seasonings of your dressing to your heart's content; however, rather than put garlic in a dressing, rub a garlic clove on the surface of the salad bowl and on slices of lightly toasted white bread slices, then cut them into croutons and slowly oven dry them until crisp or toss the garlicked bread called a *chapon* into the salad, then remove it just before serving the greens.

If using shallots, enclose them, chopped, in the corner of a kitchen towel and squeeze out their juices, even rinse the still enclosed shallots under running water if you wish. The taste of the shallots will be much softer and the dressing much less difficult to digest.

If you use dried herbs, steep them in the vinegar you are using; add fresh herbs to the already mixed dressing.

Use a glass or china bowl to serve your salad and chill it before use. A wooden bowl becomes rancid with age, even if washed regularly. Toss the greens and dressing at the table so that no wilting will occur between the time you toss and the time you serve a salad. If you dress the salad ahead of time, the salt and vinegar will team up to deflate the leaves and draw their water content out into the salad bowl.

If you prefer, instead of adding the already mixed dressing to the greens, add the dressing ingredients one after the other, starting with the oil and ending with the vinegar-and-herb mixture; in this way, the greens will be first well coated with oil and protected from the acids of the vinegar.

Serve a salad on very cold plates. Serve it at the beginning of the meal if you wish. If the meal is rich, serve it after the meat dish, in the French manner; it lightens the stomach for cheese and dessert.

Thousands of French people drink rosé wine everyday with their salade Niçoise, probably the best choice for salad, as the acid in a dressing is the downfall of any good wine, unless one has reduced some of the wine and used it instead of vinegar to make the dressing. Otherwise, serve a glass of chilled water with any salad dressed with an acid dressing.

LOW-CALORIE DRESSINGS

There are two ways to prepare low-calorie dressings, three if you want to prepare a yogurt dressing. I am not too fond of nonfat yogurt dressings because of their often chalky texture and sharply acid taste. I much prefer a salad dressing prepared with a reduced fat-free broth or stock or mango pulp.

1. *Dressings based on vinegar and a slurried broth or other liquid:*

¼ **cup vinegar of your choice**

Salt

Pepper from the mill

1½ teaspoons cornstarch

⅔ cup cold Pure Vegetable Broth (page 213) or chicken broth of your choice or water

1 tablespoon oil of your choice

Bring the vinegar, salt, and pepper to a boil in a small nonreactive saucepan; turn down to a simmer. Dilute the cornstarch with the chosen liquid and *stir, do not whisk* this into the simmering vinegar. Continue stirring well until thickened. Add the oil, then stir in any additional herbs, aromatics, and condiments. Pour into a small bottle and shake well.

This is just a simple base that you can vary with all kinds of additions to go with all kinds of salad greens and vegetables.

For salads containing grated carrots, add:

1 shallot, chopped

1 tiny clove garlic, chopped

1 tablespoon chopped fresh Italian parsley leaves

For salads containing red peppers, tomatoes, and/or artichokes, add:

1 shallot, chopped

1 teaspoon finely scissored fresh basil leaves

1 teaspoon anchovy paste

For cold meat salad, eggplant salad, or hearts of palm salad, add:

1 clove garlic, chopped

½ teaspoon chopped fresh oregano leaves

Pinch of grated lemon rind

Dash of red pepper flakes

For any salad containing ham, white meat of chicken, and/or celery, add:

2 teaspoons chopped fresh tarragon leaves

1 teaspoon Dijon mustard, or more to taste

1 tablespoon snipped fresh chives

For use on shellfish salads, especially mussels:

Cook 1 teaspoon curry powder for 1 minute in the oil over medium heat, then stir into the dressing.

For all bitter salads, add:

½ teaspoon grated orange rind

1 teaspoon Dijon mustard or more to taste

1 tablespoon Sercial Madeira

These are just a few examples; you can vary the proportions of each and everything to your taste and make a whole world of personal salads.

2. Dressings based on fresh mango pulp: Mango provides the most wonderful texture when preparing low-calorie dressings. Puree the mango with the vinegar or citrus juice of your choice, add a tad of oil, and any herbs you believe will marry well with the salad greens and garnishes you are using. See page 450 for an example.

Beware: Mango ferments rapidly once it has been processed and mixed with any acid. Because of this, make the dressing as close as possible to serving time and serve it promptly; if the dressing must wait, it should do so in the refrigerator.

Classic Salads

Potato Salad

To make a good potato salad in which the slices of potatoes do not break, you need waxy potatoes with a low starch content. The fingerlings are the very best if you can find them at farmers' markets; if not, the small red ones will do just fine.

FCR—6 SERVINGS

1 pound fingerling or small red potatoes, scrubbed

2 teaspoons salt

3 large shallots, finely chopped

1 small white onion, finely chopped

½ small red onion, finely chopped

10 small cornichons or 2 larger sour gherkins, diced into ⅛-inch cubes

½ cup dry white wine

⅓ cup cider or wine vinegar of your choice

⅔ cup pure or virgin olive oil

35 turns of the pepper mill

Light cream as needed

2 scallions, sliced into rings

1 sprig fresh Italian parsley

Put the potatoes in a large saucepan and cover them with water. Bring slowly to a boil, add 1 teaspoon of the salt, and simmer over medium heat until fork tender, about 18 minutes. As soon as the potatoes are done, drain the water, refresh them under cold water and peel them. Cool them to lukewarm and only then slice them into ⅙-inch-thick slices.

Squeeze the shallots and white onion in the corner of a kitchen towel to extract the strong juices. Put them and the red onion and cornichons in a bowl. Add the wine, vinegar, oil, and pepper, and the remaining teaspoon of salt and whisk into a well-homogenized dressing; pour over the potatoes and toss well together. Taste the salad, add more of whichever ingredients you would like. If you prefer a more fluid texture, add small quantities of light cream until you reach the texture you like best. Once seasoned to your taste, turn the salad into a bowl and sprinkle the sliced scallions rings all around the edge of the salad. Put the sprig of parsley at the center of the bowl.

Coleslaw Remoulade

FFR — 6 SERVINGS

I small head cabbage, outer leaves removed

2 heaping tablespoons mayonnaise of your choice

I heaping tablespoon Dijon or Düsseldorf mustard

2 tablespoons chopped fresh Italian parsley leaves

2 tablespoons chopped fresh chives

I Asian pear, peeled and cut into matchsticks ⅛ inch wide

Salt

Pepper from the mill

Sherry vinegar to taste

When dressing this salad with the mustard mayonnaise, remember that the salt in the mustard will draw a lot of juice out of the slaw; dress it just before serving. All salads made with mayonnaise should be consumed on the day they are made and kept refrigerated when not on the table to be served.

Cut the cabbage head into quarters. Remove the core and the large ribs from the leaves. Slice the cabbage into ⅛-inch-thick slivers. Put them in a colander and rinse under cold running water. Pat as dry as possible.

Mix the mayonnaise with the mustard; add the herbs and mix well. Toss the cabbage and Asian pear julienne into the mixture until well coated. If the sauce is not plentiful enough for your taste, add more of each ingredient. Season with salt and pepper to your taste and if you like the mixture a little more sour, add as much sherry vinegar as you enjoy. Refrigerate until ready to use and serve as soon as possible for maximum freshness and crunchiness.

Fennel and Carrot Salad with Anise Oil Dressing

FCR — 6 SERVINGS

½ cup unsaturated oil of your choice

I tablespoon aniseeds

Juice of 2 oranges

Pinch of powdered saffron

Juice of I lemon

Salt

Pepper from the mill

2 fennel bulbs, white part only, well washed and slivered

3 large carrots, very thinly sliced

Fennel greens

Prepare the oil first, and finish the dressing the next day. If you want to make this a "center of the plate" meat dish, toss some of the dressing with two sliced cooked chicken breasts mixed with 1 cup cooked cracked wheat or couscous (see page 477 or 478).

Heat the oil in a small saucepan over medium heat. Add the aniseeds and toss for 1 minute. Pour oil and seeds in a blender, and process until smooth. Refrigerate overnight. The next day bring to room temperature and strain through a China cap.

In a small nonreactive saucepan over medium heat, reduce the orange juice to 2 tablespoons. While still hot, add the saffron and 1 tablespoon of the lemon juice. Season with salt and pepper, then dilute with the anise oil to your taste. Correct the balance of the dressing with salt, pepper, and as much lemon juice as needed to your taste.

Toss the slivered fennel bulbs with one third of the dressing and the carrot slices in another third. Mix the fennel and carrots together well; if there is not enough dressing, add more. Arrange the salad on a large round platter and surround with some sprigs of fennel greens. Chop some of the fennel greens and sprinkle them at the center of the salad. Serve any leftover dressing in a small ramekin.

Chicken and Zucchini Salad with Mango Dressing

This is a center of the plate dish. To make this vegetarian, replace the chicken meat with slivers of tofu ½ × 1½ × ¼ inch, colored in hot oil for better appearance.

LFR — 6 SERVINGS

1 head Romaine, well washed and torn into bite-size pieces

1 cup cooked cracked wheat (page 477)

2 small zucchini, thinly sliced slantwise

2 nectarines, pitted and each cut into 8 slices

2 boneless chicken breasts, cooked and sliced across into slivers

2 scallions, finely slivered

1 mango, peeled

Juice and grated rind of 1 lime

Salt

Pepper from the mill

2 tablespoons unsaturated oil of your choice

Clean and crisp the Romaine leaves. Arrange on the bottom of a round country platter. Spread the cooked cracked wheat over the Romaine. Mix together the zucchini and nectarine slices and chicken slivers. Pile the mixture over the wheat. Sprinkle generously with the scallions.

Remove the mango meat by slicing along the pit. Put in a blender, add the lime rind and juice, salt, pepper, and chosen oil. Blend until smooth. Turn into a gravy boat or other small dish. Pass the salad platter and dressing together for your guests to help themselves.

Mesclun in Pistachio Oil Dressing

FCR—6 SERVINGS

¾ pound mesclun

1 tablespoon balsamic vinegar

Juice of 1 small tangerine or ½ orange

2 teaspoons fresh lemon juice

½ teaspoon finely grated orange rind

6 tablespoons pistachio oil

Salt

Pepper from the mill

Check the mesclun for wilted and yellowed leaves and wash in cold water. Spin it dry in a salad spinner. Keep refrigerated until ready to use.

For the dressing, mix together the vinegar, citrus juices and rind, and oil with salt and pepper. Whisk the dressing until it turns extremely creamy and pale green from containing millions of tiny air bubbles. Pass both the bowl of greens and that of dressing to guests so they can help themselves and toss the greens in their own plates for the sake of total freshness, for mesclun greens are fragile and wilt easily. If you prefer to toss a large bowl of greens, rub your clean hands with some of the dressing and gently toss until the greens are sufficiently coated.

A mesclun is, in the language of the French Provence, a mixture of immature salad greens of all breeds. The equivalent to mesclun exists in all other provinces of France (and, I am pretty sure, all over the temperate countries of Europe), made with different greens and called saladine, meaning young salad. Both mesclun and saladine are prepared when, after having sowed the salad seeds, a multitude of small, tender leaves of many types come up all at once in late spring through to midsummer. The fields are "cleared" of these leaves to allow full-grown lettuce to develop. These small leaves are a delight to all French people, since they announce the warmer weather.

California and, during the summer, many other colder places in the country now grow these small baby lettuces in huge quantities and send them to the large city markets. A good and elaborate mesclun can contain over thirty different types of baby greens, some green, some pale yellow, some frankly red, the seeds of which come not only from France but from Japan and the entire Mediterranean basin.

Oriental-Style Romaine and Shrimp Salad

FCR — 6 SERVINGS

½ cup peanut oil

18 small snow peas

18 large shrimp, deveined

3 tablespoons seasoned rice vinegar

1 tablespoon soy sauce, more or less to taste

1 tablespoon oyster sauce, more or less to taste

1 teaspoon sesame oil

1 teaspoon finely ground Szechuan pepper

Salt

2 heads Romaine, well washed and dried

If you prefer the pepper toasted, please do so; I prefer the intriguing flowery taste of the untoasted pepper. Devein the shrimp while still uncooked by teasing the vein out. It will come out only if filled; if it is empty, simply leave the vein in the shrimp.

Heat half the peanut oil in a large skillet over high heat. Add the pea pods and stir-fry 1 minute, then remove to a plate lined with a paper towel. Cool and refrigerate as long as needed. In the same oil, cook the shrimp until the shells turn bright red, 2 to 3 minutes on each side. Remove to a plate and remove the shells when cool enough to handle. Add the remainder of the peanut oil to the skillet. Cut up the shells with scissors and cook 5 more minutes in the oil, then cover and let steep half an hour. Strain the shrimp oil into a small bowl.

Whisk the shrimp oil, rice vinegar, soy and oyster sauces, sesame oil, and pepper into a dressing. Taste for salt, and whether you need more oil or vinegar. Marinate the shrimp for 2 hours in the dressing in the refrigerator, well covered with plastic wrap.

When ready to serve, toss the Romaine with a few tablespoons of the dressing. Mix the shrimp and snow peas and arrange on top of the Romaine. Pass the remainder of the dressing in a small bowl.

Truly Mediterranean Tomato Salad

FCR — 6 SERVINGS

2 each medium-size Green Zebra, Red Gold Stripe, and Snowball tomatoes

1 ½ tablespoons fresh lemon juice

6 tablespoons extra virgin olive oil

Salt

Pepper from the mill

Small fresh basil and chervil leaves

Remove the stem end of each tomato. Bring a pot of water to a boil and immerse each tomato separately in the boiling water for 1 to 2 minutes.

Remove from the water with tongs and rinse immediately under running cold water. Peel and cut into ¼-inch-thick slices.

Arrange the tomatoes on a large platter alternating the colors and decorate at regular intervals with some of each type of herb. Whisk the lemon juice, oil, and salt and pepper to taste into a pinzimonio-type dressing and drizzle over the tomatoes. Decorate with basil and chervil leaves.

VARIATION

Cut a ball of *mozzarella di buffala* into ¼-inch-thick slices and intersperse the mozzarella among the slices of tomatoes. This typically southern Italian specialty was introduced in California by Michael Chiarello at Tra Vigne Restaurant in St. Helena in 1989–90.

Chabot Salad

FCR—6 SERVINGS

For the dressing

1 bottle red wine of your choice

3 large shallots, extremely finely chopped

1 to 2 tablespoons plain yellow American mustard or to your personal taste

Salt

Water as needed

Pepper from the mill, used discreetly, carefully, and progressively, as some wines are peppery

For the salad

½ recipe Puff Pastry (page 1082)

6 slices Brie ½ inch thick and as long as the cheese, rind completely removed

3 white Belgian endives

3 red Belgian endives

2 tablespoons chopped fresh chives

To prepare the dressing, in a large nonreactive saucepan over high heat reduce the bottle of wine and the shallots together until only ½ cup of very concentrated liquid mixed with blackened shallots is left. Cool completely, then pour into a blender, shallots and all. Add the mustard, salt, and water to your taste until you obtain a balanced dressing, processing until smooth. Strain the dressing to discard any irregular pieces of shallots. Add pepper now, but only if necessary.

Roll the puff pastry out into a rectangular sheet ⅛ inch thick. Turn a baking sheet upside down and butter it. Lift up the sheet of puff pastry by wrapping it around your rolling pin; unroll it onto the baking sheet. Prick it all over with a fork. Refrigerate or even freeze it until well chilled. Meanwhile, preheat the oven to 425°F. Cover the pastry with another baking sheet

This is a good salad for learning a few new concepts. I first presented this with a dressing consisting mostly of reduced Cabernet Sauvignon from Beringer's Chabot vineyard, an intense Cabernet full of the deep aromas of its natural environment and of concentrated fruit. You may use any other Cabernet, Merlot, Pinot Noir, French Rhône, or Italian Barolo or Barbaresco instead; the wine certainly need not be the most expensive, but it cannot be a bargain wine either.

I must leave to you the final seasoning of the wine dressing with mustard and salt, for each and every wine will be different and the quantities I give here are bound to vary with your taste and the way the wine you used concentrated during its reduction. Do not succumb to the temptation of not reducing the wine as much as you should to "have more liquid and avoid using water" for you need to totally evaporate any trace of alcohol and totally concentrate the acids to be able to work the perfect balance of taste for the dressing. Added water here is no sin, just a necessary balancing agent.

This may sound a bit difficult, but it is a great "palate" exercise if you are a passionate and/or professional cook.

lightly buttered on its inside, using it as you would a lid. Bake the sheets together, turning over once, until the pastry sheet is golden to golden brown, as you prefer, 20 to 25 minutes. Cool the baked sheet on a rack.

Cut the sheet into 12 rectangles 3 × 1½ inches, then cut each end on a slant to make parallelograms. Slip one slice of cheese between two pieces of pastry to make napoleon-style cakes.

Clean and core the endives and separate their leaves. Crisscross the leaves as elegantly as you can on a plate. Set the napoleon in the center. Drizzle some of the dressing on the leaves and sprinkle the top of the napoleon with chopped chives. Serve rapidly for freshness.

Grains, Legumes, and Pasta

THIS CHAPTER CONTAINS INFORMATION ON THE BASIC WAYS OF PREPARING THE two most ancient foods in the world—grains and legumes—as well as on making fresh pasta and macaroni, as the colloquial expression goes, "from scratch."

To be consistent with the goal of this book—to understand the basic techniques—I have included a lot of techniques with only a few typical recipes. After you have mastered the basics, venture into the world of grains, legumes, and pasta by consulting the bibliography for the names of volumes exclusively concerned with each of these three types of foods.

To keep a measure of rationality in your own learning, it may be a good idea to start with the pulses, as grains and legumes have been called since Roman times. Once those are mastered, proceed to make a true study of the pastas.

The pasta techniques explained here work extremely well but other methods exist that are just as successful, so it is essential that after you have mastered the first steps described here you go on to consult experts on the matter in the Italian and Germanic traditions. The ideas you will find will enrich your knowledge immensely.

I would like to add an important remark concerning grains, legumes, and pastas and nutrition. You may be hesitant to consume a lot of pulses and grains and pasta, because they contain so many carbohydrates and you do not wish for you, your family, or restaurant guests to put a lot of weight on. These are complex carbohydrates and they are good carbohydrates with what modern French nutritionists call a "low glycemic index." Basically, what applies to potatoes also applies to complex carbohydrates; they themselves will not cause anyone to put weight on if no excessive amount of fat is added to them. Think, for example, of the multiple dishes of pasta presented with a sauce made with pure heavy cream and cheese. It is tempting because of course it is absolutely delicious, but if you are going to consume pasta every day and offer it to family and guests, it is essential that you also know how to prepare a fat-free or fat-controlled tomato sauce (see page 309) or one made with reduced completely defatted stock (see page 216).

To avoid using egg yolk in pasta, use the formula for pasta made of durum wheat flour (semolina) and egg whites which appears side by side with the whole-egg formula on page 499. If you prefer, you can also use the formula for macaroni on page 513.

Rice

True Rice

Among the many grains gathered in the wild by our distant prehistoric ancestresses, rice, along with wheat, has been the most important.

Karen Hess, in *The Carolina Rice Kitchen* (University of North Carolina, 1992), indicates that diverse strains of rice called *Oryza sativa* originated in India and Indonesia, while in Africa another variety called *O. glaberrina* was found in the wild. Considering that India and Indonesia are relatively close to southern China, it is probable that some of the varieties existing in both these regions arrived there around 4,000 B.C. Rice, however, did not reach Japan until 600 to 300 B.C.

Over the millennia, the numerous strains have been separated into two main groups: *Oryza sativa indica*—or Indian rice—which we now call long-grain rice, and *O. s. japonica*—or Japanese rice, which we know as short-grain rice.

How did rice arrive in America? Perhaps on a stranded ship from Madagascar carrying the rice that was to become the Carolina gold rice. Nothing, however, is certain except one fact: The black slaves taken from the western coast of Africa to South Carolina knew how to cultivate rice, and it was their work that made the first American rice plantations possible.

The largest area of rice production in the United States is now Arkansas, with one third of the totality of the national production; other rice-producing states are California, Louisiana, Mississippi, Missouri, and Texas.

Modern rices are divided into white and brown short-grain rices and long-grain rices.

White rice includes any long- or short-grain rice in which the bran and its underlying layers have been polished off. The powder that results from this polishing is called rice polish and is rose colored. It can replace cake flour very advantageously from a nutritional point of view because of its vitamin and mineral content, its pleasant taste, and light texture.

Brown rice includes any long- or short-grain rice that has not had its bran and underlying layers removed. Because of this, it is more nutritious and contains a larger percent of proteins, niacin, fiber, vitamin E, and more calcium, phosphorus, and potassium than white rice. These are extremely important for everyone's health but especially so for vegetarians. Brown rice takes one and one half to two times longer to cook than white rice.

The short-grain rices, which come mostly from cooler climates, yield grains that are starchier and tend to stick to one another. They are considered tastier than the longer grain types by some. The tastiest come from Japan, the California Central Valley, and the Po Valley in northern Italy. The Chinese and especially the Japanese people relish the stickiness of their steamed short-grain rices. The Italians use several short-grain rices to prepare their *risotti;* the more expensive are the Arborio superfino from Lombardy and the Vialone from the Veneto, south of the city of Venice. Both yield dishes with diverse tastes and textures. Although California rices are used in many restaurants to prepare risotto, their texture never rivals that of the incomparable Italian types.

Long-grain rices are usually cultivated in warm climates and yield nice, long, translucent grains almost always four to five times as long as they are wide. Even when prepared with very little fat the grains separate easily when fully cooked. They are usually used in making pilafs. The tastiest come from India. The most famous long-grain rice is the basmati rice from India, which is aged—like a good wine is—to deepen its taste and flavor. Both the long-grain Texmati rice developed in Texas from basmati seeds and the pecan rice have a delicious flavor, if a little less intense than the original basmati.

All rices, short- or long-grained, contain two starches, amylose and amylopectin. Amylose is able to retain much less water than amylopectin. This is due to their different molecular structures. The short-grain rices, which contain a large amount of amylopectin (between 80 and 85 percent), are able to absorb more water than the long-grain rices, which contain only 70 to 72 percent of it. While cooking short-grain rices you will see the liquid used to cook them turn milky and the grains become progressively stickier as they soften. On the other hand, long-grain rices will absorb all the liquid blended into them without clouding the liquid hardly at all and the grains will barely stick together. Pay attention, though, not to overmoisten the long-grain rices, for if you do, they will absorb the totality of the liquid you give them and change shape, ending up looking like small ⅓-inch-long sticks with a fork at each of their ends as the endosperm of the grain starts disintegrating.

CONVERTED AND INSTANT RICE

Rice cooks so fast and is so delicious that I strongly recommend you do not use any parboiled rice or precooked rice or any flavored mixes. They are certainly good grains and are practical to use when in a hurry, but they do not show off the delicious taste of the two different rice starches as well as the unworked rices do.

WASHING RICE

About washing rice before cooking it: In the United States and the European countries, rice was until thirty to thirty-five years ago washed before cooking to allow its grains to remain as separated as possible when cooked. The commercial conditioning of rice has been by now so perfected that this has become unnecessary for rices produced in the United States and Europe. Rice bought in a large bag from an Asian store should be inspected for stones and other impurities and washed carefully under cold running water before cooking; this washing removes excess starch, which you will see in the rins-

1½ Cups Uncooked Rice	Water	Cooking Time	Yield
Long-grain rice	2½ to 3 cups	16–18 minutes	4½ cups
Medium- or short-grain rice	2¼ cups	16–18 minutes	3¾ to 4 cups
Brown rice of either type	2½ to 3 cups	About 50 minutes	4 to 5 cups

ing water. If you do not wash the rice and pat it dry, its grains may indeed stick together while cooking.

BOILED RICE

These guidelines are based on the directions usually given by the Rice Council of America. The quantity indicated here will serve 6 people and yield 3¾ to 5 cups cooked rice, depending on the type of rice used.

Mix the rice, water, salt to your taste, and 1 tablespoon unsaturated oil or butter together in a 2-quart sauteuse pan. Bring to a boil over medium-low heat to allow the grains to swell progressively. Fluff the mixture twice with a fork in two different directions. Reduce the heat to a low simmer, cover the pot with a tight-fitting lid, and cook the length of time indicated above.

COOKING RICE IN THE MICROWAVE OVEN

If you prefer to use the microwave, please do so, but do not expect any benefit in time; the cooking times are identical. Always start the cooking on high for 5 minutes, then reduce to 50 percent power and continue cooking 15 minutes for long- and short-grain rices and 45 to 55 minutes for brown rice.

STORING BOILED RICE FOR LATER USE

If you are going to consume the rice right away, use it as it comes out of the cooking pot. Add more fat if you like and correct the seasoning very carefully.

If the rice is to be cooked ahead of time and kept refrigerated, *rinse the cooked rice under warm water, not cold water.* The warm water will wash off the jelled layers of starch surrounding the grains and keep them from sticking to one another. Rinse under warm water until the water runs clear. Let the rice drain completely. Pat it dry and store it in plastic bag(s); keep refrigerated or even, if you have to, frozen for reheating. It will keep one week refrigerated. This rinsing technique makes for perfect-looking rice, but causes an additional loss of nutrition as well as an appreciable loss of taste. Rice that has not been rinsed before refrigerating or freezing tends to clump somewhat when reheated and tastes a bit stale.

To reheat boiled rice, you can:

• Put the bag of rice in a pot of boiling water for a few minutes;

- Reheat as is for 2 minutes in the microwave oven on high; or
- Transfer the rice to a baking dish, dribble it with the oil of your choice or dot it with as much butter as you wish, and season with salt and pepper. Fluff the rice with a fork. Cover the dish with a food grade plastic wrap, punch holes in the top of the wrap, and reheat in a preheated 200°F oven for 25 to 30 minutes, fluffing it occasionally with a fork. Do not use a spoon to fluff the rice, as its edge can cut and break the kernels.

Here is a recipe to practice reheating rice:

Turkey Rice

FCR—6 SERVINGS

⅓ cup dried currants

3 tablespoons fino sherry

¼ cup canola or grapeseed oil

1½ to 2 teaspoons curry powder or to your personal taste

3 cups cooked long-grain rice (page 460)

½ cup slivered almonds, lightly toasted (page 50)

2 tablespoons chopped cilantro leaves (optional)

Macerate the currants overnight in the sherry. Heat the oil in a small skillet and cook the curry powder 3 to 4 minutes over low heat. Turn the heat off and let cool, then cover and let steep overnight in the refrigerator to infuse the oil with the curry taste.

Blend the cooked rice, the currants with any remaining sherry, and the curry oil in a baking dish. Reheat slowly in a preheated 200°F oven for approximately 40 minutes, fluffing occasionally with a fork. When ready to serve, blend in the almonds and the cilantro if used.

MODERN PILAFS OF RICE

The pilaf, as we call it now, is said to have come from Turkey and Persia, but it is really found all over southeastern Asia. A pilaf is usually made with long-grain rice which is braised in broth.

Modern Basic Pilaf

FFR WITH BUTTER, **FCR** WITH OIL

½ cup unsalted butter or ⅓ cup unsaturated oil of your choice

1½ cups uncooked long-grain rice

3 cups scalding hot broth of your choice

Salt

Pepper from the mill

This is called turkey rice because our whole family liked it to accompany the Thanksgiving turkey. It also goes well with duck and chickens of all sizes.

NOTE: *You can, if you want, prepare the rice as a pilaf with the ingredients in this recipe. See the technique below.*

These are the proportions to obtain 4½ cups of cooked rice or 6 portions. Use an enameled cast-iron pan or a good heavy-bottomed stainless steel sauteuse.

Heat the butter or oil over medium-high heat, then add the rice and sauté until the grains look as white as milk, a sign that the starches in the outside layers of each grain have seared and hardened; this searing helps to keep the kernels from sticking to one another. Add the broth.

The quantity and choice of broth is important. There should always be twice as much broth as rice. The broth can be veal or beef broth, chicken broth, duck broth, fish fumet, or vegetable broth, as you wish. However, do not use a very rich stock, but rather a very simple one, flavorful but not very gelatinous. If the stock is too gelatinous, it will not penetrate the rice grains, which will remain crunchy. A pilaf cooked with canned broth or with water in which bouillon cubes have been diluted will cook faster than one made with the richer home-made stock, so do not hesitate to dilute your own rich stock with water.

After adding the hot broth and seasoning with salt and pepper, stretch several layers of paper towels over the opening of the pot before closing it with the lid. They will keep the steam that rises from the cooking rice from falling back into the pilaf. Bake the pilaf in a preheated 325°F oven for 18 minutes. Fluff with a fork. Each grain will remain separate and be done to tenderness, and the broth will have been completely absorbed. Mold if desired in a lightly oiled or buttered mold. The mold can be held as long as needed in a hot water bath in a 175°F oven.

Pilafs of rice can be kept a nice long time in a low oven if not blended with other ingredients be they meat or fish, but if they are blended with such ingredients, *they must be served immediately.*

Shellfish and Rice Pilaf

FCR — 6 SERVINGS

24 black mussels

Salt

3 jumbo fresh scallops

4 to 5 tablespoons light olive oil as needed

6 large shrimp in their shells, deveined

2 cloves garlic, crushed

Small bouquet garni

½ cup dry white wine

1½ cups white wine fish fumet (page 543)

1 large yellow onion, finely chopped

1½ cups uncooked long-grain rice

Pepper from the mill

2 scallions, thinly sliced on the diagonal

Soak the mussels for 30 minutes in water salted with 1½ teaspoons of salt per quart. Scrub and debeard. Discard those with broken or opened shells.

If you have no fish fumet, you can blend clam juice with the mussel cooking juice, but beware of oversaltiness. Taste the mixture first and decide whether you should use 1 part mussel juice, 1 part clam juice, and 1 part water, or change the ratio to favor water. You may use alcohol-free cider instead of wine and compensate for the sweetness with lemon juice.

Remove the "feet" of the scallops. Heat 1 tablespoon or so of the olive oil in a large sauteuse over medium-high heat and sear the scallops on both sides until browned but still uncooked in their centers. Remove to a plate and cut each scallop across into two slices.

In the same sauteuse and oil, sauté the shrimp over medium-high heat until both sides of their shells have turned very red. Remove from the heat, let cool and shell, leaving only the tail fin on; remove to the same plate as the scallops.

To the same sauteuse, add the garlic cloves, bouquet garni, the drained mussels, and wine. Cover and steam just until the mussels have opened; do not overcook them. Discard any that will not open. Shell the mussels. Measure the cooking liquid and add enough fish fumet to make 3 full cups. Strain using a China cap.

Preheat the oven to 325°F. Wash and dry the sauteuse. Heat 3 to 4 tablespoons of the olive oil over medium-high heat. Add the onion and sauté until translucent, then add the rice and sauté until white and milky. Reduce the heat to medium and add the fumet mixture. Be certain that the mixture boils before covering the opening of the pot with several layers of paper towels, then with the pot lid. Bake 16 minutes in the oven. Remove from the oven, open, and blend in all the shellfish; keep covered 2 to 3 more minutes to reheat the shellfish. Correct the final seasoning with salt, if needed, and pepper. Serve immediately from the sauteuse sprinkled with the scallions.

SUGGESTED WINE: A *French Mâcon-Villages or a California Sauvignon Blanc or Fumé Blanc*

THE AMERICAN PILAU

The technique used in traditional American pilaus varies from the classic pilafs (pilau and pilaf are one and the same word) in that the rice is not hardened in hot butter or oil before being added to water to be cooked. It is immersed directly into a tasty broth flavored either with beans or shellfish and meat mixed. This type of preparation seems to have come from the Spanish paella and indeed appears in the cooking of regions of the United States which were first settled by Spanish colonists, then by French ones or vice versa. Such is the case of the South Carolina New Year dish of beans and rice called hoppin' John and the jambalaya of Louisiana. The jambalaya, the name of which comes from the Provençal *jambalaia*, which referred to a soup containing ham (*jambon* in French and *jamon* in Spanish), is definitely reminiscent of the Spanish paella; hoppin' John is not. Both, though, are considered pilaus, and in both you will see the rice added to the hot beans or to the hot shellfish stew without being seared in fat beforehand.

Hoppin' John Another Way

FCR — 6 SERVINGS

I smoked chicken

8 cups water

3 medium-size yellow onions, coarsely chopped

I large leek, white part only, well washed and thinly sliced

I large carrot, coarsely chopped

Small bouquet garni of I bay leaf, I sprig fresh thyme, and 5 parsley stems

Salt

Pepper from the mill

I cup dried black-eyed peas

Large pinch of red pepper flakes

I cup uncooked long-grain rice

This recipe is an extrapolation from the classic hoppin' John rice-and-bean dish originally made by the ancestors of the present-day African Americans. The recipe for the true traditional hoppin' John can be found in John Taylor's book Hoppin' John's Low Country Cooking *(Bantam, 1992), and you must look at it to see how much liberty I have taken with the ingredients. But I am faithfully following his technique.*

SUGGESTED WINE: *As was done in South Carolina, a nice glass of dry Sercial Madeira*

Bone the chicken entirely; keep the breasts to prepare sandwiches, bone and dice the legs entirely, and refrigerate them, covered with plastic wrap. Reserve for later use. Put all the bones in a soup pot. Add the water, bring to a boil on medium heat, and add 2 of the chopped onions, the leek, carrot, and the bouquet garni. Turn the heat down to medium-low and season with salt and pepper. Simmer until the broth tastes good and the chicken bones have fallen apart, about 1½ hours. You should obtain 6 cups of broth. If necessary, keep adding boiling salted water to the pot to maintain that volume of broth to 6 cups, which is what you will need to prepare the dish. Strain the broth into a large bowl; cool completely and when cool refrigerate overnight. The next day lift off any fat that may have hardened on the surface of the broth.

Put the peas in a 5-quart pot. Add the cold broth, the third chopped onion, and the red pepper flakes; bring to a boil slowly on medium-low heat and cook 2 minutes only. Turn the heat off and let stand 1 hour. Bring back to a boil on medium-low heat and cook until the peas are just shy of being tender, about 1½ hours. After 1 hour, add the diced chicken leg meat. You should by now have only 2 cups of broth left with the beans. Add the rice, bring back to a low simmer, and cook the rice, tightly covered and without ever peeking into the pot for 20 minutes. Using a long fork, fluff the pilau; let stand 3 minutes, still covered, then serve immediately.

A Small Jambalaya

FCR — 6 SERVINGS

4 cups water

¼ cup crab boil seasoning

I pound medium-size shrimp in their shells

This is simplified, but very good and will give you an idea of what the real jambalaya can be. The true taste of the dish comes from

¼ cup bacon fat or unsaturated oil of your choice

One ¼-inch-thick slice country ham or prosciutto, cut into ¼-inch cubes

3 medium-size yellow onions, very finely chopped

2 celery ribs, diced into ¼-inch cubes

2 cloves garlic, very finely chopped

3 tablespoons chopped fresh parsley leaves

¼ teaspoon dried thyme

3 pounds sun-ripened tomatoes, peeled, seeded, and diced into ½-inch cubes

I large green bell pepper, charred over a flame or under a broiler, peeled, seeded, and cut
    into ½-inch-square pieces

2 cups chicken broth of your choice

I dried hot pepper, finely chopped

Salt

Pepper from the mill

I cup uncooked long-grain rice

the combination of country ham and bacon fat. People with cardiovascular problems can use unsaturated oil instead of the bacon fat.

SUGGESTED WINE: *A nice supple white wine from the South. Ask your wine merchant; there are vineyards throughout much of the South.*

Bring the water to a boil. Add the crab boil seasoning, then the shrimp. Bring back to a boil and cook 2 minutes at a hard boil; drain, cool the shrimp, and peel. Store, covered, in the refrigerator.

In a stew pot, heat the bacon fat over medium-high heat, then add the ham and onions and sauté until the onions are translucent. Add the celery, garlic, parsley, and thyme and cook, stirring, over medium heat until all the vegetables are lightly browned and dry. Add the tomatoes and stir well until they lose their juices. Then add the bell pepper, chicken broth, and dried hot pepper and season with salt and pepper. Continue simmering until the mixture is well bound and almost homogeneous. Add the rice, toss it with the mixture, and cover the pot. Let cook on low heat until the rice is tender, about 25 minutes. Open the lid only then and stir in the shrimp. Cover again and let steep for 5 minutes. Serve piping hot.

MODERN PILAFS PREPARED WITH SOUP MACARONI

Small commercial soup pasta such as small orzo, tubettini, and acini di pepe can be used very effectively to prepare different pilafs. The technique is exactly the same as explained for rice; there are only two small differences:

- The pasta will be cooked in the fat the same way to harden it, but it will take on color and,
- With pasta *you must always use the same volume of broth as pasta*. Please measure accurately so you do not end up with a sticky pilaf.

Pilaf of Small Orzo with Goat Cheese, Chives, and Walnuts

With a side dish of mixed
vegetables and a green salad, this
is a good lacto-vegetarian dish.
The recipe can be considered fat-
controlled for regular diets; heart
patients should consider it full fat
because of the presence of the goat
cheese.

SUGGESTED WINE: *An
Italian Dolcetto d'Alba*

FFR to FCR—6 SERVINGS

¼ cup unsaturated oil of your choice

2 cups uncooked small orzo

2 shallots, finely chopped

2 cups broth of your choice, scalding hot

¼ cup chopped walnuts, lightly toasted (page 50)

3 to 4 ounces fresh goat cheese or to your personal taste

1½ tablespoons chopped fresh chives

Salt

Pepper from the mill

Heat the oil in a heavy-bottomed sauteuse over medium-high heat. Add the pasta and sauté until it turns golden. Add the shallots and sauté until translucent. Add the hot broth. Cover the opening of the pot with several layers of paper towels, then the pot lid. Cook on medium heat until all broth has been absorbed, 10 to 12 minutes.

Add the walnuts and goat cheese to the sauteuse and mix well, so the cheese melts completely. Add the chives and correct the final seasoning with salt, if needed, and as much pepper as you like. Turn into a heated serving dish and serve promptly.

RISOTTO

Risotto, the delicious braised rice dish from the northern provinces of Italy, is prepared with two types of rice; each can be found easily not only in all Italian neighborhoods of big cities but in many supermarkets.

USING THE CORRECT RICE   The two rices are Arborio superfino and Vialone, also called Vialone nano. Arborio is used mostly in Piemonte and Lombardy while Vialone is used in the Veneto. I suggest that you try both; it will take you no time to develop a preference. I find Arborio kernels, with their lovely pearl white centers, to be far superior to Vialone, but it has a tendency to be firm at the center one minute and overcooked with a touch of oversoftness all around the kernels the next minute. Vialone cooks very fast and is used mostly in the Venetian areas where one likes the risotto to be moister than in other regions. *Neither of these rices is washed before being cooked.*

In California risotto is often made with round California rice. This is all right but the kernels of rice too often remain too hard, and the combination of California rice with much too strong stock, offered in many Italian-American restaurants, results in a—shall I say—different risotto.

The technique of risotto making is understood somewhat differently by

Italians of diverse regional origins. My cousin Bruno, who is Milanese by birth, and a first-rate cook, taught me how to do it.

THE POT AND FAT TO BE USED Use a heavy-bottomed enameled cast-iron pan; *this pan will never be covered at any time during the cooking.* As much as you would like to use olive oil because it is healthier, if you want the true taste of risotto, you must use butter and nothing but butter or a very uneven blend of butter and oil, which should be in the vicinity of 5 parts butter to 1 part oil.

THE AROMATICS The aromatics used will vary but onions are always among them, in rather large quantity. They should be chopped—*by knife*—so finely that they almost turn into a coarse puree. They will be cooked over medium-low heat until soft and moisture free so that the butter seeps out of them and is clearly visible again on the bottom of the pan before you add the unwashed rice.

ADDING THE RICE Only now will you add the rice as it comes from the bag. Heat it deeply over medium heat so it becomes hard before you add any broth.

Cousin Bruno would never be caught in the act of stirring a risotto, as our Italian-American authorities recommend, because, he says, it can break the kernels much too easily when they reach perfect doneness. He taught me instead to fluff the kernels with a fork all through the additions of the broth. It is just as easy to keep the rice moving with a fork all around the pot and through its center as it is to stir it; and indeed, the integrity of the kernels is much more respected than it is with the wooden spoon that is used enthusiastically and much too early. In the very last stage of the cooking, Bruno switches to a wooden spoon and stirs the risotto for one to two minutes to homogenize it a bit and bring out more of the amylopectin, which gives the risotto a nice, smooth texture.

THE QUALITY OF THE BROTH AND ITS RHYTHM OF ADDITION The broth should in no way resemble the hefty and solid French veal stock appearing in this book. Use a secondary stock made from lean trimmings of veal and beef, aromatized with onions, carrots, and *always* a few pieces of celery, which is the Italian stamp of authenticity when it comes to broth (*brodo*).

Italian authorities prefer veal and beef flavor to chicken in broth prepared for the making of risotto. Duck broth, however, gives a risotto a very pleasant flavor, and if you use a vegetable or several vegetables as a garnish, it is a good idea to prepare the stock with some of those vegetables to maintain uniformity of taste throughout. As an example, look at asparagus risotto on page 469.

The total quantity of broth, which is three to four times that of the rice by volume, should be premeasured and kept in a saucepan over low heat. Add it

⅔ to ¾ cup at a time. When you reach the last stage of cooking, add the broth 2 tablespoons at a time and taste the rice to determine exactly when it is ready. Proceed to the last technique.

"CREAMING" THE READY-TO-SERVE RISOTTO This last technique is the most important for the taste and texture of the rice. Because of it, it is essential that you do not overcook the rice; otherwise, it will immediately turn into an abominable mush. Stir the risotto for one full minute, adding a nice portion of butter at room temperature as well as any garnish. Risotto in Italy always comes to the table as a perfectly homogenized mixture of rice and garnish(es) with a modest sprinkling of Parmigiano-Reggiano, or of any other preferred Italian cheese. *A risotto garnished with fish or shellfish never receives any addition of cheese.*

Here are three *risotti* for you to try:

Bruno's Risotto

SUGGESTED WINE: *Pinot Oltrepò Pavese*

FFR — 6 SERVINGS

7 tablespoons unsalted butter

2 large yellow onions, extremely finely chopped

1½ cups uncooked Arborio rice, unwashed

½ cup dry Italian vermouth

2 cloves garlic, completely mashed

4 to 6 tablespoons tomato paste or to your personal taste

¼ cup fresh basil leaves, finely julienned

3 anchovy fillets, rinsed and mashed

4½ to 5 cups hot broth of your choice as needed

¼ pound mushrooms, chopped and presautéed in butter

¾ cup freshly grated Parmigiano-Reggiano cheese

In a heavy-bottomed enameled cast-iron pot over medium-high heat, melt 6 tablespoons of the butter. Add the onions and sauté until they are dry and the butter starts to ooze out of them. Toss the rice in the hot mixture until the grains turn milky white. Add the vermouth and stir until evaporated. Mix the garlic, tomato paste, basil, and anchovies with one third of the broth and add to the rice; cook over low heat while you fluff the rice with a fork all around the saucepan and through its center until the liquid has been absorbed. Add the remaining broth in the same way in additions of ½ to ⅔ cup.

Stir the rice well with a wooden spoon as you blend in the last tablespoon of butter, the mushrooms, and any juices they may have lost as well as 2 tablespoons of the Parmigiano-Reggiano. Pass the remainder of the Parmigiano cheese in a small bowl for your guests to add more if they so desire.

Asparagus Risotto

FFR—6 SERVINGS

2 pounds small green asparagus (⅓ inch in diameter)

7 tablespoons unsalted butter

2 large yellow onions, extremely finely chopped

2 cloves garlic, finely chopped

1 ½ cups uncooked Vialone rice, unwashed

1 teaspoon ground coriander

1 large ¼-inch-thick slice prosciutto, diced into ¼-inch cubes

¾ cup freshly grated Parmigiano-Reggiano cheese plus extra to pass on the side

Pepper from the mill

Salt only if needed

SUGGESTED WINE: *Use no cilantro if you plan to drink wine and look for an excellent Soave.*

Cut the tips of the asparagus 1 inch long. Blanch 2 minutes in salted boiling water sufficient to yield 5 cups hot cooking liquid for later use. Remove them with a slotted spoon and set aside. Chop all the stems, discarding the hard root ends. Add the chopped stems to the boiling blanching water and cook 5 minutes. Remove the stems from the water with a slotted spoon and liquefy them in the blender, gradually adding 5 cups of the cooking water. Strain through a China cap to discard all fibers. Reheat in a saucepan to the boiling point.

Heat 6 tablespoons of the butter in a heavy-bottomed enameled cast-iron pot over medium-high heat. Add the onions and garlic and sauté together until the onions are dry and the butter breaks out of the mixture. Add the rice and sauté until the grains turn milky white. Gradually add the pureed asparagus liquid ⅔ cup at a time, fluffing the rice with a fork all around the pot and through its center each time.

Melt the remaining tablespoon of butter in a skillet over medium heat. Add the asparagus tips and sprinkle them with the coriander; add to the rice along with the prosciutto and 2 tablespoons of the cheese, stirring well for 1 to 2 minutes to melt. Pepper to taste and add salt only if needed. Serve immediately with a bowl containing the remaining cheese.

VARIATION

Although the flavor will not be Italian at all, you can add, instead of the cheese, ¼ cup finely chopped cilantro leaves.

Risotto with Sausage
RISOTTO CON SALSICCIA

SUGGESTED WINE: *Rosso dell'Oltrepò*

FFR — 6 SERVINGS

1 pound sweet Italian sausage with fennel seeds

6 cups hot broth of your choice

6 tablespoons unsalted butter

2 large yellow onions, extremely finely chopped

2 cloves garlic, mashed

1 ½ cups uncooked **Arborio** rice, unwashed

½ cup freshly grated **Parmigiano-Reggiano** cheese plus extra to pass on the side

6 fresh basil leaves, scissored

Add ½ inch of water to a large skillet. Prick each sausage several times with a needle. Add the sausages to the water and slowly bring to a boil. Let the water evaporate, at which point the sausages will have lost about half their fat content into the pan and started to brown. Turn them around while they cook to brown all their faces. When they are cooked, remove them to a board, let them cool, and once cold, slice them into ¼-inch-thick slices. Set aside on a plate.

Using a wad of paper towels, pat the fat off the bottom of the skillet and deglaze the pan with the broth. Keep the broth hot. Heat the butter in a heavy-bottomed enameled cast-iron pot over medium-high heat. Add the onions and garlic and sauté together until the onions are dry and the butter breaks out of the mixture. Add the rice and sauté until the grains turn milky white. Gradually add the broth 1 cup at a time, fluffing the rice with a fork all around the pot and through its center each time until each cup is absorbed. When the rice is cooked, add the sausage rounds and grated cheese using a wooden spoon and stirring well for 1 to 2 minutes to homogenize the preparation.

Serve immediately sprinkled with the basil and accompanied by a bowl of the same cheese.

Wild Rice

Zizania aquatica is the Latin name of what we know as wild rice, which is in reality an aquatic oat (the French pioneers called it *folle avoine*, which means crazy oats) that grows wild in the areas of Minnesota and Canadian Manitoba once covered by the quaternary ice cap and embedded with a multitude of small lakes and rivers resulting from the melting of millions of stranded icebergs.

Wild rice was called *tuskaro* by the Iroquois and *manomin* by the Ojibwas. Since there were unending discussions and dissensions among tribes for possession and/or rights of harvest of the most fertile waters, the French term *zizanie*, meaning discord, came to be used by the French settlers of southern Canada to indicate both the plants and the discord among the tribes. It is with that meaning of discord that the word traveled back to France and is used in modern French; the modern French word for the rice is *ris sauvage*.

Modern Native Americans living in these regions still gather *Zizania* and I was able to acquire the best I ever tasted at a gas station while passing through Minnesota; gas stations seem to be a good place to find really wild rice since I found some in three different stations, driving East to West. Approximately 500,000 pounds of the wild *Zizania* are gathered, compared to the 2 million pounds yearly cultivated in paddies since the early seventies, but there is no taste comparison possible between the slightly grayish brown wild grain and the deep brown, almost black cultivated one. The first is "wildly" delicious, the second quite nice; this is my personal taste, others may think differently.

Years ago I was privileged to meet one very lovely Native American grandmother who explained to me in detail that wild rice tastes better not when it is cooked in hot water but rather when it is slowly fluffed opened by soaking it in successive baths of hot water, each left to cool until the water is completely cold. Indeed, the fresh grassy taste is much more discernible when the kernels are opened this way, curling up slowly and naturally, and it does a lot for the cultivated variety.

Zizanie Salad

FFR to FCR—6 SERVINGS

4 ounces (about ¾ cup) uncooked preferably truly wild rice

I cup cooked brown rice (page 460), still hot from the stove

Salt

Pepper from the mill

Cooked meat of 2 Maine lobsters, cut into bite-size pieces

3 shallots, finely chopped

¼ cup cider vinegar

⅔ cup walnut oil or half walnut and half unsaturated oil of your choice

½ cup chopped pecans

2 tablespoons finely chopped cilantro leaves

¼ cup finely chopped fresh curly parsley leaves

3 scallions, finely slivered

4 each nasturtium flowers and leaves (optional)

This recipe must be considered as full fat for heart patients because of the use of lobster.

If you live in those areas where the small brown-legged glacial water crayfish are to be found, by all means use the cooked tails of as many "crawdads" as possible instead of lobster; the salad will be even more delicious and have much more character.

SUGGESTED WINE: *A dry Vidal Blanc from a northeastern vineyard*

Soak the wild rice in three successive baths of hot water to cover until each has cooled and the rice has opened up. Drain well and mix with the hot brown rice and season well with salt and pepper. Cool completely and mix the lobster meat into the rice.

Squeeze the chopped shallots in the corner of a kitchen towel to discard any harsh juices. Put in a blender with the vinegar and oil and season with salt and pepper. Blend until homogeneous, then pour into the salad mixture with the pecans and herbs. Mix well. Serve mounded on a platter sprinkled with the scallion slivers and brightened with the nasturtium flowers and leaves. Serve at room temperature.

Cooking Barley

Barley is as ancient a cereal as wheat since, according to the historian Toussaint-Samat, both could be found and were consumed in ancient Jericho in 10,000 B.C. It has been said to be the most adaptable cereal to any agricultural circumstances since it grows in a range extending from Scandinavia to the tropics. It was in great part barley which fed the Egyptian builders of the pyramids.

Barley remains in cultivation in many modern countries because of its extensive use in the making of beer, as a softener for hard flours, as a garnish for winter soups, and as a most pleasant and different starch food. During the forties the whole of Europe used hulled whole barley as a substitute for coffee; I remember my mother roasting it in an old frying pan until the house filled with its aroma. I also remember it as better tasting than any other manufactured coffee substitute we could buy nowadays; it smelled and tasted good but did we ever miss the Arabica kick!

Barley is delicious, especially in the form we mostly cook, which is pearl barley; unfortunately because of having been polished, it has lost its aleurone layer and consequently a considerable amount of its vitamin B content. This situation can be remedied by serving meat or fish and a garnish of vegetables with it.

Basic Barley

The usual proportions used to cook barley as a side dish or as a main course for 6 people are:

3 cups liquid

I cup pearl barley

The average cooking time is 35 minutes. The liquid is usually water, but if you use a light broth adapted to the meat or fish you are going to use as a vitamin B replacement, you will obtain a much more complex taste. Simply bring the liquid to a boil, add the barley, turn down to a simmer, and cook until tender.

Norwegian Barley and Shrimp

FFR—6 SERVINGS

7 cups broth of your choice

1 large bunch fresh dill, stems chopped

¼ cup unsalted butter or unsaturated oil of your choice

2 cups uncooked pearl barley

2 large European cucumbers, peeled, cut in half, and seeded

Salt

Pepper from the mill

3 tablespoons chopped fresh dill leaves

1½ cups tiny shrimp, shelled

½ cup crème fraîche, warmed but not boiled

6 thin slices gravlax or commercial smoked salmon of your choice

Mix the broth in a large saucepan with the chopped stems of the dill. Bring to a boil over medium heat and reduce to 6 cups. Strain through a conical strainer.

Heat 2 tablespoons of the butter in a large sauteuse pan. Turn the heat off and toss the barley in it without heating further. Add the reserved broth, bring back to a boil, and turn down to medium-low to simmer. Cook until the barley is tender, about 35 minutes.

Meanwhile, slice the cucumber halves into paper-thin slices. Heat the remainder of the butter in a skillet over medium-high heat. Toss in the cucumbers, season with salt and pepper. Cover and let stew over low heat until they have lost all of their moisture. Add half the chopped dill leaves. Remove from the heat and set aside.

As soon as the barley is cooked, add the cucumbers with their juices and the shrimp, transfer the pan to a dish containing hot water, and keep warm. Just before serving, transfer to a heated serving dish. Season the crème fraîche with salt and pepper and spoon it over the barley. Top the dish with the gravlax slices and sprinkle with the remainder of the dill. Serve promptly.

Here is a recipe for barley presented almost as a main ingredient. The original recipe was a soup prepared by the cook of a Norwegian freighter on which I came back from Oslo to Antwerp in September 1947, which I transformed into a main course.

If you have no homemade broth, 3 cups clam juice mixed with 1½ cups each commercial broth and water makes a good combination. Use the tiny frozen shrimp.

SUGGESTED BEVERAGE:
No wine, a light beer

Cooking Millet

Millet is no less ancient than wheat and barley; it is probably the grain first used by the earliest northern Chinese civilizations. It is now an African cereal par excellence and is mostly used in the United States by vegetarians and people following a macrobiotic regimen.

Basic Millet

6 SERVINGS

2½ cups broth of your choice, light rather than rich and gelatinous

1 cup millet

The average cooking time is 5 minutes for parching, 20 minutes for cooking, and 10 to 15 minutes for standing and acquiring full taste.

Millet is tasty plain and it is even more flavorful when parched in a skillet over medium-high heat, stirring constantly, for 5 to 8 minutes before adding any liquid. If unparched it breaks open quickly and looks and tastes different. Do not hesitate to prolong the parching for a few more minutes if needed. The more it toasts, the better it tastes and the better it keeps whole. Add the hot broth to the cereal and bring to a boil. Turn down to a simmer and cook over medium-low to low heat until tender. Taste the millet; once it is tender, let it stand 10 minutes at least for it to fully develop its taste.

Millet and Chicken Sausage

SUGGESTED WINE: *A Beaujolais Villages*

FFR — 6 SERVINGS

1 head garlic, cloves peeled

3¼ cups chicken broth of your choice or Pure Vegetable Broth (page 213)

1 tablespoon unsaturated oil of your choice

6 links chicken sausage

1 cup millet

1 fresh sage leaf, cut in half

2 tablespoons chopped fresh parsley leaves

Mix the garlic cloves and broth together in a large saucepan and bring to a boil. Reduce the heat to medium-low and simmer until the garlic is soft, 35 to 40 minutes. Transfer the garlic cloves from the broth to a blender. Measure 3 cups of the broth into the blender and liquefy. Return the mixture to the saucepan and keep warm over low heat.

Heat the oil in a large skillet over medium heat. Add the sausages and slowly brown until fully cooked. Set aside on a heatproof plate and keep warm in a low oven. Pat the fat off the bottom of the skillet with paper towels, taking care not to disturb the sausage glaze. Add the garlic broth to the skillet and deglaze completely over medium heat. Set aside in a bowl.

Wash and dry the skillet. Heat it over medium-high heat, add the millet, and parch it, tossing constantly until the grain has uniformly turned deep golden. Add the garlic broth and sage leaf and cook over low heat until the millet is tender, 18 to 20 minutes. Turn into a serving dish and top with the prepared sausages and chopped parsley. Serve with a jar of mustard.

Cooking Wheat in Its Diverse Forms

For an extended discussion of the many types of wheats and flours, see pages 1003–17 in the baking chapter.

Wheat had been cooked as a gruel of cracked kernels for millennia before it became flour with which one could make leavened bread. In Latin the porridge was called *pulmentum* (see page 1020), often a mixture of several cereals almost always containing some crushed emmer and spelt, two very simple types of wheat very much used in antiquity by the Gauls and Latins.

The names are simple; emmer and spelt crushed together were called *far*, which gives us the root of the Italian *farro*, the modern word for spelt. According to historian Toussaint-Samat, *far*, over the centuries, became more and more finely milled thanks to several inventions by the Etruscans, Latins, and Gauls. It came in three different grades, depending on the size of the particles obtained. *Far* became *farina* in Latin, which was real flour, coarser than ours, but flour (it would possibly take its place today between our coarser flours and what we know as farina, our modern cereal resulting from coarsely milled very hard flours that produce particles which remain separate after cooking). It is possible that the Italian word *semola*, which passed into modern English as semolina, may have come from the Sanskrit *similia*. Madame Toussaint-Samat gives *similia* as the Latin word for extra finely milled flour, but I have not been able to verify its existence in my Latin dictionary, possibly because it is not extensive enough.

Wheat has been cooked in whole kernels from great antiquity and the dish persisted through the Middle Ages under the name *fromentée* in medieval France and frumenty in middle English. Wheat kernels are rarely cooked whole in this country although they are delicious and have a good chewy texture which, mixed with fresh vegetables, is most pleasant. The old spelt, although difficult to find, is becoming once more popular. Looking for emmer I have never been able to find any, but that does not mean that it does not exist anymore. It is preserved in seed libraries.

Whole Wheat

If you decide to cook whole wheat kernels, 1 cup wheat berries soaked and cooked yields 2 cups cooked berries and 6 portions. First and foremost soak the kernels in water overnight to soften the several layers of its bran covering. When ready to cook the berries, wash them and drain them well.

- Use a pot which you can close tightly. Add berries and enough water to cover them plus ½ inch. Bring to a boil over medium heat, turn down to a simmer, and, as the cereal cooks over low heat, add as many additions of warm water as needed to keep the expanding wheat just covered. Add salt only when the wheat kernels are almost finished cooking, or

- In an open pot, add the kernels to a large amount of boiling water, salted with 1½ teaspoons per quart water, turn down to a simmer, and let it cook for as long as it takes to soften the grains to an edible texture. Add warm water to the pot anytime the water level drops below that of the wheat.

Whichever method is used, expect the cooking time to be between 2 and 3 hours. The time will vary depending on:

- *The type of wheat.* There are hard and soft wheats. The kernels of hard wheats are short and squat-looking while those of soft wheats are longer and thinner. Soft wheats, which contain more starch than hard wheats, will most probably cook faster. However, when experimenting with wheats bought in a vegetarian supermarket in my area, I found that the soft wheat cooked slower than the hard one; this sounded illogical, so I reasoned that the soft wheat was older than the hard one. The second factor that is important when cooking wheat then is:
- *The age of the wheat.* You'll never quite know how old the wheat you're buying is, and the older it is, the longer it will take to soften the layers of bran and ultimately the endosperm, the starchy, proteinic center of the kernel.
- *The quality of the water you use.* I recommend you use water as pure as possible, like mineral water, the formula of which is available on the label. Too many minerals in the water may harden the bran and retard the swelling of the starches in the endosperm. Wheat will absorb at least three times its own volume in water.

Do not under any circumstances use a stock or broth to cook wheat. The gelatin in the stock slows the hydration of the bran and consequently that of the endosperm; this prevents the wheat from cooking or at least delays its softening. If you like the taste of stock in your grains (it is very good), reduce some stock to a glaze and mix it into the kernels of wheat after they are fully cooked.

What to do with cooked kernels of wheat? I prefer salads to any other preparation, but you certainly can replace the dressing with a light cream sauce, or one made with a vegetable broth. Here is a salad I like very much.

A Wheat Miller's Salad

SUGGESTED BEVERAGE:
Beer is best here but a pleasant light white wine such as Portuguese Vino Verde is delightful.

FCR— 6 SERVINGS

For the warm salad

½ cup warm cooked tiny carrots, sliced on a slant ⅛ inch thick

½ cup warm cooked yellow-striped beets, sliced ⅛ inch thick

½ cup warm cooked red-striped beets, sliced ⅛ inch thick

½ cup warm cooked rutabaga, cut into 1½ × ⅓-inch sticks

½ cup warm cooked small snow peas, cut in half on the diagonal

½ cup warm ¼-inch-thick celery slices, cut on the slant and stir-fried

½ cup warm red radishes, cut into ⅓-inch-wide strips, stir-fried

2 cups warm cooked wheat kernels (page 475)

Salt

Pepper from the mill

2 white endives, leaves separated

2 red endives, leaves separated

1 bunch watercress

½ cup coarsely chopped walnuts

For the dressing

½ cup stock of your choice, reduced to 2 tablespoons glaze (optional)

1 anchovy fillet, rinsed and mashed

2 cloves garlic, mashed

1 very large shallot, finely chopped and juices squeezed out in the corner of a kitchen
    towel

1½ teaspoons Dijon mustard

¼ cup sherry vinegar

1 cup walnut oil

3 tablespoons finely chopped fresh Italian parsley leaves

3 tablespoons finely chopped fresh chervil leaves

Mix the warm vegetables and wheat kernels together. Put all the dressing ingredients in a blender and process until smooth. Dress the salad with three quarters of the dressing. Toss well and correct with salt and pepper. Pile the salad in the center of a round platter; quickly surround with endive leaves of both colors and sprigs of watercress. Drizzle the remainder of the dressing over those and sprinkle the top of the salad with the chopped walnuts.

Cracked Wheat and Bulgur

The next wheat product that you should try is cracked wheat. Cracked wheat consists, not surprisingly, of uncooked wheat kernels that have been cracked into pieces. Occasionally you can find some imported from the Mediterranean but it is rare and one mostly has to settle for bulgur.

Bulgur is made of wheat kernels that have been industrially steamed and hulled, then redried and cracked into different textures. There is fine, medium, and coarse bulgur, and regular and organic bulgur. Try all the different types you can find. Prepare bulgur as you would a pilaf of rice, using 2½ cups of light stock or broth for each cup of bulgur. The best bulgurs come from the Middle East. I have used Greek bulgur with great pleasure. Here is one of the dishes I particularly enjoyed while traveling in Greece.

The Pligouri at Delphi

FCR to FFR — 6 SERVINGS

3 tablespoons light olive oil

1 large yellow onion, very finely chopped

2 cups medium bulgur

5 to 6 cups boiling light broth of your choice as needed

Salt

Pepper from the mill

3 ounces feta cheese, crumbled

3 scallions, finely sliced

Because of the feta, this recipe should be considered full fat for heart patients.

This is a memory of a lunch served in Delphi on a terrace facing the unending and magnificent sea of olive trees, which fills the valley of Delphi below the ancient temple, their leaves scintillating in the Greek sunshine.

SUGGESTED WINE: *A Greek Retsina of your choice*

Heat the oil in a heavy pot over medium heat, add the onion, and cook, stirring, until golden. Add the wheat and toss until well mixed with the oil. Keep tossing for a few minutes. Add 5 cups of the broth. Cover the pot with several layers of paper towels and the pot lid and bake in a preheated 325°F oven for 28 to 30 minutes. Taste for doneness; the grains should be firm, al dente. Correct the seasoning with salt and pepper.

Remove from the oven and fluff with a fork. If the grain is too dry, add more broth. Turn into a bowl and sprinkle with the crumbled feta and sliced scallions.

Couscous

Couscous is made from semolina grains agglutinated to one another by the work of very dexterous women's hands. I learned to prepare it by hand in Algiers under the direction of Fatma Charif, who called it *t'am*, and I still do it with pleasure. I cannot write the instructions better than Paula Wolfert did in her book *Couscous and Other Good Food from Morocco* and urge you to refer to her description if you want to learn "the long way." The technique I learned was somewhat different but the results identical.

Those of you who are not tempted (I am not always because of the time involved, and I use instant couscous myself about half the time) by the rolling of the couscous grains in an oval basin and the multiple strainings of the coarse grains to separate them from the tiny grains of semolina will have to use instant couscous, which is sold ready to cook by simple addition of hot broth.

Couscous Fatma

FCR — 6 SERVINGS

6 chicken legs, cut into drumsticks and thighs

Salt

½ teaspoon cayenne pepper

1 teaspoon black peppercorns

6 cloves garlic, crushed

2 tablespoons finely chopped cilantro leaves

2 large, sun-ripened tomatoes, peeled, seeded, and finely chopped

3 large yellow onions, quartered, then separated into layers

Pure olive oil as needed

2 cups instant couscous

⅓ cup dried currants

½ cup whole blanched almonds, very lightly toasted (page 50)

½ teaspoon ground cinnamon

Couscous is the last dish served in a formal Mahgrebine dinner and is always accompanied by a meat sauce, here made with chicken. Of course you can use couscous by itself garnished with the herbs and aromatics of your choice or, as here, with spices and fruit. For each cup of instant couscous, use 1 to 1⅛ cups of water or broth. The swelling capability of the grains varies slightly with the brand used.

SUGGESTED BEVERAGE: *I serve chilled mint tea with a tad of sugar.*

Wash and dry the chicken pieces. Rub them with salt, then sprinkle them with the cayenne pepper. Let stand at room temperature for 30 minutes, covered. Place the pieces in a large sauteuse pan and add warm water to cover the chicken plus 1 inch. Bring to a boil, then add the peppercorns. Reduce the heat to medium-low and simmer while you mash together the garlic and cilantro. After they have turned into a paste, add them to the broth along with the tomatoes, onions, and a large splash of olive oil. Simmer until the chicken is very tender, about 35 minutes, keeping the sauteuse lid slightly askew to allow for evaporation. When the chicken is cooked, remove enough broth from the sauteuse to equal the volume of couscous, or a tad more if needed.

Mix the couscous, 2 tablespoons olive oil, the currants, almonds, and cinnamon together in an enameled cast-iron pot. Add the reserved hot broth. Fluff with a fork, cover, and let the couscous swell over very low heat for 6 to 8 minutes.

Fluff the couscous with the tines of a fork again before piling it onto a shallow round dish. Arrange the pieces of chicken around the couscous, spoon the remaining sauce into a small bowl, and serve immediately.

Semolina

As we know it in America, semolina is made from the milled midlings of durum wheat (see page 1013) ground fine enough to pass through a regular sieve.

Semolina is versatile; it is used in the making of pasta (see page 1013), dumplings, dessert puddings, bread (see page 1013), and as a support of a vegetarian diet. With an addition of eggs and garnished with cheese and vegetables it can become a delicious and complete lacto-vegetarian meal. The most celebrated dish made with semolina is the famous *gnocchi alla Romana* made from a gruel of semolina to which Parmigiano-Reggiano cheese is added and topped with more cheese and melted butter; this is as delicious as it is nourishing, especially if enjoyed in its full glory once or twice a year.

The amount of liquid semolina can absorb varies greatly and depends on how it is cooked:

- As a gruel and pudding, it will need four times its own volume of water or milk to swell to its maximum.
- When used in dumplings, however, use an equal volume of liquid, as the semolina will finish softening as it poaches in water or very light stock.

Bean Ragout on Semolina Cakes

FCR to FFR— 12 CAKES FOR 6 DINNER OR 12 LUNCH SERVINGS

For the cakes

Melted unsalted butter or unsaturated oil of your choice as needed

3 cups milk of your choice

¾ cup uncooked semolina

1 large egg plus 1 large egg white, beaten together

½ cup freshly grated Pecorino Romano cheese

Salt

Pepper from the mill

Freshly grated nutmeg

For the bean ragout

1½ cups bean cooking liquid

1 tablespoon cornstarch

2 cloves garlic, finely chopped

1 teaspoon ground cumin

1 pasilla chile, seeds removed and finely chopped

1 cup cooked red pinto beans

1 cup cooked Great Northern or cannellini beans

1 cup cooked black beans

1 cup cooked lima beans

1 cup ½-inch pieces cooked Blue Lake green beans

1 cup ½-inch pieces cooked wax beans

2 tablespoons chopped fresh Italian parsley leaves

2 tablespoons chopped cilantro leaves

¾ cup grated queso Oaxaca or other melting cheese of your choice

This recipe is to be considered full fat for heart patients because of the Pecorino cheese. Although home-cooked beans will always be superior, you can use canned beans if you like.

SUGGESTED BEVERAGE:
Dos Equis beer

Using a brush, butter or oil very lightly a (preferably) nonstick 13 × 9-inch jelly-roll pan.

Bring 1½ cups of the milk to a boil in a 2-quart enameled cast-iron pot. Turn the milk down to a simmer. Dilute the semolina with the remaining cold milk and, stirring constantly, add the mixture to the simmering milk. Bring to a boil and continue stirring until the gruel has boiled and thickened enough for a wooden spoon to stand in it. Off the heat, add the beaten eggs, the grated cheese, salt, pepper, and nutmeg to taste.

Spread the semolina evenly over the prepared jelly-roll pan. Cool completely and cut into twelve equal pieces. When ready to reheat for service, brush the cakes with butter or oil and cover with a sheet of parchment paper. Preheat the oven to 325°F, then bake 15 to 20 minutes to warm.

Meanwhile, prepare the bean ragout. Mix the bean cooking water with the cornstarch in a large saucepan and bring to a boil. Reduce the heat to medium and cook until lightly thickened. Add the garlic, cumin, and pasilla chile, then mix in all the beans and simmer a full 20 minutes. Add the parsley and cilantro.

Place two semolina cakes on each of six plates. Spoon an equal amount of bean ragout over each cake, sprinkle with the cheese, and serve promptly while bright hot.

Cooking Corn in All Its Forms

We were all happy to know that corn had been cultivated in North America for 8,000 years until an article published in the *New York Times* in March 1995 gave us more food for thought. According to the latest information, the cultivation started only around 4,700 years ago. However, experts in the distinguished discipline of paleobotany have cautioned us not to jump to conclusions, so we will simply rejoice and be grateful for corn and the bounty it represents for all of us.

You all know what a fresh ear of corn wrapped in its own husk and slowly grilled at the edge of the barbecue rack tastes like, especially when rubbed with a nice fat piece of butter. It is simply heavenly; this French-born writer, who knew corn only through the provincial *millias* (cakes) and *gaudes* (soups) of her own country, quickly succumbed to gluttony on her first meeting with fresh grilled corn way back in 1960 while attending her first American barbecue.

We also eat fresh corn off its cob in kernels, we eat it as cornmeal in mush and breads, and we eat it in grits and hominy, the preparation of which seems to be understood best by the cooks of the Deep South.

As opposed to those vegetables that traveled from Europe to the Americas after Christopher Columbus rediscovered what Leif Erikson had already discovered as Vinland, corn traveled from America to Spain, then to the Basque country and other enclaves of the southwest of France. It also reached the French Bresse, the French Alps, and the Italian Piemonte which, if one stops to reflect, is where the armies of the then King of Spain brought it. In all these parts of Europe, one still uses cornmeal for many preparations. To a mash made of cornmeal mixed with powdered milk and water, the French owe those marvels called the Bresse chickens.

Grits

Grits are made from the grinding of white corn, which grows in the South. And as far as my southern friends are concerned, the only grits worth buying are stone-ground grits. Because I do not want to lose my southern friends, I voted a long time ago for stone-ground grits, and nothing else; but my reason is selfish—I simply like them better than the boxed grits.

Stone-ground grits are never served alone, they are just one part of that wondrous meal called breakfast in the Deep South. Their grits come with country ham and lots of redeye gravy, made with the ham drippings and—coffee. If you like having a dish of just grits, because you like the taste of the pure grits, you better say nothing and do your eating in secret. I do, or often I add things I should not add such as compotes of fresh fruit which are so good. Sorry, John, here comes grits with compote. At least I use your stone-ground grits.

RATIO OF GRITS TO WATER One cup of stone-ground grits will need 4 cups of boiling water to soften properly, and this will happen in 35 to 45 minutes with you stirring at regular intervals to make sure that nothing drastic is happening at the bottom of the pot. This amount will serve 6 people.

Grits and Red Rhubarb Compote

This recipe is fat-controlled only if you use no butter.

FCR to FFR—6 SERVINGS
For the compote
6 stalks rhubarb
½ cup firmly packed light brown sugar
Tiny pinch of salt
½ pint fresh raspberries
½ pint fresh strawberries, hulled and quartered

For the grits
1 cup stone-ground grits
4 cups spring water
Salt
Unsalted butter to taste

Peel the rhubarb stalks, cut them into 1-inch chunks, and wash them well. Put them into a large saucepan, add the brown sugar and salt, and cook over low heat until the rhubarb has completely fallen apart, about 20 minutes. Take the compote off the heat and stir in the two berries. Let cool completely.

While the fruit cooks, add the grits to a bowl of cold water and stir a few seconds with your hand. All kinds of chaff will come floating to the surface. Take a paper towel and wet it lightly. Let it fall on the surface of the water and lift it immediately; the chaff will come away attached to the paper towel. Drain the grits into a large conical strainer. Repeat this operation several times until all the chaff is gone.

Bring 2 cups of the spring water to a boil in a large saucepan while you dissolve the grits in the remaining water. Stirring constantly, gradually add the grits slurry to the boiling water and reduce the heat to a simmer. Stir at regular short intervals making sure that the grits do not burn at the bottom of the pan. In 38 to 45 minutes you will have a creamy, absolutely delicious mixture, which you can salt to your taste and turn into a warmed bowl. Put the butter to melt on it and pass it around; if you are lucky your guests will not have eaten all of them by the time you pour the fresh compote into another bowl.

If there are some left, top them with a nice serving of compote.

Cornmeal

There is regular cornmeal and there is organically grown stone-ground polenta. Try both; they taste very different. So does the white finely bolted cornmeal which in the first edition of this book I used to prepare a pleasant crepe batter (see page 1023).

There is cooked cornmeal mush and there is cooked polenta. The American poet Joel Barlow did not seem to notice any difference between the two when traveling through the French Alps in 1793. He was so delighted with the local *polente* that he wrote his famous Hasty Pudding poem.

But the Italians, like the southerners with their grits, insist that there is a difference. So that you may judge, here are three recipes: one for Hush Kiddies made with plain ordinary cornmeal, one for a polenta pilaf also made with ordinary cornmeal, and the last for a serious dish of true Piedmontese polenta that I hope you will try with organic stone-ground Italian polenta bought from an Italian grocery store.

Hush Kiddies

FFR— 18 TO 24 PIECES

The hush puppies of southern fishermen. These are best for a snack or an appetizer at a barbecue. Made first, not for my own kiddies, but for two little French squirmers I was babysitting. The cornmeal fritters took care of the problem.

1½ cups cornmeal

⅔ cup sifted unbleached all-purpose flour

Dash of salt

1 tablespoon granulated sugar

¼ teaspoon ground cinnamon

¼ teaspoon finely grated lemon rind

1 large egg yolk

¾ cup milk of your choice

2 large egg whites

Unsaturated oil of your choice for deep-frying

Cherry jam or Fresh Cherry Compote (page 935)

Mix together the dry ingredients and lemon rind in a medium-size bowl. Beat the egg yolk together with the milk. Stir this into the cornmeal mixture until smooth. In another bowl, beat the egg whites until they can carry the weight of a raw egg in its shell without sinking by more than ¼ inch. Fold into the batter, overfolding slightly.

Heat 3 inches of the oil to 370°F (see page 632). Drop small spoonfuls of the batter into the hot oil and fry until crisp and uniformly gold in color, 1 minute or so. Remove to crumpled paper towels to drain and serve piping hot with the cherry jam or compote.

Polenta the French Way

FFR to FCR— 6 SERVINGS

The French of the northern Alps cook their polenta like a rice pilaf. The ragout of broad beans was once served during the medieval Foire du Lendict, the ancient two-week-long June fair celebrating spring held in the Landit plain, between Paris and the St. Denis Abbey.

For the polenta

¼ cup unsalted butter or 3 tablespoons unsaturated oil of your choice

2 medium-size yellow onions, very finely chopped

1½ cups coarse cornmeal

4½ cups boiling broth of your choice

Salt

Pepper from the mill

For the broad bean ragout

3 pounds shelled and peeled medium-size broad beans or 3 cups fresh or frozen medium-size lima beans

2 large yellow onions, sliced

Broth of your choice, to cover

1 anchovy fillet, rinsed and mashed

Few saffron threads

Preheat the oven to 300°F. In a 2-quart enameled cast-iron pan, heat 2 tablespoons of the butter or oil over medium-high heat. Add the onions and sauté until translucent. Add the cornmeal and toss together well. Add the boiling broth, season with salt and pepper, and stir well. Cover, place in the oven, and cook until all the liquid has been absorbed, 35 to 40 minutes. Add the remaining butter or oil to the polenta and fluff with a fork.

Meanwhile, mix the ragout ingredients together in a large saucepan and cook over medium heat until the beans are tender, about 30 minutes. Check for doneness and add small quantities of water or broth if necessary while cooking. The juice should just surround the beans.

Serve the beans over the polenta.

Rich Polenta from the Italian Piedmont
POLENTA GRASSA ALLA PIEMONTESE

FFR — 6 SERVINGS

4 heads escarole, washed and finely chopped

3 to 4 tablespoons unsalted butter or light olive oil as needed

2 large yellow onions, finely chopped

1 cup heavy cream

One 4-ounce piece prosciutto, ¼ inch thick

Salt

Pepper from the mill

2 cups stone-ground organic cornmeal

2 cups cold water or broth of your choice

6 cups boiling water or broth of your choice or half boiling water and half scalded hot milk

Freshly grated nutmeg

⅓ cup freshly grated Parmigiano-Reggiano cheese

Eight ¼-inch-thick slices Italian fontina cheese

Spin the greens as dry as possible. Heat 2 to 3 tablespoons of the chosen fat in a large sauteuse pan over medium-high heat. Add the onions and sauté until golden. Add the escarole and cook over medium-low heat until reduced to 2 small cups. Add the cream and prosciutto, season with salt and pepper, and cook just a few minutes. Set aside.

Dissolve the cornmeal in the cold water; stirring contantly, add the slurry to the boiling water, as well as salt, pepper, and nutmeg to taste. Cook over medium-low heat until the spoon stands up straight in the polenta mixture, about 40 minutes. Add the Parmigiano cheese.

Butter a 2-quart dish with the remaining 1 tablespoon butter or oil. Add

SUGGESTED WINE: Any light white or red wine of your choice, but a Mondeuse or a Chambave would be perfect if you can find it.

From the Italian side of the Alps and the little township of Morgex.

half of the hot polenta, spreading it out evenly over the bottom of the dish. Spread the escarole mixture on top, then spoon and spread the remainder of the polenta over the greens. Smooth well and top with the slices of fontina. Bake until the cheese has melted and starts to turn golden, about 15 minutes.

Cooking Quinoa and Amaranth

Quinoa is an ancient grain used by the Incas of the Andes. It is found in all mountain regions, the Andes as well as the Rockies and the Alps. It is a plant of the genus *Chenopodium* which is used in the French Alps as a replacement for spinach and because its high calcium content was considered prime nutrition for people suffering from lung diseases.

Amaranth—from the Greek *amaraton* meaning nonfading—belongs to a genus of plants producing bright red flowers, the seeds from which were used by the Aztecs for religious food when Cortez arrived in Mexico. The conquistador became so upset by the confection (it was cooked in sacrificial human blood) that he ordered every single plant he could lay eyes and hands on destroyed. Amaranth survived, however, and resurfaced a few years ago as the interesting and nutritious cereal that it is.

Both quinoa and amaranth do not always do well on a dinner plate because of their looks. This is why I propose here cakes made with the grains. They can be served under a vegetable ragout for a vegetarian main course or as a garnish for a nonvegetarian meal.

The ratio of water to grain for both are: in volume, twice as much water as grain. Both are cooked over medium-low heat, quinoa for 10 to 15 minutes, amaranth for 20 to 25 minutes.

Amaranth or Quinoa Cakes

FFR to FCR — 12 CAKES 3 INCHES IN DIAMETER

1 cup amaranth or quinoa

2 cups cold water

3 tablespoons unsalted butter or unsaturated oil of your choice

1 cup sifted unbleached all-purpose flour

1 teaspoon baking powder

3 large eggs, separated

1 cup milk of your choice

Salt

Pepper from the mill

¼ cup chopped cilantro leaves

Mix the grain with the water in a small saucepan. Slowly bring to a boil and let simmer until all the water has been absorbed. Add the butter, stirring gently until melted. Cool at least to lukewarm.

Mix the flour, baking powder, egg yolks, milk, salt, pepper, and cilantro together into a smooth batter in a large bowl. Beat the egg whites in a medium-size bowl to stage 3 foam (see page 166). Add the grain to the yolk batter. Mix one quarter of the whites into the batter, then fold in the remainder until completely homogeneous.

Cook the cakes for 2 minutes on each side in a hot nonstick frying pan over medium-high heat until golden on both sides.

If you want to know all about cooking all types of grains, please consult the excellent book written by my late colleague Bert Greene called *The Grain Cookbook* (Workman, 1988).

Legumes

Legumes are the seeds of different beans and peas which have been dried for preservation during the winter months.

They present absolutely no difficulty in their preparation; the only technique used to soften them is boiling. They can, after being partially boiled, be baked as in the classic American Boston baked beans.

Beans, Peas, and Chick Peas

You have a vast choice. Preferably buy organic beans; I find that they taste better and if you can choose those sold in the fall at farmers' markets, they will come from the current year crop and cook relatively faster than those bought in supermarkets which wait in storage before finding their way onto the shelf.

THE WHITE VARIETIES White beans require the longest time to cook, with navy beans often taking up to three hours, which makes them perfect for baking (see page 491). Great Northern and butter beans (originally the Soissons variety) cook faster. White peas such as chick peas (garbanzos) require long, slow cooking but black-eyed peas are ready in a relatively short time.

THE ROSE TO BLACK VARIETIES Black, pinto, pinquitos, cranberry, black runners, and kidney beans cook faster than the white beans.

THE GREEN VARIETIES Lima beans must be presoaked for 8 hours but will cook in a very short time—sometimes as little as 15 to 18 minutes—after soaking. The pale green French flageolets are very lovely, but they are expensive for they must be produced and consumed within the same year. This makes them difficult to find in this country where you will pay premium price for imported flageolets which, you will soon find out, will never cook fully. The cost of the beans is so prohibitive that few people buy them; they stay on the shelves of fancy grocery stores, whose managers may not know that their shelf life is so limited.

It is best before cooking beans to soak them overnight in cold water to cover to soften their outer skins and let the starches held in their cotyledons absorb as much water as they possibly can without being heated. If you are fairly certain that the beans are of the current year crop, you can dispense with soaking; simply put the beans in cold water, let them come slowly to a boil over low heat, and, as soon as they boil, turn the heat off and let them stand for 2 hours, until they are almost cold. Then start the real cooking in the same water. This method is advocated in many of the recipes given on market-bought bags of beans.

If the just described method is not used, *the cooking of presoaked beans always starts in fresh cold water* to allow for a continued, very progressive absorption of water and full softening of the starches. Vegetarians should cook legumes in their soaking water to keep the nutrients that leached into it during soaking. The aromatics of your choice should always be added after the boiling point has been reached to prevent their taste from permeating the beans too strongly. Starting the cooking of soaked legumes in hot or boiling water yields legumes that never soften properly and, especially in the case of red beans, may not always destroy their content of haemaglutinin, causing rapid intestinal distress.

No one type of bean will cook the same length of time ever, due to the different mineral makeups of the different soils in which they are grown. So cook gently for half an hour, then start tasting regularly; the cooking to the perfect texture can vary between 50 minutes and 3 hours. Add boiling lightly salted water as needed to always maintain enough water over the beans or other legumes. Taste often. When I was a child my mother taught me how to check the doneness of beans by blowing on a spoonful of them; if the thin skins lifted backward to form miniature curly "bonnets" looking exactly like reduced-size models of the coifs of the Sisters of St. Vincent de Paul, the beans were declared fully cooked. This rule still applies; do not let the beans fall apart completely.

Boiled legumes can be mashed to obtain delicious purees which should be well buttered and strained to discard the skins, which are not digested until their nutritional content reaches the lower intestine. This problem can be avoided by adding to each plate of ready-to-be-served beans three drops of the necessary enzyme, which is sold in health food stores under the name Beano.

Lentils and Split Peas

Unless they have been sitting in your cupboard for years, lentils and split peas need not be soaked overnight before cooking. However, note that the green and brown-black ⅙-inch-wide *lentilles du Puy* taste best if you give them a 4-hour soak in cold water before cooking them. Brown lentils also taste better after soaking for 30 minutes in barely lukewarm water before the final cooking starts. Scottish orange lentils which have been taken out of their skins cook very rapidly without presoaking. Otherwise, you can follow all the rules indicated above for beans and chick peas.

Canned Legumes

The United States canning industry is extremely successful in producing excellent canned legumes which are rarely mushy or overcooked. The canning juices of these legumes can be used in their preparation provided they are reboiled. Reboiling legumes coming from cans for 20 minutes is essential for food safety especially if you are going to use the beans in a salad; please go back to page 362 and read before you make a salad with canned beans.

The discarding of the water in which canned beans are cooked is not necessary if you are going to use canned beans for a soup or a chili. Rinsing the beans as is often done "to rinse them of salt" is not going to take the salt out of the beans, for the salt has already penetrated their starches and cannot be removed in any way.

Although I have not found a text explaining the possible hardening effect of acids on the pulp of legumes, you will notice that all baked compositions of beans and tomatoes are always prepared with beans that have been cooked until at least four fifths done.

Here are a few bean recipes:

Polka-Dot Puree of Beans

FFR—6 SERVINGS

1½ pounds dried **Great Northern** beans, soaked overnight in cold water to cover and
   drained

2 large yellow onions, peeled and each stuck with 2 cloves

2 bay leaves

2 sprigs fresh thyme

10 parsley stems

Salt

Pepper from the mill

1 pound dried black beans, soaked overnight in cold water to cover and drained

2 to 8 tablespoons unsalted butter or to your personal taste

¼ cup crème fraîche or sour cream

3 tablespoons chopped fresh curly parsley leaves

To be served with winter dishes of lamb, pork, chicken, or turkey. Use any leftover black beans and bean cooking broth as the start of an improvised vegetable soup; see the soup chapter for ideas.

Put the presoaked white beans in a large pot with enough fresh cold water to cover by 1 inch. Slowly bring to a boil over low heat. When the water boils, add 1 of the clove-stuck onions and 1 of the bay leaves, 1 sprig of the thyme, and 5 of the parsley stems all tied together into a bouquet garni. Bring to a boil and season the water with salt and pepper. Again turn down to a simmer, and continue cooking, covered with a lid left slightly askew, over medium-low heat until tender, 1 to 1½ hours.

Using another pot, repeat exactly the same operations using the black beans and the remaining aromatics. The cooking time will be only 40 to 45 minutes.

Drain both beans into two different bowls, discarding the aromatics and reserving the juices of the white beans. Put the hot Great Northern beans in a food processor with a few tablespoons of their cooking water and process into a not too stiff but not too light puree. Strain the puree through a conical strainer to discard all traces of skins. Add as much butter as you will allow yourself.

Blend all or as much of the black beans as you wish into the white puree. Correct the seasoning with more salt and pepper if needed and finally blend the crème fraîche and chopped parsley into the mixture. Serve piping hot on heated plates.

La Menouille

FFR—6 TO 8 SERVINGS

1 pound dried **Great Northern** beans, soaked overnight in cold water to cover and drained

1 medium-size yellow onion, peeled and stuck with 2 cloves

1 sprig fresh thyme

1 bay leaf

5 parsley stems

Salt

Pepper from the mill

1 pound slab bacon, cut into lardons (page 1165) ⅓ inch wide

¼ cup canola oil or unsalted butter, as preferred

2 California White Rose potatoes, peeled and diced into ½-inch cubes

1 cup dry white wine (optional)

1½ cups fresh bread crumbs from French bread

1 tablespoon finely chopped fresh savory leaves

The famous dish of baked beans made in Boston since the colonial days is one of the greatest culinary creations in the world as far as I am concerned. This sweet dish can be considered the prototype of "baked beans," be they baked the New England colonial way or any other way which consists of precooking the beans in water, then baking them with additional seasonings.

This is a main course in itself and must be served with a crisp green salad, preferably with a low-calorie dressing. It comes from the kitchen of one of my great-grandmothers and from the very northern part of France.

SUGGESTED BEVERAGE:
Beer of your choice; try the Lambic of the Belgian and French Flanders

Put the presoaked beans in a large pot. Add enough fresh cold water to cover by 2 inches and slowly bring to a boil over low heat. Add the cloved onion and the thyme, bay leaf, and parsley tied together into a bouquet garni, and salt and pepper. Cook, covered with a lid left slightly askew, until the beans are done only al dente, 40 to 45 minutes. Remove the pot from the heat, but keep it warm.

Put the bacon lardons in a cold skillet, then slowly raise the heat to medium to allow them to render their fat; toss often until the lardons are golden but not crisp inside. Remove to crumpled paper towels which will absorb their excess superficial fat. Discard the fat in the frying pan and deglaze the caramelized bacon juices in the pan with ½ cup of the bean cooking juices. Pour the deglazing into a bowl and set aside.

Clean and dry the skillet; add the canola oil and heat to high. Add the potatoes and toss them in the hot oil until they start to turn light golden but are not cooked to their center. Remove to a plate.

Preheat the oven to 325°F. Rub a 2-quart baking dish with a thin layer of the frying oil. Drain the beans completely, reserving the cooking juices. Once they appear well drained, empty them into the baking dish; add the lardons and potatoes and mix well. Mix the wine with the deglazing of the bacon and 2 cups of the bean cooking juice. Pour over the vegetables. Now add only as much additional bean juice as will cover the vegetables by ⅛ inch.

Bake, uncovered, until the juices in the dish have reduced to ⅛ inch below the vegetables, about 30 minutes. Mix the bread crumbs, savory, and a pinch of salt together and sprinkle evenly over the top. Continue baking another half hour; the liquid in the dish should by now have reduced by a full half. Remove from the oven and let stand 10 minutes before serving.

A Form of Cassoulet

This is by no means a true cassoulet; it is only a shortened version of it, but it will taste respectably authentic. No dish resembling a cassoulet can ever be produced with canned beans. You can make the confit months ahead of time if you use the high dose of salt recommended in the section on confits on page 785. If you prefer to buy canned confit from France, expect it to be expensive, but it will save you work and taste as it should. When cooking the beans immerse them in plenty of water so that you have enough bean water to moisten the dish should it dry out a little too much while baking.

Warning: Because duck and sausage are already quite salty, I am not mentioning salt and pepper again in the building of the confit. Taste the mixture at all stages of its cooking and if not seasoned enough, add salt and pepper to your taste.

SUGGESTED WINE: *Cahors from the French southwestern countryside or, if you prefer, any full-bodied red wine made in the United States from any varietal grape*

FFR—6 SERVINGS

I pound dried navy beans, soaked overnight in cold water to cover and drained

2 medium-size yellow onions, peeled and each stuck with I clove

Bouquet garni made of I bay leaf, I sprig fresh thyme, and 5 parsley stems

2 fresh pork hocks, blanched in boiling water for 5 minutes

Salt

Pepper from the mill

I recipe confited duck legs (page 790) or one I-quart can confit of duck imported from France

½ cup water

6 links sweet Italian sausage with fennel seeds

2 medium-size yellow onions, finely chopped

1½ cups tomato coulis (page 309) or vegetarian tomato sauce containing no bell peppers (page 310)

I large clove garlic, crushed

3 cloves garlic, finely chopped

1½ cups fresh bread crumbs

3 tablespoons chopped fresh parsley leaves

Put the beans in a large pot, cover them with fresh cold water to reach 2½ inches above the beans. Bring slowly to a boil over medium heat, add the cloved onions, the bouquet garni, and blanched hocks, and season with salt and pepper. Bring to a second boil, turn down to a simmer, and cook on medium-low heat until the beans are al dente, 35 to 40 minutes. Remove and dice the lean meat only from the hocks, discarding the other parts. Keep the beans warm in their cooking juices. You will drain them into a colander, keeping their juices, just before building the cassoulet.

Meanwhile, heat the confited duck legs slowly in their fat. Remove them from the fat bath and pat them dry in paper towels. Remove their skin and bones, chop the meat very coarsely and add to the hock plate. Set aside.

In a sauteuse pan or skillet add the water and sausage links. Cook over medium heat until the water has evaporated and the sausages have rendered some of their fat. Continue browning them lightly on all sides until they have rendered more fat. Remove the sausages to the same plate as the hock and duck meats, and blot the sausage fat away with crumpled paper towels. Deglaze the caramelized sausage juices with ½ cup of the bean cooking water and set aside.

Wipe the pan clean; add 3 tablespoons of the confit fat and over medium-high heat brown the chopped onions lightly. Add the tomato *coulis* and 2 cups of the bean cooking water and bring to a boil; reduce the heat and simmer for 15 minutes.

Preheat the oven to 325°F. Now build the cassoulet: Use a 2-quart heavy ceramic baking dish. Rub its surface first with the crushed garlic clove, then with a thin layer of the confit fat. Add half of the drained beans, then sprinkle them with one third of the chopped garlic. Add the boned and skinned duck legs, sausages, and pieces of hocks. Add half the mixture of tomato sauce and bean juice; top with another third of the garlic; add the remainder of the beans and the remainder of the tomato mixture. Add as much extra bean juice as needed to reach ⅛ inch above the beans and bake uncovered until the broth is level with the beans, about 45 minutes.

If the broth has dipped below the beans, add enough reserved bean juice so it comes level again with the beans. Mix the bread crumbs, the remaining garlic, and the parsley together and sprinkle evenly over the cassoulet. Cook another 30 minutes. Push the crust of crumbs down; return it to the oven and bake another 30 minutes. Check one last time that the beans are not dry, adding more reserved bean juice if necessary. Continue baking another 30 minutes and remove from the oven. Let cool 10 minutes and serve piping hot. A cassoulet is bound with just enough broth to keep the beans together and should never be "out of juice."

Curried Warm Lentil Salad

FCR—6 SERVINGS

2 cups dried green lentils, picked over

I small yellow onion, peeled and stuck with 2 cloves

I sprig fresh thyme

5 parsley stems

I bay leaf

Salt

Pepper from the mill

I clove garlic, coarsely chopped

3 tablespoons wine or cider vinegar

½ cup pure olive oil

I ½ teaspoons fresh curry powder

I scallion, thinly sliced

I red bell pepper, seeded and sliced

I yellow bell pepper, seeded and sliced

I green bell pepper, seeded and sliced

I teaspoon finely crushed dried green peppercorns

I very large shallot, finely chopped

2 tablespoons chopped fresh parsley leaves

Although this recipe calls for green Le Puy lentils imported from France, you can make it with the lentils of your choice. Simply adjust the cooking time.

SUGGESTED BEVERAGE:
Perrier or light beer

Soak the lentils in barely lukewarm water for 1 hour. Discard the soaking water and put the lentils in a large saucepan. Cover the lentils with fresh cold water to cover by 1 inch. Slowly bring to a boil over medium heat, add the onion, and the thyme, parsley stems, and bay leaf tied together into a bouquet garni, and salt and pepper. Bring back to a boil, then turn down to low heat and cook, covered with a lid left slightly askew, until the lentils are fully tender, 35 to 40 minutes. Drain the lentils of their cooking juices and keep warm.

Remove the clove from the cooked onion, then cut up the onion, letting the pieces drop into a blender. Add the garlic, vinegar, and ⅓ cup of the olive oil. Cook the curry for 2 minutes in the remainder of the oil and add to the dressing. Season with salt and pepper and process until a smooth, creamy dressing results. Correct the seasoning, then toss the lentils with two thirds of the dressing.

Mix together the sliced scallion, the sliced peppers, peppercorns, shallot, salt and pepper to taste, and the remainder of the dressing. Arrange the lentil salad on the mixture of garnishes. Sprinkle with the chopped parsley.

Euro-American Ways with Pasta

What this means is that all the noodle and pasta dishes described in this section will be exclusively Euro-American. For noodles of Far Eastern origin, please refer to the books listed in the bibliography.

Any of the dishes proposed in this section can be used for a good supper or lunch accompanied by your favorite salad. You can, if you wish, add a little more protein to any of them in the form of well-rendered bacon nicely crumbled in the American manner, or pancetta or fresh pork brisket lardons diced and sautéed golden but not crisp as the Italians and French like it, added to the sauce or directly to the noodles.

Practical Pasta Without Too Much Hand Work: Spätzle

Spätzle are daily fare in all Germanic countries; they are found everywhere, in Austria, Switzerland, Germany, and, of course, in lovely Hungary and that wonderful Alemanic-speaking province of France, the beautiful Alsace.

The dish of spätzle that follows is a variation on those I presented in my television series; they are, basically, the plain, protein-rich formula of my Lorraine great-aunt Orelly, but I have added a lot of greens to change the taste and extend the nutritional power. You can vary the herbs as you wish.

Spätzle with Radishes and Pickling Cukes

SPÄTZLE MIT RADIESLE UND GÜRKELE

FFR — 6 SERVINGS

1 bunch red radishes

3 tablespoons unsaturated oil of your choice

2 tablespoons cider vinegar

Salt

Pepper from the mill

6 pickling cucumbers (like Kirbys), scrubbed, ends removed, and sliced

1¼ cups unsifted unbleached all-purpose flour

1 cup pasta flour (fine semolina)

1 teaspoon chopped fresh thyme leaves

2 cloves garlic, mashed into a puree

6 large eggs, well beaten

⅓ to ½ cup milk of your choice as needed

As much butter as you will allow your family

2 tablespoons chopped fresh parsley leaves

SUGGESTED WINE: *Any wine you like, simple and down to earth*

Wash and clean the radishes. Slice the bulbs into ⅛-inch-thick slices. Pat dry and chop the green leaves very finely; set those aside. Heat half the oil in a large skillet over high heat, then add the radishes and vinegar and sauté until the skins turn bright red; salt and pepper well. Remove to a waiting plate.

In the same pan, add the remainder of the oil and stir-fry the cucumbers for 3 minutes, then salt and pepper them well. Remove them to a second plate to prevent the vinegar in the radishes from discoloring them.

Mix the flours in a large bowl, make a well, and add the chopped radish leaves, thyme, 1 teaspoon salt, pepper to taste, and the mashed garlic. Pour in the beaten eggs and, using a large wooden spatula, gradually draw the flour into the liquids. Stir well to develop a tad of gluten for better texture; the mixture should be thick enough to spread on a cutting board without dripping. If it drips, add some flour; if, on the contrary, the batter is too thick, dilute with the milk, adding 2 tablespoons at a time. Let stand 15 minutes.

Bring a large pot of water to a boil, salt it, and turn the heat down to a steady simmer. Spread some of the batter ¼ inch thick on a small chopping board or the bottom of a cake pan and "shave" ¼-inch-wide ribbons of batter into the water. The spätzle are done when they float to the surface of the water. Gather them up with a large, round, slotted spoon, so they can drip all their water quickly, and put them in a dish containing at least 2 tablespoons butter. Keep warm in a low oven. Keep cooking the noodles and adding them to the dish; add more oil or butter as needed but neither too much nor too little. Finally when all the noodles are cooked, reheat the radishes and cucumbers in the same pan and toss with the noodles. Serve sprinkled with the chopped parsley and accompany with a nice green salad.

Gnocchi the French Way

French gnocchi are made from unsweetened or barely sweetened cream puff dough containing fewer eggs than the regular baked formula of this pastry; they are poached in water, then baked slowly in a light cream sauce, generally well mixed with cheese, until the gnocchi puff. These gnocchi make a nice weekend supper with a green salad.

Gnocchi de Châtaignes

FFR—6 SERVINGS

I tablespoon corn or walnut oil

I large yellow onion, finely chopped

6 largest ribs of a celery heart, peeled and thinly sliced

¼ teaspoon celery salt

Pepper from the mill

1½ cups light cream

1½ tablespoons cornstarch

⅔ cup grated Cantal, Comté, or Gruyère cheese

I cup Pure Vegetable Broth (page 213) or other broth of your choice

¼ cup unsalted butter, diced

¾ teaspoon salt

½ cup sifted unbleached all-purpose flour

½ cup unsifted chestnut flour

3 large eggs, beaten separately

Heat the oil in a sauteuse pan over medium heat. Add the onion, cook, stirring, a few minutes, then cover and cook until soft. Mix into the onion the celery, celery salt, and pepper to taste. Cover and cook over low heat until the celery has fallen apart, adding a dash of water here and there if too dry. Empty into a blender and puree. Strain, then keep warm.

Meanwhile, mix the cream with the cornstarch in a small saucepan, bring to a boil, and thicken, stirring constantly. Add the celery *coulis* to the cream sauce. Keep warm. Very lightly oil a 9-inch ovenproof dish. Pour half the celery cream into the dish and sprinkle it with half the cheese. Preheat the oven to 325°F.

Pour the chosen broth into a large saucepan, add the butter, salt, and pepper to taste. Mix the flours together on a plate. Bring a pot of water to a boil, salt it lightly, and turn the heat down to a simmer.

Bring the broth-and-butter mixture to a full boil. Off the heat, add the

All these operations may seem time-consuming but the whole dish can be prepared ahead of time, kept refrigerated, and reheated in a low oven which you gradually raise to 325°F. The celery coulis can be done at any time, kept refrigerated, and reheated when needed.

Chestnut flour was one of the staples of the ancient French Vivarais and Cévennes cuisines.

SUGGESTED WINE: *Any wine you like, simple and down to earth* flours and stir into a ball. Return to the heat and dry over medium-high heat until the mixture starts to form a thin, sandy layer on the bottom of the saucepan. Off the heat again, add the eggs in three equal, successive additions. Stir after each addition until homogeneous. Season with salt and pepper.

Slip the gnocchi batter into a pastry bag fitted with a ½-inch plain nozzle. Push the batter out of the bag and, with the back of a paring knife blade, cut gnocchi ¾ inch long, letting them drop into the simmering water. Let simmer until the gnocchi return to the surface of the water, then let them float there until they start swelling, about 3 minutes.

As soon as the gnocchi are done, lift them out with a slotted spoon and deposit them in the baking dish, in one layer. Cover with the remainder of the celery sauce, then the remainder of the cheese, and bake until puffed up, about 30 minutes. Serve very hot.

Gnocchi the Italian Way

These are the potato gnocchi and if you look at the ingredients, you will realize that they are nothing but potato mixed with macaroni dough prepared by using the moisture locked in the potatoes. This moisture can present a Catch 22: too much of it and the gnocchi are too soft, too little and they are tough. Rarely, however, will they be too tough, unless you add too much flour. If they indeed are too soft, 1 to 2 tablespoons of semolina will stiffen them nicely.

Potato Gnocchi with Artichokes
GNOCCHI DI PATATE CON CARCIOFI

FFR—6 SERVINGS

6 large Yellow Finnish potatoes

Olive oil as needed

2 cloves garlic, finely chopped

2 tablespoons chopped fresh Italian parsley leaves

I medium-size yellow onion, finely chopped

I medium-size carrot, finely chopped

I celery rib, finely chopped

12 large fresh basil leaves, mashed into a puree

12 large Italian pear-shaped tomatoes, peeled, seeded, and chopped

12 trimmed baby artichokes, cut in half and blanched (page 370) 3 minutes

Salt

Pepper from the mill

2 to 2¼ cups sifted unbleached all-purpose flour or more if needed

2 tablespoons semolina

½ to ¾ cup freshly grated Parmigiano-Reggiano cheese or to your personal taste

In this recipe I yielded to the advice of Artusi in La scienza in cucina e l'arte di mangiar bene *to use potatoes with a good balance of starches and proteins. However, instead of boiling them, I bake them. Served with a salad this is a nice supper meal.*

SUGGESTED WINE: **A** *Chianti or Sangiovese of your choice*

NOTE: *To use the potato skins, roll one piece of mozzarella 2 × ½ inch into a slice of prosciutto, coat with chopped garlic and parsley mixed together and stuff into each potato skin. Heat in a preheated 300°F oven until the cheese starts melting; this will be the appetizer for your gnocchi supper.*

Preheat the oven to 400°F, prick the potatoes with a fork, and bake until tender, about 1 hour. Rub a 1½-quart baking dish generously with olive oil.

While the potatoes bake, make the sauce: Heat 3 tablespoons olive oil in a sauteuse pan, then add the garlic and brown until golden. Add the parsley, onion, carrot, and celery and cook over medium heat until nicely browned. Add the basil, tomatoes, and artichokes and cook, covered with the lid left slightly askew, until saucelike, 25 to 30 minutes. Correct the final seasoning and keep warm.

As soon as the potatoes are baked, remove the pulp from the skins (keep those and see the note below), and strain through a conical strainer, food mill, or *tamis* into a warmed bowl. Add the flour gradually, mixing it with the warm potato pulp. Season with salt and pepper, then empty the mixture onto the countertop and knead until a nice, coherent, but not too elastic dough forms. Keep the counter lightly floured if necessary.

Sprinkle a baking sheet with the semolina. Shape the gnocchi dough into strings 8 inches long and ⅓ inch in diameter. Cut into 1-inch-long pieces and roll onto the back of a fork dipped in flour at regular intervals to give it ridges. Let fall onto the semolina-sprinkled sheet. Bring a pot of water to a boil, salt it, and add the gnocchi. Simmer until the gnocchi come floating to the surface of the water. Transfer to the oiled dish and mix with the sauce. Sprinkle with the Parmigiano-Reggiano and bake until the cheese has turned golden. Serve piping hot with a nice salad.

Handmade Pasta, Wherever It Comes From

Many families own a pasta machine, as they own a bread machine. As I have stated elsewhere, the two goals of this book are (1) to teach the correct way of preparing and cooking the basic western foods, and (2) to preserve those hand techniques that are quickly disappearing, mostly because they are being replaced by machines.

In the same manner that bakers at heart have often started by making bread in a machine, I am certain that noodle makers at heart, who right now are using a one-step noodle-making machine, will, after reading this section, graduate to using their hands in combination with a noodle-kneading/rolling and cutting machine, and eventually end up using only their hands. I started making noodles with my hands when I was a child. I am pleased every so often to go back to the kneader/stretcher/cutter simply because it lets me take it a little easier.

If you graduate from the one-step machine, do not by any means discard or give it away; keep it to start your children on pasta making. Children love the miracle of seeing the pasta come out of the cutters.

Whichever way you make your pasta, it will always be better than any "fresh" pasta you will buy in a supermarket or cook out of a bag. So now, come along with me and let us try to make sense of what we do when we work by hand.

The techniques described in the coming paragraphs are combined techniques taught to me by the women of my family, by two good friends in Italy, and a few German and Austrian cooks. Do what I did; gather all kinds of little tricks and you will end up developing your own method.

The following pages offer:

- The making of pasta entirely by hand; this will effectively leave you one pound lighter in body weight.
- The making of pasta half by hand and half by machine; sorry, no weight loss with this method.

Choose right now what you think you want to learn; see below and pages 500–2 for the hand technique and pages 502–3 for the half hand/half machine technique.

Simple Egg Noodle Doughs

Each recipe yields about 1 pound or 6 servings

Whole-egg pasta (FFR)

2¼ cups unsifted unbleached all-purpose flour

3 large eggs, well beaten

½ teaspoon salt

Egg white pasta (FCR)

3 large egg whites

2 teaspoons olive oil

2 tablespoons water or more as needed

½ teaspoon salt

1¼ cups unsifted unbleached all-purpose flour

¾ cups pasta flour (semolina)

In the recipe instructions, eggs means whole eggs or egg whites mixed with water and oil, and flour means all-purpose flour or all-purpose flour mixed with semolina. These are not my favorite doughs, but they are the simplest to start with; you will find better doughs in the recipes that follow the pure technical explanations.

Stage 1: Forming the Dough and Initial Hand Kneading
Place ¼ cup of the flour in a small bowl so you can rub your hands with it if need be.

Sift the remaining flour(s) onto a counter or, even better, a wooden tabletop. Make a well in the flour, then add four fifths of the total volume of the eggs and the salt to the well. Set aside the remainder of the egg to be used later if need be.

Beat the eggs (or the egg whites, oil, and water) and salt with a fork, gradually bringing in flour from the sides into the well, until the paste has thickened enough so the liquid will not run onto the counter. Switch from a fork

A well-shaped well in a pile of flour

Bring the flour into the beaten eggs very gradually. When the mixture starts to stiffen, change from a fork to a pastry scraper.

Blend the eggs and flour together with the pastry cutter, then with your hands.

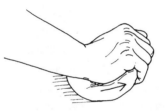

The dough ready to be worked into pasta

Dig the heel of your hand into the dough, pushing away from you. Alternate doing this between your right and left hands, creating an imaginary V on the counter.

to a pastry cutter. Bring all the flour into the already wet part and cut through the dough several times until it is evenly moistened. Start kneading with your hands until the dough forms a ball and looks homogenized, if still bumpy, about 8 minutes.

If the dough becomes stiff and refuses to bend, remedy the situation by rubbing a bit of the remaining egg mixture on your hands and kneading it in. Continue doing this until the dough becomes more and more manageable. *Do not pour egg onto the counter* or you will see your dough "squish-squash" all over the place and stubbornly refuse to accept the additional egg.

If you have added a bit too much egg, so that your dough feels too soft and tacky, reach for the bowl of flour, rub your hands with some of it, and continue kneading. Repeat as many times as needed for the dough to stiffen and reach the correct texture.

Your finished dough will not look at all like it can be rolled out and made into pasta. You are exactly right. Your hand work has just begun. If you prefer to continue by machine, go straight to page 502.

Stage 2: The Second Hand Kneading
If you decide to work the dough all the way by hand, make a note of the time. You must knead another 10, perhaps even 12, minutes.

Knead by passing the dough from one hand to the other, digging the heel of your hand into it each time. Your rhythmic movement should form an imaginary V on the counter- or tabletop. As you continue, the dough will progressively become lighter in color, more elastic, and finally very supple. You will have broken down all the long strands of gluten (see page 1009) you built up in the first stage, which are now much smaller and the change of color is due to all the air you have introduced into the dough while kneading. Cut the ball in half and reshape into two smaller balls. Put to rest for 30 minutes under a bowl turned upside down.

Stage 3: Hand Stretching the Dough into a Sheet

It is preferable to use a rolling pin that is built in one piece and without ball bearings; the ball bearings are of no help whatsoever. What works best is a dowel that is tapered at both ends. A thick unpainted broomstick will also do well.

Place one ball of the dough at a time on the counter and roll it out as you would a pie crust as far as it will go by itself. When it starts curling over ever so lightly at its edges, the time to stretch has come.

To stretch away from you, place the rolling pin in the center of the dough and your hands side by side at the very center of the rolling pin. Apply pressure only from the hand cushion below your thumb, index and middle fingers. Pressing down hard and evenly on the rolling pin, push the pin away from you and let your hands travel away from the center of the pin toward each of its ends. You will see the dough advance forward almost 2 inches if you are strong.

To stretch toward you, reverse the process, working from the center of the dough toward yourself to cover the yet unstretched part of the dough. Place your hands at opposite ends of the rolling pin and, pressing down hard and evenly, let your hands travel toward its center until they meet there; you will see the dough advance and stretch almost 2 inches toward you.

To stretch the dough evenly, each and every time you repeat these two movements, once away from you and once toward you, turn the dough 90 degrees and flip it upside down. Also, start stretching where you left off so as not to overstretch portions that have already been worked.

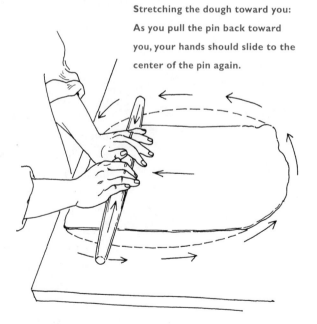

Stretching the dough toward you: As you pull the pin back toward you, your hands should slide to the center of the pin again.

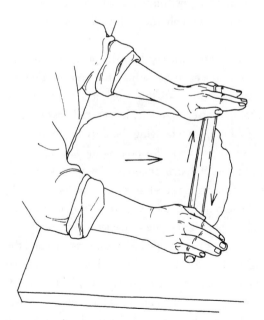

Stretching the dough away from you: Start with your hands in the center of the rolling pin. As you roll the pin forward, your hands should slide apart to the opposing ends of the pin.

– – – – indicates the line to which one must stretch to obtain a round, paper-thin, and even sheet by turning the dough 45 degrees after each outward and inward stretching series. The very edge will be cut off and used as soup pasta.

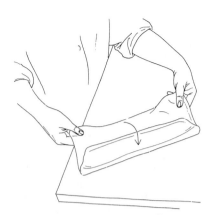

Folding the rolled-out dough upon itself across its width

When cutting pasta by hand, cut straight down using the back of the knife blade, not the tip, then shake each ribbon to obtain a noodle.

You must turn the dough upside down to make use of the moisture constantly sent toward the countertop by the pressure of your stretching. Avoid flouring the sheet of dough; the flour would absorb that moisture and this would prevent rather than help the stretching. Use the very thinnest veil of flour only if your dough is tacky.

To Cut the Noodles

When the dough is stretched to its maximum it should be less than $\frac{1}{32}$ inch thick and almost transparent. Pass a thin veil of flour over the entire circle of dough using the palm of your working hand, and fold the dough upon itself into a flat scroll 2 inches wide. Using the part of the knife blade closest to the handle, cut pieces $\frac{1}{4}$ to $\frac{1}{3}$ inch wide at a precise right angle to the counter- or tabletop. To separate, push each strip of pasta with the knife blade, to the right if you are right-handed or to the left if you are left-handed. Grasp one end of each strip, unroll it or shake it open; you will be holding a noodle. Repeat with the other pieces and let dry on a baking sheet, either rolled into nests or loose. If you use the pasta immediately, let it dry 15 minutes. If you are preparing it for a future meal, do not dry it; wrap the baking sheet in plastic wrap and freeze the pasta on it.

Working Through Stage 2 by Machine

If you do not feel that you can stretch by hand, do not hesitate to use the machine. As soon as the dough is homogeneous, cut it into three even balls and let them rest 20 minutes under a bowl turned upside down. Then pass each piece of dough several times through the rollers of a manual pasta machine.

You will have to do this quite systematically. Pass the piece first through the machine set at its largest possible opening. When it comes out, fold the pasta dough upon itself across its width. Pass the dough again through the machine, then fold the pasta upon itself across its length and pass it again through the machine, then fold it again, changing the direction of the fold each time, etc. As you successively pass and fold and pass and fold again, you imprison air between the two layers of dough, then you chase it out again by rolling the dough under pressure, but some gets forced into the dough which, you will soon see, lightens somewhat in color. As soon as it does, pass the dough through the next smaller opening. The new heavier pressure will continue to chase air out of the pasta but keep a tiny bit of it imprisoned and the dough will get lighter and lighter in color. To see how much you have worked the dough, compare it to a piece that has not been worked yet. The dough has lost all tackiness; it is as smooth as satin and is ready for stretching. After it has passed through the smallest opening, the piece will be almost as wide as the roller and three times as long. Cover with a kitchen towel and let rest until you have rolled the other pieces to the same size following exactly the same method.

Working Through Stage 3 and Cutting Noodles by Machine

While sheets two and three rest, stretch sheet one. Pass it successively through the rollers of the machine at smaller and smaller settings until it is a little thinner than ½₂ inch thick. Let the dough sheet sit a few minutes to slightly dry it, then cut through the ¼-inch-wide cutter of the pasta machine and roll the noodles into nests.

Repeat the process with sheets two and three.

You now know how to make pasta. I know that you work the whole day and making pasta is time-consuming, but never underestimate the value of a bit of handwork when you work too much, be it with your brain or physically. A good workout is not to be disdained.

VEGETABLE-FLAVORED PASTA

All kinds of flavored doughs can be made by using vegetable purees instead of water or to replace some of the eggs. To prevent the vegetable puree from containing moisture, the water must be evaporated by reducing the puree slowly. (See the recipe on page 504.)

Any time you add vegetable puree or herbs to pasta dough, the volume of egg white is reduced since some of its moisture is replaced by that of the vegetable or herbs, but the amount of egg yolk is slightly increased to maintain enough proteins for a good texture.

TO COOK THE PASTA

Boil a large pot of water. Salt the water first before adding the pasta. Cook, al dente, tasting often, 3 to 4 minutes.

Here is an example in which I use vegetables from the Basque country. For the original taste by all means use the confit fat.

Noodles with Basque Herbs and Vegetables
NOUILLES AUX Z'HERBES BASQUES

Do not use more fat in the cooking of the greens; it would interfere with the proper texture of the pasta dough. Ardi Gazna is a Basque country cheese made entirely with ewes' milk.

SUGGESTED WINE:

Beaujolais Villages, Italian or California Grignolino or, if available, Irouléguy

FFR—6 SERVINGS

For the pasta

2 teaspoons confit fat (page 787) or walnut or corn oil

2 cloves garlic, finely chopped

I large leek, white and light green parts only, well washed and finely chopped

I cup very finely chopped spinach, beet, or turnip greens

I cup very finely chopped Swiss chard leaves

Salt

Pepper from the mill

2 large eggs

3 large egg yolks

2½ cups unsifted unbleached all-purpose flour

I teaspoon salt

For the garnish coulis

Fat of your choice as needed

2 teaspoons finely chopped fresh thyme leaves

12 Italian pear-shaped tomatoes, peeled, seeded, and chopped

6 large red bell peppers, seeded and chopped

6 large yellow or orange bell peppers, seeded and chopped

Salt

Pepper from the mill

I large ¼-inch-thick slice Bayonne, prosciutto, or country ham, diced into ¼-inch cubes

2 large yellow onions, coarsely diced

½ cup diced cooked young carrots

½ cup cooked fresh corn kernels

½ cup cooked fresh green peas

½ cup cooked peeled fresh fava beans

Chopped fresh Italian parsley leaves

2 cloves garlic, finely chopped

1½ cups coarsely grated Ardi Gazna, Pecorino Romano, or Sardo cheese

To prepare the pasta, heat the chosen fat or oil in a large skillet over medium-high heat, then add the garlic and brown well. Add the leeks and greens, season with salt and pepper, and toss together well. Turn the heat down to low, cover, and cook until all the water has come out of the greens.

Remove the lid and continue cooking until the mixture is completely dry. Cool completely.

In a blender mix together the cooked greens, whole eggs, and egg yolks. Process well but avoid making too much foam. Pour all but ¼ cup of the flour onto a work surface and make a well in it. Add 1 teaspoon of salt and four fifths of the greens mixture to the well. To understand why part of the flour and part of the greens mixture are not fully used, you must be familiar with the instructions on making pasta on pages 499–503. Gather the flour into the greens mixture and start kneading the pasta dough exactly as described in these pages. When the dough is ready, cut into noodles of the size you like best.

To prepare the garnish, over medium heat, heat just enough fat to coat the bottom of a sauteuse pan. Add the thyme, tomatoes and peppers, season well with salt and pepper, and cook, covered, until all the vegetables have fallen apart. Add a tablespoon or so of water every so often if the mixture becomes too dry. Strain into a bowl, pushing the vegetable mixture hard through a conical strainer to obtain a *coulis*. Correct the seasoning carefully.

Heat just enough fat over medium heat to coat the bottom of a skillet, add the ham and onions; cook, stirring, until nice deep golden. Add the carrots, corn, peas, and fava beans, mix well, and set aside.

Bring a large pot of water to a boil; salt it just before adding the pasta. Cook the pasta 3 minutes. Drain well, add to the sauteuse containing the vegetables, mix well, and turn into a warmed pasta bowl. Top with the *coulis* and sprinkle with parsley and garlic mixed with the cheese. Serve piping hot.

NOODLE DOUGHS MADE WITH DIFFERENT FLOURS

Buckwheat, rye, and corn flours can, either separately or blended together, be used in conjunction with regular unbleached flour to prepare all kinds of pasta. But it is important to use one half to two thirds of a flour with a high protein content (approximately 11 to 11.5 percent) to compensate for the lack of body-building proteins in the weaker flours. Also, the amount of egg must be increased to make sure that the dough is water-resistant and will not get too soft while cooking.

Here is a dish in which a fresh herb pasta is mixed with a corn flour pasta and the meat of a smoked chicken. Instead of a cream sauce and plenty of cheese, stock is reduced on top of the chicken carcass for a much lighter sauce.

Two Pasta
and Smoked Chicken Dinner

This is very good for a fun dinner among friends. Make the pasta ahead. If you have only fine cornmeal, put it in a blender and process it until you obtain flour. You will use only two thirds of each pasta; the remainder will yield another meal for four people.

SUGGESTED WINE: *If you can find it, try a Valtellina or any other light Nebbiolo.*

FFR—8 SERVINGS

For the mixed herb pasta

½ cup packed mixed fresh tarragon, basil, chervil, and chives

2 large eggs

2 large egg yolks

1 teaspoon salt

2 cups unsifted unbleached all-purpose flour

For the corn flour pasta

2 large eggs

2 large egg yolks

1 large clove garlic, chopped

1 teaspoon salt

⅔ cup unsifted corn flour

1⅓ cups unsifted unbleached all-purpose flour

For the garnishes

1 smoked chicken, skin removed

2 quarts **Primary Veal Stock** (page 219) or stock of your choice

2 tablespoons cider vinegar

¾ cup dry Marsala

1 medium-size yellow onion, finely chopped

1 small carrot, finely chopped

Small bouquet garni

Olive oil of your choice as needed

2 cloves garlic, finely chopped

4 small zucchini, cut into ¼-inch-thick slices

3 dozen Red Currant or Sweet 100 tomatoes or 2 dozen regular storebought cherry tomatoes

Salt

Pepper from the mill

¼ cup chopped mixed fresh tarragon, basil, chervil, and chives

Freshly grated Parmigiano-Reggiano or other hard grating cheese

Prepare both pastas according to the techniques described on pages 499–503 a few days before you plan to serve this dish and freeze them. It will preserve the nice color of the herbs and all you will have to do about an hour before dinner is prepare the sauce and garnish before plunging the noodles into *two* different pots of boiling salted water, so you can cook each of them to the best possible texture.

To prepare the garnish, bone the chicken meat and cut into bite-size pieces. Chop the carcass into pieces. Put it into a sauteuse pan, add the veal stock, and reduce together over medium heat until 4 cups are left.

Meanwhile, in a medium-size nonreactive saucepan reduce the vinegar and Marsala, mixed together with the onion, carrot, and bouquet garni, by one half over medium-low heat. Pour the reduced stock over this mixture and reduce again together to obtain 2½ cups of finished sauce. Place the chicken meat in a large pasta bowl and spoon ¼ cup of the sauce over it. Keep warm.

Heat as much olive oil as you like in another sauteuse over medium-high heat and brown the garlic and zucchini. Bring two pots of salted water to a boil and cook each pasta in each pot. Drain both, add the green and yellow noodles in alternate quantities to the sauced chicken, and blend in the zucchini. Sauté the tomatoes over medium-high heat for 1 minute in the zucchini pan, salt and pepper and spread over the top of the pasta. Serve well sprinkled with the chopped herbs and pass the bowl of cheese and the remainder of the sauce in another bowl.

Filled Pasta

These are our ravioli, tortellini, capelletti, agnolotti. Since I do not have enough space in such a general book to go into the many details of each of these pasta presentations, here is a second edition of a recipe published in my own book *Madeleine Kamman's Savoie*. *Agneletti* in the patois of the French Alps is the same as ravioli (or agnolotti) in good Italian.

The goal of this recipe is to teach you how to make ravioli freehand. If you are disturbed by the making of the larger sheets, purchase a ravioli tray and cut smaller sheets, but I prefer the larger sheets because the loss of dough is truly minimal; the trays are not as thrifty.

Pumpkin and Hazelnut Ravioli

AGNELETTI A LA COURGE ET
AUX NOISETTES

SUGGESTED WINE: *A Chignin-Bergeron from the French Savoie if you can find it, or if not a Swiss Dézaley or a California Riesling*

FFR—6 SERVINGS

For the filling

⅔ cup cooked butternut squash pulp

I cup cooked pumpkin pulp

Salt

Pepper from the mill

I tablespoon brandy of your choice

½ cup mashed semi-dry goat cheese

½ cup unsalted butter

½ cup chopped hazelnuts (page 50), toasted

I tablespoon fresh lemon juice

Chopped fresh Italian parsley leaves

For the pasta dough

3 cups unsifted unbleached all-purpose flour

4 to 5 large eggs as needed

I teaspoon salt

Mix the squash and pumpkin together in a medium-size skillet. Season with salt and pepper and cook over medium heat until the puree turns thick and brown and caramelizes on the bottom of the pan. Stir occasionally to prevent burning. Add the brandy. Remove from the heat, let cool, and add the goat cheese. Keep refrigerated until ready to use.

Prepare the pasta as indicated on pages 499–503. Divide the dough into 4 balls and allow them to rest for 20 minutes under an upside down bowl. When rested, roll the dough out into four rectangular sheets as thin as possible and of as much the same size as possible. Place one sheet of pasta on the counter and keep the others separate and well covered.

At 1½-inch intervals, place half a teaspoonful of filling. *Do not overfill!* A half teaspoon of filling is truly enough. When done, dip a pastry brush lightly in water and lightly paint the dough between the dabs of filling in both directions: top to bottom and left to right.

Now take a second sheet of pasta and roll it around your rolling pin. Aligning the edges of both pasta sheets, gently allow the second sheet to cover the first. With your fingertips, chase the air from between the sheets and, pushing gently between the rows of fillings in both directions, seal the top sheet to the bottom one. With a pizza wheel cut along an imaginary line that passes at the very center of the stretch of pasta between the dabs of filling in both directions, top to bottom and left to right. Repeat the very same operations with the other two sheets and the remainder of the filling. Keep the agneletti on a sheet lined with a kitchen towel sprinkled with a tad of semolina and covered with another kitchen towel until ready to use.

Cook the agneletti in a bath of boiling salted water approximately 8 minutes, or longer if you prefer, keeping the lid slightly askew over the pot. To serve, cook the butter to the noisette stage (see page 32), add the hazelnuts and lemon juice and toss the well-drained pasta in the mixture. Serve on hot plates sprinkled with parsley.

Ravioli from Nice
RAIOLA

FFR—6 SERVINGS

For the pasta dough

I cup packed fresh spinach leaves, tough stems removed, well washed, and fully
   dried

3 large eggs

I large egg white or more if needed

I teaspoon salt

2 cups unsifted unbleached all-purpose flour

I cup pasta flour or superfine ground semolina

For the filling

I cup coarsely chopped cooked duck meat from the legs or any dark meat of
   poultry

I fresh uncooked sweet Italian sausage link, casing removed

¼ cup fresh bread crumbs from Italian or French bread

Salt

Pepper from the mill

I small clove garlic, very finely chopped

2 tablespoons coarsely chopped fresh parsley leaves

12 fresh basil leaves, coarsely chopped

2 tablespoons finely grated Pecorino Sardo cheese

For the sauce

2½ cups excellent stock of your choice, preferably duck or veal

2 tablespoons unsalted butter

12 walnut halves, very finely chopped

I small clove garlic, very finely chopped

12 fresh basil leaves, chopped

I cup finely grated Pecorino Sardo cheese

Cook these ravioli immediately after making them or freeze them if you do not, to preserve their lovely color. Raiola is the Provençal word for ravioli, and this dish is from the lower Alps on both sides of the Franco-Italian border, where the backcountry of Provence meets with the backcountry of Liguria. The sauce is a modern replacement for reduced heavy cream.

SUGGESTED WINE: *A Cinqueterre, a Bellet white, preferably, or rosé, if you can find these wines. Otherwise, any other dry rosé will be fine; avoid sweetish rosés.*

Prepare the pasta: Chop the spinach leaves, then put them in a blender with the whole eggs, egg white, and salt. Process on "blend" speed until the spinach leaves have disappeared and the mixture has turned green. Turn into a measuring cup.

Mix the flours together on a countertop and make a well. Add three quarters of the spinach-and-egg mixture. Gradually draw the flours into the well and start kneading. If the dough is too thin, add some more semolina; if it is too dry, add more of the spinach mixture or, if none is left, as much of another egg white as needed. Work the dough as indicated on pages 499–503. Divide the dough into four balls and allow them to rest under an upside down bowl.

Prepare the filling: To a food processor, add the duck meat, sausage meat, bread crumbs, salt and pepper to taste, garlic, parsley, basil, and finally the Pecorino Sardo. Process until you obtain a mellow stuffing. If too stiff, add more basil leaves; if too wet, add bread crumbs until you reach the consistency you prefer. The mixture should hold its shape without being stiff.

To fill the ravioli: Work with two balls of dough at a time. Roll each out into two rectangular sheets as thin as possible as described on pages 501–2. Place one sheet of pasta on the counter and keep the other well covered. At 1½-inch intervals, place ½ teaspoon of filling. *Do not overfill!* A half teaspoon is truly enough. When done, dip a pastry brush lightly in water and lightly paint the dough between the dabs of filling, in both directions, top to bottom and left to right.

Now take the second sheet of pasta and roll it around your rolling pin. Aligning the edges of both pasta sheets, gently allow the second sheet to cover the first. With your fingertips, chase the air from between the sheets and, pushing gently between the rows of fillings in both directions, seal the top sheet to the bottom one. With a pizza wheel, cut along an imaginary line that passes at the very center of the stretch of pasta between the dabs of filling in both directions, top to bottom and left to right.

Repeat the very same operations with the other two balls of pasta and the remainder of the filling. Keep the ravioli on a sheet pan lined with a kitchen towel sprinkled with a tad of semolina and covered with another kitchen towel until ready to use.

Cook the ravioli in a bath of boiling salted water approximately 8 minutes, or longer if you prefer, keeping the lid slightly askew over the pot.

To prepare the sauce and serve: While you make the pasta and ravioli, reduce the stock to 1¼ cups in a saucepan over medium heat. Mash the butter with the chopped walnuts, garlic, and basil using the side of your chef's knife blade until you obtain a homogeneous basil butter. Set aside.

Heat a serving bowl with hot water, then empty and dry it. Drain the ravioli very well. Alternate layers of ravioli with equal amounts of the hot reduced stock and small dabs of the compound butter. Sprinkle with the cheese and serve immediately.

Lasagne

The word *lasagne* comes from the Greek *laganon*, which became *laganum* or *lasanum* in Latin and is the name of an ancient Roman dish. *Laganum* may also have been the collective name for strips of pasta which were fried and used to garnish soups. The word remains in the modern southern Italian word *laganella* which means tagliatelle or flat ribbon noodles.

The Romans of imperial times may not have made pasta, but the Etruscans, their close neighbors, did. Their instruments to prepare it at home are very visible and recognizable in the famous pictures of the tomb of the Cerveteri in Caere. I was not able to find anywhere an exact indication of when large sheets of pasta, as we use them now, started to be layered with vegetable or meat garnishes as the polenta (*polenta concia*) has been for centuries in the very northern parts of Italy (see bibliography).

In the *Apicius Roman Cookery Book* by Flower and Rosenbaum (London, Harrap, 1961), one can see on page 17 a photograph of an ancient "frying pan" made of bronze which resembles the rectangular dishes in which we make our own lasagne. Such a vessel may have existed in a ceramic version since it does and is still in use in the Alemanic regions of Germany, the Alsace, and the Pennsylvania Dutch country; it is called a *Rutscher* (slider) because it is slid onto the oven shelf by its handle. The *Rutscher* was inherited from Roman times.

Provençal Lasagne

FFR — 6 SERVINGS

For the layers

I recipe Ratatouille (page 396)

2 tablespoons olive oil

2 medium-size yellow onions, very finely chopped

I pound ground veal or turkey

2 cups tomato sauce of your choice

Salt

Pepper from the mill

¼ cup unsalted butter

3 tablespoons sifted unbleached all-purpose flour

1½ cups milk of your choice, scalded

Freshly grated nutmeg

1¼ pounds aged hard cheese, sliced, or 2 cups fresh goat cheese (page 73)

¼ cup grated hard cheese

This dish requires organization; spread the work over two days:

ON DAY 1:
Prepare the ratatouille; keep it refrigerated.
Prepare the meat sauce; keep it refrigerated.

You may use the following cheeses: any Gruyère-type cheese, fontina, mozzarella di buffala, American mozzarella, Oaxaca cheese, feta, and, if you make it yourself, fresh goat cheese. If to be used, prepare a double recipe of goat cheese and drip it overnight. Slice other cheeses into thin slices if you use any of the aged cheeses listed above and keep the slices separated from one another between sheets of parchment paper. Roll the sheets of parchment enclosing the slices of cheese into a scroll and wrap this in clear plastic to prevent dehydration.

ON DAY 2:
Prepare the pasta so you can use it fresh as it comes from your workbench and put the dish together.

SUGGESTED WINE: **A Cassis or a Bandol, or a Sauvignon Blanc, Fumé Blanc, or light Pinot Noir**

For the pasta dough

2 cups unsifted unbleached all-purpose flour

½ cup pasta flour or fine ground semolina

3 to 4 large eggs as needed

Salt

Prepare the ratatouille and set aside.

Prepare the meat sauce: Heat the olive oil in a large skillet, add the onions, and cook, stirring, over medium heat until golden. Add the ground meat in successive small amounts, flattening the meat and breaking it apart with a flat wooden spatula so it can brown lightly. When the meat is evenly light golden, tilt the pan and gather the meat toward the handle of the pan. Let the fat drip into the lip of the pan and dab it off with a wad of paper towels. Add the tomato sauce, season with salt and pepper, and cook 30 minutes, stirring occasionally, until the mixture is well bound but not dry.

Melt 3 tablespoons of the butter in another saucepan over medium heat. Add the flour and cook a few minutes, stirring, to obtain a white roux. Off the heat, whisk in the hot milk; bring back to a boil, stirring constantly, and cook until thickened. Add the nutmeg, salt, and pepper, and keep the *béchamel* warm in a double boiler.

Reheat the ratatouille to lukewarm. Rub the last tablespoon of butter on the bottom and sides of a 1½- to 2-quart rectangular baking dish.

Make the pasta exactly as described on pages 499–503 just before building your dish of lasagne. Cut it into three equal pieces. Knead each through the pasta machine until smooth and satiny. Then, roll it out still using the pasta machine and thinning it to the thinnest possible thickness on your machine. Cut each band of pasta obtained in half crosswise. Now, using a dowel or rolling pin, stretch the pasta until it is as wide as you can make it and very thin, to the point you can almost read through it. The pasta will not be precooked, since it is so thin; it will cook as it bakes, absorbing moisture from the ratatouille. When cut, keep the pasta sheets on kitchen towels and covered.

Preheat the oven to 350°F. Line the dish snugly with pasta, letting any excess hang over the sides of the dish if necessary. Layer in half the ratatouille, half the meat sauce, and half of the cheese slices or goat cheese. Cover with a second layer of pasta. Top this second layer with the remaining ratatouille, meat sauce, and cheese. Add the last layer of pasta and cut off any excess pasta. Spread the *béchamel* sauce over the top of the pasta and sprinkle with the grated cheese.

Bake until thoroughly heated through and the grated cheese has turned golden, 30 to 35 minutes. Let stand 10 minutes out of the oven to firm up the lasagne before serving it.

Macaroni for All,
Especially Heart Patients

NFR — 6 SERVINGS

2 cups unsifted unbleached all-purpose flour

⅔ cup semolina

1 teaspoon salt

Lukewarm water, as needed

Mix the flour, semolina, and salt together on a work surface. Make a well, add ½ cup lukewarm water and gather into a dough. Knead until completely smooth and satiny. Let rest, covered, for 20 minutes under an upside down bowl.

The making of this dough is identical to that of regular egg noodle dough (see pages 499–503). The problem resides in trying to establish exactly how much water is going to be used, since there is not a flour that absorbs water at the same speed as another. Start with ½ cup; if you have added too much, add a little semolina, or if the dough feels too dry, rub your hands with water and knead it into the dough, continuing this technique until the dough becomes flexible and smooth.

Macaroni dough is a pasta dough made without the slightest trace of egg, which makes it perfect for those engaged in a steady battle with the cholesterol in eggs. Because our American flour is somewhat stronger than the southern Italian flour, I use a little less semolina than the recommended ratio of two parts flour to one part semolina which is traditional in the Italian Puglia.

Orechiette with
Garlic, Oil, and Hot Pepper

ORECHIETTE, AGLIO, OLIO E PEPERONCINO

FCR — 6 SERVINGS

1 recipe macaroni dough (preceding recipe)

Semolina

Salt

¼ cup extra virgin olive oil or to taste

No less than 2 and no more than 4 cloves garlic, finely chopped

No less than ½ small and no more than 1 cayenne pepper, finely chopped

¼ cup chopped fresh Italian parsley leaves

Prepare the dough as explained above. Cut the dough into long strips which you will gently roll back and forth to become strings 8 inches long and ⅓ inch in diameter. Cut these strips into ¼-inch-thick pieces. Place each little piece of dough in the center of your hand and make a little cup by pushing the flat of your thumb into the dough. Then wrap and bend the little cup upside down over the fleshy tip, your other thumb pulling it gently to enlarge it a little. Sprinkle a baking sheet with semolina and let the orechiette fall onto it gently.

Orechiette are from Puglia and this way of preparing them is from Abruzzo.

Small strips of pasta will be cut from dough and rolled very thinly with both hands.

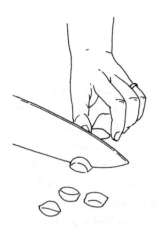

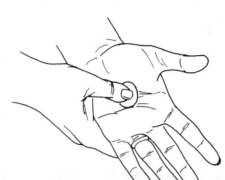

Cut the strips of dough into ¼-inch-thick pieces.

Take each piece, roll it between the palms of your hands, then flatten it with your thumb against the palm of your hand.

Turn the pasta upside down on the tip of your thumb and pull it over your thumb into the orechiette shape.

SUGGESTED WINE: *A good Rosso Barletta from Puglia or a Montepulciano d'Abruzzo*

To cook, bring a large pot of water to a boil. Add salt just before adding the pasta. Cook the pasta until done just a tiny bit over al dente, or as you prefer them.

Meanwhile, heat the oil in a large sauteuse or skillet over low heat, then add the garlic and cayenne pepper and slowly cook until the garlic has turned golden. Drain the pasta and add to the skillet at the same time as the parsley. Toss together and serve promptly. The pasta should glisten with olive oil.

Cavatelli with Escarole and Young Fennel Bulb
CAVATELLI CON SCAROLA E FINOCHIETTI

SUGGESTED WINE: *If you can find it, a Greco di Bianco from Calabria or an easier to find Orvieto*

FFR — 6 SERVINGS

1 recipe macaroni dough (page 513)

2 heads escarole

2 heads chicory

2 large fennel bulbs

Salt

¼ to ⅓ cup extra virgin olive oil or to your personal taste

2 cloves garlic, finely chopped

Freshly grated Pecorino Romano cheese

Chopped fresh parsley

Prepare the macaroni dough as described above. Cut the dough into long strips, which you will gently roll back and forth to become ¼ inch wide and 9 inches long. Cut six 1½-inch-long pieces out of each strip. Using a table knife—not a professional kitchen knife which would cut through the dough—flatten each striplet of dough toward yourself at the same time you make the dough curl around the knife blade. You will find yourself the happy possessor of a macaronilike little piece of pasta that is semitubular instead of tubular; this is the ancestor to all the modern machine-made store-bought shapes of hollowed macaroni. Cover the pasta with a kitchen towel while you prepare the garnish.

Trim the escarole and chicory of unattractive outer leaves and wash very well. Clean thoroughly, then slice the fennel bulbs into ¼-inch slivers. Bring a large pot of water to a boil, add very little salt, and blanch each green 2 minutes. Put the fennel in a large conical strainer and immerse 3 minutes in the blanching water. Drain the vegetables, let cool, then chop coarsely. Do not discard the blanching water; you will cook the macaroni in it.

Add more salt to the water, bring back to a boil, then add the macaroni and cook until done to your liking, tasting often.

Meanwhile, heat a generous amount of olive oil in a large skillet. Add the garlic and let it cook over low heat until golden. Add the greens and fennel to the pan and coat well with the olive oil. As soon as the pasta is done, drain and add it to the skillet and mix very well. Add as much of the cooking water as needed to obtain a very small sauce that just binds the pasta well. Turn into a pasta dish and serve well sprinkled with Pecorino Romano and parsley.

For a wealth of recipes prepared with pasta, consult the index.

MAKING CAVATELLI

Add rope of dough being stretched by rolling with your hands

Roll the dough with your hands into long ropes, then cut them into 2-inch-long pieces.

Cut ¾ of the way down into each piece, flattening the pasta with the blade until it makes a valleylike indentation. The dough rolls around the blade and makes a small, tubular piece of pasta.

Of River, Lake, and Sea Critters

All Manner of Cooking and
Preparing Fish

Before You Buy and
Start Cooking Fish and Shellfish

THE FOOD CHAIN HAS, OVER THE LAST FIFTY YEARS, BECOME SO LONG AND SO complicated that in America we eat fish from Hawaii and the Southern Hemisphere, and shrimp raised in the Far East. This long chain gives us considerable variety but it also presents possible dangers of contamination and toxicity due to lengthy and improper storage or handling before the fish or shellfish enters your kitchen.

The following is a list of the problems you *must* anticipate by understanding that the proper cooking of fish and shellfish is essential. Following the fashions of eating raw or rare fish and shellfish is not worth taking the risk of becoming extremely ill.

Fish Toxins and Viruses

SALMONELLA Please cook fish so it is safe, which is at least 160°F. And especially bear in mind that pets such as turtles, birds, fish, dogs, and cats can be carriers of salmonella and contaminate your family and foods.

TAPEWORM LARVAE Normal cooking disposes of these; they can also be destroyed by freezing the fish to 0°F for 24 hours and then cooking it to an internal temperature of at least 160°F.

ANISAKIASIS This is a worm found in raw fish. As a result, you must beware of sashimi, however fond of it you may be. The parasite can be passed on to humans and attaches itself to the stomach or intestinal membranes. Symptoms are cramps, heartburn, and vomiting, which occur one hour after ingesting the fish and will continue for a number of days. To prevent problems, the fish should be cooked to an internal temperature that ensures total destruction of the parasites (see page 520).

HISTAMINE POISONING This may sometimes happen after the ingestion of mahimahi and tuna, which contain histadin, an amino acid that converts to histamine while the fish is on its way to market. The poisoning manifests itself rapidly after ingestion with sweats, difficulty in breathing, and a diffuse, unpleasant headache that feels like you are wearing a tight, constricting hat. Go to a medical facility immediately. The problem is easily treated with antihistamine.

POISONOUS ROE   The roe of at least one of the Scorpanidae or sculpin family of fish—the cabezon of the California to Canada coast—are known to be poisonous; do not consume the roe of any of the sculpin family of fish.

Shellfish Toxins and Viruses

It is not without reason that the consumption of shellfish is customarily suspended outside of the months containing an "r." Marine algae by the name of dinoflagellates are consumed by the shellfish during the warmer months and fill their bodies with toxins that are undetectable, indestructible, and very dangerous to humans. Do not pick shellfish yourself between May 1 and October 31; it is a good idea anyway to purchase all shellfish, as chances are on the side of the buyer that the shellfish are uncontaminated either by toxins or by one of the hepatitis viruses. Hepatitis viruses are present in shellfish of any kind in waters located too close to human habitation and liable to be contaminated with sewage.

Important Information on the Internal Temperature of Cooked Fish

As you can see, an internal temperature of 165°F is necessary for the safe consumption of fish and shellfish. For those, however, who do their own fishing in unpolluted rivers, lakes, and oceans, the length of the food chain is considerably shortened because the fish or shellfish caught is usually consumed two to twenty-four hours after coming out of the water. In such cases the fish need not be cooked to the maximum temperature of 165°F.

To indicate the best internal temperature of fish flesh for maximum moistness and flavor, I have given in all the recipes that follow a wide range of doneness stretching from 140° to 165°F.

Most cooked fish show superior texture and taste between 140° and 145°F. Fish is not as good when cooked all the way to 165°F. Both temperatures are indicated in all recipes so the cook can, seeing both, be reminded of the two extreme situations, fish straight out of the water and fish that has passed through many hands as it has been transported from other latitudes and longitudes.

Categories of Fish and Shellfish

Fish is divided into several species:

Vertebrate or Finfish

Vertebrate fish, also called finfish, have bony skeletons and skin covered with scales of differing thicknesses protecting large fillets. These fillets are edible and choice; the head and bones, well cleaned, are used to prepare fish stock, also called fish fumet. The only parts not usable are the fins (except in some sharks used in Chinese cuisine), gills, tail, and viscera, which must be discarded, because they all contain oxidated oils that taste and smell bad.

Vertebrate fish are divided into the following categories based on environmental origin:

1. *Sea fish:* These are all fish born in ocean or sea waters and number in the many thousands of species, many of them edible, and varying in size from tiny whitebait to the largest sharks. Of these many thousands of edible species, we see only a few, which are quickly overfished; many species have become extinct, and many are hovering on the edge of extinction. Over the last forty years I have seen the size of many fish and the volume of their supply gradually decrease.

2. *Freshwater fish:* Freshwater fish are born in rivers or landlocked large bodies of water such as the Great Lakes. To this group belong all whitefish, all the species of lake and river trout, muskelunge, pike, Arctic char, and black bass.

3. *Anadromous fish:* Salmon (the true *Salmo salar* of the Atlantic Ocean and the different species of *Oncorhyncus* salmon of the Pacific), the different types of sturgeon, smelts, and striped bass, as well as the magnificent steelhead trout of the Pacific Ocean, are all born in rivers. After becoming young adults, they swim to the oceans where they will travel very long distances for several years, fattening on marine krill and plankton, before coming back to the river of their birth to spawn. Such a fish is called an *anadromous* fish. It must be caught for consumption while it travels toward the headwater of its birth river; large males only are generally kept by conscientious sport fishermen and all females carrying eggs are released. See the bibliography for a great book on the odyssey of salmon and you will understand why the Atlantic salmon especially is an endangered species.

The not-so-attractive looking but oh-so-delicious eel is a *catadromous* fish. Whereas the male eels live and reside in the estuaries of rivers, the very young females make their way to the headwaters of the same rivers, where they grow to full maturity. Once mature, they travel back to the estuaries, where they are fertilized by the resident males, and in huge numbers continue on to the Sargasso Sea in the southwestern Atlantic.

There they will release innumerable numbers of eggs which will hatch, transparent and threadlike. These infant eels will then travel back toward the estuaries of rivers where they will arrive, white, ⅛ to ¼ inch wide, and still blind. They will be gathered in masses by fishermen and prepared in many interesting dishes in the countries bordering the Atlantic. Those young males that escape capture will grow up and stay in the estuaries while the young females will fight their way toward the river headwaters, continuing the external cycle of life of their ancestors.

Shellfish

Shellfish are contained in either a hard containerlike shell or an articulated shell that bends with the movements of the animal.

1. *Mollusk* is the name given to those shellfish contained in a tight-closing shell. They include the bivalves such as oysters, clams, mussels, and scallops, the two-part shells of which are all lined with the most attractive mother-of-pearl, varying in color with the types of algae living in the water where the mollusks are born and grow and a univalve, the abalone, which has only one shell lined with beautiful iridescent mother-of-pearl.

    The shell of all bivalves is kept tightly closed by way of a strong adductor muscle that is always edible, unless it is too small to be eaten as it is in mussels and small clams. It is left attached to these shellfish and consumed with it in the raw state, but is left attached to the discarded shell when eaten cooked.

    In oysters, the adductor muscle gives additional taste to soups and chowders containing oyster stock and to sauces accompanying oysters.

    In scallops, the adductor muscle is the best and most substantial edible part of the mollusk and takes the center of the plate always; the other edible part, the coral, which is part of the reproductive system, is used to finish sauces in the cuisines of the European countries bordering seas and oceans. In North America, it can be found in Canada, but is always discarded in the United States, which is unfortunate, since it gives the finest possible taste to sauces prepared for scallops.

    In abalone, the adductor muscle keeps the shellfish attached to the ocean floor and is *the* choice piece, but it is tough if not treated properly (see page 666 for instructions).

    Cephalopods belong to a class of mollusk of the type Cephalopoda, which all have a pointed head with droopy but sharp eyes; to their heads are attached tensile tentacles. This group includes squid and octopus. Cuttlefish is a cephalopod which is also vertebrate since it sports a large inner cuttlebone, often given to canaries to sharpen their beaks. Cuttlefish belongs to the family of the Sepiidae.

2. *Crustaceans*, the shells of which are segmented to allow the fish to bend

and displace itself, include some seawater critters and some freshwater critters.

From the sea come:

- All types of shrimp from all the oceans;
- All types of lobsters, including the western North Atlantic green- and brown-tinged two-clawed lobsters of the species *Homarus americanus,* the blue-tinged two-clawed lobsters of the species *H. vulgaris* from the English Channel and North Sea, the small so-called Norwegian lobsters of the genus *Nephropsidae* (called *langoustines* in French and *scampi* in Italian), and the large and small Mediterranean furry brown lobsters (*Ursus arctus*) known as *cigale de mer* in French and *cigala* in Italian;
- All types of crabs, including the eastern Maryland blue crab, the Maine rock crab, the snow crab of Florida (also known as *tourteau* in French in the eastern Atlantic), the green crab so destructive of clam seedlings of Maine and excellent for chowders, the spider crab or *granzeola* of the Mediterranean and Adriatic seas, the Pacific Dungeness crab, and the Alaskan king crab.

From freshwater come:

- The brownish beige alpine crawfish with inner "white legs" that come from lakes of glacial origin still fed by rivers originating from live glaciers or winter snows; they can be found in all the northern states east to west;
- The deep reddish brown so-called bayou or delta crawfish with inner "red legs" from the southern and southwestern bayous or from the Sacramento delta.

    Both of these are often called crawdads or mudbugs and a few other funny names in different local vernaculars.

A Brief Look at the Structure of Fish Muscle

Land mammals used for human nutrition have extremely strong connective tissues, which they need to be able to stand on the ground for hours on end. Fish do not as they are supported by the water in which they live, a water which often changes temperature. Fish have addressed this problem of temperature change by being poi-kilothermic, which means that they adapt to these changes by varying their own body temperature in concert with that of the surrounding waters.

    Fish provide us with particularly succulent morsels for our consumption precisely because the arrangement of their muscle fibers is directly related to their rapid movement across the water. Understanding this arrangement is important because it allows us to understand why fish is so quickly over-cooked, becoming dry and unpalatable.

In mammals, muscle fibers can be many inches long; not so in fish where the fibers are no longer than ⅔ to ¾ inch. Several muscle fibers are gathered together into small bundles called myotomes. When fish is cooked enough, you can separate the myotomes and see their W-like shape, with one flexure going forward and two going backward. If you look at a salmon steak that has been cut across the grain, you can see whole successions of myotomes tightly packed against one another, pointing toward the bone at a somewhat sharp angle. Myotomes are layers or bundles of short fibers which are separated by sheets of connective tissue called myocommata which all gather to attach the muscle to the bone, in the same way that tendons or connective tissues do in meats. These myocommata are made mostly of collagen. The type of collagen present in the muscle tissue of fish converts to gelatin at a much lower temperature than it does in meats. Part of it is soluble in salted water, part in acid, and yet another part is nonsoluble and can be seen floating in fish stock. All the soluble parts will dissolve during cooking; often the conversion of collagen to gelatin is helped by the action of the acid contained in the lemon juice and wine we use during the cooking process to flavor the fish. You can observe the action of this gelatin in a cold refrigerated fish stock, which requires only 35 minutes of simmering, and has the same jellied consistency as a chicken stock which required almost two hours of cooking time. Collagen in uncooked fish is in the shape of fibrils and when cooked in water ends up as an amorphous gelatinous broth or gravy.

Nutrition

Fish is a premium source of protein since its fillets offer 15 to 25 percent proteins, and approximately 5 percent essential amino acids. Unless it has been salted and smoked it generally contains less salt than most meats. All fish offer such a good percentage of phosphorous that, where I was born, we call it brain food. If you are looking for potassium and iron, fish is also your kind of food. If you want a solid supply of calcium, eat sardines; of iodine, try oysters and clams; and just about every possible fish offers traces of cobalt, copper, fluoride, manganese, molybdenum, and selenium.

In addition, fish offers a large supply of vitamin A, especially fat fish. Most cooks using this book will probably be too young to remember the days when cod liver oil came by the spoonful on an empty stomach each and every morning; now it comes in capsules that are sources of vitamin A and D. Most fish contain vitamins from the B complex: riboflavin, niacin, B_6, and B_{12}, and in those fish roes that are edible (not all are) there is thiamine and more riboflavin.

Fat in Fish: Lean Fish, Fat Fish

Like meat, fish flesh comes in light or darker color. Fish containing mostly white muscle tissue is usually lean and contains only a small quantity of fat; this is the case of all the flatfish of the sole and flounder families. The darker the color of the fish muscle becomes, the more fat it contains, so that a snapper with its light beige meat contains more fat than sole; it is a semilean fish, as are salmon and mahimahi. Sardines, herrings, and anchovies, with their dark meats are really fat fish. Please consult the list of fish on page 526 that lists both the percentage of fat and the amount of cholesterol in each edible portion of fish.

In white fish the fat is concentrated in the liver, with less than 1 percent found in tiny droplets between the muscle fibers. In red-fleshed fish the fat is dispersed into the cells making up the red tissues. All fish fillets show both lighter and darker tissues, even in lean white fish; in white fish the dark tissues are mostly beige, but in salmon they are deep reddish brown and in tuna they look dark violaceous. There is more fat in the darker tissues of each muscle. It is believed that the fish uses this brown muscle for sustained effort when swimming over long distances; this thesis seems reasonable if one compares the brown tissue of salmon, which roams the oceans, with sole, which undulates its life away on sandy bottoms.

Almost all fatty acids contained in fish flesh are unsaturated. Since the water in which fish swim is very cold, the unsaturated fatty acids allow the fat to remain fluid at very low temperatures, so that the fish muscles can bend easily even in the coldest water.

We all know how important the famous omega-3 fatty acids are in the fight against high levels of triglycerides in the blood and the formation of dangerous blood clots. Fish present a double nutritive advantage: lots of proteins and excellent nutritionally useful oils.

Fish and shellfish can be divided into four fat categories depending on their content of fat. You will realize as soon as you look at the numbers that a particular fish or shellfish can belong to a category that contains little fat but still contains a relatively large amount of cholesterol. Looking at the respective numbers will tell you immediately which fish or shellfish should be avoided for its higher content of cholesterol if you have high blood cholesterol or cardiovascular problems.

So you can translate the grams of the metric system into ounces, always remember that:

- One ounce weight equals about 29 grams
- One hundred grams, which is a regular portion, corresponds to approximately 3½ ounces.
- Category VLF (very low fat) equals up to 2 percent fat
- Category LF (low fat) is up to 5 percent fat
- Category MF (medium fat), up to 10 percent fat
- Category F (very fat), 10 percent or more fat

Finfish	Fat Category	Fat Content (in Grams)	Cholesterol (in Milligrams)	Finfish	Fat Category	Fat Content (in Grams)	Cholesterol (in Milligrams)
Bluefish	LF	4.22	58.1	Red perch (Atlantic)	VLF	1.60	42
Catfish	LF	4.23	58				
Cod (Atlantic)	VLF	0.66	43	Salmon (Atlantic)	MF	8	60
Cod (Pacific)	VLF	0.63	37	Salmon (Pacific)	MF	3.4	52
Eel	MF	11.60	125.4	King	F	10.44*	66*
Flounder**	VLF	1.17	47.9	Shark***	LF	4.48	50.58
Grouper*	VLF	1.02	37	Smelt	LF	2.41	70
Haddock	VLF	0.71	57	Snapper***	VLF	1.33	36.5
Halibut	LF	2.58	31.75	Sole***	VLF	1.17	44
Mackerel	F	13.82	70	Striped bass	LF	2.33	80
Mahimahi*	VLF	1.1	n/a	Swordfish	LF	3.99	38.7
Monkfish	VLF	1.52	25	Trout***	LF	4	57.5
Orange roughy	MF	7.00	20	Tuna*			
Pike (yellow)	VLF	0.67	38.75	Albacore	MF	7.60	n/a
Pike (walleye)*	VLF	1.22	86	Bluefin	LF	4.90	38
Pollock (Atlantic)	VLF	0.97	70.5	Skipjack	VLF	1.01	47
Pollock (Pacific)*	VLF	0.80	71	Yellowfin	VLF	0.95	45
Pompano	MF	9.47	50	Whitefish	LF	5.83	59.75

The Market Forms of Fish

Fish is offered for sale in different presentations; it is up to you to familiarize yourself with them and to tell the fish market exactly what you want.

To purchase fish, go nowhere else but to a reputable fish store. The smell of the store will tell you everything; if it smells fresh and pleasant, this is the place to go. If it smells strong and slightly ammoniacal, go somewhere else, as the fish obviously make the store smell and you do not want fishy-smelling fish. There is fish sold in supermarkets, but I want you to look at it with a critical eye; it sits in the refrigerator case looking sad and often dehydrated, or it feels flabby when you gently squeeze the fillets with your thumb; most of the

Shellfish	Fat Category	Fat Content (in Grams)	Cholesterol (in Milligrams)	Shellfish	Fat Category	Fat Content (in Grams)	Cholesterol (in Milligrams)
Abalone	VLF	0.78	84.5	Scallops***	VLF	0.76	33
Clams***	VLF	0.97	34	Shrimp***	VLF	1.73	152
Crabs***	VLF	1.07	64	Squid†††*	VLF	1.38	223
King crab* Alaskan	VLF	0.60	42				
Crayfish*	VLF	1.06	139				
Lobster†							
Gulf spiny	VLF	1.51	70				
Homarus (Atlantic)	VLF	0.90	95				
Mussels*	LF	2.24	28				
Oysters***††	LF	2.38	55				

Sources: The numbers given in both tables represent an average between the information published in USDA Handbook Number 8 (1987), Composition of Foods: Finfish and Shellfish Products, and the third edition of *Nutrition Almanac* (McGraw-Hill, 1990).

* USDA data only.

** *Nutrition Almanac* data only.

*** Average of all existing types of fish or shellfish.

† In lobsters the meat itself is lower in cholesterol; the high amount of fat is concentrated in the soft abdominal parts such as the tomalley; the tomalley should not be used anymore because this is where the pollutants can concentrate.

†† Fat and cholesterol contents in oysters vary with the seasons. I do not know whether these figures take into consideration the difference between winter oysters, which are leaner, and spring and summer spawning oysters.

††† These figures and the fact that squid is best when deep-fried places this delicious shellfish among really forbidden food if you have high cholesterol or any cardiovascular disease.

time it is opaque and dull and when you cook it, it floods the pan with liquid and yields fibers that are stringy and dry. Or take the mussels sold under tight plastic wrap; what do you think these poor black things will taste like after three days of sitting there, their shells tightly closed because no tide comes to refresh them? Open the package, smell, and rest assured that you will lose one third of the purchase amount, which will not steam open because they have simply succumbed in their own pollution. All this definitely speaks for a good "fishman" whom you will trust and to whom you can explain your likes and dislikes. There are still plenty of them across the United States; just look for them.

The deterioration of fish occurs much faster, even under refrigeration, than it does in meats; it is caused by the combined effects of multiplying bacteria, the work of enzymes called proteases which denature and eventually completely degrade the proteins in the muscle cells, and the work of enzymes called lipases and phospholipases which help in the rapid oxidation of the fats. See below under frozen fish for an explanation of the deterioration of frozen fish.

If you are the type of cook who likes to do all the work yourself, buy the fish:

Whole or Round

Both terms are used. Such fish is offered for sale exactly as it emerged from the water, unscaled, unfinned, and uneviscerated.

This is the best fish you can purchase because *you* can determine, just by looking at it and gently poking at it, whether it is fresh or not. If it is really fresh, the eyes will be slightly pushing out of the sockets, and be bright and transparent; the whiter the eyes, the older the fish, the membranes becoming opaque with age as dehydration sets in. You will find the smell to be perfectly pleasant; it will have the smell of the ocean or river, without the slightest whiff of ammonia. If you lift one of the gills with a finger, you will see that it is dark pink to bright red; should it be bluish or brownish or badly discolored and pale, the fish is visibly too old to be tasty. If you poke the top of the fish with a finger, the flesh under the scaly robe will be firm and resistant and will not dent under pressure; if it does, do not buy the fish.

It is up to you to do what you please with the fish; you need to know how to eviscerate it, fillet it, how to skin the fillets or the whole fish, and, finally, how to make a fish fumet/stock with its cleaned head and bones.

Drawn

In such a fish, the viscera have been removed.

Before buying a drawn fish, please ask to see the inside of the fish. Look at the color of the "bloodline"; it should be dark red and not have any smell other than that of the ocean. Should you detect the slightest offending smell—and you will know immediately what I mean without further explanation—do not buy the fish. It has probably been drawn because it neither looked nor was fresh enough to be sold round.

Dressed

Such a fish has been scaled and eviscerated, the head, all fins, and the tail having been cut off.

Once dressed, a fish can be further cut in the following ways:

CHUNK OR BLOCK

A large piece of a medium-size fish such as salmon, monkfish, large striped bass, etc., is usually referred to as a chunk, while a large piece of such very large fish as tuna, shark, or large mahimahi is referred to as a block. When you want a chunk or a block of any of these fish, specify the weight and the area of the fish you prefer; the price will vary, the center cut being the most expensive and the nape just behind the head and tail regions being less expensive.

FLETCHES

Some flatfish can be extremely large; a dressed halibut, for example, can still be three feet long after its head and tail are removed. Such fish will yield 2-inch-thick fillets, called fletches, which are removed by cutting from the center of the back down against the backbone, contouring carefully toward the abdomen and along the whole length of the backbone. Fletches are usually used in restaurant operation as follows: The nape and tail parts are cubed for chowders or fish soups of all kinds while the center cuts yield slices or steaks which should be between ½ and ⅔ inch thick, no more, and cut perpendicularly, that is, at an exact right angle with the surface of the counter.

STEAKS

Steaks can be cut to your specifications; indicate your preference to the fish market. A steak is always best when ⅔ to 1 inch thick.

Steaks can then be transformed into *medallions* taken from the center cut of the fish only. Do not make medallions out of fillets by putting the fillets head to tail and pairing two pieces of meat that are dissimilar in shape and size; otherwise, the medallions will be irregular. If you go to the trouble of making medallions, pay the price for the best center cut to obtain perfect medallions. You can always offer the nape and tail parts in a chowder or as small escalopes.

ESCALOPES

If you do not wish to cube the nape and tail parts, they can also be cut into escalopes (which can also be called scallops, but I use the older term to differentiate them from the shellfish) which should be ¼ inch thick and cut on the diagonal with a razor-sharp knife. Sashimi knives from Japan are best for this operation.

FILLETS

Fillets can be lifted from the bone frame *single*, that is, coming from one side of the fish in medium-large fish (salmon, lake trout), or *butterflied*, which means that the backbone has been removed from both sides of the fish and the fillets left attached to each other to form a large M in small fish. This butterflying technique is used in smaller fish such as tinker mackerel and medium-size whiting.

All flatfish of the sole and flounder families have two double fillets instead of two single fillets. If you ask the fish market to fillet such fish for you, you should receive two double fillets each representing one side of the fish.

Such double fillets usually come from small flatfish; they can be stuffed and rolled upon themselves to form what is called a *paupiette*, which is torpedo-shaped and makes a nice portion. If gray soles, for example, are very large, do not hesitate to separate each double fillet into half lengthwise by cutting along the very visible natural line dividing each half of the fillet. You can then make two round *paupiettes* out of one fillet by spreading a bit of

Butterflied small trout, cut through the back

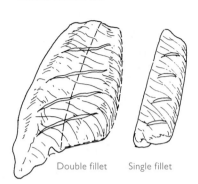

Double fillet   Single fillet

Score the skin side of the double fillet.

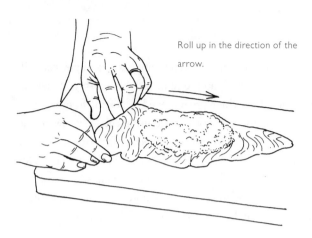

Spread the stuffing over the scored fillet.

Paupiette made from a double fillet

Paupiette made from a single fillet. Stuffed exactly as a double fillet is but standing on its side.

stuffing on the inside of the fillet and rolling the half fillet upon itself, thick end first and scored skin side facing the inside (see the recipe on page 578 for details).

STICKS OR DARNES

The center cuts of medium-size fillets of fish such as salmon can be cut into 1- to 3-inch-wide portion-size sticks called *darnes* in French culinary jargon, by cutting from the top of the fillet down toward the counter at a perfect right angle. If one prefers to use almost all the fillet and have as few small pieces as possible left over for chowders, cutting the sticks or *darnes* at an angle is the solution; you usually obtain two more portions to be served at premium price this way.

Frozen Fish

Only if fresh fish cannot be located, consider frozen fish. When you buy frozen fish, it must form a solid block, without a trace of intersticial air or frozen liquid. The presence of such frozen liquid indicates that the fish has been defrosted and refrozen.

Check on the package where the fish has been packed; it will tell you where it came out of the ocean as the processing plants are, most of the time, located on the coasts. The fish, presorted on board, are transported directly from the boat to the processing rooms. The best brands of frozen fish are located in New England, the Pacific Northwest, Canada, Norway, Newfoundland, Denmark, and Japan, all of them processing fish fished from very cold waters. All these packaged fish will mention the grade of the fish and carry a shield certifying that at least the processing plant has been passed as sanitary. *If neither origin nor sanitation shield is to be found on the package, do not buy the fish.*

Darnes of salmon cut out of a fillet

Flash frozen fish is best; the faster the freezing process, the smaller the ice crystals formed between the fibers and the better the preservation of the original state of the flesh, for important changes take place in frozen fish, which contribute to making it much less attractive for the dinner plate than the same fish in its fresh state. The freezing process, which forces water out of the flesh, is responsible for the amount of salt rising in the fibers; this salt, in turn, initiates the denaturation of the fish proteins and makes the flesh tough. Denaturation will continue while the fish waits in storage to be sold through the progressive dehydration of the flesh, as moisture travels from the inside of the package toward the outside and builds on the refrigerator coils. Several things can be done to prevent this denaturation from taking place; the fish can be frozen under pressure or in a light brine or saline that will fill the interstices in the package. In Canada, cooked lobsters are frozen in cylinders of heavy plastic containing a light brine.

Crab should be frozen this way, but it never is, so its freezing will exhibit varying degrees of success. If it is frozen at all, it should be frozen when already cooked, and consumed in a matter of one to two weeks after freezing. Dungeness crab in its shell and unshelled Alaskan king crab legs can be successfully served if frozen for a short time only. Blue crab and Maine crab legs and backfin meat are best frozen once shelled—none of these shellfish will retain their natural sweetness after having been frozen. Crab that has remained frozen too long displays almost totally dehydrated meat which shreds into long fibers and tastes stale and rancid.

The process of flash freezing that is applied to shrimp in shells is quite successful. The shrimp are spread on trays and frozen almost instantly at a very, very low temperature so that the water crystals in the meat remain extremely tiny. If such shrimp are cooked while still partly frozen, they remain sweet and delicious.

Shelled shrimp frozen the same way and cooked without defrosting by sautéing in a very hot pan or by immersing into boiling water can also be quite pleasant but are never as good as those frozen in their shells.

It is best not to use frozen scallops unless they have been flash frozen, but even then their quality is vastly inferior to the fresh ones. Scallops that have been frozen are sold swimming in their own defrosted juices. Fresh scallops are dry and shiny.

Stores selling fish that has been defrosted must label it as "previously frozen." Check yourself how dehydrated the fish or shellfish looks and how much water is visible in the dish that contains it.

Where white-fleshed fish can be frozen somewhat successfully, darker fleshed fish, which contain a lot of fatty acids, cannot, because the relatively high amount of fatty acids will react with oxygen—or oxidate—during the freezing period. The fats and fatty acids will denature and become rancid while the fish still remains frozen.

This is particularly important to remember if you have access to relatively large quantities of fish coming from sportfishing, which is frozen for you or your fisherman by people who butcher their catch poorly and throw it topsy-turvy into plastic bags. These loose bags will often contain a lot of blood; the blood oxidating faster than the muscle tissues, the taste of the defrosted fish is nothing short of a disaster and a great disappointment. Salmon frozen whole in its skin will never taste as it did when fresh and will have that awful fishy smell as it defrosts. Salmon that has been filleted, and from which the dark tissues and the skin, which both contain the majority of fat in the animal, have been removed, tastes better but still is far from perfect because of the droplets of fat in suspension between the muscle fibers. The worst instance is trout, which, once frozen, acquires a nasty taste and smell, which, because of its small size, seems even more concentrated.

If you freeze fish yourself relatively often, try to purchase a small home-style Cryovacking machine, which is quite good and affordable and will remove all air from the bag and prevent oxidation. I found it very effective.

Because of the difficulties involved in cooking fish that has been frozen, I have taken to the habit of freezing *only lean white fish* in single portions, first Cryovacked, then wrapped in aluminum foil. Each package is taken out of the foil and immersed, solidly frozen, in boiling water until it has defrosted away from the sides of the bag. The heat is turned off and the fish finishes cooking in the very hot water for another few minutes, the particular length of time needed changing each and every time with each different fish. *Check that the fish is cooked to its center.* The seasoning and garnish of such fish is always added after the cooking is completed and should be a little richer to compensate for the slight dryness of the fibers in any fish that has been frozen.

Freshness Control of Shellfish

Oysters, clams, and mussels living or being raised in the shallow waters of bays and estuaries can be contaminated by the water they live in, if those have been polluted by neighboring habitations or factory refuse. Bags of oysters, clams, and mussels come with "identification of origin" tags that, if you purchase by the bag, *you must keep*, preferably for four months after the shellfish have been cooked and consumed. This is especially important in the restaurant industry to help trace any case of hepatitis.

For home use, most of the time it will be impossible to see the tag attached to the bag. Make a mental or real note of where you bought the shellfish and on which date so you can trace the source of any sickness they may occasion.

All fresh shellfish sold in shells should be offered for sale in trays embedded in ice and placed in the usual showcase; the shells should always look moist and shiny, not dry, drab, and brittle.

Oysters sold uncooked in jars should not be consumed raw and must be used exclusively well cooked in stews and chowders.

Scallops sold fresh and not previously frozen have often been treated with an antibiotic to lengthen their shelf life. They look very translucent, sometimes with iridescent tones to the flesh. Learn to recognize them because when they cook they take on an unnatural texture and appearance and once you have cooked them, they will have none of their normal natural sweetness.

When ordering scallops, ask for "day boat scallops" which on all coasts are fished by smaller boats that go out to fish every day. They look splendid, smell like the sea, and are most expensive but well worth the cost.

Aquaculture and Mariculture

Aquaculture, the raising and producing in quantity of certain species of fish in monitored freshwater pools, and *mariculture*, the production and raising of quantities of marine species in seawater pools installed at the edge of oceans, are becoming more and more sophisticated. Such production of seafood is good for the rest and reconstitution of endangered ocean species on one side, but detrimental to the business of small fishermen whose business it has been from generation to generation to bring back excellent quality wild seafood in reasonable quantities from their daily expeditions along the coasts of all continents. If you want to find out where the problem lies, go to any library and read as much as you can on the world fish supply; you will find it disheartening.

Aquaculture and mariculture produce fish and shellfish. Oysters and lobsters raised under such conditions are tasty but the finfish has a blander flavor than that of the wild species; still, aquaculture is welcome, needed to feed our ever-increasing population and to offer fish that is clean and non-polluted. A few contamination problems manifest themselves here and there in hatchery pools, but the management of the fish is generally so careful and professional that the quality is excellent and the few problems are faced with energy and decision.

The following species are now available from hatcheries:

- Catfish, coming from Arkansas and Mississippi.
- Hybrid bass, a crossbreed of sea bass and white bass, is also in budding production in California.
- Trout comes from Idaho and Utah principally; some hatcheries are also located in Iowa, the New England states, and California.
- A variety of sea trout with a salmon pink meat somewhat similar to wild steelhead is produced on the coasts of Brittany in France.
- Salmon is raised in the Pacific Northwest, Norway, and Chile; it is, for

economic reasons, raised to a smaller size than the wild fish and does not taste as flavorful as the wild species, but it costs less than the wild fish.

- Excellent sturgeon comes from the Pacific Northwest.
- Tilapia, a fish native to Africa, and tasting somewhat like the Australian orange roughy, is now produced in small quantities in California and Arizona.
- More species of fish are in the stage of study for production in the near future, such as mahimahi in Hawaii, and Arctic char, the wonderful salmonoid of the states formerly covered by the ice cap.
- Mussels are raised in Canada on Prince Edward Island and in Maine where the pioneer of the industry, my friend Mr. Edward Myers from Abandoned Farm in Walpole, started experimenting and established the method in the early seventies.
- Spiny North Sea lobsters are produced on the coast of Brittany in France; they are large and tasty.
- Oysters. Wellfleet and Cotuit oysters are cultivated in the bays of Massachusetts. In Maine the Belon oysters cultivated by Dr. Thompson went wild and now grow to the same large sizes as they do in the North Sea, sporting the same cutting shells but absolutely delicious meat. In California both superior quality Belon and Japanese Pacific oysters are being raised at Tomales Bay, Morro Bay, and Pigeon Point. In Washington State many different oysters are being raised.
- Shrimp are being cultivated at Lake Charles in Louisiana, in Ecuador, China, and Thailand. The only wild shrimp for sale nowadays seem to be the Mexican ones.

All of these fish and shellfish are available for import into the United States or for interstate commerce. Please call the department of fisheries for information on their availability in your state. Any good "fishman" by profession will also be able to help you and procure hatchery fish for you.

Fish Handwork

It is essential that while working on fish, you wear disposable surgical gloves or you will, if you do it on a regular basis, develop some skin problems due to the effects of fish enzymes or other agents on your own epidermis. Even if you have worn gloves, wash, brush, and scrub your hands and arms afterward all the way up to your elbows with an antiseptic soap; rinse your arms abundantly with water, then rub your hands with a few drops of olive oil.

All fish cutting is to be done on a board that can be washed, then placed in the dishwasher for sterilization between each use. If you have no dishwasher, please, wash the board with soap and water, rinse, and sprinkle salt and lemon juice; let stand 10 minutes, then rinse again and air dry.

To Scale a Fish

Place newspaper on the countertop. Hold the fish tightly by the tail with your other hand. Holding a crinkle-cut cookie cutter or a specialized scraper in your working hand, scrape from tail to head as methodically as you can, passing only once over the same spot, so as not to tear the underlying skin. Pass a wad of paper toweling over the body to catch all loose scales. Rinse the fish and pat it dry. Roll all the scales up in the newspaper and discard.

To Fillet a Fish

The techniques are slightly different for round fish and flatfish, but only fillet a whole fish that has not yet been eviscerated.

FOR ROUND FISH WITH TRIANGULAR BACKBONE Place the fish on a board, the head facing your working hand, that is, to the right if you are right-handed or the left if you are left-handed. The dorsal fin of the fish will be facing you.

Place your second hand over the pectoral fin and the rounded part of the gill. Holding your knife steady, make a cut toward yourself, following the side of the gill-covering plate. As you do so and as you progress toward yourself and the nape of the fish, slowly and gradually raise the angle of your blade toward the left, pushing forward at the same time until you can feel the point of your knife hitting against the backbone and your blade is at an approximate 20-degree angle.

Let the blade flatten back to the horizontal position and slide it flush against the ribs, cutting progressively toward the tail. Lift the fillet, cut through the pin bones, and uncover the backbone completely.

Repeat the same smooth cutting motion against the belly bones as you did against the backbone. You should be holding a fillet in your second hand.

Turn the fish over and repeat the same operation on the other side, this time working from the tail toward the head.

FILLETING A ROUND FISH (SALMON OR SEA BASS)

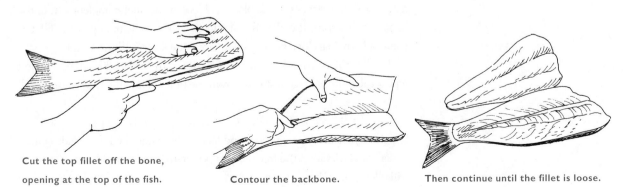

Cut the top fillet off the bone, opening at the top of the fish.

Contour the backbone.

Then continue until the fillet is loose.

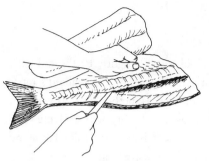

Remove the backbone from either the backside, as shown here, or the cavity side.

Slide the blade under the thin bones until you hold the backbone in your other hand.

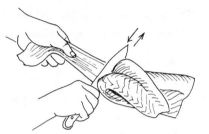

Remove the fin edge on each fillet.

Remove the skin from the fillet with long back and forth strokes of the knife blade.

FOR FLATFISH WITH FLAT BACKBONE Small flatfish of the sand dab or small flounder type are boned exactly as described above, in order to obtain two small double fillets. Since the underbelly is tougher than the top gray skin, start with the underbelly (see illustrations A and B opposite).

If the flatfish is large, proceed as follows, using a true filleting knife known as a *filet de sole*, which bends to hug and scrape the backbone with precision, so that no meat is left on it. Cut the head off, then lay the fish on its back, white belly skin up, the head pointing away from you. Now, cut along the line marking the center of the body until both fillets are separated. Starting at the head, slide the blade between the backbone and fillet and, scraping the bone with your blade parallel to the bone, slide the blade toward the tail. Two or three successive strokes of the blade will loosen the fillet completely from the bone. At this point the fillet is still attached to the side fin; open the fillet as you would the page of a book and cut along the fin (see illustration C).

To fillet the other side, turn the fish over with the head close to you and repeat the same operation starting from the tail and moving toward the head.

TO SKIN A FILLET OF ANY FISH
Lay the fillet skin down and tail end facing you. Slide the knife blade ⅓ inch under the skin. Grasp the free piece of skin with a paper towel or any rag that will allow you to hold it steady.

Proceed carefully; you do not want to break the skin and find yourself with a semiskinned fillet. Slide the blade under the skin again at a 15- to 20-degree angle, and pull tight and taut on the free skin with your other hand. Slide the knife blade into a wide left-to-right then right-to-left sweeping motion between the skin and fillet. To better see what you are doing, flip the part of the fillet already skinned forward over the yet unskinned part and continue separating the skin from the flesh. In a few seconds the fillet and skin will be separated. You will see the darker tissues of the fish; whether you remove them or not is your choice. Just skim them off gently if you do. See the illustration on the opposite page.

To Eviscerate a Fish

Insert the tip of a pair of scissors into the vent (lower abdominal opening) and cut until you reach the small tip of flesh that joins the gills to the head, just below the mouth. Cut this small pointed piece of flesh, then, still using the scissors, cut the gills out. With your working hand, gently pull the whole intestinal sac out of the cavity and place it on the table; with your other hand pull the whole body of the fish away from it. The viscera are enclosed in a membrane forming a pouch that, if you are careful, should not break. Sweep the whole pouch into the trashcan and *scrape the bloodline as carefully as you can*. This dark, livery-looking line is responsible for giving eviscerated fish a rancid fat taste so removing it as soon as you can is the smartest decision.

To Dress Small and Medium-Size Fish for Panfrying

This applies to sardines, small whiting, trout, small salmon, steelhead, etc. Very large fish should be dressed by the "fishman."

With the fish's back and dorsal fin facing you, remove the head with one solid stroke of a large cleaver or heavy chef's knife. If the fish is on the thick side (3 or more inches) use a rubber mallet or the head of a household hammer to help pass the cleaver through the bone. To do so, initiate the cut through the softer tissues with the knife blade. When you hit against the bone structure, slide the blade of your knife forward so the part of the blade that is the thickest and closest to the handle is well engaged into the meat and exactly above the nape bone. Hold the blade tightly with your left hand. Pounding on the top of the blade with the mallet, knock the thick part of the blade into and through the collarbone down to the board.

Use the same technique to remove the tail and use a very sharp pair of heavy scissors to cut off the gills. Remove the bloodline carefully.

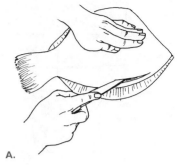

A.

Starting the filleting of double fillets in a small or large flatfish

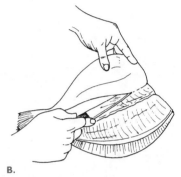

B.

Contouring the bone structure to obtain double fillet

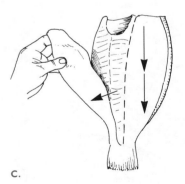

C.

To fillet a large flatfish into single fillets, cut along the dotted line and lift single fillet exactly as in illustration B above. Cut along the two long arrows and scrape in the direction of the small arrow.

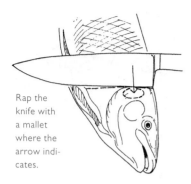

Rap the knife with a mallet where the arrow indicates.

Removing the head from a fish

To Cut Fish Steaks

There are "bone-in" fish steaks cut from medium to medium-large fish such as salmon or bass and boneless fish steaks cut out of the large fletches of very large fish.

BONE-IN STEAKS   Work at a 90-degree angle to the board; keep cutting straight or you will have irregular, bad-looking steaks. I suggest that if you work in quantity, you order whole fish from your purveyor and instruct him to cut the steaks himself of the thickness you prefer.

To cut the steaks yourself, use both a knife or cleaver and a rubber mallet or hammer. Cut through the top fillet. As soon as you feel that the blade has reached the backbone, slide the blade forward so the thickest part of the blade that is closest to the handle rests directly on top of the backbone. With a sharp stroke of the mallet over the blade, sever the backbone, as you did when cutting off the head, then gently cut through the bottom fillet.

BONELESS STEAKS   Cut straight down across the grain of large fletches at a right angle to the board and in the thickness you desire.

To Cut Fish Medallions

Medallions are prepared mostly from salmon steaks, but they can also be made with steaks of other fish such as large lake trout. For the sake of uniformity, prepare medallions exclusively with center cut steaks *no thicker than ⅔ to ¾ inch*. If the steak is thicker (this will also happen in medallions cut out of whole fillets that have not been thinned), the center of the medallion will protrude and rise when rolled.

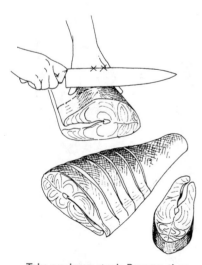

MAKING MEDALLIONS OF SALMON

Take a salmon steak. Remove the backbone and pin bones and contour the inner belly flaps.

FOR DINNER-SIZE MEDALLIONS
1. Do not cut the steak into half.
2. Work exactly the same way on each side of the steak:

Starting inside the belly opening, as close as possible to the backbone, pass a sharp paring knife under the whitish membrane, progressing steadily toward the end of the belly flap, and cut the membrane off.
3. Go back to the bone and start in the other direction working from the backbone toward the outer gray skin of the fish back.

When you are ⅓ of an inch beyond the backbone, you will encounter the pin bones; *do not cut through them*. Rather, tease them out with the back of your knife blade; they will come jutting out and stay attached to the backbone. Cut through the back skin.

Do not discard the backbone, as it can be used in the preparation of some sauces.
4. Put each side of the steak flat on the board and pass your finger over them

Remove the skin and bones; it will separate the steak into two darnes.

Flip one *darne* over.

Wrap the *darnes* around each other.

to feel whether all the pin bones have been extracted; if they have not, grasp each remaining bone with a pair of tweezers; they will come right out. It is important for the look of the medallion not to tear the meat.

5. Now set each half up on its skin side. Gently pass the blade of a sharp filleting knife between skin and light-colored muscle tissue. You must contour and include the dark muscle tissues in your cut for the steak to look uniform in color and not taste oily. If you enjoy the dark tissues, by all means leave them on each half.

6. Set both sides of the steak so they face each other again, bone side to bone side. Both belly flap sides are on your right; if you were to squeeze them together, you would have a boneless steak made of two boned *darnes*. To obtain a medallion, flip the upper *darne* upside down lengthwise, so that one belly flap now faces toward the left and one toward the right.

7. Push the two halves together so as to seal the thick parts. Now wrap the belly flap of the upper half around the bottom half and the belly flap of the bottom part around the upper part or vice versa.

You now have a well-shaped salmon medallion; you can leave it oval or shape it gently to become round. Push four toothpicks into the medallion so they crisscross at its center; they will keep the medallion together as it cooks. Let ¼ inch of each toothpick peek out of the meat, so you can easily pull them out once the meat is cooked. Count your toothpicks faithfully as you remove them and make certain that you observe the rule always to use four, so you're not chasing after a toothpick while serving.

Secure with four toothpicks.

FOR APPETIZER- OR LUNCH-SIZE MEDALLIONS

Prepare half-size medallions by rolling each *darne* upon itself, bone side in, and secure with two toothpicks.

Demi-medallions for first courses.
These small medallions are made
by wrapping one *darne* upon itself
and securing with two toothpicks.

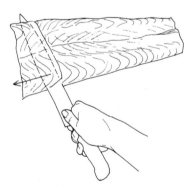

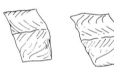

Cutting escalopes from a fillet of
salmon

To Cut Escalopes

These are mostly prepared from large Pacific salmon. Cut escalopes at an angle out of medium-large or large fillets, preferably starting from the small end of the fillet. Use a sashimi knife if you have one or a large bendable slicing knife. Cut the escalopes ¼ inch thick. Such thin escalopes will cook on contact with a hot plate and the very warm sauce spooned over them.

Fish Stock

This section is about preparing a good fish stock and good fish soups. The first reaction of the novice cook to both of these is a crinkly nose and a doubtful: Do I really have to do "that" to be a good cook? Certainly not if your work is inspired by the Far Eastern cuisines. For western-style cuisines, do it or don't, it is up to you, but you cannot expect the same results in taste and texture if you use chicken broth instead of fish fumet. As long as you are aware of the difference, the choice is entirely yours. In the recipes that follow, you can follow your own preference. I strongly urge future professionals to use fish fumet exclusively.

From several other points of view, as cooks we cannot afford to just throw away all the fish bones that cross our path; if our ancestors who lived by the oceans and seas have used them for centuries, there has to be some merit to them. A fish broth transformed into a fish soup or fish pot is economical, for if you think of it, it is made entirely with pieces of perfectly good fish that are not too presentable on a plate and the bones, which are usually given to the gulls; besides nutritionally it is extremely good and tastes absolutely glorious since over the centuries people of all cultures have devised ways of seasoning fish soups with the most delightful spices and herbs.

A fumet in the old classic cuisine was a very concentrated stock that may have been made with poultry, game, or fish. It is interesting to note that the substantive fumet in French also defines the strong, pleasant, characteristic smell of a particular food. When you first prepare fish fumet, you will understand why the name *fumet* is given to fish stock; the smell is robust and, contrary to what might be expected, quite pleasant; that is, of course, provided that the freshness of the fish is impeccable.

Due to the less than satisfying quality of the wild fish supply nowadays, the formula given here will be of the empirical type, without any indication of any quantity, so that you can prepare a small batch of fish fumet whenever you can find a few fresh fish "frames." A frame consists of a fish head with the whole backbone and viscera attached as they come off the filleting bench, fresh enough to qualify as "fumet quality" material. Fish fumet is absolutely necessary for:

- Most good western-style fish soups and chowders
- Good western-style fish sauces

Local "Fumet Quality" Fish

Only white-fleshed fish can be used to prepare a good, versatile fish stock that can be used with any fish or shellfish. *Any type of bluefish is unacceptable for fumet* because its taste is too heavy and oily. *No skin, fin, gill, tail, or any part of any viscera* may ever be used in any category of fish. *Roe is better not used,* the reason being that the roe of several fish, the frames of which are choice for fish fumet, happen to be poisonous, so abstaining altogether from using roe seems wise to prevent mistakes from happening.

Note how small the supply seems for each region. Many more species could be used, such as all the sculpin types (not using their poisonous roe, however), but we never see them and asking for them at the fish store draws nothing but blank stares or quizzical looks. All "odd fish" are thrown to the gulls as trash fish. Not so in the Mediterranean, where what Americans consider trash fish is turned into the most delicious fish soups.

EAST COAST SUPPLY
- *Sea fish:* flounder, gray sole, whiting, haddock, hake, halibut, monkfish, conger eel, ocean perch, shrimp shells, lobster abdomens (without the tomalley, which is not used anymore nowadays, because it is the liver of the crustacean in which problems of pollution may develop), oysters
- *Anadromous fish:* salmon (see note below)
- *Freshwater fish:* trout of all breeds; "ice hole"-type lake crayfish

SOUTHERN COAST AND GULF SUPPLY
- *Sea fish:* red snapper, ocean perch, pompano, grouper, shrimp shells, oysters; redfish has been depleted too much, do not use it
- *Freshwater fish:* catfish, pike, bayou crayfish

WEST COAST SUPPLY
- *Sea fish:* petrale sole, sand dabs, rockfish and all snappers, yellowtail, grouper, John Dory, shrimp shells, oysters
- *Anadromous fish:* Pacific salmon (see page 521), steelhead trout
- *Freshwater fish:* trout of all breeds, Sacramento delta and alpine crayfish from Sierra or Rocky Mountain ancient glacier lakes

LANDLOCKED STATES SUPPLY
- See the special instructions on page 544 for a fumet to be made in landlocked kitchens.

A special word on the use of salmon: Salmon is, unfortunately, all too often disregarded for fumet because of its fat content. Salmon makes a light and pleasant fumet, which, if too light for the cook's taste, can be reduced, *provided that it has been carefully and completely defatted.* Do not hesitate to use salmon fumet, but observe the very important techniques outlined on page 540 to discard the smallest traces of fat from the obtained fumet.

Fumet Texture and Taste

You have noticed that different types of fish appear in the above lists. Some of them, such as sole, flounder, ocean perch, rockfish, and grouper always give both taste and texture to a fumet, while others, such as halibut and haddock, give it only texture. It is always a good idea to use a mixture of several fish, together offering a good balance of texture and taste.

Since it is so difficult to find the exact type of fish frames one wishes for fumet nowadays, may I recommend that you prepare fumet with whatever good-quality fumet-grade fish frames you can find anytime you go to the fish store and freeze the fumet, not the frames. By doing so, you will have small stashes of different kinds of fumet which you will be able to blend to obtain the mixture you need for any dish you are preparing. Before freezing, label each jar or plastic container with a self-sticking label indicating the type of fumet and the date, such as:

Haddock fumet, 12/5/97

Frozen fish fumet should be used within 2 months of its date of preparation.

Wine in Fumet

Fish fumet should be made with dry white wine only. The following wines are the best, but not necessarily the only ones that can be used:

- Sauvignon Blanc, as low in alcohol as possible
- Chardonnay, as simple and straightforward as possible
- Perfectly dry Riesling from Alsace

If, occasionally a red wine fumet is needed, you can prepare one by using three parts red wine to 1 part white wine. This blend is necessary to raise the acidity of the red wine and extract the gelatin efficiently from the fish bones.

Do not use sweet wine, even if some well-known chef likes to use such wines for shellfish sauces. Your taste might not be the chef's taste and you may find that the sweetness of the reduced wine clashes miserably with the sweetness of the shellfish. The only sweet wine that could be used, and with lobster only, is a very old, true Sauternes, the sweetness of which has blunted considerably through aging. I doubt, though, that the price of such a bottle would be enticing to any food cost-conscious cook or chef.

Do not use dry white vermouth. When a fumet made with vermouth is reduced to make a modern sauce, the bitter taste of the herb *Artemisia absinthium*, or absinthe, which is infused in dry white wine to prepare the vermouth, surfaces and gives the fish sauce an underlying bitter taste.

Basically, if you use wine, use good, well-made wine or no wine at all; any fumet made with plain water will taste better than it would prepared with cheap, low-quality wine that turns sour on cooking and turns the cook sour on wine.

If you do not use wine, add lemon juice to the fumet before cooking it to extract the gelatin efficiently.

Cleaning Fish Frames for Fumet

Fish frames as received from the fish store are pretty discouraging to look at. If you wish them to be cleaned by the fish merchant, ask him to do so, but be prepared to pay for this service. If you clean the bones yourself:

1. With a heavy chef's knife, cut out the gills, then pull out the whole bottom part of the head; the viscera will come with it. Chop the head off; also chop off that part of the backbone which has been tainted by the viscera. Throw the unusable lot away, keeping only the upper part of the head with the nape and the cheeks and the backbone.
2. Cut off all fins and the tail. Rinse the frames carefully, so no traces of blood or dark organ tissues are visible anywhere; if some bloody area cannot be cleaned, soak the frame in lightly salted water for half an hour. Break clean frames into three smaller pieces and add those and the heads to a stainless steel pot.

These steps are absolutely necessary. Failure to take the precautions listed above will result in a bad, fishy-smelling and -tasting fumet and consequently a nasty-tasting sauce or fish soup.

Basic Fish Fumet

LFR— YIELD IS PROPORTIONAL TO THE QUANTITY OF BONES YOU WILL USE; APPROXIMATELY 2½ CUPS PER POUND OF BONES

This is a low-fat recipe if you defat the cooked fumet completely.

To as many cleaned fish frames as you can find, add 1 large or 2 smaller yellow onions, coarsely chopped; a large bouquet garni; the white part of one large leek if available, and any mushroom peelings available (optional); cold water to barely cover the fish frames plus 1 inch of dry white wine. If you do not use wine, add an additional inch of water plus the juice of half a lemon for 1 pound of fish or 1 whole lemon for up to 3 pounds.

Bring to a boil, then reduce the heat to medium and simmer 35 minutes. Push down on the frames several times with a wooden spoon or spatula to break the bones while the stock cooks; it will help release all the melted collagen. Strain through a large conical strainer and refrigerate overnight.

If fat is visible on the surface of the stock, defat completely by letting a layer of paper toweling fall gently upon the fat layer. Let the fat adhere to it, then lift the towel off and discard it; there should be no fat left; pursue each and every little bit of fat with another piece of paper towel.

Principles and Practices of Fumet Management

Once any fish fumet has reached the boiling point, do not let it boil violently or it will look and taste muddy. Do not let it cook beyond 35 minutes, or it will acquire a pronounced taste of fish bones; 35 minutes of well-regulated simmering over medium heat is sufficient to extract all the flavor from the fish. If the fumet is too thin, strain and defat it first with paper towels, then reduce it to the depth of taste you desire. Remember that *the reduction of fumet should never occur in the presence of the bones used to prepare it*.

After 35 minutes you have pretty much extracted everything the bones contain in the way of collagen, the acid from the wine and/or lemon juice helping to dissolve that collagen rapidly into the fumet.

Storage of fumet in the refrigerator is limited to 48 hours, after which the fumet must be reboiled. Fish fumet remains good and tasty if frozen no longer than two months maximum. Store refrigerated or frozen fumet in tightly covered plastic containers. Such containers have been sanitized in the dishwasher or hand washed in soapy water, rinsed with hot water, and air dried.

When using frozen fumet, put the plastic container in hot water to loosen the solid block of fumet, then turn the container upside down into a stainless steel saucepan. Remove the container and immediately bring to a full boil for immediate use.

The Preparation of Fumet in Landlocked States

The supply of fish frames and heads is so limited in landlocked areas that the preparation of fumet, fish soups, and sauces can be problematic. Two possibilities exist:

1. In landlocked areas with a supply of available freshwater fish, such as the Great Lakes, prepare the basic recipe above for fumet using whichever freshwater fish frames are available. Whitefish, pike, and muskelunge do

very well. For the liquid, use by volume: two parts water mixed with one part clam juice and one part wine, or:

2 cups water

I cup bottled clam juice

I cup dry white wine

2. In landlocked areas with no supply of available freshwater fish (the desert areas, for example), locate shrimp in shells if you really want a base for sauces. Good fish stores everywhere get them frozen from the Gulf. Purchase one pound of shrimp. Cook the shrimp over medium heat in a bit of olive oil until their shells turn red on both sides. Shell the shrimp and set them aside for a salad. Proceed as follows to prepare a fish fumet with the following ingredients; if you do not wish to use wine, you can replace it with 2 more cups of water and add the juice of 1 lemon.

The reserved shrimp shells

3 cups water

I bottle clam juice

2 cups dry white wine

I yellow onion, sliced

I leek, white and light green parts only, well washed and sliced

2 shallots, sliced

I clove garlic

Large bouquet garni

Place the shrimp shells and water in a blender and process until the shells are well broken up. Empty the mixture into a stainless steel saucepan. Add the clam juice, wine, and aromatics and bring to a boil. Turn down to a simmer and cook until 3 cups of tasty liquid is left. Strain through a conical strainer or China cap; no defatting will be necessary.

Other Substitutes for Fish Fumet

• *Court bouillon*: Refer to the section on poached fish to find the recipe for a court bouillon, the flavored bath in which such fish as salmon are poached. Add vegetables to this court bouillon and replace one quarter of the water with clam juice in which you have blended as many shrimp shells as you can find. This will give you a court bouillon that is tastier than the basic water-wine-vinegar court bouillon and will be made yet richer by the immersion in it of the fish or fish fillets you will be poaching. Use some of that court bouillon to prepare a soup or sauce and you will be surprised at how good it will taste.

- *Chicken broth or stock*: For soups of oriental origin (China, Vietnam, Thailand), you may use plain chicken broth (see the section that starts on page 547).

Fish Soups and Fish Pots

Ah, will you say, who wants to eat fish soup? The populations of countries bordering all the seas and oceans have for centuries survived on fish soups and pots and it is to them that we owe some of the most delicious and nutritious food existing. Judge for yourself with the little collection that follows.

The Oriental soups speak for themselves as being truly different from their European counterparts. Simple and direct in execution, their base is a light clear chicken or pork broth broth well seasoned with different delicious spices and aromatics.

You will notice two different methods in the European soups. The first is the chowder way, which is traceable in all preparations which originally started in many countries but were modified by the English habit of adding milk to fish broth. Such is the case of the ancient soups of the Maori of New Zealand as well as the *chaudrée* that the French Protestant immigrants brought from La Rochelle on the Atlantic coast of France below the estuary of the Loire River to what is now the East Coast of the United States; there it became chowder (just read *chaudrée* with an English or American accent) when milk replaced the wine of the French. Most of these soups are very straightforward, uncomplicated, and very light in texture and taste.

The second method is that of the *kakavia* or bouillabaisse, early descendants of the much more ancient fish soup of the "old people of the sea" of the eastern Mediterranean. This soup traveled east to west with the Greek colonizers and pops up in each and every port of modern Greece, still under the name *kakavia* and in Italian ports as *brodetto*, *zuppa di pesce*, *burrida*, and *ciuppin*, depending on which fish are included in the kettle. More often than not, the soup will take on the name of the pot in which it customarily cooks. The *kakavia* cooks in a *kakavi*, and since Marseilles was settled by Greek colonists, of course bouillabaisse was cooked originally by fishermen in a pot called a *bouillet*. These soups range from the simplest preparation, tasting thin and lean, to the richest double- often even triple-strength broth, giving a mouthful of pleasure.

On the eastern Atlantic coast, there is also the Basque *ttoro*, originally a simple kettle of boiled fish, nowadays strongly flavored by the new world peppers brought back by the great discoverers, and the *cotriade* of Brittany, so-called because the pot rested on the hearth, balanced on two crossed bars of cast iron called *cottrets*.

Fish soups number in the hundreds if not the thousands with many variations in each and every country, for this is the food of the people and of fishermen, not food for the upper classes. It varied each and every day with the catch and was made with what we call trash fish, fish that was not saleable to the more affluent part of society.

N'gao's Mother's Saigon Fish Soup

NFR — 6 SERVINGS

One 1-pound piece fresh halibut or other firm-fleshed lean fish of your choice, cut into 1 × ½-inch slivers

1 to 3 Thai chiles, to your personal taste, finely chopped

2 tablespoons nuoc mam

2 teaspoons peeled and grated fresh galangal or ginger

3 tablespoons coarsely chopped cilantro leaves

1 teaspoon grated lime rind

Juice of 2 limes

5 cups chicken broth of your choice

⅔ cup uncooked basmati rice

2 cups bottled clam juice

4 small zucchini, cut into 1 × ¼-inch slivers

3 scallions, finely slivered

Place the fish in a bowl, then add the chile(s), *nuoc mam*, galangal, cilantro, and lime rind and juice, and mix until the fish pieces are evenly coated. Let marinate together while the rice cooks.

Bring the broth to a boil in a large saucepan, add the rice, and simmer over medium heat until tender, about 15 minutes. Add the clam juice and slivered zucchini and bring back to a boil; add the marinated fish. Turn the heat off, cover and let stand for 5 minutes. Add the scallions and ladle into warm bowls.

In 1972, I received a letter from my school friend N'gao, who, at the time, lived back in Saigon with her family. In the letter she described a fish soup prepared by her mother, asking me to think of her if I ever prepared it. N'gao did not survive the events of 1973, a great emotional loss for me. Probably out of self-defense, I never tried the recipe until, one day in 1993, it fell out from between the yellowed pages of the little old cookbook my mother used in our home in France. This is N'gao's recipe. For the broth, I like a combination of chicken broth and clam juice. The number of Thai chiles used will depend on your taste for heat. The chiles, nuoc mam (a fermented fish sauce), and galangal can be found in Oriental food stores and some supermarkets and specialty food stores.

Maori-Inspired Pipi and Kowhitiwhiti Soup

The pipi I saw in New Zealand resemble, in a larger size, the telline of the Mediterranean and, in a way, the soft-shelled steamers of Maine. They can be replaced by any type of clam, including prepared minced clams. Wild watercress grows as a weed all over New Zealand, where it is thought to have arrived from Sydney in 1841, with the French ship Comte de Paris.

SUGGESTED WINE: A Cloudy Bay Sauvignon Blanc from New Zealand

FCR—6 SERVINGS

3 quarts Maine steamers or other smaller clams

Salt

2 tablespoons unsalted butter or unsaturated oil of your choice

3 large yellow onions, chopped

I cup water

2 cups milk of your choice or light cream

2 cups packed watercress leaves, well washed and chopped

2 tablespoons cornstarch

Pepper from the mill

Soak the clams for 2 hours in plenty of water salted with 1½ teaspoons salt per quart of water, to allow the mollusks to lose their sand. Scrub well and let drain in a colander. Discard any clams that will not close.

Heat the butter in a larger pot over medium heat. Add the onions and cook, stirring, until golden. Add the clams and 1 cup water. Cover the pot and steam until the clams have opened, tossing the clams several times during the steaming. Discard any clams that do not open. Remove the remaining clams from their shells, chop them coarsely, and return them to the cooking pot; add half of the milk and heat to just below the boiling point.

Bring a small pot of water to a boil, place the watercress in a colander, plunge the colander into the water, and blanch for 2 minutes. Drain well and add to the soup. Mix the cornstarch with the remaining cup of milk. Stir into the hot soup, bring back to a boil, stirring, and, as soon as thickened, turn the heat off and let stand for 5 minutes. Correct the final seasoning and serve with a crusty loaf of bread.

China Sea-Style Prawn and Lean Fish Soup

The basic broth used in this soup can be any fat-free chicken broth at your disposal; homemade broth gives better results than canned to my personal taste, but the Oriental spices are often strong enough to disguise the difference.

LFR—6 SERVINGS

3 dried Chinese black mushrooms

6 cups clear chicken broth of your choice

4 jumbo shrimp in their shells

I tablespoon dark soy sauce

2 tablespoons dry sherry

1½ teaspoons peeled and finely grated fresh ginger

One 2 × ½-inch piece fresh tangerine rind without pith, finely chopped

Fillets of I medium-size sole of any type, cut into I × ⅓-inch slivers

½ red bell pepper, seeded and cut into I × ⅛-inch sticks

2 scallions, sliced into ⅛-inch-thick slivers on the diagonal

Salt

Pepper from the mill

Soak the black mushrooms in cold water to cover until rehydrated. Remove, rinse, and chop the stems. Slice the mushroom caps into 1 × ¼-inch slivers and set aside. Strain the mushroom soaking liquid through a double thickness of paper towels.

Bring the chicken broth to a boil in a large saucepan. Add the strained mushroom soaking liquid and chopped stems. Shell the raw shrimp, add the shrimp shells to the broth, and simmer over medium heat for 20 minutes. Slice the shrimp into slivers. Mix the soy sauce, sherry, ginger, and chopped tangerine rind together and divide between two medium-size bowls. Add the shrimp to one and the sole to the other, mixing well until each is coated with the marinade. Set aside.

Strain the flavored broth through a fine strainer into a clean saucepan. Bring back to a rolling boil. Add successively the slivered mushrooms, red pepper, slivered shrimp, sole, and scallions. Bring back to a boil and remove from the heat immediately. Cover, and the fish will finish cooking in the hot broth. Correct the final seasoning to your taste. Serve in hot bowls.

Scottish Haddock and Salmon Chowder

FFR — 6 SERVINGS

1 small smoked finnan haddie fillet, about ½ pound

Skim milk

4 salmon steaks taken from the nape or tail

4 cups chicken broth of your choice

6 large leeks, white and light green parts, well washed and finely chopped

1 cup bottled clam juice

2 Yellow Finnish or Yukon Gold potatoes, peeled and diced into ⅓-inch cubes

¼ cup cornstarch

1 cup cream of your choice

2 hard-boiled eggs, coarsely chopped

3 tablespoons chopped fresh parsley leaves

Salt

Pepper from the mill

To make this soup even leaner, use only the egg white. The choice of cream is yours; you have your pick from crème fraîche to sour cream, as well as heavy cream or light cream; yogurt is not recommended for this preparation. Serve with Scottish oat cakes.

Soak the finnan haddie in enough skim milk to cover for several hours in the refrigerator; pat dry and discard the milk. Cut into ⅔-inch cubes. Skin and bone the salmon steaks; discard the skins, but keep the bones. Set both fish aside.

Bring the chicken broth to a boil in a large saucepan. Add the leeks and bring back to a boil. Loosely wrap the salmon bones in a piece of cheesecloth rinsed under cold water and squeezed dry; tie well enough so the bones will not escape. Add to the broth and simmer over medium heat until the broth is very tasty, about 30 minutes. Remove the salmon bones. Add the clam juice, bring to a boil again, and add the diced potatoes. Cook for 15 minutes over medium heat.

Mix the cornstarch with the cream and add, stirring, to the chowder base. Stir until well thickened. Bring to a rolling boil, then add the salmon, then the haddock and remove immediately from the heat. Let stand 5 minutes covered, then add the chopped eggs and chopped parsley. Correct the final seasoning and serve in hot bowls.

Ttoro des Pays Basques
BASQUE FISH SOUP

I have yet to find a completely detailed recipe which is authentically Basque because I cannot read the Basque language. This is a personal composition of what is available from the sea, and grown on or around the French littoral of the Basque country; it also reflects the information I received from several older home cooks in St. Jean de Luz and Hendaye.

You should not be surprised by the corn cubes. Called arthoua *in the Basque country, corn arrived there after the Great Discoveries and largely replaced the ancestral millet to become a staple of Basque farm cuisine. The prosciutto replaces the so-called Bayonne ham which is processed and aged not in Bayonne but in the neighboring town of Orthez.*

If you do not use wine, add 1 more cup of fish fumet or chicken

FFR—6 SERVINGS

For the corn cubes

2 cups water

½ cup cornmeal

2 large pinches of red pepper flakes

Salt

Pepper from the mill

Unsalted butter or unsaturated oil as needed

For the soup

One 5-pound striped bass, cleaned and boned

Salt

Pepper from the mill

I large sprig fresh thyme

12 large shrimp in their shells

½ cup water

I quart mussels, debearded, cleaned (page 680), and well scrubbed

4 large shallots, finely chopped

Large bouquet garni

1½ ounces fat from proscuitto or other air-dried country ham or 3 tablespoons corn oil

4 large cloves garlic, finely chopped

2 tablespoons finely chopped fresh parsley leaves

3 large yellow onions, finely chopped

I red bell pepper, seeded and finely chopped

I green bell pepper, seeded and finely chopped

3 large sun-ripened tomatoes, peeled, seeded, and cut into ¼-inch cubes

6 cups fish fumet (page 543) or chicken broth of your choice

I cup dry white wine

Make the corn cubes. Bring the water to a boil in a 1-quart saucepan. Add the cornmeal, one pinch of pepper flakes, and salt and pepper and stir constantly. Cook over medium heat until the stirring spoon stands straight in the mass of mush. Lightly butter or oil an 8-inch-square cake pan and spread the corn mush in it to an even ⅓-inch thickness. Rub with a tiny bit of butter or oil; cool completely and refrigerate. When cold, cut into ⅓-inch cubes. Set aside.

Skin the bass fillets and cut into strips ⅓ inch wide. Salt and pepper lightly, then sprinkle with the thyme, cover, and keep refrigerated until ready to use.

Heat a nonstick frying pan. Pan-broil (see page 795) the shrimp on both sides until cooked through. Shell and slice the shrimp; set the shrimp and shells aside.

Bring the water to a boil in a large pot. Add the mussels, shallots, and bouquet garni, cover, and steam till open. Discard any mussels that do not open. Shell the mussels and reserve in a small bowl; discard the shells. Reserve the mussel juices and the bouquet garni.

Cut the ham fat into small cubes; add to a cold sauteuse pan and, slowly increasing the heat, sauté until light golden. Add the garlic and parsley and sauté until the garlic is golden and fragrant. Add both peppers and the tomatoes and toss until well blended. Add the fish fumet and wine, the reserved bass bones, shrimp shells, and mussels juices and the bouquet garni. Add the remaining pinch of pepper flakes and bring to a boil. Reduce the heat to medium and simmer, uncovered, 35 to 40 minutes. Strain through a China cap, pushing on all the elements of the broth to extract as much flavor as possible.

To serve, reheat the broth to the boiling point. Add the mussels, shrimp, strips of sea bass, and cubes of cornmeal. Heat again to the boiling point. Turn the heat off, correct the seasoning, and serve.

broth. *When asking your fishmonger to clean and bone the bass, ask him to also give you the cleaned head and backbone.*

SUGGESTED WINE: *A Vin des Sables or a dry Jurançon, both from France*

La Chaudrée de La Capitaine

La Capitaine was the nickname given to one of my great grandmothers. An orphaned daughter of a captain who lost his life in the most famous cavalry charge in French history, she was widowed early from yet another captain. She raised her three sons on the profits of a small mattress-making business and by cooking very formal dinners in very upper class households. This is the way she prepared the chaudrée *of her native Poitou south of the Loire.*

This chowder is made according to one of the best rules of French cuisine, the double fumet technique, in which the soup itself is prepared with fish fumet instead of water to obtain more depth of taste. A treat for a nice company dinner; it was served with a small montagne de rôties, *or a small pile of lovingly toasted slices of robust country bread, shiny with butter. If you do not wish to use wine, use ¾ cup each more of fumet or chicken broth and of clam juice. The shellfish is not shelled; offer wet paper towels.*

FFR—6 SERVINGS

¼ cup unsalted butter plus extra for the beurre manié

½ pound yellow onions, coarsely chopped

6 leeks, white and light green parts, well washed and coarsely chopped

½ pound carrots, coarsely chopped

1 pound cleaned squid, sliced

2 large cleaned sole or flounder "frames" (page 540)

2 cod heads, cleaned

1 pound whiting, cleaned and cut into pieces

Salt

Pepper from the mill

8 cups fish fumet (page 543) or chicken broth of your choice

2 cups bottled clam juice

1½ cups dry white wine

Large bouquet garni

½ cup cloves garlic, peeled

Dash of ground cloves

½ teaspoon ground coriander

1 quart mussels, debearded, cleaned (page 680), and well scrubbed

1 quart Manila or cherrystone clams, cleaned (page 680) and well scrubbed

3 shallots, very finely chopped

Flour as needed

2 tablespoons Cognac

3 tablespoons chopped fresh tarragon leaves

Heat the ¼ cup butter in a 1-gallon pot. Add the onions, leeks, and carrots and cook, stirring, over medium heat until the onions are translucent. Add all the fish, salt and pepper lightly, and cover. Let the fish and vegetables sweat on low heat until the juices extracted from the fish almost cover the solids in the pot; keep breaking the bones as they fall apart. Add the fish fumet, clam juice, wine, and bouquet garni. Bring to a boil, then reduce the heat to medium and simmer until the soft-fleshed fish falls apart and the squid has turned hard, about 25 minutes. Continue destroying the fish pieces as much as possible during the cooking to extract as much juice as possible. Strain into a bowl through a large conical strainer or China cap.

Put the garlic cloves in a small pan; add just enough of the prepared double broth to cover the garlic. Season with salt and pepper and cook over low heat until the garlic falls apart, about 35 minutes. Whisk to puree coarsely, then add the ground cloves and coriander. Blend back into the double broth and reheat together.

Put the mussels, clams, and shallots in a sauteuse. Add 1 cup of the double broth, cover the pan, and steam open. Discard any that do not open. Leave the shellfish in their steaming pot and liquid.

Meanwhile, reheat the remaining double broth to the boiling point and prepare a *beurre manié* (see page 287) with 1 tablespoon each flour and butter per each cup of available double broth. Thicken the double broth with the *beurre manié* and pour immediately over the steamed shellfish. Reheat well without boiling. Heat the Cognac in a small pan and pour, flambéed (see page 117 for more specific instructions on this), into the *chaudrée*, shaking the pan back and forth. Serve sprinkled with the chopped tarragon. Serve with *rôties*.

SUGGESTED WINE: **A Muscadet de Sèvre-et-Maine**

About Bouillabaisse

I have tried time and again to obtain a "true"-tasting bouillabaisse in this our New World without ever being able to duplicate it 100 percent; a little something is always missing. I started blaming myself until I taught in Aix-en-Provence, used the fish of the Mediterranean and obtained that intriguing and utterly delicious taste from all that rockfish not sold in fish stores in this country. There exists no recipe written which, executed with the fish available in this country, will taste quite like the true Marseilles concoction or I would refer you to its text immediately. So, rather than trying to entertain you with yet one more not-so-authentic-tasting bouillabaisse, I much prefer to let you work on something that works out very well, one of the other fish soups of Provence, the *bourride*. I can, as I write, hear the outcry at all these egg yolks and oil. Again, you certainly are not going to have *bourride* each and every day, are you? So, why not have it once in a while exactly as it is prepared by the Provençaux?

Bourride

This fish soup will taste of the Provence, especially if you prepare it with wild fennel seeds, which are nice and pungent and should be gathered along creeks, not along the highways, to avoid tasting of car exhaust. We can at least find the fish we need to prepare it in this country: monkfish, striped bass, and whiting. And our garlic is every bit as good as that found in Provence. Notice that again I use fish fumet rather than water to start the broth. The whole dish is high in taste, if not in color. For the preparation of the aïoli, see the techniques for mayonnaise on page 340.

This is an authentically Provençal recipe which I have seen prepared by several of my friends in Provence exactly as I do it here. Some people make this soup by pouring plain water over the fish, which results in a weak broth; to alleviate this problem, they add an ounce of flambéed Pernod to the finished soup. This is a viable solution if you do not care to prepare fumet and certainly not a bad idea either, even if you use the fumet.

SUGGESTED WINE:
Châteauneuf-du-Pape Blanc

FFR—8 SERVINGS

For the fish and broth

One 3-pound chunk monkfish

One 3- to 4-pound striped bass

2 very fresh large whiting

Salt

Pepper from the mill

1 tablespoon (preferably wild) fennel seeds, crushed to powder

1½ teaspoons ground dried orange rind

3 tablespoons olive oil of your choice

2 large yellow onions, minced

1 large sprig fresh thyme

1 large Mediterranean bay leaf

3 tablespoons chopped parsley stems

6 cups fish fumet (page 543) or 3 cups water plus 3 cups bottled clam juice

2 small fennel bulbs, well washed and finely chopped

For the aïoli

8 large cloves garlic, peeled and green shoots, if any, removed

Large pinch of salt

2 large egg yolks

2 cups olive oil of your choice

Juice of 1 lemon

Lukewarm water as needed

Pepper from the mill

For the binding and presentation

8 oven-dried ⅓-inch-thick slices French bread

5 large egg yolks

Salt

Pepper from the mill

Chopped fresh parsley leaves

Bone, skin, and clean completely all the fish (or have the fish store do it for you). Reserve the heads and all bones. Cut the meat into 2-inch cubes. Sprinkle the meat with a bit of salt and pepper, half the fennel seed powder, and half the dried orange peel. Let marinate several hours, refrigerated.

Meanwhile, heat the olive oil in a large sauteuse pan. Add the onions and cook, stirring over medium heat until translucent, then add the thyme, bay leaf, and parsley stems and continue cooking until the onions turn golden, stirring occasionally. Add the fish fumet, fennel bulbs, and the remaining fennel seed powder and orange peel; bring to a boil. Reduce the heat to medium-low and simmer 35 minutes. Strain through a China cap, pushing on the solids with a ladle to extract all the flavor. Keep the broth hot.

To make the aïoli, pound the garlic cloves to a fine puree. Add the salt and the two egg yolks and mix well. Add the olive oil drop by drop until the mixture is thick and forms a paste. Gradually lighten with a bit of the lemon juice and warm water; very gradually add more olive oil to avoid "flooding" and breaking the aïoli. Continue alternating oil and lemon juice and/or water until the sauce has absorbed all the olive oil. Correct the seasoning.

Once the fumet is well flavored by the aromatics, lightly oil a sauteuse and add the marinated fish. Gently pour the hot broth over the fish maintaining high heat under the pot until the broth comes back to a boil. Remove from the heat and let stand 5 minutes.

Meanwhile put the slices of bread in an ovenproof dish. Moisten each slice with a sauce spoonful of the broth. Top with the fish. Cover with parchment paper and keep warm.

Divide the batch of aïoli into two equal parts. Put one in a sauce boat and set aside to serve warm with the fish. Whisk the 5 additional egg yolks into the second batch of aïoli. Gradually stir in half the broth, then, reversing the process, stir the lightened aïoli–egg yolk mixture back into the sauteuse, mixing well. Return the sauteuse to a medium flame and thicken until the soup coats the back of a sauce spoon by ⅛ of an inch. This operation takes only a few minutes. *Do not boil.* Correct final seasoning with salt and pepper.

Serve the soup immediately accompanied by the dish of fish sprinkled with chopped parsley and the sauce boat of remaining aïoli.

Asparagus Broth with Scallops and Smoked Salmon Quenelles

FFR — 6 SERVINGS

For the broth

I pound medium-size fresh asparagus

6 cups water

2 teaspoons salt

3 cups fish fumet (page 543), no replacement please

2 cups bottled clam juice

I cup dry white wine

I teaspoon coriander seeds, crushed

One 2 × ½-inch strip orange rind

2 shallots, finely chopped

2 medium-size yellow onions, finely chopped

¼ cup chopped fresh dill

6 teaspoons crème fraîche

For the quenelles

½ pound fresh scallops

4 ounces smoked salmon, preferably Nova Scotia

I large egg white

I large egg

¾ teaspoon salt

30 turns of the pepper mill

3 tablespoons unsalted butter, at room temperature

1⅓ to 1½ cups heavy cream as needed

There is an excellent way to prepare this soup so no work except reheating is necessary on the day you are serving. Before making the quenelles, be sure to fully understand the general techniques of making mousselines and quenelles as described on pages 690–93, as well as the explanation of making this type of paste in the food processor on pages 690–91.

SUGGESTED WINE: *A dry Tokay d'Alsace*

Peel the asparagus and slice into ¼-inch-wide elongated slivers. Bring the water to a boil, then add the salt and the asparagus. Cook 2 minutes at a rolling boil. Drain, saving 1 cup of the water for the broth. Refresh the asparagus slivers under cold water and pat dry. Set aside.

Mix the fish fumet, clam juice, wine, reserved asparagus cooking water, coriander seeds, orange rind, shallots, and onions together in a large saucepan. Bring to a boil, then reduce to a simmer, and cook over low heat until reduced to 4 cups. Strain and let drip through a conical strainer.

To prepare the quenelles, remove the feet from the scallops and place the scallops, smoked salmon, egg white, and whole egg in a food processor. Process until smooth, then separate the mixing bin from the machine and put it and its contents to chill for 2 hours, covered with plastic wrap, in the refrigerator.

After 2 hours, using a wooden spoon, cream together 2 tablespoons of the butter and the salt and pepper. Add this to the fish meat in the processor bin, reset the bin on its machine, and pulse the butter into the fish mixture until homogeneous. Finally, gradually add 1⅓ cups of the cream. If the mixture is too stiff, add the remaining cream.

Rub the bottoms of two sauteuse pans each with ½ tablespoon of the remaining butter. Using two oblong tablespoons, shape eighteen quenelles by passing eighteen successive tablespoons full of quenelle paste from one spoon to the other until each quenelle is smooth. To make the work easier, dip the spoons into cold water to clean them between each quenelle. Deposit nine quenelles into each sauteuse pan.

Bring the prepared broth back to a full boil. Reheat the asparagus in 1 cup of the broth. Very gently pour half the remaining boiling stock into each sauteuse. Put the heat on medium-low under each pan until the quenelles come floating to the surface of the broth. Using a slotted spoon, gently turn them over and finish cooking, 2 more minutes.

Divide the dill among six bouillon bowls or deep soup plates. Transfer three quenelles and an equal amount of asparagus to each bowl. Correct the final seasoning of the broth with salt and pepper and gently strain again an equal amount of broth into each bowl. Top each bowl with 1 teaspoon of the crème fraîche.

Generalities on Sauces Accompanying Fish Dishes

The ways of preparing sauces for fish are multiple. In this chapter, you will see:

- Classic sauces relying on the use of a fish fumet made into veloutés (see pages 271–76 for complete technical explanations of flour-bound sauces)
- A few emulsified egg sauces, but very few, for they have become all too rich for our modern way of life (see pages 337–40 for technical explanations)
- Some *beurre blanc*–type sauces (see technical explanations on pages 333–35)

There are, by far, more modern sauces and they are divided into these two categories:

Quick Sauces for Everyday Fish Dishes

These quick sauces accompany quickly panfried, steamed or pan-steamed, and grilled fish. Their methods of preparation will be both classic and modern and you will find:

- Noisette butter blended with lemon juice
- Compound butters
- Vinaigrette-type dressings poured over a bright hot fish to be served either hot or cold after a few hours of marination in the refrigerator.

Other sauces are the plain fish cooking juices blended with an enriching element and/or thickened with a bit of cornstarch.

In very contemporary style, you will find purees of vegetables blended with cooking juices and a pat of butter, vinaigrettes made with flavored oils, chutneys, and salsas.

More Elaborate Sauces for Elegant Fish Dishes

Prepared with fish fumet and other ingredients, these sauces deserve some explanation of their possible components:

LIQUID AROMATIC COMPONENTS

These liquid components can be: a wine (always dry), white or red or fortified; fish fumet, clam juice, or other shellfish juice; court bouillon; vinegar; or lemon juice. They are not all mixed together, of course, and the most common combinations are:

- Wine and fumet or fresh shellfish juice
- Wine, fumet, and vinegar
- Fumet and court bouillon
- Fumet, court bouillon, and citrus juice

Note that none of the formulas proposed contain only fish fumet. Fumet reduced alone tastes fishy; its texture is too thick, which makes the sauce stick to the lips, and its color is an unattractive off brown.

Every combination being possible, you will see the various elements combined, with a predominance of fish fumet, because fumet *ties* the fish to the sauce that covers it and eliminates that slight feeling of "unrelation" between fish and sauce existing in sauces that do not contain fumet, such as the true *beurre blanc*. The neutral taste of the fumet also somewhat counteracts the acids of the wine, vinegar, or citrus juice, and the slight viscosity from its gelatin content is helpful in forming an emulsion with butter or a flavored oil.

SOLID AROMATIC COMPONENTS OF FISH SAUCES

The solid components will be the following, used alone or in combination, depending on your choice: chopped onions, chopped shallots, chopped leeks, bouquet garni, chopped stems of herbs, crushed garlic cloves, chopped fresh herbs, fish bones, shellfish shells, pieces of skinless fish or shellfish, spices, hot peppers, etc.

Note that the smaller you chop the aromatics in all the dishes that follow, the more flavor they will release into your sauce. There are two different categories of aromatics, added at different times: those introduced at the onset of cooking, before the reduction starts, which will flavor the sauce by losing their essences to the reducing fumet-wine or other acid mixture, and those added as garnish to provide an element of freshness when the sauce is finished. The reduction may also be blended with a puree of vegetables or a puree of acid fruit.

The Modern Sauce Base: The Reduction

The reduction is obtained by mixing and reducing together the liquid and solid aromatic components of the fish sauce. It must be reduced by at least 50 percent, so if you start the sauce base with 1 cup of mixed liquids, you should have ½ cup before you add any enrichment.

THE ENRICHMENT OF FISH SAUCES

You can use heavy cream, sour cream, crème fraîche, or butter. Or you can, if you prefer to stay on the lean side, add light cream or, if the acidity is not important for the general character of the sauce, some plain low-fat yogurt.

For more details on sauces in general, see pages 265–354. and relate the techniques used in each of these recipes to the general explanations given in the sauce chapter.

The Diverse Techniques of Cooking Finfish

The techniques of cooking fish are divided into three main categories:

1. *Moist heat procedures* in which the fish is either cooked in an added liquid, over steam, or over very low heat using only the water present in its own fibers.
2. *Semidry/semimoist procedure* in which the fish is cooked half by searing and half by the heat gathered by its own juices.
3. *Dry heat procedure* in which absolutely no liquid is used at all and the fish is submitted to direct heat transferred by radiating or conduction heat.

Cooking Finfish by Moist Heat
Fish Poached in Salted Water or a Court Bouillon

Poaching is an ancient method that has been finally perfected as we have at our disposal sophisticated instant thermometers to measure the temperature of the liquid bath accurately. Some people call it "boiling" fish, something that should never be done unless one likes stringy fish. The technique is sometimes used for larger fish to be served hot, but most of the time it is used for fish to be served cold in summer.

To poach is to cook fish by immersing it in hot water or any combination of hot liquids, making certain that the poaching bath is held at a steady 200° to 205°F, never letting it come to a boil. Such poaching is often done in water salted at the same ratio as the sea, which is 1 ounce or approximately 2 level tablespoons of salt per gallon of water. Generally the smaller the piece of fish the hotter the court bouillon or water will be. Whole large fish may be immersed in cooler water and be brought to the final poaching temperature.

More often than not the poaching bath is not just salted water, but water strongly flavored with a mixture of aromatics and wine, vinegar, or lemon juice, a combination known as court bouillon. The aromatics have the double role of flavoring (herbs) the court bouillon and helping firm (acids) the outside tissues of the fish rapidly. Court bouillon is prepared in the same pot or poacher where the fish will be cooked.

THE POACHER

To poach a medium to medium-large fish such as striped bass or salmon, you will need a long poacher fitted with a rack that is lightly greased. The fish will first be set on the rack, then immersed in the court bouillon. If you do not own a poacher, you can improvise one with an oblong roaster fitted with a rack. To poach small pieces of fish such as steaks or medallions, you can use the basket of a round steamer and immerse the basket in a pot or sauteuse the diameter of which is 1 to 2 inches larger than the basket.

COURT BOUILLON

Different fish require different court bouillons; semifat fish such as salmon, striped bass, and snapper will take a slightly acid wine or vinegar court bouillon, while a very white fish such as the European turbot, which is sometimes available in the big restaurant cities (New York, Los Angeles, San Francisco) and the excellent Chilean sea bass should be poached in a milk court bouillon which will preserve the color of its flesh and prevent its fibers from drying excessively.

You will notice how simple the aromatics are and wonder about other choices. Leeks are always welcome; they do not appear in the recipes because they are so expensive that they are usually kept for sauces and stocks. But by all means if you have leek greens, add them to any court bouillon; it can only make it better. Beware of celery, which is a wonderful vegetable, but so strong and so persistent as an aromatic that all one can taste in fish poached in court bouillon containing too much celery is celery. And if you use a bit of court bouillon to prepare a sauce, the celery flavor surfaces even more during the reduction of the sauce base. So, if you want celery, use celery, but with the utmost discretion.

Milk Court Bouillon

FFR — ENOUGH TO POACH 1 LARGE TURBOT OR
6 CHILEAN SEA BASS STEAKS

8 cups water

1 ½ cups whole milk

4 teaspoons to 2 tablespoons salt or to your personal taste

½ teaspoon white pepper from the mill

2 thick slices lemon

This court bouillon is used exclusively to poach fish, never as part of a sauce. Do not use skim milk.

Mix all the ingredients together except the lemon. Bring to a boil and add the lemon. Let stand for 5 minutes. It is now ready to use for fish steaks. If needed to poach whole fish, let it cool to barely lukewarm before adding the fish.

Wine Court Bouillon

LFR — ENOUGH TO POACH A LARGE SALMON OR STEELHEAD TROUT
OR TO CRIMP A NUMBER OF SALMON STEAKS AND TROUT

3 quarts cold water

2 bottles dry white or red wine

6 large yellow onions, minced

1 large carrot, sliced

Large bouquet garni

3 tablespoons salt

1 ½ teaspoons white peppercorns

White wine court bouillon is used for most lean, white-fleshed fish as well as all semifat fish. Red wine court bouillon can be used for carp, salmon, and trout. Please use good if inexpensive wine, but not cheap wine.

Mix the water and wine together in the poaching vessel, then add the onions, carrot, bouquet garni, and salt, bring to a boil slowly, then reduce the heat to medium, and simmer for 20 minutes. Add the peppercorns and simmer an additional 10 minutes. *Let cool completely and strain before using.*

Vinegar Court Bouillon

LFR—ENOUGH TO POACH LARGE SALMON, STEELHEAD TROUT, ANY
LARGE LAKE TROUT, BASS, AND LARGE CATFISH. IF USED FOR LOB-
STER AND SHRIMP, INCREASE THE AMOUNT OF SALT TO
1 TABLESPOON PER QUART OF LIQUID AND OMIT THE VINEGAR.

4 quarts cold water

2½ cups white or red wine vinegar or cider vinegar

3 carrots, sliced

5 large yellow onions, minced

Very large bouquet garni

2½ to 4 tablespoons salt, to your personal taste

1 teaspoon black or white peppercorns

Pour the water and vinegar into the poaching vessel. Add the vegetables,
bouquet garni, and salt. Bring to a boil slowly; reduce the heat to medium
and simmer for 15 minutes. Add the peppercorns and simmer another 20
minutes. *Let cool completely and strain before using.*

POSSIBLE SECOND OR MULTIPLE USES OF COURT BOUILLONS
Milk court bouillon can be used within one day as many times as desired,
provided it is refreshed with more water and more milk as the day goes along,
but it must not be kept overnight; a new milk court bouillon must be prepared each and every day. The combination of milk and fish proteins makes
the mixture very perishable.

Wine and vinegar court bouillons, however, can be reused; here is how.

* *At home:* Strain the court bouillon after use and freeze in a large sterilized
  plastic container. When ready to reuse, add ⅔ cup water for each quart of
  defrosted court bouillon to compensate for the loss of volume during its
  previous use, as well as a few aromatic vegetables to "renew" the taste of
  the court bouillon. Use exactly as you would a new mixture.
* *For larger quantity production:* When poached or crimped (see page 567)
  fish is on the menu, the court bouillon is to be strained carefully after daily
  use and refrigerated carefully since it contains a lot of fish proteins. Before
  using the next day, renew the court bouillon by adding water to deconcen-
  trate the taste of wine or vinegar and a few fresh aromatics and salt and
  pepper to pep up the taste.

POACHING WHOLE FISH
PREPARING THE FISH You must purchase the fish "round" (see page 528)
and prepare it yourself. No fishman will do it the way it should be done; take
it from a cook who has had several bad experiences in this department.

* Do not scale the fish.

- Do not remove the head.
- Eviscerate the fish, making an incision 1½ inches long at the vent and cut off the end of the intestinal tract. With a pair of sharp scissors cut the gills away from the remainder of the head, grasp the gill with your gloved hand, gently pull the viscera out in their membrane, and discard.
- Pass a round-tipped dinner knife inside the cavity along the backbone to dislodge the bloodline. Run cold water through the whole body, starting at the head, until it runs clear through the vent.

The fish is ready for poaching.

If your fish has already been cleaned and has lost its head, you can, if you want, roll the fish into a piece of cheesecloth that has been rinsed and squeezed dry and tie a double layer of parchment paper around the cut stomach end; cloth and paper will replace the thick shield of scales. Chunks or blocks of fish should also be wrapped in cheesecloth for easier handling.

POACHING THE FISH Never immerse a whole fresh fish in a boiling court bouillon; otherwise, you will see the skin rupture under the pressure of the rapidly swelling tissues. Place whole fresh fish in cooled court bouillon to cover and bring to poaching temperature:

- Slowly if the fish is large to allow the tissues to heat and swell gradually,
- A little more quickly if the fish is small; since the thickness of the fillets is not considerable, the tissues will heat and set almost simultaneously.

If these two options leave you a bit perplexed, think of a trout which will poach in a total of 12 minutes and of a whole salmon which will require some 6 minutes per pound of body weight, which for an 8-pound salmon will be a total cooking time of 40 to 45 minutes. Whereas the heat must penetrate the thin trout fast, it must penetrate the salmon progressively or the outer layers will be overcooked while the inner side of the fillets close to the bone will be too rare. Maintain the poaching temperature between 200° to 205°F. The pot should be covered with the lid left slightly askew.

If a whole fish is not sparkling fresh. It happens unfortunately too often that a large fish is delivered still edible and good but not as sparkling fresh as it should be for poaching. You can safely immerse it in a *boiling court bouillon* to prevent the further degradation of quality that would take place in the meat if it had to go through progressive reheating of the court bouillon. No skin rupture will occur since the tissues have already started denaturing and dilating while the fish was in transit to the kitchen.

The sure way to check the cooking time. Measure the thickness of the fish you are poaching at its thickest part and count 7 minutes per inch for a fish up to 8 pounds and 8 minutes per inch for a fish up to 10 pounds. A fish larger than 10 pounds is usually reserved to be cut into steaks or filleted.

The internal temperature of the fillet when measured with an instant thermometer all the way to the backbone should be 140° to 165°F, no more.

SERVING WHOLE POACHED FISH To serve a whole poached fish warm, at home, lift the rack out of the poacher, slide the fish onto a platter. Skin the fish and separate the top fillets from the bone frame. Remove the backbone and replace the top fillets over the bottom ones to present the dish. Use large wads of paper towels to absorb the liquid in the platter before you garnish the fish.

To present the fish cold, let it cool completely in the fish poacher and proceed as above. Cold fillets are solid and break less easily than warm ones. Decorate the fish as you like.

POACHING LARGE CUTS OF FISH, LARGE FILLETS, STEAKS, AND MEDALLIONS Any piece of fish showing exposed tissues unprotected by skin *must be immersed in boiling court bouillon* so as to provide an immediate coagulation of the exposed meat tissues. Go back to the recipes for chowders on pages 547–53 where the fish is skinless and added to the boiling soup which is then immediately removed from the heat to prevent overcooking.

Wrapping the steaks or medallions in leaves of lettuce or other greens will protect the exposed tissues from overhardening but not interfere with the proper penetration of the heat since they are so thin.

Sven's Salmon

From Lavik on beautiful Sognafjorden in Norway, as enjoyed on June 24, 1947. Court bouillon is needed in this recipe; prepare it ahead of time.

SUGGESTED BEVERAGE: *Rather than wine, try a nice light beer or ale.*

FFR to FCR—8 TO 10 SERVINGS

1 salmon, about 10 pounds, eviscerated only, as described on page 537

1 recipe Vinegar Court Bouillon (page 562)

Salt

Pepper from the mill

1 large bunch fresh dill, stems and leaves separated

1 European cucumber, peeled and seeded

2 tablespoons cider vinegar

1 cup crème fraîche, sour cream, or plain yogurt of choice

2 tablespoons yellow mustard or to taste

½ teaspoon granulated sugar (optional)

2 tablespoons aquavit or Cognac (optional)

Measure and take note of the thickness of the salmon at its thickest part. Heat the court bouillon to lukewarm in the poaching vessel. Salt and pepper the salmon in its cavity and stuff with the dill stems. Put the salmon on the rack and immerse in the liquid. Bring to a bare boil, then turn the heat down and maintain at 205°F for 7 minutes per inch of thickness, plus 7 minutes for the pot, until the fish has reached an internal temperature of 140° to 165°F as desired. Keep the pot covered leaving the lid slightly askew.

While the fish poaches, dice the cucumber into ¼-inch cubes, salt and sprinkle with the cider vinegar. Let stand until all the water has come out of the vegetable. Drain in a colander and let drip completely. Chop the dill leaves to obtain 3 tablespoons and add to the cucumbers. Mix together well ⅓ cup of the court bouillon and the chosen cream, mustard, and the sugar, if desired. Add the cucumbers and aquavit. Correct the salt and pepper.

If the fish is served warm, reheat the sauce well without boiling it. If the fish is served cold, serve the sauce cold. For the best look, present the whole fish skinned on a platter and portion it at the table.

Poached Striped Sea Bass Anchoaïde

FCR — 6 SERVINGS

I large striped bass, 4 to 5 pounds, eviscerated only, as described on page 537

I large bunch fresh sweet basil, stems and leaves separated

I recipe Vinegar Court Bouillon (page 562)

Salt

Pepper from the mill

2 cans anchovy fillets preserved in olive oil

4 large cloves garlic, very finely chopped

6 slices French bread cut ½ inch thick on a slant

½ cup chopped fresh parsley leaves

3 large sun-ripened tomatoes, sliced in half

Extra virgin olive oil to your taste

6 lemon wedges

As enjoyed in a bistro in the Vieux Cannes on the French Riviera. Court bouillon is needed in this recipe; prepare it ahead of time.

SUGGESTED WINE: *Cassis or Bandol from France or red Grignolino from Italy or a rosé Grignolino from the Napa Valley*

Measure the thickness of the fish at its thickest part. Heat the court bouillon to lukewarm in the poaching vessel. Stuff the fish cavity with the basil stems and salt and pepper well. Set the fish on the poaching rack and immerse in the court bouillon. Bring to a bare boil and maintain the poaching temperature at 205°F for 7 minutes for each inch of thickness plus 5 minutes for the pot, until the internal temperature of the fish has reached 140° to 165°F. Keep the poacher covered with the lid slightly askew.

Meanwhile, drain both cans of anchovies, saving the oil from one. Mash half the anchovy fillets completely with 2 of the garlic cloves, 6 basil leaves, and a generous amount of pepper; this is the anchoaïde. Brush the bread slices with the olive oil from the can of anchovies on one side only; place on a baking sheet and broil, then spread with an equal amount of the anchoaïde. Set aside.

Mix the remainder of the garlic with 6 tablespoons of the chopped parsley and salt and pepper. Sprinkle over the tomato halves. Set the tomatoes on a baking sheet, drizzle their tops with virgin olive oil and broil until brown.

When the fish is done, fillet and top each slice of bread with a portion of fish. Top each portion with one of the remaining anchovy fillets and sprinkle with the remaining parsley. Serve accompanied with a broiled tomato half, a few basil leaves drizzled with fresh olive oil, and a wedge of lemon.

Poached Fresh Haddock with Radish Green Vinaigrette and Stir-fried Radishes

Inspired by the Arabic escabeche, I started presenting fish in vinaigrettes in 1970. This different vinaigrette, full of good greens and vitamins, lifts the fish out of its inherent blandness and enhances its beautiful texture.

SUGGESTED WINE:

Sakonnet's Vineyard America's Cup White

FCR — 6 SERVINGS

2 bunches round red radishes

One 4-pound piece fresh haddock, bone in and skin on

1 recipe Vinegar Court Bouillon (page 562)

For the vinaigrette and garnish

1 tablespoon fresh lemon juice or to taste

Salt

Pepper from the mill

1 shallot, very finely chopped

1 ½ teaspoons Dijon mustard or to taste

⅔ cup plus 1 tablespoon corn oil

Dash of red wine vinegar

Remove the greens from 1 bunch of the radishes, wash, and dry them. Cover the flesh of the fish entirely with these radish leaves, then wrap it in cheese-cloth. Bring the court bouillon to a bare boil in the poaching vessel, add the fish, and poach covered with the lid slightly askew at 205°F, for 8 to 10 minutes per pound, until the internal temperature of the fish reaches between 140° and 165°F.

While the fish poaches, prepare the vinaigrette and garnish. Remove the leaves from the second bunch of radishes. Wash, pat dry, and chop half of them coarsely as you would parsley. Set aside.

Mix ⅔ cup of the poaching court bouillon, the lemon juice, salt, 6 turns of the mill of pepper, and the shallot together in a small saucepan; reduce to 3 generous tablespoons over medium heat. Off the heat, add the mustard and whisk in the ⅔ cup of corn oil. Set aside.

Slice the radishes. Stir-fry them quickly in a hot skillet in the remaining tablespoon of corn oil, adding a dash of vinegar to set the color. Season with salt and pepper. Set aside.

Remove the cooked fish from the court bouillon, discard the cheesecloth, and discard the radish leaves and skin from the surface of the fish. Carve and lift portions off the bone and set each portion on an individual plate on a bed of sliced radishes. Just before serving, add the chopped radish greens to the dressing and rehomogenize well, adding a tablespoon or so of court bouillon if necessary for a looser texture. Spoon over the warm fish and serve.

Crimped Fish

Crimping is not used enough; it seems to have been a long existing English technique which is summarily described but not very much used by Escoffier. It came to me through a friend from England who, one day, served me the most delicious, moist salmon steak I ever had. I adopted the technique and have been teaching it since 1970.

Crimping fish is another way of poaching small whole fish as well as fish steaks and medallions. The poaching medium can be salt water or court bouillon, as you prefer, and the technique is as simple as can be.

Immerse the fish or portions in boiling salt water or court bouillon. Maintain high heat under the poacher so the water comes back to a boil in seconds; remove the pot from the heat and let the fish stand in the hot bath for 6 minutes per inch of thickness, uncovered but fully and deeply immersed. Simple, direct, rapid, and British, which makes you think twice about the legend, probably spread by the French, that the British cannot cook. They can too and they certainly have the art and manner of not unduly complicating matters.

Since crimping in a large bath of water can be cumbersome in a small home kitchen, the same operation can be done with much simpler equipment. You can place the fish in a shallow metal baking dish and fire a burner on very high. Put the dish on the high burner at the same time as you pour boiling water over the fish. Salt the water, and as soon as it comes back to a boil, which is almost instantly, remove the dish from the heat and let your fish stand the number of minutes necessary to firm it up. The recipes that follow will be executed half with a court bouillon in a poacher and half with this last method; as you follow them, you can interchange the poaching vessel according to your personal needs.

Crimped fish is served both warm and cold; crimped salmon steaks or medallions, or slices of Chilean sea bass presented on a cold summer buffet are always moist, tender, and most flavorful. Skate wings, however, are better warm.

East-West Crimped Skate Wings

Purchase the skate in ready-cut portions; this is the easiest way to handle a fish which is otherwise awkward. Varying with the size of the skate, wings come generally 1 to 1½ inches thick. The fish fibers are long and lean and overcooking is to be avoided at all costs. This dish must be served warm and the poacher is the most practical implement for cooking.

SUGGESTED BEVERAGE:
Warm saké

FCR—6 SERVINGS

For the court bouillon

6 portions skate wing

6 tablespoons saké

3 tablespoons dark soy sauce

Grated rind of 2 tangelos or oranges

4½ quarts water

2 cups sweet rice vinegar

2 tablespoons salt or to taste

1½ teaspoons black peppercorns

For the dressing and garnish

Juice of 2 tangelos or oranges

2 tablespoons fresh lemon juice, more or less to your personal taste

¼ teaspoon granulated sugar

6 tablespoons corn oil

Dark soy sauce

Dash of red pepper flakes

3 scallions, slivered

1 pound carrots, shredded

Sweet rice vinegar

Salt

Pepper from the mill

Fresh parsley leaves

Lay the skate portions next to one another on a lightly greased poacher rack. Mix together the saké, soy sauce, and 1 teaspoon of the grated tangelo rind; brush the mixture on both sides of the skate wings. Let marinate while you prepare the court bouillon.

Mix together the water, rice vinegar, salt, and peppercorns in a large saucepan (see the basic techniques for court bouillon on pages 560–62) and simmer for 15 minutes. Remove ⅓ cup of the finished court bouillon to a small skillet; mix in the orange and lemon juices, the remainder of the grated tangelo rind, and the sugar. Reduce to ¼ cup over medium heat, then whisk in the oil and season with as much soy sauce and red pepper flakes as desired. Blend in the slivered scallions.

Season the shredded carrots with vinegar, salt, and pepper to taste. Finally, bring the court bouillon back to a rolling boil, add the skate, and bring back to a rolling boil again, then remove the poacher from the heat and let stand 6 minutes for wings 1 inch thick and 7 to 8 minutes if they are 1½ inches thick.

To serve, remove the skate pieces to a clean cutting board. Slide a cake spatula between the skate flesh and wing cartilage and separate them. Set each edible portion on a plate; spoon some of the vinaigrette over the fish and garnish with the vinegared carrots and parsley leaves.

Walensee Trout

FFR — 6 SERVINGS

I recipe **Vinegar Court Bouillon (page 562),** boiling

6 very sparkling fresh trout, eviscerated only, as described on page 537

Salt

Pepper from the mill

8 jumbo asparagus, peeled and bottoms removed

I tablespoon fresh lemon juice or to taste

¼ cup unsalted butter

½ cup crème fraîche

I½ tablespoons chopped fresh tarragon leaves

I½ tablespoons chopped fresh chervil leaves

Bring a large pot of water to a boil and at the same time bring the court bouillon to a rolling boil. Season the trout cavities with salt and pepper. Using a trussing needle, pass kitchen string through tail and head and tie nose to tail, pulling the fish into a closed circle. Set the trout on the poacher rack.

Add salt and the asparagus to the plain water and cook until tender-crisp, al dente. Reserve ½ cup of the cooking water. Add the trout to the boiling court bouillon and bring back to a rolling boil. Immediately remove the poacher from the heat and let stand 8 minutes.

While the trout poaches, mix together the reserved asparagus cooking water, the lemon juice, and a dash each salt and pepper in a small saucepan and reduce to ¼ cup over medium-high heat. Melt and cook the butter in a small skillet until it reaches the noisette stage (see page 32). Add the noisette butter to the crème fraîche and blend gradually into the reduction of lemon juice. Correct the seasoning and add the herbs. Keep warm.

Remove the trout from the court bouillon. Skin the fish and pull out the strings. Spoon an equal amount of sauce over the top of each trout and garnish each plate with three asparagus which will be seasoned by the sauce running from the top of each fish.

A Swiss delicacy and a delicious memory of Easter 1951. Walensee is a deep green glacier lake 50 miles east of Zurich. If you are lucky enough to catch true brookies or browns, use this recipe by all means. When cooked just out of the water, the trout will split open over the dorsal fin when immersed in the court bouillon, so don't worry. If white asparagus is available, by all means use it and do overcook it a bit so it acquires that typical "melting" European texture. The best implement here is a poacher.

SUGGESTED WINE: **A Swiss Dézaley**

Chilean Sea Bass Steaks on Black Bean Salsa

Both steaks and salsa can be served either warm or cold. You can poach either in a poacher or in a metal baking dish.

SUGGESTED WINE: **A** *Chilean Sauvignon Blanc or Pinot Blanc, or the same from your favorite California vineyard*

FCR — 6 SERVINGS

I large clove garlic, crushed

½ cup corn oil

5 teaspoons sweet Hungarian paprika

Six ¾-inch-thick Chilean sea bass steaks

I cup warm cooked black beans

I cup warm cooked corn kernels

I or 2 jalapeño peppers, to your personal taste, thinly sliced

½ red onion, finely chopped

2 tablespoons vinegar of choice or to taste

Salt

Pepper from the mill

2 teaspoons Tabasco sauce, more or less to your personal taste

2 scallions, finely slivered

3 tablespoons chopped cilantro leaves

Put the garlic clove and oil in a small skillet. Heat over low heat until the garlic has turned light brown. Remove the garlic and, off the heat, stir in the paprika. Let stand 2 hours to allow the paprika taste to infuse the oil; do not strain the paprika out.

Remove 2 tablespoons of the flavored oil to a small ramekin and brush on both sides of the sea bass steaks. Marinate the fish while you prepare the salsa.

Mix the black beans and corn with the slivered jalapeño(s), red onion, vinegar, salt, and pepper. Toss with the remaining paprika oil. Set aside while you cook the fish.

Bring a large saucepan full of water to a rolling boil. Add salt and the Tabasco sauce. Arrange the steaks in a thick metal baking dish over high heat and pour the flavored boiling water over them, keeping them on high heat until the water returns to a rolling boil. Immediately remove the baking dish from the heat and let stand about 5 minutes. Transfer the steaks to a platter; sprinkle with half the scallions. Add the remaining scallions and the chopped cilantro to the salsa and arrange around the steaks. Serve immediately.

Curry of Lingcod

FFR—6 SERVICES

½ teaspoon ground cumin

6 turns of the mill of ground pepper plus more as needed

I rounded teaspoon ground turmeric

½ teaspoon ground ginger

½ teaspoon chili powder

I tablespoon ground coriander

¼ cup clarified butter (page 32), mustard oil, or unsaturated oil of your choice

3 cloves garlic, coarsely chopped

I pound silverskin onions, peeled

1½ cups water or as needed

Salt

2 pounds lingcod fillets, skinned and cut into ¾-inch cubes

I cup canned coconut milk

3 large sun-ripened tomatoes, peeled and diced into ¼-inch cubes

3 cups cooked basmati rice

Mix all the spices together well. Heat the chosen fat in a skillet, over medium heat, then add the garlic and onions and cook, stirring until golden. Remove the vegetables to a plate. Add the spices and cook the mixture until fragrant, 2 to 3 minutes. Remove a teaspoon of the spice mixture and set aside. Return the garlic and onions to the pan. Add the water to generously cover the spice-and-onion mixture and cook over medium-low heat until the onions are tender.

Meanwhile, toss the reserved teaspoon of spice mixture and salt and pepper to taste with the cubed lingcod pieces, then place in a thick metal baking dish. Bring a kettle full of water to a boil. Place the baking dish over high heat at the same time as you pour the boiling water directly from the kettle over the lingcod. Salt the water. As soon as the water comes back to a rolling boil, remove the lingcod to the curry sauce using a slotted spoon. Add the coconut milk and tomato cubes and reheat well. Serve the curry over the rice.

You can replace lingcod with any other white fish of your choice. For the best Indian taste, use mustard oil, which can be found in all Indian markets and by mail from the Napa Valley Mustard Company in St. Helena, California.

SUGGESTED BEVERAGE: *Try iced tea, but a mellow California Riesling could be pleasant.*

Crimped Pike, Bruschetta, and Basil Pinzimonio

FCR—6 SERVINGS

1 recipe Wine Court Bouillon (page 561)

Juice of 1 lemon

Salt

Pepper from the mill

⅔ cup extra virgin olive oil

Six ⅔-inch-thick slices Italian bread

2 large cloves garlic, cut in half

2 yellow pike, 2 to 3 pounds each, eviscerated only, as described on page 537

⅓ cup packed fresh basil leaves

The scene is Sora Lella, the old restaurant on the Isola Tiberina in Rome, in 1952, where the grandmother of a friend was hosting my friend and me to dinner. A wonderfully typical Roman skit happened, for Sora Lella, the restaurant owner, offered her luccio grilled, and la nona wanted it poached; so poached it came with typical Roman bruschette and the best ever pinzimonio, the oil-rich dressing flavored liberally with fresh basil. This is best prepared during the spring when the Jewish holidays bring us a good supply of pike. Both yellow and walleye pike work well. Use a poacher.

SUGGESTED WINE: A Frascati, Est! Est!! Est!!! di Montefiascone, or Castel Gandolfo

Prepare and keep the court bouillon at a rolling boil in a fish poacher while you prepare all other elements of the meal.

Put the lemon juice, salt and pepper to taste, and the olive oil in the blender and process until white. Let stand.

Toast the slices of bread under the broiler on a baking sheet just to dry their surfaces. Rub them with the garlic cloves, then brush them with a bit of the prepared dressing. Set the toasts back on a baking sheet.

Set the pike on a lightly greased rack and immerse in the boiling court bouillon. Bring back to a rolling boil and remove from the heat. Let stand 10 minutes. Remove the pike to a dish; skin and bone into fillet portions. Keep warm.

Broil the toasts until golden, another minute, and keep warm. Add the basil to the blender and process until the pinzimonio turns green. Correct the salt carefully. Serve each portion of pike on a bruschetta, spooning fresh pinzimonio liberally over the fish. The dish should be served lukewarm.

Salmon in a Pinot Noir and Blackberry Coat

FCR—6 SERVINGS

6 large red potatoes, peeled

8 cups water

Salt

Pepper from the mill

1¼ cups good California Pinot Noir or other dry red wine

4 shallots, finely chopped

½ cup fresh blackberries

¼ cup unsalted butter

This is my personal interpretation of salmon steaks prepared for us by Betty Starke from Calistoga in the Napa Valley. The sauce is sweet-sour. And, the logistics work; I have done it many times. To transform this dish into a company dinner, make

6 salmon steaks or medallions

Chopped fresh parsley leaves

6 sprigs fresh basil

medallions out of the steaks (see page 538).

SUGGESTED WINE: *The remainder of the bottle of Pinot Noir plus another one if need be*

Quarter the potatoes; round the angles of each piece of potato to prevent them from breaking off and mushing up. Place the potatoes in the water, seasoned well with salt and pepper, bring to a boil, and boil just until tender, about 20 minutes.

Put the Pinot Noir and shallots in a saucepan with salt and pepper to taste. Reduce by one half over medium heat, then pour into a blender and add the blackberries. Process until smooth, then strain carefully through a conical strainer to remove all the seeds. Return to the saucepan, bring to a boil, and whisk in 3 tablespoons of the butter. Salt and pepper well. Set aside, keeping warm.

Put the salmon steaks in a thick metal baking dish. Set the dish over high heat as you immediately pour the boiling water from the potatoes over the fish, letting the potatoes fall into a colander. Return the potatoes to their cooking pot and add the remaining tablespoon of butter. Keep warm. By then the fish will be back to a rolling boil. Remove the salmon pan from the burner and let stand 5 to 6 minutes.

Skin the salmon steaks, serve them coated with the blackberry sauce, and dot the potatoes with the chopped parsley. Brighten the plates with leaves of basil.

All Manner of Steamed Fish

In this section, you will find all the methods of steaming fish, each with two recipes for illustration.

PAPILLOTE-STEAMED FISH

This is a very old technique that I remember from my childhood. What looked like a small army of parchment paper papillotes, each enclosing a piece of fish with its garnish, were lined up on the kitchen table and my aunt was blowing air into them, using a long, straight macaroni. I remembered this with a bit of a tremor after I became a strict sanitarian, though no one in the restaurant seems ever to have become ill.

The technique is easy: *Use absolutely no liquid*; the only liquid used to cook the fish will be its own juices and those of the vegetables eventually used to garnish it.

TO MAKE THE PAPILLOTES For six papillotes, you will need two regular-size precut sheets of parchment paper, or six smaller sheets large enough to contain one steak if you cut parchment from a roll.

Fold each sheet of paper in half lengthwise. Place two or three portions of

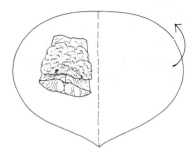

Fish and garnish

Flip the right side over the fish and
crimp the two edges of paper
together to enclose fish.

fish 1½ inches away from the fold and cut the paper around each portion, forming a half heart all around the fish and maintaining a distance of at least 1½ to 2 inches all around the fish. When you have cut the half heart, reach under the fish and pull out the undersheet and you will see your piece of fish sitting pretty on one half of a heart. The papillote can be made smaller or larger as needed for the size of the pieces of fish available.

Season the fish with whichever spices you like, top with precooked vegetables of your choice, and fold the paper over the fish, pleating it all around to enclose the fish tightly inside the papillote.

To bake, transfer each papillote to a baking sheet. Bake 5 to 8 minutes in a preheated 450°F oven. The heat of the oven is high because the paper is not a good heat conductor; the high heat will have just enough time to penetrate the paper and fish flesh and start cooking the latter. Remove the papillote from the oven and let it stand, still tightly closed, for another 2 to 3 minutes, which will finish cooking the fish and deliver it tender and moist to your plates.

If you use aluminum foil for the packages, cut squares large enough to wrap a steak in each in "drugstore fashion" and dull side out, the dull side absorbing the heat faster. Since the foil is a good heat conductor, the oven need only be preheated to 375°F. As for the papillote, put the packages on a baking sheet and bake 8 minutes, then remove the foil packages from the oven and let stand 3 minutes before opening the packages.

NO OVEN? If you have no oven, as happens quite often in small apartments, cook the papillotes or foil packages in a covered electric frying pan preheated to 400°F for papillotes and 350°F for foil packages.

Here are two recipes, one for papillotes and one for foil packages.

Bluefish and Fennel in Papillotes

This recipe comes from the Cotentin peninsula of Normandy, where it is made with mackerel fillets, which could replace the bluefish if not available. Because of this preparation, gooseberries in Normandy have been given the name groseilles à macquereau or mackerel berries. You can replace them with red or black currants or any acid berry such as wild cranberries, regular cranberries, white raspberries, cloudberries, or salmonberries.

FFR — 6 SERVINGS

¼ cup unsalted butter

2 small fennel bulbs, well washed and thinly sliced, with some of the greens

1½ teaspoons fennel seeds

Salt

Pepper from the mill

2 large sparkling fresh bluefish fillets, skinned

3 tablespoons crème fraîche, heavy cream, or sour cream of your choice

1 tablespoon cider vinegar

⅔ cup fresh gooseberries or acid berries of your choice

2 tablespoons coarsely chopped fresh parsley leaves

6 large red or Yellow Finnish potatoes, quartered and steamed until tender

Preheat the oven to 450°F and cut the papillotes (see page 573). Heat 3 tablespoons of the butter in a skillet and cook to the noisette stage (see page 32). Add the sliced fennel with some greens and the fennel seeds and sauté over medium-high heat until the vegetables soften slightly. Salt and pepper well. Cool while you put the fish on each papillote.

Top each fish portion with an equal amount of the fennel, then close the papillotes and bake 6 minutes. Remove from the oven and let stand 4 minutes. Mix the cream with the vinegar, salt, and pepper. Open the papillotes and slide the fish onto individual plates. Spoon equal amounts of the cream mixture over each portion. Heat the remaining tablespoon of butter in the same pan you sautéed the fennel and sauté the berries over medium-high heat a few seconds, then sprinkle them over the fish, along with the chopped parsley. Surround with the potatoes.

SUGGESTED BEVERAGE:
Try hard sparkling cider from Normandy or a Pacific Northwest Riesling.

Halibut Steaks in Foil Packages

FCR—6 SERVINGS

6 skinless and boneless halibut steaks, 4 ounces each and ½ inch thick

6 large slices smoked salmon of your choice

Pepper from the mill

¼ cup pure olive oil

I yellow onion, finely chopped

I clove garlic, finely chopped

I cucumber, peeled, cut in half lengthwise, seeded, and thinly sliced

I medium-size zucchini, cut in half lengthwise and thinly sliced

I tablespoon fresh lemon juice

10 kumquats, seeded and finely chopped

I tablespoon finely scissored fresh Chinese chives or regular chives

A favorite from the small weekday menu of my Boston restaurant. Use salmon of any origin; I use my own home-smoked salmon (see page 645); "belly lox" is too salty.

SUGGESTED WINE: *A Fumé Blanc from California*

Wrap each halibut steak with a slice of smoked salmon and pepper lightly. Place each steak on a square piece of foil, large enough to wrap the fish in it "drugstore fashion."

Preheat the oven to 375°F. Heat 1 tablespoon of the oil in a skillet over medium-high heat and sauté the onion and garlic until golden. Add the cucumber and zucchini slices and stir-fry 1 minute. Salt and pepper lightly. Divide this mixture into six portions and top each steak with one portion. Wrap the fish and set the packages on a baking sheet. Bake for 7 minutes. Remove from the oven and let stand another 2 minutes still tightly wrapped.

Meanwhile, mix the lemon juice, the remaining olive oil, salt, pepper, the chopped kumquats, and chives into a small vinaigrette. Open the packages and slide each portion onto a dinner plate. Spoon an equal portion of the dressing over each steak. Serve promptly.

FISH STEAMED IN A STEAMER

This is the *jing* method of cooking fish done so beautifully by Chinese cooks and which I have been very happy to see enter western kitchens in the last few years. The fish comes out of the steamer quite succulent, provided you have the right equipment and follow some rules carefully.

THE STEAMER   Steamers consist of three parts:

- A deep container which holds the water, which when heated will turn into steam, the intense heat of which will cook the fish.
- One single basket or several stacked baskets which will hold the fish to be steamed. The fish will be set in the basket as is or, if very delicate, will be wrapped in green leaves which will protect its surface from being hardened by the intense heat of the steam.
- A lid which will close tightly, trap the steam inside of the pot, and keep it under pressure all through the pot from bottom to top.

Use any steamer you own already; it can be either a metal one or a series of Chinese steaming bamboo wicker baskets set over a wok. Double-tier basket steamers are particularly practical since a dinner for six to eight can be steamed at once.

If you own a wok with its lid, you can turn it into a steamer by dropping a cake rack in the bottom, on which you will be able to set a plate or dish containing the fish and/or any other garnishes of vegetables. Chinese neighborhood kitchen equipment stores offer all kinds of inexpensive possibilities and solutions for a self-made steamer.

Restaurant-style steamers Large restaurant kitchens and some smaller ones which have been equipped the modern way often use the large steamers with horizontal sliding trays fitted with racks, in which the pressure can be regulated and a number of portions can be steamed at once. The length of the steaming can be varied to the chef's specifications for each type of food. If you work in a restaurant equipped with such a steamer, your chef will teach you how to regulate the exact pressure required for each of his/her fish dishes. Such a steamer is a *precision tool* with which one needs to familiarize oneself carefully, for one second too long can spoil a whole tray of expensive fish portions.

AN IMPORTANT CAUTIONARY NOTE   *Be careful: Steam is hotter than boiling water and can inflict deep and most cruel burns which take a long time to heal.*

It is therefore essential that when you handle the steamer you wear kitchen mittens. It is also essential that you never put your face over the steam and always open the lid so it protects your face to avoid burns.

HOW TO STEAM   Fill the bottom of the steamer one third full with lightly salted water or, if you prefer, with lightly salted water seasoned with aromatics which will release their volatile acids into the steam. These volatile acids will be carried to the fish and flavor it.

Spray the basket lightly with a bit of oil, so the fish does not stick to it. Set the basket(s) over the steam and close the lid.

When you start the steaming, the water must boil rapidly. Reduce the heat as soon as the fish has been put in; the water should be at a rapid simmer. A rolling boil will make the pot lid lift constantly and is unnecessary.

To remove the food from the steamer, turn the heat off, remove the lid so as not to burn your face, remove the basket(s), and lift the portions out of the basket(s) with a spatula or tongs with insulated handles.

Plate steaming Plate steaming consists in steaming the fish on the plate on which it will be served. It is a good technique for people living alone or cooking no more than two portions at a time. The portions can be steaks, fillets, or medallions or one small two-pound fish tied head to tail into a circle and placed at the center of the plate surrounded with vegetables. Make certain that the plate fits into the basket in such a way that you will have no difficulty removing it after the cooking is completed.

To avoid burning yourself, remove the basket from the heat. It will cool rapidly, then you can remove the plate, which stays hotter, and set it on the table.

Here are a few recipe ideas:

Steamed Salmon with Avocado Salsa

FCR — 6 SERVINGS

1 large bunch cilantro

½ small red onion, diced into ¼-inch cubes

Salt

2 Haas avocados, peeled, pitted, and diced into ¼-inch cubes

Grated rind and juice of 1 lime

Cider vinegar

2 ears freshly picked Silver Queen corn, shucked and kernels cut off

1 tablespoon finely chopped dried pasilla chile

Pepper from the mill

1 red bell pepper, optionally peeled

6 salmon medallions (page 538), ⅔ to ¾ inch thick

You can use steaks instead of medallions; I advocate medallions because you can fit six medallions into a steamer basket with a 10-inch diameter, whereas it is more difficult to do so with steaks. This avocado salsa can be replaced by any salsa of your choice. Use the amount of vinegar you prefer in the salsa.

Chop the cilantro leaves coarsely and set aside. Salt the onion and let stand 30 minutes. Drain, rinse, and pat dry. Mix with the avocado cubes, lime rind and juice, and vinegar to your taste; toss well to coat the avocado and pre-

SUGGESTED BEVERAGE: **A difficult choice: You can go from a light Zinfandel, to an oaky Chardonnay, to a fruity French Côtes-du-Rhône. Most Mexicans would probably tell you that their Dos Equis beer would be just fine.**

vent browning. Mix the corn into the avocado. Add the pasilla, black pepper to taste, and the diced red pepper. Let stand 20 minutes.

Chop the cilantro stems. Put them in the water container of the steamer and add water to fill the pot by a little more than one half and add a large pinch of salt. Bring to a boil, then reduce the heat to medium and simmer 10 to 15 minutes, uncovered.

Lightly salt and pepper the salmon pieces, then sprinkle them on both sides with the chopped cilantro leaves. Bring the cilantro water in the steamer water container to a rolling boil again. Place the salmon in the steamer basket and set in the water container. Turn the heat down to a steady simmer. Cover and steam 6 to 8 minutes, depending on the type of salmon. Check the doneness of salmon with an instant thermometer, which should record 140° to 165°F.

Finish the salsa by adding as much chopped cilantro as you personally like and toss well. Serve the salmon with the salsa and a good salad of your choice.

Steamed Mountain-Style Trout Fillets

FFR—6 SERVINGS

1 pound thin-sliced bacon

12 boneless trout fillets

Salt

Pepper from the mill

3 tablespoons peeled and coarsely chopped hazelnuts

6 tablespoons chopped fresh chervil leaves

12 light green escarole leaves, blanched in boiling salted water 1 minute and cooled completely

Large bouquet garni

1 medium-size yellow onion, coarsely chopped

2 cloves garlic, coarsely chopped

1 shallot, very finely chopped

2 tablespoons wine vinegar of your choice

¼ cup hazelnut, walnut, or corn oil

½ pound baby frisée salad leaves

12 nasturtium leaves and flowers (optional only if not available)

A good recipe for those wonderful Rocky Mountain trout fillets. This can be served either as a light dinner course or a first course for a more substantial company dinner.

SUGGESTED WINE: **A light red Zinfandel, a Beaujolais-Villages, a Mondeuse from the French Alps, or a Bourgogne Aligoté**

Render the bacon slices slowly until crisp in a large skillet. Pat them dry of all fat and crumble into small pieces.

Pat the trout fillets dry with a wad of paper towels lightly impregnated with a bit of oil. Salt and pepper them. Mix together 3 tablespoons of the crumbled bacon, the chopped hazelnuts, and ¼ cup of the chopped chervil. Sprinkle an equal amount of the mixture over what was the bone side of each fillet. Roll each fillet upon itself so the bacon and nuts are inside and wrap in one blanched leaf of the escarole.

Lightly oil the steamer basket and add the trout packages. Fill the bottom of the steamer one half of the way with water and add the bouquet garni, onion, and garlic. Bring to a boil, then reduce the heat to medium and simmer 10 minutes, uncovered, before you begin to steam the trout. Steam the fillets 8 minutes. Remove from the heat and keep warm, covered, over the water. Strain ½ cup of the steaming water into a small saucepan.

Reduce the steaming water to 2 tablespoons over high heat, then add the chopped shallot, vinegar, oil, and salt and pepper to taste and homogenize well. Add the remaining 2 tablespoons of chervil.

Toss the salad leaves with half the dressing; open the packages of fish with a pair of scissors, opening the greens around the fillets; arrange the fish and salad on serving plates, each one decorated with two nasturtium flowers and their leaves. Spoon the remainder of the dressing over the fillets.

Southeast Asian-Style Plate-Steamed Rockfish

FCR— 2 TO 4 SERVINGS

For the salad

¼ pound bean sprouts

2 medium-size carrots, very coarsely grated

I scallion, finely sliced

Tender part only of 2 stalks lemongrass, finely chopped

2 tablespoons chopped cilantro leaves

I tablespoon chopped unsalted peanuts

For the cooked dressing

2 tablespoons chunky peanut butter

I ½ teaspoons finely chopped sweetened coconut flakes

I small white onion, grated

I tablespoon nuoc mam or nam pla

Tender part only of 2 stalks lemongrass, finely chopped

Pinch of cayenne pepper

I tablespoon dark soy sauce

I tablespoon rice vinegar (optional)

This also tastes delicious cold. You may use either nuoc mam, the Vietnamese fish sauce, or nam pla, the Thai fish sauce, as you prefer. Prepare the salad and dressing first and toss the salad just after the fish has started steaming. Some better supermarkets carry the sauces required here; they are available in all Asian markets.

SUGGESTED BEVERAGE:
Many people like a hillside Gewürztraminer, so try a Stony Hill Gewürztraminer; also good with beer.

For the fish

1 rockfish or snapper, 2 to 3 pounds, eviscerated, as described on page 537,
    and fins removed

Nuoc mam or nam pla

1 bunch scallions, finely chopped

Large pinch of red pepper flakes

2 teaspoons peeled and grated fresh ginger

Salt

Blanch the bean sprouts and grated carrots 1 minute in boiling water. Reserve 6 tablespoons of the blanching water. Refresh the sprouts and carrots immediately under cold water and pat completely dry. Mix with the other salad ingredients.

Mix all the dressing ingredients together in a small saucepan with the reserved blanching water and, over medium heat, reduce to 3 tablespoons of a thickish dressing. Cool completely. Set aside.

Truss the rockfish by passing a threaded kitchen needle though its gills and tail. Pull the string taut and tie; the fish will curve upon itself and form a circle. Set it at the center of a plate with a diameter 1 inch less than that of your steamer.

Brush the fish with *nuoc mam* or *nam pla* and sprinkle it all over with the scallions mixed with the pepper flakes and ginger. Steam over lightly salted boiling water about 15 minutes. Check the fish for doneness with an instant thermometer inserted just behind the head. The temperature should be between 140° and 165°F. While the fish is steaming, toss together the salad and dressing. When the fish is done, skin and fillet it and serve with the salad.

PAN-STEAMED FISH

I discovered this technique while I was writing my book *In Madeleine's Kitchen*. It started with a chicken cutlet abandoned in a warm frying pan because of a telephone call and which ended up as tender as butter. I have fooled around with this technique for the last ten years, changing it constantly until I found the very best way to pan-steam.

The idea is to steam the fish using only the fish's own water content, steaming so the fish proteins denature just enough and the following things occur:

- The flesh turns opaque and translucent but loses absolutely no volume,
- The tissues are still full of their natural juices,
- There is absolutely *no trace* of liquid in the pan where the fish was cooked, and
- There are no beads of white collagen pearling on the surface of the fish. This last condition is the most important because if the collagen is visible, you have overcooked the fish by modern standards.

I have found over the years that each fish needs to be looked at and appreciated for the apparent strength of its fibers, the amount of fat it contains, etc. As a result, when I have an important dinner I have taken to the habit of always having one more piece of fish than I need so I can test this particular fish by cooking a piece of it first. You can employ this technique in restaurant or catering cooking, but be prepared to test each and every different fish you are cutting and to have one person whose occupation will be only cooking the fish. Also, study very carefully the synchronization of the plating for each table ordering a pan-steamed fish; if pan-steaming reveals itself logistically impossible because of the labor cost, use other less taxing methods of cooking fish.

The technique of pan-steaming varies especially with the thickness of the fish; the thinner the fish, the higher the initial heat must be. Conversely, the thicker the piece of fish, the lower the heat will be, to allow its *relatively* slow and progressive penetration toward the center of the fish. *The fish must be at room temperature for 30 minutes before you start cooking it.* This allows the fish to unchill (remember, it is around 35° to 37°F when it comes out of refrigeration) and start cooking right away.

- *For fillets up to ½ inch thick:* Use medium heat; heat the butter or oil until very warm, then add the seasoned fillets. Flip them over after 1 minute in the pan; flip again after another minute. Then cover the pan tightly with a lid one size smaller than the pan, resting it flush over the fillets, and let stand 2 to 3 minutes *off the heat*. Check for the qualities of doneness listed on page 580 and serve.
- *For steaks or medallions ⅔ to ¾ inch thick:* Heat the butter or oil over low heat, *then turn the heat off* and let the pan cool completely. Add the pieces of fish, and start the burner again keeping it on extremely low heat, turning the steaks over twice at 2-minute intervals. Remove the pan from the heat, cover with a lid one size too small for the pan, resting it flush over the fish, and let stand 2 more minutes. The internal temperature should be between 140° and 155°F for the best texture.

SAUCING PAN-STEAMED FISH Pan-steamed fish is so delicious that you can use any type of garnish, from minimalist lemon or lime juice, to a sinful little sauce, a nice and rich compound butter, or a reasonable butter oil.

Here are a few recipes as examples of what can be done:

Pan-Steamed Orange Roughy

Prepare the sauce before you steam the fish because no sooner is the fish ready than it must go to the table. If no fish fumet is available, use chicken stock, but the results will be different.

SUGGESTED WINE: *An Australian Yalumba Riesling or an Alsatian Riesling or a Napa Valley Stony Hill Riesling*

FFR — 6 SERVINGS

I pound jumbo asparagus

4 cups water

I cup fish fumet (page 543)

½ cup dry white wine of your choice

I cup bottled clam juice

3 kumquats, finely chopped, or one 2 × ½-inch strip orange rind

2 shallots, finely chopped

Small bouquet garni

½ cup crème fraîche

¼ cup unsalted butter

Juice of I Valencia orange

Fresh lemon juice

Salt

Pepper from the mill

6 orange roughy fillets, ½ inch thick at the thickest part and at room temperature

2 scallions, diagonally sliced into paper-thin slivers

2 tablespoons slivered orange rind, blanched in boiling water for 2 minutes

Peel and slice the asparagus diagonally into ¼-inch-thick slices. Bring the water to a boil and blanch the asparagus 2 minutes. Drain, reserving 1 cup of the asparagus cooking water. Rinse the asparagus under running cold water. Pat dry and set aside. Kept over hot water, the asparagus will be warm enough to add to the sauce.

Put the reserved asparagus cooking water, the fish fumet, white wine, and clam juice in a skillet together with the chopped kumquats, shallots, and bouquet garni. Reduce slowly by three quarters and strain through a China cap, pushing on the solids to extract all their essences. Reheat well, then blend in the crème fraîche and whisk in 2 tablespoons of the butter. Add the asparagus slices and correct the final seasoning with the orange and lemon juices and salt and pepper.

To cook the fillets, heat the remaining butter in a large electric frying pan to 275°F. Add the fillets and flip over once after 2 minutes, turn the heat off, salt and pepper the fillets, and cover with a sheet of aluminum foil shiny side down placed flush over them. In a minute or so, two at the most, the fillets are done. Spoon a large ladle of asparagus sauce on the bottom of each plate. Add one fillet per plate. Dot each fillet with slivered scallions and blanched orange rind mixed.

Pan-Steamed Salmon Medallions

FCR—6 SERVINGS

½ cup packed fresh basil leaves, washed and dried

½ cup corn or pure olive oil

½ cup fish fumet or substitute (page 543 or 545)

½ cup dry white wine

Juice of 1 lemon

7 anchovy fillets, rinsed and mashed

1 large shallot, very finely chopped

1 clove garlic, very finely chopped

Small bouquet garni

¼ cup unsalted butter

Salt

Pepper from the mill

6 salmon medallions or steaks, at room temperature

1 pound fresh spinach leaves, well washed and tough stems removed

This sauce is a derivative of beurre blanc, the techniques of which are outlined on page 335, but instead of being prepared only with butter, it is made with 50 percent basil oil. If you have no time to prepare the basil oil, purchase a small bottle of it. Medallions are more practical than steaks, because steaks must be skinned and boned just before serving. The spinach leaves should remain bright green and neither lose their moisture nor deflate completely.

SUGGESTED WINE: **A** *Châteauneuf-du-Pape Blanc or a rich and buttery Chardonnay*

The night before you prepare the salmon, blanch the basil leaves for 1 to 2 minutes in rapidly boiling water. Drain, refresh under running cold water, and squeeze dry. Put the basil in a blender and add the oil; process until smooth and turn into a glass jar that has been washed in the dishwasher. Cover and let stand, refrigerated, overnight. Before you start cooking the salmon, separate the clear oil from the sediment. Keep the sediment to flavor and enrich a vegetable soup or to season vegetables (use within 24 hours).

Put the fish fumet, wine, 1½ tablespoons of the lemon juice, one mashed anchovy, the chopped shallot, garlic, and bouquet garni in a small saucepan and reduce over medium heat to ⅓ cup. Remove the bouquet garni. Let cool to warm.

Off the heat, using only the heat remaining in the pan, whisk in the butter, then whisk in ¼ cup of the basil oil, to obtain a 50-50 "butter oil" sauce. Correct the seasoning with salt, pepper, and more lemon juice if desired.

Rub an electric frying pan or skillet with only a trace of the basil oil. Season the fish lightly with salt and pepper and place in the pan. Cover the pan with a piece of aluminum foil resting shiny side down and flush over the fish; set the heat as low as the pan will allow. Keep turning the medallions every 2 minutes until they look opaque and translucent and are resilient to the touch of a finger, but have not lost any water, 6 to 7 minutes. Immediately transfer to dinner plates. Rewhisk the sauce and strain 2 teaspoons of it over each steak. Wilt the spinach a few seconds in the pan in which the fish cooked with the remainder of the sauce on medium-low heat. Add a few leaves of spinach to each plate and lay one anchovy over each medallion.

Pan-Steamed Steelhead Trout Fillets in Noisette Butter

This recipe is dedicated to Debra and Greg Murphy, but it will please all the West Coast fishermen and partners who cook the steelheads coming from all the rivers running into the Pacific. The beautiful ivory-colored midwestern and eastern lake trout fillets sold in northeastern fish stores or the shad fillets of the Mid-Atlantic states will do just as well. Sorrel is now available on a regular basis in the herb section of most food stores.

SUGGESTED WINE: *Any one of the many wonderfully buttery and fruity Chardonnays of the Napa and Sonoma valleys or an older Meursault or Chassagne-Montrachet*

FFR — 6 SERVINGS

I pound Yellow Finnish or Yukon Gold potatoes, peeled and quartered

½ cup unsalted butter

1½ tablespoons fresh lemon juice

Fillets of one 6- to 8- pound trout, at room temperature and cut into serving pieces

Salt

Pepper from the mill

3 tablespoons chopped well-washed sorrel leaves

Before you cook the potatoes, round off their angles to prevent them from breaking and mushing up in the water. Immerse them in boiling water, reduce the heat to a simmer, and cook until almost tender, about 17 minutes; keep the potatoes in the warm water where they will finish softening.

Put the butter in a small skillet and cook to the noisette stage, until it turns brown and smells highly of toasted hazelnuts (see page 32). Off the heat, whisk in the lemon juice. Set aside.

Using a brush, rub the bottom of an electric frying pan with a tablespoon or so of the butter. Preheat the pan to 275°F. Add the trout fillets, season with salt and pepper, and cover with a sheet of aluminum foil shiny side down and flush over the fish. Cook, turning the fillets every 2 minutes, for a total of no more than 4 to 5 minutes. Remove the fillets to warm dinner plates, quickly whisk the sorrel into the noisette butter, add salt and pepper and spoon over the fish. Add one quartered potato per plate. There will be enough butter for both the fish and the potatoes. Enjoy; the essence of simplicity but, oh, so delicious.

PAN-SEARING/PAN-STEAMING

If this term seems confusing, it is. Pan-searing is a dry heat cooking procedure and pan-steaming is a moist heat procedure so how can both be done at the same time? Quite simply, pan-searing/pan-steaming is a technique usually applied to what is called in English "fish sticks," or in French *darnes*, cut out of the center part of larger unskinned fillets, usually 2 inches or so wide. The procedure is as follows, using fish that has been at room temperature for 30 minutes before you start cooking it.

1. Coat the skin of the fish with a thin layer of seasoned flour or cornstarch.
2. Heat a thin layer of oil in a heavy-bottomed skillet or frying pan over medium-high heat until it ripples with heat.
3. Add the fish to the skillet skin side down and sear it rapidly and deeply so the skin turns crisp.
4. As soon as the fillets turn opaque to a thickness of ¼ inch just above the

crisp skin, remove the skillet from the heat, cover it, and let the top part of the fish turn translucent in the accumulated heat of the pan. This usually requires 4 to 5 minutes. Serve promptly.

5. Be certain that any accompanying sauce, butter, or butter oil is ready before the fish goes into the frying pan, for the fish cannot wait. Sauces made with butter can go directly over the fish; sauces that are semiliquid or compotelike must be served in a ramekin on the side so as not to mar the look of the fish.

Here is the technique applied in two recipes:

French Riviera-Style Fish Sticks

FCR—6 SERVINGS

For the compote

3 tablespoons dried currants

¼ cup red wine vinegar

3 tablespoons olive oil of your choice

3 medium-size white onions, sliced

Salt

Pepper from the mill

1 tablespoon granulated sugar

2 pounds fresh, sun-ripened tomatoes, peeled, seeded, and coarsely chopped

1 teaspoon grated Valencia orange rind

Juice of 1 Valencia orange

12 long fresh mint stems, tied in a bundle

1½ teaspoons ras el hanout (page 69)

12 oil-cured olives, pitted and chopped

2 tablespoons tiny capers, drained

¼ teaspoon powdered saffron

2 tablespoons warm water

For the fish

Six 2-inch-wide sticks taken from large snapper or rockfish fillets (page 530)

2 tablespoons unbleached all-purpose flour or cornstarch seasoned with salt and pepper

2 tablespoons olive oil of your choice

Salt

Pepper from the mill

This is adapted from the recipe of a Pied Noir friend whose family moved to Nice after the independence of Algeria, hence the mixture of Arabic and Provençal spicing of the compote accompanying the fish. French quatre épices or garam masala can substitute for the ras el hanout. Prepare the compote as long as 24 hours before the salmon. As a vegetable garnish, present a tiny julienne of deep-fried leeks (see page 421).

SUGGESTED WINE: *A rosé from Provence, a Napa Valley Grignolino rosé or a Cigare Volant from Bonny Doon Vineyard*

To prepare the compote, place the currants in a ramekin. Heat the vinegar and pour it over the fruit. Let steep until the vinegar has been absorbed.

Heat the oil in a skillet over medium heat until the oil ripples, then add the onions and cook, stirring a few minutes; season with salt and pepper and cover the pan. Let the onions render their juices. Add the sugar and continue cooking until the onions have browned. Add the tomatoes, orange rind, orange juice, mint stems, and ½ teaspoon of the ras el hanout. Bring to a boil. Reduce the heat to medium and simmer until the mixture has bound and turned compotelike. Add the olives, capers, and vinegar-steeped currants. Simmer 5 more minutes and turn off the heat. Just before serving, reheat the compote, remove the mint stems bundle, dissolve the saffron in the warm water and add to the compote. Correct the final seasoning and divide the compote into six ramekins.

Dust the skin side of each piece of fish with the seasoned flour or starch. Heat the oil in a heavy skillet; when the oil ripples, sear the skin side of each piece of fish until crisp. Salt and pepper the top of the fish, cover, and turn the heat off. Let stand until the fish has turned completely opaque, with no trace of water in the skillet and no visible beads of collagen, 4 to 5 minutes. Serve immediately with the compote on the side.

Fish Sticks and Zucchini in Agrodolce

Agrodolce is the Italian for sweet-sour. This dish is from Sicily and to be served barely lukewarm. "Marrow" zucchini are so small they have not yet developed seeds. This is very ancient Mediterranean cooking in which the food looks really brown. Note that the bass will need a full 6 minutes in the covered pan.

SUGGESTED WINE: **A** *Sicilian wine, either light and red or white, Regaleali, for example*

FCR — 6 SERVINGS

2 tablespoons dark raisins

3 tablespoons boiling water

Olive oil as needed

3 tablespoons pine nuts

3 cloves garlic, extremely finely chopped

6 small marrow zucchini, cut into ⅙-inch-wide sticks

2 anchovy fillets, rinsed and mashed

Salt as needed

Pepper from the mill

1 teaspoon granulated sugar

2 tablespoons red wine vinegar

2 tablespoons unbleached all-purpose flour or cornstarch seasoned with salt and pepper

Six 3-inch-wide sticks taken from the center part of Lake or Chilean sea bass fillets (page 530)

Cover the raisins with the boiling water and let stand until they have absorbed most of the water and plumped up.

Heat a tad of olive oil in a skillet, then add the nuts and toss them over medium heat until they turn light golden; using a slotted spoon, remove them to a plate lined with a paper towel. Heat a tad more oil, add the garlic to the skillet, and toss a few seconds without browning. Add the julienne of zucchini and mashed anchovies. Toss together, taste, add salt only if necessary, and pepper well. Cover and cook over low heat until the vegetables are tender (not crisp-tender; it will not result in the right texture); off the heat, add the sugar and vinegar and toss well together. Let cool to lukewarm, add the reserved raisins and pine nuts, and correct the seasoning with more salt and/or sugar as needed and to personal taste.

Lightly dust the skin side of the fish sticks with the flour. Over high heat, heat 3 tablespoons oil in a heavy skillet. Sear the sticks skin side down until the skin is crisp. Remove from the heat, cover, and let stand until the flesh has turned translucent, 4 to 5 minutes; salt and pepper the top of the fish. Serve each portion topped with some of the zucchini in *agrodolce*.

OVEN-STEAMING FISH

My friend and former student Gary Danko, who is the dining room chef at the Ritz Carlton in San Francisco, mentioned to me transferring the technique of pan-steaming to the oven by using two baking pans which can contain a larger quantity of servings.

Unfortunately I never saw Gary do this, so I applied the same technique used in classic French cuisine for the poaching of chicken breast cutlets at high heat and it worked perfectly. The fish steaks must be ¾ inch thick and the technique works best with medallions, as the oily taste of the skin transfers rapidly to the flesh during the cooking. The fish must be at room temperature for at least 30 minutes before cooking it and the procedure is as follows:

1. Preheat the oven to 450°F.
2. Salt and pepper the fish medallions or steaks lightly on both sides, then set them on a piece of lightly oiled parchment paper. Prepare a second sheet of lightly oiled parchment paper for later use.
3. As soon as the oven temperature has reached 450°F, put two baking pans to heat in the oven for 4 minutes on the top and middle racks of the oven.
4. Using oven mittens, transfer the sheet of parchment on which the fish is resting to the upper rack pan. Top the fish with the second sheet of parchment, then place the second pan upside down over the first to form a lid. Bake 4 minutes at 450°F, then turn the heat off and let stand in the turned off oven another 3 minutes.
5. Remove to warm plates, garnish, and serve immediately.

Salmon Medallions with Dried Sour Cherry Dressing

FCR—12 SERVINGS

½ cup dried sour Michigan cherries

2 cups Pinot Noir or Gamay Beaujolais

12 salmon steaks or medallions

1 large yellow onion, coarsely chopped

1 leek, light green part only, well washed

Small bouquet garni

1 cup water

Salt

2 tablespoons red wine vinegar

2 shallots, finely chopped

Pepper from the mill

¾ cup walnut oil or other oil of your choice

2 tablespoons chopped fresh parsley leaves

2 tablespoons chopped fresh chives

1 pound mesclun greens (spring greens)

Place the cherries in a small bowl. Heat half the Pinot Noir and pour it over the cherries; let steep overnight, covered, at room temperature.

The next day, skin the salmon steaks, removing all brown tissues; discard the skin. Bone the steaks into *darnes*, paying particular attention to the removal of salmon pin bones (see details on page 535). Wrap the salmon *darnes* around each other to form medallions (see page 538) and secure each with four crossed toothpicks. Keep covered at room temperature.

Place the salmon backbones, onion, leek, and bouquet garni in a small pot. Add the second cup of Pinot Noir, the water, and a tiny dash of salt and bring to a boil. Reduce the heat to medium and simmer 35 minutes. Strain the resulting fish fumet through a conical strainer into a clean saucepan and defat it completely (see page 544).

To the fumet, add the Pinot Noir in which the cherries have softened, the vinegar, half the chopped shallots, a good pinch of salt, and pepper and reduce over medium-low heat to ¼ cup. Strain into a blender. Add the remaining shallot, the oil, more salt if needed, and pepper to taste. Process to a smooth dressing, pour into a bowl, and add the wine-soaked cherries, parsley, and chives. Correct the final seasoning.

Preheat the oven to 450°F, salt and pepper the fish; and oven-steam the salmon for no more than 7 minutes as described on page 587. As soon as the salmon is out of the oven, spoon 1 tablespoon of the dressing over each medallion. Dress the greens with the remainder of the dressing; serve the salmon either lukewarm or cold surrounded by some greens.

Save Your Heart Salmon Demi-Medallions

FCR—12 SERVINGS

6 center-cut salmon steaks

1 cup fish fumet (page 543) or ½ cup bottled clam juice mixed with 1 cup water

1 teaspoon curry powder

2 shallots, finely chopped

Small bouquet garni

¼ cup jellied cranberry sauce

3 tablespoons balsamic vinegar

Salt

Pepper from the mill

½ cup granulated sugar

½ cup water

36 large pretty, deep red fresh cranberries

½ teaspoon cornstarch

3 tablespoons unsaturated oil of your choice, preferably pistachio oil

36 jumbo asparagus tips, peeled

A variation of this first course dish was served at a benefit lunch for the Heart Association of the Napa Valley in 1992. I've added curry to this present version. The syrup in which the cranberries are poached should be kept refrigerated and used to prepare any red berry sorbet.

SUGGESTED WINE: A Beringer Vineyards proprietor grown Chardonnay of current release

Skin the salmon steaks and bone them, reserving the bones. Roll each *darne* upon itself, starting at the thick end, into a small half-size medallion; secure with two toothpicks (see page 538 for more detailed instructions).

Mix the fish fumet or clam juice and water with the curry, salmon bones, shallots, bouquet garni, cranberry sauce, and 2 tablespoons of the balsamic vinegar in a small saucepan. Add a dash each of salt and pepper and reduce to ½ cup over medium-low heat. Let cool to lukewarm.

Meanwhile, mix the sugar and water together in another small saucepan. Bring to a boil, then add the cranberries. When they float to the top of the syrup, transfer them to a bowl using a slotted spoon and add the remaining vinegar. Toss together and set aside.

Strain the cooled reduction of fumet through a conical strainer into a small saucepan. Mix the cornstarch into the reduction and bring back to a boil, stirring constantly to thicken. Cool completely and whisk in the chosen oil. Correct the salt and pepper.

Blanch the asparagus tips 3 minutes in boiling salted water. Preheat the oven to 450°F. Oven-steam the demi-medallions as described on page 587 for only 4 minutes. Remove from the oven, let stand for 1 minute, then remove to a platter and spoon a small tablespoon of dressing over each piece of fish. Surround the fish with the cranberries and asparagus and serve.

Fish in the Microwave

One might think that the good old microwave would zap a piece of fish in no time, but such is not the case; as a matter of fact, it takes exactly as much time to microwave fish as it does to oven-poach it. But less heat in the kitchen and fewer dirty dishes are always a plus when one uses the microwave oven.

The optimum number of portions made in the microwave at once seems to be four; two portions become overdried around their edges, six end up being half cooked.

The best types of fish for the microwave are—to my personal taste—the flatfish that yield relatively thin fillets, although sticks or *darnes* of fish taken from thicker fillets can also be prepared successfully.

THE TECHNIQUE

Arrange the fish on a 10-inch *nonmetallic* plate, their thick part facing toward the outside of the dish and their thinner parts meeting at the center of the dish. If the fillets are very tapered at one of their ends, fold the thinnest part under the middle of each fillet to obtain a more or less uniform thickness of the whole piece.

Cover the plate with a well-stretched piece of microwave-quality plastic wrap and *punch eight holes* over the thickest part of the fish using a ⅛-inch-thick trussing or knitting needle.

One pound of fillets usually serves four people, so purchase that amount, not worrying whether it's a little above or a little below.

BEST HEAT, COOKING, AND RESTING TIMES Fish tastes best when microwaved on *high power*.

The cooking time is divided into two parts, the actual cooking time in the oven and a resting period, during which, the heat continues to penetrate the fish and finishes cooking it. Keep the fish covered during the resting period and be careful when you uncover it, for the steam is extremely hot.

For fillets, steaks, and medallions Cook 3 minutes for thin folded fillets, plus a maximum of 3 minutes resting time after taking the fish out of the oven.

Cook 4 minutes for steaks and medallions, plus 3 minutes resting time after taking the fish out of the oven.

For whole smaller fish Whole smaller (up to 3 pounds) or medium-large round-bodied finfish must be sewn together by passing a needle threaded with light kitchen string through the head and tail, then pulling it tight, which rolls the fish into a circle, and tying it. The diameter of the dish on which the fish will cook must be one inch larger than the fish itself so it does not touch the sides of the dish.

If the fish is flavored with any aromatics, the aromatics must be enclosed in its cavity so their flavor will penetrate through the flesh as the fish cooks.

The plate must be covered with a sheet of well-stretched microwave-quality plastic wrap well-anchored around and under the plate. Punch ten holes in the plastic over the fish with a ⅛-inch trussing or knitting needle.

The most important part of microwave cooking for a whole fish is the resting time, which can be almost as long as the cooking time. The resting time is the equivalent for microwaved fish of the poaching time for crimped fish after the crimping vessel has been removed from the heat (see page 567). The fish must remain tightly covered for the flesh to finish cooking to the bone, otherwise it will be rare and not detach from the bone easily.

FOR A WHOLE FISH WEIGHING
- 1 pound: 5 minutes cooking time on high power, plus 8 minutes resting time
- 1½ pounds: 8 minutes, plus 6 minutes resting time
- 2 pounds: 12 minutes, plus 10 minutes resting time
- 2½ pounds: up to 15 minutes, plus 10 to 12 minutes resting time
- 3 pounds: up to 18 minutes, plus 10 minutes resting time

The larger the fish, the more difficult it becomes to evaluate the length of the cooking and resting times, so be ready with your instant thermometer and measure the heat at the very center of the back, where the fish is the thickest. As soon as it reads 140° to 165°F, it is done. Check several times if need be and each and every time recover the fish tightly and carefully.

It is difficult to cook a whole fish larger than 3 pounds in a microwave oven because of the smaller size of most microwave ovens which do not accommodate larger baking dishes.

SAUCING MICROWAVED FISH
I recommend to prepare the sauce ahead of time by the conventional methods. If you make a roux, make it on a stove burner; you will lose more time opening and closing the microwave oven door than you will preparing your sauce as usual. You can use any type of sauce you like, from the classiest to the simplest. I personally believe that the simplest is the best and I like very much to go with a compound butter or a butter oil.

Here are two recipes to practice on:

MICROWAVING A SMALL FISH

Pass the needle through the head.

Pass the needle through the tail.

Tie the string ends together so that the head is brought up snugly against the tail.

Orange Roughy Fillets with Sweet-Sour Grapefruit Sauce

If butter is not on your list of indulgences, you can use the oil of your choice instead; pistachio oil is particularly delicious, so are oregano and cilantro oils. As a vegetable garnish, consider some fresh snap or snow peas quickly stir-fried while the fish cooks.

SUGGESTED WINE: *A California Knights or Alexander Valley Sauvignon Blanc or an Alexander Valley Viognier*

FFR to FCR — 4 SERVINGS

2 grapefruit

I Valencia orange

I lime

½ teaspoon brown sugar

Salt

Pepper from the mill

¼ cup unsalted butter or 3 tablespoons unsaturated oil of your choice plus ½ tablespoon for greasing the pan

4 orange roughy fillets (about I pound)

2 tablespoons chopped cilantro leaves

Lift enough of the rind without any pith from each type of fruit to obtain three strips 2 × ½ inch. Cut into superfine ¹⁄₁₆-inch-wide julienne; blanch 1 minute in boiling water. Drain and set aside for later use.

Grate ¼ teaspoon of each type of rind remaining on the fruit and place in a small, heavy, nonreactive saucepan. Juice all the fruit and strain the juices over the grated rinds. Remove 2 tablespoons of the mixture to a small bowl and set aside. To the saucepan add the brown sugar, salt, and pepper and reduce to 2 tablespoons over medium-low heat. Off the heat but while the saucepan is still lukewarm, whisk in the butter. Keep warm.

Rub a baking plate or dish with the remaining ½ tablespoon of the butter or oil. Salt and pepper the fillets lightly on their skin side; score on the same side with a knife and fold into halves, tucking under the tapered end of each fillet.

Arrange the fillets on the plate so their thick part faces its rim and their thinner part its center. Sprinkle the fish with the reserved fruit juice mixture. Cover with tightly stretched microwave-quality plastic wrap pricked with a needle. Cook 5 minutes on high power, then take out of the oven and let stand, still covered, another 3 to 4 minutes.

Serve the fillets topped with an equal amount of the citrus sauce; sprinkle with the chopped cilantro.

Cherviled Pike

FFR— 2 SERVINGS

1 large bunch fresh chervil

Grated rind and juice of 1 Valencia orange

2 tablespoons unsalted butter

Salt

Pepper from the mill

1 pike, 2 to 2½ pounds, dressed, with head and tail left on

½ cup light cream

Chop the stems of the chervil and reserve the leaves; mix together the chervil stems, orange rind, butter, and salt to taste; pepper the mixture generously and stuff way up into the cavity of the pike. Thread a trussing needle with fine kitchen string. Pass the needle through the head and tail, pull tightly so the fish curves into a full circle, and tie. Set in a nonmetallic baking plate or dish 1 inch larger in diameter than the fish. Wrap with plastic wrap and prick with a needle.

Microwave on high 12 to 15 minutes, then turn the oven off and let rest in the oven another 12 minutes. Meanwhile, bring the cream to a boil. Place the orange juice in a small nonreactive saucepan and reduce it over medium-low heat to 1 tablespoon. Chop all the chervil leaves.

As soon as the fish has fully rested, spoon the fragrant butter from the baking dish into the cream. Add the chervil leaves and, just before serving, the reduced orange juice. Skin and fillet the pike and serve the sauce over the fillets.

In memory of a wonderful small pike which I angled myself out of Annecy Lake, a miraculous happening since I haven't caught anything since.

SUGGESTED WINE: **A Napa Valley or Alexander Valley Viognier or a French Viognier**

Single's Trout

NFR— 1 SERVING

12 seedless red grapes

12 seedless white grapes

Pinch of cayenne pepper

1 to 2 tablespoons plain nonfat yogurt, to your personal taste

½ tiny clove garlic, finely mashed

1 tablespoon chopped fresh mint leaves

Salt

1 trout, 8 to 12 ounces, dressed

2 tablespoons fresh lemon juice

Pepper from the mill

In this world where so many young people live alone, this is a nice dish for a pleasant dinner to precede a quiet evening of relaxing with music and a good book.

SUGGESTED WINE: **A pleasant soft white wine such as a Graves from France or a second-label Chardonnay from any California winery**

Cut the grapes into quarters; toss in the cayenne pepper, yogurt, garlic, mint, and a dash of salt.

Set the trout flat on a dinner plate, drizzle the lemon juice over it, and sprinkle with salt and pepper. Wrap in plastic wrap and prick with a needle. Microwave on high for 5 minutes; let rest in the microwave still covered, until the meat feels firm at its thickest part, another 3 to 4 minutes. Skin and fillet and enjoy with the grape and mint relish.

Oven-Poaching in a Small Amount of Liquid

This is the technique known in French as *pochage à court-mouillement*, still very much in use in all French kitchens which produces extremely good, even classy, sauces using both the classic and modern methods.

This technique is reserved for fillets folded over upon themselves lengthwise and fillets rolled upon themselves from their thickest end to their thinnest to form *paupiettes* which can be cooked plain or stuffed with herbs, aromatics, mousses of fish, etc. It also works with steaks and medallions, namely, all small pieces of fish.

PREPARING THE FISH

FILLETS Skin and score fillets on their skin side to prevent the bursting of connective membranes and breaking of the fillets as their fibers swell under the influence of the heat.

STEAKS Steaks must be skinless and the dark tissues should be removed to prevent the presence of the somewhat strong omega-3 oils in the sauce; this applies to all semifat or fat fish such as salmon, large bluefish, large striped bass, large Pacific rockfish, or snapper.

PREPARING THE DISH

The baking dish should be nonreactive (namely, not made of aluminum or cast iron) and conduct heat evenly. Use old-fashioned lead-free pottery, Pyroceram (Corning), or enameled cast iron (Le Creuset) preferably; baking glass is a second choice only and stainless steel does not conduct heat well enough. Butter the baking dish generously. Line with the vegetables of your choice; they can be each and every aromatic vegetable you enjoy used alone or in combination; let your taste and imagination be your guide.

If the vegetables are to be included in the sauce, they must be presautéed in a small amount of butter; if they are not, they can go into the dish raw but cubed, either into ¼-inch mirepoix or ⅛-inch brunoise.

THE POACHING LIQUIDS

The best combination is half dry white wine and half fish fumet or fumet substitute. Remember always that the substitute never yields either as good a taste or texture as fish fumet.

Do not poach in pure wine or the fish will acquire the unpleasant taste of raw alcohol. If more than ¼ cup of wine is used in a recipe, reduce the wine at least by half before using it to evaporate its alcohol.

THE POACHING TECHNIQUE

After the vegetables have been placed in the dish, arrange the fish over them, salt and pepper them, add the liquids, and place a buttered sheet of parchment paper flush on the surface of the fish. It will keep the fish from drying out.

Immediately place the dish to bake in the preheated oven. The temperature of the oven will vary from 350° to 400°F. Decide on the temperature following these guidelines:

- Delicate fish with a loose fiber structure such as young halibut, warm-water flounder, sole, and John Dory require 400°F for fast cooking.
- Solid, firm fish that does not fall apart easily such as large halibut, large gray sole, haddock, and medium-size snapper do best at 375°F.
- Firm fish such as swordfish, mahimahi, and shark will be best poached at 350°F, so that the penetration of the heat is slower and more progressive.
- Basically, the thicker and the larger the fish, the lower the heat should be, so do not hesitate to go down to 325°F if need be.

TESTING DONENESS

Fish steaks will be done in 12 minutes, fillets in 8 minutes. Any fish is done when a skewer inserted at the center of the fish comes out without bringing any fish with it and feels *warm* to the touch. The internal temperature of the fish measured with an instant thermometer reads 140° to 165°F, no more.

When you prepare a sauce with the cooking juices, do not cook the fish to its very core, but only until the skewer penetrates the meat half of the way toward the center of each piece. Drain the cooking juices to prepare the sauce but keep the fish in its baking dish still covered with its parchment paper; it will finish cooking while you prepare the sauce.

Fillets of Sole Prosper Montagné

This is an adaptation, using American ingredients, of the dish created by Prosper Montagné under the name of Sole Sylvestre. Fino or Amontillado sherry, white port, or Sercial Madeira may be used for the sauce. Positively no vermouth belongs in this recipe and please use butter and true heavy cream. This is a once in a while treat for a celebration, and must be enjoyed as conceived by its creator. I have extended the six-line recipe of Prosper Montagné, so it will make sense to any cook.

SUGGESTED WINE: **A** French Meursault of your choice

FFR — 6 SERVINGS

3 tablespoons unsalted butter

I small carrot, cut into ⅛-inch brunoise

I medium-size yellow onion, cut into ⅛-inch brunoise

I large shallot, cut into ⅛-inch brunoise

One 2-inch piece celery rib, strings removed and cut into ⅛-inch brunoise

I large fresh black truffle (optional), cut into ⅛-inch brunoise

2 large mushrooms, cut into ⅛-inch brunoise

Salt

Pepper from the mill

⅔ cup fino or Amontillado sherry

¾ cup fish fumet (page 543; use no substitute)

12 large gray sole fillets, skinned and dark tissues removed

½ cup heavy cream

½ cup crème fraîche

12 vine-ripened cherry tomatoes

6 sprigs fresh Italian parsley for garnish

Preheat the oven to 350°F. In a saucepan heat 2 tablespoons of the butter. Add the carrot, onion, shallot, celery, truffle, and mushrooms and sauté for a few minutes over medium-high heat. Season with salt and pepper, cover the pot, and continue cooking slowly on low heat for 8 minutes. Add the wine and stir for a few minutes to evaporate the alcohol. Add the fumet and bring just to the boil.

Salt and pepper the fillets, score them on the side originally covered with skin with a knife, and roll them into *paupiettes* skin side in (see page 594). Spread the prepared vegetables and their juices in an even layer in a baking dish. Add the fillets and cover with a sheet of buttered parchment paper and oven-poach about 8 minutes. Remove the fillets from the oven when half done. Keep covered. Raise the oven temperature to 400°F for later use.

Drain the cooking juices of the fish with their aromatic vegetables into a skillet, leaving the fish, covered, in its baking dish. Bring the cooking juices to a boil, add the heavy cream in three successive additions, reducing over high heat while stirring constantly with a blunt-end spatula until the sauce coats it well. Add the crème fraîche and bring back to a simmer for a few minutes. Do not boil hard anymore; correct the seasoning very carefully. Keep warm over low heat.

Meanwhile, butter a cake pan with the remaining butter and put it to melt for 1 minute in the hot oven. Add the tomatoes, roll them in the melted butter, season lightly, and bake 3 to 5 minutes.

Put two fillets on each plate, spoon 3 to 4 tablespoons of the sauce over each portion. Brighten the plate with 2 tomatoes and a small sprig of parsley.

Snapper Fillets Chambéry

FCR—6 SERVINGS

6 medium-size red snapper fillets, skinned

Pure olive oil or walnut oil

1 tablespoon each chopped fresh tarragon, chives, chervil, parsley, and basil leaves mixed together

Salt

Pepper from the mill

⅓ cup French or Italian dry vermouth

¾ cup fish fumet or substitute (page 543 or 545)

2 juniper berries, crushed and powdered with a knife

2 shallots, very finely chopped

1 tablespoon unsalted butter

1 tablespoon all-purpose flour

3 tablespoons crème fraîche

6 sprigs fresh basil

This is a typical au Vermout recipe from the alpine province of Savoie in France where the vermout (no "h" at the end) is prepared from Artemisia absinthium flowers, bitter orange rind, chamomile, aloe vera, cardamom, and aniseeds. The faint trace of bitterness in the sauce comes from artemisia.

SUGGESTED WINE: *A California meritage of Sémillon and Sauvignon Blanc or if available a Chignin-Bergeron from the French Alps*

Preheat the oven to 350°F. Brush the fillets sparingly on the skin side with olive oil, then score them, sprinkle with a teaspoon each of the herb mixture, and season with salt and pepper. Fold the fillets over, tucking the tapered end of each fillet under its thicker end. Brush the baking dish with a bit of oil, then add the fillets.

Mix the vermouth, fish fumet, juniper berries, and shallots together in a small saucepan, bring to a boil, and pour around the fillets. Cover the fillets with a sheet of lightly buttered or oiled parchment paper, bake 6 to 7 minutes, remove from the oven and drain all the cooking juices into a skillet. Keep the fillets warm under the parchment where they will finish cooking. Reduce the cooking juices at a rolling boil for 5 minutes. Reduce the heat to a simmer. Mix the butter and flour into a *beurre manié* (see page 287) and whisk into the simmering juices. Remove from the heat as soon as the sauce has thickened, whisk in the crème fraîche and the remainder of fresh herbs; correct the seasoning carefully. Serve immediately on plates or a platter brightened with a basil sprig.

Salmon Medallions in Zinfandel

A good dish for a lighthearted Saturday night with friends. The red wine-salmon combination has been a classic one for centuries in European cookery. Zinfandel is perfect with salmon but Pinot Noir, a lighter Cabernet, or Syrah will do just as well. If butter is not on your list of indulgences, replace it with pure olive oil. The salmon steaks need not necessarily be turned into medallions, but the taste of the sauce is more refined if they are, because there is no contact of the sauce with the fish skin.

SUGGESTED WINE: *The same wine as used to prepare the dish*

FFR — 6 SERVINGS

6 salmon steaks

I clove garlic, crushed

4 large yellow onions, finely chopped

I large leek, white and light green parts, well washed and finely chopped

½ pound mushrooms, finely chopped

Small bouquet garni

I teaspoon tomato paste

¼ teaspoon meat extract

I bottle excellent Zinfandel of your choice

½ cup water

I cup bottled clam juice

2 tablespoons unsalted butter plus extra as needed for the beurre manié

Unbleached all-purpose flour as needed

Salt

Pepper from the mill

I bunch fresh Italian parsley, enough leaves of it chopped to equal 2 tablespoons

2 cups rice pilaf (page 461)

Turn the salmon steaks into medallions (see details on the technique on page 538); discard the skins but keep all the bones. Place those in a saucepan with the garlic, ¼ of the chopped onions, the leek, 2 tablespoons of the chopped mushrooms, the bouquet garni, tomato paste, meat extract, 1 cup of the Zinfandel, the water, and clam juice. Bring to a boil, reduce the heat to medium-low and simmer for 30 minutes. Strain through a conical strainer into a bowl and set aside.

Heat the 2 tablespoons butter in a skillet, then add the remaining onions and cook, stirring, over medium heat until golden. Add the mushrooms, salt, and pepper, and cook until the mixture forms a fragrant compote. Set the compote aside, keeping it warm.

Preheat the oven to 400°F. Lightly season the salmon steaks on both sides. Lightly butter a baking dish; arrange the salmon steaks in the dish. Add the reduction to the dish, cover with a sheet of buttered parchment paper and cook 5 to 6 minutes, turning the steaks over once. The steaks should be two thirds done only. Remove them from the oven but keep them in the baking dish covered with the parchment paper; they will finish cooking by themselves.

Strain the fish cooking juices into a measuring cup and note their volume. Prepare a *beurre manié* (see page 287) by mashing together on a plate 1½ tablespoons butter and 1 tablespoon flour per cup of fish cooking liquid. Reheat the cooking juices just to the boiling point, whisk in the *beurre manié*, and thicken; as soon as it is thickened, remove from the heat.

Arrange the medallions on a round platter, placing at its center the bunch of parsley; top each medallion with an equal amount of the onion-and-mushroom compote. Spoon half the sauce over the medallions, sprinkle with the chopped parsley, and serve the remainder in a sauce boat. Serve with the prepared rice.

Lemon-Lime Fish Steaks

FCR—6 SERVINGS

1 tablespoon extra virgin olive oil of your choice

Salt

Pepper from the mill

6 fish steaks of your choice, preferably a white fish

½ cup fish fumet or substitute (page 543 or 545)

¼ cup dry vermouth

½ teaspoon very fine lemon rind julienne

½ teaspoon very fine lime rind julienne

½ cup sour cream

1 teaspoon fresh lime juice or to taste

1½ tablespoons chopped cilantro leaves

A recipe which in the 1971 first edition of this book was a true novelty and has since become a classic.

SUGGESTED WINE: **A** *French Aligoté or a light fruity Chardonnay from California*

Preheat the oven to 325°F. Lightly oil a baking dish with the olive oil. Salt and pepper the steaks and arrange them in the dish. Mix together the fish fumet and vermouth and add to the dish. Cover with a sheet of lightly buttered or oiled parchment paper and bake until the steaks are two thirds done, 12 to 15 minutes. Remove from the oven and set aside, still in the baking dish and covered with its parchment.

Meanwhile, blanch the lemon and lime rinds in boiling water for 2 minutes; drain. Strain the cooking juices through a conical strainer over the rinds and simmer together in a small saucepan for a few minutes. Off the heat, blend in the sour cream and reheat well without boiling hard. Add the lime juice to taste, correct the salt and pepper, and add the cilantro. Spoon over the steaks and serve immediately.

Braised Fish

The braising of fish is another old-fashioned technique which tends not to be used that much anymore, but is still used enough in the country cooking of all European nations that it must be mentioned in a basic cookbook. Larger pieces of fish may be braised as well as smaller whole fish such as trout, small bass, pike, whiting, sole, John Dory, etc. This technique is so closely related to that of oven-poaching *à court mouillement* that the two are very often confused with each other. Braised fish cannot be served for a ceremonial or formal dinner, but it certainly can be a choice morsel for entertaining friends informally.

FONDS DE BRAISE

The braising should be done in a Pyroceram (Corning) or enameled cast-iron (Le Creuset) baking dish which can be used both on top of the stove and in the oven. Avoid stainless steel, which conducts heat irregularly, and aluminum, which reacts with acids.

The vegetables used in the braising are, as they are in meat cookery, called *fonds de braise,* and consist of a mirepoix of aromatic vegetables, usually carrots, onions, shallots, and a bouquet garni, but it can include other vegetables. These vegetables are always precooked either in butter or oil before the fish is set on them.

BRAISING LIQUIDS AND FISH

The liquids used are, as in oven-poaching, wine, fish fumet or its substitutes, or a mixture of both. Tomato sauce or essence is often used, especially in Mediterranean recipes.

Although the fish can be cooked completely dressed, it is important to remember that a fish with its head on will produce a better sauce. The head, which is the most flavorful part of the fish, will lose most of its juices into the gravy and flavor it highly. Though the head is not generally consumed, it does contain two choice little pieces which are usually reserved for the cook: the fish cheeks, which are located just under the eyes—do not discard them inadvertently.

The contents of the dish—the vegetables, fish, and liquids—are brought to a boil on top of the stove before being put into the oven and covered with a buttered or oiled paper.

BRAISING TECHNIQUE

Braising is done at 325°F to allow for the even penetration of the heat to the center of the fish. The fish is basted several times with the cooking juices during the cooking. Ideally, the juices should be reduced enough by the heat of the oven to form a sauce by themselves, but this does not always happen. If it does not, the juices may be thickened with a starch slurry or a *beurre manié* if need be. In the old days, it was easy to have the sauce reduced to the proper texture by the time the fish was cooked because the fish, very simply, was overcooked, even by the greatest culinary practitioners of the classic cuisine, which made almost everyone say that "the sauce made the fish." Nowadays, we pay great attention to the texture of our fish and it is the texture of the fish which attracts the attention, so the sauce should be easy and uncomplicated.

Here are two examples of braised fish:

Braised Steelhead or Lake Trout

FFR or FCR—6 SERVINGS

5 to 7 tablespoons unsalted butter or unsaturated oil, to your personal taste

1 bunch scallions, sliced diagonally

½ pound fresh mushrooms, cut into ¼-inch thick slices

1 large leek, white and light green parts, well washed and thinly sliced

Salt

Pepper from the mill

One 6-pound trout, dressed, with head left on

¾ cup dry white wine

¾ cup fish fumet or substitute (page 543 or 545)

Fresh lemon juice to your personal taste

1½ cups rice pilaf (page 461)

Heat 1 tablespoon of the butter in a large skillet. Add the scallions, mushrooms, and leek and cook, stirring, for a few minutes over medium heat. Turn the heat down, season with salt and pepper, cover, and let the juices run out of the vegetables. Transfer the vegetables and juices to a 2-quart baking dish.

Preheat the oven to 325°F. Salt and pepper the fish in its cavity; set it on its *fonds de braise,* add the wine and fumet and bring to a boil on top of the stove. Cover with a sheet of lightly buttered or oiled parchment paper and bake about 30 minutes, basting at regular intervals with the juices in the dish. Check the doneness of the fish by using an instant thermometer which should read between 140° and 165°F, no more. Remove the top skin of the fish and, using a long cake spatula, lift off the two top fillets and place on a warm platter. Now, lift the head and bones in one piece and discard them (or keep them to make another light fumet).

Lift the two bottom fillets and put them on top of the others in the serving platter. Cover with the parchment paper and keep warm.

To finish the sauce, reduce the cooking juices, vegetables and all, to ⅓ cup then whisk in 4 to 6 tablespoons of butter. Correct the seasoning with salt, pepper, and lemon juice and serve immediately with the pilaf.

The same recipe can be executed with a whole California cabezon, the large fillets of an 8-pound anglerfish or monkfish, a buffalofish or a carp, a scrod, 6 smaller trout, 6 whiting, 6 butterfish, etc.

NOTE: *If you want to avoid the butter, you can use half butter and half olive oil or even one quarter butter and three quarters olive oil. To avoid fat altogether, reduce the cooking juices, vegetables and all, by one quarter, then measure 2 teaspoons cornstarch per cup of cooking juices, and thicken with the cornstarch slurry (see page 269 for the technique of slurry).*

SUGGESTED WINE: **A** *Sancerre or California Sauvignon Blanc*

Braised Striped Sea Bass

FCR — 6 SERVINGS

This is one of the presentations of the famous Loup de Mer, the sea bass of French Riviera waters. From a friend's kitchen in Nice. Dried orange peel or rind is sold in spice jars in supermarkets.

SUGGESTED WINE: *Bellet, Cassis for a white wine or Bandol for a red wine, or a white or red Rhône varietal from California; an Italian Cinqueterre would also be very nice*

Juice of I lime or lemon, as you prefer

2 tablespoons chopped fresh Italian parsley leaves

Dash of salt

6 turns of the pepper mill

3 tablespoons olive oil of your choice plus extra for drizzling

One 6-pound striped sea bass, dressed, with head left on

I pound sun-ripened tomatoes, peeled, seeded, and finely chopped

6 cloves garlic, crushed in their skins

I medium-size yellow onion, finely chopped

¼ teaspoon finely grated dried orange rind

I cup dry white wine

I teaspoon fennel seeds

I small bunch fresh basil leaves

I cup tomato essence (page 309)

¼ teaspoon powdered saffron

I ½ tablespoons finely chopped oil-cured olives

I cup coarse fresh bread crumbs

Preheat the oven to 325°F. Mix together the lime juice, chopped parsley, salt, and pepper with the 3 tablespoons olive oil. Enclose this mixture in the cavity of the fish, making sure that you spread it all along the backbone and very high into the cavity, so only the oil slowly escapes, not the herbs.

Mix the tomatoes, garlic cloves, onion, orange rind, wine, fennel seeds, and basil together in a 2-quart baking dish. Arrange the fish over the mixture and pour the tomato essence over the fish. Bring to a boil on top of the stove, then cover with a sheet of lightly buttered or oiled parchment paper and bake until the internal temperature of the fish reaches 140° to 165°F, 35 to 40 minutes.

Fillet the fish and transfer the fillets to another ovenproof dish. Process the cooking juices in the blender and reduce quickly by one quarter in a small saucepan over high heat. Off the heat, whisk in the saffron, then add the olives. Spoon the sauce over the pieces of fish. Sprinkle generously with the bread crumbs and drizzle olive oil over the crumbs. Broil until the tips of the crumbs turn brown. Serve immediately.

Roasting and Baking Fish

In the old days when we still cooked on the hearth, roasting meant exclusively "spit-roasting." Whole fish was skewered on a strong spit and turned in front of a hot fire until its skin had crisped and its meat was done to perfect juiciness. Nowadays, roasting and baking apply most of the time to oven roasting at a medium-high to high temperature and baking at medium temperature. In an oven the heat used to cook the fish is a combination of mostly radiant heat coming from heating elements, some convection heat coming from the heated air circulating all through the oven from bottom to top and vice versa, and conduction heat transferred by the radiating elements to all sides of the container in which the fish cooks.

This section will be concerned with:

- Spit-roasting quite large fish for feasts of 12 to 50 guests
- Roasting medium-thick fish fillets or smaller whole fish at relatively high temperatures
- Baking smaller and thinner fish fillets and larger fish at relatively low temperatures to prevent outside drying

TEMPERATURE The rule is simple, the temperature depends entirely on the size of the fish; the greater the weight of the fish, the lower the cooking temperature to allow the heat to penetrate slowly toward its center and prevent the outside tissues from being overcooked while those close to the bone remain somewhat rare.

USE OF FAT Roasted or baked fish must receive a coating of clarified butter or the oil of your choice, plain or flavored—to prevent the skin from drying out. A special spray bottle for warm liquid clarified butter or room temperature oil will allow you to spray the surface of fillets or whole fish evenly.

ROASTING FISH FILLETS

Fish fillets must be skinned and scored on their "skin side," that is, on the side where the brown tissues are visible, and brushed or sprayed with clarified butter or with an oil of your choice. They can, if you wish, be sprinkled with seasoned fine dry or fresh bread crumbs before being baked. In this case the caloric intake is relatively higher, because the crumbs themselves must also be sprayed with either liquid butter or oil, so that they may brown better and become pleasantly crisp.

OVEN TEMPERATURE 375° to 350°F for thinner fillets up to ⅔ inch thick and 350° to 325°F for thick fillets up to 1½ inches thick.

ROASTING WHOLE FISH

Set the whole fish, dressed *but with its head left on,* in the cooking vessel resting on one of its sides and cut slashes ¼ inch deep through the skin and fillets of its top side to prevent the skin from bursting. Such slashes are not necessary if the fish fillets are separated and a stuffing is slid between them, since this presentation releases the pressure and tension on the skin.

OVEN TEMPERATURE 350°F for medium-size whole fish, 325°F for large whole fish.

To test doneness, use an instant thermometer. If the fish is done, it will penetrate the fillets and reach to the bone in whole fish; if not, you will feel the resistance of the tissues that are not yet done under the tip of the thermometer. The internal temperature of a roasted or baked fish should be between 140° and 165°F.

Once defatted, the juices in the roasting or dripping pan can be deglazed and added to any sauce, or become the base a small sauce.

Here are a few recipes to practice on a variety of fish, whole or in fillets.

Spit-Roasted King Salmon for the 4th of July

FCR — 12 SERVINGS

1 medium-size salmon, 10 to 12 pounds, dressed with head left on

2 tablespoons hot pepper oil plus extra for brushing

3 tablespoons pure olive oil plus extra for brushing

5 pounds white onions, sliced

½ pound country ham, diced

½ cup chopped fresh parsley leaves

Salt

Pepper from the mill

For the barbecue sauce

Rind and juice of 2 lemons

½ cup dried currants

3 cups fish fumet or substitute (page 543 or 545)

1 cup dry white wine

4 cups plain nonsmoky barbecue sauce of your choice

Salt

Pepper from the mill

Purchase a salmon which will fit the length of your grill. The whole salmon with its head on must be exposed to the flames. Atlantic salmon and Pacific salmon, though different, are just as delicious, especially the wild Atlantic species. After the feast is over, gather all the bones and the head and make fish fumet; it will replace the supply you used in the barbecue sauce. It is a good idea to prepare the barbecue sauce a day early.

SUGGESTED WINE: A California Sauvignon Blanc, or a French Grenache rosé or a white Châteauneuf-du-Pape

Clean the salmon cavity with great care, removing all traces of the bloodline along the backbone.

Over medium heat, heat the hot pepper oil and olive oil together in a sauteuse pan. Toss in the onions, turn the heat down to low, and cook until half tender. Toss in the ham and continue cooking, covered, until the onions form a well-bound compote. Add the parsley, season with salt and pepper, and mix well. Keep warm.

Build a good fire in the grill, putting the bright hot coals in one thick line at the back and a second thick line at the front of the grill, so they will radiate toward the turning salmon. Place a long fireproof baking dish on the bottom center of the barbecue rack to catch the dripping juices and fat. Spit the salmon, securing it to the spit with tightening forks and attaching the fish all around with thick, strong kitchen string which will brown but not burn during the roasting. Cut three slashes ¼ inch deep on each side of the salmon. Start the spit motor and spray or brush the fish with hot pepper oil or, if you prefer, with olive oil. Spit-roast the salmon to an internal temperature of 140° to 165°F, 40 minutes to 1 hour, depending on the initial inner temperature of the fish. Keep your coals hot, renewing them if needed during the roasting.

Cut the lemon rinds into ⅛-inch julienne. Blanch 1 minute in boiling water and set aside. Pour the lemon juice over the currants and let macerate overnight.

Mix the fumet, wine, and barbecue sauce together in a saucepan and reduce over medium heat to 4 cups. Add the currants with the lemon juice and the lemon rinds. If the sauce is too thick, lighten with deglazed and defatted juices from the drip pan. Correct the seasoning with salt and pepper.

Set the onions on a large platter, top with the fish fillets, and sprinkle with the chopped parsley and a drizzle of barbecue sauce, passing the remainder of the sauce in a bowl.

Salt-Baked Red Snapper

FCR—6 SERVINGS

I tablespoon pure olive oil

I small yellow onion, chopped

2 cloves garlic, finely chopped

3 large red bell peppers, seeded and cut into strips

⅔ cup fish fumet or substitute (page 543 or 545)

⅔ cup dry white wine

Salt

Pepper from the mill

4 to 6 pounds kosher salt

One 4- to 5-pound rockfish, eviscerated only, as described on page 537

2 dried pasilla chiles, softened in water to cover, drained, and shredded

½ cup shoepeck corn, cooked

2 tablespoons chopped cilantro leaves or to taste

2 limes, cut into 6 wedges each

Also for larger mackerel, red ocean perch, cabezón, or any fish you like and have access to. The pasillas must have softened completely by the time you prepare the fish. One of the dishes of salt must be large enough to contain the fish with its head on.

SUGGESTED BEVERAGE: Dos Equis beer is preferable to wine.

Heat the oil in a medium-size saucepan, add the onion and garlic, and sauté until golden over medium-high heat. Add the pepper strips, fish fumet, and wine and cook together over low heat until a *coulis* results. Strain through a fine conical strainer and season to taste. Keep warm. The *coulis* should have the texture of a light sauce, coating the back of a spoon by ⅛ of an inch.

Preheat the oven to 400°F. While the pepper *coulis* cooks, pour half the kosher salt into two large baking dishes and let preheat. Meanwhile, clean the fish cavity so no traces of the bloodline are visible along the backbone. Salt and pepper the pasilla shreds and stuff into the fish cavity along the backbone.

Embed the fish into the larger dish of salt. Using oven mittens, pour the contents of second dish of salt over the fish in one regular layer. Bake until an instant thermometer inserted into the thickest part of the fish registers 130°F, about 30 minutes. Remove from oven and leave in the salt 5 to 8 minutes more.

Remove the pasilla from the fish cavity, mash coarsely, and add to the bell pepper *coulis* along with the corn and half the cilantro. Correct the seasoning. Fillet the fish and sprinkle with the remaining cilantro. Serve piping hot with the *coulis* and slivers of lime.

Roasted Mackerel in Parsley Juice

A combination of my mother's salt-baked mackerel with a more modern and leaner sauce. Mackerel may be replaced by trout, larger butterfish, pan-size Coho salmon, or small buffalofish.

SUGGESTED WINE: *A Muscadet of your choice or a light reedy young Chardonnay from France or California*

FCR— 6 SERVINGS

¾ cup fish fumet or substitute (page 543 or 545)

½ cup dry white wine

I shallot, finely chopped

I very large bunch fresh Italian parsley

2 tablespoons unsalted butter

Salt

Pepper from the mill

6 medium-size mackerel, dressed

I tablespoon kosher salt

Cornstarch or potato starch, if needed

Add to a saucepan and reduce together over medium heat by two thirds the fish fumet, wine, shallot, and 2 tablespoons chopped parsley stems. Strain through a conical strainer and set aside.

Blanch the leafy tops of the parsley for 1 minute in boiling water. Drain, refresh under cold water, and pat dry. Add to a blender together with the reduction. Process until smooth, then empty into a strainer lined with several layers of cheesecloth that has been rinsed in cold water and squeezed dry. Let drip, then squeeze the puree gently to extract as much juice as possible. Transfer the juice to a small saucepan, simmer a few minutes over medium-low heat, whisk in the butter, season with salt and pepper, and keep warm.

Preheat the oven to 350°F. Spray the bottom of a long baking dish with a bit of oil. Arrange the mackerel head to tail in the dish and sprinkle with the kosher salt. Bake until the skin is dry and starts to blister, about 15 minutes. Remove from the oven and fillet the fish. Pat off any traces of fish fat in the baking dish and if juices are present, deglaze them over high heat with a bit of the parsley sauce. Blend the deglazing back into the parsley sauce. Serve the fillets with the parsley sauce. If the sauce is too thin for your taste, thicken it with a slurry of 1¼ teaspoons of corn- or potato starch per cup of sauce.

Bachelor's Pecaned Pike

FFR— I SERVING

Unsaturated butter or unsaturated oil of your choice

Three ⅓-inch-thick slices butternut squash

Salt

Pepper from the mill

Fino sherry as needed

Fillets of one 2-pound yellow or walleye pike

3 tablespoons chopped pecans

2 teaspoons chopped fresh curly parsley leaves

I tiny clove garlic, mashed

For a single diner; many a senior citizen has expressed great fondness for this dish. You need a large round or oval ovenproof plate. A butterflied 12-ounce trout can replace the pike fillets very well and will cook even faster.

SUGGESTED BEVERAGE: **A** *small glass of fino sherry*

Heat a bit of butter in a nonstick skillet over medium heat; cook the squash on both sides until tender, 7 to 8 minutes. Season with salt and pepper, add a dash of sherry, and set aside while the fish cooks.

Preheat the oven to 375°F. Spray an ovenproof plate with a bit of melted butter or oil. Arrange both fillets head to tail on a plate, season with salt and pepper, and spray with a bit more oil or melted butter. Mix together the pecans, parsley, and garlic and sprinkle over the fillets. Spray the fillets again very lightly with butter or oil and bake until the fillets are done, 6 to 8 minutes.

Arrange the butternut squash on the same plate as the fillets and enjoy.

Broiled Fish

Broiled fish is exposed successively on each of its sides to the radiating heat of a heating element. Small fish such as sardines, trout, and smelts are broiled whole in their skins. Larger fish cut into steaks, sticks, or rolled into medallions can be broiled plain, after short marination, or under the protection of a layer of fresh bread crumbs over which melted butter or oil has been drizzled.

Broiling is usually done at home in a regular oven with a broil cycle. Please study and know how your oven functions, for there have been many more innovations in broiler building techniques than in oven building and there are many types of broilers.

BROILERS

In older gas ovens, broiling is usually done at the bottom of the oven in a special smaller broiling oven which utilizes the same heating element as the oven. Modern gas broilers are fitted with their own heating element attached to an incandescent heat plate which intensifies the heat. In most gas broilers one broils with the broiler door closed. In most electric ovens, the broiler heating element is located at the top of the oven and one broils with the door ajar. When you take possession of a new apartment or house, your best bet is to look for the serial number of the manufacturer and call their consumer services asking for new documentation on the stove you will be using.

One good way of recognizing whether you should leave the door ajar is to open the door slowly; if it stays ajar by itself at an approximate 60-degree angle, you should broil with the door in this position.

Broiling in commercial operations is done in large broilers equipped with vertical heat jets that heat from both sides of the oven, or sometimes in salamanders, or small "salamander ovens" in which a very hot gas flame can cook the fish from the top in a matter of minutes. In the vertical ovens the intensity of the heat is controlled by moving the fish closer or further from the jets, and in the salamander by moving the rack on which the fish cooks vertically down or up with a lever. If you enter the food professions you will quickly learn to use these two types of broilers.

BROILING PAN The broiling pan should be fitted with a rack on which the fish rests and from which the fat can drip down into the broiler pan. The rack must be lightly oiled and not preheated.

TYPES OF BROILING FISH

Any fish can be broiled, either cut into steaks, large, thicker fillets, or whole. The fish must be at room temperature for at least 30 minutes if thin and 45 minutes if thicker in order to broil fast and well.

Fish that can be broiled in steaks or thick fillets include: halibut, mahimahi, swordfish, tuna, shark, salmon, yellowtail, and many more. As you see they are mostly medium fat to fat fish. Fish to be broiled whole can include almost any kind of fish, since the skin acts as a protector and takes the brunt of the heat.

BROILING TECHNIQUES

Broiling consists in cooking the fish so that it browns lightly and appetizingly on the side exposed to the heat without burning and in just enough time so the juices remain contained within the fish tissues without escaping, which prevents the drying out of the piece of fish.

SEASONING THE FISH

Do not salt the fish before it is exposed to the heat of the home broiler; instead, brush or spray it with clarified butter or the oil of your choice, plain or flavored.

The broiling and seasoning sequence of any piece or fillet of fish in a home broiler is:

1. Coat with fat or oil;
2. Broil the first side;
3. Season the broiled side;
4. Turn the fish over *only if necessary,* as in thicker whole fish, chunks, or thick fillets;
5. Coat the second side with fat, broil it, and season it;
6. Serve immediately.

The presence of salt on the surface of the fish before the start of broiling is not favorable in a home oven in which the maximum output of heat by the broiler element is only 550°F.

In professional ovens where the temperature is much higher, salting can be done before the broiling starts for no sooner does the salt start to melt in contact with the moisture on the fish than the high heat evaporates it and concentrates it. This explains why fish broiled in restaurants always tastes so much more concentrated and truly better than fish broiled at home.

Beware of pepper. Grind it directly over the broiled and ready-to-serve fish. Any pepper exposed to direct heat burns badly and turns extra bitter. Taste dictates to technique here though, because many people like their pepper burned. I prefer the natural heat and flower of the pepper without the bitterness it acquires by exposure to the flame.

DISTANCE FROM THE HEAT ELEMENT

The distance between the fish and the heat element is most important. Too close to the heat and the fish will dry out and burn; too far away and it will languish and not sear fast enough.

FOR FILLETS AND STEAKS The best all-around distance is approximately 4 inches from the heat element. If the fillets or steaks are only ½ to ⅔ inch thick, it can be helpful to coat the fish with a thin layer of fresh bread crumbs which are then sprayed with some more fat or oil and will take the brunt of the heat. There is no nutritional advantage to this crumbing; the crumbs protect the texture of the fish, but add calories and fat to the dish. The same goal can be achieved by lowering the broiling pan to about 6 inches from the source of heat so the fish finishes cooking without turning it over and without dehydrating and overhardening its top.

If the fillets or steaks are 1 inch thick or a little more, spraying or brushing them with fat or oil is sufficient.

FOR WHOLE FISH Whole fish should not weigh more than 3 to 4 pounds and are best enclosed in a wire basket for easy turning. Brush or spray the skin with butter or oil. Cut three slashes ¼ inch deep through the skin and fillet. Broil 4 inches from the heat element for 7 to 8 minutes for the first side and no more than 5 for the second.

Test doneness with an instant thermometer, which should read 140° to 165°F.

To turn over thick steaks, fillets, or whole fish, put a second rack on top of the fish using mittens. Grasp both the top and bottom racks together and turn over. Remove the top rack and broil the second side of the fish.

Here are a few recipes illustrating these principles:

Broiled Lemon Sole

FCR—6 SERVINGS

1 ½ to 2 pounds thickest available lemon sole fillets, cut into 6 equal portions

2 tablespoons dark "light" soy sauce

2 tablespoons balsamic vinegar

3 tablespoons virgin olive oil

Salt

Pepper from the mill

2 cups rice pilaf (page 461)

4 scallions, finely slivered

½ teaspoon finely grated lemon rind

1 teaspoon peeled and finely grated fresh ginger

Set the pieces of fish on an oiled rack set over a broiler pan. Mix the soy sauce, vinegar, and olive oil together and divide into two equal parts; one will serve as marinade, the second as dressing. Brush the first half evenly over all six portions of fish and let marinate, unrefrigerated, for 30 minutes covered with plastic wrap.

Preheat the broiler. Broil the fish 4 minutes 4 inches from the heat. Test for doneness with an instant thermometer (140° to 165°F), salt lightly and pepper to taste, and if the fish is not quite done, finish cooking 6 inches from the heat.

To serve, rehomogenize the remainder of the dressing; add a pinch of salt if necessary and spoon over the fish. Serve with the pilaf flavored with the scallions, lemon rind, and grated ginger.

Lemon sole is a large winter flounder also known as black back flounder, which I remember fondly from my Philadelphia years. This presentation mixes Atlantic, Mediterranean, and China Sea ingredients and can be executed with any other thick fillets of fish. Light soy sauce is less salty than the regular soy sauce.

SUGGESTED WINE:

California meritage of Sauvignon and Sémillon, French Entre-deux-Mers, or Verdicchio dei Castelli di Jesi

Broiled Tinker Mackerel with Pinzimonio

FCR — 6 SERVINGS

12 tinker mackerels, dressed with heads left on

Salt

Pepper from the mill

½ cup olive oil of your choice, plus extra for spraying

2 tablespoons fresh lemon juice

24 small fresh basil leaves

Do not cut slashes into the skin of the mackerels; it is very thin and stretches nicely. Salt and pepper the fish in their cavities, then set them belly down on an oiled broiling rack; spray or brush with olive oil. Broil 5 minutes 4 inches from the source of heat. Lower the rack to 6 inches and broil until the fish feel firmed up when squeezed between your fingers, another 2 to 4 minutes. Remove from the broiler and skin the mackerels.

Mix the lemon juice with the ½ cup olive oil, season with salt and pepper to taste, and whisk until white. Spoon the pinzimonio over the fish reserving 1 tablespoon in which you will toss and season the basil leaves. Decorate the top of the fillets with the basil leaves.

In memory of all the lovely tinkers I rushed from Marblehead to my kitchen all through the 1960s and 1970s. This can be applied to small whiting, butterfish, small trout, etc.

SUGGESTED WINE: *Est! Est!! Est!!!, or Frascati, or Portuguese Vusho Verde*

Broiled Tuna Steaks Taormina

FCR — 6 SERVINGS

6 tuna steaks, about 4 ounces each and ¾ to 1 inch thick

6 tablespoons virgin olive oil plus extra for brushing

1 teaspoon very finely chopped fresh rosemary leaves

1 teaspoon finely ground fennel seeds

Grated rind of 1 large Valencia orange

1 small head each white and purple cauliflower

2 tablespoons red wine vinegar, preferably Italian

Salt

Pepper from the mill

3 tablespoons small capers, well drained

2 tablespoons chopped fresh Italian parsley leaves

1 hard-boiled egg, chopped

Trim the steaks of any skin. Spray or brush on both sides with olive oil. Mix half of the rosemary, fennel, and orange rind together. Sprinkle the steaks with two thirds of the mixture and let stand at room temperature covered with plastic wrap for 30 minutes.

A fond memory of lunch in Taormina in 1955 with Etna rumbling and spewing fireworks in the distance.

SUGGESTED WINE: *Corvo Bianco or white Regaleali*

Separate both cauliflowers into florets; blanch each color separately in boiling salted water to the texture you prefer. Mix them together when cooked, and cool completely. Whisk the vinegar together with the 6 table-spoons olive oil, salt and pepper to taste, and the remaining rosemary, fennel, and orange rind mixture until the dressing turns white. Toss the cauliflowers with three quarters of the dressing, adding the capers and chopped parsley.

Set the steaks on a lightly oiled rack; broil 4 minutes 4 inches from the heat source. Using a second rack turn the steaks over and broil 3 minutes on the second side. As soon as done to your taste, drizzle the remainder of the dressing over the fish and serve with the cauliflower salad sprinkled with the chopped egg.

Broiled Redfish Steak and Garlic French Fries

FFR — 6 SERVINGS

2 pounds ½-inch-thick redfish, mahimahi, or yellowtail fillets

Cayenne pepper

¼ teaspoon ground bay leaf

¼ cup corn oil

Salt

Pepper from the mill

12 lemon slices

1 pound freshly fried french fries

3 cloves garlic, finely chopped

2 tablespoons finely chopped fresh Italian parsley leaves

This recipe is inspired by one of my many trips to the Deep South. The choice of fries is yours; you can choose from homemade to frozen fries. If you want to make the fries yourself, see the recipe on page 425, and have them ready at the time the fish comes off the broiler.

SUGGESTED WINE: *A crisp Alsatian Riesling*

Cut the fillets into six equal portions. Set each on a lightly oiled rack placed over the broiler pan. Mix together cayenne pepper to your personal taste, the bay leaf, and corn oil and brush over the fish. Let marinate 30 minutes at room temperature covered with a piece of plastic wrap or parchment paper.

Broil 5 minutes 4 inches from the source of heat; if not quite done to your taste, lower the pan to 6 inches below the heat and finish cooking, another 2 to 3 minutes. Salt and pepper well.

Serve promptly garnished with 2 lemon slices each and with the fries tossed with the mixture of garlic and parsley as soon as they come out of the oil bath; keep the fries warm in a 200°F oven for a few minutes if necessary.

Broiled Salmon Medallions in Herb Crumbs

FFR — 6 SERVINGS

1 European cucumber, peeled, seeded, and slivered into ⅛-inch julienne

1 red onion, cut in half and sliced into ⅛-inch-thick slivers

Salt

Fresh lemon juice

Pepper from the mill

1 small clove garlic, finely chopped

1 teaspoon Dijon mustard

2 tablespoons chopped fresh parsley leaves

6 skinned boned salmon medallions or steaks

6 tablespoons unsalted butter, melted

½ cup coarse fresh bread crumbs

2 tablespoons chopped fresh dill

1 tablespoon chopped fresh chives

Steamed potatoes or rice of your choice

Put the cucumber and onion slivers on two different plates. Salt each vegetable and let it render its juices; drain each, then mix them together. Add lemon juice to taste, more salt if needed, pepper, garlic, Dijon mustard, and 1 tablespoon of the chopped parsley. Let stand while you broil the salmon.

Brush the salmon and broiling pan rack with some of the melted butter. Set the salmon on the rack. Mix the bread crumbs with the dill, the remaining parsley, and the chives. Sprinkle the medallions evenly with the herbed crumbs. Dribble the remainder of the butter over the crumbed salmon.

Broil 4 inches from the heat source for 5 minutes. Do not turn the fish over; lower the pan to 6 inches from the heat source to finish cooking the medallions, 2 to 3 more minutes, and remove from the broiler. The internal temperature measured with an instant thermometer should be between 140° and 165°F. Let stand on the rack 2 more minutes and serve with the cucumber-and-onion relish and steamed potatoes.

Of course, you can use steaks, but the taste will be less refined because of the presence of the skin. If you do not wish to bone the steaks, at least pass your knife under the skin to remove it all around the steak; you will appreciate the difference in taste. If you have a choice of salmon, wild Atlantic or Pacific Silver is the best for this preparation.

SUGGESTED WINE: *Alsatian Riesling or California Dry Riesling*

Broiled Aniseed and Saffron-Flavored Roughy

This recipe can also be used with red perch or snapper fillets and butterflied trout.

SUGGESTED WINE: *Any white or rosé Côtes de Provence or "Cigare Volant" from Bonny Doon Vineyard in Santa Cruz*

FCR—6 SERVINGS

¼ cup pure olive oil plus extra for the broiler pan

⅛ teaspoon powdered saffron

½ teaspoon finely ground aniseed

6 orange roughy fillets, as large as possible

3 small fennel bulbs, well washed and cut into ⅛-inch julienne

1 unripe pear, unpeeled, cored, and cut into ⅛-inch julienne

1 tablespoon fresh lemon juice or to taste

Salt

Pepper from the mill

2 tablespoons chopped fresh chervil leaves

Heat the olive oil over low heat in a small pan, then turn the heat off and add the saffron and aniseed; let stand 15 minutes and cool completely.

Oil a baking sheet. Arrange the fillets on the bottom of the pan. Divide the flavored oil into two equal parts. Brush one half over the fillets; let marinate 15 minutes at room temperature.

Meanwhile, mix the fennel and pear together and toss with the remainder of the flavored oil, the lemon juice, and salt and pepper to your taste. Set aside to serve as a relish with the fish.

Broil the fillets 5 minutes 4 inches away from the heat source. Season with salt and pepper, turn the heating element off, and let the fish finish cooking, 1 or 2 more minutes, in the hot broiler. The fish is done just as soon as the flesh looks pearly.

Serve the fish sprinkled with the fresh chervil and the fennel-and-pear relish.

Grilled Fish

Grilling can be done with several different implements. The most popular of all is the outdoor grill. Our beloved and popular barbecue seems to have taken a trip around the world; the Australians call it affectionately the "barbi" and even the French now never let a weekend in the country go by without lighting *zhe barbe-Q*.

Then there is the stovetop grill, which may be built into a home stovetop, or be a separate small cast-iron ribbed grill on which fish or meat steaks cook rapidly with great flavor. In professional kitchens huge and powerful gas units spew hot flames which heat heavy grates which will, in turn, transfer the heat to the food and allow professional kitchen chefs to grill many portions in a matter of minutes. Some kitchens grill on a griddle, a thick, flat, and smoothly polished stainless steel plaque on which just about everything can be either cooked (eggs for breakfast) or grilled (fish, steaks, chops, sliced blanched vegetables), depending on the temperature of the heat elements hidden under the plaque. Such an instrument is rarely available at home, but it can be improvised very easily for a very small number of portions in a nonstick electric frying pan. The technique of grilling in a nonstick frying pan is often called pan-broiling.

Read all about your outdoor grill when you purchase it and make friends with it; this wonderful instrument harbors within its dark structure many good hours of cooking outside while chatting away with friends.

PREPARING THE GRILL AND FIRE

To light a grill, follow the directions given for each particular model of barbecue. Be certain to ignite your coals with a chimney and to prod them into flaming happily with Georgia fatwood or any clean dry small kindling you can gather in your surroundings; use storebought lighter fluid only if you have no other more natural fire accelerant source. Charcoal made from any type of wood will communicate a better taste to the fish than briquets. One of the best types of charcoal is southwestern mesquite (be careful, though, it sparks considerably); eastern woods such as alder, oak, hickory, and apple wood are also most delightful. You will soon find out which works best for your personal taste. I prefer apple wood because it reminds me of the first duck breasts available after the war years which we grilled on apple wood in a wintry Normandy garden.

The fish will be cooked by the radiating heat of nicely red coals which have just turned white and by heat transferred to the fish from the grill rack, which itself becomes extremely hot from the heat released from the charcoal. Enough charcoal will be needed to cover the whole bottom of the barbecue so the fish rests on a rack well heated by an even fire all around.

The rack which will hold the fish must be rubbed with a wad of paper towels well impregnated with olive or another oil, but never butter, even if clarified, which will go up in smoke on the extremely hot grill, which is some 200°F hotter than an oven broiler. I have, when traveling the islands of the Aegean, especially on Aegina and Paros, enjoyed more than one fish with the crispest skin. It had been grilled on a rack that had been dipped into a tank of seawater and turned crusty white from the hardening salt. Having tried this in my garden using tap water seasoned with the same concentration of sea salt as seawater, I found out that the Aegean water worked better, as does Pacific water, so the nice taste and color given by seawater must come from elements other than the salt, perhaps the iodine, spores from seaweeds, and microscopic plankton.

PREPARING THE FISH

The fish need not be skinned if the fillets are relatively thin, or up to ⅔ inch thick; the skin will acquire a crispy and extremely tasty flavor which many eaters relish.

If the fish is cut into steaks from large fish such as shark, swordfish, marlin, mahimahi, ono, etc., you must remove the skin if the fishmonger has not done so; simply pass a sharp blade between skin and meat, trying not to leave more than ⅟₁₆ inch of meat on the skin. Most of the time the skin will have been removed. Failure to remove this skin will make the center of the steak buckle and act as a container which will fill with the juices of the fish as the steak overcooks at its center.

Whichever form of fish you may be grilling, spray or brush it lightly with oil, never butter or clarified butter. Small fish such as sardines, herrings, pilchards, smelts, tinker mackerels, small butterfish, etc. must be lightly oiled and enclosed in a wire fish basket or set on stainless steel wire mesh, which itself has been oiled. The basket or mesh will prevent the small fish from slipping between the rungs of the rack and allow easy turning.

Before grilling, the fish must be at room temperature at least 30 minutes covered with plastic wrap or parchment paper. Fish grilled straight out of the refrigerator will remain rare at its center.

COOKING TIME

The grill rack should be set 4 inches away from the burning coals. Do not cover the grill, except when grilling a larger whole fish.

Fish is turned only once on the grill and cooked a little over half of the total needed time on its first side and the rest of the time on its second side. Because grilling occurs outdoors, the time needed to cook the fish is slightly longer than it is for broiling in an oven.

For each inch of thickness, you may want to count 4½ minutes on the first side and 3 to 3½ on the second. *However*, not only are the inner temperature of the fish when it goes on the grill and the heat of the grill important, *but the texture of the flesh is also most important.* Make a little experiment. Grill three steaks side by side: one of mako shark, one of swordfish, and one of mahimahi, all exactly of the same thickness and at the same internal temperature before going on the grill; you will understand exactly what I mean. The shark will be done first, followed by the mahimahi, and finally the swordfish. The tighter the texture of the fish the longer it will take to reach the correct internal temperature.

Your instant thermometer remains your best friend, for 140°F is the temperature you must absolutely reach in order for your fish to be done properly if you caught it yourself. If the fish is store-bought, do not hesitate going to 165°F, but then you will be exchanging perfect texture for total safety and your grilled fish will not be as moist.

Here are a few recipes for you to practice on.

Grilled Yellowtail and Zucchini

FCR — 6 SERVINGS

3 large zucchini, cut on a slant into ¼-inch-thick slices

Salt

1 tablespoon plus ⅓ cup olive oil of your choice

1 very small red onion, diced into ⅛-inch cubes

12 fresh nasturtium flowers, stems removed and finely chopped

1 tiny clove garlic, finely chopped

1 heaping tablespoon chopped fresh Italian parsley leaves

1½ tablespoons fresh lemon juice

1½ tablespoons sweet rice vinegar

Pepper from the mill

Six ¾-inch-thick yellowtail steaks

Fire up the barbecue.

Blanch the zucchini slices for 1 minute in boiling salted water. Drain, pat dry, salt, and toss in 1 generous tablespoon of the olive oil. Set aside.

Salt the red onion well; let it sit at least half an hour to extract its hard juices. Drain through a stainless strainer, rinse, pat dry, and turn into a bowl. Mix in the nasturtium, garlic, parsley, lemon juice, rice vinegar, a pinch only of salt, and 2 turns of the pepper mill. Add the remaining ⅓ cup of oil and whisk until well homogenized. Let stand 15 minutes.

Spray the steaks with oil and salt and pepper lightly. When the coals are bright red passing to white, set the steaks on the hot rack which has been lightly rubbed with oil and grill 3½ minutes on the first side and 2½ on the other. Remove to a plate, correct the seasoning if necessary, and let stand 2 more minutes while you grill the zucchini slices 1 minute on each side. Correct the seasoning of the zucchini. Serve the fish and vegetables with the well-rehomogenized dressing.

Watch the pepper in the dressing, the nasturtium itself being slightly peppery. This recipe also works for thresher shark, mahimahi, and swordfish.

SUGGESTED WINE: *A cool climate American Sauvignon Blanc, or French Sancerre or Quincy*

Grilled Wild Trout

FFR — 6 SERVINGS

Corn oil as needed

1 large freshwater trout of your choice or as the luck of the fisherman will provide, 3 to 5 pounds dressed with head left on

½ cup unsalted butter

Salt

Pepper from the mill

Fresh lemon juice

This is the essence of simplicity. To aid in grilling, use an oblong wire basket. Any sweet cold water fish will serve just as well: steelhead, Mackinaw, Dolly Varden, large brown trout, and especially the precious Arctic char (Salmo salvellinus).

SUGGESTED WINE: *The best buttery Chardonnay you can find from Corton-Charlemagne to the best of the Napa and Sonoma wines*

Fire up the barbecue. Rub the basket all around with a thin layer of oil. Also lightly oil the fish's surface. If the fish has been cleaned so that the belly is split open, do not cut slashes in its robe; if it has been cleaned the European way with the belly is still closed, cut slashes ¼ inch deep on one of its sides.

Once the coals are red, starting to turn white, place the grill basket on the grill and grill 8 minutes on each side, turning the fish regularly every 4 minutes. Use an instant thermometer to check that the internal temperature reaches 140° to 165°F.

Put the butter in a small saucepan set at the edge of the grill and let it cook to the light brown stage, then season with salt and pepper and whisk in lemon juice to taste. Fillet the fish and serve the fillets basted with the flavored butter and nothing else. The fillets may be skinned or served with the skin on if you prefer.

Bora Bora Mahimahi

From the kitchen of my schoolfriend Malilé who was raised in "Bora Bora of the sublime sunsets." The green peppercorns came from the garden of the cook; replace them with any other green peppercorn—those from Ponape in the South Pacific are the best. Omit the coconut for fat-restricted diets. And be aware that pineapple cores vary in acidity from sharp to semisweet, so the taste of the dish may vary somewhat each time you make it.

FCR—6 SERVINGS

I fresh pineapple, peeled but left uncored

Sweet rice vinegar as needed

Salt

Freeze-dried green peppercorns from the mill

½ cup corn oil

Three ¾-inch-thick mahimahi steaks

½ small white onion, finely chopped

½ teaspoon peeled and grated fresh ginger

I scallion, white part only, sliced paper thin

I tablespoon unsweetened shredded coconut

SUGGESTED WINE: *French Graves or Entre-Deux-Mers, or California meritage of Sauvignon and Sémillon, or California Johannisberg Riesling*

Slice the pineapple into ⅓-inch-thick slices. Using a cutter, remove the core of each slice and put all the cores into a blender. Blend to a mash and pour into a tea strainer placed over a bowl to collect the juices. Press on the pulp to obtain as much juice as possible. This juice will replace part of the vinegar; if it is not acid enough, blend it with some rice vinegar to obtain 3 full tablespoons of acid, then add salt and pepper to taste, and blend in the oil. Homogenize until the dressing turns white.

Remove 3 tablespoons of this dressing and brush it in a thin layer over both sides of the steaks. Let stand covered with plastic wrap or parchment paper, unrefrigerated, until the coals are red, starting to turn white.

While the fish marinates, finish the dressing by adding the onion, ginger, scallion, and grated coconut. Let stand until the fish is ready. Correct the salt and pepper.

Oil the grill rack and set 4 inches over the hot fire; arrange the fish on it. Grill the fish 4 minutes on the first side and 3½ on the second. Remove from the heat and keep warm for another 2 minutes while you grill the pineapple slices 1 minute on each side.

Serve the fish surrounded by the pineapple slices and well-rehomogenized dressing.

Grilled Poor Man's Lobster Kebabs

FCR — 6 SERVINGS

2 cups cold light chicken broth of your choice

1½ cups coarse polenta

½ cup fine polenta

6 cups boiling light chicken broth of your choice

Salt

Pepper from the mill

Sweet paprika

1 tablespoon finely ground pasilla chile

1 canned chipotle chile, finely mashed

Corn oil as needed

2 pounds monkfish fillets, cut into 1½-inch cubes

1 large ripe (but not overripe) papaya, peeled, seeded, and diced into ⅓-inch cubes

1 large avocado, peeled, pitted, and diced into ⅓-inch cubes

1 red bell pepper, preferably peeled, seeded, and cut into ⅓-inch squares

½ large sweet onion of your choice, diced into ⅓-inch cubes

Tabasco sauce

1½ tablespoons red wine vinegar

2 tablespoons chopped cilantro leaves

If you are pressed for time, purchase the Italian polenta ready in a sealed plastic bag; it works better for this preparation than the instant polenta. If you cook the polenta in a shallow sauteuse pan, you will gain time; when you test the polenta for thickness, tilt the pan and bunch the polenta into its lip. If a spoon stands in the polenta, it is ready.

SUGGESTED BEVERAGE: *No wine, but rather the delicious, cool beer of your choice*

In a large saucepan, mix the cold broth with both the polentas, then stir into the boiling broth. Continue stirring until the mixture comes back to a boil and cook, still stirring, until a spoon stands in the polenta. Season with salt, pepper, and paprika to taste, then add the pasilla and chipotle, mix well, and continue to cook a few minutes. Rub two 8-inch-square cake pans with corn oil and pour half the polenta into each. Let cool completely. When cold, cut into 1¼-inch cubes. Spray the cubes with corn oil.

Sprinkle the monkfish cubes lightly with paprika, salt, and pepper and toss into just enough corn oil to coat. Skewer the polenta and cubes of monkfish alternately on six skewers. Let stand, covered, while you prepare the relish.

Mix together the papaya, avocado, red pepper, onion, Tabasco to taste, vinegar, and cilantro. Correct the salt and turn into a serving bowl.

Set the skewers to grill on a hot, lightly oiled rack set 6 inches over red coals starting to turn white until the monkfish feels slightly springy when pushed with the finger and the polenta hot, turning the skewers every 2 minutes; the total time will vary from 6 to 8 minutes. Serve with the relish.

Basque-Style Sea Bass

LOUBINES BASQUES

FCR — 6 SERVINGS

2 tablespoons corn oil

I large yellow onion, chopped

2 red bell peppers, preferably peeled, seeded, and coarsely chopped

2 yellow bell peppers, preferably peeled, seeded, and coarsely chopped

Salt

Red pepper flakes

2 cups tomato essence (page 309) or the same amount canned tomato puree plus I
  cup water

2 anchovy fillets, rinsed and mashed

2 cloves garlic, mashed

I teaspoon finely grated lemon rind

I large sprig fresh French thyme, bruised with the back of a knife

2 teaspoons unsweetened cocoa powder of your choice

A loubine is the fish Provence calls loup, *a type of sea bass we replace with striped bass in this country.*

Grill two smaller fish, arranging both head to tail in an oblong basket, exactly as described in the Grilled Wild Trout recipe above, reducing the total cooking time to barely 15 minutes. Serve with the following sauce:

SUGGESTED WINE: *French Vins des Sables, Irouléguy, Jurançon Rouge, or Jurançon*

Heat the oil in a skillet over medium heat. Add the onion and cook, stirring, until golden, then add the peppers, blend into the onion, and cook 1 minute. Season with salt and pepper flakes, cover, and cook over low heat until the juices of the peppers have run out into the pan. Add the tomato essence and bring to a boil. Add the anchovies, garlic, lemon rind, thyme, and cocoa. Reduce the heat to medium and simmer until well bound. Remove the thyme and strain through a conical strainer into a warm bowl, pushing on the fibrous material in the strainer to extract all the flavorful juices. You can also process the sauce in a blender if you prefer and strain. Serve with the fish.

STOVETOP GRILLING

At home this is done on a ribbed cast-iron grill; the best are stovetop grills made in France by Le Creuset and can be purchased from cookware stores across the nation. Two models are made, one for meats with very small ribs and one with larger and rounder ribs, usually used for fish. However, I have grilled fish on the meat model and vice versa with great success. If you can afford one of each, you will be set for life; I am still using my mother's blackened grill, which is fifty years old.

The only disadvantage of these ribbed grills is that they are pricey; if you cannot afford one, you can use an electric frying pan heated to its maximum temperature. In this case you must use fish that cooks fast at a lower temperature, like fillets of flatfish, since the pan never heats up as much as any grill.

I have used these grills in my restaurants with great success. In larger kitchens, the grilling of fillets and steaks of fish can be done on the griddle.

Whichever style of grill you use, *you will need excellent ventilation*, with a fan pulling out the smell and eventual smoke so your kitchen and house are not permeated with strong fish smells. If your kitchen is not ventilated properly, do not grill in the house; rather, use a barbecue grill on the balcony of your apartment, in your garden, or at the entrance of a garage. Stovetop grilling without good ventilation can be as noxious and potentially dangerous as grilling on a barbecue pit in your kitchen would be.

Heat the grill until it is so hot that it looks somewhat white. Roll up a thick wad of paper towels and moisten well with oil. Rub the oil over the grill; when the grill shows a few wisps of smoke, it is ready to receive the fish.

The only disadvantage of stovetop grills is that they are too small to allow the preparation of more than four portions. Remember this fact when you decide on a menu.

Here are a few recipes for the stovetop grill.

Lime-Marinated Shark Steaks

FCR — 4 SERVINGS

1 tablespoon fresh lime juice

1 tablespoon tomato essence (page 309) or tomato juice

2 tablespoons olive oil of your choice

4 thresher shark steaks, skinned

For the guacamole

3 large, ripe Haas avocados, peeled and pitted

Juice of 1 lime

1 teaspoon grated lime rind

Salt

¼ large red onion, finely chopped

2 medium-size sun-ripened tomatoes, peeled, seeded, and cut into ¼-inch cubes

1 to 2 tablespoons chopped cilantro leaves, to your personal taste

1 teaspoon to 1 tablespoon chopped jalapeño pepper, to your personal taste

1½ teaspoons very coarsely grated frozen bittersweet chocolate

Light olive oil as needed

If shark is not available, try halibut, swordfish, tuna, or mahimahi. The condiment is a simple variation on the classic guacamole.

SUGGESTED BEVERAGE:
No wine, but rather Dos Equis beer

Mix together the lime juice, tomato essence, and olive oil and brush the steaks on both sides with it. Let marinate for 30 minutes at room temperature covered with plastic wrap or parchment paper.

To prepare the guacamole, completely mash two of the avocados with the lime juice and rind. Dice the third and add it to the puree; set aside. Salt the onion and let stand 15 minutes. Drain off any rendered juices, pat dry, and add without rinsing to the avocado puree. Add the tomatoes, cilantro, jalapeño, and grated chocolate. Correct the salt. Keep refrigerated until ready to serve.

Heat the grill till white hot. Moisten a thick wad of paper towels with olive oil and pass it over the grill. Brush off any excess marinade from the surface of the fish, then grill the steaks 3 minutes on the first side and 2 on second side. Remove from the heat and let stand another 2 minutes. Beware of overcooking the very tender shark meat, which is done extremely fast. When pushing on top of a steak, it should still spring a bit under the finger. The instant thermometer should read 140° to 145°F, no more; at 165°F they will be overdone. Serve with the guacamole.

Pacific Fish with Vanilla Fruit Relish

Simple and quite pleasant. The elements of the relish were part of a very popular first course salad offered in my first restaurant in Boston twenty years ago; this relish can be used also with shrimp and lobster.

SUGGESTED WINE: *Mellow white Zinfandel or white Cabernet; also Grignolino or Grenache rosé*

FCR — 4 SERVINGS

For the relish

2 tablespoons sweet rice vinegar

I large shallot, extremely finely chopped

Salt

Pepper from the mill

I tablespoon pure vanilla extract

I slightly underripe, deep orange papaya, peeled, seeded, and diced into ¼-inch cubes

I large, almost ripe but still firm mango, peeled, pitted, and diced into ¼-inch cubes

2 kiwis, peeled and diced into ¼-inch cubes

2 slices fresh pineapple, peeled, cored, and diced into ¼-inch cubes

2 tablespoons chopped fresh chives

To grill the fish

Pure olive oil

4 halibut steaks, ¾ to I inch thick, skinned

Salt

Pepper from the mill

Mix all the relish ingredients together and let stand at room temperature until ready to serve.

Oil the halibut steaks. Heat the stovetop grill until white hot. Rub with a wad of paper towels moistened well with olive oil. Grill the steaks until an instant thermometer reads 140° to 165°F, 4 minutes on the first side and about 3½ on the second. Salt and pepper the fish generously and serve with the relish.

Swordfish in Neapolitan Sauce

PESCE SPADA CON SALSA NAPOLETANA

FCR — 4 SERVINGS

2 tablespoons white raisins

Boiling water

Olive oil of your choice as needed

2 large cloves garlic, finely chopped

2 tablespoons pine nuts

2 pounds fresh, sun-ripened tomatoes, peeled, seeded, and coarsely chopped

I rounded tablespoon tiny capers, drained

I anchovy fillet or more, to your personal taste, rinsed and mashed

I sprig fresh oregano or savory

1½ tablespoons chopped pitted oil-cured olives

Light olive oil as needed

Four 1-inch-thick swordfish steaks, skinned

Salt

Pepper from the mill

I recipe Deep-fried Zucchini (page 423)

Put the raisins in a small bowl and cover with boiling water. Let stand while you prepare the remainder of the dish.

Heat 2 tablespoons olive oil in a sauteuse pan, then add the garlic and pine nuts. Sauté until light golden over medium-high heat, then immediately add the tomatoes and cook over low heat until most of the water has evaporated and the sauce is light orange in color and supple in texture. Add the capers, anchovy, oregano, olives, and drained raisins; mix well. Remove from the heat and let stand 10 minutes to blend the flavors well.

Heat the stovetop grill to white hot. Rub with a wad of paper towels well moistened with olive oil. Brush the steaks with a thin layer of olive oil. Grill 4 minutes on the first side and 3½ on the second. The internal temperature should be 140° to 165°F. Remove from the heat and let stand a few minutes before serving. Salt and pepper to your taste, remove the oregano sprig, and pass the sauce on the side in a small bowl, along with the deep-fried zucchini.

From a small Naples trattoria where the walls were worn with age and the chairs ready to crumble, but the dish was so fresh and zesty that I went back to enjoy it several times. Use the fresh tomatoes of August and September. The original of this sauce was light orange hued, fluffy, and utterly delicious.

SUGGESTED WINE: *Lacryma Christi del Vesuvio red or white*

Grilled Sardines with Leek Fondue

SARDINES GRILLÉES À L'EMBEURRÉE
DEPOIREAUX

A recipe from the Atlantic coast of France in the vicinity of La Rochelle, native city of Huguenot Mr. Revere, father of Boston's Paul, whose French family name was originally Rivoire. Northern Europeans slather their grilled sardines with fresh unsalted butter. The leeks absorb quite a bit of the butter; use unsaturated oil if necessary.

SUGGESTED WINE: *Any humble white or red wine of your choice*

FFR — 4 SERVINGS

12 large leeks, white and light green parts, well washed and cut into
   ⅛-inch-thick slices

6 tablespoons unsalted butter or more if desired or needed

Salt

Pepper from the mill

8 large sardines or pilchards, drawn (with heads left on)

1 tablespoon unsaturated oil of your choice

Blanch the leeks for 2 minutes in boiling salted water, then drain and let drip completely dry. Roll the leeks into a towel to absorb any excess water. Heat the butter in a large skillet or small sauteuse, then add the leeks and salt and pepper to taste, and toss in the butter. Cook gently over low heat until only a thickish compote of overcooked, delicious leeks is left; turn into a small bowl and keep warm.

Heat the stovetop grill to white hot. Rub the sardines well with the oil. Grill 2 to 3 minutes on each side. Skin the sardines or leave it for your guests to skin themselves. Serve with the leek compote.

Ma and Pa Electric-Grilled Perch Fillets

Dinner in a matter of minutes, perfect for senior citizens who prefer relaxing to long dinner preparations.

SUGGESTED WINE: *Any mellow white wine from anywhere*

FCR — 2 SERVINGS

2 tablespoons unsalted butter or unsaturated oil of your choice

2 fennel bulbs, well washed and slivered

Salt

Pepper from the mill

2 red perch or rockfish fillets, skin left on

1 to 2 tablespoons Pernod (optional), to your personal taste

1½ tablespoons chopped fennel greens

Preheat a nonstick electric frying pan to 375°F. Heat the butter and add the fennel strips. Sauté until well coated with the butter, then season with salt and pepper. Cover the pan and let steam until crisp-tender. Remove to a plate and keep warm.

Raise the heat to the highest level and let the pan heat until the light goes off. Place the fillets skin side down; grill 3 minutes. Turn over using a spatula, season the cooked side with salt and pepper, and cook 2 minutes. Add the Pernod and light with a long match, keeping long hair and dangling sleeves away from the pan (see page 720 for more details on flambéing). Remove the fillets to warm plates and serve sprinkled with the chopped fennel greens and garnished with the fennel strips.

Panfrying Fish

It often happens when a word is adapted from one language to another that its meaning changes. This is precisely what happened to sauté when it passed from the French to English sometime between the end of the eighteenth and early nineteenth century.

Sauter, or faire sauter, or faire un sauté in French does not refer to the same cooking technique as is meant when the term sauté is used in English. A sauté in French refers to a certain way of cooking young meats using the semimoist and semidry procedure that you will find on page 840.

In English—or perhaps only in American English—sauté refers to what is called in French sauter à la poële, which means cooking a food in hot butter or oil in a frying pan in such a manner that the food ends up nice, brown, and crisp. Faire sauter à la poële implies that in order to crisp and brown the food properly, one flips the food in the pan, making it jump (the original meaning of sauter), to ensure that all its surfaces have been exposed to the hot frying medium and browned properly on all sides.

Considering that necessity of crisping the food on all of its surfaces, the English term panfrying is perfectly adequate and understandable by all, which is why I am using it here. For vegetables such as potatoes or other small vegetables that are tossed in the pan, which makes them jump, to prevent them from attaching to its bottom, the English sauté may make sense. For fish or meat, however, which are not tossed as vegetables are, but rather, most of the time, turned over once with a spatula, panfrying is definitely more appropriately descriptive. Although experienced cooks and chefs definitely can turn crisped fish over by flipping the pan, I recommend using a spatula, because it is safer, especially for beginners.

Since fish contains a large amount of water, cooks have for centuries coated fillets, escalopes, and steaks with plain flour, a breading, or a pastella, the role of which is to absorb the water which will bind with the flour, harden in the hot fat or oil, and eventually turn into that irresistible well-known golden to golden brown crispy crust.

FLOUR

Use flour that is as absorbent as possible. All-purpose flour is fine but a mixture of half all-purpose and half cake flours is more efficient. The mixture must always be seasoned with a bit of salt and pepper. White pepper tastes more refined and less aggressive with white-fleshed fish and black pepper is definitely better adapted to red- or dark-fleshed fish.

BREADING

The breading consists of two parts: the anglaise and the bread crumbs.

Anglaise is a beaten mixture of whole egg lightened with a bit of water and oil; seasonings can be added, they can be varied forever. For diets lower in cholesterol, it is feasible to bread only with egg white beaten with a small amount of unsaturated oil and water. The oil acts as a foam retardant and suppressant (see egg foams, pages 162–69) and allows the beaten egg white to spread on the food without difficulty.

Whole-Egg Anglaise

You need a supple brush that will bend along the fillets or pieces of meat, a small bowl to beat the ingredients together, and two pieces of parchment paper.

FFR—SUFFICIENT FOR 12 FISH FILLETS, 12 CHICKEN CUTLETS, OR 6 CHOPS

I large egg
I teaspoon unsaturated oil of your choice
I teaspoon water
Good pinch of salt
I turn of the mill of white or black pepper
¼ cup flour of your choice
I cup semicoarse fresh or fine dry bread crumbs

Mix the egg, oil, water, salt, and pepper together until the mixture is fully liquefied. This mixture is called the anglaise; some people, among which I number, like it well beaten and fluid so the resulting breading is thin and crisp. Others like it beaten only lightly so the egg lies thicker on the fillets and attracts more bread crumbs. The choice of style is yours as well as the choice of fresh or dried bread crumbs. The crumbs can be replaced by other things such as ground nuts, cereals, etc.

VARIATION

EGG WHITE ANGLAISE: Use the same recipe, but substitute 1 egg white for the whole egg and increase the water to 2 teaspoons.

HOW TO BREAD FISH WITHOUT BREADING YOURSELF
Sift the flour onto a sheet of parchment paper. Spread the bread crumbs over a second sheet. Have these sheets and the container of anglaise all lined up on the table.

With surgical gloves on, flour the fish; pat it smartly between your hands to discard excess flour. Brush the anglaise on the fish if you want a thin breading (or dip it into the anglaise if you prefer a thicker breading). Invert the egg-brushed side onto the bread crumbs; brush the second side with anglaise and turn over into the crumbs, paying special attention to the sides of each piece, which should also be well covered.

Set the breaded fish on another piece of parchment paper, covering only half the sheet. Fold the other half of the paper over the fish and apply a little pressure with one hand to secure the breading to the anglaise. Pat the pieces of fish to discard any excess crumbs. The breaded fish may wait in the refrigerator covered with parchment paper for 2 to 3 hours. If never frozen before it can be frozen for as short a time as possible, up to two weeks, to prevent oxidation of the fats in the fish. Fish tastes best when panfried in clarified butter, pure olive oil, or grapeseed oil.

Pastella

FFR

¾ cup sifted cake flour

¾ cup sifted unbleached all-purpose flour

2 large eggs

1½ to 1¾ cups water or fat-free cold chicken broth of your choice

Large pinch of salt

Pepper of your choice from the mill

Flavorings of your choice

Mix the flours together. Put the eggs, two thirds of the water, the salt, and pepper to taste in a blender and liquefy. Gradually add the flours until a fluid batter slightly thicker than crepe batter results. Let stand 2 hours covered and refrigerated. When ready to use, test the thickness of the batter on a small piece of meat; add more liquid or more flour as needed for proper texture.

Very lightly floured pieces of fish or meat are dipped into the pastella, shaken gently to drip as much of the paste as possible, and lowered into hot fat or oil.

Here are a few recipes to practice with. Some are prepared with floured fish, some with breaded fish, and some with fish dipped into a pastella.

This Italian-style mixture is sufficient for 6 thinner fillets of any fish or 12 half fillets or 12 small, flattened chicken cutlets, or escalopes of fish or veal. Flavorings can be anything from chopped herbs which are added after the pastella has been mixed to a bit of the spirit of your choice which is added during the mixing. Variations of strength in flour will cause this and any other batter to have different textures. If too thick, lighten with milk or any other liquid; if too thin, add some more flour, stirring the existing batter into the additional flour. The blender or food processor can be used here since a gluten structure is not necessary as it is in crepe batter (see page 1022).

Fillets of Pompano with Florida Butter

*To lighten and decholesterolize
this dish, simply panfry the fillets
in oil and serve them with lime
quarters or any nonfat tartar
sauce you like.*

SUGGESTED WINE: *A
French Sancerre, Quincy, or a
fruity California Sauvignon Blanc
from Carneros or a hillside
vineyard*

FFR—6 SERVINGS

⅓ cup water

1 tablespoon fresh lime juice

¼ teaspoon finely grated lime rind

Salt

Pepper from the mill

½ cup unsalted butter

Chopped cilantro leaves

2 to 3 tablespoons unsaturated oil of your choice or clarified butter (page 32)

2 tablespoons each cake and unbleached all-purpose flours mixed together

1 ripe Haas avocado (optional), peeled, pitted, and sliced paper thin

6 pompano fillets

Mix the water, lime juice, lime rind, a good pinch of salt, and pepper together in a small saucepan. Reduce to 3 tablespoons over medium heat. Turn the heat off; let cool a few minutes, then whisk in the butter, tablespoon by tablespoon. Add as much cilantro as you like.

Heat the oil in a large buffet-style electric frying pan preheated to 425°F. Mix the flours with a large pinch of salt and several turns of the pepper mill. Coat the fish fillets with the mixture, tapping off any excess. Panfry the fillets until golden on each side, 3 to 4 minutes. If you wish, top each sautéed fillet with a slice of avocado and serve the lime-flavored butter in a bowl for your guests to help themselves to as much or as little as they wish.

Nostalgia for Australian Orange Roughy

*This recipe happened in my
wintry New England kitchen
after I came back from sunny
Queensland, Australia, in a
raging snowstorm.*

SUGGESTED WINE: *A
Cloudy Bay Sauvignon Blanc
from New Zealand*

FFR—6 SERVINGS

3 tablespoons chopped macadamia nuts

2 tablespoons unsalted butter or oil if preferred

1 large, slightly unripe mango, peeled, pitted, and diced into ¼-inch cubes

Salt

Pepper from the mill

Juice and seeds (membranes removed) of 2 passion fruit

1 tablespoon fresh lemon juice or to taste

2 tablespoons each unbleached all-purpose and cake flours mixed together

6 orange roughy fillets

1 tablespoon chopped fresh chives

Toss the macadamia nuts in the butter over medium-high heat; do not let them color too much. Strain through a tea strainer to drip most of the butter into a small bowl you will reuse to fry the fish.

Mix the nuts, mango, salt and pepper to your taste, passion fruit juice and seeds, and lemon juice together and set aside.

Preheat a large buffet-style electric frying pan to 425°F. Flour the fish fillets. Add the strained butter to the pan and, when hot, panfry the fillets until golden on each side, about 5 minutes altogether. Add the chives to the relish and serve quickly.

Basel-Style Salmon
BASLER SALM

FFR — 6 SERVINGS

½ cup unsalted butter

6 cups minced yellow onions

Salt

Pepper from the mill

½ cup German Riesling

1 tablespoon sweet Hungarian paprika

⅓ cup oil of your choice

Twelve ¼-inch-thick salmon escalopes

2 tablespoons each cake and unbleached all-purpose flours mixed together

1 recipe Anglaise of your choice (page 626)

2 cups fresh bread crumbs

Lemon quarters

A variation on the nice old salmon recipe that made having dinner at the Drei Koenige in Basel in the 1950s such a pleasure.

SUGGESTED WINE: *A Swiss Dézaley or a Napa Valley Château Woltner St. Thomas*

Heat half the butter in a large sauteuse pan. Toss the onions into the butter to coat them well and cook, stirring, over medium heat until light brown; season with salt and pepper, then cover and let the onions form a delicious compote over low heat. Keep warm.

Meanwhile, mix together the wine, paprika, and a pinch each salt and pepper in a small saucepan and reduce to 3 tablespoons over medium heat. Whisk in the remainder of the butter and keep warm.

Preheat the oil to 425°F in a large buffet-style electric frying pan. Dredge the escalopes in the flour, tapping off any excess, then brush them with the anglaise and dredge them in the bread crumbs. Add the escalopes to the pan and brown rapidly, 2 minutes on the first side and 1 on the other.

Serve two escalopes per plate on a bed of the onion compote and pass the paprika butter for your guests to help themselves to. Also pass a plate of lemon quarters for those who find enough fat in the onions and the breading.

Panfried Pecaned Catfish and Sauce Piquante

The hatchery catfish is really very good but its taste will never equal that of my first taste of true channel catfish, in Chamberlain, South Dakota.

SUGGESTED BEVERAGE: A good New Orleans or other beer of your choice

FFR—6 SERVINGS

For the sauce

¼ cup unsalted butter

3 tablespoons unbleached all-purpose flour

2 cups tomato essence (page 309) or 2 cups canned tomato puree lightened with
    1 cup water

½ cup dry white wine

Tabasco sauce

Chopped fresh parsley leaves

Chopped fresh chives

Salt

Pepper from the mill

3 tablespoons peanut oil or other oil of your choice

6 catfish fillets

2 tablespoons cake flour

1 recipe anglaise of your choice (page 626)

¾ cup ground pecans

Heat the butter in a heavy-bottomed saucepan. Add 2 tablespoons of the all-purpose flour and cook, stirring, over low heat until dark brown. Off the heat, whisk in the tomato essence and wine. Bring to a boil, then reduce the heat to medium and add the Tabasco sauce to your taste. Simmer until the mixture looks like a well-bound, not-too-thick ketchup and has reduced by a good one third. Add the parsley and chives to your taste and correct the final seasoning. Keep warm.

Preheat the peanut oil to 425°F in a large buffet-style electric frying pan. Mix the remaining tablespoon of all-purpose flour with the cake flour, and season lightly with salt and pepper. Dredge the fillets in the flour, tapping off any excess. Brush the fillets with the anglaise. Mix the remaining dredging flour and the pecans together and dredge the fillets with this mixture. Cook the pecaned fillets in the oil until golden and crisp, 2 minutes or so per side. Serve with the piquante sauce.

Almost Chinese Fried Fillets of Petrale Sole

FCR — 6 SERVINGS

3 tablespoons dark soy sauce

3 tablespoons hoisin sauce

1 tablespoon dry sherry

2 teaspoons peeled and grated fresh ginger

12 petrale sole or small other sole or flounder fillets

1 recipe Pastella (page 627)

½ teaspoon grated lemon rind

1 small garlic clove, finely chopped

2 scallions, finely chopped

¼ cup unbleached all-purpose flour

Salt

Pepper from the mill

6 tablespoons unsaturated oil of your choice or unsalted butter for frying

1 tablespoon chopped fresh Italian parsley leaves

1 tablespoon chopped cilantro leaves

Meyer or other lemon quarters

Use several frying pans if needed.

SUGGESTED WINE: *A light Gewürztraminer of your choice*

Mix the soy sauce, hoisin sauce, sherry, and ginger together. Brush the mixture over the fillets and let marinate for 30 minutes, covered with plastic wrap, at room temperature.

Prepare the pastella and flavor with the lemon rind, garlic, and scallions. Let stand for 30 minutes, then strain through a conical strainer.

Season the flour with salt and pepper. Preheat the oil to 425°F in each of three large buffet-style electric frying pans. Scrape the marinade from the surface of the fillets and dredge lightly in the flour, tapping off any excess. Coat with the pastella.

Panfry the fillets about 2 minutes on each side until golden. Serve sprinkled with the parsley and cilantro and the lemon quarters on the side.

Potato-Crisped Roughy with Nashi Salad

FCR—6 SERVINGS

2 brown Japanese pear-apples of medium-dry texture

¼ teaspoon each grated lemon and orange rinds

1½ teaspoons fresh lemon juice

2 tablespoons fresh orange juice

2 tablespoons pistachio oil or extra virgin olive oil

Salt

Pepper from the mill

1 tablespoon each cake and all-purpose flours mixed together

6 orange roughy fillets

1 recipe anglaise of your choice (page 626)

1 cup instant mashed potato flakes

2 to 3 tablespoons unsaturated oil of your choice

2 teaspoons chopped fresh Chinese chives

Dice the pears into ⅓-inch cubes; place them in a small bowl and toss together with the citrus rinds and juices, pistachio oil, and salt and pepper to your taste. Let marinate while you cook the fish.

Lightly salt and pepper the flour mixture, then dredge the fillets of roughy in it, shaking off any excess. Brush with some of the anglaise, then coat with a layer of potato flakes on each side.

Heat the unsaturated oil to 400°F in a large buffet-style electric frying pan and fry the fillets until golden, about 2 minutes on each side.

Serve with the pear salad seasoned at the last minute with the Chinese chives.

General Rules for Deep-frying All Foods

Safety first. Do not start deep-frying without a box of baking soda on hand to smother a possible fire. Never sprinkle a burning oil bath with water, for the oil will splatter, dispersing the flames instead of containing them.

And a good tip . . . There should always be onions in your kitchen, for should a stovetop fire occur, two quartered onions added to the center of the flames will immediately starve them of oxygen. This is a tried and true method that comes from old Europe where chimney fires were numerous, and many larger fires were avoided by applying this method.

BEST OILS TO USE

Deep-fried foods have become anathema in our lean modern society, even though we are still fed more deep-fried chicken, fish, clams, and fritters than any other nation in the world.

I figured that if they worked so well to bake chicken, instant mashed potato flakes would also work to prepare panfried fillets. Be sure to use potato flakes, not "buds."

A nashi is a type of Japanese pear-apple available in Australia; you may use any kind of brown-skinned pear-apple instead.

SUGGESTED WINE: *Try to find one of the excellent Rieslings of the Australian Barossa Valley; some excellent labels are Yalumba, Orlando, Henschke, and Springton; any Alsatian Riesling will also do well.*

Up until quite recently, deep-frying was done in animal fats, usually rendered beef or veal kidney suet (to learn how to render fat, see the rendering of duck fat on page 779). My restaurateur aunt used to deep-fry her potatoes in clarified butter. Nowadays, vegetable oils are almost exclusively used; they are less saturated, require no rendering, and the manufacturers stabilize and winterize them so they neither oxidate nor partly solidify when standing in a cold cupboard. It is most unfortunate that the very best oils for deep-frying are palm and coconut oils, which give incomparable color and crispness to the fried foods plus quite a delicious taste. However, both of these oils must be forgotten because of their high saturated fat levels.

The very best oil for deep-frying may very well be grapeseed oil which has been used in France for at least thirty years now and on which in-depth research is in motion in the United States. Grapeseed oil, which seems to have the lowest level of saturated fatty acids, smokes very little, and yields a nice crisp product. Pure olive oil can also be used as well as corn oil; I am hesitant to use canola oil. Much laboratory work has gone into lowering its erucic acid content to a level where it is supposedly inoffensive, but I personally would rather have no erucic acid at all in my oil.

Whichever frying medium you choose, heat it to 370°F and fry a small piece of bread in it before using it for the first time. This step, which helps remove any off taste in the frying fat, can be eliminated if you know your oils are of very high quality.

CARE AND PROPER USE OF THE OIL BATH

Once the frying oil has been used once, do not store it at room temperature. As soon as it has cooled, strain it back into a glass container to discard all the particles fallen from the fried food. If left in the oil, these particles will burn when the oil is reheated for reuse; also, burned particles will turn rancid on standing. Cover the glass jar(s) with an airtight seal and keep them refrigerated.

Do not use an oil bath more than twice without adding some fresh oil to it; it lengthens its life. For fish you may use oil that has already been used to deep-fry vegetables in fritter batter. Once a bath has been used for fish, it may not be used for any other food. A potato fried in a bath can remove partly the taste of onions, but never that of fish.

THE FRYING KETTLE;
TEMPERATURE CONTROL

Fry in a deep kettle with straight sides in 4 inches of oil. Do not fill the fryer more than half full with oil, and handle it with quiet motions to avoid spilling. Do not deep fry in a frying pan with a handle that can be misplaced, catch on something or someone brushing against it, and cause dangerous spilling. The best fryer is an electric one controlled by a thermostat, but a large kettle with side handles is perfectly acceptable if a thermometer is used so that you can check and control the temperature of the bath.

If you have no thermometer, the degree of heat of the oil can be monitored by using a crust of bread. If the oil shivers around the bread, the temperature is between 365° and 370°F; if the oil looks like it is boiling rapidly, the temperature ranges between 375° and 380°F; if the bread turns brown almost instantly and the oil smokes, the temperature is between 385° and 390°F.

Immerse food to be fried between 365° and 370°F; the addition of room temperature food will make it drop to 350°F, so maintain the heat under the kettle to bring the temperature back to 360° to 370°F.

Do not fry too much food at a time or the oil will cool off too much, not sear properly, and the food will be saturated with fat and become soggy; the same will happen if the bath is not hot enough when you first immerse the food.

Rather than drop breaded food into the oil, it is preferable to use a frying basket; all specialized frying kettles come with a basket. If you have no basket, add the food to be fried in small quantities and gently, so the oil does not come splattering out of the kettle.

If a food is coated with a fritter batter or a pastella, lift each piece on the two prongs of a long-handled kitchen fork and immerse it; do not pierce the coated food. Remove the fried food from the bath either with a basket or a slotted spoon; let it drain on several layers of crumpled paper towels.

SERVING FRIED FOODS Serve fried foods on a white napkin folded on a serving platter. If the food must wait, store it, *unsalted*, in a 225°F oven. *Always salt any fried food just before serving* or it will turn soggy and limp as the salt, always thirsty for water, will penetrate the crisped outside layer of the food and absorb some of the steam under it.

COATINGS FOR FRIED FOODS

To coat foods for deep-frying, dip into seasoned flour, brush with anglaise (see page 626), then coat with bread crumbs (see page 626), or dip the foods into a fritter batter, which differs from a pastella (see page 627) in that its egg whites are beaten and folded into the egg yolk base. *Always flour food to be fried in a fritter batter* before coating it to prevent the batter from sliding off, as the fine particles of dry flour absorb some of the liquid in the batter.

Here are two recipes, the first is for a classic European fritter batter, the second for a Japanese tempura-style batter which is extremely light and pleasant.

Savory Fritter Batter

FCR

2 large eggs, separated

2 cups water or light beer or half beer and water

2 tablespoons unsaturated oil of your choice

1½ cups sifted unbleached all-purpose flour

½ cup sifted cake flour

½ teaspoon salt

Liquefy the egg yolks, water, and oil in a blender. Gradually add both flours and the salt and process until a batter forms. Turn into a large bowl. If you have no blender, mix the flours together in a bowl and make a well in the center. Beat the egg yolks, water, and oil together. Gradually whisk the mixture into the flour until perfectly smooth.

Beat the egg whites with an electric mixer or by hand in a medium size bowl until they can carry the weight of a raw egg in its shell without it sinking into the foam by more than ¼ inch. Stir a saucespoonful of the egg foam into the flour batter, then fold in the remainder.

This quantity will coat 24 small bite-size pieces of fish, meat, or savory preparation for hors d'oeuvres. The absorbency of any flour varying always, please add more flour if the batter is too light or more liquid if it is too heavy.

Tempura-Style Frying Batter

FFR — 1½ TO 2 CUPS

1 large egg plus 1 large egg yolk, cold out of the refrigerator

⅔ cup ice cold water

½ cup cake flour

6 tablespoons unbleached all-purpose flour

⅔ cup self-rising flour

Beat the egg and egg yolk together until liquid, then blend in the water; cover and refrigerate 2 hours before using.

Mix the flours together in a bowl. Cover and *store in the freezer* 45 minutes to 2 hours before using.

To combine, pour the egg-and-water mixture into the flour and, using chopsticks, mix until the batter is still rough, imperfectly mixed, and shows lumps, as would a muffin batter. If the batter is elastic, discard it, as it will not adhere well to the foods to be coated. *Use the batter as soon as it is mixed,* which means that all your vegetable and fish offerings must be ready to be dipped before you start mixing the batter.

The following recipes are for deep-fried fish. For deep-fried meats, see page 806, for deep-fried vegetables, page 421, and for fruit fritters, see page 957.

With the forever changing qualities of flours, finding the correct flour for tempura batter is always a bit of an adventure. Here is a formula which I have found to work to my taste.

For the batter to coat evenly, flour the tempura components with all-purpose flour. When you prepare the batter, be certain to use flour that has been in the freezer at least 45 minutes, in essence, flour which is too cold to retain its gluten-developing capability (see page 1008). In mixing the batter, leave the batter lumpy, a guarantee that no gluten strands will form; gluten would interfere with the batter adhering properly.

Home-Style Fish and Chips

FFR—SERVINGS TO YOUR DISCRETION

Garlic cloves as needed

Chopped fresh Italian parsley leaves as needed

1 potato per person, scrubbed, dried, and cut into ¾-inch cubes

Unsaturated oil of your choice for deep-frying

One 4-ounce skinless fish steak of your choice per person, cut into ¾-inch cubes

Corn flour as needed

Salt

Pepper from the mill if you like it

Ketchup, vinegar, and/or butter as you prefer

If my grandmothers and my Scottish landlady tasted these fish and chips, their eyebrows would go up, but corn flour is one of my culinary discoveries in the United States and I like to coat fish in it for deep-frying. My husband, Alan, is insane enough to enjoy his "chips" with butter.

SUGGESTED BEVERAGE: *A nice cool or room temperature ale as you prefer*

Chop as much garlic and parsley as you like to obtain a persillade. Pat very dry with paper towels and keep refrigerated.

Peel the potatoes only if you want; the deep-fried skins taste very good. Heat the oil to 365°F (see page 633). Add no more than the equivalent of two potatoes at a time and cook until the potatoes are tender but not brown, 5 to 6 minutes. Remove the potatoes from the bath to drain on crumpled paper towels.

Reheat the bath to 370°F. Fry the potatoes a second time until they are golden. Be careful—this occurs extremely quickly; do not overbrown. Spread the potatoes on a baking sheet and keep at 225° to 250°F until ready to use.

Toss the cubes of fish in the corn flour. Add the equivalent of two steaks only at a time to the fryer and cook until golden and crisp, 3 to 4 minutes. Drain the fish on paper towels. Mix with the potatoes, salt, and toss with the persillade. Serve immediately and enjoy with vinegar, ketchup, or butter as you like.

Fried Smelts

FFR—6 SERVINGS

Unbleached all-purpose flour

Salt

Pepper from the mill

3 pounds small smelts, dressed, with heads left on

Unsaturated oil of your choice for deep-frying

This spring dish invariably evokes memories of my grandmother Marguerite cleaning buckets of goujons, those tiny, silvery blue river fish now decimated by pollution. Use the smallest smelts you can find; whitebait, or any fillet of a flatfish cut into little strips 2 × ½ inches, called goujonnettes, will do just as well.

SUGGESTED WINE: *Any ordinary good white or red or rosé wine*

Season the flour with salt and pepper. Toss the smelts into the flour. Coat well and tap off any excess. Heat the oil to 365°F. Deep-fry about ten fish at a time until golden and crisp, 3 to 4 minutes. Keep in a 225°F oven until all the fish have been cooked. Serve with any condiment you like.

Snail Fritters

FFR — 2 DOZEN APPETIZERS

24 snails

¼ cup dry white wine

I large shallot, very finely chopped

¼ cup Dijon mustard

Unbleached all-purpose flour

Freshly grated nutmeg

I recipe Savory Fritter Batter (page 635)

I clove garlic, finely mashed

2 tablespoons chopped fresh curly parsley leaves

Unsaturated oil of your choice for deep-frying

Drain the snails from their can so the juices collect in a saucepan. Add the wine and shallot to the juices and reduce over medium heat to 4 tablespoons of liquid and solids. Add the mustard to obtain a strong-tasting dip. Set aside.

Pat the snails completely dry. Roll the snails in the flour mixed with a good dash of nutmeg, tapping off any excess. Season the finished fritter batter with the garlic and parsley. Heat the oil to 360°F. Dip the snails into the fritter batter and deep-fry 6 to 8 snails at a time until the fritters are golden. Serve on a folded napkin with a small bowl containing the mustard condiment.

Snails are not too popular, mostly because too few people know how good they can be. Use the canned medium-size "Burgundy"-type snails.

SUGGESTED WINE: *A nice crisp and dry Alsatian Sylvaner or Riesling*

Almost Japanese Fish and Chips

FFR — 4 SERVINGS

Unsaturated oil of your choice for deep-frying

12 slices zucchini, cut ¼ inch thick on a slant

2 small fennel bulbs, sliced into ¼-inch-thick rings, rinsed in cold water, and patted dry

I red bell pepper, cut open flat (page 367), seeded, recut lengthwise into strips 1½ inches wide, rinsed, and patted dry

6 very large crimini mushroom caps, cut into ¼-inch-thick slices

½ cup cake flour

4 ocean perch fillets, skin on, cut into ¾-inch-wide sticks

I recipe Tempura-Style Frying Batter (page 635)

Salt

Pepper from the mill

Preheat the oil to 370°F. Mix all the vegetables together and dredge in 5 tablespoons of the flour, tapping off any excess. Divide the vegetables into four equal portions.

Toss the fishsticks with 3 more tablespoons of the flour and divide into four portions.

A variation on the Japanese tempura using Mediterranean vegetables. This dish is not easy to make in larger quantities at home. Preparing this tempura for à la carte service follows the usual rules of preparation for this type of service. You can, if you want, serve with the usual Japanese condiments (see bibliography).

SUGGESTED BEVERAGE: *Green tea or Japanese beer*

Dip the frying basket into the hot oil. Dip one portion each of vegetables and fish into the tempura batter, then place in the fry basket and deep-fry until barely golden. Drain on paper towels and serve immediately in a small basket lined with more paper towels. Repeat this procedure with the remaining three portions. Put salt and pepper on the table for guests to sprinkle on the tempura themselves.

Salted, Pickled, and Smoked Fish

No sooner was early man conscious of the fact that he had to store food during the warm seasons if he hoped to be fed during the cold ones, than competition for supplies of salt started among tribes, as salt was the key to year-round protein supplies.

Fish was salted and dried in Egypt, Mesopotamia, China, and the Indus Valley as far back as the fifth millennium before Christ, and until the Middle Ages more salted than fresh fish was consumed. We now consume more fresh fish than we do salted, but the tang of salt and smoke still remains in our subconscious and there is not one of us who does not relish kippers and bloaters, lox, gravlax, seviche, or escabeche.

The popularity of salted fish came from two facts: It kept a long time since all water mobility in the fish tissues had been suppressed by the salting and, consequently, the activity of microorganisms such as bacteria, yeasts, and molds was reduced to a minimum. Also, much reduced in volume and safe for transport, fish could be taken on long-distance trips. There developed during the Middle Ages a large traffic of salt fish coming from the Mediterranean to northern Europe and from the Atlantic toward Central Europe and northern Italy; the villages on both sides of the two Saint Bernard passes were known for the high and mighty smells of the salted fish passing borders in both directions.

According to historian Toussaint-Samat, the cod banks of Newfoundland were discovered by the Basque whalers quite possibly before Leif Eriksson reached those waters; the rumor of these whalers' activities prodded French King Francis I to send explorers toward the northwestern Atlantic. When Jacques Cartier arrived at the mouth of the St. Lawrence, he indeed found a considerable flotilla of Basque fishing ships, and launched France on its way to becoming one of the "salt cod powers." Another powerful incentive had been given to other European sovereigns by the Dutch who had made their original fortunes and developed into a great naval power by fishing herring, brining it, packing it in barrels, and sending it all over Europe.

We use only a small amount of salted fish nowadays. The Scandinavian and other countries situated along the shores of the North and Baltic seas are the countries to visit if you like superior pickled or smoked fish. I strongly urge you to try brined fish from all the northern countries of Europe and compare the tastes and textures; there is much to learn there.

Meanwhile, how about pickling, and curing by salt ourselves? I generally prefer to purchase salted, pickled, and smoked fish, but I have had a good measure of success with the following techniques.

SHORT PICKLING OF RAW FISH VS. SHORT PICKLING OF COOKED FISH

SEVICHE AND ESCABECHE According to A. J. McClane, seviche is Peruvian; it consists of pickling fish and shellfish in pure citrus juice, a technique which has spread all over Latin America. Other food historians have related the origin of the Spanish escabeche, which is the pickling of pre-cooked fish in a salad dressing-type marinade, back to the Persians, who called it *sisquihb*. From the Persians it would have passed to the Arabs, and from the Arabs to the Spaniards, who made it escabeche. If the second theory is true, isn't it interesting that both the words *seviche* and *escabeche* contain some of the same consonants and vowels?

Seviche and escabeche indeed have similar traits, but in seviche the fish "cooks" as its proteins denature under the effect of citric acid, while in the escabeche the fish is first seared in hot oil, then finishes cooking in the hot marinade. The textures of seviche and escabeche are totally different and so are their tastes.

Seviche

LFR—8 APPETIZER SERVINGS

I large white sweet onion, cut into ⅛-inch cubes

I large clove garlic, finely minced

¼ teaspoon grated rind Florida juice orange

3 tiny dried Tabasco peppers (piments oiseaux), chopped into a powder

½ teaspoon ground coriander

Tiny pinch of ground true cinnamon

Salt

Pepper from the mill

One 2 × ½-inch strip Florida juice orange rind

⅔ cup fresh pink grapefruit juice

⅓ cup fresh lime juice

⅓ cup fresh lemon juice

I½ pounds calico scallops, feet removed

2 large Haas avocados, peeled, pitted, and diced into ¼-inch cubes

2 tablespoons pineapple vinegar

½ cup fresh but not too ripe ¼-inch pineapple cubes

2 tablespoons chopped fresh cilantro leaves

You can experiment with different fish such as snapper, healthy sole, corvina, Chilean sea bass, lake trout, etc., and all kinds of diverse lemons. The orange rind and the grapefruit juice temper the harsh acidity of the lemons and limes and provide a very slight bitter undertone. If you cannot find pineapple vinegar, replace it with sweet rice vinegar.

SUGGESTED WINE: *A nice crisp white Chilean wine*

Spread the chopped onion and garlic in a single layer over the bottom of a shallow baking dish and sprinkle with the grated orange rind, Tabasco powder, coriander, cinnamon, and salt and pepper to taste. Let stand until the juices are running out of the vegetables.

Meanwhile, mix the orange rind strip and grapefruit juice together in a small saucepan and reduce to ⅓ cup over medium heat. Mix this reduction with the lime and lemon juices and cool completely. Strain over the prepared onions, then mix in the scallops. Cover with plastic wrap, punch a few holes in the plastic, and refrigerate for 12 hours, tossing at regular intervals.

Just before serving, mix the avocado cubes with the vinegar, salt, pepper, pineapple cubes, and cilantro leaves. Drain the scallops from their marinade and arrange them in a small shallow serving dish, surrounded by the avocado salsa. Serve with a bowl of large tortilla chips.

Fatma's Algerian Escabeche

FCR — 6 SERVINGS

I cup olive oil

2 pounds fresh large sardines or pilchards, dressed

Unbleached all-purpose flour as needed

Salt

6 large cloves garlic, finely chopped

I small red onion, finely chopped

I small carrot, finely chopped

I teaspoon sweet Hungarian paprika

I teaspoon ground cumin

4 to 6 tiny dried Tabasco peppers (piments oiseaux), to your personal taste, chopped into a powder

I teaspoon fresh thyme leaves or ½ teaspoon dried

I Mediterranean bay leaf, crumbled

⅔ cup cider vinegar

⅓ cup water

Pepper from the mill

Heat ⅓ cup of the oil in a large skillet. Toss the sardines in just enough salted flour to coat them lightly. Fry the sardines on both sides over high heat until golden, about 3 minutes per side. Remove to a cutting board and let set until cool enough to handle. Bone each fish, then replace the top fillet on the bottom fillet. Arrange the sardines head to tail in a large dish. Cool completely.

Add the remaining olive oil to the pan; add the garlic and cook, stirring, over medium heat until beige, then add the onion and carrot and sauté until wilted. Add the paprika, cumin, Tabasco powder, thyme, and bay leaf. Remove the pan from the heat, let it cool to lukewarm, and whisk in the

From Fatma Charif who in 1974 spent a lot of time furthering my culinary education in Algiers. You can use any small fillet you like such as Mediterranean mullet, fillets of ocean perch, smelts, fillets of tinker mackerel, etc.

SUGGESTED WINE: *Any everyday wine of your choice*

vinegar and water; bring back to a high boil and continue boiling happily for 10 to 12 minutes. Season with salt and pepper and pour bright hot over the cool sardines.

Cool to room temperature and cover with plastic wrap; punch small holes in the plastic and marinate 24 to 36 hours in the refrigerator. Serve chilled with good crispy bread.

FULL PICKLING Any fish to be pickled for longer preservation, two to three months, must first be cured in brine. May I suggest, considering the difficulty of finding the totally fresh fish that is needed for pickling without problems, that you do not launch yourself into long-term pickling, unless:

- You have done this with professionals or older people who have done it for years, and/or
- You live at the seashore, in a cold climate, and have the proper refrigeration and cold storage.

If any of these things apply, prepare the brine by mixing together:

2½ cups kosher salt or more if needed

¾ to 1 cup firmly packed brown sugar

4 quarts water

1½ cups white vinegar of your choice or a strong citrus juice such as lemon or lime

To make sure that you have enough salt, dissolve the salt and sugar first in the water and add a large egg in its shell. If the egg floats just below the surface of the water, showing only somewhere between a dime and a quarter's worth of its shell, the brine's salt concentration is high enough; if the egg does not float this way, add more salt, stir to dissolve, and keep testing in this way until the egg floats. Then add the other ingredients and any spices and aromatics you like.

The fish is brined in this mixture in the refrigerator until its skin shows the slightest trace of discoloration, a maximum of two days; then it can be pickled and kept in glass jars which are best kept refrigerated.

Brining minimizes water mobility in the brined food and prevents bacterial development. There is so much salt in the brine that it is impossible for microorganisms in the fish to absorb the water in it and continue a normal life cycle; on the contrary, it is the water in the bacteria and other microorganisms which, following biological law, will flow from the protoplasm of the bacteria into the brine, and leave all microorganisms totally dehydrated and unable to function. The result is a fish that will keep about 3 months well refrigerated.

However, due to the many types of fish existing and the various degrees of efficiency of refrigerators, your good sense must prevail. It is up to you to discard any brined fish that shows gas bubbles or aggressive smell.

Chtimi Roll Mops

You are a Chtimi when you are
born in the very northern part of
France, usually with a strong
taste for the fattest herrings from
the Channel. For the cornichons,
see page 315, or use imported
cornichons. Use full herring with
egg and sperm sacs.

NOTE: *The milt is often pureed
into the pickling vinegar; this is a
matter of personal taste.*

SUGGESTED BEVERAGE: *In
many Flemish-French families
this is accompanied by homemade
beer.*

FFR — 12 SERVINGS

8 cups water

⅔ cup kosher salt

½ cup firmly packed brown sugar

⅔ cup cider vinegar

½ teaspoon ground allspice

Dash of ground cloves

Dash of freshly grated nutmeg

6 very fresh large herrings, preferably with milt

Whole milk

1 large red onion, finely chopped

12 very small French cornichons, finely diced

⅓ cup Dijon mustard

⅓ cup sweet yellow mustard

For the final pickling

2 cups water

2 cups cider vinegar

Large bouquet garni

1 teaspoon black peppercorns

Mix together the water, salt, sugar, vinegar, and spices. Clean, scale, and
bone the herrings into fillets, then line them up and their milt in a large glass
baking dish and cover them with the brine. Let marinate in the refrigerator
until the skins start discoloring, a maximum of 2 days. Drain completely and
pat the fillets and milt dry. Rinse and dry a baking dish and arrange the fillets
in it again. Cover the fillets generously with milk and let stand 2 hours, under
refrigeration.

Prepare the pickling ingredients: Salt the chopped onion lightly and mix
with the chopped cornichons; add both the mustards and mix well. Remove
the fillets from the milk and pat dry again. Using tweezers, remove all bones
if possible. Spread each fillet on its meat side with an equal amount of the
mustard mixture and roll each fillet upon itself. Place the fillets and milt in a
wide-mouth glass jar with a tight-fitting lid, just large enough to contain the
mops with 1 inch of space left.

For the final pickling, bring the water and vinegar to a boil, then add the
bouquet garni, and peppercorns, reduce the heat to medium, and simmer 10
minutes; strain the hot vinegar mixture over the roll mops and milt. The fish
is ready in 24 to 36 hours and will keep a good 2 weeks refrigerated.

Sanitation I recommend consuming these and any other type of home pickled fish as rapidly as possible. It is up to you to check that no bubbles, which

mean bacterial development, appear in the jar; if they do, discard this and any other pickled product.

DRY CURING

Fish that are, according to the modern lingo of the kitchen, "laxed" or smoked must undergo a dry salt curing period.

GRAVLAX *Gravlaks* in Norwegian, *Gravadlax*, in Swedish and *Gravlax* in Danish all refer to the same way of curing a salmon (or *Lachs*, *Laks*, or *Lax* in the Germanic languages) in a "ditch" (*Graben*, *Grav*, or *Gravad*); salmon was originally cured by salting it mildly and burying it in the ground. I have seen it done this old-fashioned way in a sandbox in a remote village of the Sogne-fjorden in 1947. The principle used in the old days combined the dehydrating effect of the salt cure with weighting the fish—either with soil or any other weight—which accelerates the penetration of the salt into the salmon tissues. The storage place being deprived of air (anaerobic), aerobic bacteria perish and the salmon can keep a rather long time in a low temperature environment. If you are worried about parasites, freeze the finished gravlax—not the fresh fish—for five days.

This is my personal recipe for a gravlax which I like very much; if it does not appeal to you, go back to the classic Scandinavian cure which uses only salt, sugar, and crushed fresh dill; it appears in any of the Scandinavian books listed in the bibliography. If Jack Daniel's is a tad too smoky for your taste, use any spirit of your choice: Armagnac, Cognac, blended Scotch whisky, single malt whisky, or aquavit.

MMK's Gravlax

FFR— 18 TO 24 FIRST-COURSE SERVINGS

1 medium-size Atlantic salmon, about 10 pounds, dressed

⅓ cup fine sea salt

½ cup sugar, white or firmly packed brown, or half and half to taste

Grated rind of 1 orange

Grated rind of ½ lemon

1 teaspoon crushed allspice berries

½ teaspoon each crushed black and white peppercorns

1 large bunch fresh tarragon, bruised with the back of a knife

1 large bunch fresh chives, bruised with the back of a knife

2 ounces Jack Daniel's

Fillet the salmon, removing all the bones but trying not to bruise the fillets when you pull the pin bones out. Cut away the belly flap on each fillet. (See the techniques on page 535.) Mix the salt, sugar, orange and lemon rinds, all-spice, and peppercorns together; divide into two equal parts.

Arrange one third of the herbs on the bottom of a large stainless steel or glass baking dish; place one of the fillets on top skin side down; sprinkle with one part of the cure and one third of the Jack Daniel's. Press the cure well into the fillet and cover with another third of the bruised tarragon and chives. Press the remainder of the cure into the meat side of the second fillet and sprinkle with one third of the Jack Daniel's. Put the salted side directly on top of the layer of herbs to reform the fish. Wrap the salmon tightly in a single layer of cheesecloth that has been moistened and squeezed dry to apply pressure on the fish. Top the fish with the remainder of the herbs and Jack Daniel's and place an empty baking dish on top of the salmon; fill the latter with as many full cans or bottles as you can, to weigh the fish down as much as possible. Let cure 5 days in the refrigerator, turning the fish over every 12 hours and discarding the curing liquid which will escape from the fish tissues after 2 days. Remove the weights and cheesecloth after the second day, but continue the cure until no more liquid comes out of the fish fillets.

On the fifth day, remove all the herbs and scrape the fillets gently with the back of a knife. *Observe* the texture of the salmon; it should be dry and, since it has lost most of its moisture, the fat should glisten at its surface and prevent your knife from sticking to the meat.

Slice it into superthin slices at a very low angle so as to obtain as large slices as possible, and serve with the following dressing or any other dressing of your choice.

If the salmon does not slice evenly, it is not dry enough. Wrap the fillets separately in one layer of snuggly fitting plastic wrap; with a pin, punch multiple tiny holes in the plastic, and keep aging it until it slices perfectly. Refrigerated, the salmon will keep aging and become drier. Consume within 2 weeks. In cool Scandinavia, the salmon is consumed even much older. *Check that the temperature of your refrigerator does not reach above 40°F.*

Gravlax Sauce

FFR — 12 SERVINGS

1 cup heavy cream or ½ cup sour and light cream mixed together

¼ cup sweet yellow mustard or to taste

Sugar

Salt

Pepper from the mill

Jack Daniel's or other spirit of your choice

2 tablespoons chopped fresh chives

Mix the cream and mustard together. Add all the seasonings to your taste and the Jack Daniel's and let stand, covered, in the refrigerator for at least 2 hours. Add the chives just before serving.

SMOKED FISH

Another way of preserving fish even longer than brining and pickling it is to smoke it. Our taste for smoked meats is universal, wherever we may come from, probably because our collective memory subconsciously remembers our ancestral great hunts and long sessions of meat and fish curing and smoking. The smell and taste of sweet smoke is one of the most comforting to us because we all know that it means survival through both warmth and food available year-round.

To smoke fish properly, you must be equipped for it and I strongly recommend that if such is not your case, you go directly to excellent professionals who smoke fish safely and deliciously. There are many brands in the United States, some coming from Europe, all of them extremely reliable and smoked in different styles that will make you want to try them all.

The general technique consists in dry curing *large*, well-prepared fillets— meaning totally and smoothly boned and trimmed of the belly flap. Salt is rarely used alone; most of the time it is flavored with diverse spices, as in the gravlax above. The Scots like a completely different flavoring from that of the Scandinavians, the Irish, the Canadians, and the many producers in the United States.

This not being a specialized book, but a general one, may I recommend that you check the bibliography of the fish section where you will find several books dedicated to smoking fish and in which the different styles are investigated.

If you want to smoke at home, follow these directions:

DRY CURE AND COLD SMOKE METHOD This is my favorite way to smoke and is generally used for *larger fillets*, averaging 8 pounds; the successive steps are:

1. Scale but do not skin the fillets. Cut several ⅛-inch-deep slashes into the skin to allow the penetration of salt on the skin side.
2. Cure under a simple spray of seasoned salt on the skin side and an ⅛-inch-thick layer of the same applied to the meat side of the fillet overnight or up to 10 hours, no more, in a cool room or cellar.
3. Rinse the cured fillets in fresh water and pat dry.
4. Dry the fillets on a rack exposed to a steadily running fan until a thin layer of dried tissues is visible on the surface of the fillet, 5 to 6 hours; this can be done by putting the rack on the refrigerator shelf closest to the refrigerator cooling fan. Turning the rack at regular intervals will expose both sides of the fillets an even length of time to the drying air.

5. Finally, cold smoke the fish (see below) at a temperature varying from 75° to 85°F for 36 hours. The smoky taste can be varied by using different woods; you will develop a taste either for hickory, alder, oak, apple, or other fruit woods. I prefer apple wood to any other.

BRINE CURE AND COLD SMOKE METHOD This works for smaller fillets, up to 3 pounds, scallops, and large shrimp or prawns. It employs a brine instead of salt (see page 641), following the same drying and smoking directions as explained above after the brining has been completed.

SMOKERS AND SMOKING METHOD While the fish cures, sit with the directions for your smoker and study how to proceed with the equipment you own.

Since many books offer only hot smoking methods, which correspond to completely cooking the fish, you should know that by placing a tray of ice between the source of smoke and the rack carrying the fish, you can cold smoke and obtain fish looking and tasting every bit as good as the fish offered by the best smokehouses. The smoking is done at a low temperature, between 75° and 85°F, for a short time, so that the fish is not cooked but only well penetrated by the smoke on its surface. This ice-tray method allows you to poach the smoked fish in a soup or chowder, or finish cooking it and serve it with a relish or sauce. Bear in mind always that fish that has been brined and smoked cooks twice as fast as fresh fish, and need only be added to a hot soup or sauce to be cooked perfectly.

Gravlax smoked this way can be served as is, sliced thinly as ordinary gravlax (page 644).

Vesiga and Caviar

Caviar is prepared from the roe of different types of sturgeon coming from the Caspian Sea which borders on Russia and Iran. Sturgeon are not endowed with a true backbone but with a notochord, or flexible rodlike structure, which, once pulled out of the carcass, can be dried and is used in Russian cookery to prepare a soup and the salmon specialty called *coulibiac*. Escoffier, on page 302 of the French edition of his *Guide Culinaire* (Flammarion, Paris, 1921 and 1948), gives a detailed explanation of how to prepare this dried notochord which is called *Vesiga* by Russian cooks. A less detailed explanation is to be found in the American translation of *Le Guide Culinaire* (Crown Publishers, 1969), on page 273.

Approximately one hour after the notochord has been pulled and the fish has been hanging, the sac containing the roe is removed from the carcass and treated as follows:

The eggs are gently stirred and washed over screens of mesh slightly larger than the eggs, through which the latter fall, into a container. After being washed, the eggs are drained thoroughly for a good 15 minutes, then mixed with the finest sea salt.

If there are dedicated sportsfishermen in your family, you can prepare a caviar with the roe of sturgeon, salmon, and steelhead and large trout that is quite creditable and in any case far better than the artificially colored lump-fish caviar available for sale in supermarkets and specialty shops.

To prepare good caviar *you must weigh* the well-drained eggs and use ½ ounce of fine sea salt (3 teaspoons) per pound of eggs. Once the eggs have been carefully mixed with the salt, they must be packed all the way up to the top of a jar presterilized in the dishwasher and sealed in such a way that there is absolutely no air between the lid (which also should be sterilized by boiling in water) and the caviar. Store in the coldest part of the refrigerator set at its highest setting so the temperature inside the refrigerator is no higher than 35°F. Please use a refrigerator thermometer, and observe the low temperature or the caviar will spoil and all your work will be for nothing.

After a week of refrigeration, the caviar is ready to consume. Please do so on the same day as you open the jar, for the minute you open it, the caviar starts to acquire off tastes. If you have a pound or even more, which can easily be the case, simply plan a feast. If some caviar is left, repack it in a smaller sterilized container filled up to the lid and keep refrigerated. Use preferably to add to a fish sauce.

Russian and Iranian Caviars

These caviars are so expensive by now that they are almost unaffordable. These are the categories that you will be able to find, with this terminology usually applied:

- An *original* is a 4-pound tin of caviar as purchased by the great caviar houses of the major capital cities in the world and served in the best restaurants in the world. The names that appear below are those of five different types of sturgeon producing caviar. The originals usually carry the name of the district where the fish was caught. *Malosol*, from the Russian *malo*, "little," and *soleny*, "salt," is only lightly salted with no more than 3 to 4 percent salt.
- *White almas*, or the roe of the albino beluga sturgeon. Only about ten pounds are produced each year and the House of Caviar in Geneva has the monopoly over its sale. If you win at the lottery, call them; one quarter pound of almas will be delivered to you in a 24-karat-gold tin, crated in a leather-lined chest, with a solid gold spoon attached; this charming investment will come to you in exchange for the small amount of $5,000 or so.
- *Beluga* is always *malosol*; its grains are grayish and supremely delicious.

- *Sevruga*, also always *malosol*, comes from smaller fish, so that the grain is smaller, but extremely flavorful.
- *Osietra*, with brown grains often flecked with gold, is *malosol* and quite delicious.
- *Sterlet* comes from the fish of the same name and has golden grains. It is *malosol* but is not exported out of Russia and the only place you would be liable to enjoy it would be at a state affair in Moscow or St. Petersburg. It was the caviar reserved for the tsars of Russia. During Shah Mohammed Reza's regime, sterlet processed in Iran would eventually find its way to foreign countries at astromonic prices. I enjoyed some once, compliments of a work friend of my husband who brought it back from Teheran in the early sixties.

When any caviar is preceded by the term *payusnaya*, it means that the caviar is "pressed" or a mixture of eggs and crushed eggs which form a spreadable mixture. This is delicious and not to be disdained in any case, the more so that it is less expensive. It will, more than probably, also be saltier since the crushed eggs are more perishable.

TO SERVE CAVIAR

Caviar speaks for itself. Serve it in its original little container embedded in crushed ice.

Besides the caviar, put nothing more on the board than unsalted butter, unsweetened toastlets, and a bucket of ice containing the best possible French Champagne. Wash down each toastlet lightly brushed with butter and topped with a neat little pile of caviar with a great mouthful of Champagne.

Excellent American Caviars

Besides these expensive foreign caviars there are, since the 1970s, some excellent, affordable American caviars coming from salmon, whitefish, lumpfish, carp, etc. And there is true sturgeon caviar also, coming from Oregon at less than half the cost of Russian and Iranian caviars. I have tasted some of the latter; as much of a purist as I may be, they are truly delicious, so go USA All the Way—and, for more in-depth information on caviar, see the bibliography.

Cooking Crustaceans

Lobster, crab, and shrimp are crustaceans, the shell of which is articulated and always tinted by the compound pigment astaxanthin, of the same family as the carotene in carrots. When the shellfish is submitted to heat for cooking, the brown, green, and often blue colorations of the shell which are the xanthin part of the pigment are bleached while the astacin part, which is very stable, retains its bright red color and gives most crustaceans their appetizing bright red, orange, or pink colors.

ABOUT CRUSTACEANS AND NUTRITION

Crustaceans are expensive and justifiably considered food for entertaining and not for daily consumption. Another reason they should be limited in your diet is their high content of cholesterol, which, while almost reasonable in Atlantic spiny lobster at 70 milligrams per portion of 3½ ounces of meat, becomes more serious in Atlantic cold water lobster at 95 milligrams and downright unreasonable in sweetwater crayfish at 139 milligrams per portion. The crustacean with the least amount of cholesterol is king crab from Alaska, with 42 milligrams per 3½-ounce portion.

The solution to this problem is to consider these delicious critters as once-in-a-while treats. You will notice that many of the recipes are full-fat formulas, which will appear to add insult to injury. However, all crustaceans are delicious enough to be enjoyed once in a while with plain lemon juice or any of the little fat-free relishes found all through the book by anyone with a cardiovascular problem.

Lobster

Ask the fish market for female lobsters if you want the coral, which is made up of thousands of eggs colored deep green by the pigment ovoverdin; when added to a hot sauce the coral turns to the "cardinal red" color that gave its name to the classic French dish lobster cardinal. Females are easily recognizable: Turn the lobster on its back; at the limit of its tail and abdomen, on its underside, are two thin and feathery atrophied legs, barely ⅛ inch wide, which it uses to push its eggs, ready to hatch, under its tail shell. By comparison the same pair of legs in males is hard-shelled and almost ¼ inch wide. In both, the tomalley, or liver, of the lobster used to be a delicious addition to any sauce, but the pollution of bays has taken its toll and it seems prudent not to use the tomalley, which some authorities say may carry a great concentration of not-so-charming pollutants. Too bad.

The cost of lobster has become somewhat forbidding and they should really be reserved for small-size entertaining; the recipes that follow will be for only four persons. If you plan an eight-guest dinner, simply double the recipe.

ATLANTIC LOBSTERS

The best lobsters (*Homarus americanus*) come from the North Atlantic coast of North America from Canada to New Jersey. Except for the coloration of their shells, they are in every way identical to the northeastern European lobster (*H. vulgaris*). Both are fitted with two claws, one large one for crushing, the other for cutting. Having enjoyed each of these two types quite a bit, I can say that they are both superior to any other lobster if cooked properly and served *hot*. Their respective tastes are certainly different but their quality identical if they are tasted at the seashore. Any lobster of any geographical location which travels, especially by air, loses at least 50 percent of its flavor and acquires a cottony texture during the plane ride; the texture repairs itself somewhat while the lobsters sojourn in saltwater market basins but the taste never quite recovers its splendid original flavor.

BOILED—OR STEAMED—ATLANTIC LOBSTERS Atlantic lobsters are excellent boiled. Measure the amount of water sufficient to cover the lobsters and bring to a "raging" boil; add 1 tablespoon salt per quart of water. You can, if you enjoy it, add a bag of shellfish "boil" (a packet of spicy seasonings) to flavor the bath. Immerse the lobsters, live, into the water head first and keep the pot on the highest possible heat, covered.

Before you immerse lobsters in water, grasp each just below the abdomen with a kitchen towel and pacify it by rubbing the top of its head with your thumb, until the critter becomes totally immobile.

The following sizes of lobster must boil the following lengths of time *after the water comes back to a boil*; these timings take into consideration the fact that the lobster starts cooking as soon as it is immersed in the water.

- "Chickens," 1 pound: 5 minutes
- "Eights," 1⅛ pounds: 6 minutes
- "Quarters," 1¼ pounds: 8 minutes
- "Large" weight, 1½ to 2 pounds: 8 to 10 minutes
- "Jumbo" weight, more than 2 pounds: 12 minutes

As you can see, the heavier the lobster the shorter the cooking time proportionally.

Giant twenty-pound lobsters, which are fifty to eighty years old, still can be found and can be purchased in Boston and Maine; boiled for 45 minutes to 1 hour they are excellent, tender, contrary to what is believed, and relatively less expensive than smaller-size lobsters for salads.

Boiled lobster is served with plain melted butter or any flavored oil of your choice (see page 304).

Steamed lobsters are cooked, covered, in the basket of a steamer suspended above rapidly boiling water. The cooking time is 1 to 2 minutes less than for boiled lobster, because steam is hotter than boiling water.

TWICE-COOKED ATLANTIC LOBSTERS This technique of cooking lobster was passed on to me by my former student Gary Danko, dining room chef at the Ritz Carlton in San Francisco. The lobsters, preferably "quarters," are immersed in boiling salted water and are boiled no more than 3 minutes after the water comes back to a boil. They are then shocked in a tub of ice cubes to cool the meat rapidly and firm it up. After the lobster is shelled, it is firm all around and almost cooked but not quite, so that when the lobster is reheated, either over low heat in a skillet or in a 350°F oven, it finishes firming up and can be sauced as desired, or tossed with a mixture of vegetables, or pasta. This is probably the very best basic preparation of lobsters for à la carte service in restaurants, for the lobsters can be boiled ahead of time and always taste fresh and tender.

Lobster in Lettuce Cream

FFR— 4 FIRST-COURSE SERVINGS

2 large lobsters

Saltwater bath large enough to cover the lobsters

10 tablespoons unsalted butter or ½ cup corn or pure olive oil

1 cup bottled clam juice

½ cup dry white wine

1 large yellow onion, chopped

½ small carrot, chopped

Bouquet garni of fresh parsley and chervil stems, 1 bay leaf, and 1 sprig fresh thyme

3 shallots, very finely chopped

1 large head Boston lettuce

⅓ cup crème fraîche or to taste

Salt

Pepper from the mill

Chopped fresh chervil leaves

⅓ cup cooked baby peas

Fresh chervil pluches (small sprigs)

This modern-style recipe contains several important techniques: cooking the lobsters, preparing lobster fumet, making lobster oil or butter, and using a puree of vegetables to thicken a sauce. You'll need two large bags of ice.

SUGGESTED WINE: **A** *mellow* meritage of Sauvignon Blanc and Sémillon from California or a Château Carbonnieux from France

Crush the ice while still in the bags. Empty the first bag into a very large container. Pacify and boil the lobsters 3 minutes after the second boil. Deposit the cooked lobsters onto the ice and pour the contents of the second bag of ice evenly over them. Let cool completely, then shell, store the meat in a covered nonreactive container, and keep refrigerated. Keep both tips of the heads and both tail fans for plate decoration and the inner parts of the abdomen and small legs for the broth. Crush the remaining shells and set aside.

Preheat the oven to 350°F. Add the crushed lobster shells to a small baking dish along with the butter. Bake until the butter has turned deep orange, 30 to 35 minutes. Drain the butter completely into a small bowl. Set aside.

Put the baked crushed lobster shells, the chopped inner parts of each abdomen cleaned of the spongy gills, the chopped small lobster legs, clam juice, wine, onion, carrot, bouquet garni, and shallots into a large saucepan.

Add enough water just to cover all the solid ingredients; bring to a boil, then reduce the heat to medium and simmer 35 minutes, pushing and crushing all the parts of the fumet mixture while it cooks to release their flavors. Strain through a China cap, letting the fumet drip into a saucepan. Reduce over high heat to 1 cup.

Wash and dry the whole lettuce leaves, then chop them finely, ribs and all. Bring the lobster fumet to a boil and add the lettuce. Empty into a blender and puree; strain through a China cap into a clean saucepan or sauteuse. All of this can be done up to 12 hours ahead of time.

At service time, preheat the oven to 325°F. Reheat the lettuce sauce base. Whisk in the crème fraîche and half the lobster butter, then correct the sauce seasoning carefully. Add a small sauce spoonful of sauce to each of four soup plates, then set half a lobster body and one claw on the sauce. Brush the lobster with a bit of the remaining lobster butter and put a sheet of parchment paper over the lobster. Reheat the plates in the oven until the lobster pieces are hot. Add chervil to taste to the remaining sauce and spoon over the lobsters; dot with peas and drops of the remaining lobster butter. Decorate two plates with the reserved head shells and two with the reserved tail fans. Dot the plate with chervil *pluches* and serve.

GRILLED AND BAKED ATLANTIC LOBSTERS To grill or bake a lobster, it must be cut in half while it is alive. Scientists assure us that the nervous system of lobsters is not developed enough for them to feel pain. Very nice, indeed, but still unnerving. So be fast. Use a very sharp and very big knife that will cut without hesitation in the interest of the lobster and the well-being of your hands.

Use 1½-pound female lobsters. Put each on a cutting board. Hold the tail fast under a towel with your second hand. Just behind the eyes, you will see a small horizontal line. Plunge the tip of your blade into it in the direction of the line, not perpendicular to it; this severs the spinal cord and stops any possible pain. Any movement in the lobster from this point on is only nervous reflex. Cut the abdomen in half lengthwise, starting at its base and ending

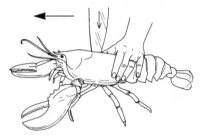

CUTTING A LIVE LOBSTER IN HALF FOR GRILLING

Plunge the knife down here to kill the lobster, following the small arrow; then cut the abdomen following the long arrow.

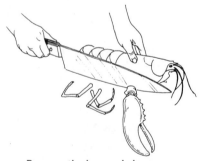

Remove the legs and claws.

Crack the claws using the heavy topside of the knife blade.

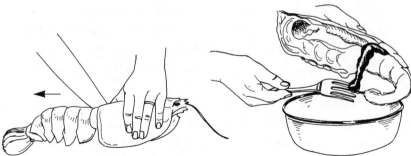

Cut down the tail, slicing the lobster in two in the direction of the arrow.

Remove the vein but keep the dark green coral.

between the eyes. Still holding the tail, push the tip of your knife through the cartilage of the main articulations of the claws. Twist to remove the claws and crack them open by rapping them with the back of your knife blade. Turn the lobster around and cut through the whole tail, also lengthwise. Remove the stomach-gravel bag just behind the eyes and the intestinal tract. Save the tomalley *only if you are certain that the waters where the lobster was caught are unpolluted,* and save the bright green coral.

Grilled Lobster with Cardinal Coulis

FFR—2 MAIN-COURSE OR 4 FIRST-COURSE SERVINGS

I cup bottled clam juice

⅔ cup dry white wine

I teaspoon tomato paste

I large shallot, finely chopped

Small bouquet garni

Two I½-pound live lobsters

⅓ cup plus I tablespoon unsalted butter

Dash of Cognac or Armagnac

2 tablespoons crème fraîche

Salt

Pepper from the mill

I red bell pepper, peeled, seeded, and cut into ¼-inch-wide julienne strips

Skin with ¼-inch flesh attached of I zucchini, cut into ¼-inch-wide julienne strips

Start a fire in your grill. Put the clam juice, wine, tomato paste, shallot, and bouquet garni in a small saucepan; reduce over medium heat to a small cup of liquids and solids mixed. Strain the obtained *coulis* through a China cap into a clean small saucepan and set aside.

Cut and clean the lobsters and crack the claws open with the back of your knife (see page 652). As soon as the coals are white, put the claws on to grill 2 minutes on each side. Brush the meat of the lobster tails with a tablespoon of the butter, melted, and grill 4 minutes, then turn over and finish grilling another 2 to 3 minutes; keep the claws on the grill so they continue cooking.

Meanwhile, reheat the *coulis.* Cream ¼ cup of the butter with the coral. Add half the hot *coulis* to the butter, which will turn red, then, reversing the process, pour the red *coulis*-butter mixture into the remainder of the *coulis.* Heat the Cognac and add, flambéing (see page 117), to the *coulis.* Whisk in the crème fraîche and correct the final seasoning.

Push the cooked lobster pieces to the sides of the grill. Heat the remainder of the butter in a skillet at the center of the grill and stir-fry the pepper and

Purchase two 1½-pound lobsters, asking the fishman for female carrying coral; the coral is visible through the underside membrane of the tail.

SUGGESTED WINE: *An opulent Chardonnay from California or an older Meursault*

VARIATION

Instead of being grilled, the lobster can be baked at medium-high temperature, and yield the same number of portions. Preheat the oven to 375°F. In a skillet, heat 2 tablespoons oil and sear the cracked claws. Remove them to a larger baking dish and cook in the oven for 3 minutes. Meanwhile, sear the lobster halves in the same skillet and finish cooking them in the oven for 8 minutes. Proceed as for the grilled recipe.

Cut the tail into medallions.

zucchini quickly; season well. Transfer the lobster halves to plates, filling each half head with one quarter of the vegetables. Shell the claws and set one on the vegetables. Spoon half the *coulis* over each lobster tail and claw. Enjoy right then and there.

STEWED ATLANTIC LOBSTERS To be used in stews, lobsters have to be cut while alive as for grilled and baked lobster recipes, but the tail is cut differently. Put the lobster on a board. Hold down the tail with a thick towel and sever the spinal cord by plunging the tip of the knife into the natural horizontal line existing just behind the eyes as shown on page 652. Remove the claws by twisting the knife blade into the cartilage of each articulation and severing them; crack the claws with the back of your knife blade.

Turn the lobster around. Slide the knife blade between each of the tail articulations and cut through to remove each "steak" or "medallion." Finish cutting the head; remove the stomach-gravel bag behind the eyes and the intestinal tract. Save any tomalley—provided the lobster comes from totally unpolluted waters—and the coral.

Lobster Civet

A modernized formula that goes way back to the Middle Ages when vinegar was used instead of wine. Use the tomalley only if you obtained the lobster directly from a fisherman at the seashore and if it is firm, pale green, and without any trace of smell. Otherwise, use only the coral.

SUGGESTED WINE: *The same wine as used in the making of the sauce*

FFR— 4 SERVINGS

Unsalted butter as needed

I large carrot, chopped

I large yellow onion, chopped

½ celery rib, chopped

I½ cups excellent dry red wine of your choice

2 medium-size shallots, finely chopped

2 cloves garlic, chopped

I teaspoon tomato paste

⅛ teaspoon commercial meat extract

Small bouquet garni

I pound silverskin onions, peeled

Salt

Pepper from the mill

I cup large cooked lima beans

Two I½-pound live lobsters

2 tablespoons pure olive oil

I ounce Cognac, Armagnac, or other spirit of your choice, heated

½ cup fish fumet or substitute (page 543 or 545)

Unbleached all-purpose flour as needed

Chopped fresh parsley leaves

I cup cooked rice of your choice

Heat 1 tablespoon of butter in a large skillet, then add the carrot, onion, and celery and cook a few minutes, stirring, over medium heat. Add the wine and bring to a boil. Add the shallots, garlic, tomato paste, meat extract, and bouquet garni. Reduce to ¼ cup over medium-low heat and set aside.

Heat another tablespoon of the butter in a medium-size skillet over medium-high heat, add the silverskin onions and sauté them until light golden. Season with salt and pepper, then add the lima beans and mix well. Set the mixture aside, keeping it warm over a hot water bath.

Cut and clean the lobsters as described on page 652. In a skillet, heat the olive oil over medium-high heat; toss in the lobster pieces and cook until they are bright red. Sprinkle with salt and pepper. Discard the oil and flambé (see page 117 for more detailed instructions) with the Cognac. Add the wine reduction and fish fumet. Simmer over medium-low heat for 5 minutes or more if needed.

Remove the lobster pieces to a serving dish; discard their shells. Thicken the wine gravy with a *beurre manié* made of 2 tablespoons of butter and 1 tablespoon of flour per cup of gravy. Cream the reserved tomalley and coral together, if any, with another tablespoon of butter; add half the lobster gravy, then, reversing the process, add this mixture to the remainder of the gravy. Bring back to a boil and add the onions and lima beans. Mix in the lobster meat and turn into a serving dish. Sprinkle with parsley and serve over rice of your choice.

SPINY LOBSTER TAILS

Large lobster tails from Florida, Gulf, and South American spiny lobsters are almost exclusively offered for sale frozen. This type of lobster is best served *cold* and should really be reserved for salads.

These lobster tails have the reputation of being tough, but they are only if overcooked. They are best boiled in salted water for a bare 5 minutes, their exposed meat neatly wrapped in aluminum foil so the water does not rush to their center through the intestinal tract. After the 5 minutes or so of boiling, the heat should be turned off and the lobster tails cooled in their court bouillon. Removed from the court bouillon, they keep for 2 full days or more in high speed refrigeration.

Small lobster tails from South African and Australian and New Zealand rock lobsters are best broiled 3 to 4 minutes on each side and served with the compound butter of your choice. No recipe is really necessary for this very elementary technique.

Smoked Lobster Salad

FCR—6 DINNER FIRST-COURSE OR LUNCHEON MAIN-COURSE SERVINGS

4 each white and red endives

2 large Florida or Gulf lobster tails

I recipe Court Bouillon (page 561), boiling

9 tablespoons avocado oil as needed or other oil of your choice

3 tablespoons sweet rice vinegar

I clove garlic, mashed

Salt

Large pinch to ⅓ teaspoon red pepper flakes

Soft center part of 2 small, thin stalks lemongrass

Cilantro leaves

I very small red onion, sliced and salted

Remove the core of each endive and pull into leaves. Arrange the leaves, alternating colors, around a platter, leaving the center free.

Wrap the meat side of the lobster tails in aluminum foil. Immerse in the boiling court bouillon and cook 4 minutes after it returns to a boil.

While the lobster cooks, light wood chips of your choice in the smoker. Remove the lobsters from the court bouillon with a slotted spoon and, using surgical gloves, carefully unwrap the lobster and shell it while still warm. Brush the lobsters with a very thin layer of avocado oil, place on the smoking rack, and cover with a tightly closed tent of foil. Smoke 5 minutes only to finish cooking the lobster and obtain a light smoke taste. If smoking in a barbecue, place wet wood chips over the hot coals and close the lid. Smoke only 2 to 3 minutes.

Meanwhile, prepare a dressing with the rice vinegar, garlic, salt to taste, and the remaining avocado oil; homogenize well with a whisk.

Cool the lobster completely and slice it into thin slices. Put the slices in a baking dish and sprinkle with the red pepper flakes and lemongrass. Add a third of the dressing, turn the pieces over, and add another third of the dressing. Let stand 10 minutes.

Arrange the lobster salad at the center of the dish, separating the lobster from the endive leaves with large leaves of cilantro and the red onion rings. Rehomogenize the remainder of the dressing and dribble it over the endives. Serve promptly.

Larger lobster tails partially cooked in court bouillon and finished cooking on a covered barbecue are perfect for an end-of-the-winter salad. Or, use the small rectangular stovetop smoker to obtain a light smoke on the outside of the lobster.

SUGGESTED WINE: *A Theo Faller or Zind-Humbrecht Gewürztraminer from Alsace*

Freshwater Crayfish or Mudbugs

There are over 300 species of crayfish throughout the world, and basically two types of crayfish, or mudbugs as they are affectionately called by every kid who was born in crayfish country, exist in the United States. Both of them comprise a number of subspecies, with complicated Latin names.

Astacus astacus could be called the alpine crayfish since it lives in mountain creeks and lakes, especially those of glacial origin. They can be found where the glacial cap spread during the last significant period of glaciation. All the northern states of the United States and the southern provinces of Canada, parts of Appalachia, the Rockies and Sierras creeks and lakes have a subspecies of one name or another. They are grayish and often give the impression of being transparent, so thin can their shells be. They are small and pinch fingers with glee, and they taste as delicious as they pinch viciously. The French call these *écrevisses à pattes blanches* or white-legged crayfish because their legs are grayish white.

The western delta crayfish and the Louisiana bayou crayfish (*Cambarus*) are of different species but each is a good inch to an inch and a half longer than the alpine critter and with a reddish brown shell that is prickly to the touch. If your finger gets caught in a pincer of one of these little monsters, you will be pierced to the blood—nothing dangerous, just pesky; bleed the wound as much as you can as you run cold water over it. Then dip your finger into lemon juice. The French call the delta and bayou crayfish *écrevisses à pattes rouges* or red-legged crayfish because the inner side of the legs is indeed reddish to frankly red.

All are best cooked in a wildly boiling, highly spiced court bouillon for a good 10 to 12 minutes, then shocked in ice so they cool fast and keep well. The best crayfish are never part of a complicated dish, but are prepared in a southern-style crab boil and always the object of a feast. A mudbug feast in the Napa Valley is always a grand occasion with lots of fun, fast shelling and everyone literally stuffing themselves unreasonably, which, of course, results in the consumption of a few glasses of nice and crisp Chardonnay. In more elaborate cooking styles, crayfish can become a mousseline (see page 690), a gratin in the French style, and an étouffée in the Cajun style (see the bibliography for recipe references).

Crayfish that have cooled can be kept refrigerated at 40°F for one more day; the following day, I like to make a few fritters with the remaining tails, but you can also use the tails in a mixed vegetable salad served in an artichoke bottom with a nice dressing. Here are fritters with a dip of rouille. Harissa is the Arabic hot pepper paste; you can replace it with any hot pepper of your choice mashed.

Deep-fry and enjoy immediately.

SUGGESTED WINE: *Any humble dry white wine that you like*

Crayfish Fritters

FFR—6 APPETIZER SERVINGS

3 cloves garlic, well mashed

½ teaspoon harissa or to taste

I teaspoon sweet Hungarian paprika

I heaping tablespoon chopped cilantro leaves

I cup mayonnaise of your choice (pages 340–44)

Unsaturated oil of your choice for deep-frying

3 pounds crayfish tails, cooked

About I tablespoon cake flour

I recipe Savory Fritter Batter (page 635)

Add the garlic, harissa, paprika, and cilantro to the mayonnaise. Mix well and let stand 15 minutes to blend the flavors.

Heat 2 inches of oil to 370°F. Toss the tails with the flour and shake in a colander to discard any excess. Toss into the fritter batter. Using a fork, lift successively 10 crayfish tails out of the batter and drop into the hot oil. Deep-fry until golden. Serve on crumpled paper towels and dip into the mayonnaise.

Crabs

There are crabs for each and every possible use.

SOFT-SHELL CRABS

Blue crabs (*Callinecter sapidus*) are the source of the very best soft-shell crabs, crabs that have molted their old hard shell but have not yet hardened their new one. The period of molting lasts from late April to the beginning of July. There are two sizes of shedders, the larger ones with a shell about 3 inches wide, and the small, barely 2-inch-wide crabs. It is bad enough to gather shedders, but gathering them that small is ecologically unsound; use the larger ones.

Shedders should be alive when you purchase them; they will come in large, thick boxes, packed in straw. To clean them, refresh them in water salted with 1 teaspoon salt per quart. Pat them dry; lift and cut off the mantle, or pointed apron of the underbelly, and remove any matter under it. Cut off the eyes and push on the shell to extract any remainder of yellow matter from under the shell and, finally, cut the two hard tips at each extremity of the shell. Flour the crabs lightly and immediately add them to hot butter. Fry a few minutes on each side and serve, with more melted butter and lemon juice or plain lemon juice if you prefer. For fancier recipes, see my book *In Madeleine's Kitchen*, pages 222 and 223.

PREPARING SOFT-SHELL CRABS

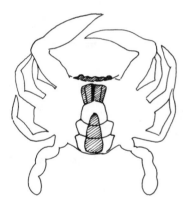

Remove the mantle and cut the eyes.

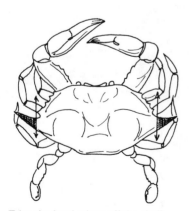

Trim the hard edges off the shell.

If you want to avoid butter, you can grill shedders. Brush them lightly with olive oil and grill them at the outskirts of the fire; the intense heat will kill them immediately. Lemon juice or, if you like it, cocktail sauce is the best accompaniment.

For a good crab soup, use *green crabs* from New England; you will be giving the soft-shelled clams on which they feast a well-deserved break. The soup is absolutely delicious and inexpensive, as Mainers will be glad to sell the crabs to you at a most advantageous price.

For beautiful backfin meat that can be sautéed lightly in noisette butter and sprinkled with lemon, or for the best soft-shelled crabs, there is nothing like the blue crabs that roam the shallows of the Atlantic coast.

For crabcakes prepared with Atlantic salmon and blue crab backfin meat done in a very different manner, a bit expensive but absolutely perfect as a first course for entertaining or for the dining room of a nice restaurant, see page 695.

DUNGENESS CRABS

Dungeness crabs (*Cancer magister*) roam the Pacific coast from Alaska to Baja California. I am particularly fond of it because it reminds me so much of our French *tourteau*. Not only are the legs tight with solid meat, but the backfin meat, though not as delicate as that of the blue crab, has more character and is most tasty. The crab's Latin name is very evocative of this splendid critter.

At the Crab Feast

FFR—6 SERVINGS

½ cup prepared southern-style crab boil spice mixture

¼ cup red wine vinegar

1 medium-size white onion, finely chopped

Salt

Pepper from the mill

1 teaspoon dried basil (do not use fresh)

¾ cup pure olive oil

6 Dungeness crabs, 2 to 3 pounds each, well washed in salted water

In a very large pot, bring enough water to cover the crabs to a furious boil. Add the crab boil and reduce the heat to a simmer while you prepare the dressing.

Place the vinegar, onion, salt and pepper to taste, basil, and oil in a blender and process until liquefied and homogeneous; keep in the blender until ready to serve.

Add the crabs one by one to the water bath and bring back to a high boil.

From January to the middle of March, there are in the Napa Valley three important crab feasts, two in St. Helena and one in Calistoga. This is one of the ways the crab arrives on the table. Use your favorite brand of crab boil.

SUGGESTED WINE: *One usually drinks what appears on the table, but, if you are choosy, bring an Alsatian Gewürz-660*

Cook 12 to 15 minutes after returning to a boil. Remove the crabs from the water to a colander and drain well over the kitchen sink. Cool to warm.

Place each crab on its back. Pull off the mantle and discard it. Remove the gills and "butter" (this yellow material is the liver and the same as the tomalley in lobster and should be used only if you are certain that the crabs come from nonpolluted waters). Keep the butter and, if you enjoy it, add as much as you like to the dressing.

Cut each crab in half; cut the legs and remove the backfins from the shell; discard the shell and pat the backfins dry with paper towels. While the crab parts are still lukewarm, toss them all into the dressing. Serve immediately.

Dungeness contains so much meat that one always cooks more than one can enjoy in one day. This is how leftovers are often presented.

Grilled Crabs with Aïoli

FFR — AS MUCH AS YOU WILL HAVE LEFT OVER

6 whole cooked crabs

Mayonnaise as needed

Several cloves garlic, mashed

2 tablespoons chopped fresh parsley leaves per cup of mayonnaise

2 red, yellow, and green bell peppers

You can use any mayonnaise to prepare the aïoli, even store-bought. Fire up the barbecue and use it when the coals turn white. For great reserves of this dish, a visit to Tra Vigne Restaurant in St. Helena or Stars Restaurant in San Francisco is recommended.

SUGGESTED WINE: *Any nice dry white wine or light fruity red wine you like*

Put the crabs on the grill to heat their shells, then turn them over to heat their legs, leaving them on until they are nice and warm. Clean the crabs as described in the preceding recipe.

Mix as much mayonnaise as you like with as much mashed garlic as you like and the chopped parsley. Blend well.

Grill the whole peppers until their skins blister and peel them when cool enough to handle, then cut them open and remove the seeds. Cut them in strips and toss in a bit of the aïoli. Serve the peppers and remaining aïoli with the crabs.

ALASKAN KING CRAB

Alaskan king crab (Paralithodes camtschaticus) from Alaska, a large beast which can weigh as much as twenty pounds, is a very expensive delicacy. It has a number of long, thick legs which are sold mostly frozen or poorly defrosted in fish markets across the continental United States. If you buy Alaskan king for a special occasion, buy a larger box solidly frozen, and defrost it only halfway in the refrigerator. Fire up the barbecue and put the legs, in their shells, on the hot fire, turning them regularly for about 6 to 7 minutes; the meat will finish defrosting as it reheats and less of the juices in the flesh will be lost. Cut the legs open with shears and pull out those long strings of delicious meat. Lemon juice is sufficient to enhance it, but if you want a great meal, prepare any of the *beurre blanc*–style sauces on pages 335–37.

STONE CRAB

Stone crabs (*Menippi mercenaria*) from the southeastern coast of the United States are large crabs, one claw of which is collected by twisting it off the crabs' bodies; the crabs are thrown back into the ocean and grow new claws called retreads. This may seem cruel but at least the crabs are not pushed to the edge of extinction and can continue reproducing.

Stone crab claws cannot be found in any other form than cooked and fresh in Florida and the two Carolinas; in any other part of the United States they are available cooked only on special order. Stone crab claws are never frozen because after freezing, the meat sticks so powerfully to the shell that the two can hardly be separated.

Stone crabs are best served cooked fresh and cold, just as is, without any sauce, or with lemon juice; mayonnaise and any of its variations are also good. You can reheat them by arranging them in a steamer or colander placed over steaming water and serve them with melted butter or a pinzimonio (see page 405). Or, you can grill them as for Alaskan crab (see page 660), but in my personal opinion, they taste better cold.

Shrimp

Each and every coastal region of the United States offers different types of shrimp with different textures, tastes, and looks. In English-speaking European and Asian countries large shrimp are called prawns.

SHRIMP AND NUTRITION Each and every type of shrimp is excellent but for its cholesterol content. In general, though only containing about 2 percent fat, two shrimp are nevertheless a "cholesterolic" disaster, with 153 milligrams of cholesterol per 3½-ounce portion. If your health requires it, enjoy shrimp with lemon juice or a fat-free tomato-based sauce and only once in a while.

WAYS TO USE SHRIMP

Most shrimp in the United States are sold without their heads, the exceptions being the Lake Charles shrimp of Louisiana and the small Maine shrimp. This is too bad as shrimp heads make a good broth to be used either for a chowder or a sauce, and can produce excellent shrimp butter or oil (see page 304).

Do not discard shrimp peelings; have a bin in your freezer in which you accumulate them until you have enough to prepare fumet (see the replacement fish fumet on page 545). Or simmer the shrimp peelings in ordinary clam juice or chicken stock or a mixture of both cut with one third water and you will obtain a broth good enough to prepare a shrimp or fish soup or sauce.

Court Bouillon for Shrimp

LFR

For 2 pounds shrimp any size

2 cups water

4 cups bottled clam juice

2 cups dry white wine

Small bouquet garni

6 black peppercorns, cracked

Pinch of salt

For 5 pounds shrimp any size

4 cups water

8 cups bottled clam juice

4 cups dry white wine

Large bouquet garni

12 black peppercorns, cracked

2 teaspoons salt

This same court bouillon can be used to poach scallops and is good enough to use as the base for a sauce. Keep frozen between poachings and renew with smaller amounts of water, clam juice, and wine in the same proportions as in this recipe. (See the theory of court bouillon on page 560). If an herb is going to be used in the dressing or sauce accompanying the shrimp dish, add its chopped stems to the court bouillon.

Mix all the ingredients together and bring to a boil. Reduce the heat to medium-low and simmer 30 minutes. Strain through a conical strainer.

The best way to consider shrimp from the culinary point of view is to go by size.

TINY OR SMALL SHRIMP

If you live at the seashore, purchase whichever small shrimp come into season while they are alive and jumping. And keep them restrained with a pot lid, because when they warm up they really jump. Cook them in a court bouillon as in the following recipe. If they are already dead, consider them fresh as long as they look firm and, especially, smell frankly of seawater. If the smell of seawater has passed, and they bend easily or give under the pressure of two fingers, do not buy them as the meat will be mushy when cooked.

Buying small shrimp in the shell is not necessarily the best bet at the seashore; you can save time buying them already cooked if you know that the fisherman who boiled them used today's shrimp catch, not yesterday's. In big cities inland, you will have no choice; tiny shrimp come frozen and most of the time are sold swimming in their defrosting water, but the meat is so firm that the shellfish is still good for salads and small sauced dishes.

Marinated Maine Shrimp in Artichoke Bottoms

FFR—6 FIRST-COURSE SERVINGS

I recipe **Court Bouillon for Shrimp** with cilantro stems added (page 662)

4 pounds **Maine shrimp** in their shells

Salt

I tablespoon **dark soy sauce**

2 tablespoons **hoisin sauce**

½ teaspoon **peeled and grated fresh ginger** or more, to taste

2 tablespoons **sweet rice vinegar**

2 teaspoons **regular or hot sesame oil** or to taste

⅔ cup **corn or sunflower oil**

2 **scallions**, finely sliced

I teaspoon **untoasted Szechuan peppercorns**, finely chopped to powder

2 tablespoons chopped **cilantro leaves**

6 large **artichoke bottoms**, cooked in water to cover until tender

2 **red bell peppers**, peeled, seeded, and slivered

2 **orange bell peppers**, peeled, seeded, and slivered

Cilantro leaves

Bring the court bouillon to a boil in a large pot. Rinse the shrimp in water salted with 1½ teaspoons per quart, then drain in a colander and add to the court bouillon. Bring back to a boil, then take the pot off the heat and let the shrimp cool in the court bouillon.

While the shrimp cool, place the soy and hoisin sauces, the ginger, vinegar, and oils in a blender and homogenize until whitish. Pour into a bowl and add the scallions, salt to taste, the peppercorns, and chopped cilantro. Let stand while you peel the shrimp.

As you peel, add the shrimp to the dressing, toss well, and let marinate for an hour at room temperature, then refrigerate another hour. When ready to serve, lift the shrimp out of the dressing with a slotted spoon, let drip, and add to the artichoke bottoms. Toss the peppers with the remainder of the dressing. Divide the pepper salad among six plates, add one filled artichoke bottom per plate, and dot each plate with cilantro leaves.

MEDIUM-SIZE SHRIMP

Medium shrimp are best for sauced dishes. They should be slightly undercooked (see the illustration to the right) in court bouillon then added to a light sauce where they will be mixed with vegetables or with a pasta and finish cooking. The recipe on the next page is an example. Medium shrimp are also very good for fritters, or in the tempura, as in the recipes on page 635.

If one wishes to devein medium-size cooked shrimp, after peeling the

A tad time-consuming to peel the shrimp but very delicious—and also fine using already cooked shrimp. For a full luncheon or summer dinner course, double the ingredients. Only one pound of shelled cooked tiny shrimp is necessary for this recipe.

SUGGESTED WINE: *A mellow Riesling or Gewürztraminer*

TESTING SHRIMP FOR DONENESS

Uncooked shrimp in shell

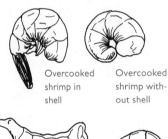

Overcooked shrimp in shell

Overcooked shrimp without shell

Shrimp with and without shell cooked just right; by the time it is plated, it will be done.

shrimp, pass the tip of a knife, special or regular, all along the back of the shrimp. Open it up and discard the dark vein.

Shrimp Copenhagen

FFR — 6 FIRST-COURSE SERVINGS

½ pound fresh spinach leaves, well washed, blanched 1 minute in boiling salted water, and tough stems removed

2 tablespoons chopped fresh dill

18 medium-size shrimp, cooked in Court Bouillon for Shrimp (page 662)

1 tablespoon fresh lemon juice

1 tablespoon Cognac or aquavit

3 tablespoons unsalted butter or 2½ tablespoons unsaturated oil of your choice

½ pound small mushrooms, sliced

Salt

Pepper from the mill

Few gratings of nutmeg

2 tablespoons unbleached all-purpose flour

1¼ cups hot Court Bouillon for Shrimp (page 662), fish fumet (page 543), or Secondary Stock (page 220)

⅓ cup crème fraîche

This dish was served as one of the warm little dishes that followed the cold smørrebrød at the Sunday dinner table of the Danish farm where I picked potatoes in my youth. The greens replace a pastry shell.

SUGGESTED WINE: **A** *mellow Riesling*

Lightly butter or oil six 3-ounce custard cups; line them with the spinach leaves and dill. Marinate the shrimp for 15 minutes in the lemon juice and Cognac mixed together.

Heat 1 tablespoon of the butter or oil in a skillet on medium-high heat, then add the mushrooms, salt and pepper to taste, and nutmeg and toss well. Turn the heat down to low, cover, and steam until the mushrooms have rendered their juices; raise the heat to high and evaporate all the juices until the mushrooms brown well. Cool, add to the shrimp, and toss well.

Heat the remaining 2 tablespoons of butter or 1½ tablespoons of oil in a small saucepan. Add the flour and cook, stirring, over medium heat to golden; off the heat, whisk in the court bouillon; return to the heat and thicken, stirring constantly. Simmer and skim until 1 cup of sauce is left. Strain the sauce over the shrimp and mushrooms. Add the crème fraîche and reheat to just below the boiling point. Correct the seasonings and spoon an equal amount of the composition into the prepared ramekins. Serve immediately.

LARGE AND JUMBO SHRIMP

Large and jumbo shrimp are mostly for grilling on white coals, although they can be used whole and cold in strikingly pretty salads or cut up and warm in pasta dishes.

Jumbo shrimp must be deveined; use the European method. Before you cook and shell the shrimp, look for the black dot indicating the position of the vein at the center of the meat where the head was removed. If the vein needs removal because it is filled, gently dig around the black dot until you can grab on to it between your parer's blade and your thumb and tease the whole vein out; it will come without difficulty. If the vein does not come, it is empty and need not be removed. The result of deveining this way is a beautiful-looking shrimp with a smooth, round back.

Charcoal-Grilled Shrimp and Fruit Platter

FFR—6 FIRST-COURSE SERVINGS

12 jumbo shrimp, peeled and deveined

12 thin slices pancetta

2 Asian pears, preferably brown skinned for firmness

1 ripe pineapple

1 ripe but not yet soft papaya

Fresh lime juice

Corn or other unsaturated oil of your choice in an oil spray bottle

Pepper from the mill

2 limes, quartered

You may use bacon or pancetta as you prefer, but pancetta brings the necessary salt to showcase the sweetness of the shrimp without the smoke of the bacon.

SUGGESTED WINE: *Any Mediterranean white wine; a white Retsina from Greece tastes great with this dish*

Fire up the barbecue. Let the coals turn white. Wrap each shrimp in a slice of pancetta, covering the shrimp meat very well. Let stand, covered, for 30 minutes at room temperature.

Meanwhile, peel, core, seed, and slice all the fruit into ⅓-inch-thick slices. Dribble lime juice over the Asian pear slices.

Grill the shrimp at the center of the grill 3 minutes on the first side and 2 on the second. Spray the fruit slices with a bit of oil and grill at the edges of the grill until golden on both sides. Serve two shrimp and as many slices of each fruit as available per person. Pass the quartered limes for dribbling over the fruit and shellfish.

Mollusks

Mollusks include sea and land snails, abalone, oysters, black mussels and green lip mussels of the southern Pacific, clams, and scallops.

THE NUTRITIONAL VALUE OF MOLLUSKS

Contrary to crustaceans, most mollusks are both lean and low in cholesterol if they are served without rich sauces or butter-saturated crumbs. The only problematic mollusk is abalone which registers at 89 milligrams of cholesterol per 3½-ounce portion but abalone is so rare a treat that one need not worry about an occasional serving in a lifetime!

Mollusks are otherwise gems of human nutrition, with high protein contents, lots of good mineral salts, great taste, and great texture if cooked properly. A dozen oysters easily replace the best beefsteak; take it from a survivor of World War II who made it thanks to thousands of oysters.

Abalone

Abalone can come two ways, whole and fresh in its shell, or already pounded and ready to cook.

Abalone has only a top shell, oblong and ranging from two inches in length to ten inches. It is attached to rocky outcrops on the bottom of the Pacific Ocean along the colder parts of the West Mendocino and Oregon coasts. Abalone fishing is strictly restricted to a small number of a prescribed size per day. The mollusk adheres by its "foot" or tough, large muscle to the rock and must be pried from it. The only edible part is the foot. It is known as a univalve because there is only one shell covering its whole body. This shell, once cleaned, reveals the most gorgeous greenish to bluish mother-of-pearl which can offer large bumps that can be cut out and mounted in gold for rare pieces of exquisite jewelry.

Here is how you get it from shell to ready to cook. With a long thin-bladed and very sharp knife, sever the large foot or adductor muscle. It is surrounded by a tight belt of strong connective tissue. Refrigerate the foot two hours so it is nice and firm. Cut across the muscle to obtain slices ¼ inch thick. On a cutting board, pound the slices with a wooden mallet until you have broken all the fibers, which are extremely strong and tough. The slice should look somewhat like a tightly woven lace. Take a 4-inch round plate, place it upside down over each slice, and cut all around it. This disposes of the circular band of connective tissue. If you leave that band of hard connective tissue around each slice, it will tighten up as it cooks, transforming your slice of abalone into a small shallow cup, which will cook irregularly.

Abalone, of course, is sold in slices already pounded, but where the surrounding band of connective tissues has not been removed, please do so.

There is definitely an economy of time purchasing ready-cut slices, but not of funds, the time necessary to pound the shellfish being costly.

The best treatment for abalone slices is to flour and bread them, and cook them until golden in clarified butter; they can also be deep-fried in olive oil.

Here is a recipe that comes from the first edition of this book and which has met with great success over the years.

Abalone Bliss

FFR — 6 LUNCHEON MAIN-COURSE SERVINGS

1 large egg

1 teaspoon pure olive oil

1 teaspoon water

Salt

Pepper from the mill

Unbleached all-purpose flour

12 slices abalone, trimmed of connective tissues and pounded

6 tablespoons chopped cooked Dungeness backfin crabmeat

1 cup fresh bread crumbs

¼ cup clarified butter (page 32) or unsaturated oil of your choice

3 tablespoons Noisette Butter (page 32)

2 limes, cut into 6 wedges and seeded

2 lemons, cut into 6 wedges and seeded

Serve this delicate preparation with a light salad for a luxurious lunch. Overcooking means losing the shellfish, so be fast . . . a large buffet-size electric frying pan set at 350°F gives the very best results. Also, go for broke with the butter, since abalone is so rare—and be a Spartan again the next day.

SUGGESTED WINE: **A** *luscious Mark Kreydenweiss Kastelberg Riesling from Alsace*

Beat the egg with the oil and water and a dash each of salt and pepper to obtain an anglaise. Sift a spray of flour on a sheet of parchment paper. Put six slices of the abalone on the paper and brush a ⅓-inch-wide band of anglaise on its edge. Place 1 tablespoon of the crab (no more or the taste of crabmeat will overpower that of the abalone) in the center of each slice. Top with a second slice of abalone, sealing the two together well. Repeat with the remaining crab and abalone.

Flour the top of the abalone packet. Season the bread crumbs with salt and pepper. Brush the patties with the anglaise on both sides and coat with the bread crumbs. Air dry 15 minutes, turning over once. Meanwhile, preheat the clarified butter in an electric frypan to 350°F. Cook the packets in the butter, 1½ to 2 minutes on each side, until both sides are pale golden.

Serve very quickly basted with 1½ teaspoons of noisette butter each and accompanied by a lime and lemon wedge.

Oysters

Oysters are one of the luxuries of life; thousands of kitchen middens found all over the world brimming with millions of discarded shells tell us that much. Oysters are bivalved mollusks, which means that the mollusk itself is protected by a two-part container which must be pried open if one wants to consume its contents.

American oysters are divided into eastern and western oysters. Native to the eastern shores is the genus *Crassostrea virginica*, recognizable by its thick, elongated shell, with a slightly elevated upper valve. To this type belong the Apalachicola, Blue Point, Cotuit and Wellfleet, Chesapeake Bay, and Chincoteague, plus a few others coming from such small areas of production that they cannot be found but locally.

Cultivated in New England, California, and the Pacific Northwest is *Ostrea edulis*, the European-born flat oysters which in Europe are represented by the light beige-colored Belons and blue-green Marennes from France as well as the Colchester, Whitstable, and a few others in England, Belgium, and Holland. Rounder than the *Crassostrea* and with a curly, brittle, and cutting shell, *Ostrea edulis* has such a flat lid that it may sometimes appear slightly concave. *Ostrea edulis* has not always been successful in aquaculture in Maine, but it is there that it has taken to the wild very successfully. Once shucked, a Maine wild *edulis* stares at the cook with the beautiful blue-green color that the true Marennes usually acquire from ingesting the one-celled diatom *Navicula ostrearia*.

The native western oyster is the beautiful but tiny (as wide as a quarter) *Ostrea lurida* with its attractive green mother-of-pearl and gently iodic taste, which makes for such splendid chowders and sauced dishes.

The whole length of the American West Coast is full of experimenting oyster enthusiasts who produce Belon and Japanese (*Ostrea gigas*) oysters in Bodega Bay and the Puget Sound. To these belong the Western Belons, Bodega Bay, and Quilcene oysters.

A third category of oysters, called *gryphea* or Portuguese oyster in Europe and *Ostrea angulata* by marine biologists, is not to be found in the United States, but you may want to investigate it when visiting France. These oysters are cultivated in *claires*, which are fattening ponds watered by the regular tides and in which the oysters develop to their market size, to be sold as *fines de claires* if still lean or, if a bit fatter, as *speciales*, both words meaning an oyster fattened in a *claire* as opposed to the wild deep-sea oysters which are called *huître de pleine mer* (literally, deep-sea oyster). Although there are probably some adventurous oyster people working on adapting the Portuguese oysters to the coast of Washington, I have never been able to purchase any in this country.

KEEPING OYSTERS

If you happen to have purchased a large quantity of oysters which will have to be kept a few days, stack the oysters on top of one another, deep valve down so they retain all their juices. If the shells dry out, the oysters are in trouble, and the mollusks may die and become unconsumable.

Prepare a saline solution of ½ tablespoon salt per quart of water and pour as much of that saline over the oysters as will cover them. Let the oysters rest in the saline for two hours so they can open their shells and clean themselves. Drain all the water.

Restack the oysters so their lid valve is up and pour another clean saline solution to cover them. The oysters will be fooled into reacting as if they were in the ocean. Keep the oysters in saline well refrigerated between 35° and 40°F, and *change the salt bath each and every day.* Do not keep the oysters more than three days this way. Oysters to be served on the half shell should not be kept in salt water; they should come straight from the ocean to your kitchen. Oysters that have been kept in saline should be served cooked.

SHUCKING OYSTERS

When shucking an oyster, wrap it in a kitchen towel with its pointed end peeking generously out of the towel; if you miss and slip, the tip of your blade will go into the towel, not into your hand. Slide the tip of your oyster knife into the visible seam of both valves at the tip of the oyster and continue sliding it into the shell parallel to the top valve and scraping against it, in order to leave no meat or as little meat as possible on the upper valve.

If you serve the oysters on the half shell, loosen the adductor muscle from the bottom valve to prevent diners struggling at the table to loosen it themselves. If you plan to cook the oysters, tease their adductor muscle as cleanly as you can from the oyster body (use it in the making of your sauce, stew, or soup), and drain each oyster on a conical strainer placed over a bowl to gather the juices. Keep shelled oysters and oyster juices in closed dishwasher-sterilized containers embedded in crushed ice and in a 40°F refrigerator.

OYSTER SEASON

It is better to consume oysters in the cold months of the year when they look and taste just right and are not all too fat. The best months are November through April. After April the oysters get fat and develop their spat which, once ready, is sent floating away to attach itself to whatever rock, shell, or stick will receive it and allow millions of baby oysters to develop their shells. From late August on the oysters resume their normal life cycle to become normally plump by mid-October to November. November is definitely the better date.

Place the oyster in a towel, then place the blade of an oyster knife in the weakest point between both valves.

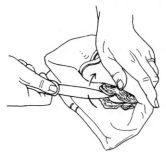

Slide the tip of your oyster knife into the shell, parallel to the top valve, twisting upward and scraping against it.

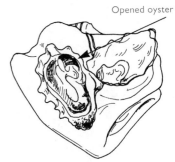

Opened oyster

The arrow indicates the position of the adductor muscle. The meat seen on the lid, if any, is used in stews and sauces.

All of the above-mentioned oysters can be enjoyed on the half shell with rye bread and a mignonette prepared this way.

Oysters on the Half Shell with Oyster Liquor Mignonette

FFR—6 DOZEN-OYSTER SERVINGS

I cup dry white wine

2 tablespoons sherry vinegar

2 shallots, very finely chopped

6 dozen oysters

Salt if needed

Cracked white pepper from the mill

Crushed or shaved ice

Seaweed

Reduce the wine and vinegar together by half in a small saucepan over medium heat. Add the shallots and let steep off the heat while you shuck the oysters.

Shuck the oysters over a bowl fitted with a conical strainer to collect all the juices dripping from the shells. Be sure to leave at least half the original quantity of juice in each oyster so the oysters do not dry out or appear dry.

Mix the collected oyster liquor with the mignonette and season with salt and pepper. Divide the condiment into six ramekins and serve with the oysters; a few drops of the mixture enhance the natural taste of the shellfish.

Fill six plates with crushed or shaved ice, arrange the oysters on the ice, and serve chilled. Decorate the edges of the plate with seaweed.

BROILED OYSTERS

Baking dishes full of oysters that have been deeply cooked under a crust of bread or cracker crumbs are not tops for the taste of oyster. But since they are popular presentations, please refer to the bibliography; many trustworthy American cookbooks offer this type of dish.

Here is a presentation in which the oysters do not cook, but simply poach under a silky sauce and feel like velvet on the palate.

The term mignonette comes from the name customarily given in French to cracked white pepper. This mixture is preferred to other condiments by passionate oyster afficionados.

SUGGESTED WINE:

California stainless steel-fermented light Chardonnay, French Muscadet sur lie, or dry Alsatian Riesling or excellent Sylvaner

Broiled Oysters for Toni

FFR — 6 APPETIZER SERVINGS

3 dozen medium-size oysters

Kosher salt

Chardonnay as needed

Best quality fish fumet (page 543) only, no substitute, as needed

3 shallots, finely chopped

Small bouquet garni

1 carrot, diced into ⅛-inch brunoise

1 white turnip, peeled and diced into ⅛-inch brunoise

10 French cornichons, diced into ⅛-inch brunoise

Heavy cream as needed

6 tablespoons unsalted butter

1 tablespoon Dry Sack sherry

Salt (optional)

White pepper from the mill

Shuck the oysters over a bowl fitted with a conical strainer to collect all their juices. Set aside the adductor muscle from each oyster. Put the oysters in a container and their juices in another; keep both covered in the refrigerator. Scrub the bottom shells and dry well. Pour a layer of kosher salt in a sheet or jelly-roll pan, arrange the oyster shells in the pan, and put in a preheated 250°F oven to dry and warm. Scrape any meat on the top shells and add it to the reserved adductor muscles, then discard the top shells.

Measure the oyster liquor. In a saucepan place the oyster liquor, the same volume of Chardonnay, the same volume of fish fumet, the shallots, bouquet garni, and adductor muscles. Slowly reduce by one half over low heat.

Meanwhile, blanch the carrot and turnip brunoises for 1 minute in boiling salted water. Drain well and empty into a small nonstick skillet; dry over low heat, tossing well. Cool and mix with the diced cornichons; set aside.

Strain the oyster juice reduction. Measure the reduction. Add one third of the reduction to a sauteuse and reduce almost to a glaze; add the same amount of cream as the original addition of the oyster reduction and reduce over medium-high heat until the sauce lightly coats the spatula. Repeat this same double operation twice more, turn the heat off, and whisk in the butter. Add the sherry, salt if needed, and pepper to your taste. Drain and add all the oyster liquor surrounding the oysters in their container. Reheat the sauce to almost boiling.

Fire the broiler. Spoon 1 teaspoon of the hot sauce into each oyster shell and add a large sprinkling of the brunoise; top with an oyster, then top the oyster with as much sauce as it takes to cover it. Repeat till all the shells are used up. Broil the oysters 4 inches away from the broiler or salamander until the sauce has browned lightly. Serve immediately.

Toni was Anthony Spinazzola, restaurant reviewer of the Boston Globe *from the 1960s to the middle 1980s who wrote the first review of my Boston restaurant; it made this small restaurant run by young, just graduated students an international success. I wrote this recipe for the 1994 Winter Culinary Festival organized by Toni's family for the benefit of the Anthony Spinazzola Culinary Scholarship Fund. Use preferably Apalachicola, Kent Island, Cotuit, Kumamoto, Bodega Bay, or Maine Belons, all of medium size.*

SUGGESTED WINE: **A** *California barrel-fermented Chardonnay that has undergone malolactic fermentation, or an opulent Montrachet "family" white in the vintage of your choice. A Blanc de Blancs French Champagne or a Napa Valley Schramsberg or Wesport Rivers Riesling sparkling wine from Massachusetts*

Shuck and drain the oysters; keep the liquor for a chowder or sauce for another dish. Pat the oysters dry, then flour them lightly with cake flour. Dip into the frying batter featured on page 635 or fine cornmeal and deep-fry in a hot oil (365°F) bath (see page 632 for more detailed instructions). Serve without any sauce but rather a small dish of balsamic or other vinegar of your choice or lemon quarters.

SIMPLE OYSTER STEWS

Oyster stews are done in a jiffy and without complications. I would like to recommend, however, that instead of adding the oysters to the light cream with all their liquor, you first reduce the liquor with a bit of dry white wine; here is a recipe:

Plain Oyster Stew

SUGGESTED WINE: *A Schramsberg Blanc de Blancs from Napa Valley or a Blanc de Blancs from Champagne*

FFR — 6 SERVINGS

3 dozen oysters, shucked, reserving all their liquor

Chardonnay as needed

2 cups light cream

Dash of Worcestershire sauce

Dash of Tabasco sauce

2 tablespoons fino sherry

White pepper from the mill

1 tablespoon finely chopped fresh tarragon leaves

Salt

Heat six small soup bowls in the oven. Keep the oysters chilled until ready to use.

Measure the oyster liquor and add to it in a medium-size saucepan an equal volume of Chardonnay. Reduce by half over medium heat. Blend in the cream and heat to just below the boiling point. Add the remaining ingredients, except the oysters and salt. Put six oysters in each of the bowls. Bring the soup as close to a boil as possible, then ladle over the oysters. Return the bowls to the oven for 2 minutes, then taste, and salt only if necessary.

Smoked Oyster Stew

Wonderful as a first course in the winter months.

FFR — 6 SERVINGS

3 dozen oysters, shucked, reserving all their liquor

Chardonnay as needed

Two 3½-ounce cans smoked oysters, drained of their oil and finely chopped

3 leeks, white part only, well washed and finely chopped

2½ cups light cream

1 tablespoon unsalted butter

Dash of red pepper flakes

2 tablespoons chopped fresh parsley leaves

SUGGESTED WINE: *Any French Chablis*

Heat six small soup bowls in the oven. Keep the oysters chilled until ready to use. Measure the liquor and add to it in a medium-size saucepan an equal volume of Chardonnay, along with the smoked oysters, one of the chopped leeks, and ½ cup of the light cream. Reduce to half the original volume of liquid over medium heat and strain through a conical strainer. Discard the solids.

Heat the butter well in a medium-size skillet over medium-high heat and sauté the remaining two leeks until golden. Add the strained reduction and the remainder of the cream and reheat to the boiling point. Add the pepper flakes. Place six shucked oysters in each bowl and ladle the hot broth over the oysters. Return the bowls to the oven for 2 minutes. Sprinkle with chopped parsley and serve with crisp bread.

Scallops

If you wish to know what a scallop in its shell looks like, you will have to go to a fish pier in Boston, Portland, Maine, or New York, where they are unloaded by the ton directly from the Georges Bank, off the coast of Maine, and Canada. Scallops from deep waters have smooth gray or white shells. On the continental shelf of the eastern Atlantic and in the Pacific many of the scallop shells are prettily ribbed and colored brick red or pink. And while tiny, lacy scallop shells of the tenderest pink litter the beaches of the South Atlantic in Brazil, others coming from deep water can have shells as wide as 5 inches, with an adductor muscle almost 2½ inches in diameter. Scallops snap their shells closed, expelling a jet of water which sends them flying through the water and across the ocean floor.

What is called a scallop—the edible portion of it—in our country is only the adductor muscle of the mollusk. When I was a child, my mother always bought large red-shelled scallops from the Channel for Sunday dinner and prepared both the adductor muscle and the coral in a delicious sauce, using whatever juices the animal still retained within its folds. Since their shell gapes slightly open at all times, scallops retain very little juice. When sauced they must be combined with mussels or clams which provide the juice for a sauce.

BUYING SCALLOPS

Be very careful—most scallops offered for sale have been shucked, soaked in water, and have acquired an engaging white color, virginal indeed, but treacherous as the scallops proceed to lose all their water and boil instead of searing. Mousselines prepared with this type of shellfish are always shaky (see page 690). Scallops fresh out of the shell are never pure white. Their color varies from ivory to beige and even a pale coral color.

Purchase darker fleshed scallops brought back by "day boats" which were dredged up in the wee hours of the morning and on the market shelves by the late afternoon or, latest, the next morning. Those scallops sold in large 5-pound containers and dripping with water are good only for chowders or old-fashioned baked recipes.

Since scallops, to be delicious, must never be cooked deeply, you will not see here any of the classic recipes for gratinéed scallops in which the mollusks end up overcooked and rubbery and in which "the sauce really makes the fish."

Each scallop is made of a large number of vertical fibers held together by a circular membrane, to which is attached a small tendon called the foot of the scallop. In any size scallop the foot must be removed because it becomes terribly tough as the scallop cooks; however, it should not be discarded but used to flavor the base of any sauce or chowder. If you prepare a small sauce, its base should be clam juice since scallops are a type of clam.

THE NUTRITIONAL VALUE OF SCALLOPS We consume only the adductor muscle of the scallops, skipping altogether the coral that contains the cholesterol. Adductor muscles contain a total amount of fat of no more than 2 percent with only 33 milligrams of cholesterol per 3½-ounce portion. Go ahead, enjoy scallops to your heart's content.

LARGE SCALLOPS

Large day-boat scallops are for searing and grilling, either on a barbecue or on a stovetop grill.

Searing large scallops should be done very rapidly over high heat in a non-stick skillet barely rubbed with a paper towel very lightly saturated with the oil of your choice. Let the first side of the scallop sear to golden, turn it over, and season, then let the scallop sear on its second side. When it is done, the scallop will be "poached," meaning not deeply cooked, at the center and warm; if you want the scallop slightly more cooked, which is still delicious, press on it with a metal turner to drive the heat toward the center for 30 seconds or so on each side. Such scallops are perfect for an everyday meal with plain lemon juice and stir-fried vegetables. For a more formal company dinner, here is a recipe:

The large scallops from the American coasts of the Atlantic Ocean are simply called sea scallops (*Pecten magellanicus*) and, from the Pacific coasts from Alaska to Baja, rock scallops (*Hinnites giganteus*). The shell of both species grows from 4 to 6 inches wide and their adductor muscle varies in diameter from 1 to almost 2 inches. Both species have strong fibers that can turn tough very rapidly if overcooked. They should be reserved for searing and grilling either on a barbecue or on a stovetop grill.

Seared Scallops with Lemon Oil and Dried Sour Cherry Dressing

FCR—6 SERVINGS

½ cup corn or sunflower oil

Finely grated rind and juice of 1 lemon

2 tablespoons dried sour Michigan cherries, finely chopped

½ cup plus ⅓ cup fresh or bottled clam juice

½ cup dry white wine

1 very large shallot, finely chopped

Very small bouquet garni

Salt

White pepper from the mill

18 large deep-sea scallops, feet removed

2 tablespoons chopped fresh chives

18 purple garlic chive flowers

18 long sprigs fresh chives

In the execution of this recipe, you can roughly mix the lemon oil and acid part of the dressing so they are barely combined and the lemon oil remains very visible; the plate will look pretty but the wine and food pairing will be more difficult (see page 109 for details on this subject).

SUGGESTED WINE:
California dry white Riesling or Alsatian Riesling

Heat half the oil in a small pan until hot but not smoking, then turn the heat off, add the grated lemon rind, and let stand until cool; mix in the remainder of the oil. Scrape into a small bowl, cover, and keep refrigerated overnight. Toss the cherries with 2 teaspoons of the lemon juice. Let macerate overnight, covered.

Reduce ½ cup of the clam juice, the wine, shallot, and bouquet garni in a saucepan over medium heat until 3 tablespoons of liquid are left after pressing on the shallots; strain into a small bowl. Add the remaining lemon juice and the prepared lemon oil less 1 tablespoon and mix until a well-homogenized dressing results. Add the chopped cherries and correct the seasoning with salt and pepper.

Heat six luncheon plates in a low oven. Over high heat, heat a large nonstick skillet lightly brushed with a wad of paper towels barely moistened with the reserved tablespoon of lemon oil. Sear the scallops 2 minutes on the first side, then turn over and season; sear the second side, pushing down on the tops of the scallops with a turner only if desired.

Arrange three scallops on each plate. Spoon 3 teaspoons of dressing around the scallops. Sprinkle well with the chives and set a small bouquet of garlic chive flowers and chive sprigs in the center of the plate, between the scallops. If desired, deglaze the searing pan with the remaining ⅓ cup of clam juice to obtain 2 to 3 tablespoons of glaze. Brush it lightly over the scallops.

Grilling large scallops can be done either on a stovetop grill or on the barbecue.

The cardinal rule in scallop grilling is not to sear the shellfish to the point where the grill marks are so deep and blackened with carbon that the result is deeply cooked scallops with a bitter aftertaste. Grilled scallops are best by themselves, or with a bit of flavored oil or compound butter, and a garnish of stir-fried vegetables.

There is a modern presentation making the rounds in these midyears of the 1990s, which consists of serving seared or grilled scallops in a few spoonfuls of very concentrated broth. This is interesting, but only if the broth is really concentrated so the grilled taste of the shellfish leaches into the broth and sustains the opposition between the seared concentrated taste of the scallop surface and the sweetness of its meat. Please do not serve one of those grayish spineless liquids which contributes no taste and destroys the whole dish; let the scallops emerge from the broth by at least two thirds of their height.

Here is an example:

Grilled Scallops in Asian-Flavored Broth

FCR — 6 SERVINGS

2 cups fish fumet or substitute (page 543 or 544)

2 cups fresh or bottled clam juice

2 cups dry white wine

18 large deep-sea scallops, feet removed and reserved

½ small carrot, chopped

1 very small white turnip, peeled and chopped

1 large leek, white and light green parts, well washed and chopped

Small bouquet garni

1 large slice fresh ginger, peeled

Soft part of 2 stalks lemongrass

8 sprigs cilantro

Salt

Pepper from the mill

¼ pound snow peas

2 tablespoons red pepper oil, homemade or store-bought

⅓ pound fresh water chestnuts, peeled and diced into ¼-inch cubes

1 large red bell pepper, peeled (optional), seeded, and diced into ¼-inch cubes

Put the fish fumet, clam juice, and wine in a large saucepan. Add the scallop feet, the carrot, turnip, leek, bouquet garni, ginger, 1 stalk of the lemongrass,

Have the broth ready and the vegetables ready to be stir-fried before you start the final cooking of the scallops. If freshwater chestnuts are not available, use a small firm jícama instead.

SUGGESTED WINE: *A simple white wine such as an Entre-Deux-Mers or a simple California Sauvignon Blanc or Chardonnay* and 2 sprigs of the cilantro. Bring to a boil, then reduce the heat to medium. Simmer until 1½ cups of excellent and flavorful broth are left. Strain through a conical strainer, pushing on the vegetables to extract as much flavor as possible. Correct the final seasoning and keep warm.

Preheat the barbecue or stovetop grill; in a low oven warm six soup bowls. String and slice the snow peas crosswise at a slant to obtain small sticks ¾ inch long. Heat 1 tablespoon of the pepper oil in a skillet and stir-fry, adding first the snow peas for 30 seconds, then the chestnuts for 1 minute, and finally the red bell pepper for another minute. Season with salt and pepper and keep the vegetables warm.

Cool the skillet completely, then add the second tablespoon of oil and toss the scallops in the skillet to coat them lightly. Remove them from the pan and grill them 2 minutes on each side on the white hot grill; push down on the scallops a few seconds more with a turner if you wish them slightly more cooked.

Arrange three scallops on each bowl, surround with stir-fried vegetables, and add ¼ cup broth. Dot each plate with 1 sprig cilantro. Serve hot.

MEDIUM-SIZE AND SMALL SCALLOPS

Medium-size scallops come from smaller specimens of the larger types described above on page 674. Their fibers being softer and more delicate than those of the larger scallops, they are, once cut in half horizontally, better used in stir-fried or poached preparations. Poaching for small scallops means simply immersing into a hot broth just before serving, most of the time in a chowder-type soup.

The small scallops we call bay scallops are no more than ½ inch in diameter, sometimes even a bit less, and can be found from New England to Florida. They are, from north to south: the little northern scallop (*Argopecten circularis*) found along the northernmost coasts and the Peconic Bay scallops on Long Island; from Cape Hatteras to Florida, the two types called *Pecten irridians* and *P. dislocatus*; and the calico scallops which appear in abundant supply in our supermarkets in the spring are of the species *Argopecten gibbus*. A few other species of bay-type scallops are imported from South America and more recently in large quantities from China.

Scallops of this size must be stir-fried on high heat in a wok or heavy, well-heated skillet. Stir-frying is especially useful with the smaller scallops which have been whitened by soaking them in water; cooking in hot oil brightens their taste and prevents the shellfish from turning hard through overcooking. Stir-frying is also excellent for sliced medium-size scallops surrounded by a small light sauce, or used for a salad.

The secrets of stir-frying are:

- The use of a very hot wok or an unconditionally *flat-bottomed* skillet of a heavy material that conducts heat very efficiently and rapidly. An old cast-iron pan is perfect and so are the modern Le Creuset or Calphalon-type pans.

- The skillet or sauteuse pan must be almost too large for the quantity of shellfish to be cooked, so that the cook can toss the food back and forth over the whole surface of the pan bottom, keeping it constantly in contact with the hot pan and cooking it on all of its outer surfaces while keeping it tender and juicy inside.

- The oil used must be able to sustain very high temperatures, so use grape-seed oil preferably, but corn oil also will do well.

- The shellfish is always the last of all the ingredients cooked in the recipe; if it were done first, it would overcook in its own accumulated heat, and its juices would break through the thin outer layer of seared tissues by the time the vegetable garnish had cooked.

- All elements of a dish are cooked separately, removed to different plates and tossed together for a final quick burst of heat and seasoning just before serving. Or the vegetables can be added one after the other, starting with the most fibrous which takes the longest time to soften, and ending with the least fibrous or softest one.

- Add as little oil as you wish, but some oil must be added to the wok or skillet for each new vegetable; it coats the vegetables and prevents them from coloring too much or sticking to the hot pan.

- Who says stir-frying is just for Chinese cooking? You can stir-fry using western seasonings only. But you can also add any Asian seasoning you personally like. Note, however, that the little cornstarch and chicken broth slurry of the Chinese can be skipped. All it does is add more "slip" to the dish by coating all the elements and making them rounder in the mouth.

Basic Scallop Stir-Fry

FCR—6 SERVINGS

I pound medium-size scallops, feet removed and cut into ¼-inch-thick slices, or bay scallops, feet removed

I teaspoon fennel seeds, ground or very finely chopped

Grapeseed or other unsaturated oil of your choice as needed

6 young carrots, sliced ⅛ inch thick on a slant

6 young purple-top turnips, I inch in diameter, sliced ⅛ inch thick on a slant

I small zucchini, cut into ⅛-inch-thick slices

I fennel bulb, quartered and cut into ⅛-inch-thick slices

8 large red radishes, cut into ⅛-inch-thick slices

I to 2 tablespoons cider vinegar, to your personal taste

½ cup chicken broth of your choice (optional)

My children were raised on a lot of these stir-fries, the colors of the vegetables usually "selling" the dish to them. If the total preparation of the vegetables takes up too much of your time, use whatever vegetables you can find already peeled and trimmed offered for sale fresh—not frozen—in plastic bags and slice them. For the seasonings, follow your own preferences.

½ teaspoon cornstarch (optional)

1 tablespoon chopped fennel greens

Salt

Pepper from the mill

SUGGESTED WINE: *Any simple, pleasant wine, preferably white, that you enjoy*

Spread the sliced scallops in a baking dish; sprinkle the fennel seeds evenly over them, and toss; add 1 tablespoon of the oil to the scallops and toss again. Let stand, covered, at room temperature while you stir-fry the vegetables.

Heat a dab of oil in the wok or skillet over high heat. Add the carrots and stir-fry 1 minute; remove to a plate. Repeat the same operation in turn with the turnips, zucchini, and fennel bulb. Remove each to a different plate.

Repeat the same operation for the radishes, adding a dash of vinegar to the pan to prevent them from turning bluish.

Finally, stir-fry the scallops 1 minute or so and return all the vegetables to the pan, stir-frying the mixture until it is well heated. The scallops should be opaque and the vegetables quite crunchy. If desired, mix the chicken broth and cornstarch together and add to the wok or skillet in the last minute of stir-frying. Turn into a shallow dish and sprinkle with the fennel greens. Season with salt and pepper or any other seasoning or condiment you like.

Mussels and Clams

Mussels are black shelled and elongated in shape; there are several species of which only a few are truly delicious and edible. Very popular in all European countries, from the Mediterranean to the North Sea, mussels are just about the leanest seafood going, registering a 5 percent total fat content and 28 milligrams of cholesterol per 3½-ounce portion of meat. Mussels are the seafood par excellence for heart patients, and steamed *plain* or with onions, shallots, and dry white wine, they offer not a royal but almost an imperial meal, which was not disdained by Roman emperors (see recipe No. 433 in the *Book of Apicius*).

The modern way of growing mussels on plastic mesh bags filled with large gravel has increased their production in Maine and along the coasts of California and Washington State. Slowly but surely, mussels which, I was once told by an old Mainer, were "poisonous," are becoming the basis of popular dinner dishes.

However, mussels now as then *can be poisonous* if picked in the wrong season or at the wrong place. Please *do not collect mussels yourself* anymore; buy them from a reliable fishmonger who knows they are clean and come from nonpolluted waters. Mussels feed on dinoflagellates called gonayaulax, which in the warm season can be seen floating at the surface of the sea, the famous "red tides." Dinoflagellates ingested by mussels produce a toxin in the shellfish which is fatal when in turn the shellfish are ingested by humans. Mussels are for consumption in late fall, winter, and very early spring only. Estuaries and seashores where gonayaulax can manifest themselves are constantly monitored and bans are proclaimed in the newspapers when a red tide occurs; all mussels then disappear from stores until they are safe again.

The large green lip mussels which are flown to us from New Zealand and the southern Pacific are delicious also; they look and taste striking in salads.

Black mussels are delicious consumed raw *only at the seashore at the proper times of the year and coming from unpolluted waters. Never consume a mussel raw that you have picked yourself*; go to the nearest mussel farm and purchase a bag or two; the farmers will know the latest information on their state of health.

Clams are nutritionally just as desirable as mussels, with only 2 percent fat and 33 milligrams cholesterol per 3½-ounce portion. There are *soft-shell clams* which are mostly steamed, served piled on large platters at all eastern seashore restaurants and dipped in melted butter. Soft shells are recognizable by the black syphon which protrudes from their shells.

Hard-shell clams come in several sizes, from the huge quahogs of New England, which are ground and sold by the ton, canned for the production of commercial chowders. The smaller quahogs, called littlenecks and cherrystones, can be consumed on the half shell with cocktail sauce or a mignonette prepared with some of their own juices as explained for oysters on page 670 or stuffed with a nice bread stuffing and baked.

When overseas, do not miss experimenting with clams everywhere you go, especially in France; try clovisses, palourdes, and praires on the half shell, and the wonderful cockles of the Channel which are sold throughout Normandy and on the northern coasts of England, France, Belgium, and Holland, steamed accompanied with mountains of the best french fries and delicious sparkling hard cider.

PURCHASING AND CLEANING MUSSELS AND CLAMS

When contemplating the preparation of mussels or clams, please go to a reputable fishmonger who will order them in mesh bags for you and deliver you a fine and healthy product. The shellfish will come either scrubbed or not. Most of the time they've been scrubbed. If they have not been, scrub yourself: Pull off the wiry brownish ligament that peeks out of the shell and is called the byssus, or beard; simply pull until it comes out and scrub the shells with a plastic scrubber until all traces of marine life have disappeared. Prescrubbed mussels and clams will cost more but that is time gained against money spent.

I cannot insist enough on the damage done to mussels and clams which are sold in supermarkets in plastic trays tightly wrapped in clear plastic. Ask the attendant when the shellfish arrived at the store and on which day it was put out for sale. If it was only today, use the shellfish after scrubbing it and giving it a double bath in *salted water*, but if they came in as long as 48 hours ago, the shellfish must be purged through several saltwater baths given at 3-

The beard, or byssus, should be pulled off in the direction of the arrow.

hour intervals. Considering the time involved, it is better not to purchase mussels or clams which have been tightly packaged in plastic.

When cooking spanking fresh mussels and clams, they can be cooked slightly rare. Such is not the case for shellfish that has been under plastic for twenty-four hours, which must, after being purged, be well cooked. Purchase mussels sold in plastic net bags; their juice will be twice as strong as that of older mussels treated in saltwater. Also, they will not be broken or have gaping shells.

Cornmeal is useless to purge mussels and clams well; only saltwater will do, as the shellfish believes itself to be in the ocean, and opens its shell and cleanses itself. This tells you that salt should not be forgotten when you clean mussels and clams or they will taste flat and unsalted.

Mussels and hard-shelled clams can be steamed in white wine and the aromatics of your choice; you can go French, Mediterranean of all nationalities, Asian, etc. Serve as a plateful of fun and pleasure with crisp bread, buttered or not, as you prefer, with the steaming juices, or prepare a small sauce such as the old-fashioned poulette sauce, a white cream sauce flavored with lemon juice.

The steaming technique is exactly as described in this recipe.

Poulette of Mussels, Clams, Scallops, and Mushrooms

FCR—6 SERVINGS

2 quarts black mussels

2 dozen cherrystone clams

I large yellow onion, chopped

2 large shallots, chopped

I medium-size leek, white and light green parts, well washed and chopped

2 tablespoons coarsely chopped fresh parsley stems

¾ cup dry white wine

¾ cup fish fumet or substitute (page 543 or 544)

6 white peppercorns, cracked

I pound button mushrooms, trimmed

Salt

Pepper from the mill

I cup light cream or milk of your choice

Cornstarch as needed

I tablespoon unsalted butter

½ pound bay scallops, feet removed

Fresh lemon juice

1½ cups steamed or boiled long-grain rice

Chopped fresh parsley leaves

This recipe is modernized and lightened: The egg yolks and roux have been removed, and there are no bread crumbs to add more calories.

SUGGESTED WINE: *A nice French Vouvray Sec*

Scrub and debeard the mussels, then scrub the clams. Put them both through two saltwater baths (see page 680). Place in a two-handled kettle with a lid. Add the onion, shallots, leek, parsley stems, wine, fumet, and peppercorns. Cover the kettle, set over medium-high heat, and steam until the mussels start to gape open. Grasping the handles of the pot, toss the shellfish to bring them from the bottom of the pot to the top or vice versa. Remove the mussels as they open so they do not harden. Clams will open more slowly and will be removed last. Discard any mussel or clam that has not opened. Shell the remaining mussels and clams and put them in a large bowl. Reduce the steaming juices over high heat by one quarter, then strain through a tea strainer, which will retain all the sand, into a 1-quart measuring cup.

Put the mushrooms in a saucepan with salt and pepper to taste and approximately ¼ cup of the steaming water. Bring to a simmer and cook 5 minutes, until all the mushroom liquor has mixed with the water. Drain the liquid into the measuring cup containing the shellfish juices. Add the mushrooms to the bowl containing the shellfish.

Measure the total amount of liquids (the mixed juices plus the cream). Dissolve 1 tablespoon of cornstarch per cup of liquid in the cream only. Bring the juice mixture to a boil; reduce to a simmer and, using a wooden spoon, stir the cream into the juices, continuing to stir until the sauce has thickened, about 5 minutes.

When the sauce is almost ready, heat the butter in a large skillet and stir-fry the scallops 1 minute or so. Add the shellfish, mushrooms, and scallops to the sauce and finish the dish with lemon juice to your taste, and salt and pepper as needed. Serve over the rice dotted with the parsley.

Baked Clams and Mussels

FFR to FCR—6 APPETIZER SERVINGS

For the mussels

12 green lip mussels

Kosher salt

1 cup dry bread crumbs

3 large cloves garlic, finely chopped

2 tablespoons chopped fresh parsley leaves

¼ teaspoon dried oregano

Pure olive oil as needed

For the clams

12 littleneck clams

⅔ cup dry crumbs made from barely sweetened corn bread

2 cloves garlic, finely chopped

Mussels and clams can also be baked. In this case they will be opened raw on the half shell, and a mixture of crumbs, seasonings, and aromatics will be sprinkled generously on each of them. Baking in a hot oven will result in a splendid tray of the most pleasant appetizers. Here is a tray of mussels and clams that you can arrange on platters to be passed around.

Use butter or light olive oil or a combination of both as you prefer.

2 tablespoons chopped fresh parsley leaves

¼ teaspoon rubbed sage

Melted unsalted butter or olive oil as needed

SUGGESTED WINE: *Any California Sauvignon Blanc, or a French Sancerre or Quincy*

Preheat the oven to 400°F. Set the mussels on one side of a baking sheet or jelly-roll pan filled with kosher salt for the stability of the shellfish. Set in the oven until the shells open but the mussels remain rare. Remove the top shells gently, scraping the meat into the bottom shells. Sever the adductor muscle to separate the shellfish from the bottom shell. Mix the crumbs, garlic, parsley, and oregano together and spread over the meat of the mussels. Dribble olive oil over the shellfish and return the shells to the pan.

Shuck the clams while still raw, severing their adductor muscles; discard the top shell and return each clam to its bottom shell. Mix together the stuffing ingredients and sprinkle over the surface of the clams. Dribble melted butter over the clams and set on the second half of the jelly-roll pan.

Bake until the toppings are golden and crisp, about 10 minutes. Serve alternated on a country platter.

Cephalopods
Squid, Cuttlefish, and Octopus

These all too unpopular mollusks belong to the cephalopods. All are characterized by possessing a head with many tentacles, a skin that moves easily over its muscle tissues, and the capability of developing from the smallest baby size to a gigantic fish distinguishing itself by its amazing voraciousness.

The meat of squid, cuttlefish, and octopus is delicious only if cooked either very quickly or for a nice long time. Anywhere in between and it will be hard and unpalatable.

All fish in this category are sold cured and cleaned, except sometimes for their skin, which is easy to pull off, either when the squid or octopus is uncooked or cooked. Where octopus heads are always cleaned completely, those of squid are not always and you will have to make sure that the "beak" (a round muscle with a black needlelike point) has been removed. Cuttlefish is not readily available in this country but I suspect that it is sold prepared in the newfangled "squid steaks." Squid steaks are sold in western supermarkets. They are made of chopped squid meat, probably held together with egg white and shaped into steaks. Fried golden and crisp, they are quite popular.

A NUTRITIONAL WORD OF CAUTION To add insult to injury, squid, with 2 percent fat, but a whopping 233 milligrams of cholesterol per 3½-ounce portion, tastes really at its best when deep-fried. Numbers are not available for octopus or cuttlefish.

Fisherman's Calamari
CALAMARI ALLA PESCATORA

Don't feel bad when you enjoy this immensely delicious and appetizing dish; just make fat-free yogurt your main protein for the next day. Guests must sit down and wait for this delight to come straight from the kitchen. Californians may want to try Meyer lemons.

SUGGESTED WINE: *Any uncomplicated dry white wine from California, Italy, or southern France*

FFR—6 APPETIZER SERVINGS

3 pounds fully cleaned baby squid bodies

Unbleached all-purpose flour as needed

Pure olive oil for deep-frying

Salt

Lemon quarters, seeded

Make sure that the beak and other elements have been removed from the squid heads and that the bodies are totally empty of any material. Slip off any traces of gray skin. Leave the tentacles attached to the lower part of the head. Cut the bodies into rings ¼ inch wide. Pat the squid dry and divide into six portions. Place each portion successively into a brown paper bag filled with flour and shake well. Empty into a colander and shake again to discard any excess flour.

Heat 4 inches of oil to 365°F in a deep kettle (see page 632 for more detailed instructions). Deep-fry one portion at a time and drain on crumpled paper towels. Guests must salt the fish themselves as they eat it, in order to prevent sogginess. Enjoy with lemon juice.

Octopus and Citrus Salad

Octopus always comes frozen from the Atlantic or the Mediterranean. Soak it for 30 minutes in cold salted water, rinse the inside of the head well, and proceed as follows.

SUGGESTED WINE: *White Lacryma Christi del Vesuvio from Italy*

FFR—6 MAIN-COURSE SERVINGS

1 recipe Court Bouillon for Shrimp (page 662)

5 pounds frozen octopus, defrosted and cleaned

Balsamic vinegar

Fresh lemon juice

12 oil-cured black olives, chopped

2 anchovy fillets, rinsed and mashed

1 large clove garlic, mashed

Virgin olive oil as needed

¼ teaspoon each grated lemon and grapefruit rinds

Salt

Pepper from the mill

1 each white and pink grapefruit, peeled and sectioned

1 large red onion, sliced and salted

Fresh basil leaves

Bring the court bouillon to a boil in a large pot. Add the octopus meat, bring back to a boil, and simmer over medium heat until tender. You will have to check as the time will vary widely with the thickness of the tentacles; the meat is done when the skin slips off easily.

Remove all the skin, keeping the suction cups of the tentacles which are delicious and look good sprinkled on the salad. Cut the tentacles into ¼-inch-thick slices and the heads into strips. Put the meat in a large bowl and the tentacles in a smaller one.

Reduce ½ cup of the court bouillon to 3 tablespoons over high heat, then add balsamic vinegar and lemon juice to your taste, the olives, anchovies, and garlic. Whisk in enough olive oil to balance the acid and let the dressing ripen for 1 hour. At this point rehomogenize it, add the citrus rinds, and correct with salt if needed and pepper. Marinate the octopus meat in as much of the dressing as you like for 2 hours in the refrigerator.

To serve, line the edges of a platter with alternating sections of white and pink grapefruit, slices of red onion, and small basil leaves. Pile the octopus meat in the center topped with a few scissored leaves of basil and the tentacle suction cups; serve the remainder of the dressing in a bowl. A loaf of crisp Mediterranean bread is a must.

Gastropods
Snails

Outside of the small black snails known as periwinkles, which are usually boiled in salted water flavored with seaweed, sea snails are not considered as food. Land snails are known as gastropods because they have no legs and utilize the strong muscle of their abdomen to move themselves. The only edible snails in the United States are the small gray snails of California which, come the rains of spring, seem to congregate on wild fennel stalks. If you want to consume them, you must be certain that the area in which you gather them is not polluted by any chemical fallout or other such delight. If you are, put the snails in a large clay pot, cover it with a lid secured with a heavy weight, and starve the snails at least six weeks; they will build their overwintering window of calcium carbonate and slowly purge themselves of poisonous material they may have ingested. When you are ready to cook them, salt them first, so they purge themselves, completely rinse them several times in running cold water, and boil them in a court bouillon for 45 minutes. You can then transform them into the following suggested preparations:

- Escargots in Bourguignon butter; see the classic French recipes in any book.
- Snail soup, see page 259 of my own book *In Madeleine's Kitchen*.
- Snail Fritters, see page 637 of this book.

Batracians
Frogs

Frogs are known as batracians. Preparing frog legs in the United States is a major problem because at this time, there is no aquaculture of frogs yielding small frog legs. The majority of frogs to be found come from Asia and undergo quite a number of crossings of oceans before they finally land in this country. Most of them are tough old bullfrogs, which will make a good broth if they are not yet dehydrated by extra long freezing. So no frogs in this country.

If you can find small, good, fresh frogs out of a fresh pond, gather them at night with a flashlight. Do not kill them, but rather pinch their legs and cut them off, then throw the frogs back into the water where they will grow "retreads" as stone crabs do and continue reproducing normally. Skin and soak the legs in water, pat them dry, and store overnight in the refrigerator. You can then:

- Make fritters as on page 637.
- Prepare them in any of the ways of the classic French cuisine: panfried with persillade butter, with a sauce poulette (see page 681), etc.
- Prepare them in the Alsatian manner as indicated on pages 232 and 234 of my book *When French Women Cook*.

Specialties Prepared with Ground or Pureed Fish

Most of the ancient civilizations of Europe and the Orient have quite a repertory of fish presented in ground or pureed form. Many of these preparations are first courses and work well for entertaining. I include in this section two recipes which can be prepared ahead, allowing the hosts some time for drinks with guests before dinner.

For Oriental ground fish dishes, consult the list of Thai and Vietnamese books mentioned in the bibliography. For fish and crab cakes, see the section on crustaceans on page 648 and the recipes on page 695.

This section is entirely dedicated to French mousseline and quenelle paste and fish pâtés. I have dedicated quite a bit of space to them because they employ a technique that is in danger of disappearing in this country (though not in Europe) due to our obsession with lean and healthy foods. I have developed these precise techniques myself over the last thirty years. As described here they are foolproof and have become relatively rapid to execute. You will find that with very slight variations on classic techniques and the modern simplifications brought on by the food processor, the very same batter can be used for all three categories of presentation.

Knowing the Difference

A *mousseline* is made with a very light paste of fish (or meat) enriched with eggs, butter, and cream. Although the word *mousseline* refers to this mixture molded in special small metal pans or ramekins, mousseline can also be mixed with pieces of fish or shellfish to make delicious fish or shellfish cakes.

A *quenelle* is made of a fish (or meat) paste identical to that of a mousseline, but this paste is not as rich and contains less butter and less cream, so it is more solid and can be poached in a liquid instead of being baked in a mold or ramekin.

A *pâté* is made of a fish (or meat) paste (see the terrine recipe on page 881). The fish paste is mixed with eggs, butter, cream, and bread crumbs and molded into a loaf pan, so it can be sliced when served—either warm or cold. Fish pâtés are excellent as a first course that can be made ahead of time. In the last ten years, plain mousseline or quenelle pastes have been used to make pâtés to avoid the heaviness brought by the bread crumbs.

The basic elements used in the composition of mousselines, quenelles, and pâtés of fish are divided into solid ingredients, liquid ingredients, and seasonings, spices, and garnishes.

The Solid Ingredients

It is essential that the fish or shellfish be extremely fresh, *raw*, and free of skin, brown tissues, and bones. For mousselines and quenelles, the cleanest, most agreeable taste is always obtained by using a fish that has literally just jumped out of an ocean, lake, or river. Cooks living by the sea, a lake, or major river will have a privileged situation.

A mousseline is made by using the principle that the more viscous the collagen or liquid tissue that binds the fish fibers together, the better butter and heavy cream will stay in suspension in the quenelle paste and form a smooth, even paste with a firm and airy texture.

In fish fillets that are not so fresh and have been waiting to be sold in the fish store, dehydration takes place at the same time as autolysis, the softening of the muscular tissues, which happens very fast in fish, and causes the meat to rapidly become flabby. Any mousse or quenelle made with such fish will lack firmness, not hold butter or cream well, and will not acquire a perfect texture.

Fish fillets that are very fresh never have the slightest tinge of grayness; they are firm and always have a pinkish or solidly white hue to their color. The best fish to use is a super fresh one that you fillet yourself or ask the fish store to fillet to order for you.

The most desirable fish to use in mousselines and quenelles are, in order of preference, pike, all salmons, with preference going to *Salmo salar*, the Atlantic salmon, and Pacific silver salmon, lake trout, Arctic char, freshwater trout, healthy gray sole, petrale sole, winter flounder, red snapper, and medium-size halibut. The most desirable shellfish are Maine lobster, deep-sea scallops, Louisiana crayfish—as large as possible and caught early in the season before the water warms up too much—rock lobster or spiny lobster (clawless lobster), and large shrimp or prawns. For any mousse, lobster from cold waters will always be superior to lobster from warmer waters and, for the same reason, shrimp caught in winter will be superior to shrimp caught in the warmer months.

It is entirely possible to make a mousseline with a fish whose natural texture is not as firm as that of the species mentioned above, provided one adds alternately with heavy cream:

- 3 to 4 tablespoons double strength fish fumet (see page 689) enriched with 2 to 3 teaspoons gelatin per pound of fish meat.
- Or 3 to 4 tablespoons warm fish fumet thickened with ½ teaspoon cornstarch, then cooled.

The same reinforcements may be used for fish that is only fresh, not sparkling fresh.

While experimenting for the sake of learning myself whether either of these methods would be helpful, I have been able to prepare a mousseline with fish that had been flash frozen and defrosted in the refrigerator. This information is for those cooks who have only frozen fish at their disposal, for mousselines made with frozen fish usually show a slight grain if the fish was not of top quality when frozen or was defrosted outside of the refrigerator, its natural juices lost in the defrosting dish. It is interesting to note that frozen shrimp have such tough fibers that they can be made into a mousseline without the addition of double strength fish fumet.

Although this is not a subject about which I like to write, I urge cooks to inspect all fish fillets for traces of parasites that feed by sucking the fish liquid collagen. Parasite-infested fish makes a poor mousseline with an unsteady, slightly granular texture. This, of course, speaks in favor of hatchery fish which are strongly controlled and always healthy. Hatchery fish are always sparkling clean but healthy wild fish caught from live wild waters will always be better tasting. There are advantages to each.

The Liquid Ingredients

EGGS

Egg whites only were used in most classic recipes for mousselines and quenelles, probably to secure a perfect white color. A wonderful conversation with André Soltner thirty years ago put me on to using part egg white with part whole egg for better color in mousselines made with white fish. The cook should be warned, however, of a possible problem resulting from the use of egg yolks with deep-sea scallops, shrimp, and lobster. Once in a great while the yolks will provoke massive syneresis (the erratic separation of an apparently perfect mousseline batter upon baking and *not because of overheating or overcooking*). This—possibly enzymatic—reaction does not always occur, but it has happened enough times during my years in the kitchen that I stopped preparing shellfish mousselines with egg yolks for restaurant consumption.

HEAVY CREAM

In the last fifty-four years, I have made mousselines with many types of cream, from light cream to thick crème fraîche, and these are my conclusions.

Light cream may be used by those who would like to enjoy a mousseline without clogging their arteries. The resulting mousseline is nice, but it does lack "slip" on the tongue and is by no means as good as it should be; it is only an acceptable product.

The best mousselines are made with pasteurized heavy cream containing 34 to 38 percent butterfat; sterilized cream may be used, but pasteurized is better. The American heavy cream is perfect and gives by far the best results. Many contemporary French chefs in France use the fluid yet unripened *fleurette*, which has the same texture as American heavy cream and which, formerly, was used almost exclusively for dessert and pastry work.

However, the crème fraîche craze is such that I feel compelled to say a word about it. Yes, you may use some crème fraîche, if you think the taste "does something" for the finished product. If you are smart, however, you will limit your use of crème fraîche to no more than one third the total volume of cream and before using it, you will dilute the crème fraîche with one fifth of its volume of regular 4 percent homogenized milk to return it to a more liquid texture. For example, if you prepare a mousseline batter requiring a total of 2 cups of cream, you will need 1⅓ cups regular heavy cream plus ½ cup crème fraîche diluted with 2½ tablespoons of 4 percent milk.

DOUBLE-STRENGTH FISH FUMET OR FISH ESSENCE

If, as explained above, the quality of your fish necessitates the use of a mixture of gelatin or starch with double-strength fish fumet, prepare the fumet as follows. Mix about 1 pound fish bones (heads are best) with 1⅓ cups fish fumet and ⅔ cup dry white wine. Cook 35 minutes as you would a regular fumet (see page 543) and strain well. Use as much of this cold double-strength fumet as you need for the mousseline and keep the remainder for use in the sauce.

Why not take simple fish fumet and reduce it until thick? Try it if you have the time and an excess of fish fumet at your disposal. The result is neither the best-smelling nor best-tasting mixture, for as the gelatinous texture thickens, so do the taste and smell, and not in the most attractive manner. The simple "fish essence" I recommend here is better—Escoffier also thought so and taught me that fact on page 14 of *Le Guide Culinaire* (Crown Publishers, American edition).

ers, American edition).

BUTTER

Whipped or creamed butter is used to give slip on the palate to mousseline or quenelle pastes made with fish that, due to its natural texture, would yield a dry and somewhat unpalatable paste once cooked.

The Seasonings and Spices; Garnishes

The most frequently used seasonings are, per pound of processed meat, 1½ teaspoons salt and 35 turns of a French pepper mill (but beware: All pepper mills do not grind exactly the same).

The seasonings go into the fish puree at the same time as the butter. If more salt is needed when the mousseline batter is finished, dilute any addition in a tablespoon or so of cream and fold the mixture into the paste. A pinch of nutmeg is often used, and chopped fresh herbs can also be added to the paste.

In the days of rich cuisine, a garnish of fish, shellfish, or diced vegetables was often enclosed in the center of the mousseline; these garnishes would be cooked and tossed with a bit of sauce first, so that they would just reheat as the mousseline baked. This is done less and less nowadays.

Small dices of raw shellfish can also be added to a mousseline paste; these should be tossed in egg white before being folded into the finished paste, so egg and fish proteins bond in the mousseline and remain well encased in the mousseline if it is cut into portions or sliced. This technique is still in use; see the recipe on page 694.

Mousseline Mixing Techniques

There are different ways of preparing mousseline pastes.

THE QUICK, ONE-STEP
FOOD PROCESSOR METHOD

If you have never made mousseline paste, start this way; the results are nice and the work minimal.

Process the ice-cold fish combined with the chosen egg mixture until completely pureed. As soon as this is done, remove from the processor and strain the puree if you wish (remember that deep-sea scallops never need straining). Cool the puree again in the refrigerator for at least 30 minutes.

Put the entire quantity of *room temperature butter* needed into the processor along with the salt, pepper, and any other spices you may be using; process to cream and aerate the butter. Then gradually return the fish meat to the food processor, processing until fish and butter form a homogeneous paste. Now add the ice-cold cream in four successive additions and in a steady stream each time. Remember that the machine should be on all the while you are adding the cream *but must be stopped any time you are not,* so as not to overwhip the cream already integrated into the paste.

Between each addition, bring the paste up from the bottom of the container to the surface with a rubber spatula, except after the last addition, for the paste should by then be completely finished and homogenized. Total mixing time: 6 to 8 minutes.

THE FOOD PROCESSOR—ELECTRIC MIXER COMBINATION

This is the method I use all the time and prefer to any other; do not worry about its apparent difficulty. Once you have done it, you will be able to do it faster and faster. I remember an emergency situation, when I made a batch of five pounds in seventeen minutes.

1. *The rapid puree of the fish or shellfish.* Process the fish and chosen egg mixture in the food processor until completely smooth. *Only if needed* (scallops never need straining), strain the puree into a stainless steel or glass bowl using a drum sieve (the French *tamis*) and a wide, thin plastic scraper. When you strain fish or other proteinic purees, do not put the whole amount of paste on the surface of the sieve, but rather strain it tablespoon by tablespoon, always pushing it toward yourself without ever changing direction in your movement. It is the fastest way to strain and the easiest, for a large mass of proteinic material such as fish puree passed through a strainer with small holes will denature and turn gummy and elastic if moved back and forth in two or more directions.

Deep chill the puree in its bowl, embedding it in a second bowl filled with plenty of ice cubes and a bit of salted water. *The fish puree must become ice cold.*

To clean the *tamis,* flush the puree still remaining in the strainer mesh under a jet of *cold* water; it will flush away immediately. If you do so under hot water, the puree will cook into the mesh and there will be no end to your scrubbing.

2. *Adding the butter and cream in an electric mixer.* The best model of electric mixer existing for this procedure is a Mixmaster or one of the old models of Hobart K45 with the glass bowl in which the beater rests at the center of the mixing bowl. Watch those mixer bowls with a little hump at the center of their bottom; the mixing there is irregular and some of the mousseline paste will remain unhomogenized. In such mixers you will have to stop the mixing of the cream at regular intervals, lift the beaters out of the paste, and, with a rubber spatula, *gently* bring the unhomogenized paste to the surface of the bowl so it will rehomogenize into the paste when beating starts again.

Cream the *room temperature butter* (it should be plastic, neither too soft nor oily) with the salt, pepper, and any other spice used until smooth. Keeping the mixer on medium creaming speed, add the ice-cold fish puree, generous tablespoon by generous tablespoon, until all has been added. Continue beating until the mixture develops some elasticity; you will see this happen as the liquid collagen and the butter form an emulsion in which the broken fish fibers are held in suspension. The development of elasticity is to be compared to the development of gluten in bread; it happens under the mechanical action of the mixer whip. *Do not overwhip* or overdevelop the elasticity, or you will have to add more cream than is called for to soften the paste, thus blunting the good taste of the fish. As soon as you see the fish puree stick in blocks to the beaters, you are ready to add the cream.

Please, before you add the cream, go back to page 28 and read all about whipping cream again if you are not clear on the logistics of this delicate operation.

Your goal is to whip the *ice-cold cream* into the fish puree without it breaking and separating. Were you to add warm cream, which has lost its capacity of foaming, you would be left with whey containing islands of fish puree. Add the cream in four successive additions and in a steady ¼-inch-thick stream, until all the cream has been incorporated. Between each addition, bring the machine to high speed for 30 seconds, so as to homogenize the paste.

TESTING THE PASTE

Now test the paste: Prepare a small quenelle of paste, using 2 teaspoons dipped into cold water; gently drop the paste into a bath of *barely simmering* salted water, not boiling, which would make the water content of the quenelle also come to a boil and literally explode and fall apart. Simmer until, when tested with a finger, the test quenelle feels springy under pressure. Cut the quenelle in half, taste it, and check for these possible problems:

- The quenelle is good and homogenous but a bit too "solid": You must add more cream.
- The quenelle does not look granular but the fish can still be perceived in tiny particles on the tongue and between the front teeth: Add more cream.
- The quenelle is not seasoned enough: Spread a tablespoon or so of cream on top of the finished paste, sprinkle the needed seasoning on it, and quickly fold into the paste.

Your next question is, "how much cream?" Unfortunately, there is no way to know exactly, because no one cream and no one fish puree ever have the very same texture in any batch of paste. Very gradually add as much as is needed until a new test gives you that wonderfully airy texture of the perfect quenelle. Trust yourself, you will know. You cannot miss it; all of a sudden, it is there, the tested paste is light and airy, almost trembling and looks completely homogeneous when cut with a knife, with only a few tiny air bubbles here and there.

To help you in the recipes that follow I have given the amount of cream in a range—for example, 2½ to 3 cups heavy cream.

Test after adding the lesser amount and go to the higher amount only if necessary. How much is truly needed depends on the quality of your fish and the fat content of your cream, and both will vary every time you prepare a new batch.

Mousseline Baking Techniques

Pack the paste, without leaving any air holes, into generously buttered ramekins or paper cups 1 to 3 ounces in capacity. One 1-ounce mousseline makes a cute and delicious little appetizer, two 1-ounce mousselines or one 2-ounce mousseline a lovely first course. A 3-ounce mousseline, well garnished with vegetables, could constitute a main course in the United States but mousselines should really be served only as appetizers and first courses.

Bring a large kettle of water to a boil and preheat the oven to 325°F. Set the mousselines into a baking dish, then set the baking dish on the oven rack. Pour boiling water into the dish to ¼ inch below the rims of the ramekins or cups only now; should you fill the bath before putting it in the oven, you can slosh water onto the tops of the mousselines and onto your feet and legs. Cover the mousselines with a sheet of parchment paper to prevent a dry skin from forming on the top. The cooking time varies from 7 to 8 minutes for 1-ounce cups to 10 to 12 minutes for 2-ounce cups to 14 to 17 minutes for 3-ounce ramekins. The mousselines are usually done when the parchment lifts off easily. The mousseline is then unmolded, and a sauce can be placed under or over the mousseline(s) as you prefer.

SHELF LIFE OF MOUSSELINES

The shelf life of a mousseline paste prepared ahead of time is 24 hours, to be absolutely safe. It is good to know that mousselines can be made and kept in a very cold refrigerator a whole day ahead of time. After baking, their shelf life increases another 48 hours and you can serve them cold with a very lightened mayonnaise-derived sauce, a light vinaigrette, or a relish.

Fish Pâtés to Be Served Cold

Old-fashioned fish pâtés contained, besides a large amount of eggs, cream, and butter, a relatively larger amount of bread softened in milk and recooked, called *panade*, or a good dose of *pâte à choux* as described on page 1105. The results were overfat loaves in which the taste of the fish was much too light and diffuse. Today, a pâté is a simple mousseline paste containing a reduced amount of egg and stabilized with a small amount of oven-dried bread cubes soaked in milk. It is still a rich composition, but better balanced, with a rich fish taste and not nutritionally unreasonable if enjoyed once in a while.

Here are two recipes, one for a mousseline, the other for a pâté.

Three-Fish Mousseline

FFR—12 TO 16 FIRST-COURSE OR 8 MAIN-COURSE SERVINGS

For the mousseline

½ pound large deep-sea scallops, feet removed (save for the sauce) and diced

½ pound halibut fillet, skin and bones removed, diced

3 large egg whites

¼ pound smoked salmon of your choice, in one piece

6 tablespoons unsalted butter, at room temperature

1½ to 2 teaspoons salt, to your personal taste

35 turns of the pepper mill

2 to 3 cups deep-chilled heavy cream as needed

For the sauce

2 cups fish fumet (page 543)

2 cups fresh or bottled clam juice

2 cups dry white wine (Sauvignon Blanc or Chardonnay)

Feet of the scallops

4 large shallots, finely chopped

I large leek, white part only, well washed and finely chopped

Stems of a bunch of fresh dill, chopped

Small bouquet garni

⅓ cup heavy cream

6 to 12 tablespoons unsalted butter, to your personal taste, at room temperature

⅓ to ½ cup crème fraîche, to your personal taste

Sweet yellow mustard

2 to 3 tablespoons chopped fresh dill, to your personal taste

Fresh lemon juice

If you serve this composition as a luncheon main course, foresee a light jardinière of vegetables as an accompaniment (see page 382). *Use "day boat," large deep-sea scallops which have not been previously frozen, and either Scottish or Nova Scotia smoked salmon, if you do not smoke your own fish.*

This is serious culinary work, so please understand the techniques described in this recipe as outlined in the preceding pages before you start working; you will gain time, make no mistakes, and not lose any of the pricey ingredients.

SUGGESTED WINE: *A very buttery Chardonnay from California, or Les Resses Pouilly-Fuissé from the Madame Ferret vineyard in France*

To prepare the mousseline, process the scallops and halibut together in a food processor with 2 of the egg whites until smooth. Empty the puree into a non-reactive bowl; place this in another bowl filled with ice. Refrigerate for 2 hours, covered with plastic wrap.

Dice the smoked salmon into ¼-inch cubes and toss with the remaining egg white. Butter the ramekins evenly.

Add the butter, salt, and pepper to the cleaned food processor and pulse for several seconds, until the butter is soft. Add the chilled fish puree, generous tablespoon by generous tablespoon, until completely homogenized. Add the cream in four additions in a steady stream, testing the texture of the paste once or twice during the mixing.

Gather the smoked salmon cubes on a slotted spoon, leaving the excess egg white in the bowl; this can be discarded. Fold the salmon into the mousseline. Pack the finished mousseline into the prepared ramekins. Cover with a sheet of parchment paper and cook immediately or keep refrigerated for no longer than 24 hours before cooking.

Bake in a preheated 325°F oven in a hot water bath until the parchment paper lifts from the surface of the mousselines without difficulty, 12 to 17 minutes, depending on the size of ramekin (see page 693).

To prepare the sauce, mix together the fumet, clam juice, and wine in a large sauteuse pan. Add the scallop feet and all aromatics, bring to a boil. Reduce the heat to medium and simmer until reduced to 1½ cups of solids and liquids mixed.

Do not strain the reduction. Bring it back to a small boil, then add the heavy cream and continue reducing, about 15 minutes; strain the sauce through a conical strainer into a clean saucepan. Over very low heat, whisk in the room temperature butter. Mix the crème fraîche and mustard together in a small bowl, then gradually add half the prepared sauce base to this mixture. Reverse the process, whisking the warm cream mixture into the remainder of the base. The sauce will be light in texture. Add the dill and lemon juice to your taste and keep very warm without boiling.

Adjust the taste of your sauce with seasonings or lemon juice to show off both the mousseline and the wine. Garnish with light vegetables of your choice. Serve the sauce either over or under the mousseline.

Maddie's Salmon and Crab Cakes

FFR—12 CAKES

For the cakes

½ pound salmon meat, skin and bones removed

I large egg

3 tablespoons unsalted butter, at room temperature

¾ teaspoon salt

15 grinds of the pepper mill

Large grating of nutmeg

I cup heavy cream

½ pound blue crab backfin meat

Cake flour for dusting

You decide whether to make this 6 or 12 servings. This is a recipe I presented at lunch for the 1989 Napa Valley auction at Beringer Vineyards. For details on making the preparation of the salmon paste easy, see pages 690–91. You will need twelve 3-inch squares of parchment paper.

SUGGESTED WINE: *A*
Beringer Vineyards private reserve
Chardonnay of the current release

For the sauce

1 cup fish fumet (page 543)

1 cup bottled clam juice

1 cup dry white wine

2 tablespoons fino sherry as needed

3 shallots, finely chopped

Very small bouquet garni

Chopped stem of 1 large sprig fresh tarragon

Several stems fresh chervil leaves

½ cup crème fraîche

Unsalted butter as needed (optional)

To complete the dish

2 tablespoons unsalted butter

12 sprigs fresh chervil

Chopped fresh chervil leaves

Process the salmon meat and egg in the food processor until smooth. Chill the meat 2 hours.

Using a fork, mash the butter with the salt, pepper, and nutmeg. Return the salmon meat to the processor, add the seasoned butter, and process until homogeneous. Gradually add the cream. Empty into a bowl and carefully fold the crabmeat into the salmon mousseline. Using floured surgical gloves, shape the batter into 12 small cakes, then flour them lightly with cake flour and deposit each onto a parchment paper square.

Mix the fumet, clam juice, wine, sherry, shallots, bouquet garni, and tarragon and chervil stems together in a medium-size saucepan and reduce by two thirds over medium heat. Strain and add the crème fraîche; correct the seasoning and add just enough more sherry to make its lovely *flor* taste barely perceptible. Reheat well and whisk in butter to your taste, but only if you want to. Correct the final seasoning. Keep warm.

To cook and present the cakes, heat two tablespoons butter in a large electric frying pan preheated to 425°F. Grasp each square of paper and invert the surface of each cake into the hot butter. Cook until golden, then remove the paper, turn over with a spatula, and cook until golden on the second side.

Ladle an equal amount of the sauce into six plates. Place two cakes on each plate. Add a sprig of chervil and a dab of chopped chervil on top of each cake.

Pâté of Salmon and Shrimp with Orange Caramel Vinaigrette

FFR — 12 SERVINGS

For the salmon pâté

1 pound **Atlantic or Pacific silver salmon fillets, skin, bones, and brown tissues**
   removed

1 **large egg**

2 **large egg whites**

8 **jumbo shrimp, peeled, deveined, and cubed**

2 **tablespoons chopped fresh tarragon leaves**

2 **tablespoons chopped fresh chives**

⅔ **cup plain cubed dry bread stuffing**

½ to ⅔ **cup milk of your choice, as needed**

¼ **cup unsalted butter, at room temperature**

1½ **teaspoons salt**

35 **turns of the pepper mill**

2 **cups heavy cream**

For the vinaigrette

Juice of 4 Valencia oranges

1 **tablespoon balsamic vinegar**

1 **tablespoon sherry vinegar**

1 **shallot, extremely finely chopped**

Salt

Pepper from the mill

⅔ **cup pistachio oil or other unsaturated oil of your choice**

1½ **tablespoons chopped fresh tarragon leaves**

1½ **tablespoons chopped fresh chives**

This is rapidly put together and quite delicious. Change the salad components as you please to follow the seasons. Use a good brand of unflavored ordinary bread stuffing as used for Thanksgiving. The salad presented here is for early spring to early summer. The recipe can be multiplied to fit larger kitchen equipment.

SUGGESTED WINE: **A** *méthode champenoise sparkling wine from California of your choice, particularly Maison Deutz, Schramsberg, or Mumm Napa*

Process the salmon with the whole egg and 1 egg white in a food processor until fully pureed. Strain if needed through a drum sieve (see proper techniques on page 691) or simply turn into a nonreactive bowl; embed the bowl, covered with plastic wrap, in a larger bowl filled with ice cubes and keep refrigerated 2 hours. Clean the food processor.

Toss the shrimp with 1½ teaspoons each of the tarragon and chives in the remaining egg white; cover and keep refrigerated. Soak the bread stuffing in the milk until the milk has been completely absorbed and the mixture forms a uniform paste. Cover and keep refrigerated.

Cream the butter, salt, and pepper together in a food processor. Add the soaked bread stuffing alternately with the cold fish and process until homogeneous. Add the heavy cream in four additions. Test for seasoning; finally, turn into a bowl and fold in the shrimp with all the egg white surrounding it and the remainder of the herbs.

Preheat the oven to 325°F. Line a 1¼-quart loaf pan with parchment paper. Pack the pâté paste into the loaf pan and fold the paper over the top of the loaf. Set the loaf pan into a small hotel pan or deep baking dish. Bring a kettle of water to a boil and pour into the pan to reach within ¼ inch of the rim of the loaf pan. Bake until an instant thermometer reads 140° to 165°F, 15 to 20 minutes. Cool in the water bath, then remove from the pan. Keep the pâté in its baking paper and wrap in aluminum foil. Refrigerate 24 hours before serving.

To prepare the dressing, reduce the juice of 3 of the oranges in a small nonreactive saucepan over medium heat until it starts caramelizing at the bottom of the saucepan. Off the heat, dissolve the brownish juice completely with the remaining fresh juice. Add the vinegars, shallot, salt, and pepper, then whisk in the pistachio oil and homogenize well. Add the fresh herbs. Serve with the pâté cut into ⅓-inch-thick slices.

Possible vegetable garnishes:

- *Winter to spring*: Slivered fennel and slivered artichoke bottoms dressed as you please.
- *Spring to summer*: Asparagus and sliced crimini (brown) mushrooms dressed as you please.
- *Summer to fall*: Slivered zucchini and fresh tomatoes with basil, lemon, and olive dressing.
- *Fall to winter*: Mixed white and red endives dressed with the orange dressing from the pâté.

Quenelles

For a recipe for quenelles, see page 887.

All Manner of Cooking Meats

About Meats:
Definitions and Warnings

THIS CHAPTER IS DEDICATED TO MEAT AS A MAJOR SOURCE OF PROTEINS IN human nutrition.

The word *meat* refers to the muscle part of husbanded or wild animals as they are sold to us in markets and specialty shops (or as some of our family hunters detail their spoils after a successful hunt) and as they have been changed by the reactions that occur in the muscle after slaughtering (for an in-depth explanation of these reactions, see pages 716 to 718).

Beef as sold in modern markets or by modern purveyors is mostly obtained from steers and heifers, although in less expensive grades it will come from younger cows. Veal is obtained from young animals three weeks to three months old, while calf is obtained from animals three to eight months, and pork from either male or female pigs between the ages of eight months and one year. Lamb should normally be obtained from animals no more than six months old, but it is not rare for it to come from animals older than a full year, when it is then mutton.

Unless I indicate otherwise, for example, "offals" or "variety meats," by using the word *meat* I shall always mean the muscles from the different parts of the carcass of any animal used.

Because of the ever increasing population and the large urban concentration of millions to be fed, the shipping of meats over much larger distances is much more common nowadays than it was when each village had one butcher and each city sported well-organized corporations, hansas, and guilds of professional butchers, each doing its very best to offer quality and freshness. The food chain is now so long and so complicated in America that we eat lamb and venison raised in New Zealand and Australia.

Sometimes a piece of meat will reach our home or restaurant kitchen with a hidden bacteriological problem which will eventually result in our being ill for a few days. The tragic deaths of several young children after eating hamburger in a chain restaurant sent me to the library, and here is the list of problems you must anticipate by understanding that the proper cooking of meat is essential. It is nice to want to follow the fashion of eating very rare beef or venison, but it is now unsafe. I apologize to all my readers for such unpleasant writing but being a teacher I consider it my duty to draw the attention of readers to problems that can have significant consequences.

In meats you must watch for the following problem organisms:

IN BEEF E. coli 0157:H7 (there are several coli, but this seems to be a particularly dangerous one), called the "bad bug" in popular language, requires you to cook your hamburger to 160°F. E. coli damages the lining of the intestines and provokes small hemorrhages, which send infected blood to the small intestinal arteries.

E. coli survives refrigeration and freezing and can continue living happily at 44°F. Any food can be contaminated with it—undercooked hamburger and roast beef, unpasteurized milk, unpasteurized cider processed from unwashed apples which fell on soil contaminated by the manure of sick cows, vegetables grown in soils fertilized with cow manure. There is no way a farmer, however careful and conscientious, can know which cow is contaminated and which is not. So it is up to you to cook the beef you buy properly.

What makes ground beef even more susceptible to E. coli contamination than a solid piece of meat is its passing through the blade(s) of a meat grinder. The blades of a grinder must be sanitized after each use, a sanitary standard that is not always observed and which offers E. coli an opportunity to develop within the grinder components and to contaminate successive batches of ground meat. See the sections on ground meats on page 867.

IN PORK AND VENISON Trichinella spiralis is still found in these animals even if porkers are raised in cleaner environments nowadays. Trichinellae, microscopic nematode worms, transmit the disease known as trichinosis, settling in human muscles and making a person extremely sick for several weeks.

According to information gathered in all modern food science books, the minimal temperature to which any cut of pork should be cooked is 137°F, in order for all possible existing trichinellae to be rendered harmless. However, my ears are always very attuned to all kinds of information and I have heard enough "interesting" stories to make it a personal rule never to trust such a low temperature in pork, for if it takes care of the trichinellae problem, it does not ensure that there will not be a bacterial one.

Pork shoulder tastes best when baked slowly and deeply to an internal temperature of 160° to 170°F, but the loin and the tenderloin when cooked to this higher temperature are too dry. You may have heard that so as to be able to cook these two cuts medium rare for maximum enjoyment and total safety, you should purchase the loin and tenderloin ahead of time and freeze each for twenty-three full days at 5°F in a professional freezer equipped with a freezer thermometer. This freezing will indeed kill all trichinellae, but it will not kill bacteria, so it is not entirely safe. For that reason, loins and tenderloins should still be cooked to an internal temperature of 160°F.

IN CHICKEN ESPECIALLY, BUT ALSO IN ALL OTHER MEATS
Salmonella can be found in all meats, including meat products such as sausage and high-protein salads made with meats. Salmonella in eggs is on its way to being controlled as mentioned in the egg chapter, but you should cook whole roasted poultry to an internal temperature of 180°F regardless of whether the bird has been stuffed or not.

Beware of cross-contamination (see details on page 19), resulting from contact with pets such as turtles, birds, fish, and dogs which can be carriers and contaminate your family and yourself, which in turn can contaminate any meat. Please read as much as you can about salmonella and especially its sources.

ABOUT SAFE INTERNAL TEMPERATURES FOR COOKED MEATS
In view of what was just discussed, you will find all through this chapter, two sets of possible internal temperatures for cooked and ready-to-serve meats. One set represents the temperatures formerly recommended to obtain succulent and/or soft-textured meats. The second set follows the present recommendations given by the U.S. Department of Agriculture (see chart at right). If you raise your own free-range cattle and chickens with organic feeds, this double system will allow you to still use the classic temperatures if you prefer. But if your sources for meats are purveyors, butchers, or supermarkets, please use the USDA set of temperatures; you are in any case, and at all times, responsible for the safety of the meats you cook.

Up to the last twenty years, red meats occupied the center of the dinner plate in the majority of families. However, because of the nutritional discoveries of the last quarter century and the belief held by an increasing number of people that raising cattle may not be the most beneficial use of our environmental resources, we have started to favor poultry and fish; the length of the fish chapter partly reflects this change.

However, I shall again preach moderation and cannot insist enough that if you are not a pure vegetarian by conviction, a moderate amount of red meat well defatted can only be beneficial to your intake of natural vitamins. This chapter reflects my personal feelings on the types of meats that are best put on today's table; if you prefer to serve a wider range of red meat, by all means do so. To help you, I indicate in many of the recipes for white meats whether one of the red meats may be substituted and, if it can, which other ingredients should be used to harmonize the recipe to beef or lamb.

Besides 67 to 75 percent water, meat contains approximately 1 percent minerals, such as iron, phosphorus, and copper, and a large dose of vitamins, especially those of the B complex. The average protein content of meats, whether red or white, is around 18 percent. The average fat content is 13 percent, lower in poultry and usually higher in red meats. Nutritionally it is important to know that meat proteins, eaten in the right proportions, contain all the essential amino acids necessary for body tissues to grow and main-

The U.S. Department of Agriculture recommends the following minimum internal temperatures when cooking meats (always use a clean instant-read thermometer):

Fresh ground beef, veal, lamb, pork . . . . **160°F**

Beef, veal, lamb—roasts, steaks, chops
Medium rare . . . . **145°F**
Medium . . . . **160°F**
Well done . . . . **170°F**

Fresh pork—roasts, steaks, chops
Medium . . . . **160°F**
Well done . . . . **170°F**

Ham
Cook before eating . . . . **160°F**
Fully cooked, to reheat . . . . **140°F**

Poultry
Ground chicken, turkey . . . **165°F**
Whole chicken, turkey . . . . **180°F**
Breasts, roasts . . . . **170°F**
Thighs and wings . . . . Cook until juices run clear

Stuffing
(cooked alone or in bird) . . . **165°F**

Egg dishes, casseroles . . . **160°F**

Leftovers . . . . **165°F**

For more information call the Meat and Poultry Hotline 1-800-535-4555 or in the District of Columbia area (202) 720-3333

AVERAGE FAT AND CHOLESTEROL CONTENTS OF MOST COMMONLY USED MEATS (PER 3-OUNCE [84-GRAM] PORTION CALCULATED FOR A CONTENT OF 10% FAT ON EACH TYPE OF MEAT)

Type of meat	Total fat/grams	Cholesterol/mg	Type of meat	Total fat/grams	Cholesterol/mg
Beef			Turkey		
10% fat, lean only	8.1	78	White meat, skinless	2.1	66
			Dark meat, skinless	4.5	87
Lamb					
10% fat, lean only	8.4	84	Duck		
			Skinless meat	6.9	n.a.
Veal					
6% fat, lean only	9.0	84	Quail		
			Whole, with skin	6.0	n.a.
Pork (ham)					
10% fat, lean only	8.4	75	Goose		
			Skinless meat	6.0	n.a.
Chicken					
White meat, skinless	4.2	66	Rabbit	5.4	41 mg
Dark meat, skinless	5.4	78			

Source: Dr. Dean Ornish, *Program for Reversing Heart Disease*, Random House, New York, 1990. The unit used in Dr. Ornish's book being the ounce, the amounts of fat and cholesterol have been multiplied by 3 to obtain the full amount of each in a 3-ounce serving portion.

tain themselves in a state of good repair; meat proteins keep their whole nutritional value after cooking.

In this chapter meat recipes are grouped by techniques of cookery rather than by categories of meats with the exception of the ground meats. However, within each technique, the particularities of each kind of meat or bird are well defined and outlined. For specific recipes for chicken and other birds, domesticated or wild, veal, beef, lamb, venison, or rabbit, look under those headings in the index.

Generalities on Red Meats and Pork

The likelihood of buying an ungraded meat is small in our modern markets; nevertheless, be sure to look for the stamp on the fat side of the meat.

The round stamp tells you that the meat has been "inspected and passed," i.e., that it has been processed under the best sanitary conditions and comes from a perfectly healthy animal. The round stamp is applied by federal agents; meats cannot be sold from state to state without carrying this stamp.

The shield-shaped stamp tells you which grade of meat you are buying, whether *prime*, *choice*, or *good*.

All other grades of meats come from healthy but older animals and are sold to process as luncheon meats. Grading is done voluntarily by meat packers; however, you must appreciate whether the stamp corresponds to the quality offered for sale.

Recognizing the Quality of Meats by Sight

It is up to you to recognize the grade and quality of a piece of meat when you buy it. If, for a very special occasion, you buy a piece of prime red meat, it will show thin regular fat layers, called marbling, very visibly running through the grain of the meat. Choice meats should be used for everyday cooking and will show small or no fat deposits between the muscles fibers, and the covering of fat, called the finish, of the meat will not be thicker than ⅔ inch in beef and ¼ inch on legs of lamb, even less on lamb rib racks and French saddles (another name for the full loin). The fat of beef is pinkish, that of lamb white; both are solid and quite saturated. Meats graded "good" are usually not available in supermarkets or butcher shops, but rather from purveyors. They are mostly used for government agencies and for the making of variety meat products.

Pork as produced for modern consumption is much leaner than it used to be and as such has lost quite a bit of its old-fashioned flavor. Being much less fat, it is better adapted to grilling and can be cooked using techniques different from the old-fashioned baking. You will see recipes for pork in this chapter that will be served pink instead of the old-fashioned gray. Notice that such recipes are always accompanied by the caution to freeze the raw meat for twenty-three days before cooking to insure that all trichinellae parasites (those responsible for trichinosis) are disposed of (see page 702 for more details).

Because a butcher does not wrap the meat he sells in a tight layer of plastic wrap, any large joint of meat bought from him will be nice and dry as opposed to those you remove from plastic supermarket wrappers. The cuts in which you will most appreciate this difference are leg of lamb, rib roast of beef, and pork loin roast. Any wettish piece of meat must be dried carefully with paper towels before cooking to prevent poor, slow searing.

Primal Cuts of Beef, Lamb, Veal, and Pork

Each carcass is usually separated into four quarters known as the four primal cuts: the chuck or shoulder, the rib, the loin, and the round or leg. Out of each primal cut are detailed the different joints you can buy in a market or butcher shop. Here are the charts of the different cuts and their position in the carcass of each type of animal.

The shoulder and leg cuts contain joints that can be roasted and/or slow cooked as braises and stews, whereas the ribs and loin produce joints that

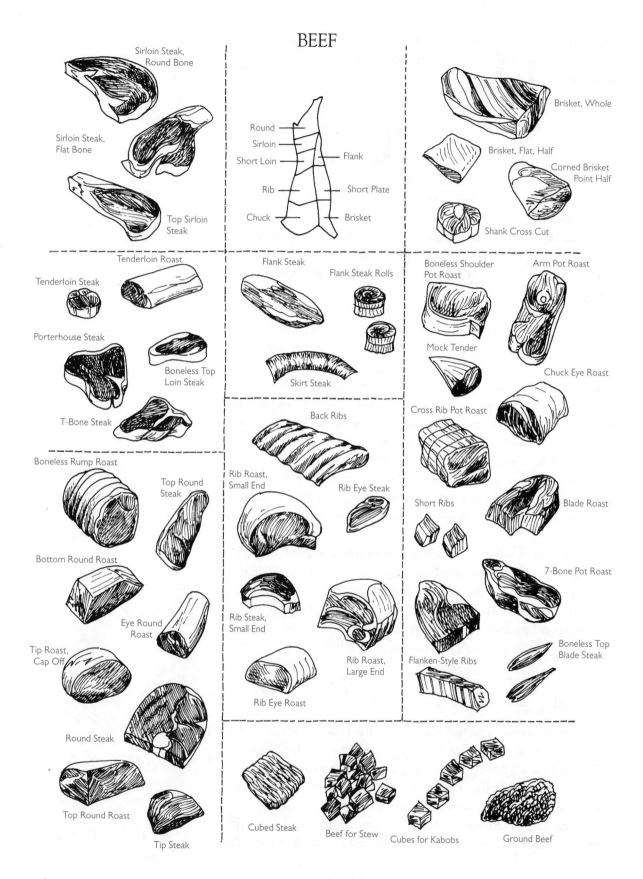

BEEF

Sirloin Steak, Round Bone

Sirloin Steak, Flat Bone

Top Sirloin Steak

Round
Sirloin
Short Loin
Rib
Chuck
Flank
Short Plate
Brisket

Brisket, Whole

Brisket, Flat, Half

Corned Brisket Point Half

Shank Cross Cut

Tenderloin Roast

Tenderloin Steak

Porterhouse Steak

Boneless Top Loin Steak

T-Bone Steak

Flank Steak

Flank Steak Rolls

Skirt Steak

Boneless Shoulder Pot Roast

Arm Pot Roast

Mock Tender

Chuck Eye Roast

Cross Rib Pot Roast

Boneless Rump Roast

Top Round Steak

Bottom Round Roast

Eye Round Roast

Tip Roast, Cap Off

Round Steak

Top Round Roast

Tip Steak

Back Ribs

Rib Roast, Small End

Rib Eye Steak

Rib Steak, Small End

Rib Roast, Large End

Rib Eye Roast

Short Ribs

Blade Roast

7-Bone Pot Roast

Flanken-Style Ribs

Boneless Top Blade Steak

Cubed Steak

Beef for Stew

Cubes for Kabobs

Ground Beef

LAMB

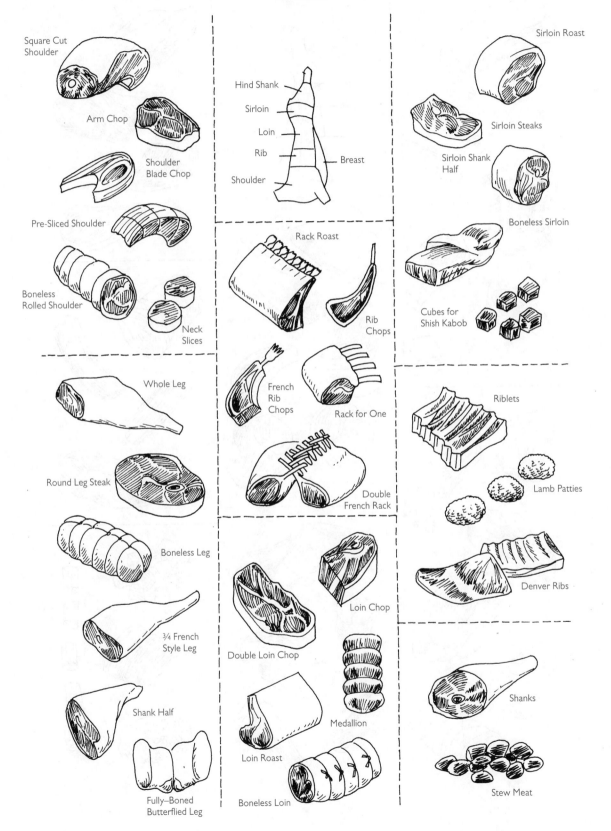

Square Cut Shoulder

Arm Chop

Shoulder Blade Chop

Pre-Sliced Shoulder

Boneless Rolled Shoulder

Neck Slices

Hind Shank

Sirloin

Loin

Rib

Shoulder

Breast

Rack Roast

Rib Chops

French Rib Chops

Rack for One

Double French Rack

Sirloin Roast

Sirloin Steaks

Sirloin Shank Half

Boneless Sirloin

Cubes for Shish Kabob

Riblets

Lamb Patties

Denver Ribs

Whole Leg

Round Leg Steak

Boneless Leg

¾ French Style Leg

Shank Half

Fully–Boned Butterflied Leg

Double Loin Chop

Loin Chop

Loin Roast

Boneless Loin

Medallion

Shanks

Stew Meat

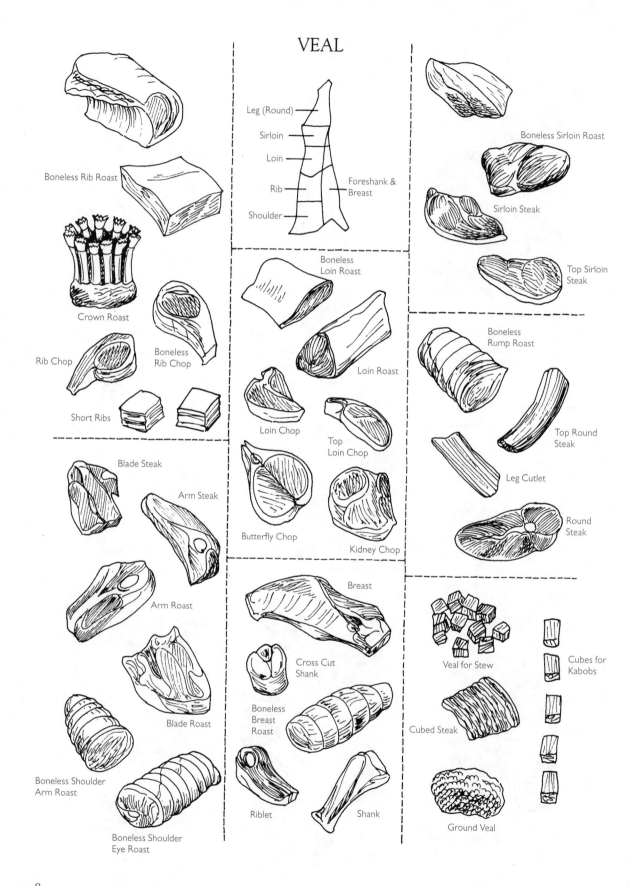

VEAL

Leg (Round)

Sirloin

Loin

Rib

Shoulder

Foreshank & Breast

Boneless Rib Roast

Crown Roast

Rib Chop

Boneless Rib Chop

Short Ribs

Blade Steak

Arm Steak

Arm Roast

Blade Roast

Boneless Shoulder Arm Roast

Boneless Shoulder Eye Roast

Boneless Loin Roast

Loin Roast

Loin Chop

Top Loin Chop

Butterfly Chop

Kidney Chop

Breast

Cross Cut Shank

Boneless Breast Roast

Riblet

Shank

Boneless Sirloin Roast

Sirloin Steak

Top Sirloin Steak

Boneless Rump Roast

Top Round Steak

Leg Cutlet

Round Steak

Veal for Stew

Cubes for Kabobs

Cubed Steak

Ground Veal

PORK

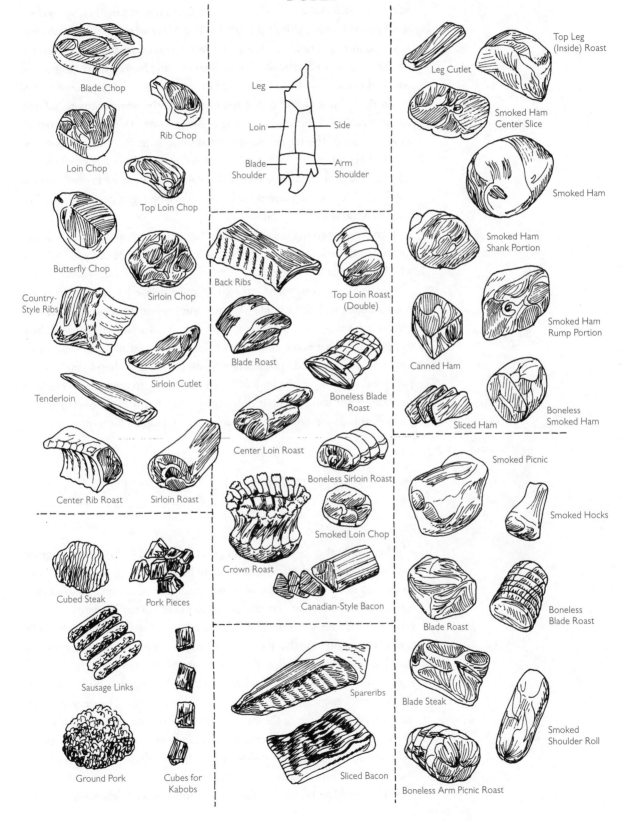

Blade Chop

Rib Chop

Loin Chop

Top Loin Chop

Butterfly Chop

Country-Style Ribs

Sirloin Chop

Tenderloin

Sirloin Cutlet

Center Rib Roast

Sirloin Roast

Leg

Loin

Side

Blade Shoulder

Arm Shoulder

Back Ribs

Top Loin Roast (Double)

Blade Roast

Boneless Blade Roast

Center Loin Roast

Boneless Sirloin Roast

Smoked Loin Chop

Crown Roast

Canadian-Style Bacon

Leg Cutlet

Top Leg (Inside) Roast

Smoked Ham Center Slice

Smoked Ham

Smoked Ham Shank Portion

Canned Ham

Smoked Ham Rump Portion

Sliced Ham

Boneless Smoked Ham

Smoked Picnic

Smoked Hocks

Boneless Blade Roast

Blade Roast

Blade Steak

Smoked Shoulder Roll

Boneless Arm Picnic Roast

Cubed Steak

Pork Pieces

Sausage Links

Ground Pork

Cubes for Kabobs

Spareribs

Sliced Bacon

should only be roasted or, if cut into steaks, grilled or panfried. If you read the sale tag of each and every piece of meat you can buy in a market, you will see it reflects this information; the label will tell you whether the meat comes from the shoulder, rib, loin, or leg, and recommended methods of cooking.

Purveyors sell full carcasses, sides, quarters, and broken down primal cuts wrapped in Cryovac. Meats purchased in Cryovac have been vacuum packed in plastic and it is essential that you check that the wrapper tightly adheres to the meat on all its sides; the aging of beef packed in Cryovac is extremely slow because of the negligible amount of oxygen in the wrapper, but Cryovacked beef does age and can be kept for two to three weeks when well refrigerated. Such is not the case with lamb which must be frozen if kept at any length in Cryovac; anaerobic bacteria develop rapidly on lamb that has been Cryovacked and spoil it.

If you cannot go to market every few days, and you purchased Cryovacked meats, use those joints in which there is a pocket of air before you use those which remain tightly sealed.

If your family is not large enough so you can use larger cuts, acquire a small vacuum sealing machine; they are quite reasonably priced. When you receive a delivery, recut the meat yourself into smaller portions and seal them in plastic bags that you can later thaw slowly in the refrigerator. When buying in a supermarket, do not hesitate to ask the butcher shop to unwrap the package and show you the underside of any meat, or to get a special cut from the refrigerator and prepare it differently from what is being offered on the shelf. This is your privilege, for you are paying top dollar for meats.

Recognizing the Quality and Types of Poultry by Sight

Chickens and other birds are sold in grades A, B, and C. Usually only grade A is available for sale; grade B birds are to be found mostly as fowl for soup, broth, and stock. Grade C are to be obtained only from purveyors and they can be used for stocks at very advantageous prices; do not hesitate to do so if you have a freezer for storage of larger amounts of stocks and broths. Any family well outfitted with a large freezer can purchase meats for stocks from a meat purveyor; see the Yellow Pages for information.

Chickens, Cornish hens, and turkeys are white-meated birds. They all should have a roundish look with a nicely plump breast. The only fat to be seen is at the entrance of the cavity, where the two fat pads are always left attached, and over the backbone; *there should be absolutely no other fat visible under the skin*. The fat of white-meated poultry is yellow, flabby, and pliable and visibly less saturated than that of red meats.

There should be no tears in the skin or pinfeathers anywhere on the bird, and when you cook and carve it, you should not find an unpleasant brown blotch along the thigh bones, which would tell you that the chicken has been processed too fast and was not given enough time to bleed completely. This does not happen in the top quality large fryers and roasters that are proudly offered by the best poultry houses in the country. The color of the meat in good, white-meated poultry is clearly visible through the skin.

Up to a few years ago, the giblets were wrapped in a bag and were to be found in the cavity of the chicken; very often nowadays, if they are present at all, the giblets are not wrapped and you may find a chicken with two hearts and no liver, half a neck or two necks. The gizzards, which gives gravy a great taste, are often not included but sold separately in trays. The turkeys of Thanksgiving still retain their giblets in a bag tucked under the neck skin.

Guinea hens and farm-raised pheasants have very dark leg meat and light breast meat. They should be evaluated as for white-meated poultry.

Squabs and quail are deep red-meated poultry; their skin is very thin and tears easily and reveals the depth of the color in their meat. They are available both fresh and frozen.

The white-feathered duck known as white Pekin always has a skin lined with a ¼- to ⅓-inch fat layer; most of it will be disposed of in slow roasting the birds. Such a duck can weigh up to six pounds.

Black-feathered Muscovy ducks, which can weigh up to eight pounds, are much leaner and an excellent source of totally fat-free red meat much less saturated than beef or lamb. Their fat can be discarded or kept for use in confits (see page 790) and their breasts can be cooked exactly like lean beefsteak. At this date Muscovies are not available in supermarkets, but can easily be bought from butchers or purveyors and stocked in the freezer.

A third type of duck exists that is available through purveyors and butchers: the Moulard duck. It is a large, very lean animal, the result in the United States of a crossbreed between a female white Pekin and a male Muscovy. These ducks are specially bred for the production of fattened livers for the restaurant industry. The term *Moulard* is an American one. In France the name Moulard is given to the offspring of a female white goose crossbred with a male Muscovy duck, because, like a mule, they are sterile and cannot reproduce themselves.

Geese are available mostly frozen from butchers or purveyors. Their deep red meat can be treated exactly like duck.

Dressed poultry is sold fully feathered but with its head, feet, and viscera still attached, while *ready-to-cook poultry* is completely cleaned inside and out and ready for trussing. A few of the better poultry houses sell their ready-to-cook birds already trussed.

Purchasing Large Amounts of Meats for the Freezer

This paragraph is for cooks who buy meats in quantity to store in the freezer for reasons of economy or availability. It may be a good idea to acquire *Specs*, the book professional cooks and chefs use to order their meats (see bibliography for details). This book outlines all the cuts available for purchase and lists them by a code number preceded by the letters IMPS (Institutional Meat Purchase Specifications). Using this book will allow you to purchase exactly the cuts you want, as opposed to purchasing a whole carcass, having it detailed, and finding yourself the proud owner of pounds of more or less fatty ground meat for which you have little use. By using *Specs*, all you have to do is find the code number for the cut you wish and list it with the grade of meat you would like. You will pay a little more, but each and every piece will be prepared as you prefer it.

How to Defrost Meats

The way you defrost your meat and poultry will affect the way it will taste cooked. Do not remove meats from the freezer to let them defrost on a kitchen counter; it's not a good idea from a food safety standpoint, not to mention that the meat will lose all its juices in the freezing bag and taste dry and unpalatable after cooking.

To defrost with no loss of juices requires some planning. Remove the meat from the freezer, wrap it in a thick kitchen towel, and *defrost it in the refrigerator* the following length of time:

- Steaks, chops, and chicken pieces: 24 hours.
- Roasts and birds: 2 to 3 days, depending on size.

Defrosted this way, meats remain very juicy, pork especially, which loses almost no juices at all. Bring the meat to room temperature for 30 minutes before cooking it; it will allow it to start cooking immediately instead of unchilling first, and only then start cooking.

A Quick Look into the Structure of Meats

The following section is about the structure of meats. If you do not feel like reading about it that's fine, but if you are a professional or intend to become one, you will find here simplified information which is directly related to the quality of the meat you buy and serve. Also refer to the bibliography for books that offer detailed information on the structure of the meat muscles. This is something we learn in cooking school and proceed to forget as soon as we are out of the "learning" world, but that we should try to remember in order to be able to read a piece of meat in greater depth.

For the sake of learning, the next time you plan to have company, order a whole tenderloin of beef with its fat cover, for this is probably where you will find the best visible lesson in reading a piece of meat. As you strip the piece of meat of fat yourself, you will better understand why meat can cost so much more if sold to you ready to cook.

Adipose Tissues Versus Marbling

The whole muscle of the tenderloin is surrounded by a large cover of fat known as the *adipose tissues*. As you remove this fat you will realize that it breaks down into smaller pieces of fat, each surrounded by very thin, transparent membranes. Here and there you will find grayish pink nuggets, which are lymph nodes. All the other large muscles in a carcass are surrounded by thick adipose tissues which protect them from bacteria as the meat hangs and ages.

You may find, if your tenderloin is of prime grade, another type of fat running through the meat fibers; separated into thin filmlike deposits that spread across the muscle tissues, this fat is called *marbling*. When the meat cooks, this fat melts and some of it will find itself suspended in droplets in the meat juices; this suspended fat will stimulate salivation and thus increase the feeling of juiciness on the taste buds and palate. Marbling is the only fat tissue in meat that is useful. In modern cookery, the adipose covering is usually removed to limit the consumption of fats.

As you remove the fatty tissues, you will find the whole muscle to be covered by a thick membrane that cooks call the *silverskin* but is known as the aponeurosis in anatomical terms. This long, bluish membrane thickens at each end of the muscle to form tendons and ligaments. This membrane must be removed so the tenderloin can roast without buckling into a semicircular shape. To do so, pass the knife blade as close as you can between meat and membrane at the center of the tenderloin; continue sliding the blade forward in both directions successively, until the meat is free of all traces of silverskin. The underside of the tenderloin reveals small pads of fats which also should be removed.

Just below the silverskin and inseparable from it by a knife (you will have removed it with the silverskin), is the epymisium. The epymisium surrounds the whole edible part of the muscle and is not visible to the unassisted eye.

Now cut the flatter end of the tenderloin, usually called the tail, and you will see the muscle fibers. They are gathered into large bundles surrounded by yet another membrane also invisible to the naked eye called the perimysium.

You can eventually see small blood vessels nestled in the tiny interstices between epimysium and perimysium and distinguish very clearly the large bundles of muscle fibers. Their size determines the so-called grain of the meat. When you next buy a rib steak and a strip steak, compare the grain of those two with that of the tenderloin; do the same with the grain of a true eye of the round or that of a blade chuck roast and you will soon understand that the finer the grain, the more tender the meat.

If you take a strong magnifying glass, you will be able to distinguish that inside larger secondary bundles of muscle fibers are primary bundles separated from one another by yet another invisible membrane, the endomysium. More than that cannot be distinguished by the naked eye, but if you have access to a microscope, you will see what scientists have described in science books: the structure of the many single muscle fibers. This structure is explained in great detail in many of the books appearing in the bibliography.

Connective Tissues

Tendons, ligaments, silverskin, epimysium, perimysium, and endomysium are all connective tissues. All connective tissues are made of several different tissues, the two most important of which are elastin and collagen. Elastin and collagen are proteins of two different types.

Elastin is useless to the cook; it neither softens nor melts, but rather contracts and shrinks when submitted to heat and remains, even after long cooking, totally inedible. You will recognize elastin as you bone meat; it is a pearly white tissue so tough that even the tip of a paring knife cannot penetrate it easily and a boning or chef's knife cuts through it only with difficulty. A large band of elastin can be found all along the backbone of any four-legged animal; in the lamb it is barely ½ inch wide while in cattle it is more than an inch wide. If you leave this band of elastin on a rib roast, it will, like the silverskin mentioned on page 713, bend into a semicircle as the elastin contracts while heating.

Collagen is the most important of all connective tissues for the cook; its complicated structure of interwoven tightly coiled fibrils breaks down into amorphous *gelatin* when the meat cooks. During cooking, the gelatin goes into suspension in the water contained in the meat and circulates freely between the meat fibers. The melted fat forms droplets which stay in emulsion in the meat juices. It is the tactile perception by the tongue and taste buds of these rich juices coating the firmer meat fibers that makes us say that a meat is tender.

The older the meat cooked, the longer it takes to break down its collagen; to understand the relation of the age of the meat to the speed of the denaturation of its collagenous tissues, simply compare the lengths of time needed to pot roast a chicken, a veal roast, and a beef roast, as well as the thickness and richness of their respective gravies. Veal, which is a young animal, yields stock much more gelatinous than that from beef because the percentage of connective tissues in muscles is larger in younger animals. The concentrations of both collagen and elastin diminish as the age of the animal increases and veal becomes steer, then beef.

Muscle Cells

The muscle cells of a meat are not visible to the naked eye; they consist of microscopic fibrils surrounded by yet another connective membrane called the sarcolemma. The sarcolemma consists of two parts: contractile myofibrils and the slightly viscous fluid sarcoplasm, which keeps the contractile myofibrils together. It also contains diverse elements that assist in transmitting nerve impulses to the muscle cells, as well as glycogen granules, which are a second source of energy for the muscle cells. Glycogen, which is stored in the muscles and the liver, is made up of repeating units of glucose, the simple sugar contained in the blood of mammals.

The structure of the muscle cells is extremely complicated; it is described here as succinctly as possible to allow the cook to understand the process of aging meats described on page 717. Muscle cells can be as long as the entire length of a muscle. They are made up of tiny fibers gathered tightly together into bands of thick and thin filaments called sarcomeres. Each sarcomere is separated from the next by a thin dark line called the Z line. The thick filaments are made of the protein myosin, and the thin ones of two different proteins called F-actin and tropomyosin. When the muscle is at rest, it contains a large amount of a chemical compound called adenosine triphosphate, usually simplified to ATP. As soon as the brain gives muscles the signal to contract, thick and thin filaments slide past one another and the heads of the myosin molecules form cross-links with the actin in the filaments, thus producing a third protein called actinomyosin. Muscle contractions are possible thanks to the oxygen brought to the muscle cells by the circulation of blood.

Color of Meats

The pigment responsible for the color of the surface of meats is called myoglobin. Myoglobin consists of an iron-containing pigment called a heme group and of an iron molecule which is attached to a protein called globin. Myoglobin takes the oxygen from the bloodstream and stores it in the muscle cells for use during contraction.

The appearance of the surface of a meat depends on its chemical state. In fresh meats as displayed for sale in butcher shops, myoglobin is purplish red. As soon as a piece of meat is cut, the surface turns bright red because the myoglobin turns into oxymyoglobin because of its exposure to the oxygen in the air. If the same piece of meat is left exposed to the air a certain length of time, the oxymyoglobin continues to oxidize and turns to the dark brown pigment metmyoglobin. Metmyoglobin is the result of the chemical modification by the oxygen of the iron molecule present in the myoglobin.

Beef, lamb, duck, and quail are all red meats but with large variations in color. Pork, chicken, and turkey have "dark" and "white" meats. In all animals the difference of color in meats is tied to the amount of myoglobin and consequently of oxygen kept in storage in the different muscles. The more myoglobin and oxygen a muscle contains, the better it can contract. This makes it easy to understand why chicken legs are made of dark meat and chicken breasts of white meat.

The cook can gather a lot of information from observing the color of any piece of meat. The depth of the red coloration also varies with the age of the animal: Young lamb is never deeper colored than a pretty rose, while mutton is frankly red, having exercised its limbs longer. The color of a leg of lamb can tell you, besides its weight, whether you are buying a leg of true lamb or that of an older lamb just about to turn to mutton. Veal is pale pink when milk fed or fed by the Provimi method (an anagram for the type of feed its receives: proteins-vitamins-minerals), but rose when free ranging and grass fed. Steer is light ruby red, but in all categories, you will find the leg and shoulder meats to be darker than the loin and tenderloin because legs and shoulders exercise more than the loin.

Aged Meats

In order to evaluate the quality of meat, you must understand that, once the animal has been slaughtered, different reactions continue to take place in its tissues which modify their composition in ways that are important for the taste and texture of the meat.

After slaughter, the temperature of the animal starts to decrease gradually, the carcass stiffening into the well-known rigor mortis, best observed in birds that have just been shot during a hunting party. This happens because there is no more blood circulation to bring a supply of oxygen to the muscle cells. These cells now exist only on the energy they can still derive from their stored sugars (glycogen). As the carcass cools, the muscle fibers contract more and more as myosin and actin cross-link. With the help of enzymes, the glycogen present in the muscles fibers is degraded to a relatively large amount of lactic acid which accumulates in the meat, since there is no more blood circulation to remove it. This is why, if a steak or roast is cooked while the meat is still in rigor, it will have a tough texture and a noticeably acid taste when cooked rare. I experienced such meats during the war, since the only little bit of meat we had was sold as soon as slaughtered and we were too hungry to let it sit and lose its rigor.

Aging carcasses are hung upside down to allow the muscle fibers to stretch again. As the meat "ages," the stiffness disappears. The speed with which rigor mortis dissipates varies with the temperature at which the meat is stored. Loss of water happens gradually, and a number of enzymes go to work and provoke the dissolution of the Z lines. This is called autolysis. You may have experienced this in tenderloins which are overaged and are so tender and so powdery dry that you almost can feel the separation of the muscle fibrils as you eat the meat. In normally aged meats, the large protein molecules are split only enough to make the meat tender.

Knowing the process of rigor mortis, you can now understand why those frozen legs of lamb found in all eastern and midwestern supermarkets imported from the Southern Hemisphere are often found to be tough. Most probably, they were flash frozen too soon after slaughtering, before rigor mortis had started. As you defrost the meat, the rigor cycle will start and if you feel and observe the meat it usually feels very tight under the hand. This is called thaw rigor and it lasts a good forty-eight hours or even longer. Do not cook such a leg of lamb; it will not be ready for consumption for at least a full week after complete defrosting. Defrost it in the refrigerator, then let it sit there another six to seven days so the enzymes can do their work; you will be surprised how good this usually tough lamb tastes and feels to the palate. This defrosting-aging technique can be applied to all other meats that you suspect to be in thaw rigor, taking into consideration the fact that smaller animals such as chickens or rabbits will soften much faster than lamb or beef. All free-range chickens, which have strong muscles from roaming the fields, should age one week to ten days in a refrigerator before being roasted. I learned from Mr. Wilson, famous for his Wilson's Fields Organic Kentucky chickens, that he aged some of his own experimental birds much longer than that.

In Colorado, Texas, and California lambs, the same phenomenon occurs if the lamb legs have been refrigerated at a very low temperature before rigor has had time to set in; this is called cold shortening. Let the legs rest a week in the refrigerator and you will have the best piece of meat ever, once you strip it of its fell (membrane) and roast it.

Have you ever cleaned a piece of tenderloin, its meat almost purple-red? Did you find it did not cut "clean" even with the sharpest knife, but showed irregular protruding of the muscle fibers, making them look almost like miniature organ pipes? The meat felt sticky and viscous to the hand and, when cooked, tasted somewhat sticky and gummy and not remarkably favorful? Scientists call such a piece of beef "dark cutting beef." Such a tenderloin comes from an animal that was so stressed, nervous, and agitated before slaughtering that its muscles were left totally exhausted of any trace of glycogen, resulting in ready-to-cook meat containing little or no lactic acid.

An identical reaction may happen in pork, which butchers then call PSE pork, an abbreviation for pale, soft, and exudative pork. That occasional extra-dry textured pork roast which every one of us has eventually experienced may be due to overcooking, but it can also be the result of such PSE pork.

To sum up the last paragraphs, a well-aged and tasty meat with good texture when cooked is the result of a combination of factors: proper hanging in the vertical position until rigor mortis has dissipated; and enough but not too much breakdown of the meat fibers by the combined influences of lactic acid, enzymes, and bacteria working as a team to modify the appearance and smell of the uncooked meat and ultimately the taste and texture of the cooked meat.

Cooked Meats

When meats are cooked, their proteins undergo a number of changes. Changes in the muscle tissues happen as soon as the inner temperature of the meat reaches between 105° and 110°F. The muscle fibers shorten considerably in length and shrink in width; the muscle fibrils pack tightly against one another, releasing the water contained in their proteins. Soon the collagenous connective tissues will soften in this water, turn into gelatin, and be released in the form of meat juices which will drip or slowly flow out of the piece of meat.

These juices will form a small gravy if the meat is cooked by one of the dry heat cooking procedures such as broiling, roasting, or baking or enrich the liquid in which the meat is cooked if the meat is poached, boiled, stewed, or braised. The gravy, broth, or sauce will acquire the characteristic texture of a plain liquid enriched with gelatin and gel when cold. The more the connective tissues denature, the more tender the meat becomes. The perception of tenderness in the mouth is helped further by the melting of the marbling fat, some of which emulsifies in the protein-laden meat juices.

THE PRINCIPLE OF "CARRYOVER HEAT" It is essential that you remember a very important physical phenomenon that takes place in meats that have just been cooked and are coming out of the oven or the frying pan.

The term "carryover heat" is given to the increase in temperature that occurs in any meat that has just been removed from the source of heat in which it cooked. Since the internal temperature of a piece of meat keeps increasing for a few minutes after removal from any oven or pan, the meat will continue cooking, and it is essential that you take this fact into consideration if you do not want to serve overcooked meat. Remember that the larger the piece, the greater the internal temperature increase. Where you can expect the internal temperature of a 2-inch-thick London broil to rise about 12 more degrees while waiting to be sliced, a small bird like a pigeon, a large quail, or a Cornish hen would see its final temperature increase 15 degrees, while the temperature of very large roasts can go up by 18 to 20 degrees.

To avoid unpleasant surprises, use an instant thermometer and remove the meat in time for it to finish cooking to the right degree of doneness off the heat. The waiting time for large roasts is explained in detail on page 747.

Choosing Meats

Two general categories of meats are found for sale: the regular meats as purchased in supermarkets and free-range meats as offered by purveyors and some butcher shops. Free-range animals are allowed to roam freely and graze, in the case of bovines and lamb, while chickens are let out of their cages to scratch for their own secret morsels. There is no doubt as to the superiority in taste of free-range veal, lamb, and chicken. Investigate both types of meats; you will find varying differences in price between both. Give a chance to each kind, using the same techniques of cookery and making a comparison for yourself without listening to other opinions.

Special Procedures: Tenderizing and Marinating

Since tender, quick-cooking cuts are not within the reach of every purse every day, many ways of tenderizing less naturally succulent meats have been tried.

I strongly urge cooks not to use meat tenderizers that contain an enzyme extracted from papaya. When such tenderizers are sprinkled on the meat, they break down the Z lines, separating the muscle cell sarcomeres only on the superficial layers of the meat; they do not penetrate into the deeper layers. As a result, tenderizers work with supreme efficiency on the surface of the meat, rendering it mushy, while the core of any joint remains as tough as ever. Nothing short of the proper cooking method can tenderize a tough piece of meat; see the following sections where different slow-cooking techniques are explained.

Meats are marinated, or steeped in an acidulated liquid, for several reasons:

- *To tenderize*; however, except in the case of thin cuts, the tenderizing is superficial.
- *To flavor*; the surface of the meat acquires a definite taste from the liquid and its seasonings.
- *To retard bacterial growth* if the meat must wait longer than expected to be cooked.

Flambéing Meats

To flavor them, their sauces, or gravies, meats are sometimes flambéed before being served; this is an old-fashioned method which is now only rarely used, but may still tickle some cook's fancy. Flambéing removes all harsh alcohol from the chosen spirit, but, while burning, leaves its flavor and aroma on the surface of the meat. All spirits must be well heated before flambéing or they will not light up.

Use only a small amount of spirit; more than one ounce is not necessary for home-cooking proportions.

Be careful: Avoid burning yourself by keeping your face well away from any flambéing pan and using a long-handled skillet or sauteuse which will keep the top of your hand from being grazed by the flames.

In a home kitchen, pour and heat the required amount of spirit into a small pot over medium heat. Light the spirit with a long match and pour it ablaze onto the hot meat. Shake the pan back and forth until the flame dies out, keeping your face well away from the flames.

The chef's method for flambéing consists of pouring the required amount of alcohol directly into the hot sautéing or frying pan and tilting the pan toward the flame of the burner so the spirit immediately catches on fire is for use only in commercial kitchens; it could be potentially dangerous in a small home kitchen where space is reduced around the burners and the side counters may be cluttered. If you use this technique, you are more than ever responsible for your own safety; make sure that nothing that can catch on fire is close at hand.

When using either of these techniques, keep a large lid at hand to cover the pan and smother the flames rapidly. A fire extinguisher would also be a smart addition to any kitchen. *Never throw water on a fire in a pan if hot animal fat is involved;* it will help spread rather than contain the flames.

Meat Handwork
Meat Cuts and Their Uses

Before you start working on meats, see pages 701–3 and consider whether you should wear protective surgical gloves. Such gloves are on sale in each and every drugstore. The thinner, more expensive ones will provide more "fingertip feeling" while you work.

Working Meats

Large roasts usually come already prepared by a butcher or supermarket meat department, but it is important to know how to remove the fat and connective tissue covering in order to limit fat intake.

TO REMOVE A RIB ROAST FROM THE RIBS This procedure applies to rib roasts of beef, veal, and pork as well as to rib racks of lamb.

Using a knife with which you are very comfortable (boning knife, short chef's knife, or larger paring knife), cut along the backbone and rib structures, separating the muscle attached to the bones gradually and neatly.

Keep the ribs to prepare short ribs or a delicious beef stock, or beef and vegetable soup. To remove the fat, go to the next step.

TO REMOVE THE FAT AND CONNECTIVE TISSUE COVERING OF A SIRLOIN STRIP, RIB, OR TENDERLOIN OF BEEF Shave the covering fat (called suet in beef and lamb, and fatback in pork by most cooks and "finish" by butchers and chefs) from the top of the roast in successive flat sheets approximately ¼ inch thick, until the underlying connective membrane, called the silverskin, has become entirely visible.

Once you have removed the fat covering, the removal of the silverskin is essential or the meat will buckle while cooking.

TO REMOVE THE SILVERSKIN The silverskin is bonded very strongly to the muscle, and the direction of its fibers does not always exactly follow that of the muscle fibers. Remove it in successive parallel strips, following the direction of its own fibers, *not that of the underlying muscle fibers*.

Pass the tip of your knife blade ⅟₁₆ inch under the silverskin, at the midlength of the roast, the cutting edge of the blade facing right or left depending on whether you are right- or left-handed. With your working hand, engage half the length of the blade under the small bridge formed by the membrane. Position the knife blade at a bare 10-degree angle, the cutting edge of the knife resting on the meat. Move the blade forward in the direction indicated by the cutting edge of the blade with smooth, wide, back-and-forth sawing motions all the way to the end of the piece of meat. To skin the other end of the strip, repeat the exact same operation positioning the cutting edge of the blade to face the opposite direction. It will be easier if you

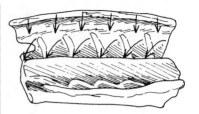

Strip detached from the chine (backbone), resting on its cover of suet. Arrows indicate the direction of the knife blade.

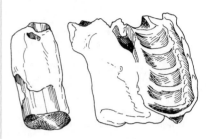

Strip separated from its suet

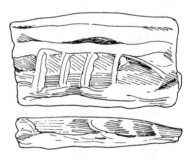

Tenderloin removed from the underside of a strip of lamb (same as for veal and beef)

REMOVING THE SILVERSKIN

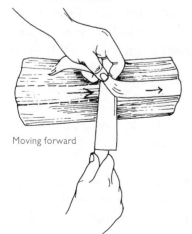

Moving forward

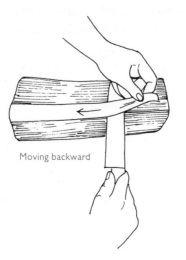

Moving backward

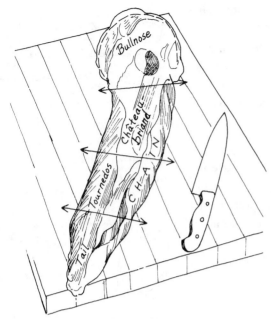

Whole tenderloin, fat removed, untrimmed

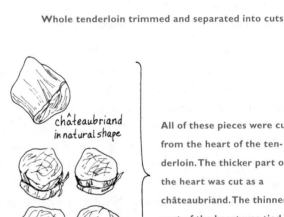

Whole tenderloin trimmed and separated into cuts

Bullnose tied for roasting. Steaks can also be cut out of it between the ties.

châteaubriand in natural shape

Tournedos rounded by tying

All of these pieces were cut from the heart of the tenderloin. The thicker part of the heart was cut as a châteaubriand. The thinner part of the heart was tied (like the bullnose), then cut between ties into four tenderloins.

Two steaks cut from the tail

grab the already loosened membrane strip with the fingers of your second hand and pull it tightly ¼ inch above the already bared strip of meat, keeping it as parallel as possible to the surface of the meat. Remove as many strips as needed to completely uncover the edible muscle part of the meat. Then, turn the roast over and remove any traces of the regular strips of fat where the rib bones originally rested.

The muscle will flatten considerably without the silverskin. To shape it again, tie it all around with individual tight ties of kitchen string, though not so tightly that they would squeeze the meat juices out of the muscle. The butcher-style tie is often not tight enough.

If roasting the whole piece of meat, each tie should be placed ½ inch from the next. The muscle will reshape into its original oval or round form.

If cutting steaks, the ties should be placed ¾ to 1 inch apart; steaks are obtained by cutting between the ties. Steaks cut from the tenderloin are called tournedos, a French expression possibly coined by the composer Rossini and meaning "cooked while one turns one's back" because Rossini liked his tenderloins very rare. Tournedos should not be more than ³/₄ inch thick.

TO BONE AND STRIP SIRLOIN STRIPS OF BEEF, VEAL, LAMB, OR PORK Veal, lamb, and pork loin can be bought double (both sides of the loin) or single (one side of a double loin that has been sawed in half through the backbone). To remove the strips of meat from the backbone, cut ½ inch deep all along the backbone, separating the meat from the bone as you go. Continue severing and separating the muscle from the backbone until you completely uncover the T-bone. At this point the meat is not on the bone anymore but hangs free by a thick bridge of fat. Pass your fingers between the fat and the meat and the strip of meat will almost miraculously detach itself from its fat covering. It will remain attached deeply to the fat only by one of its ends. At this point, working only with the tip of your blade, gently detach the muscle until it falls on the meat cutting board. Now you must remove the silverskin from the meat as described on page 721.

Strips of beef, veal, and pork must be tied as explained on page 746 when oven roasted. Whereas the sirloin of beef is mostly roasted whole, the sirloin of veal and/or pork is cut into medallions. To make medallions, tie the sirloin at ¾-inch intervals and cut between the ties. Whole strips of lamb are mostly pan-roasted or grilled. To cut them into the small steaks called noisettes, tie the loin at ½-inch intervals, then cut between the ties.

TO BONE AND DETAIL A LEG OF LAMB Use only a well-aged leg on which the fell looks somewhat dry and parchmentlike. Remove the fell, its thin layer of underlying fat, and the silverskin covering the different muscles of the leg all at once by sliding your blade under each of them, at a 10-degree angle to prevent removing too much of the muscle meat.

1. If the leg is to be roasted whole:

    Gently pass a finger between the two muscles clearly visible on the top part of the leg until you see a large walnut-size piece of fat appear; pull it out. This nugget of fat surrounds the so-called eye of the pope, which is a lymph node. If you cut through the nugget of fat, you will see the darker pink node. Pat the two muscles back together after removal.

    Now turn the leg over. You will see a blotchy red region. This is where the femoral artery has been cut; 75 percent of the time it will still contain some bright red liquid. Take a large wad of paper towels and push about 1 inch above the opening to drain all the liquid into the paper towels.

2. If the leg is to be "butterflied":

    Butterflying means boning the leg of lamb so it can lie flat with an approximately even thickness of all its muscles. This is easily done by first

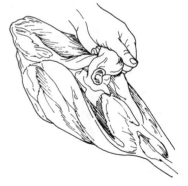

Removing the eye of the pope from a leg of lamb

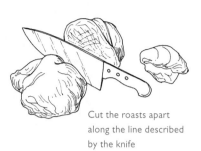

Cut the roasts apart
along the line described
by the knife

Butterflied leg of lamb with whole shank muscle beside the knife handle

Left and right, small and large roast tied for cooking; middle, shank muscles cut up to prepare a sauce

Scaloppine and small steaks cut out of the large roast muscles. The sizes of the scaloppine vary with that of the muscles out of which they are cut.

separating the meat from the thigh bone, then separating the meat from the shank bone. If you are butterflying, you can wait to remove the "eye of the pope" when you cut the meat from the bones. Leave both of the shank muscles on, as they roast deliciously. The so-called heart of the leg is a tight, round ball-like muscle thicker than the other muscles. Snip it open with the tip of your blade until it is of the same thickness as the other muscles.

3. If the leg is to be roasted for a restaurant à la carte menu or catered dinners or for a special dinner party at home:

Roasting a whole leg on the bone is often not a favorite for à la carte service because it is difficult to keep all the muscles of the leg fresh tasting and juicy throughout the serving and carving of many portions. But since a well-aged leg is an excellent tasting cut, and more affordable than loins and racks of lamb, here is a practical way to obtain fresh slices and enough meat to prepare a small sauce.

Bone the leg entirely; lay it flat on the board cut side down. Remove both the upper and the lower shank muscle; set both aside. Following the very visible dividing line between the two major top muscles, separate the leg into two parts. Roll each into a smaller roast and tie each well at ⅓-inch intervals and into a round shape. One will be larger and serve up to five portions, while the second will serve only three. After you have roasted the rolls and removed the ties, you will see that each roast will separate into individual muscles. Cut each and every muscle individually *across the grain* into thin slices, or scaloppine; serve three- to four-slice portions, depending on the size of the muscle.

With the shank muscles you can prepare excellent stews for home and bistro-style meals. To entertain at home, in catering preparations, or in classy restaurant-style food presentation, use those shank muscles to prepare an essence of lamb which can serve as a sauce. See page 296 for a typical example of such a roasted leg.

Once the two small roasts have been carved for service there will be some small amount of leftover outer cuts; they will taste excellent in lamb salads or for an everyday meal blended with risotto, a grain, or a pasta and freshly stir-fried vegetables.

Working Poultry

All birds can be trussed with or without a trussing needle. The trussing needle gives a better shape to the bird because its legs will cover the tips of the breast and prevent them from drying out while cooking. Turkeys and smaller birds are mostly trussed without a needle.

TRUSSING POULTRY WITH TRUSSING NEEDLE

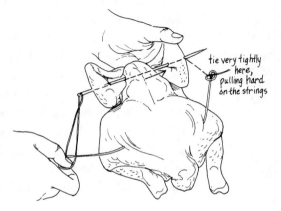

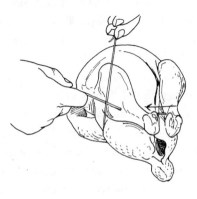

Pass the needle through the body from thigh to thigh, leaving a 6-inch tail of string.

Turn the bird over and pass the needle through the wings and neck. Tie both ends of the string together here, pulling hard on the strings.

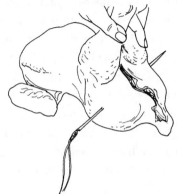

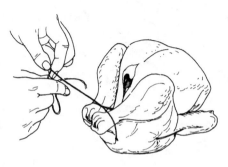

Pass the needle through the body from knee to knee.

Push the needle back through the tips of the drumsticks following the direction of the arrow and tie.

Wrap the string around the tail and tips of the drumsticks and tie again.

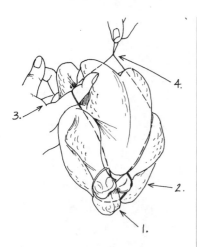

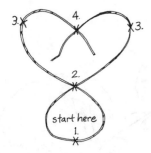

TRUSSING WITHOUT A NEEDLE

1. Tie the string around the tail and drumstick ends.

2. Pass the string under the tip of the breastbone and deep down between thigh and breast on each side.

3. Pass through the wings, folded akimbo, on both sides.

4. Tie over the wing and upper part of the neck.

Front view of the trussed bird

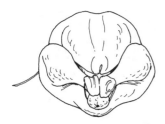

Path of the string

To truss ducks, chickens, Cornish hens, and squabs with a trussing needle:

1. Thread a long trussing needle with about 2 feet of thin kitchen thread. Put the bird on its back with the neck to your left or right, depending on whether you are right- or left-handed. With your second hand, hold the legs up as high and tightly as possible while, with your working hand, you thrust the needle into the middle of the thigh on the right side of the bone; the needle will come out at exactly the same spot on the other side. Pull the string through to the other side of the bird, leaving about 6 inches of it hanging out of the first thigh. Turn the bird on its side, breastbone facing you. Pass the needle through the second joint of the wing, then through the gathered neck skin, then through the second joint of the second wing. Pull the string through and tightly tie the free end of the string to the 6-inch piece you left at the thigh. With your paring knife, cut both ends of the string ½ inch above the knot.

2. Thread the needle again. Holding up the legs again with your second hand, use your working hand to pierce the leg a second time, this time in front of the thigh and drumstick joint; pass the needle through to the other side of the bird, leaving about 6 inches of string hanging out of the first thigh. Coming back toward yourself, pass the needle through the skin under the tip end of the far drumstick, take a stitch right through the tail, and pass the needle through the skin under the tip end of the near drumstick. Pull the string through and tightly tie the free end to the 6-inch piece you left at the joint. Finally, wrap the hanging remainder of the string around both the tail and the ends of the drumsticks and tie again.

To tie all birds however large or small without a needle: Measure enough string to go one and a half times around the bird. Tie the middle of the string around the tail so as to have the same length of string on each side, and make a knot. Cross the string over and around the ends of the drumstick, then, passing it under the tip of the breastbone, push each piece of string deep down alongside the breast on each side and finally thread the end of the string through the hole made, on each side, by each wing of the bird folded akimbo. Turn the bird over and tie both ends of the string over the upper back of the bird.

To disjoint a bird of any size:

1. Pull the legs away from the breastbone and cut through the skin between the leg and breast. Pull each leg down until it lies flat on the board. Sever the joint between the leg and the remainder of the carcass.

   If you want to separate the leg into halves, cut right through the articulation to separate each leg into one thigh and one drumstick.

2. Cut off the pointed, bony joint of each wing; set it aside for the stockpot. Now cut the second flat joint of each wing as well as the first joint, also called the drumette, of each wing; you can leave them attached to each

other or separate them as you prefer. They are both used for appetizers when separated, and for economical stews when left attached to each other.

3. The "oysters" of a chicken, duck, or turkey are the delicious little nuggets of meat located in the two depressions of the lower backbone located just above the tail (they also exist in smaller birds but are too small to be of any use by themselves). To remove them, cut straight through the abdominal cavity skins and thin rib bones until your blade meets resistance. Bend the lower end of the backbone backward until it breaks and cut through the skin that keeps it attached to the carcass; also cut off the fatty tail of the bird (remember, though, that in a whole roasted chicken it is considered a delicacy by many!). This part contains the famous delicious oysters, which in French carry the descriptive name of *sot-l'y-laisse* (translating to "a fool will leave it there") because, being so small, they are indeed easily overlooked. You can use the piece of the backbone where they are nested as is in a stew or sauté, or you can, using the tip of a smaller knife, excise each oyster from the bone and keep them frozen in a plastic bag, adding more oysters as you bone more birds. When you have accumulated four dozen, you can prepare a delicious appetizer with them (see page 808 for an example). Turkey oysters roast deliciously and should be left on the bird when only one bird is prepared. In professional kitchens where many birds are roasted, they can be removed before cooking the birds, accumulated, and used for excellent appetizers or sautéed dishes.

4. To obtain boneless cutlets: Pass your index and middle fingers under the skin so each of them rests on each breast fillet. Push up toward the neck bone until you can anchor each finger on each side of the neck. The skin will pull free, baring the fillets.

To lift the fillets from the breastbone, lay the rib cage of the bird on

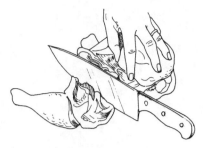

Removing a limb: A leg here, but the principle of cutting through a joint is the same for all pieces.

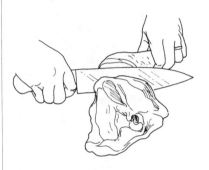

Cutting a leg into thigh and drumstick

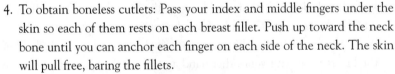

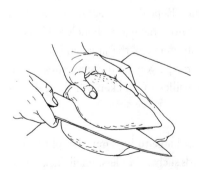

The whole breast after removing the lower back with the gizzards. Separating a cutlet (suprême) from the bone

Removing the cutlet cutting toward the right

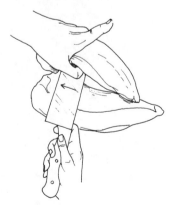

Cutting the breast free

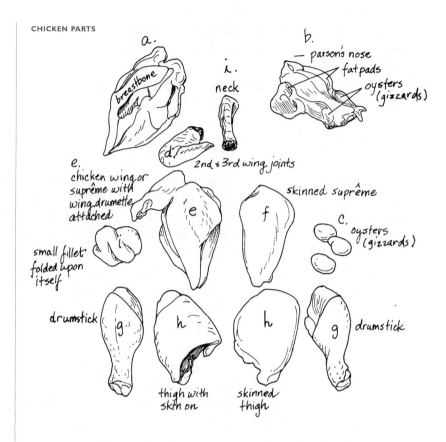

one of its sides, the shoulders facing away from you. Pass the blade of the knife 1 inch down all along and hugging the breastbone. This will separate the thicker part of the fillet from the top of the breastbone.

Now, turn the bird so the cut you just made is facing you. Take hold of the breast meat with your other hand and thrust the blade of your knife between bone and breast meat, one inch below the shoulder joint; at this point the blade will rest on the meat and the thumb of your other hand will be between the blade and the meat. With your working hand cut the meat off the carcass with one stroke of the blade toward the left and right and you will be holding a boneless fillet. Repeat the exact same operation on the other side of the bird. You now have two boneless fillets of chicken each made up of two separate muscles, the large and the small fillet. *Do not separate them* unless the recipe you are using requires you to do so. Throughout this book such a fillet of chicken will be called a chicken cutlet.

To split a bird of any type and size in half: Large turkeys must be split by the butcher using an electric saw. Smaller birds such as broilers, small ducks up to five pounds, Cornish hens, poussins, squabs, and quail should be split as follows:

Remove the backbone using poultry shears (or sharp smaller scissors for smaller birds) by cutting on each side of the tail along the backbone and the neck; keep the backbone for the stockpot. Open the bird and lay it as flat as possible cavity side down on the board; if the breasts make a hump, flatten them with one thump of your fist. Using your chef knife, cut straight down the center of the breastbone.

To "frog" a chicken, Cornish hen, poussin, squab, or quail: A bird that is "frogged" does indeed resemble a frog. It has been cut and evenly flattened so that it can be broiled or grilled uniformly, with no differences of texture and doneness.

To frog a bird, remove the backbone with poultry shears or sharp smaller scissors for smaller birds as described above for halving a bird. Open the bird and lay it as flat as possible cavity side down on the board. Cut two openings in the skin on each side of the tip of the breastbone. Push each drumstick as high as it will go, then gently slide its tip into each opening.

Remove the backbone.

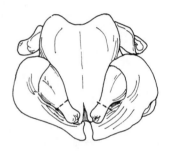

Push the legs upward and cut slits in the skin alongside the breastbone where indicated by dotted lines.

Insert the tips of the legs into the slits.

Cooking Meat with Dry Heat

There is no doubt that early man first cooked his meats using dry heat. What I want to know is, did he roast a whole animal or grill some smaller pieces placed at the end of a stick or flat on a hot stone? The idea of roasting may have come about after foraging for food following a large forest fire and finding the usually hunted deer already cooked, while that of grilling or broiling was probably adopted when a piece of meat was dropped by accident amidst the flames of a smoldering fire, retrieved with a long stick, and found to be much more appetizing and satisfying than uncooked flesh.

For the student of culinary history, one interesting question remains: Could the centuries of dominance of professional kitchens by men possibly find its origin in the times when the "hunters" were the all-important protein food providers for the clan and when the clan chief directed the ceremonial roasting of large catches? Also, do we find a remnant of these ancestral customs in the facts that butchers have always had a position of predominance in organized societies and that our family barbecuers are to this day almost always our fathers and husbands?

Broiling and Grilling

A cut of meat is broiled or grilled when it is cooked by radiant heat emitted in a gas or electric broiler, from the embers of a charcoal grill, or by the conduction heat of a stovetop ribbed grill. Practically all types of meats can be broiled or grilled.

THE TECHNIQUES OF
OVEN BROILING-GRILLING

Since no two stoves or wall ovens are identical, read the maker's instruction booklet carefully. Only one feature is common to all ovens: broiling is done with the door closed in gas ovens and with the door ajar in electric ovens, probably for ventilation reasons, to prevent submitting the heating elements to 550°F, which could damage them.

PREPARING STEAKS FOR BROILING

When broiling beefsteak(s), trim the meat of all traces of its outer fat covering and its underlying connective tissues. Steaks from which the fat covering and connective tissues have been removed flatten and become thinner. To restore their original thickness, tie them all around with kitchen string, just until they hold a regular shape. Do not tie too tightly or you will squeeze the juices out of the meat. Classic chefs wrapped the steaks into a layer of fatback; some chefs still do so with a thin rasher of bacon or pancetta.

If you prefer the taste of cooked natural fat on grilled meat, remove all but ¼ inch of the fat covering the piece of meat, then score the underlying connective tissues at regular intervals, to prevent the meat from buckling during cooking.

These are the two possible sets of internal temperatures you will be looking for when broiling beefsteaks to obtain the corresponding final degree of doneness after you have let the meat rest long enough for its internal juices to stop moving and stabilize. Choose the set you prefer; you are responsible for your own safety.

Degree of Doneness	Internal Classic Temperature	USDA Recommended Internal Temperature
Very rare (also known as "blue")	120°F	
Rare	125°F	
Medium rare	130°F	145°F
Well done	135°F	170°F

The internal temperature can be easily checked using either the so-called "button" thermometer for home cooks and the instant thermometer for professional cooks. Buttons are short-stemmed instant thermometers that should be inserted at the thickest part of a broiling steak, from its side rather than from the top. There are two types of buttons: One is made exclusively for steaks, with a dial indicating "Rare," "Medium," and "Well done," while the dial of the second type indicates both the type of meat and its desired internal temperature.

Buttons and thermometers have the disadvantage of piercing the meat and promoting a certain loss of juices. As you become familiar with grilling, work on developing enough confidence to test the meat with the pressure of your index finger. You can learn this old-fashioned method by comparing the temperature or degree of doneness indicated on the thermometer or button dial with the resilience of the meat under your finger. It is a good idea to learn simultaneously to appreciate doneness with the tip of a finger for if you are in a rush, it takes too much time to take a thermometer measurement. Classic chefs simply poke here and there and read the meat as follows: If the meat is well seared on both sides, but gives extremely easily under the pressure of your index finger, the meat is very rare; if it gives moderately, it is rare to medium rare; if it gives only a little, it is medium well done; and if it does not give at all it is well done.

BROILING STEAKS

Preheat the broiler, but put the piece or pieces to broil on a cold broiler rack resting over the broiler pan where any melting fat can collect. A cold broiler rack guarantees that the steak(s) will not start to cook at too low a heat on their bottom side.

Brush the meat with an extremely thin layer of oil of your choice if you like; it helps the meat sear faster. Do not salt or pepper. Exposed to the moisture of the meat, salt will melt and produce additional unwanted moisture and retard the browning of the meat surface. Pepper will burn and communicate an acrid, bitter taste to the surface of the cooked meat. Your goals are to handle the piece of meat so it is cooked to the desired degree of doneness inside, without it burning outside, and to keep each piece as juicy as possible.

For pieces of meat less than 1 inch in thickness cooked rare to medium rare: Place the meat 4 inches from the source of heat. Broil/grill the first side until brown, about 4 minutes. Salt and pepper the browned side, then turn it over and broil/grill until brown on the second side, 3 to 4 minutes. Salt and pepper the second side before serving.

For pieces of meat 2 to 2¼ inches thick, the technique is a bit more difficult. Expose the first side to the heat for 5 minutes, then turn down the heat to 350°F if the broiler is thermostatically controlled and cook about 3 minutes. If the broiler is not so controlled, move the cuts 8 to 9 inches away from the source of heat and cook for another 4 to 6 minutes. Season the cooked side with salt and pepper. Turn the piece over and repeat on the second side, but bear in mind that the second side will cook a bit faster than the first one. If you find it necessary, because the meat looks as if it is drying a bit too much for your satisfaction, brush it with a another very thin film of oil. Season the second side after it has finished cooking.

Remove the meat from the heat when, at the center of the piece, the thermometer registers the temperature indicated on page 703 for the degree of doneness you are looking for, remembering that the inner temperature of the meat will continue to increase during the first few minutes of the resting time.

Here is a good old-fashioned bit of information that will prove important at the beginning of your career at the broiler/grill: When each surface of the meat is exposed to the radiating heat, the meat juices travel from the searing side toward the center of the piece of meat. When you see those juices pearl on the seared second side of a steak, know that the steak is cooked rare. If the juices form a small puddle instead of pearling, the meat is done medium rare.

After removal from the source of heat, the internal temperature will increase another 7° to 12°F (this is called carryover heat), depending on the thickness of the steak(s). Letting the juices stabilize within the muscle tissues will prevent them from pouring onto the plate when the meat is cut. However, do not let the meat rest so long that its internal juices have the time to travel from the center toward the outside, abundantly breaking through the very temporary barrier formed by the seared surface of the meat. If you serve the meat after a few minutes of rest, the juices will escape onto the individual plates instead of the platter.

Châteaubriand or London Broil

FFR to FCR—RESPECTIVELY 3 TO 4 AND 6 SERVINGS

One 3-inch-long piece center cut of tenderloin or one 2-inch-thick London broil
2 tablespoons dark soy sauce
I slice fresh ginger, peeled and very finely chopped
I scallion, thinly sliced
I ½ tablespoons unsaturated oil of your choice
Salt, only if needed
Pepper from the mill

Trim either cut of meat of all fat and gristle. If using the tenderloin, flatten it with the side of your hand until it is 1¾ to 2 inches thick. Mix the soy sauce with the chopped ginger and let stand 10 minutes. Strain through a small tea strainer and brush all over the meat. Sprinkle the meat all around with the chopped scallions, then set it on a cold broiler rack; let it air dry about 45 minutes.

Preheat the broiler. Scrape the scallions away from the meat, then brush with as little oil as possible. Broil 4 to 5 inches away from the source of heat for 5 minutes on the first side. Salt and pepper the seared side, then turn over and broil until the internal temperature reads 125°F for medium rare (USDA 145°F), about another 3 minutes. Check doneness with steak button or your finger. Correct final seasoning with salt only if needed and pepper.

Let the meat rest 4 to 5 minutes before carving into ¼- to ⅓-inch-thick slices.

Traditionally a thick steak taken from the center part of the beef tenderloin, the châteaubriand used to be served with the rich béarnaise sauce on page 352. You can still prepare it that way for a very special occasion, but the following "East-West" version will taste just as interesting in a different style. The expensive châteaubriand may be replaced by a plain, lean, and delicious London broil as available in all butcher shops and supermarkets.

SUGGESTED WINE: *A full-bodied Cabernet Sauvignon from California, any excellent red Bordeaux, or a northern red Côtes-du-Rhône*

For the best look, texture, and taste, use whole broilers 2 to 3 pounds in weight. These must either be split into halves (they can be bought that way) or, if left whole, "frogged" before being broiled. (See pages 728–29 for the techniques for splitting poultry into halves and/or "frogging.")

Half a broiler usually makes a single serving. However, for senior citizens and children one broiler will offer four portions.

CHICKEN PIECES Large chicken legs sold in "family-style" trays in supermarkets can also be broiled, as can chicken wings and wing drumettes. Chicken breasts do not fare as well under the broiler and taste much better cooked on a stovetop ribbed grill.

Broiled Chicken with Herb Butter

FFR to FCR—6 TO 8 SERVINGS

2 teaspoons chopped fresh tarragon leaves

1 tablespoon chopped fresh chives

1 tablespoon chopped fresh Italian parsley leaves

1 tablespoon coarsely chopped fresh basil leaves

½ teaspoon finely chopped fennel seeds

¼ cup unsalted butter or 3 tablespoons olive oil of your choice

Salt

Pepper from the mill

3 broilers, 1½ to 3 pounds each, split or frogged (pages 728–29)

3 tablespoons boiling water

2 tablespoons fresh lemon juice or to taste

This recipe can also be used for the outdoor grill. You can replace the butter with olive oil in the herb mixture.

SUGGESTED WINE: *Any California white Zinfandel if you like a mellow wine or, for a drier wine, a Sauvignon Blanc from California, or the French Beaujolais of your choice if you prefer a red wine*

Mix all the herbs and fennel seeds together. Cream the butter with the thumb pad of your working hand or a knife blade, mixing it gradually with the herbs and salt and pepper to your taste. If using oil, mix the herbs, seeds, and oil together and refrigerate until semisolid before using.

Rub the flavored butter or oil evenly under the skin of each chicken or chicken half, spreading the mixture as uniformly as possible over the breast and leg meats. Set the chickens on a cake rack placed on a broiler pan.

Broil the "cavity" of each chicken first, about 15 minutes, the first 5 minutes on high heat 4 inches away from the broiler flame and the next 10 minutes either at 350°F in a gas oven or 8 to 9 inches away from the source of heat in an electric oven. Turn the chickens skin up and repeat the same procedure until the skin is golden and crisp. Brush the skin at 5-minute intervals with the butter or oil melting in the broiler pan. The total broiling time should be 25 to 30 minutes for chicken halves and up to 35 minutes for frogged chickens. Check doneness with a thermometer; the internal temperature should not be less than 170°F, both in the breast meat and at the thickest part of the leg (USDA 170°F in the breast and 180°F in the leg).

When done, remove the chicken to a platter. Discard the fat in the broiler pan. Add the boiling water and lemon juice and dissolve all the pan juices. Add more salt and pepper to the small gravy if needed and dribble it over the cooked chicken pieces. Serve rapidly for totally delicious freshness of taste.

Bourbon Chicken Wing Appetizers

FCR—6 SERVINGS

2 dozen chicken wings

3 tablespoons Jack Daniel's or bourbon of your choice

I teaspoon grated lemon rind

Juice of I lemon

3 tablespoons unsaturated oil of your choice

I tablespoon sweet Hungarian paprika

I cup fine bread crumbs

Salt

Pepper from the mill

Wash the wings and pat them completely dry. Cut the wings apart along their three successive joints. Save the bony tips for your next batch of chicken broth. Place the flat joints and drumettes in a glass dish. Whisk the Jack Daniel's, lemon rind and juice, and oil into a dressing and toss it over the wings. Marinate overnight, covered, in the refrigerator.

Thirty minutes before serving, transfer the wing pieces from the marinade to a stainless steel cake rack and let drip dry completely. Mix the paprika, crumbs, salt, and pepper together in a brown paper bag. Add the well-dripped wings and toss together to coat the wings evenly.

Set the wing joints on a cold broiler tray and broil 5 inches from the heat source until crisped and golden, 3 to 4 minutes on each side. Serve piping hot with cocktails or the dry white or red wine of your choice.

OTHER MEATS
Thinner steaks, thick loin lamb chops, free-range veal chops, and pork chops can also be broiled, but you will find they taste much better when grilled on a stovetop ribbed grill or a charcoal grill.

GRILLING ON A STOVETOP RIBBED GRILL
The stovetop ribbed grill is perfect for the preparation of quick dinners and the recipes that follow purposely reflect the everyday character of these meat dishes.

If you still own the old-fashioned cast-iron griddle of your grandmother, please bring it out of storage. It is in every way as good a piece of grilling equipment as the stovetop ribbed grill which was designed in France in the late fifties, and the many American versions that have been designed in the last twenty years. There are two types of ribbed cast-iron grills: the round one which can be heated on one burner only and the rectangular one that can be heated over two home or professional burners.

It is wise to condition any new cast-iron grill before using it the first time. To do this, rub it with a mixture of unsaturated oil and coarse salt to remove all traces of industrial oil, then heat the grill over medium-high heat until it smokes. The grill is ready for use when the smoke dissipates. Keep the kitchen window open and/or an exhaust fan on through the whole operation.

After each use, scrub the grill well with a steel brush, then rinse it, dry it well, and coat it with a very thin layer of oil. To prevent this oil from oxidizing, heat it again until the smoke dissipates, let it cool, then store till the next use.

CHOICE OF MEATS FOR THE RIBBED GRILL
The following small pieces of meat can be prepared on the stovetop grill:

- All steaks of beef from all cuts, ⅓ to 1 inch thick
- Small duckling cutlets (skinless fillets of commercial white Pekin ducks)
- Skinless chicken cutlets, also called magrets
- Butterflied quail
- Veal rib or loin chops ⅔ inch thick
- Slices of Boston pork butt ⅓ inch thick

Here are a few recipes:

Grilled Blade Steaks
CROQUE AU SEL

FCR—6 SERVINGS
6 blade steaks
Kosher salt as needed
Pepper from the mill
Cold unsalted butter (optional)

Cut away all the fat and connective tissues surrounding the steaks. Remove the strip of central connective tissue to obtain two strips of meat about ⅔ inch wide.

Preheat a ribbed grill over medium-high until white hot. Sprinkle the grill with enough kosher salt to make it appear gray. When the salt starts jumping, add the steaks. Grill 4 minutes on the first side and 3 on the second for

These humble steak strips are my favorite memory from my mother's kitchen. Blade steaks owe their name to the tough connective membrane passing through their center. On the East Coast, they are still sometimes called chicken steaks.

SUGGESTED WINE: *An excellent California Pinot Noir*

medium rare (the steaks taste best when medium rare). Remove the steaks from the heat, pepper well, and, if desired, rub a bit of cold butter over the surface of each strip.

Grilled Canton Duck Cutlets with Orange Bourbon Sauce

FCR—6 SERVINGS

¾ cup ruby port

I tablespoon balsamic vinegar

6 skinless duck cutlets (breast halves), tendons removed

½ teaspoon grated orange rind

I ⅓ cups fresh orange juice

I tablespoon bourbon or scotch whisky

I tiny clove garlic, finely chopped

I tablespoon chopped fresh Italian parsley leaves

I tablespoon unsalted butter (optional)

Salt

Pepper from the mill

I piece duck skin 2 inches square or I tablespoon unsaturated oil of your choice

½ cup duck or chicken stock of your choice or water

Mix the port and vinegar together in a small saucepan over high heat, reduce to 2 small tablespoons of thick glaze, and cool. Set the cutlets on a rack and brush the glaze thinly over all sides. Let stand at room temperature for 30 minutes, covered with a tent of aluminum foil.

Without washing the saucepan in which the port and vinegar were reduced, add to it the orange rind and juice and reduce to ¼ cup over medium heat. Add the bourbon to the reduction during the last few minutes of cooking. Turn off the heat and whisk in the garlic, parsley, and butter. Season with salt and pepper; keep warm.

Preheat the grill to white hot over medium-high heat. Rub the piece of duck skin fat side down on the grill till the grill glistens. Grill the cutlets 3 minutes on the first side, turn over, salt and pepper, and grill on the second side 2 to 3 more minutes, keeping the cutlets medium rare and pushing each of them down with a metal turner for a few seconds to send the heat toward their center. The internal temperature should be 145°F. Season the second side. Remove to a platter. Remove the grill to a heatproof pad using potholders and slowly pour the stock or water onto the grill; it will boil hard for a few seconds. Using potholders lift the grill and empty the dark reduced stock or deglazing water into the orange sauce. Mix well and dribble the sauce over the cutlets.

This recipe can also be used for butterflied quail. Keep the duck legs to bake or prepare confit with them; stock can be made with the carcass and the fat can be rendered to cook confits. Keep one small piece of skin to rub on the grill. Use 5½- to 6-pound regular ducks ordered from a butcher.

SUGGESTED WINE: *Light young American Zinfandel or Pinot Noir, French Beaujolais-Villages, or an Italian Lambrusco*

Grilled Veal Rib Chops

FFR — 6 SERVINGS

I cup Secondary Stock (page 220) or chicken stock or broth of your choice

I tablespoon tarragon mustard

I tablespoon chopped fresh tarragon leaves

I tablespoon unsalted butter (optional)

I tablespoon olive oil of your choice

6 veal rib chops, trimmed of fat and connective tissues

Salt

Pepper from the mill

In a small saucepan over medium heat, reduce the stock to ⅓ cup. Put the mustard and tarragon in a small bowl and whisk in the hot reduced stock and butter, if used. Keep warm.

Heat the grill over high heat until white hot. Moisten a wad of paper towels with the oil and rub quickly over the grill. Grill the chops 3 minutes on the first side and 2 to 3 minutes on the second. Season both sides only after the meat is off the grill. Spoon 2 teaspoons of the tarragon sauce over each chop.

Veal is baby beef, so cook it no deeper than medium rare; it will retain all its juiciness and be delicious. Free-range veal is best for this preparation.

SUGGESTED WINE: *A good Pinot Noir from California or France*

Neil's Pork Grillades

FFR — 6 SERVINGS

2 tablespoons olive oil of your choice

I large clove garlic, finely chopped

I shallot, finely chopped

6 sun-ripened Roma or plum tomatoes, peeled, seeded, and chopped

I tablespoon chopped fresh chervil leaves

I tablespoon chopped fresh tarragon leaves

I tablespoon Noisette Butter (page 32; optional)

Large pinch of cayenne pepper

I tablespoon tiny capers, drained

Salt

Pepper from the mill

6 slices pork shoulder butt, trimmed into grillades

Heat 1 tablespoon of the olive oil in a skillet, then add the garlic and shallot and toss 2 minutes in the hot oil. Add the tomatoes and let cook, stirring occasionally, until they form a well-bound sauce, about 10 minutes. Off the heat, add the chervil, tarragon, noisette butter, if used, cayenne pepper, and capers, and season to taste with salt and black pepper.

Heat the grill over medium heat until white hot. Moisten a wad of paper

Purchase a small Boston butt and have the butcher cut it into ⅓-inch-thick slices. Completely defat the slices by removing the fat inside and out; you will end up with fat-free strips of pork that are the "grillades."

SUGGESTED WINE: *Beaujolais-Villages, a light young Zinfandel, Valpolicella, or typical Chianti* towels with the remaining tablespoon of oil and rub it quickly over the grill. Grill the strips of pork 5 minutes on the first side. Turn the strips over, salt and pepper their cooked side, and finish cooking 3 to 4 more minutes on the second side. The grillades should be well browned and crisp on both sides, with an inner temperature of 160°F (USDA 170°F).

Remove the strips to a serving platter, season the just cooked side with salt and pepper, and dribble the tomato fondue over the pork.

Grilled Chicken Cutlets in Vinegared Red Pepper Coulis

FCR—6 SERVINGS

2 large red bell peppers

I dried pasilla chile, seeded

I cup Secondary Stock (page 220) or chicken stock or broth of your choice

2 tablespoons red wine vinegar

Salt

Pepper from the mill

I tablespoon chopped cilantro leaves

I tablespoon unsaturated oil of your choice

6 boneless skinless chicken cutlets

Chicken cutlets are done just as soon as they resist under the pressure of your finger, but check the internal temperature with an instant thermometer; it should be between 155° and 165°F (USDA 170°F).

SUGGESTED WINE:

Beaujolais-Villages, or California Gamay Beaujolais

Cut the peppers open, completely remove the ribs and seeds, and cut into slivers. Place them in a medium-size saucepan. Chop enough of the pasilla to the consistency of powder to obtain 1 tablespoon, then add it to the saucepan together with the stock and vinegar. Season to taste with salt and pepper. Bring to a boil, reduce the heat to a simmer, and cook over medium heat, stirring occasionally, until reduced to the consistency of a sauce. Strain to remove the pepper skins. Add the cilantro.

Heat the grill over medium-high heat until white hot. Moisten a wad of paper towels with the oil and rub it quickly over the grill. Grill the cutlets 3 minutes on one side, then turn them over and salt and pepper them. Grill the second side another 3 minutes, pushing on the cutlets with a flat spatula to force the heat rapidly to the center. When done, remove to a platter and salt and pepper the other side. Serve with the prepared pepper sauce, on the cutlets or on the side.

CHARCOAL GRILLING

Charcoal grilling is the simplest and possibly the most delicious way to grill. To understand the technique better, read this entire section, recipes included, before you light the grill.

You can use any barbecue grill at your disposal, including those small hibachis on which one can usually prepare only two portions of meat. Be careful with them, though, as they can be difficult to control; the meat may cook extremely fast, or painfully slowly.

It is essential that you use no starter fluid, which can communicate a chemical taste to your meat. Lump charcoal is by far the best fuel; it is not difficult to locate in any good local hardware store or even in large supermarkets. It seems easier to find in the West than in other parts of the nation; its main quality is that it burns "hotter." Try mesquite charcoal, which burns so extremely hot that it sears very rapidly and delivers a meat with a pleasantly flavored seared surface. Be careful when you light it for it also sparks a lot.

If no lump charcoal is available, briquets are the next best choice; some are made of agglomerated pure charcoal powder, others contain part charcoal powder, starch, and coal powder. Train your nose to recognize the smell of mineral coal as opposed to that of charcoal; it is easily recognizable. When using the latter, heat the coals long enough so all traces of red flames or red glowing have disappeared. Briquets containing coal powder must glow white before the meat is put on to cook to prevent any possible coal aftertaste on the fully cooked meat.

I personally prefer charcoal to gas-fueled barbecues, but I must give gas its credit for being the most convenient, even if the slight aftertaste of wood essences is missing from the surface of the grilled meats. Some gas barbecue chefs like to replace it by coating their meats in a thin layer of Liquid Smoke. I prefer not to, because there is a better way, which consists of smoking the pieces of meat to be grilled a few minutes in one of those convenient small stovetop smokers. The meat does not start to cook and can be grilled normally on the gas flame afterward, but the familiar little wood taste will be on its surface.

Fire the coals at least 45 minutes before your planned meal time. This is best done by packing the bottom of a fire-starting "chimney" with loosely crumpled newspaper topped with a few sticks of Georgia fatwood or ordinary kindling and filling the chimney two thirds of the way up with wood charcoal. A chimney is easy to locate in any hardware store, and if you cannot find one, you can make one yourself by cutting two rectangular openings each 3 × 2½ inches and facing each other for good ventilation, out of an empty two-pound coffee can; use metal shears and gardening gloves to protect your hands.

When the wood or briquets are burning orange, empty the contents of the chimney into the barbecue and add more charcoal if your grill is large. Wood charcoal is ready for grilling when it glowers deep crimson. Rub the grill rack with a wad of paper towels moistened with unsaturated oil and put the rack over the fire. Add the meats only when the rack has thoroughly heated.

For additional wood flavor on the meat, lightly moisten wood chips and add them to the coal just before you start grilling. Hickory, alder, apple, and maple will each impart a different and delicious flavor to any meat. Be careful using grapevine cuttings. Chop them as finely as you can and add sparingly to the coals as they flare up and crackle spectacularly even when moistened.

The best cuts of meat to be charcoal broiled are:

- Any cut of steak
- Pork chops and grillades of pork shoulder
- Thick loin and rib chops of veal and lamb
- Completely boned loin strips of veal
- Butterflied leg of lamb and fully boned long strips of lamb loin
- Any dark-meated chicken part
- Cutlets of chicken and duck breast
- The thick, so-called magrets or fully boned breasts of large Moulard and Muscovy ducks
- Quail
- Baby back ribs of pork
- Beef short ribs

Any of these pieces of meat can be marinated in a dry or liquid marinade before being grilled. Large pieces with less tender textures such as short ribs of beef are best preroasted, then basted with a marinade or barbecue sauce before finishing the cooking on the charcoal grill.

Beware of cross-contamination: To prevent cross-contamination (see page 19), two platters or trays are needed; one to carry the uncooked meats to the grill and a warmed *clean* one to carry the cooked meat back to the table. Also, *never* use the marinating liquid as a barbecue baste, unless it has been boiled first.

MARINADES FOR BARBECUED MEATS

The two marinades featured in the recipes below have been among my favorites for many years. You can create many such marinades yourself by changing the aromatics and herbs in the dry marinade and the juices in the liquid marinade.

Marinades for charcoal-grilled meats are very concentrated and of small volume; even more concentrated are the wine glazes used in this section and the section on roasting starting on page 744. As a matter of interest, compare these wine glazes with the "long," much more liquid marinades used in the section on braising and stewing starting on page 815. All barbecue marinades must be very reduced to minimize the amount of water they contain, allowing the flavoring ingredients to form a glaze around the meat.

Magrets of Muscovy Duck

FFR — 6 SERVINGS

For the dry marinade

2 tablespoons kosher salt

1 tablespoon coarsely ground Aromatic Pepper (page 57) from the mill

1 tablespoon finely chopped garlic

2 tablespoons chopped fresh Italian parsley leaves

1 teaspoon finely chopped fresh thyme leaves

1 teaspoon chopped fresh rosemary leaves

½ teaspoon ground allspice

1 tablespoon seeded and very finely chopped dried pasilla chile

For the meat

2 magrets of Muscovy duck

1 piece duck skin 2 inches square or 1 tablespoon unsaturated oil of your choice

Mix together all the ingredients of the dry marinade.

To remove the skin of each magret, slide the tip of a paring knife under the skin at the tapered end of the magret; snip the skin away with your working hand, while you gradually wrap the skin backward around your other hand as you progress. At the thickest end of the magret, the skin is so tightly attached to the muscle that you will have to remove it slowly and carefully to prevent tearing the muscle fibers. Set aside a piece of the skin to use to oil the grill.

Turn the skinned magret over, and you will find the "small fillet"; slide the blade of your parer forward under the whole length of the long white tendon clearly visible on it. The thicker part of the magret contains a sheet of silverskin large enough to necessitate its removal. Slide your blade between the meat and the silverskin and bare the latter along its whole length. Then slide your blade under the silverskin and remove it carefully. You now have two flaps of meat: Push them tightly together.

Sprinkle each side of each magret with one quarter of the marinade. Let marinate overnight, covered, in the refrigerator. Bring back to room temperature 45 minutes before cooking.

Preheat the grill; when the coals are white hot, stick a piece of the duck skin fat side down on the prongs of a long-handled fork, and rub it over the grill. Grill the magrets 4 to 5 inches from the coals for 5 minutes on the small fillet side first, pushing on the meat to drive the heat rapidly toward its center. Repeat the same operation on the second side. Check doneness with a meat thermometer and turn over again if more time is needed to finish the cooking. The magrets are rare when the internal temperature reaches 125°F (USDA 140°F). Remove from the heat; rest a few minutes, letting the internal temperature rise to 130° to 135°F (USDA 170°F) while the juices settle.

This recipe also works for flank steak, London broil, all beefsteaks, thick lamb, veal, and pork chops, and all poultry parts. The elements of the dry marinade may be changed to reflect your personal taste.

A single breast fillet of chicken is called a suprême in French and a cutlet in English; in the same manner the single breast fillet of a larger Muscovy or Moulard duck is given the name of magret. Muscovy and Moulard ducks, which at this date can be obtained only from butchers or specialty food stores, provide some of the leanest and most delicious red meats existing.

A magret can weigh over a pound, and if your table companions have normal appetites, use only two magrets, three if some of them come to the table with a larger hunger.

SUGGESTED WINE: *Full-bodied Zinfandel, mature Pinot Noir, mature northern Côtes-du-Rhône, mature California Cabernet Sauvignon, or Pomerol*

Carve into ⅙- to ⅛-inch-thick slices at a 20-degree angle, starting from the thinner end of each magret. The highest temperature a magret should ideally reach is 140° to 145°F. Above that it becomes tough and unpalatable.

Barbecued Chicken

FCR—6 SERVINGS

For 2½ cups fat-free barbecue sauce

2½ cups Secondary Stock (page 220) or any broth of your choice

2½ cups peeled and finely crushed fresh tomatoes or Pomi-style canned strained tomatoes

1 large yellow onion, chopped almost to a puree

1 shallot, finely chopped

2 cloves garlic, mashed to a paste

3 tablespoons firmly packed brown sugar of your choice

3 tablespoons cider vinegar

Very large pinch of cayenne pepper

3 tablespoons Worcestershire sauce

1 tablespoon dried pasilla chile chopped to a powder

1 teaspoon sweet Hungarian paprika

¼ teaspoon Liquid Smoke (optional)

Salt

For the chicken

4 quarts water

1¼ cups kosher salt

1 cup firmly packed brown sugar

3 broilers, 2½ to 3 pounds each

Salt

Pepper from the mill

This recipe can also be applied to:

- Chicken legs
- Baby back ribs and short ribs of pork
- Butterflied leg of lamb
- Pork slices from the shoulder butt
- Beef flank steak
- Beef short ribs preroasted 40 minutes in a 400°F oven

This plain barbecue sauce can be replaced by your own favorite sauce. Items grilled with homemade barbecue sauce must be generously salted before cooking while whole broilers are best brined as recommended below. This relatively heavy salting rebalances the relatively pronounced sweet-sour taste of the sauce.

Pomi tomato puree (Parmalat brand) is imported from Italy in special cardboard boxes which can be kept at room temperature. Check the date on the box before buying and using. If you wish to prepare a larger amount of sauce, quadruple the amount of all the ingredients and pack the finished sauce into 2-cup Mason jars and can or freeze them. Any amount left over from an opened 2-cup container must be reboiled before refrigerating or refreezing. It will last for one week in the refrigerator.

Mix all the sauce ingredients together in a saucepan. Bring to a boil, then turn down to a simmer and let the mixture reduce by half. Correct the seasoning to your taste. Place the mixture in a blender and process until completely smooth. Strain through a conical strainer. Cool completely, stirring once in a while to dissipate air bubbles; correct final seasoning. Set aside ¾ cup of the sauce for the chicken and refrigerate or freeze the rest.

Mix the water, salt, and sugar together in a large bowl or pot. Immerse the whole broilers for 30 minutes in this brine, then dry the broilers inside and out. Remove their backbone and cut each into half (see page 728). Brush both sides of each half with a very thin layer of the barbecue sauce and set to marinate on a stainless steel cake rack set over a sheet pan. There should be just enough sauce on the broilers so it does not drip into the pan. Keep refrigerated at least 2 hours. Bring back to room temperature 30 minutes before grilling.

Preheat the grill. Grill the chicken 5 inches over charcoal or briquets that are turning white for 8 minutes on the cavity side first. Turn the chicken halves over and grill 5 minutes on the skin side. Raise the grilling rack another 2 to 3 inches and continue grilling on the skin side until the chicken's natural juices come out clear when each leg is pierced at its thickest part with a skewer. The skin should be nice and brown but not burned and the meat inside juicy and tender (see also the USDA recommended inner temperature on page 703). Let the chicken rest on the serving platter a few minutes before serving. Season with additional salt and with pepper only if desired.

SUGGESTED WINE: **Any** *mellow white wine such as Chenin Blanc,* **meritage of** *Sémillon and Sauvignon Blanc, California Grignolino rosé, white Zinfandel, Italian Lambrusco or Valtellina*

Butterflied Leg of Lamb in Citrus Marinade

FFR to FCR — 6 TO 8 SERVINGS

Oriental-style marinade

Grated rind of 1 orange

Juice of 5 large navel oranges

2 cloves garlic, coarsely crushed

One ¼-inch-thick slice fresh ginger, peeled and coarsely chopped

2 tablespoons fresh lemon juice

3 tablespoons dark soy sauce

3 tablespoons hoisin sauce

1 whole leg of lamb, 6 to 7 pounds

Salt

Pepper from the mill

This recipe also works for:
- *Completely boned and skinned loin strip of veal, preferably free range*
- *Turkey breast pounded to a thickness of 1½ to 2 inches*
- *All chicken parts*
- *Thick pork and veal chops*

SUGGESTED WINE: **An** *opulent Pinot Noir, well-rounded Cabernet Sauvignon, or the first-growth Beaujolais known as Fleurie, or an Italian Barolo*

In a small stainless steel saucepan mix together the orange rind and juice, garlic, and ginger and reduce to ⅓ cup over medium heat. Strain out the rind and ginger, then add the lemon juice, and soy and hoisin sauces. Mix well.

Completely strip the meat of all fell and underlying fat (see page 723). Remove all the bones (see page 724) and flatten the leg completely, patting it out to an even thickness. Place the leg on a stainless steel rack set over a sheet pan; brush with a thin layer of the marinade. Let marinate refrigerated for 2 hours; bring back to room temperature 30 minutes before cooking.

Preheat the coals to glowing red. Stick a piece of lamb fat on the prongs of a long-handled fork and rub it over the hot grill. Grill the leg 5 minutes on each side 4 to 5 inches from the coals. Raise the grilling rack to 8 inches above the coals and cook until the internal temperature reads 125°F, a few more minutes on each side. Remove from the heat leaving the thermometer in the meat, salt and pepper immediately on both sides, and let rest until the thermometer reads 130° to 135°F (USDA 145° to 160°F). Slice into thin slices, salt and pepper the slices, and serve promptly.

Napa Grillades

A recipe not to be used with thin cuts of veal such as scaloppine, but with

- *All thick cuts of steaks*
- *Thick, preferably free-range, veal steaks cut from the top round*
- *Boneless strips of rack or loin of lamb*

SUGGESTED WINE: *A young, truly fruity Cabernet Sauvignon or Syrah, or Chianti Classico*

FFR to FCR—6 SERVINGS

1½ cups mellow Cabernet Sauvignon

2 large whole flank steaks

1 clove garlic, finely chopped

3 tablespoons finely chopped fresh Italian parsley leaves

1 tablespoon unsaturated oil of your choice

Salt

Pepper from the mill

Reduce the wine to 2 generous tablespoons of very thick wine glaze in a small stainless steel saucepan over medium heat.

Remove all fat from the steaks. With a very sharp knife cut ⅛-inch-deep slashes edge to edge into both sides of each steak to obtain a crisscross pattern forming ½-inch squares. Brush a thin film of the wine glaze on both sides of each steak, then coat each with the mixed garlic and parsley. Let marinate 2 hours in the refrigerator, covered with a tent of aluminum foil. Bring back to room temperature 30 minutes before grilling.

Preheat the coals to glowing red. Using a mitten so you don't burn yourself, rub the hot grill with a thick wad of paper towels saturated with the oil. Grill rapidly 3 to 4 minutes on each side, 4 inches from the coals. Remove the meat from the heat when an instant thermometer reads 125°F. Leave the thermometer in and let the meat rest a few minutes. Season with a relatively large amount of salt and only a tiny bit of pepper. Cut the steaks into paper thin slices as soon as the internal temperature reaches 130°F (USDA 145°F).

Roasting Meats

When we spit roast over our barbecue pits or in a modern rotisserie oven, letting a nice little electric motor rotate the piece of meat or bird(s) over hot coals, we imitate our distant ancestors. More ancient ways of spit roasting can be seen in old European kitchens such as that of the Hospices de Beaune in French Burgundy, where the 1700s' mechanical spit still functions and is in use, and in many of the country kitchens of remote valleys of central Italy. Closer to us in time and spirit, the American Indians and mountain and pioneer men and women spit roasted by passing a long stick of green wood through their catch, setting it over two sets of crossed green wood boughs and turning the meat by hand. I was one of the many awed kids who during World War II watched several women of my family replicate this ancestral cooking method to roast illegally poached rabbits in forest clearings, far from indiscreet eyes.

In modern roasting we slowly bake meats in our barbecue pits, spit roast them over dancing flames of hot coals, or oven roast them in our modern thermostat-controlled ovens utilizing the currents of hot convected air and the radiating heat of the heating elements. Only when roasting a large standing rib roast or a large turkey do we use also the conduction heat of the pan, when the meat or bird is set directly on the bottom of the roasting pan.

The best roasting is done on a spit because any steam rising from the joint escapes into the ambient air. In an oven, steam condenses and produces a small but appreciable amount of moisture which retards the browning of the roast.

Meats contain sugars and proteins; as they roast, their proteins slowly coagulate and release sugar- and amino acid-laden water. The sugars (glucose and others) react with some of the amino acid groups (lysine, tryptophane) which are part of the meat proteins. As the water in the drippings evaporates in the oven, successive reactions take place which lead to the formation, on the bottom of the roasting pan, of caramel from the sugars; at the same time, the breaking down of the amino acids through several other reactions results in the formation of brown pigments called melanoidins. Their delicious taste and lovely brown color are responsible for the deep flavors and shades of brown of different roasted meats. The longer the roasting time, the more intense the reactions and the more taste and color in the gravy. In meats roasted to the well-done stage, the taste is ultimately more in the gravy than it is in the meat. About halfway through the total roasting time, the meat will give off its particular aroma, very special to each and every type of meat and the result of the formation of volatile compounds released as the heat breaks down the amino acids, which react with a number of other components and generate a meatlike aroma.

As the coagulation of the outside of the roast progresses and moisture evaporates, progressive shrinkage can be observed. In institutional cooking, large roasts are often cooked at a lower temperature to prevent such shrinkage and coax a few more portions out of a joint, a technique that results in the meat neither looking nor tasting as good as it does when roasted at a higher temperature.

From a nutritional point of view, red meats are rich in vitamin B. Rare meat remains rich in the B vitamins. Whether rare or well done, the nutritional value of the proteins in meats remains the same.

The tenderness of a piece of roasted meat depends on many factors such as the animal's diet and age, as well as the length of time it has aged (see page 716); it will also depend on the amount of collagen and fat it contains and, last but not least, on the skill of the cook.

TYING ROASTS AND TRUSSING BIRDS

While roasts baked the old-fashioned way with their natural layer of fat left on need not be tied, roasts that are completely defatted must absolutely be tied with 1/10-inch-thick string, spacing the ties 1/2 inch apart, for as soon as a muscle has been stripped of its outside connective tissues, it flattens out and loses its original shape. This is especially important for long, thin muscles such as loins of veal which have been completely stripped of their fat and connective tissue coverings. You can tie such a roast using either the so-called butcher tie, in which the meat is tied with one long string, or you can use separate ties; I personally prefer individual ties which allow you to better control the uniformity of the piece of meat and insure its even roasting along its entire length.

Important: When you tie a piece of meat, do not squeeze it too tight. It is all right for the meat to show light string "scars" as it swells during the first half hour of roasting, but if your ties are very tight, the meat will start losing its juices before roasting.

REPLACING THE NATURAL SUET ON A DEFATTED ROAST

Completely defatted roasts must be coated with a very thin layer of olive oil or any other unsaturated oil.

They can also be coated with a thick reduction of wine and/or different compositions of chopped fresh herbs or a combination of both. If using reduced wine, it is essential that the wine be reduced to a thick syrup; a full bottle of wine should be reduced to no more than 2 generous tablespoons. A very expensive wine is not recommended for such a reduction; a pleasant, good quality wine is sufficient. Remember, though, that a wine that does not taste good to drink will still not taste good as a glaze on a lean piece of meat.

If you especially like one of the many newfangled prepared mustards available to the modern cook, by all means use it to coat meats that are to be roasted but sear the meat lightly before you apply it, to prevent losing good meat juices which will be drawn out of the meat by the high salt contents of the mustard.

THE ROASTING PAN

Oven manufacturers usually provide stoves with a roasting pan fitted with a rack and deep enough to accumulate the fat of nondefatted roasts or fatty birds. If you have inherited an oven which has lost its roasting pan, improvise one by placing a cake rack over a rectangular or oblong metal baking dish or cake pan.

OVEN AND MEAT THERMOMETERS

Invest in an oven thermometer and an instant meat thermometer. Both are affordable and the accuracy of each can be tested by dipping the needle part of the thermometer in boiling water for 2 full minutes. It should read 212°F.

ROASTING OR BAKING?

Notice the two different terms: roasting and baking. In the old days one meant roasting when the meat was spit roasted over the dancing flames of the hearth and baking when the meat was cooked slowly in the "used" heat (read dying heat) of the bread baking oven. Nowadays, we can either roast or bake by varying the temperature of our modern ovens.

If you want to roast to obtain a succulent meat, you must either spit roast or oven roast at a high temperature (400°F); if you prefer to roast to obtain a good, average tasting meat and a good gravy, you must oven bake at medium temperature (325°F). This distinction seems simple, but there is a slight complication: the choice of cut. Some cuts taste best when roasted, others when baked. Refer to the section on roasting and baking beef that follows; the recipes mention the different cuts that can be used and the best temperature to be applied when preparing each of them.

A BASTER

Meats are not basted with their own melted fat anymore, but we still use a metal baster. It is the best instrument to remove melted fat from a roasting pan so that it does not burn and smoke in the pan. Plastic basters tend to lose their shape when subjected to the high heat of the melted fat.

ROASTING BONE-IN OR BONELESS MEATS

Bones conduct the heat toward the center of the meat. For that reason boneless meats do not roast as fast as pieces with the bone in. This is particularly true of a leg of lamb and a standing rib roast.

CARRYOVER HEAT AND RESTING TIME

Remember that after any meat comes out of the oven, it will continue to cook from its own accumulated heat or carryover heat and may, depending upon its size, see its inner temperature go up by an additional 10° to 15°F as it rests. Taking this important point into consideration, remove the roast or bird from the oven in time and keep it resting while you prepare the gravy. The resting time will vary from 5 to 7 minutes for a small 3-pound roast, to 12 to 20 minutes for a 7- to 8-pound roast.

Resting the meat also allows the pressure on the internal juices to diminish slowly and gives the proteins in the meat fibers time to reabsorb them, thus preventing that disheartening rush of juices out of the meat when slicing and carving. Anytime you see more than a few tablespoons of red juice on the meat platter, you have carved the meat too soon after removing it from the oven. There is no way to repair the meat slices, which will be slightly dry, but you can use these juices in your gravy.

HELPING THE FORMATION OF THE GRAVY

For all roasts but especially for roasts that have been completely defatted, once the outside layers of the meat have browned well and drippings have started to coagulate at the bottom of the roasting pan, add small amounts of lightly salted water in increments of ¼ cup to prevent those drippings from burning and being lost.

In the case of roasts carrying their natural fat, use the metal baster to pump the fat out from the bottom of the roasting pan and replace it with a small amount of lightly salted water.

In both cases the salted water can be replaced by the stock of your choice. Light stock is preferable as thick, rich stock will thicken to a glaze and may burn as fast as the natural drippings of the meat. You can always finish the gravy with rich stock during the final deglazing of the roasting pan.

TO DEGLAZE   Dissolving the browned pan deposits of a roast with a liquid is called deglazing.

Here are my deglazing liquids of choice for the following meats:

- Roast beef, any light stock or lightly salted water
- A defatted rack of lamb will yield no gravy and requires a small sauce
- Leg of lamb, light stock or lightly salted water
- Veal loin or pork loin roast defatted in the modern way will have almost no pan deposits to make a gravy from and will need a small sauce
- Pork shoulder roast baked at 325°F, a light stock or broth or lightly salted water as preferred for a thicker or thinner gravy
- Turkey and chicken, any light stock or plain turkey or chicken stock
- Ducks and game birds, a rich veal stock or a strongly reduced stock made from their own neck, wing tips, and giblets when available

To deglaze, remove all excess fat from the roasting pan. If you like the taste of fat, leave 2 tablespoons of the liquid fat in the gravy; it will not be detrimental to your health provided you do not make it a practice to enjoy such a gravy each and every day. Once or twice a month is fine.

Try to completely defat turkey and chicken gravies since the taste of their fats is not especially attractive; duck or goose fat tastes very good, but 1 tablespoon of it in a roast duck gravy is sufficient.

Defatted leg of lamb roasted bone-in will release only a very small amount of gravy; so will a completely boned leg of lamb rolled into two smaller roasts (see Meat Handwork on page 720). *Please leave absolutely no fat in lamb gravy*, as it is heavy and unpleasant.

To remove the fat from the surface of a gravy, let a sheet of paper toweling fall onto the surface of the gravy and absorb the fat; lift the paper and discard it.

Depending on the size of the roast or bird, you will obtain a varying amount of pan deposits. Bring the deglazing liquid to a boil and gradually add it to the pan, scraping at the deposits as you do so. If the deposits are too abundant to loosen up easily by simply scraping, put the roasting pan over the medium-high flame of a burner and scrape over the heat. As soon as the deposits have completely liquefied, strain the deglazing into a measuring cup using a China cap or fine-meshed conical strainer.

TO MAKE A GRAVY You will need 1 cup of liquid to deglaze the pan and serve 6 to 8 people. Discard most of the fat in the pan first. If you prefer your gravy plain and unthickened, dilute it with the very best available stock and completely skim off any fat left at its surface. Served unthickened gravy is known as *jus* (in French recipes, it is also called *jus de viande*, literally, meat juices), which explains the restaurant menu expression "*au jus*." A well-prepared *jus* is very brown, very tasty, and slightly viscous.

To thicken a thoroughly modern and light gravy, potato starch is added. Although you can also use the same amount of cornstarch, the gravy will be more attractive with potato starch, which is clearer and shinier once it has boiled. For each cup of gravy to be thickened, mix 1¼ teaspoons potato starch with 2 tablespoons cold stock, broth, or lightly salted water. Bring the deglazing to a simmer—not a high boil—stir in the slurry of potato starch, and simmer, stirring constantly, until the gravy is shiny and thickened, which takes all of 2 minutes.

The old-fashioned *beurre manié* (see page 287 for more details) is still used by cooks who enjoy the taste of butter in their gravy. For each cup of gravy, mix 1½ tablespoons unsalted butter with 1 tablespoon all-purpose flour and whisk into the simmering gravy. Stop the cooking as soon as the gravy thickens. *If you use butter, do not keep any fat from any kind of meat or poultry in the gravy.*

To best serve the gravy, heat a sauce boat or bowl with hot water. Discard the water, dry the boat or bowl completely, and strain the gravy into it.

TO USE THE JUICES FLOWING FROM A ROAST THAT HAS BEEN CARVED TOO EARLY These bright red juices are not to every diner's taste. Do not throw them away, though. Pour them into a skillet and reduce them to a thick brown glaze, identical to the drippings in the roasting pan. Add a few tablespoons of broth, stock, or lightly salted water, strain, and stir into the gravy you've just prepared.

ROASTING AND BAKING BEEF

For roasting and baking, use cuts of beef graded "prime" only occasionally and "choice" most of the time. Some stores offer only beef graded "good"; in this lesser grade, it is best to buy only the most tender cuts: tenderloin, sirloin strip, and rib.

The names of the cut may vary from one state to another, depending on local vocabulary. While everyone knows a rib or a strip of beef from seeing it in the supermarket all the time, other cuts are often hard to identify. To prevent confusion, I will indicate the code numbers (see page 712) of all cuts that may be unfamiliar to the cook or even to the supermarket meat cutter.

Give this code to any true butcher in a true butcher shop, and he/she will know how to read and understand it and pass it on to the purveyor, so that you will receive exactly the piece of meat you want, not a frustrating piece of "whatever," as is often the case in supermarkets.

Aged beef being more tender than beef that is bought and cooked on the same day, consider aging larger celebration pieces of beef. It is only possible if you have an additional refrigerator or a walk-in refrigerator in which to let the piece(s) sit and change flavor gradually. Unwrap the beef and place it on a stainless steel rack placed over a roasting pan; cover it with a tent of aluminum foil well vented at both ends and extending at least 1 inch away from the sides of the meat and 2 inches above its top. For the "American taste," let the piece age only four to five days; you will obtain tender meat without what you would call an "off" taste. For the "French taste," you can go to a full week; for the "English taste," up to ten days. The longer the aging, the more fat you will have to trim from the surface of the roast if the meat is to be roasted with some of its fat covering on, for the fat covering oxidates as the meat stands and acquires a slightly rancid flavor. The two end slices may, if you age to the French taste, dehydrate considerably and look dark and dry; slice them off before cooking. If you age to the English taste, a blue mold called whiskers may start developing; trim the meat wherever it is present. The longer the meat stands, the more water and weight it will lose, the better its flavor and texture will be, and *the faster it will cook*, since there is less water in the meat and since enzymes have been at work softening the fibers for a while already.

Primal cuts of rib and sirloin strip of beef for roasting or detailing in steaks are sold in Cryovac packaging which is supposed to be under vacuum (see page 710). The roasts are packed in boxes in which the meat is often tossed in such a way that the pieces can hit one another during transportation and break the vacuum seal. You will know this has happened when the bag does not adhere to the meat and dark blood has accumulated in the bag. Use those joints first. Very little aging takes place in meats that are Cryovacked, but I have kept such beef two weeks in an excellent refrigerator at 41°F and obtained extremely tender and flavorful meat.

The tenderness of a cut of beef determines whether it should be roasted at 400°F or baked at 325°F. Tenderloin, sirloin strip, and rib roasts that have been completely defatted should be roasted at 400°F, or spit roasted.

When roasting at this temperature, the browning of the meat happens rapidly, especially if it has been stripped of all fat and connective membranes and isn't salted until the roast already looks light brown. At this temperature with these cuts, shrinkage is significant, the flavor highly concentrated, and the contrast between the "brown flavor" of the outer layers with the juiciness of the center is a delight to the palate. Such roasts lose no more than 3 tablespoons of very concentrated drippings, not sufficient enough to provide a good gravy and are to be enjoyed for their own juiciness or with a separate small sauce.

A standing rib roast that has not been defatted is best baked at 325°F. So are rump, true eye of the round, and blade roasts. Since their major virtue is their excellent taste rather than their tenderness, it is best not to defat these cuts before baking them.

When roasted at this temperature, the proteins in the outside layers of meat exposed to the oven heat do not denature as quickly and there is time for a handsome amount of juice to escape. If the meat is salted before roasting starts, the salt has an additional slight dehydrating effect on the surface of the muscle fibers, and being naturally attracted to any moisture helps draw relatively abundant good juices from the meat. The meat will darken gradually; as soon as the browning is completed and the temporary sealing of the juices within the roast is achieved, the Maillard reaction speeds up, darkening the drippings rather rapidly. From then on, it is important to watch that the drippings don't become too dark and burn slightly or the resulting gravy will be slightly bitter. Add small amounts of stock for a rich, heavier gravy or extremely light broth or lightly salted water for a lighter gravy to the roasting pan to prevent this from happening.

When removed from the source of heat, the meat juices will continue traveling under pressure between the muscle fibers. As the pressure diminishes, the muscle fibers' proteins will start rebinding the water contained in those juices, but not all of the juices will rebind and you will see a bit seep out of the resting roast. Do not discard these juices; add them to the already prepared gravy and simmer 2 to 3 minutes after this addition.

Here are recipes that illustrate these guidelines:

Roast Beef with Gravy and Yorkshire Pudding

FFR — NUMBER OF SERVINGS VARIES WITH THE NUMBER OF RIBS USED

1 standing rib roast

Salt

Pepper from the mill

1½ cups lightly salted water

Potato starch or cornstarch as needed

For the Yorkshire pudding

3 cups sifted unbleached all-purpose flour

5 large eggs, separated

Salt

Pepper from the mill

2½ to 3 cups skim milk, light broth, or water as needed

Ask the butcher to order for you IMPS No. 103 rib primal and tell him the number of portions you need.

This recipe can also be executed with:

- *Rump roast, always available in any butcher shop*
- *True eye of the round roast, always available in any butcher shop*
- *Sirloin butt roast boneless— IMPS No. 182*

Buy an expensive festive rib roast oven-ready from a good butcher only. Once baked, the rib is presented standing on one of its ends, carved by first detaching the meat from the rib rack with a long sharp-bladed knife, then cutting slices transversally at a right angle to the bones. This cut will yield up to twenty boneless portions; smaller roasts can be cut out from the whole rib rack to serve the following numbers:

- *3 ribs will serve about 6 portions*
- *4 ribs will serve about 8 portions*

SUGGESTED WINE: *Any excellent full-bodied Cabernet Sauvignon or exceptional Pinot Noir from the United States, an excellent red Medoc or Côte de Nuits of your choice, or Cabernet Sauvignon or Shiraz from Australia*

CARVING A STANDING RIB ROAST

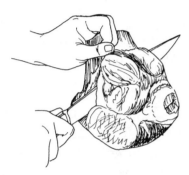

With the roast on its side, separate the beef from the rib bones, moving the knife downward between the meat and bone.

Stand the roast on one of its flat planes and slice from the rounded outside cut toward the rib. When your blade reaches the rib, each slice will separate.

Preheat the oven to 325°F. Set the roast rib side down on a roasting pan. Season well on all sides with salt and pepper. As the meat bakes, remove the liquid fat from the roasting pan with a metal baster. Bake approximately 20 minutes for the first pound and 15 minutes for each additional pound, checking doneness with an instant thermometer. Remove the roast from the oven when the thermometer inserted at the heart of the eye muscle registers 120°F for rare (final temperature after resting about 130°F) or 125°F for medium rare (final temperature after resting 135°F; the USDA required temperature is 145°F for medium rare). Cover the meat with aluminum foil to keep it warm while it rests and until the Yorkshire pudding is fully baked or, if no pudding is prepared, up to 30 minutes.

Start mixing the Yorkshire pudding batter as soon as the beef has started to bake. Resift the flour into a large bowl, then add the egg yolks, seasonings, and one third of the chosen liquid. Stir together with a wooden spoon until smooth; gradually add the remainder of the liquid. Keep covered.

As soon as the inner temperature of the roast beef is 90°F, whip the egg whites until a raw egg in its shell sinks into the foam by no more than ¼ inch. Gradually beat the semiliquid batter into the egg whites until the foam has dispersed into the batter. Let rest while the roast finishes baking.

Skim the fat from the drippings in the roasting pan as completely as you can with a sauce spoon, reserving 1 tablespoon of it. Add the salted water to the pan and scrape to dissolve the solidified meat juices; strain this concentrated deglazing through a conical strainer into a measuring cup. Do not wash the roasting pan.

Mix 2 tablespoons of the concentrated gravy and the reserved beef fat together in the roasting pan, spreading the mixture over the bottom of the pan. Beat the pudding batter well to rehomogenize it and add it to the roasting pan. Bake at 400°F until puffed up, 15 to 20 minutes, then reduce the temperature to 350°F and bake until golden and crisp, another 8 to 10 minutes.

While the pudding bakes, finish the gravy. Unless you like the taste of beef fat, of which, in spite of your previous degreasing, there will be a small amount left on the surface of the gravy, use a baster to remove the fat-free concentrated gravy to a small saucepan. Dilute this deglazing with as much salted water as needed to obtain a gravy that pleases your taste. Bring to a simmer over medium heat. Measure 1¼ teaspoons of the starch of your choice per cup of simmering gravy and dissolve it in 2 tablespoons cold salted water. Add this slurry, stirring, to the simmering gravy until it has thickened. Correct the seasoning and simmer 2 more minutes.

Carve and serve ⅛- to ¼-inch-thick rib slices and portions of the pudding on heated dinner plates and spoon gravy over the meat.

Roasted Sirloin Strip of Beef with Madeira-Mushroom Sauce

FCR— 10 TO 12 SERVINGS

1 whole sirloin strip of beef, fat and silverskin removed

2 tablespoons light olive oil

2 cloves garlic, very finely chopped

¼ cup chopped fresh Italian parsley leaves

Salt

Pepper from the mill

3 cups Primary Veal Stock (page 219)

2 tablespoons unsalted butter

½ pound each chanterelles and black chanterelles, cleaned and quartered

1 pound fresh boleti or shiitake mushrooms, cleaned and diced into ½-inch cubes

2 tablespoons Sercial Madeira or fino sherry

Tie the roast with kitchen string at ¾-inch intervals. Rub the roast all around with the olive oil. Mix the garlic and parsley together; reserve 2 tablespoons of the mixture. Sprinkle the roast all around evenly with the remainder of the mixture. Let stand at room temperature 30 minutes before roasting. Roast in a preheated 400°F oven approximately 12 minutes for the first pound and 10 minutes for each additional pound, until an instant meat thermometer reads 125°F for rare for a serving temperature of 130°F, or 130°F for medium rare for a serving temperature of 135°F (USDA 145°F). Salt the roast only after it has seared well and pepper only in the last few minutes of roasting.

While the roast cooks, reduce 2 cups of the veal stock to 1¼ cups in a small saucepan over medium heat. Set aside. Heat the butter in a large skillet over medium-high heat until light brown, then toss the mushrooms in the hot butter and salt and pepper well. Turn the heat down to medium-low, cover, and cook until the mushrooms have lost all their moisture. Raise the heat back to medium high, add the remaining garlic and parsley, and continue cooking until all the water has evaporated and the mushrooms are coated with butter. Pour the reduced veal stock over the mushrooms and simmer a few minutes on low heat. Set aside, keeping warm.

When the roast is done, remove it from the oven and let it rest for 15 minutes. There will be only a very small amount of fat-free very concentrated drippings in the roasting pan. Remove the roast to a carving board, and deglaze the roasting pan with the remaining cup of veal stock, reducing it by two thirds over high heat. Stir the deglazing into the mushroom sauce and reheat to the boiling point. Add the Madeira and correct the final seasoning.

Serve slices of beef on heated plates and spoon the mushroom gravy over the meat.

This recipe can also be executed with a completely defatted rib roast or tenderloin of beef, each roasted at 400°F.

The boneless strip loin of beef—cut IMPS No. 176 strip loin boneless—also known as sirloin strip, is an expensive roast and can be bought from a supermarket or a butcher. It can be roasted at 400°F either with its fat covering on or, as in this recipe, completely stripped of its fat. A whole strip, once defatted and roasted, will serve about twelve people, half a roast up to eight. If you cannot get wild mushrooms, use regular brown or white mushrooms as available in all supermarkets. As an exercise for student chefs or any keen-by-avocation cook, this recipe can be prepared using the Classic Espagnole Sauce on page 284 instead of the reduced veal stock used here.

SUGGESTED WINE: *As you prefer, Heitz Cellars Martha's Vineyard or Bella Oak Cabernet Sauvignon, Beringer Vineyards Private Reserve Cabernet Sauvignon, Mondavi Opus One or other good California Cabernet Sauvignon of your choice; or any Saint-Estèphe or Vosne-Romanée as old as you can find, or afford*

California Spit-Roasted Tenderloin of Beef

This recipe will bring California to your celebration dinner, and can also be used for:

- A rib of beef completely trimmed of fat and tied
- A sirloin strip completely trimmed and tied

Purchase an IMPS No. 189A, full tenderloin defatted, from a butcher. In the last five years what seems to have been sold as tenderloin in supermarkets is only what in colloquial butcher language is called the bullnose or thick end of the tenderloin, which once cleaned up will serve only 4 to 5 people.

SUGGESTED WINE: *An excellent Cabernet Sauvignon either from California or Australia or an excellent French Medoc*

FCR—8 TO 10 SERVINGS

1 bottle light Cabernet Sauvignon

1 tablespoon dark soy sauce

3 large cloves garlic, finely chopped

¼ cup finely chopped fresh Italian parsley leaves

2 teaspoons finely chopped fresh oregano flowers or 1 teaspoon leaves

½ teaspoon finely chopped fresh rosemary leaves

½ teaspoon finely chopped fresh summer savory leaves

¼ teaspoon ground allspice

1 whole tenderloin of beef, 5½ to 6 pounds, fat and silverskin removed

Salt

Pepper from the mill

For the sauce

Olive oil as needed

Fat-free trimmings from chain and tail of the tenderloin (page 722)

5 cups Primary Veal Stock (page 219)

2 cups Cabernet Sauvignon of your choice

3 shallots, finely chopped

2 to 6 tablespoons unsalted butter, to your personal taste

Pour the bottle of Cabernet into a large saucepan, bring to a boil, reduce to a simmer, and cook over low heat until 2 tablespoons of thick and syrupy glaze remains, about 40 minutes. Add the soy sauce, cool completely, and set aside.

Mix the garlic, herbs, and allspice together, then spread evenly on a sheet of parchment paper or clear plastic wrap. Set aside.

Completely trim the fillet of beef of all remaining fat and silverskin until the muscle fibers are exposed all around the piece of meat. Pull off the long 1-inch-thick muscle or "chain" found along the tenderloin, clean it of fat, and cut it into ½-inch cubes; set aside.

At the bullnose (the thick end) the tenderloin divides into three muscles. The large and long tenderloin tapers to a point in the center; on one side is the true filet mignon (called that because it looks like a miniature tenderloin) and what, on the other side, appears to be a third muscle is really part of the main muscle of the tenderloin separated from it by a band of fat. Remove all silverskin and fat all the way to the end of the tip of the bullnose. Push all three now fat-free muscles together and tie them at ½-inch intervals. Push the center and tail parts of the tenderloin upward toward the already tied bullnose so the muscle becomes almost evenly thick along its entire length. Tie at ½-inch intervals. The thinner end of the tenderloin tapers into a flat piece called the tail. Cut it off and dice it into ½-inch cubes; add them to the cubed chain. Set aside.

Brush the tied tenderloin all over with the reduced Cabernet and soy sauce. Roll the meat over the herb-sprinkled paper and coat evenly on all sides. Set on a stainless rack and refrigerate, covered, with a tent of aluminum foil until ready to cook.

Prepare the sauce. In a 1-quart sauteuse pan or medium-size skillet, heat the olive oil on medium-high heat. Add the reserved cubed meat trimmings and brown them. Discard the browning fat and add 1 cup of the stock. Over medium heat, reduce to a thick glaze that will coat the meat. Add the remainder of the stock in four successive additions of 1 cup each, reducing each time until the glaze coats a spoon with ½ inch of shiny laquer. Strain through a conical strainer or China cap into a small saucepan; you should have about 1 cup of excellent beef essence.

Meanwhile, reduce the 2 cups Cabernet and the shallots to ¼ cup over medium heat in a small saucepan. Strain into the essence and simmer together 5 to 10 minutes to blend the flavors. Correct the seasoning and add as much butter as needed to temper the acidity given to the sauce by the wine; it will vary between 2 and 6 tablespoons.

To roast, remove the tenderloin from the refrigerator 30 minutes before roasting. Start a fire in the barbecue pit using half each briquettes and mesquite wood, placed so they radiate behind the roasting piece of meat and extend at least 4 inches beyond and in front of the roast. When the fire is hot and ready, pass a spit through the roast and attach on both sides with special balancing forks so the roast does not flop around while roasting. Roast to an internal temperature of 115° to 120°F. You must use an instant meat thermometer; it is impossible to predict an exact or even approximate roasting time; it will vary with the weather conditions of the day. Salt the meat only when the internal temperature reaches 100°F and pepper only a few minutes before removing from the spit. Let rest 10 minutes before carving to reach a temperature of 130°F (USDA 145°F).

Slice the roast, set it on a clean platter. Pass the sauce in a sauce boat.

ROASTING VEAL

Butchers can now provide two types of veal, each expensive for different reasons:

- Provimi veal, named for the diet of *proteins*, *vitamins*, and *minerals* given the young animal, resulting in perfectly pale pink veal.
- Range-fed veal, taken from a young animal who besides being allowed to normally suckle its mother during its short life is allowed to roam and graze freely. Its meat will be somewhat darker than that of Provimi veal and most delicious.

Because of the nature of my work, I have to use both types of veal as a matter of comparison for my students. I strongly urge you to try each, and read everything you can find on the techniques used to raise the animals before you make up your mind on which you prefer.

My personal philosophy on roasted veal is to use only the very best cut—the sirloin strip—and to reserve it for very special occasions. Shoulder roasts should be baked, pot-roasted, or braised rather than roasted at a higher temperature.

To obtain a loin of veal, ask your butcher for IMPS cuts:

- No. 332 for a *loin trimmed, double,* which will yield two roasts to serve a total of 10 to 12 people, or
- No. 333 for a *full loin trimmed, single,* yielding one roast that will serve 6 people.

Each side is made of two muscles: the sirloin strip situated above the T-bone and the tenderloin situated underneath. In classic cuisine, the sirloin strip and the tenderloin were boned, them wrapped into each other and tied to form a long roll which was then casserole roasted or braised. This piece is so expensive that it is rarely sold for home cooking nowadays in the United States. Refer to the section on meat handwork (see page 720) and be prepared to do the butchering yourself for, unless you are a millionaire, you will not want to pay the price for the cleaned loin(s) if the butcher does it for you.

Each side of the loin will provide enough extras to make the following additional culinary preparations:

- Stock, prepared with the bones and trimmings containing too many connective tissues to be used otherwise.
- Each tenderloin offers two additional portions of meat (see the recipe for pan-roasted tenderloin on page 797 for a good way to use them).
- Enough lean meat trimmings to prepare either a sauce to be served with each side of loin, or six to eight portions of small meatballs for pasta dishes or appetizers (for a recipe, see page 874).
- One veal kidney pie made with each kidney (see page 896).
- Excellent rendered veal kidney suet for a very occasional treat of old-fashioned french fries (see page 425) or fish and chips (see page 636); this is your decision, and if you decide to try it, use the fat only once and discard it.

Strip the loins of all fat and connective tissues as indicated on page 723. After cleaning and stripping a loin you will see it flatten to a piece no thicker than a large steak. To round its shape again, tie it with thin kitchen string at ½-inch intervals. You will notice that smaller loin strips will take proportionally almost as much time to cook as larger ones.

Treat roast strip loin of veal as you would tenderloin of beef; veal is baby beef and should be served cooked medium rare. The roast should be removed from the oven at an internal temperature of 120°F to be served at 130°F (USDA 145°F) after 5 to 8 minutes of rest.

The meat must be roasted coated with lightly toasted crumbs, chopped nuts, aromatics, and herbs alone or in combination, which prevent the outside from experiencing unpleasant dehydration. A thin layer of olive oil can replace the crumb coating; the cooking then will be faster by approximately 3 minutes.

Here is a recipe to practice on:

Riviera-Style Veal Roast

FFR to FCR — 6 SERVINGS

For the roast

1 loin strip of veal, single, entirely trimmed of fat and connective tissues

2 cloves garlic, very finely chopped

3 tablespoons finely scissored fresh basil leaves

3 tablespoons chopped fresh Italian parsley leaves

Spray bottle filled with olive oil

2 tablespoons very finely chopped pine nuts

3 tablespoons finely ground Pecorino Romano or Sardo cheese

¼ cup dry bread crumbs made from Italian bread

Salt

Pepper from the mill

For the sauce

1 tablespoon olive oil of your choice

Fat-free meat trimmings from the loin, cut into ½-inch cubes

5 cups Primary Veal Stock (page 219)

2 tablespoons unsalted butter (optional)

Salt

Pepper from the mill

You will need a small sprayer containing olive oil to spray the roast. The sauce is a typical single veal essence (see page 296 for details); 2 tablespoons of it per person will be entirely sufficient.

SUGGESTED WINE: *Italian Dolceacqua, a Mourvèdre/ Cinsault blend from California, or a Domaine Tempier Bandol from France*

Tie the strip at ½-inch intervals to reshape it to a perfect round.

Mash the garlic, basil, and parsley leaves together into a paste. Mix half the mixture with a bit of olive oil; set aside and keep the remainder of the herb paste for the sauce. Mix together the pine nuts, cheese, and bread crumbs; sprinkle evenly on a sheet of paper and set aside. Rub the oil-herb mixture all over the meat and roll the flavored roast in the crumb mixture. Set on a stainless steel rack placed over the roasting pan and let stand at room temperature for 30 minutes.

Heat the olive oil in a sauteuse pan over medium-high heat; brown the cubes of veal. They may brown readily or, depending on the type of veal you use, the meat juices may flood the pan. If they do, patiently let them come to a brown glaze, then brown the pieces of meat evenly. When the cubes are golden brown, remove the pan from the heat. Lift the pan to a 30-degree angle and block it in this position by resting it on the edge of a chopping block. Gather all the meat cubes to the raised side of the pan. In a few minutes you will see the browning fat drip into the lip of the pan; pat entirely off, using a large wad of paper towels. Return the pan to the flat position on the burner; add 1 cup of the veal stock and scrape the pan bottom to completely deglaze it, add the remainder of the stock at once and bring to a boil; turn down to a simmer and reduce to 1 generous cup of veal single essence, 45 minutes to 1 hour. Strain through a China cap or conical strainer into a small saucepan. If used, mash the butter with the remaining paste of herbs or add plain herb paste to the sauce and let steep while the loin roasts.

Preheat the oven to 500°F. Spray the crumb-coated meat with a little more olive oil and put it in to roast on the upper rack of the oven. Immediately reduce the oven temperature to 400°F. Roast about 18 minutes, until an instant thermometer registers 120°F. Let rest about 8 minutes, covered with aluminum foil, till an internal temperature of 130°F (USDA 145°F) is achieved. Reheat the sauce. Slice the roast, salt and pepper the slices, and serve on a platter, passing the sauce in a sauce boat.

ROASTING LAMB

Lamb should always be less than a year old and mutton is over that venerable age. The lamb usually sold in supermarkets is way over five months old, and its age can be roughly determined by the weight of a leg. An early season leg does not weight more than five pounds while a fall/winter leg will easily climb to seven, even, in extreme cases, eight pounds. The darker the color of the meat and the thicker the fat covering on the leg, the older the animal. The "eye" of rib and loin increase in size and color in the same manner as the months go by in the life of the animal.

The western states and progressively more of the central and eastern states produce excellent, truly young lambs which allow cooks to produced wonderful roasts done to a delicate pink. Never undercook true young lamb so that it remains so rare it deserves the qualification of "blue" lamb, for such meat develops little flavor, its texture is somewhat chewy, and its taste unpleasantly acidic. True older lamb, which hopefully will one day be given its true name of mutton, can be roasted slightly rarer than lamb, but never blue, and is in a different way just as delicious as true lamb, if well prepared.

All through my years as a restaurateur I have served medium-rare lamb and converted a lot of guests over to lamb who had resisted it because they had always been served well-done lamb. Well-done lamb is unpleasant, as the taste of the cooked and crisped lamb fell and suet permeates the meat. To make older lamb or mutton acceptable to the majority of diners in the United States, its meat should be entirely trimmed of fat and connective tissues for any and all of its methods of cooking.

Do not hesitate to let any cut of lamb age a bit in a tent of aluminum foil in your refrigerator. If you have walk-in refrigeration, purchase lamb legs one week before they are to be used and hang them without covering them; they will become most tasty and tender as butter, even when they come from larger older animals. All you have to do is remove the dried-out fell carefully.

Remember that lamb cannot be aged in Cryovac wrapping. If you keep lamb in Cryovac wrapping, keep it frozen, defrost it slowly, and use it as soon as defrosted.

WHOLE LAMB If you happen to have a big clan reunion or feast coming, consider roasting a whole 4- to 5-month-old lamb as is done is Greece or the Maghreb (the Mediterranean coast of Africa). All you have to do is stuff the cavity with the herbs of your choice and slowly spit roast it over a good open fire.

For a leg of lamb roasted whole and served without sauce or gravy, order cut IMPS No. 1233A, leg, lower shank off, single, or IMPS No. 233C, leg, shank off, single.

In the following Provençal recipe, the gravy will be absorbed by the potatoes as the dish roasts.

Roasted Leg of Lamb and Potatoes
PROVENÇAL TIAN D'AGNEAU

FCR — 8 SERVINGS

I whole leg of spring lamb, 5 to 6 pounds

4 large cloves garlic, finely chopped

2 teaspoons finely chopped fresh rosemary leaves

2 teaspoons finely chopped fresh summer savory leaves

2 teaspoons finely chopped fresh thyme leaves

⅓ cup finely chopped fresh Italian parsley leaves

Olive oil of your choice in a spray bottle

I clove garlic, peeled

6 large Yellow Finnish or Yukon Gold potatoes, peeled and cut into ⅛-inch-thick slices

Salt

Pepper from the mill

I½ to 2 cups light broth of your choice as needed

4 sun-ripened pear tomatoes, peeled and sliced

½ cup water

This recipe can also be used to bake a whole shoulder of veal (see page 774). It is one of the many variations of a traditional Provençal dish.

A tian in the Provençal language is a brown earthenware baking dish; over the centuries, tian has become the name of any dish prepared in such a dish, so that there are tians of all kinds of meats and vegetables. Those of lamb are particularly typical and popular. You will need a tian or a baking dish and a roasting pan fitted with a rack.

Strip the lamb leg all around of fell, fat, and connective tissues, all the way down to the bare muscle. Mix the chopped garlic and all the herbs together. Rub half the mixture all over the leg. Set on a stainless steel rack fitted over a roasting pan, spray with olive oil, and set aside while you prepare the vegetables. Preheat the oven to 400°F.

SUGGESTED WINE: *A Châteauneuf-du-Pape or Hermitage from France or Clos Pegase Hommage Cabernet Sauvignon from California*

Crush the whole garlic clove and rub a 2-quart baking dish with it. Let the garlic juice dry; spray the baking dish with olive oil. In a large bowl toss together the sliced potatoes and the remaining herbs, and season with salt and pepper. Arrange the potato slices in four layers and add the broth to barely cover. Put the potatoes on the bottom rack to the left side of the oven at the same time you put the leg of lamb on the upper rack on the right side. Let them cook separately for 35 minutes.

Add the tomato slices to form a circle all around the dish of potatoes. Transfer the leg of lamb to rest on the center of the potatoes and finish baking together. Add the water to the juices that have deposited in the meat roasting pan and reduce to a tablespoon or so of concentrated liquid over medium heat. Brush this liquid over the meat as it finishes baking. Roast until an instant meat thermometer registers 125°F at the center of the roast by the bone. The total roasting time from start to finish will be about 1 hour and 15 minutes. Remove the roast from the oven and let rest, covered with aluminum foil, until the internal temperature reads 135°F (USDA 145°F). Carve the roast and serve with portions of the tomato-and-potato *tian* on heated plates.

WHOLE LEG OF LAMB ROASTED WITH GRAVY OR SAUCE Order cut IMPS No. 233E, hindshank, heel attached, which is a whole leg with all its muscles intact, or IMPS No. 233, legs. This item is delivered as two legs attached together. Have the butcher separate the legs and saw off the heel for you. If you use only one leg, keep the second frozen for later use.

Either of such legs will allow you to prepare a sauce from the shank muscles, and bone the remainder of the leg to obtain two small rolled roasts, one slightly larger than the other; for this technique see pages 723–25.

Once roasted, you will separate all the muscles and slice each against the grain, so that there is very little meat left over.

When using this method with several legs for larger parties, all the ends of the small roasts are kept to prepare modern dishes of part grain, part vegetable, part meat as can be found on pages 407–11 under the heading of Stir-fried Vegetables.

Roast Leg of Lamb from Antibes

FCR — 8 TO 10 SERVINGS

I whole leg of lamb, completely stripped of all fat, fell, and connective tissues and
butterflied (page 723)

Salt

Pepper from the mill

¼ teaspoon coriander seeds

¼ teaspoon fennel seeds

Any leg of lamb prepared as described here can also be spit roasted on your barbecue. The city of Antipolis, now Antibes, on the French Riviera, used to be celebrated for its excellent Roman garum, made of fermented tuna.

¼ teaspoon celery seeds

1 tablespoon chopped fresh dill

2 teaspoons finely chopped fresh yellow celery leaves

2 teaspoons chopped fresh oregano leaves

2 teaspoons finely chopped fresh mint leaves

2 teaspoons finely chopped Italian parsley leaves

3 anchovy fillets, rinsed and mashed to a paste

1 large clove garlic, rinsed and mashed to a paste

Olive oil as needed

5 cups Primary Veal Stock (page 219)

The anchovies and garlic used here are most probably a modern replacement for the garum.

SUGGESTED WINE: *Barolo or Barbaresco of your choice or a rich Zinfandel from California such as Ravenswood*

Lay the butterflied leg flat on the table, the bone side facing you. Salt and pepper the meat. Divide the leg into two parts from its flatter center out, and roll and tie them into two smaller roasts with kitchen string at ½-inch intervals. In a mortar or spice mill, crush all the seeds to a powder, then mix that with the chopped herbs and mashed anchovies and garlic, adding as much olive oil as needed to make the mixture spreadable. Set 1 tablespoon of this mixture aside, then spread a thin layer of it all around both roasts. Let stand for 40 minutes at room temperature on a roasting pan fitted with a rack and while you make the sauce.

Dice the lower and upper shank meat into ½-inch cubes. Heat 2 tablespoons of the olive oil in a sauteuse pan and brown the meat cubes over medium heat until evenly golden. Discard the fat in the pan completely and deglaze with 1 cup of the stock. Reduce to a glaze over medium heat. Gradually add the remainder of the stock in 3 to 4 additions, reducing between additions, until you obtain a generous cup of lamb essence. Set aside. Strain into a small saucepan using a China cap and the reserved tablespoon of herb mixture.

Preheat the oven to 450°F. Put the roasts in the oven and immediately turn the temperature down to 400°F. Roast until the internal temperature registers 125°F on an instant thermometer, about 30 minutes for the smaller roast and 35 minutes for the larger one. Remove from the oven and let rest, covered with aluminum foil, until the internal temperature of both roasts registers 135°F (USDA 145°F). Slice and serve on hot plates with a garnish of the Mediterranean vegetables of your choice.

ROASTED RACK OF LAMB Finding a rack of lamb in a butcher shop is almost as easy as it is difficult to find leg of lamb prepared to one's specifications.

The rack of lamb comes from the foresaddle of lamb (IMPS No. 202) which extends from the neck to the thirteenth rib. It is separated from the remainder of the carcass, known as the saddle, between the twelfth and thirteenth ribs, the latter remaining attached to the saddle. After cutting off the uneven neck, one obtains a double rack known as the bracelet (IMPS

No. 203), consisting of the ribs and of the rib plates. The bracelet is separated from the chuck or shoulder by cutting across the foresaddle between the fourth and fifth ribs.

After purchasing the rib racks from purveyors, butchers separate the whole rack into two single sides. Each side consists of the plates, which start just about 4 inches from the tip of the eye of the rib and are nowadays cut with power saws. This leaves the butcher with a single rack of lamb well covered with lamb suet.

The next step consists of "frenching" the rack, which means removing most or all of the fat covering and stripping away the membrane that covers the rib. Make a cut through the fat all the way down to the bone 2½ inches from the tip of the eye of the rib. Now, still working on the fat side, stand the rack on its side and push the tip of a knife between each of the ribs at the same level, so that all the cuts will be aligned in one straight line.

Turn the rack to the other side and you will see the cuts you just made between the ribs. Now cut the membrane at the very center of each rib and pull the whole covering off. The covering of fat and membranes will come off in one piece still attached to each other, leaving the ribs completely clean and bare of any tissue. All that is left to do is remove as many layers of fat as you like from the top of the meat.

If you decide to remove all the fat, you will soon see two muscles appear; one is the rib cap and it is separated from the rib eye by a thin band of fat. Do not worry about that fat; leave it there for if you attempt to remove it, you will separate the rib cap and rib eye. On top of the rib eye you will see a very thin layer of silverskin; remove it carefully with the tip of a small parer. The rack is ready to roast.

Here is a recipe that is a variation on a classic of Normandy cookery:

Blonville Easter Rack of Lamb

FCR—6 TO 8 SERVINGS, DEPENDING ON THE APPETITES

2 single racks of lamb, frenched as described above

Salt

Pepper from the mill

2 tablespoons unsalted butter

2 large cloves garlic, very finely chopped

¼ cup finely chopped fresh curly parsley leaves

¼ cup dry bread crumbs

3 tablespoons Dijon mustard

FRENCHING A RACK OF LAMB

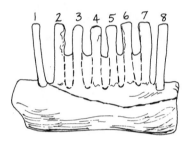

Look at the illustration. Ribs 1 and 8 are completely frenched. Ribs 2–7 must be finished and all the tissues between them removed. The meat you remove can be used to make a sauce or two patties.

This recipe is full of childhood memories; the smell of it filled the kitchen of my friend Henriette when we came back from Easter Mass. It was traditionally served with the first tiny green beans of the season, butter-fried potatoes, and soft béarnaise prepared with soft spring tarragon.

Preheat the oven to 450°F. Season the rack of lamb with salt and pepper to taste. Heat the butter in a large nonstick frying pan over medium-high heat and sear the top of the meat until light golden. Remove from the pan; do not discard the butter. To the pan add the garlic and parsley and toss until the garlic starts developing its flavor, 1 or 2 minutes. Mix in the bread crumbs and cool.

Brush the top of each rack of lamb with 1½ tablespoons of the mustard, then spread the prepared topping equally over the two racks. Set the racks on a roasting pan. Turn the oven down to 400°F and roast until an instant meat thermometer registers 120°F, 20 to 25 minutes. Remove from the oven and let rest until the inner temperature has reached 130°F (USDA 145°F). Slice between the ribs.

SPIT-ROASTED RACK OF LAMB If you wish to spit roast a rack of lamb, you must leave a layer of fat ⅛ inch thick over the rack before roasting it. Keep a roasting pan below the racks to gather the fat and prevent a lot of smoke.

ROASTING PORK

Pork is marketed between the ages of five months and one year; great care is taken not to keep the animal any longer than necessary to avoid the development of excessive fat. The best pork available is light pink; the rosier the meat, the older the animal. Extensive marbling is not desirable, as the meat does not contain the large amounts of collagen necessary to emulsify the relatively large streaks of fat.

The loin of pork (IMPS No. 410 and 412) can be roasted at the relatively high heat of 375° to 400°F. Such a loin can be served at an internal temperature of 160°F, as recommended by the USDA.

There seems to be a certain modern enthusiasm about completely defatting and roasting a pork loin to medium rare only. Its meat may be more tender, but it does not in any way taste as good as pork that is baked at a lower temperature with some of its fat cover on. The reason is the complete removal of the fat which carries most of the taste and flavor in pork. So, if like me, you prefer a slowly baked piece of pork, refer to the section on baking on page 773 for other techniques and recipes.

Here is a recipe to practice roasting pork at high temperature:

SUGGESTED BEVERAGE OR WINE: *Normandy or English hard cider. I personally prefer a small Pomerol or a really nice Cabernet from Sonoma such as Simi or Jordan.*

Roast Pork Loin with Mustard and Currant Sauce

The roast will have to be boned entirely, cleaned of all silverskin and fat, and tied with kitchen string as indicated on page 721, then marinated overnight.

SUGGESTED WINE: *A happy Beaujolais or lighter Zinfandel*

FFR — 8 SERVINGS

I side of boneless loin of pork, about 5 pounds

I teaspoon ground cinnamon

I teaspoon ground allspice

I teaspoon ground coriander

I teaspoon ground cardamom

⅛ teaspoon freshly grated nutmeg

⅛ teaspoon ground ginger

Large pinch of ground cloves

2 cloves garlic, very finely chopped

2 tablespoons finely chopped cilantro leaves

I½ tablespoons dark soy sauce, nam pla, or nuoc mam

2 tablespoons dried currants

I tablespoon vinegar of your choice

I cup boiling veal or chicken stock of your choice

2 teaspoons cornstarch

2 tablespoons cold veal or chicken stock of your choice

Dijon mustard

Salt

Coarsely cracked black pepper

Strip the pork loin completely of fat and silverskin. Tie the loin at 1-inch intervals to shape it evenly round. In a small cup mix together the spices, garlic, and cilantro. Spread evenly on a sheet of parchment paper. Brush the meat with the soy sauce, then roll the roast in the mixture of spices and herbs to cover its entire surface evenly. Put the roast on a stainless steel rack resting over a roasting pan, cover loosely with plastic wrap, and let marinate overnight in the refrigerator. Soak the currants in the vinegar overnight.

Bring the meat back to room temperature for approximately 45 minutes. Preheat the oven to 375°F. Roast the meat to medium rare, when an instant meat thermometer registers 150°F, about 30 minutes. Let the roast rest 10 minutes, covered with aluminum foil, to allow the internal temperature to reach 160°F as recommended by the USDA.

Deglaze the roasting pan with the boiling stock, scraping to dissolve the few meat juices at the bottom of the pan. Add the currants and any vinegar left over; simmer, stirring, 2 to 3 minutes. Dilute the cornstarch in the cold stock; turn the gravy down to a simmer and stir in the starch slurry. Continue stirring until the gravy boils and thickens. Remove the pan from the heat and whisk in as much mustard as you like. Correct the seasoning with salt and pepper.

For more pork recipes, see the section on baking meats starting on page 771.

This very ancient meat cooking technique is found in the cuisines of ancient civilizations along the shores of the Sea of China and in the vicinity of salt mines exploited in Italy. It is probable that many other countries that produce a large amount of salt, either from mines or from the purification of seawater, also treasure some recipe or another for a food cooked in deep salt.

Red meats are truly roasted in salt, since the salt is heated in a 400°F oven before the meat is buried in it.

The principle of roasting in salt is related to pressure cooking. In the recipe that follows the fillet of beef is wrapped in grape leaves which will act as a protector for the meat in the same way the skin of the chicken does in the recipe for chicken poached in salt on page 856. The salt will draw the moisture out of the leaves, which will wilt and dry by the time the meat is cooked. The meat, however, will only lose an insignificant amount of its juices; at the same time, it will acquire a pleasant tangy taste from contact with the grape leaves.

Fillet of Beef Roasted in Salt

FCR — 6 SERVINGS

For the roast

Two 5-pound boxes kosher salt

1½ cups Primary Veal Stock (page 219)

¼ teaspoon grated lemon rind

2 tablespoons capers, drained

1 tiny clove garlic, mashed

1½ tablespoons chopped fresh Italian parsley leaves

Pepper from the mill

1 head fillet of beef, about 2¼ pounds

18 to 20 fresh or canned grape leaves, thoroughly dried

For the mushrooms

6 small boleti or large shiitake mushrooms

2 tablespoons olive oil of your choice plus extra as needed

Salt

Pepper from the mill

1 medium-size yellow onion, finely chopped

1¾ cups fresh Italian bread crumbs

3 paper-thin slices prosciutto, very finely chopped

2 tablespoons finely chopped fresh Italian parsley leaves

2 tablespoons finely scissored fresh basil leaves

2 tablespoons chopped pine nuts

Purchase the fillet in the supermarket if you wish; you will be offered the thickest part of the fillet or "bullnose." This section is better than the center cut of the fillet which is a little too narrow for this preparation. You will have no problem wrapping the meat in the canned leaves. If wrapping it proves difficult with fresh leaves, pass a needle and a thread into each row of leaves until you obtain a small rug of leaves slightly wider than the roast, which you can then wrap around the meat. Tie the meat at ¼-inch intervals and pull out the threads.

SUGGESTED WINE:
Châteauneuf-du-Pape, Barolo, or Barbaresco of your choice or a well-breathed Brunello

Preheat the oven to 425°F. Pour the salt into a large braising pot and preheat in the oven until unbearably hot to the top of the hand. Meanwhile, in a saucepan reduce the veal stock to 1 cup over medium-low heat. Add the lemon rind, capers, garlic, parsley, and pepper to taste. Keep warm in a hot water bath to prevent further reduction.

Clean the fillet, removing all traces of fat and silverskin between the muscles. Tie the roast with fine string at 1-inch intervals to make it easy to wrap. Blanch the fresh grape leaves for 1 second in boiling water so they can bend easily. Cool them, then remove their stems and central rib. (If you are using canned leaves, skip these steps.) Roll the meat into the leaves and tie as described in the introduction to this recipe.

Using a large measuring cup with a handle, remove two thirds of the hot salt to a baking dish. Arrange the meat on the bottom layer of salt and immediately cover it with the reserved salt. Turn the oven temperature down to 400°F and roast about 25 minutes. Remove the meat from the salt, keep wrapped in the leaves, and let rest 5 minutes to reach an internal temperature of 130°F (USDA 145°F).

To serve, remove all the strings and leaves, slice, and serve with the caper sauce and the garnish of stuffed mushrooms.

You can prepare the mushrooms ahead of time and bake them on a lower shelf of the same oven in which the beef will cook.

Wash and dry the mushrooms; cut the edible part of their stems into ¼-inch dice and set aside. Using a melon baller or Parisian spoon, remove all the foamy "tubes" inside the cap of each mushroom and discard them.

Heat 2 tablespoons olive oil in a skillet and sear the boleti 1 to 2 minutes on each side over medium-high heat. Remove them to a fireproof baking dish, hollow side up, and season with salt and pepper. To the same oil in which the caps were seared, add the onion and sauté until translucent. Add successively more oil if needed, the mushroom stem dice, bread crumbs, prosciutto, parsley, basil leaves, and nuts; toss together until well mixed. Season with salt and pepper; cook a few minutes and spoon an equal amount of the mixture into each boleti cap. Drizzle more olive oil over the top of each mushroom and bake 10 to 15 minutes in the same oven as the beef.

ROASTED POULTRY

There are two types of poultry: the white-meated poultry such as all types of chickens and turkeys and the red-meated poultry such as duck, goose, guinea hen, raised pheasant, squab, pigeon, and quail.

The rule to remember is the following: Too small a bird does not roast well in the oven because its flesh is cooked before its skin has time to turn the expected appetizing golden color; try roasting quail and pigeon in a 375° to 400°F oven and you will soon discover that the skin remains flabby with a lot of fat still not rendered properly. Such little birds cooked whole are best spit roasted.

Large birds also do not turn out the very best when they are roasted at a high temperature. Try to roast a medium turkey weighing 12 pounds at 375° to 400°F and you will find that the breast is too done just below the skin and remains too red by the breastbone and at the leg joints. The solution is, of course, to bake the turkey at a lower temperature which will insure the even penetration of the heat through to the bones. The same applies to large roasters and capons weighing between 5 and 6 pounds.

From all these caveats can be deduced the fact that the best oven-roasted birds are chickens weighing between 4 and 4½ pounds and guinea hens weighing up to 3½ pounds. Any bird used for oven roasting can also be spit roasted.

Duck in the United States presents a bit of a problem because it is raised so very fat that if you roast it at a high temperature, its fat burns in the roasting pan and smokes the whole kitchen up. Muscovy ducks can be roasted at high temperature and remain rare, but with all due respect to French cooks and chefs, I care only for the breast meat of these birds when they are roasted, for their legs are stringy and should really be baked in fat as a confit (see page 785). Goose, which contains so much fat, should be baked very slowly, and you will find a recipe for goose on page 784.

It is essential that any bird that will be roasted or spit roasted be trussed. I know that the subject of trussing has given rise to all kinds of discussions in culinary circles, but it makes sense that a trussed bird will cook more evenly than a nontrussed one, in which the tips of the breast fillets will always be drier than they should be. Also, does a roasted chicken, the legs of which have not been tied properly, really look good on a platter? A comparison between a trussed and a nontrussed bird provides the answer in one look.

Since it takes all of three minutes to truss a chicken once one has mastered a technique, please refer to pages 725–26 to find the two methods that are mostly used and try to learn one of them; your birds will definitely taste and look better.

FINAL INTERNAL TEMPERATURE AND AVERAGE ROASTING TIMES FOR DIFFERENT BIRDS It will be up to you to decide to which internal temperature the birds you are roasting or baking must be brought to, depending on their origin. The lowest possible temperature of the breast meat is 150°F, the temperature at which the bacteria are killed (USDA recommends 170°F). Measure it by passing the stem of an instant thermometer between the breast meat and the breastbone all the way through to the hump of the breastbone. If the birds you bought have traveled long distances before reaching your kitchen, it is a good idea to bring the temperature of the white meat all the way up to 170°F; this is best done by covering up the breast with a sheet of aluminum foil, shiny side out (to reflect the majority of the heat away from the meat) so the internal temperature progresses slowly from 150° to 170°F without further damage to the white meat.

The leg is done when a skewer inserted at the very center of the thigh releases perfectly colorless and clear juices. Any trace of blood, red or pink, means that the bird is still undercooked. If you also check the temperature of the leg by passing the instant thermometer between the leg and the rib cage, it should register 170°F (USDA 180°F) or very close to it. Although some people like to consume chicken still showing a trace of red when the leg is separated from the carcass, I find it more prudent to have the leg meat done until it just has turned beige at the knee-thigh joint.

Checking the general doneness of a whole bird is done by grasping the chicken with both hands protected by two clean kitchen towels and tilting the bird forward to let all the juices in the cavity flow into the roasting pan. If these juices are colorless and clear, the bird is done. Generally a bird that does not release any juice is overcooked.

Here are the average roasting times for different unstuffed oven-roasted birds; notice that the larger the bird, the shorter the cooking time proportionally:

- Chickens, 4½ pounds, 18 minutes per pound
- Guinea hens, 2½ to 3½ pounds, 18 minutes per pound
- Cornish hens, 1½ to 2 pounds, 20 minutes per pound

For small birds that are spit roasted, notice the relatively longer cooking time required. These red-meated little birds are best when medium rare, which the safe internal temperature of 140° to 165°F does not deliver. Know where your birds came from; if you cannot find out, do not take a chance and braise or pot roast them. They will be delicious and safe (see page 828).

- Quail, 25 to 30 minutes per bird
- Squab, 30 to 35 minutes per bird

California Garden Roast Chicken

FCR — 4 TO 6 SERVINGS

One 4½-pound roasting chicken

8 cups water

3 tablespoons sea salt

2 teaspoons granulated sugar

1 to 2 lemons

1 large sprig each fresh rosemary, tarragon, oregano, and thyme

3 cloves garlic, peeled

Pepper from the mill

This chicken will taste even better if you spit roast it in your barbecue. If you spit roast, the roasting time will be 1½ times longer than in the oven. We usually accompany this chicken with a great salad of Romaine with Parmigiano-Reggiano dressing and garlic croutons.

Wash the chicken abundantly inside and out in cold running water and pat it dry with paper towels. Mix the water with the salt and sugar and stir well to dissolve. Immerse the chicken in the brine and let stand at room temperature 35 to 40 minutes. Remove the chicken from the brine and dry it with paper towels.

Preheat the oven to 375°F. Quarter one of the lemons and squeeze all the juice into the cavity. Place the lemon peels, all the herbs, and garlic in the cavity and season with salt and pepper. Gently truss (see page 725) the chicken so as not to lose the lemon juice. Set the chicken on a rack set over a roasting pan and roast until the juices from the cavity run clear and the thermometer inserted between thigh and breast reads 170°F (USDA 180°F), approximately 1 hour and 15 minutes.

Remove the chicken to a platter. Add broth or water to the roasting pan, deglaze well, scraping up any brown deposits, reduce a bit over medium heat, and add more lemon juice if you want. Correct the seasoning with salt and pepper. Strain the gravy through a conical strainer into a gravy separator and pour the lean gravy into a warmed sauce boat.

SUGGESTED WINE: *An Italian Lambrusco, a Joseph Phelps Vin du Soleil Rosé, or a Bonny Doon Le Cigare Volant, or a Côtes de Provence red or rosé*

Almost Wild Spit-Roasted Quail

FCR — 6 SERVINGS

12 large quail
12 large cloves garlic, crushed
12 fresh sage leaves
24 juniper berries
Salt
Pepper from the mill
Olive oil of your choice

Wash the birds inside and out and pat them completely dry. Push 1 garlic clove, 1 sage leaf, and 2 juniper berries into the cavity of each bird. Season the cavity with salt and pepper. Truss with thin kitchen string using the needleless method outlined on page 726. Brush each bird with olive oil and allow the flavors to penetrate the birds for 24 hours in the refrigerator. Bring the birds back to room temperature 35 to 40 minutes before cooking.

Build a mesquite wood or other wood fire in your barbecue to white hot. Spit the quail so each pair of drumstick ends fits into the neck cavity of the next quail. Secure well with forks and spit roast until the breast is plump but gives in under the pressure of thumb and index finger, 25 to 30 minutes. Quail must be medium rare (internal temperature 145°F) not "blue" rare, since it belongs to the "red-meated" birds.

Serve with a bowl of warm lemonized water and a towel for finger cleaning since quail are finger food.

Quail run year-round on my hill in the Napa Valley, but we look at them with great love, hatching their eggs when a wildcat kills their mother, and buying raised quail for our table. This is the way to make raised quail taste wild. Serve with a fresh mesclun salad seasoned with a lemon juice, garlic, mint, and olive oil dressing.

SUGGESTED WINE: *A Napa Valley Syrah or Sangiovese or a red Vin du Mistral from Joseph Phelps*

Roast Stuffed Cornish Hen

FFR—6 SERVINGS

6 rock Cornish hens

½ pound rich cream cheese

¾ cup Grape Nuts cereal

⅓ cup crème fraîche

⅓ cup dried cranberries, finely chopped

4 ounces pork sausage, casing removed

I large yellow onion, very finely chopped

2 shallots, very finely chopped

Salt

Pepper from the mill

⅔ cup chicken broth or stock of your choice

Perfect for a "fancy" winter dinner party. Stuff the birds just before you start the roasting. Go back on your diet tomorrow; just treat yourself happily tonight, the more so with a puree of chestnuts or butternut squash nicely buttered and sherried (see page 413).

SUGGESTED WINE: *Any Beaujolais of your choice or a Meridian Pinot Noir*

Wash and dry all the birds with paper towels. Cream the cheese, then add the Grape Nuts, crème fraîche, and cranberries and incorporate well. Set aside.

In a nonstick frying pan, crumble the sausage and brown it lightly over medium heat until all the fat has escaped into the pan. Remove the sausage to a plate with a slotted spoon and discard half the fat. In the remaining fat over medium-high heat, sauté the onion until translucent. Add the shallots and sauté until both vegetables start browning. Let cool, then blend the onion mixture and sausage into the cream cheese stuffing. Season with salt and pepper.

Preheat the oven to 350°F. Salt and pepper the hens in their cavities. Divide the dressing into six equal parts and stuff each part into one of the birds. Truss the birds. Roast on a rack placed over a roasting pan until the temperature of the dressing registers 180°F on an instant meat thermometer and the juices run clear out of the leg of the largest bird when pierced with a skewer, about 45 minutes.

Deglaze the juices in the roasting pan with the broth, reduce a bit over medium heat, strain through a conical strainer into a gravy separator, and pour the lean gravy into a warmed sauce boat.

Mimi's Poor Man's Guineas

FFR—6 SERVINGS

3 guinea hens, 2½ to 3 pounds each

Salt

Pepper from the mill

2 cloves garlic, mashed

2 shallots, finely grated

3 tablespoons finely chopped fresh Italian parsley leaves

A recipe from the French Poitou as prepared by my great-grandmother. As a vegetable use the gratin of celery on page 441.

3 tablespoons finely chopped fresh chives

I anchovy fillet, rinsed and mashed

Finely grated rind of I lemon

2 tablespoons walnut oil

I cup dry red wine such as Cabernet, Syrah, or Pinot Noir

½ cup chicken broth of your choice

SUGGESTED WINE: *A Saint-Emilion of your choice, or a lighter Côtes-du-Rhône, or an excellent well-aged Pinot Noir (Burgundy or California)*

Wash and pat the guineas dry with paper towels. Salt and pepper them in their cavities. Mix the garlic, 1 grated shallot, the chopped herbs, anchovy, lemon rind, and walnut oil together in a small ramekin. Freeze for half an hour to harden the oil, then divide into twelve pats. Gently separate the skin from the meat with your finger, then spread the oil mixture under the breast and leg skin of each bird. Truss the birds and let them marinate in the refrigerator at least half a day.

Preheat the oven to 375°F. Place the guineas on a rack in a roasting pan and roast until the juices run clear out of a leg pierced by a skewer, 45 to 55 minutes. While the birds roast, mix the remaining shallot and the wine together in a small saucepan and reduce by half over medium heat. Add to the roasting pan during the last 5 minutes of roasting. When the guineas are done, add the chicken broth to the roasting pan and deglaze, reducing a few minutes over medium heat. Strain the gravy into a gravy separator and pour the lean gravy into a warmed sauce boat. Serve promptly.

Baking Less Expensive Cuts of Meat

"Baking" is an old-fashioned expression that means roasting at a medium to medium-low temperature. The expression is left over from the days of bread ovens, when cooks, to utilize the "leftover" heat of the oven, would put a piece of meat in to roast in an uncovered dish immediately after removing the last loaves of bread from the oven. The modern word *baking* comes from the old High German *bahhan* and the old English *baken* which have respectively become *backen* and "to bake" in the modern form of each language. The same Indo-European origin can be found in the Greek root word for roasting which is *phogein*, in which "p" and "g" take the place of "b" and "k" in the Germanic languages.

The outside layers of any piece of meat baked in a medium oven will not seal as fast as they would if roasted at a higher temperature; there will be time for more juices to escape from the roast, releasing a larger amount of gravy. If the meat is sprinkled with salt, the salt will attract the moisture on the surface of the meat, somewhat denaturing the proteins of the muscle fibers and accentuating the small gaps between the superficial layers of muscle fibers. If you observe larger pieces of beef or pork that are roasting a relatively long time, you will see large drops of meat juices pearling at their surface and slowly dripping into the roasting pan.

The Maillard reaction (see page 745 for a more detailed explanation) will take place at a slower pace because the caramelization of the juices at the surface of the meat is delayed by the slower heat of the oven. Eventually, though, the dripping will stop, as it does in high-heat roasting, as soon as enough superficial dehydration and caramelization of the sugars in the meat juices has taken place on the surface of the meat. Baked roasts offer perhaps a bit less juiciness, but their "brown flavor" is excellent and the relatively larger amount of drippings allows the preparation of a more plentiful and delicious natural gravy, making a sauce unnecessary.

As you will notice below, with the exception of the prime rib given as an example on page 751, all the cuts of meat that are usually baked come from the less tender, more exercised parts of the animal: the shoulder, or chuck, and the leg, or round. Since they are not as tender as the fillet, rib, or sirloin strip, it is necessary to cook them slowly and a relatively long time so the fibers have time to soften gradually.

BAKING LESSER CUTS OF BEEF

In the recipes that follow I use rump and true eye of the round roasts, but any part of the chuck and round can be baked in the same manner.

In these less tender cuts, do not strip the roast of all its outside connective tissues and fat finish. Shave off some of the superficial fat, but be sure to leave at least ⅙ inch of fat around the muscle. This will keep the meat moister; the connective tissues surrounding the meat soften enough while baking so they can be easily sliced through. You will see the gravy drip mostly from the bottom of the roast and its two ends.

Any less tender cut of beef will be very tasty if brought from the refrigerator to room temperature for 30 to 40 minutes and baked approximately 20 minutes per pound to rare and 24 minutes per pound to medium rare. Each and every piece will vary a bit, so use your instant thermometer for accurate information. Carryover heat happens with baked meats exactly as it does with roasted meats, so do not forget to take into consideration the temperature increase of 10 to 15 degrees as the roast rests after baking. Stop the baking when the internal temperature is 125°F for a rare meat and 130°F for medium rare (USDA 145°F).

Baked Rump Roast or True Eye of the Round

FFR — 6 TO 8 SERVINGS

One 3-pound rump roast or ½ true eye of the round

Salt

Finely ground thyme

The purchasing cuts numbers are, for the rump roast, IMPS No. 113, square cut chuck, and, for the true eye of the round, IMPS No. 171C, eye of the round.

¼ to ½ teaspoon finely ground bay leaf, to your personal taste

Beef or veal stock of your choice as needed

Potato starch as needed

1 tablespoon unsalted butter (optional)

Preheat the oven to 325°F. Trim the outer surface of the roast, leaving only ⅛ inch of fat. Sprinkle the roast on all its faces with salt and the ground herbs mixed together. Bake on a roasting pan fitted with a rack to an internal temperature of 125°F. Let the roast rest until the temperature is between 135° and 140°F (USDA 145°F) before slicing.

To prepare the gravy, remove as much fat as possible from the roasting pan. Add broth as needed. Put the roasting pan over medium heat and deglaze well, scraping up all the browned bits. Pour the gravy into a measuring cup or a gravy separator; let the lean part settle. Gently pour the lean drippings from the gravy separator or siphon them out with a baster into a small saucepan. Using 1¼ teaspoons of potato starch per cup of gravy, dilute the starch in a tablespoon of cold stock. Bring the gravy to a good simmer and stir in the slurry of starch until the mixture comes back to a boil. Whisk in the butter only if you wish. Correct the seasoning with salt and pepper.

BAKING LESSER CUTS OF VEAL, LAMB, AND PORK

As is the case with beef, the cuts best adapted to baking will be those coming from the shoulder and the round.

VEAL Large roasts are usually rolled from the shoulder; they will bake to some of the best-tasting and most tender meats ever. The roasts to ask for are IMPS No. 1309R, chuck, square cut, boneless, tied, or IMPS No. 310, shoulder clod. Both must be specially ordered from a butcher as they are rarely sold in the supermarket.

The first cut is best for a large number of guests since the whole piece can, depending on the size of the animal, reach 10 to 22 pounds before being detailed into smaller roasts. When ordering this cut from your butcher tell him the number of guests at your table; he will recommend the necessary size. Three to 4 pounds will serve six easily, 4 to 6 pounds will be best for eight.

The shoulder clod is better adapted to home use since it varies from 2 to 6 pounds; it will generally be sold whole, prepared for roasting with a thin layer of fat left on the meat. Do not remove it.

A rump roast is perfect for six portions, the whole true eye of the round for nine to ten, even twelve if there are children at the table. These two roasts are the most perfect candidates for a good dish of mashed potatoes as vegetable garnish (see page 387).

SUGGESTED WINE: *Any red wine of your choice; best would be a good Côtes-du-Rhône, a medium-weight Cabernet Sauvignon, or any good Pinot Noir*

Baked Veal Shoulder and Vegetables

This presentation is a classic of Loire Valley cookery and is served on the first Holy Communion in many farm and little town households.

SUGGESTED WINE: A Vouvray Sec or, if red wine is preferred, a Chinon or Bourgueil

FCR—8 SERVINGS

Salt

One 5-pound rolled veal shoulder roast, skin removed

2 cups Primary Veal Stock (page 219) or excellent chicken stock

Pepper from the mill

1 pound baby carrots, peeled

1 pound baby turnips, peeled

1 pound baby potatoes, peeled

2 teaspoons each chopped fresh tarragon, chives, chervil, and curly parsley leaves

1 tablespoon unsalted butter (optional)

Preheat the oven to 325°F. Salt the roast. Bake it, turning it over twice while baking and brushing it regularly with small amounts of the stock. Pepper the meat during the last half hour of baking.

Blanch each vegetable separately for 3 minutes in boiling salted water. Add them to the roasting pan when the roast is half done and finish baking together so the vegetables are glazed with gravy.

The meat is done when a skewer inserted at its center comes out freely and an instant meat thermometer registers 135°F. The roasting time is 23 minutes or so per pound. Remove from the oven and let stand, covered with aluminum foil, until its inner temperature reaches 145° to 150°F (USDA 160°F). Remove the vegetables to a heated platter.

Add the remainder of the stock to the gravy and deglaze over medium heat, reducing to approximately 1½ cups. Pour into a gravy separator or measuring cup and siphon the lean part of the gravy into a small saucepan. Add the fresh herbs and, if desired, fluff in the butter. Turn into a heated sauce boat and serve with the roast and its garnishes.

LAMB   The best baking cut of lamb is the shoulder which should be fully boned, rolled, and tied. Once rolled the shoulder can be sliced thin; though it is definitely not as desirable as the leg, it still offers a very nice and appealing serving of medium-rare meat.

The code number for a shoulder is IMPS No. 208, square cut shoulder, boneless, tied.

Tarpeius's Shoulder of Lamb

FFR to FCR—6 SERVINGS

1 boneless lamb shoulder, about 3 pounds

Pepper from the mill

1 tablespoon plus ½ cup dry vermouth

2 teaspoons finely chopped fresh savory leaves

2 medium-size white onions, peeled

Leaves of 2 large sprigs fresh thyme, very finely chopped

½ teaspoon finely chopped fresh oregano leaves

2 anchovy fillets, rinsed and mashed

Nuoc mam or nam pla as needed

1¼ cups white grape juice

1½ tablespoons fresh lemon juice

2 soft dates, mashed to a paste

1 generous tablespoon virgin olive oil

⅓ cup Vin Santo or Amontillado sherry

Salt

Sprigs fresh savory and oregano

Remove most of the fat covering the meat, leaving only a ⅛-inch layer. Roll and tie the shoulder at ½-inch intervals with fine kitchen string. Put 10 turns of the pepper mill, 1 tablespoon of the vermouth, and 1 teaspoon of the savory leaves in a small bowl. Chop the onions so finely that they turn into a puree. Add half the onion mash to the pepper mixture, along with half the thyme, ¼ teaspoon of the oregano leaves, and 1 of the mashed anchovy fillets. Mix well until homogeneous, then add just enough *nuoc mam* to make a spread. Coat the roast evenly with the mixture; set on a rack placed over a roasting pan, and let air dry for 1 hour.

Preheat the oven to 325°F. Bake the roast until it has an internal temperature of about 160°F and is so well done that a skewer inserted at its center comes out freely, about 30 minutes per pound. Remove the roast to a slicing board and keep warm covered with aluminum foil.

While the meat bakes, put the grape and lemon juices in a medium-size saucepan and reduce by one third over medium heat. Off the heat, add the remainder of the savory, onions, thyme, oregano, and anchovy, the mashed dates, a few drops of *nuoc mam*, the olive oil, and the chosen wine. Set aside.

Discard all the fat from the roasting pan; deglaze with the remainder of the vermouth, boiling hard and stirring constantly for a few minutes. Add the date mixture and reduce together by at least one half over medium heat or until the resulting sauce is syrupy. Strain into a small sauce boat. Correct the seasoning with salt and pepper, if needed.

Slice the meat; serve it on a round dish basted with the sauce and sprinkled with pepper. Brighten the plate with the sprigs of herbs.

This is an adaptation of Apicius's recipe number 367 as published in the Flower and Rosenbaum edition of this ancient Roman cookery book. The original formula calls for the herb rue, now considered unsafe for consumption and for which I have substituted dry vermouth. The mixture of oregano leaves, anchovy, and nuoc mam replaces the Latin fermented fish condiment called garum or liquamen. The grape juice blended with a tad of lemon juice replaces the caroenum of the Latins, which was must (grape juice in fermentation) reduced by one third to one half. The Romans prereduced this mixture and then used it to deglaze the natural gravy of the meat. As presented here the sauce ends up being a well-balanced sweet-salty-sour-bitter compound. If it tastes too strange to you, cut the sauce with lemon juice until it tastes frankly sweet-sour. The short and concise Roman recipe does not mention straining the sauce; I chose to strain it since the Romans had a strainer called a colae. As a vegetable, consider the Braised Fennel on page 401.

SUGGESTED WINE: *Lacryma Christi del Vesuvio, a Greek Kokkineli*

PORK Two cuts of pork can be baked at a medium-low temperature with the most delicious results: fresh ham and Boston butt. The IMPS numbers to be used for ordering are, for the ham, IMPS No. 401, ham, regular, which will have its full rind and all its bones from shank to hip bone, or IMPS No. 402, ham, skinned, in which only a collar of rind located around the shankbone will be left on the ham; the fat will be trimmed to no more than ½ inch thick. For the butt, order IMPS No. 406A, Boston butt, boned, tied.

Some authors advocate roasting a fresh ham at high temperature; this is not advisable because of the large mass of the meat. The result would be a ham medium rare at the bone and overcooked just below its golden crust. A medium temperature is absolutely necessary for such a large joint.

Here are two recipes, one for a large group, the other for a family dinner:

Itterswiller Schinken

FFR— 15 TO 18 SERVINGS

1 whole fresh ham, all skin removed but for 2 inches of rind left over the hock

Whole cloves as needed

Kosher salt as needed

Semicoarsely ground black pepper from the mill

1 teaspoon ground allspice

1½ cups dry Riesling

2 shallots, very finely chopped

One ¼-inch-thick slice honey cake

1½ cups Secondary Stock (page 220) or chicken stock of your choice

Dijon or Düsseldorf mustard

Note the exact weight of the ham carefully. Turn the ham over and check the large bone (femur) area for splotches of blood coming from the severed femoral artery. Should some be visible, crumple a paper towel and, with your other hand, apply it against the splotch; with your working hand, starting 2 inches above the splotch, apply pressure against the meat as your fingers move toward the towel, pushing hard against it. This will take care of this small problem. Discard the towel and rinse the ham. Pat it *completely* dry.

Check that the thickness of the fat covering the ham is no more than ¼ inch. Cut a crisscross pattern ¾ inch square into the fat on the diagonal and push 1 clove into the center of each square. Mix the salt, pepper, and all-spice together in a small cup and apply to the whole ham surface not covered by rind, especially to the heel where the meat is exposed. Set the ham on a roasting pan fitted with a rack. Let sit for 24 hours in the refrigerator so the flavors can penetrate the ham.

Bring the ham back to room temperature for 1 hour. Preheat the oven to 325°F and bake 40 minutes for the first pound, then 30 minutes for each

The pièce de résistance of an Alsatian wedding dinner in 1973. You may use gingerbread, honey cake, or pain d'épice to thicken the gravy. The classic accompaniment in my family is a dish of Soured Turnips as per the recipe on page 394. The hock is the lower part of a ham, 2 inches wide about its pointed end.

SUGGESTED WINE: *Riesling of your choice, from Alsace if you like it dry, California if you like it mellow, or Germany if you like it slightly sweet* additional pound until the internal temperature registers 160°F on an instant meat thermometer. Remove from the oven, cover with aluminum foil, and let rest until the internal temperature has risen to 170°F.

To prepare a gravy, put the wine and shallots in a medium-size saucepan over medium heat and reduce to ¾ cup. Crumble the honey cake into the reduction and let stand while deglazing the roasting pan. Remove as much fat as possible from the roasting pan. Add the stock to the pan and bring to a boil over medium heat, scraping well to dislodge all traces of caramelized drippings. Pour the gravy into a measuring cup or gravy separator. Let the fat settle at the top and separate the lean meat juices. Add the meat juices to the saucepan containing the wine reduction, bring to a boil, stirring, and reduce over high heat until the gravy has thickened to a syruplike consistency. Strain through a conical strainer into a clean saucepan; off the heat, whisk in as much mustard as you like. Reheat to just below the boiling point. Correct the seasoning with salt and pepper and serve over the sliced ham.

Stuffed Pork Butt

FFR—6 TO 8 SERVINGS

One 3- to 4-pound pork butt roast
I pound chicken sausage, casings removed
½ small yellow onion, grated
I small shallot, grated
24 pistachios, peeled and very coarsely chopped
¼ cup chopped fresh chives
3 dried apple slices, diced
I large egg white, lightly beaten
4 large cloves garlic, finely slivered
Salt
Pepper from the mill
Quatre épices or other spice mixture of your choice
Dijon mustard
1½ cups fresh bread crumbs
Grapeseed or olive oil as needed
1½ cups sweet or hard cider
Fresh lemon juice

The authentic Normandy recipe for this calls for pork sausage in the stuffing and crème fraîche in the gravy, just in case you would like to try it.

SUGGESTED BEVERAGE OR WINE: *Preferably Normandy or English hard cider but a mellow California Riesling will be very pleasant*

Place the piece of pork on a cutting board, the fattiest side down. Cut 1½ inches deep into the meat lengthwise, then cut 1½ inches deep across the meat to the left at the bottom of the existing cut. Now cut 1½ inches deep across the meat to the right. Open the piece of meat flat on the board and smooth it with the flat side of a chef's knife blade.

Mix the sausage meat, onion, shallot, pistachios, and 2 tablespoons of the

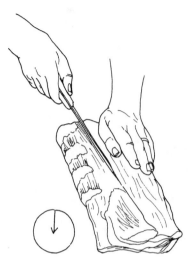

Notice placement of knife and hand

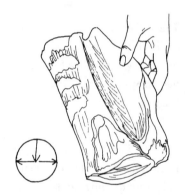

Roast cut open on one side; the
same operation will be done on the
other side.

chives together in a bowl. Blend the apple cubes with the egg white, and mix into the stuffing until homogeneous. Spread the forcemeat evenly over the meat, then roll up the meat and sew it closed with a large upholstery needle and heavy white thread.

Preheat the oven to 325°F. Remove all fat from the surface of the meat. With the tip of a paring knife, cut small openings into the roast at regular intervals; insert a garlic sliver in each cut. Salt and pepper the outside of the roast and sprinkle it evenly with *quatre épices* to your taste. Set the roast on a roasting pan fitted with a rack and bake 1 hour. Remove the pork from the oven and brush with mustard. Spread the bread crumbs over a sheet of waxed paper and roll the roast in the crumbs. Spray the crumbs with the oil of your choice for better coloration and finish baking, approximately another hour, until the internal temperature registers 160°F on an instant meat thermometer. Remove from the oven and cover with aluminum foil until the internal temperature has risen to 170°F.

Deglaze the pan with the cider and reduce by half over medium heat. Pour the gravy into a measuring cup or gravy separator and let stand until the fat has collected at the top. Pour or siphon the lean gravy into a saucepan. Reheat well and correct the seasoning with salt, pepper, lemon juice to your personal taste, and the remaining 2 tablespoons chives.

BAKED POULTRY

Although we always talk about "roasting" a turkey or a capon, we almost always end up baking them. Both turkeys and capons are much too large to be truly oven roasted at a high temperature; you will notice, if you do, that the outside skin will be overcrisp with a slightly overcooked breast, while the meat that is close to the center bones will, more often than not, end up being a little too rare. If you want to really roast a turkey or a capon, use the spit of your barbecue.

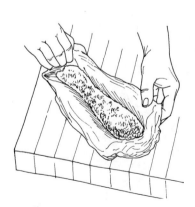

Stuffing in place

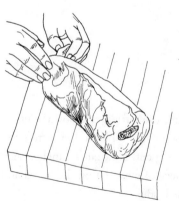

Closing the roast around the stuffing

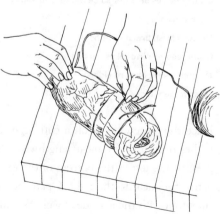

Tying the roast

Remember that when baked stuffed, large birds should not be filled until just before the baking starts to prevent the development of dangerous bacteria (for details, see page 364).

Farm-raised ducks and geese are roasted in a lower oven to allow for the slow and gradual melting of their copious amounts of fat; any higher temperature will cause the fat to burn and fill kitchen and home with acrid blue smoke. Even baked at a very moderate 325°F both duck and goose lose so much fat that it accumulates in the roasting pan and must be siphoned off with a baster to prevent its burning, smoking, and spoiling the taste of the meat juices.

Duck and goose fat can be gathered and carefully strained into clean jars to be used later for:

- The making of confits (see page 785)
- Frying the most deliciously sinful potatoes for an occasional treat, and
- Preparing regional dishes such as cassoulet and choucroute (see pages 492 and 403).

Ducks should never be stuffed because they give off way too much fat, and if you stuff a goose, make sure to use a nonabsorbent stuffing of fruit or non-starchy vegetables since any starchy material will become undigestible from soaking up fat.

COOKING TIMES FOR BIRDS 10 TO 14 POUNDS

- For the first five pounds, bake 20 minutes per pound
- For the sixth to the tenth pound, bake only 10 minutes per pound
- For any additional pound over 10, bake only 6 minutes per pound

BIRDS OVER 14 POUNDS

- For the first five pounds, bake 15 minutes per pound
- For the sixth to the tenth pound, bake only 12 minutes per pound
- For the eleventh to the fifteenth pound, bake only 9 minutes per pound
- For the fifteenth to the twentieth pound, bake only 6 minutes per pound.

The reason for decreasing the length of the baking time as the baking progresses is that the larger a bird is, the faster it will bake proportionally. A large mass of whatever heat-conductive material always absorbs heat proportionally faster than a smaller one, so that large birds will cook proportionally faster than smaller ones.

This method prevents birds from being vastly overcooked.

Large birds are done when a skewer inserted at the thickest part of the thigh releases clear and almost colorless juices. The temperature measured with an instant thermometer should be between 165° and 180°F (USDA 180°F).

Neil's Thanksgiving Turkey

FCR — 10 TO 12 SERVINGS

One 12-pound fresh turkey

Large bouquet garni of parsley stems, 1 Turkish bay leaf, and 1 sprig fresh thyme

Salt

Pepper from the mill

5½ cups turkey giblet broth or other stock or broth of your choice

1 pound sweet Italian sausage, casings removed

5 tablespoons unsalted butter or olive oil

2 large yellow onions, finely chopped

4 very large shallots, finely chopped

2 celery ribs, finely diced

2 cups oven-dried cornbread cubes

2 cups oven-dried whole wheat bread cubes

2 large eggs, beaten

1½ tablespoons all-purpose flour

¼ cup dry sherry

The method used in this recipe is my son Neil's, who is the family champion of turkey baking. Prepare a nice broth with the turkey giblets the day before you bake the bird. Our favorite vegetable garnish for this bird is a medley of chestnuts, celery root, baby onions, and Brussels sprouts, etuvéed in butter (see page 391).

SUGGESTED WINE: *This festive bird will take any wine you like, from the most opulent to the simplest. Enjoy making the choice yourself.*

Wash the turkey inside and out and dry completely with paper towels. Preheat the oven to 325°F. Stuff the bouquet garni into the cavity of the bird; salt and pepper well, and truss without stuffing the bird. Set the bird on a roasting pan fitted with a rack and bake 1½ hours in the middle of the oven.

Meanwhile, add ½ cup of the giblet broth to a skillet. Crumble the sausage into the broth and gradually heat over medium heat to allow the fat to separate from the meat. When the broth has evaporated and the meat has browned, discard the fat; remove the sausage to a large bowl. Do not wash the skillet.

Heat 2 tablespoons of the butter in the same skillet over medium heat. Add the onions and toss until the caramelized sausage drippings in the pan have colored them; add the shallots, season with salt and pepper, and cover until the vegetables have softened. Add the celery dice and toss in the pan until soft. Remove the vegetables to the bowl containing the sausage, also adding the bread cubes, 2 cups of the broth, and the eggs. Work with a spoon or spatula until homogeneous; if using your hand to mix, use a protective glove. Adjust the seasoning.

Butter or oil a 1½-quart baking dish with 1 more tablespoon of butter or oil. Pack the dressing into the dish. As soon as the turkey has cooked for 1½ hours, grasp it firmly on each side with both hands protected by two clean kitchen towels and tilt it to pour the gravy accumulated in its cavity into a measuring cup. Drizzle about half of the turkey juices over the stuffing. Return the bird to its rack and cover the breast with aluminum foil shiny side up.

Now rearrange the oven, placing the dish of stuffing on the upper rack and to the left side and the turkey on the lower rack and to the right side.

Continue baking another hour until both the dressing and bird are done; the stuffing should register a temperature of 180°F and the juices should run clear out of the turkey legs.

Let the bird rest under aluminum foil while you prepare the gravy. Remove as much fat as possible from the roasting pan. Deglaze what is left in the pan with 3 cups of the broth, reducing by one third over medium heat as you do so, and pour into a gravy separator. Empty the lean gravy into a saucepan, bring to a boil, turn down to a simmer. Knead together the remaining butter and the flour, then whisk into the simmering liquid. Add the sherry and simmer 15 minutes. Strain through a conical strainer into a gravy boat.

ABOUT CAPONS What is nowadays called a roaster should not be confused with a capon; a roaster or large chicken weighing approximately 6 pounds has its virtues but never offers the extreme delicacy and tenderness of a true capon, or castrated male chicken. The capon is easily recognizable by its large size, which can reach 8 pounds, the well-rounded contour of its body, and the extremely fine grain of its skin, which is lined with a fine even layer of natural fat. In my personal opinion, kosherized capons are the best tasting; order from a butcher who will know which brands offer the best birds. Capons have become rare in regular food markets.

The Treat of a Capon

FCR—8 SERVINGS

One 7- to 8-pound capon

One 2 × 1-inch piece fresh ginger, peeled

1½ teaspoons salt

20 turns of the pepper mill

Pinch plus ½ teaspoon 5-spice powder

2 cloves garlic, mashed

1 bunch fresh scallions, white part finely chopped and green part cut paper thin on a slant (keep separate)

Peanut oil as needed

2 ounces dried Chinese wood ear mushrooms

1 pound crimini mushrooms, stems discarded and caps sliced

1 pound fresh shiitake mushrooms, stems discarded and caps sliced

Soy sauce

¼ cup dry sherry

A new twist for a classic western bird.

SUGGESTED BEVERAGE OR WINE: *If some readers would like to serve a Gewürztraminer, it will blend nicely with the faint flavor of the 5-spice powder; I prefer jasmine tea.*

Wash the capon inside and out and dry completely with paper towels. Preheat the oven to 325°F. Cut the ginger piece in half. Finely grate one half, cut the other half into 2 slices. Mix the grated ginger with the salt, pepper, a large pinch of 5-spice powder, half the garlic, and the scallion whites. Pack the mixture into the cavity of the capon, pushing it well against the breast-bone on both sides of the cavity, then truss the bird. Brush the bird with a thin layer of peanut oil, place in a roasting pan fitted with a wire rack, and bake until it registers an internal temperature of 170°F (USDA 180°F) on an instant thermometer and the juices run clear when the thigh is pierced with a skewer, about 2 hours.

Meanwhile, soak the wood ear mushrooms in enough water to cover plus ½ inch and rehydrate them fully, then drain and reserve the clear soaking water, discarding any grit at the bottom of the bowl.

Heat 3 tablespoons of the peanut oil in a small skillet over medium heat and add the ½ teaspoon 5-spice powder and the remaining ginger and garlic. Turn the heat off and let steep 15 minutes. Strain the oil into a small container. Reserve 1 tablespoon of the fragrant oil for later use.

Heat the remainder of the fragrant oil in a larger skillet over medium-high heat and sauté both fresh mushrooms. Add the wood ear mushrooms when the others release their juices. Continue to cook, now on high heat, until most of the juices have evaporated, then season with salt, pepper, and soy sauce to taste. Stir in the sherry. Remove from the heat and set aside.

When the capon is done, defat its pan drippings completely. Add the wood ear mushroom soaking water and deglaze well over medium heat. Add the remaining tablespoon of fragrant oil and cook together for 2 minutes. Strain the sauce through a conical strainer into a small bowl. Detail the capon into eight servings and serve surrounded by the mushrooms; dribble the sauce over the pieces of meat and sprinkle with the slivered scallion greens.

ABOUT BAKED DUCK AND GOOSE The recipes that follow are for duck and goose to be served well done and with a very crisp skin. If you wish to cook the breast of either bird rare to medium rare, see page 767.

Citrus Duck

Please do not be frightened by the long list of ingredients or the length of the instructions. Spread the work over two days and all you will have to do is bake the ducks and blend all the elements of the sauce before dinner.

The mixture of citrus fruit in this recipe duplicates very closely the taste of the true Bigarade orange. The bitter-sour Bigarade, which up to fifty years ago grew

FFR — 6 TO 8 SERVINGS

2 ducks, 5 to 6 pounds each
2 tablespoons corn oil
4 cups Primary Veal Stock (page 219)
2 tablespoons julienne of Valencia orange rind
½ teaspoon julienne of lime rind
½ teaspoon julienne of lemon rind
1 teaspoon julienne of white grapefruit rind
½ cup fresh Valencia orange juice
2 teaspoons fresh lime juice
1 teaspoon fresh lemon juice
2 tablespoons fresh white grapefruit juice

2 teaspoons Grand Marnier

4 teaspoons Cognac

2 Valencia oranges, cut in half

Salt

Pepper from the mill

¼ cup dry white wine

2 teaspoons granulated sugar

2 teaspoons sherry vinegar

1 to 2 tablespoons unsalted butter for sauce enrichment (optional),
     to your personal taste

Valencia orange and white grapefruit sections

Day One

Remove the second joint and the tip of the wing of each duck. Discard the wing tips; chop all the flat joints in half crosswise. Chop the necks into 1-inch chunks, cut the gizzards in half crosswise, rinse, and pat dry.

Heat the corn oil in a large skillet over medium heat and brown the wings, necks, and gizzards to a deep golden. Remove to several layers of paper towels and pat off the fat. Discard the oil from the skillet, patting it off gently with paper towels to avoid dislodging the glaze in the pan. Add the veal stock, bring to a boil, return the pieces of duck to the pan, and reduce to a generous cup of single duck essense over medium heat. Strain through a conical strainer and refrigerate.

Blanch the citrus juliennes for 1 minute in boiling water. Drain, pat dry, and keep ready to use in a covered plastic container. Strain the citrus juices together and keep ready to use in a covered plastic container.

Day Two

Preheat the oven to 400°F. Mix the Grand Marnier and Cognac together. Rub each duck with half the mixture and let air dry on a rack in a roasting pan for 1 hour. Place 2 orange halves, salt, and pepper into the cavity of each duck. Roast the ducks in the 400°F oven for 20 minutes, then prick their skins on both sides just below the breast meat to allow the fat to escape. Reduce the oven heat to 325°F and continue roasting another 1½ hours. Use a baster to siphon off the fat as it melts and gathers in the roasting pan. After removing the fat and at half-hour intervals, grasp each bird with a clean kitchen towel and pour the juices accumulated in its cavity into the roasting pan to obtain deep brown caramelized drippings. The birds are done when the juices run clear when the thickest part of a thigh is pierced with a skewer. Remove them from the oven and keep them warm under aluminum foil.

Remove all possible traces of fat from the roasting pan and deglaze with the wine. Strain through a conical strainer into a gravy separator. Reheat the duck essence, then gently pour the lean gravy into the essence. Simmer together for 15 minutes.

wild in many Mediterranean gardens, is slowly disappearing. Although our Seville orange is one of its descendants, it is much sweeter. Positively do not use any kind of marmalade, as it leaves traces of sugar in the sauce, which are not true to taste. The dark caramel dissolved with vinegar is called a gastrique. At first sight this word seems related to the adjective gastric, as in gastric juices. I have searched for it in all the classic cookbooks without success. It does not seem to have appeared in print until Henri-Paul Pellaprat introduced it as a variation in the making of the sauce for Canard à la Bigarade (duck with orange sauce). Modern Raymond Oliver used it liberally. To my knowledge the word remains undefined in French dictionaries and I would gladly be enlightened by any food historian.

Use the regular white-feathered yellow-billed white Pekin ducks, as large as you can find them, and for a vegetable accompaniment consider the grilled sweet red bell peppers on page 433.

SUGGESTED WINE: *Try a nice mellow California or German Riesling; I find it more harmonious with this dish than any other varietal red wine as is usually advocated.*

Cook the sugar to a deep caramel (see page 938) in a small skillet. Cool completely and dissolve with the vinegar. Add the fruit juices and reduce by half over medium heat. Add the mixture to the prepared sauce, along with the blanched rinds. Simmer another 2 to 3 minutes. Whisk in the butter only if you like (the butter will soften any slightly acidic edge brought by the fruit juices) and correct the salt and pepper if necessary.

Serve the ducks decorated with orange and grapefruit sections and pass the sauce in a sauce boat.

Tante Else's Gans

A happy memory of Christmas 1948 in northern Germany. The Viking influence on the food is visible in the use of aquavit. You may use any other apple you like if Fujis are not available.

SUGGESTED WINE: *The mellow German Riesling of your choice*

FFR—6 TO 8 SERVINGS

2 to 3 tablespoons unsalted butter, to your personal taste

12 Fuji apples, peeled, cored, and each sliced into 8 slivers

4 to 5 tablespoons aquavit, to your personal taste

One 10-pound goose

Salt

Pepper from the mill

6 large Yellow Finnish or Yukon Gold potatoes, peeled and diced

¼ cup rendered goose fat

1 cup chicken or Secondary Stock (page 220)

½ teaspoon caraway seeds

Watercress sprigs

Heat as little butter as you can in a large skillet over medium-high heat. In three successive batches, sauté the apples until very brown on both sides but still crisp inside. Off the heat, add 2 tablespoons of the aquavit, mix well, and cool completely.

Preheat the oven to 325°F. Wash the goose inside and out and dry with paper towels. Remove and set aside all fat from the goose cavity. Rub the inside of the bird with a generous tablespoon of aquavit, season with salt and pepper, and stuff with the apples. Truss the bird and place in a roasting pan fitted with a rack. Bake, breast up, 2¼ to 2½ hours, pricking the skin on each side of the bird just below the breast meat and siphoning off the fat from the pan at regular intervals. The bird is done when it registers an internal temperature of 180°F on an instant thermometer and the juices run clear when the thickest part of a thigh is pierced with a skewer.

Parboil the potatoes 1 minute to prevent discoloration. Panfry slowly in ¼ cup hot goose fat over medium heat until nice and golden; this may take as long as 40 minutes (see the technique of panfrying potatoes on page 415).

Remove as much fat as possible from the roasting pan and deglaze with the stock over medium heat. Pour into a gravy separator, let settle, then pour into a saucepan. Add the caraway seeds and reduce by one quarter. Add 1 to

2 tablespoons aquavit to the boiling gravy, just before taking it off the heat and serving.

Detail the goose into 8 portions; arrange on a platter and surround with the potatoes and sprigs of watercress. Serve the gravy in a sauce boat.

MEATS BAKED IN FAT

A look at the menus of most well-known restaurants nowadays reveals the almost certain presence of a confit.

DEFINITION OF A TRUE CONFIT *Confire* in French means to preserve; as one preserves fruit by cooking it in sugar, one preserves meat first by curing it, to extract its perishable juices, then cooking it in a bath of fat. The technique is extremely ancient and seems to be so universal that it might date back to the Stone Age when meats were cooked in water in a large animal skin stretched like a pouch over an open fire. This technique was still in use among the Indians of the Plains when Europeans arrived in North America. When one cooks meat this way and lets it simmer a long time, the water eventually evaporates, leaving the meat to finish cooking in its own fat (see the recipe for rillettes on page 791). The meat is succulent but cannot be kept a long time and remains perishable. If one salts the meat to cure it before cooking it in fat, it can keep a longer time.

In the Old World meats salted for long storage may have come from the Semitic civilizations, who koshered their meats to purify them before cooking. It might also have come from the Celts, who salted their meats, proof of which can be found in the way the Loire Valley people, who apparently never had any contact with Semitic populations, cure their *rillons* and *rillauds* (pork ribs) in salt before cooking them in lard. A quick look into the foods of the Italian Piemonte, of the Greek Peloponnesus, or of Hungary reveals the same curing and cooking and/or storing in fat.

The goal of curing in salt is to make water unavailable to microorganisms eventually present in the meat. The salt denatures the meat proteins as it binds the water contained in the microorganisms and in the proteins. Without water microorganisms cannot live and proteins cannot function. A confit will keep about six months.

SALT CURING In modern cookery, there are two ways of salting meats for confits:

- *Traditional method, for long-term preservation and cassoulet making:* Use ⅓ ounce kosher salt to salt each pound of meat, and cure 36 to 48 hours.
- *Modernized method, for short-term preservation and salad making:* Use ⅙ ounce kosher salt to salt each pound of meat, and cure 24 to 36 hours.

Note that the meats and salt must be weighed with a scale to prevent over- or undersalting.

FLAVORING THE MEATS Confited meats are not only cured in salt, they are often flavored with diverse spices. The spices used in the confits prepared in the southwestern provinces and regions of France seem to come from the Arab world, as these regions were infused with Arab populations after a large band of Arab invaders was routed by Charles Martel (prime minister of Pepin the Short, himself father to Charlemagne) not too far from the modern city of Poitiers in A.D. 732. These warriors took refuge and went into hiding in the countryside stretching between the Charentes, the Central Mountains, and the Pyrénées.

The following is my favorite mixture of spices for confit and came originally from the village of Beynac in the Perigord.

For the confit spice mixture

1 teaspoon ground cumin

1 teaspoon ground coriander

1 teaspoon ground cinnamon

¾ teaspoon ground allspice

¼ teaspoon ground cloves

½ teaspoon ground ginger

½ teaspoon freshly grated nutmeg

1 Turkish bay leaf, finely crumbled

¾ teaspoon finely crumbled dried thyme

This mixture should be sprinkled sparingly on the meats, covering all the surfaces, before you add any salt. The amount given above is sufficient for two to three confits, each with six to eight serving-size pieces of meat.

If this mixture is too elaborate for you, by all means, use those spices you like or no spices at all.

OTHER FLAVORINGS Large amounts of garlic cloves or small white onions or shallots can also be used to flavor a confit; they will give both traditional and lighter modern confits quite a lovely flavor. In modern confits, these onion family members can be used in salads.

You can also use fresh herbs, the flavor of which intensifies as it transfers itself to the meat as it cooks slowly and to the very caramelized juices in the bottom of the baking dish. No such caramelized drippings are to be found in the old-fashioned confit because the larger amount of salt removes all the juices from which they could form during the curing period.

Salads made with meats confited after curing in light salt can be seasoned with those caramelized drippings.

For the long preservation confits, the fat itself will become one of the major flavors. Indeed, if you keep a confit for more than six weeks and up to six months, you will, as soon as you open the jar in which it is stored, detect the typical smell of fats that have oxidated. Not only is the smell typical but so is the taste communicated to the confited meats by the fat.

THE BATH OF FAT The fat bath is usually a rendered animal fat, the most popular and the least damaging to health being duck fat. It is easy when baking a duck to siphon off all the fat rendered into the roasting pan and store it to prepare confits. A bath of fat can be used a maximum of three times and must then be discarded. After each use, it must be strained while still warm through a fine-meshed China cap. Keep well covered and frozen between uses in dishwasher-sterilized jars. After 6 months the fat-oxidation taste becomes gradually more noticeable.

If you prefer goose, chicken, or pork fat, these are acceptable also, each of them alone or in combination.

STORING AND RENEWING TRADITIONAL CONFITS When you intend to store the meats for longer periods, always pour enough fat over them to cover by one inch; you want as little air as possible to reach them. Seal the top of the jar and keep in a cold cellar or the lower shelf of the refrigerator.

If the confit is not used within six months, bring the jar to room temperature. Place it in a bath of hot water to melt the fat. Transfer the meats and fat to a sauteuse pan and recook over medium-low heat for 35 to 40 minutes, which will stop any possible bacterial growth. This recooking is called "renewing" the confit, which will insure its safe storage for another 4 to 6 months.

For best flavor, though, a confit is always best consumed between the third and fifth months after its initial cooking.

NUTRITION AND CONFIT However one may favor confit and however less saturated the fat of duck may be, confit must be considered a gastronomic treat and nothing but. Confits of pork or other meats cooked in a bath of pork fat or other heavily saturated fat are not for everyday consumption and must be avoided by people with heart problems. Such people should not have confit more than once a year and it should be a confit of duck made with duck fat, because of its lesser saturation and excellent flavor. Corn oil flavored with garlic of course comes to mind as a substitute. Vegetable shortening is not acceptable as it is partially saturated. Also, the quantity of salt used for curing should be the lower one, as indicated on page 785.

TYPES OF MEATS FOR CONFITS Basically all meats can be confited in their own or another fat. Customarily and primarily, ducks and geese are used, but confits are entirely feasible with a turkey, large roaster chicken, capon, and rabbit using either duck or chicken fat; pork shoulder and ribs are best confited in lard.

WHY BAKE A CONFIT? In traditional cuisine, the confit was cooked in the kettle hanging over the flame of the hearth. At the end of the nineteenth century it passed to the top of the stove with delicious results, but a bit of a mess in the kitchen. To this day the duck is often half cooked on top of the stove, topped with rendered fat, sealed in jars, and the cooking finished in a canner.

Since our ovens are so well calibered, it is now much easier to bake the meats in their bath of fat, keeping the temperature of the oven low to medium-low to obtain a slow, deep cooking of the meats, which can, as a consequence, be transferred and kept in their preserving glass jars without danger of spoilage. Still, sterilizing the jars in the dishwasher before they receive the cooked meats remains a necessity.

ACCOMPANIMENTS FOR CONFITS Since any version of confit tastes from a bit salty to frankly salty, any accompaniment served with it should offer a sweet-sour or frankly sour flavor able to temper the high salt. This is why the modern confit is so well adapted to salad presentation.

In the two recipes that follow, the traditional confit is served with an orange-and-tomato compote and the modern one as a salad.

Confit of Rabbit Legs on a Bittersweet Salad

A thoroughly modern preparation which mixes southwestern French and modern American cuisines. This formula does not use the rabbit loins; see page 804 for a quick recipe to use them and the recipe for rillettes on page 791 to use the remainder of the rabbit. Wash all the bitter salad greens thoroughly but quickly as too much water renders them extra bitter.

FFR — 6 SERVINGS

Legs and bones of 3 young rabbits

2 teaspoons finely chopped fresh savory leaves

2 teaspoons finely chopped fresh oregano flowers

Large pinch of cayenne pepper

Kosher salt as needed

6 boiling onions

6 shallots

8 cups rendered duck fat

1 medium-ripe Bosc pear

½ cup dry white wine

2 tablespoons balsamic vinegar

1 teaspoon sweet yellow mustard

½ cup walnut oil or olive oil of your choice

Pepper from the mill

2 cooked medium-size yellow Chiogga beets

2 cooked medium-size red Chiogga beets

2 large yellow Belgian endives, cleaned

2 large red American endives, cleaned

1 small head very pale chicory (called frisée), cleaned and separated into leaves

1 small head escarole with as white a center as possible, cleaned and broken into bite-size pieces

1½ tablespoons finely scissored fresh chives

Remove the legs and shoulder joints from the rabbits. Mix the chopped herbs with the cayenne pepper and press against the surface of the rabbit legs. Weigh the rabbit legs and enough salt to obtain ⅙ ounce salt per pound of rabbit. Coat the meats well with the salt and place in a glass baking dish. Cure, covered with plastic wrap, for 24 hours, in the refrigerator.

Bring a pot of water to a boil. Add the onions and shallots in their skins and blanch for 3 minutes. Rinse under cold water and peel. Cut a small cross in the root end of each; add to the glass dish containing the rabbit legs. Cover the dish with plastic wrap and cure another twelve hours.

Preheat the oven to 300°F. When ready to confit, discard any juices that have accumulated in the curing dish. Pat the meat, onions, shallots, and curing dish dry with paper towels. Return them to the dish and cover completely with the melted duck fat to reach 1 inch above the meat. Bake until a skewer inserted into one of the legs comes out without difficulty, 1½ to 2 hours.

Pour 1 inch of kosher salt in a 1-quart saucepan; add the pear and cover it with enough salt so the pear disappears in it. Bake in the salt side by side with the rabbit for 30 to 40 minutes. Remove from the oven when a skewer inserted into the pear comes out without difficulty. When the salt is cool enough to touch, remove the pear, brushing off the salt (see page 701 for safety tips). Cut the edible parts of the pear, skin still on, into small cubes and add half to a blender.

When the confit is done, remove the pieces of rabbit to a plate and keep warm, covered with aluminum foil. Drain and strain the fat into a bowl or jar. Leave only the caramelized rabbit juices in the dish. To the rabbit juices add the wine and balsamic vinegar. Bring to a boil over medium heat and simmer until reduced to ⅓ cup. Strain into a measuring cup and remove the small layer of fat at the surface of the reduction. Pour the reduction over the pear in the blender, add the mustard and walnut oil, season with salt and pepper, and process into a dressing. Add more of the pear and salt if the dressing is too sour.

Remove the confited onions and shallots from the fat bath, pat dry, and slice. Slice the beets and mix with the onion and shallot slices. Mix with a bit of the dressing. Toss the greens with as much dressing as needed and arrange on six luncheon plates. Top each portion with the sliced vegetables and a rabbit portion. Dribble a teaspoon or so of the dressing over the meat and sprinkle with the chopped chives. Serve promptly.

Traditional Confit of Duck with Tomato-Orange Confipote

A confipote *is a modern French preparation which is half preserve* (confiture *in French*) *and half a traditional compote of mixed fruit. Use either sun-ripened tomatoes or canned stewed tomatoes seasoned with a bit of sugar. For use of the duck cutlets, see the sections on grilled and panfried meats on pages 729 and 795. You may remove the thigh bone before serving; it pulls out easily.*

SUGGESTED WINE: *A generous wine such as Cahors or a Mas de Daumas Gassac*

FFR—6 SERVINGS

Legs from three 5- to 6-pound ducks

½ recipe **Confit Spice Mixture (page 786)**

Kosher salt as needed

36 cloves garlic, peeled

8 cups rendered duck fat

For the confipote

3 pounds fresh tomatoes, peeled and seeded, or two 29-ounce cans stewed tomatoes

3 Valencia oranges

1½ tablespoons granulated sugar

Salt

1 Meyer lemon or ½ regular lemon

1 teaspoon finely ground dried pasilla chile

2 teaspoons finely scissored fresh basil leaves

Balsamic vinegar

Pepper from the mill

Weigh and note the total weight of the duck legs. Sprinkle the legs on both sides with the confit spices. Weigh enough kosher salt to obtain ⅓ ounce per pound of meat. Sprinkle the legs with the salt on both sides, set them in a flat glass baking dish with the garlic cloves, and cover the dish with plastic wrap. Cure for 36 hours in the refrigerator.

Preheat the oven to 275° to 300°F. Drain the totality of the colored water that has accumulated at the bottom of the dish. Pat the legs, garlic cloves, and the curing dish dry; return the legs and garlic to the dish and cover with the duck fat. Bake until the cloves of garlic have turned deep golden, 2 to 2½ hours. When the meats are done, let them cool in the fat until they can be handled without danger of burns. Transfer the meat to a large canning jar and strain the fat over the meat so it covers it by a generous inch. Cool completely, seal, and store for up to 6 months in a cold, dark place such as a cellar or the bottom shelf of a refrigerator until ready to use.

Prepare the *confipote* on the day you will serve the confit. Put the tomatoes in a large saucepan. Slice 1 of the oranges, then cut each slice into dice and add to the tomatoes. Bring to a boil, add the sugar and salt to taste, and turn the heat down to a simmer. Grate the rinds of the remaining oranges and set aside. Squeeze the juice of the remaining oranges and the lemon and add to the saucepan. Cook until a compote forms. Ten minutes before the end of the cooking add the pasilla and just before serving add as much grated rind as you like. Recut the julienne of basil at a right angle to obtain small dice and mix into the preparation. Correct the acidity of the *confipote* by adding balsamic vinegar to your taste; correct the final seasoning with salt and pepper and keep warm.

To prepare the confit for serving, melt the fat by immersing the jar into a pot of hot water; slowly bring the water to a boil. Remove the jar from the water, then, using tongs, remove the duck legs from their fat. Let the fat drip from them and pat them as dry as possible with paper towels. Crisp them on their skin side only and very slowly in a nonstick pan. The skin must turn russet in color and be extremely crisp. Serve with the *confipote*.

Rillettes (also called Poillettes)

FFR — 18 APPETIZER SERVINGS

3 pounds lean Boston pork butt or 1½ pounds butt mixed with 1½ pounds skinned goose or duck leg meat

1 pound sow-belly, fatback, or uncooked duck fat, diced into ⅓-inch cubes, or half and half of two of them

2 tablespoons fine salt

½ tablespoon black peppercorns

Bouquet garni of 2 Turkish bay leaves, 2 sprigs fresh thyme, and 20 parsley stems

4 fresh sage leaves or 2 teaspoons rubbed sage

2 sprigs fresh summer savory

Place all the ingredients in an 8-quart pot, then add water, leaving 1½ inches of the meats uncovered. Bring to a boil over medium-low heat. Skim and turn down to a simmer. Cook 2 to 3 hours, uncovered, over low heat. When the water has almost completely evaporated and the meats are overdone, falling apart, and starting to brown at the bottom of the pot, stir them often with a wooden spoon to turn them into a hash. Let cool in the pot until semisolid, then turn into one or two terrines and let stand until cold. Cover well with plastic wrap and chill for 48 hours at 35°F before serving to develop full flavor. Bring back to room temperature before serving. The shelf life is one week refrigerated. Do not freeze, as the fat oxidates too fast.

This recipe is from my aunt Claire Robert, a native of the French département of Indre-et-Loire. Rillettes are a specialty of the Loire Valley and its surrounding regions. They are very ancient, and in this region probably originated at the hearths of the troglodyte dwellings along the Loire and its tributaries. The Dordogne, which also has prehistoric caves, prepares rillettes mixing pork with goose or duck. All rillettes are delicious when spread generously on country bread. Washed down with a glass of Bourgueil, Chinon, or Cahors wine, they are a sinful delight to enjoy once a year as a sort of "gastronomic Beltane."

Pan-Roasted Meats

This technique of cooking meats applies almost exclusively to beefsteaks 1½ to 2 inches thick of the type loosely termed London broil when they are cooked in a heavy skillet of plain cast iron, black-surfaced enameled cast iron, copper-dressed stainless steel, or an electric frying pan with a nonstick coating.

Those pieces of beef usually pan roasted belong to cuts readily available and very well labeled in supermarket meat counters; they are:

EXPENSIVE CUTS YIELDING USUALLY 2 TO 4 SERVINGS

- Center cut of tenderloin, also known as châteaubriand, trimmed to the bare muscle, cut to a length of 3 to 4 inches and flattened with a meat bat or the side of the hand to a thickness of 1½ to 2 inches
- Châteaubriands are quite often cut from double-thick sirloin and rib steaks which are cut against the grain of the meat and, as a result, are not as attractive as the less expensive pieces indicated below and not worth the difference in price.
- Large magrets from Muscovy ducks

AFFORDABLE CUTS YIELDING 4 TO 6 SERVINGS

- London broil cut from the chuck (the most common)
- True London broil consisting of the very tender rib cap or rib lip, which has been separated from the eye of the rib (you can do this only when you purchase a large rib roast and lift the cap yourself)
- True London broil made from flank steak
- London broil cut from the sirloin butt
- Half blade roast completely trimmed of its tough outside layer of connective tissue

Note that the most tender cuts will be the true rib cap or flank London broil that you will be able to cut across the grain by aligning the length of the piece of meat with that of your cutting board and slicing into ⅛- to ¼-inch slices.

London broil cuts from the chuck and sirloin butt will have to be sliced as thinly as possible to prevent them from being perceived as somewhat tough since the slicing is done against the grain.

THE TECHNIQUE

Preferably use a nonstick pan and have a pot lid just large enough to fit inside the pan and flush over the piece of meat at your fingertips. Moisten a crumpled paper towel with a little oil and rub it all over the bottom of the pan. Heat the pan thoroughly.

Sear the meat over high heat to brown the first side. Turn it over and salt the seared side. Still on high heat, sear the second side to the same color, then turn and salt. Reduce the heat to medium and let the meat cook 3 more minutes on each side. Finally, push the lid tightly onto the surface of the steak until you hear it sizzle, to cook the center of the meat. At this stage of the cooking the meat juices have concentrated at the center of the cut due to the regular turning of the piece; if the meat is allowed to remain too rare and cut without allowing it to rest a few minutes to allow the juices to settle, they will flow out of the meat and spoil its texture.

Remove the cooked meat to a plate and let rest a few minutes while you deglaze the pan and prepare a small gravy. The gravy must be small and no more than a glaze for the slices that you are about to cut.

Here is a recipe appropriate for all the cuts mentioned above:

London Broil London Style

FCR—6 SERVINGS

I Châteaubriand or London broil of your choice, 2 to 2½ pounds

2 tablespoons scotch whisky of your choice

I small yellow onion, finely chopped

I large shallot, finely chopped

⅛ teaspoon celery salt

I clove garlic, finely chopped

½ cup dry white vermouth

¼ cup water or very light broth of your choice

I tablespoon chopped parsley stems

½ teaspoon grated orange rind

Juice of 2 oranges

I tablespoon Worcestershire sauce

I teaspoon unsaturated oil of your choice

Salt

Pepper from the mill

Dash of fresh lemon juice

I tablespoon unsalted butter (optional)

I½ tablespoons chopped fresh Italian parsley leaves

SUGGESTED WINE: *My English friends enjoy Beaujolais with this steak; I enjoy Bonny Doon's Le Cigare Volant from Santa Cruz.*

Completely strip the steak of all fat and connective tissues; brush on all sides with the whisky. Let stand while you prepare the deglazing mixture. In a small saucepan, mix together the onion, shallot, celery salt, garlic, vermouth, water, and parsley stems; reduce to ⅓ cup over medium heat and strain through a conical strainer, pushing on the vegetables to extract all flavor. Set aside.

Mix together the orange rind and juice and Worcestershire. Set aside.

Preheat a nonstick skillet over high heat and brush with the oil. Sear the meat until brown, then turn over and salt. Sear the second side, then turn over and salt. Let cook another 4 to 5 minutes on each side, then using a lid, push hard on the meat to finish cooking its center. Remove the steak to a carving board, and let rest 3 to 4 minutes, to reach an internal temperature of 130°F (USDA 145°F).

Over medium-high heat, deglaze the pan with the prepared reduction, gradually adding the orange and Worcestershire mixture. Reduce until the short sauce turns syrupy; correct its seasoning with salt, pepper, and lemon juice. Add the butter if desired. Slice the meat and spoon ½ tablespoon of sauce over each portion. Garnish with the parsley.

Muscovy Magret

FCR — 4 SERVINGS

1 cup Primary Veal Stock (page 219) or duck or chicken stock of your choice

1 magret of Muscovy duck

Salt

Pepper from the mill

1 ounce Armagnac

½ ounce fresh foie gras (optional), mashed to a puree

¼ cup fresh corn kernels

2 teaspoons chopped fresh chervil leaves

2 teaspoons chopped fresh chives

In a small saucepan over medium heat, reduce the stock by a third. Cut a ¼-inch-wide crisscross pattern down into the fat of the magret without damaging the underlying meat.

Put the magret in a skillet and add just enough water to cover the layer of fat, but none of the lean meat. Over medium-low heat, slowly bring to a boil and simmer until the fat starts to melt. Continue to cook over medium-low until the fat covering is golden brown and crispy and the fat is melting abundantly in the skillet. Spoon off the fat as it melts to prevent it from burning; when the fat is well colored, turn the magret over and let it brown only on its second side. Salt and pepper it well. Now turn the magret over a second time and salt and pepper its underside. Using a lid small enough to fit inside the skillet and flush over the meat, push on the magret for 1 minute to force the heat to its center. Check the inner temperature of the magret with a steak button or instant thermometer. Remove the magret to a plate and let rest a few minutes loosely covered with a sheet of aluminum foil. Serve when the thermometer reads 135°F (USDA 145°F).

Meanwhile, discard any traces of fat from the pan and deglaze it with the reduced veal stock over medium heat, scraping well. Heat the Armagnac in a small pan and pour it flambéing into the sauce (read about this special technique on page 720). Off the heat, whisk in the foie gras. Let stand a few minutes, then strain into a clean saucepan using a conical strainer. Gently poach the corn kernels in the sauce over low heat, but do not allow the sauce to boil anymore.

Slice the magret paper thin and dribble the corn gravy over it. Sprinkle with the chives and chervil mixed together. Serve promptly.

Buy the magret from a butcher who will know where to order it for you. IMPS numbers do not exist for these birds which have only recently become popular. You can either cook the magret exactly as described for the London broil above, or you can use this recipe, which comes from the French Landes, south of the wine country around Bordeaux. As a vegetable, consider a mixed ragout of mushrooms.

SUGGESTED WINE: *Any of the great Medoc crus or the best California Cabernets in their best vintages; also any good red wine from the Côte de Nuits or an Étude or Saintsbury Pinot Noir*

Pan-Broiled and Panfried Meats

Pan-broiling and panfrying meats is not identical to sautéing meat, which is described on page 840. As a longtime teacher, I know that many cooks and chefs thoroughly dislike using the term "panfrying" and prefer "sautéing," but sautéing, when applied to meats, is a completely different technique and an imprecise translation of the French *sauter à la poële* which means "tossing" in the pan while frying in a fat medium. The *sauté* used as an adjective usually applies to vegetables, as in *pommes de terre sautées* or sautéed onions, for example, which are not stirred, but tossed in the frying pan to expose all their surfaces to the hot fat.

Pan-broiling and panfrying should be done in a heavy frying pan or skillet made of plain or enameled cast iron, stainless steel dressed with copper, or plain aluminum coated with nonstick material. It is essential in these two techniques to studiously avoid thin metal, which does not conduct heat evenly.

Pan-broiling is best done in a nonstick pan since hardly any fat is used to cook the meat; true panfrying is done in a thin layer of fat, which in modern cuisine is generally oil, although some cooks still use clarified butter for the white meats.

Since one 10-inch frying pan can cook only three steaks comfortably, use two pans side by side or purchase a rectangular "buffet-style" electric frying pan, which can take care of up to six tenderloin steaks or five larger steaks at once.

CHOICE OF MEATS FOR PAN-BROILING AND PANFRYING Tenderloin, sirloin and rib beefsteaks, rib and loin chops of veal and lamb, scaloppine of lamb, thin pork cutlets, thinner pork chops, and boneless white meat of chicken and boneless breast meat of regular ducks are favorites for pan-broiling and panfrying. Rabbit loins are also excellent.

All meats to be cooked in this manner must be completely skinned, defatted, and cleaned entirely of all their connective tissues, and have been at room temperature for 35 to 40 minutes.

PAN-BROILING AND PANFRYING RED MEATS Bring the meat to room temperature for 30 minutes and trim it properly. *Do not flour, salt, or pepper it.* Heat the pan over high heat and sear one side until brown. Some of the meat's red juices will start to appear on the unseared side; at this point, turn the meat over and only now salt the seared side. You will see the bundles of muscle fibers slightly separate. The heat of the pan searing the second side of the meat will cause the juices to travel upward where you will soon see them pearl on the surface of the meat. At this point any piece of red meat is done rare. To obtain medium rare, reduce the heat to medium, turn the meat over once more and season the second side; let it cook 1 more minute for medium rare, 2 to 3 for well done, but remember that a well-done piece of red meat is ruined; a lamb chop should be pink as should a veal chop. However, keep in mind the USDA internal temperatures on page 703 and check with an instant thermometer.

The thicker the piece of meat, the more the question of cooking the center of it properly gathers importance. If the meat must cook a few minutes longer after searing, turn the heat down to medium or the outside of the meat will overcrisp while the center will stay raw. Panfried meats are perfect with baked potatoes.

Onion Steaks

SUGGESTED WINE: *A simple Cabernet Sauvignon, either from Bordeaux or California, or a Côtes-du-Rhône such as Gigondas*

FFR — 6 SERVINGS

3 tablespoons unsalted butter

6 large yellow onions, thinly sliced

1 tablespoon unsaturated oil of your choice (optional)

6 sirloin strip steaks, ¾ to 1 inch thick, completely trimmed of fat and gristle

Salt

⅓ cup dry white wine

1 teaspoon vinegar

¼ teaspoon meat extract

Pepper from the mill

Finely chopped fresh Italian parsley leaves

In a large skillet, heat the butter over medium-high heat. Add the onions and sauté until translucent. Cover and let simmer over medium heat for a few minutes. Uncover and toss again until moisture-free. Remove the onions to a plate. Do not wash the skillet.

If needed, add the oil to the skillet and sear the steaks until brown over high heat. Turn over, salt the seared surface and cook, still on high heat, until the second face has browned. Reduce the heat to medium and finish cooking to preferred doneness, checking with an instant thermometer for medium-rare, 130° to 135°F (USDA 145°F). Remove the steaks to a warm platter. Pour off the cooking oil completely and replace with the wine, vinegar, meat extract, and prepared onions. Cook rapidly over high heat, stirring well, until only enough moisture is left to bind the onions well. Turn the heat off and adjust the seasoning with salt and pepper. Serve the steaks topped with the onions and sprinkled with the chopped parsley.

Modern Peppered Steaks

FFR — 6 SERVINGS

½ cup sifted unbleached all-purpose flour

I large egg

½ cup milk of your choice

Salt

Pepper from the mill

I tablespoon olive oil of your choice

¼ cup chopped cilantro leaves

I large red bell pepper, peeled, seeded, and coarsely chopped

I large yellow bell pepper, peeled, seeded, and coarsely chopped

I canned chipotle chile, finely chopped

¼ cup medium-dry sherry

2 tablespoons unsalted butter

6 center cut tenderloin steaks, ¾ inch thick, completely trimmed of fat and gristle

The crepes as used here are called chemises because they dress up the steaks; this is a good dish for entertaining elegantly and rapidly. The crepe batter can be made 24 hours ahead of time, as can the pepper compote. As a vegetable, consider a medley of corn and wild mushrooms.

SUGGESTED WINE: *You will need a French Côtes-du-Rhône or a California Syrah. Cabernet Sauvignon and peppers of any type do not get along.*

Resift the flour into a small bowl. Beat the egg and mix in the milk, then gradually stir into the flour until a smooth batter results. Season with salt and pepper, then add the olive oil and cilantro and let stand 30 minutes.

Mix together all the peppers and sherry in a small saucepan. Add ½ tablespoon of the butter and cook over low heat until a very thick compote results, about 30 minutes. Cool completely. Cream the remaining butter, mashing it with a fork, and gradually mix it with the compote. Keep warm.

Preheat an 8-inch nonstick skillet over medium-high heat. Ladle 2 tablespoons of the batter into the lip of the pan and steer the batter to slowly cover the bottom of the pan. Cook 1 minute and turn over, either flipping the crepe or turning it with a spatula. Cook 1 minute on the second side and remove from the pan. Repeat 5 more times. Pile the cooked crepes on a plate, separated from one another by a sheet of parchment paper, and keep the plate over hot water.

Heat a nonstick electric skillet or other large skillet over high heat. Sear the tenderloins on one side until brown. Turn over and salt the seared side. Sear the second side until brown and turn over, salting the second side. Cook another 2 minutes or so, until the tenderloins are rare to medium rare, 130° to 135°F (USDA 145°F). Set each crepe on a dinner plate and place a steak on the lower edge of each crepe.

Pepper the cooked steaks well and spread an equal amount of the compote over each. Flip the top of each crepe over each steak and serve promptly.

Tournedos of Veal with Zucchini-Basil Sauce

This modern sauce is made with zucchini juice and basil oil. Notice that the deglazing added to it ties the meat and vegetal essences together. Use free-range veal if you can find it. The cut to be ordered from a butcher carries IMPS No. 1306, rib chops; the 6- to 8-ounce caliber is best. The vegetable garnish could be a dish of crisp deep-fried zucchini sticks (page 423) or braised fennel bulbs (page 401).

SUGGESTED WINE: *A lovely Pouilly-Fumé or California Fumé Blanc; if red is preferred, a Cabernet Franc such as Chinon or Bourgueil*

FCR — 6 SERVINGS

1 very large red bell pepper
Salt
2 bright green zucchini, 1 inch in diameter
1 cup packed fresh basil leaves
¼ cup extra virgin olive oil
6 bone-in veal chops
⅔ cup Primary Veal Stock (page 219) or other rich stock of your choice
Pepper from the mill
2 scallions, white part only, thinly sliced on a slant
10 hazelnuts, toasted (page 50), peeled, and coarsely chopped

Peel the red pepper with a paring knife. Remove all the seeds and inner ribs and cut into quarters. Using a round cutter ⅓ inch wide, cut small confetti out of the quarters. Bring a small saucepan of water to a boil, add salt, place the confetti in a strainer, and immerse in the boiling water for 1 minute. Remove to paper towels and pat dry.

Wash the zucchini and remove their skins with a paring knife leaving ⅛ inch of white pulp attached. Put in a blender and puree coarsely; squeeze the mash through several layers of cheesecloth to extract the juices and reduce these by one third over medium heat.

Blanch the basil leaves 1 minute in boiling water. Squeeze dry, then put in a 1-cup blender jar, add the olive oil, and process until a pale green paste results. Line a tea strainer with two layers of cheesecloth and empty the basil puree into it. Let drip at least 1 hour over a bowl.

Detach the eye of each veal chop from the rib and backbones; gently remove the fat and connective tissue coverings without destroying the "lip," or large piece of meat situated just below the fat. Wrap the lip tightly around the eye and tie with a piece of kitchen string or secure with toothpicks. Keep at room temperature 20 minutes before cooking.

In a small saucepan blend 1½ tablespoons of the veal stock with the zucchini juice and 1 tablespoon of the basil oil; reheat gently over low heat. Skim off any trace of cellulose released from the zucchini juice.

Heat another tablespoon of the basil oil in a nonstick skillet over high heat. Sear the tournedos of veal on the first side until golden, then turn over and season the seared side with salt and pepper. Sear the second side until also golden, then turn and sprinkle with salt and pepper. The meat should be medium rare with an internal temperature of 135°F (USDA 145°F); if it is less done, turn the pieces of meat over once more. Remove the chops to individual plates, placing the tournedos at 10 o'clock.

Deglaze the pan over medium-high heat with the remainder of the stock. Spoon large drops of the basil mixture around the chops; now dribble smaller drops of the veal deglazing, and yet smaller droplets of pure basil oil. Dot the plate here and there with a few red pepper confetti and sprinkle the meat with slivers of scallion and a large sprinkle of the toasted hazelnuts. Serve rapidly with fried zucchini placed as a bush at 4 o'clock (see page 423) or with two fennel bulb halves, each placed on one side of the tournedos.

Panfried Baby Lamb Strips and Baby Artichokes

FCR — 6 SERVINGS

3 tablespoons pure olive oil

I lemon

I tablespoon chopped fresh mint leaves

I tablespoon chopped fresh Italian parsley leaves

I small clove garlic, very finely chopped

I double 7-rib rack of lamb or, if unavailable, 6 large lamb chops, trimmed of fat and
   gristle

Salt

Pepper from the mill

½ cup Primary Veal Stock (page 219) or other stock of your choice

Fresh chervil leaves

This recipe calls for two sides of the true baby lamb rack, IMPS No. 204, rib rack, boned, to obtain two strips 1 to 1¼ inches in diameter (see Meat Handwork on page 720). Such racks are for sale in the supermarkets of all lamb-producing areas; if not available, order from a butcher or use lamb chops instead. As accompaniment, present the baby artichokes on page 372.

SUGGESTED WINE: **A** *lighter style Pomerol or a Markham Winery Merlot*

Heat the olive oil in a small skillet over medium heat. Lift two strips of lemon rind from the lemon with a potato peeler, rinse under cold water, pat dry, and add to the hot oil. Turn the heat off, cover, and let stand at least 1 hour. Squeeze the juice of the lemon and set aside in a small cup.

Mix the mint, parsley, and garlic together on a piece of parchment paper and rub evenly and on all sides of the lamb strips. Heat 1 tablespoon of the prepared lemon oil in a nonstick skillet and sear the lamb on both sides over high heat. Salt and pepper well, turn the heat down to medium, and finish cooking to an internal temperature of 135°F (USDA 145°F).

Remove to a small platter and cover lightly with aluminum foil. Deglaze the pan over high heat with the stock and reduce to ¼ cup. Add lemon juice to taste and another drop of the lemon oil and spoon over the strips of lamb. Present the strips on a platter separated by the artichokes. Dot the plate with tiny droplets of lemon oil and a few chervil leaves. Serve sliced.

PANFRIED WHITE MEATS

Before the advent of nonstick pans, white meats were floured and seasoned before being panfried. Now, however, while it is still essential to season them because of their blandness, flouring is no longer necessary. Once in a while, if you do not mind the calories, try flouring them to experience the old-fashioned delicious super-thin outside crust created by the flour absorbing the meat's juices.

As a panfrying medium, clarified butter or the "super butter" now sold to chefs under the name of Plugras presents a definite taste advantage, but from the nutritional point of view, unsaturated oils are a wiser choice. Use any mono- or polyunsaturated oil you like, any olive oil of your choice being the best.

VEAL AND TURKEY SCALOPPINE AND ESCALOPES Scaloppine are slices of veal or turkey ⅛ inch thick, cut across the grain in the width of the muscles. They cook almost instantly without producing almost any gravy. This necessitates the preparation of a small, rapid sauce. Escalopes, also cut across the grain the width of the muscle, are approximately ⅓ inch thick; they release enough juice to build a small gravy.

Scaloppine and escalopes, if cut with the grain of the meat, following the length of the muscle, will buckle and shorten while cooking and become tough.

The best cuts for preparing scaloppine and escalopes of veal are the top and bottom of the round, the top of the round, commonly called "veal top," being the best. Any butcher will understand what you mean when you order a veal top or a bottom round of veal; each comes in a Cryovac bag. Buying veal scaloppine or escalopes already sliced is not always a good decision for many meat cutters do not cut the muscles in the correct direction; if you order scaloppine make sure you do so from an established butcher who knows the difference and specify the thickness you prefer.

For cooks who cut their scaloppine themselves, this slightly difficult job becomes much easier if you partially freeze the meat so it stiffens enough for you to cut straight slices of an even thickness. An electric meat slicer is also of great help.

Any part of the turkey breast can be used for escalopes. Since turkey breasts offered for sale whole come mostly from 10- to 12-pound birds, the escalopes will be small. Cut them ⅓ inch thick and gently flatten with a meat bat or the flat side of a cleaver blade to a thickness of ¼ inch; they will, while cooking, thicken back to approximately ⅓ inch. Escalopes cut out of the smaller veal tenderloin must also be cut across the grain but at a 30-degree angle, to obtain larger pieces.

There is a difference of taste between turkey and free-range veal; but it may happen in very affordable restaurants that turkey escalopes will be served instead of very pale young veal. The turkey is much better from the nutritional point of view because of its very low content of saturated fats and cholesterol.

Because of the different textures each meat possesses, veal should be panfried at a slightly higher temperature than turkey. If the frying pan has a thermostat, chose 425°F for veal and 400°F for turkey. After cooking, the meat will be at an internal temperature of 135°F, reaching 145°F by the time you serve it.

CHICKEN CUTLETS Chicken cutlets are boneless breasts of chicken; there are two cutlets per chicken. See pages 727–28 for detailed explanations. Whole chicken cutlets must be flattened with the flat of a cleaver blade or a meat bat and seasoned before being panfried to prevent blandness once cooked. A thick aluminum pan coated with nonstick material is the best; the initial heat of the frying pan should be no higher than 375°F, or else the long, delicate muscle fibers will seriously toughen. In order to avoid cutlets that are overcooked on the outside and underdone inside, it is necessary, once the browning has been completed, to push on the meat with a lid that fits inside the pan and flush over the cutlets; the pressure will send the heat of the pan to the center of the cutlet. A chicken cutlet is done in a matter of 5 to 7 minutes and larger cutlets will cook proportionally faster than smaller ones.

Chicken cutlets can be filled with a filling that may swell under the influence of the heat. The best way to keep the cutlet looking good and evenly shaped is to sew it closed with *white* thread (other colors have an interesting way of leaching their color into the meat). Leave a two-inch tail of thread on both sides of the opening, making convenient handholds for pulling the thread out when the cooking is done. Note that a meat filling always consists of already cooked meats, in thin slices or chopped. If the filling is cheese, nuts, or precooked vegetables, just pressing the pockets closed will be sufficient; the liquid collagen will, as it coagulates, keep both sides sealed together. If you must sew the cutlets, remember the basic rule: *For safety reasons, the needle is either in your hand or attached to your apron, but never left lying on the cutting board or on the table*.

Escalopes of Veal Riviera Style

FCR — 6 SERVINGS

2 small top rounds of veal, I pound each

I tablespoon olive oil plus more as needed

I cup Primary Veal Stock (page 219) or best chicken or turkey stock

Salt

Pepper from the mill

⅓ cup dry white wine

I to 1½ teaspoons anchovy paste, to your personal taste

⅓ teaspoon finely grated lemon rind or more to your personal taste

Juice of I lemon

6 pitted black oil-cured olives, finely chopped

2 tablespoons coarsely chopped fresh Italian parsley leaves

This recipe also works with chicken cutlets and turkey escalopes. As a vegetable, consider a stir-fried medley of bell peppers and fennel.

SUGGESTED WINE: *Any of the rosés of the Côtes de Provence, light Gigondas, lighter Châteauneuf-du-Pape, any good dry California rosé*

Cut the veal tops into slices ⅓ inch thick and flatten them to ¼ inch with a meat bat or the flat of a cleaver blade. Line the slices on a baking sheet or jelly-roll pan lined with plastic wrap; cover them with plastic wrap while they wait.

Cut the uneven end pieces of the meat into small cubes. Heat 1 tablespoon olive oil in a 9-inch skillet, then brown the veal pieces to golden over medium-high heat. Add the veal stock and reduce to ½ cup over medium heat. Strain into a small bowl using a conical strainer and set aside.

Heat a large skillet or electric frying pan on high heat; moisten a crumpled paper towel with a tablespoon of olive oil and rub over the entire surface of the hot pan. Fry the escalopes till golden, about 2 minutes per side, seasoning each side with salt and pepper after it is seared. Remove to a platter and keep warm.

On high heat, deglaze the pan with the white wine, reducing it to 2 tablespoons. Add the reduced veal stock, anchovy paste, the lemon rind, lemon juice to taste, and any juices that may have escaped from the waiting cooked scaloppine. Mix well, give several good boils, and correct the final seasoning with more salt and pepper if needed. Spoon the sauce over the escalopes and sprinkle with the mixed olives and parsley.

Scaloppine of Turkey in Corn-Milk Gravy

FCR—6 SERVINGS

2 cups fresh corn kernels, yellow, white, or mixed

2 cups milk of your choice, scalded

I tablespoon unsalted butter

I pound black chanterelle mushrooms, hard part of the stems removed

Salt

Pepper from the mill

I tablespoon pure olive oil

I2 turkey scaloppine

⅓ cup chicken or veal stock or broth of your choice

Hot salted water as needed

Juice of I lemon

I teaspoon chopped fresh parsley leaves

I teaspoon chopped fresh chives

This is inspired by a dish prepared in my Boston restaurant. Whole 4 percent milk is best for preparing the corn milk. If your finances are in great shape, replace the black chanterelles with two black truffles. You may use yellow or white corn or a combination of both. Notice that because of its extreme blandness, the white meat is seasoned before cooking, which will allow it to absorb more of the taste of the salt and pepper. The texture of the corn milk depends on the fullness of the kernels; it is up to you to modify the texture to your preference by adding as much hot salted water as needed to obtain the texture you prefer.

Put 1½ cups of the corn kernels in a blender or food processor. Pour in the scalded milk and process until a puree results. Pour into a saucepan, bring to a boil, turn down the heat to medium-low, and simmer approximately 30 minutes. Rinse a large piece of cheesecloth under cold water and squeeze it dry. Line a strainer with the cloth folded over three times, set it over a bowl, and pour in the corn milk. Let drip until most of the milk has passed through, then squeeze gently to extract as much liquid as possible out of the fibrous material. Set aside; you should have approximately 1 cup of excellent, flavorful corn milk, the thickness of which will vary with the type of corn you have used. If you have more, use 1 cup and keep the remainder to enrich a vegetable soup.

Heat the butter in a nonstick skillet over medium-high heat. Add the mushrooms and salt and pepper to taste and sauté for 2 minutes. Cover, turn the heat down to low, and let the mushrooms lose all their juices. Remove the lid, raise the heat again, and let the juices evaporate completely. Stir in the remaining corn kernels, let heat through, then turn into a bowl and keep warm while the turkey cooks.

Without washing the pan, add the oil and heat the pan over medium-high heat. Salt and pepper the scaloppine and panfry them until golden, about 2 minutes on each side. Pour the corn-and-chanterelle mixture onto a platter. Arrange the cutlets on the mixture, cover with a sheet of aluminum foil to keep warm. Deglaze the pan in which the cutlets cooked with the stock and reduce to 3 tablespoons on medium-high heat. Add the corn milk without reducing anymore; correct the texture with hot salted water, if needed, to obtain the texture you prefer. Correct the final seasoning with salt, pepper, and lemon juice to temper the extreme sweetness of the corn. Drizzle a bit of the corn-milk sauce over the meat and sprinkle with the herbs. Turn the remainder of the corn-milk sauce into a small sauce boat. Serve with haste.

Chicken Cutlets with Hazelnuts and Chervil

FCR — 6 SERVINGS

6 chicken cutlets, trimmed of skin, fat, and tendons

¼ cup finely chopped fresh chervil leaves

Salt

Pepper from the mill

3 tablespoons hazelnut oil or other oil of your choice

¼ cup hazelnuts, peeled and chopped

Juice of ½ lemon

Coat the unflattened chicken cutlets with half the chervil, then season them with salt and pepper. Heat a large skillet on medium-high heat. Add 2 tablespoons of the hazelnut oil and brown the chicken until golden, about 2 minutes on each side. Reduce the heat to very low. Cover with a lid small enough to fit inside the pan and rest flush over the cutlets. Without pushing on the

This is another dish to be served in a great hurry to preserve the texture of the white meat of chicken. If hazelnut oil is not available, heat 2 tablespoons vegetable oil in a skillet and cook the hazelnuts in it over medium heat until a powerfully nice smell develops; do not burn the nuts. A plain pilaf of rice is best as accompaniment.

SUGGESTED WINE:
Adelsheim Vineyard white
Riesling from Oregon

cutlets, let stand 4 minutes; the cutlets will be done and juicy, with an internal temperature of 165° to 170°F. Transfer the cutlets to a serving platter.

Add the last tablespoon of hazelnut oil to the pan over medium heat. Toss the hazelnuts in it until they turn honey colored. Add the lemon juice and season with salt and pepper, then spoon the mixture over the cutlets. Sprinkle with the remainder of the chervil. Serve in all haste.

PANFRIED BREADED MEATS

The same basic anglaise or breading used for fish is used also for meat, so refer to page 626 for more information. You will find many variations to these basic formulas, some offering different types of herbs, some of nuts.

Often the white meats are presoaked in milk before being breaded, a useful technique that provides additional moisture to very small pieces such as rabbit loins which might dehydrate too much when panfried over high heat.

Here are two recipes:

Old Giovanni's Rabbit Cutlets

This recipe also works well with chicken cutlets and turkey escalopes. It is from St. Vincent d'Aosta in northwestern Italy and is slightly modified by introducing almonds in the breading. As a use for the legs of the rabbit see the confit on page 839. For vegetable accompaniment, use the Mediterranean medley of stir-fried vegetables on page 410.

FCR—6 SERVINGS

Boneless loins of 3 rabbits
I cup milk of your choice
I large egg, beaten
I teaspoon water
I teaspoon plus 2 tablespoons pure olive oil
Salt
Pepper from the mill
½ cup coarse fresh bread crumbs
¼ cup blanched almonds, chopped
I ½ tablespoons unbleached all-purpose flour
I large lemon, cut into 6 wedges and seeded

SUGGESTED WINE:
Chambave from the Valle d'Aosta
or a nice Lambrusco

Place the rabbit loins on the cutting board, cut a long slit two thirds of the way into each loin, and open it up like a book. Gently pound with a meat bat or the flat of a cleaver blade to an even ⅛ inch thickness. Put the cutlets in a large baking dish and cover with the milk. Let steep, refrigerated, for 2 hours, turning over once.

Beat the egg, water, 1 teaspoon of the olive oil, and salt and pepper to taste until almost liquid. Set aside. Put the bread crumbs and almonds in a blender or food processor and process until the mixture is fine and even textured.

Remove the cutlets from the milk and pat dry. Flour the cutlets very lightly, patting them smartly to discard any excess flour. Spread the crumb mixture evenly on a sheet of waxed paper. Brush the anglaise on the first side of each cutlet, then invert and push lightly into the crumbs. Turn the cutlets over and repeat the same operations on the second side.

Heat the remaining 2 tablespoons of olive oil in an electric skillet to 375°F and panfry each cutlet until golden, 2 to 3 minutes on each side. Correct the seasoning, remove to a platter, and serve with wedges of lemon. The inner temperature of the meat will be safe.

Modern Cordon Bleu

FCR — 6 SERVINGS

6 large chicken cutlets, trimmed of skin, fat, and gristle

6 paper-thin slices deli-style smoked turkey, about 2 × 3 inches

4 ounces fresh American or French goat cheese

½ small clove garlic, mashed

I tablespoon chopped fresh Italian parsley leaves

Salt

Pepper from the mill

I ½ tablespoons unbleached all-purpose flour

I recipe Anglaise (page 626)

½ cup medium-coarse fresh bread crumbs

Open a pocket in the thickest part of each of the cutlets. Lay the cutlets in one line on the left side of your cutting board, open side facing out. Next to each cutlet, place one slice of turkey.

Mash together the goat cheese, garlic, and parsley. Shape the mixture into 6 even-size cigars half as wide as the cutlets and almost as long as the slices of turkey. Place each cigar on one slice of turkey and wrap the turkey loosely around it. Stuff the cigars into the cutlets and press closed. Pass a white thread through both sides of the opening to prevent gaping while cooking. Leave 2 inches of thread at each end of the cutlets.

Salt, pepper, and flour the cutlets as lightly as possible, patting them smartly to remove any excess flour. Beat the egg, water, a dash of salt and pepper, and 1 teaspoon of the oil together until almost liquid. Spread the bread crumbs on a sheet of waxed paper. Brush the anglaise on one side of each cutlet, then invert into the crumbs and push lightly. Brush the second side with the anglaise and invert again into the crumbs. Press on the cutlets to push the crumbs against the cutlet.

Heat the remaining 2 tablespoons of olive oil in a large nonstick skillet over high heat. Add the cutlets and brown well on both sides over medium-high heat. Reduce the heat to medium and cook another 3 to 4 minutes. Season with salt and pepper. Pull the threads off and serve immediately.

The classic Cordon Bleu came from Switzerland and was prepared with boiled ham and Gruyère, a combination that gave birth to multiple variations. Here is one with goat cheese and smoked turkey. For more choices with diverse American cheeses, see the first edition of this book. As a vegetable accompaniment, consider a salad of bitter greens.

SUGGESTED WINE: **A** *Joseph Phelps red Vin du Mistral*

Cutting a pocket into a chicken cutlet and finished cutlet with pocket cut in

Deep-fried Meats

For a general discussion of the techniques used in deep-frying, please refer to pages 632–34.

Very few meats are deep-fried nowadays outside of chicken, an occasional little bird such as a quail, and the all-American breakfast steak still to be found in some small towns of the Central Plains when crossing the country by car. Appetizer fritters are slowly disappearing in favor of lighter tidbits made of healthy laxed salmon and small tortillas topped with a vegetable salsa.

Here are just a few recipes as examples:

Breakfast Steaks

From a roadside breakfast, somewhere in Illinois in 1964; the home fries were bad and the small, deep-fried steaks were juicy and delicious. This recipe can be executed also with chicken, turkey, or veal cutlets and escalops.

SUGGESTED WINE: *The steaks were awkward with coffee. In case you prepare these for an impromptu lunch, enjoy a Beaujolais-Villages.*

FFR — 6 SERVINGS

Unsaturated oil of your choice for deep-frying

1 large egg

1 teaspoon water

1 teaspoon plus 1 tablespoon vegetable oil

Salt

Pepper from the mill

Unbleached all-purpose flour

6 small tenderloin steaks, 1½ inches in diameter and ¾ inch thick, cut out of the thin part of the cut

½ cup fine dry bread crumbs spread on a sheet of waxed paper

2 tablespoons unsalted butter

2 teaspoons fresh lemon juice

1 tablespoon finely chopped fresh Italian parsley leaves

6 large eggs, fried sunny side up

Preheat 3 inches of oil to 360°F. Beat together the egg, water, 1 teaspoon of the oil, and a dash each of salt and pepper. Flour the steaks all around; pat smartly to remove any excess. Brush the edges of the steaks all around with the egg mixture; roll each steak into the crumbs to coat their edges. Now brush one side of each steak and invert into the crumbs, pushing lightly; turn over, brush the second side and invert again into the crumbs. Pat gently to discard excess crumbs. Let air dry 10 minutes on a rack.

Cream the butter, then add a dash each of salt and pepper, work in the lemon juice and parsley, and divide into six patties. Immerse the steaks in the hot oil three at a time and fry until golden, 2 to 3 minutes. Top each steak with a fried egg and a dollop of the compound butter.

Chicken Liver Fritters

FFR—6 APPETIZER SERVINGS

½ pound chicken livers, trimmed and cut into 4 pieces each

2 tablespoons dry sherry or Madeira of your choice

Salt

Pepper from the mill

I cup plus 3 tablespoons sifted unbleached all-purpose flour

I tablespoon finely chopped fresh tarragon leaves

2 tablespoons unsaturated oil of your choice

½ cup water

½ cup light beer

2 large egg whites

Unsaturated oil of your choice for deep-frying

Toothpicks

If beer is not agreeable, replace it with an additional ½ cup of water.

Marinate the liver pieces in the sherry for about 2 hours in the refrigerator.

Put ¼ teaspoon salt and 35 turns of the mill of pepper in a medium-size bowl. Add 1 cup of the flour, the tarragon, and oil. Gradually whisk in the water and beer, proceeding slowly to prevent lumps. Strain the mixture through a conical strainer into a clean bowl. In a large bowl, beat the egg whites almost until stiff peaks form. Gradually beat into the batter.

Preheat 4 inches deep of oil to 360°F. Drain the chicken livers and pat them dry. Coat them with the remainder of the flour, patting them to remove any excess. Dip in the fritter batter. Dip a two-pronged fork into the hot oil, then use it to lift each piece of liver out of the batter and into the oil; cook 6 to 8 pieces at a time until golden, 2 to 3 minutes. Drain on paper towels, transfer to a serving plate, and pass accompanied with toothpicks.

Juicy Quail

FFR—6 DINNER SERVINGS

12 plump California quail

12 cloves garlic, crushed

12 small sprigs fresh thyme

Salt

Pepper from the mill

3 shallots, very finely chopped

I cup Cabernet Sauvignon

1½ tablespoons dark soy sauce

Unsaturated oil of your choice for deep-frying

With many thanks to Russell, who taught me the trick of fried quail. For lunch or a salad, use only six birds. Quail are finger food; present small bowls of warm water with a slice of lemon and a clean towel.

Stuff the cavity of each quail with 1 garlic clove and 1 sprig of thyme, then season well with salt and pepper. Truss, then cover with plastic wrap and refrigerate overnight to let the seasonings penetrate the meat.

In a small nonreactive saucepan over high heat, reduce the shallots and Cabernet to ¼ cup of liquids and solids. Strain through a tea strainer into a ramekin and mix in the soy sauce.

Set the quail on a rack and brush with the mixture. Let air dry 1 hour. Preheat the oven to 400°F and bring 4 inches deep of oil to 370°F. Add 3 quail at a time to the oil and fry until nice and deep golden, about 4 minutes. Remove to a baking sheet or jelly-roll pan and keep covered with aluminum foil until all the quail have been fried. Finish cooking the quail in the hot oven until the breast of the largest bird starts showing slight resistance to pressure when squeezed between the thumb and index finger; the birds will be medium rare and register 130° to 135°F between the thigh and breast on an instant thermometer (USDA 145°F). For well-done meat, leave in oven a few more minutes.

Fried Chicken Fingers and Funny Salsa

This is fun food for summer days; enjoy! Use more or fewer chiles as you prefer. You can use "chicken oysters" also if you have some frozen (page 727).

SUGGESTED BEVERAGE: *The beer of your choice*

FFR—6 SERVINGS AS A PICNIC MAIN COURSE

For the salsa

I medium-size red onion, diced into ¼-inch cubes

Salt

3 canned chipotle chiles in adobo, finely chopped

2 tablespoons adobo sauce

½ cup water

4 teaspoons unsweetened cocoa powder

I red bell pepper, seeded and diced into ¼-inch cubes

I yellow bell pepper, seeded and diced into ¼-inch cubes

I ripe avocado, peeled, pitted, and diced into ⅓-inch cubes

I ripe mango, peeled, pitted, and diced into ¼-inch cubes

I large sun-ripened tomato, peeled, seeded, and diced into ⅓-inch cubes

2 tablespoons chopped cilantro leaves

For the chicken fingers

6 chicken cutlets, trimmed of skin, fat, and gristle

Unsaturated oil of your choice for deep-frying

2 cups unbleached all-purpose flour

½ teaspoon ground allspice

I teaspoon ground cumin

3 tablespoons corn oil

Salt

Pepper from the mill

1 ½ cups pale ale or 1 ½ cups milk of your choice

3 large egg whites

Place the onion in a colander and salt lightly. Set aside. Mix the chiles and adobo sauce together. Combine the water and cocoa in a small saucepan and cook over medium-high heat until slightly thickened, about 2 minutes. Cool completely and mix into the chiles. Add the bell peppers, avocado, mango, and tomato, season with salt, and mix well.

When the red onion has lost its juices, drain, pat dry, and add it to the salsa. Correct the final amount of salt and mix well. Let the mixture macerate at least 1 hour at room temperature and just before serving with the chicken fingers mix in the cilantro.

Remove the small fillets from the cutlets (see page 728). Flatten the large fillet of each cutlet to ¼ inch thickness with a meat bat, the flat of a cleaver blade, or the side of your hand and cut each into six fingers on the diagonal. Preheat 4 inches of oil to 360°F.

Mix ½ cup of the flour with ¼ teaspoon of the allspice and ½ teaspoon of the cumin. Set aside. Put the remainder of the flour in a bowl and add the remainder of the allspice and cumin and the oil. Season with salt and pepper. Gradually whisk in the ale, proceding slowly to prevent lumps. Beat the egg whites in a large bowl. When they almost reach stiff peaks, beat in the prepared batter.

Toss the chicken fingers and small fillets in the flavored flour. Shake well in a large strainer to discard any excess flour. Dip a two-pronged fork into the hot oil, then dip each finger in the batter with it and drop each finger into the hot oil and fry until golden. Fry only a few fingers at a time. Drain on paper towels and serve immediately with the salsa.

Stir-fried Meats

Stir-frying is the most delightful and rapid way to prepare a quick dinner that balances one's nutrition and introduces a lot of taste, texture, and nutritional diversity to the plate all in one stroke, since a good stir-fry consists of two thirds fresh vegetables and one third to one quarter meat. The meat can be varied easily and the vegetables mixed in such a way that white, yellow, and leafy vegetables are represented all together. Such mixtures of vegetables offer vitamins and fiber while the meats offer some of the proteins and vitamin B that is needed to feel well.

Stir-fries are a good way never to "forget" vegetables in the vegetable bin of your refrigerator. Check your bin twice a week and imagine a nice stir-fry with whatever you have at hand, deciding which meat will go best with the present combination. Of course it goes with stir-fries as it goes with any other food, too many stir-fries can become monotonous, so be sure to alternate styles.

IMPLEMENTS FOR STIR-FRYING

If you can acquire a Chinese wok, you will be set for life; if your stove does not offer enough heat to use one, electric woks exist at reasonable prices and they work very well. A large electric frying pan set at its highest heat setting or a heavy-bottomed skillet used on a high gas burner will do almost as well.

To stir-fry ingredients, you will need a blunt-end wooden spatula or a Chinese stir-frying spoon, and, to remove the meat and vegetables from the pan, a slotted spoon.

THE SEQUENCE OF A STIR-FRY

Stir-frying, like all cooking methods, has a drawback. The cooking time of the food is extremely short, but the time required to slice or dice all the ingredients into small pieces is not. However, the cutting need not be an agonizingly long affair. If you learn to wield the chef's knife or Chinese cleaver from a good practitioner, it will take you no more than a few weeks to become as fast as your master.

To gain time, line the vegetables on the kitchen counter in small bowls or on plates in order of cooking time, so all you have to do is toss them into the pan as their turn to cook comes. Harder root vegetables will go first and soft green ones last.

Those convenient bags of frozen vegetable medleys, after a day of hard work, will come in handy, if not deliver the very best texture. Separate the vegetables into categories, so the longest to cook goes first into the pan and the softer ones last. Add frozen vegetables to the pan frozen; they will instantly lose their moisture but they will take a few more seconds to cook than the fresh ones.

The next element to go into the pan will be the sauce, if you use one; it's not absolutely necessary but helps to give slip on the palate to fibrous vegetables. The sauce consists of chicken or vegetable broth mixed with a bit of cornstarch to bind the mixture together and in Chinese-style dishes only, of a small amount of soy sauce. For people allergic to soy sauce, it can be replaced by a mashed anchovy dissolved into the chicken broth. Once the vegetables are all cooked and sauced, transfer them to a large plate to wait for the meat to cook; they will continue to cook from their own accumulated heat.

It seems as if I am using a topsy-turvy way to add the sauce, but if the meat is beef and is submitted to the additional heat needed to introduce the sauce, it will overcook and be tough; similarly, the white meat of poultry will be stringy and ruined, so I always add the meat last so it can cook alone without overcooking. All meats must be cut into ½-inch cubes or into 1½ × ⅛-inch slivers. Beef can be used plain or marinated in aromatics and spices; poultry, which toughens so easily, is often *velvetized* or velveted.

To velvetize a meat, beat 1 large egg white in a small bowl until liquid, then beat in 1 tablespoon dry fino sherry and ⅔ teaspoon salt. Sift in 1 tablespoon cornstarch and stir until perfectly smooth.

Mix in 1 pound of cubed white meat of poultry. Let marinate at least 30 minutes (but you can leave it to marinate in the refrigerator for a much longer time if you wish). When ready to start cooking, separate the pieces from one another on a large plate.

Have a colander ready while you bring a pot of water to a boil; lightly salt it as soon as it boils. Turn the water down to a simmer and let the meat slide into the water for 20 seconds. Drain the meat into the colander placed over the sink. Shake to drain rapidly. (For an extensive explanation of this technique refer to the beautiful work of Barbara Tropp in *The Modern Art of Chinese Cooking*.)

Velvetized meat is not cooked to its center; be fast and immediately add the meat from the colander to the wok or pan and conclude the cooking with 1 to 2 minutes of stir-frying in oil. Return the vegetables to the pan, stir-fry another 30 seconds to reheat them to their centers, and serve immediately.

Serve stir-fries on preheated plates so as not to destroy one of their great charms, their very hot temperature which accentuates the fresh taste of the vegetables.

DO NOT USE TOO MUCH OIL   Use the oil of your choice, peanut, corn, or pure olive, but the best for stir-frying is grapeseed oil. It is a relative newcomer to the United States that has been used for frying in France for a good twenty years, and has a very high smoking point. Never use butter, clarified or not; the high heat of the wok will burn it.

It is not so rare to see attractive recipes for "lean" stir-fries literally floating away in oil; remember to limit the amount of oil as much as you can by drizzling the oil from the lip of the pan in as small a quantity as you can. The ingredient that will actually require the majority of the oil used in the dish is the meat.

Here are three examples, one made with beef and a small sauce, one with plain turkey meat and no sauce, and one with velvetized chicken meat. Try to imagine similar dishes made with slivers of veal loins, slivers of leg of lamb, and slivers of rabbit loins and legs. To do so, think of the climates in which those animals are raised and of the vegetables they produce, that could accompany those meats well.

ROUNDING OFF A STIR-FRIED MEAL
Think of a starch since you already have meat and vegetables taken care of. Rice, either steamed, pilafed, or risottoed, will be perfect but so will pasta of any kind, and any grain you like.

Velvetized Chicken Stir-fry with Ratatouille Vegetables

This recipe can also be prepared with slivered sirloin strip of beef, slivered veal loin, or turkey breast. This is not a common texture for the vegetables usually making up a true ratatouille (see page 396), but this preparation is, in a different way, just as attractive in its modern crunchy form. If you cannot find small eggplant, use a large one, discarding all the seeds and soaking the remaining parts in salted water for 30 minutes. Pat dry before stir-frying.

SUGGESTED WINE: *Any good Côtes de Provence, white, red, or rosé*

FCR — 6 SERVINGS

For the pesto

1 cup packed fresh basil leaves

2 small cloves garlic, chopped

½ cup extra virgin olive oil

¼ cup freshly grated Pecorino Romano or other hard grating cheese of your choice

For the stir-fry

2 cloves garlic, mashed

2 tablespoons finely chopped fresh Italian parsley leaves

2 pounds chicken breasts, trimmed of skin, fat, and gristle, and cut into
  1½ × ⅛-inch slivers

1 large egg white

1 tablespoon Pernod or ouzo or broth of your choice

1 tablespoon cornstarch

Salt

Olive oil as needed

2 small Japanese or 3 small Italian eggplant, cut into ½-inch cubes

1 large red onion, coarsely chopped

1 tablespoon red wine vinegar

2 medium-size green zucchini, cut into ½-inch cubes

2 medium-size yellow zucchini, cut into ½-inch cubes

2 large red bell peppers, seeded and cut into ½-inch squares

2 sun-ripened beefsteak tomatoes, peeled, seeded, and cut into ⅛-inch-wide wedges

Pepper from the mill

2 scallions, slivered

Prepare the pesto: Mix the basil leaves, garlic, oil, and cheese together in a blender and process until a thick paste results. Turn into a small bowl and set aside (you will need approximately half of it only; store the remainder for a dish of pasta).

Mash the garlic and parsley together. Toss the chicken slivers into the mixture to coat them well. In a large bowl beat the egg white until liquid, then beat in the liqueur, sprinkle the cornstarch over the surface, and whisk until smooth. Add the chicken to the velvet and marinate 1½ hour in the refrigerator and ½ hour at room temperature. Bring a pot of water to a boil, add salt, and turn down to a simmer.

Preheat the wok over high heat. Dribble a bit of oil all around the pan. Stir-fry the eggplant until they color well, 1 to 1½ minutes; add the onions and vinegar and stir-fry 30 seconds; add the green zucchini and stir-fry another 30 seconds; add the yellow zucchini and stir-fry another 30 seconds. Toss in successively the bell pepper and tomato wedges, salt and pepper the mixture well, toss for 2 minutes, and remove to a waiting platter. Wipe the pan dry.

Put the chicken in a colander and immerse 1 minute in the simmering water. Drain well while you heat 1½ tablespoons of oil in the pan almost to the smoking point. Add the meat and stir-fry 1 minute. Return the vegetables to the pan and reheat all together until bright hot. Stir in the scallion slivers. Remove to a serving platter and dribble dollops of pesto all over the top of the dish. Serve immediately.

Steak Stir-fry

FCR—6 SERVINGS

1 pound steak meat of your choice, cut into slivers

2 tablespoons dry Sercial Madeira or fino sherry

1 clove garlic, mashed

1 teaspoon soy sauce of your choice or 1 anchovy fillet, rinsed and mashed

½ teaspoon cornstarch

½ cup cold Secondary Stock (page 220) or other broth of your choice

Grapeseed or other oil of your choice

Two ⅛-inch-thick slices fresh ginger, peeled

⅓ pound carrots, cut into halves lengthwise, then into half moons ⅛ inch thick

¼ pound superfine or regular green beans, strings removed and cut on a slant into
    1-inch pieces

¼ pound brown mushrooms, sliced ⅛ inch thick

¼ pound bean sprouts

Salt

Coarsely cracked black pepper

1 scallion, slivered on a slant into paper-thin slices

Use any quality of steak you like but be careful to cut the lean meat into 1½-inch strips with the grain of the meat and recut those into ⅛-inch-thick slivers across the grain.

SUGGESTED BEVERAGE:
Beer or, if you prefer, Gewürztraminer, or even Oolong tea

Mix the steak slivers, Madeira, and garlic together very well. Refrigerate and let marinate in a bowl for 2 to 3 hours. Gradually dilute the soy sauce and the cornstarch in the chosen broth; set aside for later use.

A few minutes before serving, heat the wok or frying pan over high heat. Drizzle a bit of oil evenly into the pan. Toss in the ginger and fry for 1 minute, then remove. Add in succession the carrots, green beans, mushrooms, and bean sprouts and stir-fry 1 minute each. Stir the ingredients of the sauce together well again, add to the wok, and stir until the mixture coats the vegetables. Remove the vegetables to a waiting platter and keep warm.

Clean the pan with a wad of paper towels and drizzle 1½ tablespoons oil into the pan; heat almost to the smoking point over high heat, add the beef, and stir-fry to medium rare, or as well done as you prefer. Return all the vegetables to the pan and reheat a few seconds, stirring wildly. Season with salt and pepper and serve immediately sprinkled with the slivered scallions.

Stir-fried Curry from Martinique

FCR—6 SERVINGS

1 pound turkey tenders (small fillets), cut into slivers 1½ × ⅛ inch

2 cloves garlic, mashed

2 tablespoons light rum (optional)

1½ teaspoons curry powder

Pinch of cayenne pepper

Grapeseed or other oil of your choice as needed

2 large green bell peppers, seeded and cut into ¼-inch-wide slivers

2 large not too ripe mangoes, peeled, pitted, and cut into ½-inch wedges

Six ⅓-inch-thick slices not too ripe fresh pineapple, cut into triangular wedges

2 scallions, sliced into ¼-inch-thick slivers

2 to 3 tablespoons unsweetened large toasted coconut flakes, to your personal taste

Toss the slivered turkey together with the garlic, rum, curry, and cayenne pepper. Marinate for 2 hours, 1½ hours in the refrigerator and ½ hour at room temperature.

Heat the wok or pan over high heat. Drizzle a small amount of oil into the pan and add the green peppers, stir-fry 30 seconds, add the mango wedges, stir-fry another 30 seconds, stir-fry the pineapple wedges another 30 seconds. Remove to a waiting platter.

Clean the pan with a wad of paper towels and add 1½ tablespoons oil. Heat to the smoking point and stir-fry the marinated turkey slivers 1 minute. Return the vegetables and fruit to the pan, adding the scallions; stir-fry together another brief minute and serve immediately sprinkled with the coconut flakes over a plain pilaf of rice.

Moist Heat Meat Cooking Methods

All the techniques explained and illustrated in this section are for meats that are cooked in the presence of a liquid. They include:

- Braising and stewing
- Pot-roasting and sautéing
- Poaching
- Steaming and pan-steaming

This recipe can also be used with small cubes of lamb or veal loin. The spices here are those used in Martinique in many dishes originating in the homes of Indian families who immigrated to the French West Indies in the 1840s.

SUGGESTED BEVERAGE:
Beer of your choice

Braising and Stewing

Braising comes from the French word *braise*, which means smoldering coals, and is the name given to an interesting process for cooking meats in a small amount of liquid in a tightly covered pot called a *braisière*. In centuries past and as recently as the early 1900s when people still cooked on the hearth, braising roasts and stewing cubed meats in good stock was done by cooking with fire under, on top of, and all around the pot which, especially designed for this function, had a deep concave lid. The pot was embedded in embers and more embers filled the lid, and coals were banked all around the pot. I remember my great grandmother doing this. The meat rested on several layers of aromatics mixed with raw ham and veal slices called *fonds de braise* (to be roughly translated as "base of the braise" and the main aromatic taste enhancer).

Nowadays the procedure has been oversimplified to such a point that it is totally misunderstood. The results are either washed-out meats and watery gravy because the pot used is not adequate, or meats that are, so to say, confited in stock and come out glazed and delicious, but not tasting at all like braised meats. A short study of the elements and principles of braising will forever banish these shortcomings and restore the knowledge of how one should truly braise.

CHOICE OF BRAISING POT FOR HOME USE AND RESTAURANT PRODUCTION

A braised meat cooks under pressure, and it is essential to choose a pot that will keep the pressure as even and constant as possible; such a pot should be thick and just big enough to contain the piece of meat. There should be absolutely no space or, at least, as little space as possible between the lid and the meat, so as to imitate the old-fashioned *braisière* in which the concave lid came very close to touching the top of the meat. The difficulty with modern pots is that they often have sides too thin to conduct the heat evenly.

The best pots nowadays for cooking perfect braises at home are the very thick copper pots, enameled cast-iron pots, and the old-fashioned cast-iron pots, well seasoned with age. Do not throw your grandmother's cast-iron pots away!

For restaurant production, when medium-large quantities are involved, rondeaux made of heavy material are best; for very large production, meats can be braised in the electric cooker known as the Swiss skillet or tilting skillet, which, besides being used for cooking stocks and panfrying larger quantities of steaks or chops is also deep enough to braise large numbers of roasts or stew large quantities of cubed meats.

Since none of the modern pots have concave lids, it is essential to compensate for this deficiency by fitting a large piece(s) of heavy aluminum foil snugly over the cooking meat and its cooking liquid. The foil should be shaped like an inverted lid, its center part resting on the meat and liquid with the excess foil hugging the sides of the pot and hanging over its rim and crushed flat and snuggly all around and against its outside. Not only is the meat covered with the foil, it is double covered by the pot lid which seals the heat into the pot and makes sure that the edges of the aluminum foil stay put inside and outside the pot. The inverted aluminum foil lid has the double duty of:

• Catching any steam that might condense on the pot lid and fall back into the sauce.
• Putting the contents of the pot under the heaviest steam pressure possible.

Should the condensation be allowed to fall back into the cooking liquid, the latter would never concentrate and the result would be a boiled piece of meat instead of a braise.

If the braising liquid of a meat or vegetables contains an acidic liquid such as wine and/or vinegar, a piece of parchment paper needs to be first stretched over the contents of the pot to isolate the acidic liquid from the aluminum and prevent reactivity between the two (this situation happens in coq au vin, bourguignon, and any other braises marinated in wine as well as German and Alsatian sauerkraut).

WHAT HAPPENS WHEN YOU BRAISE?
I have purposely kept my wording very simple and as nonscientific as possible so my text can be accessible and make sense to all cooks. Every cook, professional or not, deserves a good, well-prepared braise.

When a piece of meat is seared and acquires a brown crust, its natural juices, travel toward the center of the piece and concentrate there. After the meat is put to braise in the oven, the pressure and the heat around the piece become increasingly intense, causing the collagen to gelatinize (or break down into gelatin).

When the temperature has reached its maximum at the center of the meat, the pressure of the steam is such that it bears down on the meat fibers and slowly pries them open; the meat juices now make their way from the center of the piece toward the outside, break through the seared surface, and mix with the cooking stock, which is generally the richest possible stock.

If you were to open the pot at this time, you would notice that the liquid in the pot has increased and that the piece of meat is at this point nothing more than a tremendously tight bundle, or series of tight bundles, of moisture-deprived fibers. Because of the inner lid of foil, the meat is in such tight surroundings that the pressure will continue increasing in the pot and slowly the meat juices, this time mixed with the stock, will find their way back inside the meat and make it deliciously tender. The next time you braise a piece of meat, notice how the quantity of liquid in the pot has diminished after the meat is perfectly cooked, which is when a skewer inserted at the center of the piece of meat goes in and comes out freely. As you slice the

The pot is completely covered by the foil. Now you can put the lid on.

meat you will clearly be able to see the liquid in suspension between the muscle fibers and notice a great difference of texture from the unfortunate stringy pieces of meat that you may have ended up with in former braises or stews. This difference is especially visible in stews such as the classic Milanese osso bucco, the classic lamb stews such as the navarin, and boeuf bourguignon.

ARE BRAISES AND STEWS OBSOLETE?

"I do not prepare stews and braises because they are so labor-intensive and so fattening" is heard all over the land. Indeed, a delicious, well-prepared braise requires time and to-the-letter observance of some seemingly difficult cooking techniques. There is no doubt that larding (the passing of long strips of pork fatback called lardons through a piece of meat to help add moisture to the coarse-textured meat fibers of lesser cuts) has fallen into desuetude not only for its labor-intensiveness, but also because modern American meats have nothing in common with the meats used in Europe nowadays nor with those prepared in the eighteenth and nineteenth centuries, during which the techniques of braising were refined.

Modern American meat animals are raised so scientifically that indeed pork fat lardons can be forgotten without worry; our beef is too marbled at an early age and contains enough fat for the cook to concentrate on getting rid of it, rather than adding it to obtain a delicious stew or braise. Again, as I've said in many other sections of this book, I am for moderation and all in favor of a good stew or a braise on late fall and winter days; a stew at regular intervals is not going to hurt anyone in any way, people with very serious heart problems excepted.

THE MODERN TECHNIQUES

The most important part of preparing a braise is to realize that it can be done over two days and that no additional butter or saturated fats besides those contained in the meat need enter its composition, unless you wish it to. The browning of the meat and that of the aromatic vegetables can be done in the oven with the help of a very small amount of unsaturated oil.

The flavor of a braise comes in large part from aromatic vegetables, the browned meat, and a delicious wine marinade that gives a lot of body and taste to the cooking juices. Even if you are not a wine drinker, do not hesitate to use wine here; the ready-to-eat braise will contain only an infinitesimal amount of alcohol.

MODERN WINE MARINADE

I would like to emphasize strongly that the bulk of the tenderization of a piece of meat does not come from marination but, first and foremost, from proper cooking techniques. A great deal of time has been spent on this subject by food scientists and I would like you to refer to the bibliography for information on the research of this subject. If a marinade has a tenderizing effect, it is only a very small one affecting the outer layers of the meat.

Meats for braising, more so red meats than white ones, are often marinated in wine, a mixture of wine and vinegar, or a mixture of vinegar and water, but *never vinegar alone*, which is too pungent.

The classic cuisine used to offer two types of marinade. The uncooked marinade was preferred in everyday cuisine and the cooked marinade in refined cuisine. I have decided to remove raw marinades from my kitchens and use only a cooked marinade, the reason being that a meat marinated in raw wine always results in a sauce that is acid and difficult to finish and a meat texture which, to my taste, is far inferior to that of a meat marinated in a cooked marinade. Last but not least, meats marinated in raw wine are more taxing to the digestive system.

The cooked marinade has lost almost all of its alcohol and its acidity has been tamed by the sweet juices of the aromatics, such as carrots, onions, and shallots.

All-Purpose Cooked Marinade

NFR—8 CUPS

2 tablespoons pure olive oil

2 shallots, sliced

1 medium-size carrot, sliced

2 medium-size yellow onions, sliced

¼ celery rib (optional), sliced

2 tablespoons chopped parsley stems

6 cups dry white wine or 5 cups dry red wine plus 1 cup white wine

1 small Mediterranean bay leaf, crumbled

1 large sprig fresh thyme, chopped

2 cloves

6 white peppercorns, cracked

Any part of this marinade not used can be stored in a sterilized glass jar and frozen for up to one year for later use. Notice the ratio of 1 part white wine to 5 parts red wine used for a red wine marinade. Vinegar is often used but in the small quantity of 1 part vinegar—or even less—to 6 parts wine. The herbs and aromatics indicated are passe-partout *("good for every use") herbs which can be used with any meat without problem. If you feel like using other herbs, such as rosemary and savory, or citrus fruit such as lemon or orange, and spices such as juniper berries, do not hesitate. Simply add what you like to the marinade before cooking it and see the recipes that follow as examples.*

Heat the olive oil in a sauteuse pan over medium-high heat and lightly brown the shallots, carrot, onions, celery, and parsley stems. Add the wine, bay leaf, thyme, and cloves and bring to a boil; reduce the heat to a simmer and cook uncovered 20 minutes. Add the peppercorns during the last 5 minutes of cooking. Cool completely.

If you wish to obtain a venison taste in beef or lamb to imitate true, all too expensive braised deer or chamois, add the following combination to the marinade immediately after it has finished cooking but is still boiling hot to evaporate the alcohol in the spirits:

1 ounce Cognac, Armagnac, malt whisky, or bourbon of your choice

1 ounce dry Sercial Madeira

1 ounce dry fino sherry

1 ounce white port

Mix the marinade well after the addition.

MARINATION TIME   A whole piece of meat of 3 to 4 pounds should marinate no less than 24 hours, a larger one up to 4 days and should be turned every 12 hours.

ADDITIONAL AROMATICS
The fonds de braise   A *fonds de braise* is a mixture of additional vegetables sautéed lightly in oil or butter that is placed under the meat in the braising pot. These can include thickly sliced shallots, onions, and carrots and garlic cloves crushed in their skin. Thick slicing is essential so the vegetables do not fall apart in the gravy and mar it with tiny pieces.

Fat-free pork rind   Yes, pork rind! Do not throw your arms up; pork rind is mostly protein. In areas where you can find pork rind in the supermarket, the use of a large piece completely trimmed of its layers of fat is beneficial, especially if you have no time to prepare your own stock. Cook the pork rind starting with cold water; slowly bring the mixture to a boil and simmer until the rind becomes translucent; any fat that remained on the piece will have melted completely and be in the water. Place the rind at the bottom of the braising pot and top it with the already browned vegetables. As the braise cooks, the pork rind will slowly melt into the gravy and give it excellent shine and viscosity, which will replace thickening the gravy with flour and butter. Use one larger piece fitting the center of the pot at home and smaller pieces placed at regular intervals in the professional tilting skillet.

Avoid large fresh bones   Avoid adding large fresh bones to the braising pot, as they will not have time to release sufficient amounts of gelatin and add any texture to the gravy. And if they cook one tiny bit too long, they will communicate that awful bony taste which will ruin the gravy altogether.

The bones of small animals such as rabbits, chicken, and pigeons are all right.

RED MEAT BRAISES
Beef, lamb, and red-meated birds such as duck, goose, squab, and quail are the best red meats for braising. Duck and goose, however, are very fat indeed and as nice as they may taste braised, they are, in my opinion, better off roasted or baked.

BEEF AND LAMB Cuts of beef and lamb for braising need not be the most tender; the extravagant days of braised tenderloin and sirloin strips are gone forever because of their high cost. The best cut to use for both beef and lamb is the chuck or shoulder. Lamb shoulder is lean enough and beef chuck has relatively fine fibers separated by tiny streaks of suet; don't push the panic button about that suet, though, as it will melt while the meat cooks and you will remove it completely after cooking.

Positively do not use round of beef, the fibers of which are coarse and deliver a very dry braise and an average gravy.

The grade of the meat you use should preferably not be below U.S. Choice or Good, but I have had good success with Standard meats.

QUALITY OF STOCK OR BROTH The stock, besides the quality of the meat, is the most important element of a braisage. The better it is the tastier and the more tender the meat will be. Use, in order of my preference:

- Primary veal stock (see page 219)
- Secondary stock (see page 220)
- Any stock made with any type of poultry
- Water plus commercial meat extract wisely dosed
- Canned stock containing as little salt as possible

RED MEAT BRAISING SEQUENCE Please reread the general principles of braising starting on page 815 to understand what happens in a piece of red meat while it's being braised.

One to four days before cooking, if you wish, place the meat in a cooked marinade.

The day before you serve the braise:

1. If the meat has been marinated, dry it well and rub it with oil before browning it. Sear whole small pieces of meat on all sides in oil on top of the stove over medium-high heat. Whole large pieces of meat are best seared on all sides in a preheated 450°F oven until a brown crust of caramelized juices has formed.
2. Sauté the vegetables of the *fonds de braise*. If you use a pork rind, precook it, then place it in the bottom of the braising pot and spread the vegetables of the *fonds de braise* over it.
3. Strain the marinade, if you have used one, pushing hard on it to extract all the liquid from the solids. Add all of its aromatics and spices to the braising pot on top of the *fonds de braise*. Reduce its liquid to 1 cup for each 3 pounds of meat and strain it again through a very fine mesh tea strainer to catch those purple solids, which are made of agglutinated blood corpuscles and other materials. Left to cook with the meat, they are responsible for a muddy sauce, with three times as many of those tiny floaters as there should ever be.

4. Add the piece of meat on the vegetables and pour in enough best possible stock plus the reduced marinade to half cover it. Bring to a boil and add a bouquet garni and any other condiments or aromatics you like. Cover the meat flush with a sheet of parchment paper if your stock or marinade contains any acidic components, then with aluminum foil, forming an upside-down dome lid. Tuck the edges of the foil tightly against the outside of the pot, then cover with the pot lid.

5. The same day, braise the meat. It is preferable to cook it in a preheated 325°F oven rather than on top of the stove. The cooking time depends on the size of the piece, but is never less than 1¼ to 2 hours. In any case, the meat is done when a skewer inserted in its thickest part comes out freely. *Do not forget to turn the meat over several times while it braises.* Remove the cooked meat to a bowl, cool, and seal the bowl with plastic wrap only if serving on the next day. Strain the cooking juices into a large gravy separator using a conical strainer or China cap and let the fat come to the top; defat completely.

6. For delayed completion: If you are going to serve the braise the next day, do not discard the foil lid. Store the gravy in a wide-mouth measuring cup and refrigerate it overnight. Refrigerate the meat wrapped tightly in clear plastic. The next day, remove the layer of solid fat from the top of the gravy, discard it, and reheat the meat slowly in its cooking juices with the foil and pot lid on, which will take about 30 minutes.

7. In a saucepan over medium-high heat, reduce the gravy to the consistency you like. If the gravy was made with veal stock, it probably will need no thickening after reduction. If it was made with any other stock or broth, thicken it with a *beurre manié* (see page 287) or a slurry of potato starch (see page 269).

Note the application of all these rules in the recipes that follow.

REHEATING AND FREEZING BRAISES The finished braise often tastes better after being reheated. Do not hesitate to prepare braised meats ahead of time, but only up to the stage when you thicken the gravy; you can refrigerate it up to three days and keep it frozen up to six months.

Horseradish Braised Beef

Serve this braise with any homemade egg pasta (see page 499) or commercial macaroni.

SUGGESTED BEVERAGE:
A great Bavarian lager beer

FFR—6 SERVINGS

I recipe **All-Purpose Cooked Marinade (page 818)** made with dry white wine

I whole sprig fresh **marjoram** or ½ teaspoon crumbled dried

I teaspoon **ground ginger**

I **Mediterranean bay leaf**, crushed

One 3- to 4-pound piece **beef chuck blade roast**

Unsaturated oil of your choice

Salt

Pepper from the mill

I medium-size **carrot**, sliced

I medium-size **yellow onion**, sliced

One 8 × 4-inch piece **pork rind**, cooked (page 819; optional)

4 cups **Primary Veal Stock (page 219)** or best available stock

I teaspoon **meat extract**

Bouquet garni of a few parsley stems and I sprig fresh thyme

Butter and **flour** as needed if making a beurre manié (page 287; optional)

2 tablespoons **cream-style horseradish**

2 tablespoons **sour cream** or **crème fraîche**

Watercress bouquets

Assemble the ingredients of the marinade in a saucepan, add the marjoram, ginger, and bay leaf, bring to a boil, and cook 20 minutes over medium-low heat. Cool completely; marinate the meat 24 hours in the refrigerator, turning the piece over three times.

Preheat the oven to 450°F. Drain the meat and pat dry; rub it lightly with oil, season it with salt and pepper, and set it in a roasting pan. Surround it with the carrot and onion and brown it in the oven, about 20 minutes, turning it over once. Meanwhile, strain the marinade, keep its aromatic vegetables, and reduce the liquid in a small saucepan over high heat to 1 cup. Strain the reduction through a tea strainer or China cap.

Turn the oven down to 325°F. Arrange the ingredients in the braising pot in the following order: pork rind if used, carrot and onion mixed together, marinade vegetables, meat, reduced marinade, stock to cover the meat halfway, meat extract, and bouquet garni. Bring to a boil, then cover the meat with a sheet of parchment paper, then a sheet of aluminum foil resting over the meat and forming an inverted lid, and finally the pot lid. Braise until a skewer inserted through the thickest part of the meat comes out clean, 2½ to 3 hours. Turn the meat three times during cooking.

Remove the cooked meat to a cutting board and keep warm covered with its foil. Strain the sauce through a conical strainer and defat entirely. In a small saucepan over high heat, reduce it by one third. Thicken with a *beurre manié*, only if desired. Blend in the mixed horseradish and sour cream. Correct the final seasoning to your taste.

Slice the meat, set on a platter, baste with some of the sauce, turn the remainder into a sauce boat, and decorate the dish with watercress.

Shoulder of Lamb Braised in Zinfandel

FCR — 6 SERVINGS

1 recipe All-Purpose Cooked Marinade (page 818) made with Zinfandel

4 cloves garlic, mashed

4 juniper berries, crushed

1 sprig fresh rosemary or ½ teaspoon dried, crumbled

1 small bunch fresh basil

Bouquet garni of parsley stems, 1 Turkish bay leaf, and 1 sprig fresh thyme

1 shoulder of lamb, 3 to 4 pounds

4½ tablespoons chopped fresh Italian parsley leaves

1 ounce dried boleti

¼ cup pure olive oil

1 medium-size carrot, thickly sliced

1 yellow onion, thickly sliced

3 medium-size sun-ripened tomatoes, peeled, seeded, and coarsely chopped

4 cups best available stock

1 teaspoon meat extract

1 ounce brandy of your choice or gin

Salt

Pepper from the mill

¼-pound slab pancetta, cut into ⅓-inch cubes

A nice accompaniment would be a simple risotto flavored with Mediterranean herbs (see page 466). Boleti are the largest cèpes or porcini, which grow during the summer in temperate climates and during the winter in Mediterranean climates.

SUGGESTED WINE: **A Ravenswood Zinfandel**

In a medium-size saucepan, combine the ingredients for the cooked marinade, add 2 cloves of the mashed garlic, the juniper berries, rosemary, basil, and bouquet garni. Bring to a boil, reduce the heat to medium, and simmer for 20 minutes. Cool completely and set aside.

Shave most of the fat from the top of the lamb shoulder and remove the shoulder blade to obtain a relatively even opening in the center of the meat. Mix 3 tablespoons of the parsley and remaining garlic together into a persillade. Spread one third of it inside the shoulder; keep the remainder covered and refrigerated in a small bowl. Reshape the shoulder so the opening is no longer visible and tie at ½-inch intervals with thin kitchen string. Place the shoulder in a glass bowl just big enough to hold it, pour over the marinade, and marinate 24 hours in the refrigerator, turning it over three times during the marination. Soak the boleti overnight in just enough water to cover them.

Lamb shoulder with the shoulder blade bared but still attached to one end of each muscle

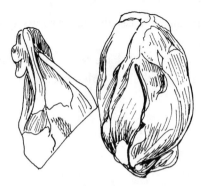

Shoulder blade and reshaped boneless shoulder

Shoulder stuffed and tied

The next day, preheat the oven to 450°F. Remove the shoulder from the marinade and pat completely dry. Rub with some of the olive oil, then the remainder of the persillade. Put the carrot and onion in a roasting pan, toss with a bit more of the olive oil, set the shoulder over the vegetables, and sear and brown in the oven, about 20 minutes, turning it once.

Turn the oven temperature down to 325°F. Meanwhile, strain the marinade into a small saucepan, reserving the vegetables, and reduce its liquid part by one third over medium heat. When the meat is seared, add the vegetables from the marinade to the braising pot along with the tomatoes. Strain the reduced marinade over the meat using a tea strainer, then add enough stock to cover the meat halfway, the meat extract, brandy, and salt and pepper to taste. Bring to a boil on top of the stove, then put a sheet of parchment paper flush over the meat; add a sheet of aluminum foil resting flush on the parchment and clinging snuggly up the sides of the pot to form an inverted dome lid. Finally cover the pot with its lid and braise until a skewer inserted at the center of the meat comes out freely, or about 1¼ hours. Remove the meat from its pot and set on a cutting board covered with its foil lid.

Heat the remaining olive oil in a medium-size skillet over medium-high heat. Sauté the pancetta cubes until barely golden. Pat dry in paper towels. Strain the gravy through a conical strainer and return to the braising pot. Drain the boleti over a small bowl; rinse the rehydrated mushrooms in clear water, pat them dry, then chop and add them to the pot. Strain and add the boleti soaking water to the gravy, taking care not to include any gravel. Reduce the sauce by one third over medium-high heat. Correct the seasoning with salt and pepper.

Serve the lamb shoulder sliced and garnished with the diced pancetta, the boleti lifted out of the sauce, and the remaining 1½ tablespoons parsley. Pour the remainder of the sauce into a sauce boat and serve with risotto.

Confit de Pigeons

FFR — 6 SERVINGS

Six ¾-pound squabs

½ cup duxelles (page 1064)

6 slices fresh foie gras (page 898), 2 x 1½ inches

3 large truffles, peeled (reserve the peels) and 1 cut into 6 even slices

3 tablespoons clarified butter (page 32)

5 tablespoons Armagnac

1 medium-size yellow onion, sliced

1 medium-size carrot, sliced

Small bouquet garni made of parsley stems, 1 Turkish bay leaf, and 1 sprig fresh thyme

Salt

Pepper from the mill

3 to 4 cups Primary Veal Stock (page 219), to your personal taste

2 tablespoons tawny port

2 tablespoons unsalted butter

Bone the squabs through the back (see page 883), leaving only the drumstick bones in. Stuff each bird with 1½ tablespoons each of the duxelles, 1 slice of the foie gras, and 1 slice of truffle. Dice the remaining 2 truffles and set side. Sew the skin closed over the back of the bird using a fine needle and white thread. Tie the tips of the legs together with fine kitchen string. Heat the clarified butter in a braising pot, over medium-high heat and brown the squabs on all sides. Spoon out the remainder of the butter and flambé the squabs with the Armagnac (see more detailed information on this technique on page 720).

Preheat the oven to 325°F. Remove the squabs to a plate. Toss the onion, carrot, and bouquet garni into the pot and cook, covered, for a few minutes over medium-low heat. Set the squabs on top of the vegetables, sprinkle with salt, pepper, and the chopped truffle peels. Pour in stock to cover the squabs halfway. Bring to a boil, then reduce the heat to a simmer. Cover the squabs with a sheet of aluminum foil, resting it on the birds to form an inverted lid, and the pot lid. Braise in the oven for about 1 hour; the birds should be well done.

Remove the squabs to a board and keep them warm covered with the foil. Strain the cooking juices through a China cap into a gravy separator or measuring cup and let the fat and pure gravy separate. Return the fat-free gravy to the pot. Add the diced truffles and port, and reduce to 1¼ cups over medium heat; finally, whisk in the raw butter. Correct the final seasoning.

Set each squab on a portion of gratin and baste with a generous teaspoon each of the sauce. Pass the remainder of the sauce in a sauce boat.

The name of this dish is a misnomer for a true braise. It is expensive and challenging but the results are worth the effort. Please, no substitute ingredients for the truffles or foie gras; the cost will be less if you use Oregon black truffles which have a delightful aroma and flavor. If truffles or foie gras are not possible, simply prepare three times as much duxelles for the stuffing, and the pigeons will be delicious in a different way. Serve with the gratin of potatoes and celery root on page 441. Be careful, your sewing needle must be either in your hand or attached to your apron, never on the table.

SUGGESTED WINE: **A** *Pomerol Château Petit-Village, an old Châteauneuf-du-Pape, or a great old California Zinfandel*

Roast Pork Braised in Milk

Do not use the center cut of the loin; cut IMPS No. 406, Boston butt tied and rolled tightly is better. Cooking pork in milk is a technique used both in the French Alps and the Basque country. As a vegetable serve a medley of stir-fried bell peppers of your choice.

SUGGESTED WINE: *A white meritage of California Sauvignon Blanc and Sémillon is excellent.*

FFR—6 TO 8 SERVINGS

4 cups whole milk

½ teaspoon dried rosemary leaves

¼ teaspoon dried thyme

¼ teaspoon dried sage

1 Mediterranean bay leaf

1 tablespoon chopped parsley stems

1 boneless pork blade roast, 3 to 4 pounds

Salt

Pepper from the mill

Pinch of cayenne pepper

1 tablespoon corn oil

2 medium-size yellow onions, sliced

1 medium-size carrot, sliced

1 teaspoon cornstarch

¼ cup sour cream

1 heaping teaspoon Dijon mustard or more to your personal taste

1 tablespoon chopped fresh chives

In a large saucepan, bring the milk to a boil, then add the herbs, reduce the heat to medium-low, and reduce to 3 cups.

Set the pork in a roasting pan in a preheated 400°F oven for 20 minutes, seasoning with salt, black pepper, and cayenne pepper twice during the process, and turn the meat over once.

Heat the oil in the braising pot over medium-high heat and sauté the onions and carrot slices 2 minutes. Add the pork, half cover with milk, and bring to a boil. Cover with a sheet of parchment paper resting flush on the meat, then with a large sheet of aluminum foil resting on the parchment and climbing snuggly up the sides of the pot to form an inverted dome lid. Reduce the oven temperature to 325°F and bake until a skewer inserted at the center of the roast comes out freely, 1½ hours to 2 hours. Remove the cooked meat to a platter. Clean its surface of all milk solids.

Strain the cooking juices through a China cap into a gravy separator. The juices will be clear as the straining will discard the milk solids. Gently pour the meat juices into a small saucepan, leaving all the fat in the separator. Bring the juices to a boil, turn them down to a simmer. Make a slurry with the cornstarch and a bit of water and stir into the simmering meat juices until the gravy thickens. Blend in the sour cream and mustard. Reheat to just below the boiling point. Add the chives and correct the seasoning. Slice the meat, dribble a bit of the sauce over the slices, surround them with the stir-fried peppers, and pass the remainder of the gravy in a sauce boat.

Brown stews are prepared with cubed pieces of beef, veal, lamb, or venison, cut-up chicken or rabbit, or small birds. While in a true braise a roast or bird(s) is half covered with stock, in a stew the cubes of meat are, according to the consecrated expression, "barely covered" with it.

The cooking principles governing brown stews are identical to those for braises. Stews are better when braised in the oven, but they can also be cooked on top of the stove.

The cook has two choices: Either brown the meat without flouring it and obtain a strong sauce that may be thickened after completion of the cooking, or sprinkle the browned meat cubes with flour before adding the stock. The sauce obtained with the second procedure is thickened by the time the cooking is finished, but it is not nearly as strong and flavorful; the meat cubes, however, may be a tad more flavorful. Cooks can suit themselves as to their favorite formula.

You may have run across the word *daube* applied to a beef stew. A *daube* is a Provençal stew made with marinated then floured but unbrowned beef cubes or slices. The meat and its accompaniment of vegetables are barely covered with stock and braised in the oven in a pot hermetically sealed with a paste of flour and water. The best implement for this type of stew, if you are intrigued by the principle, is a medium-large bean pot, safely glazed without lead. This last point is worth paying attention to since the pot is left to cook in a 250° to 275°F oven for approximately 7 hours.

Guinness Beef Stew

FCR—6 TO 8 SERVINGS

4 pounds beef chuck

Pure olive oil as needed

2 tablespoons unbleached all-purpose flour

12 large yellow onions, sliced

Salt

Pepper from the mill

½ teaspoon ground ginger

2 cloves garlic, sliced

2 tablespoons blackstrap molasses

8 ounces Guinness stout

3 cups stock of your choice

Small bouquet garni of parsley stems, I Turkish bay leaf, and I sprig fresh thyme

I dime-size piece lemon rind

2 tablespoons chopped fresh Italian parsley leaves

A variation on the Belgian carbonnades de boeuf. *The final sauce is a bit bitter; if you prefer it sweeter, use light beer instead. As an accompaniment, choose a pasta, the gnocchi on page 496, or simple rice. This recipe can also be executed with boned turkey legs and thighs cut into ½-inch-thick pieces.*

SUGGESTED WINE: *The same kind of stout or beer you used in the making of the stew*

Cut the beef into ½-inch-thick slices, removing all traces of fat. Heat just enough olive oil to coat the bottom of a large skillet over medium-high heat. Brown the meat slices on both sides. Once browned, sprinkle the slices with the flour and toss around in the skillet a few minutes to cook the flour. Remove the slices to a plate.

Preheat the oven to 325°F. Without washing the skillet, add the onions and toss over medium heat until they start browning. Transfer the onions and meat to the braising pot, arranging them in alternating layers. Salt and pepper each layer. Mix the ginger, garlic, molasses, and stout together and pour over the meat. Cook down over high heat until the liquid is reduced by half. Add enough stock to barely cover the meat again and bring to a boil; add the bouquet garni and lemon rind. Cover the stew with parchment paper, then a large sheet of aluminum foil, resting shiny side up on the meats and forming an inverted lid, and finally the pot lid. Braise until a skewer inserted at the center of one piece of meat comes out freely, 1½ to 2 hours.

Uncover, taste the gravy, and correct the seasoning; spoon off any trace of fat from the surface of the stew. Sprinkle with the chopped parsley and serve piping hot.

WHITE MEAT BRAISES

The components used in the braising process for white meats are the same as in brown braises, with the following details being important enough to pay them special attention:

- The pork rind is most useful, but not absolutely necessary.
- The vegetables of the *fonds de braise* are quickly sautéed, without allowing them to color.
- The meats primarily used are a veal roast or a white-meated bird. In the old days some veal roasts, such as the top round known in French as *fricandeau*, were "piqued," which means larded all over with tiny lardons of fresh fatback passed ¼ inch down into their surface at regular ½-inch intervals with a special needle. The roasts were not seared but glazed after the cooking was completed, which is difficult to do in one of our powerful broilers and which should be altogether skipped rather than ruin the wonderful texture of the meat by overexposure to radiating heat.
- White-meated birds can be seared in a preheated 375°F oven to tighten their skins lightly, but it is not a necessity.
- The stock used must be white, so the secondary stock on page 220 made only with white poultry carcasses and a large veal bone is perfect. The more gelatinous the stock, the better. If you do not use a pork rind, just add 1 teaspoon of gelatin per cup of broth used.
- An old-fashioned technique called *tombage à glace* can be used, but is not a must in any way, to intensify the gelatin content and taste of the stock used to complete the braisage: Set the white meat on the vegetables of the

fonds de braise and add about ½ cup of stock. Let it reduce to 1 tablespoon over medium-high heat; repeat with two more successive additions of ½ cup stock each for good concentration and light coloration of the juices at the bottom of the pan.

PROCEED TO THE BRAISAGE   Add the braising stock to cover just a bit more than halfway up the piece of meat or bird. Cover with a sheet of parchment paper (it protects the skin of fine birds), then a sheet of aluminum foil, forming an inverted lid (see page 815), and then the pot lid. Braise in a preheated 325°F oven.

BASTING THE MEAT   Baste the piece of meat or bird every 15 minutes with the braising juices, so that the gelatin forms a light coating. The braising time for white meats is short compared to that of red meats. A 4½-pound chicken is ready in just above an hour and a 6-pound capon in 1½ hours at most from the time it starts braising. A veal roast weighing 4 pounds will be done in about 2 hours.

THE DIFFERENCE BETWEEN RED AND WHITE BRAISES   In veal, which is really an immature red meat, the exchange of juices between the meat and the gravy happens partially and the braise is not truly a pure braise but a half-breed between casserole roasting (see page 836 for an explanation) and braising.

In white birds, the exchange of juices between the meat and the gravy does not and should not occur at all; if you overcook the braise, the exchange will happen and the bird will fall apart when you lift it out of the braising pot.

TO GLAZE OR NOT TO GLAZE?   Braised white meats look pale and, according to the pure classic techniques, should be glazed. This is feasible *only* if you have a broiler that functions on a thermostat and can radiate heat at about 350°F. Set the meat in its pot on the lowest rack of the oven and baste it with the juices as many times as is necessary to obtain a lovely golden color. *This is not a necessity; rather than ruin the texture of your meat, skip this step.*

Braised Veal Bracelet

Read this introduction carefully. This dish is expensive but excellent for entertaining a larger group served with one or several purees of vegetable (see pages 389–91).

Purchase or order from the butcher cut IMPS No. 305, bracelet double. The bracelet is the double rib rack of veal which in beef is the rib roast. To bone the bracelets, repeat exactly the same operation on each side of the bracelet: Cut along and down the backbone from end to end, progressing carefully downward until you hit the ribs. Turn your blade parallel to the ribs, the sharp edge looking toward the rib ends; take hold of the muscle with your other hand and, with your working hand, separate the meat from the rib cage, hugging the bones carefully. If you concentrate, it will take you no more than 10 minutes to finish this operation.

You are now holding a boneless rib roast ready to be prepared for braising. Remove all excess fat between rib eye and brisket and leave the brisket attached; you will wrap it around the eye to obtain a perfectly round roast which you can tie at ½-inch intervals with fine kitchen string. After repeating the same operations on the second side, you will have two roasts ready to cook. You need a large round or oval pot and, if you wish, a piece of caul fat.

FFR — 12 TO 14 SERVINGS

1 pound chicken sausage, casings removed

1 large egg

¼ cup chopped fresh French tarragon leaves

Pinch of cayenne pepper

¼ teaspoon freshly grated nutmeg

2 prepared rib roasts of veal, as explained at left

1 tablespoon unsalted butter

2 yellow onions, thickly sliced

1 carrot, thickly sliced

1 large pork rind, cooked in water (page 819; optional)

½ cup dry white wine

½ cup dry Sercial Madeira

8 cups Primary Veal Stock (page 219)

Cornstarch as needed

Put the sausage, egg, half the tarragon, the cayenne pepper, and nutmeg in a food processor and process until a fine-textured puree results, about 45 seconds. If you have no food processor, mash them together for 5 minutes with the sides of your knife blade. Spread half the sausage between the eye of each rib roast and its brisket, leaving 2 inches of the brisket uncovered. Roll up each roast tightly and tie at ½-inch intervals with fine kitchen string or, better, roll tightly in a piece of caul fat and tie.

Sear the meat in a preheated 375°F oven for 15 minutes. Turn the oven down to 325°F. Heat the butter in the braising pot over medium-high heat. Sauté the onions and carrot a few minutes. Add the pork rind if used, then set the two pieces of meat in the pot leaving 1 inch between them. Add the white wine and Madeira and reduce to a glaze over medium-high heat. Add 1½ cups of the stock and reduce to a glaze. Add enough stock to half cover the meat and bring to a boil. Cover the meats with a large sheet of parchment paper, then a sheet of aluminum foil, resting directly over the meats and forming an inverted lid, and finally the pot lid. Braise 45 minutes without opening the pot. Braise, covered, another 45 minutes, basting the meat with its own juices every 10 minutes and turning the pieces of meat each and every time you baste. Uncover the pot, switch it to the lowest rack of the oven, and set the oven to broiler function at 325°F and, basting every 3 minutes, glaze for a total of 12 minutes. Your roasts should be ready and a skewer inserted at each of their centers should come out freely. Keep warm in the braising pot.

Using a conical strainer, strain the juices into a gravy separator, then pour the lean gravy into a measuring cup leaving behind the fat. Reduce one quarter of the gravy to glaze in a large skillet on high heat, stirring constantly with a blunt-end spatula. Repeat with another quarter of the gravy, then blend in the remaining plain gravy. Use the final gravy as is or thicken it with 1¼ teaspoons cornstarch per cup of gravy. Serve the roasts sliced, sprinkled with the remaining tarragon, and basted with a bit of the gravy. Pass the remainder of the gravy in a sauce boat.

SUGGESTED WINE: *Alsatian Riesling of your choice or a Napa Valley Stony Hill White Riesling*

Braised Roaster

FCR— 6 SERVINGS

One 4½- to 5-pound roaster, washed and patted dry

2 cloves garlic, crushed

1 sprig each fresh rosemary, thyme, and savory

2 sprigs fresh lavender with flowers on

Large bouquet garni of parsley stems and 1 Turkish bay leaf

Salt

Pepper from the mill

2 tablespoons unsalted butter

4 medium-size white creaming onions, thickly sliced

4 shallots, thickly sliced

2 cups Secondary Stock (page 220)

3 tablespoons crème fraîche

½ teaspoon fresh lavender flowers

1½ teaspoons chopped fresh chervil leaves

Good entertaining at less expense and in less time than a piece of veal. The perfect accompaniment would be artichoke bottoms topped with some of the chicken sauce (see page 373).

SUGGESTED WINE: A *French dry Jurançon or a California white* meritage *of Sémillon and Sauvignon Blanc*

Remove all traces of fat from in the chicken cavity. Stuff it with the garlic cloves, herb sprigs, and the bouquet garni. Salt and pepper the bird's cavity and truss. Set the bird on a roasting pan fitted with a rack and sear in a pre-heated 375°F oven for 15 minutes.

Turn the oven down to 325°F. Meanwhile, heat the butter in the braising pan over medium-high heat and sauté the onions, then the shallots for a few minutes. Set the roaster on top of the *fonds de braise* and add the stock. Bring to a boil, then, if you want, cover with a sheet of parchment paper, then, in any case, a sheet of aluminum foil, forming an inverted lid, and then the pot lid. Braise the chicken 15 minutes, then remove the lids and baste with the cooking juices. Repeat this operation two more times. Finally, finish braising, another 25 to 30 minutes; the chicken is done when one of the thighs, pierced to its center with a skewer, releases colorless juices.

When the roaster is done, pour the cooking juices into a small saucepan and reduce them, the onion, shallots, and all, to 1½ cups over high heat. Pour into a blender and liquefy. Add the crème fraîche, season with salt and pepper as needed, and, at the last minute, add the lavender flowers and chervil. Serve cut up into eight portions, basted with some of the sauce, and surrounded by the artichokes.

STEWING WHITE MEATS:
BLANQUETTES AND FRICASSEES

White stews are known as blanquettes or fricassees and can be prepared with any of the following meats:

- Shoulder of veal
- Shoulder of lamb
- Chicken legs *only*. The white meat of chicken is much too fragile to be able to simmer for a longer time in any liquid. If you like white meat better than dark meat, refer to the panfrying, poaching, and pan-steaming techniques (see the index).

In blanquettes and fricassees the meats are not cooked under pressure but rather are simmered in a chosen liquid that just covers them. They are cooked in sauteuse pans or small rondeaux, the lid of which is kept slightly askew while the meat simmers. This prevents the formation of a lot of steam, which would condense on the lid and dilute the taste of the cooking liquid. The meat juices slowly pass into the cooking liquid but, since the cubes or pieces of meat are not under pressure, do not return into the meat; as a result, great care has to be taken not to overcook the meat.

THE DIFFERENCES BETWEEN A BLANQUETTE AND A FRICASSEE In a blanquette, the plain meat is completely immersed in cold water or, in better kitchens, stock. The stew is brought to a boil, then turned down to simmer until the meat is tender. Cooked this way, the meat loses a lot of its juice to the poaching liquid, which, if it is water, then turns into stock.

To prevent the meat from losing too many good juices, many cooks sear the cubes of meat—plain or floured—lightly and add hot stock, which helps to retain more juice in the meat and still gives an excellent sauce. If the cook chooses to sear the floured meat, the blanquette becomes a white fricassee.

A brown fricassee also exists, especially for chickens and Cornish hens. In that case the floured meat is seared to a lovely deep golden to light brown color and is prepared with brown veal stock, which yields a deep golden sauce.

As opposed to the smaller reduced sauces of the braises and brown stews, the sauces of blanquettes and fricassees are white or deep golden veloutés thickened by flouring the meat, or with a white to golden roux, or with a *beurre manié* (see page 287). In modern leaner cuisine the thickener is often a slurry of cornstarch. These sauces are finished with an addition of crème fraîche or a liaison of yolks and cream. You can decide which you prefer. I take the middle way of using a slurry of cornstarch to thicken the sauce and enriching it with a most reasonable amount of crème fraîche.

Here is a blanquette of lamb served as a casserole:

Lamb and Fennel Stew

ABBACHIO E FINOCCHI

FCR—6 SERVINGS

2 tablespoons pure olive oil

3 pounds boneless pink shoulder of spring lamb, completely defatted and cubed

Salt

Pepper from the mill

4 cups Secondary Stock (page 220) or white stock or broth of your choice

2 medium-size yellow onions, peeled and each stuck with 2 cloves

I small carrot, halved

½ teaspoon chopped fresh rosemary leaves

Medium-size bouquet garni of parsley stems, I small Turkish bay leaf, and I small sprig
fresh thyme

6 fennel bulbs, well cleaned and trimmed

2 tablespoons chopped fennel greens

2 tablespoons cornstarch

I heaping tablespoon crème fraîche

3 ounces Italian fontina, grated on the coarsest blade of the grater

This blanquette-type stew comes
from the Italian Val Veni, one of
the valleys around Aosta. The
lamb can be replaced by veal,
pork, or the dark meat of chicken.

SUGGESTED WINE:
A charming Soave

In a sauteuse pan, heat the oil over medium-high heat. Sear the cubes of
lamb without letting them brown, then salt and pepper the meat well. Tilt
the sauteuse to bring the meat toward the pot handle, spoon out the oil, and
reserve it.

Add enough of the stock to the sauteuse to just cover the meat and slowly
bring to a boil. Add the clove-stuck onions, the carrot, rosemary, and bouquet garni and simmer over medium heat until a skewer inserted into a piece
of meat comes out without difficulty, 40 minutes or more if needed, testing
often from 40 minutes on.

Cut the fennel bulbs into half lengthwise, then cut into ⅓-inch-thick
slices. Add the reserved oil to a large skillet, heat to medium-high, then add
the fennel and stir-fry until it starts to lose its crunch. Add about ½ cup of the
stock and cook until soft, 10 to 12 minutes.

Remove the cooked meat to the skillet containing the fennel and mix
well, then add the fennel greens and set aside. Strain 2 cups of the cooking
stock into a saucepan using a conical strainer. Remove and cool completely ½
cup of it. Place the cornstarch in a small bowl and gradually add the cold
stock. Bring the stock in the saucepan to a visible simmer and add the cornstarch slurry, stirring constantly. Continue to simmer for 5 minutes. Remove
½ cup of the sauce to a bowl and add the crème fraîche; gradually whisk half
the sauce into the bowl, then, reversing the process, whisk the enrichment
into the remainder of the sauce. Reheat just below the boiling point. Correct

the seasoning. Using a conical strainer, strain the sauce over the mixture of meat and fennel, and turn into a baking dish or casserole.

Top with the grated fontina, broil until the cheese is barely melting, and serve.

A Well-Prepared Coq au Vin
UN COQ AU VIN SOIGNÉ

FCR—8 SERVINGS

For the garnish

Raw unsalted butter as needed, 8 to 10 tablespoons

30 small silverskin onions, peeled, with a small cross cut into their root end

Salt

Pepper from the mill

One ½-pound slab fresh pork brisket or, if unavailable, pancetta

½ cup water, if using brisket

1 pound button mushrooms

For the fricassee

½ cup clarified butter (page 32)

1 medium-size carrot, cut into salpicon

2 medium-size yellow onions, cut into salpicon

2 shallots, cut into salpicon

2 tablespoons coarsely chopped parsley stems

2 cloves garlic, crushed in their skins

2 bottles Bourgueil or other Cabernet Franc of your choice

1½ cups Primary Veal Stock (page 219)

Small bouquet garni of 10 parsley stems, 1 small Turkish bay leaf, and 1 good sprig fresh thyme

6 very large chicken legs, skin left on but trimmed of as much fat as possible

Salt

Pepper from the mill

Ground dried thyme

Ground dried bay leaf

8 slices French baguette, cut as wide as possible on a slant

1 clove garlic, peeled

Unbleached all-purpose flour as needed

Unsalted butter as needed

⅓ of a small chicken liver, trimmed of fat and pureed

2 tablespoons crème fraîche

¼ cup Cognac, Armagnac, or whisky of your choice

1 tablespoon chopped fresh chives

1 tablespoon chopped fresh Italian parsley leaves

This is a brown fricassee. This is an authentic and old recipe, without any shortcuts, as is clearly apparent. The great aunt who trained me in the kitchen made a national reputation with it. She received it from the chef who trained her as a young woman in the kitchen of a Loire Valley castle. The chef, born in the second decade of the 1800s, and whose name remains unknown to me, was reputed to have worked in Carême's kitchen.

The word soigné in kitchen language means finished with the greatest care. Please use only large chicken legs, the breast meat is destroyed by the long simmering in wine. To lighten the work, prepare the garnishes the day before. The liver replaces the chicken blood used in the Loire Valley to thicken the sauce.

Ground bay leaf and thyme from commercial spice jars are all right here as freshly ground herbs may be too strong and overbearing.

Day 1

Heat the butter in a large skillet over medium heat. Add the silverskin onions and cook, stirring occasionally, until they start to soften; raise the heat to medium-high and brown until uniformly deep golden. Season lightly with salt and pepper and empty into a bowl. Do not wash the pan.

If using brisket, cut it into lardons 1 × ⅓ inch. Add ½ cup water to the skillet in which you browned the onions. Bring to a simmer over medium heat and let cook until the water has evaporated and the fat releases from of the lardons. Raise the heat slightly and brown the lardons until light golden but not crisp. Using a slotted spoon, transfer them to crumpled paper towels to absorb the excess fat. Put in a small bowl, cover with plastic wrap, and refrigerate until ready to use.

If using pancetta, also cut it into lardons. Place them in a medium-size saucepan, cover with cold water, and turn the heat to high. Cook until the water turns salty. Drain the lardons and pat dry. Heat 1 tablespoon of the butter in the skillet in which the onions cooked over medium heat and brown until light golden. Drain and store as for the brisket above.

Discard any pork fat in the skillet, replace it with another tablespoon of butter, and heat over high heat. Add the mushrooms and sauté for 1 minute on high heat. Season with salt and pepper, reduce heat to low and cover them a few minutes, until they have lost their juices. Raise the heat to high again and evaporate all these juices until the mushrooms are well browned. Add to the same bowl as the onions and cover; refrigerate overnight.

Day 2

Heat ¼ cup of the clarified butter in a large skillet over medium-high heat. Add the carrot, onions, shallots, parsley stems, and crushed garlic and sauté until golden brown. Gather the vegetable salpicon in one part of the skillet and, lifting it up at an angle, squeeze the butter out of the vegetables. Turn the salpicon into a clean sauteuse, add the wine, stock, and bouquet garni, and reduce to 4 cups over medium-high heat.

While the wine reduces, season the chicken legs with salt and pepper and sprinkle them lightly with the thyme and bay leaf. Let stand at room temperature, covered, until the wine mixture is properly reduced. Empty into a bowl.

Clean the sauteuse, heat 3 more tablespoons raw butter and slowly brown the chicken legs very thoroughly on all sides over medium heat; discard the butter. Add the reduced wine mixture and bring to a boil. Reduce the heat to a simmer and cook, covered with the lid slightly askew, until the chicken is tender when tested with a skewer, 35 to 40 minutes.

While the chicken cooks, dry the baguette slices for 10 minutes in a preheated 350°F oven. Rub them with the peeled garlic clove and fry them in the remaining ¼ cup of clarified butter over medium heat. Set aside.

Remove the chicken legs to a large ovenproof country dish. Measure the

NOTE: *Depending on the body of the wine you are going to use, the finished sauce might still show a pinch of acidity. This can be repaired by adding meat extract until the taste of the sauce is exactly what you want.*

SUGGESTED WINE: *Bourgueil, Chinon, or the American Cabernet Franc of your choice* amount of cooking juices. For each cup you have, mash together 1 tablespoon each flour and unsalted butter to make a *beurre manié* (see page 287). In a medium-size saucepan, bring the cooking juices to a small boil, and whisk in the *beurre manié* until no lumps are visible. Add the refrigerated garnishes to the sauce, bring back to a simmer, and cook together a full 5 minutes over medium heat. Strain the sauce through a conical strainer into another saucepan and add the garnishes to the chicken legs.

Put the chicken liver in a blender and add the crème fraîche. Start the blender, gradually pour in the hot sauce, and process until smooth. Strain into a clean saucepan using a China cap. Heat the chosen spirit in a small pan, light it, and whisk it, flambéing, into the finished sauce. Correct the seasoning and ladle evenly over the chicken and its garnishes, sprinkle the dish with the chives and parsley mixed, and decorate with the slices of baguette.

Semimoist Semidry Meat Cooking Techniques
Pot Roasting: The French Way

This technique, excellent for smaller roasts, birds, and large chops, is known in classic technical terms as *cuire à la casserole* (to cook in a covered sauteuse). Birds and small roasts will cook best in an enameled braising pot, chops in a round copper or heavy-bottomed sauteuse.

Brown the meat first so as to concentrate the juices toward the center of the piece. Add very little stock or none at all, in any case never more than ½ cup, cover the pan and complete the cooking in a preheated 325°F oven. The meat juices will break down into water and gelatin and steam and travel from the center of the piece to the pot where they will make a lovely gravy. Baste the meat once in a while with the butter or fat and meat juice mixture in the pot.

Make sure that birds are evenly browned; if the skin seems too thin and you fear it will tear during the browning, sear the bird in a hot oven. Defat the cooking juices before serving in the same pot in which the meat or poultry was cooked. If there is not enough gravy, add a little veal stock or the best available broth.

Provençal Chicken with 40 Garlic Cloves

LE POULET AUX QUARANTE GOUSSES D'AIL

FCR—4 TO 6 SERVINGS

One 4½-pound chicken

2 small sprigs fresh rosemary

2 small sprigs fresh thyme

2 fresh sage leaves

I Turkish bay leaf

Salt

Pepper from the mill

Virgin olive oil as needed

40 cloves garlic, blanched 2 minutes in their skins in salted boiling water

I large bunch fresh Italian parsley stems, coarsely chopped

I celery rib from the middle of the heart, coarsely chopped

I pound baby potatoes, unpeeled, or 4 large potatoes, peeled and turned (page 384) into smaller pieces

⅔ cup Primary Veal Stock (page 219) or chicken stock

This recipe is for Bob Thompson of St. Helena, California, to enjoy with his Sauvignon Blanc. The pot used in the old days was a clay pot sealed with a paste of flour and water known as lutage.

SUGGESTED WINE: *Cassis, Bandol, or Bellet White, or a French Pouilly-sur-Loire, or a California* meritage *of Sauvignon Blanc and Sémillon, or Sauvignon Blanc as fruity as possible*

Wash the chicken inside and out and pat it completely dry. In its cavity place 1 sprig each of the rosemary and thyme, 1 sage leaf, the bay leaf, and season with salt and pepper. Truss.

In an enameled cast-iron pot just large enough to contain the chicken, pour in ¼ inch of olive oil. Over medium heat, slowly brown the chicken on all sides with the lid on, but slightly askew. Remove the browned chicken to a plate and cover with a sheet of aluminum foil. Discard the browning oil and add another full cup of olive oil, the blanched garlic, all the remaining herbs, and the celery. Return the chicken to the pot, put the lid on, and place in a preheated 325°F oven for 45 to 50 minutes, basting the bird every 10 minutes with the oil.

When the chicken is almost cooked, remove most of the clear olive oil to a large skillet and heat it well over medium high heat. Add the potatoes and fry until pale golden, then reduce the heat to medium-low to allow them to cook to the center. Check the doneness of the chicken and as soon as the juices run clear from the thigh or cavity, raise the heat under the potatoes to medium high again and finish cooking them until blond all around. Drain the potatoes on crumpled paper towels.

To the chicken pot, still containing the chicken, add the stock and give a few high boils to blend it into the chicken gravy. Serve the chicken in the pot and carve at the table, giving each guest a favorite piece of meat, along with garlic cloves and potatoes, and two spoonsful of gravy. Each should squeeze the garlic pulp over the potatoes and enjoy this unequaled delicacy of the Provençal culinary repertory.

Pot Roasting: The American Way

This is the classical *poëlé*. Whenever you see a recipe for "poëléd" meat (see description below) the following procedure will be applied, although this technique is often confused with the French method of pot roasting. The technique is not used very much anymore and its name is a misnomer which I prefer not to translate for it cannot really be translated accurately.

Use a heavy-bottomed braising pot just large enough to contain the piece to be *poëléd*. Salt and pepper the meat and roll it either in butter or in olive oil. *Do not sear it.* Set the meat on a bed of sautéed aromatic vegetables and cover the pot. Bake in a preheated 325°F oven, basting the meat with the fat in the pot every 15 minutes.

Check the doneness with a skewer: When you can insert it halfway into the meat, uncover the pot to let the meat, which will be rather pale, take on even coloration all around. Turn it three times every 5 minutes for approximately 15 minutes, until a skewer penetrates it completely and comes out without resistance.

Vegetables may be added to the cooking pot. There will be some gravy; if more is desired, add a little veal stock.

In this procedure, approximately the same amount of meat juice escapes into the pot as remains in the meat. It is an ideal cooking method for any small roasts of veal, lamb, and pork, for brisket of beef, and flank steak rolled upon itself, or for rabbit, as in the recipe that follows.

Charlotte's Rabbit and Charles's Farci

LE LAPIN DE CHARLOTTE ET
LE FARCI DE CHARLES

FCR — 6 SERVINGS
For the rabbit
¼ cup walnut oil
¼ cup unsalted butter
3 pounds large white onions, cut into quarters
One 3-pound rabbit
Salt
Pepper from the mill
Large sprinkle of quatre épices (page 71)
½ cup Primary Veal Stock (page 219), Secondary Stock (page 220), or any good chicken stock
1 teaspoon chopped fresh Italian parsley leaves

This recipe is from one of my grandmothers, whose family came from L'Ile Bouchard in the Loire Valley. As an accompaniment she served my grandfather's farci, one of the many versions of this old Celtic dish coming from his birth province of Poitou. Prepare and bake the farci before the rabbit and put it in to reheat on the oven shelf below the rabbit 20 minutes before serving, taking care to

1 teaspoon chopped fresh chives

1 teaspoon chopped fresh chervil leaves

1 teaspoon chopped fresh tarragon leaves

For the farci

Salt

1 large head white cabbage

2 cups packed cleaned and chopped Swiss chard leaves, preferably white

2 cups packed cleaned and chopped spinach leaves

2 cups packed cleaned and chopped soft-leaf lettuce

1 ¼ cups unbleached all-purpose flour

Pepper from the mill

Freshly grated nutmeg

3 large eggs or their whites only

1 ¼ to 1 ½ cups milk of your choice

3 to 4 tablespoons walnut or pure olive oil, to your personal taste

One 2-ounce slice pancetta, cut into ¼-inch cubes

3 medium-size leeks, white and light green part, well washed and thinly sliced

Preheat the oven to 325°F. Heat the walnut oil and butter in an oval braising pot large enough to contain the rabbit when bent to follow the shape of the pot. Add the onions and sauté them over medium-high heat until they start to color. Add the rabbit, well seasoned inside and out with salt, pepper, and *quatre épices*.

Cover the pot and bake 15 minutes. Baste with the mixture of oil and butter seeping out of the onions, then turn the rabbit over and cook another 15 minutes. Baste once more. Leave the pot uncovered and raise the oven temperature to 350°F; cook another 10 to 12 minutes on each side, basting with the oil-and-butter mixture. The rabbit is done when it has taken on a lovely golden color on both sides and the onions have turned golden brown. For accurate checking, a skewer inserted into one of the legs should come out without resistance.

Remove the rabbit to a cutting board and cover with a sheet of aluminum foil. Spoon out as much of the oil-and-butter mixture from the pot as you can, add the stock, and give it a few boils on top of the stove. Meanwhile, carve the rabbit into two legs and two shoulders; the two loin fillets should be removed from the backbone from the neck down to the rump; do not forget the ribs and the kidneys. Turn the onions into an oval serving dish and present the rabbit pieces on them, sprinkled with the chopped herbs. Serve with the farci.

To prepare the farci, bring a large pot of water to a boil and salt it lightly. Remove the first eight outer leaves of the cabbage, cut off their ribs, and blanch the leaves 1 minute in the boiling water. Remove to a colander using

position the rabbit and farci on opposite sides of the oven (if the rabbit is on the right side of the oven the farci must be on the left side and vice versa, each on its respective rack).

SUGGESTED WINE: *A Chinon or Bourgueil from the Loire Valley, a light meritage or light Cabernet, Cabernet Franc and Merlot from California*

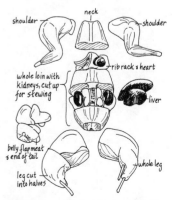

Rabbit carved into serving pieces, whether cooked or uncooked

a slotted spoon and let drip; when cold, blot dry in a kitchen towel. Cut the remainder of the cabbage into quarters, remove the core in each of them, and cut the remainder of the leaves into a fine chiffonnade (see page 17).

To the same boiling water, add the chopped cabbage and all the greens; blanch for 2 minutes. Drain in the colander and let drip completely, then pat completely dry in tea towels.

Put the flour into a bowl; make a well in the center and add salt, pepper, and nutmeg to taste. Add the eggs and whisk together, gathering half the flour. Add the milk and continue homogenizing until a smooth crepe batter results. Let stand for 15 minutes.

Heat 2 tablespoons of the oil in a large skillet over medium heat and cook the pancetta, stirring, until it starts turning golden. Add the leeks and cook, stirring, until they turn translucent. Add all the blanched greens, salt, pepper, and nutmeg to taste and mix well. Cook together on low heat until the vegetables have lost half of their volume, about 10 minutes. Let cool completely, then mix into the prepared batter. Correct the final seasoning by adjusting the salt, pepper, and nutmeg.

Preheat the oven to 325°F. Rub a 10-inch porcelain or Pyroceram pie plate with a generous tablespoon of the oil. Line the plate with the cabbage leaves, letting those that are large hang over the lip of the plate. Spoon the mixture of batter and greens into the plate and flip the ends of the cabbage leaves over the composition; drizzle the top with a bit of oil. Bake until a skewer inserted at the center of the pie comes out clean and feeling hot to the top of the hand, 40 to 45 minutes. Serve in wedges with the rabbit.

Sautéing Chicken and Thick Chops the French Way

This technique has a confusing name. Almost every cook, seeing the term "sauté," is tempted to panfry the meat involved, but that is not what this technique is all about (see pages 795–96 about panfried meats).

This technique is very popular in France because it is fast, yields delicious meat, and lends itself to so many variations of tastes and combinations of vegetable garnishes that Escoffier listed sixty-four chicken sautés in his *Guide Culinaire*. The technique also works for larger veal rib chops (see page 843) that have been boned and turned into tournedos and to veal and lamb shoulder chops and sweetbreads of lamb (see page 906).

THE CHOICE OF COOKING VESSEL

The proper pot is a sauteuse with straight sides and a thick bottom. You can also use a heavy-bottomed skillet or a large buffet-style electric frying pan, but in either of these two cases, use a double layer of aluminum foil to cover the pan and leave a small space open along the edge of the pan to allow for a slight amount of evaporation. Regulate the size of the pot to the number of pieces you are sautéing; the pieces of meat must have enough space to lie flat in the pan and apart from one another by at least ¼ to ⅓ inch. There should be only one single layer of meat.

SAUTÉED CHICKEN

In the classic cuisine, the chicken was cut up into four to six pieces and both dark meat and white meat were sautéed; it often happened that as the white meat cooked side by side with the dark meat, its texture was totally destroyed by simple overcooking. Escoffier explains clearly that the white meat should be seared, then put to wait on a plate, to be finally returned to the pan to finish cooking during the last five minutes of cooking the legs.

In spite of the great respect I have for the old master's techniques, I have come to the conclusion that even when the white meat is finished cooking as thus described, its texture is quite perfect, but—and this is a big drawback— the taste of the sauté is unbalanced because the legs have acquired quite a bit of flavor from their cooking broth and eventual vegetable garnish, while the breast meat has not. The final result is extremely flavorful dark meat and bland white meat. My proposed solution is to use only chicken legs and to keep the white meat for other techniques in which it can showcase its delicacy more efficiently (see particularly the section on pan-steaming, page 858).

Depending on your personal taste, you can sauté a chicken to obtain a browned bird in brown gravy or a whiter bird in a lighter colored gravy. When the meat is browned deeply, the small gravy obtained will also look golden brown and, if you wish to extend the quantity of gravy, you must do so with the primary veal stock on page 219.

When the meat is browned very slowly and superficially, so that the meat turns only a bare golden and the chicken skin is just stiffened, the gravy obtained will also be much lighter in color also and is best deglazed with secondary or any other white poultry stock or broth of your choice, or even cream.

SAUTÉED VEAL OR PORK CHOPS AND SWEETBREADS

For these three meats, use the brown style and primary veal stock.

GENERAL SAUTÉ SEQUENCE

1. Brown or stiffen the meat in the butter or oil of your choice and to the color desired. Adapt the choice of oil to the origin of your dish, olive oil for Mediterranean dishes, butter for northern European dishes, corn oil for true American dishes, and, if you prepare a sauté with Chinese ingredients, peanut oil. Salt and pepper the meat as you sear and turn it in the

hot fat to color it evenly. Use medium-high heat if you want a lot of good browning and only medium heat if you prefer little color.

2. Discard the browning oil. Add ½ cup of the proper type of stock, or ¼ cup each stock and wine, or ¼ cup each *verjus* (see page 43) and stock. Cover the pan, leaving the lid on all through the cooking but *ever so slightly askew* to allow the steam to escape and the gravy to thicken. Turn the pieces of meat every 5 minutes for even cooking. Add the vegetable garnish in time for it to be cooked (not too crunchy for this preparation) at the same time as the meat is. A total of approximately 30 minutes is sufficient for chicken. For veal the time will be 20 to 25 minutes, for pork chops and shoulder chops, 30 to 35 minutes. Sweetbreads will be done in 25 minutes if you like them somewhat firm and 35 to 40 if you like them tender in the old-fashioned way.

Sautéed Chicken with Beets and Verjus

For a definition of and a recipe for verjus, see pages 42–43. You can also purchase verjus from a fancy food store or, if you live close to vineyards, pick two bunches of grapes when they are already juicy but still green. Crush the grapes and strain the acidic juice through a tea strainer before using it. For a recipe that makes use of the beet greens, see page 398.

SUGGESTED WINE: *A very mellow Chenin Blanc from California or a Vouvray moelleux*

FCR — 6 SERVINGS

12 small yellow Chiogga beets

12 small red Chiogga beets

Salt

Pepper from the mill

2 tablespoons vinegar of your choice

3 tablespoons grapeseed oil

6 medium-size chicken legs, cut into drumsticks and thighs

1 cup verjus

¼ teaspoon finely grated lemon rind

1 tablespoon fresh lemon juice

⅓ cup Primary Veal Stock (page 219) or other stock of your choice

Chopped fresh Italian parsley leaves and chives mixed together

Cut the beet greens ¾ inch above the roots. Scrub the roots. Bring a large pot of water to a boil, add salt and pepper to taste and the vinegar. Add the yellow beets and cook until soft enough that their skins can be slipped off easily and the roots have turned a translucent deep yellow. Remove from the bath with a slotted spoon and immerse in cold water. Immediately add the red beets to the water bath and cook and cool in the same manner. Slip the peels off all the beets, remove any black traces from them, and set aside in two different bowls.

Heat the grapeseed oil in a large sauteuse pan or electric frying pan. Salt and pepper the chicken pieces, then cook them over medium-high heat, until golden brown, about 12 minutes, on all sides. Discard the oil; add ½ cup of the *verjus*, cover the sauteuse, leaving the lid ever so slightly askew, and cook over medium heat until the chicken is 90 percent done. Add the whole beets and the remainder of the *verjus*, the lemon rind, and lemon juice, cover again, and finish cooking together; the beets should be fork tender. Remove the chicken and beets to a round country dish; add the stock to the pan and deglaze well over medium-high heat, reducing lightly to obtain a short gravy. Correct its seasoning and dribble it over the pieces of chicken. Sprinkle with parsley and chives.

Veal Chinoiserie

FFR — 6 SERVINGS

I teaspoon Szechuan peppercorns

6 large center cut rib veal chops, I inch thick, turned into boneless veal chops by the butcher

2 tablespoons dark soy sauce

I tablespoon Chinese rice wine or dry fino sherry

6 tablespoons peanut oil

I cup Primary Veal Stock (page 219) or best available stock of your choice

½ teaspoon cornstarch

Two ⅛-inch-thick slices fresh ginger, peeled

2 cloves garlic, slivered

½ cup fresh water chestnuts, peeled and sliced ⅛ inch thick

4 large shiitake mushrooms, stems removed and cut into slivers ¼ inch thick across the caps

I red bell pepper, seeded, cut into strips I inch wide on the diagonal, then into diamonds

I yellow bell pepper, seeded, cut into strips I inch wide on the diagonal, then into diamonds

6 leaves Romaine lettuce, cut across the leaves into I-inch-wide bands

2 scallions, cut on the slant into ¹/₁₆-inch-thick slivers

Salt

⅓ cup very coarsely chopped cilantro leaves

Heat a skillet over medium heat, then add the Szechuan peppercorns and toast them gradually until their outer skins burn off. Empty the toasted peppercorns into a conical strainer and shake over a trashcan until the burned-off skins have been completely discarded. Using a chopping knife, crush the black center kernels almost to a powder and set aside.

Place the boneless chops on a cake rack set over a baking sheet or jellyroll pan. Mix the soy sauce and rice wine together and brush some of the mixture very lightly on both sides of the chops. Let marinate 45 minutes to 1 hour at room temperature.

Order the cut IMPS No. 1306, rib chops. Since the boning of these chops is difficult, have the butcher turn them into boneless veal chops for you. Future food professionals can benefit by doing the boning themselves, removing all fat finish and silverskin, defatting the rib cap, and shaping tournedos by wrapping the eye of the rib into the cap (see Meat Handwork, page 720). Secure the two muscles together with toothpicks first, then with kitchen string. Pull the toothpicks out once the string is securely surrounding the tournedos.

SUGGESTED WINE:
Gewürztraminer of your choice

Heat 3 tablespoons of the peanut oil in a heavy-bottomed sauteuse pan large enough to contain the 6 chops in a single layer. Without wiping the marinade off and on high heat, sear the chops on each side; sprinkle each chop sparingly on one side only with a tiny bit of the Szechuan pepper. Discard the browning oil and replace it with ¼ cup of the veal stock. Cover the pan, leaving the lid slightly askew; turn the heat down to medium and when the gravy has thickened add another ¼ cup of the stock. Turn the chops over and let cook another 5 to 6 minutes. Remove the chops to a plate; they should be rare, and will continue cooking to medium rare from their own accumulated heat by the time you serve them (with an internal temperature of 135°F, USDA 145°F). Keep them warm, covered with a sheet of aluminum foil.

Let the pan cool a minute or so, then add another ½ cup of cold stock and over medium heat scrape to dissolve the gravy in it. Cool the deglazing completely. Put the cornstarch in a small bowl, dilute it with the cold deglazing and set aside. Quickly rinse the sauteuse under hot water and dry it well.

Heat the remaining 3 tablespoons peanut oil in the just washed sauteuse over medium-high heat. Add the ginger slices, fry 1 minute, then add the garlic slivers and fry 30 seconds more. Using a slotted spoon, discard both. Raise the heat to high and in rapid succession add the chestnuts and stir-fry 30 seconds; add the mushrooms and stir-fry 1 more minute; add the bell peppers and stir-fry 1 more minute. Continue stir-frying a few more seconds as you add the Romaine mixed with the scallions. Season with salt and as much as you desire of the remaining Szechuan pepper.

Stir the mixture of cornstarch and stock again and toss into the sauteuse until the sauce thickens. Remove to a serving platter. Arrange the tournedos on top of the vegetables and their sauce and serve, sprinkling the cilantro leaves on the side of each tournedos already seasoned with the hot pepper.

Poached Meats

Poaching is so mystifying to many a cook that I have seen extraordinary things done under the guise of poaching, such as boiling chickens in great huge vats of water at a rolling boil, until the substance was completely gone out of the poor beasts.

A poached meat is cooked by immersion in a boiling liquid, but after the second boil has been reached, the temperature of the liquid must be reduced to and must remain at between 190° and 205°F. The danger zone is reached when:

- The temperature of the bath dips to below 190°F, in which case the meat languishes in the water and cooks so slowly that lots of its good juices have time to escape into the cooking water or broth or,
- When the water temperature creeps toward 205°F; for the seven little degrees between 205° and 212°F can sneak up on you so very fast that it

often feels like all you have to do is turn your back and the water will start to boil again.

To prevent this from happening, anchor an instant thermometer attached to a string to the handle of the vessel in which you are poaching and let its stem hang constantly in the water or broth so you can refer to it.

If the poaching liquid is allowed to boil, the meat will lose a lot of its juices and eventually toughen to become boiled meat instead of tender poached meat.

POACHING RED MEATS

With the current great focus on barbecuing, spit roasting, and grilling meats, poaching has been almost totally forgotten as a cooking technique for red meats, although it does offer some of the most delicious and leanest dishes.

POACHED RED MEATS DEFINED   Do not confuse *poached* beef or lamb with *boiled* beef or lamb. In boiling the meat will lose most of its juices to its water bath which will become a stock or broth. If the water is cold at the time of immersion, more juices will be lost to the water and the broth will be superior; however, if the water is boiling at the time of immersion, the boiled meat will be somewhat superior in taste and texture and the broth weaker. We are all familiar with the boiled dinners of our mothers and grandmothers, surrounded as they were by their garnish of root vegetables; we are also familiar with the less than attractive appearance of boiled meats.

To obtain a poached piece of red meat, add the prepared meat to the boiling liquid, keep the heat high under the pot, and, at the first indication of a boil, turn the liquid down to poaching temperature (190° to 205°F). The piece of meat will cook for a limited amount of time, its juices will travel toward the center of the piece, but once the meat is cooked and removed from its cooking liquid, the juices will not have time to travel back toward its outside layers until you let the meat rest as you would any roast and carve it. The look of the meat will be the same as that of boiled beef, brownish gray, but the surprise will come when you slice the meat and its rare or medium-rare center appears. Salt and pepper the meat only after it has finished cooking.

CHOICE OF CUTS FOR POACHING   The best cuts for poaching are the same as those usually roasted. The sirloin strip, sirloin tip, and rump are the best; the rib is too fat and the round too coarse grained. All these cuts are affordable and clearly marked in the supermarket.

CHOICE OF COOKING LIQUID   If you prepare a piece of beef, the best medium is a good broth which will flavor the outside cuts. Primary veal stock (see page 219) and secondary stock (see page 220) both work well, but if you feel like preparing a beef or lamb stock or using a ready-made broth, that is also acceptable.

When you poach a piece of beef, if you use any of the broth for a sauce, it will be only a small amount, and you will want to save the rest of the poaching broth for soups, the deglazing of gravies, etc. If you have no immediate use for the remainder of the broth, strain it carefully through as fine meshed a strainer as is available, cool it rapidly in a bath of cold water, and freeze it for later use (see page 216 for freezing directions).

POACHED RED MEATS AND NUTRITION   Poached red meats are as succulent, if not as tasty, as roasted meats since no brown flavor is present, as is the case with roasted meats. Since they must be trimmed of all traces of fat and connective tissues before going into their cooking bath, poached meats are also somewhat "healthier" and offer an excellent change from grilled meats. The best condiment for poached red meats is not a sauce, but any chutney or other condiment that you like, preferably one containing a good amount of mustard. As for the accompaniment, if you really want to stay on the lean side, cook the vegetables of your choice in the poaching broth while the meat rests; otherwise, think of a delicious dish of potatoes, rice, pasta, or spätzle.

Note that lamb must be poached in water, as its taste will taint any stock and make it unusable for any other use. The lamb poaching water along with the bones of the lamb can be used afterward to prepare a bean soup.

THE TECHNIQUE MODERNIZED   Use a stockpot with two handles.

After trussing the meat into as regular a shape as possible, cut the last piece of string long enough so that you can attach the meat to the handle of the pot in which you will poach it, and not let it fall to the bottom, where it would doubly cook in contact with the hot metal.

If you prefer, use a pasta cooker with a basket that does not touch the bottom of the pot but that is deep enough for the piece of meat to be totally immersed in the broth or stock. Whichever pot you are using, proceed as follows for best results:

Attach an instant meat thermometer to the other handle of the poaching vessel. Bring the stock, broth, or water to a full boil in another vessel. You will need 4 to 5 quarts of liquid altogether, so that the meat is truly surrounded with plenty of liquid.

Arrange the meat either on a string or in a basket set inside the poaching vessel and pour the boiling liquid over it, making sure that the liquid covers it completely. Turn the heat to medium at first, then check the temperature of your instant thermometer and regulate the heat to keep the temperature between 190° and 205°F; it should be between medium-low and low.

The cooking time is 15 minutes per pound for rare (125°F to 130°F) and 17 minutes for medium rare, 135°F (USDA 145°F).

Here are two recipes, one for a roast beef, the other for a leg of lamb:

Roast Beef on a String

FCR—6 SERVINGS

4 quarts stock or broth of your choice plus extra as needed for the potatoes

One 3-pound sirloin strip roast in one piece, completely trimmed of fat and connective tissues

12 small red potatoes, peeled and parboiled for 5 minutes in boiling salted water

1 tablespoon unsalted butter or pure olive oil

Salt

Pepper from the mill

¼ cup Dijon mustard

3 tablespoons tiny capers, drained

1 tablespoon chopped fresh Italian parsley leaves

1 tablespoon chopped fresh chives

1 large bunch watercress

Bring the stock or broth to a boil in a large saucepan. With kitchen string, tie the roast into a regular shape. Place it in the poaching vessel (see page 846). Attach an instant meat thermometer to one of the pot handles. Pour the boiling stock over the meat so it is completely covered. Check the temperature and raise or lower the stovetop heat as necessary to maintain it between 190° and 205°F. Poach for 45 minutes, then lift the meat out of the broth and check the doneness with a meat thermometer. It should read 130°F for medium rare.

Remove the cooked meat to a plate and let rest 15 minutes covered loosely with a sheet of aluminum foil which will bring the internal temperature to 135°F (USDA 145°F).

During the last 15 minutes of poaching, place the parboiled potatoes in a sauteuse pan so they form a single layer. Cover them barely with stock and bring to a boil. Finish cooking at a steady simmer over medium-low heat, rolling them at regular intervals for even cooking. Add the butter or oil to the stock when only a few tablespoons of stock are left and keep rolling the potatoes in this light glaze. Season well with salt and pepper.

Mix the mustard with the capers, herbs, and enough broth to make a semiliquid condiment. Add salt if needed, pepper generously, and turn into a small bowl.

Cut the beef at the table, adding 3 potatoes, 2 tablespoons of the condiment, and a nice bunch of fresh watercress to each plate.

As was served in some of the many bistros of Les Halles, when this huge market was still at the center of Paris. If sirloin strip is too expensive, use sirloin tip. If you like marrow, add a long marrow bone cut into sections to the broth, toast long slivers of French baguette, spread the cooked marrow on each toast, salt and pepper it, and serve the toasts alongside the sliced meat.

SUGGESTED WINE: *A young Pinot Noir from Carneros or a Beaujolais-Villages*

Viking Leg of Lamb

FCR—8 TO 10 SERVINGS

6 quarts water

Stem from 1 large bunch fresh dill

1 Turkish bay leaf

1 sprig fresh savory

1 small leg of lamb, 4½ to 5 pounds

¼ cup unbleached all-purpose flour

Salt

Pepper from the mill

½ teaspoon caraway seeds, crushed

½ cup chopped fresh dill

Rind of 1 orange or peels of 12 kumquats

6 large white onions, diced into brunoise

2 tablespoons cider vinegar

⅓ cup sweet yellow mustard

I adapted this recipe from a picture I saw in a Norwegian magazine; a somewhat similar preparation is one of the mainstays of old English cookery. If using a New Zealand leg of lamb, defrost and age it a total of one week in the refrigerator before cooking (see Aged Meats, pages 716–18). As a vegetable, use a stir-fried cabbage with caraway.

Front view: string starts under the leg, crosses in front, and ties behind the shank

Back view: ends of string tie together under the leg just below the shank

Bring the water to a boil in a large pot, add the dill stems, bay leaf, and savory. Simmer 20 minutes over medium heat while you prepare the meat. Tie an instant thermometer to one of the handles of the pot so its stem is completely immersed in the water.

Trim the meat completely of fell and suet, down to the bare muscle. Remove the hip bone. Set the leg on the table top side up. Pass a long piece of kitchen string behind the shank bone, cross it at the middle of the leg, and bring one of its ends to pass exactly over the muscle that originally covered the hip bone so that it can keep the muscle tucked in place. Now turn the leg over and as you bring the string up, cross it over the middle of the leg again to finally bring it around the shank; tie as firmly as you can.

Season the flour with salt and pepper and mix in the caraway seeds and 2 tablespoons of the chopped dill. Apply the mixture all round the leg. Dampen a large piece of cheesecloth and squeeze it dry. Stretch the cloth flat on the counter and sprinkle it evenly with the remainder of the flour mixture. Wrap the leg as smoothly as possible in the cloth; gather the excess cloth around the shank bone and tie it as tightly as possible with kitchen string.

Immerse the leg in the boiling water and consult the thermometer to regulate the heat so the water remains between 190° and 205°F. Poach 15 minutes per pound and remove from the bath when the internal temperature is 125°F. Let rest 15 minutes, covered loosely with a sheet of aluminum foil, to obtain a final internal temperature of 135°F (USDA 145°F).

While the meat cooks, chop the rind or peels; mix with the onions, season with salt, pepper, and vinegar, and let steep 30 minutes. Drain well, then add the mustard, the remainder of the chopped dill, and a few tablespoons of the lamb cooking broth to obtain a semiliquid condiment. Correct the seasoning.

To serve, remove the cheesecloth, wipe the surface of the meat with paper towels, and slice. Serve on individual heated plates with the condiment served on the side.

SUGGESTED BEVERAGE: *No wine; rather a good Scandinavian ale*

WHITE MEATS POACHED IN WATER

White meats here means mostly chicken and Cornish hens. Veal is a white meat, but the closest it comes to being poached is in the blanquette described on page 832, even if the sauce is finished as that of a stew.

SIZE AND CHOICE OF BIRDS Chickens for poaching should be the same size and quality as for roasting, four to a maximum of five pounds.

Meal-fed chickens have very soft meat, but can taste somewhat bland; you will find out, if you try both types, that the best poachers are free-range chickens. Be sure to let such "runners" sit long enough in the refrigerator—a few days—so that their flesh has time to soften before you cook them.

PROTECTING THE WHITE MEAT OF POACHED CHICKENS Gone are the days when a chicken to be poached in liquid was wrapped in a large sheet of pork fatback, although it is not rare to see chickens prepared for poaching this way in Europe. A more common way to protect the delicate white meat from the intense heat of the stock is to pass a compound butter under the skin of the bird to moisten and aromatize the meat and to wrap the bird in a sheet of parchment which covers its breasts and legs completely. The parchment is safely tied around the breasts and legs of the bird with kitchen string.

A NEW TECHNIQUE I have, since 1970, replaced fatback and parchment paper with "cook-in" bags; regular storage plastic bags do not work. It is not really such a new idea, only an excellent modern replacement for the occasional pig's bladder still used as a tight glove into which the Europeans slip a chicken to poach. Cook-in bags allow the cook to poach in salted water, which is economical compared to stock and helps save good stock for the making of light white sauces or in the making of pilafs and risottos. Should the bag break or leak, the salted water will not damage the taste of the chicken as bland unsalted water will. The poaching is done between 190° to 205°F, until the juices which accumulate in the bottom of the bag turn clear. A small sauce can be built by blending the cooking juices with a bit of stock and crème fraîche.

There is a slight inconvenience to plastic bags; it is extremely difficult to chase all the air out of them. If any air remains, the bag will inflate, and the chicken float to the surface of the water bath. To keep this from happening, rub the bird either with soft butter or olive oil which will make the plastic adhere to its skin; then push the air toward the outside of the bag and tie the bag very tightly with a plastic-covered metal tie found in the box of bags. Also, the bird will not float upward, if you keep the critter pressed down in the water with a lid just about a size smaller than the lid of the pot.

If you cook several birds and must keep them warm for a little while, cook them only till three quarters done, remove the pot from the heat, and let it stand, covered. You will find that the birds not only keep nice and hot, but finish cooking perfectly in their own accumulated heat.

Handle these boiling hot bags carefully; use strong tongs to remove them from the hot water bath. If you have not yet developed a cook's "asbestos fingers," put on a pair of plastic gloves and have a small pile of kitchen towels at your disposal to hold the bird and protect your hands from their heat. You are responsible for setting your equipment in such a manner that you will not get burned.

The bird is ready to serve as it comes out of the bag and need not rest.

WHEN TO USE STOCK   If you cannot locate a cook-in bag, go back to sliding a compound butter under the skin of the chicken and wrapping it in parchment paper prior to immersing it in stock, not water. Simply wrap the bird in a piece of parchment paper large enough to cover the bird from shoulder to tail, and tie with kitchen string once over the shoulder and once over the knees.

Here are two typical recipes:

Poached Rock Cornish Game Hens

Start this preparation several hours before you begin the cooking to allow the flesh of the bird to become infused with the taste of the cilantro.

SUGGESTED WINE: **A** *pleasant Gewürztraminer not too perfumed or a pleasant Pinot Gris or an Italian Pinot Grigio*

FFR—6 SERVINGS

3 rock Cornish game hens

3 tablespoons unsalted butter

1 tablespoon seeded and very finely chopped pasilla chile

¼ cup finely chopped cilantro leaves

Salt

Pepper from the mill

Olive oil as needed

4 quarts water

2 large carrots, cut into brunoise

3 leeks, white part only, well washed and cut into brunoise

One 2-inch-long piece daikon, peeled and cut into brunoise

1 celery rib, cut into brunoise

1 cup best chicken or veal stock or other stock of your choice

⅓ cup heavy cream

1 tablespoon Chinese oyster sauce

2 tablespoons grapeseed or pure olive oil

½ pound small chanterelle mushrooms

I red bell pepper, seeded and cut into strips ½ inch wide, then into diamonds

I small bok choy, ribs and leaves coarsely slivered

Cilantro leaves

Wash the game hens thoroughly inside and out and pat completely dry.

Mash together 3 tablespoons butter, the pasilla, 2 tablespoons of the cilantro, and salt and pepper to taste into a soft compound butter. Divide the mixture into 6 equal portions. Slip a portion under the skin on each side of each bird, and massage them so the compound butter covers the top of each breast and leg. Salt and pepper the birds in the cavity, truss them, and very lightly oil their skin all around. Keep refrigerated covered with plastic wrap until ready to cook. Remove from the refrigerator 45 minutes before cooking.

In a large pot with handles, bring the water to a boil and add 2 tablespoons salt. Tie an instant thermometer to one of the handles of the poaching vessel and let the stem of the thermometer hang fully immersed in the water.

Meanwhile mix together the brunoised vegetables. Put one third of them into each of three small cook-in bags. Place a Cornish hen in each bag and arrange the brunoise to cover the whole bird. Seal the bags carefully (see page 849). Immerse the bags in the boiling water, regulate the temperature of the bath so it stays between 190° and 205°F and poach until the juices of the birds run clear, 40 to 45 minutes.

Remove the birds from the poaching liquid to a platter and take them out of their bags. Empty their juices, along with the brunoise into a skillet, blend in the stock and cream, and reduce over medium-high heat until the sauce coats a spoon lightly. Stir in the oyster sauce. Spoon half the sauce into the bottom of a round, flat dish. Cut the Cornish hens into breast and leg portions and arrange on the platter.

Heat the grapeseed oil in a wok or skillet over medium-high heat. Quickly stir-fry the chanterelles for 1 minute, then the red pepper for 1 more minute, then the bok choy for 2 more minutes. Season well. Off the heat, toss in the remainder of the brunoise sauce and arrange around the meat. Dot the meat with cilantro leaves and serve.

Poached Chicken in Vietnamese Flavors

Modernized from a specialty of my Vietnamese friend N'gao.

SUGGESTED BEVERAGE:

Jasmine or lotus tea

FCR — 4 TO 6 SERVINGS

One 4½-pound roasting chicken

3 dried star anise

I rounded teaspoon 5-spice powder

One ¼-inch-thick slice fresh ginger, peeled and coarsely chopped

3 thick basil stems, crushed

2 cloves garlic, I crushed in its skin, I finely chopped

Salt

Pepper from the mill

3 small zucchini, finely sliced

3 scallions, thinly sliced on a slant

I tablespoon peanut oil

2 tablespoons unsweetened large coconut flakes

⅓ cup packed fresh green basil leaves

Nuoc mam as needed

Juice and pulp of I lime

Large pinch of cayenne pepper

Meat of I cooked lobster, diced into ⅓-inch cubes

6 fresh opal basil leaves, cut into thin chiffonnade (page 17)

Wash the chicken thoroughly, then pat dry. Add the star anise, 5-spice powder, ginger, basil stems, crushed garlic, salt, and pepper to its cavity. Truss the chicken and shake it well to distribute the aromatics all around the cavity. Refrigerate overnight, covered with plastic wrap. Bring back to room temperature 45 minutes before cooking.

Mix the zucchini, 2 of the scallions, the chopped garlic, salt, and pepper together in a small cook-in bag. Rub the chicken with oil and roll it into the coconut flakes. Place the chicken in the bag and arrange the vegetables so they completely cover the bird. Tie the bag tightly closed (see page 849).

Attach an instant thermometer to one of the handles of a cooking pot filled with 4 quarts of water so its stem is completely immersed in the water. Bring to a boil. Carefully immerse the chicken in its bag. Cover it with a lid fitting just inside of the pot and regulate the temperature under the pot so the water stays between 190° and 205°F. Poach the chicken until the liquid in the bag runs clear, about 1 hour and 15 minutes.

Empty the contents of the bag into a bowl. Clean the surface of the chicken of all traces of vegetables and coconut and keep it warm under a sheet of aluminum foil. Pour the vegetables in a blender and add the green basil leaves, *nuoc mam*, lime juice and pulp, and cayenne pepper. Process until smooth, adding enough of the chicken cooking water to lighten the mixture if it is too thick. Correct the final seasoning with more salt, *nuoc mam*, and pepper.

Put the lobster meat in a cook-in bag. Seal and immerse it in the hot water to reheat. To present the dish, spoon a ladleful of the sauce on the bottom of each individual dish. Detail the chicken into six to eight serving pieces. Place one or two pieces of chicken on each dish and top with several cubes of lobster and drizzle some more of the sauce lightly over them. Sprinkle with the remaining scallions and the opal basil chiffonnade. Pass the remainder of the sauce in a small bowl.

CHICKEN CUTLETS OVEN-POACHED IN BUTTER OR OLIVE OIL

Chicken cutlets become stringy and tough when subjected to the slightest excess of heat, but there are a few techniques that can be used to keep them perfectly tender, juicy, and delicious.

One of them consists of arranging the cutlets in a sauteuse pan and pouring boiling salted water or broth over them, then maintaining a low temperature until they have cooked to the desired texture. This technique is fraught with danger as one second too long in the water can result in tough cutlets which have lost their moisture.

Another technique consists of immersing the cutlets in 200° to 205°F water or broth and letting them poach until done; the danger is either the same as for the first technique, or possible undercooking.

These two immersion methods are also awkward as you must lift the cutlets out of the liquid to test each and every one of them. Because of these problems, professional cooks prefer to use a third technique which consists of placing the cutlets in a baking dish and poaching them in very little butter or oil in a very hot oven, preheated to 450° to 500°F. This technique, used in classic French kitchens, will require all your attention while you are executing it, but the cutlets, being more accessible, are easier to test.

SEQUENCE FOR POACHING CHICKEN CUTLETS IN BUTTER OR OIL

1. Rub an enameled cast-iron baking dish with butter or oil. Sprinkle medium-large, evenly sized and shaped chicken cutlets with salt and finely ground white pepper and roll them in the measured butter or oil. Lay them flat on the bottom of the baking dish, small fillet side down. Feel any cutlet with the tip of a finger before you start cooking; it will have a soft, spongy texture.

2. Cover the cutlets, first with a sheet of parchment paper resting flush over the meat, then with a sheet of aluminum foil, dull side up. Put the dish in the preheated oven. Cook the cutlets 5 to 6 minutes; pull the oven rack halfway out of the oven, turn the cutlets over, *and turn the oven off*. Leave

the cutlets 3 more minutes in the oven, covered; they should then be completely cooked and resilient under the touch of a finger. If they are, remove the dish from the oven. Remove the foil but leave the cutlets another 30 seconds under the parchment to allow any steam to dissipate. The second sides of the cutlets cook in a shorter time, exactly as happens in egg custards (see page 142).

But remember that there will be a small amount of carryover heat and if you wait too long to remove the cutlets from the hot dish, they will harden.

It is a good idea while you are learning to cook one more cutlet than you need as a test piece. If you cut through its center just as it is done, you will find it solidly compact, barely pink, and moist with the protein-laden juices still visible at the surface of the fibers. Should you leave the cutlets too long in the hot pan, these meat juices will leach to the bottom of the pan, starting to form a gravy and, in the process, turn the cutlets into nothing more than hardened muscle fibers tautly packed against one another.

Remember the rule: *Properly oven-poached chicken cutlets show absolutely no trace of chicken juices in the poaching dish.*

The cutlets are poached by bringing their own water content to poaching temperature; since the cutlets are covered, the technique could just as well be called oven-steaming. The internal temperature should be 155° to 160°F (USDA 170°F).

Oven-poached cutlets used for a warm meat course are usually served with a compound butter, a butter oil, or a flavored oil as illustrated further on in the section on pan-steaming chicken cutlets (see page 858). In the classic cuisine, they were more often than not used for the type of dish called *chaud froids*.

No basic cookbook should be without instructions for a *chaud froid*, however old-fashioned the technique may be. A *chaud froid*, French for what could be literally translated as a "hot cold dish," took its name from the fact that a normally warm sauce (the *chaud* element) is prepared with a stock rich in gelatinous material (the *froid* element), cooled over ice, and, while it is still viscous, gently layered upon a chilled roast, bird, or small pieces of meat such as chicken cutlets. Meats prepared as *chauds froids* are, after being coated with the sauce, covered with a layer of gelatinized clarified stock called aspic. A *chaud froid* is easy to execute provided that you organize yourself fully before starting any operation.

Before we start, here are some *chaud froid* tips:

- The stock used to prepare the sauce need not be clarified (see page 230) but it must be entirely fat-free; if it is not, the bubbles of fat will harden as they cool, and the surface of the finished product will be dotted with multiple tiny eyes of hardened fat.
- All the components of a *chaud froid*—meats, sauce, and aspic—should be lightly oversalted when warm as seasonings don't taste as strong once chilled.

- To prevent either a *chaud froid* sauce or an aspic from jelling too fast, divide the volume of each into three parts. Jell two parts and keep one fluid. If the jellied sauce or aspic becomes too thick, loosen it with some of the still fluid mixture and stir gently until viscous enough again to coat the meat.
- Do not stir either *chaud froid* or aspic quickly, nor whisk either of them; otherwise, bubbles or foam will form throughout their texture, which will not allow either to lie flat and evenly on the food to be coated.
- The food to be coated should show no traces of any kind of fat or the *chaud froid* will not adhere properly. Wipe any meat cooked in fat or oil completely before coating it.
- Have a large platter able to contain all the pieces at once; refrigerate the finished *chaud froid* on the top shelf of your refrigerator until ready to serve.
- You will also need a baking sheet or jelly-roll pan lined with parchment paper and a stainless steel rack to rest over the sheet pan.

Here is a recipe which can be executed relatively fast, with pleasant and refreshing ingredients for an elegant summer buffet table.

Tarragon Chicken Chaud Froid

FFR — 12 SERVINGS

12 medium-large chicken cutlets, trimmed of skin, fat, and tendons

Salt

Finely ground white pepper

¾ cup fresh lemon juice

Olive oil as needed

6 cups fat-free Secondary Stock (page 220) or chicken stock of your choice

¾ cup chopped fresh tarragon leaves

8 teaspoons unflavored gelatin

4 teaspoons cornstarch

4 cups heavy cream

3 cups clarified aspic (page 232)

12 slices carrots, cut into flower shapes with a fancy cutter and blanched 1½ minutes in boiling salted water

Green leaves of 2 leeks, well washed, then cut into elongated leaves, six 1 inch long, and six 1½ inches long, and blanched 1 minute in boiling salted water

Preheat the oven to 475°F. Season the cutlets with salt and pepper, then rub them on both sides with the lemon juice. Rub a very thin layer of oil in the bottom of an enameled cast-iron baking dish. Add the chicken cutlets, cover with a sheet of parchment paper, then a sheet of aluminum foil dull side out.

The quantities of stock, gelatin, cream, and aspic as given here are, on purpose, very generous to prevent the beginner from running short in the middle of a delicate procedure. Gather any excess of coating ingredients together in a saucepan, add to them a garnish of cooked baby peas, corn, diced carrots, turnips, artichoke bottoms, and chopped fresh tarragon, and serve as a lovely soup.

SUGGESTED WINE: *Any bubbly of your choice*

Oven poach 5 to 6 minutes, then turn the cutlets over, cover, turn the oven off and poach, another 2 to 3 minutes. Remove from the oven, remove the foil, and let stand 30 seconds under the parchment. Remove to a plate and cool completely. Wipe off any trace of oil from the cutlets and set them on a stainless steel rack placed over a baking sheet or jelly-roll pan lined with parchment paper.

Bring 3½ cups of the stock to a boil in a saucepan. Add the tarragon and let simmer over medium heat until reduced to 2½ cups. Mix the remaining cold stock with the gelatin, then blend into the hot stock, stirring well to dissolve the gelatin completely. Mix the cornstarch and cream together, blend into the simmering stock, and thicken. Strain the sauce to discard the tarragon, correct the seasoning with salt and white pepper, and chill over ice until the sauce reaches a viscous coating consistency.

Spoon the viscous—*not thick*—*chaud froid* evenly over the cutlets. Deep chill the cutlets. If you are short of sauce, melt any that has fallen on the parchment paper while coating, then bring back to coating consistency over ice and finish coating the cutlets. They should be covered with a ⅙-inch-thick layer of *chaud froid*. Change the parchment under the cutlets, saving the jelled sauce on it.

Cool 2 cups of the aspic over ice. As soon as it has reached the consistency of oil, spoon half of it evenly over the coated cutlets. Chill the chicken again. Ten minutes later, dip the carrot flowers in aspic; let any excess aspic drip back into the bowl. Using a skewer as a helper, on which to poise the thin pieces of vegetable, gently place one carrot flower 1 inch from the thin tip of each cutlet.

Now, separate the two thick layers of each leek leaf by passing the blade of a parer horizontally between them; the leaves will become supple and bendable. Dip one long leaf in the aspic and place it to the left of the carrot, then dip one short one and place it to the lower right of the carrot. Cool the remainder of the aspic and spoon another layer of it over the whole cutlet to finish fixing the decorations.

To serve: Using scissors, trim any traces of jelled sauce away from the edge of each cutlet. Arrange the cutlets on a very flat platter. Collect all the remaining aspic in a bowl, melt it over hot water, cool it again to a viscous consistency, and pour it evenly on the bottom of the platter to make what is called a *miroir*, or aspic so clear that it reflects the pieces of meat.

Store the dish in the refrigerator for as little time possible or the top of the aspic will dehydrate and look dull.

Birds Poached in Salt

The difference between poaching in salt and roasting in salt is one of temperature. Whereas in roasting the salt is hot when the meat is embedded in it (see page 765), in poaching the meat is set in cold salt and the baking temperature is only 325°F. This technique is best applied to fat birds such as capons and ducks which will slowly drip their fat into the salt and emerge from the pot nicely browned. Serve any condiment you like with the bird; it should be plentiful as the bird will have absolutely no gravy.

Duck with Crimson Mustard

FFR — 4 TO 6 SERVINGS

¾ cup dried sour cherries

24 kumquats

1¼ cups port of your choice

2 dozen fresh or frozen loose raspberries

1 tablespoon sweet yellow mustard or more, to your personal taste

1 tablespoon firmly packed brown sugar (optional), or to taste

Salt

Pepper from the mill

One 5-pound duck

Bouquet garni of sprigs fresh rosemary, thyme, and savory and 1 Turkish bay leaf

10 pounds kosher salt

1 tablespoon olive oil

3 heads escarole, coarsely chopped

If you wish to serve six to eight, simply double the recipe using two identical pots and setting one on the upper rack and one on the lower rack of the oven. To prepare two ducks at once you would need a large rectangular restaurant-size roasting pan. The cherry condiment needs overnight steeping.

SUGGESTED WINE: *If served without the mustard, any of the good Cabernets of California or a Saint-Emilion; with the mustard, a Côtes de Provence, or Le Cigare Volant from Bonny Doon would be better.*

Chop the cherries coarsely. Peel the skins from 12 of the kumquats and chop the skins. Discard the pulp. Place the skins and cherries in a bowl. Bring the port to a boil and reduce to ¾ cup. Pour over the cherries and the skins of the 12 kumquats and let macerate overnight. The next day, crush the raspberries and push the pulp through a fine-meshed strainer into the cherry mixture. Add the mustard and brown sugar and season with salt and pepper to obtain a fruit mustard. Process to a smooth texture in a blender. Turn into a bowl and keep refrigerated until the duck has cooked.

Preheat the oven to 325°F. Chop the remaining whole kumquats. Stuff into the duck cavity along with the bouquet garni and season with salt and pepper; truss (see instructions on page 725). Pour one third of the cold salt into an oval enameled cast-iron pot. Cover the duck completely with the remaining cold salt, cover the pot, and bake for 2 to 2½ hours.

A few minutes before taking the duck out of the oven, heat the oil in a large sauteuse pan over medium-high heat and stir-fry the chopped escarole until wilted. Season with salt and pepper and turn into a serving platter.

When the duck is cooked, turn the pot upside down onto a large cutting board, break the salt, and brush off any trace of it from the skin. Detail into four to six portions, arrange those on the platter over the escarole, and serve with the crimson mustard.

Pan-Steamed Chicken Cutlets

This technique can be used only with chicken cutlets. It is fast, yields perfect texture, and requires a minimum of fat or no fat if you prefer, and only a plain old skillet, frying pan, or electric frying pan. This is the perfect way to prepare chicken cutlets to be used in a salad.

Since the cutlets from regular chickens are not that terribly deep in taste, it is a good idea to either cook them in a very small amount of a flavorful fat or to coat them with all kinds of herbs or spices. Cutlets from free-range chickens will have a more meaty flavor and a firmer texture.

As you read the cooking sequence, you may wonder why this technique is called pan-steaming when no true steam is used. It is simply because during the cooking time, the water content of the meat gradually attains a temperature high enough to denature and cook the muscle fibers of the cutlets, with just the barest hint of steam visible on the lid that covers them. The technique could just as well be called pan-poaching, as the preceding technique was called oven-poaching.

SEQUENCE FOR
PAN-STEAMED CHICKEN CUTLETS
Please follow these directions exactly.

1. Start the cooking in a *cold pan* lightly rubbed with the chosen fat. If you use butter, rub the raw unmelted butter on the bottom of the pan; if you prefer the flavor of noisette butter (see page 32), cook the butter to the noisette stage, turn the heat off, and *wait until the pan is cold again to cook the meat.* Always start cooking in a cold pan rubbed with creamed butter or oil.

2. Add the well-seasoned chicken cutlets to the cold pan. Now and only now, turn the heat on as low as you possibly can; an electric frying pan should be set just below 275°F.

3. As you turn the heat on, cover the cutlets with a lid that fits inside the pan, one just large enough to cover them tightly; in an electric frying pan use a sheet of aluminum foil dull side out and cut to fit exactly over the cutlets and in the shape of the pan. Cook 2 minutes. Turn the cutlets over, cover, and cook another 2 minutes. The internal temperature should read 155° to 160°F (USDA 170°F).

   Continue this turning over until the cutlets are resilient to the finger, then quickly remove to lukewarm dinner plates; the carryover heat will do its work on the plates where they will finish cooking. Do not platter these deliciously melting little pieces of meat as their texture will suffer from being displayed, waiting to be decorated, and being passed around the table.

4. Last but not least, since the cutlets are best served without waiting, have

all vegetable garnishes, any relish, compound butter, or butter oil prepared to flavor them ready before they are. Remember the basic rule: *The garnishes must wait for the chicken*.

Here are two recipes, one prepared with noisette butter, the other with a butter oil.

Pan-Steamed Chicken Cutlets with Bitter Greens Cream

FFR—6 SERVINGS

2 heads chicory, well washed and finely chopped

2 heads escarole, well washed and finely chopped

Salt

Pepper from the mill

⅔ cup heavy cream

1½ tablespoons unsalted butter

1 large clove garlic, finely chopped

6 chicken cutlets, trimmed of skin, fat, and tendons

⅓ cup freshly grated Parmigiano-Reggiano cheese

SUGGESTED WINE: **A** *Lambrusco or Sangiovese*

Add the chopped greens to a nonstick 10-inch skillet, toss with salt and pepper to taste, and cook over low heat, covered, until the juices are running out of the greens and they have completely wilted. Empty the greens into a colander and gather their juices in a bowl. Set the greens in a dish and keep warm.

Mix the greens juices and cream together in a small saucepan and reduce over medium heat to ⅓ cup of slightly thickened sauce.

Wipe the skillet clean with paper towels and add the butter. Cook to the noisette stage (see page 32), then toss in the garlic, turn the heat off, and let the pan cool completely.

Season the chicken cutlets with salt and pepper, then arrange them in the skillet. Cook them over very low heat, covered as directed on page 858, turning every 2 minutes until resilient to the finger.

Arrange an equal amount of greens on each plate. Top with one chicken cutlet. Meanwhile, raise the heat under the skillet, add the cream sauce, give 2 or 3 boils, and spoon over the cutlets. Sprinkle an equal amount of the cheese over each cutlet and serve immediately.

Pan-Steamed Chicken Cutlets in Chive Butter Oil

As an accompaniment use a pilaf of pecan-flavored rice and any fresh vegetables of your choice. Do not use mascarpone to fill the cutlets, as it will melt out of the cutlets very fast.

SUGGESTED WINE: *An Alsatian Edelzwicker*

FCR — 6 SERVINGS

½ cup plus 2 tablespoons dried cranberries, very finely chopped

Finely grated rind of 1 lemon

Melted orange, lime, or lemon marmalade, to your personal taste

Juice of 1 lemon

Salt

Pepper from the mill

2 tablespoons cream cheese

6 chicken cutlets, trimmed of skin, fat, and tendons

1 tablespoon unsalted butter, softened

1 tablespoon light olive oil

2 tablespoons chopped fresh chives

Place ½ cup of the cranberries in a small bowl, together with ¼ teaspoon of the lemon rind and just enough water to cover. Let the dried fruit rehydrate at room temperature and absorb all the water; mix at regular intervals, adding a dash more water if and when necessary. Blend in the melted marmalade, lemon juice, and salt and pepper to your taste. Macerate overnight in the refrigerator, covered. When ready to use, mix well, and bring to room temperature if you like.

Mix the remaining cranberries with the cream cheese, a dash of grated lemon rind, and salt and pepper to taste. Let blend overnight in the refrigerator, covered.

When ready to cook the cutlets, cut a pocket into each of them (see page 805), stuff each with one sixth of the cheese mixture, and press the edges of the cutlet closed.

Cream the butter in a small bowl until very white and creamy, then gradually cream in the oil and chives. Melt in a skillet without letting the mixture brown, then set aside until the pan is cold. Salt and pepper the cutlets, roll them in the cold butter mixture, place them in a single layer in the pan. Cook over very low heat, covered with a lid resting flush over the cutlets, turning the cutlets every second minute till they are resilient to the touch of a finger. Serve immediately with the prepared relish.

Truly Steamed Meats

Pan-steaming is probably the very best way to cook the white meat of chicken because of its fragility when exposed to the high heat and pressure of a true steamer. It is not impossible to truly steam white meat, but a few seconds of inattention can deliver disastrously toughened, unpalatable meat.

This is why I prefer to pan-steam chicken cutlets and only steam whole chickens or their drumsticks and thighs.

THE STEAMER

If you can acquire a true steamer fitted with a deep flat-bottomed basket in which to arrange the meat to be steamed, you will be in possession of a very useful implement that will last you a lifetime. Some steamers will be fitted with one of several deep flat-bottomed baskets, that can be set way above the steaming liquid. Investigate the Chinese bamboo steaming baskets which are quite handy and not expensive.

If you have no steamer, you can steam in a wok. The wok lid is usually adequate to allow good pressure to build underneath it. Many woks come with a rack which fits a little more than halfway down the wok but high enough above any liquid to steam foods properly.

In the absence of both steamer and wok, simply use a colander. A regular 10-inch colander fitted into a 4- to 5-quart double-handled stock or stew pot can very easily be used to steam a whole chicken up to 5 pounds.

For smaller pieces of meat, ingenuity is of the essence and putting money away to purchase a good steamer would be a worthwhile goal. Still, you can make do until you have that valuable piece of equipment.

The smaller flat-bottomed-type colander that is 8 inches in diameter and used generally for draining noodles and rice is perfect for steaming either 2 chicken cutlets or 6 chicken thighs. Such a smaller colander can fit snuggly into a 4½- to 5-cup capacity saucepan.

A regular 10-inch rounded colander fits well inside a 4- to 5-quart two-handled soup or stew pot and can be used to steam 4 to 6 chicken cutlets, depending on their size, and 6 to 8 chicken thighs. Arrange the cutlets and thighs so 2 or 3 are on the bottom of the colander and another 2 to 4 arranged all around its bending sides with a little space between each piece of meat to allow the steam to penetrate between them and over them. Most pieces will either have their skin on or be wrapped in a vegetable leaf (see below), which will sink into the holes of the colander and help keep the pieces from sliding. Check once in a while to make certain that the pieces have not fallen upon one another; if they have, remove the colander from the source of steaming water, rearrange the pieces, and replace over the colander over the steaming bath.

In any case, should the upper holes of the colander reach above the pot rim, cover them tightly with aluminum foil to prevent some of the steam from escaping. The pot lid always comes last.

THE STEAMING LIQUID

The steaming liquid can be plain water, a stock or broth, or a mixture of any of these with wine. All can be flavored with herbs. If the steaming liquid is water, the juices from the bird will fall into the water and flavor it. As a result, if you add herbs to it, you can obtain a small light broth flavored with meat juices and herbs. This can be used either to build a small sauce or as the base of a dressing, once it is reduced.

There is no need to put a large amount of liquid in the bottom of the steamer; two inches are amply sufficient, since the vapor condenses on the lid of the steamer and eventually finds its way back down into the liquid.

THE PRINCIPLE OF STEAMING

Steamed food, unlike boiled and poached foods, are not brought in direct contact with water, but rather in contact with the steam produced by the liquid simmering in the lower part of the steamer. It is essential when steaming to keep the pot lid tightly on and to make sure that the liquid stays at a steady simmer. If it comes to a high boil, it could pop the lid off. Keeping the lid on ensures that the pressure and slightly higher temperature in the steaming compartment of the pot remains constant and that abundant steam always surrounds the cooking meat. Depending on the regularity of the simmer and the tightness of the pot lid seal, the meat may cook slightly faster or slightly slower than it does when immersed in water.

PROTECTING THE MEAT
FROM INTENSE HEAT

The skin of birds to be presented whole is a good protection and should be left on; it can be removed if desired by the cook when the meat is seasoned.

SPECIAL FOR CHICKEN PARTS

The skin of small pieces—thighs and drumsticks—is better removed before steaming and replaced with leafy vegetables or thick layers of herbs which will have the double duty of protecting and flavoring the meat. Although chicken cutlets can be steamed wrapped in vegetable leaves, it is preferable to pan-steam them. The steam temperature is so intense that they can be overcooked in a matter of seconds.

It is essential as you steam chicken parts that the basket be set absolutely flat over the simmering water, for should the basket be tilted, the parts will slide toward one another and the cooking will be irregular.

STEAMING CHICKENS FOR LARGE PARTIES

For those cooks who have to steam a larger number of birds at one time for a large party, using a Swiss tilting skillet is a good solution. Place six to eight (depending on the size of the skillet) empty sauce containers upside down on the bottom of the skillet. Add 3 inches of liquid to the skillet, place as many stainless steel racks on the inverted containers as needed, and set the birds or chicken pieces on the racks. Cover the opening of the skillet with aluminum foil and the skillet lid. Depending on the size of the skillet, you can steam from eighteen to twenty whole chickens.

SAUCE, DRESSING, OR CONDIMENT?

If you wish to prepare a sauce with the juices of a steamed chicken, it is a good idea to put the bird into a snuggly fitted plastic cook-in bag at an angle so juices will gather in one corner. Reduced, these juices can be blended with vinegar or lemon juice to prepare an excellent dressing which peps up the very moist but often somewhat bland meat. To obtain good cooking juices, it is essential to salt and pepper the bird in its cavity.

You have several choices. You can prepare a sauce or dressing using some of the steaming medium. If you prefer a condiment, you can use homemade or ready-made. I have indicated all through this book diverse condiments for boiled and poached meats and fish; they can be used as well for steamed meats.

Here are two recipes, one for a steamed whole chicken, the other for dark meat chicken parts.

Steamed Chicken in Celadon Dressing

FCR — 4 TO 6 SERVINGS

One 4½-pound roasting chicken

Salt

Pepper from the mill

Very large bouquet garni of parsley stems, I sprig fresh tarragon, I sprig fresh thyme,
    and I Turkish bay leaf

I tablespoon pure olive oil

3 tablespoons chopped fresh chervil leaves

2 tablespoons cider vinegar

½ cup hazelnut oil

Mesclun made of lamb's lettuce and baby chicory

This recipe can also be applied to Cornish hens.

SUGGESTED WINE: *A very well-chilled California Riesling or a dry French Jurançon*

Season the inside of the bird with salt and pepper, stuff in the bouquet garni, and truss the chicken. Rub it with the olive oil and put it in a cook-in bag, forcing the air out of the bag as much as possible and tying it tightly just above the tail bone.

Bring 2 inches of water to a boil in the bottom of a steamer. Put the steamer tray in place, place the chicken on top of it, and cover tightly with the steamer lid. Steam until the juices in the bag are clear, about 1 hour.

Empty the juices into a small saucepan and reduce them to 2 tablespoons over medium-high heat. Add the chervil, vinegar, and hazelnut oil. Empty into a blender and process until pale green. Taste the dressing and correct for the proper balance of salt and acid by adding more salt, pepper, vinegar, or oil as needed.

Carve the chicken into four or six serving pieces and arrange them on a platter. Surround with the mesclun. Drizzle the dressing over the chicken and greens and serve.

Steamed Chicken Thighs in Saffron Orange Coats

FCR — 6 SERVINGS

1 anchovy fillet, rinsed and mashed

Salt

Pepper from the mill

1 small vial powdered saffron

Grated rind of 1 navel orange

1/4 teaspoon fennel seeds, finely ground

2 tablespoons finely chopped fresh Italian parsley leaves

1 clove garlic, finely mashed

12 large chicken thighs, trimmed of skin and fat and bone removed

1 bunch green Swiss chard

3 cups chicken stock of your choice

Juice of 2 oranges

2 tablespoons unsalted butter

Mix together the mashed anchovy, a touch of salt, 20 turns of the pepper mill, a pinch of saffron, half the grated orange rind, the ground fennel seeds, half the parsley, and the garlic in a small cup. Sprinkle the mixture on both sides of the chicken thighs.

Blanch 12 large leaves of chard in salted boiling water for 2 minutes. Remove the center rib and wrap each thigh in a leaf. Bring the chicken stock to a visible simmer in the bottom of the steamer. Arrange the thighs in the steamer basket and cover. Steam until a skewer inserted in the center of one of the thighs comes out freely, about 35 minutes.

For a small sauce, remove half the chicken broth from the steamer to a small saucepan. Add the orange juice and reduce to ½ cup over medium-high heat. Whisk in the butter and the remaining orange rind, parsley, and the remaining saffron; correct the final seasoning.

To serve, open the packages of chicken with scissors, arrange them on a platter, and spoon some of the orange sauce into the opening of the leaves.

As an accompaniment, serve stir-fried bell peppers of all colors mixed with yellow and green zucchini (see technique on page 407), adding the remainder of the Swiss chard used to wrap the chicken thighs.

SUGGESTED WINE: *A lovely Ravenswood Zinfandel or a Côtes-du-Rhône Saint-Péray*

Microwaved Meats

Having been raised on slow-cooked foods which acquire a deep flavor while cooking, I am not one to cook in the microwave, which I otherwise use with enthusiasm to melt chocolate, defrost and reheat frozen foods, etc.

The microwave oven generates short radio waves, which do not cook meats by way of gradual heat penetration from the outside as in a conventional oven would, but by immediate penetration to about a depth of 2 inches. When the microwaves pass through the water contained in foods, they cause the dipolar water molecules to oscillate. This oscillation is so rapid that intense heat is produced, which is transferred to the food. You must have noticed how very hot coffee or any food turns out when reheated or cooked in a microwave oven. Their respective containers are warm only because they have absorbed some of the heat from the food they contain.

According to some food scientists meats cooked in the microwave retain more of their vitamin content; since there is no loss of water whatsoever, any vitamin that is water soluble will indeed remain in the meat.

Best Type of Meat for the Microwave

Meats do not brown when cooked in the microwave, which presents a significant disadvantage for red meats which are usually brushed with coloring agents to attain the proper look of a roasted meat. The look is not quite there, however, and the true roasted taste, with its fantastic combination of flavors and textures, between the browned outside and the rare, juicy center, is simply not there. The same applies to stews where, in spite of everything being cooked carefully, the meat, sauce, and vegetable garnishes each pull the palate in different directions instead of forming a well-centered whole. The only piece of meat which, in my opinion, microwaves true to taste and texture is the chicken cutlet.

High or Moderate Power?

I have done a lot of testing, comparing my results with those obtained by following manufacturers' directions, and have found that the power of the oven should be 50 percent, which is half as high as generally indicated.

The best possible number of cutlets to cook at once seems to be four, which came out of the oven with perfect look, taste, and texture and done evenly from their outside to their center. When six cutlets were cooked, the test yielded meat that was hard and tough on the outside and too pink in the center, while two cutlets looked very good but were uniformly tough through to their centers.

When you microwave chicken cutlets, be sure that the meat is done to its very center. Each and every microwave oven model delivers a slightly different heat power. The destruction of bacterial content in cooked foods depends not only on the degree of heat applied but also on the duration of this application. In a microwave, the heat is high, without a doubt, but the duration of the cooking time is quite short; as a result, it is important that you serve chicken cutlets sliced on the diagonal, so you are able to insure that absolutely no pinkness is left in the meat. The meat should look pearly white but still show traces of moisture between its fibers, with an internal temperature between 155° and 160°F (USDA 170°F).

I never cook vegetable garnishes with the cutlets, preferring to microwave the cutlets by themselves while I stir-fry the vegetables on the stove. The results are perfect cutlets with properly cooked meat and vegetables.

Here is a recipe which you can use as a model to create many others that will answer to your taste.

Microwaved Fenneled Chicken Cutlets

SUGGESTED WINE: *Any mellow white wine of your choice, American or French*

FCR—4 SERVINGS

2 medium-size fennel bulbs with greens, well washed

½ teaspoon fennel seeds

⅓ teaspoon salt

¼ teaspoon freshly ground black pepper

¼ teaspoon very finely chopped fresh rosemary leaves

2 teaspoons very finely chopped fresh tarragon leaves

2 teaspoons very finely chopped fresh chervil leaves

4 medium-large chicken cutlets, trimmed of skin, fat, and tendons

3 tablespoons virgin olive oil

I clove elephant garlic, finely minced

8 large sun-ripened Italian plum tomatoes, peeled, seeded, and sliced ¼ inch thick

2 tablespoons finely chopped fresh Italian parsley leaves

Large pinch of cayenne pepper

Remove and chop the very fine greens of the fennel bulbs to obtain 2 full tablespoons. Mix with the fennel seeds, salt, pepper, rosemary, tarragon, and chervil. Coat each chicken cutlet on all sides with one quarter of the mixture.

Rub a microwaving dish with 1 tablespoon of the olive oil and arrange the cutlets in it so they form a cross, pointed tips toward the center of the dish. Cover tightly with microwave plastic wrap and punch eight small holes in it with the tip of a parer. Let the cutlets marinate in the herbs while you prepare the vegetable garnish.

Slice the fennel bulbs into ⅛-inch-thick slivers. In a nonstick skillet, heat another tablespoon of olive oil over medium-high heat, add the fennel, and stir-fry until it starts to soften. Remove to a plate and keep warm. In the same skillet, heat the remaining tablespoon of olive oil, add the garlic, and toss rapidly until it turns light beige. Add the tomatoes and toss for 2 minutes in the hot pan; turn the heat down to medium, cover, and cook until the tomatoes form a compote.

Set the chicken cutlets in the microwave oven. Cook for 4 minutes at 50 percent power, then turn over and cook another 3½ minutes, still at 50 percent power. The cutlets should be resilient to the touch and have lost absolutely none of their juices. Slice the cutlets into slivers starting at their larger end and arrange on the bed of fennel. Spoon the compote of tomatoes over the sliced meat and sprinkle with the chopped parsley and the cayenne pepper. Serve very rapidly.

Using Ground Meats

I have made a special section for ground meats because they are a world unto themselves, one that includes the most humble and the most noble dishes. The cooking techniques used to cook ground meats are varied and most of them already have been explained in detail; those techniques that remain to be fully explained will find their place here.

The public attention given to cases of serious sickness due to the bacterial content of some ground beef has demonstrated how important it is for the cook to take all necessary precautions in the use of ground meats. I offer here some guidance to solve a problem that is very serious and needs to be treated with care and understanding.

When you handle ground or pureed meats, wear surgical gloves (you can buy them inexpensively in any drugstore), not only to protect your hands from the bacterial content of the meat, but to protect the meats from any bacterial contamination of your hands. This is especially important when you mix meat loaf and meatballs, shape hamburgers, fill small ramekins with pureed meats, etc.

Ground meats, because they are cut into small particles, offer a larger surface of living space to bacteria. Ground meat will always contain more bacteria than a solid piece of meat, especially after passing through the blade of the grinder.

Strict federal regulations mandate the way prepackaged ground meats should be prepared and sold, and, all in all, supermarkets do a very good job of following these regulations. When a whole or half carcass is detailed by the butcher shop or the supermarket, the parts that will become ground meat must be taken off the bones within twenty-four hours, and ground within the four hours of its removal from the bones. The choice of cut is decided upon by the butcher and you will find in the showcase a relatively large selection of meats originating from different cuts, labeled, hopefully, with the name of the cut and with the descriptor "freshly ground."

Be aware that "freshly ground" legally means ground within those four important hours while "ground fresh daily" is more ambiguous.

Ground Beef

If you make a study of the types of ground beef offered by any supermarket, you will notice that the package will sometimes say "ground beef" which probably means that the shop gathered different pieces of different cuts and mixed them together to obtain a good blend of textures and tastes. More often than not, though, it will indicate the cut—"ground round," "ground chuck," "ground sirloin."

Another thing to look for on the packaging is the amount of fat contained in the ground meat. It must be mentioned by regulation; if it does not, go straight to the window and not only ask why, but demand that all the ground meats be sold with a mention of the percent of fat they contain. Compliance is high nowadays, but once in a while the content of fat is forgotten on the label. You can gauge the approximate content of fat in a ground meat by its color; if it contains 30 percent fat, it will be much paler than if it contains only 15 percent. The meat containing 15 percent will feel drier on the palate than the meat containing 30 percent; the greater amount of fat remaining in it after cooking will rightfully be perceived as more slip on the palate.

The following are the best possible scenarios for buying ground beef:

THE IDEAL IS Having your own grinder and, as a consequence, being totally in charge of the sanitary conditions in which you will grind your beef. This will allow you to buy a piece of meat of the weight you need in the cut you prefer, and to use as much fat as you like and/or must use. *The piece of meat you buy must have some fat or the cooked meat will be very dry.* Grind red meats twice for the proper texture in hamburgers, meatballs, etc.

Even if your grinder is clean as you take it out of its storage box or bag, wash it again in scalding water and air dry all its components before using them.

A special note for caterers and family-owned fast-food restaurants: Your best bet is to own your own grinder (the grinding attachment to a solid mixer is perfectly adequate) and grind your own meat *as needed,* sanitizing the grinder components in the dishwasher everytime you use them during the day. You will get the proper rhythm as your food operation develops its daily routine. Do not allow your personnel to become negligent when it comes to sanitizing a grinder; the future of your operation may depend on it. One instance of negligence may cause you unimaginable troubles.

Meat ground in a sanitized grinder can be used for hamburger, which still must be cooked to an internal temperature of 170°F as recommended by the USDA. There cannot be any exception to this rule.

IF YOU HAVE NO GRINDER You can either chop the meat finely by knife on a sanitized board or ascertain when the butchers start working in the butcher shop of your market. Go to the shop before the grinder has been activated and have the butcher grind a whole piece of meat that you have chosen in the cut you desire with the amount of fat you want or need to use. The internal temperature after cooking should also be 170°F. I am not in favor of using the food processor to grind meats. Because of its speed, one often overgrinds and finds puree in the bottom of the bin with irregularly ground meat in its upper part. This is a personal opinion; feel free to use the processor if you like its type of efficiency.

IF YOU MUST BUY YOUR GROUND BEEF ALREADY GROUND Do so, but make certain that if it is used for hamburgers they are well done. Use a steak button to ascertain this fact.

IF YOU ONLY WANT TO PREPARE MEATBALLS OR MEAT LOAF In this case you can use any preground meat, but make sure that the meatballs or meat loaf is well done, which is no hardship since they taste good only if they are well done anyhow. Well-done meatballs can be prepared with ground turkey also.

IF YOUR BUDGET DOES NOT ALLOW YOU TO BUY THE MORE EXPENSIVE GROUND BEEF Buy a lesser quantity of the more expensive meat and add to it stretchers such as eggs or egg whites, soft whole wheat bread crumbs soaked in milk, cooked bulgur, wheat germ, etc. All of these give your ground meat preparation a pleasant, moist texture and nutritional enrichment.

In commercial operations, hamburgers should not receive any such additives but be made of pure ground beef. The additives are only for home situations and are to be blended into the ground meat just before the cooking starts.

ABOUT STEAK TARTARE Steak tartare, previously prepared to be consumed uncooked, should unconditionally not be served any longer, whether at home or in food service.

Ground Mutton

Ground mutton—or red-meated sheep above one year old—is subject to the same grinding rules as indicated above for beef.

Ground Veal, Hand-Chopped Veal, and Lamb

If you wish to use veal in the making of meatballs or meat loaf, make sure that you use meat from the shoulder, the shank (osso bucco), the neck, and the meaty layers of meat covering the breast. The coarser the grain of the meat, the drier the meat will be, and often in Scandinavian recipes you will see butter or cream added to the mixture, while in Italian recipes the ground mixture often contains a bit of olive oil and many eggs.

Veal, being a young meat, is very perishable and it would be best if you either grind it yourself or have the butcher grind it for you first thing in the morning before he uses his grinder for any other meat.

In the preparation known as *pojarski*, which was originally created in Russia from the tenderloin of veal by a train station restaurateur named Mr. Pojarski, the expensive cuts of veal, such as the tenderloin, the loin, and the eye of the ribs can be used. They must then be chopped by hand on a sanitized board until they form a homogeneous rough puree. Resist the temptation to prepare *pojarski* in the food processor, as the meat would be pureed too finely.

Delicious *pojarski* can also be made with lamb loin and tenderloin (see page 874).

Ground Poultry and Processor-Pureed Poultry and Veal

Ground poultry is a relative newcomer in markets. As it is extremely perishable, I would recommend that you grind your own turkey and chicken meat, adding as much fat, such as butter and cream, as you wish for better palate slip in the cooked product.

Some brands of poultry offer very well-prepared, appetizing trays of ground poultry, with a clear indication of the safe date of use. I have used these for well-done meatballs and meat loaf with excellent results. Avoid using ground poultry for grilling, broiling, and panfrying; stewing offers a longer cooking time which results in a better tasting and safer product.

Chicken, veal, or lamb meats can be pureed to the smoothest texture in a food processor or blender to prepare the very rich quenelles and mousselines of the French and Middle European cuisines. These dishes are prepared exclusively for expensive restaurant presentations or celebration or special reception meals in home kitchens and they are to be served in tiny portions as delicious appetizers, with a nice garnish of salad or fresh colorful vegetables.

Ground Pork

Pork is extremely perishable and serious butcher shops keep two grinders, one for all other meats and one for pork alone to prevent cross-contamination, not only by bacteria but by possible parasites (see page 702).

If you like to use pork in meatballs or meat loaf, prepare the forcemeat with all the other ingredients first, then grind and add the pork to the mixture just before you start to cook it. Any ground meat preparation containing ground pork must be deeply cooked.

Ground Meat Recipes

HAMBURGERS

Our hamburgers received their name from the German Hanseatic city of Hamburg, where the steak is always served ground. The tradition probably came through the Vikings who established several shipping ports along the coast of the Baltic Sea and extended their commerce eastward along the Russian waterways and all the way down to the Black Sea. If you look at the food of these regions, they all offer dishes prepared with ground and chopped meats, as do the cuisines of the Scandinavian countries.

Follow the directions given on page 868 for grinding the hamburger meat. All the recipes for steaks offered in the sections on grilling, broiling, pan-broiling, and panfrying are appropriate for hamburger patties 3 inches in diameter and ½ to ¾ inch thick. Please read the directions given above, as you are responsible for cooking hamburger as it should be to an internal temperature of 170°F.

MEATBALLS AND MEAT LOAF

The composition of these two preparations is often very similar and can be made with any combination of meats. If you look through the cuisines of different ethnic groups, you will find that some seem to prefer veal meatballs ground very, very finely, while others prefer pork meatballs hand chopped rather than ground.

It is essential that the meat be ground at least twice; Italian meatballs are ground at least three times.

Besides the meat, the composition always contains additional ingredients which all have a role. In veal meatballs or meat loaf, the Scandinavians like to add a small amount of oil to supplement the meat which is otherwise quite dry and can lack slip on the palate once cooked. Most meatball compositions contain egg protein which adds solidity to the product, especially when the meatballs are used as the garnish of a clear soup. If cholesterol is an issue, use the egg white plus a tablespoon of unsaturated oil to replace each egg yolk for each pound of ground meat.

It is not unusual to see fresh bread crumbs soaked in milk or half-and-half added to a meatball or meat loaf formula. The crumbs absorb a large part of the meat juices, give the texture of the finished product mellowness, and make for easier cutting.

As already mentioned, precooked cereals such as bulgur, millet, amaranth, and quinoa can be added to a forcemeat to allow for reduction of the amount of meat.

You can make up your own meatball or meat loaf combinations by blending meats containing lower amounts of cholesterol and saturated fats with meats which contain a relatively large amount of it.

TESTING GROUND MEAT MIXTURES FOR SEASONING

Do not taste the raw mixture; instead, cook a heaping teaspoon of it in hot oil until thoroughly done and then taste it to find out how much more seasoning is needed. If preparing ground meat dishes to be served cold, proceed the same way, but cool or even chill the cooked patty in the freezer for a few minutes before tasting it, as the cold will mute the strength of the seasoning.

A Meat Loaf from East Prussia

I have adapted this recipe to modern nutritional demands by replacing the ground pork with ground turkey, and removing the egg yolk. For accurate taste, panfry a nugget of the forcemeat and taste, then adjust the seasoning. As a vegetable, consider étuvéed red cabbage.

SUGGESTED BEVERAGE: **A nice lager from eastern Germany**

FCR—6 SERVINGS

2 slices whole wheat bread, as rich as possible, crusts removed
¼ cup milk of your choice
½ pound freshly ground turkey breast
½ pound freshly ground beef chuck
I large egg white
I tablespoon unsaturated oil of your choice
I medium-size yellow onion, finely grated
2 anchovy fillets, rinsed and mashed
⅛ teaspoon ground bay leaf or I small fresh Turkish bay leaf, crumbled
⅛ teaspoon dried thyme or ¼ teaspoon fresh leaves
Salt
Pepper from the mill

For the condiment
I small white onion, finely chopped
Salt as needed
Granulated sugar as needed
⅓ cup Düsseldorf mustard
2 heaping tablespoons tiny capers with their brine
Grated lemon rind and juice as needed

Preheat the oven to 325°F. Crumble the slices of bread into the milk and let stand 10 minutes. In a large bowl mix together the bread-and-milk mixture, the two meats, the egg white, oil, onion, anchovies, bay leaf, and thyme and season with salt and pepper. Using surgical gloves, mix together extremely well and turn into a small nonstick loaf pan. Bake until the fat runs clear and an instant thermometer inserted at the center of the loaf comes out without resistance and registers an internal temperature of at least 165° to 168°F, 55 to 60 minutes. Drip any melted fat out of the loaf pan and let stand 10 minutes; then unmold the meat loaf onto a platter.

Meanwhile, to prepare the condiment, put the onion in a small bowl, sprinkle it with a bit of salt and sugar, and toss well; let stand until the onion has lost its juices. Remove the onion from the bowl and pat it dry. Wipe the bowl dry with paper towels, return the onion to the bowl, and add the mustard, capers with as much of their brine as you like, lemon rind and juice, and additional sugar to your taste. Mix well and serve with the meat loaf.

Meatball Stew

FCR — 6 SERVINGS

½ pound each turkey breast, fat-free veal shoulder meat, and Boston pork butt, each
    ground twice or chopped by knife extremely finely

½ cup fresh white bread crumbs

½ cup half-and-half or milk or cream of your choice

1 large egg white

1½ teaspoons dried mixed Provençal herbs or 1½ tablespoons chopped fresh

1 large shallot, finely grated

1 medium-size yellow onion, finely grated

2 large cloves garlic, mashed

Salt

Pepper from the mill

Unbleached all-purpose flour as needed

2 tablespoons unsaturated oil of your choice

3 leeks, white part only, well washed and finely sliced

1½ cups Secondary Stock (page 220) or stock or broth of your choice

1½ cups tomato coulis (page 308) or tomato sauce of your choice

3 tablespoons finely scissored fresh basil leaves

Freshly grated Parmigiano-Reggiano or Pecorino cheese as needed

These delicious little meatballs call for a dish of any grain or pasta you like or can be a pleasant hors d'oeuvre served with steamed small red potatoes cut into halves and hollowed out to receive a meatball with a bit of its sauce.

SUGGESTED WINE: **A** *Corsican Patrimonio or any of the lovely rosé wines of California*

Wearing surgical gloves, mix the three meats, bread crumbs, half-and-half, egg white, herbs, shallot, onion, and garlic together in a large bowl. Season with salt and pepper. To test the seasoning, cook a teaspoon of the mixture in hot oil thoroughly and taste. Adjust the seasoning if necessary.

Preheat the oven to 325°F. In a small bowl mix together the flour, a dash each of the salt and pepper, and strain through a conical strainer onto a large platter or baking sheet. Shape small meatballs 1 inch in diameter and roll in the flour. Heat the oil in a large sauteuse pan over medium-high heat and brown the meatballs on all sides until deep golden. Remove to a waiting plate. Discard the fat in the pan. Without cleaning the pan, sauté the leeks over medium heat until wilted; cover them for a few minutes until they release their juices. Return the meatballs to the pan, add the stock and tomato *coulis*, and bring to a boil. Cover the pan with a sheet of parchment paper then a sheet of aluminum foil, forming an upside-down lid, and finally the pot lid. Braise over low heat on top of the stove for 45 minutes to 1 hour; the meatballs are done when an instant thermometer inserted into the center of one of them comes out without resistance and registers an internal temperature of 165° to 168°F. Defat the sauce as much as possible and serve the meatballs in a deep country dish, well sprinkled with the basil and cheese.

Pojarski and Bitoques

FFR— 6 SERVINGS

1¾ pounds tenderloin of veal, chicken cutlets, or center cut of beef tenderloin or
    boneless fat-free lamb loin (approximately 2½ cups packed 1-inch cubes)
10 thin slices white bread, crusts removed
½ cup heavy cream
¾ cup unsalted butter
1 teaspoon salt
¼ teaspoon freshly ground white pepper
Unbleached all-purpose flour
1 recipe Anglaise (page 626)
1½ cups fresh bread crumbs
Clarified butter (page 32) as needed
⅓ cup Noisette Butter (page 32)
Fresh lemon juice for veal and chicken only

Cut the meat into very small pieces and chop it by hand into a fine paste. This is best done by chopping left to right or vice versa, then turning the direction of the meat and repeating until the meat forms a uniform sheet that, in spite of being chopped, hangs from the blade of the knife without breaking.

Tear the bread and soak it in the cream. With an electric mixer cream the butter in a large bowl. With the mixer still on creaming speed, add the meat 2 or 3 tablespoons at a time. Add the soaked bread bit by bit, then the salt and pepper. Continue beating until the mixture is homogeneous.

Wearing surgical gloves, shape twelve cutlets ⅓ inch thick and 2 inches long from the mixture. Flour the cutlets, brush them with the *anglaise*, and

This is the famous pojarski *mixture which so enchanted Auguste Escoffier, presented here with very little modification, extra rich and very evocative of the opulence of the late Imperial table of Russia. Since the formula is sinfully rich, I suggest dividing the forcemeat into 12 smaller cutlets instead of six larger ones. Resist the temptation of grinding the meat instead of chopping it by hand; if you do, you will lose all the meat juices while cooking. Cook all the cutlets and keep any leftover cooked (not uncooked) cutlets to enjoy cold.*

The same preparation made with tenderloin of beef is called bitoques. *The lamb version (to be made with sirloin strip) has no special name and is my idea; it is appreciated by people who really do not like medium-rare lamb. Serve this type of preparation with salted but unbuttered baby green beans.*

coat with the bread crumbs. Heat the clarified butter in a large skillet over medium-high heat. Add the cutlets and cook until well done and golden on both sides. For veal and beef the internal temperature should be at least 165°F, for chicken 180°F. Season with salt and pepper and serve basted with the noisette butter and lemon juice to taste.

Fresh Homemade Sausage

By sausage, I mean ground fresh pork or other meat mixed with selected spices of your choice. Fresh sausage is prepared today, served over the next two days, and kept in a very cold refrigerator, the temperature of which is never higher than 35°F.

Basic fresh sausage mixture is seasoned only with salt and pepper, so you can vary the taste by adding any other seasonings. Sausages intended to be smoked and cooked are discussed briefly in the section on cured meats (see page 910) and must contain a cure mixture.

Home-Style Sausage

FFR—SIXTEEN 2-OUNCE PATTIES

Basic pork mixture, regular formula

3 pounds net weight deep-chilled Boston pork butt (with its full amount of sinews, bones, traces of blood, and blood vessels completely removed, but fat left on)

4½ teaspoons salt

1 teaspoon freshly ground Aromatic Pepper (page 57) or to taste

¾ cup ice water

Lighter formula

2 pounds fat-free duck meat or dark turkey meat

1 pound unrendered fresh duck fat (see note below)

4½ teaspoons salt

1 teaspoon freshly ground Aromatic Pepper (page 57) or to taste

½ cup ice water

When all the implements are cold, grind the meat (and fat) into the mixer bowl. Season with salt and pepper. Refrigerate the meat, covered with plastic wrap, while you prepare the spice mixture. Keep the ice water chilled in a separate cup.

In the different spicing variations that follow, note that the dosage of the spices represents my taste; feel free to use more of any spice or to add any other spice you like, provided it is in harmony with the origin of the sausage forcemeat.

SUGGESTED WINE: *For the pojarski, a simple Pouilly-Fuissé from the Ferret vineyards or Edmunds St. John Viognier from California; for bitoques or lamb bitoques, a Saint-Amour Beaujolais or a Petite Syrah from California*

This sausage forcemeat is meant to be ground with the small die of a regular grinder, not chopped by hand or processed in a food processor. Note that all implements to come in contact with sausage meat—knife, grinder die and other parts, mixer bowl and blades—should be boiled or put through the sanitizing cycle of the dishwasher, then cooled to extremely cold in the refrigerator before grinding the meat. You must wear surgical gloves during the whole process.

NOTE: *To gather unrendered duck fat to prepare sausage, keep all the fat from ducks you roast frozen in a plastic bag. Keep the bag wrapped in aluminum foil to prevent oxidation.*

SUGGESTED WINE: *If the sausage is served for lunch or dinner, choose a simple red or white wine from the country of origin of the sausage.*

Dried herbs and garlic are used on purpose because there is no water mobility in them, consequently much less possibility for bacterial development. The herbs will rehydrate by absorbing some of the water in the mix.

American sausage

2 teaspoons rubbed sage

¼ teaspoon ground ginger

¼ teaspoon ground nutmeg

½ teaspoon ground thyme

Italian sweet sausage

1 teaspoon fennel seeds, finely chopped

½ teaspoon dried oregano

½ teaspoon dried basil

¼ teaspoon freshly ground black pepper

½ teaspoon granulated sugar

Italian hot sausage

2 teaspoons dried red pepper flakes

1 teaspoon granulated sugar

½ teaspoon ground coriander

¼ teaspoon ground nutmeg

Basque chorizo (from the Basque provinces on French Territory)

Replace the water with chilled dry white wine

1 teaspoon garlic powder

1 dried cayenne pepper, finely powdered

½ teaspoon dried thyme

Basque kainkas (from the Basque provinces on French Territory)

2 teaspoons garlic powder

¼ teaspoon aniseed

¼ teaspoon cayenne pepper

For all these compositions, finish the sausage as indicated below:

Remove the bowl containing the basic mixture from the refrigerator. Pour the water over the sausage forcemeat and sprinkle the spices over the water. Whip on medium-low speed to homogenize the mixture and distribute the spices evenly. Leave the mixture in the mixing bowl, cover again with plastic wrap, and refrigerate overnight.

The next morning, cut as many square sheets of parchment paper as you plan to make patties. Wearing surgical gloves, shape the patties 3 × ½ inch. Set each on a square of paper, and keep chilled until ready to cook.

To cook, add a ¼ inch of water to a large skillet or electric frying pan.

Grasp one square of paper and its patty, invert it into the cold pan, and remove the paper. Gradually heat over medium-low heat until the fat starts melting into the water, then turn the patties over and repeat with the second side. Finally, let the sausage patties finish cooking until the hot water has completely evaporated and the patties have browned on both sides in their own fat and have reached an internal temperature of 180°F. To serve, remove to paper towels to absorb superficial fat and serve bright hot.

Pleurines in Mustard Sauce

FFR—SIXTEEN 3-OUNCE PATTIES

1 ½ pounds caul fat

3 pounds net weight Boston pork butt with its full amount of fat, sinews, bones, traces of blood, and blood vessels completely removed

4½ teaspoons salt

1 teaspoon finely ground Aromatic Pepper (page 57)

¾ cup French, Canadian, or English hard cider

1 medium-size yellow onion, very finely chopped

1 teaspoon fennel seeds, finely crushed

4 cloves garlic, mashed

½ cup washed, patted completely dry, and chopped fresh Italian parsley leaves

12 large fresh Italian parsley leaves, washed and patted completely dry as needed

For the sauce (optional)

2 tablespoons pork fat or butter for authenticity or unsaturated oil of your choice for health reasons

4 yellow onions, very finely chopped

1½ cups broth of your choice

Yvetot or Dijon mustard

2 tablespoons crème fraîche (optional)

Salt

Pepper from the mill

Soak the caul fat in cold water for 30 minutes, changing the water several times. Rinse under running cold water, then cut into 5-inch square pieces. Place them on a baking sheet or jelly-roll pan lined with parchment paper and cover with plastic wrap to keep moist and pliable.

When all the implements are cold, grind the meat into a mixer bowl, adding the salt and pepper. Pour the cider over the forcemeat. Sprinkle in the onion, fennel seeds, garlic, and chopped parsley and mix until homogeneous on medium-low speed with an electric mixer. Cook a nugget of the mixture, taste it, and correct the seasoning if needed.

Shape the mixture into 2½ × ½-inch patties. If you wish larger patties, cut

These round sausage patties come from a village on the Normandy coast. Anywhere else in France they would be called crepinettes *because the forcemeat is wrapped in caul fat (called* crépine *in French), which makes their outside look enticingly appetizing.* Pleurine *is the ancient French name which has fallen more and more in desuetude in France, but is still current in the lower valley of the St. Lawrence where the* pleurine *is served with a white onion sauce; the Norman sauce is strong and mustardy. Pleurines are mostly served for lunch with a puree of either white beans or potatoes (see page 490 or 387). Prepare these tonight and cook them no later than for lunch tomorrow because of their fresh herb content. Caul fat can be ordered from any good butcher. Freeze what you do not use immediately for up to six months.*

SUGGESTED BEVERAGE:

Normandy, Canadian, or English hard cider

the caul fat into larger pieces. Put a parsley leaf in the center of each square of caul fat, top with a patty, and wrap by folding the four corners of the caul fat over the meat.

Add ¼ inch of water to two large skillets. Place half the *pleurines*, seam side down, in each pan and cook over medium-low heat until the water has evaporated and one side of each patty is golden. Turn over and brown on the other side. Cook to obtain well-done meat (internal temperature 180°F) all through the patties. Remove to crumpled paper towels to absorb any fat and keep warm.

While the *pleurines* cook, heat the chosen fat for the sauce in a sauteuse over medium heat, add the onions, and cook, stirring, until they have lost all their moisture and are soft and translucent. Raise the heat to medium high and brown until golden. Push the onions toward the handle of the pan, tilt up the pan, and spoon or wipe off any fat coming out of the vegetables. Set aside.

Discard the fat in the *pleurine* pan and deglaze the plentiful meat juices with the broth. Add to the onions, mix well, and cook a few minutes together, until the broth seems absorbed by the onions. Add mustard to your taste and crème fraîche if you wish. Season with salt and pepper. Serve the *pleurines* on a bed of the onion sauce.

Meat Terrines, Pâtés, Saucissons, and Galantines

This is a synopsis of the techniques involved in the preparation of terrines, pâtés, saucissons, and galantines. These preparations are not totally out of fashion and out of the modern kitchen, but they have undergone quite a number of changes with the advent of the modern kitchen equipment and of the care about proper nutrition.

DEFINITIONS

A *terrine* is nothing more than a fancy meat loaf cooked in an earthenware or other ovenproof dish, chilled and served cold as an appetizer, usually with a small salad or a pickle, sometimes with a special sauce called Cumberland sauce. A terrine can be served hot if desired, but it will then require a regular meat sauce, preferably an essence of the main meat contained in the preparation. I personally prefer a terrine cold and as an appetizer in small quantity.

A *pâté* is a terrine mixture baked in pastry. It is always a striking-looking achievement, but only for the eyes; it is otherwise extremely heavy and difficult to digest. If you want more information on pâtés, see the first edition of this book; they will not appear here because so very few chefs, cooks, and diners are interested in them anymore.

A *saucisson* is a terrine mixture shaped into a large sausage by stuffing it into a natural skin or a plastic cook-in bag; it is generally poached. A saucisson is still an interesting preparation as a small appetizer, but, being cooked in a cook-in bag, it retains more fat than a terrine which, after being baked in a loaf pan, loses a greater amount of its fat content.

A *galantine* is a very large cooked sausage, the forcemeat of which contains the meat of one or several birds or other meats. The skin of one of the birds is used as a container for the forcemeat. In modern restaurants, galantines are used exclusively in cold buffet displays, but in the home they cut a royal figure when served hot with a lovely sauce or cold as a first course. There is no beating around the bush: They are much work.

COMPOSITION OF A FORCEMEAT

THE PRIMARY MEAT OF A FORCEMEAT The main meat of a terrine, saucisson, or galantine gives the preparation its name. A "terrine of duck" contains twice as much duck as the other meats in its composition, called secondary meats. The weight of the main meat should represent two thirds of the total weight of all the meats.

This is approximately how much pure meat you can glean from the animals that are the favored sources of the main meat for forcemeats:

- One rabbit, about 3 pounds, yields 1 generous pound
- One hare, 6 to 7 pounds, yields 2 generous pounds
- One duck, 4 to 5 pounds, yields 1½ to 1⅔ pounds
- One small turkey, capon, or fowl, 5 to 6 pounds, yields 2 pounds
- One pheasant, 3½ pounds, yields 1 to 1½ pounds, depending on its age

THE SECONDARY MEATS The so-called secondary meats deepen and refine the taste of the forcemeat with their diverse flavors and textures. They are generally lean veal from the shoulder and semilean/semifat pork from the shoulder butt. The weight of the secondary meats should represent one third of the total weight of all the meats.

A GOOD TERRINE FORCEMEAT MUST RECEIVE A GENEROUS AMOUNT OF FRESH FATBACK Fatback is the name given to the fat covering the back of the pork; this fat must neither have been cured nor salted in any way. Any cured or salted fat has seen its water content captured by the salts, which you can plainly see resting in crystals on the surface of the meat. The water locked in fat tissues gives a terrine its "slip" on the tongue and palate so you would defeat your own purpose by using salt pork or bacon.

The weight of the fatback used must be half the total weight of the meats.

BINDING AGENT AS FAT REPLACEMENT If you are of the modern school that prefers less fat, you will have to substitute something for the fat. Remember never to remove the total amount of fatback or the terrine will be too dry.

The binder of choice used to make sure that a terrine is firm and cuts well is eggs. In the regular full-fat formula 2 to 3 eggs per each pound of meat are used. To lighten the formula, you can replace each ½ pound of fatback with 2 eggs. If the egg yolks are objectionable, you may replace each egg yolk in the formula with 1 teaspoon of the unsaturated oil of your choice.

Does this all sound terribly complicated? Just take a look at the three formulas given below as examples, and you will immediately see how things fall in line:

Full-Fat Formula	Leaner Formula	Fat-Controlled Formula
1 pound duck meat	1 pound duck meat	1 pound duck meat
¼ pound veal meat	¼ pound veal meat	¼ pound veal meat
¼ pound pork meat	¼ pound lean pork meat	¼ pound lean pork meat
¾ pound fatback	⅓ to ½ pound fatback	¼ pound fatback
5 large eggs	7 large eggs	8 large egg whites
		8 teaspoons unsaturated oil

SEASONINGS Since terrines, pâtés, saucissons, and galantines are mostly served cold, they must be seasoned more heavily than foods that are served warm. The minimum amounts of seasonings, spices, and aromatics *per pound of finished forcemeat*, that means the total weight of the meats and eggs, are:

- 1½ teaspoons salt
- 35 turns of the mill of aromatic pepper
- ⅓ teaspoon spices
- 2 shallots, peeled
- 1 medium-size yellow onion, peeled

Additional salt will be needed for the ingredients used as a garnish.

GARNISHES The garnish of a terrine consists of whatever meat, nut, or vegetable—diced, sliced, or otherwise cut—you can add to the forcemeat to give it more taste and a colorful appearance. Remember that the more garnish you add, the drier the terrine will feel on the palate. Limit the amount of garnishing material to one third the weight of the completed forcemeat.

PREPARATION SEQUENCE OF A TERRINE, SAUCISSON, OR GALANTINE FORCEMEAT

1. *Cutting the meats:* Trim the meats of all fat, tendons, and connective tissues. Cut them and the fat into 1-inch cubes, then weigh them.
2. *Marination:* Marination in wine and liqueur(s) is extremely important for the taste of the finished product. Any wine used must be a dry one and preferably have been reduced over medium heat for 20 to 25 minutes to remove the alcohol and concentrate its flavor.

  You can marinate the meats in reduced dry wine or a mixture of wine combined with Cognac, Armagnac, Scotch whisky, or bourbon.

Here are the best marriages of wine and meat for marination; all these wines are best used in their driest form.

Dry white wine: rabbit, capon, fowl (another name for a stewing hen, and the best type of chicken for a terrine), turkey

Dry red wine: fowl, duck, squab, quail

Dry sherry: duck, fowl, capon, turkey, especially when Chinese spices are used

Sercial Madeira: rabbit, fowl, turkey, squab, quail, pork, veal

Port: duck, squab, quail, fowl

Always remember to marinate the elements of the forcemeat and the garnish an equal amount of time, so there is no difference of taste between them.

3. *Grinding the forcemeat:* Please use a meat grinder rather than a food processor. Divide the bulk of the meats into two equal batches. Use the small grinding die and grind half the meats twice and the other half only once. Clean the grinder by passing onions and shallots through the machine and letting them fall into the bowl.

4. *Homogenizing the forcemeat:* Beat the forcemeat with an electric mixer as you add the eggs one by one and the mixed seasonings very gradually.

5. *Testing the forcemeat:* Cook a small patty of it in hot oil, then chill it well. Taste carefully, and correct the seasoning carefully.

IMPORTANT: All terrines, galantines, and saucissons must be cooked to an internal temperature of 180°F.

Barnyard Buddies on a Three-Way Street

FFR — 16 SERVINGS

Shopping list

One 3½-pound rabbit

One 4- to 5-pound duck with liver

1 turkey tender (small fillet of the breast)

¾ pound boneless veal shoulder meat

¾ pound boneless Boston pork butt

1½ pounds fresh fatback

1 dozen large eggs

For the forcemeat

Meat from the rabbit, coarsely diced

Meat from the duck, less the fillets, coarsely diced

Turkey tender, coarsely diced

½ pound veal meat, trimmed of all fat and coarsely diced

½ pound Boston pork butt, trimmed of all fat and coarsely diced

1¼ pounds fatback, coarsely diced

2 medium-size yellow onions, coarsely diced

4 shallots, coarsely diced

8 to 10 large eggs as needed

½ cup Cognac or Armagnac

Salt

Pepper from the mill

1 tablespoon peanut oil

This is the full-fat version of this recipe. Please refer to the guidelines on page 879 to transform this into a leaner or fat-controlled version. Please read the recipe to the end. Add the ingredients in the order they are called for. The last three sections of the recipe explain how to use the forcemeat in three different styles (the three-way street).

For the garnish

Duck fillets, cut into strips

I large egg white, lightly beaten

⅓ cup chopped fresh Italian parsley leaves

Salt

Pepper from the mill

For the seasoning and marinating mixture

I ½ teaspoons Chinese 5-spice powder (page 68)

I ¼ cups fino sherry

¼ cup dark soy sauce

I teaspoon ground ginger

4 cloves garlic, finely chopped

Put the diced meats, fatback, onions, and shallots for the forcemeat in a large bowl and the duck strips for garnish in a small one. Mix the 5-spice powder, wine, soy sauce, ginger, and garlic together. Divide the mixture between the two bowls, combining well to coat. Marinate 2 full days in the refrigerator, covered with plastic wrap, turning every 12 hours.

Prepare the garnish: Dip the strips of marinated duck in the lightly beaten egg white, then roll them in the parsley. Season with salt and pepper and set aside on a plate or sheet.

Using the small die of the grinder, grind half the forcemeat once, then grind the remainder twice. Transfer to a large bowl, add any of the marinade liquid that might be left over, and, with an electric mixer, whip on medium speed, adding 8 eggs, one after the other, the Cognac, and salt and pepper as needed. Test the forcemeat for seasoning and texture (see page 881) and add more eggs, salt, pepper, and any spice if needed. *Refrigerate until chilled.*

To present the forcemeat/garnish as a terrine: Preheat the oven to 350°F. Brush two 1-quart loaf pans or long terrine pans with a thin layer of peanut oil. Line with parchment paper, then brush the parchment lining with the remainder of the oil. Build the terrines by packing alternating ¾-inch-thick layers of forcemeat and garnish, starting and ending with a layer of force-meat. Cover with the terrine lid or with a sheet of parchment, then with aluminum foil. Bake in a hot water bath (see page 976) to 180°F, until the meat juices run clear. Cool for 20 minutes, then drain off the liquid fat around the terrine; reserve about 1 cup of it. Cut a piece of cardboard that fits just inside each terrine, wrap it tightly in foil, then in parchment, place it flush against the surface of the terrine, and apply moderate weight (you can use 8-ounce bottles full of juice or mineral water). Cool at room temperature another 30 minutes, then refrigerate, still under weight, for at least 24 hours. The ter-rines need to rest at least 2 days, well covered and refrigerated, before reach-ing full flavor, and 4 days would be better. If the fat extracted by the weight does not reach the top of the loaf pan, melt the reserved fat and pour it on top of the terrine; it will prevent oxidation of the loaf.

When ready to serve, bring the terrine to room temperature, pass a knife along the sides of the loaf and unmold it. Scrape any remaining fat off. Remove the paper and slice into ⅓-inch-thick slices. Serve with cornichons (see page 315) and a sparkling little salad.

Any left over should be well wrapped; it will keep one full week refrigerated at 35°F. You can also reheat slices in a frying pan to an internal temperature of 165°F.

To present the forcemeat/garnish as a galantine: You will need the skin of one duck, hopefully without tears and in one piece. This is obtained amazingly easily by boning the duck through its back.

Cut a long slit on each side of the backbone, from neck to tail. Using a sharp knife (some people use boning knives, I prefer a very sharp parer), gently separate the meat from the underlying carcass, baring gradually the rib cage and the shoulder and leg joints on each side. Separate each from the carcass by cutting the tendons that keep each joint attached to the carcass.

Now work to reach the breastbone, proceeding very carefully to cut the breast meat very slowly from the breastbone until only the breastbone is attached to the skin. Snip away at that skin on each side successively and without fear, for the skin is thicker than you think, until it falls on the table. Gently lift the breast fillets from the skin.

The shoulder and the legs are still attached to the skin on each side. Proceed exactly the same way with each joint: Separate the skin from the meat and start pulling the joint inside out. As you pull, the skin will look like an inside-out glove finger; all you have to do is cut it as closely as you can around

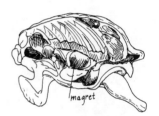

Having cut through the skin along the backbone, one side shows the rib cage.

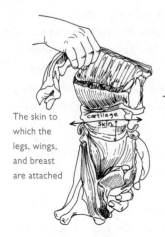

The skin to which the legs, wings, and breast are attached

The rib cage and breastbone ready for the stockpot

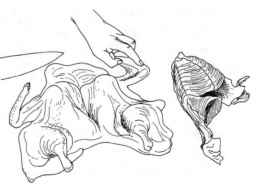

Cutting the wing tips and eventually the meat of the thighs

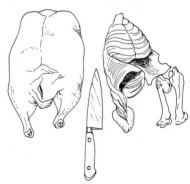

The skin with breasts and drumsticks still attached, ready to be stuffed as a *galantine*

the end of the wing tip and drumstick. On each side, the skin of the shoulder joint looks like a glove finger, and so will the skin of each leg.

You are now contemplating a whole duck skin. If you see a tiny tear here or there, do not worry; any tear can be sewn closed if need be with a fine needle and white thread.

Gently shave off (do not scrape, as that would break the skin) any blob of fat present on the skin with a very sharp paring knife. Salt and pepper the skin and brush it with beaten egg. Cover the skin with a sheet of parchment paper (it will prevent the skin from toughening) and prepare the forcemeat as indicated in the recipe you are using. The parchment will be removed before filling the skin.

To shape the forcemeat so that it can be fitted inside the skin without difficulty, spread a sheet of plastic wrap on the counter or tabletop. Arrange the forcemeat and garnish in layers at the center of the piece of plastic and close the plastic over the forcement on each side, forming a large sausage. Semifreeze this sausage and, when it is stiff enough to handle, remove it from the plastic, transfer it to the center of the skin, and sew the skin closed over the forcemeat, using a white thread.

Now, to make sure that the galantine will stay well put together and that your carefully prepared arrangement of layers will not move, brush a large piece of cheesecloth with oil. Align the edge of the cheesecloth nearest to you with the visible outer edge of the skin and roll the filled skin into the cheesecloth. Although it is feasible for one person to do this, it ends up being much easier if performed by two: One person on one side of the table pulls on the center part of the cheesecloth, while the second person on the other side of the table rolls the filled skin forward from both its sides as tightly as possible with each of his/her hands.

When rolled, the galantine looks like a very messy, blobby sausage. Turn that formless sausage so that the ends of the cheesecloth face you on one end and your partner on the other. Each of you must now start turning your end of the cheesecloth clockwise as tightly as possible. The galantine will transform into a huge, regularly shaped sausage as you twist. Tie each end of the cheesecloth with many turns of string, constantly passing each tie above the already existing ones before you knot the string. The galantine is now ready for baking or poaching.

ROASTING AT 375°F OR BAKING AT 325°F The choice of temperature is yours; generally, use the higher temperature for duck and the lower for white meats:

Brush the outside layers of the cheesecloth generously with oil so it does not burn while the meat cooks. Put the galantine on a rack placed over a roasting pan and roast or bake on the middle rack of the oven. Turn it at regular intervals while it bakes. The cooking time varies from 1¾ to 2½ hours, depending on the temperature used and on the size of the galantine. The meat is done when an instant thermometer reads 180°F.

A roasted or baked galantine may be served warm, in which case you can prepare a small essence of duck with the neck and wings of the duck and primary veal stock (see page 219); add the defatted deglazing of the galantine to the prepared sauce. Or you can serve the galantine cold with a few green leaves, pickles, and mustard, and make a cold jelly with the defatted gravy diluted with veal stock. The quantity obtained will be too small to clarify, but delicious. Chill in a shallow pan and cut into ¼-inch dice.

POACHING Bring a large container (the best vessel to poach a galantine in is a fish poacher) of water or light broth to a boil, salt it well, and add a bouquet garni and any spice you desire. Immerse the galantine in the boiling stock, reduce to a simmer as soon as the broth has reboiled, and poach 1½ hours. When the poached galantine is done, let it cool in its cooking bath, and when it is cold, unwrap it from its cheesecloth. Then, to pack its center well, wrap it very tightly in plastic wrap first, then in several layers of aluminum foil. No need to pack under weight; the excess fat has escaped into the cooking broth. Refrigerate at least 48 hours before serving.

To present the forcemeat as a saucisson: Cut open two small cook-in bags on the right side, and again on the bottom so you obtain a large, single, flat sheet of plastic. Lay the flat sheets on a table or countertop. Shape half the forcemeat into a large sausage and set it on one of the plastic sheets. Roll the forcemeat into the sheet and, with the help of another person, twist the sheet clockwise at each end of the saucisson as described for a galantine (see page 884). You will see it shape up by itself. Tie very carefully with several turns of kitchen string. Cut the plastic ends in half lengthwise and tie again and again around each separate end to prevent the forcemeat from leaking out under the pressure of the hot water. Wrap the saucisson in a triple layer of cheesecloth. Repeat with the remaining forcemeat and the other sheet of plastic.

Bring a large pot of water to a boil, reduce the heat to a simmer, and add the saucisson(s). Let poach until an instant thermometer reads 180°F, 45 to 60 minutes. Let cool in the water; when cold, unwrap from the cheesecloth, rewrap in plastic wrap and several layers of aluminum foil, and refrigerate at least 48 hours.

Serve the saucisson(s) sliced with a sparkling little salad of your choice.

Shelf life: Terrines and saucissons have a shelf life of one week, if kept well wrapped and refrigerated at 35°F. Another way of prolonging their shelf life is to add a tiny amount of curing salt to them. A galantine has the same shelf life when prepared to be served cold. Any leftovers from terrines, galantines, and saucissons can be served hot, reheated to 165°F. You are responsible for proper refrigeration and reheating. Any such product with the faintest off-smell must be discarded.

Quenelles and Mousselines

The preparations that follow are extremely rich and are worth making *only* if they are made correctly *and* with the proper ingredients; no substitutes can achieve what butter, cream, and a good understanding of proper technique can. If you are in any way not allowed to consume rich foods or object to rich foods out of personal conviction, please skip this section; you will neither like it nor be able to use it.

The techniques for making quenelles and mousselines of poultry, veal, or duck being exactly the same as those used for preparing quenelles and mousselines of fish and shellfish, please refer to pages 690–98 for a complete explanation of the successive steps. Once the very visible and relatively large connective tissues are carefully removed from the meats, there is less of a need for straining the meats than there is for straining fish (because of the bones) and that step can be skipped.

The addition of fish fumet in fish preparations can be replaced by an equivalent addition of chicken, veal, or duck glaze, which will enliven the taste of the paste and give it firmness while cooling to the correct eating temperature.

The pastes used for making mousselines and quenelles can be made with more or less cream, and/or with or without butter, depending on how much natural fat the meat contains.

The quenelles in the first recipe are made without butter, because there is enough fat in the chicken leg meat and because they need to be less fragile, being, as they are, shaped between two spoons by hand instead of molded. They also need be a little firmer if they are to be added as a garnish to a clear soup or stew.

In the duck and quail mousseline—a modernized version of the famous Boudin Blanc of Christmas on page 890—there is a good amount of both butter and cream, and in the mousseline made exclusively with the white meat of chicken on page 888, there is a noticeably large amount of each. Both meats are made of very long fibers containing relatively little viscous collagen and water, but the duck meat contains much more natural fat than does chicken. In the mousseline made only with white meat, the larger amount of butter is used to give "slip" to the texture of the long fibers and prevent a "powdery," dry feel on the tongue and palate.

A Chicken Quenelle Appetizer for a Celebration Dinner

FFR — 6 TO 8 SERVINGS

4 large chicken legs, skinned, boned, trimmed of all gristle and sinew, and cut into cubes, net weight 1 pound

2 large eggs

1½ teaspoons fine sea salt plus extra for the mushrooms

35 turns of the mill of Aromatic Pepper (page 57) plus extra for the mushrooms

⅛ teaspoon freshly grated nutmeg

2 ounces dried morels, rehydrated in very light chicken broth of your choice to cover

2 tablespoons unsalted butter

½ pound button mushrooms

½ pound dried chanterelle mushrooms

3 cups heavy cream

3 tablespoons chopped mixed fresh tarragon, chives, chervil, and parsley leaves

Fresh chervil leaves

This is a delicious small appetizer; if you prefer, you can add those quenelles mixed with tiny vegetables as a garnish to a clear soup, or use them to garnish chicken stew.

SUGGESTED WINE: *A very nice Meursault-Genevrières from Burgundy or a Beringer or Kistler Chardonnay turned buttery by a few years of aging*

Chill the chicken meat at 35°F for 2 hours. Place the cold meat in a food processor, add the eggs, salt, pepper, and nutmeg and process until smooth. Return to the refrigerator and chill for another hour.

Drain the morel rehydrating liquid into a bowl, straining it through a coffee filter to remove any sand. Wash the morels and pat them very dry. Heat 1 tablespoon of the butter in a nonstick skillet over medium-high heat and sauté the morels a few minutes; remove to a plate. Add half the remaining tablespoon butter to the pan, sauté the button mushrooms for a few minutes, salt and pepper them, and cover them a few minutes so they lose their water. Add their water to the morel-soaking liquid and mix the button mushrooms with the morels. Repeat the same operation with the chanterelles. Reduce the mixed mushroom juices to ¼ cup in a small saucepan over medium heat. Return the mixed mushrooms to the skillet, add 1 cup of the cream, and cook gently over medium-low heat until the cream has turned medium thick. Bring the mixture back to a light coating consistency by adding the reduced mushroom juices and season with salt and pepper. Keep warm.

Meanwhile, fill a sauteuse pan two thirds full with water and bring to a boil, then reduce the heat to a gentle simmer; do not salt yet.

Return the chicken puree to the processor. Process again, gradually adding 1½ cups of the heavy cream in a steady stream until the mixture is well homogenized. Remove the mousseline to a bowl; pour the remaining ½ cup of cream over the mixture and sprinkle the chopped herbs over it; fold in the herbs and cream.

Add 1 tablespoon salt to the simmering water. Depending on the size of your sauteuse, you may have to proceed in 2 or 3 successive poachings. Using two teaspoons dipped into the hot water, shape 36 small torpedo-shaped quenelles by passing the quenelle paste several times from one spoon to the other until the shape is regular. Ease each quenelle down into the simmering water. Maintain the simmer and cook, uncovered, until the quenelles come floating to the top of the water, then gently turn them over with a slotted spoon and poach them a few more minutes. The quenelles are done when their thicker middle is resilient to the touch (USDA 180°F).

Spoon an equal amount of the mushroom ragout into 6 large soup plates and add 6 well-drained quenelles to each plate. Decorate with the chervil and serve promptly.

Mousselines of Chicken in Lemon Oil and Citrus Dressing

This is another appetizer, small enough to be executed with the help of a small food processor such as an Oscar. Divide the work over two days.

SUGGESTED WINE: *A Vinho Verde from Portugal*

FFR—6 SERVINGS

1 lemon

1 lime

¼ cup plus extra for blending unsaturated oil of your choice

2 tablespoons mashed ripe mango pulp

2 tablespoons mashed ripe pineapple pulp

6 baby carrots, peeled

6 baby purple-top turnips, peeled and cut into halves

1 small bright zucchini, barely 1 inch in diameter, ends removed

1 small yellow zucchini, barely 1 inch in diameter, ends removed

Salt

½ small cauliflower, cut into tiny florets

1 large stem broccoli, cut into tiny florets

1 large red bell pepper, peeled, seeded, and cut into lozenges

½ pound net weight white chicken meat

3 large eggs

½ cup unsalted butter

17 turns of the mill of Aromatic Pepper (page 57)

Large pinch of cayenne pepper

⅛ teaspoon freshly grated nutmeg

2 cups heavy cream

1 head Lola Rossa lettuce (red-tipped curly lettuce)

2 scallions, sliced paper thin on a slant

Day One

Grate the rinds of the lemon and lime finely. Heat the oil to 350°F; off the heat add the rinds, let cool at room temperature, and store, covered, in a sanitized jar. Squeeze both juices, mix half of each with the mango and pineapple pulps, and store in two other jars.

Cut the carrots on a slant into thin slices. Cut the turnips halves thinly into half moons. Cut both zucchini into halves and recut into thin half moons.

Bring a large pot of water to a boil and add 1½ teaspoons of salt per quart. Place the carrots, turnips, and zucchini in a large colander, immerse for 30 seconds in the boiling water, and immediately rinse under cold water. Pat dry with paper towels. Repeat the same blanching and shocking in cold water procedure for the cauliflower and broccoli florets. Finally, immerse the pepper lozenges in the boiling water for only 15 seconds before rinsing in cold water. Pat all the vegetables dry one last time. Store the vegetables and bell pepper in 2 different bowls to prevent the latter from staining the white pulps of the first.

Day Two
Cube the chicken meat and process it to a fine puree with the eggs in a food processor. Cool over ice, covered, for 2 hours.

Preheat the oven to 325°F. In a small bowl, cream the butter and flavor with the pepper, cayenne pepper, and nutmeg. Turn the well-creamed butter into the food processor and gradually pulse in the chilled puree of chicken until completely homogeneous. Continue processing continuously for another minute, then, still processing, gradually blend in the cream in a continuous stream until well blended.

Lightly oil eight 2-ounce timbales. Fill to the top with the mousseline and set in an ovenproof baking dish. Bring a potful of water to a boil. Lightly oil a sheet of parchment paper and place over the mousselines, cutting one of the corners of the paper. Pull the middle rack of the oven out, place the dish full of mousselines on it and pour the water through the cut corner of the paper into the bottom of the baking dish so the timbales are three quarters immersed. Gently push the rack back into the oven and bake until the parchment paper can be lifted from the mousselines without sticking to them anymore. Remove from the oven and let cool a few minutes in the hot water bath, then remove from the water and cool on the counter to lukewarm.

Meanwhile, prepare the dressing. Add the fruit puree and juice mixture, salt, and pepper to a blender; strain 1 to 2 tablespoons of the prepared citrus oil into the mixture, process, and taste. The taste of the oil should be just a touch too perceptible and slightly bitter. Now add enough plain oil so that the bitterness disappears and only the citrus flavor reaches the taste buds. Strain through a very fine strainer to discard any solids. Mix the dressing with the vegetables. Adjust the salt and pepper.

Arrange one or two leaves of lettuce as a doily at the center of each of six or eight 10-inch plates, leaving 1½ inches of white porcelain passing all around. Unmold one mousseline on the lettuce and arrange equal parts of the vegetable mixture around each mousseline. Drop some of the scallion slivers randomly over the plate and dribble tiny droplets of the remaining citrus oil on top of each mousseline and on the white of the plate; serve immediately.

Christmas Boudin in Mexican Flavors

FFR—6 SERVINGS

One 6-pound white Pekin duck (not Muscovy or Moulard)

4 quail

I large rib veal chop

6 tablespoons pure olive oil

5 cups Primary Veal Stock (page 219) or duck stock made with the duck

2 quail carcasses

6 cloves garlic, cut into brunoise

4 large red bell peppers, seeded and cut into strips

Salt

Pepper from the mill

I dried pasilla chile or less, to your personal taste, chopped to powder

3 pounds red onions, quartered and slivered

Vinegar of your choice to taste

6 large eggs

⅔ cup plus 2 tablespoons unsalted butter

⅓ teaspoon freshly grated nutmeg

¼ teaspoon ground cumin

2 cups heavy cream

I box salted sausage casings

Chopped cilantro leaves as needed

Cilantro leaves

Day One

Bone all the meats: Lift the breast meat from the duck and quails as well as the eye of the rib chop; set aside for use in the mousseline. Set aside the neck and wings of the duck and 2 quail carcasses to prepare the duck essence; if you need to prepare a duck stock, set aside the duck carcass and the other 2 quail carcasses.

Completely defat the veal chop bones and chop into small pieces. Chop up the duck wings and neck and quail carcasses with a cleaver. Heat 2 tablespoons of the olive oil in a large sauteuse; brown the bones over medium-high heat on all sides to deep golden. Tilt the pan, gathering the bones toward the pan handle; blot up any fat, using crumpled paper towels. Cover

Try this as a main course for Christmas Eve; it should be preceded by oysters and followed by a salad and a very light dessert. Do not use a large magret of Muscovy or Moulard duck; their deep red meat tastes better grilled or pan-roasted. Use the wings and neck of the duck, the quail bodies, and the completely defatted bony parts of the veal chop to prepare the small essence used here. If you have no veal stock, use the unbrowned carcass of the duck and those of two quail to prepare your own stock; see page 220 for directions. The sauce obtained from such a stock will be redder and lighter in color than the sauce proposed here.

The sausage casings can be ordered from any good butcher.

SUGGESTED WINE: *An older Chardonnay with quite a bit of butter and a definite hint of dry sherry in its aftertaste, or an older Rioja of your choice* the bones with 4 cups of stock and reduce to 1 generous cup of duck essence. Strain into a clean saucepan, using a conical strainer.

Reduce the remaining cup of stock to 3 tablespoons heavy meat glaze; over low heat, empty into a ramekin, cover, and refrigerate overnight.

Heat another 2 tablespoons of the olive oil in a small saucepan over medium heat, add the garlic brunoise, and sauté until beige to light golden. Remove the garlic to a paper towel, blot off any fat, and store overnight in a covered small ramekin.

Toss the bell pepper strips into the oil remaining in the same saucepan; season with salt and pepper, add the powdered pasilla, and cook, covered, over very low heat until the peppers have disintegrated into a fluid mush. Puree in a blender or food processor and strain through a conical strainer to discard all traces of skins. Blend as much of the pepper puree as you like into the prepared duck essence so the sauce remains fluid and pretty looking and tasting. Correct the salt and pepper, cool, and refrigerate overnight in a 2-cup bowl.

Heat the remaining 2 tablespoons of olive oil in a sauteuse pan and add the red onions and vinegar; toss over high heat until the onions start to color. Reduce the heat to medium-low and let the onions color slowly. Finally, cover the pan and let the onions cook to a delicious brown compote; correct the seasoning. Remove to a bowl, cool, and refrigerate overnight.

Day Two
Skin the breast fillets of all the birds. Remove the tendons visible in the small fillets and at the thickest part of the large fillets. Scraping along to disengage the bluish sheet of connective tissue (you will make a large cut in the large fillet in the process; this is normal). Remove all traces of connective tissue around the eye of the rib chop. Dice all the meat into ½-inch cubes. Refrigerate the meats 1 hour. Process the meat and the 6 eggs in a food processor to a fine puree (divide into 2 equal batches if your processor is small). Remove to a sanitized bowl and set over ice, covered with plastic wrap, for 2 more hours.

To finish the mousseline, mellow the meat glaze by immersing the ramekin into hot water until the glaze is viscous. Cream ⅔ cup of the butter in a small bowl with 1½ teaspoons salt, 35 turns of the pepper mill, the grated nutmeg, and cumin. Remove to the food processor and gradually pulse in the meat puree. When combined, process 30 seconds to completely homogenize as you let the meat glaze flow into the forcemeat. Gradually add two thirds of the heavy cream. Test the seasoning by thoroughly cooking a small nugget of the mousse in a tad of barely simmering water. Add more salt and pepper if needed, and the remainder of the cream.

Wash the sausage casings abundantly inside and out in cold water, letting the water run from the spigot into the casings. Pat them dry. Tie a knot at the end of three feet of casing. Stuff the mousseline into a pastry bag, pushing it way down to the very end of the nozzle. Bunch the casing over the nozzle so that the knot at the end of the skin is flush against its opening and the mousseline. Keep the bag on the table and push the forcemeat into the casing. Try to avoid forming air bubbles and make sure the skin is not taut and overfilled to prevent bursting while cooking. Tie a knot at the other end of the sausage skin and twist the long white sausage into as many 4-inch-long links as you can. Tie lightly between the links.

Bring a large pot of water to a boil. Set the whole length of boudin on the bottom of a stockpot or steamer; pour the boiling water gently over the boudin. Set the heat so the water barely simmers very gently and cook 6 to 7 minutes. Using a clean sewing needle, prick each sausage lightly in four different places to release pressure on the skins and continue poaching another 15 minutes or so. Let stand in the hot water until the water's temperature is 170°F. Remove from the water, cool in ice water, and keep refrigerated in a very cold refrigerator until ready to use.

When ready to serve, reheat the compote of onions, reheat the sauce, and adjust its seasoning. Gently peel the sausage skin from around the links. Slowly brown the links in the remaining 2 tablespoons of butter over medium heat to reheat them thoroughly to their centers so their internal temperature is 165°F.

Serve each link on a bed of onion compote and dot the whole plate generously with the copper-colored sauce. Sprinkle with chopped cilantro and dot the edges of the compote with a few more whole cilantro leaves. Pass the remainder of the sauce in a small sauce boat.

Variety Meats
Brains

Variety meats, also known by the much less elegant name of offal, still aren't very popular in the United States. At least now one has an acceptable reason for not eating them—variety meats are very high in cholesterol. Any recipe for variety meats will a priori be a full-fat recipe.

I have elected not to prepare brains anymore, for many reasons, one being their lamentable state of disrepair when they are offered for sale; they in no way compare with the beautiful look of brains in European markets which should be avoided for health reasons. As a result brains cook very poorly and are not worth the time spent on them.

Heart

Heart still numbers among the least expensive meats. Veal hearts are tender enough to be cut into very thin slivers, which can be stir-fried in oil. Since a veal heart does not weigh more than one pound, you will need two to three hearts to serve six people. Lamb hearts are smaller, weighing a third of a pound, and five to six hearts are needed to prepare a dish for six. Beef heart is huge and not particularly good tasting, but it can be stuffed and braised for a very inexpensive dinner. I prefer not to use pig heart; if you do, you should braise it. See the braising procedure on page 820. Before cooking heart in any manner, remove all traces of blood vessels and of the powerful ligaments that make the organ function; they are tough and even long cooking will not soften them.

Sautéed Heart Scaloppine

FFR — 6 SERVINGS

2 veal hearts or 6 lamb hearts

2 tablespoons pure olive oil

1 tablespoon finely chopped shallots

3 tablespoons broth of your choice

1 pea-size drop semisolid meat extract

1½ teaspoons finely chopped garlic

2 tablespoons finely chopped fresh curly parsley leaves

Salt

Pepper from the mill

SUGGESTED WINE:
California Gamay Beaujolais or French Beaujolais-Villages

Trim the hearts of blood vessels and ligaments and cut into ⅛-inch-thick slivers.

Heat the oil in a heavy-bottomed skillet, add the heart slivers, and stir-fry over high heat 2 to 3 minutes. Remove to a platter and keep warm. Add the shallots to the pan and stir-fry 1 minute. Off the heat, add the broth, meat extract, garlic, and parsley. Return the meat to the pan, season with salt and pepper, and toss everything over medium heat one more minute. Serve piping hot.

Kidneys

Buy veal or lamb kidneys; the others are not worth the time of modern cooks who go to work daily. Take the time and precaution to smell the kidneys you buy and never ever buy those wrapped in plastic. The smell of uric acid betrays an old kidney that no proper cooking procedure can make good tasting. Purchase kidneys from a butcher who understands that they are perishable and delicate and takes proper care of them.

Lamb and veal kidneys have no unpleasant smell or aftertaste once cooked, provided they have been cleaned properly and the cooking technique is quick and does not overcook the fragile tissues. Although stewed lamb kidneys as prepared in England for beef or lamb and kidney pie are quite edible, they do not in any way compare with kidneys that have been grilled or quickly sautéed.

An excellent veal kidney is pink or very pale red rather than purplish. The average weight is ⅓ to ½ pound. One kidney can serve two people when sautéed in slivers or cubes and mixed with a garnish such as mushrooms, and four veal kidneys are sure to serve six people adequately.

An excellent lamb kidney is barely 2 inches long, 1½ inches wide, and pale pink.

To clean kidneys, remove all outer membranes and as much of the central fat pad as possible using tiny manicure scissors.

To grill veal and lamb kidneys, cut each veal kidney in half; grill lamb kidneys whole (see below). Clean carefully and sear over high heat 2 minutes on each side in clarified butter or oil. Skewer each kidney half lengthwise and sprinkle with fresh bread crumbs. Broil on each side for a maximum of 3 minutes. Serve with a butter sauce of your choice.

Lamb kidneys are at their peak of flavor when grilled or broiled. The easiest way to prepare them is to skewer them whole. Lamb kidneys look like huge beans; cut each lengthwise starting on the concave side but leave about ⅓ inch uncut on the convex side to serve as a hinge. Open the kidney as flat as you can, so it will be almost 3 inches wide. With your skewer, take a large butterfly-fashion stitch about ¼ inch wide at the center of each half. As the kidney cooks, the edges will curl up slightly, forming a small natural container in which the seasoning of your choice can be deposited just before serving.

Sautéing veal kidneys is, in my opinion, the best way to cook veal kidneys; it can also be used for lamb kidneys. Remove all traces of outer skin and inner fat. Cut the kidneys into ⅛-inch-thick slivers or ½-inch cubes. Sauté quickly in hot oil or fat until the meat turns grayish, at which point it is cooked enough. Drain into a colander and let drip completely. Discard the juices that have run out of the meat; they carry elements which could eventually give the dish an unwelcome strong taste.

A sauce can be made with stock and reduced wine, using the thickening method one desires, but one rule must be applied scrupulously: If the sauce must boil, *never add the kidneys to it before it has boiled.* Boiled kidneys are as tough as rubber. Should they boil by accident, do not serve them as a sauté, but let them stew about 1 hour so that the long cooking softens the toughened tissues again. Serve them as stewed kidneys or use them for a kidney pie.

Skewered Lamb Kidneys

SUGGESTED WINE: *Light California Zinfandel or vin de pichet de Châteauneuf-du-Pape*

FFR—6 SERVINGS

¼ cup olive oil

12 large mushroom caps

12 lamb kidneys, trimmed of membranes and ready to cook

Salt

Pepper from the mill

1 cup fresh bread crumbs

¼ teaspoon each chopped fresh oregano, basil, rosemary, mint, and lavender flowers

Heat the oil in a skillet over high heat. Sauté the mushrooms until they have lost all their moisture and it has evaporated. Cut the kidneys open but leave the halves attached. Alternating mushrooms and kidneys, thread 2 mushrooms and 2 kidneys on each of six skewers. Brush with a third of the oil in the skillet, season with salt and pepper, and sprinkle with the bread crumbs. Broil 4 inches away from the broiling element, 3 minutes on each side, starting with the cut side. Add the herbs to the oil still in the skillet and reheat well. When the kidneys are ready, dribble the oil over them and serve immediately.

Veal Kidneys in Mustard Sauce

FFR—6 SERVINGS

2 tablespoons unsaturated oil of your choice

Salt

Pepper from the mill

4 veal kidneys, trimmed of membranes and fat and very thinly sliced

2 ounces Cognac, Armagnac, or bourbon of your choice

⅔ cup best stock of your choice

1½ teaspoons hot honey mustard

1½ teaspoons Düsseldorf mustard

3 tablespoons unsalted butter, at room temperature

2 tablespoons chopped fresh Italian parsley leaves

6 slices French bread, crusts removed and toasted

Both regular and hot sweet mustard from Germany can be found on all supermarket mustard shelves.

SUGGESTED WINE:
California meritage *Blanc of Sémillon and Sauvignon Blanc*

Heat the oil in a large sauteuse pan. Salt and pepper the kidneys lightly. Raise the heat to high under the pan, add the kidneys and stir-fry 1 minute, until they turn gray. Flambé with 1 ounce of the Cognac (see page 720 for more detailed instructions on this technique), let the flames die out, immediately turn into a colander, and let drip thoroughly.

Add the stock and remaining liqueur to the pan and reduce to ½ cup over medium-high heat. Turn the heat all the way down. Off the heat, add the mustards, blend well, and return to the heat. Do not boil. Turn the heat down to low. Return the kidneys to the pan and, while shaking the pan back and forth over the heat, fluff in the raw butter tablespoon by tablespoon. Correct the seasoning and add parsley. Serve on toasts.

Veal Kidney and Mushroom Pie

This is a good recipe to use veal trimmings left from the boning of full loins and not used to prepare a sauce.

SUGGESTED BEVERAGE: A good Irish stout or British ale

FFR—8 SERVINGS

½ cup dried boleti mushrooms

⅔ cup water

½ recipe pastry of your choice (see index)

Unsaturated oil of your choice as needed

I pound fresh brown mushrooms, quartered

Salt

Pepper from the mill

2 veal kidneys, trimmed of membranes and fat and cut into ½-inch cubes

2 cups veal cubes from trimmings or from shoulder

I tablespoon unbleached all-purpose flour

I ½ to 2 cups warm Secondary Stock (page 220) or other stock of your choice

I clove garlic, chopped

I shallot, chopped

Small bouquet garni of 5 parsley stems, ½ Turkish bay leaf, and I sprig dried thyme

2 tablespoons skim milk

Soak the dried mushrooms in the cup of water overnight; they will absorb all the water. Prepare the chosen pastry and keep it well chilled. Heat ½ tablespoon of the oil over medium-high heat in a nonstick skillet or sauteuse pan and sauté the fresh mushrooms and cook until all their moisture has evaporated. Season with salt and pepper and remove to a plate. Do not clean the pan.

Add a little more oil to the pan, heat over high heat, and add the kidneys. Sauté for 1 minute, season with salt and pepper, and drain into a colander; discard the drippings. Add another tablespoon of oil to the pan and brown the cubes of veal meat well over medium-high heat. Add the flour to the pan, toss to coat the pieces of meat, and cook until light brown. Off the heat, stir in the stock, then bring to a boil and add the garlic, shallot, and bouquet garni. Add the kidneys, veal cubes, and both types of mushrooms, cover, leaving the lid slightly askew, and simmer for 1 hour over medium-low heat. Defat as much as possible, turn into an 8-inch baking dish, and cool completely.

Preheat the oven to 375°F. Roll out the pastry to a thickness of ⅛ inch. Cut a 9-inch lid from the pastry and fit it over the stew. Cut a vent at the center of the pie. Brush with the milk and decorate if desired with pastry cutouts. Bake until golden, 25 to 30 minutes.

Calf's Liver and Other Livers

By far the best of all livers is that of the calf. The color of calf's liver should never be reddish or purplish but a deep light rose. The French call calf's liver with a light coloration *blond;* it has a fine flavor and is very tender if not overcooked. Cut it into ⅓-inch-thick slices, flour or coat with egg wash and anglaise (see page 626), and quickly panfry on both sides to serve medium rare.

Beef, lamb, and pork livers are also available but not really choice, especially after long stays in freezers. If price is an issue, it is better to have calf's liver once in a while than to prepare other, less appetizing livers.

Chicken livers and the livers of other poultry can be very pleasant and a goose or duck liver added to a pâté or terrine works wonders. Great care has to be taken to remove all traces of biliary ducts before using poultry livers since it is not unusual to find some left on by the butcher. When sautéing chicken livers, do not overbrown them or the outside will be overcooked while the centers remain, if not underdone, at least quite rare when they should be pink.

Poultry livers benefit from being flambéed with a little Cognac or brandy and seasoned with some port, Madeira, or sherry.

Fegato

FFR — 6 SERVINGS

1 pound calf's liver, outer membrane removed, cut into ⅓-inch-thick slices

Juice of 1 lemon

3 slices white bread, crusts removed

½ teaspoon fennel seeds

¼ cup chopped fresh Italian parsley leaves

¼ cup unbleached all-purpose flour

Salt

Pepper from the mill

1 recipe Anglaise (page 626)

3 tablespoons best available olive oil

2 small cloves garlic, slivered

6 slices lemon

An Italian approach to liver that is delicious.

SUGGESTED WINE:
Valtellina

Sprinkle the liver with the lemon juice. Let stand 30 minutes. Put the bread slices and fennel seeds in a food processor and blend well to break the seeds into tiny pieces. Mix the crumbs with the chopped parsley.

Pat the liver slices dry. Dredge in the flour, shake off any excess, and season with salt and pepper. Brush the liver slices with the anglaise and coat with the flavored bread-crumb mixture.

Heat the olive oil in a large skillet over medium-high heat. Sauté the garlic in olive oil until blond; remove the garlic using a slotted spoon and set aside. Brown the liver slices in the same oil until golden on both sides. Serve piping hot topped with the lemon slices and reserved garlic slivers.

Sautéed Chicken Livers

FFR — 6 SERVINGS

I cup heavy cream

2 tablespoons Sercial Madeira or fino sherry

2 large Oregon black truffles, scrubbed, unpeeled, and very finely diced

Salt

Pepper from the mill

I ½ tablespoons unsalted butter

I small yellow onion, very finely chopped

I ½ pounds chicken livers, trimmed of any membranes

I ounce Cognac or brandy of your choice

I recipe plain boiled rice (page 460)

Oregon black truffles are very affordable and to be found in specialty stores. If you cannot find them, use any other presautéed mushroom that you particularly like.

In a small saucepan, mix the cream, Madeira, and diced truffle (or sautéed mushrooms) together if used; add a pinch of salt and pepper and bring to a boil, then turn down to a simmer. Cook over medium-low heat until reduced to ½ cup. Correct the seasoning and keep warm.

Heat the butter in a large skillet over medium-low heat; add the onion and cook until softened without allowing the onion to take on any color. Raise the heat to high, add the livers, and sauté, tossing often, until seared on all sides. Sprinkle with salt and pepper, then turn the heat down to low. Heat the Cognac in a small pan. *Very carefully*, pour flambéing (see page 720 for more detailed instructions on this technique) over the livers, shaking the pan back and forth and keeping your face away from the flames. You are responsible for your own safety while flambéing the livers. Cover the pan and cook on low heat for another 4 minutes. Uncover the pan and add the prepared cream mixture. Toss over medium heat until the livers are well coated with the cream. Serve over the boiled rice.

True Foie Gras and Poultry Liver Mousses

Foie gras is the liver of duck and geese which have been forcefed (the English term "crammed" is also used) for a period of six weeks in order to create very fat livers which are a true and very addictive delicacy. I will not preach here for or against foie gras; some people will make a religion of never consuming it. That is fine and I respect their opinion, but any enthusiastic home cook and certainly any chef deserving her or his title should know how to cook a foie gras perfectly. It took me years to achieve this goal, for the simple reason that I never had enough capital to cook too many until the last fifteen years.

Ancient tomb paintings from Sakkara, on display at the Musée du Louvre in Paris, show geese being forcefed by Egyptians during the third millennium B.C. Today's forcefeeders are mostly women and those I have observed at work in France have always been gentle people, many chatting to the birds and stroking their back plumage. The birds, contrary to what one might imagine, always seem eager to receive their *patée* of corn kernels, pork fat, and salted water and push at one another for access to the feeder and to their water trough.

The Egyptians fed the birds figs, an experiment which has been duplicated in southwestern France in the last few years and yielded livers just as pretty as those fattened on corn. Foie gras is also produced in Alsace, Hungary, Bohemia, Israel, and, in recent years, New York State and California. Foie gras is "the real thing"; other poultry mousses, however good and well prepared, are only second rate if delicious replacements.

The Romans served foie gras warm and so did the French southwestern cooks, but it was a practice that remained rare in restaurants located in other regions until Chef Freddy Girardet resurrected the custom in the early 1970s. For more information on the history of "cramming" and on other ethnic ways with foie gras, consult Maguelonne Toussaint-Samat's *History of Food* listed in the bibliography, and in French *La Célébration du Foie Gras* by Marie Luce Cazamayou.

There is a difference between the foie gras obtained by fattening the livers of Moulard ducks and those obtained by fattening the livers of Muscovy ducks; like each and every cook you will have your preference and soon realize which of the two is superior for cold presentations and which for warm. You must buy one of each to experience the difference yourself.

To order foie gras from anywhere in the United States call D'Artagnan in Jersey City, New Jersey, (201) 792-0748 or (800) DAR-TAGN.

When buying foie gras, pay attention to these details:

- Is the color dark and irregular or an even deep ivory-rose?
- Are there traces of blood just below the surface of the liver?
- Are there greenish traces of bile around the area where the choleduct was excised?
- Winter foie gras will always be firmer than summer foie gras.

A dark foie gras may come from an animal that was not bled properly and any trace of bile will make the foie gras taste slightly bitter, which is an absolute no-no.

Foie gras is sold in several grades. Those you should buy are grade A prime, which must be absolutely perfect, and grade B, which is also good, but smaller and often shows a few undesirable traces of bile or blood. The weight of a duck liver varies between 1 and 1½ pounds. Expect prime to be somewhat more expensive than B and all foie gras to be generally pricey.

MODERN WARM FOIE GRAS

To cook foie gras that is to be presented warm, do not clean the inner parts of the foie gras, rather, remove only the visible parts of the large arteries and the few small outside fat pads from both lobes. Cut the foie gras into ⅓- to ½-inch-thick slices across the large lobes and on a slight slant to obtain slices approximately 3½ to 4 inches long. If you cook professionally, use the large lobes and keep the small ones to prepare parfaits (see page 900).

Over high heat preheat a nonstick pan with a very thick "dressed" (meaning lined with copper) bottom (a thin pan will not do). You can also use an old-fashioned cast-iron pan, but be careful not to preheat the pan too much for all liver contains a large amount of glycogen which is a form of sugar (polysaccharide) and which, like all sugars, can burn and make the liver look black. An overheated pan can also melt the fat very rapidly out of the liver. A most unpleasant combination of tastes can be communicated to the liver coming from the acrolein resulting from burned sugar and from strongly oxidated fats.

Add the foie gras to the pan and sear it well. As soon as it is brown, turn the heat down to medium for 1 or 2 more minutes. Turn the liver over and repeat on the other side; if you have difficulty obtaining good coloration, push on the liver with a large turner for a few seconds at a time, but be careful not to keep it on too long to avoid burning the surface. Salt and pepper the cooked foie gras on both sides.

Contrary to many modern chefs who serve foie gras with fish or shellfish or old-fashioned ones who slather a beefsteak or roast with it, I like my foie gras plainly and simply by itself. You can also try it with lemon juice, a vinaigrette of excellent vinegar and fresh herbs that is not finished with oil but some of the melted foie gras fat (one more reason not to burn that fat during the cooking). A favorite of mine is a tiny condiment made with a *coulis* of rhubarb and a sweet white dessert wine. Serve in small metal or porcelain pans called cassolettes which will keep the liver warm.

Classic Parfait de Foie Gras

FFR — 16 TO 20 SERVINGS

3 foie gras as perfect as possible or 8 to 10 small lobes, 3 to 3½ pounds total net weight

Sea salt

Aromatic Pepper (page 57) from the mill

Ground allspice

Tio Pepe sherry

Day One

Cut off a sliver about ⅛ inch thick all around the rims of each lobe of each liver and separate the lobes to allow the blood contained in the capillaries and other vessels to leach into the water. Soak the livers in cold water to cover salted with 1½ teaspoons salt per quart of water (please count) for 5 hours on the bottom shelf of the refrigerator. Bring back to room temperature and let stand until the livers are pliable, about 1 hour.

Place each liver on a clean kitchen towel. Working on its inner side, slit each lobe ⅓ inch deep in a straight line following the long side of the lobe and on both sides of the very visible artery. Grasp the artery in your other hand, pulling gently to create just a bit of tension on it. With your working hand and using the back of a paring knife blade, push the liver tissues to disengage the entire length of the artery (this will prevent you from cutting the artery). Gradually this will lead you from the artery to the capillaries; you must continue until you have removed all the capillaries. If on the way you locate a splotch of blood, moisten another clean towel with some of the salted water and blot it gently until it has been absorbed by the towel. The liver will look terrible because the tissues have been disturbed; it will seem like a quake has passed through them. Don't worry, as one side will remain smooth. Repeat what you have done with all the lobes of all the livers.

When all the lobes have been cleaned, weigh them carefully. Now weigh out the salt you will need, figuring one fifth of an ounce (5.5 to 6 grams) per pound. Mix the salt intimately with 35 turns of the pepper mill per pound and ⅛ teaspoon allspice per pound. Sprinkle this mixture evenly on both sides of each piece of foie gras.

Line the terrine with clear microwave-quality plastic. Sprinkle sherry on the bottom of the terrine and cover the bottom with the best-looking lobe arranged with its best side down and as flat and even as possible. Continue adding layers of livers, seasoning as you go and sprinkling each layer with sherry. Arrange the last layer in such a way that its smooth surface is on the outside. Fold the plastic tightly over the last layer of foie gras. Refrigerate overnight.

Day Two

Remove the terrine from the refrigerator 45 minutes before baking it. Preheat the oven to 300°F. Bring a kettle of water to a boil; turn the water off and let the kettle stand 5 minutes. Pour one inch of water into the baking dish. Add the terrine, then add more water from the kettle until it covers the sides of the terrine to just below the terrine rim. The water temperature will have gone down to 176° from 178°F. Bake the terrine. The temperature of the water bath will go down further; maintain it between 156° and 160°F

At first sight, this recipe will seem absolutely impossible, but I have taught it to as many nonprofessional as professional cooks who have had great success with it. Many thanks to Patricia Wells for indicating a very correct and usable range of initial water temperatures in Simply French *and to Gary Danko for using microwave quality plastic wrap instead of the stiff parchment paper.*

If you cook professionally and serve hot sautéed foie gras, use the large lobes for sautéing and the small lobes plus any other good looking odd piece to prepare this parfait.

This is for a terrine 12 to 13 inches long and 3½ to 4 inches wide. Also, you need an accurate scale.

SUGGESTED WINE: *The best Gewürztraminer you can find, or of course, a good or great Sauternes* until the inner temperature of the foie gras is between 100° and 110°F. With an instant thermometer, check the internal temperature rather than the clock or you are in danger of overcooking the liver; the baking time will vary from 23 to 30 minutes.

Most unfortunately, the slightest amount of excessive heat destroys foie gras and renders it pasty so that cooked to an internal temperature of 120° to 150°F, it will lose its delicate and silky texture and progressively more of its flavor. It is entirely up to you to make the decision as to whether you want to use the classic temperatures indicated here or not.

Remove the terrine from the water bath. Drain the liquid fat and juices from the terrine into a container and let it settle. Lift the top of the plastic wrap and return enough fat to the terrine to half cover the livers; fold the plastic wrap back over the livers. Cut a piece of thick cardboard to fit inside the opening of the terrine and wrap it entirely with aluminum foil; when the livers are just warm, set it over the livers and put weight on top of this cover (the weights can be a full bottle of wine or several unopened cans that would fit into the terrine). The fat will squeeze up and over the cover. Let cool completely at room temperature and refrigerate overnight. Remove the weights and let ripen for two to four days in a refrigerator at 35°F.

Serve in slices ⅓ inch thick on chilled plates with the unsweetened Pain Français on page 1052, nothing else. The foie gras will keep one week unopened. Consume quickly after opening.

A Newfangled Terrine of Pears and Foie Gras

FFR — 16 TO 20 SERVINGS

4 cups Primary Veal Stock (page 219)

¼ cup Tio Pepe sherry

12 large sweet but not quite ripe Bosc pears, unpeeled, stems removed

I tablespoon corn oil

I tablespoon hazelnut oil

Salt

Pepper from the mill

I recipe Classic Parfait de Foie Gras (page 900) or other foie gras

I large loaf any good not too sweet white bread

Bring the stock to a boil in a small saucepan and reduce to 1¼ cups. Add the Tio Pepe and cool completely.

Cut the pears into slices ¼ inch wide and as straight as possible from top to bottom of the pear. Do not yet remove their cores. Heat the oils together in a heavy skillet over medium heat; brown the pear slices on both sides so they

As I imagined it for a dinner at Beringer Vineyards in 1990. You will need a modern small, narrow loaf pan approximately 12 inches long and 2 inches wide. Please use the stock listed; others will not work because of their lack of viscosity and proper taste. The stock need not be clarified. Prepare this terrine in the morning and serve it at dinner, keeping it deep chilled in between.

SUGGESTED WINE: *A Blanc de Blancs Champagne or a light Sauternes* are as uniformly golden as possible. Season with salt and pepper, then remove to crumpled paper towels which will absorb the coating oil. Recut the pears into as long as possible rectangular pieces that will fit into the loaf pan, discarding the cores.

Line the loaf pan with clear plastic wrap and embed it in ice. Have the flavored stock in one bowl, next to a bowl of ice and an empty bowl. Unmold the foie gras terrine and cut it into ¼-inch-thick slices. Recut those slices into pieces wide enough to fit into the loaf pan.

Now start building the new terrine: Throughout the building of the terrine you will pour successive small amounts of the stock into the empty bowl and stir each over the ice until viscous. Brush the bottom and sides of the loaf pan with thickened stock. Line the pan bottom with slices of foie gras touching one another but not overlapping. Brush the foie gras with the viscous stock; now arrange a tightly packed layer of pears and brush with stock. Continue alternating layers of pears and foie gras until the loaf pan has been filled. Push down gently as you go along with the top of your hand protected by a piece of clear plastic. You should preferably end with a layer of foie gras. When the terrine is full, dribble more viscous stock wherever you see an opening to be filled (although there should really be none). Wrap the loaf pan tightly with plastic wrap and refrigerate until solid, at least 4 hours.

To serve, use a thin, very sharp knife dipped in hot water and dried. Cut into ¼-inch-thick slices, and serve these slices on toasted slices of white bread cut to the same size as the slices of the terrine. This must be served within 24 hours of its making.

Mousse of Blond Livers and Figs

FFR— 16 TO 20 SERVINGS

6 midget dried Black Mission figs or 3 regular dried figs of your choice

2 to 3 tablespoons California angelica or oloroso sherry as needed

1¼ pounds light-colored duck or fowl livers

2 tablespoons plus ½ cup duck or goose confit fat (page 779), at room temperature

1 small yellow onion, very finely mashed

1 large shallot, very finely mashed

Salt

Aromatic Pepper (page 57) from the mill

Pinch of ground allspice

1½ ounces Gentleman Jack or bourbon of your choice

6 tablespoons unsalted butter

⅓ cup heavy cream

2 tablespoons crème fraîche

Large pinch of grated orange rind

To be served in a small crock to spread on crackers or toasts. Any good butcher can order the pale-colored livers for you. Do not be offended by the duck fat, it is less saturated than butter. Prepare today, serve no later than tomorrow, and discard any part left over the day after tomorrow.

SUGGESTED WINE: *Pineau des Charentes*

Cut the dried figs into halves and scoop out the seeds. Dice the skins into ⅛-inch pieces, macerate overnight in enough sherry to barely cover.

Clean all traces of membranes from the livers. Heat the 2 tablespoons of duck confit fat in a skillet over medium-high heat, then add the onion and sauté 2 minutes. Add the shallot and sauté another 2 minutes. Add the livers and sear on both sides until gray outside but still rare at the center. Season with salt, pepper, and allspice.

Heat the bourbon in a small saucepan over low heat with a long match, carefully light and *very carefully* pour flambéing into the skillet (see page 720 for more detailed instructions on this technique). Shake the skillet back and forth until the flames die, keeping your face away from the flames. You are responsible for your own safety while doing this. Remove the livers to a large flat dish where they can cool rapidly. When cold, place in a blender and puree. Strain through a fine conical strainer. Cool the puree over ice.

Cream the butter with a pinch more salt and pepper. Gradually cream in the remaining ⅓ cup of confit fat. Add salt to taste. In another bowl, whip the two creams together until they barely start mounding. Taste the liver puree, the butter-fat mixture, and the cream mixture; they should all have the same level of salt, pepper, and allspice; correct now if such is not the case.

On creaming speed, gradually add the liver puree to the butter-fat mixture. Remove the bowl from the mixture. Pour the cream over the puree. Drain the pieces of figs, pat them dry, and sprinkle them and the orange rind over the cream. *By hand,* fold the liver puree, cream, and figs into one another until homogeneous. Do not overfold or the mixture will separate. Pack into a small crock and chill. When chilled, melt the remaining duck fat and spoon over the surface of the mousse. Serve deep chilled within 24 hours.

Sweetbreads

Wild guesses are always being made as to what sweetbreads really are. Every organ is cited, except the right one, which is the thymus gland of lambs, calves, and less than one year old steer. In animals older than a year the gland shrinks and disappears. This is why one never finds beef sweetbreads.

Sweetbreads are a true delicacy as well as a good source of protein, but, alas, also the richest source of cholesterol. To boot, they are so perishable that they should be prepared without fail on the day they are purchased. Veal sweetbreads are available frozen in boxes of five separate pounds which are of great quality and must be defrosted under running water. All sweetbreads, fresh or defrosted, must soak in cold water for at least 4 hours, and the water must be changed as soon as it has colored pink.

Sweetbreads have two parts, a thinner long lobe called the throat sweetbread and a large fat, oval-shaped one called the heart sweetbread. Their long soaking in water is an absolute must and will result in your bringing to the table absolutely white sweetbreads inside and outside, which is very important for the appetizing value of your dish.

After being soaked, sweetbreads must be blanched, starting in cold water and letting the temperature of the water increase very gradually. The heat makes the inside tissues swell, and any burst of heat will cause the outside conjunctive membrane to rupture. Once the boiling point has been reached, let the sweetbreads poach 2 minutes if they are to be truly braised or simply cooked in stock, and for 5 minutes if they are to be sliced and sautéed in butter (breaded or not) or grilled.

Drain the sweetbreads and rinse them thoroughly under cold running water. With a paring knife, remove all the sinews and blood vessels. Do not remove the conjunctive membrane that encases the tissues, which by now looks like a bloated balloon; if you do, the sweetbreads will fall apart into small pieces before you finish cooking them, which they should not. That membrane will be removed when the sweetbreads are fully cooked, for it is full of collagen, which helps the gravy thicken when it turns to gelatin. Also, the membrane becomes so very thin after cooking that it becomes imperceptible.

Place the sweetbreads between two flat cake serving trays, set a 4-pound weight over the top plate, and refrigerate for 4 hours. The sweetbreads will lose any blood they still contain and flatten to an even thickness of about ¾ inch. They will look better for presentation, and will also be easier to cook as the heat will penetrate them evenly.

If you wish to braise sweetbreads, you can do so by observing the technique outlined in the section on braised white meats on page 828. Nowadays, the sauces for braised sweetbreads consist exclusively of the reduced braising juices mixed with aromatics and a dab of enrichment; egg yolk sauces for sweetbreads must be completely disregarded as dangerous to one's survival! Topping cholesterol-laden meat with cholesterol-laden sauce is not exactly a dream of modern nutrition.

Sweetbreads in Light Tea Smoke

SUGGESTED WINE: *An older Fumé Blanc*

FFR — 6 SERVINGS

2 dozen baby artichokes, thoroughly cleaned

Salt

Juice of 1 lemon

1 tablespoon oolong tea leaves

2 tablespoons pure olive oil

4 pairs veal sweetbreads, blanched for 2 minutes in boiling water and trimmed of
thicker membranes

1 medium-size carrot, thickly sliced

1 large yellow onion, thickly sliced

Small bouquet garni of 5 parsley stems, 1 Turkish bay leaf, and 1 sprig fresh thyme

2 cups excellent Primary Veal Stock (page 219) or stock of your choice

1 ½ tablespoons chopped fresh chives

1 tablespoon Noisette Butter (page 32)

Pepper from the mill

Remove all the outer leaves from the artichokes until the hearts are no more than ⅔ inch thick. Trim their bottom ends and blanch for 3 minutes in boiling salted water to which the lemon juice has been added. Drain and rinse in cold water. Spread the tea leaves on the bottom of an old skillet (using an old skillet is recommended because it may warp). Stretch a large sheet of aluminum foil over it, tuck it around the edges of the pan, and punch small holes in the foil. Set the artichokes on the foil, cover the skillet with another large sheet of foil arranged like a big bubble around the artichokes, and seal well all around the pan. Heat the skillet on medium-high heat until the tea starts to smoke. Turn the heat off and let the artichokes smoke, 3 to 4 minutes. Remove from the pan.

Heat the olive oil in a braising pot over medium heat and lightly brown the sweetbreads in it. Remove to a plate. Add the carrot, onion, and bouquet garni, toss in the oil, and return the sweetbreads to the bed of vegetables. Add just enough stock to half cover the sweetbreads and cover the pot with a sheet of parchment paper, a sheet of aluminum foil forming an inverted lid, and the pot lid. Bring to a boil on top of the stove, then bake 30 minutes. Uncover, add the artichokes, cover again, and finish cooking, another 15 minutes; the sweetbreads are done when a skewer inserted at their center comes out freely. Remove all the membranes from the sweetbreads. Strain the stock through a conical strainer and reduce it to 1 small cup over medium-high heat. Toss the sweetbread pieces and artichokes together into the stock adding the chives and noisette butter. Correct the seasoning and serve rapidly.

Simply Grilled Sweetbreads

FFR — 6 SERVINGS

2 large zucchini, sliced

Salt

6 pairs sweetbreads, blanched and trimmed of thicker membranes

4 cups salted water or broth of your choice

Pepper from the mill

Olive oil

3 lemons, each cut into 6 wedges

Chopped fresh Italian parsley leaves

SUGGESTED WINE: *An older buttery Chardonnay*

Start a nice fire in your barbecue.

Set the zucchini slices in a colander and salt generously. Let them sit until they lose most of their juices. Pat dry and set aside. Bring a pot of water to a boil and turn down to a simmer.

Add the sweetbreads to the simmering water and cook 15 minutes. Let cool completely in the water and slice into ⅓-inch-thick slices. Salt and pepper the slices, then brush them lightly with olive oil. Also brush the slices of zucchini with olive oil. When the coals burn deep red, oil a special vegetable grilling griddle lightly and set it on the barbecue rack. Grill the sweetbread and zucchini slices a few minutes on each side until tender and deep golden. Serve on a large platter with the lemon wedges and sprinkled with the parsley.

Tongue

The availability of fresh tongue seems to have increased over the years. Yet another unfortunate source of fat and cholesterol, tongue is one of the most delicious and tender meats existing.

Although veal tongue is delicious braised as suggested for the sweetbread recipe on page 906, it is wiser to simmer it in a nice court bouillon containing a very large amount of fresh herbs. Do not attempt to remove the strong glove of skin that covers the uncooked tongue; it will come off by itself when the tongue has been fully cooked. Rest at ease as to the cleanliness of the tongue; it is sold to you sanitized and properly scrubbed.

The best sauce for a poached tongue is a vinaigrette-style dressing chockful of green herbs.

Tongue in Green Sauce

FFR — 6 SERVINGS

4 veal or 12 lamb tongues

Salt

Pepper from the mill

Large bouquet garni of 5 parsley stems, 1 Turkish bay leaf, and 1 sprig fresh thyme

2 yellow onions, peeled and each stuck with 2 cloves

7 tablespoons cider vinegar

1 heaping tablespoon prepared mustard of your choice

⅔ to 1 cup grapeseed oil as needed

⅓ cup chopped mixed fresh curly parsley, chives, chervil, and tarragon leaves plus 1 heaping tablespoon chopped fresh summer savory leaves

2 medium-size heads frisée lettuce, cleaned, dried, and separated into leaves

Put the tongues in a large pot and cover generously with water. Bring to a boil, then reduce the heat to a simmer and cook 10 minutes, skimming well. Add salt, pepper, the bouquet garni, onions, and 4 tablespoons of the vinegar. Simmer until a skewer can penetrate the largest tongue and come out freely, about 1 hour. Remove 1 cup of the poaching liquid to a small saucepan and reduce to 3 tablespoons over medium heat. Mix with the remaining 3 tablespoons vinegar and the mustard. Gradually whisk in enough oil to make a dressing resembling a light mayonnaise. Salt and pepper well and, just before serving, add all the herbs.

Remove the skin from each tongue and cut veal tongues into ¼-inch-thick slices and lamb tongues in half lengthwise. Serve the tongue on the lettuce seasoned with the prepared dressing.

Tripe

Tripe is the general name given to the stomach lining of cows and other bovines. Depending on which part of the animal's stomach it comes from, it bears a different name. Honeycomb tripe, which comes from the largest part of the stomach, is easily recognizable by its thickness and its internal layers of tissues which closely resemble a honeycomb. This is the best known and, as it is the meatiest of all, the most desirable of all the kinds of tripe. Pocket tripe and smooth tripe, although their flavor does not differ from that of honeycomb, are thinner.

Tripe is sold already cleaned and blanched, but it is a good safety measure to blanch it again, starting the blanching in cold water. Tripe must cook such a very long time that your best bet may well be to put it in a low oven overnight.

Tripe can be boiled in a court bouillon until tender. The court bouillon

From the mining country of the northernmost part of France and a nineteenth-century Sunday noon dinner of the miner families after Mass. One cooked red beans and potatoes in the poaching liquid to make a soup for the evening meal.

SUGGESTED BEVERAGE:

The usual beverage was homemade frenette, *a low-alcohol beer made with ash tree leaves, which is nicely replaced by Flemish Lambic.*

may contain some wine, but preferably no vinegar, which tends to toughen the tripe, and you may add to it all the vegetables used in a regular stock. If you like vinegar in a tripe soup, boil it a few minutes and add it to the finished soup, ready to serve.

Once cooked, tripe can be cooled, cut into strips, and breaded for pan-frying, or brushed with melted butter and broiled. In either case, serve it with a highly seasoned sauce containing a lot of pepper or mustard. Any leftover tripe, with its own cooking broth, will make an excellent soup, such as the celebrated Philadelphia pepperpot. Strain the cooking broth to discard the vegetables and replace them with freshly diced vegetables such as potatoes, carrots, corn, and bell peppers. Some marjoram enhances the taste of a tripe soup considerably.

Fireman's Apron
TABLIERS DE SAPEURS

FFR — 6 SERVINGS

3 pounds honeycomb tripe

Bouquet garni of 5 parsley stems, I Turkish bay leaf, and I sprig fresh thyme

One 2-pound bag prepared soup vegetables, coarsely cut

Salt

2 teaspoons black peppercorns

Dijon mustard

Pepper from the mill

2 cups dry white wine such as Beaujolais Blanc or light Pouilly-Fuissé

Unsaturated oil of your choice for deep-frying

2 large eggs

2 teaspoons peanut or light olive oil

2 teaspoons water

Unbleached all-purpose flour as needed

2 cups fresh bread crumbs

Tartar sauce of your choice

A specialty of the canuts (silk workers) of the city of Lyon, this recipe is one of the glories of Lyon's ethnocuisine. It was kept alive and popularized by one of the greatest mères cuisinières of this city, Madame Lea, whose restaurant was known as Au Tunnel.

The name of this dish comes from the shape of the pieces of tripe, which resemble the fireproof aprons of firemen.

SUGGESTED WINE: *Let the Beaujolais red or white flow freely.*

Blanch the tripe for 20 minutes starting in cold water. Discard the water and rinse the meat very well. Return to the pot, and add water to cover, along with the bouquet garni, soup vegetables, salt to taste, and peppercorns. Bring to a boil, then turn down to a simmer and cook until the tripe is tender, 4 to 5 hours. Drain the tripe, reserving the liquid for a future soup.

Pat the tripe dry and cut into rectangular pieces 4 to 5 inches long and two thirds as wide. Mix mustard to taste with the wine and salt and pepper. Pour over the pieces of tripe and let marinate 3 hours or more in the refrigerator.

Preheat the oil to 375°F (see page 634). Mix the eggs, oil, and water together until well homogenized. Pat the tripe pieces dry again. Dredge in the flour, tapping off any excess. Dip into the eggs, then coat with the bread crumbs. Deep-fry until golden. Drain on paper towels and serve piping hot with tartar sauce.

Cured Meats

Early man probably smoked before he cured. Many old houses with large country chimneys still show the hooks on which hams, shoulders, sausages, and salami were hung. Hanging and smoking without first curing with salt, however, leaves the door open for too much spoiled meat, because smoking does not entirely stop water mobility in the muscle tissues.

This discovery by early man made salt an important commodity and was the reason why "salt roads" were already so well established in the most ancient civilizations. Taxes were never popular in France, but no tax was as hated as the infamous *gabelle*, or tax on salt; some historians have seen in the *gabelle* one of the causes of the great French Revolution of 1789. This tax had simply become a symbol of excessive taxation. My great grandmother, whose own great grandfather had been a mature man in 1789, still talked about the hated *gabelle* and how one had fought the *gabelou* so hard in her family, whose main source of business had been spices and mustards. The colloquial word *gabelou* (from *gabelle*) used to designate a border customs officer or inspector, is still in the vernacular and does not show signs of disappearing in spite of the European Community.

Curing at home is not easy, but a good little "duck" or "goose" ham cured and aged in a dry refrigerator that works well and does not sweat moisture can bring a nice sense of accomplishment in a new discipline. If you want to learn how to cure and smoke hams and sausages, you must learn from a professional source which will give you an in-depth education in this subject. Because of the many chemical transformations happening in cured meats, I would like you to refer to the one volume I recommend on this subject in the bibliography, which is dedicated entirely to making cooked and smoked sausages, and curing and smoking meats and fish. My reason for not addressing this subject in more depth is simple: I can teach you how to cook foods; another expert will be able to teach you how to cure and smoke the same foods.

Here is a recipe on which you can try your hand:

Duck Magret Ham

You will need a scale. To prepare such a magret or a series of several magrets together the ratio of kosher salt to be used is 4.25 percent of the total weight of each

I large magret from a Moulard duck

Kosher salt as needed

Large pinch of ground thyme

Large pinch of ground bay leaf

5 fennel seeds, crushed

5 coriander seeds, crushed

2 juniper berries, crushed

Set the magret in a small dish or if you have several magrets place them all *skin side down* in a stainless steel hotel pan or glass baking dish. Mix the salt and spices together and spread evenly all over the meaty part of the magret. Let cure 24 hours in a cool room; the salt will slowly dissolve on the meat.

To dry the magret, roll it up tightly to resemble a salami and tie into that shape at ⅓-inch intervals, with kitchen string. Wrap the magret in a single layer of cheesecloth and age in a very dry refrigerator for at least 4 weeks.

Serve the magret meat sliced very thin as you would good Italian prosciutto, accompanied by a fresh loaf of country bread, a nice pat of butter, and a small colorful vegetable salad.

piece of meat. Do not use the total weight of all the magrets because some are heavier than others and the heavier ones will need more salt than the lighter ones. Check the weight of each magret on the price tag, then weigh the amount of salt necessary for each magret of duck. If the amount of spices varies a bit from magret to magret, it matters less but the correct weight of salt is important.

SUGGESTED WINE: *Any dry white wine of your choice*

Fruit and
the Cook

THE FIRST TREAT A CHILD ALWAYS REMEMBERS IS A NICE, RIPE PIECE OF FRUIT, probably because of its bright coloring and, of course, because the color corresponds to a certain sweet-sour flavor very particular to each fruit, for which the little person will develop a special like or dislike.

The pollination of flowers that results in the development of fruit covers hundreds of pages in manuals of botany, and the little bit of information I am giving here comes from my old college book *On Anatomy and Physiology of Plants* (A. Obré, Hachette, 1947). Rejoice, as I shall leave all the true biology behind and concentrate only on the part that involves fruit, fruit sugars, and starches as they can be used by the cook for different desserts or fruit sauce preparations.

Fruit are the result (in certain genuses of plants) when the female ovules of a flower are fertilized (pollinated) by male pollen. There are, as usual in nature, some fruit which are not the result of fertilization, such as oranges and bananas. They carry the extraordinary name of parthenocarpic fruit, which simply means born without fertilization.

After pollination occurs, hormones are secreted that cause the ovary walls to thicken significantly. The cells divide and multiply rapidly inside the ovary walls, but all you have to do is look at any developing fruit to realize that however fast the cell multiplication may be, the maturation of the fruit is extremely slow. Cells at the time of fertilization measure between a hundredth of a millimeter and one millimeter; the size of any fruit will give you an idea of how much those cells have increased in size by the time maturation is completed. The water absorbed through the roots of the plant will travel upward to the fruit. Simple sugars will be the immediate products of photosynthesis. The structural framework of fruits is built from these sugars. The simple sugars glucose and fructose as well as the double sugar sucrose will accumulate in the cell sap. Organic acids will also form in the tissues in the course of the normal metabolic processes, and when starch forms, it will be organized into small grains. The proportions of all these different constituents will change with the metabolic activity of the plant, with the biggest changes occurring during the ripening of the fruit.

At the same time and in the interest of self-defense, the fruit develops alkaloids and astringent compounds such as tannins which are supposed to keep humans, beasts, birds, and insects away. The tannins are what you taste when eating a grape and, having swallowed the juice, you are left with the grape skin on your tongue: It makes you pucker as the tannin it contains deposits on your large papillae and along the sides of your cheeks and tongue. You have eaten, I am sure, pears and apples that were not ripe enough and thrown them away with an exclamation of anything but delight.

I remember the days when as a child growing up, I used to choose a particularly pleasing looking fruit—apple, pear, or peach—and enjoy observing daily as it developed on the tree. From a tiny, hard, deep green fruit full of chlorophyll, it was weeks until the fruit was 2½ inches across, and the green disappeared gradually as the chlorophyll faded, letting the other characteristic yellow, orange, or red pigments synthesized by the fruit appear.

If you have lived in the country, you must have noticed that the fruit known as pomes, which are apples and pears, are usually picked when they are full size but still green. If they are not picked then, the ripening accelerates so quickly that they will do what you can see them do in untended orchards, namely start to rot and finally fall to the ground.

In the final stage of maturation, the starches in those fruits containing starch (apples, bananas) break down into sugars, and in fruit containing less starch (nectarines, peaches, plums, apricots) into sugar dissolved in a large amount of juice. This brings on a softening of the pulp and the almost total mellowing of astringency as the tannins disappear. All these changes are the result of many enzymatic reactions.

While still unripe, fruits contain pectic substances capable of jelling a liquid. From these pectic substances a large molecule called protopectin is synthesized which prevents the fruit juices themselves from gelatinizing. Two enzymes called pectinase and esterase are responsible for the synthetization of soluble pectin. It is the presence of pectin in ripe fruit which helps us make good jellies. When making jelly, however, it is essential not to use fruit that is beyond the peak of ripeness, for as soon as the fruit softens too much, the pectin turns into pectic acid, which prevents the fruit from jelling when cooked. (For more information on jellies, see page 966.)

At its peak of ripeness, a fruit is extremely susceptible to being stung by insects in search of sweet nourishment, and every little insect bite or sting will turn into one of those brown spots, to which molds will attach themselves, damaging pulp and skin and bringing on a rapid and final spoiling of the fruit.

You also must have noticed the smells that develop from ripening fruit. After the fruit is picked, the pulp continues to soften, the tannins disappear, and those strong lovely smells are the result of 100 to 200 different volatile substances combining together. Bananas are in the 200-some volatile substances category, which accounts for the high smell of the kitchen when a banana turns brown or when you bake banana bread.

You know what happens if a friend brings you a basket of fruit. The fruit ripens faster than you expect. This quick ripening is due to the fact that each piece of fruit, packed close as it is to another piece of fruit, produces ethylene, which softens the cellulose structure of each and every fruit. You can use this effect to your advantage, hastening the ripening of a piece of fruit by placing it in a brown bag with an already ripe piece of fruit.

You also know how disappointing a market-bought fruit can be in taste and texture, simply because it was picked too early to have received enough nutrients for its cells to fill with sweet juices. Not only do commercial fruit handlers keep the fruit in storage anywhere from weeks to months by reducing its oxygen supply from the normal 21 percent to a meager 2.5 to 5 percent or by increasing its supply of carbon dioxide, but when the fruit is ready to be released for sale, it is subjected to a supply of chemically produced ethylene which immediately results in overripening with rapid spoilage.

What to do? Enjoy those fruits that bear storage (apples and pears for long storage and citrus fruits for shorter storage) with a modicum of elegance during the winter months and enjoy the others only in season. Buy your fruit from farmers' markets. However small your garden may be, grow a tree or two; you can even grow small fruit-bearing trees in large buckets on balconies in suburban areas and, if you look at the terraces on some of New York City's skyscrapers, you will see fruit trees blooming in the spring and bearing a few beloved fruits later in the season. In cold climates, dwarf trees can be brought inside and continue growing in the warmth of a sunny room.

Also preserve fresh fruit, either by canning it or by making jams and preserves. For a list of the exact seasons for all fruit available in the United States, consult the charts published in *Cooking for All Seasons* by Jimmy Schmidt (Macmillan, 1991).

Types of Fruit and How to Handle Each

Pome is the name given to fruit in which the edible, fleshy part completely surrounds the seeds, which themselves are enclosed in cells called carpels.

TO RIPEN PEARS AND APPLES Pears and apples bought green can be enclosed in a brown bag containing a banana and will ripen in two days.

Apples (Malus communis)

Apples are indigenous to the area around the Caspian Sea and were already part of the human larder in the Stone Age. Archaeologists were able to deduce from their fossil remains that apples were, even then, dried for winter months' food, as they still are in New England and east of the Mississippi farms.

The Egyptians were already cultivating apples in the Fayum in the twelfth century B.C.; the Greeks may also have cultivated them and the Romans knew some thirty-seven varieties of this, the most popular fruit.

The gardens of temperate Europe from north to south and west to east offer thousands of varieties of apples, some of which carry the most romantic names such as White Astrakan, Beautiful Girl, Beautiful Yellow Flower, etc.

Apples arrived in New England with the first English settlers, and by 1649 land was considered a legitimate payment for apple trees. Apples were spread all through the United States by travelers and settlers who helped their propagation, the most famous of them being Jonathan Chapman, better known as Johnny Appleseed, who almost single-handedly covered the states of Ohio and Indiana with extensive apple orchards. Apples crossed the Mississippi rapidly and reached California in 1853 and the Yakima Valley of Washington State in 1875.

An apple a day, with its 10 percent content of carbohydrates, vitamins B and C, calcium, iron, potassium, phosphorous, and enough acids and pectin to be beneficial to the human body, can really keep the doctor away.

The best apple is picked by hand, gently detaching its stem from the tree branch to which it is attached, just as it is starting to release its perfume, which will increase as the fruit stands at room temperature. If you want a crisp apple with a maximum of flavor, store it in a cool room; the refrigerator is too cold and masks the perfume of the fruit.

EATING APPLES The best eating apples will crack and pop under the pressure of your front teeth, releasing a slightly sweet-sour juice which will run into your mouth as it spurts from millions of vacuoles filled to the brim with their thirst-quenching liquor. You will notice how tight the pulp is and how it resists and crunches under your bite.

If you have a tree producing eating apples and wish to keep the fruit for a while, dip their stems into melted hard wax; it will prevent excessive evaporation of the fruit moisture. Store these apples in a very cool room on shelves, nicely separated from one another to prevent contamination, should one go bad prematurely. Stored this way, fresh apples will still taste nice and crunchy at Christmas and, if you have New England Russets or any of its sister or cousin breeds, very close to spring. Preserved this way, apples were the one fruit that prevented millions of European children from becoming anemic during the two world wars.

The best eating apples are Fuji, Jonagold, Baldwin, Cortland, Winesap, Golden Delicious, and Red Delicious; which is the best depends entirely on your personal taste.

COOKING APPLES Of course you can always eat a cooking apple, but as you do so, you will find that it feels softer to the point of sometimes feeling mushy under the tooth compared to the eating varieties. Their cell walls being softer, these apples release their juices faster when baked or cooked into applesauce.

The best cooking apples are Rome Beauty, Baldwin, Gravenstein, McIntosh, Northern Spy, Cortland, and New England Russet.

PIE APPLES have some of the qualities of both eating and cooking apples, with a firmness that will keep the pieces of fruit whole all through the baking, but also allow it to mellow completely. This is important because any pie in which the apples are not completely cooked is short of perfection. Pie apples make better eating apples than the softer "cooking-only" apples.

The classic American pie apples are Greening, Pippin, and Granny Smith. Fuji, recently adopted from the Japanese production, makes the very best open-face tarts.

CIDER, BRANDY, AND VINEGAR APPLES Sweet or fermented, so-called hard cider can be made from crushing just about any apple, a blend of sweet fruit and more acid fruit being ideal. Apples used for the making of cider need not be the beauty queens of the apple world; if you go to England or Normandy and look at the making of the cider in both countries, you will understand what I mean. The apples are of all possible breeds, mounded into what anywhere else would be considered hills, and certainly not looking their most appetizing. But what comes out of the press is mighty good and will, after a few days, turn from sweet to hard cider.

Hard cider in its turn is distilled into applejack in the United States and in France into Calvados which undergoes a double distillation. If no spirits are wished, some of the cider is left to sour and will, after a few months, turn into cider vinegar, which must be carefully decanted to discard the lees at the bottom of the large bottles, called demijohns in the wine country.

Pears (Pyrus communis)

Pears originated in western Asia, probably also along the Caspian Sea. The ancients recorded a lot of interesting information about their pears, the propagation of which was originally done from wild seeds. From a maximum of forty varieties known in the ancient world, we have progressed to 5,000 now existing across the world. We see only very few of these delicious pears in the United States due to the large storage space they require. In the southern Napa Valley, one can, come late August, see some abandoned old orchards faithfully dropping hundreds of pounds of beautiful, ripe pears to the ground. No one pays attention to them, except a few fanatics of pear jam, among them the writer of this book (see page 983 for the "half sugar" jam recipe, which makes the delight of my breakfast almost year-round).

If you have a tree and pick pears, do so when they turn pale green. Stand them on a shelf and let them ripen to the degree you prefer. Keep them from insects and flies by putting them under muslin "food umbrellas" as are used usually to protect picnic foods. Insects like to sting pear skin, which smells so delightful, break it, and thus leave an entrance for bacteria which makes the fruit start rotting and prevents it from ever reaching peak flavor. Such damage happens fast. Any such pear, if reasonably ripe, can be used for sautéing or grilling as a vegetable (see page 434) or, if ripe enough, to make pear butter (page 946).

If you have a tree of French butter pears (the French Beurrée Hardy)—I have seen quite a few along my travels through the United States and, now that we can see those pears in markets, you will be able to identify them on the tree if you have one—do not hesitate to dip their stems in melted hard wax, store them on shelves in a cold room (leaving space between them) and you will have fresh butter pears at Christmas. The only disadvantage will be a few small lignous stones in the still juicy and fragrant pulp.

Commercially, pears are stored for months at 30° to 35°F and are brought to 65°F for twelve days before being offered for sale. The only way to ripen them well is to put them in a brown bag with a ripe banana. Watch them, though, they will then ripen very fast and lose their fragrance rapidly.

Anywhere you may be, market or farm, you can, besides looking at the color of the fruit, test its ripeness with your thumb; if it sinks slightly into the pulp around the bottom of the pear, the fruit will be ready for eating or using within a day. Any fruit that does not pass this test will be too hard to eat or cook.

FOR EATING   Use Comice, French butter pear, Bartlett green, Bartlett red, Bosc, and Anjou. Remember, though, that, if a pear does not drip juice when cut, it is not ready to eat.

FOR TARTS AND PIES   Use Bartlett or Anjou.

FOR POACHING OR COOKING   Use Bartlett green, Anjou, or Seckel. If a pear is too hard for poaching in syrup, peel and core it, and blanch it 1 minute or so in water acidulated with lemon juice, then bake it in a preheated 325°F oven in a buttered dish generously sprinkled with sugar or dribbled with honey. Keep adding small amounts of water to the dish as the baking progresses to prevent hard-cooked fruit that does not ever soften. The fruit, although never perfect, is at least edible, especially if you add to its syrup a dab of Grand Marnier or pear brandy.

POIRÉ AND PEAR BRANDY PEARS   A cider-type drink called poiré can be prepared from abundant, quickly ripening pears which one could never use fast enough otherwise. The pears are crushed exactly as apples are for cider and the juice is fermented. If pears are not abundant enough, they are mixed with apples and the resulting drink is called Maude. The Bartlett pear is the best for this production.

The pulp of "William Pear"—the American Bartlett-type pear—can be distilled to obtain the famous pear brandy called *eau de vie de poire* in France and *Birnengeist* in the German-speaking countries.

Drupes

Drupe is the name given to any fruit producing only one large seed surrounded by a hard protective pit, surrounded itself by an edible, colorful, and juicy part called the pericarp. The almonds in the pits of drupes should not be eaten, as many contain the poisonous amygdalin. In making jams, only two almonds per batch of four pounds of fruit may be used for faint flavoring.

If picked directly from the tree, drupes should be gathered at the peak of ripeness for a maximum of flavor, smell, and look. They are sold in such a state only on farmstands; all drupes for sale in supermarkets have undergone periods of storage of variable duration and never quite ripen to their peaks of flavor, sweetness, and fragrance. Those still in the supermarket fruit section in the late season of each respective fruit present an unpleasant (either hard or mushy and starchy) texture, which tastes flat. Such fruit will not cook well. It is wise to buy drupes in the following time windows:

- *All peaches and nectarines:* Last week in June to the first week in September; a number of varieties come in season one after the other. You can consider peaches and nectarines offered for sale after August 20 in the East and Midwest and September 10 in the West to be a loss of valuable cash.
- *Apricots:* Last week in June to third week in July. Those sold in August are from storage and are either hard or mushy.
- *Cherries:* All types are good from mid-June to mid-July.
- *Green and all shades of red or purple round plums:* July through September.
- *Italian-Alpine elongated purple prune plums:* Mid-August to October 10.
- *Damson black plums:* August through the first week of September.

TO RIPEN MOST DRUPES SO THAT THEY TASTE NICER AND SWEETER Enclose as many as you will need in one to two days in a brown bag together with a ripe banana or peach and check every 12 hours. This home-style ripening method works especially well for nectarines and peaches.

APRICOTS (PRUNUS ARMENIACA)

Often said to have originated in Armenia, the apricot really comes from China where it grew in the wild. It probably traveled to Armenia along the Silk Road, transported by Arab caravans; its name derives from the Arabic *al-birquq* and, according to legend, it was brought to Greece by Alexander the Great. It was not until the fifteenth century that the apricot was fully accepted by western European countries, but it then became such a coveted possession that to this day many European gardeners exchange pits with much enthusiasm. When in Europe, try the musk apricot of Spain and the ruby-cheeked Provençal Bergeron sold in all markets of France come the third week of June. The apricots we find in American markets come from California and may be cultivars of the English Blenheim.

All apricots can be eaten raw and all can be cooked or dried. The Blenheim, which does not soften too much, makes excellent tarts and excellent jams.

CHERRIES
Cherries are divided into:

SOUR CHERRIES (*Prunus cerasus*), also known as the morella or morello cherry. It is mostly cultivated in the Mediterranean Basin, where it already existed in ancient Egypt. The Romans had ten varieties of it and it is still cultivated and used by Italian cooks. Such black sour cherries (*amarene*) are sold in Italian grocery stores preserved in thick syrup in attractive white and blue jars. They are most delicious on double vanilla ice cream. They also can be found on all French open air markets under the name of *griottes* from mid- to end of July.

The red sour cherry from Michigan often called red morello (*cerise de Montmorency* in France) is derived from the black sour cherry and is the best pie cherry ever. It is now sold dried and can be used in many desserts such as *clafoutis*, sauces, or dressing for the salmonidae fish or other fish, see pages 588 and 675.

SWEET CHERRIES (*Prunus avium*) grow wild in the Caucasus but can still be found in many European forests. Since they are well hidden, the discovery of a large tree with its bright to dark red fruit is always a welcome surprise. Called *merises* in France and *visciole* in Italy, this wild fruit is gathered with enthusiasm, turned either into the best pies and jams or preserved in Maraschino or sweetened kirschwasser for an exquisite after-dinner delicacy.

There are many varieties of sweet cherries in the United States, but the choice seems to be reduced when it comes to supermarket availability. Farmstands are the best sources of good, juicy cherries, especially when it comes to the white sweet cherries such as the Queen Anne, with their tender, very juicy flesh. Full of calories and excellent to eat raw, sweet cherries make delicious jams if cut with a bit of lemon juice and rind.

PEACHES (PRUNUS PERSICA)
Peaches come originally from China where they grow in the wild, and were also one of the Silk Road travelers. Its arrival in ancient Persia is evoked in its Latin name. Alexander the Great brought peaches back to Greece from his Indian campaigns and from there they spread all over the Mediterranean. It is from Spain that they reached South America, then California.

YELLOW PEACHES There are two types of yellow peaches grown in the United States. Those with a pit adhering to the flesh are called clingstones and are said to be the best for pies, ice cream making, cooking in compotes, making sauces for duck, and all types of jams.

Those with a nonadhering pit, or freestones, should be reserved for poaching, canning, pickling, and brandying.

All peaches, whether cling- or freestone, are excellent for eating fresh for dessert, preferably peeled; and they are second only to apples in nutritional value.

The best peach to be grown in southern gardens is probably the Belle of Georgia; there is a large number of peach cultivars grown in all the states of the Union where the climate is favorable. Your local farmer will always be your best source of good peaches; ask him what the best use of his peaches is, beside eating raw.

WHITE PEACHES These are supremely delicious when eaten raw and peeled, and are to be found more abundantly in California. Cultivars that came originally from Japan and the Far East are usually freestones and good for poaching, sautéing in butter, and grilling (Babcocks especially).

Cultivars that originated in the Mediterranean, especially the French Frejus, make stunning jams and, although awkward to eat because of their most generous juiciness, they are probably the most extraordinary in taste and perfume. Even in France they have become somewhat difficult to find, because they do not fit within the norms of the agribusiness, but they can be found on farms in the warm states; do not miss tasting them.

In season, all peaches shipped outside of their warm growing regions will probably have to be given a final ripening in a brown bag using an already ripe peach to initiate the last stages of ripening. Checking the fruit every third hour is prudent.

PLUMS (PRUNUS)

All plums are of the genus *Prunus;* they come from all corners of the world in thousands of cultivars. They seem to favor strongly mountainous areas in the Orient, Europe, and both Americas. Plums must be picked as soon as their "bloom" (the white dust of natural yeasts visible in the dark skin) has developed completely and as soon as they are soft to the touch; it is important not to let them fall onto the ground where an attack by ants is immediate and forceful.

The small round yellow plums such as the yellow Mirabelle of eastern France, northern Switzerland, and Italy can occasionally be found in a local farm market but remain very rare in the United States. If to be found, they will make excellent open face tarts in the French manner, jams, and the best Germanic-style *Mirabellenkuchen*.

Oblong prune plums such as the Italian prune plum are the very best for pies and *clafoutis* because they juice just enough without flooding the pastry crust and pie plate. They can also be pickled and brandied.

Large round red plums such as the Santa Rosa and all its light or dark red-skinned derivatives are best sliced in modern salads; they can also be brandied, pickled, turned into plum butter, and sauces for duck and desserts such as rice pudding.

The medium-size green or yellowish green Reine Claude, originally from France and occasionally found in farms and farmers' markets, as well as the round or pointed green gage, originally from England, are probably the best eating plums when fully ripe. They also yield excellent jams and make delicious salads when tossed with diverse greens.

Berries, Grapes, Figs, and Melons

Berries, grapes, and figs are, as I was taught by my very first teacher, "false fruits," the true fruits being the seeds which are hidden in the single berry of a grape, for example, or the multiple berries of a raspberry. A raspberry is, in reality, made up of many little drupes clustered together; a strawberry is the swollen receptacle of the strawberry flower on which the seeds or achenes (the dried ovaries of the flower each containing a tiny seed) are attached.

BLUEBERRIES, HUCKLEBERRIES, AND BILBERRIES

Blueberries—the *bleuets* of French-speaking Canada—belong to the genus *Vaccinium*; there are nine species of blueberries growing wild in North America either as high bushes or low bushes. The blueberries we can buy in markets come from different states of the Union and all belong to the species *Vaccinium australe*, which itself is comprised of ten different varieties. All have many tiny seeds.

Huckleberries have only one central seed and belong to a cousin genus of the blueberry, *Gaylussacia*, of which four different varieties can be found. Huckleberries are related to the European bilberry (*Vaccinium myrtillus*), which is abundantly found in all the mountains of Great Britain, Europe, and Asia.

All are well known to hikers for their capacity to quench a thirst rapidly. They are excellent as breakfast or dessert fruit, alone or in combination with other red berries, and make excellent pies and jams. Huckleberries and bilberries combine well with red wine to make sauces for venison and game birds.

CRANBERRIES

The wild Arctic cranberries as found all over Alaska and in all the lower mountainous areas of the eastern United States and Canada as well as Scandinavia that were once covered by the Quaternary Ice Sheet are of the species *Vaccinium vitis-idaea* and known as lingonberries. They have nothing in common with our North American cultivated cranberries (*V. macrocar-*

pon). Both are good for the same types of preparations: pies, sauces, and, if macerated in vinegar for several months, excellent flavored vinegar.

GRAPES

The best known of all berries and the most cultivated the world over, grapes have relatively few culinary uses outside of their presence in a few desserts and as a garnish in some game and poultry dishes. Grapes can be:

- Eaten raw as a snack or after a meal (choose from one of the table grape varieties).
- Squeezed, its unripe berries yielding an acid juice used to make *verjus* (see page 41).
- Crushed, fermented, and pressed, its ripe berries used to make wines in California, Oregon, Washington, Idaho, Montana, Arizona, New Mexico, Colorado, Texas, Oklahoma, Arkansas, Missouri, Iowa, Illinois, Wisconsin, Michigan, Indiana, Ohio, Tennessee, Mississippi, Alabama, Florida, Georgia, South and North Carolina, Virginia, West Virginia, Pennsylvania, New Jersey, New York, Connecticut, Rhode Island, and Massachussets.
- Cooked with sugar to make jelly. The most flavorful are the Labrusca grapes for the American taste and the Vinifera grapes for a European taste.
- Made into a dense, brownish sugar that stains the teeth called grape sugar; it is made from the juice of grapes and is full of vitamins and iron.

KIWI

New Zealand's "Chinese gooseberry" (*Actinidia sinensis*) is now cultivated in the United States in relatively large quantities. Outside of giving a tremendous appearance to fruit salads, it makes a pleasant jam and is delightful consumed raw with sugar that has been mashed with grated lime rind. Kiwi, like pineapple, contains an enzyme that prevents gelatin from setting.

STRAWBERRIES (FRAGARIA)

Unless you grow your own strawberries, you have absolutely no idea what a truly delicious strawberry tastes like. The problem with strawberries is that taste has been sacrificed to the selection of strains that will not bruise, will pack well for the market, and will look red and delicious when in reality each berry is nothing more than a bundle of colored fibers with almost no taste whatsoever. The problem is compounded when those "selected" berries are picked too early and as a result never ever ripen; even food sections in newspapers have commented about this problem lately.

So start a strawberry patch and find a seed provider that sells ancient heirloom seeds. Once you succeed in producing a few plants from seed, those plants will multiply by sending out shoots called stolons which will become new plants, and you will be in strawberry business, producing enough fruit for fresh desserts, tarts, pies, ice cream, and jam.

If you live in European mountainous areas, during the summer months you can still find relatively large amounts of the true wild strawberry, *Fragaria vesca*. Let it melt on your tongue and you will have an idea of the true taste of strawberries that are sun-ripened.

RASPBERRIES (RUBUS IDAEUS)

Raspberries grow wild in most temperate forests of the Old World. They were brought to northern America in the early 1800s and immediately thrived, especially in mountainous areas. They are easy to propagate by separation of a root carrying a live stem, and grow very fast and produce abundantly; if you find a plant at the edge of a forest clearing, you can easily transplant it into your garden. If you do not cut it back regularly, it will spread wildly. A wild plant I transferred from the forest to my garden in New Hampshire covered one good quarter of its surface after four years of growth.

Raspberries are mostly red, but some of its cousins such as the cloudberry (*Rubus chamaemorus*) and the wonderful salmonberry (*R. spectabilis*) are respectively ivory-white to exactly salmon-orange, or bright ruby red in Alaska.

Raspberries are first and foremost for eating raw, crushing the berries on the palate to release all the wonderful flavors and perfume; they can also be pureed and strained to make refined dessert sauces or the wonderful *rod grod* of the Scandinavian countries or *rote Grütze* of northern Germany. They can be set on tart shells filled with luscious heavy sour cream or crème fraîche, and can be made into the most delicious jams or thick jellies.

RED, WHITE, AND BLACK CURRANTS; GOOSEBERRIES

Red currants (*Ribes rubrum*), white currants (*R. candidum*), and black currants (*R. nigrum*) are favorite berries of northeastern Europe as are gooseberries (*R. grossularia*). There are a few red and white currants to be found in several areas of the United States, mostly on farms or in farmers' markets.

The black currant is unfortunately not to be found in the United States because of its role as carrier of the white pine blister rust, which destroyed many trees earlier in this century.

All currants can be used to prepare a wonderful Germanic *Kuchen* using a shell of sweet yeast dough or *brioche* filled with either red currants, or red and white currants mixed, or gooseberries (in German respectively *Johannisbeeren* and *Stachelbeeren*). The name *Johannisbeeren* comes from Johann since the berries are usually ripe on June 24, name day of St. John or Johann in German, and the *Stachelbeeren* owe their name to the tiny needles that cover them and which soften during baking.

The French from Normandy have a special way of preparing mackerel using either a puree of or sautéed gooseberries, which give them their French name of *groseilles à maquereau*.

The juices of all currants, diluted with water and sweetened, makes a delightful summer drink; it also makes excellent Russian kissels or, as mentioned above, the Northern Germanic *Grütze*.

FIGS (FICUS CARICA AND F. SATIVA)

Ficus carica is the wild ancestor of *F. sativa*, the Mediterranean domesticated fig which grows on both sides of the Mediterranean Basin and all the way to the Canary Islands to the west and to Iran to the east. The fig is one of the three basic foods of ancient Rome, along with the grapevine and the olive. If you visit Rome, make a point of finding the plant of each of them which grows at the center of the ancient Roman Forum.

The Black Mission figs and many others were brought to California by the Spanish fathers in the late 1700s at the time of the creation of the missions. Besides the Black Mission figs we also have white figs (Kadota and Honey).

If you plant a tree in California, its size will double each and every year. Among the hundreds of varieties of figs existing, choose preferably a double crop tree which will give you a first crop in late June to mid-July and an even more abundant one in September to October. To have the most delicious fresh figs, let the fruit dry a week on the tree and each morning spread a sheet under the tree, shake it well, and collect the figs; if you let them fall, ants and squirrels will gather the figs, not you. Use only figs that are whole and have not been bitten into or gnawed at.

Figs can be used to prepare exquisite Italian appetizers; try rolling half a ripe fig in a small slice of prosciutto or wrapping the same in a thin small slice of pancetta and grilling this little gem a few minutes on each side over the barbecue. Figs are as interesting as they are delicious in modern salads, especially duck salad, in the making of pies, tarts, and jams, and they bake beautifully in the fortified wine of your choice. The resulting baked figs are exquisite on double vanilla or pistachio ice cream.

MELONS (CUCUMIS MELO)

It is not yet clear whether melons came to us from Asia or Africa. All archaeology can offer in the way of information is that there were melons in Egypt and that they were cultivated by the Romans from the first century A.D.

There is great confusion in the names of melons grown in America. What we call a cantaloupe really is a netted melon, so-called because of the reticulations visible on its rind; the true cantaloupe, on the contrary, has a smooth greenish yellow skin that is ridged, so that one tends to cut the portions following those ridges. The name cantaloupe probably reflects their origin, which is Italian, Cantalupo being the name of a suburb of Rome where the popes maintained a resort villa and where monks grew melons from the time of the Renaissance on.

Melons always make a very refreshing dessert. In Italy, portions of melon are commonly offered wrapped in the delicious prosciutto di Parma, while in

France the glorious Charentais melon is served by the half which is filled with either port or Muscat wine from the Languedoc (Frontignan).

The best American melons are the cantaloupe, the honeydew, the casaba, and the crenshaw, plus a number of varieties that come with names that vary depending on where you live. Besides being enjoyed raw, lightly salted or sprinkled with lemon and pepper, all juicy melons at peak of flavor make the very best jam; they can also be pickled.

Choosing a melon is, to say the least, difficult, for some melons develop their smell long before they are fully ripe. It is a good idea to tap the melon to see if it sounds hollow, which indicates ripeness, and to check for small fissures around the stem end. One fissure no longer than ½ inch generally indicates a perfectly ripe melon.

Melons bought at farmers' markets will always be far superior to the melons piled up on the stalls of supermarkets, which have been kept in storage for weeks on end.

Watermelons come in many shapes and dimensions with shocking pink or yellow flesh. They do not seem to ever suffer from storage; they taste good for a large part of the year with a peak of flavor and sweetness starting at midsummer. Those varieties of watermelon which have firmer flesh can be turned into jam and their rinds pickled.

Citrus Fruit (Citrus)

The sweet orange originated in China and India (*Citrus aurantium sinensis*) and is probably another traveler of the Silk Road, since its name is derived from the Arabic *narandj*. The Arabs are responsible for the propagation of the orange tree all around the Mediterranean Basin; the Romans did not plant orange trees before the first century A.D. The sweet orange has several Latin names; it can be called *C. aurantium dulcis* or *C. aurantium vulgaris*. To the sweet oranges also belong the mandarin (*C. reticulata* var. *nobilis*) and tangerine (*C. nobilis*).

The following sweet oranges are grown in the United States:

- Valencia, in Florida and California, is used for its juice.
- Navel, in California, is used as a dessert or snack food.
- Temple, in Florida, is a crossbreed between the sweet orange and the tangerine and is used as a dessert fruit.
- Satsuma, in Florida a yellow-skinned mandarin, is a dessert fruit and at the peak of ripeness its skin is especially delicious when used to flavor a custard.
- Tangelo, in Florida, with its deep orange skin, is a crossbreed between a white grapefruit and a tangerine and is used as a dessert fruit.

All these fruits blended with one another can make an exquisite marmalade.

Citrus aurantium bigardia or *amara* is the bitter orange of the Mediterranean which is used for the preparation of orange flower water and, in mixture with the sweet orange, to prepare the brown so-called vintage marmalades of Scotland and England.

Some authorities place the blood oranges among the bitter oranges, some do not. The most common blood orange in Spain is the Sanguinello, the juice of which is tomato red and so sour that it must be sweetened, and the Tarroco, which looks exactly like our sweet tangelo but is slightly sour-bitter. The blood orange of California is the Moro, the coloration of which is maroon-red, with a slightly bitter-sour taste. These characteristics make them an excellent fruit to introduce in a modern salad. See page 445.

KUMQUATS (CITRUS JAPONICA)

Kumquats also came from China, and are grown in abundance in Japan, Indochina, the island of Java, and the hills over the Central Plain of northern California.

Once seeded, they make a nice marmalade, but their best uses are in relishes and salad dressings and in garnishes for salads, where the somewhat gingery taste of their skins is absolutely wonderful. A cranberry-and-kumquat sauce to accompany the Thanksgiving turkey can be improvised and is absolutely delicious.

GRAPEFRUIT (CITRUS AURANTIUM VAR. GRANDIS, C. GRANDIS, C. DECUMANA, OR C. MAXIMA)

The grandfather grapefruit is the pummelo sometimes called pomelo, which was developed from the East Indian shaddock, taken to and cultivated in the West Indies by East Indian immigrants in the nineteenth century. Now we have yellow-fleshed grapefruit with yellow skins and pink- as well as ruby red-fleshed grapefruit with pink-cheeked skins.

Grapefruit is mostly consumed as a fresh fruit in the morning sprinkled with brown sugar and grilled; its juice is also consumed at breakfast and slivers from the fruit are used in fruit or green salads. The skin of the grapefruit is valuable candied as a confection and as a flavor giver to custards when infused in the milk used to make it.

LEMONS (CITRUS LIMON) AND LIMES (C. AURANTIFOLIA)

These have the highest content of ascorbic acid of any fruit. The paler the skin of a lemon is, the higher its content of acid. The Meyer lemon is probably a descendant of the sweet lemons of Egypt and is considerably less acidic than the supermarket-ubiquitous Eureka lemon, so much so that it can be eaten by the slice and is delicious and refreshing in salads.

The tiny limes known as Key limes (from the Florida Keys) make the best cream pies, for which a large number of different recipes exist (see the bibliography) or can be found on cans of condensed milk.

All lemons and limes are taste brighteners for fish and the white meat of chicken. Their rind is one of the most delightful flavoring agents for desserts and can also be candied. Besides, lemons and limes make a delicious marmalade alone or in combination with one another and/or grapefruit and/or any type of orange.

Avocado (Persea americana)

The avocado captures the imagination of children with its other common name, alligator pear. It is native to Central America and Mexico. Mexico produces tiny avocados resembling gherkins, while the California Haas avocado is rough-skinned and dark and the Florida avocado is large, smooth-skinned, and shiny. Avocados can be kept unpicked indefinitely on their birth trees, since they do not start to ripen until they are picked; once separated from their source of water they continue multiplying their cells and, five days later, they are full of flavor. They should never be refrigerated.

Avocado is used mostly in salads and the famous guacamole of Mexico; since it oxidates and browns rapidly, it must be generously sprinkled or mixed with lime juice.

Bananas (Musa paradisiaca and M. nana) and Plantains (M. paradisiaca)

Both are grown in all tropical countries and are by now a huge industry. Picked and shipped green, they ripen under strict temperature and humidity controls. Left to ripen on a counter a banana will overripen in a matter of a few days and is then used to best advantage to prepare cakes and quick breads. There are also red bananas, sweeter and more tender than the yellow ones, with a delicate vanilla flavor; they shine as stars in a tropical fruit salad.

Plantains are those long bananalike, almost always hard and green fruits found in better green grocery stores. When in their climate of birth or left at room temperature at great length in the warmer climate regions of the United States, they will eventually turn black and ripen fully. For recipes using such ripe plantains, consult the bibliography. I have been quite unsuccessful at ripening them to a black skin with a completely soft texture in the colder climate of the northeastern United States, where they turned a pale yellow at most after being kept for several weeks. At this point I have done what I was taught to do in Martinique and Guadalupe, I used them to prepare the best gratins (see page 434) and french fries (page 425).

Pineapple (Ananas comosus)

Pineapples originally came from South America where the best is the white-fleshed pineapple of the area of Belem in Brazil. White pineapples ripen better after being picked than do yellow-fleshed pineapples grown on most of the archipelagoes in the Pacific Ocean. Once picked and shipped far away, a Hawaiian pineapple, which is so delicious when picked ripe in Hawaii, has difficulty ripening and, more often than not, is served unripe and acidic to the great gastric distress of humans.

Pineapple is used in desserts, salads, and as a softener for tough meats; however, it should be remembered that its softening enzyme, bromelin, does not work to any depth but only on the surface of the meat. The same bromelin will prevent a gelatin dessert from setting unless you puree the pineapple, strain its juice, and boil it to kill the enzyme, or, more simply, use canned pineapple juice that has been sterilized. Pineapple is excellent served grilled with barbecued chicken.

Mango (Mangifera indica)

Mangoes are becoming more and more popular for their wonderful capacity to enhance a salad. You can also use them to prepare a wonderful nonfat salad dressing (see page 446) and ice creams and sorbets. Mangoes ripen very well by simply standing them at room temperature until soft; their color will turn from yellow to orange when they do so and their wonderful smell will remind you that they should be used rapidly.

A *warning*: If you prepare a dressing with a mango or a papaya which you intend to use on fish or shellfish, do not pour it over the fish, but rather pass it in a bowl for your guests to help themselves. Both fruits contain an enzyme (papain), which turns the outside layer of fish or shellfish to mush in a matter of two hours.

Papaya (Carica papaya)

Papaya is the best breakfast fruit, seasoned with lime juice, and can easily be ripened at home at room temperature. See immediately above for the warning about the enzyme papain, which, like the bromelin in pineapple, softens the outside of meats and can ruin the texture of fish and shellfish.

For information on other fruit, consult *Uncommon Fruits and Vegetables* by Elizabeth Schneider.

Dried Fruit

From times almost immemorial, at least since the Stone Age, fruit has been dried as storage food for use during the bad weather months of the year.

Drying a fruit, by whichever method used, removes enough of its moisture content so that no bacteria, molds, or yeasts can grow in it anymore and render it harmful for consumption. Nowadays we have two types of storage fruit: dried fruit, which retains 10 to 20 percent of its moisture content, and dehydrated fruit, which retains only 2.5 to 4 percent. Drying is done mostly by sunlight and dehydrating in dehydrators. Both techniques yield different types of storage fruit.

Apples are dried by evaporation as they lie sliced on slatted wooden trays while hot air passes through the fruit and evaporates its moisture; they can also be sun-dried. Apricots are blanched one minute, then cut into half and sun-dried. Figs and dates are left to dry partially on the tree, then picked and sun-dried on wooden slats. Grapes, cherries, nectarines, peaches, and prune plums are also sun-dried.

If you decide to dry your fruit yourself, you must live in the inner valleys of California or in the southwestern states where the climate is dry with very low or no air moisture. Most of the fruit sun-drying done in Europe takes place in the dry air of the Mediterranean Basin. If you live in a climate that is colder or humid and if you have access to a large amount of fresh fruit, you will be able to dehydrate your own fruit using one of our modern fruit and vegetable dehydrators. Since not one of these very useful machines is exactly identical to the other, you will have to follow the directions of the manufacturer; they are usually quite clear and explicit.

If, living in the inner valleys of California or one of the southwestern states, you are able to dry your own fruit relatively easily and fast in the fierce afternoon sun, there are a few precautions to take:

First, the fruit has to be cleaned properly, then sulfured by enclosing it in a sulfuring box in which you will burn sulfur so its fumes deposit on the fruit and prevent it from oxidating. Then the fruit must be dried in the sunshine, in wooden trays 2 inches deep, well covered with solidly anchored double layers of cheesecloth to prevent insects and dust from reaching it. Finally you can let the afternoon sun do its work and, when it is finished, you must pasteurize the fruit by baking it in your oven for a full 15 minutes at 175°F.

I did all that the first year I lived in California with the fruit of an apricot tree turned wild and of an even wilder Italian plum tree, which had escaped the destruction of the bulldozers during the building of the condominium in which I then lived. I was thrilled. I picked baskets of each fruit, brought them back to my postage stamp-size kitchen, and went through all the ceremonials listed above, nearly suffocating on the sulfuring because, at the time, I did not know that I was allergic to sulfur. Never mind; in a few days I gathered the proudest two pounds each of apricots and prunes that ever reached my cupboard. They never proved their keeping quality, as we ate them all like candy.

Most dried fruit found in regular markets—apricots, peaches, nectarines, prunes, light raisins, white figs, and pears—are treated with sulfur dioxide to preserve and enhance their true colors; only dark raisins and some soft pitted prunes are not and sometimes (not always) currants. You may want to pay attention to this fact if members of your family are allergic to any derivative of sulfur. Read everything printed on all boxes of dried fruit carefully to prevent extreme discomfort and sometimes dangerous reactions to sulfites. If you operate a restaurant or food manufacturing business, pay particular attention to this problem; it is easier to adapt a recipe to commercially available nonsulfured dried fruit than it is to deal with a lawsuit brought by an allergic customer.

The dried fruit found in health food stores are of course free of sulfur, but their color is forever altered by oxidation. Although their taste is somewhat different from the sulfur-treated fruit, they are very good when rehydrated and cooked into compotes; it is a good idea to mix all dried fruit together for a more diversified taste. A very thick compote of rehydrated unsulfured dried fruit makes a wonderful filling for a light biscuit cake such as the *génoise* on page 1133, of which children are usually very fond.

The best way to rehydrate dried fruit, when no allergy to sulfur has to be considered, is to pour boiling water over the fruit to just cover it and to gently simmer it for no more than 20 minutes. Let the fruit cool in its juice and keep it overnight in the refrigerator. Notice that no sugar is added to the fruit before stewing it because sugar has a hardening effect on the fruit. To sweeten dried fruit, remove some of the cooking water to a small saucepan, adding just enough sugar to sweeten the fruit, then heat gently to dissolve the sugar and let the syrup cool before blending it back into the bowl of fruit. Honey can replace sugar, but in that case, the mixture of fruit water and honey must be brought to a full boil, then turned down to a simmer and cooked a full 20 minutes to destroy any bacteria or botulin toxin which may be present in the honey. The honey syrup must be cooled completely before being blended back into the dish of fruit.

Another way to cope with the presence of sulfur is to soak the fruit in two successive baths of water, which are discarded before finally stewing the fruit in a very small amount of fresh water. This method is useful in relieving digestive distress in people not allergic to sulfur, but it doesn't help those who are sensitive and allergic to it. Also, the texture of the fruit after this treatment is that of a thick compote in which the fruit has lost its original shape.

Dried fruit are often macerated in a small amount of warm water or a liqueur or brandy before being used in a dessert or a cake batter. Do not macerate sulfur-treated fruit in any strong liqueur or alcohol as they will turn leathery and lose their mellowness.

Here are two sweetmeats prepared with dried figs and dates:

California Garden Sweets

FCR—6 TO 12 SERVINGS

12 large, moist dried Black Mission figs

1 cup blanched slivered almonds

½ teaspoon fennel seeds

10 dried lavender flowers (optional), crumbled

1 tablespoon fortified wine of your choice

Salt

Liquid honey as needed, about ⅓ cup

Confectioners' sugar

I prepare these figs each year with the almonds, figs, fennel, and lavender growing in my garden. They are best prepared at the end of the year when the large dried Mission figs arrive from California for the holiday baking. These will easily replace a chocolate candy. Do not make the almond paste too liquid as it will render the stuffing of the figs difficult. If you don't have a food processor you can use a 7-ounce bar of Odensee almond paste, to be found in any supermarket.

Soak the figs 5 minutes in two successive baths of cold water. Discard both waters and pat the figs dry. Snip away their stems and roll the fruits in your fingers until they have completely softened. Flatten the figs so their root end and cut stem are each at the center of one of their two sides. Cut a semicircular opening on the stem side no longer than ½ inch. Pass a finger into each fig to make a receptacle in which you will stuff the almond filling.

Put the almonds in the food processor, pulse twice to chop them coarsely. Add the fennel seeds, lavender, and wine in which you will have dissolved a few grains of salt. Process until the almonds form a good meal. Meanwhile, bring the honey to a boil over medium heat and simmer it 20 minutes over low heat. Cool it completely and teaspoon by teaspoon add enough of it to the almonds until a tender but not too liquid paste forms. Remove the paste from the processor, divide into twelve small balls, and squeeze one of them into each prepared fig. Close the opening of each fruit and gently flatten and shape it to make it as evenly thick and round as possible. Place upright in a baking dish.

Preheat the oven to 175°F and bake the figs 15 minutes. Let them cool and dust them with confectioners' sugar. Keep at room temperature and serve on the same day as prepared.

Christmas Dates
TORPILLES DE NOËL

FCR—12 SERVINGS

One 7-ounce bar Odensee almond paste

⅓ cup chopped walnuts

Confectioners' sugar as needed, about ⅓ cup

1½ to 2 tablespoons dark rum to your personal taste

Salt

From my home in Paris where I was in charge of preparing these each and every year. During the war, they became preciously rare and, because of their shape, we gave them the name of torpedoes.

24 dried large Deglet Nour dates, as soft as possible

2 cups granulated sugar (for an optional glaze)

Grate the almond paste into a bowl. Put the walnuts, ¼ cup of the confectioners' sugar, and 1½ tablespoons of the rum in which you will have dissolved a few grains of salt in a food processor. Process until the mixture forms a paste. Pour the almond paste over the walnut paste and process together until a stiffer moldable paste is obtained. Taste for sweetness and rum flavor. If too bland, add sugar a teaspoon at a time and more rum a few drops at a time, plus a gew grains of salt.

Remove the paste to the table and knead it a few minutes to homogenize it. Make a long roll 1 inch in diameter, cut into twenty-four even-size pieces, and shape them into torpedoes each as long as a date. Choose the best-looking face of each date and cut a long slit from one end of the fruit to the other, remove the pit, and stuff a nut torpedo into each fruit. The nut paste should be apparent. With the back of a knife trace parallel lines on the surface of the paste on the diagonal.

If you love sugar work, cook the granulated sugar to the hard crack stage (see page 938). Lightly oil a cookie sheet, dip the dates into the sugar syrup, and deposit them onto the oiled sheet to completely cool.

Present the nuts on a plate in those same pleated paper cups as used by chocolatiers to present their chocolate candies. Keep at room temperature and serve on the same day as prepared.

Cooking Fresh Fruit

Serving fresh fruit needs no instruction, but we are less familiar with cooked fruits other than stewed prunes and an occasional poached pear. Poaching is a good method to use, for this gentle cooking helps to keep the shape of the fruit and adds to its lusciousness, but fruit can also be grilled, baked, or roasted.

Most poachable fruits are of temperate origin while tropical fruits are usually consumed raw, as are most citrus fruit.

Peeling Fruit;
The Browning Effect of Enzymes

Before being poached, a fruit must be peeled as fits its nature:

CITRUS FRUIT

To peel a citrus fruit when you will be using the rind, lift the rind off with a potato peeler, applying just enough pressure to engage the outer layer of the rind and not the white cottonlike cellulose. It is not the cottonlike cellulose that is bitter, but the oil contained in thousands of small sacs visible at the surface of the rind, so you must not cut through those sacs or bitterness will result.

After cutting wide strips into fine julienne strips, you should blanch them to remove some of that oil and prevent the bitterness that too much of it would give to candied peel.

To remove the cellulose skin of a citrus fruit, start by removing a small quarter-size piece of pulp at each end of the fruit, so it can stand on the cutting board without rolling back and forth. Now begin to remove the white skin from top to bottom; start cutting at the top of the fruit with the wide part of your blade that is closest to the handle of your knife and work your way down the rounded surface of the fruit, slowly passing from its wider part to the tip of the blade. This way you will slice the pith off following the curve of the fruit, retaining its shape without showing those ugly flat planes and surfaces that beginners usually do. The fruit will look elegant only if your hand is steady and if all traces of white cellulose are removed. Make an effort to be light-handed and if you are not happy with your first try, look how different your second and third fruit already are and feel encouraged.

DRUPES

To remove the skins of peaches, apricots, and nectarines (and tomatoes also), remove their stems and immerse them in boiling water for 45 seconds. Immediately plunge the fruit in cold water; it will stop the cooking of the first layers of pulp and build a layer of steam between the skin and pulp which will allow you to lift the skin off without damaging the appearance of the fruit pulp. Some drupes have red cheeks from the presence in their skins of pigments called anthocyanins. Blanching causes these pigments to transfer to the pulp, which gives the poached fruit a very pretty appearance.

POMES

When you peel a fruit such as an apple or a pear, the fruit pulp exposed by the knife will brown rapidly. This is caused by the presence of enzymes, which, combined with the oxygen in the air, provoke an oxidation of the phenol-type material present in the fruit pulp. An antioxidant will stop or slow enzymatic reactions. Rub the fruit immediately with lemon juice; its citric and ascorbic acids will go to work at once. As soon as you immerse a fruit in a hot sugar syrup the enzyme is destroyed by the heat and the browning stops.

Peel pears and apples very gently with a vegetable peeler or a paring knife to remove a very thin layer of skin, applying minimum pressure. Remove apple cores with a corer and pear cores with the small scoop of a melon baller or Parisian spoon dipped in lemon juice.

Peaches can also turn brown, but not as fast. You may rub them with lemon juice if you plan to poach them. If you are going to macerate them in wine, immediately sprinkle them with sugar. The sugar will draw some of the fruit juices but it will also build a protective layer of concentrated sugar all around the fruit.

Thickness of Poaching Syrups

Poach the following fruit in syrups of different density, depending on their nature:

APPLES   Use a light syrup—⅓ to ½ cup of water per cup of sugar, which in larger quantity corresponds to 8 to 10 ounces of water for each pound of sugar.

APRICOTS, PEACHES, CHERRIES, AND PEARS   Use a medium syrup—½ to ¾ cup of water per cup of sugar, or in larger quantity 8 to 12 ounces of water per pound of sugar

BANANAS   Use a medium or heavy syrup—1 cup of water per cup of sugar, which corresponds in larger quantity to an equal amount of sugar and water since both sugar and water have the same density; the same weight of sugar and water will fill the same volume.

Instead of water, you may use wine or a fruit juice, or a combination of both as the poaching liquid. If the wine is sweet, reduce the amount of sugar. Too much sugar in a syrup will shrivel the fruit and draw the juices out of it, but not enough sugar will cause the fruit to break down completely and mush up; the best example is the apple, which falls apart when cooked without sugar and becomes applesauce.

Cooking a Sugar Syrup

Before you even start, be aware that sugar syrup burns very deeply and is very dangerous. Be certain that the burner on which you are working is steady and that there is absolutely no chance that the pot or skillet in which the syrup cooks will tip off the burner and spill its hot contents over the stove, counter, or your hands. Flat electric cooking plates and coils are safer than home-style gas burners with high-sitting grates.

It is your responsibility to protect yourself from burns by working cautiously and without rash movements and by wearing a smock with loose sleeves to protect your skin. If you have very sensitive hands, you should wear protective gloves that are thick enough to resist penetration by the syrup. Specialized pastry and cake stores may carry gloves for working with sugar.

The first step to successful sugar cookery is a heavy-bottomed perfectly clean pot. Any trace, even the smallest, of dried food or fat may provoke the crystallization of the sugar. Even if your pot seems clean, wash it again, rinse it several times, and dry it *with paper towels exclusively*. The cleanest kitchen towel always contains undetectable but chemically active fat residues.

Mix the sugar with the water, add a pinch of cream of tartar or one drop of lemon juice. If you leave this mixture to stand, it will form a saturated solution; while some sugar granules will dissolve in the water, others will sink to the bottom of the pot and dissolve only if subjected to heat. When heated, all of the sugar will dissolve resulting in a transparent solution. The sugar bought in stores is called sucrose, a double sugar. An acid (cream of tartar or lemon juice) added to a cooking sucrose solution will break the sucrose down into two single (also called simple) sugars called glucose and fructose. This reaction is known as *inversion* and prevents the recrystallization of the sucrose, either while cooking or during the cooling period.

To cook the sugar accurately, use a candy thermometer; place it in the sugar solution before the cooking starts. As soon as sugar solution has reached the desired temperature we call it a syrup. Remove the thermometer and immerse it in hot water to keep the sugar from hardening on it.

As soon as the syrup comes to a boil, steam will rise from the cooking solution; after a few minutes of cooking over medium heat, bubbles will appear, very close to one another and very small, a sign that the water has completely evaporated and the sugar itself has started to cook. Sugar refined in the United States is usually so clean that barely any scum forms. Should some materialize at the edges of the syrup, remove it with a clean silver spoon. Do not let the flames rise around the pot, for this extreme heat will start the sugar caramelizing at its edge. Should this happen, wrap a linen cloth dipped into ice water around the prongs of a fork and rub all around the inside of the pan to remove all traces of burned sugar; then *do not touch the syrup anymore*, simply let it cook.

As sugar cooks, it reaches higher and higher temperatures and passes through successive "stages." In recipes you will still sometimes see the expression, "Cook the syrup to the thread stage" or "the ball stage." The old-fashioned way of testing the temperature of a syrup was with the tips of the fingers. The fingers were dipped into ice water before being dipped into the syrup. As the sugar reached various temperatures, it would form a thread or ball when pulled or rubbed between the thumb and index finger.

Stages of Cooked Sugar

From 260° to 310°F, the sugar passes successively from the light to the medium to the hard crack stages. From 260°F on, the stages of cooking are separated only by intervals of *seconds*. From the hard crack stage on, the syrup forms a brittle sheet that cracks and breaks when dropped on a cold plate. It starts coloring and reaches caramel at 350° to 355°F. Caramelized sugar is recognizable by its candylike smell, the result of its chemical components. If cooking is continued too long, caramel converts to suffocating smoke and burns, its residue pure black carbon.

Poaching Fruit

Using a nonreactive stainless pot, prepare enough syrup so the fruit will bathe completely in it; you should use at least a depth of 3 inches of syrup for flat fruit such as pear halves and a depth of 4 inches for whole pears and large peaches 2½ inches in diameter to be completely immersed. Any syrup left over can be stored and used to prepare sorbets after having measured its concentration of sugar with a saccharometer, also called a hygrometer. This instrument can be found easily and at very little expense in good kitchen equipment stores. Also, any leftover syrup will have acquired the taste of the fruit poached in it and will be delightful used on pancakes.

Mix sugar and water in the proportions indicated on page 937, bring the mixture to a boil, turn it down to a simmer, and stir in a few drops of lemon juice. You may flavor the syrup with vanilla or any other spice of your choice.

Lower the fruit in the syrup using a slotted spoon. Keep tipping the fruit over and over again every 2 minutes until a sewing needle inserted at its thickest part comes out without difficulty and without your being able to perceive any change of texture between the outside part of the fruit and its center. This is a very important point, for should you remove the fruit before it is fully poached, its center will turn brown as soon as the fruit is removed from the syrup. This happens commonly with pear halves in which the center is thinner than the sides and bottom of the fruit and consequently is cooked sooner than they are. Do not cook too many pieces of fruit at once to be certain that the fruit has ample space to be in complete contact with the syrup. Once the fruit is done, transfer it to the serving dish in which it will be served or, if you do not wish to have any syrup around the fruit, deposit it gently onto a stainless steel griddle placed over a bowl, into which the syrup can drip.

When fruits are poached in a syrup made with wine, they are often cooled in the syrup in which they cooked, which then becomes a sauce for them. The most common fruit presented in this manner is the classic pears poached in red wine or port, which look quite lovely floating in their crimson syrup. This technique should be used when preparing this type of dessert for a larger dinner party or for large quantity production in restaurant service or catering, for as long as the syrup is around the fruit, no oxidation can occur.

Here are two examples of desserts prepared with poached fruit:

Apricots Jolie Madame

FFR—6 SERVINGS

1 cup granulated sugar

1½ cups water

One 1-inch piece vanilla bean

12 large, ripe but firm apricots

½ cup finely ground blanched almonds

½ cup chopped peeled pistachios

¼ teaspoon pure bitter almond extract

2 to 3 tablespoons liquid honey, to your personal taste

½ cup heavy cream

1 tablespoon confectioners' sugar

2 tablespoons kirsch or Apry (a pleasant apricot liqueur)

Prepare a sugar syrup with the sugar and water (see pages 937–39). Cut the vanilla bean open and scrape the seeds into the syrup. Cut the apricots into halves and remove their pits, but do not peel them; the skin will keep the fruit from falling apart during poaching. Immerse half of the apricot halves in the barely simmering syrup and poach gently until a large needle inserted in the center of an apricot half comes out without difficulty, 3 to 4 minutes. Do not overcook the fruit. Repeat with the remaining apricot halves. Remove the apricots to a large flat dish and chill completely round side up. Reserve the cooking syrup.

Mix together the almonds, pistachios, and almond extract; bind with just enough honey for the mixture to hold together. Fill the cooled apricot halves with a nugget of the mixture. Whip the cream to the Chantilly stage (see page 30), sweeten with the confectioners' sugar, and flavor with the liqueur of your choice.

Set four apricot halves into each of six dessert dishes; baste each serving with 2 tablespoons of the reserved cooking syrup and top with 2 tablespoons of the whipped cream, or pass the whipped cream in a bowl for your guests to help themselves.

Dubonnet Pears

FFR—6 SERVINGS

2 cups red Dubonnet

½ cup fresh orange juice

One 2 × ½-inch strip orange rind

1¼ cups granulated sugar

6 ripe Bartlett pears

1 lemon, halved

To core the whole pears, pass an apple corer into the center of each pear without reaching as far as the neck of the fruit, twist the corer in one direction and the pear in the opposite direction as you remove it; you will find the seeds and carpels in the corer.

1 cup heavy cream

2 tablespoons Curaçao

1 tablespoon very finely minced candied orange peel

1 tablespoon confectioners' sugar (optional)

6 tablespoons finely chopped peeled pistachios

Mix the Dubonnet, orange juice, orange rind, and granulated sugar together in a large heavy-bottomed saucepan. Bring to a boil, then reduce the heat to medium-low and simmer 5 minutes. Peel and core the whole pears carefully. Rub with the lemon and immediately immerse in the simmering syrup. Simmer until a large sewing needle inserted at the thickest part of the largest pear comes out without difficulty, 8 to 10 minutes. Chill the pears in the syrup, preferably overnight.

Remove the pears from the syrup and set them on a stainless steel griddle set over a bowl so they drip their juices and are not slippery when you fill them. Cut a small slice off the bottom of each fruit so it can stand easily. Reduce the syrup in a small saucepan over medium heat to 1 cup. Whip the cream to the Chantilly stage (see page 30). Add the liqueur, candied peel, and confectioners' sugar, if desired. Put the cream into a pastry bag fitted with a ½-inch nozzle. Pipe a large rosette of cream in each of six dessert dishes. Set one pear into each dish and sprinkle with the chopped pistachios. Pass the reduced syrup in a sauce boat.

Serving Peeled Fresh Fruit as Juice-Steeped Fruit Salads or Wine-Marinated Fruits

If you have a source of extremely ripe and delicious fruit, slice them and serve them either macerated in citrus juices and a liqueur of your choice as is done in France or marinated in delicious wine as is done in Germany.

There are really no stringent rules to observe, outside that of peeling the fruit elegantly without leaving ridges or angles on its surface so the salad you serve is a joy for the eyes as well as for the palate. Immediately after being peeled and sliced, those fruits which oxidate easily (pears, apples, bananas) should be sprinkled with fresh citrus juices. You can, if you prefer, use the crystals of citric acid sold in small boxes in supermarkets, but I prefer mixed fresh lemon and orange juices. Berries, which are usually quite tart and the colors of which are very stable, need no citrus juice addition.

Summer drupes which are just ripe often do not peel as easily as wished; it will then be wise to blanch them in boiling water for 45 seconds to remove their skins. The hot water will also kill the enzymes at their surface and prevent the fruit from darkening.

Serving whipped cream with fruit salads is not necessary, unless you specifically like and enjoy it.

Summer Berry Salad

NFR—6 TO 8 SERVINGS

½ pint fresh strawberries, washed, hulled, and sliced

I pint fresh raspberries, sorted and brushed of any traces of soil

½ pint fresh cloudberries, salmonberries, or white raspberries, sorted and brushed of any traces of soil

½ pint fresh blueberries, sorted, washed, and patted dry

½ pint fresh blackberries, brushed of soil, rinsed, and patted dry

½ pint fresh boysenberries, brushed of soil, rinsed, and patted dry

I ½ tablespoons superfine sugar

¼ cup crème de cassis liqueur

Mix the berries together in a large bowl. Keep them chilled. Half an hour before serving them, sprinkle the berries with the sugar and add the liqueur. Toss three times at regular intervals before serving.

Summer Fruit Salad

Summer fruit salads may contain peaches, yellow and white; nectarines, yellow and white; apricots; plums of all kinds and colors; and summer melons. Here is one made with nectarines and the first kiwis of late summer, which is striking to look at and delicious.

NFR—6 TO 8 SERVINGS

6 fully ripe nectarines, peeled

6 kiwis, peeled

I ½ tablespoons superfine sugar

¼ cup Apry (apricot) liqueur

Cut the nectarines and kiwis into quarters, alternating the colors in a serving dish for a lovely bright pattern; keep refrigerated. Half an hour before serving, sprinkle with the sugar and add the liqueur. Tilt the dish and spoon the mixture of nectarine juices, liqueur, and sugar over the fruit several times before serving.

Winter Fruit Salad

The fruits of winter are pineapple, pears of all kinds, kiwis, and winter melons, to which you can add the tropical papaya and mango toward the end of the

NFR—6 TO 8 SERVINGS

I pineapple, peeled, cored, and sliced

4 kiwis, peeled and sliced

2 late winter mangoes, peeled, pitted, and sliced

2 ripe Bosc pears, peeled, cored, and sliced

Juice of I navel orange

2 passion fruits

I cup water

½ cup granulated sugar

½ cup fresh cranberries, sorted and washed

Arrange the pineapple, kiwi, mango, and pear slices in an elegant pattern in a crystal dish. Put the orange juice in a measuring cup; cut the passion fruits open and squeeze their juices into the orange juice and mix well. Sprinkle this mixture over the fruit. Cover with plastic wrap and let macerate in the refrigerator while the cranberries cook.

Mix the water and sugar together in a small, heavy-bottomed saucepan; bring to a boil, then simmer for 5 minutes. Add the cranberries; as soon as they come floating to the surface of the syrup, lift them out with a slotted spoon. Cool them and arrange over the tropical fruit. The juice seeping from the cranberries will drip into the underlying fruit. Tilt the crystal dish and baste the fruit several times with the mixture of fruit juices. Serve within a half hour.

winter and the early spring and around Thanksgiving and Christmas poached cranberries. With such a mixture of fruit, which have many different flavors, do not use a single brandy which will be sure to clash with some of the fruit. Rather, choose liqueurs containing a lot of essences of herbs such as Chartreuse or Benedictine and brandy or a liqueur of tropical fruit such as passion fruit liqueur.

Kotja's Riesling Marinated Peaches

FCR — 6 SERVINGS

9 ripe white peaches

9 teaspoons superfine sugar

I bottle German Spaetlese Riesling

Bring a pot of water to a boil and immerse the peaches for a few seconds; cool them down under cool running water, then peel them immediately. Halve and pit the fruit, then sprinkle each peach half, inside and outside, with approximately ½ teaspoon of the sugar. Place the peaches, pit side down, in a shallow dish and pour the Riesling on top. Refrigerate at least 5 hours. Shake the dish gently at regular intervals to mix the fruit juice and wine.

This recipe offers a truly marinated fruit in a relatively large amount of wine. It was first made for a visit by Dr. Konstantin Frank who in the late 1950s and early 1960s introduced vinifera grapes in New York State. The euphoric effect of this type of marinated fruit had a splendid effect on the whole table. Use fragrant fresh white peaches if you can find them, but the euphoria is the same with yellow peaches.

Fruit Purees and Fruit Mousses

The best fruit mousses are made with a puree of fruit and plain whipped cream; quite calorific, I know, but well worth having at least once a year. If too rich for your taste or diet, just thicken the fruit puree as you would a pudding and chill it; you will obtain what in Imperial Russia was called a kisel. Here is a very pleasant example:

Four-Fruit Kisel

NFR—6 SERVINGS

I pint fresh strawberries, hulled

I pint fresh raspberries, sorted and brushed of any traces of soil

¾ cup pitted sweet dark cherries

1½ cups cherry juice

I teaspoon fresh lemon juice

½ cup granulated sugar

Salt

I tablespoon potato starch

I tablespoon water

6 tablespoons vodka of your choice (optional)

In the classic kisel (also spelled kissel) the fruit was cooked at least 15 minutes with water. To preserve the fresh fruit taste, I prefer to blend the uncooked fruit puree with cherry juice. The texture of this fruit preparation is quite thin when hot; it thickens upon cooling.

Puree the strawberries, raspberries, and cherries together in a blender. Strain through a conical strainer directly into a saucepan; discard all the seeds and traces of cherry skins if any. Blend in the cherry and lemon juices, sugar, and a few grains of salt; bring to a boil over medium heat. Turn down to a simmer while you mix the potato starch and water into a slurry. Stir the slurry into the simmering kisel, continuing to stir until the mixture reboils and thickens lightly and its color turns clear and translucent. Cool to lukewarm and pour into six tall dessert dishes or fancy stemware. Chill at least 2 hours before serving.

Just before bringing to the table, spoon 1 generous tablespoon of vodka on the surface of each portion of kisel.

Fruits that do not oxidate or oxidate very slowly can be pureed in the blender or food processor; the obtained puree is then strained and used either for a kisel or a mousse. Those fruits that oxidate easily such as pears and apples are better cooked to neutralize the enzymes that provoke their oxidation; they can then be transformed into a puree the color of which will be stable.

However, it may happen that the fruit will not cook gracefully or that if cooked it will lose a great deal of its flavor; such is the case with bananas, for example. In this case the oxidation is stopped with a nice addition of lemon juice to the uncooked fruit.

While cooking a puree of fruit, do so on medium-low heat and stir often to prevent the fruit from attaching to the bottom of the pan. Also watch for those exploding "bubbles" which happen when the puree thickens and becomes viscous; they splatter and can provoke burns on hand or face. Stirring with a long handled wooden spoon with your face away from the pot will be helpful.

Apple Puree

(ALSO CALLED PLAIN APPLESAUCE)

NFR — 4 CUPS

2 pounds McIntosh or Jonathan apples, peeled, cored, and cut into cubes

I teaspoon finely grated lemon rind

Juice of I lemon

½ teaspoon ground cinnamon

Granulated sugar as needed

¼ cup water

Apple cider if needed

I ½ tablespoons unsalted butter (optional)

Place the apples, lemon rind and juice, cinnamon, and sugar to taste in a stainless steel sauteuse. Add the water and bring to a boil; reduce the heat to medium-low and simmer, covered, until the apples have fallen apart, which will take only a short time. Remove the lid and let cook gently until reduced to the texture you prefer; the time it takes to reduce the puree to texture will vary with the quantity of water the apples contain and the texture you prefer. If the puree becomes too thick for your taste, add apple cider to bring it back to the consistency you like. If, on the contrary, it is too thin, put it back on the stove and let it reduce further, watching that it does not caramelize on the bottom. If caramelization happens, use the puree for a dessert. In any case, whisk the butter into the finished puree, if you wish.

This is a French version from Normandy. If you want, you can finish the applesauce with a pat of very fresh unsalted butter.

Homemade Apple Butter

NFR — 2 CUPS

4 cups Apple Puree (above)

¾ cup apple cider

¼ cup cider vinegar

½ teaspoon ground cinnamon

¼ teaspoon ground cloves

¼ teaspoon ground allspice

⅓ cup firmly packed light brown sugar

Pinch of salt

Place all the ingredients in an enameled cast-iron pan. Bring to a boil, then reduce the heat to a slow and steady simmer. Reduce the mixture, stirring occasionally, until no liquid separates from the apple butter. If dropped onto a plate, the apple butter should form a round droplet that does not flatten. Pass through a blender to equalize the texture by destroying the always present small bumps in the preparation.

Pour into a sterilized 2-cup jar and keep refrigerated between uses.

Pear butter can be made following this recipe also.

Zwilling Apfelmus

Apfelmus *is applesauce in Schwyzer Tuetsch; this dessert is one of my favorites and made of two intertwined mousses, one of apples, the second of apple butter.*

FFR — 6 SERVINGS

1½ cups apple puree (page 945)

1½ cups apple butter (page 945)

1⅓ cups heavy cream

Pinch of salt

2 tablespoons confectioners' sugar

2 tablespoons Calvados or applejack

Place the apple puree and apple butter each in a separate bowl. In a large bowl, beat the cream to the Chantilly stage (see page 30), adding the salt, sugar, and chosen liqueur. Fold half the cream into each of the purees.

Spoon half of each mousse in each of six 6-ounces glasses. Using a knife blade, swirl the mousses into each other. Chill before serving.

Pear Butter

This recipe can be executed with pears that are damaged but in no way are overripe. It will produce enough pear butter to fill several canning jars which must then be processed in a boiling water bath and kept in a refrigerator after final cooling. This method of cooking the butter prevents the always possible scorching that can happen when cooking on top of the stove.

LFR — FOUR TO FIVE 8-OUNCE JARS

12 cups (3 quarts) quartered and cored but unpeeled pears

4 cups water

Juice of 1 lemon

Granulated sugar as needed

1 tablespoon ground ginger

Put the pears, water, and lemon juice in a 6-quart pot. Bring slowly to a boil, then reduce the heat to a simmer and cook until the pulp is soft, 25 to 30 minutes, stirring often. Puree the obtained mixture in several batches, using the food processor. Strain through a conical strainer to discard all traces of skins, which have lost all of their flavor in the cooking water.

Preheat the oven to 300°F. Return the puree to the same pot or another smaller one. Add sugar to the ratio of half as much sugar by volume as there is pulp ready to cook (½ cup sugar to each cup of pulp) and the ginger; bring to a boil, stirring while the sugar melts. As soon as the butter boils, transfer it to the middle rack of the oven. Bake until no water separates from the butter, stirring at regular intervals.

Sterilize the jars, dome lids, and screwtops (see page 975). Fill the hot jars with the hot butter. Seal and process in boiling hot water bath (see page 976) reaching 2 to 2½ inches above the top of the jars for 20 minutes. Remove from the water bath, turn upside down 1 to 2 minutes, then let stand upright at room temperature until the dome lids have clicked into the concave position; you will not be able to move the lids anymore with pressure from your hand, a proof that the vacuum has been completed. Please check this carefully as you are responsible for the proper sterilizion of that butter. Keep refrigerated.

Banana Mousse

FFR — 6 TO 8 SERVINGS

¼ cup unsalted butter, at room temperature

6 tablespoons granulated sugar

3 tablespoon dark rum (optional)

5 large bananas

2 tablespoons fresh lemon juice

1 ounce unsweetened chocolate

1 cup heavy cream

Use only very ripe bananas, full of sugar (black) spots, and mash them with a fork; they will liquefy too much if you use a blender or a food processor.

Cream the butter with 5 tablespoons of the sugar, then add 2 tablespoons of the rum and continue beating until fluffy. Peel and mash 3 of the bananas with 1 tablespoon of the lemon juice. Grate the chocolate into the banana puree. Blend the banana puree into the creamed butter. Whip the cream until it starts to mound and fold it into the banana-chocolate puree. Turn into a nice crystal dish and deep chill.

Before serving, peel and slice the remaining 2 bananas, sprinkle them with the remaining sugar, and the remaining lemon juice and rum mixed together. Arrange the slices on top of the chilled mousse before serving.

Mousses Made of Fruits That Do Not Oxidate

Most red berries do not oxidate nor do blue- and blackberries, so that one might think that the fresh puree can be used uncooked. However, cooking the puree with some sugar removes the edge of the natural acids and keeps the mousse from acquiring a faint cheeselike flavor when the cream comes in contact with the acid of the berries. This can happen with raspberries especially and almost always when using strawberries that have been picked too early.

One good way to avoid problems of this nature is to use berries frozen in syrup or, if using other fruit, fruit that has been dried and the color of which has been stabilized by the use of sulfur dioxide. With both these types of fruit, the sugar content of the fruit, which is raised in the frozen fruit by the addition of a sugar syrup and in the dried fruit by dehydration, lowers the acidity of the fruit pulp. The two recipes that follow are typical examples:

Strawberry Mousse

FFR—12 SERVINGS

1 quart fresh, fully ripe strawberries, hulled

6 tablespoons confectioners' sugar

1 tablespoon fresh lemon juice

2 to 3 tablespoons raspberry brandy or raspberry liqueur, to your personal taste

1¼ cups heavy cream

Puree the strawberries. Pour into a medium-size saucepan and add the sugar and lemon juice. Cook over low heat until reduced to 1 cup, stirring occasionally. Stir the brandy in. In a medium-size bowl whip the cream to the Chantilly stage (see page 30), then fold into the fruit puree. Pour into a serving dish and deep chill.

Apricot Mousse

FFR—6 TO 8 SERVINGS

13 ounces large dried American apricots

6 tablespoons granulated sugar

½ cup water

2 tablespoons kirsch

1 cup heavy cream

2 tablespoons chopped peeled pistachios

Cover the apricots with cold water and soak overnight at room temperature. Discard the water, rinse the fruit, and drip it dry in a colander. Place in a large saucepan and add the sugar and water. Cook over medium heat until the apricots are mushy. Strain through a conical strainer to remove all the skins. Chill.

Stir the kirsch into the puree. Whip the cream to the Chantilly stage (see page 30) and fold into the apricots. Serve deep chilled, sprinkled with the pistachios.

Baking and Roasting Fruit

We have baked apples for many centuries and made brown betty, which is another classic way to bake fruit topped with delicious crumbs, for at least three. In the last few years roasting fruit has become so extremely popular that making a distinction between baking and roasting is necessary.

This is always very successful for a dinner party, but it will be delicious only if you can find sun-ripened strawberries from a farmer's market.

Oven-Drying Fruit

Thin ⅛-inch-thick slices of different fruit are nowadays baked in a very low oven, the temperature of which ranges from 175° to 220°F. The baking lasts from 2 to 4 hours, depending on the moisture content of the fruit. This is truly a type of drying and the results are very interesting chips of all colors, crispy on the outside with a bare hint of moisture at their centers and a great concentration of their fructose; these are often used as garnish for rich custards. However new the idea may seem, all European village women did exactly the same thing in their ancient bread ovens using the long-lasting "leftover" heat of the oven after baking breads and cakes. There is no need to keep these only as garnish for rich desserts; they will accompany a roast duck or Boston butt of pork very well.

I have prepared such chips for my grandchild and she has loved them; they are a wonderful replacement for commercial candies. The vitamins are not plentiful but the taste is explosive and attractive to all ages and the look on a plate is irresistible.

There is really no technique involved other than putting the thin slices of fruit on a nonstick baking or cookie sheet and letting the heat of the oven do its work. One peek into the oven every 20 minutes is important to survey the progress of the operation as well as to turn the slivers of fruit over.

Blanc Manger with Oven-Dried Fruit

FFR — 12 SERVINGS

4½ cups heavy cream

1½ envelopes unflavored gelatin

⅔ cup granulated sugar

⅛ teaspoon salt

½ cup milk of your choice

½ cup kirsch or maraschino

½ teaspoon pure bitter almond extract

2 ounces bittersweet chocolate

Four ⅛-inch-thick slices pineapple, skin and core removed and cut into quarters

Twelve ⅛-inch-thick slices papaya, peeled

Juicy red seeds of 2 pomegranates

Divide the cream, gelatin, sugar, salt, and milk in half. Keep each in separate containers. Scald half the cream, then soften half the gelatin and salt in half the milk. Add the milk-and-gelatin mixture to the hot cream and stir until dissolved. Cool and add ¼ cup of the kirsch and ¼ teaspoon of the almond extract. Stir over ice, and as soon as the cream starts to set, ladle

For the idea of using oven-dried fruits as a dessert garnish, I am indebted to and thank Nancy Silverton. The blanc manger is a dessert that I served in my Boston restaurant, and the oven-dried fruits give it a modern direction. Prepare the blanc manger the day before your party and keep it well covered with plastic wrap. Oven-dry the fruit the day of your party and keep them in a dry room to prevent them from losing their crispness. For another recipe of blanc manger with cherries, see my book In Madeleine's Kitchen, *page 457.*

into 12 Champagne cups. Cover with plastic wrap and refrigerate until fully jelled.

Grate the chocolate with a potato peeler and add 1 teaspoon of the chocolate to each cup, sprinkling it evenly over the layer of cold cream.

Repeat the steps outlined in the first paragraph with the remaining cream, gelatin, salt, milk, kirsch, and almond extract. Cool and ladle into the cups on top of the chocolate. Cover again with plastic wrap and return to the refrigerator until ready to use.

Preheat the oven to 200°F. Spread the slices of fruit over one or two baking or cookie sheets. Bake the slices of fruit until they are nicely dried. Keep in a cool and dry room.

To serve, arrange a few of the different slices of fruit over the blanc manger and dot with a few pomegranate seeds. Serve rapidly to prevent the moisture in the pomegranate seeds from mellowing the slices of fruit.

Baking Fruit

To bake means to cook in an oven at moderate temperature, between 300° and 325°F. The fireproof dish containing the fruit is rubbed with butter or any other oil or fat of your choice. The fruit, whole, sliced, or cubed, is put to bake in the preheated oven and is enjoyed by itself or with cream, yogurt, or plain curdled fresh milk.

Here are two country-style examples:

Golden Pears with Clabbered Goat's Milk
POIRES MORDOREES AU LAIT DE CHÈVRE CAILLE

This recipe, which I inherited from my great grandmother, is ancient. This is one of the many versions of this rustic dessert existing in the food lore of the French province of Poitou. The clabbered milk must be prepared first. Junket tablets are available in all good supermarkets, specialty stores, health food stores, etc.

FFR—6 SERVINGS

For the clabbered milk

4 cups goat's milk or other milk of your choice

¼ cup nonfat plain yogurt

¼ tablet junket

2 tablespoons water

For the baked fruit

1 tablespoon unsalted butter

6 ripe Bosc pears, unpeeled

¼ cup water

¼ cup liquid honey

Empty the milk into a large saucepan. Check its temperature with an instant thermometer; if it is lower than 76°F, bring it slowly to this temperature on very low heat. Meanwhile, whisk the yogurt; crush the junket in the water and add to the yogurt. Blend the mixture into the milk. Cover with a piece of cheesecloth to prevent insects and dust from falling into the clabbering milk and let stand 3 hours in a cool room until ready to serve.

Preheat the oven to 325°F. Divide the tablespoon of butter into 6 very small pieces. Flatten each on the bottom of a baking dish at regular intervals. Wash and core the pears using an apple corer; twisting the pear in one direction while you twist the corer in the other, pull the core out. Remove one small slice of pear from the bottom of each fruit so it can stand in the dish without wobbling. Add the water and honey to the dish. Bake, basting the pears with the syrup at regular intervals, until a needle pushed into the thickest part of the largest pear comes out without difficulty, about 1 hour. Cool to lukewarm.

Pour the cooking syrup into a small pitcher. Cut each pear in half lengthwise. Mash the pulp as you would mash a baked potato, with some of the syrup poured from the pitcher. Stir the clabbered milk and spoon 1 large sauce spoon of it over each pear half.

Baked Quetches

FFR — 6 SERVINGS

2 tablespoons unsalted butter

30 large Italian prune plums as ripe as possible

¾ cup granulated sugar

Chilled or frozen lemon yogurt of your choice

Preheat the oven to 325°F. Butter a 9-inch porcelain pie plate with the butter. Cut a cross ½ inch deep into the top of each plum and extract the pit. Stand each plum in the dish, cut side up and looking like the corolla of a tulip. Sprinkle with all the sugar and bake until the juices have thickened into a deep red, heavy syrup, about 1 to 1¼ hours. The plums must be golden brown and their tips must look candied.

Serve lukewarm with the chilled or frozen yogurt.

This preparation comes from Lorraine where it is called la chaudée, because it is eaten hot out of the oven. There are two chaudées; this one is crustless. To prepare a chaudée à croûte, line the plate with a ⅛-inch-thick layer of sweet yeast dough or brioche dough (see page 1045), fill it with the plums, and let the dough double in bulk around the pie plate before baking.

SAVORY VARIATION: *Using only ⅓ cup sugar, bake the plums until the juices have reduced and serve with a duck baked also at 325°F and its well-defatted gravy.*

Miss J's Baked Apple and Fennel Slices

From Marseilles; this savory dish was created by one of my cousins to accompany panfried whiting fillets.

VARIATION: *The same dish can be prepared with butter and served with chicken or duck.*

FFR—6 SERVINGS

Olive oil, light or fruity, as personally preferred

3 large fennel bulbs, cut across into ¼-inch-thick slices

6 Gravenstein apples, peeled, cored, and cut into ¼-inch-thick slices

1 tablespoon granulated sugar

Salt

Pepper from the mill

½ cup fresh bread crumbs

Preheat the oven to 325°F. Rub a 2-quart baking dish generously with olive oil. Bring a large pot of water to a boil and blanch the fennel slices for 4 minutes; they will be half cooked and their rings will separate.

Remove the core from each slice of apple using a small cutter or a paring knife. Arrange the apple rings on the bottom of the dish, slightly overlapping one another. Drizzle with olive oil and the sugar mixed with salt and pepper to your taste. Toss the fennel slices with salt and pepper, then pack it in one single layer over the apples. Sprinkle with the bread crumbs and drizzle generously with olive oil. Bake until both fruit and vegetables are very tender and the layers have reduced to a thickness of a bare inch, about 1 hour. Serve piping hot. If the dish appears at any time to be too dry, add a tablespoon of water here and there during the baking.

Baked Figs with Wine and Butter Sauce

This demands an excellent ice cream (see techniques and basic formula on page 145) flavored with 1½ teaspoons aniseeds and ¼ teaspoon powdered saffron, both infused in the mixture of cream and milk before cooking the custard.

FFR—6 SERVINGS

2 tablespoons unsalted butter

1 dozen large ripe Black Mission or honey figs, washed

½ cup granulated sugar

1 cup sweet wine such as oloroso sherry, California Angelica or Essencia, Sauternes, or port of your choice

Preheat the oven to 325°F. Butter a stainless steel baking dish using all the butter. Cut each fig into ¼-inch-thick slices, without cutting through the stem and separating the slices; fan the slices so the figs can lie flat in the baking dish. Sprinkle with the sugar and bake until the figs start losing their juices, about 15 minutes. Turn over using a spatula and baste the figs with the juices in the pan, adding gradually one third of the wine; continue baking until the figs have browned, another 20 to 25 minutes or longer if needed. Remove the figs to a buttered plate.

Transfer the baking dish to a stovetop burner. Add the remaining wine and deglaze all the juice in the pan. Strain the juices through a conical strainer into a small pitcher. Keep warm in a pan of hot water.

Serve the figs and a scoop of ice cream of your choice (if you do not like the above suggestion) basted with the delicious wine sauce.

Roasting Fruit

The technique is identical to that for baking, the only difference being the higher temperature of the oven. Roasting works better with very juicy fruit such as peaches, nectarines, and ripe figs.

The oven should be preheated to 375° to 425°F and the fruit will cook fast, taking on a lovely color and remaining very succulent inside. Such fruit can be served either as a dessert or an excellent accompaniment to various white meats, mostly turkey, chicken, and duck.

Salt-Roasted Peaches

NFR—6 TO 12 SERVINGS

10 pounds kosher salt

6 large ripe white or yellow peaches of your choice, washed and dried, stems left on

Pour half the salt into an enameled cast-iron round stew pot and the other half into a 3-quart baking dish. Put both dishes in the cold oven and set the oven to 400°F. When the salt is also at 400°F when tested with an oven thermometer, deposit the peaches into the stew pot and, using a large ladle, transfer the hot salt from the baking dish to cover the peaches completely. Put the stew pot lid on. Return the stew pot to the oven for 20 minutes, then remove the pot from the oven, open the lid, and let stand for 5 minutes.

Using a sauce spoon, gently push the salt away from the peaches and lift the peaches out of the hot salt. Put thick kitchen mittens on so as not to burn your fingers. Brush the salt completely away from the peaches, then remove your gloves and peel the peaches. Deposit them whole on a baking or cookie sheet lined with a sheet of parchment paper. The peaches will not taste salty, rather they will be very peachy and concentrated; they have many uses:

1. They can accompany a dish of duck prepared with a duck essence (see page 293), or any other poultry, or even pork.
2. They can constitute a dessert unto themselves accompanied by a raspberry sauce (see page 963), or other fruit sauce.
3. Chilled and halved, they can become the receptacle for a delicious scoop of ice cream of your choice, preferably one with a light flavor such as dou-

In his book Cooking for All Seasons, *my former student and collaborator Jimmy Schmidt transferred the salt-roasting technique applied to meats for centuries by the Chinese and southern Italians to fruit. I have enjoyed it so much that I have used it and introduced it to all my students at the School for American Chefs. Here are peaches prepared this very unusual and delicious way. Nectarines and pears can be cooked like this also. The salt can be stashed away and reused provided any lumps formed by water oozing from the fruit are removed.*

ble vanilla, lemon, verbena (see page 146), or any other fresh herb of your choice.

4. They can be brandied; here is the recipe:

Brandied Peaches

NFR— I QUART

I 2 freestone peaches white or yellow, salt roasted (preceding recipe)

I ½ cups water

I ½ cups granulated sugar

½ cup brandy of your choice

You will need a 1-quart canning jar with a dome lid and screw top, everything sterilized in the dishwasher or in boiling water. You can choose Cognac, Armagnac, an excellent Italian Grappa, 80-proof peach brandy, any malt whisky of your choice, or any great Spanish or Portuguese brandy.

Peel the roasted peaches, cut them in half, and remove the stones. Arrange them rounded face up in a sterilized 1-quart glass jar with lid.

Mix the water and sugar together in a saucepan, bring to a boil, and simmer for 5 minutes. Pour the brandy over the peaches and slowly add enough syrup to cover the top of the peaches and reach within ½ inch of the rim of the jar. Roll the jar of peaches back and forth in your hands to bring air bubbles to the surface and make sure that there is enough syrup to cover the peaches. Seal the jar with the dome lid and well-tightened screw top.

Bring a large pot of water to a boil. Put a rack into a stew pot high enough to contain the jar. Set the jar on the rack and surround it with a towel so it does not move. Pour the boiling water around the jar and to reach 2 inches above it. Bring back to a rolling boil, cover the pot, and process for 20 minutes. Remove the jar from the bath, using a jar lifter, as soon as the processing time is up and deposit it on a wooden board. Cool to room temperature in a relatively temperate corner of the kitchen to prevent sudden retraction of the glass and shattering due to contact with cold air from an air conditioning vent, for example. You will at some point hear the dome lid retract and "click," signifying that a vacuum seal has been achieved. Store the peaches in a cool room until Christmas and enjoy them then.

When you open the jar, make certain that you hear the noise made by the air entering the jar as you break the vacuum (as occurs with all canned products); if you do not, do not use the peaches. Refrigerate the peaches once the seal is broken, and eat within 2 days. You are responsible for the safety of your canning; please pay attention to all possible details.

Roasted Papaya Slices

FCR—6 SERVINGS

2 ripe papayas

Canola oil

Salt

Pepper from the mill

Preheat the oven to 400°F. Peel the papayas and remove their pips. Cut them into wedges 1 inch wide, spray them with canola oil, and place them on a nonstick cookie or baking sheet. Season with salt and pepper and roast them until they have shrunk somewhat, 20 to 25 minutes, turning them over several times. Serve as a side dish.

Whole Roasted Figs with Goat Cheese and Frisée

FFR—6 SERVINGS

6 small portions young frisée or white leaves from center of regular head chicory,
   washed and spun dry

1½ tablespoons balsamic vinegar

Salt

Pepper from the mill

6 tablespoons virgin olive oil

6 large ripe Black Mission figs

6 thin slices semiripened goat cheese

2 tablespoons chopped fresh chives

Preheat the oven to 400°F. Arrange one small portion of frisée on each of six lunch plates. Mix the vinegar with salt and pepper to your taste. Add the olive oil and whisk until the emulsion has turned foamy and pale.

Cut a cross in the root end of each fig. Set the fruits in a nonstick 9-inch cake pan and bake until the juices start running out of the fruit, 10 to 12 minutes.

Top each plate of salad greens with a slice of goat cheese and top the cheese with a warm fig. Whisk the dressing again and spoon 2 tablespoons of it over each fig; as it flows down, the dressing will cover the cheese and the greens. Sprinkle with the chopped chives and serve quickly.

This is a good recipe for a pork roast well seasoned with sweet spices (see page 764).

This is a small appetizer course.

Panfried Fruit

Some of the very rich desserts of the classic cuisine are prepared with fruit that is sliced and panfried—some would say sautéed (see page 840). The technique is as simple as it is for vegetables; heat the butter (not oil in this case, which is reserved for vegetables) until its foam starts to recede, then add the fruit and over high heat toss the fruit in the hot butter until its moisture evaporates—the time this will take depends entirely on the type of fruit. Peaches will take longer than apples and pears because of their juiciness; it will also depend on the variety of fruit used, as some peaches are drier than others, and so are some apples and pears.

If fruits are sautéed in butter to concentrate their juices and eventually to bring them close to the caramel stage, it is usually because one intends to flambé the fruit with a liqueur or brandy. Here is a recipe for pears:

Hot Pears on Chilled Pudding

The meeting of ice cold and hot on a dessert plate is always a pleasure; here is one version of it.

VARIATIONS: The very same preparation can be served over ice cream and/or made with peaches and Southern Comfort, bananas and rum, apricots and Apry liqueur, apples and Calvados or applejack, or plums and slivovitz.

FFR—6 SERVINGS

⅔ cup uncooked Italian Arborio rice

1½ cups water

4 cups milk of your choice, scalded

1 vanilla bean, cut in half lengthwise

⅛ teaspoon salt

¼ cup unsalted butter

6 tablespoons granulated sugar

½ cup heavy cream, whipped to the Chantilly stage (page 30)

4 large ripe but not soft large Bosc pears, peeled, cored, and cut into ¼-inch-thick slices

¼ cup green Chartreuse

Put the rice and water in a large saucepan; slowly bring to a boil, then simmer for 5 minutes. Drain any water left in the rice and replace it with the scalded milk; add the vanilla bean halves and salt. Transfer the mixture to the top of a double boiler (or improvise one if you have none), cover the rice, and steam it over simmering water until it has completely swollen, about 1 hour. Stir gently every so often.

When the rice is soft or done to your personal taste, remove the vanilla bean halves, mix in 2 tablespoons of the butter, and fold in half the sugar and the whipped cream. The pudding should be soft, so it solidifies somewhat upon cooling. Turn into a dish and cool completely at room temperature. Cover with plastic wrap and store in the refrigerator.

When ready to serve, spoon the chilled pudding into six compote serving dishes. Heat the remaining butter in a large skillet until it turns almost to the noisette stage (see page 32). Add the pears and toss them in the pan over high heat until they start to color. Add the remaining 3 tablespoons of sugar, toss 1 minute more, then add the Chartreuse and let it heat a few seconds. Turn off the heat, but keep the pan on the burner.

Now, keeping your face carefully away from the pan and stove and striking one of those long matches usually used for barbecues, light the liqueur in the pan and flambé (see page 720) the pears, shaking the pan back and forth over the burner, until the flames die out. You are responsible for your own safety when flambéing. Spoon an equal amount of hot pears over the chilled portions of pudding. Serve immediately.

Deep-frying Fruit

All fruit can be deep-fried; please refer to the chapter on deep-frying (see page 632). The technique consists of flouring the pieces or slices of fruit, dipping them in the fritter batter described on page 635, and dropping the fritters into oil preheated to 370°F. The fritters are then drained on crumpled paper towels and dusted with confectioners' sugar.

Resist the temptation of serving a *chaudeau* or sabayon with this dish as is done in the Germanic countries; although it tastes really delicious it is a bit too rich. Just know that it can be done.

Grilling Fruit

I have already written about this subject in a general manner in the chapter on vegetables (see page 434).

Here is a nice appetizer done with grilled pears and blue cheese that is always met with great enthusiasm:

Pear and Gorgonzola Another Way

FFR — 6 SERVINGS

3 ripe but not soft Bosc pears, unpeeled

2 tablespoons walnut oil

12 large light green leaves from center of a head of escarole

2 ounces cream cheese

6 ounces Gorgonzola cheese

4 walnut halves, finely chopped

Pepper from the mill

Salt only if desired

This is barbecue fare. If you really like bitter greens, you can use radicchio leaves if you prefer, but their bitterness added to that of the grill marks may be a bit too pronounced for everyone's taste.

Cut 6 round slices a scant ¼ inch thick from the top of each pear. When you reach the part containing the core, remove it using a melon baller or Parisian spoon. Cut another 6 slices ¼ inch thick out of the bottom of each pear. Brush with some of the oil and grill all the slices on each side at the edge of the hot barbecue or on a stovetop grill. This will require no more than a minute on each side.

When the pears are ready, put each large slice of pear on one leaf of escarole. Mash together the cream cheese, Gorgonzola, chopped walnuts, and a little salt and pepper to taste. Divide the mixture into 6 portions and drop one in the hole of each pear slice. Top each nugget of cheese mixture with one of the small grilled slices of pear. Close the leaf of escarole over the pears. Brush the sandwiches very lightly with the remaining oil and grill 1 minute on each side at the edge of the barbecue to prevent burning and bitterness of the greens. Serve lukewarm on small appetizer or butter plates.

Other fruit can be grilled to be served with diverse meats:

- Pineapple slices with barbecued tenderloin of pork
- Mango halves with barbecued chicken
- Peach or nectarine halves with duck or any smoked bird

Churned Fresh Fruit Sorbets

Sorbet mixtures are prepared by blending together a fruit puree or juice with a heavy syrup made with the same weight—which also happens to be the same volume—of sugar and water, both these ingredients having the same density. Sorbets contain no cream or milk as opposed to American sherbets which do.

To Prepare the Syrup

Clean a stainless steel saucepan as much as you possibly can; rinse it a number of times and dry it with a wad of paper towels.

If your budget allows it, try to prepare this syrup with spring water. I always use Evian because I lived for so long in the Alps that for me, Evian is the paragon of good waters. Mix the water and sugar together and bring to a boil. Reduce to a simmer and cook over medium heat for 5 minutes. This syrup can be kept refrigerated for as long as 2 months in a large container. To be sure that the syrup is usable, write on a label the date on which it was prepared. If for any reason you have doubts about the syrup's reusability, add ½ cup of water to it, bring it back to a boil, and simmer it again for a full 5 minutes, or discard it.

The Puree of Fruit

On page 960, you will find approximate quantities to prepare some of the most popular sorbets. I want to emphasize the fact that these quantities can only be approximate, for there is no fruit that will ever contain the very same quantity of sugar and water as another fruit of the same variety. As there are people who weigh more than others because their bodies retain water or store fat, there are fruits that are gorged with water because of rain while they were ripening and others that have high concentrations of sugar because they ripened under a blazing sun. So consult the list of possible proportions if you want; I personally prefer to teach you a trick which will always give you a very delicious sorbet. Then we shall also discuss a more scientific approach.

How Much Syrup for How Much Fruit?

To be able to evaluate this within a reasonable range of accuracy, you need the following material:

- A narrow, deep container,
- An uncooked egg in its shell (please wash that egg very carefully several times and dry it with paper towels), or
- A saccharometer,
- An ice cream machine which will churn the sorbet at a steady regular rhythm will ensure that the crystals of ice will be tiny and the texture of the sorbet absolutely silky.

Mix whichever amount of fruit puree you have with about one third of its volume in syrup, stirring well to mix intimately. Add the clean egg and see whether it floats; a patch of the egg's surface should show, an area somewhere between the size of a dime and that of a quarter. If it does not, gradually add more syrup until the small white eye of the shell appears.

In a more scientific manner, you can evaluate this by using a saccharometer. A saccharometer is an instrument which, floated in a sugar solution, measures the density of the solution. The density relates to the amount of sugar the solution contains. Saccharometers offered for sale in all kitchen equipment stores may be graded either in Baumé degrees or by density. To be able to use either of these measurement systems, you must know that to prepare sorbet mixtures, the degree Baumé 17 corresponds to density reading of 1.1335 and the degree Baumé 18 corresponds to a density reading of 1.1425. To obtain a good sorbet, the saccharometer should float between those two numbers; so, add sugar syrup to the fruit puree until the saccharometer indicates that level. A little more complicated than the egg floating method and all in all not that much more accurate. But I am sure that hardcore scientists would find a difference between the textures of two sorbets made with identical fruit puree but each with one of those two methods.

The last operation before churning consists of adding some lemon juice to the sorbet mixture to brighten its taste and set its color. Then the mixture must be deep chilled for several hours. Just before you start the churning you can, if you so desire, add a tad of light corn syrup and a very tiny pinch of salt. I usually forget to add the corn syrup and my sorbets always come out very well, so consider this optional.

BUDGET SORBETS   The sorbets described above are really fruit ices and extremely rich in flavor; they are also expensive. If you are on a budget, do not hesitate to dilute the fruit puree with one third of its volume in spring water.

Basic Churning Mixtures

To each of these proposed mixtures, add 1½ tablespoons fresh lemon juice before churning:

- **Apricots:** 1 pound pitted apricots, net weight, poached 5 minutes in 1⅓ cups syrup; add the lemon juice, puree in a blender, and strain.
- **Banana:** 5 medium-size peeled bananas pureed in a blender with the lemon juice; blend with 1⅓ cups syrup and strain.
- **Strawberries:** One 24-ounce bag frozen loose strawberries barely defrosted, pureed in a blender with 2½ cups syrup and the lemon juice.
- **Raspberries:** One 24-ounce bag frozen loose raspberries barely defrosted, pureed in a blender with 2¼ cups syrup and 1 tablespoon only of lemon juice.
- **Mango and passion fruit mixed:** The pulp of 2 large ripe mangoes plus the juice of 3 passion fruits to which enough water is added to make 1 cup, pureed in a blender with 1 tablespoon each fresh lime and lemon juice and 1¼ cups syrup. Strain before freezing.
- **Melon:** 1 very ripe peeled cantaloupe pureed in a blender with 1 cup syrup and ¼ cup tawny port or walnut wine and the lemon juice.
- **Peaches:** 6 large white peaches, roasted in salt (see page 953) and peeled, then pureed in a blender with 1¼ cups syrup and the lemon juice.
- **Cranberries:** The juice of two 10-ounce packages fresh cranberries fully cooked with 2 cups water and dripped completely overnight, blended with 2 cups syrup and the lemon juice.
- **Pears:** 4 ripe pears, peeled and pureed with 2 tablespoons lemon juice and 3½ cups syrup.
- **Pineapple:** The meat of 1 large pineapple, core and skin removed, pureed in a blender with 3½ cups syrup. No lemon juice is needed.

To Churn a Sorbet

Prechill the ice cream machine according to the manufacturer's instructions. Add the sorbet mixture and churn until it turns opaque and to superfine ice.

Two things can happen, in spite of all your measurements, scientific or empiric:

- The machine stops but the sorbet is too crystally. Let it mellow again, stir a bit more syrup in it, and churn again.
- The machine does not seem to want to stop because the sorbet is too soft and does not set well. Simply add more fruit puree very gradually until the mixture firms up and really freezes.

Serving Sorbet

Keep the fruit mixture deep chilled until about half an hour before you want to serve the sorbet; during that same span, chill the machine and churn the sorbet so that it is ready to serve at just about the same time as the machine stops.

Another school of thought prefers sorbets to be aged a few hours before serving them. Try both and simply decide which you personally prefer.

Still-Frozen Sorbets

Before I lived in California where the fruit can really reach peak of ripeness, I was, like all people who live from the Midwest to the eastern seaboard, very frustrated with the flavor of the fruit to be bought in regular markets. Of course there were always a few old farms in the surroundings that offered delicious white or yellow peaches once a year, but really nothing as grandiose as what can be found on the West Coast or in the desert states.

Also, I had a restaurant for a year before I could even think of affording an ice cream machine. The combination of both situations led me to use my head and find a way to prepare good sorbets; none of the methods which I called the "freeze and slush and freeze and slush again technique," which consists in partly freezing a sorbet mixture, then beating it with a fork or an electric mixer, really gave me good results. Until one day, longingly thinking of the wonderful French black currant sorbets, I hit on the idea of mixing Maine huckleberry (not blueberries) puree with melted Canadian black currant jam and straining the mixture to perfect smoothness; people loved it. The sorbets obtained were somewhat heavier in texture than those made with syrup and churned, but basically they were very nice and certainly nicer than what could be obtained from purees of canned fruit or from imperfectly ripened fruit.

Here is the formula: For each pound of fresh fruit puree, use 24 ounces of jam or jelly of the same fruit or a comparable fruit. Use your palate; however, if your fruit is very sweet—it does happen after all even in the worst of climates—you may have to experiment a bit and use less jam. The quantity of jam or jelly can dip all the way down to 18 ounces per pound of fresh fruit at the height of summer.

These sorbets are perfect for those who do not own an ice cream machine for they can be still frozen without crystals. If they show crystals, they contain too much fruit puree, and the obvious remedy is to melt the mixture, cool, add a little more jam or jelly, mix very well, and put back in the freezer.

The smooth texture is the result of the cooked sugar in the jam as well as the pectin which acts as a stabilizer by absorbing the water contained in the fruit puree.

Freeze in shallow plastic trays and keep covered with plastic wrap; when fully frozen double wrap in aluminum foil.

Sanitation

Serve sorbets within 24 hours of their making; they will taste fresher and not gather bacteria. Keep them frozen up to the minute you are going to serve them.

Here is the most favorite sorbet recipe ever served in both my restaurants:

Apricot Sorbet

NFR—6 TO 8 SERVINGS

½ pound best California dried apricots

Juice of 2 lemons

Tiny pinch of salt

24 ounces excellent quality apricot jam

¼ cup kirsch

Soak the apricots overnight in water to cover. Discard the water and rinse the fruit well.

Mix the apricots, just enough water to cover them, the lemon juice and salt in a large saucepan. Bring to a boil and cook until the apricots break down and lose their shape. Add the jam and melt into the apricots. Cool to lukewarm for easier handling.

Puree the apricot mixture in a blender. Strain it through a conical strainer into a stainless steel or plastic tray to discard all traces of skins. Mix in the kirsch. Cover the tray with plastic wrap and aluminum foil and freeze. Ripen overnight and serve within 24 hours with the raspberry sauce on page 963.

Fruit Sauces for Desserts

Fruit sauces do not present the slightest technical difficulty. They are fruit purees often flavored with a liqueur or brandy. If such a puree is a bit too thin, you can thicken it with 1 teaspoon cornstarch per cup of sauce.

If, on the contrary, the puree is too thick to flow, you must dilute it. If the puree has been made with frozen fruit, which is very economical, you can use some of the freezing syrup to dilute the puree. If the puree has been made with fresh fruit, dilute with a fruit juice that is in taste harmony with the puree, or with spring water.

Fruit sauces are very pleasant spooned over rice pudding, upside-down vanilla custard, molded English custard or Bavarian cream, ice cream, and many other desserts.

SHELF LIFE OF FRUIT SAUCES Pure fruit sauce can be kept refrigerated for 4 days in a well-covered container. Fruit sauces containing a starch binder or thickened with cake crumbs will keep only 2 days.

Apricot Sauce

NFR— 1½ TO 2 CUPS

½ pound dried apricots

Sugar of your choice

2 tablespoons kirsch, rum, or brandy of your choice

Soak the apricots in water to cover overnight at room temperature. Discard the soaking water, rinse the apricots, and drip dry in a colander. Place in a sauteuse and cover with enough cold water to just cover the fruit. Bring to a boil, then turn down to a simmer and cook until the fruit is tender. Drain and reserve the cooking water. Puree the apricots in a blender, then strain through a conical strainer to remove the skins. Add enough of the cooking water to the puree to obtain the desired consistency. If there is no cooking water, which may happen, use spring water. Sweeten to taste and flavor with the desired liqueur.

Raspberry Sauce

NFR— 1½ CUPS

Two 10-ounce packages frozen raspberries in syrup, thawed

Sugar of your choice

Fresh lemon juice

2 tablespoons kirsch or Framboise liqueur

Drain off the raspberry juices and reserve. Puree the berries in a blender and strain through a conical strainer to discard the seeds. Add enough of the reserved syrup to the puree to obtain the desired consistency. Add sugar to taste and stir well to dissolve it. Brighten the color and taste with as much lemon juice as you like. Flavor with the kirsch.

Strawberry Sauce

NFR — 1 ½ CUPS

3 cups individually frozen unsweetened strawberries, thawed

1 tablespoon fresh lemon juice

Sugar of your choice

2 tablespoons kirsch, Framboise, Triple Sec, or Curaçao

Puree the strawberries in a blender with the lemon juice. Strain through a China cap or very fine-meshed tea strainer to remove as many seeds as possible. Sweeten to taste and flavor with the desired liqueur.

Cherry Sauce

NFR — 1 ½ CUPS

½ pound juicy ripe Bing cherries

½ pound juicy sour red cherries

¾ cup granulated sugar

½ cup fresh orange juice

1 dime-size piece lemon rind

Pinch of ground ginger

2 tablespoons kirsch or cherry brandy

Pit the cherries, mix them with the sugar and orange juice in a large saucepan, and bring to a boil. Reduce the heat to medium, add the lemon rind and ginger, and simmer 6 to 8 minutes. Puree in a blender and strain through a China cap to remove any trace of skins. Add more sugar if needed and flavor with the liqueur of your choice.

Orange Sauce

NFR — 1 ½ CUPS

1 cup fresh orange juice

One 12-ounce jar Scottish orange marmalade

2 tablespoons Cognac

Mix the juice and marmalade together in a medium-size saucepan, and bring to a boil. Turn down to a simmer and cook together until the sauce coats the back of a spoon by $\frac{1}{10}$ inch, 10 to 15 minutes. Strain to remove any orange peels. Flavor with the Cognac.

Strawberries Madeleine

FFR—6 TO 8 SERVINGS

1 quart fresh, ripe strawberries, hulled and washed

¼ cup Framboise or kirsch

1½ to 2 cups Raspberry Sauce (page 963) to your personal taste

2 large egg yolks

2 tablespoons granulated sugar

½ cup milk of your choice, scalded

1 teaspoon unflavored gelatin

1 tablespoon water

½ cup heavy cream, whipped to the light Chantilly stage (page 30)

¼ cup chopped peeled pistachios

Macerate the whole berries in 3 tablespoons of the Framboise for 2 hours in the refrigerator. Prepare the raspberry sauce.

With the egg yolks, sugar, and milk, make a stirred English custard (see page 140). Soften the gelatin in the water and add it to the custard. Flavor with the remaining Framboise. Stir over ice cubes until the mixture starts thickening. Whisk in the whipped cream until the color is uniform. Pour the custard cream into a crystal dish. Refrigerate to jell, but the mixture will stay quite soft. Arrange the berries on top of the custard cream. Spoon the raspberry sauce on top and sprinkle with the chopped pistachios.

If you can find fresh Louisiana berries, use them, as they are the tastiest in the nation. The same recipe can be made with fresh raspberries.

Fig Fritters with Orange Sauce

FFR—6 SERVINGS

24 fresh figs, ripe but not oozing juices

Flour for dredging

For the frying batter

2 large eggs, separated

¾ to 1 cup milk

3 tablespoons granulated sugar

1¼ cups sifted unbleached all-purpose flour

¼ teaspoon salt

Unsaturated oil of your choice for deep-frying

½ recipe Orange Sauce (page 964), kept warm

Slice each fig from the root to the stem in ¼-inch-thick slices, but without cutting all the way through. Sprinkle with flour to coat well, shaking off any excess.

In a large bowl, mix together the egg yolks, milk, and sugar. Stir in 1 cup of the flour. In a medium-size bowl, whip the egg whites and the salt until they can hold the weight of a raw egg in its shell without sinking more than ¼ inch and fold into the batter.

Preheat at least 4 inches of oil in a frying kettle to 370°F (see page 632). Dip the floured figs into the batter and deep-fry in the hot oil until uniformly golden. Let drain on crumpled paper towels and serve drizzled very lightly with the warmed orange sauce.

Jams, Marmalades, and Jellies

The ancient techniques of preserving fruit were multiple. Some fruits were pickled, while others, like whole clusters of grapes, were immersed in water and kept in containers sealed as tightly as the technical knowledge of the time allowed. In the Roman cookery book of Apicius, a recipe—probably borrowed from another opus written by the Latin author Apuleius and entitled *Geoponica*—instructs the reader to gather figs, apples, plums, pears, and cherries with their stems on and to immerse them in honey, so they do not touch each other. Whole quinces—with their twigs and leaves—were kept fresh for a long time by covering them either with honey or *defrutum* (grape must reduced to a thick consistency).

Published at the very end of the fourteenth century, the *Ménagier de Paris* (see the bibliography) preserved walnut meats in honey, alternating cooking the meats in the honey with periods of the walnuts resting in the cooked honey. Once the honey had turned thickish and a deep, rich brown, the mixture was poured into pottery jars which were kept as tightly closed as possible in a cool place; the *Ménagier* warned to check the jars every week to make certain the mixture was not spoiling.

I remember preparing this same very time-consuming concoction around 1945 in the Loire Valley. As soon as the honey reached the desired thickness the preserved walnuts were poured into small canning jars which were then sealed, immersed completely in water, and brought to a rapid boil to put them under vacuum and prevent them from spoiling. These preserves kept for months, even years, in the dark, cold cellar of a former convent dating back to the 1400s.

Cane sugar was brought to the Mediterranean Basin by the Arabs who taught the whole basin how to prepare sweetmeats and preserve fruits. It was the Italians of the Renaissance who first wrote about the art of making fruit jams and jellies with cane sugar, in a manner pretty much resembling what we do today. You may be interested to know that in 1552, the famous Nostradamus (born Michel de Nostredame) of the no-less-famous predictions, wrote a book, concerned partly with the making of jams, jellies, and candied fruit, which he called the *Excellent Opuscule*. In it, he stated that "If one is not too frugal in one's use of sugar, one can, anywhere, make fruit jams and jellies in every point as good as they are made in Provence, Genoa, Venice, and the Middle East."

Elizabethan England's country gentry seems to have made the very best jams and jellies and you may want to consult the interesting *Elinor Fettiplace's Receipt Book of Elizabethan Country House Cooking*, edited by Hilary Spurling which still exists in several editions.

Colonial American cooks, relatively close to the sources of Caribbean cane sugars as they were, and having brought from England their many formulas for good fruit preserves, produced jams and jellies every bit as good as were made on the Continent in the eighteenth century. On this subject, you may want to consult *The First American Cookbook* authored by Amelia Simmons and published in 1796 in Hartford, Connecticut (see the bibliography), for her colonial recipes. They yield delicious jams and jellies which, very well covered, keep fresh for months in a modern refrigerator.

Cane sugar, sold in loaves that had to be crushed at home until quite recently (the last ones I ever saw were sold, wrapped in blue paper through which just the tip of each white loaf peeked, in large Paris apothecaries and fine groceries in the early 1940s), was available to the upper classes from the sixteenth century on. Jams made with the fruit produced in Louis XIV's garden (called *Le potager du Roi*), which can still be visited in Versailles, adorned the table of the king daily.

Cane sugar remained an expensive rarity for the common folks of Europe and until the production of beet sugar began during the last few years of the eighteenth century, all jams were made with honey. But as soon as the affordable beet sugar became available sugar-made jams and jellies replaced those made with honey or must, even in the most modest of farming households. Honey-sweetened jams are rarely prepared nowadays.

Here is an ancient recipe made partially with grape juice (replacing grape must) and partially with honey:

Cotignac

NFR—SIX TO EIGHT 4-OUNCE JARS

1½ pounds (net weight) ripe quinces, peeled, cored, and cut into thick slices

2 oranges, peeled to the blood

⅓ cup cider vinegar

About 6 cups fresh white grape juice (from 3 to 4 pounds fresh grapes)

1 pound liquid honey

This recipe is from my great grandmother's kitchen, who herself got it from her own great grandmother, which would bring this recipe's date of origin to between 1695 and 1725. It is typical of all preserves made before the Renaissance, and comes from the French province of Poitou. If you replace the honey with sugar, the mixture, once fully cooked, will be stiff enough to be poured into a square 8-inch nonstick cake pan and, when completely cooled, turned over and cut into cubes. Dusted with confectioners' sugar it makes a healthy confection for children.

This can become a great accompaniment to roast chicken or turkey when reheated and mixed with ⅓ cup thick chicken stock and Dijon mustard to your personal taste.

Put half the quinces into a 3-quart sauteuse pan; add water to reach ½ inch above the fruit. Bring to a boil, then turn down to a simmer. Cook until the quince slices are tender, about 40 minutes; drain through a large conical strainer, reserving the cooking water. Set the quinces aside.

Put the cooking water back into the sauteuse and add the remainder of the quince slices. Section and seed both oranges over them to gather the dripping juices, and let the sections of orange drop into the pot. Add the vinegar and enough grape juice to reach ½ inch above the fruit. Bring to a boil, then turn down to a simmer. Cook the fruit until the texture is identical to the fruit of the first batch, about 40 minutes.

Sterilize the jars, new dome lids, and screw tops (see page 975). Return the first batch of quinces to the sauteuse pan, stir in the honey and enough grape juice to reach ½ inch above the fruit. Finish cooking together at a steady, low simmer, stirring at 10-minute intervals, until the fruit has fallen apart and forms a puree. Let this puree simmer another 10 minutes, until it is topped by a very thin layer of mixed honey-and-juice syrup. This last operation may take up to 1½ hours altogether, perhaps even longer. Pour the cotignac into the sterilized jam jars to within ⅛ inch of the rims and seal. If upon cooling it becomes too thick to spread, bring it back to a boil and add boiling water to your taste. Very good on very lightly buttered walnut bread toast.

This cotignac was stored in a cool cellar and was supposed to keep 6 months. Nowadays, safety requires processing it 5 minutes in a hot water bath to sterilize it, which will prolong its shelf life considerably.

If you read the introduction above, you can sense the care taken by ancient cooks in the production of preserved fruit, to keep it stable, so it would neither mold nor spoil. In one word, their difficulties are ours, for how many times has a beginner in the kitchen enthusiastically started making jams or preserves to see them remain liquid and never jell, and start molding within a few weeks?

If a jam does not jell well, the water mobility in it remains high and becomes a breeding ground for bacteria and molds which will spoil its taste and render it dangerous for consumption. In earlier times, when less was known about the nasty effects of some microorganisms, we simply removed the mold with a spoon and reboiled the jam thoroughly for about 20 minutes. The result was a fruit jam whose fresh taste had been completely destroyed. We know enough nowadays to immediately dispose of any jam containing any trace of mold.

Indeed, molds are bad enough, but another lethal bacterial guest, *Clostridium botulinum,* which secretes a deadly toxin called botulin, is even more dangerous because its presence cannot be detected by sight or smell. I have already referred to it on page 362 and several times in this book. However, read this warning again and understand how this organism survives. *Clostridium botulinum* is to be found in the soil, particles of which eventually enter in contact with fruits and vegetables. It settles down to live between 70° and 110°F and thrives without oxygen (it is anaerobic) in the live tissues (parenchyma) of leaves.

Live clostridium is destroyed when it boils at 212°F for a relatively short time, but its spores are not and they must be submitted to a temperature of 242°F at length to become inactive. It is these heat-resistant spores that are responsible for the production of botulin which, in the majority of cases, is fatal if ingested. Since C. *botulinum* spores thrive in a moist environment, cans of vegetables and fruits in syrup are prime environments for them to live and secrete their deadly poison. The same can eventually happen with jams prepared with lower contents of sugar and acid, so be vigilant in the way you measure, cook, preserve, and store your fruit products.

It is comforting to know—even if it remains active at refrigerator temperature—that C. *botilinum* remains inactive in frozen foods, and that its growth is impossible in food containing less than 35 percent moisture. You will see on page 983 how low-sugar jams are put under vacuum by the boiling water bath method, then stored in the freezer as soon as cold, as a double guarantee that the preparation will remain stable in an environment cold enough not to allow C. *botulinum* to develop in the jars.

You will, in each of the categories of sugar-preserved fruit that follow, find instructions on how to store them to prevent spoilage; however, I shall not be the one to prepare your jams, jellies, and preserves, and ultimately you are the one responsible for the sanitation of the material you use to prepare jams and jellies and for the proper preparation, preservation, and storage of the finished product.

For a confirmation of the principles that I outline here, please acquire the excellent book called *Putting Food By*, written by Ruth Herzberg, Beatrice Vaughan, and Janet Greene, first published in 1973 by the Stephen Greene Press. It is an important book, now available in paperback in many successive editions put out by Bantam Books. In it you will find the best directions for processing fruit in syrups, which will not be included in this book.

If you wish to establish a cottage industry making jams and jellies, go to the agricultural, food, and health departments of your state to investigate the conditions you must fullfill to enter such a business. Become familiar with your legal responsibilities before you start spending any cash on equipment. The rules and regulations are multiple and slightly different in almost all states and must be investigated in depth everywhere.

Modern Principles of
Making and Storing Jams and Jellies

The proper jelling of jellies and jams can present a few pesky problems and it is not rare for an enthusiastic jelly maker to go through a lot of work preparing the fruit and following the recipe scrupulously to end up with only a big disappointment: The jelly did not jell.

If this happens to you, first, stop being angry at yourself and thinking you did something wrong; generations of cooks before you have encountered this problem. All fruits vary in size, shape, dimension, and of course in taste. For example, take a truly sun-ripened strawberry in its gorgeous crimson robe with a fragrance so intense it can make you giddy; if you place this berry between your tongue and palate and crush it slowly, it is possible that your whole head will start to buzz as your tastebuds, your nose, and your brain react to the experience, which is so overwhelming that all you can say is "Oh." Oh yes, indeed, but when did you last taste such a strawberry still warm from the sunshine?

I need not belabor my point: Good, fragrant just-ripe fruit will give you good jellies and jams which will jell without difficulty; lesser quality fruit that has been in storage for a while or has been picked green and as a consequence will never ripen properly carries the greater possibility that it may not jell well. The conclusion is clear: Make jellies and jams or preserves only with fruit that you buy at farmstands or have grown in your own garden and allowed to develop a good pectin content, for pectin is the magic substance and in it resides the source of the jell you are looking for.

In ripening fruit there is no pectin, only its precursor, protopectin and two enzymes, called esterase and pectinase. As the ripening progresses these enzymes go to work and transform the protopectin into pectin. Once developed, the pectin is to be found in the pulp, skin, and cores of most fruits, not the juice. It develops in the membranes surrounding the fruit cells and keeps them tightly packed and attached to one another, exactly as collagen in meats keeps the long muscle cells cemented together. When the fruit reaches the just-ripe stage it contains its maximum pectin content. As soon as over-ripeness sets in, the sugars break down and the flesh of the fruit turns too soft as pectin is changed into pectic acid, which is of no use to you as a jelly maker.

By now, you understand that to make successful jellies, jams, and preserves, you need just-ripe fruit. But this is not the only substance you need; you must have the acids contained in the fruit which will, in cooperation with sugar, pectin, and heat, help form the jell you are looking for. The pectin jell will not form with artificial sweeteners.

Fruits contain a number of acids. The citric acid of citrus fruit is a good and useful acid, as are the malic acid of apples and the ascorbic acid of many berries. The tartaric acid of grapes, however, can be bothersome for it can cause a successful jelly to become granular while in storage.

During your years of schooling you surely have heard a teacher or two talk about the pH of some substance or other. Many teachers will assume that students innately know what pH stands for, but just in case it has eluded you so far, it is shorthand for "potential of Hydrogen" and is a rating of the acidity or alkalinity in any substance. It is measured on a scale from 1 to 14, with the *lower* numbers representing the *higher acidity*, the *higher* representing *higher alkalinity* and 7 being neutral, neither strongly acid nor strongly alkaline. Any fruit with a pH 7 contains an equal amount of acid and base. Here is a short list of fruits with an indication of their pH range; you will see lemons at the top with high acidity, as you might have expected.

pH Levels of Fruit

Scientists have established the fact that a 3.0 to 3.5 pH will yield the best gelation; problems will start already with a 3.5 pH. Looking at the list you can already gather the fact that, for example, plums that are not too sweet and just ripe with a probable pH of 3.4 to 3.5 will jell better than plums that are very ripe and show a pH of 4.0. The same will apply to peaches, which have a bad reputation as jellers because not only do they have a low level of acid but a lower level of pectin.

Now what happens if all you have is a batch of fruit that is slightly overripe? You can simply add lemon juice to the batch to raise its acidity. If, on the other hand, you have a batch that is not ripe enough and very acid, you can add a little more sugar. Most of the time the batch of fruit you buy or pick will have some just ripe, some overripe and they will balance one another naturally, as long as the majority of the batch is made up of just-ripe fruit.

Here is a short list of good jellers which combine good acidity with high pectin:

- Apples of all types, including and especially crab apples
- Quinces
- Cranberries, both the cultivated cranberries and the wild cranberries of northern climates
- Blackberries, especially the wild ones
- Gooseberries, either red or green
- Currants, red, black, or white
- Plums of most types, especially the prune plums
- Some grapes, especially the Concord and all grapes of the American *labrusca* type

If, for one minute, you think about the taste of each of these fruits, you will find that some of them are frankly acidic, others much less so. Quinces and ripe, juicy plums may not taste that acidic but the skins of plums are, as are the cores and skins of quinces, which also contain a very large amount of pectin. For this reason, when making plum jams, one never peels the fruit and when preparing quince jelly the skins and cores are tied into a layer of

pH LEVELS OF FRUIT

- Lemons: 2.2 to 2.8
- Gooseberries: 2.8 to 3.0
- Raspberries: 2.8 to 3.6
- Plums: 2.8 to 4.0
- Apples: 2.9 to 3.7
- Grapefruit: 3.0 to 3.7
- Oranges: 3.0 to 4.0
- Rhubarb: 3.1 to 3.2
- Blackberries: 3.2 to 4.0 and above
- Cherries: 3.2 to 4.0
- Blueberries: 3.3 to 3.5
- Peaches: 3.4 to 4.0 and above
- Pears: 3.6 to 4.4 and above

cheesecloth and added to the pot in which the quinces are cooking in water.

Other fruits contain much less pectin; they are:

- Strawberries
- Raspberries
- Cloudberries
- Blueberries, huckleberries, and bilberries
- Salmonberries
- Cherries, sweet or sour
- Figs, white or black
- Grapes of the originally European *vinifera* type
- Pineapple
- Rhubarb
- Most melons
- Rose hips
- Pears

Most of these fruits—though not all of them—will have to be combined with some high pectin fruits or processed with the specially prepared pectin found in supermarkets under different names.

HOW PECTIN GOES TO WORK
TO MAKE A JELLY

Gelatin occurs when a mesh forms, trapping a liquid. When a fruit or berry is heated by itself for jams or with water for jellies, the pectin, a long stringy molecule, is extracted from the pulp, skin, and, in pomes, from the cores. These long strands of pectin do not bond to one another, but rather to water. As you add quite a large amount of sugar, the dissolving sugar attracts the water (present in the fruit juices or as added water), leaving the pectin somehow stranded. The pectin would be in danger of separating (precipitating) from the mixture were it not for the natural fruit acids and/or added lemon juice. The acids prevent the pectin from precipitating, and as the latter absorbs water, a solid mass of jelly forms.

The more jams and jellies you make, the more you will realize that all fruits produce jellies of different strengths. For instance, an apple jelly is elastic and rather strong. However, since not every fruit produces such an elastic jelly, you will often see recipes mixing apples, berries, and drupe-type fruits together to help develop a jelly with a stronger structure.

COMMERCIAL PECTINS Some commercial pectins are made with the leftover pomace of apples that were crushed to obtain cider, while others are made with the white pith of citrus fruits. Commercial pectins can be bought either as a powder, which requires being dissolved in water, or as a semiliquid contained in a pouch. I personally prefer the semiliquid product, but this choice is entirely personal and you certainly can use the one you prefer.

Many scientists believe that powdered pectin makes jellies and jams that are stable.

When using a commercial pectin, you must follow the directions of the manufacturer very carefully for best results when making jellies from scratch. Pectins can also be used to rescue jellies that have not fully jelled; see page 998 for an explanation on how to do this.

The Implements Needed to Process Jams, Jellies, and Preserves

KITCHEN SCALE

WHEN MAKING OLD-FASHIONED JAMS AND JELLIES Once you have cleaned and dried the fruit, and removed skins, pits, cores, and pips or seeds only when necessary, please weigh the fruit as precisely as possible on a kitchen scale. Measuring in cups is not recommended with this old-fashioned technique.

WHEN MAKING MODERN JAMS OR JELLIES WITH COMMERCIAL PECTIN You will find recipes included in the package of pectin and I recommend that you follow to the letter the quantities of sugar, fruit, and acid recommended for best success, each product varying a little from the next.

The quantity of fruit needed is usually indicated twice in the directions, first, the quantity of whole fruit to buy, the second the volume of prepared, ready-to-process fruit the purchased fruit should yield in order to use the recommended dose of pectin. May I suggest that you always buy ½ pound of fresh fruit more than is required by the pectin manufacturer so you can select the best quality fruits out of the batch; you can always use the less perfect specimens in a fruit or mixed salad.

COOKING POT

The perfect cooking pot for jams and jellies is a low-sided pot with a large, flat bottom for better exposure of the mixture to heat.

If you are going to process a large amount of fruit, let us say 5 pounds and over, you will need that old-fashioned pot known as a jelly kettle, which is made of unlined copper.

If you are going to process 2 to 3 pounds of fruit, you will need a 4- to 5-quart sauteuse pan or pot, preferably one made of stainless steel with a copper-dressed bottom. If you are going to process an occasional batch of 1 to 2 pounds of fruit, a 3- to 4-quart sauteuse pan or pot of the same construction will be sufficient. *Small batches are always easier to handle and more successful than larger ones.*

Basically, use whatever pot you have, but:

- Pay attention to the fact that the fruit should reach no higher than halfway up the sides of the pot.
- Use only copper or stainless steel; enameled cast-iron or nonstick pans retain traces of fat that are not beneficial during the cooking of the preserves and aluminum is not recommended when cooking acid fruits or fruit acidified with citrus juices.

SKIMMER

Use a stainless steel slotted spoon or, better yet, a flat, round skimmer made of stainless steel mesh, which will remove the foam easily and lightly without removing too much of the fruit mixture.

TO HOLD THE FRUIT WHILE IT WAITS TO BE COOKED OR MACERATES

Use exclusively glass, ceramic, or Pyroceram bowls or containers.

TO STRAIN THE JUICE OF FRUITS FOR THE MAKING OF JELLY

Use a large China cap or conical strainer completely lined with a large piece of finely woven cheesecloth that has been boiled in water, cooled, and squeezed dry before being arranged in the strainer so that its ends hang over and outside the strainer. The best cloth to use for this operation is what is usually known as mortuary cloth. You can order one large box from a drugstore; it will cost you a little money but it will last you for years and you will be able to use it to strain other compositions such as refined sauces. An old-fashioned jelly bag is also excellent for this operation.

TO PREPARE FRUITS FOR THE MAKING OF JELLIES OR JAMS

Wash and dry the fruits. A food mill is very useful, but you can also use a grinder or simply chop the fruit by hand, making sure—if, of course, applicable to the fruit you are processing—that you collect all the juice that escapes from the fruit in the same bowl that contains the chopped fruit.

TO MEASURE THE FINAL TEMPERATURE OF JAMS AND JELLIES

A simple American candy thermometer immersed in the batch of jam or jelly will give you the temperature of the jam.

Any old-fashioned jam or jelly made only of fruit and sugar must be brought at least to a final temperature of the degree of boiling water at the altitude at which you live plus 9 degrees Fahrenheit. For example, if you live at sea level, the water will boil at 212°F, and the final temperature of any jam cannot be less than 212°F plus 9°F, or 221°F.

Here are the corresponding temperatures in Centigrade and Fahrenheit in the range of temperatures in which you will need to check any jam or jelly in the last stages of its cooking. I have indicated those ranges in both the metric and Fahrenheit systems because some very beautiful jams exist in European books published in English in metric measurements.

After the list of temperatures, you will find the two useful formulas to convert any temperature from Centigrade to Fahrenheit and vice versa, in case you have to read a temperature below or above the temperatures indicated in the list.

1. To convert from Centigrade into Fahrenheit: Temperature in degrees Centigrade $\times$ 9/5 + 32 = temperature in degrees Fahrenheit.

2. To convert from Fahrenheit to Centigrade: Temperature in degrees Fahrenheit $-32 \times$ 5/9 = temperature in degrees Centigrade. For another formula, see "Temperature" in the glossary.

CHOICE OF SUGAR

You can use cane sugar or, if working overseas, beet sugar. Both work exactly the same way; having used both, I prefer cane sugar.

STORING JARS AND HOW TO USE THEM

The most practical are the so-called Mason or Kerr or Ball jars or any other brand offering the sames sizes and shapes. They have a wide mouth and are covered with a thin, so-called dome lid which is tightened strongly with a screw top.

All jars before receiving a fresh quantity of jam or jelly must have been *sterilized* in the dishwasher or by being boiled in water for 15 minutes. The lids must be new, never used before dome lids, sterilized in boiling water for 5 minutes, as must the screwtops. Both jars and lids must air dry before being used. If you dry them even with a freshly laundered kitchen cloth, they may be exposed to some residual bacteria.

Mason-type jars come in 4-, 8-, and 12-ounce capacities. Considering that the consumption of jams and jellies is much reduced nowadays, I recommend using only the 8-ounce (half-pint) jars for family use. Prepare larger jars only if you run a food service.

Please refer below to the general explanations for jams, jellies, and preserves to learn how to fill and sterilize the contents of the jars.

BOILING WATER CANNER AND STERILIZER

Buy a canner fitted with a rack in which you will immerse the jars of those fruit products that contain lower amounts of sugar. Read carefully the details on processing jams in this canner on page 976.

CENTIGRADE FAHRENHEIT EQUIVALENTS

Centigrade	Fahrenheit
87.7°	190°
90°	195°
100°	212°
102°	215.6°
103°	217.4°
104°	218°
105°	221°
107°	224.6°
109°	228.2°
110°	230°
112°	233.8
115°	239°

IDENTIFICATION TAGS

Please buy self-stick labels on which you will identify: the fruit used and the manner of preservation, the date of confection of the preserve, and the exact contents of the product. Here are examples:

APRICOT JAM
July 10, 1995
50% apricots, 50% sugar by weight

APPLE QUINCE JELLY
October 5, 1995
50% juice, 50% sugar by weight

APPLE RHUBARB JAM
October 20, 1995
60% fruit, 40% sugar by weight

Label immediately, especially for jellies; listing the exact contents will allow you to correct any jam or jelly that turns out too soft or too hard.

Making Jams

Jams are usually made with cut-up or chopped fruit, cooked with sugar until the fruit is translucent and the syrup properly thickened. Some fruit, such as apricots and peaches, fall apart when stirred during the cooking and will require little cutting or chopping. Others, such as pears and Italian prune plums, will have to be cut into small cubes or into quarters. Whereas apples, which contain a good amount of pectin, can be turned into jams without the use of commercial pectin, pears, many drupes, and berries cannot, and if you want to avoid long reducing of the jam and a candied taste in the fruit, you will have to use a modern recipe containing added pectin.

JARS AND THEIR LIDS While the jam cooks, sterilize the jars, dome lids, and screw tops. See page 975.

BOILING WATER BATH PROCESSING With very few exceptions, jams must be processed in a boiling water bath and I recommend that you do so for total safety. The goal of processing is to completely remove any trace of air from the jar and to sterilize the whole mass of jam in each jar.

If you are a young cook, you may never have seen your mother or grandmother processing vegetables in an old-fashioned laundry tub (which in retrospect was very wrong and dangerous). I have, and remember it with total lack of fondness. It was a mess; the jars had to be wrapped in towels to prevent them from knocking one another around while sitting in the boiling water for what seemed to be a tremendously long time. And after the boiling time was over, we had to remove all this stuff from the pot and invariably burned our fingers.

It is so easy and not at all expensive to go to a hardware store and purchase a deep "boiling water bath" canning kettle. The canner will be fitted with a basket which sits a good inch above the bottom of the container and keeps the jars from jiggling and possible shattering. The rack is separated into compartments, into which you will put one jar of still hot jam or preserves. In another very large pot, heat lots of water until it starts simmering and tiny bubbles detach themselves from the bottom of the pot. Put the heat on under the canner and immediately pour enough of this simmering water into the canner to cover the jars by at least 2½ inches, being careful to first pour between the jars rather than on their lids. *Bring the water to a full boil*, then cover with a lid. There must be plenty of empty space—at least 4 inches—remaining between the water and the rim of the canner to allow the water to boil fully under the lid. Continue boiling hard. Assuming that you are using half-pint (8-ounce) jars, set a timer for:

- 5 minutes for old-fashioned weight for weight jams, which contain a little more sugar by weight than fruit (described on page 978).
- 10 minutes for classic American jams, containing ¾ pound sugar for each pound of fruit or modern American jam made with pectin (see pages 981–82).
- 20 minutes for half sugar jams containing ½ pound sugar for each pound of fruit (described on page 983).

Think of the altitude at which you live when processing jams in a boiling water bath. The canning times given here are for sea level canning where the water boils at 212°F. You must increase the canning time if you live at high altitude. Use one of the following measures, depending on where you live.

- If the canning time is less than 20 minutes at sea level, add 1 minute for each 1,000 feet of altitude (305 meters).
- If the canning time is more than 20 minutes at sea level, add 2 minutes for each 1,000 feet of altitude (305 meters).

For example, if you live at 4,000 feet (1,219 meters), you will need to process jams requiring 10 minutes of boiling at sea level for 14 minutes, the 10 minutes required at sea level plus 4 minutes for each of the four additional thousands of feet.

STORAGE Store in a cool cellar or on the lowest shelf of a refrigerator. After a jar of jam has been opened, it must be consumed within 3 weeks of its opening and be kept refrigerated at all time between uses.

Please read all instructions referring to each type of jam and in each recipe before starting to work, including troubleshooting.

TROUBLESHOOTING Rather than explain what could go wrong before the recipes, I have explained it after each type of recipe so you can relate what you did and why the jam, preserve, or jelly is short of perfection.

OLD-FASHIONED "WEIGHT FOR WEIGHT" JAMS

These usually contain only fruit and sugar with an addition of lemon juice to further acidify the mixture.

Wash the fruit under running clear water, then dry it as much as possible. Check the skins for blemishes and cut them off if the fruit is not going to be peeled, or peel the fruit. Remove the cores and pips or remove the pits. Weigh the ready-to-cook fruit, then place it in a glass or ceramic bowl.

Weigh out the exact same weight of sugar as that of the ready-to-cook fruit. For this reason, this type of product is often called "weight for weight" or "pound for pound" jam. If you take into account the amount of natural sugar in the fruit, you will realize that the total weight of sugar is greater than that of the fruit pulp. The keeping capacity of such jams is excellent, as the water mobility is significantly reduced.

The fruit is macerated in the sugar for 24 hours, which will extract its juices and begin to extract the pectin it contains. After 24 hours, cook the jam until a drop of its syrup holds its shape on a cold plate or mounds well in the lip of a spoon.

While the jam cooks, sterilize the jars, lids, and rings (see page 975). Drain the jars upside down onto a clean towel and air dry the lids and screw tops a few minutes before filling with the jam.

Ladle the cooked jam into the sterilized jars. Fill the jars within ⅛ inch of the jar lip. Clean the jar lip all around the inside and outside with a clean paper towel dipped in boiling water or brandy. Put the dome lid on and tighten the screw top around it. These jams were in earlier times sealed with melted paraffin and covered with parchment paper, elegantly ruffled at the edges by our grandmothers and great grandmothers.

For complete security, process in a boiling water bath the length of time needed for the altitude at which you live (see page 976). After processing, as the jam cools, you will hear the dome lids click as the vacuum is completed. The lid should now be concave and not move at all when you push on it.

Keep the jars at room temperature in the cooler corner of the kitchen for 24 hours. Check the texture of the jam; it should barely move. If it slides easily down along the side of the jar, it is undercooked and will be too thin to spread pleasantly on bread.

To correct this situation, unseal all the jars and return the jam to a clean cooking pot. Resterilize the jars, screw tops, and *a completely new set of dome lids*. Bring slowly to a boil, then continue cooking until the doneness test is achieved. Repeat the whole cycle of operations described above.

OTHER TROUBLESHOOTING It often happens that such jams end up being too thick the first time or two you prepare them because of your lack of experience in judging the degree of doneness and texture of the jam. To prevent this from happening, let ½ cup of the finished jam cool a few minutes at room temperature, then put it in the freezer until cold, about 10 minutes. If the jam turns stiff, add enough boiling water to it, tablespoon by tablespoon, to bring it back to the consistency you like. Note how much additional water you used for that ½ cup, then transfer the bulk of the jam to a clean pot using a ½-cup (4-ounce) ladle. Count the number of ladles you transfer. Multiply the amount of water you used in the test by the number of ladles of jam counted. Mix this amount of water into the bulk of the jam and reboil 5 minutes. Ladle into resterilized jars with new dome lids, and screw tops.

It is possible that a jam will crystallize as it sits in storage. This can be caused by significant sugar content or overcooking. When you open a jar of such jam, top it with many tablespoons of boiling water as you need to dissolve the crystals and mellow the texture of the jam.

After a jar of jam has been opened for consumption, use it within 3 weeks of its opening date and keep it refrigerated at all times between uses.

Eighteenth-Century Apricot Jam
WEIGHT FOR WEIGHT OF FRUIT AND SUGAR

NFR—SIX TO EIGHT 8-OUNCE JARS

2 pounds apricots (net weight), washed, dried, pitted, and cut in half, skins left on
   (3½ cups packed)

2 pounds (4 cups) granulated sugar

Tiny pinch of salt

Juice of 2 lemons

½ teaspoon unsalted butter

½ cup peeled pistachios

Cognac as needed (optional)

You will need 2½ pounds of apricots to obtain 2 pounds net weight after pitting.

Arrange the apricot halves and sugar in alternating layers in a 3- or 4-quart sauteuse pan, ending with a layer of sugar. Let macerate a full 24 hours at room temperature, covered.

When ready to proceed, stir the mixture thoroughly, adding the salt. Bring to a boil and add the lemon juice and butter. Let cook 30 to 40 minutes over medium-low heat, stirring often to break up the apricots and prevent scorching. Skim as much as needed, although the presence of the butter will greatly reduce the amount of foam.

Test the doneness of the jam by dropping a large drop of the syrup onto a cold plate; if it mounds, the jam is ready. Test the temperature of the jam with a candy thermometer; it should read 230° to 239°F.

While the jam is cooking, toast the pistachios in a preheated 175°F oven on a baking sheet for 15 minutes. Rub them in a towel to remove any loose skins. Stir the hot nuts and Cognac, if used, into the hot jam just before ladling the mixture into the prepared jars as instructed on page 975.

Although I have prepared and stored this jam with success and no spoilage ever without boiling water processing, I still recommend processing the sealed jam jars in a boiling water bath for total safety. See page 976 for full instructions.

Beware: It is not uncommon for apricot jams not to set completely until several days after their confection; instances of apricots completely setting two weeks after their cooking are not rare. Give this jam a chance to rest a few days in a cold, dark place before testing its texture.

CLASSIC AMERICAN JAMS

In the making of classic American fruit jams, you use only ¾ pound of sugar for each pound of ready-to-cook fruit. Since the water mobility is slightly increased in the finished product, the cooked jam should be processed in a boiling water bath.

Two-Peach and Citrus Jam
60% FRUIT AND 40% SUGAR BY WEIGHT

NFR— SIX TO EIGHT 8-OUNCE JARS

Finely grated rind and juice of 1 lemon

Finely grated rind and juice of 2 Valencia oranges

1 pound just-ripe white peaches

2 pounds just-ripe yellow cling peaches

2¼ pounds (4½ cups) granulated sugar

Tiny pinch of salt

½ teaspoon unsalted butter

Bring a pot of water to a boil. Place the citrus rinds in a tea strainer and immerse for 1 minute in the boiling water. Drain and empty into a large glass bowl, reserving the blanching water. Strain the citrus juices into the same bowl using the same tea strainer.

Place each of the white peaches on a slotted spoon. Lower it for 1 minute into the same boiling water used to blanch the citrus fruit. Rinse it under cold water and peel immediately. Roughly cut the fruit up directly into the bowl holding the citrus juices. Mash coarsely with a potato masher. Repeat the same blanching operation with the yellow cling peaches, but cut them instead into ½-inch cubes. Mix in the sugar and salt and let the whole mixture macerate for 12 hours at room temperature.

Empty the peaches and juices into a large stainless steel sauteuse pan and rapidly bring to a boil. Reduce the heat to medium-low and simmer until a drop of the syrup placed on a cold plate mounds nicely or until the jam mounds at the edge of a spoon. For peaches containing a lot of juice, this may take as long as 1 hour. Check the temperature often; the final temperature should be at least 221°F and no more than 230°F.

While the jam is cooking, sterilize the jars, new dome lids, and screw tops (see page 975). Ladle the bright hot jam into the jars to within ⅓ inch of the rims, seal with the dome lids and screw tops, and process in a boiling water bath for the length of time needed for the altitude at which you are working (see page 976).

TROUBLESHOOTING FOR PEACH AND ANY OTHER JAMS These guidelines apply especially to peach jams, but can be applied identically to all other jams.

Peaches seem difficult to cook into jams because of the small amount of pectin and the large amount of juice they contain. If a peach jam or any other jam fails to jell properly, repair it as follows:

First, let the jam sit a few days under vacuum in the vegetable bin of a dry refrigerator. It is very possible that the jam will firm up. But if after a few days it has not and still sloshes around in the jar, empty the jam back into a sauteuse. Immediately wash and sterilize the jars again as well as a new set of never used dome lids but the same screw tops.

Add ½ cup sugar mixed with ½ cup water to the jam and bring to a boil; cook 5 minutes over medium heat, stirring to make sure that the sugar has melted.

Once the sugar has melted, bring the jam to a hard boil and, stirring constantly and vigorously, add the contents of a pouch of liquid pectin. Stir one more minute and ladle the jam into the prepared jars. Cover with the lids and screw tops and resterilize another 10 minutes in a boiling water bath.

MODERN AMERICAN JAMS MADE WITH COMMERCIAL PECTINS

The making of fruit jams with commercial pectin is a good preparation for the more difficult making of fruit jellies.

To prepare jams made with commercial pectin I use liquid pectin sold in pouches. The cooking is extremely rapid, the weight of the sugar very close to that of the fruit, and the added pectin makes the jam extremely stable. Jams made with commercial pectin must be processed in a boiling water bath.

Prepare the fruit and measure the sugar and lemon juice (if the fruit is not an acid one). Cut one corner of the pouch(es) of pectin and stand it up straight and ready to use in a 1-cup measuring cup. Mix the fruit and sugar together, add the butter to minimize foam, and bring to a full rolling boil on high heat. Stirring constantly and very hard, mix in the pectin and acid, if applicable, bring back to a rolling boil, and cook 1 full minute, no more. Skim off any traces of foam and ladle the jam into the sterilized jars.

Although you can seal the jars immediately, turn them upside down for 5 minutes, turn them right side up again, and expect a good vacuum to build, I strongly believe that processing this type of jam in a boiling water bath is very important for total safety. See page 977 for boiling temperatures and times.

Four-Fruit Jam

WEIGHT OF SUGAR SLIGHTLY MORE THAN
WEIGHT OF READY-TO-COOK FRUIT

NFR — EIGHT 8-OUNCE JARS

2 pouches liquid pectin
2 cups sour cherries, red or black, pitted and crushed, or substitutes
I cup crushed just-ripe strawberries
I cup crushed red currants or blackberries
I cup thick fresh raspberry puree
3½ pounds (7 cups) granulated sugar
½ teaspoon unsalted butter

Sterilize the jars, lids, and screw tops (see page 975) and keep ready to use. Cut one corner of each pouch of pectin open and stand up both pouches, ready to use, in a 1-cup measuring cup.

In a large sauteuse pan, mix together the cherries, strawberries, currants, raspberry puree, sugar, and butter. Bring the mixture to a full, hard boil, stirring constantly. Still stirring vigorously, add the contents of each pouch of pectin; continue boiling hard and stirring 1 more minute. Skim any foam off the jam and ladle into the prepared jars to within ⅛ inch of the rims. Seal with the dome lids and screw tops and process immediately in a boiling water bath for the length of time necessary for the altitude at which you work (see page 976). Remove from the bath and cool to room temperature. Store in a cool, dark, and dry place.

TROUBLESHOOTING FOUR-FRUIT JAM, OR FOR ANY JAM MADE WITH COMMERCIAL PECTIN It is extremely rare, especially if you follow the directions well, for a jam made with commercial pectin to fail to jell. The most common reason is overcooking the jam, though it can also be an insufficient amount of pectin, or a lack of balance among the pectin, sugar, and acid in the jam. Go back to page 971 and read again about the balance of sugar, pectin, and acid.

This was the favorite jam in my French home and was made without pectin. It tasted good but was half as bright in color as this present version. Because of the scarcity of sour cherries, you may use dark sweet cherries; you will then have to add the juice of 2 lemons to acidify the mixture. You will need 2 pints of raspberries to obtain 1 cup of strained thick raspberry puree.

When France went on her *cuisine minceur* kick in the 1970s, a jam called *confipote* was initiated by most jam manufacturers in the country and became a great favorite of mine. The weight of sugar used is only half that of the net weight of the ready-to-cook fruit. The name *confipote* is fitting since the product is really halfway between a jam and a French country-style fruit compote.

But be careful: Due to the lower amount of sugar in the jam, it is imperative not only to process 8-ounce jars of the product for 20 minutes at sea level (see page 976 for directions for processing at higher altitudes), but also to keep the jars of processed *confipote frozen* until you are ready to defrost and consume it.

Once open, the product should be eaten within 10 days and kept constantly refrigerated when not being served. Do not serve the jam directly from its storage jar; always spoon out an amount slightly less than what you believe you will need into a small serving dish and keep the remainder of the jar refrigerated. If some of the jam in the serving dish has not been consumed, do not return it to the jar; cover the serving dish with plastic wrap, store it in the refrigerator overnight, and use it the next day. The reason for this is to avoid introducing any bacteria to the jam by way of an unsterilized spoon or dish.

Low-Sugar Plum Jam
CONFIPOTE DE PRUNES
65% FRUIT AND 35% SUGAR BY WEIGHT

NFR—SIX TO EIGHT 8-OUNCE JARS

3 pounds Italian prune plums, pitted and cut up

Juice of 2 lemons

1 cup water

1½ pounds (3 cups) granulated sugar

½ teaspoon unsalted butter

You need to buy 3½ pounds whole prune plums to yield 3 pounds ready to cook.

Sterilize the jars, new dome lids, and screw tops (see page 975) and keep ready.

Mix the plums, lemon juice, and water together in a large sauteuse pan. Bring to a boil and cook 15 minutes over medium heat. Add the sugar and butter, mix well, and continue cooking over medium-low heat, visibly simmering, until the mixture is thick and all the skins have blended into the pulp. The jam should mound high when taken on a spoon, with a temperature of 220° to 221°F at sea level.

Ladle the jam bright hot into the prepared jars to within ⅛ inch of the rims and seal with the dome lids and screw tops. Process in a boiling water bath for the length of time necessary for the altitude at which you work (see page 976), then cool to room temperature. When cool, store in the freezer; keep frozen until ready to consume.

TROUBLESHOOTING CONFIPOTE DE PRUNES OR ANY OTHER CONFIPOTE No difficulties are to be expected from this simple preparation. If, when cooled, you find it too soft, recook it a while. If, however, you find it too stiff, remelt it, adding boiling water until you reach the consistency you like. Process again and store as indicated above.

Making Preserves and Conserves

These types of fruit confections are holdovers from the techniques of the eighteenth century. They have been supplanted by jams and jellies, especially since the use of commercial pectin has made them easier and less time-consuming to prepare.

OLD-FASHIONED PRESERVES

A preserve is a jam in which whole small fruit, or quarters of larger fruit, are cooked in a sugar syrup. Once cooked—that means when the fruit is fully candied in sugar and sinks into the syrup—the fruit is taken out of the syrup and drained until no more syrup drips from it. The syrup is then reduced further to obtain a greater concentration of sugar. Fruit and syrup are then blended together in the proportion of two parts fruit to one part syrup.

A conserve is a preserve containing one or several nuts and raisins or currants; the recipe for apricot jam on page 979 is a half-breed of jam and conserve. Conserves have, for all practical purposes, disappeared, but like preserves they are most pleasant served over ice cream or a fluffy rice pudding.

Do not expect preserves or conserves to have the same bright fruit taste as jams, especially those jams that are made quickly with commercial pectin. The fruit in preserves and conserves is deeply cooked and their taste, as a result, is less fresh. Preserves and conserves will give you an idea of the products our ancestors so relished. The last days before school started were dedicated to preserve and jelly making and were always extraordinarily happy occasions.

There are two ways of making preserves. One consists of cooking the fruit in a syrup, the other in macerating the fruit in pure sugar, which will draw the juices out of the fruit and form a syrup in which the fruit will cook.

PRESERVES MADE WITH A SUGAR SYRUP

Nowadays this type of preserve is usually made exclusively by artisans who are trained professionally and have access to manuals, techniques, and implements which cannot be used at home.

Practiced at home, the technique is awkward for modern minds used to blindly following recipes, for it is you, the cook, who must establish the recipe, basing your calculations for the amount of sugar and water to be used on the weight of the ready-to-cook fruit and its water content. It is no more complicated than doing an elementary school sum, but we are no longer used to it. The preparation of these preserves at home is to a point experimental; I remember my great grandmother calling them "guessing game jams."

All fruit treated in this manner must be just-ripe and pitted and/or peeled if needed. If used whole they should be small rather than large. If they are large, they must be cut into quarters, cored when appropriate, and, if they oxidate easily and have to wait before going into the syrup, they must be kept in acidulated water and blanched before being immersed in the syrup.

THE SYRUP Weigh the ready-to-cook fruit; depending on the juiciness of the fruit, you will need anywhere from the same weight of sugar as of fruit, to only half as much. For drier fruit such as pears, you will need 1½ cups of water per pound of sugar. For very juicy fruit like cherries and strawberries, the only additional water required will be the small amount needed to help the sugar melt into a syrup before adding the fruit. More liquid will be gleaned from the fruit losing some of its juices into the syrup.

Important: To prevent the fruit from turning hard while cooking, do not bring the syrup to a boil before adding the fruit. Simply melt the sugar over low heat, so it is still cool when you add the fruit. Slowly bring the mixture to a full boil, then turn the heat down to medium-low and cook together to the proper degree.

If you observe the rule that the fruit is cooked properly when it sinks into the syrup, you will rarely have to reduce the syrup before adding it to the jars. If you have to reduce the syrup, it is essential that the fruit be kept hot while you do so; put the fruit in a heatproof dish covered with tightly stretched microwave quality plastic wrap and keep it waiting in a 225°F oven. When the syrup is reduced, pack the fruit to reach two thirds of the way up the sides of each jar and top with the syrup, filling each jar up to ¼ inch from its rim.

Shake the jar to balance the fruit in the syrup. Process in a boiling water bath for:

- 30 minutes if you used half as much sugar as fruit by weight.
- 20 minutes if you used the same weight or close to the same weight of fruit and sugar, plus any time adjustments you need to make for high altitudes (see page 976).

Then *freeze* these products for complete safety; they will defrost without damage to the fruit or syrup. Once opened, keep the preserves refrigerated and use within a few days. As with half-sugar jams, never serve these preserves directly from the jar (see page 983).

There is sometimes a relatively large amount of syrup left after making preserves. You can keep the syrup frozen and use it later, diluted to preserve some of the same fruit, or you can keep the syrup to make a sorbet or a pancake syrup. The syrup will keep well; if and when it crystallizes, discard it.

Here is a recipe for a pear preserve from the eighteenth century; it calls for *roussettes*, another name for Bosc pears:

Candied Bosc Pears
ROUSSETTES CONFITES

NFR — SIX TO EIGHT 8-OUNCE JARS
12 small, ripe Bosc pears, peeled, quartered, cored, and weighed
Juice and rind of 1 lemon
Same weight of granulated sugar as of ready-to-cook pears
1 ½ cups water per pound of sugar

As soon as the pears are peeled, drop them into a bowl of water mixed with most of the lemon juice. You need to keep a few drops of juice to cook the sugar syrup.

Using a potato peeler, lift one thin curl of lemon rind from one of the half lemon skins.

Bring a pot of water to a boil, then blanch the pears for 2 minutes, 6 pear quarters at a time. Remove them to a clean kitchen towel. With the last batch of pears, also blanch the curl of lemon rind.

Mix the sugar and the needed quantity of fresh cold water in a large, flat-bottomed sauteuse pan. Stir and dissolve the sugar into the water, then add the pears and lemon rind. Slowly bring to a boil, then turn down to low heat, and simmer without stirring until the pears are translucent and sink into the syrup. They should be soft enough for a large needle to penetrate the largest of them easily but be candied throughout. If they are not, they will turn brown from the center out and spoil the preserve.

While the pears cook, sterilize the jars, new dome lids, and screw tops (see page 975). Set the oven at 225°F. Remove the pears to a baking dish, cover the dish tightly with microwave quality plastic wrap, and set the pears to wait in the oven. Measure the temperature of the syrup; if need be, reduce the syrup over low heat until its temperature is 8 to 9 degrees Fahrenheit above the normal boiling temperature required for the altitude at which you work.

Transfer 6 to 8 pear quarters to each jar to fill it two thirds of the way up. Pour the syrup over the fruit to within ¼ inch of the jar rim. Seal the jars. Process 20 minutes or whatever is correct required for your altitude in a boiling water bath (see page 976). After removing from the water bath, shake the jars gently so the pears are centered in the syrup by the time they are cold. *Keep frozen until ready to use.*

This recipe will not work with pears that are hard and have just arrived from a supermarket. Ripen them in a brown bag with a ripe banana, checking them often. Do not process them until they give slightly when pressed gently at their bottom.

Melon Preserve

NFR— FIVE 8-OUNCE JARS

2 or 3 ripe cantaloupes, depending on size

1 ½ pounds (3 cups) granulated sugar

1 lemon

1 ¼ cups water

½ whole nutmeg

It is essential that the melons be at the peak of ripeness—juicy, flavorful, and extremely aromatic. Supermarket cantaloupe does not work well; use farmers' market melon or some from your fields or garden. This recipe is for summer melons, not for winter melons.

Sterilize the jars, new dome lids, and screw tops (see page 975). Peel the melons and remove the seeds and the softer pulp that lines their center. Cut the meat into ½-inch cubes and weigh it to obtain 2 pounds of pulp.

In a large, flat-bottomed sauteuse pan, mix the sugar, a squeeze of lemon juice, the water, melon cubes, and nutmeg together. Bring to a boil, then reduce the heat to low and simmer until the melon cubes sink into the syrup and are cooked to their very centers when tested with a large needle. Drain the cubes on a drum sieve placed over a bowl. Place them in a baking dish, cover the dish tightly with microwave quality plastic wrap, and keep warm in a preheated 225°F oven.

Remove the nutmeg from the syrup and, if the syrup needs reducing, bring it to 8° to 9°F above the boiling temperature required for your altitude (see page 974).

Fill the jars two thirds full with the melon cubes, then pour in enough syrup to reach to ¼ inch below the rim of each jar. Shake the jar to balance the pieces of melon through the syrup. Seal the jars. Process in a boiling water bath for 30 minutes or whichever time is correct for the altitude at which you live. Cool completely and *keep frozen until ready to use.*

TROUBLESHOOTING FOR PEAR AND MELON PRESERVES AND ALL OLD-FASHIONED PRESERVES *Be careful:* Preserves are wonderful but they will mold and ferment before any jam will. This can happen when some of the fruit is not evenly done through to its core or the syrup was not reduced enough. You must be strict in discarding any preserve or conserve that looks and/or smells suspicious. The long canning time followed by freezing should, in principle, take care of *Clostridium botulinum*, its spores, and toxin.

MODERN PRESERVES

Since the old-fashioned preserves never quite completely "preserve" the fresh true taste of the fruit, I prepare sour cherry preserves with pectin and find them more delicious than any cherry preserve I ever made in Europe. You can follow the same recipe exactly using small strawberries, about ½ inch in diameter. Do not use wild strawberries or the cultivated variety of strawberries called *fraise des bois;* they are too small and shrink and lose completely the wonderful flavor they have in the raw state.

Modern Cherry Preserves

You will need 3½ pounds of cherries to obtain 3 pounds net weight after pitting the cherries with a pitter; leave the cherries whole. Use dry pectin. No water is needed; the juices of the cherries and the sugar will form the syrup. There is no need to check the preserve texture on a plate as is done in old-fashioned jams.

NFR — SIX 8-OUNCE JARS

3 pounds (net weight) pitted cherries

2 ounces powdered pectin

½ teaspoon unsalted butter

2½ pounds (5 cups) granulated sugar

Sterilize the jars, new dome lids, and screw tops (see page 975). Put the cherries in a large flat-bottomed sauteuse pan. Sprinkle in the pectin, stirring. Rapidly bring the mixture to a full, irrepressible boil that wells up over the whole surface of the pot. Continuing to stir and boil hard, add the butter, then the sugar in one continuous rain. When the sugar has all been added, continue boiling hard and stirring *only 1 more minute*. Remove from the heat, skim off any traces of foam, and ladle into the prepared jars to within ⅛ inch of the rims. Seal with the dome lids and screw tops. Process for 15 minutes or whatever is correct for your altitude in a boiling water bath (see page 976). Cool and keep refrigerated overnight to check the texture. If well jelled, freeze until ready to use.

TROUBLESHOOTING FOR CHERRY PRESERVES AND ALL MODERN PRESERVES   Imagine that the preserve has not set, which is quite unlikely, but still could happen. The only reasons why it would not set well could be either too little pectin or sugar. If the preserve once cold slides along the sides of the jars, empty all the jars into a sauteuse pan. Set the stove flame on medium-high. As you start stirring, gradually add ½ to ¾ ounce additional powdered pectin. Bring to a high boil. Immediately stir in 1 cup sugar and, after the addition, boil 1 more minute, no more. Skim the foam off and ladle into the resterilized jars, using new, never used dome lids. Reprocess for 15 minutes in a boiling water bath.

PRESERVES MADE BY MACERATION
OF THE FRUIT

To macerate a fruit means to soak it either in a liqueur or spirit, or to layer it in a bowl with sugar to extract its juices. Another type of maceration happens when you make marmalades of citrus fruit. The fruit is mixed with water and brought to a boil; this softens the rind. As the fruit sits in the water for 12 to 24 hours the pectin slowly leaches out of the white pith into the water. The fruit is boiled a second time and left to macerate another 12 to 24 hours. Finally the sugar is added and the marmalade cooked until the rinds are fully immersed in the syrup and a drop of the syrup mounds on a plate.

The recipe that follows is typical of a preserve in which the fruit is cooked two times, first in a sugar syrup, then, after maceration of the poached fruit overnight, in currant jelly.

Strawberries Preserved in Currant Jelly

NFR — SIX 4-OUNCE JARS STRAWBERRY PRESERVES, PLUS FIVE
8-OUNCE JARS STRAWBERRY JELLY

3 pounds (net weight) fully ripe strawberries, ¾ inch across, washed (4 to 4½ cups)

3 pounds (6 cups) granulated sugar

1⅔ cups water

Few drops of fresh lemon juice

24 ounces excellent quality commercial currant jelly (four 6-ounce jars or 3 cups)

Empty the washed berries onto a terry towel and pat gently until very dry. Hull the berries. Mix the sugar, water, and lemon juice together in a large, flat-bottomed sauteuse pan. Bring to a boil and cook without stirring until the temperature of the syrup measured with a candy thermometer registers 238° to 239°F (see Cooking a Sugar Syrup on pages 937–38).

While the syrup comes to the correct temperature, melt the currant jelly in a large sauteuse pan over low heat; keep it warm. Add the berries to the boiling sugar syrup. Shake the pan back and forth gently to keep the berries immersed in the syrup and to prevent them from breaking. Working over medium-high heat, bring the mixture back to a full boil that will fill the whole surface of the cooking vessel. Stir by sliding a blunt-end wooden spatula under the berries and pushing it from side to side of the pan, changing direction often. This allows the berries to roll over the spatula and not be crushed. Let cook, stirring at 1-minute intervals, until the berries look candied and have acquired a uniform color that blends completely with that of the syrup, 8 to 10 minutes. Skim off any foam.

Place a drum sieve (*tamis*) or the stainless steel basket of a round steamer over a large bowl and, using a stainless steel slotted spoon, deposit the strawberries on the *tamis* and let them drip well; they will look deflated. Once drained, add the berries to the pot containing the hot currant jelly and mix gently. Let cool and macerate, covered, overnight in a cool but not cold place; the remaining juices of the strawberries will mix with the currant jelly. Add any juice that has dripped out of the berries to the leftover sugar syrup. Cool the sugar syrup. Store it overnight in a cool place (and use it to make the strawberry jelly on page 996).

The next morning, bring the mixture of currant jelly and strawberries back to a boil over medium heat. Reduce the heat to medium-low and simmer for 30 minutes, longer if the berries are large. Your goal is to candy the berries to their very centers. The preserve is ready when the berries stay immersed in the currant syrup without floating to the surface. Shake the pan back and forth several times during the cooking to mix the berries back into the jelly.

You must use sun-ripened strawberries, as this recipe will not work with supermarket berries. However, it works well with frozen loose strawberries allowed to superficially defrost before adding them to the sugar syrup.

Since there are few red currants to be found across the United States, I have replaced the currant jelly my mother used to prepare herself to make this strawberry preserve with commercial currant jelly. If you have access to currants, by all means prepare your own jelly; the technique is described on page 992.

Sterilize the jars, new dome lids, and screw tops (see page 975). Ladle the hot mixture into the prepared jars to within ¼ inch of the rims; seal with the dome lids and screw tops and process 20 minutes or whatever is correct for your altitude in a boiling water bath (see page 976).

MARMALADES AND CONSERVES

Here are two typical examples, one a marmalade made with citrus fruit, the other a conserve made with ripe mangoes.

All Citrus Marmalade

NFR — SIX 8-OUNCE JARS

I white Florida grapefruit

I lemon (a Meyer lemon is best if you can find it)

I large lime

I California blood orange or, if unavailable, I navel orange

I Florida Valencia orange

I tangelo

I mandarin orange

2 tablespoons balsamic vinegar

Granulated sugar as needed

I teaspoon angostura bitters

This is a master recipe for all marmalades of whichever citrus fruits you may use. I have made many variations over the years and always loved the results.

The successive soakings and boilings of the fruit slices in the juice-and-water mixture are used to extract as much natural pectin from the fruit skins as possible and to soften the rinds. It is up to you to do the mathematics of calculating the amount of sugar and water to be used.

A warning: It is easy to reduce a marmalade too much; see the troubleshooting tip at the end of the recipe.

Squeeze the juices out of all fruits into a measuring cup, straining out the seeds. Set aside.

Cut the whole skins of all the fruits into slivers ¼ to ⅛ inch wide, placing them all in a quart-size measuring bowl. Pat them flat into the bowl without packing them too much.

On a writing pad, add the volume of collected juices to the volume of rind slivers. Multiply this quantity by three; that will give you the total amount of water that you should now measure out and add to a gallon-size sauteuse pan. Add the mixture of juices and rinds to the water. Let macerate, covered, 24 *full* hours in a cool place (do not skimp on the time).

The next day, bring the mixture to a boil; turn it down to a good simmer and cook gently over medium heat for 20 minutes. Turn the heat off, let cool, and let the fruit macerate again in a cool place for a second period of 24 hours.

Sterilize the jars, new dome lids, and screw tops (see page 975). Measure the final volume represented by the liquid and the slivered fruit rinds mixed. In another cup or container, measure out the same volume of sugar and set it aside.

Return the fruit-and-juice mixture to a large sauteuse pan. Bring to a boil, turn down to medium-low heat, add the vinegar, and simmer gently for 10 minutes. Add the sugar, bring back to a boil, and finish cooking on medium-low heat until the fruit rinds have turned translucent and the syrup surrounds all the rinds, 35 to 40 minutes. Stir in the angostura bitters. Test the doneness of the syrup on a cold plate. If it mounds, the marmalade is ready.

Ladle the hot marmalade into the prepared jars; seal and process 20 minutes or whatever is correct for your altitude in a boiling water bath (see page 976). Remove from the water bath and let stand until cold. Then keep refrigerated or frozen.

TROUBLESHOOTING MARMALADE This type of preparation can pose only one problem: overcooking. To prevent this from happening, turn ½ cup of the finished marmalade into a small container and cool it rapidly in the freezer. When cold, judge its texture; if too thick, bring some water to a boil and add as much boiling water to the marmalade as needed to make it more fluid. Give one last boil after adding the last bit of water.

Mango Conserve

NFR—ONE 12-OUNCE JAR

3 tablespoons dried currants

¼ cup dark rum

1 pound almost ripe mango pulp, cut into slivers ⅛ inch thick

1 pound (2 cups) granulated sugar

1 tablespoon fresh lemon juice

12 smallest size cashew nuts

Macerate the currants in the rum and the slivers of mango in the sugar overnight in the refrigerator in two separate containers.

Wash a 6-cup stainless steel sauteuse pan or skillet twice with soap, rinse it abundantly, and let air dry. Add the mango and sugar and lemon juice; bring to a boil and cook over low heat until the slivers look candied and translucent and remain immersed in the syrup. The cooking time is in the vicinity of 35 to 40 minutes but no exact time can be indicated since it will depend entirely on the texture of the mangoes you have used.

Meanwhile spread the nuts on a baking sheet and dry them in a preheated 175°F oven for 30 minutes. When the slices of mango have sunk into the syrup, add the currants and nuts, give one last hard boil, and mix well. Turn into a bowl and keep refrigerated in the full amount of syrup until ready to use.

TROUBLESHOOTING MANGO CONSERVE Brace yourself; anything can happen in the way of texture since the mangoes we find in the United States have traveled far and vary a lot in their ways of ripening. I do not recommend making a larger amount of this conserve, if only for its price, but for one special dessert it is most delightful.

This is a conserve, but not one to store or keep. Prepare it, cool it, and serve it over your best ice cream flavored with double vanilla, ginger, or coconut. The recipe is from Martinique. It is erratic in the way it jells; some types of mangoes jell very well, others only a little. The fresh mixture is good anyhow. Prepare it in the morning, keep it refrigerated, and use it that same night as a perfect topping for vanilla ice cream.

Jellies

I remember all the women of my family getting together to make jelly because each and every one of them had trouble making it alone. Eventually, taking a trick from Great-grandmother and blending it with two more from Grandmother, and one from Mother, we all got there, but talk about a session in washing pots and pans! The missing ingredient was definitely the knowledge of which fruits jell better, how much water to use to release a good juice full of pectin, and how to add acid to fruits that are very sweet and contain very little acid.

Before we go on further in these explanations, please refer to page 972 and read the paragraph in which I explain the way cooking softens pectin, then come back to me for a double experiment.

TO EVALUATE THE AMOUNT OF PECTIN CONTAINED IN A GIVEN FRUIT JUICE

So that you can learn how to evaluate the amount of pectin contained in a given fruit juice, I would like you to engage in a small experiment with ingredients you have in your refrigerator and cupboard.

Melt 3 tablespoons of whatever commercial jelly you have in the house, preferably apple or currant. Take two 6-ounce wineglasses and label them 1 and 2 with a marker.

In glass number 1, put 2 tablespoons of the melted jelly plus 1 tablespoon boiling water. Stir well to homogenize so completely you cannot see any traces of jelly anymore, then let cool. Add 3 tablespoons vodka, stir well, and let stand.

In glass number 2, put 1 teaspoon of the melted jelly and 2 teaspoons plus 2 tablespoons of boiling water. Again, stir completely to homogenize, let cool, then add 3 tablespoons vodka, stir well, and let stand.

Five minutes later, examine the two glasses carefully; this is what you will see:

- *In glass number 1:* You can see that the liquid is almost clear but that there is a shadow barely the size of a penny at the bottom of the glass, made of either one larger piece or several smaller pieces of something. The something is the pectin contained in the jelly which has fallen (precipitated) to the bottom of the glass.
- *In glass number 2:* You will see a mixture of jelly water and vodka which is cloudy, but with absolutely nothing at the bottom of the glass. Because so little jelly was used, there is not enough pectin in glass number 2 to allow it to precipitate.

Now, instead of using jelly melted in water use 3 tablespoons of any fruit juice mixed with 3 tablespoons of vodka to see how much pectin the juice contains. With apple juice, for example, you will see a mass of pectin in one solid piece. That means that when you make jelly with apple juice, just adding sugar and lemon juice, the mixture will jell very well upon standing and cooling.

If, however, you test a juice and the pectin precipitates out in small pieces separated from one another, jelly made from the fruit will not jell or jell only partially. To obtain a jelly that is tender but firm enough to hold its shape well with this fruit, you will have to use commercial pectin.

Making Jellies

Cooking the fruit is absolutely necessary in making jelly. For use in jelly, pectin must be extracted from fruits with water and heat, meaning that the fruit must be cooked. If you use a plain uncooked fresh apple juice to make apple jelly because you think that it may taste fresher, you are making a mistake because you absolutely need heat and the correct cooking time to extract the full amount of pectin from your fruits.

In the making of jellies, the fruit is cooked twice: A first cooking of the chopped fruit in water extracts the pectin and acid from the fruit. The second cooking happens when the juice of the fruit is mixed with enough sugar and additional acid and heated properly, obtaining a mixture that jells upon cooling.

The degree of maturation of the fruit is an important consideration in making jelly. Since acid is one of the key ingredients for the success of jelly, make it a practice to use two thirds ripe fruit for their sugar content and flavor and one third still slightly underripe fruit for their acid content.

THE FIRST COOKING

The big question is always how much water is needed to extract the pectin of each fruit. Opinions differ somewhat, but all in all the consensus is the same.

To make things easier, it is best to measure ready-to-cook fruit in quarts (increments of 4 cups). The boiling time is much longer for pomes than it is for drupes and berries. Here is a list of the fruit considered best for making jelly with the amount of water and the cooking times they require per quart of ready-to-cook fruit.

- **Apples,** coarsely chopped, peels and cores left on
    Water: 1 cup per quart
    Cooking time over medium-low heat: 10 minutes, covered, to extract the moisture from the fruit plus 10 more minutes, uncovered and stirring occasionally to promote the extraction of the pectin
- **Quinces,** coarsely chopped, peels and cores left on
    Water: 2 cups per quart
    Cooking time over medium heat: 25 minutes, covered
- **Drupes** (such as plums, cherries, and grapes of the Concord type—other

types do not work well without added commercial pectin), chopped as finely as possible, peels left on, all pits removed with the exception of grape pips

Water: ¼ cup per quart

Cooking time over medium heat: 15 minutes, covered

Peaches can also be turned into jelly but will require the addition of lemon juice, sugar, and commercial pectin because they lack both pectin and acid content. As for pears, their juice must be mixed with quince juice, which somewhat masks the fine pear flavor but boosts the pectin level.

- **Berries** Please use only those berries which contain a lot of pectin: currants (red, white, or black), gooseberries, blackberries, and cranberries of all types. For strawberries, raspberries, and blueberries you will have to add not only commercial pectin but also lemon juice.

  Water: ¼ cup per quart

  Cooking time over medium heat: 10 minutes, uncovered

  Pay special attention not to overcook berries or to cook them over too high heat. Their pips contain quite a bit of tannin (phenolic compounds) which will leach into the juice, giving it an unpleasant, semibitter, semiastringent taste.

STRAINING THE COOKED JUICE

When the fruit has undergone its first cooking in water, you must strain the mash in such a way that the juice will drip through and remain as clear as possible. You can either use a jelly bag hanging from the spout of the spigot directly over a glass or ceramic bowl standing in the sink, or you can line a China cap with a double layer of fine cheesecloth, empty the mash into it, and let it drip over a deep container (if metal, only use stainless steel). Both jelly bag and cheesecloth should be rinsed under hot running water and squeezed as dry as possible before using. Whichever method you choose, do not push on the mash to extract the juice faster, for tiny particles of fruit pulp will pass into the juice and make it cloudy.

On the other hand, the more tiny particles of pulp a juice contains, the better the jelly will taste. So it is up to you to choose what you like best: a jelly that is clear, beautiful to behold, and tastes delicious or an ever so slightly cloudy jelly that tastes even more delicious and looks a little less elegant.

OPTIMUM QUANTITY OF JUICE TO USE

It is recommended by all authorities in the kitchen sciences not to make batches of jelly with more than a quart of juice at a time because gelation is not as fast, nor is it as successful and, more often than not, needs to be "redone" with added commercial pectin. All in all it is a loss of time greater than doing two successive batches from the start.

The following amounts of sugar apply per cup of fruit juice to the different fruit listed below:

Pomes

Apples: cup for cup

Quince: ¼ cup sugar per cup of juice

Drupes

Concord grapes: ¼ cup sugar per cup of juice

Plums: ¼ cup if the plums are very ripe, but 1 full cup if the plums are a mix of half ripe and half unripe plums

Cherries, peaches: Use the amount of sugar recommended by the maker of the commercial pectin absolutely needed to prepare the jelly.

Berries

Currants, cranberries: cup for cup

Blackberries, raspberries, gooseberries: ¼ cup sugar per cup of juice

Strawberries: Use the amount of sugar recommended by the maker of the commercial pectin absolutely needed to prepare the jelly.

The final cooking time varies with the fruit, and you must consider this important point: Sugar and fruit means that the sugar will, while cooking, be in the presence of acid and consequently will invert, that is, break down into its two constituent sugars, glucose and fructose. This requires a certain amount of time to happen uniformly throughout the pan. If you cook the jelly too fast, it will not happen completely and it is very possible that your jelly may crystallize as it sits in storage. In the recipe for strawberry jelly on page 996, this reaction may very well happen, because the amount of water in the sugar syrup is relatively small.

WHEN IS THE JELLY DONE?

Cook the mixture to the "jelly stage," which is 219° to 220°F on a candy thermometer. You can recognize this stage yourself just looking at the jelly. Take some of it on a spoon at regular intervals and pour it from the side of the spoon, not from the tip. When the jelly stage has been reached, the mixture "sheets," which means it pours from the spoon in a sheet that stretches downward along the length of the spoon bowl.

TROUBLESHOOTING   For jelly troubleshooting guidelines, see immediately after the recipes on pages 998–99.

STORING JELLY

Pour the jelly into the sterilized jars to within ¼ inch of their rims, seal with new dome lids and screw tops, and process in a boiling water bath for 5 minutes or the length of time needed at the altitude at which you live (see page 976).

If you prefer, instead of using a boiling water bath, put paraffin on to melt in a double boiler while you make the jelly. Preferably use a small pitcher with a well-designed and defined pouring spout. As soon as the jelly has been ladled into the jars, top it with a ¼-inch-thick layer of hot paraffin making it cling well to the sides of the jar to seal.

Do not store jellies for great lengths of time; they taste best when consumed within 4 months of their confection. Jellies should be stored in a cool, dark place, and transferred to the refrigerator once they are opened.

Strawberry Jelly

NFR—FIVE 8-OUNCE JARS

5 to 6 cups strawberry-flavored syrup
¼ cup fresh lemon juice
3 ounces powdered pectin
I cup granulated sugar

This is a learning recipe. In the recipe for Strawberry Preserves in Currant Jelly on page 989, the cook finds him/herself with a large supply of strawberry-flavored syrup that is not used. Cool that syrup completely; you will have between 5 and 6 cups of it. This jelly must be consumed rapidly (see explanation below) and needs no boiling water bath treatment.

Sterilize the jars, new dome lids, and screw tops (see page 975). Pour the cold strawberry syrup into a sauteuse pan, add the lemon juice to the syrup, and set over medium heat. Immediately start adding the pectin to the heating syrup, stirring constantly. When the syrup boils irrepressibly, add the sugar in one continuous rain. Boil hard *only 1 more minute* and stop the cooking. Skim if needed. Strain (see page 974), ladle into the prepared jars to within a ¼ inch of their rims, seal with the dome lids and screw tops, cool to room temperature, and store.

This is a very delightful jelly, with a but. It contains very little water, and as a result there is some danger that, if stored at any length, it will crystallize, a fact that is the more possible because the jelly is made with pectin, which needs liquid to remain stable. To prevent this, keep one jar for yourself and give the remainder to family or friends for immediate use, telling them the jelly should be consumed within 2 weeks; after that period, you will see the jelly weeping a little. Enjoy, keeping it refrigerated between uses. It really is delicious. I have been successful in keeping several jars of this type of jelly frozen for 2 months but each defrosted jar was consumed within a few days.

Apple, Basil, and Lemon Jelly

NFR—SIX 8-OUNCE JARS

3 pounds unpeeled, uncored Granny Smith apples, chopped into ⅓-inch cubes
3 cups water
½ cup packed fresh basil leaves, washed, dried, and chopped

Very finely grated rind of 1 lemon

1 tablespoon fresh lemon juice

1 cup granulated sugar per cup of obtained juice

Place the apples in a large sauteuse pan. Add the water, cover, and cook 10 minutes over medium-low heat. Uncover the pan and mash the apples as much as possible with a potato masher. Add the basil leaves and lemon rind, stir to distribute through the fruit, and cook another 10 minutes.

Immediately turn the fruit mash into a jelly bag or cheesecloth-lined China cap set to drip into a glass or ceramic bowl (see page 974). Let drip until all juice has passed through.

Meanwhile sterilize the jars, their new dome lids, and screw tops (see page 975). Measure the obtained juice, pour into a sauteuse pan, and add the lemon juice and sugar. Bring to a boil, then cook over medium-low heat until the temperature reads 219° to 220°F on a candy thermometer, about 20 minutes, until the jelly "sheets" when poured off the side of a spoon (see page 995).

Skim well and immediately pour the jelly into the prepared jars to within ¼ inch of their rims; seal with the lids and screw tops and/or paraffin (see page 996); let stand overnight in a cool place. If the jelly has firmed up, sterilize for 8 minutes in a boiling water bath. If it has not, see page 998.

Wild Blackberry and Cranberry Jelly

NFR — SIX 8-OUNCE JARS

3 quarts wild blackberries

2 quarts fresh cranberries, broken in the food processor or coarsely chopped

1¼ cups water

3½ cups granulated sugar

Place the blackberries and cranberries in a large sauteuse pan. Crush them well with a potato masher, then add the water. Bring to a boil, then simmer, covered, over medium heat, for 10 minutes. Put the mash to drip in a jelly bag or China cap lined with cheesecloth. You should obtain approximately 2 quarts of juice. Use 1 quart and store the other to process later exactly the same way.

Sterilize the jars, new dome lids, and screw tops (see page 975). In a large sauteuse pan, mix the 1 quart of juice with the sugar. Bring to a boil, then cook 15 to 20 minutes over medium-low heat to the jelly stage (219° to 220°F on a candy thermometer, until the jelly "sheets" when poured off the side of a spoon; see page 995). Skim well and immediately strain into the prepared jars to within ¼ inch of the rims. Seal with lids or paraffin (see page

These berries can be collected almost anywhere in the United States in great big quantities come mid-August and until Thanksgiving; they are delicious and inexpensive.

996) and let stand in a cool place overnight, or check the texture immediately with ¼ cup of jelly (see just below).

TROUBLESHOOTING IMMEDIATELY AFTER COOKING: Pour ¼ cup of the jelly into a small glass custard cup and put it in the freezer 6 to 7 minutes. It should be set. If it is not, it may be because you cooked it too long. So do not attempt to recook the jelly by itself, for, if you think about it, the jelly is nothing more than a sugar syrup flavored with fruit extract. As any sugar syrup would, it will, if you continue to cook it, thicken and harden, so that instead of jelly, you will obtain something halfway between jelly and sugar candy.

If you think that you have overcooked the jelly (it is very stiff and pours very sluggishly when cold), bring it to a boil and very gradually add a small amount of boiling water to it until the temperature of the batch is 220°F, no more.

TROUBLESHOOTING AFTER OVERNIGHT REST Some cooks like to leave the jelly in jars (but un-water-bath processed) at room temperature overnight to check the texture the next day.

If the jelly flows nicely, like a thick fruit puree but without sluggishness, you are probably lacking both enough acid and sugar for the pectin to jell properly. Rather than fiddle with the amounts of those two, resort to a true life and money saver—your friendly commercial pectin.

Empty the thick juice into a sauteuse pan. Sterilize the jars again as well as *new, unused* dome lids and the screw tops. Add 2 tablespoons fresh lemon juice and 1 additional cup of sugar to the fruit juice. Stirring constantly and vigorously, bring the mixture to a rolling boil; add 1 pouch of liquid pectin and continue cooking at the same heavy boil *only 1 minute*. Skim and strain into the prepared jars. This time the jelly will be firm.

PROCESSING JELLY IN A BOILING WATER BATH Jelly stored under paraffin cannot be processed. The paraffin isolates the surface entirely from air and allows the jelly to remain unspoiled for 4 to 6 months.

Any jelly that has been allowed to cool overnight completely for the sake of checking its texture and is found to have jelled properly must be processed 15 minutes, or the necessary length of time at the altitude at which you live, for the heat to reach to the center of the jars.

Any jelly that has been "rescued" with an addition of commercial pectin can be handled like freshly made jelly and processed 10 minutes.

JELLY THAT HAS MOLDED OR FERMENTED AFTER STORING No rescue mission possible here; the jelly must be discarded. It has spoiled because it was either stored in a too warm and possibly too moist place, or it was stored in not-well-sterilized jars or with defective dome lids. Please do not allow anyone to even taste it; you do not know what could be in there. Reread the safety warnings on page 968.

NO-WORRY JELLIES MADE WITH COMMERCIAL PECTINS

Excellent jellies can be made with commercial pectins. They are extremely stable and can be frozen after processing in a boiling water bath without breaking down, which natural jellies sometimes do.

If you decide to prepare such jellies, follow the directions given by the pectin manufacturers; their recipes are really very good and easy to follow.

Cooks
in the Bakery

THIS SECTION CONTAINS INFORMATION ON THE BASIC INGREDIENTS USED to bake and the elementary principles of baking breads, pastries, and cakes. Any cook, whether a home cook or professional, should know the basics of bread and cake baking, not only for the simple and satisfying sake of knowing, but because baking is a thrill for the spirit, mind, heart, and palate. In the bibliography, I have provided a list of several excellent specialized books on the subjects of bread, cakes, and pastries which present a large variety of recipes and variations on the mother recipes I provide here.

For cooks who must cook at higher altitudes, refer to pages 1152–53 before you try any recipe.

Basic Ingredients:
Flours and Yeasts
Wheat and Wheat Flours

Two wild seeds—einkorn and emmer, both belonging to the genus *Triticum*—are the wild ancestors of the modern wheats on which a large part of the nutrition of the western world has rested since the development of agriculture. Both of them grew wild in a large area stretching from the Balkans to Iran; their descendants slowly spread over the ancient Mediterranean world and in roughly 12,000 years reached from the tell of ancient Jericho to Australia, where wheat arrived with the British colonists around 1800.

The flours used presently in the United States for the making of breads and pastries come from *Triticum aestivum*, the common wheat, and *T. compactum*, also called club wheat.

Since most of us live so far away from the regions of cultivation of wheat—so far that we have no idea what wheat or other western cereals look like—make it a point to search your countryside for wild barley and wheat. More often than not there will be a few ears, sprouted from kernels carried many miles by strong winds to some vacant field in the most unexpected of neighborhoods, thriving in small clumps of several stems. Sit down, rub one of the sheaths between both hands, and you will find a number of kernels.

In health or vegetarian food stores you will find barrels of diverse types of wheats. Acquire a small bag of berries, soak a few in water, and sprout them. Cut several through their natural crease at the different stages of the sprouting and observe. If you are impressed, consider taking a trip to the wheat fields nearest to you just about a week before harvest. The sight of millions of undulating wheat sheaths and the rustling of the breeze through vast expanses of fragrant fields baking under an immense and deep blue sky will wrench your heart and elevate your soul.

The Wheat Kernel

The outer membrane of each wheat kernel, which scientifically is called a caryopsis—the lofty name given to all seeds in which the outer membranes adhere tightly to the center of the kernel—can be white or reddish russet and is called the bran. It is made of six successive membranes of cellulose and hemicellulose tightly pressed against one another. Each layer has a name: The epidermis is the outermost, followed from the outside to the inside by the epicarp, the endocarp, the testa, the episperm, and finally the aleurone, the innermost single layer of cells that adheres tightly to the kernel center, or endosperm. The bran represents approximately 5 percent of the whole berry and is nutritionally undigestible bulk containing some iron.

The endosperm contains starch cells with thin cellulose walls embedded irregularly in a matrix of proteins. Depending on the type of wheat, the endosperm may represent up to 92 percent of the volume of the wheat kernel.

The embryo, as its name implies, is a microscopic plant complete with root, stem, and two tiny leaves that is contained in a small sac called the germ, located at the pointed end of the wheat kernel. The germ provides all the nutrients needed for the future stem of wheat to get itself started. You will, as you cut through the kernel, cut the small plant in half but will be able to see its parts with a strong magnifying glass. It is no wonder that wheat was considered a deity in all of the ancient civilizations, since each wheat berry contains an eternal cycle of life. The embryo contains a lot of unsaturated fats, which unfortunately oxidate rapidly, and are more often than not removed during the milling process to avoid giving the flour a rancid taste; it contains also proteins, B-complex vitamins, and iron, and represents 2 to 3 percent of the kernel.

Of Many Wheats and Many Flours

Wheat is grown in many parts of the United States—the immense bread basket of the Midwest, the Pacific Northwest, the cooler parts of northern California, and in several parts of the southern states.

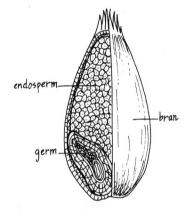

endosperm

bran

germ

CROSS SECTION OF A WHEAT KERNEL

There are several ways of categorizing flours. One can concentrate on the color of their outer bran membranes (white or red wheats) and the season in which they are sown and grown (spring and winter wheats).

Winter wheats are always sown in the fall, the exact time varying with the climate and the latitude. It is August in Canada and northern Montana, September in Wyoming and Nebraska, October in Oklahoma and November in northern Texas). Winter wheats are harvested in early summer.

The areas where spring wheats are grown are more difficult to establish with accuracy. Depending on the exact location, latitude, and altitude of the growing fields and on the general climate of a precise area, some spring wheats are sown in the spring while others are sown in the fall. As a consequence they will be harvested at diverse times of the summer.

In the last but most important of the categorizations, wheats are separated into hard and soft wheats, which differ by the way their starches are bound to the matrix of proteins in their kernels.

In hard wheats, proteins and starch particles are packed closely together, with so very little air space between them that the starch grains, which are small, cannot be separated easily from the proteins. It is this type which will produce bread flours. To familiarize yourself with hard wheat flour, rub bread flour between your thumb and index finger and you will feel its larger gritty particles; if you pinch the flour tightly between your fingers, it will not clump easily but fall into a coarse powder onto the work surface.

In soft wheats, the grains of starch are larger, more numerous, nicely rounded, and sit comfortably surrounded by larger air pockets; they are not tightly attached to the matrix of proteins and can separate easily from it. Such wheats will produce flours best used to prepare pastries, biscuits, and cakes. Try taking a small pinch of pastry flour between your first two fingers and you will find that it clumps much better than bread flour.

Selected very soft wheat flours are also used to make cake flour. Cake flour is so soft that when you press a bit between two fingers, it will form a very visible small clump, which will keep its shape as it falls to the countertop, after rapidly absorbing any tiny amount of moisture present on the surface of your skin.

About the Milling of Wheat

Milling will turn hard and soft wheats into flours. It is a very complicated process during which the premoistened grains of wheat will pass through a series of diverse mechanical rollers and/or machines which will produce successive and progressively finer "streams" of flours. Any future professional cook or baker should read and understand wheat milling as described in the food science books listed in the bibliography on page 1176.

If you have access to flour that is stone-ground by a true independent miller, you will have a treat when making breads. Search your area well, as there are dedicated millers all over the United States.

All cooks already know that the basic flours we can buy are: whole wheat flour, which comes to us truly whole with its bran, endosperm, bran, and germ included; and white flours. The largest percentage of white flours available are sold in bags carrying the label "patent flour." This means that the flour contained in the bag has been milled from a blend of the best streams of flours produced by the mill, and sifted to separate it from larger and uneven particles remaining after the last milling. Flours made from these larger particles are called clears and are used in the manufacture of breakfast cereals.

In modern milling the sifting is followed, sometimes even replaced, by passing of the flour meal through a large separator, in which the flour is wildly aerated by a central column of forced air. The air stream directs the lightest, starchiest particles toward the upper part of the container; they will be used to produce soft pastry and cake flours. The heavier particles, which contain mostly proteins, fall downward toward the bottom of the container and are used to produce strong bread flours and strong all-purpose flours.

The average yield of extraction of flour from grain in the United States is 70 to 72 percent for white flours and very close to 100 percent for whole wheat flours.

Strong Flours

Flours as they come to us prebagged at the mill can have diverse degrees of strength. Strong flours are mostly milled from hard wheats and are mostly used in the making of breads.

The strength of a flour is directly related to its composition, more specifically to the amount of proteins it contains. The strength of a flour can be measured scientifically as the percent of the production of carbon dioxide in a given dough and the amount of the same gas lost from the same dough during its fermentation.

Whereas the amount of sugar contained in a dough determines how fast the carbon dioxide will develop in it, the percent of proteins contained in the flour used to prepare the same dough is determined by the amount of carbon dioxide this dough will retain.

The Players in Bread Making

There are several types of proteins in flour; some of them are soluble in one liquid or another, others are not.

Please familiarize yourself with the cast of characters that will be your kitchen companions when you make a loaf of bread; they are a motley crew, but all have very important roles:

- The flour proteins or gliadins and glutenins. There is really not one single protein called gliadin and one single protein called glutenin, but rather complex mixtures of protein fractions called the gliadins and the glutenins.
- The gliadins are soluble in 70 percent alcohol solutions and insoluble in water. They are shaped in clusters of neither round nor oval particles which are crisscrossed with long chains of insoluble glutenins. Sometimes the glutenins are almost straight; sometimes they are so long that they fold upon themselves.
- There is you and your hands putting energy into making the dough when kneading it; you are important, for you can make or break that loaf of bread, as you will see later.
- There is the water that you will add to the strong flour to make the dough.
- There is sulfur which is an intrinsic part of the glutenins to which it is attached in the form of "disulfides." Disulfides are small clusters of two atoms of sulfur each, hence their name.
- There are sulfhydryl groups, each made of one atom of sulfur and one atom of hydrogen. These sulfhydryl groups exist attached to the proteins in flour and/or in doughs. In doughs they may come from the proteins of milk, eggs, or other proteinic products usually used in the making of doughs.
- And last, there is the natural unsaturated fat that is contained in wheat flour.

What you want to do is make a dough that holds its shape while rising properly and retains as much carbon dioxide as possible for the dough to be leavened and subsequently baked into a good solid loaf. The one element you need to obtain these results is missing from the cast above and you are going to make it yourself. Its name is gluten. Everyone talks about gluten a lot, but few people know what it really is and what it really does. It's a wonder that everyone talks about it so much, while understanding it so badly. So let's investigate.

Here is, first, what *should* happen and, second, what *should not* happen when you prepare a bread dough. Note that this is not a recipe, it is an experiment which will allow you to understand the interrelation of physics and chemistry in the making of leavened doughs. Recipes for diverse breads start on page 1036 and for filo and strudel on page 1100.

You must use either a bread flour with 12.5 to 13 percent proteins or a very strong all-purpose flour containing at least 12 percent proteins, because there is a (very) rough equivalent concentration of gliadins and glutenins in both of them.

Pour 3 cups of flour on a work surface and make a large well in the center of it, at least 9 inches in diameter. Add 1⅔ cups water at room temperature. Gather about 1¼ to 1½ cups of flour from the inner rim of the well into the water and mix it into a soft batter. Work it a few seconds and pretty soon you will see that it is elastic and can be pulled up from the bottom of the well a good 9 inches without breaking. At this point this fluid elasticity is mostly due to the gliadins being slightly unfolded by your pulling of the batter, but it is also partly due to a new protein that is starting to develop in the presence of the water, and with the help of your handwork. Now continue adding flour, and, if need be, the remainder of the water to the well. Make a dough that you will knead lightly for 4 minutes into a not too smooth ball of dough.

This ball is more or less keeping its shape and is already elastic; it is much stiffer than it was before. If you cut this piece of dough in half, you will see in the dough a few irregularly parallel lines aligned very closely with each other. Your kneading has helped distribute the water molecules through the dough and has promoted cross-bridging between the molecules of gliadins and glutenins, thus creating a third protein, the popular and all-important gluten.

At this point, the gluten is not quite fully developed but you can see all kinds of patterns in the dough, resembling a magnified version of one of those small spools of hair that you remove from your hairbrush, interspersed with places where the dough looks filled with little lumps. What you are seeing (imperfectly only for to have a very clear picture of it you would need an electron microscope) is the gluten in formation; you will notice that if you were talking about hair rather than gluten you would say that it is kinky. Feel free to say the same about the gluten; the term is perfectly acceptable.

FULL GLUTEN FORMATION

Now continue kneading the dough until these patterns disappear. The dough should be worked and kneaded around 10 minutes altogether, so you must continue kneading another 5 to 6 minutes. All the while you are kneading, your working hands will be throwing the molecules of gluten into a tizzy of stress. Stop the kneading and let the dough rest one minute until it has regained its original shape, then cut it in half. Look at one of the cuts: Parallel lines have aligned themselves into what will appear to you to be dozens or so of lines, but which are in reality a wealth of microscopic long molecules of fully developed gluten, tied together by disulfide bonds and looking by now to the naked eye somewhat like hair that has been brushed, if not in the neatest manner. The disulfide bonds, of course, are not visible, but the accumulation of the long molecules upon one another certainly is, and the lines they form are often referred to as "gluten strands" by bakers.

This is how you obtained those gluten strands: While you kneaded, you pushed on the dough, exerting force on it and stressing it to the point of almost breaking it. This disrupted the disulfide bonds but formed other bonds with the hydrogen in the sulfhydryl groups existing in the dough. As soon as you released your pressure you could see the elasticity in the dough as it slowly returned to its round shape, a sign that the disulfide bonds could go back to their original position among the gluten molecules.

The fact that the dough can be pushed and stretched proves that the gluten is elastic. Because the dough was—after you stopped working—able to return to and retain its ball shape, without collapsing on the work counter, proves that the gluten is also plastic. A substance is plastic or has plasticity when it is able to retain a shape or be molded into a shape.

So now that we have a dough full of good gluten, what is the effect of the fat existing naturally in the flour on the gluten developed in a dough by kneading? Some authors explain that the fat links up with the glutenins and gliadins, thus allowing the gluten to develop gas retention capabilities. Yet others think that this fat ties up with the gelatinizing starches once the dough is put to bake. Both may be right; scientists are still working daily on gluten research and its mysteries have not yet been fully elucidated.

What you must remember from the above explanations is that there are in flour two types of proteins called the gliadins and the glutenins, which when hydrated with water and given a good workout—either by hand or by mixer—will cross-link with each other and unite to form a third protein called gluten, without which no good bread dough can ever be made. There is no gluten in inert flour. You make it yourself when you knead flour and water together into a dough.

OVERWORKING A DOUGH:
THE DEMISE OF GLUTEN

It is essential that you look at the clock or set a timer when you knead a bread dough. It seems that 10 is the magic number when it comes to the number of minutes a bread dough of home size should be kneaded. Professional bakers who work in larger quantities know how to knead the correct amount of time in their large mixers.

If at home you knead between 9 and 10 minutes, you will obtain a dough that has the perfect balance of plasticity and elasticity. But to complete the exercise, let's continue kneading that ball of dough more than 10 minutes, all the way to a full 20 minutes. As you work, you will see the dough become progressively stickier, almost sweaty if the kitchen is warm. Instead of remaining elastic, the dough, however well shaped, will become incredibly stretchable, as the glutenin and gliadin molecules lose their ability to crosslink. The gluten slackens and loses its plasticity and elasticity, which are replaced by an amazing stretchability as the dough collapses visibly, unable to retain its shape anymore.

Why? Because while you overworked the dough, many molecules of water worked their way between the molecules of gluten, reaching the disulfide bonds and helping them form numerous sulfhydryl groups, eliminating the possibility of cross-linking which produces the elasticity.

Your dough is not usable for bread anymore, but you could use it for making something else, filo or strudel (see pages 1100–4). Basically when you make these two types of dough, you build gluten for the first 10 minutes of kneading and destroy it to force the dough to become stretchable during the last 10 minutes of kneading.

GLUTEN CAPABILITIES

Why is gluten so precious that we go to so much trouble to build it properly in our bread doughs? Because of its elasticity and plasticity. Thanks to gluten we can mold our breads into fancy shapes if we desire, for the gluten provides structure to our breads and rolls.

Thanks to its elasticity, gluten allows a dough to retain the carbon dioxide that results from fermentation. This capability develops early on in the development of gluten from its mother proteins. As soon as the flour which is to become a dough has been hydrated, tiny vacuoles form in the dough, to later grow during dough fermentation as the carbon dioxide pushes on their walls, distends them, and leavens the bread.

While the bread bakes, the carbon dioxide will distend the walls of the vacuoles further as it expands in the heat of the oven, to finally escape into the atmosphere. As the bread bakes the walls of the distended vacuoles will set in the heat of the oven yielding a true loaf of bread with large holes.

GLUTEN INHIBITORS

There are ingredients which are inhibitors of gluten. Gluten is sensitive to additions of vinegar with 5 percent acidity and lemon juice and will lose some of its plasticity. You will find out that strudel and filo doughs, which need to be stretchy, often contain added vinegar or lemon juice to soften their gluten structure and destroy the plasticity of gluten, replacing it with a degree of elasticity and stretchability.

Sugar and salt are also gluten inhibitors; sugar competes with the proteins for water and affects the development of the flour-water complex. In doughs that are sweetened, the texture of the gluten is much softer for this very reason. As an example, Danish pastry comes immediately to mind. As for salt, it reacts with the proteins in such a way as to make the gluten less elastic.

Finally, butter is also a gluten inhibitor because it coats the gluten strands and softens them considerably. As an example, see the recipe for croissants on page 1095.

Soft Flours

Soft flours are milled from soft wheats or, with the help of a separator, from the low-protein fractions of some hard wheats. Their water-absorbing capacities and gluten-producing capabilities are low. They are used for that reason in pastry and biscuit making where the need for water is limited and the presence of gluten totally unwanted.

The softest of all flours is the highly bleached cake flour, which when one desires a very light cake with large volume yield and very soft crumb, seems the best resource. In the recipes for pastries and cakes, I often give two sets of formulas for the same preparation, to be made with two different flours. May I suggest that you try both and compare the results. Soft flours used in the making of pastry generally require less shortening than unbleached all-purpose flour, for since they contain less protein, they need not be softened as strongly as all-purpose flour.

Matured Flours, Bleached and Improved Flours

One of my many great aunts, who lived on an isolated farm in Lorraine, made her own bread from flours produced by a rural miller and baked it in the communal oven of her village. Every third month, she bought flour which she stored in huge barrels, lined up in order of purchase from left to right and stored in her cool, dry pantry. When the flour arrived from the miller it was almost as yellow as our present semolina. To aerate it, she would take a long paddle and stir the flour in each and every barrel at least once a week; until it had turned a wonderful, soft, and luminous ivory-white she would not use the flour. When a flour had reached the correct color, she made a test loaf. If the loaf was compact and somewhat sticky when cooled and sliced, it was promptly relegated to the toasting tray and finally ended up in the crumb box. The flour had failed examination and had to wait longer to be used, until it could make a "true loaf of bread with big holes." Such flour, which is too young and not oxidized enough to develop a solid gluten structure, is called "bucky" and was as much a feature of Colonial and Federal America as it was of the early twentieth-century French countryside.

"Aerating the flour" is an old-fashioned country expression for what we call nowadays letting the flour proteins oxidate. As my aunt's flour rested for weeks, often months, after going through the milling process, the yellow carotene-xanthophyll pigments in the new flours were naturally bleached by light and oxygen to that lovely ivory-white and the sulfhydryl groups (see paragraphs above to know what sulfhydryl groups are) in the flour decreased appreciably, resulting in a bread dough that did not stretch and produced honest solid loaves of bread with big holes. The holes could be so big that I remember vividly passing one or two of my young fingers into them to see whether there was something in there; one day I found a small medal of the Holy Spirit.

The unbleached flours that we can buy in markets have been aged with the help of potassium bromate which accelerates their aging process. I prefer them to the bleached flours because their color is more natural and they really can bake a true loaf of bread, even if the holes in the bread are not as big as they need to be to host the Holy Spirit

By law only benzoyl peroxide is allowed for the bleaching of flours produced in the United States. It modifies the yellow color of young flours to that pallid white that is—say the flour people—desired by modern bakers.

Other improving agents can be used to accelerate the maturing of flours; most are gases which act immediately upon contact with the flour. Among them are chlorine gas used for cake flours, chlorine dioxide, nitrogen di- and tetraoxide, and nytrosil chloride. Yet other conditioning agents are added to doughs in the making of commercial baked goods. The functions of these chemicals may vary, but basically most of them bring on a reduction of thiol groups and encourage protein cross-linking (thiol groups are groups of two atoms, one of sulfur and one of hydrogen, existing on protein molecules). For a more detailed explanation of thiols, see the bibliography on page 1176, particularly Harold McGee's book *On Food and Cooking*.

The only bleached flour I use is cake flour when I am looking for a large volume yield.

Organic Flours

Any reader who wishes to become a great specialized baker should know that there is a significant difference between supermarket flours and organic flours milled from wheats grown in soils that have been improved exclusively with natural fertilizers.

Organic flours will vary in taste, texture, and smell according to the soil in which they were grown and the climate and the weather in which they mature. The weather from year to year will change and with it the quality of the organic flours. I was raised with bread made exclusively with organic flours and am always mentally and emotionally looking for their deep taste and chewiness. I suggest that you try baking the same bread with organic flour and with regular supermarket bread flour on the same day for a very interesting comparison of tastes and textures.

If you want to get seriously involved in baking your own bread, consult the diverse lists of sources for organic flours in the bread books listed in the bibliography.

Other Flours

Rye flour is used to prepare northern and central European breads. It can be obtained in a diverse range of colors, such as white, medium, or dark. The darker flours contain more bran. The dominant protein in rye flour is prolamine which cannot produce a structure as strong as that developed by gluten. As a result, if you want rye bread, you will need to mix 50 percent rye flour with 50 percent hard wheat flour, the hard wheat flour providing the loaf with gluten and solidity.

Corn can make delicious breads, but its main protein, zein, is also unable to build a good structure, which is why you always see modern corn breads made with a mixture of cornmeal and flour.

Spelt is not known enough in American homes. I am familiar with it because, from time immemorial, it has been a favorite in France. Every so often, it appears at the bakery or on a private table to the great pleasure of all. Spelt can be found relatively easily in health food stores and will make a delicious foccacia which needs very little yeast to rise beautifully. The protein content of spelt will vary by the bag, but will be at least as high as that of unbleached bread flour (about 11.5 percent). Expect spelt to be expensive and reserve it for special occasions.

Diverse Flours Available

The following is a list of the different types of flours mostly used in baking and to be found in supermarkets, health food stores, and/or with specialty flour purveyors. I have added to each flour description a short list of their best utilizations.

DURUM FLOUR AND SEMOLINA (PROTEIN CONTENT 12 TO 13 PERCENT) Durum flour has a very high protein content and is milled almost exclusively for the making of macaroni and pasta, never bread. It is milled quite coarsely as you can see when you buy a bag of "pasta" flour; it is bright yellow and it makes the very best pasta and spätzle. Durum flour is different from semolina flour; where durum flour is really a fine flour with coarse particles, semolina is milled from middlings of durum and has an even coarser texture than durum which results in the correct use of the term "grains of semolina" rather than semolina flour. You can make excellent pasta by blending semolina with all-purpose flour. Semolina can also be added in part to bread doughs prepared with all-purpose flour to give the baked product a chewier texture; use 25 percent semolina and 75 percent unbleached all-purpose flour.

WHOLE WHEAT FLOUR (PROTEIN CONTENT ABOUT 13.3 PERCENT) Whole wheat flour is also called graham flour, as in graham crackers; it derived that moniker from the name of the Presbyterian minister Sylvester Graham, of Philadelphia, who extolled the virtues of whole wheat flour in the late 1800s. Whole wheat flour contains all the elements of the wheat kernel and must be kept cool or refrigerated to slow down the process of oxidation in the wheat germ oil.

Most whole wheat flours are left unbleached, but some brands sell it bleached. You may want to check the bag, for a bleached whole wheat flour is less desirable than an unbleached one, because a large portion of the good wheaty taste is damaged by the bleaching.

Whole wheat is best used to make whole wheat breads and rolls. Because the bran cuts through the gluten strands of the dough, an appreciable part of the content of the carbon dioxide contained in the dough after fermentation can be lost, and because the wheat germ oil contained in the dough softens its gluten structure considerably, it is always necessary to blend whole wheat flour with the same amount of a strong white bread flour or unbleached all-purpose flour to make a good, solid dough.

BREAD FLOUR (PROTEIN CONTENT ABOUT 12 PERCENT) Bread flours milled from hard spring and hard winter wheats are recognizable by their slightly ivory color and coarse, gritty texture; they are used for breads leavened with yeast. The large amount of proteins in those flours make them choice material for making bread, hence their name; please go to pages 1006 to 1010 for an explanation of the relation of flour proteins to gluten.

FLOUR (THE PROTEIN CONTENT VARIES FROM 10 TO 11.5 PERCENT) Flours simply labeled "Flour" are made exclusively from the endosperm of wheat kernels. They may be enriched with B complex vitamins and iron, in which case the bag will carry the mention "enriched." They may also be "bleached," in which case the bag will carry the mention "bleached" or they may be unbleached, in which case the bag will say "unbleached."

These flours can be used for almost anything, but they will produce very average breads and slightly heavier cakes. To make a better bread with these flours, add ¼ cup semolina for each pound (4 cups) of flour. To make better pancakes, muffins, and biscuits with these flours, soften each pound with ¼ cup cornstarch.

ALL-PURPOSE FLOUR (PROTEIN CONTENT 10 TO 10.5 PERCENT) All-purpose flours are blends of soft wheat flours or hard wheat flours. Their qualities will depend on the geographic origin of the wheats used. All-purpose flours made in the northern states are strong enough to make yeast breads, while all-purpose flours from the South are softer and better for biscuits and quick baking-powder leavened breads. Any cook and baker who would like to familiarize her-himself with both types should try the following brands:

• for northern bleached all-purpose flour: Pillsbury, Gold Medal

- for northern unbleached all-purpose flour: Ceresota, King Arthur, Heckers, Gold Medal
- for southern bleached all-purpose flour: White Lily. There may be an unbleached all-purpose flour under another label, but I have not been able to find one.

SELF-RISING FLOUR (PROTEIN CONTENT 9 TO 10 PERCENT)
There are several brands of soft unbleached flour blended with salt, baking soda, and another leavening agent such as sodium acid pyrophosphate or monocalcium phosphate or a blend of both. It is essentially a biscuit mix. I prefer the southern flour to the northern flour.

Self-rising flour can be prepared at home by blending 2 tablespoons baking powder mixed with 2 teaspoons salt into 1 pound of flour, or blend of flours of your choice.

PASTRY FLOUR (PROTEIN CONTENT 8.5 PERCENT) Pastry flour can usually be purchased only from specialty purveyors; it is more difficult to find in a supermarket. To make pastry flour yourself, all you have to do is blend all-purpose flour with cake flour. With all-purpose northern flours, the blend by volume is roughly two thirds all-purpose to one third cake flour, but since flours vary so much in softness or hardness this is not a standard measurement and you will have to experiment a bit. In the South the all-purpose flour sold in bags usually makes a perfectly lovely pie. For southern flours which may be a little harder, use three quarters all-purpose flour blended with one quarter cake flour.

The softer the flour you use to make pastry, the less butter or shortening you will need to make the pastry; conversely, the harder the flour the more butter will be needed to coat the gluten strands that will form when you work the flour, shortening, and water together.

Please refer to the pastry section on page 1057 to learn how to make pastry with both all-purpose flour and pastry flour.

CAKE FLOUR (PROTEIN CONTENT 7 PERCENT) Cake flours are extremely finely milled soft flours, their texture almost as fine as that of talcum powder. The chalk white appearance speaks for the fact that they are chemically bleached.

There are no unbleached cake flours. Cake flours are compounded by mills to contain only very soft flours which result in very tender cakes with maximum volume. Please refer to the section on cakes on page 1121 for more details and information on this subject.

INSTANTIZED FLOUR Instantized flour, which came on the market in the sixties, flows freely when poured into a cup and never clumps because it has been treated by water or steam to provoke an agglomeration of several flour particles into particles roughly four times larger than their original size. This is similar to what happens when you make couscous from scratch with semolina. Such flour will hydrate faster when a liquid is added to it; never clumping into lumps, it is useful to cooks who like to prepare meat gravy by shaking flour directly into the gravy pan, then adding water. Instantized flour should not be used for baking, but if you like it, it can be used for crepes and pancakes.

Quality of Flours Used to Test Recipes in This Chapter

For recipes calling for unsifted flour, the flour has been scooped directly out of the bag and leveled with a spatula. This is mostly the case for breads leavened with yeast which must be kneaded where any remaining clumps of flour will be destroyed by the powerful stress you will be exerting on the flour while kneading.

For recipes calling for sifted flour, sift it directly into a measuring cup, letting it mound over the rim of the cup, then level it with the rim of the cup, using a spatula. This is mostly the case for pastries and cakes. Sifting flour for these preparations is absolutely necessary to eliminate any little clumps of flour since the manual work in pastry and cake making must be gentle and soft.

The differences in weights and densities of the diverse flours are shown below as a matter of comparison among the three types of flours most used in home baking. The numbers cited here represent the average weight of one cup in each category blended each from three different brands available in supermarkets across the nation.

If you try to check these measurements, you may not derive exactly the same numbers due to the capacity of flour to retain moisture. Try doing it on a dry day and on a wet day; the difference is notable.

Unbleached all-purpose flour:
1 cup unsifted, scooped with a cup = 137 grams = 4.6 ounces
1 cup, sifted directly into a cup = 112 grams = 4.1 ounces

Bread flour:
1 cup unsifted, scooped with a cup = 144 grams = 4.9 ounces
1 cup, sifted directly into a cup = 124 grams = 4.3 ounces

Cake flour:
1 cup unsifted, scooped with a cup = 108 grams = 3.8 ounces
1 cup, sifted directly into a cup = 96 grams = 3.3 ounces

In professional baking all quantities are weighed, never measured by volume.

The nutritional label on each bag gives important information about the composition of the flour it contains. Most important is the percentage of proteins because too little protein results in a poor bread and too much in a tough pastry or heavy cake. You can check the amount of protein in any flour bought in any bag under any label by doing the following calculation.

The size of the portion is given in three different measurement systems: first by volume or ¼ cup, then by weight in the American weight system, which is 1 ounce, and, finally, in parentheses, in the metric system. That last measurement, which is in reality 28.349 grams and too complicated to be used in its exact form, is always rounded to 28 grams, or 29 grams, or even 30 grams.

Below that you can find the number of grams of protein the portion contains. If you calculate the following ratio you will find the percentage of proteins contained in the flour.

$$\frac{\text{\# of protein grams in 1 oz flour} \times 100}{\text{\# of grams in 1 ounce}} = \text{percent of proteins in the flour}$$

Example: A flour contains 2 grams of protein per ounce or for each 28 grams. Divide 2 by 28 and multiply by 100 and you will find that the flour contains 7 percent proteins. Check on page 1015 and you will see that the flour you bought is really cake flour and appropriate for the preparation of light cakes.

This percent will vary depending on whether the flour packer has used 28, 29, or 30 grams as the equivalent of 1 ounce, so you will not really know the precise percent, but the result of the calculation will be close enough to allow you to check that the flour you are using is in the correct range. In the same example if 29 grams represents 1 ounce, the result is 6.8 percent, and if 30 grams, 6.6 percent, which are both still in the correct range.

If you find that a flour contains too few proteins for what you plan to prepare, compensate either by blending in some stronger flour or adding a little semolina. If the flour is too strong, either select a less strong flour than the recipe calls for or soften the flour by blending it with cake flour, or a pure starch like corn or potato starch.

Variations in Flours

Once you start baking, you will realize that supermarket flours are not always identical; as a result, more often than not, there will be small variations in the quality of your baked goods. In my years of demonstrating all over the United States, I have had some interesting experiences balancing the formulas of cakes and the texture of breads with flours that not only were different in each and every state, but within one brand. Take comfort in the fact that you are not alone; all bakers are in the same boat. Several factors cause these differences, the milling of the flour being one of them in spite of the efforts of milling companies to produce as consistent a product as possible.

Yeasts and Their Functions

In Greek *sackaron* means sugar and *mykes* mushroom; *cerevisiae* is the gene-tive of the Latin word for beer and *Saccharomyces cerevisiae* is what you reach for on the supermarket shelf when you buy yeast.

Saccharomyces is a genus of one-celled plants, deprived of chlorophyll, which, given the right type of food (starches and sugars) and the right amount of moisture in the form of pure water or as water bound into milk or eggs, lives and reproduces best between the temperatures of 85° and 115°F; the upper and lower extremes vary with the type of yeast. The reproduction of yeast cells is simple. When the yeast cell is ready to divide, it grows an excrescence called a bud. When the excrescence is as large as the yeast cell itself, the cell divides.

Before being added to a dough in the making, yeast is best softened and generously hydrated with water. If activated with milk, the milk should, with very few exceptions, be scalded and cooled to the correct temperature first, because of the enzymes it contains. Yeast feeds on maltose as it exists natu-rally in flours, or on sucrose—our regular sugar—as it is added to some doughs to give them a sweet taste. With the help of the enzyme invertase, yeast transforms sucrose into the simple sugars glucose and fructose and with the help of the enzyme maltase, it metabolizes maltose. The fermentation of a dough (which causes the rising) really starts when the yeast releases the enzyme zymase and brings on the further breakdown of glucose and fructose into carbon dioxide and alcohol. Fermentation as it happens within a dough is anaerobic.

When the dough is kneaded by hand or machine beaters, open spaces called cells form in the dough. Those cells will fill with the released carbon dioxide; the carbon dioxide will expand during fermentation and baking, dis-tend the cells, and leave empty holes in the baked product. Bakers say that the carbon dioxide "leavens" the dough.

The strength of those cells (meaning their capacity to distend as the car-bon dioxide expands) is directly related to the protein content of the flour; the higher the percentage of proteins in the flour, the stronger the cell walls will be and the more they will be able to expand to leaven the bread. The two most important proteins are the glutenins and gliadins which will, in the presence of water and mechanical action, interact to form another protein, the all-important gluten (see page 1008 for the explanation of the formation of gluten).

Excellent bread can be produced without the addition of sugar (these are called lean doughs), by letting the yeast break the natural sugars and starches existing in the flour into simple sugars; the fermentation will start more slowly and the fermentation time will be considerably longer, but the taste of the bread will be more complex and satisfying. In commercial baking, the fer-mentation of lean doughs is accelerated by the addition of so-called dough conditioners containing inorganic salt which facilitates the growth of the yeast and helps control the pH (see this word in the glossary).

The fermentation in breads containing large additions of sugar (rich doughs) will start rapidly but it ends up being slower than in lean doughs, because the hygroscopic sugar competes for water in the dough and in the yeast cells (osmosis).

Since the very same problem occurs with salt, because it also competes for water, the addition of salt to sweetened doughs should be done after the fermentation is well underway, at the same time the larger amount of flour is added.

The three different types of yeast available and predominantly used are:

COMPRESSED YEAST Compressed yeast comes in 1-inch square cakes made of a mixture of yeast cells in starch and containing 65 to 70 percent moisture. To activate a cake, it should be crumbled and dispersed into 85° to 110°F water. The shelf life of compressed yeast is relatively short and it should not be used unless it is smooth, white to very light tan, and smells frankly of yeast and nothing else. Any cheesy smell or darkening of the yeast cake means that it must be discarded. Compressed yeast must be kept refrigerated and well wrapped in its original foil paper. If a cake has been partly used, the remainder must be tightly wrapped in plastic wrap and kept refrigerated.

DRIED YEAST Dried yeast, which contains only 6 to 8 percent moisture, has a much longer shelf life than compressed yeast. In dried yeast, the yeast cells are live but in a state of suspended activity. Dried yeast can be kept in the refrigerator over a year. It is believed that yeast doughs leavened with dried yeasts rise slightly less than those prepared with cake yeast. When this happens, it is usually because the temperature of the water used for rehydration was lower than it should have been. If indeed the water temperature is too low, agents called glutathiones leach out of yeast cells, which have been bruised or torn during dehydration, and weaken the gluten strands developed in the dough while kneading, thus inhibiting the rise of the baked good. By personal taste and experience, I find the taste of yeast breads made with dried yeast more flavorful. The rehydration temperature of dried yeast is between 110° and 115°F and must be strictly observed.

INSTANT AND RAPID RISE YEASTS are dried yeasts containing 4 percent moisture: Both these yeasts are sensitive to heat. For that reason it is recommended by their manufacturers to mix flour and liquid together for a minute or so, then add the yeast, without mixing it previously in water.

Any yeast subjected to a temperature higher than 140°F will die. Again, for a good rise, keep the temperature of the yeast-activating liquid no higher than 115°F.

Other Leaveners:
Baking Soda and Baking Powders

Many modern baked goods are leavened with chemical compounds; the most commonly used are baking soda, and single-acting and double-acting baking powders. Their respective leavening capabilities are described in the sections on quick breads, biscuits, and cakes on pages 1111, 1112, and 1114.

Ancient Unleavened Flatbreads

Early womenfolk gathered the grains that grew wild on the large expanses of tall grass after the retreat of the last glaciation. These cereals were parched to remove their undigestible husks, and at first were probably eaten from the hand, as we do to this day with nuts. Later they would be crushed with stones, to obtain a mixture of coarsely cracked kernels and flour, which mixed with water was probably drunk rather than eaten. As the technology evolved and cereal meals became finer and finer, the gruel came to be cooked and was spread on hot stones to dehydrate. Both ancient Egyptians and Greeks baked such flat or slightly mounding cakes on primitive griddles topped with a ceramic bell. In ancient Greece *artos,* or leavened wheat bread, was enjoyed only for religious feasts. By the time of Pericles and the construction of the Parthenon, women ground the grains, and made at least fourteen different kinds of breads across Greece and Asia Minor.

It was probably the Greeks who invented the true bread oven, preheated with a wood fire. After the cinders were removed, the loaves were placed on the bottom, or *sol,* of the oven (from the Latin *solum*) and slowly baked. This type of bread oven still exists all over Europe and produces old-fashioned loaves at many community celebrations.

Flatbreads cooked under bells or in the embers were called *maza* by the Greeks, and consisted mostly of coarsely milled barley mixed with water. *Maza* was topped with the *opson,* or garnish of vegetables and meats.

The Romans did not start baking breads until 600 B.C., having nourished themselves before that time with a porridge made of parched cereals; this porridge was to survive in the *pulmentum* of the Roman legions which is the ancestor of our modern polenta. Today's pizzas and focaccias, although now leavened with yeast, are direct descendents of *maza,* as the millet flour gave way to wheat flour.

The Gauls, Celtic forebears of the French, learned their bread making and leavening techniques from the many Greeks living in Gaul in the first century A.D. and from the Romans. They used flour made from spelt (an early wheat with bent whiskers and bearing only two light red kernels) to make round, soft loaves which have many descendents in provincial France.

Scottish oat cakes are, along with the rye flatbreads and crackers of Scandinavia, some of the most obvious remains of ancient northern European unleavened flatbreads. The focaccia on page 1042 passed through the ages from Rome to most of the provinces and colonies of Rome to America, arriving with a fanfare in the last few years.

Celtic Oat Cakes

LFR — 16 CAKES

2½ cups rolled oats

2 tablespoons unsaturated oil of your choice

1 teaspoon salt

1 cup boiling water

½ cup steelcut oats

Put the rolled oats in a large bowl. Add the chosen oil and salt to the boiling water. Using a wooden spoon, gradually add the mixture to the oats and gather into a ball. Then knead by hand until cool.

Preheat the oven to 250°F. Spread the steelcut oats evenly on a countertop; roll the dough out into a large rectangle over the oats and to an even thickness of ¼ inch. With a 3¼-inch round crinkle cutter cut out sixteen cakes.

Line a 17 × 12-inch jelly-roll pan with a sheet of parchment paper; arrange the cakes on the paper and bake them until their edges start to curl up, about 1 hour. Cool and enjoy.

The original recipe is made with bacon fat or lard and still in use in Scotland and Wales. It is excellent served as bread with salmon chowder and for breakfast with bitter orange marmalade and a dab of butter. The steelcut oats, which are Irish, may be replaced by the same amount of additional rolled oats, but they do add a pleasant crunch to the cakes.

Brittany Buckwheat Galettes

FFR — 2 DOZEN GALETTES

1 cup buckwheat flour

½ cup sifted unbleached all-purpose flour

3 large eggs

Salt

Pepper from the mill

1½ to 2 cups water as needed

3 tablespoons unsalted butter, melted

Mix both flours together in a medium-size bowl and make a well in the center. Beat the eggs, salt and pepper to taste, and 1 cup of the water together in another bowl. Pour this in the center of the well and, using a whisk, gradually gather the flour from the sides of the bowl into the center until the liquid and flour form a homogeneous batter. Dilute with more water if necessary to obtain a batter with the texture of unwhipped heavy cream. Let rest 2 hours

These galettes are usually made of pure buckwheat, but the difference in texture between Breton and American buckwheat necessitates the addition of more egg protein and some white flour. As late as the beginning of this century, these galettes replaced bread.

Serve with nicely browned sausage as offered on page 875.

in the refrigerator. Bring back to room temperature and whisk in the butter.

Heat a 10-inch nonstick pan on medium-low heat for a full 5 minutes. Holding the pan at a 45-degree angle to the burner, add one 2-ounce ladleful of batter in the lip of the pan and, gently oscillating the pan to the left, let the batter flow back and cover the entire bottom. Return the pan to the burner, cook 1 minute, then turn over with a spatula and finish cooking 1½ to 2 minutes on the second side. Enjoy nice and hot. Repeat with the remaining batter.

French and European Crepes, American Pancakes

Of the three recipes that follow, two are unleavened batter breads. *Pannequet* is the phonetic translation in French of the English word "pancake" and this is the name given mostly to savory crepes. They appear in the cooking of all nations under different names. Blintzes, *blini, blinchiki, plattar, Pfannkuchen, palacsinta* or *palatschinken*, and tortillas are all variations of the same theme as interpreted in different countries and even regionally within countries. In the German part of Switzerland they are called *Omeletten*, which always gives rise to confusion with true omelettes. The cereal grain used in pancake batter and the consistency of the batter vary, while the other basic ingredients are invariably milk or cream and eggs, sometimes butter, and sometimes baking powder (usually in Anglo-Saxon countries), while fresh yeast is used liberally in the countries of Eastern Europe. While pancakes are mainly breakfast fare in England and America, all over Europe they are served either as an hors-d'oeuvre or for dessert. For centuries they have been used to transform leftovers into enjoyable dishes that may be served to company.

Basic Flour Crepes, Dessert Crepes, and Cornmeal Crepes

FFR — 18 TO 24 CREPES 8 TO 10 INCHES IN DIAMETER

FOR EACH RECIPE

For basic flour crepes

¾ **cup sifted unbleached all-purpose flour**

3 **large eggs**

1 **cup milk of your choice**

2 **tablespoons unsalted butter, melted, or unsaturated oil of your choice**

Salt

For dessert crepes

¾ cup sifted unbleached all-purpose flour

I tablespoon confectioners' sugar

2 large whole eggs plus 2 large egg yolks

I cup less 2 tablespoons milk of your choice

¼ cup unsalted butter, melted

Salt

2 tablespoons liqueur of your choice

For cornmeal crepes

½ cup white bolted cornmeal

¼ cup sifted unbleached all-purpose flour

3 large eggs

I cup milk of your choice

2 tablespoons unsalted butter, melted, or unsaturated oil of your choice

Salt

The mixing and cooking are identical for each of the three formulas: Pour the flour (or flour and sugar mixed, or cornmeal and flour mixed) into a medium-size mixing bowl. Make a well in it, then add the eggs and simply break them with a wooden spatula, wire whisk, or an electric mixer on low speed. Mix the eggs and flour until the mixture is shiny and shreds. The gluten should develop just enough in the flour (see page 1008 for a complete explanation of gluten) to give the crepes a certain plasticity so they can be flipped easily. Do not whip the mixture too much; if you do, long strands of gluten will form and the batter will be too cohesive to absorb the milk. Add the milk gradually, then the melted butter, salt to taste, and any other flavoring used.

The finished batter is lighter than heavy cream and must be strained through a conical strainer to remove very small flour lumps. Let the batter stand 10 to 20 minutes to allow the starches to absorb some of the milk and swell, or the first crepes will be thinner than those that follow. Before cooking a crepe, stir the batter to avoid the slighest separation. Any batter left over can be stored in the refrigerator and used within 24 hours. The batter will have separated but can easily be remedied by whisking it a few seconds.

Each of these batters can be made ahead of time and kept frozen for later use. Defrost in the refrigerator 4 hours before using.

The best pans for cooking crepes are 8-, 9-, or 10-inch nonstick ones. Preheat the pan 5 minutes on medium heat; when about to cook the crepes, raise the heat to high.

Tilt the pan forward so the handle is at a 45-degree angle to the burner. Using a large serving spoon or small ladle, pour the batter into the front lip of the pan, then slowly tip the pan backward, spreading the batter gently from one side to the other over the whole bottom of the pan. The batter will run

To flip a crepe, hold the pan at this angle, then, just below the level of your waist, with a fast upward movement, quickly bring the pan up to horizontal. This sharp movement will make the crepe flip.

This is my favorite American-style pancake. The batter is leavened with the beaten egg whites and a tiny amount of baking soda activated by the lemon juice. The texture of the egg whites will be far superior if you beat them by hand either in a copper bowl or in a glass bowl with ¼ teaspoon cream of tartar. A long buffet-style nonstick electric frying pan will allow the cook to prepare six cakes at once.

and deposit evenly and a characteristic pitting will develop as tiny air bubbles are caught between the pan and batter. For a nicely shaped crepe, do not tilt the pan wildly back and forth in all directions.

If the pan is not hot enough, no pitting will occur. If the pan is too hot, the batter will immediately fold back upon itself as you tilt the pan back. The crepe will be thick since the batter will cook too fast, and you will need twice as much batter to make an inferior grade of crepes.

The crepe is ready to be flipped when tiny droplets of butter appear at its surface. To turn it, you must flip it. Flipping is no great achievement, just fun. Hold the pan just below waist level. Shake the crepe gently from left to right until one third of it comes to hang over the lip of the pan. Give one upward tilt to the wrist, and the crepe will flip and fall right back into the pan. Do not aim for the ceiling; 4 to 5 inches above the pan is impressive enough. Cook 1 to 2 minutes on the second side.

Crepes taste best plain sprinkled with lemon juice and sugar or spread with the jelly or jam of your choice. If you wish to prepare fancy flambéed crepes or savory crepes filled with diverse garnishes, see the bibliography.

Cotton Cakes

FFR — TWELVE 4-INCH CAKES

4 large eggs, 3 of them separated
2 tablespoons granulated sugar
Salt
I cup light cream
I tablespoon fresh lemon juice
2 cups sifted unbleached all-purpose flour
I teaspoon baking soda
¼ teaspoon cream of tartar
Unsaturated oil of your choice as needed
Pure maple syrup

In the large bowl of an electric mixer, ribbon (see page 163) the 1 whole egg and 3 egg yolks heavily with the sugar and salt to taste on medium-high speed. Combine the cream and lemon juice and with the electric mixer still on medium high, add the mixture to the eggs. Reduce the electric mixer speed to low, combine the flour and baking soda and add to the bowl. Mix until completely combined.

In another large bowl, preferably using a large balloon hand whisk, beat the egg whites until just mixed; add the cream of tartar. Continue whipping the egg whites until they can hold the weight of a raw egg in its shell without sinking more than ¼ inch into the foam. Mix in 1 heaping sauce spoonful of egg whites into the flour mixture, then fold in the remainder.

Preheat a nonstick frying pan or a cast-iron griddle rubbed with a paper towel lightly impregnated with unsaturated oil on medium-high heat. Drop the batter by large spoonfuls onto the cooking surface to make 4-inch cakes. Cook until their tops are full of bubbles ready to break (do not wait until they break or the cakes will be dry), then turn them over and cook 1 to 2 minutes more. Serve piping hot with warmed maple syrup.

Clafoutis

Sweet crepe batters are also used for the country desserts called *clafoutis* (*clafouti* in the singular), which are nothing more than unleavened fruit cobblers. The batter is never made according to fixed rules but rather left to the cook's fancy and mood. A *clafouti* contains as much fruit as you can afford to include in it. It is a great dessert for the summer months and a good way to save money by using cut-up bruised and partly overripe fruit.

To be able to cut a *clafouti* into wedges, pour one third of the batter into a buttered pie plate and bake it 5 minutes in a preheated 375°F oven until firm, but without turning it over. It will form a firm bottom for the confection. Failure to do so will result in the fruit falling to the bottom of the plate, sticking there, and making serving difficult. Once the bottom is firm, add the fruit and the remaining batter and finish baking in the oven until the batter is firm and the fruit juices well reduced. *Clafoutis* are usually juicy enough to be able to wait to be served without hardening and drying as crepes often do, but they are at the peak of flavor when lukewarm and generously sprinkled with confectioners' or brown sugar; any leftovers taste good the next morning as a breakfast offering.

Italian Plum Clafouti

FFR — 6 SERVINGS

1 pound Italian prune plums

½ cup sifted unbleached all-purpose flour

3 tablespoons granulated sugar

Salt

2 large eggs

2 heaping tablespoons sour cream

⅔ cup milk of your choice

Finely grated rind of 1 lemon

1 tablespoon unsalted butter or unsaturated oil of your choice

Confectioners' or brown sugar

Only use the bluish Italian prune plums; any other type will juice hopelessly. If you wish to use some spirit, replace 3 tablespoons of the milk with an equal amount of slivovitz or French quetsche. Grated lemon rind is another excellent flavoring if the spirit is not available or wanted.

Cut open the plums and remove the pits, but do not peel them, so as to preserve the fresh sweet-sour taste. Place the flour, 2 tablespoons of the sugar, salt to taste, eggs, and sour cream in a medium-size bowl and mix by hand or with a mixer until smooth. Add the milk and lemon rind, and give one last good beating.

Preheat the oven to 375°F. Butter a 9-inch pie plate. Pour in one third of the batter and bake until the batter has set, about 10 minutes. Remove from the oven and top with the fruit, arranged in concentric circles. Sprinkle with the remaining 1 tablespoon sugar, cover with the remainder of the batter, and bake until set and light golden, about 40 minutes. Sprinkle with the sugar of your choice as soon as it comes out of the oven. Cool to lukewarm and serve.

American-Style Popovers and Yorkshire Pudding

FFR — 8 POPOVERS OR 1 YORKSHIRE PUDDING TO SERVE 6 TO 8

1 cup sifted unbleached all-purpose flour

2 tablespoons unsalted butter, melted, or bacon grease plus 1 tablespoon for greasing

1 cup milk of your choice

Salt

Pepper from the mill

2 large eggs

Plain bread crumbs and/or hard grating cheese as needed

Place the flour in a medium-size bowl and make a well in it. Add the chosen fat and, using a small whisk, gradually blend in the milk, salt and pepper to taste, and each egg separately until the mixture has the texture of heavy cream. Let stand 10 minutes. Preheat the oven to 450°F.

If making popovers, grease each cup with a bit of fat. Coat the cups with bread crumbs or half hard grating cheese and half crumbs. Pour the batter into each cup, filling it three quarters full. If using a pan, grease it or pour into it the drippings from any piece of meat you may have been roasting, then pour in the batter. Bake 15 minutes at 450°F, then turn the oven down to 350°F and finish baking, another 20 to 25 minutes, without ever opening the oven. Before removing from the oven, use a trussing needle or the stem of an instant thermometer to punch a hole or two into the center of each popover to release any steam and prevent deflation. Serve hot as a side dish with roasted meats.

You will need 8 deep custard cups or one 8-inch-square pan. For a different old-fashioned English popover recipe, see page 751. The bacon fat or butter can be replaced by the same amount of unsaturated oil.

NOTE: *The cooking time of the popover mixture will be the same in an 8-inch pan, but if you have used a roasting pan with a larger surface it will decrease the total baking time by approximately one quarter.*

Basic Blini Batter

FFR — THIRTY-SIX 3-INCH BLINI

1¾ cups lukewarm milk of your choice

1 envelope dried yeast

1 teaspoon granulated sugar

2 cups sifted unbleached all-purpose flour

2 large eggs, separated

½ teaspoon salt

¼ cup heavy cream

Handle this batter very gently to avoid toughening it. To make the starter, mix 1 cup of the milk, the yeast, sugar, and 1 cup of the flour together and let rise loosely covered for about 1 hour, at room temperature. As the yeast wakes up and feeds, the mixture will become frothy and bubbly.

Gradually add the rest of the flour and the egg yolks, then the remaining milk. Add the salt. In a medium-size bowl with an electric mixer at high speed, whip the egg whites to soft peaks. In a small mixing bowl, whip the cream at medium-high speed until it begins to mound. Fold the egg whites and cream into each other. Slowly pour the batter into the cream and egg-white mixture, whisking constantly but gently. Let the batter stand another hour at room temperature before using.

Blini are usually cooked in tiny crepe pans not easy to locate in the United States. Use a cast-aluminum pan or cast-iron griddle. An electric frying pan does not get hot enough for *blini*, even at 425°F.

Cooking *blini* falls somewhere between cooking a crepe and a pancake. Grease the pan—even if it is a nonstick one—by rubbing it with a wad of paper towels impregnated with a bit of oil. Preheat the pan for 5 minutes on high heat. Depending on the size of your pan, pour one or several serving spoonsful of batter into the pan and cook until bubbles start breaking on the uncooked side, but the batter is still wet. Then turn the *blini* over with a spatula and finish cooking. The total cooking time is 1½ to 2 minutes on the first side, and only 1 minute for the second side.

BLINI AND CAVIAR *Blini* are more often than not used to serve caviar. Use as much of the caviar of your choice (see page 646) as you can afford.

Blini are also very pleasant as small hors-d'oeuvres. Their batter can be enriched with grated vegetables such as carrots, zucchini, peeled peppers of all colors which are spread over the top of each *blini* just before it is turned over. A small garnish of sour cream or crème fraîche flavored with chives or chervil on top of each cake finishes the presentation nicely.

Although blini *are prepared with yeast, they appear in this section because they are cooked in a pan like pancakes.*

Making Yeast-Leavened Breads

This section is dedicated to all those who would like to become old-fashioned bread bakers.

The material that follows is organized by technique, starting with the most elementary and ending with the most sophisticated. May I suggest to all beginners to learn these methods in this order, so that the different tastes and textures of the breads obtained can be evaluated as the learning progresses. It will allow the palate to become attuned to the many differences between baked products and increasingly able to really appreciate and enjoy the old ways of making bread and rolls.

Before you start baking, you must have read the general instructions on the types of flours and yeasts, pages 1003–19.

General Principles of Making Bread Dough

FLOURS USED FOR MAKING BREADS

Bread doughs are prepared either with bread flour or with all-purpose flour. All-purpose flour that feels too soft to bake a loaf of bread can be strengthened by a small addition of semolina. Rye and whole wheat flours both must be blended with bread or all-purpose white flour in order to be able to develop the structure of a properly leavened bread.

ACTIVATION OF A BATTER

Yeast is activated by mixing it preferably with water or, in rich breads, scalded and cooled milk.

When one introduces the mixture of yeast and liquid into flour, the batter is then said to be activated, as the yeast starts feeding on the sugar and starches existing naturally in the flour; food scientists sometimes speak of this operation as the "inoculation" of the batter, which sounds almost medical, but is a very apt description of what happens. As the yeast starts feeding, the batter starts bubbling with more or less effervescence, depending on its stiffness and the age of the yeast. If it does not bubble within 20 minutes in a room at 70° to 72°F, the yeast is too old or dead, and the operation must be started again with new yeast.

Important: Always remember never to use any salt when you reactivate yeast. Salt will compete with the yeast cells for water, making it difficult for them to absorb any of it and consequently feed on the nutrients in the flour and start their life cycle. Salt will be added later at the same time as the large amount of water needed to make the dough.

At this stage:

Flour + Liquid + Yeast = Inoculated or Activated Batter

EFFECTS OF MECHANICAL ACTION ON AN ACTIVATED BATTER: GLUTEN FORMATION

What happens in the activated batter that you cannot see with the naked eye is fascinating.

First, the yeast starts to feed on the sugars; also, as the flour is hydrated, microscopic fibrils of protein stretch out of the moistened flour to meet one another and start to form a net.

The starches and proteins in the flour will, at first, absorb all the water you give them. This initial addition of water to the batter is known as the "bound water." If you do not add enough water and immediately start working the mixture, the result will be a stiff, unmanageable ball of gray cementlike dough. Not adding enough water initially is the most common mistake when you first start to make bread. Be generous at first so that when yeast, proteins, and starches have absorbed all they want, there is still enough water flowing freely through the young dough so you can work it effectively. The hard wheat flours will absorb a lot more water than the softer wheats and the more you work the dough, the more elastic it will become. As you gradually add successive quantities of water and flour and continue working, you will soon obtain an irregular ball of dough that is plastic enough to roughly hold its shape.

Do not worry about adding too much water; if you do so, you can correct the situation by adding more flour until the texture of the dough has become plastic again.

If you have added too little water to start with, break the hard dough into one-inch lumps and sprinkle them abundantly with water until you can bring the lumps back together and continue your work.

PROPER KNEADING

At this point, you can start kneading. This is the most important technique in bread making, the one which will yield a good, average, or poor bread. I am very partial to kneading by hand, being lucky enough to have strong hands that can handle a relatively large ball of dough. The dough hook of mixers can do the same work, but what is missing with the hook is the physical feel of texture changes in the dough as the kneading progresses. If you are making bread for yourself, use only your hands; if you are or become a commercial baker, obviously you will have to switch to a powerful mixer for large quantity production.

I like to knead with each hand alternately, passing the dough from one hand to the other. Whichever style you choose, raise your wrist up and down and push the dough very rhythmically. Do not knead way down into the work table; rather, send the dough sliding parallel to the counter or tabletop as the heel of your hand pushes halfway down into the ball of dough, without tearing or overstretching it. Then, bring the part that finds itself under your fingers back over the part that is under your palm and roll the dough com-

KNEADING BREAD DOUGH

Rough dough just gathered into a ball and ready to be kneaded

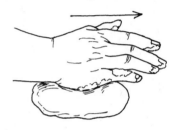

Crushing the dough forward

Pulling the front of the dough backward to fold over upon itself, top view

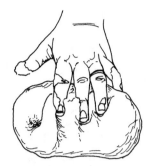

Pushing the top of the dough into the bottom, front view

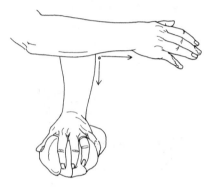

Crush, pull, and push the dough alternating from right to left hand, creating a V on the counter in front of the cook; each hand first goes forward, then backward in movement.

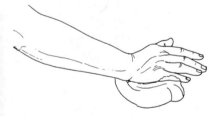

After repeating the crushing series 4 to 5 times with each hand, place the heel of your hand on the dough and roll forward with your fingers extended. Repeat this motion rapidly for 10 minutes, still in a V pattern.

pletely over in the last few seconds of the movement; the swift passing of the dough from one hand to the other will quickly become a reflex. A personal rhythm will come automatically to you; it will "kind of make you dance inside," as one of my ancient great aunts used to say, swinging her hips happily as she kneaded her sturdy loaves of Lorraine bread.

From the wettish and irregular ball that it was before kneading, the dough will become more and more elastic. The harder the flour used, the more elastic the dough will become and you can feel this elasticity develop. Under the strength of your kneading hands you are forcing the two proteins glutenin and gliadin to absorb water; in doing so they cross-link to form the all-important gluten. You will see its long strands appear through the dough, which will stick less and less to the hands as this happens. It is important that you understand that gluten does not exist in flour until your vigorous kneading of the dough makes glutenin and gliadin interact in the presence of water and create it. The gluten will give your dough its texture and allow it to stretch under the pressure of the carbon dioxide resulting from yeast fermentation—the bubbles of carbon dioxide left in the dough will leaven the bread.

Be certain that you do not add too much flour in the process of kneading the dough, which should not be dry, but still ever so slightly tacky to the touch. Gluten usually develops completely after about 10 minutes of kneading. Even if it is still slightly tacky, the dough is ready when, pushing into it gently with your thumb, it leaves an impression at least ⅛ inch deep, which remains at least a full minute before ever so slowly blending back into the surface, though still leaving behind a visible trace. I urge you *not to worry about that slight tackiness*; it will disappear as the dough rises because the always extremely water-hungry gluten will absorb any small amount of water you have left in the dough during fermentation. That slight tackiness in the dough will reward you with a wonderful loaf with a crispy outside that will crunch nicely under the tooth. Note that a dough is sticky when it clings to your hand but tacky only when touching the dough with a finger; the latter sticks for a few seconds to the dough but pulls free and clean from the dough ball.

Underkneading the dough results in a wet, coarse, doughy bread that does not hold its shape properly. Proper kneading for the proper length of time yields the proper type of dough, which has a firm structure and will rise generously, keeping its shape beautifully. Overkneading beyond 10 minutes slackens the gluten and makes the dough first gummy, then sticky to the point of appearing almost shiny wet, as well as unable to hold its shape without flattening.

This slackening of the dough is due to a complex reaction between sulfur derivatives in many of the components of the dough and water. See page 1009 and the bibliography for more scientific explanations.

At this point of the making of the dough:

Activated Batter + Kneading = Gluten Formation and Unfermented Young Dough

FERMENTATION AND RISING

Once you have finished kneading the dough, you should lightly grease it to prevent superficial dehydration and deposit it in a bowl (pottery or glass which absorb heat better than metal) that has also been ever so lightly greased, then let it rise, covered with a light cloth, in the coziest corner of your kitchen, away from cooling drafts. Yeast likes a pleasant temperature, between 70° and 85°F, and you will soon determine the best location in your own kitchen, a spot where the dough won't be too cold and ferment too slowly, or too warm and ferment too fast.

The finished dough should be smooth, feel slightly tacky, and retain the imprint of a thumb.

The initial stages of fermentation are slow; the rhythm will accelerate when the millions of yeast cells bud and divide into new yeast cells, and the multiple small air pockets you created in the dough through your kneading fill with the by-products of their life functions: carbon dioxide and alcohol. Most of the carbon dioxide will remain in the dough and stretch the gluten your kneading created in the walls of the air cells, and the alcohol, which slowly evaporates out of the bowl in which the dough is fermenting, makes the dough smell quite good. The totality of the alcohol will evaporate during the baking of the bread.

The physical and chemical changes in the dough are multiple. As explained on page 1018, enzymatic reactions break down the compound sugars and starches in the flour, changing them into simple sugars which the yeast will use as food. If you have used unscalded milk in the making of the dough, you may see the gluten structure slacken a bit. Salt makes the gluten less extensible, while fats have a slowing effect on the fermentation, so that very rich doughs will rise proportionally slower than lean ones containing no fat. Whole eggs and egg whites give color and body to the dough, and you will often find that a dough containing gluten-softening acid ingredients like buttermilk or yogurt will be reinforced by an addition of semolina or one or several eggs.

Let the fermentation proceed until:

- The dough has doubled in bulk for lean doughs, made without fat and with bread flour, and not quite doubled in bulk if the dough is lean but made with all-purpose flour and some fat.
- The dough is 1½ times larger than its original bulk, if you are handling a rich dough containing a large amount of sugar and fat. The richer the dough, the slower the fermentation which scientists call a "young fermentation" (see page 1019 for a full explanation). The sugar in the dough competes with the gluten for water absorption and the fat coats the gluten strands and prevents them from elongating and gathering strength.

Generally, a dough has fermented enough when, sinking a finger 1½ inches into its bulk, it retains the impression. When you deflate a dough, notice that the ever so slightly tacky texture has disappeared and the raised dough is now perfectly dry and supple, because the gluten has absorbed the totality of the water available in the dough.

Any fermented dough will contain several acids, such as the lactic acid generated by bacteria present in the flour, butyric acid which gives the dough a smell resembling that of butter, and, in much smaller quantities, some pyruvic acid, acetic acid, and a couple of others with unpronounceable names.

Overfermented doughs not only turn unpleasantly acid, but their gluten structure stretches and collapses. As you will see below, sourdough breads are made with overfermented starters, which communicate their sour taste to the bulk of the dough (see page 1051 for a recipe). A slightly overfermented dough need not necessarily be lost; adding some fresh flour and water, kneading it again for a few minutes, and giving it a shorter second fermentation will result in a good bread with a lot of interesting flavors. However, don't try to rescue a dough that has been altogether forgotten and has completely deflated and tastes sour to the point of being sour-bitter.

This of course brings to mind the important question: Exactly how long should one let any dough ferment and rise? This is unfortunately one of those instances in which I can only give you approximate information since the rising time depends on:

- The ambient temperature in the room where the rising takes place, and
- The strength and density of the flour(s) used.

Be prepared to study the temperature and humidity of your kitchen or bakery room and realize that your dough will rise at a slightly slower rhythm if it is made with hard flour (bread flour, semolina, etc.) than if it is made with softer all-purpose flour.

Professional bakers who have thermostatically controlled proof-boxes and humidity control can establish the time of rising of their doughs with greater accuracy.

Rest assured that you will have no problem if you use your eyes and nose fully, and your taste buds properly, as already explained above. Also, for one reason or another, we must carry in our hearts and minds quite a bit of inborn wisdom inherited from generations of baking ancestors, for over the last thirty-five years, I have never seen one student overferment a dough, and I have never overfermented one.

PUNCHING THE DOUGH DOWN;
SECOND RISING

Gently punch down the fermented dough and listen to all the hissing and puffing as the carbon dioxide is released; smell also, it is a true pleasure. Gently knead the dough again for a few seconds.

Punching down and rekneading are necessary to evenly distribute gas pockets, the water resulting from fermentation, and the large quantity of yeast cells that came to life during the fermentation process.

If your dough has been made with a strong bread flour or even with unbleached all-purpose flour, if the temperature of the kitchen is not too warm, and if you have the time, do not hesitate to give it a second rising; it will be much shorter than the first since there is so much more yeast now living in the dough, and it will result in an appreciable increase of taste in the finished product. See especially the European bread making techniques on pages 1035–38 and the sourdough bread making techniques. But remember always that a second rising depends mostly on the ambient temperature; if it is very warm to hot and if a first rising brings on enormous carbon dioxide and alcohol development, skip the second rising or go directly to a cool-rise instead.

COOL-RISE

If you want, the second rising can indeed be done in the refrigerator overnight. More often than not, I punch my doughs down at night just before retiring and put them in a refrigerator set at its warmest possible setting to undergo a second or third rising. Since for yeast this is very cool, this additional rising is very slow and the dough is ready for shaping and proofing the next morning. This is especially good for the rich *brioche* on page 1045.

PROOFING

After the dough has been fully fermented, deflated, and rekneaded a few minutes, it is shaped into the final form you wish to give it: loaves, rolls, sticks, *baguettes*, etc. The proofing (or proving, both expressions being used) allows the shaped product to again rise until 1½ to 2 times larger than its original volume, depending on the fat content of its dough. This proofing is most important because the distribution of the gas achieved by this last rising sets the final volume of the air cells and consequently the crumb texture of the baked product. Give it plenty of attention and follow directions for proofing closely. The proofing of croissants, for example, is the most critical stage in the preparation of these rolls.

It is easy to recognize after baking whether a bread has been overproofed. A normally proofed bread will have a narrow bottom with sides that round up immediately and no angle between the bottom of the bread and its top. Overproofed breads—and rolls, too—have a very flat bottom, a sharply marked, sloping 45-degree angle between bottom and sides, and a not so round body lacking volume. To go back to the same example, overproofed croissants will, while baking, stretch their structure to the utmost limits and end up flattening as they cool on a rack.

To resume the above information:

Fermented Shaped Dough + Proofing = Bread Ready to Bake

DOCKING, OVENSPRING, AND BAKING

Breads made at home are best docked before proofing and breads made in commercial bakeries can be docked after proofing, just as they are ready to go into the oven.

Since the surface of a proofing bread generally becomes slightly dehydrated you must dock it; otherwise, it will crack just above its base and look tortured and unappetizing. Docking means cutting ¼- to ⅓-inch-deep slashes into the loaves with a razor blade or, better yet, a serrated knife. These cuts will allow for the pressure of the expanding carbon dioxide and of the steam coming from the boiling of the water in the dough and let the crust expand.

In very large professional brick ovens, steam injectors deliver steam over the breads at regular intervals during the first ten minutes of baking. At home, this can be replaced by a spray bottle filled with water. The bread must be sprayed every three minutes during the first third to half of its total baking time to soften the crust; this will allow it to expand regularly and retain a beautiful shape.

Lean bread doughs tend to be baked at 425°F and rich doughs at 375°F, although there are variations. Hopefully you have an oven with a glass door so you can observe what happens after five minutes of baking. If the temperature of rich dough is higher than 375°F the center of the baked product does not fully bake and is heavy and doughy. Again croissants are the best example here.

The heat of the oven provokes dilation of the carbon dioxide and expansion of the steam and, in a last frantic bout of activity of the yeast, the bread swells by one third of its proofed, unbaked volume in a matter of 7 to 10 minutes. This last rising is called *ovenspring* and is a joy to behold. The lovely smell that almost simultaneously accompanies ovenspring is that of the last of the alcohol evaporating.

While the dough gathers internal heat, the following changes occur. At 120°F the yeast decreases activity and between 135° and 140°F succumbs to the heat of the oven. At 150°F the starches in the flour mixed with the water contained in the dough thicken and gelatinize. Browning occurs after the water contained in the dough has reached the boiling point of 212°F; browning is due partly to caramelization of the sugars, partly to the dextrinization of the starch in the flour, and also to the Maillard reaction taking place between the starches and proteins in the dough.

Once the shape of the bread is well set and the crust has browned and firmed up, the spraying can be discontinued and the temperature of the oven reduced to 350°F for lean doughs and 325°F for rich doughs to allow the crust to thicken and the soft center to finish cooking.

Bread and rolls are baked when they sound hollow when tapped with the finger, are properly browned, and no smell of alcohol can be detected anymore on opening the oven door. This test is usually sufficient; however, if you are uncertain, check with a skewer, which should come out dry and burn the top of your hand when put in contact with it for a split second.

Once removed from the oven, all breads must be allowed to cool on racks, which will allow for steam evaporation and complete hardening of the crust.

The fermentation of a yeast-leavened dough can be postponed by freezing. Freezing can be done at any stage of the bread preparation. Freezing the dough before fermentation requires a minimum amount of space in the freezer. Label packages of dough in the following manner:

Type of dough:	**Sourdough, or San Francisco sourdough, or croissants, for example**
Date:	12/12/96
Next step:	Defrost and ferment

Baked breads can of course be frozen. They must be defrosted and reheated all at once at the temperature at which they were baked or their texture will lose some of its original qualities through dehydration, however small.

The Methods of Making Breads

The following methods and techniques are listed in their order of difficulty and refinement; it is preferable for beginners to practice each method in this order and to study the differences of textures and tastes obtained from each.

ABOUT FLOURS AND THEIR WATER ABSORPTION CAPACITY
Each and every flour varies in its capacity for absorbing moisture and because of this variations in bread texture may result. This is where your own personal judgment comes into play. When making bread, add the smallest amount of water recommended in the ingredients list and, only if the texture of the dough is too hard, gradually add more water as needed.

You will rapidly be able to judge, just by looking at it and feeling it with your hands, when a dough is too tight and needs more water, or has absorbed just enough water, or has become too soft and needs to be adjusted with the addition of flour. A tight dough is dry to the touch, feels heavy and unpliable, and looks actually like a rock.

ABOUT ADDING LIQUID INGREDIENTS TO TIGHT DOUGHS
Water, milk, wine, fruit juices, and eggs are the liquid ingredients used in bread recipes. If a dough in the making becomes slightly tight, dip both your hands into water and continue kneading until it has been absorbed by the dough. Repeat the operation until the dough is moist enough to be considered slightly "tacky." (See page 1030 for the definition of tacky.)

If you have made a dough that is definitely too tight, do not throw it away, salvage it. Cut the dough into 1-inch pieces, sprinkle them with water, and gather up the pieces, gently kneading them together. Repeat with additions of water until the dough has absorbed enough to be supple and manageable.

ABOUT ADDING FLOUR TO TOO-WET DOUGH Gradually add small amounts of flour, kneading normally until the dough shapes up and feels tacky to the touch.

BATTER METHOD

This method is often used in the booklets put out by flour and yeast manufacturers. The bread is done very quickly and, considering the short time involved in making it, quite appetizing looking and pleasing. Observe its texture though; it is coarse, with relatively large air cells, and, due to the large amount of yeast leavening in a small amount of flour, the taste is a bit yeasty.

Kneading is omitted and replaced by beating of the batter with mixer beaters, or the vigorous beating with a wooden spatula. Such breads contain a lot more fat than is usually the case in bread formulas. Here is a recipe that you will be able to prepare successfully on your very first try.

Quick All-Purpose Batter Bread

You can change the flavorings to your taste; see the suggestions at the end of the recipe.

BEST FREEZING STAGE:
This bread is good for the quick fun of making it and for breakfast, but it is not worth freezing.

FFR — 1 LOAF; 8 SERVINGS

¾ cup milk of your choice, scalded

4 teaspoons granulated sugar

1 envelope dried yeast

1 teaspoon salt

2 large egg whites, lightly beaten

1 large egg

¼ cup plus 3 teaspoons olive or other unsaturated oil of your choice

2½ to 3 cups unsifted unbleached all-purpose flour

½ teaspoon dried ground orange peel as sold in spice jars

1 teaspoon crushed fennel seeds

Pour the scalded milk into a large mixing bowl and let it cool; an instant thermometer inserted in the milk should read 110° to 115°F, no more. Add the sugar and yeast and stir well. Let stand 10 minutes. Mix the salt, beaten egg whites and egg, and ¼ cup of the oil together in a small bowl. Place 2 cups of the flour in with the milk; gradually add the mixture of liquid ingredients using a wooden spoon or an electric mixer on low speed. Add the flavorings. Add the rest of the flour as needed, stirring or mixing on medium-high speed until the batter shreds from the mixer beaters or a wooden spoon. Turn the batter into a large greased bowl and let rise until doubled in bulk, 45 minutes to 1 hour in a room at 70° to 72°F.

Preheat the oven to 375°F. Punch the dough down, then beat it with a wooden spatula for a few minutes and turn it into a 5 × 9-inch nonstick loaf pan greased with 1 teaspoon of the oil. Let rise again until the dough is almost doubled in bulk and level with the rim of the pan. Brush the bread top with the remaining olive oil. Bake 30 to 35 minutes, until a skewer inserted into the dough comes out clean and hot when tested on the top of the hand. Unmold and cool on a cake rack.

To vary the flavor, omit the orange peel and fennel seeds and add one of the following:

- 1 teaspoon confit spices (see page 786)
- ¼ cup diced Gruyère or cheddar cheese
- 1 teaspoon aniseeds and ¼ teaspoon saffron threads
- 2 tablespoons finely chopped fresh herbs such as the four French *fines herbes* (see page 65) or any single herb; a mixture of dill and a few caraway seeds is especially interesting
- 2 tablespoons chopped fresh parsley leaves mixed with a large garlic clove, finely chopped.

Beaten Kugelhopf
ABGESCHLAGENER KUGELHOPF

FFR—1 LARGE BUNDKUCHEN CAKE; 12 BREAKFAST SERVINGS

½ cup dark raisins

¼ cup dark rum

⅔ cup milk of your choice, scalded and cooled

2 tablespoons granulated sugar

4 teaspoons dried yeast (or 1⅓ envelopes)

1 cup unsalted butter, at room temperature

1 teaspoon salt or more to your personal taste

6 large eggs

2⅔ to 3 cups sifted unbleached all-purpose flour

½ cup blanched whole almonds

This kugelhopf recipe, by now almost 200 years old, came from the Alsatian home of one of my grandmothers; here it is reworked as an American batter bread. The lower quantity of flour is usually sufficient, but several times I have had to use the larger one. The batter is quite soft. You need a large Bundt cake pan or two 1½-quart Alsatian Kugelhopf molds.

BEST FREEZING STAGE:
Baked. Recrisp for 10 minutes uncovered in a 275°F oven.

Soak the raisins in rum overnight; the rum will be absorbed.

Cool the milk to 110° to 115°F. Add 1 tablespoon of the sugar and mix well. Sprinkle the yeast over the mixture and let stand 10 minutes.

Meanwhile, cream the butter and the remaining sugar together until white. Season with salt, then add the eggs one at a time, beating well between each addition. Add the milk and yeast mixture to the egg-and-butter mixture and blend well.

Gradually add the flour, mixing on low speed if using an electric mixer, then beat on medium speed for 2 minutes. Stir in the soaked raisins. The batter will resemble cream whipped to the barely mounding stage. Preheat the oven to 375°F. Butter the cake pan generously. Sprinkle the almonds evenly over the bottom and fill gently with the batter. Let the batter rise until it reaches just below the rim of the pan, about 1 hour in a room at 70° to 72°F, longer if the room is colder.

Bake the kugelhopf 30 to 35 minutes, until a skewer inserted at its center comes out clean and feeling hot to the top of the hand. Unmold and cool on a cake rack.

FULL COOL-RISE METHOD COMBINED WITH THE AMERICAN SPONGE METHOD

Notice that the milk is not scalded in this method, and that there is no rising at room temperature. Rather the rising—called cool-rising—happens entirely in the refrigerator.

The manner in which this bread dough is mixed is a combination of American and European methods. The yeast activity is initiated in the European way by mixing the yeast with warm water and milk and adding approximately half the flour, leaving the resulting batter to rise slightly before adding the remainder of the flour. The initial batter is called a sponge in the United States and in many Germanic and Anglo-Saxon countries, or sometimes a starter. The rising on cool-rise is a practical American method.

ABOUT PARTIAL COOL-RISE: There is another use of cool-rise. Any dough can be prepared ahead of time, using any method, go through a first rising at room temperature, then be put to "cool-rise" for a second rising in the refrigerator. The *brioche* recipe on page 1045 is an example.

American Currant and Curry Bread

FCR or FFR—I LOAF; 8 SERVINGS

½ cup dried currants
3 tablespoons cold water
I cup warm water (110° to 115°F)
I envelope dried yeast
I cup milk of your choice
2 tablespoons firmly packed light brown sugar
4 to 5 cups unsifted unbleached all-purpose flour as needed
¼ cup unsaturated oil of your choice or melted butter, cooled
I tablespoon salt
2 tablespoons curry powder

Soak the currants overnight in the cold water. The water will be completely absorbed.

Add the warm water to a large mixing bowl, sprinkle the yeast over it, and let stand while you heat the milk to 115°F. Add it, the sugar, and 3 cups of the flour to the bowl and stir or mix with an electric mixer at medium speed until smooth. Let stand until the batter starts bubbling gently, about 30 min-

This makes a very nice cream cheese, ham, and endive sandwich or grilled chicken, young greens, and mango sandwich. Frozen and sliced very thin while still half frozen, it can be oven dried and served as a crouton with a salad of tropical fruit. If you remove the curry and currants, you will obtain a plain white bread for toasts and croustades (see page 1160).

BEST FREEZING STAGE:
Baked and wrapped in aluminum foil. Defrost and reheat at once for 25 minutes in the foil at 350°F. Remove the foil and crisp the bread crust for 5 minutes.

utes. Pour in the oil and gently work it into the dough until fully incorporated.

Pile another cup of flour on the countertop, creating a well in its center. Empty the fermenting batter into the well, add the salt and curry, and knead until the dough is smooth and will retain the trace of your thumb. If the dough is still too sticky, add as much as another ¼ cup of flour.

Drain and pat the currants dry, toss them with 2 tablespoons of the flour. Knead them into the dough. If the dough turns slightly sticky, add 2 more tablespoons of flour and work a few minutes until smooth again.

Shape the dough into a rectangle. Cut this into two smaller rectangles and flatten each to an even thickness of ½ inch using the extended tips of your fingers. Roll each thinned rectangle into a large cigar, and set each into a small 3 × 7-inch nonstick loaf pan greased with a very thin layer of oil. Cover each with an aluminum foil tent and refrigerate. Let rise until doubled in bulk, at least 48 hours; bring back to room temperature while you preheat the oven to 375°F. Bake 25 to 30 minutes, until a skewer inserted to the center of the bread comes out clean and hot to the top of the hand. Unmold immediately and cool on a rack. Consume the bread within the next 24 hours for best flavor, but it keeps fresh a long time wrapped in foil and refrigerated.

DIRECT MIXING METHOD

If you use milk as an ingredient, scald it first and let it cool to 110° to 115°F. Dissolve the yeast in the liquid ingredient(s)—not including the eggs—heated to a maximum temperature of 110° to 115°F; beat in half the flour, then hand knead the remainder of the flour into the dough.

Practice on the following recipe and when it has cooled, slice one braid or roll and notice how much finer-textured the crumb is and how much less yeasty the taste is than in the batter breads.

Semisweet Braids

FFR—2 LARGE BRAIDS

1⅓ cups milk of your choice, scalded and cooled to 110° to 115°F

2 tablespoons granulated sugar

1 envelope dried yeast

4 large eggs, beaten

1 cup unsalted butter, at room temperature

2 teaspoons salt

5 to 6 cups unsifted unbleached all-purpose flour as needed

1 large egg yolk

2 tablespoons cold milk of your choice

BEST FREEZING STAGE:
After baking

Mix the warm milk and sugar together in a large mixing bowl; sprinkle the yeast over the surface and let stand 10 minutes. Add the beaten eggs, butter, and salt and mix well. Add 3 cups of the flour and mix well with an electric mixer at medium-low speed. Let this starter stand 30 minutes to initiate the fermentation.

Put 2 more cups of the flour on the counter and make a well in it.

Pour the already rising starter into its center; gradually work the flour into the dough by hand. Knead until smooth but ever so slightly tacky, no more than 10 minutes. Add more flour or more water, whichever if needed. Place the dough in a lightly greased bowl and let rise in a cozy place, covered, until doubled in bulk; the time will vary with the temperature of the room in which the bread rises (1½ to 2 hours in a 70° to 72°F room).

Punch down and cut the dough into two equal pieces. Reshape each half into a ball, then, using a lightly floured rolling pin, roll each ball into a rectangle ½ inch thick on a lightly floured counter. Cut each rectangle into three equal pieces lengthwise. Roll each piece so it becomes a cigar 1 inch wide but tapered at each of its ends. Braid the three cigarlike pieces together, tucking the ends of each braid under the ends of the loaf. Set both breads on a large greased baking sheet lined with a sheet of parchment paper. Let rise again uncovered until almost doubled in bulk, 35 to 40 minutes, in a 70° to 72°F room. Mix the egg yolk and cold milk together; brush over both breads. Bake in the preheated oven at 375°F for 40 to 45 minutes, until a skewer inserted in the bread comes out clean and dry and hot to the top of the hand. Cool on a rack.

VARIATION: Cut and shape the dough into 24 small balls which can be baked as small dinner rolls in greased muffin tins. Also the dough can be flavored with whichever spice or herbs you like.

FLOATING SPONGE METHOD

The term "starter" is used interchangeably with "sponge." This old-fashioned way of inoculating a batter with yeast comes from Europe, particularly from France, where it is still in use in many pastry shops for the preparation of white sandwich bread, brioches, Savarins, etc. It is also used for flatbreads such as pizzas and fougasses, sisters to Italian focaccias.

The method consists of weighing or measuring the total amount of flour to be used, and separating out one third of it to prepare a sponge. The smaller amount of flour is mixed with the yeast and enough water to make a soft ball, which is immersed in water no warmer than 110°F. It is essential that this ball of dough not be worked hard and remain soft, with no gluten development at all, for, if it is tight and rubbery, the ball will be too tight and heavy for the warmth of the water and the water itself to penetrate it and begin fermentation.

If the starter has been well prepared, the yeast will ferment rapidly; you will see the ball of dough expand exactly like a dried sponge does when set in water. If the sponge does not expand, the yeast has lost its potency and the sponge must be discarded. Needless to say, this method comes from the days when yeast could be irregular in quality and need not necessarily be used nowadays, but it is a very good way to start the fermentation, which continues readily once the whole bread mix has been prepared.

Country Whole Wheat and Walnut Bread

LFR—2 LOAVES, EACH 8 SERVINGS

3 cups unsifted whole wheat flour

2 cups unsifted unbleached all-purpose flour

½ cup unsifted semolina

1 tablespoon granulated sugar

1½ teaspoons salt

1 envelope dried yeast

Warm water (110° to 115°F) as needed

Unsaturated oil of your choice

¾ cup broken walnut meats

White bolted cornmeal

Divide the whole wheat flour in half; process each half in the food processor until the flour is twice as fine as it was originally. Empty 2 cups of it onto the countertop. Mix it with 1 cup of the all-purpose flour and the semolina, sugar, and salt. Prepare a large well in the flour.

Mix the second cup of all-purpose flour, the rest of the whole wheat flour, the yeast, and approximately 1⅔ to 1½ cups water into a not too tight ball. Fill a medium-size bowl with lukewarm water 110° to 115°F. Immerse the ball of dough in the water and let stand until the sponge comes floating to the surface. When it does, spread your fingers open, pass your hand under the sponge, let it drip well, then deposit it at the center of the well of mixed flours on the countertop. Gradually mix the sponge into the flour mixture, adding as much lukewarm water as needed to make a quite moist ball of dough. Knead (see page 1029) until the dough retains a ¼-inch-deep impression of your thumb, about 10 minutes. The dough should be slightly tacky, neither smooth nor dry.

Rub a 3-quart bowl with oil and coat the dough lightly with more oil. Deposit the dough in the bowl, cover with a towel, and let rise until doubled in bulk, at least 2 hours in a room at 70° to 72°F. Punch down the dough gently, knead a few minutes more adding the walnuts, and let rise again in the refrigerator overnight until almost doubled in bulk.

Divide the dough in half. Shape each half into a rectangle 1 inch thick. Bring both sides of the rectangle together and pinch them closed. Roll back

Try making this bread once with regular whole wheat flour and once with white whole wheat flour to see the difference in the dough.

If you have worked with the French whole wheat flour and liked it, remill regular whole wheat flour in the food processor with the goal of obtaining a finer flour approximating farine intégrale. *Mixed partly with all-purpose white flour with semolina or pasta flour, it will give the bread a French-style structure.*

The French technique of using water in the quantity the flour itself will absorb naturally is applied here rather than a premeasured amount of water as in the recipes above; using this technique, the baker is more in control, being able to feel and appreciate the texture of the progressively building dough.

BEST FREEZING STAGE: *After baking and full cooling. Recrisp 10 minutes in a 275°F oven.*

and forth to even the loaves to a 3-inch diameter. Roll the ends of the bread to form two pointed ends called *croutons* and place on a baking sheet well sprinkled with cornmeal. Dock with long diagonal slashes ⅓ inch deep.

Let stand at room temperature until the breads are almost doubled in bulk. Do not overproof to avoid a flat bottom and a not so pretty look. You are on your own for this last rising, which is quite rapid if your room temperature is high. It may vary from 30 to 45 minutes.

Preheat the oven to 425°F. As you put the loaves on the oven rack, spray each with fresh water and close the door. Repeat this operation every 3 minutes, three to four times. After the last spraying, dust the top of the loaf with all-purpose flour.

When the loaves have reached their final and maximal size, turn the heat down to 325°F and continue baking until the loaves sound hollow when tapped with your finger. It may take as long as 50 minutes, sometimes even 1 hour to finish baking the loaves—go by the color of the loaves as well as their sound. Remove from the oven and cool on a rack.

Koeta

This very old pizzalike flatbread is from the French Alps. Identical yeast-leavened flatbreads exist under different names in all the provincial and regional cuisines of France and Italy. Usually made with leftovers of dough after the loaves of bread were weighed and baked. You can use any cheese from California's Teleme to Tome de Savoie, Italian Stracchino, or fontina, and Vermont mild cheddar.

BEST FREEZING STAGE: *Do not freeze the completed koeta. Make the dough, freeze it, defrost it, and let it rise, but prepare the vegetable filling as described above while the dough rises.*

FFR—6 TO 8 SERVINGS

I cup unsifted unbleached all-purpose flour

I ½ teaspoons dried yeast

⅔ cup warm water (110° to 115°F) as needed

2 cups unsifted bread flour

I teaspoon fine salt

I teaspoon caraway seeds

2 tablespoons walnut oil

White bolted cornmeal

I ½ teaspoons kosher salt

I teaspoon coarsely cracked black pepper

2 tablespoons roughly chopped fresh parsley leaves

3 strips bacon

I bunch turnip or mustard greens, chopped

2 tablespoons unsalted butter

6 small purple-top turnips, peeled and cut into ⅛-inch-thick slices

Pepper from the mill

2 cups apple cider

I to 2 tablespoons cider vinegar, to your personal taste

6 or 8 long slices melting cheese of your choice

Mix the all-purpose flour and yeast. Moisten with as much of the water as you need to gather it into a soft ball. Fill a large bowl with water no warmer than 115°F and immerse the "sponge" in it. Let rise to the surface of the water.

Meanwhile, mix the bread flour, fine salt, and caraway seeds together on a countertop and make a well in it. As soon as the sponge is floating, spread your fingers open, pass your hand under the sponge, let it drip well, and transfer it to the center of the well. Gradually mix the sponge into the flour, adding as much warm water as needed to make a slightly wet ball of dough. Knead into a 95 percent smooth and elastic dough, about 10 minutes. The finished dough should be ever so slightly tacky to the touch (remember that tacky does not mean sticky) and retain a ⅙- to ¼-inch-deep imprint of your thumb.

Pour the walnut oil into a bowl. Roll the ball of dough into the oil, cover with a towel, and let rise until doubled in bulk in a warm corner of the kitchen. When doubled, rework the dough a few minutes, incorporating the oil into it. Let rise again until almost doubled in bulk again, about 30 to 40 minutes in a room temperature of 70° to 72°F.

Preheat the oven to 425°F. Sprinkle a baking sheet with cornmeal. If need be, very lightly flour both countertop and rolling pin and roll the dough out to an 8-inch-wide circle. Transfer it to the sheet and with your hand gently flatten it to a 12- to 14-inch circle ⅓ inch thick. Let rise 20 minutes, then punch holes in it at regular intervals with a fork and sprinkle with the kosher salt, cracked pepper, and chopped parsley leaves; bake until crisp outside and soft inside, 20 to 25 minutes. Cool on a rack.

While the bread rises, render the bacon in a medium-size skillet over medium-low heat until crisp. Drain the bacon on paper towels and crumble. Do not wash the skillet and in it stir-fry the greens on high heat until tender; set them aside. Add the butter to the same pan, heat until the foam starts to recede, then add the turnips and season with salt and pepper to taste. Cover and étuvé (see page 391) them until soft. Gradually add the cider, cooking uncovered, on low heat until the turnips are well done and surrounded with a thin layer of cider syrup. Add the vinegar, toss well, and cook a few more minutes. Correct the seasoning.

Cut the cooled *koeta* in half crosswise to obtain a large sandwich. Spread the greens on the bottom layer, top with the crumbled bacon, then the turnips and the cheese and the other half of bread. Using a large knife, cut into six or eight portions, each containing a slice of cheese and serve while the vegetable garnish is still lukewarm.

Brioche

The origin of the name *brioche* as I try to pinpoint it here is the result of my own deductions based on my training in the philology of Germanic languages. The origin of the word remains undefined in the French edition of the *Larousse Gastronomique*, the two-volume version of the French Larousse dictionary, and possibly to the most prominent French food historians. The best ancient *brioches* have always been recognized as having been made in

Normandy, where for a long time the language was not pure French but peppered with many northern Germanic words, due to the extensive invasions of that region by the Norse (A.D. 850 to 920), who gave it its current name. *Brioche* is probably such a word and derived from the same root as the modern German *brechen*, which in English means to break, both derived from the Old English *brecan* and the Old High German *brehhan*. The word *brioche* (contained in the modern German past participle of *brechen*, *gebrochen*) probably refers to the way the dough was deflated and allowed to rise again several times when it was made with bread leaven instead of the yeast we use today. The French technical expression for our colloquial "punch down" is *rompre*, which can mean both to break and to punch down. Another remnant of this old German root is to be found in the name of the *pain brié* (broken bread) of the little Norman city of Honfleur, the dough of which was originally "broken" by beating it with the heel of a wooden shoe, an action done nowadays by a cutter fitted into a round revolving bowl containing the dough. In the Norman-French verb for break, *brier*, the consonants *g*, *hh*, or *ch* have probably disappeared because they were difficult for native Romance language speakers to pronounce. The *i* was probably added to render the word as fluid to pronounce as the *ch* does in the modern German *brechen*.

There are two types of *brioche* doughs. The ordinary *brioche* is made with a ratio of 50 percent butter to the weight of the flour. The very rich and outrageously delicious mousseline *brioche* is made with equal weights of flour and butter. The *brioche* is reputed as being difficult to make, which is not true, if you understand the principles well.

Brioche should be handmade, if only for the joy of the way it feels to handle that delicate dough and also because it is important to learn how to develop just enough gluten to give the bread body, without making the dough stiff and rendering it unable to absorb the relatively large quantity of butter it is supposed to receive.

When the gluten has been developed too much, it becomes quite apparent after the *brioche* has risen. The batter will appear "separated," with thousands of droplets of butter floating between thousands of tiny pieces of dough, or lining the bowl. When such a product is baked, a toughish *brioche* ends up frying in the clarified butter that oozes out of the dough. It will overflow its molds onto the oven floor, and burn and smoke up the kitchen. If you see such a problem arise, you can salvage the batter by adding first a bit of milk, then flour until the batter is smooth and even textured again. How much flour depends on the degree of separation of the butter from the batter. Such a *brioche* will not be your best, but it is still civilized and quite edible. Read the techniques explained here carefully.

THE CHOICE OF FLOUR IS IMPORTANT It is essential to blend flours to obtain a flour the texture and average protein content of which is somewhat equivalent to the French-type 45 flour. The best combination I have used is unbleached all-purpose flour blended with one quarter of its own volume in cake flour. The number 45 in France corresponds to an extraction of 70 percent. As a matter of comparison, all French breads are made with flour classified 55, sometimes 65, which corresponds to extractions of 75 to 80 percent. Many American bakers use bread flour; the combination I offer yields a lighter texture.

THE TEXTURE OF THE BUTTER IS ALSO IMPORTANT The butter must have the same texture as the batter, so it can cream and emulsify perfectly into the batter without turning oily and eventually melting.

To prepare a good *brioche*, learn to make a *brioche* mousseline by hand; this is the most difficult to achieve and since it is exactly the same technique as for the ordinary *brioche*, you will learn the way "by hand" for both at the same time.

Handmade Brioche

FFR— I LARGE MOUSSELINE BRIOCHE

For the floating sponge

I envelope dried yeast

½ cup sifted unbleached all-purpose flour

Warm water (110° to 115°F) as needed

For the bulk of the dough

½ cup sifted cake flour

I cup sifted unbleached all-purpose flour

3 large eggs, beaten

2 tablespoons milk of your choice, at room temperature

2 to 3 tablespoons granulated sugar, to your personal taste

½ teaspoon salt

½ teaspoon orange flower water or I teaspoon ground cardamom

I cup unsalted best quality butter, at room temperature but still waxy, plus 1½
   tablespoons to grease the mold

For the glaze

I large egg yolk

2 tablespoons milk of your choice

Prepare the sponge starter: In a small bowl mix the yeast and flour together. Gradually add enough warm water to make a medium-firm ball. Let warm water from the spigot run gently into the bowl to cover the sponge. Leave the bowl on the kitchen counter. The sponge will be ready to use when it floats to the surface of the water in a scant 8 to 10 minutes.

This brioche *is to be molded into a French tall cylindrical mold No. 150 (meaning 15 centimeters in diameter). If you want to make small brioche with cute heads, prepare this same recipe using only ¼ pound butter, and see page 1047 for instructions on how to shape the rolls. You will need twelve small brioche molds 2 to 3 inches in diameter. You can also use large muffin tins, although they are not as elegant. If you use the rich mousseline formula for brioche with a head (in French brioche à tête) the heads have difficulty staying straight on top of the bottom. This happens to the best bakers because the dough is really too soft for this type of equilibrium, but the brioches look tipsy and really engaging.*

BEST FREEZING STAGE:
Either when just made and before rising or after baking

Prepare the bulk of the dough: Mix the flours together in a large bowl, empty onto the countertop, and make a large well in the center. Add the eggs, milk, sugar, salt, and the chosen flavoring. Gradually work the flour into the liquid ingredients to make a soft ball. By the time this is ready, the sponge will also be. Spread your fingers open, pass your hand under the sponge, and let it drip a few seconds. Drop the sponge on top of the regular dough and mix them together, using your fingertips to pull the dough 2 inches above the counter several times to build a small amount of gluten.

Now, cut the butter into 4 equal pieces. Place one piece at the four poles of the *brioche* dough and, using your thumbs, cream the butter until its texture is the same as that of the dough. Mentally divide the dough into four equal parts. Working very fast with your fingertips, gradually blend and emulsify each little mound of creamed butter into one quarter of the dough; the butter must disappear altogether into the dough, which itself must turn very pale yellow, almost white. Gather and homogenize the dough by pulling it energetically away from the counter 2 minutes or so to give it more elasticity, *but do not overwork* or the butter will break out of emulsion during the fermentation of the dough and while baking.

Using a pastry scraper, transfer the dough to a bowl and let it ferment, covered, at room temperature (72°F) until it has risen to 1½ times its original volume, about 2½ hours. Deflate the dough, rehomogenize it well with a few flip-flops of the hand, and put it to continue fermenting overnight on the lowest shelf of the refrigerator, covered.

The next morning, grease the mold, turn the dough into it, and let proof until the dough rises within ½ inch of the rim. Preheat the oven to 425°F. Beat the egg yolk and milk together. Brush the top of the bread twice with the egg wash. Bake the *brioche* 5 minutes at 425°F, reduce the heat to 375°F, and finish baking until an instant thermometer inserted in the center of the *brioche* comes out hot and dry, another 20 to 25 minutes. Unmold the *brioche* immediately and let cool on a rack. It is wise to slightly overbake rather than underbake it so the crust is well set all around and stands firm when unmolded.

Use the following dough weights to shape the following sizes.

Brioche	Diameter	Dough Weight
No. 100	10 cm	3½ ounces
No. 120	12 cm	5 ounces
No. 140	14 cm	8 ounces
No. 160	16 cm	10 ounces
No. 180	18 cm	12 ounces
No. 200	20 cm	1 pound

Mixer-Made Ordinary Brioche for Quantity Production

48 SMALL BRIOCHES TO BE MOLDED IN 2- TO 3-INCH BRIOCHE MOLDS OR 4 SHEETS OF LARGE MUFFIN TINS, OR SEVERAL LARGE BRIOCHES MOLDED EACH IN A FLUTED BRIOCHE MOLD

For the sponge starter

3½ to 4 cups sifted unbleached all-purpose flour

1 ounce instant yeast or 2 envelopes regular dried yeast

Warm water (110° to 115°F) as needed

For the bulk of the dough

2 cups unsalted butter

2¼ to 2⅓ cups sifted cake flour

1¾ to 2 cups sifted unbleached all-purpose flour

12 large eggs

½ cup granulated sugar

2 to 2½ teaspoons fine salt, to your personal taste

1 cup milk of your choice, scalded and cooled

For the egg wash, also called dorure

2 large egg yolks

¼ cup milk of your choice

Prepare the sponge: Mix together the flour and yeast in a large bowl. Add enough warm water (110° to 115°F) to obtain a semisoft batter. Let stand, covered lightly, at room temperature until the dough is bubbly and has doubled in bulk, about 45 minutes.

Prepare the bulk of the dough: Using the paddle attachment in an electric mixer, cream the butter until fluffy and white. Using a spatula, remove the butter to a plate and divide into four equal parts. Keep at room temperature, away from heat.

Resift the flours together into a mixer bowl. Add the eggs, sugar, salt, and milk. Using the paddle attachment, beat on slow speed until the liquid ingredients are well blended with the flour. Add the sponge to the mixer bowl; beat on low speed until the dough and sponge are well mixed, then gradually add the butter 4 ounces at a time, mixing on medium speed until completely homogenized after each addition.

Divide the dough into two large stainless steel bowls and let rise, covered, at room temperature to 1½ times the original volume, about 1½ hours. Rehomogenize the dough, deflate gently, cover with clear plastic wrap, and let rise overnight on the lowest shelf of the refrigerator.

To make a brioche with a head, either in a large or small size: Shape balls to fit each size of mold adequately. Divide each ball into two parts, one representing three quarters of the dough, the other only one quarter. Roll the smaller part into a pear shape with a small conical end. Set the large piece of dough in its greased mold and, using your index finger, dig a conical hole into the dough. Drop the pear-shaped piece of dough into the hole, narrow end down. Let rise at 72°F room temperature until 1½ times its original size. The smaller part will become the head of the *brioche.*

Preheat the oven to 425°F for larger *brioches* and 400°F for small rolls. Beat the yolks and milk together, then glaze the *brioches* with the *dorure* twice. Bake for 10 minutes, then, for both large and small *brioches*, reduce the oven temperature to 375°F. Let bake until the crust is dark brown and shiny. Test a large cake by inserting an instant thermometer into the center of the cake; it

GIVING A HEAD TO A *BRIOCHE*

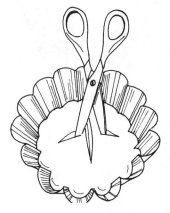

Cut a deep cross into the large part of the dough.

Insert a pear-shaped piece of dough into the cross, thin end first. Let it rise freely.

Brush with egg wash and, before baking, cut the dough with scissors all around the head where indicated.

Fully baked *brioche*

should come out clean and hot to the top of the hand. The baking time of larger cakes will vary with the size of each cake; check carefully with the stem of an instant thermometer. The small cakes will be ready in 25 minutes.

MAKING BREAD WITH A LEVAIN

For other points of view on this way of making bread, see the bibliography, especially the excellent books of bakers Joe Ortiz, Daniel Leader, and Nancy Silverton. This last technique of making breads is the most elaborate and the most ancient after the flatbreads. It was practiced in the days when professional and commercial bakers did not yet exist, and is said to have been discovered by the Egyptians. How, one still does not know exactly, but it is easy to imagine that, having baked what was probably thought to be a spoiled flatbread inflated with carbon dioxide from fermentation, the resulting loaf, full of holes, was pleasing in looks and softer in texture than any flatbread and the process was duplicated from then on.

The following is a home method to produce two types of what was called through all my years growing up in Europe a levain by the many women who, up to the late 1930s, still made their own bread. Professional bakers divide the making of a levain into two separate operations: the making of the chef and the making of the levain.

STARTING A CHEF AND A LEVAIN FROM GRAPE JUICE OR OTHER LIQUID A chef is a mixture of flour and liquid which, left to stand, will ferment into a dough that turns sour.

Once the chef has soured, it is fed more flour and becomes a levain. Here are different ways of making a chef in the home or a small cooking operation.

My favorite way uses freshly fermented grape juice, only because my great grandmother used to do it like this. I live in an area where picking a few bunches of grapes is an easy endeavor since there are grapevines everywhere. If you can, pick yourself two large bunches or the equivalent in smaller bunches. The grapes may be of any variety, red or white. I walk through the vineyards that have already been picked for wine making and take the small bunches of grapes called grapillons from the second crop, a few of which are more often than not left for the starlings and cowbirds. If you have a home grapevine growing on some arbor or above a door, you have what you need; pick the grapes at their peak of ripeness, when the skins still show their powdery covering of natural yeasts. If, at fruit stands, you can find grapes that come from neighboring farms in the fall, they are just as good. The supermarket grapes, which have been stored for a long time, may or may not work.

Stem the berries into a small bowl. Crush them well with your hands, so they are really empty of juice and the skins sink limp and crumpled to the bottom of the bowl. Cover with a double layer of cheesecloth and let stand three days at 72° to 75°F. *Do not add extra sugar, honey, or any other sweetener.*

Within three days, the skins will have risen to the surface of the juice, which will be hidden under them and separated from them by a layer of carbon dioxide. Push that little "cap" away and you will find bubbles in large quantity; what you have is not grape juice anymore but a new wine in the making which is still barely sweet. Empty this into a strainer placed over a bowl and strain, pushing on the skins to squeeze out all the liquid.

Now take 1 cup of flour and dilute the flour with as much of the fermented juice as it will take to make a dough that is *mollet*, that is, neither too liquid nor too tough, just to the point that it keeps its shape nicely.

Let the chef ferment again, loosely covered, until it smells and tastes good and sour, which may require another two days or more. When it is ready, add another cup of flour, and on the next day add one more cup of flour, letting what is now the levain ferment a full day each time. Add water each time also to keep the chef soft and mellow.

Another way to start a chef consists of mixing together

I cup unsifted unbleached all-purpose flour

¼ teaspoon ground cumin

½ teaspoon dried yeast

and warm water (110° to 115°F) as needed to obtain the same *mollet* dough; the cumin is used here to help develop more sourness. Let the chef stand, covered, at room temperature until sour, two days at least, then each of the two following days add one more cup of flour and more water as needed to reform a *mollet* dough. The obtained levain will be usable on the fourth day. This technique was given to me by my French baker in the French alpine city of Annecy.

There are numerous other ways of preparing chefs and levains, such as combining flour with a mixture of honey and water, whey from cheese making, plain milk, the soaking water of dried raisins, or grape berries wrapped in cheesecloth.

RENEWING A LEVAIN AND KEEPING A CHEF ALIVE After you have made a levain, use two thirds of it—or approximately 2 cups—to prepare a loaf of bread, then, over the next three days, add 1 cup of flour each day together with enough tap water to the remainder to renew the levain. Use the levain again on the fourth day after you refreshed it and continue using this technique every time you bake bread. If the levain tastes and smells slightly less sour at times, do not hesitate to let it ferment more than one day at a time before adding flour.

KEEPING A LEVAIN Professional bakers use different methods to store their chefs and levains. The method I describe here is strictly a home-style keeping procedure that I have used for years with great success. My latest chef was started in 1989 after my first "crush" (read harvest) in California and is still healthy and going.

Store your chef or levain in a large container with a lid on the bottom shelf of your refrigerator. As it sits, it will become more and more sour and the liquid part of it will separate from the flour, the hydrated flour settling at the bottom of the container as the liquid rises toward its top.

When ready to use the chef, take three quarters of it and turn it into a levain by adding flour and water to it as needed as described on page 1049.

Use only two thirds of the finished levain to prepare your bread. Mix the remaining third with the remainder of the chef still in its container. Add a little water to obtain a *mollet* dough. Store in the refrigerator until ready to use again.

THE EFFECT OF SALT ON A LEVAIN Salt does have a deleterious effect on yeast development, as explained on page 1019. However, should your levain be working too fast and bubbling all over the place, stir a tiny pinch of salt into it. The fermentation will slow down as the yeast activity is reduced by the salt stealing the water away from the numerous yeast cells with which it has come into direct contact. Otherwise, if the fermentation is nice and slow, be careful not to add any salt.

ABOUT THE SAN FRANCISCO SOURDOUGH STARTER *Saccharomyces cerevisiae* is not the yeast present in the famous San Francisco sourdough starter, because it is highly sensitive to and cannot live in the presence of a very large amount of acid. Instead, San Francisco sour starters and doughs harbor another *Saccharomyces*, called *S. exiguus*, which distinguishes itself by its inability to assimilate the maltose existing in flour and by its uncanny capability of thriving in an extremely acid dough, about 9 to 10 times more acid than a conventional dough.

Conventional so-called sourdough starters made in climates where *S. exiguus* cannot develop contain, besides lactic acid, only pyruvic, propionic, valeric, and isovaleric acids. In the proper climatic conditions, *S. exiguus* coexists in symbiosis with a lactobacillus (on the West Coast it is *Lactobacillus San Francisco*), or rod-shaped bacterium, that feeds only on the maltose rejected by the *exiguus* and produces as much as 50 percent lactic acid and 50 percent acetic acid. This pair thrives only in cool climates ranging from 50° to 65°F, which explains why it is to be found in the San Francisco area where the fog sent ashore by the cold Pacific Humboldt current keeps the temperature cool and pleasantly humid. This explains also why western Oregon, Washington, and Alaska benefit from the same combination and all offer excellent sourdough breads. The very same situation exists in many of the mountain ranges of the world, wherever a valley has the same type of foggy cool climate giving rise to an identical symbiosis between a local *exiguus*-type yeast and a local lactobacillus.

These climatic conditions being essential for the pair to thrive, disappointments are common when a San Francisco sourdough starter, nursed year after year in the proper climate is transported to a drier and sunnier one. As one feeds the starter with local flour and water, the *exiguus* and lactobacillus gradually die out, soon to be replaced by the local strains of *Saccharomyces*.

I have been successful in keeping a true San Francisco starter active in the French Alps in a valley where it rained a lot and where the climate was cool and almost identical to that of the San Francisco climate year around. On the other hand, in the Napa Valley, I have seen starters of wild local *S. exiguus* made in the colder months from starters exposed to the cold fog coming from the Pacific Ocean, lose their intense sourness in the heat of summer, with the latter coming back as soon as the foggy mornings and cooler temperatures of the next fall returned to the correct range.

Now that you can understand what happens to your levain starter, enjoy making sourdough bread with the yeast that will thrive in your climate. There are different ones everywhere which will make the bread taste as it should naturally in your location.

As a matter of interest for those home bakers who are able to capture a *Saccharomyces exiguus*/lactobacillus in their local surroundings during the cool months of the year, but lose it steadily during the summer months' heat, keeping the starter constantly in the vegetable bin of a refrigerator offers a temperature close enough (50° to 65°F) to the climate of San Francisco. As a result, home bakers may want to try keeping a sourdough. The sourdough chef must be used and renewed. Each and every time it is renewed, it should be left to grow at room temperature (70 to 72°F) for about 6 hours, then returned quickly to the vegetable bin of the refrigerator to develop lactic and acetic acid again.

It is also important to know when using San Francisco-type sourdough that in any dough containing a large amount of the combination of lactic and acetic acids, you will see the gluten seem to develop normally as the dough is kneaded, but as the fermentation gradually takes place, its strands will shorten, almost dramatically, and the dough will acquire a slacker texture. You will see the crust of the bread pull apart rapidly as soon as the bread, having been put to bake, goes into ovenspring. This can be minimized by using a bread flour containing 14 percent proteins.

I have taken to the habit, when baking with a San Francisco-type sourdough (though it does not always give me the volume I wish), of preparing a plain dough made with 2 cups flour and 1 teaspoon regular yeast (*S. cerevisiae*). I then blend that ready-to-use regular dough with a ready-to-use San Francisco-type sourdough made of 4 cups flour kneaded with a San Francisco-style sour starter (*S. exiguus*) and allow that hybrid dough to proof on cool-rise (see page 1033). This imparts a respectable share of sour taste to the final loaf of bread but the final product is never quite as sour as any of the commercial products.

If you would like to try this, sourdough starter can be purchased from the San Francisco Sourdough Company in San Francisco and the Gold Rush Sourdough Company in San Raphael, California.

True French Breads

Please read the general instructions on pages 1028–34 before making and baking these breads.

True French bread contains neither sugar nor milk. It is a white bread with a long-baked crispy and crackling crust, which makes the best sandwiches with butter, salami, or boiled ham, or country pâté, as on page 881. There is no way to indicate exactly how much water is to be used since each and every flour absorbs it differently.

If the dough turns out a little too wet, simply add flour. If, on the other hand, the dough is tough because you added too little water to start with, stop working it immediately, and follow the instructions on page 1035 for repairing a tight dough.

BEST FREEZING STAGE:
Fully baked

NFR—2 BÂTARDS, OR 4 BAGUETTES, OR 8 FICELLES, OR 2 CROWNS

4 cups unsifted bread flour

2 cups ready-to-use levain (page 1049)

1 tablespoon salt

1 cup warm water (110° to 115°F) plus more as needed

2 tablespoons oil of your choice, preferably light olive or corn oil

White bolted cornmeal

Pour the flour onto a work surface and make a well in it. Place the levain in the well. Dissolve the salt in 1 cup of the water and add to the well. Gather the flour, levain, and salted water together and start mixing together with your hands. Add as much additional warm water as needed to make a ball of dough that is neither too dry nor too wet. Knead until the dough retains the trace of a thumb but is still ever so slightly tacky to the touch, no more than a full 10 minutes.

Rub a large bowl with the oil; turn the ball of dough on all sides into the oil and cover the bowl with a towel. Let rise slowly covered until doubled in bulk in a cozy part of the kitchen, about 3 hours, more if needed. Punch down and let rise again; this time the full rising will take only 1 to 1¼ hours.

Lightly grease one 7 × 14-inch baking sheet for *bâtards* and crowns or two 7 × 14-inch baking sheets for *baguettes* and *ficelles*. Sprinkle each with cornmeal.

Punch the dough down. Reknead it for just a few minutes.

Preheat the oven to 425°F.

Shape, dock, proof, bake, and spray with water as indicated below:

To make bâtards: A bâtard is a large loaf, 2½ to 3 inches in diameter when baked. Cut the dough into two portions. Roll each into a rectangle 14 × 17 inches and roll the dough back upon itself, tapering the ends of each loaf into conical croutons. Arrange the breads well separated on a sheet. With a razor blade or serrated knife, cut diagonal slashes ⅓ inch deep through the top of each loaf. Let proof until doubled in bulk in a room at 70° to 72°F, 35 to 45 minutes. Bake, spraying three to five times at 425°F for 20 minutes, then another 15 to 20 minutes. Tap on the back; a hollow sound means that the loaves are done.

BREAD SHAPES

Boule, also called *pain de campagne*

Bâtard

Crown

Baguette

Ficelle

To make crowns: Cut the dough in half and roll out each into a rectangle 14 × 17 inches. Roll each piece back upon itself as for the *bâtards*, tapering the ends. Turn each loaf into a circle, intertwining the two tapered ends by passing one over the other. Dock the breads ½ inch deep at regular intervals all around the top of each crown. Arrange on two baking sheets. Handle the proofing, baking, and spraying exactly as for the *bâtards* described on page 1052.

To make baguettes: A *baguette* is that well-known long loaf of bread no more than 2 inches in diameter when baked. In French bakeries it is about 32 inches long. You will not be able to make yours longer than 17 inches for home baking sheets. They can be longer if baking on professional sheets and in professional ovens. Cut the dough into four portions. Roll each into a rectangle 7 × 17 inches and roll it back tightly up on itself, tapering the ends of the loaves into croutons. Arrange on one sheet. Dock by cutting diagonal slashes ⅓ inch deep into the top of each loaf with a razor blade or a serrated knife. Let proof until almost doubled in bulk at 425°F all through the baking time and spraying four times during the first 15 minutes of baking. Bake until one of the *baguettes* sounds hollow when tapped on its bottom, 25 to 30 minutes.

To make ficelles: The *ficelles* you will make will look quite authentic since those sold in French bakeries are only half as long as *baguettes*. Cut the dough into eight portions and roll each out into a rectangle 4 × 17 inches. Roll each rectangle back tightly upon itself to make a ¾-inch-wide loaf, tapering it at each end to make the croutons. Arrange on two sheets and dock ¼ inch through the top of each loaf. Let proof until almost doubled in bulk. Bake at 425°F for 20 to 22 minutes, spraying three times in the first 10 minutes of baking. The *ficelles* will be done and crisp.

Cool all types of breads on racks.

Swiss Whole Wheat and Rye Bread
SCHWEIZER KORN UND ROGGEN BROT

LFR — 2 LOAVES, EACH TO SERVE 6 TO 8 PEOPLE

1 cup unsifted unbleached all-purpose flour

2 teaspoons dried yeast

½ teaspoon ground cumin

Warm water (110° to 115°F) as needed

1½ cups unsifted bread flour

1 cup unsifted medium rye flour

1 cup unsifted whole wheat flour

2 cups ready-to-use levain (page 1049)

4 teaspoons salt

2 tablespoons walnut oil

1½ cups coarsely cracked wheat (bulgur), barely moistened with a bit of water

White bolted cornmeal

This was my most favorite bread when I lived in Switzerland. It is excellent spread with butter and sandwiched with air-dried mountain ham or prosciutto. Serve a bowl of small French cornichons on the side. The baking of these loaves is long and progressive to insure good even crumb in the baked dough.

BEST FREEZING STAGE: *Fully baked*

Prepare a small starter with the all-purpose flour, yeast, and cumin powder. Add as much warm water as needed to make a soft dough. Let rise until doubled in bulk, 2½ to 3 hours.

Mix the bread flour, rye, and whole wheat flours together on a work surface and make a well in the mixture. Place the levain and starter in the well. Dissolve the salt in the water and pour into the well. Work everything into the flours, adding as much warm water as needed to make a ball of dough that is neither too dry nor too wet. Knead until the dough retains the ever so slight trace of a thumb but is slightly tacky, no more than a full 10 minutes.

Rub a large bowl with the walnut oil. Roll the ball of dough into the oil to coat it well. Let the dough rise, covered, until almost doubled in bulk, about 2 hours. Dry the cracked wheat in paper towels, and toss in 1 or 2 tablespoons flour; knead the cracked wheat into the dough; let rise again, still covered, until almost doubled in bulk, another 1½ hours. Punch down and shape into two round loaves, each 6 to 7 inches in diameter.

Sprinkle a large baking sheet with cornmeal; set the loaves on the sheet, dock a circle 1½ inches inside the rim and ½ inch deep and let them rise a third time until almost doubled, about 45 minutes. Preheat the oven to 375°F. Bake, spraying the loaves with water four times at 3- to 4-minute intervals until ovenspring is completed. Continue baking until a skewer inserted in one of the loaves comes out hot and dry, another 35 to 40 minutes. Cool on racks.

VARIATION: For rye bread to be served with oysters on the half shell, replace the whole wheat flour with a second cup of rye, omit the cracked wheat, and add 2 tablespoons pure olive oil to the dough when mixing. Let rise, then shape into 3 small loaves; fit each into three 5¾ x 3¼-inch loaf pans. Proof until the dough is within 1/4 inch of the rim of each pan. Spray with olive oil; do not either dock or spray with water. Bake at 375°F until an instant thermometer inserted in the bread comes out clean, about 35 minutes.

Bruno's Panettone

FFR — 3 RICH CAKELIKE BREADS EACH TO BE BAKED IN ONE
1-QUART TALL PYREX GLASS BOWL, FOR A TOTAL OF 24 SERVINGS

For the chef

1 cup unsifted unbleached all-purpose flour

2 teaspoons dried yeast

1 cup lukewarm water (90°F)

For the levain

1 cup unsifted unbleached all-purpose flour

2 tablespoons granulated sugar

⅔ to 1 cup lukewarm water (90°F) as needed

For the intermediate dough

5 large egg yolks

1 large egg

1¼ cups granulated sugar

1½ cups sifted unbleached all-purpose flour

1½ teaspoons salt

¾ cup unsalted butter, "just melted" and barely lukewarm

For the final dough

½ cup dark raisins

⅓ cup finely diced citron

4½ teaspoons orange flower water or orange liqueur

¼ cup dry Marsala

3 tablespoons unsifted cake flour

¾ cup unsalted butter, at room temperature, plus 3 tablespoons to grease the glass bowls

1½ cups unsifted unbleached all-purpose flour

1½ teaspoons salt

1 tablespoon dried ground orange peel as sold in spice jars

1 tablespoon dried ground lemon peel as sold in spice jars

1 tablespoon aniseeds, finely ground

Confectioners' sugar

Note that three glass bowls will be needed. I have chosen this recipe because it involves all the steps of rich bread baking from the chef through to the baked product without taking days to prepare. For the preparation of this bread, I am using the techniques explained in great detail on pages 241–243 of Le Ricette Regionali Italiane, by Maria Gosetti della Salda, Milan, Italy, 1967. The amount and choice of ingredients were recommended by my Milan-born cousin Bruno Asnaghi. I have adapted the proportions to American unbleached all-purpose flour. The cake flour in the recipe is used exclusively to coat the raisins and citron and prevent them from falling to the bottom of the bread.

BEST FREEZING STAGE:
Fully baked

Make the chef: Mix the flour, yeast, and water together in a medium-size bowl until homogeneous. Cover with a piece of cheesecloth and let ferment and rise 3 full hours at room temperature in the warmest corner of the kitchen.

Make the levain: In a large bowl mix together the flour and sugar. Make a well in the center of the flour and to it add the chef; gradually blend the chef into the flour, adding also water as needed until the levain is homogeneous. Cover with the same cheesecloth and let ferment and rise overnight in a cooler corner of the kitchen.

Make the intermediate dough: Put the egg yolks and the whole egg in a large bowl. Beat them into a thick omelette batter, then stir in the sugar and whisk until the mixture turns semithick and foamy (no need to reach the ribbon stage, though).

Make a well in the flour and salt mixed together, gradually add the beaten eggs, then the levain, using a wooden spatula and lifting the dough to aerate it at the same time. Continue beating gently as you introduce the melted, barely lukewarm butter into the dough. When the dough is homogeneous, cover it with the cheesecloth and let it rise at room temperature in the warmest corner of the kitchen until doubled in bulk. Gently punch the dough down and let it rise again to the highest volume it will go, 1 to 1½ hours.

Make the final dough: While the intermediate dough rises, soak the raisins and citron in the mixed orange flower water and Marsala. Cover and let soak until the intermediate dough has risen for the second time. Drain the fruit from the flavorings keeping any liquid left at the bottom of the bowl; pat the fruit dry, toss it into the cake flour to coat well, and set aside.

Cream the ¾ cup butter with the tips of your fingers and divide it into four equal parts. Set aside at room temperature.

Make a well in the remaining flour, mix in the salt, fruit, and the ground flavorings; add the already risen dough to the center of the well together with any remaining liquid flavorings. Gradually bring the dry flour into the intermediate dough. As soon as all the flour has been incorporated, put one part of the butter at the four poles of the dough (see *brioche* dough techniques on page 1046); using your fingertips, cream each quarter of the butter into one quarter of the dough. Beat with a few strokes of the hand, then return to a large clean bowl and let rise another 1½ hours. Punch the dough gently down and aerate it with a few slaps of the hand, but do not knead it.

Butter each glass bowl with 1 tablespoon each of the remaining butter and line its bottom with a circle of parchment paper. Add one third of the dough to each bowl. Let proof until the dough reaches about ⅓ inch above the rim of each bowl, 40 to 45 minutes.

Preheat the oven to 400°F while the cakes are proofing. Using a razor blade dipped in flour, cut a semicircular line ⅛ inch deep into the top of each cake. Put the cakes to bake 20 minutes on the middle rack of the oven. Turn the oven down to 325°F and continue baking another 20 minutes. Turn the oven off and let the cakes finish cooking in the dying oven another 5 to 10 minutes. The cakes are done when a metal skewer inserted at the center of each comes out dry and burning to the top of the hand. Remove from the oven, unmold on a cake rack, and cool completely.

Wrap the cakes in aluminum foil and store 2 days in a bread box before serving. Serve lightly dusted with confectioners' sugar.

Making Pastry and Pies
The Role of Flour Proteins in Pastry Making

Gluten, explained on pages 1008–10, plays a most important role in the making of pastry; if you overwork the pastry, its gluten content will overdevelop and the pastry will be tough, sometimes even unworkable. If, on the contrary, the dough is worked too lightly, it will not be cohesive and will crumble, tear, and be quite difficult to roll out. The perfect technique develops just enough gluten to obtain a manageable dough that will remain flaky after baking.

Pastry Flour

Pastry is best made with pastry flour. Pastry flour, which is made from softer grains, produces a more tender pastry. Since it is not always available, the same result can be obtained with all-purpose flour that has been blended with cake flour; however, if only all-purpose flour is available, pastry can still indeed be made. While it is not necessary to sift flour before making bread and pasta because kneading destroys any lumps of flour, it is when making pastry because the pastry must be handled gently and lumplets of flour could remain in the finished pastry, giving it an unpleasant texture and taste.

To measure the flour, spread a piece of waxed or parchment paper on the counter. Put the measuring cup on the paper and sift the flour directly into the measuring cup and level with a long spatula. If not needed the flour on the paper can be returned to the flour bin. Do not succumb to the temptation of scooping the flour on the paper directly into your measuring cup; it has already packed down from falling on the paper and from being retransferred into the cup. Sift new flour into the cup again, then mix the flour left on the paper back into the flour bin.

Fats in Pastry

Fats act as a softener on the gluten strands. When gluten strands are coated with fat, they do not cling to each other anymore to form a solid structure; rather, they slide against each other, forming short separated strands. This is why fat is often referred to as "shortening." Fat gives the crust some of its flakiness. The colder and the harder the fat used, the flakier the crust will be. Melted butter and oil produce a sandy and mealy crust, because they are distributed into the flour and water paste in droplets. Cold raw butter, on the contrary, is distributed in the crust in solid particles which when flattened by the rolling pin separate the gluten layers. The results are the small flakes visible after the pastry has baked (see page 1060).

In our days of extreme fat anguish, many will avoid a nice little slice of pie. The scarcity of such indulgences would seem to speak strongly in favor of butter as shortening for pie crust, for if we are going to have a slice of pie twice a year, is there really any problem in consuming the 1 to 1½ tablespoons of butter it contains? Probably not for those persons whose hearts are perfectly healthy and working like clockwork, but for those who already have suffered damage, other solutions must be investigated.

Butter, which is 80 percent fat, delivers a pastry with a slightly firm and flaky texture and is positively unbeatable for taste and color of the baked product. Do not add additional salt to your pastry if you use salted butter, which you really should avoid, for it makes sense that unsalted butter that has not sold within the allowed time limits would be salted and sent back out for sale. Freshness of butter is an absolute condition for a great pie, since the slightest amount of oxidation is so easily detected in the final baked product.

Vegetable shortening which has been touted as the absolute best fat for the flakiest of pastries is unfortunately partly saturated, from the mere fact that it has been hydrogenated; also it results in a crust that colors poorly.

Water and Other Liquid Ingredients

Eggs are considered liquid ingredients. The coagulation of their proteins makes the pastry firmer and more resistant to the penetration of any moisture seeping from the fillings.

Water acts as a solvent for the salt and sugar. It allows the starch cells of the flour to dilate and the gluten to develop. Exactly how much water is needed to make a pastry dough cannot be predetermined. It depends on many factors, among which are the moisture-absorbing power of the flour, the ability of the cook to feel when the dough in the making has received enough water and her/his dexterity in introducing the water into the mixture of flour and butter. Chilled water retards the formation of the gluten strands.

You may have seen pastry recipes calling for lemon juice or vinegar. These ingredients, as well as sour cream or soured milk, are often used because their acid content works as an additional softener on gluten strands.

Special Equipment

To make pastry, all you need are your bare hands, a countertop, and a rolling pin. A marble slab is a help but not a necessity. The food processor is useful in the preparation of oil crusts for galettes, reserved for people who must mind their cholesterol.

The Principles of Pastry Making: Short Pastry

This pastry is all-purpose; it can be used for savories as well as for dessert pies, quiches, flans, and tarts. The recipe makes two single-crust 8-inch pies, or one double-crust 9- or 10-inch pie, or 24 paper-thin tartlet shells.

RATIOS

FAT TO FLOUR The weight of the all-purpose flour in this recipe is approximately 6 ounces and the weight of the butter 4.5 ounces, 75 percent of the weight of the flour. Why so high? Because all-purpose flour is strong and makes a pastry that needs to be shortened much more than true pastry flour does, so that the strands of gluten produced cannot lengthen and bind tightly together. If you decide to use pastry flour, as indicated in the second formula, you will use a ratio of 50 percent, which will make the weight of butter half that of the flour, as is done in Europe. It is a good idea if you watch your intake of butter to use pastry flour or a mixture of all-purpose and cake flour.

FAT TO WATER Notice the ratio of butter to water. In a basic short pastry, it is always two to one. If you have a recipe based on 1 cup butter (8 ounces), remember that the total amount of water should never exceed ½ cup (4 ounces). It is possible to complete a short pastry with less water than this, but if more is used, the pastry will be too wet, the reason being that butter contains some water. If you become confused when working with weights, instead of volumes, remember that 2 cups of water weigh a pound (see page 11).

Basic Short Pastry

Using all-purpose flour containing approximately 10.7 percent proteins:

1½ cups sifted unbleached all-purpose flour

½ teaspoon salt

9 tablespoons unsalted butter, chilled and cut into tablespoon pieces

3 to 4½ tablespoons chilled water as needed

Using a combination of all-purpose and cake flours to obtain a flour with approximately 8.3 percent proteins:

1½ cups sifted unbleached all-purpose flour

½ cup sifted cake flour

½ teaspoon salt

6 tablespoons unsalted butter, chilled and cut into tablespoon pieces

2 to 3 tablespoons chilled water as needed

Starting first *fraisage*

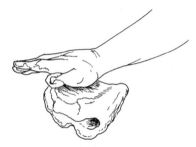

Starting second *fraisage*

Halfway through second *fraisage*

Pastry dough ready to rest, with gluten test; the hole made by a finger will not close.

HAND TECHNIQUE

Sablage Put the flour on a countertop; make a well in the center and put in it the salt and butter. Working with the tips of your fingers, squeeze the flour and butter together until the mixture forms particles the size of a large pea. In culinary jargon, this is called *sabler,* which means "to reduce to sand," but *extremely coarse sand.*

Now, add the water 1 tablespoon at a time. Mix it into the mixture with the tips of the fingers of both your hands extended down toward the counter in such a way as to form a natural pastry cutter, imitating the wire pastry cutter you may have seen older pastry cooks use. The palms must face each other. Rapidly push the forming dough from left to right, throwing it up from the counter and fluffing it about 2 inches above the countertop. The more water you introduce into the flour-and-butter paste, the more difficult it becomes to break the lumps until large clumps form that cannot be broken anymore. This is the signal that you have added enough water. Gather the lumps into a ball.

Fraisage Holding the dough lightly in your working hand, gently use it as a mop to gather all the loose particles of dough remaining on the counter. Put your right hand and wrist flat on the counter in front of the whole ball of dough; leave the heel of your hand in contact with the counter, but extend the rest of your hand upward at a 45-degree angle with the counter, your fingers remaining together and fully extended forward. *Do not knead.* Lifting your hand 1½ inches off the counter in that precise position, let the heel of your hand go up then down onto the pastry, sliding pieces of it the size of a small egg *forward only, not sideways,* and flattening each piece of it on the counter. Flatten the dough as it moves forward; do not bear down or you will tear or break it. When all the dough has been handled this way, gather all the pieces to reform another ball and repeat the operation. This must be done quickly and is called *fraiser.* It flattens the originally pea-size pieces of butter into extremely thin sheets between layers of flour-and-water paste, gives the pastry homogeneity, and, most important, develops just enough gluten to give the dough a certain plasticity for easy handling. When the pastry bakes, the thin sheets of butter will melt and be absorbed by the starches in the flour. The water will turn to steam which will fill the spaces left by the absorbed fat and push the walls of these small interstices away from each other to form flakes in the pastry. The fat will coat the small gluten strands in the pastry also and prevent them from hardening into a tough pastry. This procedure is skipped in the great majority of popular American cookbooks and is entirely responsible for most crusts not holding their shape because the tiny amount of gluten developed by *fraisage* cannot be obtained by simply mixing the ingredients together, whether in a bowl or by hand.

EGG PASTRY: For each of the basic recipes on page 1055, add 1 large beaten egg instead of water to the dough, adding it tablespoon by table-spoon as needed to avoid an excess of liquid in the dough. Pastries made exclusively with egg yolks are not recommended anymore for health rea-sons, which is just fine since they are not that tasty. If your filling is going to be very moist, always make the dough with a whole egg; the pastry will be more resistant to moisture.

SOUR CREAM PASTRY: Replace the water with 2 to 3 tablespoons pure sour cream containing no modern stabilizers—not crème fraîche; the pastry will be fragile and extremely flaky.

CREAM CHEESE PASTRY: Add 2 ounces (¼ cup) pure cream cheese to the basic recipe during the sablage and use only 1½ to 2 tablespoons water.

SANDY PASTRY: Use the same basic recipe but melt the butter and add it at the same time as the water.

NUT PASTRY: Two to 4 tablespoons of ground nuts can be added to basic pastry dough. Work the flour, less 2 tablespoons, with the nuts until an even meal is obtained. Use one quarter less butter because nuts contain oil, and liquid as needed. The best nuts to use are walnuts, hazelnuts, pistachios, and almonds. When using almonds, also add 1 drop of bitter lemon extract.

TESTING FOR GLUTEN AND REFRIGERATION
Once it has been properly fraised, shape the pastry into a circular 3-inch cake about 1 inch thick if you are making a single-crust pie. If you are making a double crust, cut the pastry into two pieces, one representing two thirds of its volume, the second one third.

Test the gluten development by gently poking your finger into the larger piece of pastry. If the hole remains, you may use the pastry after 15 minutes of refrigeration. The more that hole closes, the more gluten you have developed and the more the dough needs to rest in the refrigerator.

A nice stay of several hours is best for any pastry; not only does it relax any gluten development, but it also allows the water to be completely absorbed and the small particles of butter in the dough to firm up again. This last point is very important, because unrelaxed gluten would toughen up while baking, delivering a tough pastry which would sweat melted butter.

ROLLING THE PASTRY OUT
To roll the pastry out and place it into a pie plate, first let it stand a few min-utes at room temperature. Flour the countertop and rolling pin lightly, then, using the rolling pin, tap the dough gently to soften it a bit, making it easier to roll out; keep it very even in thickness. When you are ready, roll out from the center toward the edge, lifting the rolling pin off the pastry to change its position; never roll back and forth from the center to the edge and vice versa,

as that immediately starts gluten development. After each rolling out, turn the dough 30 degrees and roll again from the center out until you obtain a circle of the desired width ⅛ to ⅙ inch thick. You will see the dough progressively flatten into that circle, advancing about 1½ inches forward after each rollout. Continue rolling until the pastry is no more than ⅙ inch thick and extends 1¼ inches beyond the rim of the pie plate, unless otherwise instructed.

FITTING THE PASTRY IN A PIE PLATE OR RING

The best pie plates are:

- Nonstick pie plates 9 or 10 inches in diameter and approximately 1 inch deep
- French white fireproof china plates
- So-called flan rings set on an unbendable baking sheet, or
- For upside-down pies, a deep, 8-inch round baking dish

To be avoided at all costs are:

- Double-bottomed American cake pans with detachable bottoms or
- French fluted pie plates with detachable bottoms because between the double thickness of metal there is a thin layer of air that breaks the heat conduction and results in uneven heat penetration toward the center of the plate and a soggy-bottomed pie.

Fitting dough into a pie plate: The index finger of one hand pushes the dough against the middle finger of the other hand. Notice the important position of the fingers working from inside the pie plate.

Lightly butter the pie plate or pastry ring and the baking sheet on which it rests. Certainly there is already enough butter in the pastry, but this supplementary layer is insurance that the pastry will adhere to the sides of the plate or ring without falling forward over its bottom or slacken against it.

Sprinkle a tiny amount of flour over the surface of the pastry. Fold the pastry in half, then in half again, to obtain a triangular piece of dough. Place the tip of the triangle at the center of the pie plate. Unfold the pastry.

The next step requires caution; if your nails are pointed and sharp and you adjust the fitting of the pastry with your fingers extended forward, they might cut neat little slits in the pastry that may break open while the pie bakes. Instead, open your working hand and look at your palm, close your fingers loosely over the palm and, keeping your palm up, use the front side of the first two segments of your index finger to fit the pastry tightly into the angle between the sides and the bottom of the plate or ring, and smoothing the pastry over the whole bottom. Pass any overhanging dough over the rim with the help of your other hand.

If you are using a pie plate, cut off any excess dough with scissors, and squeeze the edge of the dough between your thumb and index finger to obtain a fluted rim. If you use a pie ring, roll the pin once over the edge of the ring to cut off the excess pastry. With your left hand push the dough over the edge of the ring while you pinch it with a pie crimper, or flatten it with the dull side of a knife blade or the tines of a fork.

STORING AND FREEZING SHORT PASTRY

It is preferable to make pastry 24 hours ahead of time; it will oxidate and bake to a better color. To store, wrap the dough in clear plastic and keep refrigerated. All pastries freeze well wrapped in aluminum foil. Frozen short pastry dough takes about 2 hours to thaw. Thawing may be done at room temperature.

PASTRY MADE IN THE FOOD PROCESSOR

If you are short of time and like the texture of pastry made in the food processor, by all means use it. Use any of the basic formulas indicated above. Whisk together the flour and very cold butter. When a coarse meal forms gradually, add the water 1 tablespoon at a time until a ball of dough forms. Flatten the dough to a 1-inch-thick cake and keep cool until ready to roll out.

ONE-OPERATION PIES AND TARTS

The crust and filling of a one-operation pie are cooked simultaneously. The temperature of the oven must be high at the beginning to bake the crust very quickly and seal it against the penetration of moisture from the filling. Bake on the lowest rack of a preheated 400°F oven for 10 to 15 minutes. Then move the pie to the upper middle part of the oven and finish baking at 350°F, usually for an additional 20 to 30 minutes. Here is an example:

Endive Pie

FFR — ONE 8- OR 9-INCH PIE; 6 SERVINGS

12 Belgian endives
½ tablespoon unsalted butter plus more as needed
Salt
Pepper from the mill
1 squeeze of fresh lemon juice
6 slices hickory-smoked bacon
1 cup heavy cream
½ recipe Basic Short Pastry (page 1059)
Chopped fresh Italian parsley leaves or 6 thin slices fontina cheese

This is wonderful for brunch or lunch. Endives are expensive, so if you must, you can obtain a similar taste by cooking one cleaned and chopped head each of curly endive and escarole (see the directions for étuvéed vegetables on page 391).

SUGGESTED WINE: *Beringer meritage of Sauvignon Blanc and Sémillon*

Wash the endives rapidly, letting the water run into their leaves. Squeeze dry in paper towels; cut the endive tips only if damaged and remove their root cones. Rub a small sauteuse pan with ½ tablespoon of the butter. Place the endives in the pan in a pinwheel formation. Season to taste with salt and pepper, sprinkle with lemon juice, cover, and cook over very low heat until tender, about 30 minutes. Turn the endives several times during the cooking and add small amounts of water if needed to keep them from sticking; the endives should cook without a trace of caramelization.

In another pan, render the bacon until crisp, drain out with paper towels, and crumble. Set aside. In a small saucepan, reduce the heavy cream by half. Set aside.

Preheat the oven to 400°F. Roll the pastry out (see page 1061) to barely ¼ inch thick and ¾ inch wider than the pie plate. Fit the crust into a buttered pie ring or plate 8 to 9 inches in diameter, then flute or crimp the edge. Sprinkle the bacon over the pie bottom, then top with the endives arranged in a pinwheel. Pour the reduced heavy cream over the top and season with salt.

Bake on the bottom rack of the oven 20 minutes at 400°F, then another 30 minutes at 325°F. The pie will be golden with barely any cream left; serve topped with chopped parsley or the fontina, which will slowly melt over the hot endives. Serve when cooled slightly.

BLIND-BAKED PIES AND TARTS

A pie is baked "blind" when its empty crust is baked first, to be filled afterward with a precooked filling.

If your crust is very soft and does not contain much gluten, roll it out ¹⁄₁₆ inch thick. Set it in the buttered pie plate or ring, prick it very heavily with a fork, and refrigerate for 1 hour. Then bake it on the top shelf of a preheated 425°F oven for 7 to 8 minutes. If the bottom of the crust lifts or bubbles up, prick it again with a fork to let the air escape. This is the very finest crust for fruit tarts—paper thin and especially delicious if you sprinkle it with a little sugar, which will caramelize while baking. The pastry shell will be golden, elegant, and fragile.

If you prefer, use the classic method of fitting a sheet of aluminum foil, dull side out, ⅛ inch thick snugly inside the unbaked shell and filling it with 4 to 5 cups of dried beans or, better, those heavy aluminum nuggets sold for this purpose. Bake in a preheated 425°F oven for 7 to 8 minutes, then remove the beans and foil and continue baking for another 4 to 5 minutes. This crust will be much easier to handle especially if baked with the aluminum nuggets which heat deeply so that the crust cooks from its top and its bottom sides all at once. It browns inside once the pie weights are removed. This method, in spite of its apparent complication, is easier than the first for beginners.

Mushroom Tart

FFR—ONE 8- OR 9-INCH TART; 6 SERVINGS

½ recipe Basic Short Pastry (page 1059), rolled out, fitted into an 8- or 9-inch pie plate, and blind baked (above)

1½ tablespoons light olive oil

SUGGESTED WINE:

California meritage *of Sauvignon and Sémillon, French Seyssel, or Quincy*

I large shallot, finely chopped

I pound mushrooms, minced

Fresh lemon juice

Salt

Pepper from the mill

2 tablespoons Madeira or fino sherry or freshly grated nutmeg to taste

¾ cup heavy cream or ⅓ cup melted meat glaze (page 286)

I tablespoon chopped fresh curly parsley leaves plus more for sprinkling if cheese isn't
   used

⅔ cup freshly grated Gruyère or Emmenthal cheese (optional)

Set the prebaked pie crust aside.

Heat the oil over medium-high heat, add the shallots, and sauté a few
minutes. Add the mushrooms and lemon juice, season with salt and pepper,
and toss until the mushrooms give up their moisture and the liquid has evaporated. Add the Madeira and let evaporate, or season with nutmeg. Add the
cream and cook gently over low heat until it coats the mushrooms; if you use
the meat glaze, pour it over the mushrooms during the last 5 minutes of baking. Correct the seasonings and add the parsley.

Pour the filling into the prepared shell and dot with more chopped parsley
if you serve it without the cheese. Otherwise, preheat the broiler and sprinkle
the cheese over the mushrooms. Protect the edge of the pastry with a strip of
aluminum foil and broil until golden, about 2 minutes. Serve warm.

Nova Scotia Quiche

FFR—ONE 9-INCH QUICHE; 6 SERVINGS

I cup light cream

2 teaspoons chopped fresh tarragon leaves

2 teaspoons chopped fresh chervil leaves

2 teaspoons chopped fresh chives

½ recipe Basic Short Pastry (page 1059)

6 thin slices smoked Nova Scotia or other favorite smoked salmon

2 large eggs

I tablespoon chopped fresh curly parsley leaves

Salt

Pepper from the mill

SUGGESTED WINE:
*California Fumé Blanc or
Sancerre*

In a small saucepan, scald the cream, remove from the heat, and add the tarragon, chervil, and chives. Let them infuse for 1 hour.

Preheat the oven to 400°F. Roll the dough out (see page 1061) and line a
9-inch pie plate. Arrange the salmon slices over the bottom of the crust. Mix
the cream, eggs, parsley, and very little salt and pepper together in a small

bowl. Pour over the salmon, then bake on the lowest rack of the oven for 10 minutes. Reduce the temperature to 300°F and bake on the middle rack another 20 to 25 minutes, until the egg custard is set. Serve piping hot.

TARTLET SHELLS

Buy or borrow 24 small tart pans. Butter 12 pans very lightly. Cut 12 circles from half the rolled-out dough as close as possible to the pan size. Fit each piece of dough in a pan. Lightly butter the second set of pans *on their bottoms*, then force each one into those pans lined with pastry, so the dough is squeezed between the two pans. Scrape the excess pastry off the edges of each set of pans with the dull side of a knife blade. Fill the upper set of pans with weights. Bake 5 minutes in a preheated 425°F oven. Remove the weights and upper pans and continue baking for another 3 to 4 minutes. The shells will be paper thin, golden, and done. Repeat the process to make the other 12 shells.

Tartlets of Asparagus Tips

SUGGESTED WINE: *Please follow your own taste. Many people do not believe that asparagus and wine should be consumed together. This is a matter of personal judgment.*

FCR—24 TARTLETS

2 pounds jumbo asparagus

¼ cup best possible balsamic vinegar

Juice of ½ lemon

Juice and 1 teaspoon finely grated rind of 1 small Valencia orange

½ cup hazelnut oil

Salt

Pepper from the mill

1 recipe Basic Short Pastry (page 1059), rolled out, fitted into tartlet pans, blind baked (page 1064), and still warm

¼ cup chopped fresh chervil leaves

Warning: Fill the tartlets with the asparagus just before serving.

Cut the tips of the asparagus off; plunge them 1 to 2 minutes into salted boiling water, refresh under cold water, pat dry, and set aside. Bend the stems of the asparagus; they will break when the stems stop being edible. Peel the stems and slice them ¼ inch thick. Blanch the stem pieces 1 long minute and refresh under running cold water. *Pat completely dry.* Reserve 1 cup of the asparagus blanching water.

Place the reserved blanching water, vinegar, lemon and orange juices, and orange rind in a small, heavy-bottomed, nonreactive pan; reduce to 3 tablespoons over medium-high heat. Cool the pan to warm and fluff in the oil using a stainless steel whisk 2 tablespoons at a time until completely homogenized. Season with salt and pepper. Toss the asparagus slices in the balsamic-orange dressing and spoon into the prepared tartlets. Top each tartlet with one asparagus tip and a sprinkling of the chervil. Serve immediately.

TWO-CRUST FRESH FRUIT PIES

Two-crust pies were plentiful in ancient Latin cooking and many of them have survived in the present Italian repertory of delicious savory pies made with vegetables, cheese, and diverse meats, as well as in that truly wonderful sweet two-crust pie full of chard leaves, Parmigiano-Reggiano cheese, eggs, apples, and pignoli nuts that is one of the glories of Provençal cuisine.

The American imagination, always ready for new ideas and new combinations, seems to have the monopoly on fruit pies. I was dazzled by the array of fruit pies to be found on Pennsylvania tables when I arrived in the United States and even more impressed when visiting Alaska—all these wonderful wild berries imprisoned in buttery crusts!

To make a good fruit pie, you basically have to know little more than what you already know.

Double-Crust Fresh Fruit Pie Pastry

FFR—ONE 9-INCH DOUBLE CRUST

2 cups sifted unbleached all-purpose flour

⅛ teaspoon salt

½ cup cold unsalted butter, cut into tablespoon pieces

¼ cup ice cold water or more if needed

Resift the flour with the salt onto the countertop. Make a well and add the cut-up butter. *Sabler* the butter into the flour until it is broken uniformly into small pea-size pieces. With the fingers of both hands extended down toward the counter, palms facing each other and looking like a pastry cutter, add the water tablespoon by tablespoon, rapidly pushing the forming dough from left to right and about 2 inches above the counter. As you introduce the water, lumps will form that cannot be broken anymore. Gather all the lumps together and *fraiser* the dough twice. Do not knead! Test the amount of gluten in your pastry by sticking a finger in it. If the hole made by your finger does not close, your pastry is ready. If the hole closes, let it rest several hours in the refrigerator before using it.

Cut the dough into two parts, one representing two thirds of the pastry, the other the remaining third. Shape the pastry into two round cakes ⅓ inch thick and place each between two layers of plastic wrap. Keep refrigerated while you prepare the filling.

WHICH PIE PLATE?

Use exclusively dishes that are deep and will be able to contain the large amount of filling. Nine-inch pie plates made of white Corningware and French fluted porcelain plates of the same size are the very best; they bring

You need a pastry with a modicum of solidity, which will not be all too softened by the juices running out of the fruit. Although the fragile pastries offered on page 1059 are perfectly usable and most pleasant for deep dish pies, I recommend that, for a two-crust fruit pie, you prepare this formula; an all-purpose flour crust will be more resistant to abundant fruit juices. In this recipe I use the technical pastry language explained on pages 1057–59. If you are not familiar with it, go back to these pages and familiarize yourself with their content before you start working.

BEST FREEZING STAGE:

Freeze in single or double recipes (for single-crust or double-crust recipe), wrapped in plastic and foil. To defrost: Remove the foil and wrap the dough in a terry towel. Let defrost overnight in the refrigerator. Recipes made with any pastry are best baked and consumed on the same day.

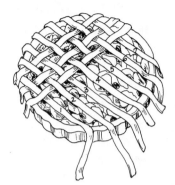

Mentally number your lattice strips
as shown in the drawing.

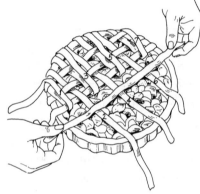

Weave the even and uneven strips
together.

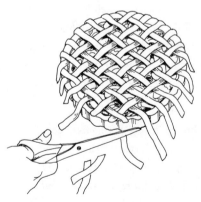

Once all the strips are woven, cut
off the ends.

no metallic taste to the fruit juices escaping from the pie and conduct the
heat in such a fashion that the bottom of the pie is always nicely cooked.
Butter the plate very evenly with a full tablespoon of butter; this sounds like
a lot of butter, but it is an insurance that the pastry will brown well under
the fruit.

ROLLING THE PASTRY OUT

Bring the larger piece of pastry out of the refrigerator. Let it warm up for 2
minutes. Lightly flour the countertop and your rolling pin. Remove the plastic and roll from the center out, turning the pastry 30 degrees to the right or
left—as you prefer—every time you roll it out so that the pastry will remain
evenly round. You should continue rolling until the pastry is no more than ⅛
inch thick, and extends 1¼ inches beyond the rim of the plate; you can test
that by setting the plate over the pastry.

Wrap the pastry around your rolling pin and set it evenly in the plate (see
page 1062) so it extends over its edges; fit the pastry snugly into the bottom
and along the sides of the plate so no air is left in between. Return the pie to
the refrigerator.

Roll the smaller piece of pastry to reach all the way over the edge of the
pie plate and keep it refrigerated between two pieces of plastic while you prepare the filling.

FRUIT FILLINGS

Pies can be filled with just about every fruit under the sun, more so the mod-
erate-climate fruit than the tropical ones, which are better arranged
uncooked on open-faced tarts. All juicy fruit is good, from berries of all types
to apricot, peaches, apples, pears, and that wonderful stalk, the rhubarb.

To make certain that the fruit will not overly juice, it is customary to mix
it with a thickener which can be flour, as in the old days, cornstarch, or
instant tapioca. Use approximately the following proportions; I wish I could
be more scientific about the amounts to be used, but you must know by now
that variations are multiple and that not one fruit will contain the same
amount of juice every time you use it, so these are guidelines only. But one
fact is certain, the more acid the fruit, the stronger the starch should be. For
each 4 cups of fruit, which is the average measure of fruit needed for a 9-inch
pie, use:

- *For apples:* 1 to 1¼ tablespoons all-purpose flour or 1½ tablespoons corn-
  starch.
- *For cherries:* 2½ to 3 tablespoons instant tapioca.
- *For all berries, black, blue, or bright red:* 3 to 4 tablespoons all-purpose flour.
- *For peaches and apricots:* 2 tablespoons all-purpose flour.
- *For rhubarb used alone or with another fruit:* ¼ cup all-purpose flour.

To introduce the starch into the fruit, put the fruit in a bowl. Mix the amount of sugar and starch you need together and toss the mixture evenly into the fruit. Immediately empty the prepared fruit into the crust.

PUTTING THE TOP OF THE FILLED PIE ON

For a full top: Wrap the smaller rolled-out pastry over your rolling pin and deposit the top crust, well centered, over the bottom crust. Cut the outer crust to be even with the top crust and fold both over together (you should have a double thickness of crust all around the edge of the pie). Now twist and flute the edge of the pie as you prefer, but make certain that it is well sealed. Cut a few slits into the top crust to allow for the evaporation of steam while the pie bakes.

For a lattice top: Cut the top piece of pastry into strips ⅓ inch wide using a pizza wheel.

Start weaving the lattice. Place half the strips in one direction on the fruit, spacing them ¾ inch from each other. Now number those strips mentally into strips 1, 3, 5, 7, and 9 and the other strips 2, 4, 6, 8, and 10.

Place the remainder of the strips at a right angle to those already on the fruit. Weave by passing strips 2, 4, 6, and 8 under 1, 3, 5, and 7, and vice versa every time you add a new strip. This is best done by flipping 1, 5, and 7 backward while you add a new perpendicular strip, then flipping them forward. At the next strip flip 2, 6, and 10 backward, then flip them forward over the perpendicular strip again. Continue alternating the strips until the whole pie is covered with a latticework. Pinch the lattice to the edge of the pie without stretching or the latticework will pull and break while baking because any pastry shrinks while baking. So weave those latticeworks very loosely.

BAKING

The baking time of a fruit pie is important. To achieve a good coagulation and browning of the bottom, put the pie to bake in a hot oven between 400° and 425°F depending on the juiciness of the fruit (400°F for apples, for example, but 425°F for very juicy berries) for 15 minutes. Then turn the heat down to 375°F to let the juices of the fruit reduce for another 15 minutes. Finally, to make sure that the pie is well "set," to use the common expression, let it finish cooking in the oven turned down to 325°F.

Here are two recipes to practice on, one for the winter and one for the summer.

Bring the edge of the bottom pastry over the ends of the strips and flute with your fingers. This step is the same when crimping a double-crust pie; both layers are folded forward and fluted together.

Cranberry Apple Pie

FFR—ONE 9-INCH DOUBLE-CRUST PIE; 8 SERVINGS

1 recipe Double-Crust Fresh Fruit Pie Pastry (page 1067)

One 12-ounce package (2½ cups) fresh cranberries

4 tart pie or baking apples of your choice, peeled, cored, and diced into ⅓-inch cubes

Grated rind of 1 orange

Juice of 2 oranges

Grated rind of 1 lemon

1½ to 2 cups granulated sugar, to your personal taste

1 teaspoon ground cinnamon or cassia

2½ tablespoons unsifted all-purpose flour

3 tablespoons unsalted butter

½ cup heavy cream, whipped to the Chantilly stage (page 30) with

    1 tablespoon Grand Marnier

Make the pastry and roll it out between two sheets of plastic wrap as described on page 000.

Crush the cranberries for 30 seconds in the food processor. In a large bowl, mix them together with the apples, grated orange rind, orange juice, and grated lemon rind. Set aside. Mix the sugar, cinnamon, and flour together in a small dish and set aside.

Rub the pie plate with 1 tablespoon of the butter. Remove the larger piece of pastry from the plastic wrap and roll it out ⅛ inch thick. Arrange it snuggly into the pie plate. Roll out the second piece of pastry so it is ready to use.

Preheat the oven to 400°F. Sprinkle the flour mixture over the fruit and mix well. Immediately transfer to the pie plate and dot with the remainder of the butter cut into small dice. Cut the pastry so it follows exactly the outer edge of the pie plate. Using a pizza wheel, cut the second piece of pastry into strips ⅓ inch wide and weave into a lattice on top of the fruit as described on page 1069. Secure the lattice to the edge of the pastry, leaving it slack for the pastry to shrink as it bakes.

Bake for 15 minutes at 400°F. Turn the oven down to 350°F for another 15 minutes and finish baking yet another 15 minutes at 325°F. Cool to barely lukewarm or room temperature before serving, if desired, with the whipped cream flavored with Grand Marnier.

Summer Garden Tutti-frutti Pie

FFR—ONE 9-INCH DOUBLE-CRUST PIE; 8 SERVINGS

For the pastry

1¾ cups sifted unbleached all-purpose flour

¼ cup finely ground almonds or pistachios

⅛ teaspoon salt

Use any tart baking apple available to you in your neck of the woods and frozen cranberries if you cannot find fresh ones. You need a 9-inch porcelain or Pyroceram pie plate.

This pie makes good use of all the summer fruit that ripens at once and too fast in our fruit baskets. If the fruit listed below is not available, simply replace it with

7 tablespoons cold unsalted butter plus I tablespoon to butter the pie plate

I teaspoon pure almond extract

¼ cup cold water

For the filling

I cup sliced ripe peaches

I cup sliced ripe greengage plums

I red Black Friar or other black or red plum, sliced

½ cup red raspberries

½ cup pitted red sweet or sour cherries, as you prefer

¼ cup orange juice

2½ tablespoons instant tapioca

1¼ to 1¾ cups granulated sugar, to your personal taste

Small pinch of salt

2 tablespoons unsalted butter, cut into ⅓-inch cubes

any other juicy fruit available in your bowl.

Using the pastry ingredients listed above, make the pastry as directed on page 1067. Roll two thirds of the pastry out into one round sheet ⅛ inch thick and the remainder into another smaller round sheet of the same thickness. Keep refrigerated between two pieces of plastic wrap until ready to use.

Mix the fruit and orange juice together in a large bowl. Mix the tapioca, sugar, and salt together in a small bowl. Keep ready to use.

Preheat the oven to 425°F. Butter the pie plate with the reserved tablespoon of butter, remove the plastic from the larger piece of pastry, and fit it snugly into the pie plate. Combine well the fruit, orange juice, and tapioca mixture and empty the mixture into the pie crust. Dot with the butter. Immediately top the fruit with the second piece of pastry; trim and flute the edge of the pie and cut a few slits in the top as artistically as you wish to allow steam to escape.

Bake for 15 minutes at 425°F, turn the oven down to 350°F and bake another 15 minutes. Finish the baking for 15 minutes at 325°F. Just before the last 15 minutes of baking, brush the top of the pie with a trace of water and sprinkle it with a heaping tablespoon of sugar. Serve by itself at room temperature.

Sweet Pie Pastry

This is one of the multiple versions of the Italian *pasta frolla* which was probably brought to France from Italy by Italian chefs during the sixteenth century. It was an expensive crust to prepare and reserved for high-class tables until beet sugar made in Europe (Prussia and France) replaced cane sugar in the first decade of the nineteenth century; Carême was one of the first chefs to use this type of sweetened pastry to prepare some of his "architectural" pastry creations.

Note that in this section, even more so than in any other, the technical details have been repeated at length both in the instructional text and in the recipes. The reason is that sweet pastry is not ever easy to prepare and handle. Too many elements can vary from one pastry to the next: the texture and density of the flour, the size of the crystals of sugar, the percent of water contained in the butter, the ambient temperature, and, last but not least, the temperature of the pastry cook's hands.

Remain as cool and collected as you can when learning to make sweet pastry by hand. If you have warm hands, your best bet is to use the food processor method below. I am naturally not machine oriented but I consider the processor the best implement ever to make sweet pastry, especially if you reach the point of having to prepare it in larger quantities.

Sweet Pastry
(PLAIN RECIPE, HANDMADE)

FFR — ONE 8- TO 10-INCH PIE CRUST OR 2 DOZEN COOKIES

10 tablespoons unsalted butter, at room temperature but still waxy

Large pinch of salt

⅓ cup granulated sugar

1⅓ cups unsifted unbleached all-purpose flour

1 large egg, beaten

Flavoring of your choice (see below)

BEST FREEZING STAGE:
Before baking. Wrap in plastic wrap and aluminum foil. Defrost 24 hours before using, removing the aluminum foil and replacing it with a terrycloth kitchen towel.

Work this pastry at room temperature with a wooden spoon. Cream the butter until plastic, neither soft nor oily. Stir the salt and sugar into the butter until the mixture looks even textured but the crystals of sugar are still very visible. Add the flour, flattening it into the butter-sugar mixture with the spoon; finally add the egg and flavoring and mix until homogeneous, no more than 1½ to 2 minutes. *Do not overwork the pastry.* Flatten it into a ¼-inch-thick cake, wrap between two sheets of clear plastic and refrigerate 1 hour.

Sweet Pastry
(BASIC RECIPE, PROCESSOR MADE)

FFR — ONE 8- TO 10-INCH PIE CRUST OR 2 DOZEN COOKIES

10 tablespoons unsalted butter, at room temperature but still waxy

Large pinch of salt

⅓ to ½ cup granulated sugar, to your personal taste

1 large egg, beaten

Flavoring of your choice (see below)

1⅓ cups sifted unbleached all-purpose flour

BEST FREEZING STAGE:
Before baking. Wrap in plastic wrap and aluminum foil. Defrost 24 hours before using in the refrigerator, wrapped in a terrycloth kitchen towel.

Place the butter, salt, sugar, egg, and flavoring in a food processor and process until smooth; add the flour through the funnel and process until a ball of dough forms, 15 to 30 seconds.

The dough will be very soft and cookielike. Place it on a sheet of clear plastic wrap. Stretch a second sheet of wrap over the dough and flatten it to a thickness of ⅓ to ½ inch in a round and regular shape. Refrigerate for 1 hour.

Whether you are working by hand or with the food processor, it is essential not to cool the pastry longer than 1 hour. If you cool it longer, it will turn into a hard piece of concretelike material that will break at any attempt to roll it out. If you do refrigerate the dough too long, let it mellow a bit at room temperature before you roll it out.

Roll the dough out to a thickness of ⅛ to ⅙ inch between the two sheets of plastic wrap, then lift the top sheet and invert the dough into your pie plate; fit it in as well as you can. By now, the dough will have become too soft for the top plastic sheet to be lifted without tearing the pastry. Refrigerate the crust again until the plastic lifts easily. Finish arranging the edges of the pastry in an attractive pattern, using either a pastry crimper, the tip of a knife, or the tines of a fork.

FLAVORINGS FOR SWEET PASTRY

You can use any of these flavorings: 1 teaspoon grated citrus rind of your choice, 1½ teaspoons of any extract, or 1 tablespoon of any liqueur. If the pastry is a little too soft after you add the flavoring, sift 2 tablespoons of flour over the counter and imprint the flour into both sides of the pastry before you wrap it in clear plastic.

SWEET PASTRY MADE WITH NUTS

Use the same formula, but remove 2 to 3 tablespoons of the butter and replace one quarter to one third of the total amount of flour with the same quantity of any finely ground nut of your choice. If you use hazelnuts, walnuts, or macadamia nuts, you can reduce the butter to 9 tablespoons. The tenth tablespoon of butter will be replaced by the oil in the nuts, because of the large quantity of oil they contain.

Great Grandma JJ's Cheese Tart Modernized

FFR to FCR—ONE 9-INCH TART; 6 TO 8 SERVINGS

Two 2-pound containers plain natural yogurt processed without starches or
    stabilizers and with the fat content of your choice

1 recipe sweet pastry of your choice (page 1072 or 1073)

1½ ounces excellent white chocolate, melted

¾ cup granulated sugar

⅛ teaspoon salt

Grated rind of 1 lemon

1 envelope unflavored gelatin

One 6-ounce package frozen raspberries in syrup, defrosted

2½ cups any fresh red, blue, white, or black berries of your choice, stems removed and
    washed

According to my mother, the original recipe was prepared with double-thick crème fraîche and full-fat fresh white cheese straight from the barn of my great grandmother Jeanne, who was born on the crest of the Vosges Mountains where the Lorraine meets the Alsace. Prepared without a crust and with nonfat yogurt, the filling of this pie would make a pleasant dessert for people with cardiovascular problems. This tart must be served the same day as it is filled. The best combination of berries is red currants with sweetened raspberry sauce.

The day before you plan to serve the tart, rinse a large piece of fine cheese-cloth under cold water, squeeze it completely dry, and line a colander with it. Empty the containers of yogurt into the colander and let drip over a large bowl until it has lost a good third of its volume. Tie together the four corners of the cheesecloth, remove it from the colander, and finish dripping it by hanging it over the handle of the kitchen faucet, gathering the remainder of the whey in a bowl placed in the sink, under the dripping cheese. When only 3 cups of firm curds are left, the cheese is ready to use. Reserve ⅓ cup of the whey.

Prepare and blind bake the pastry (see page 1064) in a 9-inch porcelain or Pyroceram pie plate. Let the pastry cool completely in the plate, then brush its bottom and sides with the cooled melted chocolate. Let stand until the chocolate has set completely, about 30 minutes.

Put the yogurt cheese in a mixing bowl, add the sugar, salt, and lemon rind and beat until light and fluffy. Dissolve the gelatin in the reserved whey, heating the mixture over a double boiler until the grains of gelatin have completely disappeared. Remove from the heat, cool a few minutes, then gradually whisk in about 1 cup of the whipped yogurt cheese. On medium speed, beat the gelatinized cheese into the bulk of the yogurt. Pour evenly into the pie crust and refrigerate, covered with a tent of aluminum foil, until the yogurt has set completely.

Drain and reserve half the syrup from the raspberries; puree the remaining contents of the package. Strain through a conical strainer to discard all seeds and add some of the syrup if you prefer a more liquid texture. Toss the raspberry puree into the fresh berries.

To serve, cut the pie into wedges and top each wedge with a large serving spoonful of berries in raspberry puree.

Salt-Baked Peach Tart

FFR—ONE 9-INCH TART; 6 TO 8 SERVINGS

Three 4-pound boxes kosher salt

12 ripe yellow freestone peaches

½ cup unsalted butter, at room temperature but still waxy

½ cup granulated sugar

Pinch of salt

2 large eggs

1 teaspoon pure almond extract

⅓ cup finely ground almonds

1 cup sifted unbleached all-purpose flour

⅔ cup heavy cream

3 tablespoons firmly packed brown sugar

This technique of baking peaches is a creation of Jimmy Schmidt in Cooking for All Seasons. It draws some water out of the peaches but also concentrates the flavor and color of the fruit.

Preheat the oven to 400°F. Empty the salt into one or several deep baking dishes. Place the salt in the oven for 20 minutes. When the salt is hot, use oven mitts to remove the dish from the oven; bury the whole peaches in it and bake another 20 minutes. Remove from the oven, let cool a few minutes, then remove the peaches from the hot salt and peel them. Separate them into halves and discard their pits.

Meanwhile prepare the pastry: Place the butter, sugar, salt, 1 of the eggs, and the almond flavoring in a food processor and process until smooth. Add the almonds and flour through the funnel and process until a ball forms, about 2 minutes. Flatten into a ¼-inch-thick round cake between two sheets of clear plastic wrap and refrigerate until it firms up a bit, 20 minutes or so.

Lower the heat to 375°F. Roll the pastry out to a thickness of ⅙ inch between the two sheets of clear plastic wrap. Remove the top sheet of plastic wrap and fit into a 9-inch nonstick pie plate. Remove the remaining plastic (see details on page 1073), crimp the edges, and arrange the peach halves on the bottom, letting each half overlap the other.

Bake until the pastry is well set, about 20 minutes. Beat the second egg, the cream, and brown sugar together and pour over the peaches, letting the custard flow under and between the fruit. Bake until the custard is set, another 15 minutes or so. Serve at room temperature.

SWEET PASTRY AS COOKIES: SHORTBREAD

The best shortbreads are made in what used to be the Viking countries. Denmark, Finland, Scotland, and French Normandy would be hopelessly tied for the top award if there were one.

What is most important in making shortbread is to keep the granulated sugar unmelted in the dough until it reaches the oven. All the little holes you see when happily crunching through a piece of shortbread are left by the crystals of sugar melting and producing first moisture then steam during baking. Here is the technique, used in making a cookie which originated in Jersey and passed to Normandy under the name of *suichette*, the Normand pronunciation of the English "sweet cake." Use whisky or bourbon if you have no Calvados. Orange flower water is sold in small bottles in fancy grocery stores. Kept in a dark cupboard, it lasts for years. If no orange flower water is to be found, use 1 teaspoon grated orange rind, but keep the lemon extract. Learn the hand techniques first, then you can use the food processor.

Suichettes

BEST FREEZING STAGE: *In rolls, ready to cut into cookies, wrapped in plastic wrap and aluminum foil. Remove the foil and wrap in a terrycloth towel. Defrost overnight in the refrigerator.*

FFR — 4 DOZEN ROUND COOKIES ¼ INCH THICK

⅔ cup sifted cake flour

1⅔ cups sifted unbleached all-purpose flour

⅔ cup plus 2 tablespoons granulated sugar

½ teaspoon salt

1 tablespoon Calvados, Cognac, or whisky

1½ teaspoons orange flower water

1 teaspoon pure lemon extract

2 large egg yolks, broken

¾ cup cold unsalted butter, cut into ½-tablespoon pieces

1 cup coarsely chopped almonds

Mix the flours, ⅔ cup of the sugar, and the salt together in a large bowl. Make a well in the mixture, add the Calvados, orange flower water, lemon extract, and egg yolks. Fluff together 1 minute with your fingertips.

Add the butter and, as you would for short pastry (see page 1060), gradually crush it into the dry ingredients, without letting it become oily or letting the sugar melt.

Gather the dough into a ball, *fraiser* once or twice (see page 1060) and shape into two rolls ¾ inch in diameter and about 9 inches long. The exterior of the dough should just start to feel slightly moist. Wrap in a sheet of parchment paper (do not use plastic wrap; the pastry will sweat and the sugar melt) and refrigerate 2 hours.

Unwrap the parchment from the shortbread rolls and spread out on a work surface. Distribute the chopped almonds and remaining sugar evenly over it. Brush each roll of dough with as little water as possible and roll into the nuts to coat it completely. Wrap the roll in parchment paper again and refrigerate for 30 minutes.

Preheat the oven to 350°F. Line two baking sheets with parchment paper. Cut the dough into ¼- to ⅓-inch-thick slices. Set on the parchment paper and bake until set to the center and uniformly blond in color, about 25 minutes or longer if needed. Cool on a rack before serving.

Pie Pastry for Heart Patients

Many heart patients and elders cannot ever enjoy a slice of pie because of the large amount of saturated fats contained in regular pastry. I have devised two different pastries, each made with unsaturated oil which will certainly not replace "Mother's pie crust" but will constitute a nice change from graham cracker, vanilla cookie, or oat bran crusts made with margarine.

The most obvious oils are light olive, corn, canola, and grapeseed oils. The heavy oils such as walnut, hazelnut, and pistachio are expensive, but they come mostly in small bottles and you can purchase one of them and stash it in a corner of your refrigerator between uses, for making what I call cracker pies or bread pies. The best taste is obtained with the following oils in the following order: pure pistachio oil, pure hazelnut oil, pure walnut oil, and virgin olive oil (extra virgin is too strong for dessert pies); pure olive oil, corn oil, canola oil, and grapeseed oil have less flavor. Where the first three are best for desserts, the last four are my choices for savory pies and tarts. Grapeseed oil works for any pie sweet or savory.

Cracker Pie Crust

FCR — TWO 9- TO 10-INCH GALETTE CRUSTS

1½ **cups sifted cake flour**

2½ **tablespoons light oil of your choice or 2 tablespoons any heavy nut oil**

1½ **tablespoons granulated sugar**

¼ **to** ½ **teaspoon salt, to your personal taste**

3 **to** 3½ **tablespoons cold water as needed**

Put the flour in a food processor and process 15 seconds. Add the oil, sugar, salt, and 2 tablespoons of the water and process with two successive bursts of 15 seconds each. Gradually add more water if needed; the dough is ready when it appears to have separated into thousands of ¼-inch balls. Empty them onto the countertop and give one quick, small soft *fraisage* (see page 1060) with the heel of your hand. Flatten into a ½-inch-thick round piece and refrigerate for at least 1 hour to firm up before using, wrapped in waxed or parchment paper. This crust freezes very well before rolling out and baking, wrapped in clear plastic and aluminum foil. Defrost it in the refrigerator, removing the foil and replacing it by a terrycloth kitchen towel.

To bake the two galettes that follow, you can use either the removable bottom of a 9- or 10-inch springform pan, or the bottom of a 9-inch nonstick pie plate. In both cases, the excess pastry must be trimmed all around the galette before baking it to obtain the right galette look. Serve any such galette lukewarm, as the cold pastry becomes too crispy.

This pastry is best prepared in the food processor using the metal blade, not the plastic blade usually reserved for making dough, because the sharp metal cuts through the dough and prevents gluten strands from forming.

Cracker Pear Galette

FCR—ONE 9- OR 10-INCH GALETTE; 6 SERVINGS

½ recipe **Cracker Pie Crust** (preceding recipe)

3 ripe Anjou pears, peeled, cored, and very thinly sliced

2 to 3 tablespoons granulated sugar, to your personal taste

½ teaspoon ground ginger

I tablespoon Grand Marnier

½ cup ginger marmalade, melted and strained through a conical strainer

Flatten any excess crust paper thin, cut it into small squares, bake, and use as crackers.

Preheat oven to 375°F. Roll the crust out to ¼-inch thickness. Set at the center of the detached bottom of a 9- or 10-inch springform pan and with your fingertips gently spread the crust from its center out to an even thickness of ⅛ inch. Cut away any excess dough. Arrange the sliced pears on the crust in concentric circles, alternating the thin and thick ends of each pear slice for better appearance. Mix the sugar and ginger together and sprinkle over the pears. Bake until the pears are nice and soft, about 45 minutes. The edge of the galette will caramelize all around.

Stir the Grand Marnier into the warm jam. Remove the cooked galette from the oven to a wire rack and dribble the sauce over it. Serve lukewarm.

Apple Galette

FCR—ONE 9-INCH GALETTE; 6 SERVINGS

½ recipe **Cracker Pie Crust** (page 1077)

¾ cup orange marmalade, melted and strained through a conical strainer

3 large Granny Smith apples, peeled, cored, and thinly sliced

I tablespoon granulated sugar

I tablespoon Calvados, Cognac, Armagnac, Scotch whisky, or bourbon

Use a 9-inch nonstick pie plate.

On a lightly floured countertop, roll out the pie crust to a thickness of ¼ inch. Put it into the bottom of a 9-inch nonstick pie plate and pat it to a thickness of ⅛ inch, letting it extend all around ¼ inch up the side of the plate. Brush it with half the marmalade.

Preheat the oven to 375°F. Arrange the apple slices over the marmalade in concentric circles, alternating the thin and thick ends of the apple slices for better appearance. With a sharp knife, trim and discard the ¼ inch of pastry around the plate side; there will now be pastry only under the apple slices. Sprinkle the apples with the sugar and bake until they are tender and lightly colored, 35 to 40 minutes. Upon removing from the oven, mix the remainder of the strained marmalade with the chosen liqueur or spirit and dribble over the apples. Serve lukewarm.

Bread Pie Crust

FCR — ONE 9-INCH PIE CRUST

I cup sifted cake flour

⅔ cup sifted unbleached all-purpose flour

I tablespoon granulated sugar

I teaspoon dried yeast

⅓ cup warm water (110° to 115°F)

¼ teaspoon salt or to taste

¼ cup nonfat milk or more if needed

2 tablespoons walnut oil or other unsaturated oil of your choice

Resift and mix the two flours together in a small bowl. Empty the flour onto a countertop. Make a large well in the center of the flour and add the sugar, yeast, and water. Gather one third to one half of the flour from the inner lip rim of the well into a small batter, then let double in bulk, covered with a clean kitchen towel, about 20 minutes.

When the batter is nice and swollen, add the salt, milk, and walnut oil and gather all the ingredients together quickly into a light dough. Let double in bulk again, covered, at room temperature, 40 to 45 minutes. Cover with a floured towel and refrigerate at least 2 hours to firm up. Use no later than the next day. When ready to use, punch down, roll out to ¼ inch thickness, then fit into a nonstick pie plate until ⅛ inch thick.

This crust is what our French wartime pies were made of between 1941 and 1945, when there was no butter, no cream of any kind, and no cream cheese, and flour was so rare that such a treat came once in a great while. The amounts of both liquids used at each of the stages of the making of this dough varies with the absorption capacity of the flour used; apply your good judgment and use the amount of water your flour demands. This pastry was tested several times with several unbleached all-purpose flours and the two leading brands of cake flour. The amounts of liquids used here are averages of all the amounts used with all flours.

An Italian Prune-Plum Pie Vintage 1943

VINTAGE 1943 ZWETSCHKE WEIHE

FCR — ONE 9-INCH PIE; 6 SERVINGS

I teaspoon unsaturated oil of your choice

I tablespoon granulated sugar

I recipe Bread Pie Crust (preceding recipe)

1½ pounds Italian prune plums, washed, cut into halves, and pitted

2 to 3 tablespoons liquid honey, to your personal taste

Large pinch of salt

Grated rind of I lemon

1½ teaspoons cornstarch

I tablespoon water

Preheat the oven to 400°F. Rub a 9-inch nonstick pie plate with the oil and sprinkle with the sugar. Lightly flour the countertop and rolling pin. Roll out the bread pie crust ¼ inch thick and fit it into the plate. Gently pat the dough to thin it to ⅛ inch to cover the bottom and sides of the plate. Arrange the plum halves in concentric circles on the bottom of the crust. Bake on the bottom rack of the oven until the plum juices start running out, 20 to 25 minutes.

Turn the oven temperature down to 375°F. Beat the honey, salt, lemon rind, cornstarch, and water together into a slurry. Drizzle between the plums. Bake on the top rack of the oven for another 20 to 25 minutes or more if needed for the plum juices to be well bound. Remove from the oven and cool to lukewarm. Serve from the pie plate.

Puff Pastry

To teach puff pastry or not to teach puff pastry, that is the question! Because of its high content of butter and the relatively long time it takes to prepare it, American cooks have tended, in the last few years, to abandon "puff" completely and to replace it with dainty little pieces of commercial filo sheets, held together with minimal layers of butter. This move would make a lot of sense, if what was found quite often inside these artistic pieces of filo were not relatively generous dabs of superrich custard, crème brûlée, cold sabayon, or other luscious "smoothies," dastardly loaded with egg yolks and heavy cream. We seem to be doing nothing more than coming full circle, exchanging loads of saturated fats in the pastry for loads of saturated fats in the filling.

Since this book is being rewritten with the preservation of authentic western techniques of cooking and baking in mind, I include here some of the techniques for making real puff pastry, which are in danger of being lost.

If there is a single "creator" of the puff pastry his/her name remains elusive, though several names have been suggested. The two main fats used by the Greco-Romans were olive oil and lard. Since they seem to have been making a type of sheet pastry, either they already made a kind of puff pastry using lard or they were making the pastry still used nowadays in the making of the cornucopia-shaped *sfogliatelle* of the Italian Campania, which is a cousin of filo, or they could even have made both.

I do not believe, as did Waverley Root, that what we know today as puff pastry is of Middle Eastern origin; the technique is altogether too different from the techniques used to prepare either filo, *sfogliatelle*, or the thin sheets of Arabic pastries such as *warka* and *trid*. After the fall of the Roman Empire and the Germanic invasions of Europe, the Dark Ages settled over the peoples of northern Europe (which starts north of the Loire River). While people living southwest of the Loire would have seen their knowledge of the ancient Greco-Roman leafy pastry enhanced and/or modified by the survivors of the A.D. 732 Arabic incursion into France, those living north of it may have transformed the practice into a new technique which allowed them to use the firm, saturated lard.

It is impossible to pinpoint when exactly this might have happened. One cook must have folded a leftover of his daily lard pastry into a neat package to discover that, when she or he rolled and baked it, it rose somewhat during baking. Butter extremely slowly but very definitely came to replace lard and walnut oil in the cuisines of northern and central Europe in a movement that probably started as early as the twelfth century, when monks began to engage in commercial cheese making. Where there is cheese, there is cream, and from cream comes butter. The descriptions of the *pastez* of meats in the fourteenth century books of Taillevent, the *Ménagier de Paris,* and Maître Chiquart bring no help in a search for the first appearance of butter in pastry, for no precise description of the preparation of the paste used to make the pâtes exists. Is it possible that among all those, one pastry would have been made with butter and turned to obtain leaves and that it would have puffed prettily when baked? According to Maguelonne Toussaint-Samat there is documentation proving that King Louis XI of France (1423–1483) loved his marzipan turnovers made with puff pastry. That would have been before the arrival in France of one of the Italian chefs who is supposed to have "invented" puff pastry. The puffing butter pastry must have traveled from royal and princely households to other royal and princely households, then to a multitude of less noble other pastry kitchens all over Europe, all the while pastry chefs everywhere added details and perfected the formula each in his own way. Both versions I am giving here contain details passed on to me by expert bakers from France, Switzerland, Germany, Denmark, and Norway.

May I recommend that you start with the old-fashioned technique so that you fully understand its basic principles; the modern technique will then feel and appear very familiar when you use it in your daily work.

In puff pastry the ratio of butter to flour is supposed to be identical; however, there will be small variations in the weight of the flour depending on its moisture content on the day you use it. Do not even give a thought to that.

The ratio of water to butter is greater than it is in short pastry; for each pound of flour worked with 1 pound of butter the ratio of water should be between 10 and a maximum of 12 ounces of water or 1¼ to a maximum of 1½ cups, depending on the moisture contained in the flour and the humidity of the day. If the flour is very moist, it will absorb less water than if it is very dry.

Classic Puff Pastry for Home Use

The best butter to use is ideally one that you make yourself by churning it in the food processor and rinsing it thoroughly. You will need 3¼ cups heavy cream to obtain ½ pound of butter.

FFR — APPROXIMATELY 1¼ POUNDS

⅔ **cup sifted cake flour**

1⅓ **cups sifted unbleached all-purpose flour**

1 **cup unsalted butter at refrigerator temperature**

½ **to ⅔ cup ice water as needed**

½ **to ¾ teaspoon salt, to your personal taste**

READYING THE INGREDIENTS

Sift the flours together in a bowl. Refrigerate it, covered, for at least 1 hour. This will prevent rapid development of gluten which must be avoided at all costs before giving the turns. If you live in a cold climate and keep your flour in a cool room, this is not necessary.

If you have warm hands, soak them 5 minutes in cold water and dry them. Work the butter with your hands until it becomes malleable and waxy, but not oily. When it is waxy, put it in the corner of a clean linen towel. Run the water very cold and wash the butter to remove the whey from it; although not totally necessary, this procedure cleans the butter of off tastes due to bacterial fermentations in the whey and suppresses most of the acidity in the butter, which could result in a dough that is too soft. The whey is completely discarded when the rinsing water runs clear. Pat the ball of butter dry and shape it into an even-sided cake ⅓ inch thick. Wrap the butter in plastic wrap and refrigerate until ready to use, not on the refrigerator shelf but in the *vegetable bin*, where it is not too cold and where the butter will not turn firm again.

Measure the larger amount of water indicated in the list of ingredients, never more.

Step 1: Making the Détrempe

The *détrempe* is, in French classical baking jargon, the name given to the ball of flour-and-water paste constituting the first element of a puff pastry. This ball of dough should not be stiff, because later you are going to enclose the ball of butter you prepared in it and, if it is too stiff and hard, the butter will not incorporate easily; rather, it will slide out.

Resift the cooled flour onto the counter. Make an 8-inch well in its center. To the well add ¼ cup of the water and the salt. Stir together, gradually bringing flour into the water until the mixture looks like crepe batter. Add the rest of the water tablespoon by tablespoon, fluffing the mixture with your fingertips as you would for short pastry, until the lumps of dough will not be broken anymore by the fingertips. Stay between ½ cup and ⅔ cup.

Gather all the lumps into one ball. Wipe all the dough particles off the counter, using the dough ball as a mop. Holding the dough in both hands, bend it back upon itself twice in a row to bring the wetter inside toward the outside. *Do not knead or handle it anymore, whether it is smooth or not.* What is essential at this point is that the *détrempe* contain as little gluten as possible.

Variation of technique for making the détrempe: You may have heard of kneading a *détrempe* for 20 minutes before enclosing the butter in it. This method is perfectly correct, for the more you knead a dough beyond 10 minutes, the more the gluten strands lose their rigidity as they shorten. At 20 minutes, they will have completely slackened and the *détrempe* will assimilate the butter very easily. The pastry will also tend to be more tender. This technique is used in Switzerland and Denmark.

Bending the *détrempe* back on itself

Remember to choose:

- Either no kneading at all, or
- 20 full minutes of kneading,

but *never* in between. Cut a cross ⅓ inch deep in the top of the dough, and refrigerate it, *uncovered,* for 30 minutes; not covering the dough prevents condensation buildup on the wrapper. The dough will not have the chance to dry out in such a short time.

***Détrempe* resting; notice the cross cut into its center**

Step 2: Making the Pâton

After 30 minutes, remove the butter from the refrigerator. Put it side by side with the *détrempe* and stick a finger into each. Your finger should penetrate both the *détrempe* and the butter at the same speed, which indicates that their textures are identical or very close to being that.

With the heel of your hand, gently flatten the *détrempe* into a 6-inch circle. Flatten the butter into a 4½-inch circle. Lightly flour the butter, place it on top of the *détrempe,* and pull and fold the pastry in small pleats over the butter, with as little overlapping of the pleats as possible; seal well at the center to avoid a hole through which the butter would be peeking. If it does, pull a small tongue of dough from the four center pleats of the dough to cover it. The dough and butter package is now a *pâton.* Gently flatten it with your fingers to become a rectangle 5 × 6½ inches and approximately ⅔ inch thick. Let stand at room temperature for 5 minutes, the rolling pin resting on it, which will indicate to you or any colleague taking over your job in a bakery that the *pâton* is ready to be rolled out.

Butter being enclosed in the *détrempe*; the lines in the opening show the butter still to be covered by the dough.

Turns I and II

To give turns to a puff pastry means rolling it out six times exactly as described below.

The basic rule in giving the turns is to roll the pastry out *only in its length,* rolling away from yourself first, then toward yourself without ever changing the width of the pastry. Should the pastry become too narrow (and this may happen at the beginning until you get the hang of it), place the rolling pin

Butter enclosed in the *pâton*

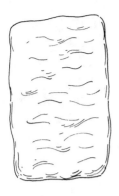

Pâton shaped into a rectangle by hand and ready to be extended with a rolling pin

diagonally across the upper part of the pastry and gently roll it wider; repeat the same operation across the lower half of the pastry. Correct the width so it is even from top to bottom.

Set the rolling pin at the center of the *pâton*. Roll the *pâton* from the center away from you, then from its center toward you, until it is three times as long as it was, keeping it 4½ to 5 inches wide and never less than ½ inch thick. Do not bear down into the dough; make the dough travel *parallel* to the countertop. You want to flatten the butter between the two layers of dough and keep it, as much as possible, *in one unbroken sheet*. Do not roll the dough in small, hesitant strokes but in one decisive one. If you have to make two strokes, lift your pin from the pastry between strokes and set your pin down where you ended the first stroke before you give the second; this will help maintain even thickness all through the length of the dough.

If the *pâton* becomes wider than 4½ to 5 inches, block it on each side by placing the rolling pin parallel to the edge of the dough and tapping it gently. The edge will straighten up.

Now fold the dough in three and turn it 90 degrees. The rectangle of pastry should be exactly the same size as it was when you started giving the first turn.

Notice that the pastry looks like a closed book ready to be opened, with the first flap of pastry looking like the cover of the book; it should *not* look like an opened book. Whether you are right- or left-handed does not matter; the edge of the *pâton* should always be on your right.

With a bit of pressure applied with the rolling pin at the top and bottom

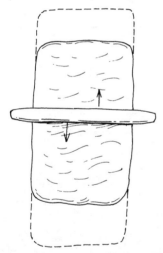

The *pâton* fully extended into a long rectangle: Following the dotted lines, extend the *pâton* northward, from the center of the pastry outward. Lift the rolling pin and start back again from the center out to extend the *pâton* southward.

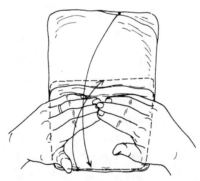

Giving the first turn: Bring the bottom third of the pastry to rest over its center third (south to north), then bring the upper third of the pastry over the bottom third (dotted line, north to south). Finally, turn the pastry 90 degrees from left to right or vice versa.

After being given a full "turn," the pastry looks like a book ready to be opened; notice its three thick layers (a, b, and c).

of the pastry, pinch the layers of dough together slightly to prevent the butter from escaping. Roll out the dough again and fold it a second time, exactly as described above. You will have given the dough two turns.

Should the pastry become too narrow again, you can do two things:

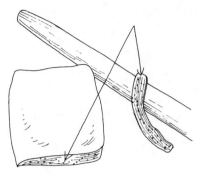

- Place the rolling pin diagonally across the pastry and gently roll it back to its required width, repeating the same operation on the other half of the pastry, as explained above, or
- Tap its top gently with the rolling pin to flatten it until it reaches 6 inches.

To keep track of the turns, punch two small depressions at the surface of the dough with a fingertip. This will remind you that you have given two turns.

Put the dough on a lightly floured plate or small baking sheet, cover it loosely with a sheet of aluminum foil, and put it to cool in the *vegetable crisper* of the refrigerator. Should you put it on a rack in the cold part of the refrigerator, the butter—which is still in a thick layer after only two turns—would harden and break through the layers of *détrempe* as soon as you start working again. Let the dough rest for 1 complete hour, or longer if you wish.

To know whether you need to give a half turn, cut a thin layer of pastry off one of its ends. If larger pieces of butter are visible, you should give a half turn.

Turns III and IV

Set the dough on the counter again so it looks like a book ready to be opened. Give two more turns exactly as described above, punch four small depressions in the dough to remind you that you have given four turns, and put the pastry to rest, again in the vegetable crisper, never less than 30 minutes so that the gluten produced by the mechanical action of your rolling motion has time to loosen up again. You may leave it for a longer time without adverse effects, but never for less.

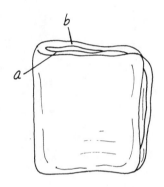

If you give a half turn, it will have only two thick layers (a and b).

"Butter Checks," the Possible Half Turn

While you give the turns, it may happen, and probably will before you get used to making the pastry, that the butter will "break out" of the dough layers. It happens even to experts, so do not worry.

If the tear is small, sprinkle it with a little flour. If it is an inch long or so, cut off a small piece of paste at the bottom or top edge. Flatten the little piece and use it to patch the hole. Continue working as if nothing has happened.

Also at the beginning of your career as a pastry cook, when your arms are not terribly strong, it may happen that the incorporation of the butter into the dough is irregular. You must check whether this is the case or not after turn IV, by cutting a sliver ¼ inch wide at either end of the dough. If, between the layers you still can see small dots of butter as thick as ⅛ to ¼ inch, you must give what is called a *half turn*.

Before putting the dough to chill after turn IV, roll out the dough about 4½ inches in each direction and fold the paste over once instead of twice. Let

Flatten the pastry with a rolling pin to return it to the proper width after each and every full or half turn.

it rest in the crisper for a good 30 minutes before giving the last two turns. The dough will be perfect; it never fails.

There is no need to put a mark on your pastry after you have given a half turn; you will know by the way it is folded that you have given 4½ turns.

Turns V and VI

Give the last two turns exactly as you did the first four. After the sixth turn is completed, trace an X on the pastry; this means that after its 30-minute rest in the refrigerator, the pastry is ready to use.

The Value of a Last Long Rest

You need not necessarily use the pastry this very moment; it can remain in the refrigerator overnight without problems. You will find that if you give the pastry a 24-hour rest, it will be firmer because it is colder, and easier to handle.

The Logistics of Rising Puff Pastry

You have, while giving the pastry six turns, produced 730 layers of flour-and-water paste enclosing 729 layers of butter* (plus a few more if it has been necessary to give a half turn) that ought to give you some idea of how very thin the sheets of butter and paste are. At the same time, you have enclosed air between the layers. When you cut the pastry you will feel its resistance under your knife blade. When you bake the pastry in a very hot oven, the thin layers of butter will melt and be absorbed by the flour-and-water paste layers. The pressure of the steam produced by the evaporation of the water contained in the dough will push those layers apart at the same time as the imprisoned air will expand under the effect of the heat and also contribute to pushing the layers apart. The result will be lovely puff pastries.

If you give more than 6½ turns, the layers of butter will start integrating into the flour-and-water paste and the dough will, after 8 turns, become an overrich short pastry, which will not puff half as much as it should in the oven. The quality of a puff paste can be judged by the length of its flakes. Long, uninterrupted flakes give a tender but solid crust. When the butter is introduced in the paste in smaller pieces the flakes are smaller and the product somewhat more fragile.

Classic Puff Pastry for Larger Production

If you intend to produce larger quantities of puff pastry, the volume system of measurements would be quite awkward and time consuming. Use equal weights flour and butter and 6 to 8 ounces water per pound of flour used. Use

---

*Madame Lucie Belime-Laugier, *Les Clés de la Cuisine Française*, page 139.

commercial pastry flour or any blend of flour that you may prepare and personally prefer. Weigh the flour or mixture of flours, sift it directly onto the workbench, and make the *détrempe*. If you give the turns by hand, the technical details given on pages 1082–86 remain valid. If you use a laminator (sheeter), set it according to its manufacturer's directions.

BEST FREEZING STAGE:
Uncooked puff pastry freezes perfectly well; you may freeze it in one piece, or you may cut it into shapes such as patty shells, vol-au-vent, or fleurons, those moon-shaped puff pastry croutons still used quite often for the decoration of fish and meat plates.

ROLLING OUT PUFF PASTRY

Roll out the dough when it is deep chilled and very stiff. You will need a lot of strength in your forearms. The important rule when you roll out puff pastry is *never to roll the pin back and forth on the pastry* to prevent the development of gluten.

Set your rolling pin at the very center of the dough. Apply pressure semilightly downward and relatively forcefully forward, meaning away from yourself. On reaching the end of the pastry, lift the rolling pin off, reposition it at the center of the dough, and again roll semilightly downward and strongly, this time toward yourself.

Since you are trying to obtain a sheet ⅓ to ¼ inch thick and very even, you should roll out equidistantly in each and every direction, which means that you must turn the sheet 90 degrees to change the direction each and every time you roll it out to extend it a bit more. When the sheet has reached the final thickness and size you are looking for, refrigerate it for a good 20 minutes on a sheet pan lined with parchment paper before cutting it.

CUTTING, DECORATING, AND BAKING

Before you cut the pastry, line the needed number of baking sheets with parchment paper; this will keep the bottoms of the pastries from browning too much. Preheat the oven to 425°F.

Cut the dough neatly, perpendicular to the countertop, so as not to produce stragglers which would burn easily and prevent the paste from rising evenly. After cutting patty shells or squares of dough, place them *upside down* on the parchment paper. This will keep the baked product from being narrower at the top than at the bottom, since a slight shrinkage always occurs at the top of the pastry sheet when it is first cut.

If you do not own pastry cutters, cut rounds with a coffeepot lid. With the tip of a paring knife, cut small indentations ⅛ inch deep into the pastry at the edges to replace the scalloped edge the cutters give; this process is called *chiqueter*. Use the same procedure when you cut the dough with a knife following a paper pattern. For a lovely finished color, brush the top of the pastries before baking with an egg yolk glaze made of 1 egg yolk mixed with 2 to 3 tablespoons milk.

To decorate the top of pastries, a technique called *rayer* is used to trace superficial parallel lines with the dull side of a knife blade after you have applied the egg yolk glaze. Many pastry chefs are extremely artistic and draw flowers and leaves on their pastries using the tip of a small paring knife.

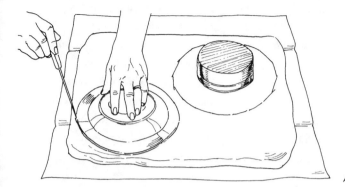

Cutting the top and bottom from the dough

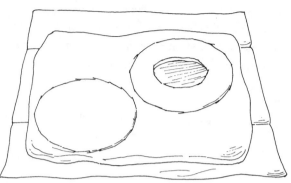

Cutout in top of *vol-au-vent*

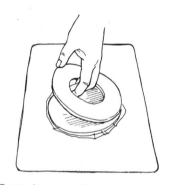

Pastry bottom with lid being put on

How to "*chiqueter*"

Rayage of the shell and bottom center, which will become the lid

Among the oldest pastries still existing to this day and going very far back are the *vol-au-vent* and patty shells, the *vol-au-vent* itself being a larger patty shell; they date back to the early seventeenth century. The name *vol-au-vent* comes from the lightness of the pastry which, in centuries past, was said to be light enough to "fly in the wind." Where patty shells are easy enough to cut with special cutters, cutting shells for *vol-au-vent* requires a bit of supplementary knowledge.

Keep the countertop and rolling pin as lightly floured as possible through these operations: Roll out the pastry ½ inch thick. Cut two round pieces using an 8-inch saucepan lid as a pattern. Wrap the first circle of pastry over the rolling pin and transfer it, upside down, to a baking sheet lined with a sheet of parchment paper. Brush the circle with egg yolk glaze.

With a 4-inch plain cutter or coffeepot lid, cut a smaller circle in the center of the second circle of pastry; remove the small circle and set it aside. Lightly flour the top of the ring that is left, fold it upon itself into quarters, and place this small piece anywhere on top of the first circle. Now open the ring and gently press the ring and circle edges together. Indent the edges (*chiqueter;* see left). Brush the top circle with egg yolk glaze without dripping any along the sides of the pastry; decorate both the ring and the bottom of the shell by striating them with the dull side of the tip of a knife. Refrigerate while you work on the lid. Now, brush the reserved small circle of pastry with the egg wash, indent its edges, and striate its top; once cooked this circle will be used as a lid for the *vol-au-vent*. Bake both the shell and its future lid at the same time side by side on the same sheet pan.

Once the pastry is baked and golden, remove the thin layer of browned pastry to be seen inside the *vol-au-vent* and discard any wet pastry inside the shell. Return the *vol-au-vent* to the turned off oven for a few minutes to dry it well inside; the pastry is then ready to fill. The lid will be ¾ to 1 inch thick and baked all the way through. If too high, cut it in half crosswise and use only the top part.

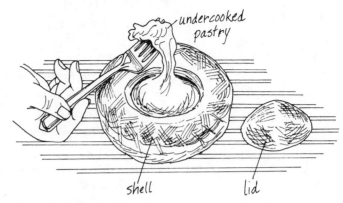

Finished *vol-au-vent* with the lid being removed

Removing undercooked pastry

A patty shell is made in the same way, with the exception that the second circle, being less wide, need not be folded but can be set upside down directly on the bottom pastry which has been brushed with glaze.

For lunch or dinner shells, use a 3½- to 4-inch cutter or coffeepot lid, and cut shells from a pastry rolled ⅓ inch thick. For cocktail shells, use a 2½-inch cutter or pot lid and cut shells from pastry rolled ¼ inch thick. Bake on the upper rack of a preheated 425° oven for 20 to 25 minutes for the smaller shells and 25 to 30 minutes for the larger ones. Remove the lids and uncooked inside dough, and let dry in the turned off oven for 4 to 5 minutes.

Wrap any solid piece of pastry in plastic wrap and a double layer of aluminum foil. To defrost, remove all wrappers and bundle the dough in a terrycloth kitchen towel, which will absorb the thawing condensation. Defrosting should be done entirely in the refrigerator; it will take 5 hours for about 1¼ pounds of pastry made with the ingredients of the recipe on page 1082.

Cutouts should first be set at regular intervals on one or several baking sheets each lined with parchment paper, then covered with plastic wrap and deep frozen. Once they are solid, they can be transferred to boxes or wrapped in packages which can be stored for several months in the freezer.

Preheat the oven to 425°F as soon as shells or cutouts come out of the freezer. To bake them, transfer them, frozen solid, to a sheet lined with parchment paper; quickly glaze them with egg wash and put them in immediately to bake, turning the oven down to 400°F as soon as the dough is in the oven. Bake until fully risen and golden, about 25 minutes.

Rectangular Apricot Tart

C A I S S E T T E   A U X   A B R I C O T S

Well-drained canned apricots can also be used.

FFR—6 TO 8 SERVINGS

1 recipe Classic Puff Pastry (page 1082)

1 large egg yolk beaten together with 2 tablespoons milk of your choice

1 recipe Pastry Cream (page 1107)

2 pounds ripe, fresh apricots, poached in syrup (page 940)

Superfine sugar

1 cup apricot jam, melted, strained through a conical strainer, and mixed with
   1 tablespoon kirsch

2 tablespoons chopped peeled pistachios

Roll the pastry out to a sheet ¼ inch thick. Transfer to a baking sheet lined with parchment paper. Cut a square of pastry 10 × 10 inches. Remove any extraneous pastry and keep it for cheese twists (see page 1094).

Fold the square into a triangle. Cut a band 1 inch wide along each of the two short sides of the triangle, stopping ¾ inch short of cutting the summit of the triangle. Open to a square again. Brush the bottom of the square sparingly with the egg yolk wash without letting any of the mixture drip over the edges of the pastry. Bring the 1-inch-wide edge to rest over the opposite side of the square, twisting the ends into a small bow as you do so. Pat gently in place. *Chiqueter* the edges approximately ⅛ inch deep (see page 1088); glaze the edge with the egg wash and freeze overnight, loosely covered with plastic wrap.

Fill the bottom of the frozen pastry ¼ inch deep with the cooled cream. Arrange the apricot halves on top. When ready to bake, preheat the oven to 425°F. Bake until the pastry is pale golden and fully puffed and about firm, about 30 minutes. Sprinkle with superfine sugar and bake until brown, another 5 minutes. Remove to a rack and brush the hot apricots with the cooled melted apricot jam mixture. Cool completely and sprinkle with the chopped pistachios.

Modern Puff Pastry

FFR—SMALL RECIPE: 1¼ POUNDS; LARGE RECIPE: 2½ POUNDS

Small recipe

½ cup sifted cake flour

1½ cups sifted unbleached all-purpose flour

½ to ¾ teaspoon salt, to your personal taste

1 cup cold unsalted butter, cut into 1½-tablespoon chunks

⅓ to ½ cup ice water as needed

Large recipe

I cup sifted cake flour

3 cups sifted unbleached all-purpose flour

I to I ½ teaspoons salt, to your personal taste

2 cups cold unsalted butter, cut into I ½-tablespoon chunks

⅔ to I cup ice water, as needed

Mix the flours and salt together intimately in a bowl and empty the flour mixture onto the countertop. Make a well and add the butter. Cover the butter with flour, then mash the butter into the flour with your fingers until the particles of butter are the size of macadamia nuts or large hazelnuts.

Mix in the ice cold water 1 tablespoon at a time (2 at a time for the larger recipe), introducing it with your fingertips extended downward in imitation of a pastry cutter. Press the small balls of dough that will form into a large one. With the heel of your hand, lightly *fraiser* (see page 1030) the balls into a large piece only once and gather it into one large ball. Shape into a rectangle 6½ × 5 inches. Refrigerate 1 hour covered with plastic wrap in the vegetable crisper.

Give the dough six turns, two at a time, as described fully on pages 1084–86, resting the plastic-wrapped pastry no less than 30 minutes in the vegetable bin of the refrigerator between each two turns.

SPECIAL DIFFICULTIES WITH
MODERN PUFF PASTRY

Turns I and II are especially difficult when you make puff pastry this way, because the butter at this point is irregularly integrated in the water-and-flour paste. If in one or two places the butter is not covered enough with the paste, do not hesitate to take a piece of dough from a region where the dough is more plentiful, flatten it carefully, and cover the bare butter with it. The second turn will already be easier and from turn III on you are sailing.

Chocolate Puff Pastry

FFR— I¼ POUNDS PASTRY

I¾ cups sifted unbleached all-purpose flour

⅓ cup Dutch-processed cocoa powder, unsifted

¼ to ½ teaspoon salt, to your personal taste

I cup cold unsalted butter

⅓ cup ice water or more if needed, but never more than ½ cup

I½ teaspoons fresh lemon juice (optional)

Resift the flour and cocoa together. Then proceed exactly as described on page 1090 in the recipe for modern puff pastry. The water must be added very gradually; lack of success and heaviness often result from adding too much

This technique is almost exclusively used nowadays and is a combination of the techniques of short pastry (see page 1059) with the turns of the full puff pastry. Do not start making this pastry if you have not read the complete techniques for giving turns (pages 1084–86). Any recipe larger than offered here need be given turns in a "sheeter," the professional electric machine that gives turns in a matter of seconds.

BEST FREEZING STAGE:
Before baking, wrap in plastic wrap and aluminum foil. Defrost 24 hours before using, removing the aluminum foil and replacing it with a terrycloth kitchen towel.

This is as easy to do as the modern puff pastry above, provided your flour is not too strong (read page 1066 about strong flour). As much as I am reticent to give brands, you will generally have the easiest time using Pillsbury unbleached flour together with Van Houten cocoa.

water too fast. If your flour is very strong, add the lemon juice with the first few tablespoons of water.

You may experience the same difficulties as mentioned in the modern puff pastry recipe while giving the first two turns (see page 1091).

Chartreuse Napoleons

FFR — 8 SMALL NAPOLEONS 1 X 2½ INCHES

½ tablespoon any butter or oil for the baking pan

1 recipe Chocolate Puff Pastry (page 1091)

2 cups whole milk

8 large egg yolks

⅔ cup granulated sugar

Large pinch of salt

1½ envelopes unflavored gelatin

1 tablespoon water

¼ cup green Chartreuse

One 3½-ounce bar bittersweet chocolate of your choice (page 49)

Confectioners' sugar

You will need two 17 × 10¾-inch jelly-roll pans and parchment paper.

For best organization and serving texture have the pastry and cream deep chilled and make the chocolate curls ahead of time. Garnish and finish the napoleons 1 hour before serving them; keep them in a very cold or air-conditioned room no more than 1 hour. If the pastries have to wait more than an hour, refrigerate them but expect them to lose some of their crispness as they absorb moisture.

The idea here is to keep the puff pastry under pressure so its leaves cannot rise but will bake against one another and, when done, yield a very thin sheet of pastry with leaves tightly packed against one another that will resist penetration by moisture.

Preheat the oven to 425°F.

FOR HOME PRODUCTION

Cut two sheets of parchment paper to the same dimensions as the bottom of a 17 × 10¾-inch jelly-roll pan. Rub traces of butter over the underside of the pan and cover with one of the sheets of paper which now will stay in place.

Roll the pastry out into a rectangular sheet ¼ inch thick. Wrap the pastry around a lightly floured rolling pin. Transfer it to the papered pan and unroll it on the pan. Refrigerate for 5 minutes. Remove the pastry from the refrigerator and roll the pastry out, still on the baking sheet, from the center toward the edges to a thickness of ⅙ to ⅛ inch. With a very sharp knife, cut the excess pastry off at the edges of the pan. Using a fork, punch holes in the pastry at ½-inch intervals in both directions. Cover the sheet of pastry with the second prepared parchment, then the second jelly-roll pan; the two pans will fit into each other and will be upside down.

Turn the two sheets right side up, holding them together. Weight the empty top pan with one large baking dish. Bring a large amount of water to a boil. When the water boils, set the baking arrangement on the middle shelf of the oven and fill the baking dish halfway with boiling water. Bake for 15 minutes, then remove the pan of water and check the pastry. It should have set already. Turn the sheets over together, so the two sheets are now upside down, and set the same pot of water on the bottom of what is now the top sheet. Finish baking another 8 to 12 minutes. The pastry should be completely done. Turn the oven off and let the pastry dry another 5 to 10 minutes in the dying heat. Remove the pastry sheet to a rack and cool completely.

FOR LARGER PRODUCTION

Proceed exactly as described above using two large sheet pans lined with large sheets of parchment and two small hotel pans filled halfway with boiling water to put pressure on the pastry squeezed between the sheet pans. The sheets of pastry will be extra thin and well done and will not absorb humidity from the cream filling.

You can, if you prefer, simply place a pastry rack over each sheet of pastry to allow it to rise evenly throughout. With this less complicated method, the puff pastry will rise to an even thickness of ¼ inch, but you will find this thicker pastry more prone to absorb humidity from the cream filling.

To prepare the filling: Scald the milk. In a sauteuse pan, and using a blunt-end wooden spatula, lightly ribbon the egg yolks with the sugar and salt until the mixture turns whitish but not foamy. Very gradually stir in the milk to temper the egg yolks. Finish cooking on high heat, stirring constantly (see page 142 for reasoned technique), until the foam recedes to the edges of the sauteuse. Turn the heat off, whisk rapidly until very foamy, and strain into a bowl through a China cap. Dissolve the gelatin in the water over a double boiler and, off the heat, gradually blend the melted gelatin with one half of the custard. Mix and homogenize the gelatinized and nongelatinized parts of the custard. Stir in the Chartreuse. Refrigerate while you cut the sheets of pastry into smaller portions. The custard must be solid before you can use it.

Using a serrated knife held at a 5-degree angle, slice the sheet of pastry into twenty-four 1 × 2½-inch rectangles. When cold and solidified, spoon the custard into a pastry bag fitted with a ¼-inch-wide nozzle. Pipe one layer of custard over 16 rectangles of pastry. Let firm up again in the refrigerator, then place two garnished layers on top of each other; top the second layer with one plain sheet of pastry. Each napoleon will have three layers of pastry enclosing two of cream. Set on a sheet and let sit in a cold pantry or room, but not the refrigerator.

Melt the bar of chocolate (see page 1138). Spread the chocolate on a clean baking sheet and as soon as it has lost its shine and looks dull, shave small curls of chocolate. Dust lightly with confectioners' sugar, then set the curls on top of the napoleons.

Cheese Twists

FFR — VARIABLE YIELD

Cutouts of puff pastry (page 1089)
Freshly grated Parmigiano-Reggiano cheese
1 large egg yolk beaten with 2 tablespoons milk of your choice
Freshly grated Gruyère cheese

Piece the cutouts of puff pastry together forming as regular a sheet as possible. Sprinkle generously with Parmigiano cheese and give two turns. Refrigerate several hours, then roll out on a lightly floured countertop with a lightly floured rolling pin into a sheet ¼ inch thick; brush with the egg wash and sprinkle with Gruyère. Flatten the pastry to ⅛ inch by rolling the pin over the Gruyère. Refrigerate another 20 minutes, then, using a crinkled pizza wheel cutter, cut into ¾-inch-wide strips 5 inches long. Twist and set on an ungreased nonstick baking sheet. Let rest in the refrigerator at least another 20 minutes before baking in a preheated 425°F oven until golden, 8 to 10 minutes. Cool on a rack before serving and serve barely lukewarm for best flavor. Preferably, do not freeze.

The Hybrid Yeast and Turn-Leavened Doughs: Croissants and Danish

Croissants and Danish pastry both belong to a special category of doughs which undergo a double leavening process by yeast fermentation, then again by receiving six full turns, exactly as for puff pastry.

Because of the relatively large amount of gluten which will develop in these doughs while giving the turns, the basic dough is not kneaded. Instead, before receiving any addition of butter, it is crashed on the countertop with a certain amount of strength. A small amount of gluten develops each and every time it hits the counter. As the throwing progresses, the dough flattens a little more every time it lands on the hard surface, exposing a little more surface to its resistance.

The first stage of the yeast fermentation happens in the refrigerator and lasts about one hour. The second stage lasts at least another 24 hours, again in the refrigerator and happens while the dough is "ripening." This fermentation is in some way identical to the "cool-rise" described on page 1033, and the flavor of these two baked products develops slowly. In the Danish, the end of the fermentation takes place during proofing (see page 1033).

It is important to check the taste/quality of these doughs relatively often during the cool-rise, for should the pastry be kept refrigerated too long, the yeast will consume all the sugar and the dough will have a sour, overfermented taste, due to all the carbon dioxide, alcohol, and acid that have formed as waste matter during the yeast fermentation.

You will see three different methods used during the second fermentation of Danish, croissants, and the famous *Kouign Amann* or butter cake of Brittany.

Croissants

FFR—8 LARGE OR 12 MEDIUM CROISSANTS

For the floating sponge

¾ cup sifted unbleached all-purpose flour

1 envelope dried yeast

3 tablespoons granulated sugar

For the dough

1¼ cups sifted unbleached all-purpose flour

½ cup unsifted cake flour

½ to ¾ cup milk of your choice, scalded and cooled to 110° to 115°F

¾ teaspoon salt

1 cup cold unsalted butter

For the glaze

1 large egg yolk

2 tablespoons milk of your choice

To prepare the floating sponge: Mix the flour, yeast, and sugar together in a medium-size bowl. Add just enough water to make a soft ball. Cut a cross ⅓ inch deep into the ball and cover with lukewarm water (105° to 110°F). Let ferment until the ball comes floating to the surface of the water, which requires no more than 15 minutes on the counter of a kitchen at 70° to 72°F.

To prepare the dough: Combine the flours and make a well in the center. Add the minimum amount of milk and the salt. As soon as the sponge comes floating to the surface of the water, spread your fingers open, pass your hand under the sponge, let it drip well, and add it to the well. Gather the mixture into a soft ball of dough, adding the remaining milk if necessary. Grasp the dough in your working hand and crash it on the counter from a foot above it; after it hits the counter, grasp it with your other hand and repeat the operation. Continue crashing, alternating hands, until the dough does not stick to the countertop anymore. Flatten into an 8-inch circle ⅓ to ½ inch thick. Refrigerate 1 hour.

Knead the butter with your bare or gloved hands until mellow but not

To taste like a true croissant, this dough must stay on cool-rise on the middle shelf of the refrigerator at least 2 days—3 would be even better—before being cut and baked. After 1½ days, snip and taste little pieces from the bottom or top edge of the package of dough every 8 hours to make sure that there is still some sugar left in the dough; if the sugar level has perceivably diminished and acids are present, bake the croissants as soon as possible or they will taste cheesy. If the dough does taste cheesy, unfold it, sprinkle its surface with sugar, refold the dough, pushing a little hard on the sugar to force it into the dough, and give one half turn. When you roll it out, the sugar will have melted into the dough. If you have to do this operation, bake the croissants within half a day at the most.

BEST FREEZING STAGE:
After the six turns

oily; you will see drops of cloudy water fall on the counter; it is the whey contained in the butter. Flour the butter and enclose it in the dough as described on page 1084. Let rest 5 minutes and give six turns (see page 1084), refrigerating the dough in the vegetable crisper at least 30 minutes between each two turns. Let the finished dough rest two days in the refrigerator, sealed in a Ziploc-type bag, before baking to develop the flavor fully.

Lightly flour the counter and rolling pin. To shape the croissants, roll the dough into a rectangle ⅛ inch thick. Cut the dough into 6 equal rectangles, then cut each rectangle into two elongated triangles. Pass the rolling pin to flatten and equalize the base of each triangle, then roll up the pastry tightly from the center of the base toward the point. Bend both ends to form a crescent, being sure that the point is well tucked under the belly of each roll. Twist both ends at the same time in opposite directions. Place all the croissants on a baking sheet lined with parchment paper.

Option 1: You Want to Freeze the Croissants
Freeze them on the baking sheet; when they are frozen, transfer them to boxes or bags. When ready to bake, allow them to defrost and proof all at once, at room temperature in a cool kitchen, the night before and bake them the next morning. Do not keep frozen longer than 4 months.

Option 2: You Want Fresh Croissants the Next Morning
Refrigerate the baking sheet overnight; the croissants will rise somewhat. If they are not fully raised, remove them from the refrigerator and let them proof again until they are 1½ times as large as they were originally. Then glaze them with the egg yolk mixed with the milk and bake in a preheated 375°F oven until doubled in size and golden, about 25 minutes.

Option 3: You Want Croissants in the Next Two Hours
Let the croissants proof in a warm place, covered, until they are 1½ times their original size. Brush them with the glaze and bake in a preheated 375°F oven until doubled in size and golden, about 25 minutes.

Whichever method you have used, the croissants are done when they are deep brown and look crispy outside, not before, or they will deflate unmercifully before your very eyes.

IMPORTANT FOR THE SUCCESS OF YOUR CROISSANTS Cool on a rack and check your work.

The proofing of croissants is *extremely difficult* and important. If you overproof, allowing the croissants to truly double in bulk, the ovenspring will bring on an overstretching of the gluten strands which will collapse as soon as the baked croissants change atmospheric pressure by passing from the hot oven to the relatively cool kitchen. If your croissants show a very flat bottom that forms a visible angle instead of a rounded bottom presenting almost no angle between the rolls' sides and their bottoms, they are overproofed. Underproofing is a lesser evil than overproofing if you want to avoid the mushy center of overproofed croissants. Do not accuse the recipe, as most students tend to; watch that last rising like a hawk!

Danish Pastry

FFR—36 AVERAGE-SIZE PASTRIES

For the floating sponge

2 cups sifted unbleached all-purpose flour

¼ cup granulated sugar

2 envelopes dried yeast

½ cup water

For the dough

2½ cups sifted unbleached all-purpose flour

½ cup sifted bread flour

2 teaspoons salt

½ cup milk of your choice, scalded and cooled to 110° to 115°F

1 tablespoon fresh lemon juice or yogurt whey

2 large eggs plus 2 large egg yolks, lightly beaten

2½ cups unsalted butter, at room temperature but still waxy

For the glaze

1 large egg yolk

2 tablespoons milk of your choice

Sugar to taste

One of the many versions of the Danish Wienerbrod, adapted from the recipe of my friend Jutte from a village in Jylland.

I have tried to make this Danish closer in texture to the true Danish Wienerbrod by using a small amount of bread flour, since Danish home-style flour is somewhat harder than ours. Danish must be proofed in the refrigerator to prevent the pastries from rising to enormous sizes and from losing traces of the layers you created in it when "turning" it. Expect this dough to be crispier than the one usually sold in U.S. bakeries.

Gather all ingredients for the sponge into a soft ball. Immerse in lukewarm water (105° to 110°F), until the sponge bobs to the surface, about 15 minutes in a room at 70° to 72°F.

Meanwhile, prepare the bulk of the dough. Mix the flours together on a countertop, then make a well in the center. Place the salt, milk, lemon juice, and beaten eggs in the well, mix together, and gather into a ball. As soon as the sponge floats, spread your fingers open, pass your hand under the sponge, lift it out, and let it drip well. Blend into the prepared dough.

Crash the dough onto a countertop ten to twenty times, adding as you do so ¼ cup of the softened butter tablespoon by tablespoon, continuing to crash the dough. *Positively do not knead.* Crash steadily for 10 to 12 minutes, until the dough is smooth and leaves your hands and counter freely, without sticking. Shape the dough into a rectangle 8 × 6 inches. Flour lightly, set on a baking sheet, and cover with a tent of aluminum foil. Refrigerate for 1 hour.

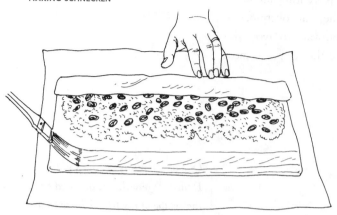

Pastry sheet spread with filling being rolled up. The edge is painted with egg wash to help secure the seam.

The rolled pastry being cut into *schnecken*

Flatten the dough to a 10-inch circle. Knead the remainder of the butter and flatten it to an 8-inch square. Flour the butter lightly and enclose it in the dough (see page 1084). Let rest with the rolling pin poised over it another 5 minutes; then give the first two turns (see page 1084), wrap, and refrigerate 40 minutes in the vegetable crisper between turns. Repeat the same operation twice, giving two more turns each time for a total of six turns. Let the dough age overnight—or a maximum of 24 hours—covered with loose plastic wrap on the middle shelf of the refrigerator before using it, so it is cold and easy to work with.

TO CUT AND SHAPE THE DOUGH

Cut the dough into halves or thirds horizontally and work with each piece separately to prevent them from warming too fast. Flour the counter and rolling pin lightly and roll each piece out into a rectangle ¼ inch thick.

To make schnecken: Brush the pastry sheet with soft room temperature butter creamed with a bit of sugar and cinnamon and a few raisins. Roll the sheet up like a jelly roll. Cut rolls no less than ⅔ inch long and no more than 1 inch thick. You can, in the French manner, use a ⅛-inch-thick layer of cooked and cooled pastry cream flavored with rum instead of the butter and cinnamon (see pastry cream, page 1107).

To make bear claws: Make a roll 1¾ inches wide, then flatten it and cut pieces 3½ inches long. Cut three slits on one side of the roll and bend the roll backward on its unslit side; the "claws" will open up as you bend.

To make pinwheels: Cut the dough into 4-inch squares. Cut through the four corners of each square and bring each alternating point to rest at the center of the square; secure these points by pushing down, then top with either a

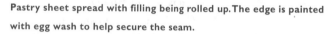

Pastry rectangle cut for bear claws with filling in place. Pull the far side of the rectangle over the filling, press the edges together, and cut where indicated.

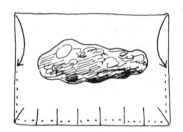

Gently pull the ends of pastry in opposite directions, fanning out the "claws."

Pastry square cut for pinwheel

teaspoon of jam, or of cream cheese mixed with the same amount of almond paste and sugar to your taste, or of plain cream cheese mixed with sugar to your taste and a few drops of almond flavoring.

TO PROOF AND BAKE

Line baking sheets with parchment paper. Line the pastries up on the sheets leaving 2 inches between each piece. Refrigerate 2 hours. Let stand 15 minutes at room temperature while you preheat the oven to 375°F. Mix together the glaze ingredients and brush over the pastries. Bake for 20 to 25 minutes; the pastries are done when they are deep golden. Cool to lukewarm on racks. Serve preferably on the same day.

TO FREEZE AND DEFROST

Freeze on sheets lined with parchment paper. When solid, remove from the sheets and pack in boxes or in well-sealed plastic bags. To defrost, line up on sheets as described in the paragraph above. Bring back to room temperature for 15 minutes, glaze, and bake about 30 minutes at 375°F .

Brittany Butter Cake
BRETON KOUIGN AMANN

FFR—ONE 9-INCH CAKE; 8 SERVINGS

1⅓ cups unsifted all-purpose flour

2 tablespoons cake flour

¾ teaspoon orange flower water

½ envelope dried yeast

½ to ⅔ cup lukewarm water (110° to 115°F)

¾ cup very fresh lightly salted butter

¾ cup plus 3 tablespoons granulated sugar

1 large egg yolk, beaten

Mix the flours together in a bowl, then add the orange flower water, yeast, and water. Work into a soft dough and flatten into a round, ½-inch-thick cake, 7 inches in diameter. Set on a lightly floured plate. Cover with a tent of aluminum foil and let rise until doubled in bulk at room temperature. Refrigerate 30 minutes to firm up the dough.

Reserve 1 tablespoon of the butter to grease the pie plate. Knead the remaining butter with your thumbs or fingers to make it soft and pliable, then shape it into a ½-inch-thick cake, 5 inches in diameter. Flour the cake of butter. Enclose it in the dough (see page 1084). Let stand 5 minutes.

Give the dough a total of four turns at 30-minute intervals and between each turn, sprinkle 3 tablespoons of the sugar evenly over the whole surface of the flattened and stretched dough before folding it. Refrigerate the dough between each set of two turns.

Rub an 8- or 9-inch pie plate with the reserved tablespoon of butter and sprinkle with 2 tablespoons of the remaining sugar. After the last 30 minutes of rest in the refrigerator, flatten the dough evenly into the pie plate, teasing it gently all the way around from its center to its side so it is evenly thick and round. Trace a ¼-inch-deep crisscross pattern into the top of the cake and keep it at room temperature until the cake has risen within a ¼ inch of the rim of the pan.

Preheat the oven to 375°F. Brush the top of the cake with the egg yolk and sprinkle it with the remaining tablespoon of sugar. Bake 25 to 30 minutes. The top of the cake should be nice and brown and a lovely thin layer of buttered caramel will have built up on its bottom. Unmold while lukewarm. Enjoy the cake nice and fresh on the day you bake it. Kids of all ages love it.

The Stretched Doughs: Filo and Strudel

To these doughs also belong the noodle doughs; to find them go to the section on grains on pages 499–503.

Filo

4 cups sifted unbleached all-purpose flour

1 teaspoon salt

1 tablespoon fresh lemon juice

1 cup lukewarm water plus 2 to 3 more teaspoons, if needed

3 tablespoons pure olive oil

3 tablespoons grapeseed oil

Oil of your choice or clarified butter as needed

Resift the flour on the counter, add the salt, and make a well in its center. Add the lemon juice and 1 cup lukewarm water. Bring the flour into the water; as soon as the mixture forms a ball, start adding the oils by making a hole in the dough with one of your thumbs, pouring in 1 tablespoon of the oil, and kneading it in; repeat the same operation five more times, kneading the dough as you go along.

To knead, pass the dough from one hand to the other in a rhythmic fashion, digging into the dough with the heel of your hand and bringing the front of the dough back, folding it over itself.

You may get tired; in this case, work only with one hand, using your fingers to keep the dough constantly in motion. If you work with your right hand, your thumb will initiate the movement by pushing the dough toward the fingers, which will bring it back to the thumb in a continuous motion. If you work with your left hand, your fingers will initiate the movement, which will be taken over by your thumb, etc.

Working with one hand is only a relief measure against fatigue; return to alternating hands as soon as you can. After a total of 20 minutes of kneading, roll the dough out into a long cigar and cut it into 15 identical balls of dough. Flatten them gently to ⅔ inch and set on a baking sheet lined with parchment paper ever so lightly floured. Brush with oil again and cover with a thick kitchen towel.

Turn the oven on at 140°F for exactly 2 minutes. Turn it off and put the dough to rest at least 1 hour in the cozy oven.

To roll the pastry out and build a pie made with filo: Work on a sanitized countertop floured with an almost imperceptible veil of cake flour and on which you will have plenty of space to work. Flatten and extend each piece of dough as much as you can with the heel of your hand, trying to give it as regular a shape as possible. Once each ball of dough is flattened into a disk ¼ inch thick, roll it out as thin as possible (use the pasta stretching technique on page 501), turning it by quarters of a turn while rolling. Brush the top of the pastry with oil. Finish by stretching each sheet of pastry with the tops of your hands, working from the center out, into a piece large enough to fit the bottom of a 1-quart glass baking dish and hang over its edges. Arrange each sheet on top of the other in the dish, oiling or buttering each sheet.

When the first eight layers are ready, cover them with a moist towel and refrigerate while you work the remaining seven balls to obtain seven sheets, which will become the top of your "pita" (recipe follows).

This is one of the ways of making filo and building a pie made with filo. There are many others and none of them is easier than the one I am proposing here. It is a nice challenge and pleasing when the pita comes out of the oven all golden, but if you are baking to make a living, by all means use commercial filo leaves.

Preferably, do not freeze.

Try at least once in your life to prepare filo yourself. Do not be discouraged if you cannot make it as thin as the sheets you buy in commercial packages; your equipment, which is your hands and your rolling pin, is not to be compared with that of the commercial factories.

The principle of this dough consists in developing a maximum amount of gluten with long long strands by kneading the dough 10 minutes and then to shorten these strands of gluten, adding oil and continuously kneading for another 10 minutes. You will, as you work, soon see the dough loosen up and soften more and more in your hands as you reach the total kneading time of 20 minutes. To roll the dough out, you will need a dowel or long, thin broomstick. Greek cooks like to let the dough relax for a long time, some for 24 hours, others for a few days in the refrigerator. A long stay in the refrigerator makes for an easier stretching.

When prepared entirely with unsaturated oil, this pastry is acceptable for heart patients.

Summary Berry Pita

BEST FREEZING STAGE:

After the pita is finished; defrost and bake at the same time by baking at 375°F for 10 minutes, then reducing the heat to 300°F. The total baking time will vary from 1 hour and 20 minutes to 1½ hours.

Summer Berry Pita

FCR—6 to 8 servings

2 pounds fresh rhubarb stems

2 to 2½ cups granulated sugar, to your personal taste

½ cup water

2 pounds frozen loose raspberries

2 pounds frozen loose strawberries

Pinch of salt

1 tablespoon pistachio oil or pure olive oil

3 tablespoons grapeseed oil or pure olive oil

1 recipe Filo (page 1100) or 1 pound commercial filo leaves

½ cup chopped peeled pistachios

Peel and cut the rhubarb stems into 1-inch-long pieces. Place in a large saucepan and add 2 cups of the sugar and the water. Bring to a boil, turn down to a simmer, and cook over low heat until very soft, then stir in both berries and salt. Cook on low heat until a thick, almost dry compote—halfway to fruit leather—is obtained in which positively no syrup is visible anymore. Cool completely. Mix the oils together in a cup and warm them in a small pot of hot water.

Brush a 1-quart glass baking dish with oil, then place one sheet of stretched filo over it. Oil this, then set another sheet of filo on top, oil it, and continue this way with the next five sheets. Do not oil the top of the seventh sheet, but sprinkle it with half the pistachios mixed with a rounded tablespoon of the sugar and top it with a dry eighth sheet of filo. Spread the compote evenly over the top.

Using scissors, cut the edges of the filo layers under the compote, leaving a ½-inch edge that you will flip over the fruit. Then top with another dry sheet and sprinkle it with the remaining pistachios and another rounded tablespoon of sugar. Cover with the remaining leaves, brushing oil over the top of each of them.

Preheat the oven to 300°F, score the top of the filo ¼ inch deep and into diamonds, and bake approximately 1 hour on the middle shelf of the oven so the bottom of the pita does not brown faster than the top. The pie should be the color of golden honey. Serve lukewarm.

Strudel

This pastry is already familiar to many cooks and bakers and will seem easy compared to filo. The technique is approximately the same as for filo, but instead of being stretched into smaller sheets, the pastry is stretched into one large sheet that is set on a work table covered with a lightly floured cloth.

Here, I give you the technique and recipe for a strudel-type pastry from the southwest of France, where an identical pastry exists and is used to make the famous *pastis* and *tourtières*. If you want to use this strudel for a person on a fat-restricted diet, use unsaturated oil.

A Snake Full of Mushrooms
SERPENT AUX CÈPES

FFR — 8 TO 10 APPETIZER SERVINGS

For the filling

2 tablespoons olive oil

3 cloves garlic, finely chopped

¼ cup chopped fresh Italian parsley leaves

2 pounds Boleti eduli (porcini or cèpes) or other mushroom of your choice,
   cleaned (net weight)

Salt

Pepper from the mill

1 pound fresh goat cheese

1 tablespoon unbleached all-purpose flour

1 tablespoon chopped fresh tarragon leaves

1 tablespoon chopped fresh chervil leaves

1 tablespoon chopped fresh chives

For the strudel dough

1 cup sifted bread flour

1½ cups sifted unbleached all-purpose flour

1 large egg, beaten

3 tablespoons walnut oil or melted duck confit fat (page 791)

1 tablespoon fresh lemon juice

1 teaspoon salt

½ cup lukewarm water

1 cup toasted bread crumbs from whole wheat bread

The best taste comes with the Boleti eduli. You can, however, use the mushroom of your choice. Preferably, do not freeze; it tastes best when baked as soon as it is put together.

SUGGESTED WINE: *Any before dinner drink or, if served as a first course, a dry Jurançon or a Cahors*

Heat the oil in a large skillet over medium-high heat; add 2 cloves of the garlic and the parsley and sauté until light brown. Add the mushrooms, season with salt and pepper, and sauté until light golden. Cover the pan and let the juices run out of the mushrooms; strain them into a small bowl through a conical strainer. Continue browning the mushrooms until dry and golden. Set aside on a plate.

Mash the goat cheese with the flour, herbs, and remaining chopped garlic clove. In a small saucepan over high heat, reduce the mushroom juices to 2 tablespoons and add to the cheese mixture. Spoon into a pastry bag and set aside.

Combine the two flours on a countertop. Make a well in the center. Add the egg, 1 tablespoon of the walnut oil, the lemon juice, salt, and water. Progressively bring the flour into the well, and as soon as the flour has been completely absorbed, start kneading as explained in the filo recipe (see page 1101), until the dough is smooth and elastic for a full 20 minutes. Rub a plate with a bit of oil, place it over a pot of water at 110°F, put the dough on it, and cover it with an inverted bowl. Let stand 30 minutes. Keep *warm*, not cold, not hot.

Stretch a tablecloth over a card table and flour lightly. Put the pastry on it and roll it out with a very lightly floured rolling pin as far as it will naturally let itself be rolled, then brush with some more of the oil. Now stretch it over the backs of your hands and those of a helper while you both turn the dough clockwise and gently pull it from under and from the center toward the outside. Be careful not only to stretch but also move your hands steadily toward the outside of the sheet.

Continue the stretching until the dough has pulled thin enough to cover the whole surface of the tablecloth. Anchor the pastry at the four corners of the table and let the unstretched pastry hang from the edges of the table. Brush the stretched pastry again very lightly with the oil or confit fat and, starting at the end closest to you, sprinkle one third of its surface with the bread crumbs.

Squeeze the cheese-and-herb mixture over the crumbs. Sprinkle the mushrooms evenly over the cheese. Cut all thick unstretched pastry edges with scissors and, holding the tablecloth with both hands, roll the sheet of pastry forward, enclosing cheese and mushrooms, until you obtain a big cigarlike package. Twist both ends tightly closed and tuck them under the ends of the cigar.

Preheat the oven to 375°F. Transfer the strudel to a buttered unbendable baking sheet and brush it with the remaining oil or confit fat, roll it into a loose coil and bake until deep golden, approximately 40 minutes. Serve lukewarm.

Steam-Leavened Dough: Cream Puff Dough (Pâte à Choux)

Cream puff dough was being made in Italy long before it arrived in France in 1540 by way of one of the pastry chefs in Catherine de Medici's retinue. Signor Popelini proceeded to make and sell considerable amounts of a certain cake, quite newfangled to the French, which became so popular that it is still made in some of the smaller towns of the French countryside. The cake was called *popelin*, which the country soon transformed into the easier to pronounce *poupelain*, and is a large cream puff filled with pastry cream and the candied fruit so dear to the Italians. My childhood was graced with many *poupelains* made by my great grandmother Marie.

The dough originally carried the name *pâte à chaud* (hot mixed dough) because it was cooked on the open fire, then baked in the dying heat of the bread oven. It is now called in French *pâte à choux* (cream puff dough) for the simple reason that in France it is never used for anything else but to make cream puffs, or *choux à la crème*, and a few other starchy preparations usually served as vegetables. Any cream puff-type cake is really a biscuit, since it is cooked in two stages, the first over an open flame, the second in an oven.

Preferably, do not freeze.

Pâte à Choux for Poupelains, Pastries, and Shells

FFR — 12 TO 18 CREAM PUFFS OR SMALLER ÉCLAIRS, DEPENDING ON
SIZE, OR ONE LARGE *POUPELAIN* TO BE BAKED IN A 10-INCH FRENCH
PORCELAIN FLUTED PIE PLATE

1 cup water

½ cup cold unsalted butter, diced into ⅓-inch cubes

½ teaspoon salt

1 tablespoon granulated sugar

1 cup sifted unbleached all-purpose flour

4 to 5 large eggs, never more

2 teaspoons pure vanilla extract

1 large egg yolk mixed with 2 to 3 tablespoons milk of your choice

BEST FREEZING STAGE:
Cream puff dough can freeze, but it is so quickly done that it is best to prepare it fresh every time one needs it.

In a medium-size saucepan mix together the water, butter, salt, and sugar. Bring slowly to a boil over medium heat to give the butter time to melt. As soon as the boiling point is reached, the mixture will foam up like milk due to the presence of casein in the butter. Remove the pot from the heat and add, all at once, the sifted flour. Stir and mix until a ball forms.

Replace the pot over medium heat and dry the paste, i.e., keep it constantly in motion on the bottom of the pan so that as much of its surface area as possible is exposed to the heat. Hold the pan handle with your left hand, a wooden spatula in the right hand as you do this. In three strokes, flatten the paste against the bottom of the pan, bringing it as you do so against the side of the pan closest to you. With one flip of the spatula, throw the bulk of the paste back against the opposite side of the pan. Repeat this operation until the butter starts oozing in tiny bubbles out of the paste. To reach this stage may take 3 to 5 minutes, depending on your dexterity. On the bottom of the pan, a film of paste will coagulate and appear slightly sandy. *Do not let it burn.*

While you work and acquire a tired arm, you extract excess water from the paste. The large amount of water used to make the paste was added only to make mixing easy and to give the starch cells in the flour a chance to start swelling. The more water you extract from the paste, the more eggs it will be able to absorb and the lighter and more voluminous the baked product will be. Old-fashioned Austrian cooks gave the paste the picturesque name of *Windnudeln* (wind noodles); in modern German, cream puffs have remained *Windbeuteln* (wind bags). The "wind" can exist only if the paste can absorb enough eggs. When the paste is really dry, remove the pot from the heat.

Beat the eggs lightly to avoid immediate coagulation of the whites on contact with the hot pot. Add the value of 1 egg at a time, stirring as fast as possible until it has been absorbed into the paste. Repeat until 4 eggs have been added. The texture of cream puff dough is correct when the paste falls from the spatula in a heavy, smooth, shiny mass. If it is thicker, add half or the entirety of the fifth egg. Add the flavoring.

The dough is best used as soon as it is finished, but it can wait an hour at room temperature, no longer. Rub the surface of the paste with a piece of butter to prevent a dehydration skin from forming.

TO BAKE THE DOUGH

Fit a round plain nozzle into a pastry bag; twist the part of the bag just above the nozzle and stuff it in its cone. The thickness of the material will keep the paste from flowing onto the table. Open your left hand wide and wrap the top of the bag backward over your extended fingers. With a large spoon or spatula, fill the bag with the dough. Close the bag and apply pressure. The paste will fall into the nozzle as the bag untwists. Squeeze the bag with your right hand while you guide it with your left hand or vice versa.

Line a baking sheet with a sheet of parchment paper. Pipe small balls ¾ inch in diameter for cocktail puffs and 1 to 1½ inches for cream puffs and shells. Leave 3 inches between puffs, for they will triple in size while baking. The top of each puff must be smooth; any *toupé* of paste left twisting on top of a puff will dry out and burn before it has time to rise.

If you have no pastry bag, you may also shape the puffs with a spoon. Use 1½ tablespoons of dough for cocktail puffs and 3 tablespoons for cream puffs. Pass the dough from one tablespoon to another to shape shells, which once baked will be oval.

Before baking the puffs, brush them with the egg yolk glaze. Make sure that no egg yolk rolls down onto the base of a puff or the pastry will rise unevenly on the side where the egg reached the baking paper.

Bake the puffs on the upper middle rack of a preheated oven. Keep the heat steady between 375° and 400°F for 20 to 30 minutes according to the size of the puffs.

The puffs must be dry and brown before being removed from the oven, or they will flatten without hope at room temperature. Cool the puffs on a cake rack, not on a plate, where they would become soggy from absorbing each other's steam. Preferably, do not freeze as the dough easily absorbs tastes.

WHAT MAKES THE SHELLS PUFF?

The large amount of water contained in the egg whites makes the shells puff. In the warm oven flour and eggs will form a solid structure of coagulated proteins and jelled starches; the steam produced by the evaporation of the water contained in the egg whites applies pressure on the protein walls and distends them. When the steam has almost completely evaporated, a large hole is left at the center of the puff and the puff is cooked. If the paste has not been dried enough, the puffs must, before being used, be "emptied" of the imperfectly baked dough at their center. By the time you have emptied 1 dozen puffs, you will quickly realize that you could have obtained 3 to 4 more puffs out of the wasted paste, had you not underdried it.

Pastry Cream

FFR — FILLING FOR 2 DOZEN PASTRIES

6 large eggs, separated

⅔ cup granulated sugar

¼ teaspoon salt

½ cup sifted cake flour

2 cups full-fat milk, scalded and completely cooled

I tablespoon pure vanilla extract

I envelope unflavored gelatin, softened in I tablespoon water mixed with 3 tablespoons liquor of your choice

I ½ cups heavy cream

In a large saucepan, ribbon the egg yolks, half the sugar, and salt together well (see page 163). Sift in, then blend in the flour tablespoon by tablespoon. Gradually whisk in the cooled milk, scraping well the whole surface of the pot bottom. Bring slowly to a boil, over medium heat, stirring constantly and very quickly. The increase of heat must be regular and not too fast, to allow the starch cells in the flour to dilate gradually. As the mixture starts to thicken, whip faster and faster to break up any lumps that may form. As soon as the cream boils—*it must boil visibly and the boil must reach the center of the pot*—remove it from the heat. Add the vanilla and softened gelatin and stir well to dissolve the gelatin. Strain through a conical strainer into a mixing bowl and keep warm over a pot of hot water.

Slowly start whipping the egg whites to the soft peak stage at the same time as you cook the remainder of the sugar to the thread stage. When the sugar reaches the thread stage (see page 938), gradually pour the syrup into

Pastry cream is the traditional filling for pastries made of cream puff dough. This flour-bound cream offers another illustration of the principle that egg yolks mixed with flour can and must boil. Pastry cream is made following the technique of stirred pudding (bouillie).

This recipe is for an all-purpose pastry cream made by combining several classic methods. It gives a light and pleasant cream, the taste of which can be varied. The teaspoon of gelatin will cause the cream to appear rather stiff when refrigerated but at room temperature it will be mellow and remain very light. The egg whites are whipped into an Italian meringue to heat them for sanitation purposes (see page 194). This cream is used to fill pastries such as cream puffs, éclairs, and tarts.

the whipping egg whites and continue whipping until they are cold. Immediately fold into the pastry cream and let cool completely.

Whip the heavy cream slightly stiffer than the Chantilly stage (see page 29) and fold it into the cream. Turn the cream into a clean bowl, refrigerate it immediately, and keep it refrigerated at all times. Use the cream within the next 24 hours.

To fill cream puffs: Turn the cream into a pastry bag fitted with a 1¼-inch nozzle. Hold the cream puff with your second hand and the bag with your working hand. Pierce the cream puff with the nozzle and squeeze the cream into the shell until you can feel the pressure against your second hand. To fill éclairs, see page 1109.

FLAVORINGS FOR PASTRY CREAM
Flavor the master recipe abovewith:

ALMONDS: Make the pastry with almond milk (see page 50) and flavor additionally with ¼ cup of the almond liqueur of your choice; or flavor with 2 teaspoons pure almond extract.

COFFEE: Add instant coffee powder to taste to the hot milk before making the custard.

CHOCOLATE: Add 3 ounces melted bittersweet chocolate to the pastry cream before adding the egg whites.

CITRUS: Add 2 tablespoons grated rinds of 2 lemons or limes or 1 orange to the scalded milk before making the custard.

BUTTERSCOTCH: Replace the granulated sugar with the same amount of firmly packed dark brown sugar and add 2 tablespoons unsalted butter to the hot custard before folding in the egg whites and cream.

LIQUEURS: Add up to ¼ cup of any liqueur to taste to the custard before adding the egg whites and cream.

Fondant

NFR—I POUND
I pound (2 cups) granulated sugar
I cup water acidulated with no more than 2 drops fresh lemon juice

This icing, the traditional icing for pastries made with cream puff dough, is also usable as a filling for chocolates, and can be shaped into patties and chocolate dipped.

A marble slab is most useful in the making of fondant; if you do not have one, wash a large enameled broiler pan with soap

Wash a saucepan with soap and water, rinse abundantly, and dry with paper towels. Add the sugar and acidulated water. Cook to 238°F on a candy thermometer over medium-high heat. Pour immediately onto the prepared slab or pan. Let cool until warm only to the top of the hand (110° to 115°F); the sugar syrup will wrinkle lightly if you tilt the pan slightly. Working back and forth with a spatula, bring the mixture constantly from the outside toward the center of the pan until milky white. The more you stir, the tinier the sugar crystals and the smoother the fondant will be. Let the mixture rest 2 minutes, then knead with the heel of your hand until a ball forms. This can be kept 4 months in a well-covered jar on the bottom shelf of a refrigerator. To use, melt and simply brush over the tops of pastries.

To flavor fondant, it is recommended you use only the strongest extracts, added drop by drop to fondant that has been remelted over low heat until you obtain the taste you are looking for. The pure extracts mostly used are vanilla, lemon, lime, orange, hazelnut, pistachio, mint, or coffee.

Coffee fondant can be made by using extra strong coffee such as espresso or very dark roast coffee instead of water to cook the syrup. In this case freshly brewed coffee gives a better flavor than instant coffee dissolved in water.

Chocolate fondant, also called chocolate mayonnaise, being used mostly in the decoration of cakes, can be found on page 1146.

Éclairs with a Twist

FFR — 2 DOZEN MINIATURE ÉCLAIRS

I recipe Pâte à Choux (page 1105)

½ recipe Pastry Cream (page 1107), flavored with chocolate and ¼ teaspoon ground cinnamon, or to taste

I recipe coffee-flavored Fondant (preceding recipe) made with I cup strong coffee instead of water

Prepare the baking sheet(s). Preheat the oven to 375°F. Fit the pastry bag with a ⅓-inch nozzle and pipe as many sticks 2½ inches long as possible at ½-inch intervals. Pass two tines of a fork ¹⁄₁₆ inch deep into the top of each éclair to allow the pastry to rise generously. Bake 12 to 15 minutes. Cool completely on a rack.

After the pastry cream has properly cooled, fill the pastry bag with the cream. Punch a hole with the tip of the nozzle at one end of each éclair and pipe the cream into the éclair until you feel the pressure of the cream against the sides of the cake. Set back on the rack.

Prepare the fondant and let it cool to mellow. Brush it over the surface of each cake and let dry. Serve as soon as possible after finishing. Although éclairs taste best when enjoyed very fresh, refrigerate them if they have to stay at room temperature more than one hour after being filled. Please do not freeze.

and water. Dry it with paper towels only, and freeze it for 2 hours. Or, if your freezer is not large enough to house the pan, chill the pan until it is as cold as you can make it by filling it with a large plastic bag full of ice cubes.

Such small pastries carry in French the genteel name of reductions. A plate of such small pastries is usually served at first Holy Communion or wedding banquets. If only vanilla cream is used to fill cream puff–style pastries, the taste is nice, but that is all. I prefer something a little more exotic.

Cream Puff Dough
Used for Savories
Gougère Bourguignonne

When a cream puff dough is going to be used for a savory dish, it never contains sugar and only a smaller amount of butter. Here is a recipe for a cheesecake often served at wine tastings in Burgundy. I use chicken stock rather than water or milk; it is more in character with the remainder of the ingredients. This was called a poupelain au fromage by my great grandmother.

FFR — 4 DOZEN SMALL GOUGÈRES OR I LARGE ONE

I cup chicken stock or broth

6 tablespoons cold unsalted butter, diced into ⅓-inch cubes

¼ teaspoon freshly grated nutmeg

Pinch of cayenne pepper

½ teaspoon salt

Freshly ground black pepper from the mill

I cup unsifted unbleached all-purpose flour

4 large eggs

¾ cup grated Gruyère cheese

I large egg yolk beaten together with 2 tablespoons milk of your choice

½ cup diced Gruyère cheese

Prepare the dough exactly like you would cream puff dough (see page 1105): mix the chicken stock, butter, and seasonings together in a large saucepan. Bring slowly to a boil, then remove from the heat and add the flour. Stir until a ball forms, then dry the paste as described on page 1106. Add the whole eggs one by one, incorporating each completely before adding the next one. Add the grated cheese to the finished batter.

Preheat the oven to 375°F. Butter an unbendable pizza pan and rinse it under cold water. With a large serving spoon, drop large spoonfuls of batter on the pan, attaching them to one another to form a crown. Brush with the egg yolk glaze; sprinkle the diced cheese over the top of the cake. Bake until deep golden, 35 to 40 minutes.

Serve lukewarm. The cake will rise considerably in the oven and deflate rather fast as it cools since it is weighted by the cheese. Please do not freeze.

Fried Cheese Puffs

FFR — 3 DOZEN

Prepare the batter for the *gougère* (preceding recipe), using only 3 eggs. Drop the batter by nuggets approximately the size of a walnut into oil heated to 360°F (see page 632). Slowly increase the temperature of the oil to 380°F. The puffs will bob up by themselves. Serve piping hot on a folded napkin. Salt lightly.

Another way of utilizing cream puff dough is to prepare French-style gnocchi; see the grains chapter for instructions, on pages 496–97.

Leavening Batter with Baking Soda or Baking Powder: Quick Breads, Muffins, and All-American Biscuits

It would be a good idea if, for the sake of good nutrition, you reserve sweetened breads, muffins, and delicious rich biscuits for the weekend; their problem is that they are seductively quick to make and so pleasant to enjoy.

The key to these lovely treats is the different baking powders employed to make them rise. Baking powders are chemicals or compounds of chemicals combined in such a way that they will produce carbon dioxide either when they come in contact with the water contained in a batter or with the heat of the oven, or both.

A number of baking powders different from the three described below exist for use in commercial baking. If you want to bake on a commercial scale, consult the books listed in the bibliography for more details.

Leavening with Baking Soda

To become active, baking soda must come in contact with an acid. Lemon juice, vinegar, molasses, honey, sour cream, buttermilk, applesauce, or yogurt are mostly used because their concentration is high enough to react with baking soda. Other fruit juices may not be concentrated enough to do so. In older recipes it was common to be directed to dissolve baking soda into the acidic liquid before adding it to a batter; the result was loss of carbon dioxide to the atmosphere, and nice and heavy cakes which I am old enough to remember very vividly. Baking soda is now ground so fine that it can be added to the dry ingredients entering the batter, with considerably less carbon dioxide lost.

When a batter containing baking soda and an acid are mixed, carbonic acid is produced which rapidly breaks down to carbon dioxide and water. This reaction is accelerated by the heat in the oven. Both the water, as it turns to steam, and the carbon dioxide contribute to dilation of the cells in the batter.

Care must be taken not to exceed the quantity of baking soda usually indicated in recipes, for any excess baking soda not fully neutralized by an acid will remain in the cake or bread, in the form of baking soda, leaving in it a nasty soapy taste. For each ½ teaspoon baking soda used, a batter should contain 1 cup sour or soured liquid to neutralize the soda.

Good for All "Pain d'Épices"

FFR to FCR — I LOAF; IO TO I2 SERVINGS

1½ cups sifted unbleached all-purpose flour
¾ cup unsifted medium rye flour
½ teaspoon salt
I teaspoon baking soda
I teaspoon crushed aniseeds
¼ teaspoon ground allspice
¼ teaspoon ground cardamom
¼ teaspoon ground coriander
¼ teaspoon freshly grated nutmeg
⅛ teaspoon ground cloves
½ cup soft unsalted butter or ⅓ cup unsaturated oil of your choice
½ cup liquid honey
½ cup unsulfured blackstrap molasses
⅓ cup nonfat plain yogurt, well stirred
I tablespoon fresh lemon juice

Good for all, because if you replace the butter with ⅓ cup of unsaturated oil, heart patients can enjoy the cake fully.

In this honey-molasses quick bread several acids are combined to make certain that the batter is acidified enough to neutralize the taste of the baking soda. A good trick is to use unsulfured blackstrap molasses which has such a strong taste that it will totally hide any off taste of soda in a cake.

BEST FREEZING STAGE:
Fully baked, wrapped in plastic and foil

Grease or butter an 8½ × 4½ × 2¾-inch loaf pan. Preheat the oven to 350°F.

Mix all the dry ingredients together.

In a large bowl, cream the butter, then gradually add the honey, molasses, yogurt, and lemon juice. Fold in the dry ingredients ½ cup at a time. Turn into the prepared pan and bake until a skewer inserted at the center comes out clean and feeling hot to the top of your hand, 50 to 55 minutes. Cool on a rack.

Wrap the cake in aluminum foil and let it mellow in the refrigerator for 2 days before eating. Slice while cold. No butter is needed on top, but if you succumb, enjoy.

Leavening with Single-Acting Baking Powder

Baking powder until twenty years ago came in two versions, single-acting powder and double-acting. We are now mostly left with the double-acting. It is important to still have some knowledge about single-acting though, for should one run out of double-acting powder it is easy to make your own single-acting baking powder by blending together, by volume, two parts cream of tartar with one part baking soda.

It is also a good idea, if you cook and bake a lot, to prepare a little stash of this mixture by mixing the following quantities:

6 tablespoons cream of tartar

3 tablespoons baking soda

1 ½ teaspoons cornstarch

Considering that 1½ to 2 teaspoons of this baking powder are sufficient to leaven 1 cup of flour, this quantity is enough to leaven several breads or cakes. The cornstarch is used to absorb moisture and keep the other ingredients dry which prevents them from reacting together, since this type of baking powder reacts and produces carbon dioxide as soon as it comes in contact with moisture. Since the reaction happens very quickly, it is important to have the cake or loaf pan greased and the oven preheated before you make the batter, which then must be quickly transferred to the pan and put to bake without delay. Any wait will result in a not so light quick bread.

Black Walnut and Dried Sour Cherry Quick Bread

FFR — 1 LOAF; 8 SERVINGS

⅓ cup dried sour cherries

1 tablespoon unsalted butter

½ cup chopped black walnuts

2 tablespoons unsifted unbleached all-purpose flour

2¼ cups sifted unbleached all-purpose flour

2 teaspoons single-acting baking powder

½ teaspoon salt

½ cup firmly packed dark brown sugar

1 large egg, beaten

½ cup milk of your choice

Toss the cherries with barely enough cold water to cover and let steep overnight.

Grease an 8½ × 4½ × 2¾-inch loaf pan with the butter. Preheat the oven to 325°F. Pat the cherries dry and toss them and the walnuts in the 2 tablespoons of flour. Mix together the remaining flour, the fruit and nuts, the baking powder, and salt.

In a small bowl, with a wooden spoon or electric mixer, whip the sugar and egg together until light and fluffy, then blend in the milk. On slow speed

If black walnuts and dried sour cherries are not available you can use English walnuts and raisins, or pine nuts and dried currants, or almonds and dried cranberries or chopped apricots.

There is no danger of any off taste in a bread made with this formula since the acid, sodium potassium tartrate, created when baking soda comes in contact with the water in the eggs and milk, has no unpleasant flavor. Bake the bread at 325°F to prevent the floured fruit and nuts from collecting toward the bottom of the bread; this will ensure that the bread batter travels upward at approximately the same speed the fruit and nuts travel downward.

or by hand, blend the mixed dry ingredients into the liquid ingredients. Pour into the pan and bake immediately until a skewer inserted in the center comes out clean and feeling hot to the top of your hand, 50 to 55 minutes. Cool on a rack.

Double-Acting Baking Powder

This is the baking powder sold almost exclusively in markets nowadays. It is known as SAS or SAS–phosphate powder. This powder is so compounded that two successive reactions take place in the batter, resulting in two successive emissions of carbon dioxide.

The first takes place as soon as the baking powder finds itself in contact with the water contained in the liquid ingredients of the batter, exactly as for the single-acting baking powder. The reaction is rapid; as much as 70 percent of the total amount of carbon dioxide can be emitted before the batter reaches the oven, depending on the chemical used to trigger the reaction. The second reaction does not begin until the batter is heated in the oven.

As with baking soda, any excess of double-acting powder will result in a baked product with an off taste; observe a maximum ratio of 1½ teaspoons double-acting baking powder per cup of flour.

If you are interested in the exact chemical reactions, refer to the books listed in the bibliography.

MUFFINS MADE WITH WHITE FLOUR(S)

The recipe that follows serves as a technical example for all muffins made with white flours. You can use the same basic ingredients and techniques and just change the garnish as you please.

Before you do anything, butter the muffin tins generously and preheat your oven anywhere between 375° and 425°F, no more; baked in this range of temperature a tray of muffins will require 20 to 25 minutes' baking time.

Muffins are treacherous all the way through their making; work the batter too much and you get a mortarlike muffin, because as you stirred with the idea of having an "oh so smooth batter" you developed gluten in a goodly amount and what will happen? Once baked this smooth batter will show the telltale signs: a hard, shiny, pointed top and, as you break the muffin open, long vertical tunnels right through the middle of the little cake.

Always remember that when you hear the word *muffin*, you must automatically think "lumpy batter," stirred 15 to 18 strokes maximum. No smoothness is needed; on the contrary, you are looking for a definite coarseness, obtained by stirring the ingredients together until just blended, period. The result will be a nice sloping top, looking like some large gravel has been caught under its surface, and a good soft and light crumb, however coarse looking. So please count your strokes until you are able to recognize by sight that your batter is ready to bake.

Whether to use melted butter or vegetable shortening is your decision; I am for butter since I make muffins rarely. If you want them more often, replace the butter with an unsaturated oil.

The method I used here is different from that used by most people. It consists of introducing unmelted butter into the flour-and-sugar mixture, breaking down the pieces of butter as is done in pastry making with the tips of fingers until the butter is in tiny particles and the mixture of dry ingredients and butter is reduced to a fine meal. This technique gives a very even distribution of the butter in the batter. All liquid ingredients are mixed together then added last.

Also important is the way you introduce the fruit and nut garnishings into the batter, which is during the last three strokes of the mixing, always tossed first with a bit of flour to prevent them from sinking. A lot of personal freedom exists as to the amount of dried fruit and nuts that may be added as a garnish to the batter; any quantity from ¼ cup to 1½ cups is acceptable.

The way you fill the prepared tins is also important. Lift the batter out of the bowl with a large spoon and let it settle gently into the tins, filling each three quarters full; do not pour from way above, nor scrape the bowl with intensity or one or two of your last muffins will be tougher than the remainder of the batch.

The last pitfall: Remove baked muffins from their tins rather rapidly; if left in the pans for more than 2 minutes, they will start sticking. It is preferable to use nonstick tins, but also brush the tins evenly with a tad of unsaturated oil.

Bartlett Huckleberry and Citrus Muffins

FFR to FCR—1 DOZEN

1⅓ cups dried huckleberries

Unsaturated oil of your choice to very lightly grease 12 tins

½ cup cold unsalted butter, cut into ½-inch cubes

2 tablespoons plus ½ cup unsifted cake flour

1⅓ cups sifted unbleached all-purpose flour

½ cup granulated sugar

¾ teaspoon salt

½ teaspoon each finely grated lemon, lime, and orange rinds

2 large eggs

½ cup milk of your choice

4 teaspoons double-acting baking powder

This basic recipe was given to me by my neighbor in Bartlett, New Hampshire; I rearranged the mixing technique to obtain the texture I was looking for.

BEST FREEZING STAGE:
Athough muffins can be frozen once fully baked, they taste best when consumed lukewarm immediately after baking.

NOTE: *For people on strict "save your heart" diets, why not use 4 to 5 tablespoons grapeseed oil instead of the butter?*

Soak the huckleberries for 1 hour in barely enough water to cover. Oil the muffin tins. Preheat the oven to 400°F. Remove the butter from the refrigerator and wrapper. Remove the berries from the water, pat completely dry, and toss with the 2 tablespoons of the cake flour.

Mix the all-purpose flour with the remaining cake flour, ¼ cup of the sugar, the salt, and grated rinds. Drop the butter cubes into the dry ingredients. Using your fingertips or a pastry cutter, mash together to obtain a very fine meal. Beat the eggs, milk, and the remainder of the sugar together.

Now sprinkle the baking powder over the flour mixture and stir in the egg mixture with no more than 10 strokes. Add the huckleberries and finish stirring with another 4 to 5 strokes.

Fill the muffin tins three quarters full with a large spoon letting the batter fall gently into each tin. Bake 25 minutes or so, until a skewer inserted into one of the muffins comes out dry. Remove from the oven, unmold immediately, cool on a rack, and serve barely lukewarm.

MUFFINS MADE WITH OTHER FLOURS AND CEREALS

Muffins are now made with all kinds of flours, cereals, and brans. They are very nutritious and present no difficulty other than those already outlined for white flour muffins.

All kinds of formulas exist, some made with cereals blended with flour or whole wheat flours, some made of pure bran. These batters, being somewhat heavier than the white flour-based batters, make it necessary to keep the amount of garnishes lighter. Here is a recipe for a very low-fat muffin made with oatmeal and whole wheat flour which tastes good with Scottish orange marmalade.

Oatmeal Muffins

In case anyone is allergic to sulfur, replace the apricots with dark raisins or soft pitted prunes untreated with sulfur dioxide.

LFR — 12 MUFFINS

2 tablespoons unsaturated oil of your choice

4 dried apricots, cut into ¼-inch cubes

½ cup unsifted cake flour

1½ cups quick-cooking oats

½ cup unsifted whole wheat flour

½ teaspoon salt

½ cup firmly packed light brown sugar

1 tablespoon baking powder

1 teaspoon dried ground orange peel as sold in spice jars

1 teaspoon crushed fennel seeds

1 teaspoon ground ginger

½ cup nonfat plain yogurt

½ cup skim milk

I large egg white, beaten

Grease 12 muffin tins with the unsaturated oil. Preheat the oven to 400°F.

In a large bowl, mix the apricot pieces with the cake flour. Blend in the oat flakes, whole wheat flour, salt, brown sugar, baking powder, orange peel, fennel seeds, and ginger. Mix well.

In a small bowl gradually dilute the yogurt with the milk and beaten egg white. Stir the mixture into the dry ingredients using no more than 12 to 15 strokes. Spoon the batter into the prepared muffin tins, filling them three quarters full, and bake 15 to 18 minutes, until a skewer inserted into one of the muffins comes out dry. Unmold as soon as out of the oven and cool on a rack.

Corn Muffins

FFR to FCR — 12 MUFFINS

3 tablespoons corn oil or ¼ cup melted clarified butter (page 32)

I cup milk of your choice

I tablespoon fresh lemon juice

2 large eggs or 2 large egg whites

2 tablespoons granulated sugar

1½ cups cornmeal

¾ cup sifted cake flour

¾ teaspoon salt

I tablespoon seeded and coarsely chopped dried pasilla chile, more or less to your

   personal taste

I tablespoon baking powder

½ cup blanched white or Silverqueen corn kernels

Grease the muffin tins with 1½ tablespoons of the corn oil or 2 of the butter. Preheat the oven to 400°F.

In a medium-size bowl, beat the milk, lemon juice, eggs or egg whites, sugar, and the remaining oil or clarified butter together until homogeneous.

In a large bowl, mix the cornmeal, flour, salt, pasilla, and baking powder together. Blend the moist ingredients into the dry ones with only 10 efficient strokes of a wooden spoon. Add the corn kernels and mix in another 5 strokes.

Spoon into the prepared muffin tins, filling them within ¼ inch of their rims and bake 18 to 20 minutes, until a skewer inserted at the center of a muffin comes out clean. Unmold as soon as out of the oven and cool on a wire rack. Serve lukewarm.

Corn muffins can range from uninspiring to heavenly buttery if the cook gives in to the seductive marriage of the tastes of corn and butter. You can in this recipe replace the corn oil with butter if you prefer. Please put a bit of butter on the table for those who will wish to enjoy it. Good with a dish of western beans.

Leavening with Self-Rising Flour: Biscuits

Self-rising flour is readily available in any store; it contains both baking powder and salt. However, it is not rare that a small town or rural store will not carry it. You can make it yourself by mixing together:

¾ cup sifted cake flour

1¼ cups bleached all-purpose flour

4 teaspoons baking powder

1 teaspoon salt

After you have made this blend, strain it twice to make sure that the baking powder is distributed evenly. You can if you want prepare a larger amount; the mixture will not spoil since it is dry. Store in a well-closed canister and label.

Biscuits are great fare for breakfast and after you have tried them once, you will be an expert both at preparing them and consuming them. Most people in this country use vegetable shortening to prepare biscuits; in some biscuits I do, but in the most delicious sweetened ones, to be enjoyed at tea or a fancy brunch or as shortcake with berries, I much prefer the rich taste of butter.

Making biscuit dough seems easy at first but there are a few pitfalls to be avoided, such as kneading the dough too much or not enough. Developing a small amount of gluten to give the biscuit structure is essential, for without this structure the biscuit will flatten and look rather ill. Developing the gluten too much results in a hard biscuit outside and a mealy center. The solution is not to knead with your whole hand, but simply to *fraiser* with the heel of your hand, as is done for pastry (see page 1030). Think of it: This dough is very similar to that of pastry.

The softness of the flour you are going to use is extremely important and it is not by accident that the South has the best biscuits; they also have the best flour with which to make them in the whole nation. Do not hesitate to have southern flour shipped to you; it is well worth it.

When you cut the dough with a metal cutter, do not forget to dip your cutter into flour each and every time you cut a biscuit. If you do not, your cutter may leave a straggler of dough and the biscuit will not rise straight.

After you have cut the dough and gotten as many biscuits as you can, push all the pieces of dough against one another to again obtain a full surface. *Fraiser* only once with the heel of your hand and reshape to be ½ inch thick. Cut as many more biscuits as you can; a few cutouts will be left over. Bake them for the children at the same time as the pretty biscuits; they love this kind of little treat.

Most recipes call for milk; try using the same amount of water, yogurt, whey, or buttermilk. You will be surprised how different the textures can be.

BEST FREEZING STAGE:
Although biscuits can be frozen, their texture slowly alters if kept frozen too long. Freeze on sheets, remove to thick plastic bags, and wrap in foil. When ready to bake (no later than 3 weeks after freezing), put on a baking sheet lined with parchment paper and bake, solidly frozen, for twice the length of time of fresh biscuits, less 5 to 8 minutes depending on size.

Traditional Biscuits

FFR— 10 TO 12 BISCUITS 2 INCHES IN DIAMETER

2 cups sifted (preferably southern) self-rising flour

I teaspoon granulated sugar

⅓ cup vegetable shortening or 7 tablespoons unsalted butter, at room temperature but
**   still waxy and cut into tablespoons**

⅔ to ¾ cup milk of your choice as needed

Preheat the oven to 450°F. Mix the flour and sugar together. Using the fingertips of both your hands, mash the pieces of shortening into the mixture until a very coarse meal results. Gradually bring in the milk and work lightly until the dough forms a ball. Transfer the dough to the countertop and *fraiser* ten times (see page 1032), working the ball of dough with the heel of your hand, not with a kneading motion. Gather into a ball and flatten into a disk as close as possible to ⅓ inch to ½ inch thick.

Stamp out with a biscuit cutter dipped into flour after cutting each biscuit. Set the biscuits on an ungreased sheet side by side touching one another and bake until light golden, 14 to 15 minutes. Cool to lukewarm on a rack and serve immediately.

NOTE: *If you do not mind another tablespoon or so of butter, you can brush the top of each biscuit with a bit of melted butter.*

Tea Biscuits or English Scones

FFR— I DOZEN SCONES OR MORE IF CUT SMALLER

2 cups sifted self-rising flour

¼ cup granulated sugar

I teaspoon ground ginger

Grated rind of I orange

½ cup plain yogurt

I large egg

7 tablespoons unsalted butter, at room temperature but still waxy

Preheat the oven to 450°F. Mix the flour with 2 tablespoons of the sugar. Add the ginger and orange rind; mix well again. Beat the yogurt and egg together until liquid; set aside. Using the fingertips of both hands, rub the butter into the flour mixture to obtain a very coarse meal. Gradually add the mixture of liquid ingredients until the dough makes a ball. *Fraiser* ten times (see page 1030) and pat into a 9 × 2-inch rectangle. Cut into triangles, brush lightly with a bit of water, sprinkle with the remaining 2 tablespoons of sugar, and bake on an ungreased baking sheet until light golden, 12 to 14 minutes. Cool on a rack and serve barely lukewarm.

Scones are the glory of British teatime when served barely lukewarm with clotted cream and a great big dollop of raspberry preserve. Use pure yogurt made only of clabbered milk and without stabilizers.

Biscuits for Sunday Breakfast on the Hill

To make yogurt cheese, drip
yogurt overnight (see page 1074).
Keep some of the abundant whey
or collect some in a larger pot of
plain nonfat yogurt, where the
whey squeezes out of the curd
after a portion has been used. Its
bright yellow color is normal, just
spoon it out.

FFR—I DOZEN 2-INCH BISCUITS

I cup sifted bleached all-purpose flour

¾ cup sifted cake flour

2 teaspoons baking powder

¼ teaspoon baking soda

I teaspoon aniseeds

Large pinch of saffron threads, powdered

¼ cup granulated sugar

½ teaspoon salt

½ cup unsalted butter, at room temperature but still waxy and cut into tablespoons

3 tablespoons yogurt whey

3 tablespoons heavy cream

Preheat the oven to 450°F. Mix the flours, baking powder, baking soda, aniseeds, saffron, 2 tablespoons of the sugar, and the salt. Using the fingertips of both hands, mash the butter into the flour to obtain a coarse meal. Add the whey and heavy cream mixed together, and work lightly into a dough. *Fraiser* (see page 1030) six to ten times. Pat into a cake ½ inch thick and dip a 2-inch cutter into flour each time you cut a biscuit. Brush with water and sprinkle with generous pinches of the remaining 2 tablespoons of sugar. Bake on an ungreased baking sheet side by side and touching one another until golden, 14 to 15 minutes. Cool on a rack and serve barely lukewarm.

American Biscuits Versus European Biscuits

Etymologically, the word *biscuit* means twice cooked. You will see this name applied also to the cakes described on pages 1118–20. The Italian *biscotti*, the French *biscottes*, and the German zwieback are true biscuits. Their dough is first shaped into loaves, baked, and cooled completely. Then the loaves are cut into ⅓-inch-thick slices, which, dried in a slow oven, become "biscuits" that can be kept a long time in a canister.

You can make *biscotti* with either semisweet or sweet yeast dough and *brioche* dough in the French and German manners, or you can prepare them from a baking powder leavened dough as in the Italian *biscotti* that follow.

Crunchy Biscotti

FCR — 48 BISCOTTI ⅓ INCH THICK, 2½ INCHES LONG

2 cups sifted cake flour

2½ cups sifted unbleached all-purpose flour

2 teaspoons baking powder

2 cups granulated sugar

Large pinch of salt

1 large egg beaten lightly together with 3 large egg whites

¼ cup dry Marsala

1½ cups nuts of your choice, whole if pistachios, pine nuts, or hazelnuts, broken in large
   pieces if macadamia nuts, walnuts, or pecans

Preheat the oven to 325°F. Sift together again the two flours and the baking powder. Make a well in the flour, add the sugar, salt, egg and egg whites, and Marsala and gradually gather the flour into the liquid ingredients. Work it to develop a little body and as you do so, gather the nuts into the dough. Shape into four loaves each 7 × 2½ × ¾ inches. Put to bake on a baking sheet lined with parchment paper until blond and just done, about 30 minutes; a metal skewer inserted at the center of the largest loaf should come out dry and feeling hot to the top of the hand. Cool completely, then slice into ⅓-inch-thick slices and return to the oven preheated to 275°F. Dry until uniformly beige in color, turning the biscuits over several times at regular intervals, another 10 to 15 minutes.

The true biscotti as they are still made in Tuscany, adapted from the Italian recipe of family friend Rosa Lantermo. The cakes are first baked, cooled, and sliced, then the slices are dried in a slow oven. You can use any nuts you like; I like peeled pistachios. Biscotti are best dunked in Vin Santo or any fortified wine you like, but they do fine with cappuccino and good Darjeeling tea also. Be careful; these are really crunchy. For softer biscotti, use 3 whole eggs plus 1 egg white.

BEST FREEZING STAGE:
Biscotti need not be frozen. Make the dough, bake the cookie, and store in metal canisters—they keep a very long time.

Baking Cakes

Coming as I do from Europe, I always have had a lot of trouble understanding why quick breads, which contain so much sugar, can be called breads. For me and pretty much all Europeans, they are a heavier form of cake, truly cakes not breads.

What really makes the difference between a bread and a cake is the texture of the crumb, which, instead of being solid and resilient as it is in yeast breads or coarse as in muffins and quick breads, is very small and light. This type of crumb is a combination of different elements entering the composition of a cake batter.

FLOUR

Flour starches and gluten mix with egg proteins to form the structure of a cake. Use the flour called for in the recipe, always sifted. Too much flour will result in a heavy, compact cake; not enough flour will result in a cake that collapses in the oven before its baking time is completed. Incorporate or blend flour into batters gently by hand or at most using the slow speed of a mixer to prevent too much gluten development, which will result in tunnels in the cake and "buckly" cakes which mound on the top instead of being perfectly flat on both sides.

Once a recipe has been tested with one type of flour you must execute it with the flour recommended or face rebuilding the recipe yourself if you do not like the texture of the cake. You should never hesitate to do so bearing in mind that: 1 cup sifted unbleached all-purpose flour can be replaced by 1½ cups sifted cake flour.

EGGS

Eggs are considered part of the liquid ingredients of a cake batter. They give the batter taste, color, and richness. Last but not least, they give it volume; this fact is especially visible in old-fashioned spongecakes and pound cakes.

SUGAR

Sugar sweetens the batter and gives it color as it bakes and browns in the oven. The more sugar a cake contains, the more the gluten development of the flour will be slowed down, and the longer the egg and flour proteins will need to coagulate in the oven. A cake containing 1 cup or more of sugar per cup of flour is called a high-ratio cake. High-ratio cakes have a fine texture because the cell walls of their batters take a very long time to stretch.

FAT

As in pastry dough, fat coats the gluten strands (see page 1008 for a full explanation of gluten), allowing them to slide against one another. Fat tenderizes the cake batter. The most tender cakes are made with vegetable shortening, but the most flavorful are made with butter. The creaming of either shortening or butter introduces air into the batter; that air is an important leavening agent.

LEAVENING AGENTS

Double-acting baking powder is the leavener of choice for modern American cakes. For an explanation of the way double-acting baking powder works, please go back to page 1114.

Foam cakes are leavened solely by the beating of eggs and/or the creaming of butter. The leavening is provided by the steam that results from the vaporization during baking of the water contained in the butter and eggs and the dilatation of the air beaten into the eggs and butter. Very often a cake will be leavened by both beaten eggs and creamed butter.

A BIT OF TROUBLESHOOTING Use the baking temperature indicated in each recipe and make certain that the thermostat of your oven is accurate or you may have some unpleasant surprises. A cake baked in a too hot oven will crack at the top; if baked in too low an oven it may flow over the edges of the cake pan onto the bottom of the oven. Old-fashioned pound cakes are almost always cooked so they develop a crack at the top, because in the eighteenth century, people baked them in the bread oven which was too hot for their rich texture. But some cooks (among them this writer) are not willing to abandon this little anachronistic particularity.

If the cake does not measure up to the volume you were expecting it to develop, watch your beating; you may not have beaten the eggs enough. This is the most common mistake when making a *génoise*.

If your cake sticks to the pan, blame only your lack of greasing and lightly flouring the pan. Of the two possibilities, lack of fat on a cake pan is responsible for many more failures than poor flouring.

A brittle crust on top of a cake means that there is too much sugar in the formula. Just so you know, this is a normal characteristic of some old-fashioned Italian and French cakes.

Too little sugar, on the contrary, will result in a cake that has coarse crumbs and a hard cardboardlike top.

Watch the amount of baking powder used; too much of it leaves an unpleasant, almost bitter taste on the palate.

General Baking Procedures

PREHEATING THE OVEN AND PREPARING CAKE PANS

Before you start mixing a cake, preheat the oven to the required temperature. *Unless otherwise directed in the recipe*, grease the cake pan(s) applying soft butter generously to the bottom and sides of the pans. Use your fingertips or a pastry brush, never waxed paper or the pan will be unevenly buttered. Flour is also often sprinkled in cake molds; it slightly slows down the rising of the batter up the sides of the cake pan (giving time to some heavier cakes, like pound cakes, to rise and set slowly at their centers). In very foamy batters containing a lot of air (*génoise*) the sides of the pan are often not floured to allow the batter, which is delicate, to rise fast and set just as fast.

BAKING AND RISING

Whatever the type of cake, the same physical transformation takes place in a batter when it bakes. The heat provokes the dilatation of the air and/or carbon dioxide in the cell walls of the batter at the same time as it causes the vaporization of the water. The combined effect of gas dilatation and steam pressure stretches the starch and egg protein walls. When most of the steam has evaporated, the cake is baked. Test its doneness by inserting a metal skewer at the center of the cake. If it comes out dry, shiny, and too hot to be bearable for more than a few seconds when applied to the top of your hand, the cake is done.

Position the cake in the right place in the oven: Some cakes must bake on the middle rack of the oven, a few on the bottom rack. Follow the directions in each recipe you use, but remember that the middle rack is the cake-baking rack most of the time. If your cake is to bake in two layers, the pan containing one goes toward the back of the oven on the left-hand side and the other on the right-hand side toward the front of the oven. Never let pans touch each other as both layers will bake unevenly where the pans touched.

COOLING AND UNMOLDING CAKES

Most cakes are cooled in the baking pan, but not a *génoise*, which should be unmolded as soon as it comes out of the oven. Let a pound cake cool in its pan for 10 minutes. Invert chiffon and angel cakes as they come out of the oven by putting the cone in the center of the tube pan over an upside-down funnel, set over a cake rack. The cake will unmold perfectly as it cools and retracts from the sides of the pan.

CUTTING A CAKE INTO LAYERS

The techniques used here come from Switzerland. Slice a cake into layers only when it is completely cold. Cut two or more pieces of parchment paper or aluminum foil. Put the cake on one of them.

Exactly in front of you, cut a small vertical groove 1/16 inch deep in the side of the cake; it will help you match the layers when you reassemble them. Holding a very sharp knife in your right hand with the correct grip (see page 15), press the tip of the blade against the side of the cake, while the three last fingers of your cutting hand remain motionless on the countertop.

Rest your left hand on the top of the cake and with it turn the cake around in a circle. The tip of the knife will trace a line all around the cake. Fit a strong but thin thread into this line. Cross both ends of the thread, and pull to separate the layers. Slide the second piece of parchment paper or foil between the layers and lift off the top layer. Repeat with all the layers and keep each of them on its sheet of parchment, where they will be spread with filling.

If a cake contains nuts, separate the layers with a knife instead of a thread.

FILLING A LAYER CAKE

Spread the filling on each layer separately, then lift the piece of paper on which the layer rests and let it slide gently on top of the bottom layer. Match your layers by making sure that the vertical groove visible on each layer is aligned in a straight vertical line.

ICING A CAKE

To ice a cake, set it on a cake rack or a lazy Susan if you have one. Melt 2 to 3 tablespoons jelly (currant for berry cakes, strained apricot jam for other cakes), and brush it on the surface and around the sides of the cake to trap the crumbs and keep them from breaking through the icing. Pour a thin icing at the exact center of the cake top and let it drip around the sides. To ice with a thick icing, spread the icing on the sides first, bringing the icing to rest on the top edge of the cake. When ready to ice the top, start at the edge first, moving toward the center, spreading with a cake spatula to obtain a smooth surface. Dip a very large clean spatula in hot water, drip it completely, and apply it gently over the surface to even it completely, let cool, then finish decorating the top of the cake.

TRANSFERRING A CAKE TO A SERVING PLATTER

Cross two long spatulas under the cake, take hold of their handles in each hand with confidence, lift the cake (it will not break or collapse), and deposit it at the center of its serving platter without problem or complication. If this method does not appeal to you, decorate the cake on a cardboard base; cardboard bases are available for sale in kitchen equipment stores.

SPECIAL EQUIPMENT FOR CAKE MAKING

You will need cake pans and loaf pans. I prefer sturdy aluminum, but the modern nonstick black pans are also very good. Have two each 8-inch, 9-inch, and 10-inch springpans, plus a 9-inch and a 10-inch form; 8 × 8 × 8-inch square pans or 9 × 9 × 9-inch square pans are also useful. Aluminum pans are expensive, but they will last you a lifetime. You will need a large cake rack to cool cakes; long-bladed cake spatulas, one medium and one large; parchment paper; a long, serrated knife to cut cake layers; if you find it necessary, a lazy Susan to decorate cakes; and a brush, quite necessary, if you want to imbibe a cake with a liqueur and sugar syrup.

Classification of Cakes

BUTTER OR SHORTENED CAKES

These can be made using two different methods: the one-bowl method or the creaming method. Whichever is used, the recipe always begins with: Cream the butter, add the sugar.

ONE-BOWL METHOD The general practice is to use vegetable shortening as the fat in the preparation of these cakes, but you can also use butter.

Mixing Pattern: Mix the dry ingredients into the liquid ones or vice versa. A typical example of such a simple cake is the *pain d'épices* on page 1112.

Ratio of Ingredients per Cup of Sifted Unbleached All-Purpose Flour:

¾ cup granulated sugar

¼ to ⅓ cup shortening

⅓ to ½ cup milk of your choice

¾ to 1 teaspoon baking powder

2 large eggs

Leavening Agent: 100 percent baking powder

Baking Temperature: 350°F

CREAMING METHOD Use vegetable shortening or butter or a combination of both.

Mixing Pattern: Cream the chosen fat, add the sugar and beat until fluffy. Add alternately dry and liquid ingredients.

Ratio of Ingredients per Cup of Sifted Unbleached All-Purpose Flour: same as for the one-bowl method

Leavening Agents: 15 percent air introduced by creaming the fat and sugar together, 85 percent baking powder

Baking Temperature: 350°F

Quick Berry Cassette

BEST FREEZING STAGE:
*Freshly baked and unfilled.
Defrost, then fill.*

FFR—ONE 9-INCH-SQUARE CAKE; 8 TO 10 SERVINGS

I tablespoon unsifted cake flour to flour the cake pan

⅓ cup vegetable shortening or ½ cup unsalted butter

¾ cup granulated sugar

1⅞ cups sifted cake flour

Large pinch of salt

2 teaspoons baking powder

⅓ cup milk of your choice

2 large eggs

1½ tablespoons kirsch or 2 teaspoons pure vanilla extract

For the garnish

I cup heavy cream, whipped to the Chantilly stage (page 30)

Granulated sugar to your taste

I cup each ripe strawberries, raspberries, red currants, and wild blueberries

⅔ cup currant jelly, melted and cooled to barely lukewarm

I tablespoon kirsch

Grease and flour a 9 × 9 × 2-inch cake pan; preheat the oven to 350°F.

Cream the chosen fat, then add the sugar and beat 2 minutes with an electric mixer until light, fluffy, and white. Meanwhile, sift together the flour, salt, and baking powder. Beat the milk, eggs, and kirsch together. Alternately blend the dry and liquid ingredients into the butter-and-sugar mixture; beat the batter 2 minutes on medium speed, until it ripples, and turn into the prepared cake pan. Bake about 30 minutes, until a skewer inserted at the center of the cake comes out dry. Unmold when lukewarm and cool on a rack.

When cold, slice off a ¼-inch-thick layer from the top of the cake. Using a fork, empty the cake to obtain a shell with a bottom and sides ⅓ to ½ inch thick. Fill the shell with the cream whipped stiffly with sugar to your taste and top the cream with the mixed berries. Just before serving, spoon some of the jelly mixed with the kirsch over each portion of cake.

With the top and center of the cake, prepare toasted cake crumbs and keep for any dessert strudel preparation to deliciously replace the regular bread crumbs.

Danish Holiday Almond Cake

FFR — 3 DOZEN SQUARES FOR PETITS FOURS,
OR 1 ROUND 10-INCH CAKE WITH 18 TO 24 SERVINGS

1 cup plus 1 tablespoon unsalted butter

1 tablespoon unsifted cake flour for the cake pan

Large pinch of salt

1 cup granulated sugar

10½ ounces almond paste (not marzipan), finely grated

2 teaspoons orange flower water or 1 tablespoon kirsch

5 medium-size eggs

1 cup sifted cake flour

½ teaspoon baking powder (optional)

Confectioners' sugar

This cake, a cousin to the French pain de gênes, is truly delicious and a treat to have once in a while. Please respect scrupulously the egg sizes given here. The cake is so delicious by itself that any icing seems to damage rather than enhance its flavor. For a recipe of the same cake made with ground pistachios, see my book Madeleine Kamman's Savoie. *To make petits fours, bake the cake in a 9 × 9 × 2-inch square cake pan.*

Preheat the oven to 325°F. Butter the cake pan with the 1 tablespoon of butter and dust it with the single tablespoon of cake flour. Set the pan upside down and slam it once to remove all traces of excess flour.

In a large bowl, cream the remaining cup of butter until white, then add the sugar and almond paste together and beat until fluffy and white again, 2 to 3 minutes on medium-high speed. Turning the speed down to low, add the orange flower water, then 1 egg at a time. Beat again on medium-high speed after each addition until the batter returns to white foaminess. Finally, resift the cake flour mixed with the baking powder (if used) directly over the batter and fold into the batter. Turn into the prepared pan and bake 40 to 45 minutes. The cake is done when it is golden brown and a metal skewer inserted into its center comes out dry and feeling hot when applied to the top of the hand.

Unmold immediately onto a rack and let cool completely before cutting. Trim off the edges if you desire petits fours and cut into as many 1-inch squares as you can manage. Dust with confectioners' sugar. If you prefer bringing the round cake to the table whole, put a decorative doily on it and dust with confectioners' sugar, then lift off the doily; its decorative pattern will be reproduced on the cake by the sugar.

Please do not freeze.

POUND CAKES AND TRUE MADELEINES

A pound cake is a type of butter cake; its recipe always starts with "Cream the butter." It owes its name to its composition, which is one pound each flour, sugar, eggs, and butter. In French this cake is called *quatre-quarts* or "four quarters" for ¼ pound of each main ingredient. The only liquid ingredient is the eggs and all the ingredients are always weighed, taking the weight of the eggs as a base for the other ingredients. If you want to prepare the cake by weight instead of by the always approximate volumes, proceed as follows:

- Weigh a very light transparent plastic measuring cup and take note of its weight.
- Break the eggs into this cup and take note of the total weight of the cup and the eggs. To know the total weight of the eggs, subtract the weight of the cup from the total weight.
- Match the weight of each of the other main ingredients (flour, butter, and sugar) to the weight of the eggs.
- When you weigh the flour, always use two thirds unbleached all-purpose flour and one third cake flour.

Mixing Pattern: Cream the butter until fluffy, add the egg yolks and sugar, beating after each addition. Fold in the dry ingredients; fold in the beaten egg whites.

Ratio of Ingredients per Cup of Sifted and Mixed Flours (⅔ unbleached all-purpose flour and ⅓ cake flour):

½ cup unsalted butter

½ cup granulated sugar

2 large eggs

Leavening Agents: Air introduced by creaming, 25 percent; egg white foam, 75 percent; in modern baking and optional: an additional 10 percent leavening power coming from the carbon dioxide produced by ½ teaspoon of baking powder.

Baking Temperature: 300°F. If a traditional cracked top is desired, start the baking at 325°F and turn the oven down to 300°F as soon as the crack has formed.

Plain 18th-Century Pound Cake or Madeleines

FFR — TWO 7⅜ × 3¾ × 2¼-INCH LOAVES; 32 SLICES

1 cup unsalted butter plus 1 tablespoon to grease the pans

2 medium-size eggs

3 large eggs

Finely grated rind of 1 lemon

2 tablespoons dark rum

1 cup granulated sugar

¼ teaspoon salt

1½ cups sifted unbleached all-purpose flour plus 1 tablespoon to dust the pans

1 teaspoon fresh lemon juice

⅔ cup sifted cake flour

Preheat the oven to 300°F. Cream the 1 cup butter until white on medium speed with an electric mixer. Grease the two small loaf pans each with ½ tablespoon of butter.

When the butter is well aerated, add 1 whole medium egg and 1 medium egg yolk. As you crack the eggs, drop the whites in a large bowl. Beat until the mixture rehomogenizes. Turn the speed down and add the 3 large egg yolks, one at a time and beating after each addition. Add the lemon rind and rum and continue beating the batter a minute or so longer.

Whip in ⅓ cup of the sugar and the salt on medium-high speed until the batter has rehomogenized and all traces of sugar crystals have disappeared. While the sugar homogenizes into the batter, dust each cake pan with ½ tablespoon of the flour. Now, add the remaining ⅓ cup sugar and whip another minute; you should still see a few crystals of sugar in the batter. Transfer the creamed batter to a large bowl. Wash the mixer bowl and beaters carefully with soapy water and rinse well. Wipe dry with paper towels and add the egg whites. Beat them until a small foam (stage 1) forms, then add the lemon juice and continue beating until the foam is perfectly white, looks smooth, and is strong enough to carry the weight of a raw egg in its shell without its sinking into the foam by more than ¼ inch.

While the whites whip, mix the 1½ cups all-purpose flour and the cake flour intimately, sift two thirds of the mixture over the butter/egg/sugar batter and, using a large rubber spatula, fold it in; do not overfold. Now add one quarter of the egg whites, folding. Slide the remainder of the egg whites over the batter, resift the remainder of the flour over the egg whites, and fold all layers together until the batter is perfectly homogenized; it should take you no more than a long minute and the batter should be soft and fluffy, not tough and deflated.

Turn half of the batter into each of the prepared pans and bake 1 hour to 1

This is my mother's family recipe, which dates back to the end of the eighteenth century; its old-fashioned texture resembles the Gâteau à la Madeleine *published by* Menon in Les Petits Soupers de la Cour. *Madeleine Paumier was the young girl who, in Commercy, presented the first known Madeleines to King Louis XV of France. You can, indeed, make delicious Madeleines with this cake batter. Bake them in the traditional shell molds well buttered and dusted with flour, in a 350°F oven to obtain the famous "buckle" on each little shell-shaped cake.*

Since we have excellent electric mixers, I use mine for the creaming of the butter and sugar and the beating of the egg whites. However, it is imperative that you reread and apply the technique of folding as described on page 168, since the flour and the egg whites are introduced into the batter by folding. Any stirring or beating in the presence of the flour will result in gluten development (see page 1008) and a mortarlike cake.

hour and 15 minutes. Check the doneness by inserting a skewer into the center of the cake. If it comes out clean and feels hot to the top of the hand, the cake is done. Let cool a few minutes in the pan, then unmold and cool completely on a rack before wrapping or cutting. The crust should be golden brown and the center soft.

Wrap the cold cakes in plastic wrap, then in aluminum foil, and refrigerate or freeze. Bring back to room temperature before cutting.

FOAM CAKES

TRUE SPONGECAKES   These cakes are called in French *biscuits* (meaning twice cooked) because when they were originally made, the egg yolks and sugar were whipped together in a copper bowl nestled in the lukewarm embers of a fire. This procedure started the poaching of the yolks and trapped tiny bubbles of air into the thick foam before the beaten egg whites and the flour were added to finish the batter. The beaters of the electric mixer provide enough friction heat to replace this cumbersome old technique.

Mixing Pattern: The first direction always given is: Ribbon the egg yolks and sugar together. Beaten egg whites and dry ingredients should be incorporated together into the base of yolks. This Swiss method preserves one quarter more of the volume of the egg whites than the French method in which whites and dry ingredients are added alternately.

Ratio of Ingredients per Cup of Sifted Unbleached All-Purpose Flour:

4 large eggs, separated

½ cup granulated sugar

¼ to ½ cup unsalted butter (the butter is optional since a true spongecake is butterless)

Leavening Agents: Beaten egg yolks and egg whites exclusively

Baking Temperature: It will vary from 325° to 375°F, depending on the composition of the cake.

Ladyfingers

FFR — 2 DOZEN

3 large eggs, separated

⅓ cup granulated sugar

Pinch of salt

1 teaspoon pure vanilla extract

1 teaspoon hot water

⅔ cup sifted unbleached all-purpose flour

Prepare

I pastry bag fitted with a ½-inch nozzle

4 bands parchment paper 4 inches wide and as long as your baking sheet

I large sheet parchment paper covered with a ⅛-inch-thick layer confectioners'
   sugar

2 lightly greased baking sheets

Preheat the oven to 375°F.

In a large bowl, ribbon the egg yolks, sugar, salt, vanilla, and water together very heavily (see page 163). In a medium-size bowl beat the egg whites until their foam can carry the weight of a raw egg in its shell without its sinking into the foam by more than ¼ inch. Mix one quarter of the total volume of the whites into the egg yolk base. Slide the remainder of the whites onto the surface of the yolks. Sift the flour again on top of the whites, then fold in the whites and flour together until the mixture is homogeneous.

Stuff the mixture into the prepared pastry bag. Pipe 6 ladyfingers 3 inches long on each parchment band. Holding each end of the band, invert it onto the parchment covered with confectioners' sugar. Don't worry: The strips of dough will adhere to the paper. When you lift up the paper band, the top of the ladyfingers will be coated with sugar; they need be coated on one side only. Transfer the paper bands of ladyfingers to the greased baking sheet; the greased sheet will keep the paper band in place. Place on the middle rack of the oven and bake at 375°F for 7 minutes, then at 325°F for 5 more minutes. The ladyfingers will be uniformly blond and set throughout.

As soon as baked, remove from the oven and transfer the bands of paper and cakes to the countertop. Align the first ladyfinger of each band with the edge of the counter and pull each band forward so each ladyfinger rolls over the edge of the counter; each cake will loosen from the paper by itself. Cool the biscuits on a cake rack.

Place sheets loaded with sugared ladyfinger bands in the refrigerator if they have to wait to be baked. Cooling retards the deflation of the whites.

Do not freeze ladyfingers; they keep several weeks in a tin.

Praline Chocolate Cake

Do not freeze the filled and decorated cake.

BEST FREEZING STAGE:
Fully baked, wrapped in plastic and aluminum foil

FFR—ONE 10-INCH CAKE; 12 SERVINGS

4 ounces unsweetened chocolate

¼ cup unsalted butter

5 large egg yolks

⅔ cup plus 1 tablespoon granulated sugar

½ teaspoon salt

1 tablespoon pure vanilla extract

7 large egg whites

1 cup sifted cake flour

1½ cups toasted (page 50) slivered blanched almonds

1 cup heavy cream

Confectioners' sugar

3 tablespoons water

3 tablespoons kirsch

½ cup apricot jam

Preheat the oven to 350°F. Generously butter a 10-inch round cake pan.

Melt the chocolate and butter together in a double boiler over hot water (see page 1138); mix well, then let cool and keep ready to use. In a large bowl, ribbon (see page 163) together the yolks, ⅔ cup of the sugar, the salt, and vanilla. Mix in the cooled chocolate mixture and set aside. In another large bowl, whip the egg whites until they can carry the weight of a raw egg in its shell without its sinking by more than ¼ inch into the foam. Mix one quarter of their volume into the chocolate-yolk mixture, slide the remainder of the egg whites on top of the lightened batter, and sift the flour again on top of the whites. Fold all the ingredients together until homogeneous. Turn into the prepared pan and bake until a skewer inserted in the center of the cake comes out clean and feels hot to the top of your hand, 35 to 40 minutes. Cool completely.

To make the almond cream filling, chop ½ cup of the almonds to semifine texture in a food processor or by hand. In a medium-size bowl, whip the cream to the mounding stage, sweetening it to taste with confectioners' sugar as you whip. Fold the ground almonds into the cream; the cream will finish stiffening as you do so.

Mix together the water, kirsch, and the remaining tablespoon of sugar. Stir well to dissolve the sugar completely. Split the cake into two layers (see page 1124). Set the bottom layer on a serving platter and moisten with half the kirsch syrup. Spread almond filling evenly on the bottom layer; top with the second layer. Moisten the top layer and sides with the remainder of the syrup. Refrigerate, covered, and let mellow half a day before finishing.

Melt the apricot jam, then strain through a conical strainer and brush evenly on the top and sides of the cake. Immediately sprinkle with the remaining toasted sliced almonds; dust with confectioners' sugar. Serve within 8 hours.

WHOLE-EGG SPONGECAKE—GÉNOISE This type of cake started being made around the beginning of the nineteenth century and slowly replaced the old-fashioned separated-egg biscuits as described on page 1130. It was apparently the first spongecake/biscuit made with butter. By now it has to be the best-known European cake; it is called the gateau in England, and *Genueser* (Genovese batter) or *warme Teigmasse* (warm batter) in the Germanic countries.

Mixing Pattern: Heavily ribbon (see page 163) whole eggs and sugar together. Fold in the flour, then fold in the butter if butter is used. (Butter is used less and less in the *génoises* currently made in Europe and which go to the freezer by the thousands. This probably accounts for the diminishing quality of some European cakes, for low-fat cakes do not freeze too well.)

Ratio of Ingredients per Cup of Sifted Flour:

4 to 6 large eggs
½ to 1 cup granulated sugar
½ cup unsalted butter or less or even no butter at all

If the baked cake is to be "punched" (moistened) with a liqueur syrup, use little or no butter; if it is not, use as much butter as you like. This general practice is due to the fact that the drier the cake, the more syrup it will be able to absorb. Do not confuse the relatively large amount of syrup used for "punching" a baked cake with the vanilla extract or the tablespoon of liqueur used when mixing its batter to flavor it and tame the strong taste of the egg yolks.

Leavening Agent: 100 percent egg foam

Baking Temperatures: 325°F for the 4-egg *génoises* with little or no butter and 350°F for the 6-egg *génoises* including butter

The *génoise* is one of the most difficult cakes to prepare and I have seen more problems with this cake than with any other. I strongly believe the major difficulty is that the technique of folding is not well understood. Remember, when you prepare this cake that *the folding motion starts at the very center of the bowl*, not on one side of the bowl; please read the detailed folding instructions on page 168 very carefully and practice the movement in an empty bowl before you begin your first *génoise*.

Génoise

FFR — ONE 9- OR 10-INCH CAKE

Plain 4-egg génoise

4 large eggs

1 cup sifted unbleached all-purpose flour

½ cup granulated sugar

¼ teaspoon salt

1 tablespoon pure vanilla extract or liqueur of choice

From no butter up to ½ cup unsalted butter, melted and cooled

Fine 6-egg génoise

6 large eggs

1½ cups sifted cake flour

1 cup granulated sugar

¼ teaspoon salt

1½ tablespoons pure vanilla extract or liqueur of choice

6 to 8 tablespoons clarified butter (page 32), to your taste

Cocoa génoise

6 large eggs

½ cup sifted cake flour

1 cup sifted unsweetened cocoa powder

1 cup granulated sugar

¼ teaspoon salt

1½ tablespoons pure vanilla extract

½ cup clarified butter (page 32)

For the 4-egg génoise: Butter and lightly dust with flour the bottom only of a 10-inch round pan. Preheat the oven to 325°F.

For the 6-egg and cocoa génoises: Use a 9-inch springform pan if you like a high cake, or a 10-inch springform if you like a slightly lower one. Lightly grease the bottom only of the pan; cut a circle of parchment paper large enough to cover the bottom of the pan and reach ½ inch above the separation line of the bottom and sides of the pan. Preheat the oven to 350°F.

Warm the unbroken eggs in warm water. Sift the flour (together with the cocoa for the cocoa *génoise*) again. Warm the mixing bowl and beaters with boiling water; dry both. Start beating the eggs immediately (Mixmaster speed 9, KitchenAid speed 6, handmixer "high" speed).

Add the sugar gradually in a stream. Add the salt; within 2 minutes the batter will start swelling considerably. Continue beating until a light ribbon forms; at this point the mixture will be lukewarm to the fingers. The eggs have somewhat poached and the sugar has formed a syrup, trapping the already dilating air into a foam. Add the flavoring and continue beating until cold.

The ribbon by now should be fat (not thin and round) and when the beater is lifted about 4 inches above the mass of foam, it should fold back and forth upon itself as it slowly falls back into the bowl, resembling precisely a silk ribbon falling onto a table in slow motion. The batter should look yellowish white and have millions of tiny air bubbles, but no large pockets of air. The batter is on the edge of passing into soft peaks. Do not let it do that; stop right now. If you pursue the beating longer, the cake will look and taste cottonlike. If you have a large electric mixer the batter will be done in 12 to 14 minutes; if you have a hand mixer it will take up to 20 minutes. You can also work by hand in a European copper bowl, set over a very low burner, using a large balloon whisk; it will take you no longer in the copper bowl than it will in the electric mixer.

Return the already sifted flour (or flour and cocoa for cocoa *génoise*) to the sifter. Sift one third of its total volume on top of the egg foam. *Fold* the flour into the foam, using a large rubber spatula or your working hand with fingers fully extended. If you use your hand (which was done until large rubber spatulas appeared), the top of your hand should be facing you. Repeat the same operation with the other two thirds of the flour. Do not add the flour in more than three additions or the cake will be overfolded.

Gently pour half the butter on top of the batter. Try to catch it with your spatula before it has time to fall to the bottom of the bowl. Fold *only* until the butter is incorporated; repeat with the remainder of the butter.

Holding the bowl very low over the prepared cake pan, pour the batter into it very slowly. When all the batter is in the pan, grasp the pan with both hands and rap it once only on the counter to break and dislodge any larger air bubbles. Bake the cake on the lowest rack of the oven. Air dilatation and steam pressure will cause the cake to rise regularly and evenly. The cake is done when it has settled within the pan and its edges recede ever so slightly from the sides of the pan, 40 minutes or so. Do not, however, let the cake shrink too much from the pan sides or it will start to dry out. *Invert on a cake rack as soon as removed from the oven.*

Mousseline Buttercream, the Classic Filling for Génoises

Génoises are usually filled with a classic preparation that is nowadays considered a no-no for one's health but which, like everything else, is not going to hurt anyone if enjoyed once in a while. Why so much bother for a once-in-a-while cake? Simply because such a cake is one of the pleasures of life; a sliver of it is really pure joy, especially when the cream is nicely flavored with a great liqueur or chocolate. There are across Europe about twenty different formulas for buttercream. The one below is the most classic and probably the smoothest and best.

FFR — 2½ TO 3 CUPS

½ cup granulated sugar

¼ cup water

2 drops fresh lemon juice

1 cup freshest unsalted butter

5 large egg yolks

Flavoring (1 to 3 teaspoons extract, 2 to 2½ tablespoons liqueur, or 2 to 4 ounces bittersweet chocolate, to your personal taste)

In a small heavy-bottomed saucepan cook the sugar, water, and lemon juice together to the thread stage at minimum and the soft ball stage at most (230° to 234°F; see pages 937–38 for detailed discussion on how to cook a sugar syrup); the rule usually followed is to cook it to 232°F. While the sugar cooks, cream the butter in a large bowl and keep it ready to use.

Clean and dry thoroughly the mixer beaters and start whipping the yolks in a small bowl until they are foamy and very pale yellow. Keep the electric mixer on medium-high speed and pour the hot syrup in a thin stream into the yolks. Continue beating until the mixture forms soft peaks and is completely cold.

Reduce the mixer speed to medium (creaming No. 7 on Mixmasters) and pour half the yolk mixture into the creamed butter (you need not wash the beaters). Beat until rehomogenized. Add any flavoring now, then scrape the remainder of the yolks into the mixture. Scrape the sides of the bowl often and continue beating until the cream is smooth.

You should obtain a perfectly velvety cream that is light and very white. In case it breaks, it will be because your flavoring added too much liquid to the cream and upset the balance of the emulsion. Simply add 1 to 2 more tablespoons butter and the cream will be as good as new. If you wish to flavor with chocolate, melt the chocolate: Let it cool to barely lukewarm, then whip it into the cream. If you want a liqueur and chocolate, add the liqueur after the chocolate.

Any buttercream is safe to consume since you cooked the egg yolks with the bright hot sugar syrup; however, consider it a perishable food that must be kept refrigerated at all times, either in its storing container or on a finished cake. If you have to use a cream that has hardened in a hurry, place the bowl over another bowl filled with warm water. Let the bottom of the cream mellow, then pass it through the mixer for 2 to 3 minutes and the cream will be ready to spread.

ABOUT CHOCOLATE AND GANACHE

Before discussing ganache, it is important that you understand the difference between melting chocolate and tempering chocolate. To do both well, you will need a very accurate instant thermometer; check its accuracy by dipping it in boiling water.

Because of cost, practice with ordinary semisweet chocolate until you are good enough to use any of the imported premium dark chocolates, made with 31 to 40 percent cocoa butter and at least 16 percent cocoa, and white chocolate, made of approximately 30 percent cocoa butter or cocoa butter and dairy butter (not vegetable shortening) mixed, 30 percent sugar, and 30 percent cream or milk.

If you want to become as proficient as a professional at chocolate work, you must go beyond the basics covered here and learn from and practice with a chocolate professional.

Both in the United States and overseas, the composition of all dark and white chocolates varies with the manufacturer. Most chocolate houses publish the composition of their chocolates on the wrapper of the large bars sold to professional bakers and pastry chefs. A large bar is in the long run less expensive than several 3-ounce bars; cut off the weight you need for each use and store the remainder tightly wrapped in a dry place at a temperature as close as possible to 65°F (74°F maximum). If chocolate is stored at too high a temperature, the cocoa butter will melt, showing whitish gray streaks called bloom.

All fats have crystalline structures. In dairy butter the crystals are so very fine that they are not perceived by the taste buds, but if you crush a tiny particle of lard between your tongue and palate, you will perceive its crystals. Refrigerated olive oil acquires a crystalline structure in which the crystals are large and very visible.

When cold or cool, as a component of chocolate together with sugar and the proteins and starches contained in cocoa, cocoa butter is crystalline. The structure of cocoa butter is a combination of four different types of crystals, all identified by the first two letters of the Greek alphabet followed by different numbers. When cocoa butter is warmed, its structure becomes amorphous and it looks like oil.

The bulk of what one should know about working with chocolate mostly concerns the changes of structure in the fats contained in the cocoa butter and their transformations as chocolate is melted and/or tempered.

MELTING CHOCOLATE Chocolate melts when left to stand in a very warm room or when deliberately melted to be incorporated in desserts such as mousses, ice creams, buttercreams, cakes, etc. Chocolate needs only to be melted, never tempered, when incorporated into desserts.

The cardinal rule of melting chocolate is, do not allow any trace of water or steam to come in contact at any time with the melting or melted chocolate, or it will harden or "seize." This hardening of the chocolate will happen as the sugar contained in the chocolate attracts the extraneous moisture and thus disrupts the structural arrangement of the fat crystals present in the chocolate. For this reason, never melt chocolate with a liqueur.

Cool melted chocolate before adding it to whipped egg yolks. Adding hot chocolate to yolks will poach them, stiffen the mixture, and render the incorporation of egg white foam into it difficult.

To melt dark chocolate for use in any dessert recipe: Chop the chocolate into ¼-inch pieces, place in a perfectly dry bowl, and set the bowl over and above water preheated to 160°F. Immediately turn the heat off under the water. Stir with a wooden or plastic spoon or a small rubber spatula until the chocolate has completely melted and its temperature is as close as possible to 90°F and never higher than 115°F. Stirring is essential to prevent the cocoa butter from cooling rapidly and marring the chocolate with visible streaks of its forming crystals.

To prevent seizing, wipe the bottom of the bowl in which the chocolate is to be melted to remove all traces of condensation. If a drop or two of water falls into a batch of melting chocolate, use a paper towel to blot off the water. If you can see a visible change in the structure of the underlying chocolate, use a spoon to remove that part of the chocolate that is affected. If you do not remove the affected chocolate and stir its whole mass, you will see the disturbance spread through the whole bowl and the chocolate turn granular.

If, in spite of all precautions, the melted chocolate seizes, gradually stir small quantities of any good tasting oil (hazelnut and pistachio oils are the most pleasant) into it until its texture comes back to reasonable smoothness. No whole butter can be used since it contains water.

To melt white or milk chocolate for use in any dessert recipe: Proceed exactly as for dark chocolate, keeping the temperature of the water bath at 140°F. Stir until two thirds of the chocolate has melted; remove the bowl from the warm water, wipe the bottom of the bowl dry, and continue stirring until all the chocolate has melted. The temperature of melted white or milk chocolate ready to use should be 87°F. If you overheat white chocolate, it will break into melted cocoa butter and streaks of thick sugar syrup mixed with cocoa butter and lose most of its fine cocoa butter flavor. Since white chocolate in this state is a broken emulsion, you may be able to return it to a workable texture by stirring in liqueur or light cream at the same temperature as the chocolate in successive increments of one to several teaspoons. I have had good success with this method, but it is a fickle process which depends on the quality of the white chocolate and it does not repair the loss of true cocoa butter flavor; if you are successful, use the chocolate immediately.

Observe any excess amount of chocolate that has been melted, not used, and allowed to cool completely to a solid texture again; it will look somewhat gritty and will show "bloom" and porosity. This imperfect appearance explains why one does not simply melt chocolate to coat candies or dried fruit. Chocolate destined to coat candy must be tempered.

TEMPERING CHOCOLATE The goal of tempering chocolate is to obtain a melted chocolate which once cold will remain shiny and hard and offer that delightful "snap" we all enjoy so much when biting through a piece of chocolate candy. The cardinal rules of tempering are:

- Temper in a dry room no warmer than 65° to 70°F; moisture and drafts are not conducive to good tempering.
- Bring the melted chocolate to a high melting temperature, let it cool to a medium temperature, then reheat it again to a high temperature. The last reheating is the most important; it allows crystal Beta 3-VI—the only one among the four types of crystals existing in cocoa butter able to provide shine and snap—to reach its melting point. If that last reheating is not achieved, the tempering is not successful.

Tempering dark chocolate Dark chocolate used to cover chocolate candies is called couverture. It is a special chocolate with a content of cocoa butter varying between 31 and 40 percent.

Divide the total amount of chocolate couverture you need in two parts, one representing two thirds of the total weight of chocolate and the other one third. Melt the first part to 120°F, stirring with a wooden spoon or rubber spatula to prevent blooming. Now add the unmelted chocolate; stir constantly, until the temperature of the chocolate has dipped to just below 80°F. As soon as this happens, reheat the chocolate to its optimum temperature of utilization, which for dark couverture is between 89° and 90°F, never more.

Other methods, each applying the principles explained above, are used to achieve perfect tempering; the method given here is the most practical.

Tempering milk and white chocolates The method to be used is the same as described above and the three successive temperatures to be reached are 115°F for the first two thirds of the chocolate, cooling to 85°F after the addition of the second part of the chocolate, and reheating of the final mass to 87°F.

Coating with white chocolate is anything but easy, and more often than not white coating is prepared with compound white chocolate containing vegetable shortening. You can coat chocolate candies with compound white chocolate without tempering it; just heat it to 100°F.

COATING CANDIES AND DRIED FRUIT The temperature of the room in which you coat should be 65° to 70°F, no higher. Maintain the temperature of the chocolate as indicated above by keeping the container at the proper coating temperature for each type of chocolate (over warm water or on one of those pads used to heat dinner plates). Professional chocolatiers have baths regulated by thermostat. And, most important, make certain that the temperature of the candy centers and dried fruit is no lower than 65° to 70°F or you will see streaking on the surface of the candy.

Chocolate-Coated Soft Prunes

This is a delicious treat for kids.

FFR — 24 PRUNES

12 ounces dark chocolate couverture or premium dark chocolate or milk chocolate

Two 9-ounce cans soft pitted prunes

Temper the chocolate as indicated above. Line a small sheet pan with parchment paper. Working in a cool room, dip the prunes in the chocolate, then, with the help of two small forks, deposit them on the parchment paper. Refrigerate them a few minutes to set the chocolate rapidly, then let them stand in a room with a temperature of 65° to 70°F until dry and shiny.

MAKING GANACHE In our days of reasonable eating, ganache is possibly the best loved chocolate filling and icing for modern *génoises* and spongecakes. There is no doubt that this delicious composition is the best ever "chocolate fix" and, enjoyed once in a while, offers an incomparable treat. It is a mixture of finely chopped chocolate and heated heavy cream or crème fraîche, which is whipped until it cools enough to turn plastic and be spreadable between cake layers or around a whole cake.

The final consistency of a ganache depends on the content of cocoa butter in the chocolate and on the amount of heavy cream used. You can vary taste and texture to fit your own requirements by using diverse chocolates and either the classic amount of cream or less, as you prefer.

Ganache should be prepared with high quality chocolate so the glorious taste of the chocolate comes through unadulterated. It is not rare in the different schools of pastry and confections of Europe to find ganaches flavored with freshly ground coffee, a vanilla bean split in half, or even tea. These flavoring elements are infused in the hot cream and strained out. The flavored cream is then pasteurized again by being held at 160°F for 15 seconds to a full minute before being mixed with the chocolate.

Ganache for Icing and Filling Cakes

FFR—GARNISH FOR ONE 9-INCH CAKE

8 ounces premium dark chocolate or premium white chocolate

I cup heavy cream or crème fraîche

Chop the chocolate as finely as possible. Heat a large mixer bowl with hot water from the tap and dry it completely. Add the chocolate, which will immediately start to melt. Bring the chosen cream to 175°F, pour the cream over the chocolate, and let stand a few minutes. Start the mixer on medium speed and beat until the mixture thickens and keeps the ripples made by the mixer blades. Use immediately to fill or ice a cake.

Stay in the vicinity of the mixer bowl while ganache is whipping and stop the mixture as soon as the proper texture has been reached, or you may see it "break," especially when white chocolate is used. If breakage happens, heat a few tablespoons more cream to barely lukewarm and gradually whip them into the broken ganache, beating on low speed. This is only a quick repair and you must use the cream quickly.

Any ganache should be used the day it is made and any cake garnished with it should be served the same day and be kept refrigerated until 20 minutes before serving.

Ganache for Chocolate Candy Centers

FFR—2 DOZEN CENTERS ¾ INCH IN DIAMETER

Use the same technique and the same amount of chocolate but reduce the amount of cream to ¾ cup or even ½ cup, as preferred. Chill until solid. Using a melon baller or Parisian spoon, cut balls, roll a few seconds between the palms of your hands to round, and bring to 65° to 70°F before coating with the tempered chocolate of your choice.

To learn more about chocolate and chocolate work, see the excellent books listed in the bibliography on page 1175.

Here is a *génoise* made with heavy cream, garnished with chocolate chips and iced with a white chocolate ganache.

A Génoise for Toni

FFR—ONE 9-INCH CAKE; UP TO 16 SERVINGS

Toni is Toni Spinazzola, whose extraordinary reviews brought international success to my Boston restaurant. The plain cake, once fully baked, can be frozen. Do not freeze the iced cake.

For the génoise

¾ cup heavy cream

4 large eggs, warmed in their shells in warm water

Pinch of salt

I cup granulated sugar

I teaspoon ground cinnamon

2 ounces unsweetened chocolate, chopped into ⅛-inch pieces

1¼ cups sifted cake flour

For the decoration

6 ounces excellent white chocolate

¾ cup heavy cream, scalded

4 ounces bittersweet chocolate

Confectioners' sugar

Preheat the oven to 325°F. Butter a 9-inch pan and flour its bottom only. In a small bowl whip the cream until mounding well but not stiff. Ribbon (see page 163) the eggs, salt, sugar, and cinnamon together in a large bowl. While the mixture is whipping, mix the chocolate pieces with the flour. When the ribbon is reached, fold in the flour-chocolate mixture in two additions, then fold in the whipped cream until the batter is homogeneous; do not overfold.

Pour into the prepared pan and bake on the lowest rack in the oven until the sides of the cake start to recede from the edges of the pan, about 40 minutes. Remove from the oven, unmold, and cool completely on a rack.

Chop the white chocolate as small as possible. Place the chocolate in a medium-size bowl, pour the warm cream over it, let stand 5 minutes and start the mixer on low speed. Beat on medium speed (up to 15 minutes) until the mixture thickens. Spread the thickened mixture on the sides and top of the cake.

Melt the bittersweet chocolate in a small bowl placed over and above hot water. Stir until smooth and spread very thinly over a chilled baking sheet. Let the chocolate sheet cool until it appears dull and is plastic. Using a pastry scraper, scrape off long chocolate curls. Decorate the top of the cake with the curls and dust with confectioners' sugar.

CHIFFON CAKES

Chiffon cakes are made with oil exclusively. In spite of being a little sweet, though not as much as angel food cake, they offer a good opportunity to make a very nice cake for heart patients; in it the egg yolks are replaced by another protein (see below).

Mixing Pattern: Blend together the dry ingredients; mix in the oil, egg yolks for the saturated recipe, or well-drained yogurt cheese or well-drained white cheese made from skim milk (page 73) for the unsaturated recipe, and other liquid ingredients. Bake in an *ungreased* tube pan only.

Ratio of Ingredients per Cup of Sifted Cake Flour:

¾ cup granulated sugar

1½ teaspoons baking powder

¼ cup unsaturated oil

3 large egg yolks or 2 tablespoons packed drained chosen cheese

5 tablespoons water

4 large egg whites

Leavening Agents: Egg foam 50 percent; baking powder 50 percent

Baking Temperature: 325°F for three quarters of the baking time and 350°F for the last quarter

A Bigarade Chiffon Cake for Heart Patients

FCR — I CAKE; UP TO 20 SERVINGS

1½ cups nonfat plain yogurt

½ cup nonfat milk

½ cup unsaturated oil (grapeseed, canola, light olive, or corn)

Grated rind of 2 oranges

Scant ⅓ cup fresh orange juice

1 teaspoon angostura bitters

8 large egg whites

¼ teaspoon cream of tartar

2½ cups sifted cake flour

1½ cups granulated sugar

3 teaspoons baking powder

½ teaspoon salt

For the icing

2 cups confectioners' sugar

2 tablespoons Grand Marnier

Fresh orange juice, if needed

½ cup toasted (page 50) chopped peeled hazelnuts

This is a cake for heart patients to enjoy without hesitation. The yogurt cheese replaces the proteins normally supplied by egg yolks and the orange juice-and-bitters mixture substitutes for the needed water. Preferably, do not freeze.

Turn the yogurt into a stainless steel conical strainer lined with cheesecloth. Set the strainer in a large measuring cup, close the cheesecloth over the cheese, and let drip overnight in the refrigerator. You should obtain about ⅓ cup of yogurt cheese. Measure out 4 packed tablespoons of it.

Preheat the oven to 325°F. Have a large tube pan ready.

Place the measured yogurt cheese in a small bowl and gradually stir in the milk and oil; set aside. In another small bowl combine the orange rind, juice, and bitters. Mix well. In a large bowl, beat the egg whites and cream of tartar together until the foam can carry the weight of an uncooked egg in its shell without the egg sinking into the foam by more than ¼ inch.

While the egg whites whip, combine the flour, sugar, baking powder, and salt in another large bowl; mix very well and make a well in the center. Pour in the yogurt and orange mixtures and homogenize well, using a wooden spoon. Mix one quarter of the beaten whites into the batter, then fold in the remainder until the batter is uniformly colored.

Pour into the ungreased tube pan. Bake 50 minutes at 325°F, then another 10 to 15 minutes at 350°F to color the cake. Test doneness by inserting a skewer into the center of the cake; it should come out clean and hot to the top of the hand. Turn the mold over a funnel and let stand until the cake separates from the sides of the pan; when the sides are free, set the tube pan, still upside down, on a cake rack. The cake will slowly fall onto the rack by itself. Do not hurry the process.

To prepare the icing, mix the confectioners' sugar with the Grand Marnier and orange juice if needed until smooth. Drizzle the icing evenly over the top of the cold cake. Sprinkle the hazelnuts over the icing before it sets completely.

VARIATIONS: You may use the following ingredients for variations of this cake to replace the orange rind, orange juice, and bitters.

- ¼ cup apple juice and ground cinnamon to taste
- 3 tablespoons pineapple juice and 2 tablespoons dark rum
- ¼ cup pear puree and 2 tablespoons pear brandy or Grand Marnier
- ¼ cup cherry juice and 2 tablespoons kirsch
- ¼ cup raspberry puree and 2 tablespoons raspberry brandy
- If you use no alcohol, just add ¼ cup fruit juice
- For the icing, adapt the nuts to the fruit and liqueur used, such as pecans for apples, walnuts for pears, macadamias for pineapple, pistachios for cherries and raspberries, etc.

Mock Fondant

NFR—ENOUGH ICING TO DRIP OVER I TUBE CAKE

2 cups sifted confectioners' sugar

I teaspoon fresh lemon juice

Fruit juice or water as needed

Put the sugar into a medium-size bowl. Using a wooden spoon gradually add the lemon juice, then very gradually enough of the chosen liquid or juice for the sugar to turn into an icing that will coat the spoon by ⅛ inch and flow slowly when poured or drizzled over a cake.

This is the easiest icing to prepare and it can be adapted to all possible tastes by using juices of diverse fruit.

Royal Icing or Egg White Icing

NFR—ENOUGH ICING TO DRIP OVER I SHEET OF CLASSIC ALLUMETTES (SEE BELOW)

2 cups sifted confectioners' sugar

I to I ½ large egg whites

3 drops fresh lemon juice

Mix the sugar together with enough egg whites and the lemon juice to obtain a glaze consistency.

This is obtained by mixing confectioners' sugar with eggs whites and lemon juice. Please do not use this icing if it is not to be cooked. Use it exclusively in pastries—such as puff pastries— which are glazed before being cooked and on which the icing bakes to a very pleasant crispy layer.

Classic Allumettes

FFR—24 ALLUMETTES FOR TEATIME

I recipe Modern Puff Pastry (page 1090)

I recipe Royal Icing (preceding recipe)

Preheat the oven to 400°F. Roll the pastry out into two rectangular sheets ¼ inch thick. Chill the sheets 15 minutes. With a pizza wheel, cut the sheets into rectangles 1 × 3 inches, called *allumettes*, and transfer them to a pastry sheet lined with a sheet of parchment paper.

Using a tiny pastry brush, spread the icing over the *allumettes*, taking care not to let it drip along the edges of the cakes. Chill another 15 minutes, then bake until the icing looks uniformly beige, 12 to 15 minutes. Cool on a rack and enjoy while fresh and barely lukewarm.

Chocolate Mayonnaise Icing

For cakes that have been first glazed with a strained jam or jelly, which will prevent cake crumbs from pitting the chocolate icing.

FFR — 1½ TO 2 CUPS

5 ounces best bittersweet chocolate, broken into pieces

½ cup hot water

⅔ cup granulated sugar

1 drop fresh lemon juice

Melt the chocolate in a double boiler over simmering water. Add 1 tablespoon of the hot water and stir to homogenize the mixture. Meanwhile, put the remaining water, the sugar, and the lemon juice in a small heavy-bottomed saucepan and cook to 238°F (see cooking a sugar syrup, page 937).

Remove the melted chocolate from the heat. Using a wooden spoon, very gradually stir the hot sugar syrup into the chocolate, stirring as if you were adding oil to a mayonnaise. Keep stirring until the icing cools to barely lukewarm.

To ice a cake with this icing, slowly pour the icing at the very center of the cake. Now put the oven on at 100°F for 2 minutes and turn it off. Open the door and set the cake in front of the opened oven for a few minutes so the icing dries out gradually and stays shiny. Any cold air blowing on this icing before it has dried will dull it. Once the icing is dry, the cake can be refrigerated.

FLOURLESS CAKES: THE TORTEN

Flourless cakes are called *Torten*; they are some of the most delicious cakes existing, made as they usually are with ground nuts and egg whites or separated eggs. Once again there is no certitude as to where exactly these cakes, basically made with a meringue mixed with nuts and sometimes crumbs, originated. Some think of Meyringen in Switzerland as the birthplace of meringues, while others maintain that meringue "happened" at the beginning of the seventeenth century in France where a flat dish of baked egg whites and sugar flavored with orange flower water, musk, and ambergris was all the rage. One thing is certain, these cakes reflect a great spirit of economy on the part of the bakers who first thought to not use the flour that was much needed for bread to make their cakes, and instead used old bread crumbs. Vienna seems to have been the champion of this type of cake since the eighteenth century.

There are two types of *Torten*, whole-egg *Torten* and egg white *Torten*.

WHOLE-EGG TORTEN Whole-egg *Torten* are spongecakes (see page 1133), made with nuts or nuts mixed with bread crumbs instead of flour.

Mixing Pattern: The technique is familiar. The egg yolks are ribboned with sugar and the beaten egg whites topped with ground nuts are folded into the ribboned mixture.

Ratio of Ingredients per Cup of Ground Nuts:

3 large eggs, separated

⅓ **cup bread crumbs or cake crumbs, toasted or not toasted, as preferred**

⅓ **cup granulated sugar**

Leavening Agent: 100 percent egg foam

Baking Temperature: 350°F

EGG WHITE TORTEN

Mixing Pattern: The egg whites are beaten until they are firm enough to carry the weight of a raw egg in its shell without its sinking into the foam by more than ¼ inch; the nuts mixed with the sugar are folded into the whites until the mixture is homogeneous.

Ratio of Ingredients per Cup of Ground Nuts:

3 large eggs, separated

⅓ **cup plus 1 tablespoon granulated sugar**

Leavening Agent: 100 percent egg white

Baking Temperature: 325°F

Canadian Torte

FFR— 1 DOUBLE-LAYER 8-INCH CAKE OR ONE SINGLE-LAYER
9-INCH CAKE; 16 SERVINGS

For the cake

6 large eggs, separated

⅔ **cup maple or granulated sugar**

¼ **teaspoon salt**

1 teaspoon instant espresso granules

¼ **teaspoon maple flavoring**

2 cups finely ground walnuts

⅔ **cup plus 3 tablespoons vanilla wafer crumbs**

For the buttercream

¼ **cup granulated sugar**

⅔ **cup pure dark grade B maple syrup**

9 large egg yolks

1½ **cups unsalted butter or more if needed**

1 tablespoon pure vanilla extract or 2 tablespoons Cognac

Use maple sugar if you can find it in your neck of the woods. Please do not freeze this cake.

For the decoration

1 recipe praline made with walnuts (page 51)

½ cup granulated sugar

12 walnut halves

Preheat the oven to 350°F. Grease two 8-inch cake pans or one 9-inch springform pan. If using the latter, cut a circle of parchment paper large enough to reach ¼ inch above the separation line between the bottom and side of the pan and fit into the lightly greased bottom of the pan.

In a large bowl, ribbon (see page 163) the egg yolks and sugar together until pale and lemon colored. Add the salt, coffee, and maple flavoring and continue to beat the eggs until they spin a very thick and heavy ribbon. In another large bowl, whip the eggs whites until they can carry the weight of a raw egg in its shell without sinking more than ¼ inch into the foam. Lighten the base of yolks with one quarter of the whites, then slide the remainder of the whites over the batter, sprinkle with the walnuts and crumbs mixed together, and fold until the batter is homogeneous.

Pour into the prepared pan(s) and bake until a skewer inserted at the center comes out clean and hot to the top of the hand, 25 to 30 minutes if using 8-inch pans and 35 to 40 if using a 9-inch springform pan. Cool on a rack and unmold. When cold, slice the larger cake in two layers (see page 1124).

To prepare the cream, bring the sugar and maple syrup to a boil in a small, heavy-bottomed saucepan and cook to 232°F (see page 938). Meanwhile, start whipping the egg yolks in a medium-size bowl. Once they are pale and yellow, gradually add the hot syrup, continuing to whip on high speed until the mixture has quadrupled in volume and is cold.

Meanwhile, cream the butter in a large bowl and, when it is nice and fluffy, pour the cold yolk mixture into the butter. Whip, gradually adding in the vanilla, until the mixture forms soft peaks. Finish with 1 or 2 more tablespoons of butter if the cream show signs of instability.

To finish the cake, fill the cake with half the buttercream. Spread a quarter of it all around the sides and top of the cake. Pipe the remainder into twelve rosettes of cream all around the top of the cake. Crush the praline coarsely and coat the sides of the cake with it. Surround the cake with a large band of parchment paper and press gently to imprint the praline into the buttercream.

Cook the remainder of the sugar into a blond caramel (see page 938). Dip the walnut halves into the caramel to coat each very well, then cool on a very lightly buttered sheet. Top each rosette with one caramel-dipped walnut meat. Refrigerate until ready to serve; bring back to room temperature before serving.

Chocolate Torte

FFR — ONE 10-INCH CAKE; 10 TO 12 SERVINGS

Meringue layers

3 large egg whites

Pinch of salt

Pinch of cream of tartar

⅓ cup plus 1 tablespoon granulated sugar

1 cup finely ground hazelnuts

½ teaspoon grated orange rind

Preheat the oven to 325°F. Butter and flour a large baking sheet, shaking the excess flour off. Using the bottom of a 10-inch pan, trace two circles on the sheet.

In a medium-size bowl, beat the egg whites with the salt, cream of tartar, and 1 tablespoon of the sugar. As soon as they are stiff enough to carry the weight of a raw egg in its shell without its sinking more than ¼ inch into the foam, fold in the remaining sugar thoroughly mixed with the hazelnuts and orange rind. Spread half the meringue on each of the two circles drawn on the baking sheet in an even ⅛-inch-thick layer. Bake until the layers are golden and done, 20 to 25 minutes. Loosen them immediately with a long spatula and gently slide them onto a rack to cool completely.

Génoise

⅔ cup sifted unsweetened cocoa powder

3 tablespoons unsifted cake flour

Pinch of salt

4 large eggs

½ cup granulated sugar

2 teaspoons pure vanilla extract

¼ cup clarified butter (page 32)

Preheat the oven to 350°F. Butter and flour the bottom of a 9-inch pan. Sift the cocoa, flour, and salt together. In a large bowl, ribbon (see page 163) the eggs and sugar together very heavily. Add the vanilla and ribbon again until the ribbon falls into the batter, folding very slowly upon itself and the batter shows no traces at all of larger air bubbles. Fold in the dry ingredients, then the butter.

Turn the batter into the prepared pan and bake until the cake has settled into the pan and slightly separates from the edges of the pan, 30 to 35 minutes. Unmold immediately onto a cake rack and cool completely.

There are two ways to enjoy this cake, the Swiss way, serving it with crisp meringue layers, and the French way, refrigerating the cake overnight to allow the meringue to absorb moisture from the buttercream and cake. You can use a number of liqueurs besides the tangerine recommended here: green Chartreuse, Grand Marnier, Kahlúa, kirsch, reduced port, etc.

Each component—meringue, cake, and buttercream—is described separately with its own list of ingredients and can be made individually at different times. The meringue layers will keep very dry in a large round canister containing a small plastic bag of cornstarch punched with several tiny holes. The buttercream must be made on the day the cake is put together.

Please do not freeze this cake.

Buttercream

⅓ cup granulated sugar

2 tablespoons water

3 large egg yolks

2 tablespoons Mandarin Napoléon or Grand Marnier

½ cup unsalted butter, at room temperature

In a small, heavy-bottomed saucepan, cook the sugar and water to 232°F (see page 938). In the meantime, beat the egg yolks in a medium-size bowl until they spin a light ribbon. As soon as the sugar is cooked, pour it in a thin stream into the egg yolks, beating continuously until barely lukewarm. Beat in the liqueur and beat until cold and thick. Cream in the butter tablespoon by tablespoon until the cream is well emulsified. If 1 more tablespoon of butter is needed, do not hesitate to add it.

Assembly

6 tablespoons Mandarin Napoléon or Grand Marnier

2 tablespoons granulated sugar

3 tablespoons water

Confectioners' sugar

24 peeled pistachios

With a serrated knife, using small cutting motions so as not to break the meringue, slowly trim off the edge of each meringue layer until it exactly matches the size of the cake. Place one meringue layer, smooth side down, on a cake platter. Spread it evenly with half the buttercream.

Mix the liqueur, sugar, and water together and mix until the sugar has dissolved. Brush half this syrup on one side of the cake. Invert this moistened side on top of the creamed meringue. Now brush the other side of the cake with the remainder of the syrup. Gently spread the remainder of the buttercream on top of the cake and carefully invert the second meringue layer on top of the cream. When ready to serve, sprinkle the top of the cake with confectioners' sugar. Trace a crisscross pattern through the sugar with the back of a knife blade and set one pistachio at the center of each diamond formed by the crisscrossed lines.

Pistachio Raspberry Roll

FFR — 12 SERVINGS

Four 10-ounce boxes frozen raspberries, thawed

6 large eggs, separated

⅔ cup granulated sugar

Pinch of salt

If pistachios are too expensive or time consuming, use almonds and add 1 teaspoon pure almond extract to the batter. The syrup from the raspberries mixed with a

2½ tablespoons kirsch, Framboise, or brandy

2 cups ground peeled pistachios

¾ teaspoon baking powder

1½ cups heavy cream

Confectioners' sugar

1 pint fresh raspberries

Fresh mint leaves

few tablespoons of lemon juice can be made into a refreshing sorbet. The baking powder is in the batter to slightly dry it. Please do not freeze this cake.

Quickly drain the thawed berries from their syrup and immediately puree in a blender. Strain and place in a large, heavy-bottomed saucepan. Over medium heat, cook down to ¼ cup of thick puree. Cool and set aside.

Preheat the oven to 325°F. Fit a sheet of parchment paper into a lightly greased 15 × 12-inch jelly-roll pan. Butter the paper.

In a large bowl, ribbon (see page 163) the egg yolks, sugar, and salt together. Add 1 tablespoon of the kirsch and continue beating until the ribbon is extremely heavy. In another large bowl, whip the egg whites until they can carry the weight of a raw egg in its shell without sinking more than ¼ inch into the foam. Mix one quarter of their volume into the yolks. Slide the remainder of the whites over the yolk mixture. Sprinkle with the ground pistachios and baking powder mixed together, and fold until homogeneous. Pour the batter evenly into the prepared pan. Bake until golden, 12 to 15 minutes. Remove from the oven and cover the cake with two layers of moist paper towels. Let stand until cool.

Whip the cream to the Chantilly stage (see page 29), blending it with the

ROLLING UP A JELLY ROLL

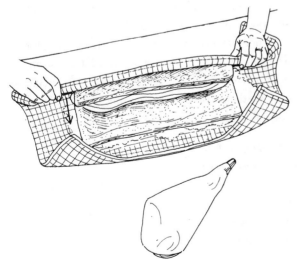
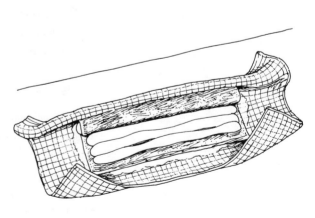
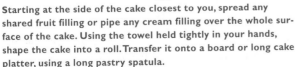

Starting at the side of the cake closest to you, spread any shared fruit filling or pipe any cream filling over the whole surface of the cake. Using the towel held tightly in your hands, shape the cake into a roll. Transfer it onto a board or long cake platter, using a long pastry spatula.

cold raspberry puree and the remaining kirsch. Sweeten to taste with confectioners' sugar.

Put a clean kitchen towel on the countertop, sprinkle it lightly with confectioners' sugar, and turn the cake upside down into the sugar. Remove the baking paper and trim the edges, using a sharp knife. Spread the raspberry cream over the cake, leaving 1½ inches of cake free of cream on the longer side of the cake closer to you. Roll the cake over lengthwise using the towel held tightly between your hands to roll it forward. If the shape is slightly irregular, shape it with your hands. Sprinkle with confectioners' sugar and arrange the fresh raspberries and mint leaves all along the top of the cake.

Because of the size of this book already, I am not offering any instructions for petits fours and cookies. However, all the techniques needed to be able to prepare petits fours have been explained in both the egg and the baking chapters. See the bibliography for an excellent volume dedicated entirely to these delicacies.

For Cooks Who Will Have to Bake at High Altitudes

Bakers born in mountainous regions have no difficulty adjusting their recipes, because the women in their families have done it for generations. Such is not the case for the people who move to a mountainous area or the young traveling cook who arrives in Colorado and starts baking biscuits in the middle of the Rockies. These were towering biscuits; the experience was repeated when I forgot completely that the little town in Wyoming I had settled in for vacation sits way up there, around 3,200 feet.

When thinking "altitude baking," bear in mind that texture problems start happening around and above 3,000 feet or 1,000 meters, and get steadily worse as the altitude climbs. Let's take the case of my biscuits and examine what I should have done to make sure that they looked as "civilized" as ever. Here is the original formula:

2 cups sifted unbleached all-purpose flour

2 teaspoons double-acting baking powder

Salt

3 tablespoons granulated sugar

⅔ cup shortening or ½ cup unsalted butter

4 to 5 tablespoons water as needed

Plain and simple, to be baked at 425° to 450°F.

They rose so high they almost had holes in their sides and they had the funniest truncated look. All I had to do was change a few amounts in the recipe and they would have been as normal as ever. Which amounts then?

First the baking powder. Since carbon dioxide encounters less pressure from its surroundings in altitude, the amount of baking powder used should have been decreased because there was less pressure to overcome on the surface of the biscuits. It is clear that my biscuits were bound to "overstretch" and they did, and beautifully so. I should have reduced the amount of baking powder by ⅛ teaspoon. Had I been at 5,000 feet, it would have been a reduction of about ⅙ teaspoon and around 7,000 feet ¼ teaspoon.

At the same time, it would have been smart to increase the liquid and use approximately 3½ teaspoons more because, in altitude, water vaporizes (sublimates into steam) at a lower temperature. Had I been at 5,000 feet, it would have been an increase of 2½ tablespoons and at 7,000 feet of 3½ tablespoons. I could also have reworked the original recipe, replacing additional water with one egg white or half of a whole egg, both containing proteins which would have reinforced the structure of the biscuit dough and prevented it from rising wildly.

Notice that I did not mention egg yolks alone; since to strengthen the structure of the biscuits it also helps to remove some fat from a high-altitude recipe, using egg yolks, which contain a lot of fat, would not make sense. But, indeed, if you remove a small amount of fat, such as 1½ teaspoons per cup of flour, the product will be more stable with less possibility for the dough to overstretch.

And finally, I should have reduced the amount of sugar by half to two thirds, to have no more than 1½ tablespoons sugar in the dough because water evaporating faster in high altitude helps the sugar concentrate faster. Here is the reworked recipe:

2 cups plus 1 tablespoon sifted unbleached all-purpose flour

1⅛ teaspoons double-acting baking powder

1½ tablespoons granulated sugar

7 tablespoons unsalted butter

¼ cup plus ½ teaspoon water, or 1 large egg white plus 1 tablespoon water,

or 1 large egg, beaten

Salt

If you bake cakes at high altitude, it is a good idea to increase the baking temperature by 20° to 25°F to provoke faster coagulation of the protein structure and allow the batter to set before the batter cells have had the time to overstretch; greasing the pan very generously and flouring it extremely lightly to allow the batter to slide upward rapidly and without sticking even the slightest little bit to the sides of the pan is also very useful.

Glossary

THIS GLOSSARY EXPLAINS SOME SCIENTIFIC, HISTORIC, AND CULINARY TERMS which may not be familiar to the cook. If you are a beginner cook, it is a good idea to become familiar with any word that is new to you; it will make the reading of any cookbook or food science book easier.

Words in **boldface** have their own individual glossary entries for further reference.

ACIDS IN FOODS: Any substance tasting sour such as lemon or other citrus fruits and their juices, vinegars, and reduced table wines are said to be acid because they respectively contain citric, acetic, malic, and tartaric acids. On the pH scale, acids are measured from 6 to 1 (*see* **pH**), 7 being neutral.

ADDUCTOR MUSCLE: The muscle that controls the closing and opening of the shell of a bivalve mollusk. All types of scallops as sold in the United States are the adductor muscles of diverse types of medium to large clams known as the pectenidae.

AEROBIC; ANAEROBIC: Terms applied to bacteria. Aerobic bacteria cannot survive without oxygen, anaerobic will. In food handling, the most important and dangerous anaerobic bacterium is *Clostridium botulinum* (see **botulin**).

ALBUMEN: A synonym for egg white.

ALBUMINS: Albumins are simple heat-coagulable proteins to be found in animal tissues and substances and in many plant tissues, among them blood, muscles, egg white, and milk.

AL DENTE: An Italian expression applied in all western kitchens to a pasta cooked just until enough resistance is left in it to be felt "by the teeth." Often, and by extension in modern cookery, the expression is also applied to vegetables that have been cooked crisp by steaming, boiling, or stir-frying.

ALKALINE FOODS: Another term for alkaline is basic. Milk is about neutral to slightly acidic, 6.6 to 6.9; egg whites are basic. The most common base used in cookery is sodium bicarbonate, also called baking soda. It has a soapy taste in solution and can give a cake a soapy taste if used in too large quantity. On the pH scale alkalis are greater than 7 (8.0 to 14), 7 being neutral.

ALLUMETTES: The French equivalent to the English "matchstick"; in cooking it refers particularly to the crisp ¼-inch-thick matchsticks of deep-fried potatoes. In pastry language it designates narrow puff pastry strips topped either with grated cheese and served for cocktails or brushed with icing and baked as small dessert pastries.

ALUMINUM FOIL: Use the strongest possible food-quality aluminum foil. When you cook in it, the dull side which absorbs heat should face out. When you want to protect food from further browning, the shiny side, which refracts heat, should be on the outside.

AMINO ACIDS: Proteins are made of several amino acids attached to one another. Amino acids always contain carbon, hydrogen, nitrogen, and oxygen, and sometimes sulfur. Whatever its particular composition, an amino acid will always contain one amino group (-NH) and one carboxyl group (-COOH).

AMONTILLADO: A fine dry sherry and light amber-colored wine from Montilla, a village and district south of the city of Cordoba in Spain.

AMYLASE: An enzyme responsible for the hydrolysis of starches (*see* **hydrolysis**) into **maltose** and water. This enzyme can, under certain circumstances, cause sauces thickened with a **roux** or a pure starch to lose their thickness and turn soupy in texture and sweet in taste, proof that the amylase reacted with the starch, producing maltose.

AMYLOSE AND AMYLOPECTIN: The two components of starch; the ratio of the components is 20 to 30 percent amylose and 70 to 80 percent amylopectin.

ANCHOVIES: All anchovies now come from the oceans, the Mediterranean types being extinct. Preferably use anchovy fillets preserved in salt. Rinse them carefully under running cold water. Since they remain quite salty, watch the final seasoning of your dish.

ANGLAISE: The word means "the English one" and is a seasoned mixture of egg or egg white (in modern dietetic cookery), oil, and water brushed over floured items, which are then deep-fried or panfried in clarified butter or oil. The term probably came into usage to distinguish it from the Italian way of dipping pieces to be fried in a pastella, or egg, flour, and milk batter, and from the plain French way of simply flouring before pan- or deep-frying.

ANTHOCYANINS: The blue, purple, or red coloring pigments found in fruits, vegetables, and flowers.

ANTIOXIDANTS: Chemical substances added to foods to prevent their reacting with oxygen. Antioxidants are added to fruit to inhibit browning when they are cut and exposed to air; they also inhibit rancidity in fats and oils.

APPAREIL: A French culinary term applied to a basic culinary or pastry preparation made of diverse ingredients. It can apply to a savory **forcemeat** (quenelle), to a cake batter (génoise), or to a basic confectionery mass (macaroon).

ARBORIO OR ARBORIO SUPER-FINO: The name(s) given to some of the best short-grained rices grown in the Po Valley of Italy, and used to prepare the Lombardy **risotto**.

ARMAGNAC: A French spirit prepared in the southwestern part of France, south of the Garonne River. Its bouquet and aroma make it the perfect companion to fowl, game birds, and venison.

AROMATICS: All the ingredients that contribute to enhance and develop both the flavor and the aroma of culinary preparations. Herbs, a **bouquet garni**, certain vegetables, garlic, and **persillade** are considered aromatics. The chief aromatic vegetables are all members of the onion family, in addition to carrots, celery, and mushrooms, cut into the following sizes: ⅛-inch cubes (**brunoise**); ¼-inch cubes (**mirepoix**); ⅓-inch cubes (**salpicon**); ¼-inch strips (**julienne**); and ⅛-inch strips (**paysanne**).

ARROWROOT: A fine starch extracted from the rhizomes of plants of the genus *Maranta*, especially *M. arundinacea*, which originated in Guiana and northern Brazil and has been brought to and cultivated in the West Indies and most tropical areas. East Indian arrowroot is obtained from the root stocks of *curcuma*, chiefly *C. angustifolia*. The name arrowroot may come from the fact that the Indians of the West Indies used it to dress arrow wounds.

BACTERIA: Microscopic organisms that range from harmless and useful (as in the fermentation of some foods such as cheeses) to detrimental to good health (as in the types which develop in foods and bring on food-borne illness).

BAIN-MARIE: What one calls in English a hot water bath. This word is a translation into French of the Italian *bagno maria*, derived from the name of Maria di Cleofa, a fourteenth-century alchemist. Also known by the professional name of Cleopatra the Wise, she described how she initiated and used a hot water bath in her *Treaty on Distillation* (this information is included in Waverley Root's book *The Food of Italy*). The bain-marie is used to diffuse the heat when melting chocolate and in some techniques of cooking egg-bound sauces.

BAKE (TO): To slow roast a food placed on a rack set over a roasting pan, uncovered, in an oven or ovenlike appliance preheated to 325°F or below. This term applies to meats and vegetables as well as to casserole-type preparations and to some cakes.

BARBECUE (TO): To very slowly bake a piece of meat in a barbecue pit, the meat being brushed at regular intervals with a favorite barbecue sauce and kept covered all through the baking.

The term *barbecuing* is increasingly applied to grilling meat or other foods over a wood charcoal grill. See charcoal grilling on pages 739–40.

BARDER, BARD (TO): Verb used to describe an old-fashioned technique in which a piece of meat or a bird is wrapped in a sheet of pork fat (fatback) before being roasted, so that the moisture contained in the fat can protect the outer surface of the meat or the bird skin from drying out.

Barding has, in this manner disappeared from modern cookery; rather, the pork fat is sometimes replaced by pancetta or bacon, which has more of a seasoning effect than a moisturizing one, since the curing process removes a large percentage of moisture. Some modern cooks prefer to coat lean pieces of meat with bread crumbs or a mixture of bread crumbs, nuts, and aromatics, or any of those used separately.

BASMATI: The name of the most deliciously flavored long-grain rice from India, see page 459.

BASTER: The well-known large kitchen syringe used to baste meats with their own forming gravy, another liquid, or even melted fat to prevent their outer surfaces from overdrying.

A baster is also the most inexpensive and best implement to separate the lean and fat parts of a gravy completely.

BATTER: A semiliquid mixture of flour, eggs, a liquid such as milk or water, and sometimes fat used to prepare pancakes, cakes, muffins, and quick breads of diverse categories. Also applies to frying batters.

BAVARIAN CREAM: The French *bavaroise* (twentieth-century nomenclature) or *fromage bavarois* (Carême's nomenclature in the first half of the nineteenth century) translates into English as Bavarian cream. Escoffier in *Le Guide Culinaire* prefers to use the name *Muscovite*. It is a stirred custard stabilized with gelatin and lightened with softly whipped cream, which is served chilled. The modern technique of making Bavarian cream is described on pages 149–53.

BÉARNAISE: A warm emulsified egg-and-butter sauce. Unfortunately too often called bernaise, which would mean that it comes from Bern in Switzerland, instead of béarnaise, taking its name from Henri le Béarnais, king of the former Béarn, which became a province of France after Henri ascended to the crown of France under the name of Henri IV.

The king himself had nothing to do with the creation of the sauce as you will see by reading its probable history and modern techniques on pages 344–54.

BEAT (TO): To agitate a mixture with the goal of making it smooth and introducing as much air as possible into it. When beating by hand, the mixture must be lifted up again and again with a wooden spoon or a whisk. Beating by hand is sometimes better than beating with an electric mixer; see the **brioche** technique on page 1045 as a typical example.

BÉCHAMEL: A classic white sauce made with aromatic vegetables, a white **roux**, and whole milk. It is used less and less in modern cuisine but cooks must continue to be aware of its composition and techniques since several preparations in French and Italian cuisines still use it. See pages 276–79 for more information on its origins and techniques.

BEURRE: The French word for plain butter. The word still appears in several preparations used currently in American kitchens. See the definitions and techniques for *beurre noisette* (brown butter) on page 32, *beurre blanc* (white butter) on page 332, and *beurres composés* (compound butters) on page 302. *Beurre noir* is butter that has been allowed to turn dark brown and which, knowing as much as we do nowadays about the effects of saturated fats on the vascular system, we should really not use anymore; it is very advantageously replaced by *beurre noisette*, which is no less saturated but is at least not partly burned.

BEURRE MANIÉ: A mixture of butter and flour mashed into a paste and used for quick thickening of a sauce. See pages 287–88 for the proper technique.

BINDER: Any starchy ingredient (flour, pure starches, rice) or proteinic ingredient (egg yolks, liver) that will thicken a sauce or batter.

BISQUE: The name given in the old classic cuisine to a soup also called **coulis** made with any shellfish, but primarily with sweet or brackish water crayfish. It is rarely prepared nowadays due to the high cost of shellfish, the time involved in preparing it, and the almost too opulent taste and texture of the soup. The crayfish was first **étuvéed** with a **mirepoix** and its cooking completed in **consommé.** Rice was also cooked in consommé. The shells of the crayfish and the rice were pounded in a mortar, diluted with more consommé, and strained through a very fine muslin. The soup was finished with a large amount of butter and a small amount of crème fraîche and garnished with the crayfish tails. Any cook curious to know the correct formula can consult Escoffier's clear explanations in the English translations of the *Le Guide Culinaire.*

In almost all modern cuisines the term bisque seems nowadays to be applied to all kinds of modern soups based on purees of vegetables.

BIVALVE: Any mollusk with a two-part shell, the opening of which is controlled by an **adductor muscle.** Common bivalves are mussels, clams, oysters, and scallops.

BLANCH (TO): The meaning varies. For young fresh vegetables, to cook rapidly in boiling salted water to preserve color and texture. For old pungent vegetables (cauliflower, Brussels sprouts, cabbage, leeks), to parboil in boiling water to lessen their pungency. The blanching water is discarded.

For meats, some salted meats such as bacon may be blanched to get rid of most of the salt, but in this case, the blanching starts in cold water.

BLANQUETTE: A classic white stew made with veal shoulder or the dark meat of poultry (the white meat does not stew gracefully), simmered either in water or white stock, and always with aromatic vegetables.

The white sauce of the stew is made with the cooking broth bound with a white **roux** and enriched with a **liaison** of egg yolks and cream. The classic garnishes were mushrooms and sometimes **quenelles** of white meat of chicken or veal meat. In modern cuisine, the garnish can be any vegetable you like. For detailed techniques, see pages 832–34.

BLEND (TO): To gently mix two or more ingredients together, or to process in a modern electric blender.

BOIL (TO): To cook any food by immersing it in rapidly boiling water (212°F or 100°C—at sea level and normal atmospheric pressure). Water and other liquids boil at a lower temperature at higher altitude, see page 977.

BORDELAISE: The name of a sauce made with wine from the region of Bordeaux. Up to the late years of the nineteenth century it was, following the techniques of Carême, made by Urbain Dubois and Jules Gouffé with the sweet white Sauternes. Several members of the *cuisine nouvelle* movement attempted, most of the time poorly, to resurrect this sauce.

Red wine reductions were used very early in western cuisine, especially in France and there are records of such sauces existing in the cuisines of all regions of France where red wines are made long before the advent of the classic cuisine. The Bordelaise as produced in the classic cuisine of the very late nineteenth and early twentieth centuries is a blend of *espagnole* sauce (page 284) with a reduction of good red Bordeaux wine mixed with shallots and coarsely cracked white pepper (*mignonette*); it appears in Escoffier's *Le Guide Culinaire* and in Montagné and Salles's *Grand Livre de la Cuisine* in two different but equally excellent versions.

BOTULIN: A deadly toxin secreted by the anaerobic bacterium *Clostridium botulinum.* Occasionally found in canned non- and low acid foods (vegetables, especially) that have not been processed long enough to completely kill any C. *botulinum* spore existing on the surface of a vegetable. There is no way—either by look or smell—to know whether a can is contaminated or not. It is good practice: 1. Not to taste the contents of any can immediately after opening it; and 2. To reboil the content of a can of vegetables for a full 20 minutes, which renders the toxin impotent (this is particularly important when using canned legumes).

BOUILLABAISSE: The name given in Marseilles, France, to one of the multiple versions of the ancestral eastern Mediterranean seafood soup. It was brought to this region by the Phocaean Protis and his men, who were Greeks from Asia Minor and founded the ancient city of Massilia (Mas-

salia), now Marseilles, around 600 B.C. The name of the soup is derived from the ancient three-footed cast-iron pot in which it was cooked for centuries and which, in this region, is called a *bouillet.*

BOUILLON: French for broth. Used to refer to the liquid resulting from simmering meats, vegetables, and aromatics in water until the meats have lost all their nutritional elements to the water and the broth can jell upon cooling. See also **fonds** and **stock.**

BOUQUET GARNI: A small or large bundle of parsley stems (for more flavor), a sprig of fresh or dried thyme, and a bay leaf (small if California, large if Mediterranean or Turkish), tied together and left to float freely in whatever broth, stock, or sauce it will flavor, so as to release a maximum amount of taste. The composition of a bouquet garni can vary to include other aromatics such as a leek or celery stalk, depending on the choice and taste of the cook.

BRAISE (TO); BRAISIÈRE: Originally *braiser* in French, meaning to cook in a tightly covered specialized pot called a *braisière* with just enough liquid to barely cover the meat in the case of a stew, or to reach halfway to the top of the meat if preparing a whole piece of meat or bird. The words *braiser* and *braisière* originated from the fact that, when one cooked on the hearth, the pot was buried in hot embers (*braise* in French). The techniques of braising are nowadays often ill understood and not done with enough precision for good results. Please refer to pages 815–21 for full details.

BRINE (TO): To soak a meat to be preserved or smoked in a solution of salt. See pages 641.

BRIOCHE: The famous flour, egg, and yeast cake of northern France, which is now made in one form or another throughout that country. For a discussion of its origin and making, see pages 1043–48.

BRUNOISE: Aromatic vegetables diced into ⅛-inch cubes. Their size is that small because they are usually included in a sauce accompanying a fish or white meat, more rarely a red meat.

CALORIE: The unit of measurement of the energy- (or heat-) producing contents in foods when metabolized in the body.

CALVADOS: In Normandy the brandy distilled from hard cider is called Calvados, because some of those brandies are produced in an area which acquired that same name after the wreck on one of its beaches of the ship *Calvador*, a member of the great Spanish Armada. Calvados can be replaced by applejack, our American apple brandy.

CANDY (TO): 1. To cook fruit or fruit peels in a syrup until they turn translucent; 2. To season some vegetables (sweet potatoes, carrots, butternut squash) with a brown sugar syrup, an old-fashioned delicious practice, unfortunately somewhat detrimental to the waistline.

CARAMEL: The product obtained when sugar is cooked until all water has evaporated out of it and the melted syrup has started its cycle of browning. Caramel starts coloring at 325°F and is brown when it reaches 355°F. Cooking caramel smells of delicious candy but as soon as it starts to release acrid smoke, it becomes bitter and unusable. If cooked further it will burn and turn into a grayish black crust of pure carbon.

CARAMELIZE (TO): This verb has several meanings: 1. To coat a mold or the top of a cake or confection with caramel; 2. To coat the top of a custard with sugar, then burn it to caramel with a blowtorch or under a broiler, as in **crème** brulée; 3. To inaccurately describe a gravy that has browned on the bottom of a roasting pan as a result of the **Maillard reaction.**

CARBOHYDRATES: Energy-producing foods; they include all sugars (mono-, di-, and polysaccharides), starches, and complex carbohydrates (pasta and all grains with or without their bran layers).

CARÊME, JEAN-ANTOINE (1784–1833): The most genial chef of his generation and probably of his century, he is considered the first codifier and father of classic French cuisine. Successively chef to the Prince de Talleyrand and the Czar of Russia, he wrote and illustrated several books himself, including several dedicated to pastry and cakes (1815–1833). His premature death prevented him from completing his major work, *L'Art de la Cuisine Francaise au 19ème Siècle*, which was completed by Chef Plumerey in 1835. Students of the culinary arts who wish to consult his works can find them at the Schlesinger Library of Radcliffe College in Cambridge, Massachusetts.

CAROTENE AND CAROTENOIDS: The respectively orange, reddish, and yellow pigments that give their colors to carrots and other yellow vegetables. Nutritionally carotene (or caroten) is converted to vitamin A.

CARRYOVER HEAT: Colloquial kitchen name for the heat absorbed by larger pieces of meat while roasting, which causes their inner temperature to continue rising after they have been removed from the oven. See page 747 for instructions on how to avoid overdoneness as a result of carryover heat.

CASINGS: Treated pig and sheep intestines into which fresh sausage **forcemeat** is piped to form sausage links. Modern casings are also made out of collagen gathered from the underlayer (corium part) of the hides of cattle.

CASSOULET: The star dish of the French Languedoc, which, like bouillabaisse, owes its name to the pot in which it bakes. It consists of partially cooked white beans blended with diverse meats, among them several pieces of goose or duck confit. The cassoulet in which the preparation is put to bake is a deep round earthenware container that looks like a probable descendant of the Roman *patina* (see *The Roman Cookery Book of Apicius*, the Flower and Rosenbaum edition, page 17). The cassoulet may very well predate the Roman era, and there is no doubt that it was originally made with fava beans, and it has excellent cousins in the food of Tuscany. For a discussion of the modern-day cassoulet in Languedoc, see *The Cooking of Southwest France* by Paula Wolfert. Cassoulet is wildly interpreted in modern American restaurants and rarely bears any resemblance to any of the continental versions.

CAUL FAT: The lining of the intestinal cavity of pigs and lambs. Its name in French is *crépine* and it is used to enclose pork **forcemeat** that is shaped into flat sausage patties known as *crépinettes*. Caul fat also provides an excellent wrap to keep stuffed pieces of meat together while they roast or braise.

CEPHALOPODS: Cuttlefish, squid, and octopus belong to this class of mollusks. They have tentacles attached to their head, sharp seeing eyes, and a "syphon," or pocket, that contains an inky secretion, which, when in danger, they release to darken the seawater and escape predators. That black ink is edible and used to prepare the traditional black pasta of the Italian Venetian coast. Cephalopod ink must be extracted from very fresh fish straight out of the water to really taste good.

CHAMPAGNE: Wine appellation which applies strictly to wines made by the *méthode champenoise* in the Champagne district of France, east of Paris. All other wines made by the same method anywhere in France should, by French law, be called sparkling wines (*mousseux*). More details can be found on pages 102–4.

CHÈVRE: The French word for goat and by extension the cheeses made from goat's milk. The word was adopted into the American culinary vocabulary with that meaning.

CHIFFONNADE: The fine ribbons obtained when several vegetable leaves are tightly rolled into a cigar and cut across into $\frac{1}{16}$-to $\frac{1}{8}$-inch-wide shreds.

CHILES; CHILI POWDER: Fruits or pods of plants of the genus *Capsicum*, the flavor and pungency of which vary from mild to breathtakingly pungent, depending on the amount of capsaicin they contain, which itself seems to depend somewhat on the soil and weather conditions in which the plants are grown. The capsaicin is concentrated in the white membranes and veins of the inside lining of the pods. For an excellent discussion of all chiles, see *Authentic Mexican* by Rick and Deann Bayless and *Peppers* by Jean Andrews.

Chili powder is a spice mixture consisting of ground dried chiles and several ground spices and aromatic herbs; it varies in heat and taste with the taste of the cook who prepares it.

CHINE BONE: The backbone of slaughtered animals. Against it on both sides is nestled one sirloin strip and one tenderloin.

CHINOIS OR CHINA CAP: A very fine-meshed conical strainer used for straining refined sauces and **coulis.** See **conical strainer** for a more detailed description.

CHIQUETER: French for notching a plain "free-hand" cutout of puff pastry ⅛ inch deep and at ¼-inch intervals all around its edge with the tip of a sharp paring knife. This allows the pastry to rise straight up while baking. See page 1088 for details.

CHLOROPHYLL: The green pigment matter found in most plants. During daylight hours chlorophyll is used by plants to produce carbohydrates and release oxygen as a residue. At night, when deprived of light, live plants release carbon dioxide. The entire process is called photosynthesis.

CHOLESTEROL: A steroid alcohol contained in animal cells and blood. Its accumulation on artery walls is responsible for blockages and heart attacks. A good modern diet should minimize consumption of saturated fats in butter, red meats, and full-fat milk and cheeses and maximize that of mono- and polyunsaturated oils, plenty of vegetables, legumes, and cereals offering a good supply of greens and fiber. Cholesterol is produced in the liver; it is also an essential component of cell membranes and is an important precursor to sex hormones, vitamin D, and the adreno-corticoid hormones.

CHOP: The word has two meanings: 1. As a verb, to cut food on a chopping board into smaller particles using a chef's knife while applying proper pressure; 2. As a substantive, it refers to either a rib chop cut from the rib back of any animal, with the two main muscles (rib eye and rib cap) still attached to the bone, or, a loin chop cut across the loin of any animal. In the latter case, the back (chine) bone will show its T-formation, with the sirloin strip nestled against the upper side of the T-bone and the tenderloin against its underside.

CHOWDER: This word is derived from the sixteenth- and seventeenth-century French word *chaudrée*, which is the name of a fish soup cooked in a pot called a *chaudière* by the populations of the eastern coasts of France between the Loire and Gironde rivers. Originally brought by French colonists to the northeastern coast of Canada and the United States, it became, during the last three centuries, a classic unthickened New England soup containing either fish or shellfish and always garnished with potatoes, cream, and butter. Many American fish and shellfish soup cre-

ations, such as the Manhattan clam chowder, now carry this basic name.

CLARIFY (TO): The word has two meanings: 1. As applied to butter, to separate the butter grease from the milk solids and whey contained in butter, obtaining clarified butter. See page 32 for more information; 2. To remove the floaters of fine proteins which cloud broth or stock to make a perfectly transparent aspic or consommé (see pages 230–33).

COAGULATE (TO): What happens when viscous proteins are submitted to heat and turn solid or jellylike. Coagulation is best observed in egg cookery.

COAT (TO): To cover the back of a spoon with a layer of a thickened sauce or stirred custard. The full expression is, to coat by ⅛ or ⅙ inch.

COD, AS IN SALT COD: Codfish that has been salted for preservation; used extensively in the Mediterranean Basin under the following names: *bacalao* (Spain), *bacalhau* (Portugal), *marlusso* (French Provence), and *baccala* (Italy). Not to be confused with stockfish (*estocafic* in Provence and *stoccafisso* in Italy), which is air-dried young codfish.

COGNAC: The name of a brandy distilled from wine in the area surrounding the small city of Cognac in western France. Cognac is aged in oak casks, which give the brandy its color. The best Cognac, called Grande Fine Champagne, should be used for desserts and special dishes only after you have become a crackerjack in the kitchen. Otherwise, three-star Cognac or VSOP (very superior old pale) Cognac will be adequate to finish a sauce beautifully for any meat, white or red. It must be flambéed before being added to any sauce. See **flambage.**

COLLAGEN: Protein fibers found in bones, cartilage, tendons, skin, and connective tissues of animals and fish. Insoluble in water in its natural state, it converts to gelatin when heated and simmered in liquid. This property of collagen is used to advantage in the making of broths, stocks, **fonds,** and the preparation of several types of stews.

CONDIMENTS: These pleasant preparations include any spicy sauce or relish served with meats or vegetables to perk up their natural taste; they include mustards, relishes, ketchup,

steak sauces, barbecue sauce, and horseradish.

CONFIRE (TO); CONFIT: A synonym for preserving: 1. When sugar is used, it refers to the preserving of fruit in sugar syrup, as in the French fruit confit; 2. When salt is used to cure meats in conjunction with cooking those meats in their own fat or other extraneous fats, the result is a preparation called a confit.

CONICAL STRAINER: A small wire strainer with a plastic handle made from wire mesh approximately ⅒ inch square, and a must for careful cooks who want a sauce free of flour lumps and overcooked aromatics. A strainer made of first quality stainless steel will last a lifetime. The special strainer called a **China cap** (*Chinois* in French) used to strain fine sauces has an extremely tightly woven mesh with interstices no longer than one fiftieth of an inch.

CONSOMMÉ: Broth or stock that has been clarified by simmering it with beaten egg whites, which attract and trap the impurities clouding the broth. See **clarify.**

CORAL: The egg pouch of female lobsters; dark green, it is not to be confused with the **tomalley**, which is pale green. The coral fills the lower head and abdominal cavity and extends into the "vein" of the tail; when the lobster lays the eggs, she uses her two atrophied, soft, and brushlike first legs to roll them under the sharp pointed shields that protrude on each side of her tail shell, where they hatch and from where they drop to the bottom of the ocean to grow up by themselves.

Coral turns red on contact with heat and gives a lobster or fish sauce great depth of taste and color.

CORNED: As in corned beef or other meat; refers to a meat that has been salted and cured, the expression "corned" referring to the very coarse European-style salt.

CORNICHONS: The French name of tiny pickles mixed with silverskin onions and other aromatics and preserved in seasoned pure wine or cider vinegar.

COULIS: The name given to medium-thick purees of vegetables, shellfish, and fish (see **bisque**), also to reduced stocks that have turned viscous, as well as to semiliquid purees of fruit, sweetened or unsweetened.

COURT BOUILLON: The name given to a large water bath flavored with varied aromatics and vinegar and/or white wine in which whole fish or fish steaks are poached. For the techniques of making and cooking with a court bouillon, see pages 560–64.

COUSCOUS: 1. Grains of semolina, which, when lightly hydrated and rolled in a special basin with the palms of both hands, agglutinate to form larger grains, which are steamed in a special steamer called a *couscoussière*. Ready rolled and precooked couscous is available packaged; 2. The name of one of the specialties of the Maghreb (Morocco, Algeria, Tunisia); it is a stew made in the *couscoussière* and served with couscous that has been steamed over the simmering stew.

CREAM: 1. As a verb, to stir a fat—usually butter—and sugar together rapidly with a wooden spoon or the beaters of an electric mixer until the mixture looks white, aerated, and somewhat like stiffly beaten whipped cream; 2. As a substantive, that part of milk, containing 32 to 42 percent of butterfat in emulsion, that rises to its surface after the milk, warm from the cow, cools to room temperature and stands for several hours. See page 27 for the diverse dairy creams available to the cook.

CREAM PUFF: In French *choux à la crème*, a pastry made with *pâte à choux* (formerly *pâte à chaud*), called cream puff dough in English. For techniques see pages 1104–7.

CREAM SOUP: A soup prepared by blending a **coulis** of cooked vegetables with **béchamel** sauce and **crème** fraîche.

CRÈME: The French word for cream. It appears in the names of numerous preparations, including: 1. Crème fraîche. The name given in French to matured dairy cream that has thickened and is starting to acquire a slight sour taste. The adjective *fraîche* in this context has the colloquial meaning of very slightly acid (as it does for a young white wine that is said to be *frais*); 2. Egg custard, as in *crème anglaise* (stirred custard) and *crème renversée* (upside-down custard). If the mold in which the upside-down custard has been cooked is caramelized, the custard is called *crème caramel*; 3. *Crème pâtissière* (not *pâtisserie*), a pudding like custard of egg yolks and milk

thickened by diverse means, and used by pastry chefs to fill many different types of pastries and garnish dessert preparations, hence its name.

CREPES: One- to two-millimeter-thick French pancakes used for both classic dessert and savory preparations. They are prepared in specially conditioned pans, which are presently in the process of being replaced by the non-stick modern pans that require no conditioning.

CROSS-CONTAMINATION: The passing of live bacteria from a food to another whether cooked or not when both are cut on the same board or with the same knife without the two implements being washed and sanitized in between. A classic case of cross-contamination happens when cooked roast beef is carved on the same board on which it and/or any other uncooked meat was trimmed just before.

CROUSTADE: 1. A patty shell cut out of puff pastry with a crinkled edge cutter; it is baked, emptied of its moist internal part, and filled, just before serving, with a delicate composition of delicious and opulent foods such as small **quenelles,** creamed mushrooms, sweetbreads, kidneys, or combinations of several other offals; 2. In everyday or vegetarian cookery croustades are made by flattening slices of crusted white bread with a rolling pin, fitting them into muffin tins, and baking them to light golden.

CROÛTE: French word which can designate: 1. The crust of a cheese; 2. The brown outside crust of a bread, which is to be removed before making bread crumbs with the center of the loaf; 3. In the expression *en croûte*, it refers to a **forcemeat** enclosed and baked in a pastry crust, which constitutes a pleonasm since a *pâté* is etymologically understood to be baked in a pastry crust. **Forcemeats** that are cooked in specialized earthenware terrines acquire the name of the vessel in which they are baked and are consequently called **terrines.**

CROUTON: A slice of French bread that has been toasted lightly or panfried in butter and serves as the recipient of a light stewed meat or sautéed offal or creamed vegetable. It is a smaller-size reminder of the medieval *trencher*, large slices of bread that were used as plates; 2. The rounded extremities of a long **bâtard** or *baguette*.

CRUDITÉS: French for a mixture of sliced and shredded vegetables diversely dressed and served as a first course in French homes and family restaurants.

CRUMB: 1. As a verb, to coat with bread crumbs; also to break a piece of bread or other baked good into fine particles; 2. A term of evaluation to describe the texture of a baked bread or cake, as in "the crumb of this cake is too coarse."

CRUSTACEANS: All shellfish, the shell of which is made of keratin of diverse thicknesses and articulations. Young crustaceans molt; at molting time they shed their old shell, revealing the new soft shell that will thicken relatively rapidly. Soft-shell crabs are a delicacy without peer.

CURE (TO): To rub and coat a meat or fish with a plain salt, or salt-and-sugar mixture, aromatized or not, and let it stand several days to extract its water content, a procedure which renders the muscle fibers able to withstand long preservation. The most celebrated cured fish is the ancient but still very popular gravlax.

CURING SALT: Also called pink salt in colloquial kitchen jargon, it is made of 94 percent regular salt and 6 percent sodium nitrite. Its use will turn the color of the cured muscle meat bright pink. Also used in small quantities to turn the color of sausage, baked **terrines,** and *pâté* **forcemeats** an appetizing pink-beige. It can be purchased from meat purveyors.

CURRY POWDER: This pungent mixture of numerous spices can be purchased in grocery stores already prepared. A better solution is to consult a good East Indian cookery book and learn to compose one's own fresh curry.

DANISH PASTRY: An extremely rich and delicious flour, egg, and milk dough containing a large amount of butter which is incorporated, as for puff pastry, by "rolling in" the butter in six successive turns. (See techniques on pages 1097–99.)

DECILITER: In the metric system, one tenth of a liter, and a very close equivalent to 3.5 ounces, which is 7 tablespoons, between ⅓ and ½ cup.

DEEP-FRY (TO): To cook a food coated with flour, a frying batter, or bread crumbs by immersion in an oil bath that has been preheated to 350° to 375°F.

DEFAT (TO): Or perhaps defatten; a new

word in the nutritional and culinary language, which can have two meanings: 1. To trim the fat covering off a piece of meat before cooking it; 2. A synonym for **degreasing.**

DEGLAZE (TO); DEGLAZING: To dissolve the thickish or "caramelized" brown proteinic deposits left in a pan after roasting, panfrying, or sautéing a piece of meat by adding water, broth, stock, or wine, with the goal of adding this "deglazing" to a sauce or to simply use it to prepare a gravy. All fat should be removed from the cooking pan before adding any liquid.

DEGREASE (TO): English equivalent of the French *dégraisser*, which means to skim the fat from the surface of a hot stock or other liquid. If the stock is to be used immediately after cooking it, keep the cooking vessel at a simmer, slightly off center on the burner, and spoon the fat off using the long side of a sauce spoon. If the stock or broth has been allowed to deep chill overnight, a thin layer of fat is best removed by letting a single paper towel fall upon the fat, which will adhere to it; paper and fat are then lifted off together. A thick layer of hardened fat is best removed with your hand protected by a surgical glove.

DEMI-GLACE: The most refined classic brown **mother sauce,** made by blending together equal volumes of *espagnole* sauce (see page 284) and excellent brown veal stock, then reducing the mixture by a little more that one half again, skimming as much as possible so the sauce is so clear it can be used as a mirror. It is flavored with a small amount of Sercial Madeira. The sauce is time consuming to make and better replaced by essences (see pages 293–97). In many modern professional kitchens, the term is inaccurately applied to brown veal stock reduced by half to three quarters.

DÉPOUILLER: The French word for skimming off fat, flour proteins, semisolid meat proteins, and cellulose residues that come to the surface of sauces while they simmer.

DEVILED: A literal translation of the French *à la diable*; the expression defines a way to grill a young broiler or other small bird. Its backbone having been removed, the bird is flattened and preroasted in a hot oven. Halfway through its cooking, it is brushed with mustard, sprinkled first with fresh bread crumbs, then generously with butter and put to finish cooking under the broiler or on a barbecue grill.

DEXTRIN(S): The result of the partial breaking down of starches when they are heated or submitted to the effects of acids and **enzymes.** Dextrins are often used in the preparation of commercial syrups.

DICE (TO): To cut any food into cubes. See also under **chop, brunoise, mirepoix,** and **salpicon.**

DILUTE (TO): To lessen the concentration of a liquid or semisolid preparation by adding water to it.

DISACCHARIDE: Name given to any double sugar. Disaccharides are formed when two single sugars (monosaccharides) unite, at the same time losing one molecule of water.

DOCK (TO): To cut more or less deep slashes into the top of a lean bread (see page 1033) to allow it to expand while **proofing** and baking. Docking in rich breads is usually done with scissors.

DRAWN: A fish with its scales and viscera removed, but its head and tail left on.

DREDGE (TO): To coat a food with flour, any other finely crumbed ingredient, or, in pastry work, sometimes with fine sugar.

DRESSED: This word has two meanings: 1. When referring to poultry, any bird killed, bled, and plucked, but not eviscerated; 2. When referring to fish, a fish eviscerated and scaled, with head, tail, and fins also removed.

DRUPE: Peaches, apricots, and all plums are drupes, a juicy false fruit attached to a wooden pit in which an almond is enclosed. The embryo of a new plant is to be found at the tip of the pointed end of the almond.

DRY CURE: A dry salt-and-aromatic mixture that is not moistened with any liquid (see **cure**).

DUMPLING: A small lump of soft leavened and seasoned egg, milk, and flour dough, shaped with two spoons or piped out of a pastry bag fitted with a nozzle. More often than not it is poached in simmering water but can also be given the form of a drop batter and steamed over a stew. This word could be an adequate translation for the French **quenelles** made of fish or meat.

DURUM WHEAT: An extremely hard wheat that yields about 70 percent durum **semolina** and 5 to 6 percent durum flour. Both are used in the manufacture of macaroni and pasta.

DUTCH OVEN: Not an oven in the modern sense, but a cast-iron pot used for the preparation of stews, braises, and pot roasts. The round French *cocotte* can be used as a Dutch oven.

DUTCH-PROCESSED COCOA: Refers to a process in which cocoa nibs are treated with alkali; it allows the cocoa to lose some of its bitterness and acidity and to acquire more solubility.

DUXELLES: A medium-fine shallot-scented mushroom hash often said to have been created by the seventeenth-century French chef François de La Varenne, but this is not an established fact since this writer-chef did not publish a recipe for this type of preparation in any of his books. The reason for the quasi-legend is that La Varenne worked as chef to the Maréchal d'Uxelles. It is not known whether duxelles originated in the kitchen of the Maréchal or in the Breton town of Uxel.

EGG WASH: The English equivalent to **anglaise.**

EMINCER: French for slicing meats, cheeses, or vegetables into very thin slices.

EMULSIFYING AGENT, EMULSIFIER: Substances able to promote the dispersion of oil-in-water or water-based solutions because they have two ends, one which is polar and connects with the water phase, and the other which is nonpolar and connects with the oil phase. Egg yolks, mustard, sour cream, a starch-bound liquid, and an **essence** of any meat are the emulsifiers mostly used in the kitchen.

EMULSION: The temporary mixture obtained by agitating together two antagonistic and immiscible liquids, one being water or a water-based solution, the other an oil or melted fat. There are oil-in-water emulsions, such as salad dressings and mayonnaise, and water-in-oil emulsions, such as raw butter. The basic salad dressing called vinaigrette is an unstable emulsion in which the water phase (called the dispersion phase) and the oil phase (the continuous phase) will always separate on standing, the oil floating to the surface of the water. The line that separates them is called the interface. Mayonnaise is a stable emulsion in which the oil is kept in dispersion in vinegar or lemon juice, by the lecithin contained in egg yolk acting as an emulsifier (see pages 337–40 for more details on emulsified sauces).

ENZYME: Any proteinaceous substance produced by living cells and acting as a catalyst in reactions happening at body temperature. Enzymes are not destroyed in the course of the reactions they bring about or accelerate.

ESPAGNOLE: Or *sauce espagnole*, French for the brown **mother sauce** used in classic cuisine as a base to the **demiglace** sauce and all the small brown sauces; see page 560.

ESSENCE: The word has three meanings: 1. For fish, a double **fumet** of fish (see Escoffier *Le Guide Culinaire*, page 9); 2. In modern sauce making, veal stock reduced over diverse browned meats to obtain a strongly sapid sauce which is then called an "essence of," followed by the name of the meat that has been used. There are single essences and double essences, depending on the meat that is used. For an in-depth explanation see pages 293–97. An essence as described here is not to be found in Escoffier, but it was used by eighteenth-century French cooks; 3. A strong reduction, extract, or essential oil possessing the concentrated qualities of a vegetable, plant, flower, or seed, such as essence of tomato, extract of vanilla, oil of bergamot, or essence of coffee.

ESTER: Chemically, an acid and an alcohol chemically combined. Fats are esters of glycerol and stearic or oleic acids (see pages 23–27).

ESTOUFFADE: Although the word has no definition relating to the culinary arts in the French Larousse dictionary, it is defined in the *Larousse Gastronomique* (French version) as: 1. A dish (of meats or vegetables) cooked *à l'étuvée* or *à l'étouffée*; 2. The classic brown meat stock known as *fonds brun* and used to prepare certain classic sauces, braises, and stews.

À L'ÉTUVÉE; À L'ÉTOUFFÉE: A technique that consists of cooking meats or vegetables or both mixed in their own juices in a pot that is tightly sealed. The American pot roast is a dish cooked à l'étuvée.

FACULTATIVE: In sanitation language, this adjective applies to bacteria that can maintain their life functions equally well in the presence or absence of oxygen.

FARINA: A white-colored wheat cereal made from hard wheat "middlings" (chunks of pure endosperm containing neither germ nor bran). It is enriched with vitamins and minerals.

FAT: Chemically an **ester** of stearic acid or oleic acid and glycerol. Nutritionally, one of the nutrients used by the body to produce energy. Gastronomically, the big taste and texture giver in all its forms; it fills the mouth, and by coating tongue and palate, lessens the perception of acids. Fats are solid at room temperature.

FATBACK: The solid, very white pork fat coming from the back of large pigs. It is used to give "slip" to *pâté* and terrine forcemeats and was in former times cut into ⅛-inch-thick sheets used to **bard** meats, as well as to line **terrines** and *pâté* pastries before adding their forcemeat.

FERMENTATION: In the life cycle of yeasts, the process by which those microorganisms feed on the sugars, starches, and cellulose of carbohydrates and produce carbon dioxide and alcohol. *Saccharomyces cerevisiae*, for example, leavens bread while *S. ellipsoideus* transforms sweet grape juice into dry wine.

FERMIER: French word for "made on a farm." It appears on the labels of some of the cheeses made in and imported from France, as opposed to the adjective *laitier*, which means that the cheese is pasteurized and has been made in a large dairy.

FETTUCCINE: ¼-inch-wide ribbon noodles as made in Rome and the Italian region of the Lazio.

FIBER: As in dietary fiber; a synonym for the roughage found in fibrous vegetables, grains, and the membranes of citrus fruits.

FIFO PRINCIPLE: The principle by which foods should be stored so they can be used in their order of purchase. Fifo is an abbreviation for "first in-first out."

FILÉ: Ground sassafras leaves used to give the Southern gumbos their unctuousness.

FILET: The French name for the tenderloin of beef, veal, lamb, goat, and venison.

FILLET: 1. As a substantive: One boneless and skinless side of a round fish (for example, salmon) or one boneless and skinless half side of a flatfish (like sole). 2. As a verb: the action of lifting fillets of fish from the fish backbone with a filleting knife.

FILLETING KNIFE: A thin-bladed knife, flexible and bendable, used to lift fillets of fish from a fish frame. Called a *filets de soles* knife in French kitchens.

FINES HERBES: Translated into English as "fine herbs," the French name for a mixture of chervil, chives, parsley, and tarragon, primarily in the fresh stage, but also in the dried stage.

FISH POACHER: An oblong narrow cooking vessel, straight sided, fitted with a rack and a lid, and used to poach whole fish. See page 284.

FLAMBAGE, FLAMBER: The action of heating a wine or spirit (Cognac, Armagnac, whisky, or bourbon) in a small pan, lighting it with a match, and pouring it, flaming, into a sauce while whisking. This burns the alcohol out of the wine or spirit, which otherwise would act aggressively on the palate. Care must be taken to keep face and hair at a safe distance from the lighted spirit to prevent burns. The cook must assume responsibility for his or her safety when flambéing.

FLAVONES: The pigmental matters in white vegetables.

FOIE GRAS: The livers of geese and ducks that have been force-fed a mixture of corn, lard, and salted water. A foie gras weighs from one to two pounds and is pink-beige in color.

FOLD (TO): Important way to incorporate an egg-white foam into an egg yolk foam or a flour batter without deflating it in order that it retains its full leavening power. In French cookbooks folding translates to *incorporer*. See pages 168–69.

FONDANT: The word has two or more meanings: 1. An icing for cakes or small pastries made with an inverted sugar syrup cooked to 237°F and beaten to obtain a creamy mass of superfine crystals; 2. Candies made with diversely flavored fondants, colored or not, and chocolate-coated or not.

FONDS: Whether in the singular or the plural, this French word always ends with an "s" and is a synonym for stock.

FONDS DE BRAISE: A mixture of browned vegetables (onions, carrots and sometimes other aromatics) on which meats to be braised are set. The mixture flavors the gravy of braises and of stews.

FONDS LIÉ: More commonly called *jus lié*, it is veal stock reduced by three quarters and thickened with 1¼ teaspoons potato or cornstarch per cup. *Fonds lié* is usually blended with the deglazing of panfried or roasted meats and used as a sauce.

FOOD-BORNE ILLNESS: A moniker used in sanitation manuals to define an illness acquired by two or more people having consumed the same food contaminated by bacteria or a toxin produced by bacteria.

FOOD PROCESSOR: A modern machine invented in France in the late 1960s which has come into wide use in the United States for its versatility. Fitted with diverse blades, it can do all the handwork done formerly by knives. Its fortes are the pureeing of **quenelle** pastes, the making of sweet pastry doughs and bread crumbs, and the very fine grinding of nuts.

FORCEMEAT: A mixture of ground meats, pork fatback, aromatics, spices, and sometimes a tinted curing mixture (pink salt) used to fill sausage casings and make *pâtés* and **terrines**.

FORTIFIED: This word applies: 1. To food products "fortified" with the addition of vitamins and minerals (milk and orange juice, for examples); 2. To wines high in alcohol content, made from grapes mostly grown in Mediterranean or warm climates, the fermentation of which has been stopped by an addition of brandy. Sherry, port, and Madeira, among others, are fortified wines; see pages 98–102.

FRAME: The kitchen name for a carcass of fish, noneviscerated, with head and tail on, sold by fish mongers to prepare fish **fumet.**

FREE RANGE: Applies in animal husbandry to all animals but especially to calves and chickens or other birds that have been raised in open fields, where they can respectively graze and scratch for natural feeds.

FRICASSEE: A type of stew with white or brown sauce made by simmering young poultry or veal in plain water or a stock, either being flavored with aromatics. They can be garnished with diverse vegetables and herbs. See pages 832–36.

FRITTATA: A flat Italian baked or sometimes also half-fried/half-baked omelette.

FRITTER: Sometimes called by its French name of *beignet*, which means cooked in a bath of oil. Any food coated with a batter or crumbs and deep-fried. Savory food fritters can be plain (chicken livers) or minced and bound into croquettes with other ingredients (croquettes of chicken). Dessert fritters can be made with fruit (apples or strawberries, for example) or a cold pastry cream floured, brushed with an egg wash, and crumbed (fried cream, *crema fritta, crèmes frites*).

FRUCTOSE: The natural simple sugar (monosaccharide) found in fruits. Also called levulose. When combined with glucose, it gives the double sugar sucrose. Fructose is about 1½ times sweeter than glucose; it is about 1.2 times sweeter than sucrose.

FRY (TO): To cook in a hot fat, whether one panfries in a small amount of fat in a frying pan or skillet or deep-fries in an oil bath in a deep-fryer fitted with a frying basket.

FUMET: The name customarily given to fish stock, although it can be applied to other stocks especially those made with game and venison. It is always followed by the preposition *de* in French. *Fumet de poisson* is fish stock, which is always made with water and white or red wine. See the in-depth discussion on pages 540–46.

GANACHE: A mixture of grated or finely chopped chocolate, black or white, and scalded heavy cream, whisked on medium speed until completely cool (see page 1141).

GARNISH: 1. As a verb, to add an interesting and completely edible item to a plate to make it look more attractive: herbs, flowers, and mushrooms are common garnishes; 2. As a substantive, any such edible item.

GASTRIQUE: French word, usually referring to gastric digestive juices but undefined in the French Larousse dictionary or the French edition of the *Larousse Gastronomique*. In kitchen language, the name of a small amount of sugar cooked to the caramel stage and deglazed with vinegar; this mixture is added to the deglazing of a duck roasted to prepare *canard à l'orange*. See pages 1162–63 for more details.

GEL: A colloidal suspension that has jellied.

GELATIN: A protein-based stabilizer extracted from the collagen found in the connective tissues, cartilage, and bones of animals by cooking them in hot water. Its presence in the stock causes the stock to jell upon cooling. Commercial gelatin used for desserts and aspic comes in sheets in European countries and very finely granulated in the United States and Canada, but both forms are available in fancy food stores.

GELATINIZATION: The word has several meanings: 1. The conversion of a liquid stabilized with gelatin into a gel (gelatinized) upon cooling; 2. In sauce making, the gradual absorption of a liquid by the starch granules in the flour or pure starch used to thicken that liquid. In pudding making the gelatinization changes its name to "pasting."

GÉNOISE: A spongecake now made with ribboned whole eggs, as opposed to an ordinary spongecake, which is made with separated eggs. In earlier centuries it contained pounded almonds, a version of which still exists in the delicious small *pain de gênes*, which are now disappearing from all but the wealthiest neighborhood French bakeries. It is probable that the cake originated in Genoa, hence the name.

GERM: As in wheat germ. The scutellum, or embryo, of any cereal grain after it has been separated from the bran and endosperm by milling. It is sold lightly toasted in glass jars.

GIBLETS: The neck, heart, gizzard, and liver of a barnyard bird, which are customarily included in the bag in which the bird is wrapped. See page 295 for their utilizations.

GLACE DE VIANDE: French for meat glaze.

GLAZE: This word has two meanings: 1. As a verb, to coat a meat with a gelatinous stock or a gravy and pass it under the broiler so the coating dehydrates and dresses the meat with a shiny and brown layer, or to coat a meat with a shiny sauce, or to coat a dessert with an icing or a thick syrup; 2. As a substantive, any shiny preparation used to coat a food, be it icing, sauce, or meat glaze.

GLIADIN: One of the two proteins that contribute to the formation of gluten when making bread; see **gluten** and **glutenin.**

GLUCOSE: Also called dextrose, a simple sugar which, like fructose, is naturally present in many fruits. Ripe grapes contain roughly 50 percent each fructose and glucose. Glucose is used in candy making to prevent the crystalization of sugar syrups.

GLUCOSIDES: A large number of sub-stances found mainly in plants that give them a bitter taste (ripe olives, for example). They have the property of releasing glucose when hydrated with an acidulated liquid.

GLUTEN: The protein obtained by sub-mitting a mixture of flour and water to the mechanical action of the hands or a mixer when kneading a bread or other dough. It is formed when the two proteins **glutenin** and **gliadin** crossbridge. There is no gluten in flour; rather, the baker is the gluten maker (see pages 1008–10 for a fuller explanation).

GLUTENIN: The second of the two pro-teins contributing by their crossbridg-ing to the formation of **gluten**. See **gliadin**

GLYCEROL: A trihydric alcohol. It gives texture to wines in which its more or less abundant presence is revealed when the wine slides back into the bowl of a glass forming either "legs" or "tears."

GLYCOGEN: The name given to carbohy-drates stored in the muscle tissues and the liver. Once released into the blood stream glycogen becomes glu-cose.

GOUJONETTE: From *goujon*, the French name for the small freshwater fish called gudgeon. *Goujonettes* are strips roughly the size of a gudgeon cut out of sole or flounder fillets. They are breaded and deep-fried.

GRAM: The basic metric weight measure. There are 100 grams in a hectogram, 500 grams in a European metric pound, and 2 pounds or 1,000 grams in a kilogram. The American avoirdu-pois ounce is just a little over 28 grams and can be rounded off in recipes to 30 grams. An American pound equals 454 grams.

GRATIN; GRATINÉ; GRATINER: 1. A gratin is any dish allowed to bake in the oven or brown under the broiler to develop a crispy delicious top; 2. The past participle of the verb *gratiner* is *gratiné* and refers to a dish being topped with crumbs or cheese and browned either in the oven or under the broiler; 3. The expression *au gratin* after the name of a food means that the top of the food has been crumbed and/or sprinkled with cheese and browned either under the broiler or in the oven. For the origin of the word, see page 440.

GRAVY: A gravy is not a sauce, although the words are often used interchange-ably. A gravy is made from the cook-ing juices of a meat which have been deglazed and defatted (see page 748), while a sauce is made with extraneous stock that has been thickened by one method or another. The best practice in refined cuisine is to add the con-centrated fat-free gravy to a sauce made with a stock to reinforce the taste of the sauce.

GRIDDLE: In restaurant kitchens, a large heavy metal plate, heated with its own heating element, on which one can cook a number of pieces of food at once to accelerate service.

GRILL: The word has several meanings: 1. As a verb, to cook a food over a source of radiant heat; 2. As a sub-stantive, the implement on which one grills, which can be a barbecue or a stovetop grill. Stovetop grills are sometimes called grill-pans and are heated over a radiating element which converts the heat to conduc-tion heat. Meats cooked on such a grill look and taste somewhat like meats cooked over radiating heat.

GRIND: To pass meats or nuts though a grinder or a food processor to reduce either to small pieces, ⅛ to ¹⁄₁₆ inch.

GUINEA, GUINEA HEN, OR GUINEA FOWL: A gallinaceous bird of the family of the Numidiae, originally found in Africa and southern Arabia. It has been domesticated in most countries, but tends to rapidly go back to the wild state. The taste of its meat is so akin to wild pheasant that it should be used by preference to raised pheasants. The optimum weight of a guinea is 1½ pounds.

GUMBO: An African word for okra, it is now the name of a soup of shellfish, either crab or shrimp or both, and/or bayou crawfish made in Louisiana since the beginning of the nineteenth century. It is lightly thickened with okra or the powdered sassafras leaves, or **filé**, used by the Choctaw Indians, but never both together. Although there is a Creole gumbo and a Cajun gumbo, there are as many gumbos as there are cooks.

HARICOT: 1. French for bean, descen-dant of the small *ayacotl* of Central America and Southern Mexico, not the fava bean, which was the type of bean known to the ancient and medieval worlds; 2. As in *haricots verts*, almost sweet green beans barely ¼ inch wide that are passing into the greengrocer vernacular as "verts." They can be found at the same price as the large ones at the bottom of all supermarket bins, where they slip eas-ily because of their small size.

HARICOT DE MOUTON: Modern name of a medieval stew of lamb meat cut into small pieces containing vegetables but no beans. It was already recorded in fourteenth-century French cookbooks under the name of *hericoc*; both names derive from the old German verb *hackon*, which means to chop roughly.

HAZELNUTS: Wild and cultivated round nuts rich in unsaturated oils; see page 50.

HERBS: Aromatic herbs as grown in gar-dens. The leaves are chopped and added to sauces and dressings, while the stems are chopped and used to fla-vor aromatic reductions or soups. Both leaves and stems are also used to prepare aromatic teas.

HOLLANDAISE: The **mother sauce** of all warm egg emulsified sauces; see pages 344–54.

HOMINY: Mature hard corn kernels soaked in a water-and-lye solution to separate the endosperm from the husk. Hominy grits are obtained by drying and grinding hominy, then "bolting" it, which means sifting it.

HOMOGENIZATION: A process that passes milk through very many tiny holes under enormous pressure, so as to dis-perse the fat into a large number of microscopic particles or globules; this procedure turns the milk into a stable emulsion in which the cream will not rise to the top of the container. Nutri-tionally too rich, whole milk should be used only occasionally for great celebration desserts.

HOTEL PANS: Rectangular 2½- to 3-inch-deep pans manufactured with a lip that allows them to be stacked in one another. They come in a large and small size and are used to hold many foods, especially baked dishes and gratins.

HYDROGENATION: A process that con-sists of adding hydrogen to a polyun-saturated oil under heavy pressure in the presence of a metal which acts as catalyst; the oil turns solid and becomes at least partially if not totally saturated. This is how shortening is made as the oil becomes a fat.

HYDROLIZATION: In many instances, but particularly in the making of sauces bound with a pure starch, this word refers to the splitting of the starches into sugars, which occurs when the sauce is submitted to a burst of high heat or other radical change of temperature. That the sauce has turned liquid and tastes sweetish are signs that this has happened; see pages 269–70 for details.

HYGROSCOPIC: In plain language, attracting water. This term applies especially to sugar and salt, which absorb water.

INFECTION: When talking about food-borne illness, a disease brought on by the ingestion of a food contaminated by pathogenic bacteria.

INSTANT THERMOMETER: A small thermometer with a face barely one inch in diameter, and fitted with a thin long stem, that can be inserted into a hot food and instantly registers its temperature.

INTOXICATION: A food-borne illness brought on by ingesting a food contaminated by toxins secreted by bacteria contaminating that particular food (see **botulin**).

JAMBALAYA: From *jamon*, the Spanish word for ham. A Cajun and Creole composition of rice, smoked sausage, cubed ham, aromatics, and any meat that tickles the cook's fancy.

JARDINIÈRE: French for a main course made mostly of new spring vegetables, like lettuce, new peas, new green beans, new carrots, new turnips, and flavored with bacon or salt pork, depending on which area of the country it is prepared. It may also contain baby artichokes and young celery and fennel hearts in Provence and, in Britanny, cauliflower. It can be prepared with older vegetables that have been cut up.

JULIENNE: Vegetables cut into matchsticks $\frac{1}{8} \times \frac{1}{8} \times 2\frac{1}{2}$ inches; by extension the soup *potage julienne* is garnished with such vegetables.

JUS: The word has several meanings: 1. The French word for the deglazed and defatted drippings of roasted meats. *Au jus* means a meat served with its own gravy; 2. In the expression *jus de veau*, it refers to veal stock, the cooking of which is initiated by a triple *tombage à glace,* a technique which is now obsolete; 3. *Jus lié* refers to brown veal stock reduced by three quarters, then bound with 1 ounce of arrow-

root, cornstarch, or, better yet, potato starch per gallon of reduced stock, or 5 to 5¼ teaspoons per quart.

KILOGRAM: 1,000 grams; or 2 metric pounds, each weighing 500 grams; or 10 hectograms, each weighing 100 grams.

KOSHER: From the Hebrew *kasher*. 1. When talking about a food, to prepare it at every stage in strict observance of the Jewish dietary laws; 2. When talking about salt, kosher salt is used to kosher meats and to pickle vegetables. It is a coarse salt that does not contain magnesium carbonate.

LACTALBUMIN: One of the proteins in milk.

LACTOSE: The double sugar (disaccharide) and main sugar found in cow's milk and human milk and simply called milk sugar. It is only one third as sweet as sucrose.

LARD: 1. As a verb, to insert strips of fatback into a not-so-tender piece of meat to be braised, using a special cutter with a hollow blade called a lardoir; a technique that is hardly used nowadays. Also in the classic cuisine and hardly used anymore, to wrap a tenderloin of beef entirely in a thin sheet of fatback before roasting it; 2. Rendered pork fat; 3. In French culinary texts it refers to bacon (*lard fumé*) or salt pork (*lard salé*).

LARDON, LARDOON: 1. Strips of seasoned fatback used to **lard** the outside of a meat with a larding needle or the inside of a meat with a lardoir; 2. Strips $\frac{1}{3} \times \frac{1}{3} \times 1$ inch of bacon or pancetta used to garnish a dish.

LASAGNE: 1. Wide strips of thin pasta (see details on page 512); 2. Modern Italian-American lasagne is made by baking layers of strips of pasta and diverse fillings in a rectangular baking dish; it is topped with either a white or tomato sauce and grated cheese.

LEAVENERS: 1. The air introduced into beaten eggs with a whisk or an electric mixer; 2. Yeast, baking soda, or baking powder, which all will produce carbon dioxide in a dough.

The carbon dioxide and the air contained in a batter will expand in the heat of the oven and allow the volume of the baked product to increase at least threefold, leaving empty holes of diverse sizes in the baked product.

LECITHIN: A natural emulsifier found in egg yolks, corn, peanuts, and soy. It is

extracted commercially and added to many manufactured products.

LEGUMES: 1. The name given to all dried beans, peas, and lentils; synonym of pulse; 2. French for vegetables, and then written "légume" when in the singular and "légumes" when in the plural.

LIAISON: A mixture of egg yolks and heavy cream used to enrich and further thicken white sauces (see pages 281–82 for composition and special techniques).

LIQUEUR: The result of mixing a fruit or herb brandy with a sugar syrup and sometimes food coloring. Modern liqueurs are also made with nuts and spices.

LITER: The metric unit measure for liquids, equivalent to 1.057 quarts; a liter contains 10 deciliters and 1,000 milliliters. Milliliters cannot be used to measure solid ingredients (see page 10).

LONDON BROIL: A large steak generally grilled or broiled and cut out of the rib cap, flank, or chuck of beef.

LOW-FAT MILK: Partially defatted milk containing 1 to 2 percent fat.

LOX: Yiddish word derived from the German word *Lachs* for salmon and the name of salt-cured belly of salmon. Often called belly lox, it is quite salty compared to smoked salmon.

LYCOPENE: The red pigment in tomatoes.

MACARONI: 1. Handmade eggless pasta product, originating mostly in the southern part of Italy and made from flour or a combination of flour and semolina, water, and a small amount of salt; 2. Diverse shapes of noodles, spaghetti, linguine, and many others, manufactured from durum wheat semolina or flour and sold packaged in markets.

MADEIRA, MADÈRE: Fortified wine made on the island of Madeira (territorial Portugal), located almost at mid-Atlantic (see page 100 for more details). Madère is the French for Madeira; the wine, in one of its drier versions, is used to finish a classic small brown sauce made on a base of either *espagnole* or **demi-glace** sauce and called *sauce Madère*. It is served on roast beef, small elegant **tournedos** of beef, or grenadins of veal.

MAHIMAHI: Dolphinfish harvested in all warm ocean waters; it tastes best grilled.

MAILLARD REACTION: A reaction that occurs between proteins or amino acids and carbohydrates when they are heated together. It gives meat drippings and bread crusts their beautiful brown coloration. See the chapters on roasting meats and on baking bread.

MALIC ACID: The organic acid found in apples and other pomes-type fruits.

MALTASE; MALTOSE: Maltase is the enzyme responsible for breaking down the dissacharide maltose into two molecules of glucose. Maltose is known as malt sugar.

MANDOLINE: The name given to a French slicer which can be fitted with diverse cutting blades.

MARBLING: The adipose tissues layered between the muscle fibers of prime meats and a few choice meats.

MARINADE; MARINATE: A dry or liquid flavoring for all meats and fish (see pages 817–19). To marinate is to steep or soak a piece of meat in any type of marinade.

MARMITE: French for stockpot. *Petite marmite* is a whole-meal soup containing poultry and beef and a large array of vegetables.

MARSALA: From *marsah-el-Allah*, Arabic for "garden of Allah." An Italian fortified wine made in the vicinity of the originally Saracen settlement of Marsala in Sicily (see page 100 for more details).

MARZIPAN: German word that has been adopted worldwide to designate a paste of almonds and sugar, which can also contain egg whites. It comes in many variations. In French culinary texts it is called *massepain*.

MATELOTE: The French name of a stew made with white or red wine, which includes only freshwater fish such as eel, carp, pike, and crayfish. The *meurette* and the *pauchouse*, two Burgundy *matelotes*, are made with red wine, and the Normandy *matelote* is made with hard cider and ocean fish. A great dish on which to exercise one's own creativity.

MATIGNON: A **julienne** or **mirepoix** (depending on the cook's preference) of carrots, onions, celery, and cured ham mixed with a bay leaf and a sprig of thyme, étuvéed (see **à l'etuvée**) in butter, and deglazed with a bit of white wine. In the classic cuisine it was used, without precooking, in the preparation of "poëléed" (see **poëler**) small pieces of meat.

MAYONNAISE: The **mother sauce** of cold egg emulsified sauces, it contains egg yolks, salt, pepper, and oil; it is often seasoned with prepared mustard and lightened with lemon juice or sometimes vinegar.

MEAT EXTRACT: A semisolid or semiliquid commercial product sold in glass jars to replace homemade meat glaze. For more information see page 287.

MEDALLION: 1. A piece of meat cut out of the narrower part of the tenderloin of beef or out of the loin of veal; 2. A rounded piece of fish shaped out of the two sides of a salmon steak or out of strips of salmon fillets or any other larger round fish fillets (see page 538).

MELT (TO): To liquefy a fat or a gel by heating it.

MERINGUE: The word may be derived from the little Swiss town of Meyringen, where a baker might have made it for the first time. It consists of beaten egg whites and sugar. The technique used to introduce the sugar into the whites differentiates French, Italian, and Swiss meringues from one another.

MIE DE PAIN: French for the inner soft part of a bread and, by extension, the bread crumbs made with it.

MILLING: The grinding of grains into meals or flours.

MINCE (TO): To chop into very small pieces. Not the translation of the French *émincer*, which means to slice very thinly or even sometimes in colloquial language to cut into a fine **julienne.**

MIREPOIX: Name of an aristocratic French family, which was probably given by one of its kitchen chefs to the ¼-inch cubes of vegetables used as aromatics in many stews and braises. The composition of a mirepoix can vary with the chef or the culinary writer, but it always contains carrots and onions.

MISE EN PLACE: French for assembling all the categories of basic preparations required to cook and serve the dishes of a menu at home or in a restaurant. No literal translation exists in English.

MIX: To combine ingredients by hand or with a mixer with the goal of blending them well and uniformly together.

MODE: As in *à la mode*. *À la mode* can mean: 1. In the favorite style of the moment, as in *boeuf à la mode*; 2. If followed by the name of a person, region, province, or city, it means "in

the style of" that person, region, province, or city, as in *tripes à la mode de Caen*; 3. In the United States, it applies to a serving of dessert topped with ice cream.

MOLLUSK: Soft-bodied shellfish protected by one (univalve) or two shells (bivalve). Abalone is a univalve; clams, mussels, and oysters are bivalves.

MONOSACCHARIDE: A single sugar, such as glucose.

MONOSODIUM GLUTAMATE, also known as MSG: A flavor enhancer originally from China and used in Chinese cuisine. In the West it is mostly used in processed foods. Many westerners are allergic to it.

MONTER AU BEURRE: French for increasing the volume of a sauce or gravy by whisking in raw butter as a finishing touch. This addition of butter gives the sauce shine, a fluffier texture, smoothness on the tongue, and it coats the palate in such a way that it helps smooth the acids and phenolic compounds of younger red wines that the dish might be served with.

MOTHER SAUCE: Also, but less often, called *grande sauce*. In classic cuisine and in all categories of sauces, a basic sauce to which diverse ingredients can be added to obtain variations called small sauces. *Espagnole*, its refined sister the **demi-glace, velouté, béchamel** as well as **hollandaise** and **mayonnaise** are all mother sauces. The term "leading sauce," which probably attempts to be a translation for *grande sauce*, is sometimes used in the United States.

MOUSSE: The French word for foam and by extension culinary preparations, savory or sweet, made of a thickish stabilized base which gives its taste to the preparation and whipped cream, which lightens the texture.

MOUSSELINE: This word has several meanings: 1. The name of a puree of vegetables that is rendered extremely light by whipping either in a mixer or food processor; it is sometimes creamed, as in *puree mousseline,* an extremely light puree of potatoes; 2. Small **timbales** of **quenelle** mousseline of any fish or shellfish (see pages 690–93); 3. A small sauce of the **hollandaise** family made by lightening the **mother sauce** with lightly whipped cream.

MOZZARELLA: Italian cheese made of

pasta filata, a cheese paste that pulls into strings when cooked to approximately 96° to 98°F. Originating in the Lazio and Campania and under the name of scamorza in the Abruzzi, it is made with water-buffalo milk, and is a cheese to enjoy fresh, not cooked. Mozzarella as produced in the United States is made with cow's milk, making it harder than the original and a cheese to be used in cooking (see page 84).

NAPOLEON: A pastry made with alternating layers of puff pastry and a cream of the baker's choice. Called *millefeuilles* in French, it is almost always filled with crème pâtissière and glazed on its top with **fondant**, but lighter modern versions also exist (see page 1092).

À LA NAPPE: French for a sugar syrup cooked to 212°F (100°C).

NAPPER; NAPPÉ(E): In pastry work or cookery, French for to coat, as in a meat coated with a sauce or as in the case of an upside-down caramel custard coated with melted caramel.

NEEDLE TEST: Pertains to the testing of the doneness of poached fruit; it is ready to serve when a needle inserted in the body of the fruit goes in and comes out freely.

NITRATES; NITRITES: Nitrates are salts or esters of nitric acid; when they are added to a meat pickle, they are reduced to nitrites, which are salt or esters of nitrous acid.

NOODLES: Alimentary pastes, or in Italian pasta, made with flour or a mixture of flour and semolina, whole eggs, or egg whites. See **pasta.**

NOUVELLE CUISINE: A modern style of cooking introduced by French chefs in the late 1960s and very early 1970s. It was the result of the modernization of life and also, in part, of a dietary revolution, which started in the late fifties and was first exposed to the public at large by two nutritionists, Simone Martin-Villeveille and Martine Deloge, then by chef Michel Guérard in his book *Cuisine Minceur.* It emphasized lighter foods prepared with some butter and cream, but not the ancestral abundant use of those two ingredients, and simpler and more vivid presentations than the classic formal presentations, but there was absolutely no change in the quasi-fanatic way French cooks and chefs pursued fresh ingredients; some exotic ingredients and curious combinations of flavors became popular for a while. It

was immediately popular with some French people and thoroughly hated by others, who now claim with glee that nouvelle cuisine is dead. In reality, it has rejuvenated the so-called grande cuisine and it is in the process of being assimilated in the psyche of the French nation; the majority of the population, however, has remained faithful to its beloved cuisine bourgeoise, which is simple and very far from being the rich, dietetically dangerous food that it is believed to be in the United States. See the bibliography, page 1177.

OFFAL: Also called variety meats and organ meats, offal includes the following organs: brain, tongue, sweetbreads, tripe, lungs, and kidneys. Offal must be consumed the day it is bought.

OILS: Oils are esters like fats, but they are liquid at room temperature. Their acids are generally unsaturated.

OVENSPRING: The large amount of expansion to be observed in yeast breads during the first ten minutes of their baking time. It is due to increased "budding" of millions of yeast cells and larger production of carbon dioxide on contact with the heat of the oven. As it expands, the gas stretches the walls of the dough cells and sets the shape, size, and crumb of the bread.

OXALIC ACID: The acid found in spinach, sorrel leaves, and rhubarb.

OXIDATION: 1. In chemical terms, it means the gain of oxygen or loss of hydrogen; 2. The browning that occurs in the pulp of some nonacid fruit and vegetables when they are cut and exposed to the oxygen of the air, which is an enzymatic reaction.

PAILLARD: From *paille,* the French word for straw. A ⅓-inch-thick slice of meat, usually veal or white meat of turkey, pounded very thin and rapidly grilled or pan-broiled (in just the time it takes a straw fire to burn!).

PANADE: Fresh bread crumbs cooked in milk or sometimes stock and reduced to an almost stiff texture. This preparation, rarely used anymore, was added to pike **quenelle** paste in the classic cuisine.

PAN-BROIL: To cook a piece of meat (steak, chop, or escalope of any meat) in a hot frying pan, barely rubbed with oil; it duplicates somewhat true broiling. See page 795 for a fuller discussion.

PANFRY: To cook a piece of meat (steak, chop, escalope of any meat) in a thin layer of fat in a skillet or frying pan (see page 795).

PAN GRAVY: See **deglazing** or **gravy.**

PAPAIN: A proteolytic enzyme found in the juice of papaya which breaks down the proteins of muscle fibers; it is used in some meat tenderizers (see page 719).

PAPILLOTE: As in the phrase *en papillote.* Food wrapped "drugstore fashion" in parchment paper or aluminum foil and put to bake in an oven where it will steam in its own moisture and that of any vegetable added to the package to flavor the meat.

PARBOIL: To cook partially in boiling water, in certain cases to prevent browning and discoloration, in others to shorten the last-minute cooking time.

PARCHMENT PAPER: Silicon-treated paper used in baking to line pans; it need not be buttered or greased. It keeps rich cookies from losing their shape and from sticking to baking sheets, and protects foods that are baked, steamed, or braised.

PARCOOK: 1. In home cooking, to partially cook any meat cut for stew that appears to be aging rapidly, in order to prevent it from spoiling; 2. In restaurant service, to precook steaks, chops, and other pieces of meat to accelerate service; also called marking if the meat is precooked on the grill.

PARISIAN SPOON: French version of a melon baller. It is a round scooplike knife, ¼ inch in diameter, made especially to cut small even-size potatoes called *pommes de terre à la Parisienne* out of larger potatoes when small potatoes are out of season.

PARMIGIANO-REGGIANO: The emperor of Italian hard grating cheeses made from cow's milk in the surroundings of the two cities of Parma and Reggio nel Emilia. Although foreign versions of this cheese are made in several parts of the world, they don't measure up to the original, which is truly impossible to duplicate; its price reflects this fact. It can be replaced by its neighbors grana padano and grana lodigiano from the Po Valley, which for being less pricey are still very good hard grating cheeses. See page 80 for more information.

PASTA: The Italian generic name for all forms of alimentary pastes made from a mixture of flour, **semolina,** and whole eggs or egg whites, but no water, as opposed to macaroni, which contains water and no eggs.

PASTEURIZATION: 1. From Louis Pasteur (1822–1895), French biologist and scientist, who, after studying fermentations resulting from bacterial development in diverse foods, discovered their danger to human health. He experimented and established the method for eliminating bacteria, which is now known as pasteurization. It consists of heating all milks used in the manufacture of dairy products, as well as sweet ciders, fruit juices, and bottled drinks long enough to destroy any pathenogenic and some nonpathenogenic bacteria they may contain and prevent fermentation, spoilage, and food-borne illnesses. Many other foods are pasteurized to insure their stability; 2. Raw milk can and must be pasteurized by bringing it rapidly to 160°F and holding it at that temperature for 30 seconds. As soon as the temperature of the milk has gone down to 140°F, it must, like any milk, be refrigerated in the coldest part of the refrigerator, and kept there between uses to prevent and/or minimize new growth of bacteria.

PASTING: In the thickening of a liquid with a starch, the stage at which the mixture acquires the thick texture of a pudding.

PASTRY BAG: Conical bag with a hole at its narrower end through which a decorative nozzle can be fitted; the bag can be filled with a puree or thickish cream which can then be piped out of the bag in attractive patterns. The best pastry bags are made of thin plastic material which can be sanitized easily.

PÂTE: French for many culinary pastes such as *pâte à frire*, or fritter batter; *pâte brisée*, or pie dough; *pâte à choux*, or cream puff dough.

PÂTÉ OR PÂTÉ EN CROÛTE: See **forcemeat.**

PAUPIETTES: French phonetic deformation, dating to the end of the sixteenth century, of *polpette*, the Italian word for any form of balls or cakes made from a hash of meat or fish. Paupiettes are thin escalopes of veal (now also turkey and salmon) enclosing a **forcemeat**; they are mostly *sautéed* or *poêléed*.

EN PAYSANNE: French for country style. In classic cuisine the term was applied to **mirepoix**, garnishing poached fish or white meat and its sauce or gravy. In neoclassic cuisine (1918–1960) the term was often applied also to a fine **julienne** of such vegetables.

PECORINO: A hard grating cheese derived from ewe's milk mostly made in the Roman Lazio countryside (Pecorino Romano) and Sardinia (Pecorino Sardo), but also in other regions. Pecorino-type cheeses made in the United States, mostly of cow's milk, are called Romano and do not compare in taste, texture, or quality to the original Italian products.

PERSILLADE: Chopped mixture of garlic and parsley, of coarse or fine texture, used in the southern French provincial and regional styles of cookery. In Languedoc and the southwest of France, it is mostly used uncooked, while in Provence it is preferred fried crisp in olive oil.

PESTO: From the Italian *pestare*, a verb that means to pound or crush. Pesto is made in the Liguria, especially in Genoa, of crushed fresh basil leaves pounded with garlic, **Pecorino** Sardo, either pine nuts or walnuts, and olive oil until a fragrant paste is obtained. In Italy, pesto is mostly used to season narrow ribbon pasta called trenette. A simpler version called pistou is added to a vegetable and two-bean soup in French Provence. Both are descendants of the ancient Roman *moretaria*, condiments pounded in a mortar, mentioned in the book of Apicius.

PH: pH stands for potential value of hydrogen; a scale of measurement of acidity and alkalinity in foods, with acid foods having a pH of 1 to 7, 7 being neutral and alkaline food having a pH of 7 to 14 (see **acid** and **alkali**).

PIGMENTS: Chemical substance(s) giving its dominant color to a fruit or vegetable. Chlorophyll is green, anthocyanins are deep red, bluish-red, or dark blue, lycopene is red, carotene is yellow to orange, and flavones white or off-white.

PILAF: Also pilau or pilaff, plus a few other variations. A technique of cooking rice by hardening it in a hot fat, then softening it with twice its own volume of water. See pages 461–63.

POÊLER (TO): A technique of cooking applicable to small pieces of meat and small birds which is rarely used nowadays, but appropriate for very small families (see page 838).

POLAR: In emulsifiers, the end of the emulsifier that is attracted to water is polar, while that which is attracted to fat is nonpolar.

POLYSACCHARIDES: Complex carbohydrates made of numerous monosaccharides attached to one another. Starches are polysaccharides.

PORT: Fortified wine made in the Douro Valley of Portugal; some ports are used in cooking. See pages 101–2.

PRIMAL CUTS: In meat cutting, whole carcasses are first split into half lengthwise. Each half is then cut transversely into four primal cuts: the round (leg), loin, rib, and chuck (shoulder).

PRIMEURS: French for the first spring production of any vegetable, fruit, and some wines.

PROOF OR PROVE (TO): The last rising of yeast-leavened bread products at room temperature after they have been shaped into loaves or rolls and before they are put to bake. This last rising plus the **ovenspring** give the breads their final shape and volume.

PUFF PASTRY: A rich and interesting pastry containing equal weights of butter and flour and enough water to allow a large development of steam which makes the pastry rise quite high. The way the butter is introduced into the pastry by giving "turns" is the key to success. See pages 1080–89 for techniques and explanations.

PULSE: See **legumes.**

PUREE: 1. The pulp of cooked vegetables mashed, then strained to obtain a smooth texture. If by personal taste one likes a lumpier texture, a coarser puree is obtained with a masher; 2. The uncooked or cooked pulp of fruits. A *coulis* is a puree of fruit with a loose texture; 3. A meat or fish completely reduced to a uniformly smooth paste.

QUENELLE: From the phonetic deformation of the German *Knödel* (itself possibly derived from an old Scandinavian root *knyll* in which "y" is pronounced "ü"), it has several meanings: 1. A paste made of fish, poultry, or veal meat mixed with eggs, cream, **panade,** and/or beef suet; 2. A delicious oblong dumpling made from such a paste or other more modern and lighter paste, shaped between two spoons, poached in stock, and served with a sauce and garnishes of one's choice. See the bibliography of French cookbooks on page 1168.

QUICHE: From *Küche* (in high German *Kuchen*), the Germanic word used in the Frankish-speaking part of Lorraine to name the savory pie known as quiche in the French-speaking Lorraine. It is a butter crust filled with eggs beaten with heavy cream and very smoky bacon, nothing more. The many variations on this theme imagined by American cooks of the 1960s and 1970s were revealing of the creativity of America in the kitchen.

RAFT: The unattractive gray mixture of coagulated egg white foam, aromatics, and sometimes meats that are used in the clarification of consommés and stocks; they come floating to the top of the pot when the liquid being clarified comes to a boil. See pages 230–33 for a complete explanation.

RAMEKINS OR RAMEQUINS: From the low German *ramken* or the high German *Rähmchen* for small cream. Small porcelain dishes used for baking **shirred** eggs, rich dessert creams, or tiny portions of rich, savory custards containing delicate pieces of shellfish, or any tiny rich stew of shellfish.

RATATOUILLE: From the Provençal *rattoulho* or *ratatouia*. An ancient Mediterranean mixture of vegetables cooked slowly until they make a well-bound compote. Cousin to the caponata of Sicily. Bell peppers and tomatoes are nineteenth-century additions to the list of its components; see page 396.

RAVIOLI; RAVIOLES; RABIOLES: *Raviula* is the name given in the alpine Franco-Provençal languages infused with ancient Ligurian used on both the eastern and western slopes of the western Alps to a small ball of hashed food. Is it possibly of the same origin as ravioli in Italy? In Italy ravioli were originally small egg and vegetable dumplings (gnocchi, *ravioli nudi*) poached in liquid, which more than likely became our modern ravioli when some unknown culinary genius had the idea of enclosing them between two layers of pasta dough. As a matter of interest the colloquial word *rabioles* used in some formerly Ligurian parts of France means leftovers, which are often used in high alpine villages to make *ravioles*, tiny rectangular raviolilike pasta pillows filled with finely chopped leftovers of meat mixed with cheese or plain cheese.

REDUCTION: 1. The concentrated liquid obtained by evaporation after reducing a stock, **fumet**, or a mixture of such sapid liquids. See page 292. In chemistry, a loss of oxygen and a gain of hydrogen in a chemical structure.

REFRESH (TO): To rinse just-boiled vegetables under very cold water to stop their cooking.

REMOUILLAGE: The name given in the classic cuisine to reboiling the bones used to prepare of a top quality stock. Sorting the bones and using new vegetables are musts to obtain a light but very usable broth that will not be strong enough, however, to make meat glaze. See the stock chapter.

RENDER (TO): To melt animal fats, which is done by placing the fat in cold water and boiling until the obtained liquid fat turns clear. See page 779 for an explanation on how to render duck fat.

RICOTTA: Italian for recooked. An Italian cheeselike preparation which is not really cheese since it is not fermented, but made by recooking fresh milk with the whey obtained from the coagulation of other types of large cheeses.

RISOTTO: The somewhat puddinglike Italian rice dish from the Piemonte and Veneto regions, made respectively with the Arborio and Vialone rices. For techniques, see pages 466–70.

RISSOLER; RISSOLÉ: In French *faire rissoler* means to brown a food, usually potatoes, to obtain it *rissolé*, or uniformly browned to golden.

ROLL IN (TO): An American expression equivalent to "giving turns" to puff pastry, croissants, and Danish dough.

RONDEAU: A round straight-sided pot, 2½ to 4 inches deep, depending on its diameter, and fitted with one rounded handle on each side, often used to sauté meats and poultry or to make stews and steam shellfish such as mussels and clams.

ROPE: The name of a sickness of fully baked bread in which bacteria develop and turn the center of the bread to a mushy, somewhat filmy texture. Calcium propionate is added to commercial breads to prevent this from occurring.

ROULADE: French for a food rolled upon itself or rolled into an envelope of cooked egg, meat, or pasta. It can be: 1. A large piece of meat flattened and rolled around a **forcemeat;** 2. An omelette garnished with diverse meats or vegetables, rolled upon itself, and served sliced transversely; 3. A sheet of pasta garnished with a forcemeat and rolled upon itself to form what in Italian is called a *rotolo*, which is also cut into slices transversely.

ROUX: The cooked mixture of equal amounts of butter and flour used to thicken flour-bound sauces; see page 272.

ROYAL ICING: A plain icing made of confectioners' sugar whisked with egg white and flavored with lemon juice; see page 1145.

ROYALE: A savory custard poached on a flat sheet, then cut into decorative shapes to garnish a clear consommé. A few royales are still used nowadays.

SABAYON: French translation of the Italian **zabaglione.**

SACCHAROMYCES: Diverse strains of yeasts used in the making of beer and bread. *Saccharomyces cerevisiae* is the common yeast used for fermenting breads, while S. *exiguus* is the yeast that gives San Francisco **sourdough** breads their sour taste; see pages 1018–51.

SALAMANDER: A small high-speed broiler used in professional kitchens to quickly brown or glaze certain items; it is easily replaced by the broiler at home.

SALMONELLA: There are many strains of this dangerous type of bacteria, which may be found active and alive in numerous foods. If these foods are not cooked properly, killing the salmonella, the bacteria can cause violent and painful food poisoning; they are killed at 165°F. See pages 124–25 for an expanded discussion.

SALPICON: A style of cutting vegetables; see **aromatics.**

SALTPETER: The common name of the chemical potassium nitrate, formerly used to cure meats, and limited in its use by the U.S. Department of Agriculture since 1975 because, used in too large quantities, it is poisonous. Saltpeter is still used but only in minute amounts, in the making of dry-cured salami, which it turns bright red.

In all other meat-curing processes it has been replaced by **curing salt.**

SANITIZE (TO): To clean any utensil or room with the goal of destroying existing bacteria. A pan can be clean without being sanitary. To learn more about sanitation, see the bibliography.

SAUCE: See **gravy** for the compared definitions of sauce and gravy.

SAUCE SPOON: The large oval spoon with

a long handle, usually part of basic kitchen equipment.

SAUTER (TO); SAUTÉ: 1. To cook vegetables in a frying pan in a small amount of fat, tossing them once in a while to stir them without breaking them. This technique does not apply to steaks, chops, and escalopes, which are panfried, not sautéed; 2. To cook a "sauté" of chicken, veal, or rabbit; see the explanation of this technique on page 840.

SAUTEUSE: A cooking pan with straight sides 2½ inches high, a flat bottom, and a long handle, used to cook chicken and other barnyard meat "sautés" as described on page 5.

SAUTOIR: A cooking pan with straight sides 2½ to 3 inches high, depending on the diameter of the pan, and two handles, one long and one semicircular and attached on opposite sides; if the two handles are both semicircular the sautoir becomes a **rondeau.** A sautoir is used to prepare the same types of culinary preparations as a **sauteuse** or a rondeau.

SAVORY: The word has several meanings: 1. Something pleasant or agreeable to eat; 2. A dish containing no sugar; 3. In the United States, an appetizer; 4. In the British Isles, an uncooked dish of high flavor served at the end of dinner (it can be a great Stilton); 5. The aromatic herbs summer and winter savory.

SCALD: The word has two meanings: 1. To heat milk just below the boiling point; 2. To immerse a vegetable or fruit (a tomato or peach, for example) in boiling water in order to remove its skin easily.

SCALE (TO): This word has two meanings: 1. To weigh ingredients, as opposed to measuring them in cups and spoons; 2. To remove the scales of a fish.

SCALLOPS: The word has several meanings: 1. The **adductor muscle** of the large penectidae clams or such clams in their shells; 2. Synonym for escalope, a thin slice of meat; 3. As a verb, to bake sliced (usually) vegetables alternated in layers with a sauce or cream in a baking dish, topped (or not) with crumbs; in essence, a synonym for making and baking a **gratin.**

SCORE: To cut indentations in a fish ready to be baked or roasted to allow the heat to penetrate it and to prevent its skin from bursting open.

SCUM: Impurities (proteins, cellulose) rising to the surface of simmering stocks and sauces. They must be removed using a **sauce spoon.**

SEAR: To brown the surface(s) of pieces of meats and or fish by submitting them to intense initial heat, either in a pan, on a grill, or in the oven.

SEASONINGS: Ingredients added to foods to enhance their basic taste and make them more palatable. Sugar, salt, pepper, celery salt, spices, herbs, and condiments are all seasonings. Cold deadens the effect of seasonings, and consequently more such flavorings should be used to season foods that will be served cold, deep chilled, or frozen.

SEMOLINA: The purified middlings of durum wheat (the meal obtained after the third or fourth grinding of hard wheat flours), ground to approximately 1-millimeter grains. Used to make pasta, homemade macaroni, and couscous from scratch.

SHELF LIFE: The span of time any stored item or product can keep its freshness and intrinsic qualities for safe consumption.

SHELLFISH: Shellfish include bivalves, cephalopods, crustaceans, and univalves; see page 520.

SHIRRED: Refers to an egg cooked in a special egg cup or a **ramekin;** see page 127.

SIFT (TO): To separate the fine particles of a substance from its coarse, undesirables ones (traces of membranes, lumps, etc.) by passing it through a sieve or strainer.

SILVERSKIN: The bluish, tough, flat, thin sheet of connective tissue surrounding any long voluntary muscle. Also called aponeurosis.

SKEWER TEST: The skewer test checks the doneness of meats that have been braised or pot roasted. If a skewer inserted at the center of a piece of such a meat comes out freely, the meat is done. As long as the meat lifts with the skewer, it is not. When testing a cake or bread for doneness, the skewer must be too hot to be tolerated more than a split second by the skin of the top of either hand.

SKIM (TO): To lift and discard any unwanted **scum**, foam, or fat from the surface of a stock, broth, sauce, or soup by using the "belly" of a **sauce spoon**, not its tip, to bring the matter to be removed from the center of the pot to the side.

SLURRY: A mixture of raw starch and cold liquid, it is added to a simmering liquid to thicken it; slurries are used to thicken gravies.

SMALL SAUCE: A sauce which is a variation based on one of the **mother sauces.**

SORBET: A superfine-crystalled ice made with pureed fruit and sugar syrup, fruit juices and sugar syrup, or sometimes a reduction of wine and a sugar syrup. See pages 958–62.

SOUFFLÉ: A composition consisting of a thick base, carrying the flavor of the soufflé, in which egg whites beaten to a foam will be folded; the resulting mixture will puff up in the heat of the oven (in French, *souffler*, hence its name). See pages 173–78.

SOURDOUGH: A dough used to make bread and obtained either by: 1. Letting a leaven of yeast and flour ripen for several days to sour it, and adding this leaven to the final bread dough; 2. Making a culture of *Sacchoromyces exiguus* and blending it with a final bread dough to obtain a so-called San Francisco sourdough bread. See the section on bread making, pages 1050–51.

SPATULAS: Turners and offset spatulas are for turning over meats; rubber spatulas 3½ × 2½ inches with a plastic or wooden handle are for folding; and straight, long-bladed spatulas are for spreading frostings and icings on cakes.

SPÄTZLE: The name given in areas of predominantly Alemanic and Frankish populations (Alsace, Baden, northern Lorraine, Palatinate, and Switzerland) to small flour, egg, and milk dumplings resembling fine noodles, which are poached in water and generously buttered. Their names may vary, but they all belong to the spätzle family.

SPELT: Ancient wheat of the species *Triticum spelta* which contains two russet red kernels. Its flour is available in health food stores and makes delicious bread. See page 1013.

SPIDER: A large wire spoonlike instrument used to retrieve small pieces of food from boiling water or hot fat. The wires of a spider are too widely spaced to skim a sauce or stock; this operation should be done with a sauce spoon.

SPIRITS: Distillates or mixtures of alcohol and water distilled from an alcoholic liquid (wine) or mash (of fruit or grain).

SPONGE: There can be two meanings: 1. When making bread, a small amount of dough prepared in advance to allow it to ferment and acquire complex flavors; it is later added to the bulk of the flour when the bread dough is made; 2. For *brioche* and croissants, a small amount of flour mixed with the yeast and some water to form a soft ball of dough which is immersed in warm water to **proof** the potency of the yeast and start the fermentation rapidly.

SPONGECAKE: A cake made by foaming egg yolks and egg whites separately, then folding both egg whites and flour at the same time into the foamed yolks, as opposed to a ***génoise,*** which is made by foaming whole eggs and folding in the flour, then the butter.

SPORES: The form taken by bacteria which have to face an unfriendly or hostile environment; spores have thick walls and membranes which allow them to survive high heat and live vegetatively in canned foods. See **botulin.**

SPRINGFORM: A cake pan with a detachable bottom and a clamp on its side that can be released to easily unmold a cake.

SQUAB: Possibly from the Swedish *Skvabb,* meaning soft and thick, although the origin is not certain. This word refers to a baby bird and is the name given specifically to small four-week-old pigeons. It can also be used as squab chicken, with the meaning of a baby chicken now sold in good butcher shops under its French name of *poussin.*

STABILIZER: 1. Any stiffening ingredient such as gelatin, or in commercial products agar-agar, added to mousse-type dessert preparations to keep the cream from separating from the base into which it has been folded; 2. Emulsifiers (egg yolk, mustard, sour cream) are stabilizers in the sense that they are added to an unstable emulsion to prevent the two phases from separating. See emulsions, pages 332–33.

STALING: Loss of moisture in baked goods, which causes the crumb to dry out and separate from the bread crust.

STAPHYLOCOCCUS AUREUS: A very dangerous, constant host of humans and animals. It can infect foods by direct contact with hands and implements. It is **facultative** and in a matter of two hours at the low temperature of 44°F

can multiply to a colony of 500,000 individuals per each ⅓₀ ounce of food. Three hours after ingestion it provokes severe abdominal illness. The most endangered foods are custards of all types and high-protein salads containing meats and eggs. Custards should be consumed within twenty-four hours of their preparation and be kept refrigerated at all times at 39°F; high-protein salads should be prepared and mixed only a few minutes before serving them.

STEAM (TO): To cook a food by placing it in a basket over a boiling liquid, utilizing the heat of the steam.

STEAM-JACKETED KETTLE: In large-quantity cookery, kettles that have double walls between which steam circulates to deliver a steady heat able to keep large volumes of stocks, soups, or sauces simmering evenly throughout. Most have a spigot to drain liquid and are also equipped with a tilting mechanism.

STEEL: A long round piece of metal, metal and diamond powder blend, or ceramic fitted with a handle that is used to sharpen knives.

STERILIZE: To destroy microorganisms, which can be done by using steam, a boiling water bath (hot water bath or pressure canner), or simply by washing vessels in a dishwasher.

STEW: 1. To cook small pieces of meat or poultry as in a **braise, fricassee,** or **blanquette;** 2. The stewed meat itself, its garnishes of vegetables, and its sauce.

STIR (TO): To move a liquid, plain or thickened, in a circular motion to: 1. Cool it and prevent it from cooking too fast (custards); 2. Prevent it from sticking to the bottom of the pan (sauces, soups); 3. Keep it well blended and of uniform texture and consistency.

STIR-FRY (TO): Chinese technique for cooking thin slivers of meat, shellfish, and vegetables in hot oil until the meat and fish are tender and the vegetables still crisp.

STOCK: A rich and gelatinous meat or fish broth. See **fumet.**

STOCKPOT: A tall, deep pot in which one cooks stocks, broths, and **fumets.**

STONE-GROUND: Applies to flours milled between two large, flat stones, as was done in the nineteenth century.

STRONG: As in strong flour; a flour that contains a large percentage of proteins

able to cross-bridge during the kneading of bread to produce a lot of gluten and consequently a well-structured bread with a good texture.

SUPRÊME: A French word (masculine gender) and the name given to a fillet lifted from one side of a whole breast of chicken. There are two suprêmes per breast.

SWEAT: To cook vegetables, covered, over low heat to extract their moisture content.

SWEETBREADS: The thymus gland of young calves and lambs (piglets have it too but it is integrated in cold cuts rather than sold by itself). It has two lobes: the throat and the heart sweetbreads. The gland shrivels and disappears as the animal reaches the end of its first year.

SWISS SKILLET: In professional kitchens, a large square or rectangular skillet used to cook stocks, stews, and braises, or even to panfry a large amount of small pieces of meat at once. If it can be tilted forward, it becomes a tilting skillet.

TART: A pie that has only a bottom crust; it can be sweet or savory.

TARTLET: A small individual tart of somewhat varying size that serves only one person.

TEMPER (TO): The word has two meanings: 1. In the making of egg custards, to raise the temperature of the eggs by blending them very gradually with successive small quantities of hot milk; see page 141; 2. A way to melt chocolate so that it is wholly melted and homogeneous; see page 1139.

TEMPERATURE: 1. The degree of heat an oven should be preheated to before baking diverse foods; 2. The amount of heat contained in any hot food. It is measured with an instant thermometer; 3. Temperature conversion: the measurement of temperature in all other countries in the world but the United States is done in centigrade or degrees Celsius (from Andres Celsius, the Swedish astronomer who devised the system). In the United States it is done in degrees Fahrenheit (from Gabriel Fahrenheit, a German who devised the system). To convert from one system to the other, use the two formulas below in which Tf = temperature in Fahrenheit degrees, and Tc = temperature in degrees Celsius.

$$\frac{Tf - 32}{1.8} = Tc \quad Tc \times 1.8 + 32 = Tf$$

For temperature equivalents from 1° to 212°F, see the chart on page 975. For a temperature control chart of all foods, see the chart on page 703. See also **thermometer**.

TEMPURA: In Japanese cookery, vegetables and shellfish coated with a light cornstarch batter and deep-fried. Tempura is of Portuguese origin.

TENDERLOIN: The long tender muscle resting on the underside of the **chine bone** of beef, veal, lamb, and pork. There are two tenderloins per carcass.

TERRINE: See **forcemeat**.

THERMOMETER: The instrument used to measure the heat of foods or of an oven. Nowadays every cook needs an instant thermometer, which reads the internal temperature of foods in a split second. See **instant thermometer.**

THERMOPHILIC: The term applies to bacteria that can maintain their normal life functions between 110° and 170°F.

TILTING SKILLET: See **Swiss skillet.**

TIMBALE: Small, slightly conical metal mold, in which many vegetable and dessert dishes are baked and, by extension, the name of the preparation cooked in such a mold, such as a "timbale of rice" or "timbale of carrot."

TOMALLEY: The liver of a lobster; it is pale green as opposed to the egg sac, which is dark green.

TOMBAGE À GLACE: To let broth or stock reduce to a full meat glaze. The expression was especially used in the old-fashioned *jus de veau,* the cooking of which began with a triple *tombage à glace* of the meat juices, extracted by sweating the contents of the stockpot. In the making of essences (pages 293–96), the first addition of stock to the meat is a true *tombage à glace.*

TOURNEDOS: A ¾-inch-thick steak cut from the tenderloin, said to have been so named by the composer Gioacchino Rossini because it cooks in the instant needed to turn one's back, in French *tourner le dos.*

TOURNER; TOURNÉ: Term used for vegetables that have been shaped into olive and torpedo shapes, so they can roll freely in any skillet without any angles breaking off and muddying the bottom of the pan. Vegetables are tournéed just as well with a simple parer as they are with one fitted with a semicircular blade (the French *couteau à ciseler*).

TOXIN: Poison secreted by aerobic or anaerobic bacteria; see **botulin** and *Staphylococcus aureus*.

TRICHINELLA SPIRALIS: A parasitic worm found in pork and venison, and transmissible to man in those two meats if undercooked. See page 702.

TRIPE: The edible scrubbed and cured muscles of the stomachs of beef, veal, pork, and lamb.

TRUSS: To tie a poultry bird so it forms a compact mass that will cook evenly; see page 725 for complete instructions.

TUNNELS: In baking, the elongated holes produced by the gas produced by baking powder straining to find a way out of an overbeaten muffin batter.

UNIVALVE: The name given to any shellfish consisting of one large shell covering a few organs and a powerful muscle that allows the critter to attach itself to undersea rocks. The most famous univalve is the abalone.

UTILITY KNIFE: A smaller knife with a blade 6 to 7 inches long that can be used for almost anything (*couteau à tout faire* in French).

VARIETY MEATS: Another word for organ meats; see **offal.**

VELOUTÉ: The **mother sauce** of white flour-bound sauces made with white stock.

VENISON: The meat of any big game, but especially deer.

VENT: The word has two meanings: 1. A small paper or porcelain piece sometimes placed in the center of the top crust of meat pies and *pâtés* to allow steam to escape and to prevent meat juices from bubbling up onto the top crust of the pie; 2. The lower abdominal opening of a poultry bird.

VINAIGRETTE: The classic French salad dressing, which is an emulsion made of one part acid of choice and three parts oil of choice. More or less acid can be used, and mustard and cream can be used as stabilizers.

VIRUS: Infective agents that elect living cells as their living quarters. They are responsible for hepatitis, colds, and a few childhood diseases.

VOLATILE ACIDS: Volatile acids that dissipate in the evaporation steam of the water bath in which vegetables are boiling. Their presence is the reason why vegetables are boiled in an open pot; if the pot is covered, the acids will condense on the underside of the lid, drip back down into the water, and dull the color of the vegetable.

WAXY: The term applies to low starch potatoes that contain a larger amount of proteins (like fingerling or Yukon Gold potatoes), which cut into clean slices that do not break and bake to a less mealy texture than starchy potatoes like Idaho Russets.

WHIP (TO): To beat a preparation with the goal of introducing air into it and, by extension, the balloon wire whisk often used to do so.

WHITE STOCK: A stock made from unbrowned but blanched white meats and bones.

WHOLE WHEAT FLOUR: Whole wheat kernels, bran, and germ ground into a flour.

WINE: The result of the fermentation of grape juice or other fruits. See pages 87–91. Hard cider is the result of the fermentation of apple juice.

YEAST: A microscopic single-cell vegetable which, in the presence of hydrated flour, starts its life cycle; we know it as fermentation and use it for making breads.

YOGURT: Milk of any fat content cultivated with *Saccharomyces thermophilus* and *Lactobacillus bulgaricus,* which give it its slight acid tang and viscocity.

ZABAGLIONE: A whipped custard made with egg yolks and sugar gradually diluted over heat with Marsala or any other wine, fruit juice, or liqueur. See pages 196–97.

ZEST: The thinner brightly colored outer part of the rind of citrus fruits. It contains a citrus oil particular to each fruit, and is useful as a flavoring.

Bibliography

THIS BIBLIOGRAPHY IS LONG BECAUSE I HAVE CHOSEN THE TITLES IN SUCH A way that they represent different points of view on an identical subject, or show different facets of one single subject, so the new cook and the student of culinary arts whose goal is to become a chef can gain a maximum of insight in each subject area. I have kept to the strictest objectivity in my choices. I could have included many more excellent books on each and every subject, but it is obvious that I ran out of space.

There are two reasons why this bibliography includes a number of foreign texts. First, because many cooks in America are multilingual, and because I am a translator myself, and deeply familiar with the difficulty of translating into another language the personality, knowledge, and intrinsic meanings in an author's original text. Consulting a foreign text in its language of origin when one can always proves more gratifying than consulting its translation. Texts in a foreign language are followed by an annotation: (Fr.) for French, (Ger.) for German, and (It.) for Italian, for example.

Many of the ancient books on food history can be consulted at the Schlesinger Library, Radcliffe College in Cambridge, Massachusetts; at the Library of Congress in Washington, D.C.; and at the New York Public Library in New York City in their original editions or one of their earlier editions. As much as any cook would of course prefer to own a valuable old edition of any antique cookbook, the cost will often prove prohibitive. Facsimile editions of these works are available, and are a blessing, for what counts is the content of the pages of a book, not its cover. There is no doubt that holding an ancient book can be a very emotional experience if one considers that it holds a tiny bit of each of its former owners, sometimes over many centuries. To compensate for their lack of emotional content, facsimiles often have beautifully crafted bindings.

University and college libraries have many books on food chemistry and food science as well as cookbooks and discourses on gastronomy. The shelves of many public libraries are stacked with culinary treasures; some of the greatest cookbooks of the nineteenth century, now completely unknown to most cooks, both in English and in foreign languages, can often be found there. Another source of older cookery books is used bookstores; each larger city has at least one which will gladly try to procure any title you may be looking for. Basically, anything of any century is worth collecting. As you become a skilled cook, with a larger background in cooking literature, you will develop a taste for some authors, and acquire a little stash of books that you personally like, for whatever reason.

PART I: REFERENCES AND HISTORY

General Language References:
Encyclopedia Britannica, 1974; *Encyclopedia Britannica, Micropedia and Macropedia*, 1989; *Britannica Atlas*, 1989; *Webster's Collegiate Dictionary*; *The Columbia-Viking Desk Encyclopedia*, *Encyclopédie Générale Hachette*, 1980; *Dictionnaire Larousse Universel*, *Etymologishes Wörterbuch der Deutschen Sprache*, *Dizonario Garzanti*.

History of Knowledge as It Relates to Food and Cooking:
Many great historical events had a large influence on the development of our western food. Although it is listed last because of the alphabetical order, it may be a good idea to start with Van Doren's *A History of Knowledge*, which is a perfect overview of the historical events through which humanity survived and progressed while sustaining itself with food.

Braudel, Fernand. *A History of Civilizations*, translated by Richard Mayne. New York: Penguin Books, 1993.

———. *La Méditerranée, Volume 1: L'espace et l'histoire*. (Fr.) Paris: Flammarion, 1985. *Volume 2: Les Hommes et l'Héritage*. (Fr.)

———. *The Structures of Everyday Life, Civilization and Capitalism 15th–18th Century, Volume 1*. New York: Harper & Row, 1979.

Crosby, Alfred W. *The Columbian Exchange, Biological and Cultural Consequences of 1492*. Westport, CT: Greenwood Press, 1972.

Elias, Norbert. *La civilisation des moeurs* (chapter IV on table manners). Paris: Flammarion, 1969. This book is a translation of the original German *über den Prozess der Zivilisation*. (Fr.)

Rotberg, R., and T. Rabb. *Hunger and History, the Impact of Changing Food Production and Consumption Patterns on Society*. New York: Cambridge University Press, 1983.

Van Doren, Charles. *A History of Knowledge, the Pivotal Events, People and Achievements of World History*. New York: Ballantine Books, 1991.

Food History, Gastronomic Literature, Opinions, and Points of View:
Appelbaum, Diana Karter. *Thanksgiving, an American Holiday, an American History*. New York: Facts on File Publications, 1984.

Beck, Leonard. *Two Loaf-givers, or a Tour through the Gastronomic Libraries of Katherine Golden Bitting and Elizabeth Robins Pennell*. Washington, D.C.: Library of Congress, 1984.

Brillat-Savarin, J. A. *Physiologie du Goût*. Paris: Flammarion, 1939. (Fr.)

———. *The Physiology of Taste* (There are two translations in English, one by M. F. K. Fisher and one by Ann Dreyton. Any bookstore will special order this interesting book in the version you would prefer. ND)

Farb, P., and G. Armelagos. *Consuming Passions, the Anthropology of Eating*. Boston: Houghton Mifflin, 1980.

Farrar Capon, Robert. *The Supper of the*

Lamb, a Culinary Reflection. New York: Doubleday and Co., 1969.

Fisher, M. F. K. The Art of Eating. New York: Macmillan, 1954.

Fuller, John G. The Day of St. Anthony's Fire. New York: Macmillan, 1968.

Hess, John and Karen. The Taste of America. New York: Grossman Publishers/Viking, 1977.

Hess, Karen. The Carolina Rice Kitchen, The African Connection. Columbia, SC: University of South Carolina Press, 1992.

Mintz, Sidney W. Sweetness and Power, the Place of Sugar in Modern History. New York: Viking, 1985.

Revel, Jean François. Un Festin en Paroles, Histoire littéraire de la sensibilité gastronomique de l'Antiquité à nos jours. Paris: Pauvert, 1979. (Fr.)

————. Culture and Cuisine, translated from the French by Helen R. Lane. New York: Doubleday and Co., 1982. (A translation of the above listing.)

Root, Waverley. Food, an Authoritative and Visual History and Dictionary of Foods of the World. New York: Simon & Schuster, 1984.

Root, Waverley, and Richard de Rochemont. Eating in America, a History. New York: William Morrow, 1976.

Shapiro, Laura. Perfection Salad, Women and Cooking at the Turn of the Century. New York: Farrar, Straus & Giroux, 1986.

Sokolov, Raymond. Fading Feast, a Compendium of Disappearing Foods. New York: Farrar, Straus & Giroux, 1979.

————. Why We Eat What We Eat, How the Encounter Between the New World and the Old Changed the Way Everyone on the Planet Eats. New York: Summit Books, 1991.

Tannahill, Reay. Food in History. New York: Stein and Day, 1973.

Toussaint-Samat, Maguelonne. Histoire Naturelle et Morale de la Nourriture. Paris: Bordas, 1987. Translated from the French into English by Anthea Bell under the title of A History of Food. Cambridge, MA: Blackwell Publishers, 1992.

Trager, James. The Enriched, Fortified, Concentrated, Country-fresh, Lip-smacking, Finger-licking, International, Unexpurgated Food Book. New York: Grossman Publishers, 1970.

Tudge, Colin. Future Food, Politics, Philosophy and Recipes for the 21st Century. New York: Harmony Books, 1980.

Visser, Margaret. Much Depends on Dinner, the Extraordinary History and Mythology, Allure and Obsessions, Perils and Taboos of an Ordinary Meal, New York: Macmillan, 1986.

————. The Rituals of Dinner, the Origins, Evolution, Eccentricities and Meaning of Table Manners. New York: Grove Wiedenfeld, 1991.

Weaver, William Woys. America Eats, Forms of Edible Folk Art, Museum of American Folk Art. New York: Harper & Row, 1989.

Wechsberg, Joseph. Blue Trout and Black Truffles, the Pregrinations of an Epicure, New York: Alfred A. Knopf, 1966.

Wheaton, Barbara Ketchum. Savoring the Past, The French Kitchen and Table from 1300 to 1789. Philadelphia: University of Pennsylvania Press, 1983.

Ancient Books (Original Editions and Facsimiles):

Apicius, Cookery and Dining in Imperial Rome, edited and translated by Joseph Dommers Vehling. New York: Dover Publications, 1977. Is an unabridged republication of that work originally issued by Walter M. Hill, Chicago, 1936. No original Latin text.

Apicius, The Roman Cookery Book, a critical translation of The Art of Cooking by Apicius, for use in the study and the kitchen, by Barbara Flower and Elisabeth Rosenbaum. London: Harrap, 1958. The Latin text is included as well as very interesting details of and insights into the Latin kitchen.

L'art de Bien Traiter, par L.S.R. 1674. Facsimile edition Daniel Morerette, Luzarches, France, 1978. (Fr.)

Beaton's Book of Household Management, S.O. Beaton, London, 1861; Facsimile Jonathan Cape Ltd., London, 1968.

de la Reynière, Grimod. Almanac des Gourmands ou calendrier nutritif servant de guide dans les moyens de faire excellente chère. Paris, An X1-1803 (Year 11 of the First French Republic, 1803), original edition and binding of 1803. Donated to me by Samuel Chamberlain in 1971. (Fr.)

Dubois, Urbain. Nouvelle Cuisine Bourgeoise, n.d., probably late 1850s. Paul Bernardin, Paris. (Fr.)

la Chapelle, Vincent. Chef de cuisine de Monseigneur Le Prince d'Orange et de Nassau, Le Cuisinier Moderne, 5 tomes, seconde édition à La Haye, 1742. Facsimile edition Daniel Morerette, Luzarches, France, 1984. (Fr.)

Liger, Louis. Vicaire Col 523, Le Ménage des Champs et de la Ville ou Nouvcau Cuisinier François, chez Christ. David, Libraire Imprimeur, Paris, 1739. Original edition and binding of 1739. This book was donated to me by Samuel Chamberlain in 1971. (Fr.)

Martha Washington's Booke of Cookery, in the possession of Martha Washington from 1749 to 1799, transcribed by Karen Hess, New York: Columbia University Press, 1981.

Le Ménagier de Paris, (last ten years of the fourteenth century), edited by Jérome Pichon in 1847. Facsimile edition Daniel Morerette, Luzarches, France, n.d. (Medieval Fr.)

Menon. Les Soupers de la Cour ou l'art de travailler toutes sortes d'alimens, pour servir les meilleures Tables, suivant les quatre Saisons, Tomes 1, 2, 3 and 4, Paris, 1755. Reprint Librairie Solete, Paris, 1978. (Fr.)

————. La Cuisinière Bourgeoise, facsimile of the 1774 edition printed by Francois Foppens in Brussels, facsimile Messidor/Temps actuels, 1981. (Fr.)

Rabisha, Will. The Whole Body of Cookery Dissected, printed for George Calvert at the Half-moon, and Ralph Simpson at the Harp, in St. Paul's Churchyard, London, 1682. Original edition and binding of 1682.

The Receipt Book of Harriot Pinckney Horry 1770, A Colonial Plantation Cookbook, facsimile edited with an introduction by Richard J. Hooker. Columbia, SC: University of South Carolina Press, 1984.

Simmons, Amelia. American Cookery, 1796. Facsimile of the first American cookbook, New York: Dover Publications, 1958.

The Viandier of Taillevent (middle fourteenth century), an edition of all extant manuscripts edited by Terence Scully. Ottawa: University of Ottawa Press, 1988. (Medieval Fr.)

PART II: INGREDIENTS

Buying and Purchasing References:

Pedderson, Raymond B. SPECS, the Comprehensive Food Service Purchasing and Specification Manual. Boston, MA: Cahners Books International, Inc., 1977.

Reading the title of this book, home cooks will wonder how the book can be of any use to them. It is a great book which contains just about every bit of information existing on the following ingredients: meats, poultry, eggs, dairy products, fish, convenience foods, kosher foods, fruits and vegetables, juices, jams and jellies, miscellaneous groceries (beverages, coffee, grains, pasta and macaroni products, flours, chocolate, fats and oils, flavorings and extracts, legumes, nuts, etc.). Also includes quality control, storage, and handling information, which, whether one works in a restaurant or is a home cook, has to be done the same way. The book also has a detailed index. A very reliable reference book which will last a lifetime.

Information on Diverse Ingredients:

Baked goods and the flours that make them up:

Amendola, Joseph. *The Baker's Manual for Quantity Baking and Pastry Making.* Rochelle Park, NJ: Hayden Books, 1977.

Beranbaum, Rose Levy. *The Cake Bible.* New York: William Morrow, 1988.

Brown, Edward Espe. *The Tassajara Bread Book.* Berkeley, CA: Shambala Publications, 1970.

David, Elizabeth. *English Bread and Yeast Cookery.* New York: Viking Press, 1977.

Dodge, Jim, with Elaine Ratner. *Baking with Jim Dodge.* New York: Simon & Schuster, 1991.

Henspergern, Beth. *Beth's Basic Bread Book.* San Francisco: Chronicle Books, 1996.

Leader, Daniel, with Judith Blahnik. *Bread Alone.* New York: William Morrow, 1993.

Malgieri, Nick. *Perfect Pastry.* New York: Macmillan, 1989.

Ortiz, Joe. *The Village Baker, Classic Regional Breads from Europe and America.* Berkeley CA: Ten Speed Press, 1993.

Reinhart, Peter. *Brother Juniper's Bread Book, Slow Rise Method and Metaphor.* Menlo Park, CA: Aris Books/Addison-Wesley, 1991.

Silverton, Nancy. *Breads from the La Brea Bakery.* New York: Villard, 1996.

Cheeses:

Androuet. *Guide du Fromage.* Paris: Stock, 1971. A translation of this book in English exists. (Fr.)

Chenel, Laura, and Linda Siegfried. *American Country Cheese.* Menlo Park, CA: Addison-Wesley, 1989.

Jones, Evan. *The World of Cheese.* New York: Alfred A. Knopf, 1976.

U.S. Department of Agriculture. *Cheeses of the World.* New York: Dover Publications, 1972.

Chocolate:

Medrich, Alice. *Cocolat.* New York: Warner Books, 1990.

Coffee and Tea:

Joel, David, and Karl Schapira. *The Book of Coffee and Tea.* New York: St. Martin's Press, 1975.

Fish and Shellfish:

Cronin, Isaac, Jay Harlow, and Paul Johnson. *The California Seafood Cookbook, A Cook's Guide to the Fish and Shellfish of California, the Pacific Coast and Beyond.* Berkeley, CA: Aris Books, 1983.

Friedland, Susan R. *Caviar, a Cookbook with 100 Recipes, a Guide to All Varieties.* New York: Charles Scribner's Sons, 1986.

Loomis, Susan Herrmann. *The Great American Seafood Cookbook.* New York: Workman Publishing, 1988.

McClane, A. J. *The Encyclopedia of Fish Cookery.* New York: Holt, Rinehart and Winston, 1977.

Netboy, Anthony. *The Salmon, Their Fight for Survival.* Boston: Houghton Mifflin, 1974.

Spinazzola, Anthony, and Jacques Paimblanc. *Seafood As We Like It.* Chester, CT: Globe Pequot Press, 1985.

Tennison, Patricia. *Glorious Fish in the Microwave.* Chicago: Contemporary Books, 1989.

Meats and Poultry:

Lobel, Leon and Stanley. *All About Meat.* New York: Harcourt Brace Jovanovich, 1975.

Muessen, H. J. *How the World Cooks Chicken.* New York: Dorset Press /Stein and Day, 1978.

Smith, Page, and Charles Daniel. *The Chicken Book.* Boston: Little, Brown and Co., 1975.

Oils and Vinegars:

Diggs, Lawrence J., aka the vinegar man. *Vinegar, the User-Friendly Reference Guide to Making and Enjoying Vinegar.* San Francisco: Quiet Storm Trading Co., 1989.

Jordan, Michele Anna. *The Good Cook Book of Oil and Vinegar.* Menlo Park, CA: Addison-Wesley, 1992.

Klein, Maggie Blyth. *The Feast of the Olive.* Berkeley, CA: Aris Books, 1983.

Vegetables, Fruits, Greens, and Grains; Vegetarian Cookery:

Andrews, Jean. *Peppers, the Domesticated Capsicums.* Austin: University of Texas Press, 1984.

Boswell, Jean. *Onions Without Tears.* New York: Hastings House, 1950.

Farm Journal, Nell B. Nichols, editor. *America's Best Vegetable Recipes.* New York: Doubleday & Co., 1970.

Greene, Bert. *The Grains Cookbook.* New York: Workman Publishing, 1988.

———. *Greene on Greens.* New York: Workman Publishing, 1984.

Katzen, Mollie. *The Enchanted Broccoli Forest and Other Timeless Delicacies.* Berkeley, CA: Ten Speed Press, 1982.

———. *Moosewood Cookbook, Recipes from Moosewood Restaurant, Ithaca, N.Y.* Berkeley, CA: Ten Speed Press, 1977.

Kowalchik, Claire, and William H. Hylton, editors. *Rodale's Illustrated Encyclopedia of Herbs,* Emmaus, PA: Rodale Press, 1987.

Madison, Deborah, with Edward Espe Brown. *The Greens Cookbook, Extraordinary Vegetarian Cuisine from the Celebrated Restaurant.* New York: Bantam Books, 1987.

Robertson, Laurel, Carol Flinders, and Bronwen Godfrey. *Laurel's Kitchen, a Handbook for Vegetarian Cookery and Nutrition.* New York: Bantam Books, 1978.

Schneider, Elizabeth. *Uncommon Fruits and Vegetables, A Common Sense Guide.* New York: Harper & Row, 1986.

Wild Mushrooms:

The Audubon Society Field Guide to North American Mushrooms. New York: Alfred A. Knopf, 1981.

Krieger, Louis C. C. *The Mushroom Handbook.* New York: Dover Publications, 1967.

Miller, Orson K. *Mushrooms of North America.* New York: Dutton, 1978.

Wines:

Amerine, M. A., and V. L. Singleton. *Wine, an Introduction for Americans.* Berkeley, CA: University of California Press, 1965; revised second edition, same editors, 1977.

Ensrud, Barbara. *American Vineyards.* New York: Stewart, Tabori & Chang, 1988.

Johnson, Hugh. *Wine.* London: Thomas Nelson Ltd., 1966; available also in a Simon & Schuster Fireside edition, 1987.

Lichine, Alexis, in collaboration with William Fifield. *New Encyclopedia of Wines and Spirits*. New York: Alfred A. Knopf, 1974.

Schoonmaker, Frank. *Encyclopedia of Wine*. New York: Hastings House Publishers, 1964–1965. A pocket-size edition excellent for traveling.

PART III: SCIENCE AND FOOD

Nutrition and Dietetics:

Claessens, Sharon, and the Rodale Food Center. *The Lose Weight Naturally Cookbook*. Emmaus, PA: Rodale Press, 1985.

Goodhart, Robert S., and Maurice E. Shils. *Modern Nutrition in Health and Disease*, 6th edition. Philadelphia: Lee and Febiger, 1978.

McDougall, John, M.D., and Mary McDougall. *The McDougall Plan*. Clinton, NJ: New Win Publishing Inc., 1983.

Montignac, Michel. *Dine Out and Lose Weight, The French Way to Culinary "Savoir Vivre."* Montignac USA Inc., 1991.

Ornish, Dean, M.D. *Dr. Dean Ornish's Program for Reversing Heart Disease*. New York: Random House, 1990.

Food Chemistry and Science:

The reading level of these books ranges from easy to erudite; they are listed with an approximate academic level indicated for each of them.

Bennion, Marion. *The Science of Food*. New York: Harper & Row, 1980 (undergraduate and graduate).

Birch, Gordon F., Allan G. Cameron, and Michael Spencer. *Food Science*. London and New York: Pergamon Press, 1978 (undergraduate).

Charley, H. *Food Science*. New York: John Wiley & Sons, 1982 (undergraduate).

Erasmus, Udo. *Fats That Heal, Fats That Kill*, 2nd edition. Burnaby, BC, Canada: Alive Books, 1993. The first edition of this book was titled *Fat and Oil* (high school senior to graduate).

Fennema, Owen, editor. *Food Chemistry*. New York and Basel, Switzerland: Marcel Dekker Inc., 1985 (graduate and above).

Graves, Jeanne Freeland, and Gladys Peckham. *The Foundations of Food Preparation*. New York: Macmillan, 1987 (undergraduate).

Kotschevar, Lendall H., and Margaret McWilliams. *Understanding Food*. New York: John Wiley & Sons, 1969 (high school through college sophomore).

Laugier, L. Belime. *Les Clés de la Cuisine Française*. Paris: Delagrave, 1960 (high school through college sophomore). (Fr.)

Lowe, Belle. *Experimental Cookery from the Chemical and Physical Point of View*. New York: John Wiley & Sons, 1966 (graduate).

McGee, Harold. On *Food and Cooking*. New York: Scribner, 1984 (all levels).

Potter, N. *Food Science*. Westport, CT: AVI Publishing, 1986 (undergraduate).

Sanitation:

Food Service Sanitation. Chicago: National Institute for the Food Industry, 1979 and 1985.

Graves, Jeanne Freeland, and Gladys Peckham. *The Foundations of Food Preparation*. New York: Macmillan, 1987.

PART IV: FRENCH TECHNIQUES OF COOKING AND BAKING

The classics have been listed in chronological order of publication, for the cook to be able to follow the development of western cuisine between 1900 and 1990. Food aficionados and future professionals will find the comparison between different editions of diverse books most interesting.

Home Cooking:

La Bonne Cuisine de Madame St. Ange. Paris: Larousse, 1929. (Fr.)

La Bonne Cuisine de Madame St. Ange. Paris: Larousse, 1958. (Fr.)

Courtine, Robert J. *La Vraie Cuisine Française*. Verviers, France: Gérard et Co., 1953. (Fr.)

Child, Julia, Louisette Bertholle, and Simone Beck. *Mastering the Art of French Cooking*, vol. 1. New York: Alfred A. Knopf, 1961.

———. and Simone Beck. *Mastering the Art of French Cooking*, vol. 2. New York: Alfred A. Knopf, 1970.

La Cuisine et les Pâtisseries de Tante Marie, La Bonne et Veille Cuisine Française. Paris: Taride, 1959. (Fr.)

Grausman, Richard. *At Home with the French Classics*. New York: Workman Publishing, 1988.

Mathiot, Ginette. *La Cuisine Pour Tous*. Paris: Albin Michel, 1955. (Fr.)

Restaurant-Style Cooking:

The techniques of the classic cuisine, as they are still executed both in Europe and in the United States in large culinary educational establishments and in all city restaurants in the New World, rest on the contents of these works:

Ali-Bab (Henri Babinski). *Gastronomie Pratique*. Paris: Flammarion, 1928. (Fr.)

L'Art Culinaire Français par nos grands maîtres de la cuisine. Paris: Flammarion, 1957. This volume was translated into English as *The Art of French Cooking* by Joseph Faulkner and Bart Winer as translators and editors. New York: Golden Press, 1962. (Fr.)

Carême, Antonin. *l'Art de la Cuisine Française au Dix-neuvième Siècle*, 5 volumes. Paris: Renouard et Cie, undated, but known to have been published between 1833 and 1835; the last volume is posthumous and published by Carême cooperator Plumerey. There is a copy at the Schlesinger Library, Radcliffe College. (Fr.)

Curnonsky, Maurice Saillant dit. *Cuisine et Vins de France*. Paris: Larousse, 1953. (Fr.)

Darenne, Emile, and Emile Duval. *Traité de Pâtisserie Moderne*. Includes Paillon revisions of 1957, Leduby and Raimbault revisions of 1965. Paris: Flammarion, 1974. (Fr.)

Escoffier, Auguste. *Le Guide Culinaire*. Paris: Flammarion, 1921. Translated as *The Escoffier Cookbook and Guide to Fine Art Cookery*. New York: Crown Publishers, 1969. (Fr.)

———. *Ma Cuisine*. Paris: Flammarion, 1934. (Fr.)

Lacam, Pierre. *Le Nouveau Mémorial de la Pâtisserie*, revised by Pierre Seurre. Imprimerie de Montligeon, France, 1949.

Lang, Jenifer Harvey, editor. *Larousse Gastronomique*. New York: Crown Publishers, 1988.

Montagné Prosper, *Larousse Gastronomique*. Paris: Larousse, 1938, 1960. A 1967 edition still under the pen of Prosper Montagné exists under the title of *Nouveau Larousse Gastronomique*, "reviewed and corrected" by food critic and writer Robert Courtine. (Fr.) Two very different translations of the *Gastronomique* exist.

————, and Prosper Salles. *Le grand Livre de la Cuisine*. Paris: Flammarion, 1929. (Fr.)

Nignon, Edouard. *Les plaisirs de la Table*. Paris: Nignon et Meynial, 1940–1945. Printed on WWII-quality paper. (Fr.)

Pasquet, Ernest. *La pâtisserie familiale*. Paris: Flammarion, 1964. (Fr.)

Pellaprat, Henri-Paul. *L'art Culinaire Moderne*. Castagnola, Switzerland: Kramer, 1935 and 1964. (Fr.)

Turgeon, Charlotte, and Nina Froud, editors. *Larousse Gastronomique*. New York: Crown Publishers, 1961; and Montligeon.

The five volumes that follow present a good picture of the simplification of French cuisine between 1945 and 1965, which eventually led to the nouvelle cuisine of the last twenty-five years. Madame Bertholle's book gives an excellent idea of what was happening in the professional kitchens of France during the late 1960s and early 1970s.

Bertholle, Louisette. *Les recettes des Meilleurs restaurants de France*. Paris: Albin Michel, 1972. (Fr.)

Dumaine, Alexandre. *Ma Cuisine*. Paris: La Pensée moderne, 1972. Reputed as the last classicist. (Fr.)

Mercier, Henri. *La Gastronomie Française*. Paris: Flammarion, 1963. (Fr.)

Oliver, Raymond. *La Cuisine, sa technique, ses secrets*. Paris: Bordas, 1965. (Fr.)

Point, Fernand. *Ma Gastronomie*. Paris: Flammarion, 1969. Writings of Fernand Point collected posthumously. (Fr.)

PART V: FRENCH NOUVELLE CUISINE TECHNIQUES OF COOKING AND BAKING

Home Cooking:

Among many others, these three particular books show the development of interest in electric kitchen equipment, the importance of dietetics and good nutrition, and the style of good reasonable cuisine bourgeoise still cherished nowadays in French families.

Bisson, Marie-Claude. *La bonne cuisine française*. Paris: Solar, 1980. (Fr.)

Deloge, Germaine. *Cuisine rapide et techniques nouvelles*. Paris et Bruxelles: Dupuis, 1969. (Fr.)

Martin-Villevielle, Simone. *Cuisine sur ordonnance*. Paris: Pierre Horay, 1967. (Fr.)

Restaurant-Style Cooking:

Andries de Groot, Roy. *Revolutionizing French Cooking*. New York: McGraw-Hill, 1976. This book is an excellent overview of the nouvelle cuisine at its peak in French restaurants as investigated by Mr. de Groot.

Bocuse, Paul. *Paul Bocuse's French Cooking*. New York: Pantheon, 1978.

Chaboissier, D. *La Compagnon Pâtissier, Synthèse technologique et pratique du pâtissier moderne*, 2 volumes. Paris: Editions Jérome Villette, late 1980s (French books often do not mention the date or place of publication). (Fr.)

Chapel, Alain. *La Cuisine c'est beaucoup plus que des recettes*. Paris: R. Laffont, 1980. (Fr.)

Charetton, B. and C. *Les nouvelles bases et techniques de la cuisine*. Paris: Télécuisine, 1984. (Fr.)

Girardet, Freddy, with Catherine Michel, and Judith and Michael Hills, editors. *La cuisine de Freddy Girardet*. New York: William Morrow, 1982.

Guérard, Michel. *La Cuisine Gourmande*. Paris: R. Laffont, 1978. (Fr.)

————. *Cuisine Minceur*. New York: William Morrow, 1978.

Lenôtre, Pierre. *Faîtes vos Glaces et votre Confiserie comme Lenôtre*. Paris: Flammarion, 1978. (Fr.)

————. *Faites votre Pâtisserie comme Lenôtre*. Paris: Flammarion, 1975. (Fr.)

Maximin, Jacques. *Couleurs, Parfums et Saveurs de ma cuisine*. Paris: R. Laffont, 1984. (Fr.)

Roux, M. and R. *The Roux Brothers on Pâtisserie*. London: Macdonald, 1986.

Six grands cuisiniers de Bourgogne: Jean-Pierre Billoux, Georges Blanc, Jacques Lameloise, Michel Lorain, Bernard Loiseau, Marc Meneau. France: Editions J.C. Lattes, 1982. (Fr.)

Troisgros, Jean and Pierre. *Les Recettes Originales de Jean et Pierre Troisgros, cuisiniers à Roanne*. Paris: R. Laffont, 1972 (Fr.)

Vongerichten, Jean-Georges. *Simple Cuisine, the Easy New Approach to Four-Star Cooking*. New York: Macmillan, 1990.

Wells, Patricia. *Simply French, Patricia Wells Presents the Cuisine of Joël Robuchon*. New York: William Morrow, 1991.

PART VI: UNITED STATES COOKING AND BAKING TECHNIQUES

Home Cooking:

Beard, James A. *Delights and Prejudices*. New York: Atheneum, 1986.

————. *The New James Beard*. New York: Alfred A. Knopf, 1981.

Claiborne, Craig. *The New York Times Cookbook*. New York: Harper & Row, 1961.

Cooking Alaskan by Alaskans. Anchorage: Alaska Northwest Books, 1983.

The Fannie Farmer Cookbook, 11th edition, revised by Wilma Lord Perkins. Boston: Little, Brown and Co., undated, probably 1950s.

The Fannie Farmer Cookbook, 12th edition, revised by Marion Cunningham. New York: Alfred A. Knopf, 1983.

Farm Journal Country Cookbook. New York: Doubleday & Co, 1959.

Fussell, Betty. *I Hear America Cooking*. New York: Elizabeth Sifton Books/Viking, 1986.

Hillman, Libby. *The Best From Libby Hillman's Kitchen*. Woodstock, VT: The Countryman Press, 1993.

Howard, Maria Willett. *Lowney's Cookbook*. Boston: W. Lowney Co., 1908.

Jones, Evan. *American Food, The Gastronomic Story*. New York: Vintage Books, 1981.

Kafka, Barbara. *Microwave Gourmet*. New York: William Morrow, 1987.

Kamman, Madeleine. *The Making of a Cook*. New York: Atheneum, 1971.

Lewis, Edna. *The Taste of Country Cooking*. New York: Alfred Knopf, 1986.

Rombauer, Irma von Starkloff. *Joy of Cooking*. New York: Bobbs-Merrill Co., 1963.

Shore, Debbie, and Catherine Townsend for "Share Our Strength." *Home Food, 44 Great American Chefs Cook 160 Recipes on Their Night Off*. New York: Clarkson Potter, 1995.

Weaver, William Woys. *Pennsylvania Country Cooking*. New York: Abbeville Press Publishers, 1993.

Restaurant-Style Cooking:

Bertolli, Paul, with Alice Waters. *Chez Panisse Cooking*. New York: Random House, 1988.

Brown, Evan. *Cooking with New American Chefs*. New York: Harper & Row, 1985.

Burns, Jim, and Betty Ann Brown. *Women Chefs, a Collection of Portraits and Recipes from California's Culinary Pioneers.* Berkeley, CA: Aris Books, 1987.

Desaulniers, Marcel. *The Trellis Cookbook.* New York: Weidenfeld and Nicholson, 1988.

Fearing, Dean. *The Mansion on Turtle Creek.* New York: Weidenfeld and Nicholson, 1987.

Feniger, Susan, and Mary Sue Milliken. *City Cuisine.* New York: William Morrow, 1989.

Lagasse, Emeril, with Jessie Tirsch. *Emeril's New Orleans Cooking.* New York: William Morrow, 1993.

Prudhomme, Paul. *Chef Paul Prudhomme's Louisiana Kitchen.* New York: William Morrow, 1984.

Puck, Wolfang. *Adventures in the Kitchen.* New York: Random House, 1991.

Schmidt, Jimmy. *Cooking for All Seasons.* New York: Macmillan, 1991.

Tower, Jeremiah. *New American Classics.* New York: Harper & Row, 1988.

White, Jasper. *Jasper White's Cooking from New England.* New York: Harper & Row, 1989.

In all the sections that follow, the books are classified in the alphabetical order of their authors' names:

PART VII: CUISINES OF THE WORLD

General Index:
Stein, Thelma Barer. *You Are What You Eat, and Its Glossary.* Toronto: McClelland and Stewart Ltd. 1979 and 1980.

North African Cuisines (Maghreb):
La Cuisine Tunisienne. Paris et Société Tunisienne de Diffusion, Editions Jean Pierre Taillandier, n.d. (Fr.)

Fehri, Youcef. *Grandes Recettes de la Cuisine Algérienne.* Paris: Bordas SNED, Chaix Desfosses, 1957. (Fr.)

Morse, Kitty. *Come with Me to the Kasbah, a Cook's Tour of Morocco.* Casablanca, Morocco: Editions Serar, 1989.

Wolfert, Paula. *Couscous and Other Good Food from Morocco.* New York: Harper & Row, 1973.

Middle Eastern Cuisines:
Corey, Helen. *The Art of Syrian Cookery.* New York: Doubleday & Co., 1962.

Rayess, George. *Rayess' Art of Lebanese Cooking,* translated from the Arabic by Najla Showker. Beirut: Librairie du Liban, Riad Sohl Square, n.d.

Roden, Claudia. *A Book of Middle Eastern Foods.* New York: Alfred A. Knopf, 1972.

Shaheer, Jameela. *Arab World Cookbook.* Saudi Arabia, Dubi, Lebanon: The International Bookshops, 1973.

FAR EASTERN CUISINES

On Far Eastern Ingredients:
Cost, Bruce. *Bruce Cost's Asian Ingredients, Buying the Staple Foods of China, Japan and Southeast Asia.* New York: William Morrow, 1988.

China:
Chao, Buwei Yang. *How to Cook and Eat in Chinese.* New York: Vintage Books, 1945, 1949, 1963.

Chen, Joyce. *Joyce Chen Cookbook.* Philadelphia and New York: J. B. Lippincott Co., 1962.

Chiang, Cecilia Sun Yun. *The Mandarin Way.* San Francisco: California Living Books, 1980.

Chinese Cuisine from the Master Chefs of China. Boston: China Pictorial, The People's Republic of China and Little, Brown, 1983.

Hom, Ken. *Fragrant Harbor Taste, the New Chinese Cooking of Hong Kong.* New York: Simon & Schuster, 1989.

Hsiung, Deh-ta. *Chinese Regional Cooking.* Secaucus, NJ: Chartwell Books, 1979.

Khan, Johnny. *Eight Immortal Flavors.* Berkeley, CA: Howel North Books, 1963.

Mei, Fu Pei. *Chinese Cookbook,* 2 volumes, produced by the author's Chinese Cooking Class Ltd., Taiwan, n.d.; the contents of the book indicate middle 1960s. Originally purchased at The Asian Gourmet, Framingham, MA.

Tropp, Barbara. *The Modern Art of Chinese Cooking, Techniques and Recipes.* New York: William Morrow, 1982.

India:
Day, Harvey. *Curries of India.* Bombay: Jaico Publishing House, 1963.

Devi, Yamuna. *Lord Krishna's Cuisine, the Art of Indian Vegetarian Cooking.* Old Westbury, NY: Bala Books, 1987.

Sahni, Julie. *Classic Indian Cooking.* New York: William Morrow, 1980.

Japan:
Andoh, Elizabeth. *An American Taste of Japan.* New York: William Morrow, 1985.

———. *An Ocean of Flavor, the Japanese Way with Fish and Seafood,* New York: William Morrow, 1988.

Green, Karen. *Japanese Cooking for the American Table.* Los Angeles: Jeremy P. Tarcher, Boston: Houghton Mifflin, 1982.

Rudzinski, Russ (Ryoichi Kokku). *Japanese Country Cooking.* San Francisco: Nitty Gritty Productions, 1989.

Vietnam and Thailand:
Brennan, Jennifer. *The Original Thai Cookbook.* New York: Putnam Publishing Group, 1981.

Kim, Minh. *200 recettes de Cuisine Vietnamienne.* Paris: Jacques Grancher, 1988. (Fr.)

Routhier, Nicole. *The Foods of Vietnam.* New York: Stewart, Tabori & Chang, 1989.

Pacific Rim and Australia:
Alexander, Stephanie. *Stephanie's Feast and Stories.* Sydney: Allen and Unwin, 1988.

———. *Stephanie's Menus for Food Lovers.* North Ryde, Australia: Methuen Haynes, 1985.

Carpenter, Hugh. *Oriental Recipes for a Contemporary Kitchen.* New York: Stewart, Tabori & Chang, 1988.

Hansen, Barbara. *Taste of Southeast Asia.* Tucson: HPBooks, 1987.

Holuigue, Diane. *The Clever Cook.* Sydney: Viacom International, 1994.

Symons, Michael. *One Continuous Picnic, a History of Eating in Australia.* Adelaide: Duck Press, 1982.

Israeli and Jewish Cooking:
Levy, Faye. *International Jewish Cookbook.* New York: Warner Books, 1991.

Lyons Bar-David, Molly. *The Israel Cookbook.* New York: Crown Publishers, 1964.

Nathan Gerson, Joan, and Judy Stacey Goldman. *The Flavor of Jerusalem.* Boston: Little, Brown and Co., 1974.

Nathan, Joan. *The Jewish Holiday Kitchen.* New York: Schocken Books, 1988.

EUROPEAN CUISINES

Albania:
Albanian Cookbook. Worster MA: Women's Guild, St. Mary's Albanian Orthodox Church, 1977.

Austria:

Duch, Karl, and Richard Witzelberger. *Die Wiener Mehlspeisen*. Bad Gastein, Austria: Karl Krauth, n.d., probably early 1960s. (Ger.)

Spezialitäten aus Österreichs Küche. Innsbruck: Pinguin Verlag, 1969. (Ger.)

England:

Hartley, Dorothy. *Food in England*. London: Macdonald and Jane's, 1954.

Finland:

Ojakangas, Beatrice. The *Finnish Cookbook*. New York: Crown Publishers, 1964.

France: Provincial and Regional Cookery

Bentley, James. *Life and Food in the Dordogne*. New York: Meredith Press, 1986.

Brown, Michael and Sybil. *Food and Wine of France, Bordeaux to the Pays Basque*. New York: Exeter Books, 1980.

Cuisine de Poitou et de Vendée. Benet, France: Editions du Marais, 1968. (Fr.)

Daguin, Andre, and Anne de Ravel. *Foie Gras, Magret and Other Good Food from Gascony*. New York: Random House, 1988.

David, Elizabeth. *French Provincial Cooking and French Country Cooking*. London and New York: Penguin Books, 1970.

Escudier, Jean-Noël. *La Véritable Cuisine Provençale et Niçoise*. Toulon: Editions Provencia, 1967. (Fr.)

Guillaume-Felden, Emilie. *Der Praktische illustrierte Frauen Wegweiser*. Strasbourg: Editorial Argentor, 1929, 1931. Authentic Alsatian cookery. (Ger.)

Kamman, Madeleine. *When French Women Cook*. New York: Atheneum, 1976.

———. *Madeleine Kamman's Savoie, the Land, People and Food of the French Alps*. New York: Atheneum, 1989.

La Mazille. *La Bonne Cuisine du Périgord*. Paris: Flammarion, 1929. (Fr.)

Morand, Simone. *Gastronomie Bretonne d'hier et d'aujourd'hui*. Paris: Flammarion, 1965. (Fr.)

———. *Gastronomie Normande d'hier et d'aujourd'hui*. Paris: Flammarion, 1970. (Fr.)

Olney, Richard. *Simple French Food*. New York: Atheneum, 1974.

Secrets des Fermes au Coeur de la France. Paris: Berger Levrault, 1982. (Fr.)

Wolfert, Paula. *The Food of Southwest France*. New York: The Dial Press/Doubleday and Co., 1983.

Germany:

Die gute bürgerliche Küche in allen ihren Theilen. Munich: J. Rottenhöffer, Braun und Schneider, n.d., about 1850 to 1860. (Ger.)

Hahn, Mary. *Praktisches Kochbuch*. Berlin: Mary Hahn's Kochbuch Verlag, 1953. (Ger.)

Schuler, Elizabeth. *German Cookery*, edited and translated by Joy Gary. New York: Crown Publishers, 1955.

Stuber, Hedwig Maria, *Ich helfe dir kochen*. Munich, Basel, Vienna: BLV, 1970. (Ger.)

Greece:

Chantiles, Vilma Liacouras. *The Food of Greece*. New York: Atheneum, 1975.

Skoura, Sophia. *The Greek Cookbook*. New York: Crown Publishers, 1967.

Hungary:

Lang, George. *The Cuisine of Hungary*. New York: Atheneum, 1971.

Italy:

Artusi, Pellegrino. *La Scienza in Cucina et l'Arte di mangiar bene*. Bologna: Capito, 1973 reprint. The classic Italian cookbook par excellence. (It.)

Buonassisi, Vincenzo. *Il Codice della Pasta, 1001 ricetta per prepare, macheroni, tagliatelle, gnocchi, tortellini*. Milano: Rizzoli Editore, 1973. (It.)

Bugialli, Giuliano. *Classic Techniques of Italian Cooking*. New York: Simon & Schuster, 1982.

———. *The Fine Art of Italian Cooking*. New York: Times Books, 1976.

Consulo, Felice. *Guida Gastronomica d'Italia*, Novara: Istituto Geografico de Agostini, 1975. Descriptions of dishes rather than recipes and interesting commentaries on the regions of Italy and their wines. (It.)

David, Elizabeth. *Italian Food*. London and New York: Penguin Books, 1970.

Field, Carol. *The Italian Baker*. New York: Harper & Row, 1985.

Hazan, Marcella. *The Classic Italian Cookbook*. New York: Alfred A. Knopf, 1976.

———. *Marcella's Italian Kitchen*. New York: Alfred A. Knopf, 1991.

Gavotti, Erina. *Mille ricette*. Milano: Garzanti, 1965. (It.)

Gosetti della Salda, Anna. *Le Ricette Regionali Italiane, La Cucina Italiana*. Milano: Casa Editore, 1975. Recipes from all regions of Italy. (It.)

"In Bocca," a series of cookbooks each covering one of the regions of Italy. Palermo: Il Vespro, 1978–1979. All recipes are written in Italian and in the dialect of each region, then translated into very understandable, if grammatically not too correct English. Rare books, difficult to find, but treasures. (It.)

Root, Waverley. *The Food of Italy*. New York: Atheneum, 1972.

Rosetto Kasper, Lynne. *The Splendid Table, Recipes from Emilia-Romagna, the Heartland of Northern Italian Food*. New York: William Morrow, 1992.

Russia:

Bremsen, Anya von, and John Welchman. *The Russian Cookbook*. New York: Workman Publishing, 1990.

Scandinavia:

Hazelton, Nika Standen. *Classic Scandinavian Cooking*. New York: Charles Scribner's Sons, 1987.

Spain:

Casas, Penelope. *The Foods and Wines of Spain*. New York: Penguin Books, 1985.

Garcia, Clarita. *Clarita Cocina, Great Traditional Recipes from a Spanish Kitchen*. New York: Doubleday and Co., 1970.

Switzerland:

Bührer, Peter. *The New Swiss Cuisine*. Lucerne: Medon Verlag Ag, 1991. In English.

Fülscher, Elisabeth. *Kochbuch*. Zurich: Im Selbstverlag von Elisabeth Fülscher, 1966. (Ger.)

Guggenbühl, Helen. *Schweizer Küchen Spezialitäten*. Zurich: Schweizer Spiegel Verlag, 1966 (Ger.)

NORTH AND SOUTH AMERICA

Canada:

L'Art Culinaire au pays des Bleuets et de la Ouananiche. Ottawa: Fondation Culinaire Régionale Saguenay-St. Jean, 1967. (Fr.)

Benoît, Jehane. *Secrets et Recettes du cahier de ma grand-mère pour la canadienne d'aujourd'hui*. Montreal: Beauchemin, 1964. (Fr.)

Vers une nouvelle cuisine québécoise. Quebec City: Institut de Tourisme et d'hôtellerie du Québec, 1977. (Fr.)

Wine, Cynthia Berney. *Across the Table, an Indulgent Look at Food in Canada*. Scarborough, Ontario: Prentice Hall Canada Inc., 1985.

Mexico:

Bayless, Rick, with Deann Groen Bayless. *Authentic Mexican. Regional Cooking from the Heart of Mexico*. New York: William Morrow, 1987.

Kennedy, Diana. *The Cuisines of Mexico*. New York: Harper & Row, 1972.

———. *Mexican Regional Cooking*. New York: Harper & Row, 1978.

South American Cooking:

Karoff, Barbara. *South American Cooking, Foods and Feasts from the New World*. Berkeley, CA: Aris Books, 1989.

Leroux, Guy, and Clea de Oliveira. *La Cuisine Brésilienne*. Papeete, Tahiti: Les Editions du Pacifique /Distribuidora Record, 1980 (Fr.)

Ortiz, Elizabeth Lambert. *The Book of Latin American Cooking*. New York: Alfred A. Knopf, 1979.

Index

Page numbers in *italics* refer to illustrations and tables.

marinated vegetables, 404–407
  broccoli in pinzimonio,
    405–406
  eggplant, 405
  Greek-style artichokes,
    404–405
  pickled striped beets, 407
  red peppers, 406
marinating, 719–720
marjoram, 62
marmalades, 966, 990–991
  all citrus, 990–991
marmite, la, 228–229
Marsala wines, 100–101
Marseilles cuisine, 952
Martinique, 57, 433, 991
  stir-fried curry from, 814
masala, garam, 68–69
mashed anchovies, 56
mashed potatoes, 387–388
Massachusetts, 534, 650
Massialot, François, 257–258
matured flour, 1011–1012
Maude, 920
mayonnaise, 332, 337–344
  aïoli, 343
  artichoke, 343
  avocado, 343
  basic, 340
  caviar and lobster, 343
  chocolate, icing, 1146
  cooked, 342
  cucumber and dill, 344
  egg-free pseudo-, 342–343
  gribiche, 343
  hard-cooked egg yolk, 341
  herb, 343
  history of, 336
  mousquetaire, 343
  pepper, 343
  quantity production, 341
  remoulade, 344
  safety with, 337–338
  separation of, 338–339
  shallot and mushroom, 343
  storage of, 340
  Swedish apple, 343
  theories and basic techniques
    with, 338–339
Mazarin, Jules, 255
measurements, 8, 9, 10–13, 10, 11,
    12, 13
  of butter, 31, 31

meat, 699–911
  adipose tissue vs. marbling of,
    713–714
  aged, 716–718, 750
  any, stock in a hurry, 217
  baked in fat, see confit(ed)
  basters, 9
  basting of, 829
  boiled, 845
  broiled, 729–734; see also pan-
    broiled and panfried meat
  broths, 212, 214–215
  "carryover heat" in cooking of,
    718–719, 747
  choice of, 719
  cold, dressing for salads with,
    447
  color of, 715–716
  connective tissues of, 714–715
  cooked, 718–719
  cooked with dry heat, 729–814
  cooked with moist heat,
    814–836
  cured, 910–911
  definitions and warnings about,
    701–704
  defrosting of, 712
  in double consommé, 232–233
  extracts, 55
  fat in, 704, 705, 713, 720, 721,
    817, 868
  flambéing of, 720
  flavoring of, 786
  foie gras, 898–903
  free-range, 719
  galantines, 879, 880
  generalities on, 704–710
  glaze, 55, 221, 286
  gravies for, 748–749
  grinders, 7, 868–869
  handwork with, 720–729, 721,
    722, 723, 724
  marinating of, 719–720
  microwaved, 864–867
  muscle cells of, 715
  nutritional value of, 704, 846
  pan-roasted, 791–794
  pâté, 878, 880
  pot roasted, 836–840
  purchasing large amounts of,
    712
  red, wine with, 113
  roasted vs. baked, 747

salt curing of, 785
saucissons, 878–879
sautéed, 840–844
semimoist semidry cooking
    techniques for, 836–864
steamed, 860–864
stews, 815, 817, 827–828,
    832–836
stocks, 215–221
structure of, 712–719
temperatures for cooking of,
    702–703, 703, 730
tenderizing of, 719–720
terrines, 878, 879–880, 882–883
toxins in, 702–704, 867
white sauces and, 289
whole-meal vegetable and,
    soups, 227–229
see also baked meat; barbecued
    meat; beef; braised meat;
    deep-fried meats; grilled
    meat; ground meat; lamb;
    mutton; pan-broiled and
    panfried meat; poached
    meat; pork; poultry;
    quenelle(s); rabbit; roasted
    meat; sausages; stir-fried
    meats; variety meats; veal
meatball, 871
  stew, 873–874
meat loaf, 869, 871–872
  from East Prussia, 872–873
Meaux mustard, 42
medallions, salmon, 538–540, 539,
    540
  broiled, in herb crumbs, 613
  with dried sour cherry dressing,
    588
  pan-steamed, 583
  save your heart demi-, 589
  in Zinfandel, 598–599
Medici, Catherine de, 255, 1104
Medici, Marie de, 255
Mediterranean:
  herbs from, 61, 63
  nuts from, 51
  vegetables from, 365, 366
  wines from, 88
Mediterranean cuisine, 404
  mashed anchovies in, 56
  medmadmash, 388
  olive oil in, 35
  seasoning in, xvi

truly Mediterranean tomato
salad, 452–453
medmadmash, 388
Melanie's stuffed zucchini, 440
melanins, 360
Melbourne pavlova, 193
melon, 927–928, 972
preserve, 987
sorbet, 960
*Ménage des Champs et de la Ville ou
Nouveau Cuisinier François,
Le* (Liger), 258
Ménagier de Paris, Le, 41, 61, 70,
251–252, 966, 1081
Menon (chef), 259–260, 304, 1129
menouille, la, 491
meringue(s), 192–195
French, 192–194
Italian, 194–195
Melbourne pavlova, 193
mushrooms, Italian, 195
old-fashioned floating island,
193–194
Merlot wines, 95
mesclun in pistachio oil dressing,
451
metric measurements, 8, 9, 10–13,
10, 11, 12, 13, 31
Mexican flavors, Christmas boudin
in, 890–892
Mexican pea puree, 236
Mexico, 63, 117, 930
herbs from, 62
Michigan, 922
microwaved fish, 590–594
cherviled pike, 593
orange roughy fillets with sweet-
sour grapefruit sauce, 592
single's trout, 593–594
microwaved meat, 864–867
description of, 865
fenneled chicken cutlets,
866–867
microwave oven:
cooking fish in, 590–594
cooking rice in, 460
Middle Ages:
galangal in, 61
mustard in, 44
salt fish in, 638
sauces in, 251–254, 277
vinegar in, 41
Middle Eastern cuisine, 69

mignonette, 56
oyster liquor, oysters on the half
shell with, 670
mikado sauce, 351
milk, 27
almond, 50, 53
butterfat in, 27
clabbered goat's, golden pears
with, 950–951
corn, velouté, 238–239
-corn gravy, scaloppine of turkey
in, 802–803
court bouillon, 561
in emulsified sauces, 331–332
ewe's, 74
goat's, 74
homogenized, 28, 332
roast pork braised in, 826
see also Bavarian creams; cream;
custards; ice cream; potted
creams
millet, 474–475
basic, 474
and chicken sausage, 474
mills:
food, 6
pepper, 9
Mimi's poor man's guineas,
770–771
mincing, 17
mint:
family, 61–62
and garlic oil, 307
relish, New South Wales, 318
mints, 61
mirepoix, 16–17
Mississippi, 458, 533
Miss J's baked apple and fennel
slices, 952
Missouri, 458
mixed greens, étuvéed, 398
mixed herb pasta, in two pasta and
smoked chicken dinner,
506–507
mixed roasted roots and squash,
428
mixed so-called wild mushrooms,
sautéed, 414
mixed vegetable ragout, 395
mixer-made ordinary *brioche* for
quantity production,
1046–1048
mixers, electric, 6–7

beating egg whites with,
166–167, *166*
mousselines and, 691–692
MMK's gravlax, 643–644
mock fondant, 1145
Moctezuma II, Aztec emperor, 47
Moctezuma's ice cream, 148
*Modern Art of Chinese Cooking,
The* (Tropp), 811
modern basic pilaf, 461–462
modern cherry preserves, 988
modern cordon bleu, 805
modern cream of leek, 244
modern oxtail soup, a, 242–243
modern peppered steaks, 797
modern puff pastry, 1090–1091
Mohammed Reza, shah of Iran,
648
molded scarlet custard, 144
Molière, 44
mollet eggs, 130–131
mollusks, 522, 666–683
nutritional value of, 666
see also specific mollusks
Moluccas, 68
monkfish, *526*
in *bourride*, 554–555
monosodium glutamate (MSG),
55, 363
monounsaturated fat, 24–25, *25*
monounsaturated oils, xiii
Montagné, Prosper, 133, 150, 265,
279, 308, 344
fillets of sole, 596
Montana, 1005
morel mushrooms, spring, 72
Morocco, 70
mortars and pestles, 9
mother sauces, classic flour-bound,
275–288
Moulard duck, 711, 740
foie gras of, 899
mountain-style trout fillets,
steamed, 578–579
mousquetaire, 343
moussaka soufflé, 183
mousse(s), 199–203
apricot, 948
banana, 947
basic proportions for, 201
of blond livers and figs,
903–904
cakes, frozen, 203–205